Physiological
Psychology

Physiological Psychology

ROBERT B. GRAHAM

East Carolina University

Wadsworth Publishing Company
Belmont, California
A Division of Wadsworth, Inc.

Psychology Editor: Kenneth King

Development Editors: Mary Arbogast and John Bergez

Editorial Assistant: Michelle Palacio

Production Editor: Vicki Friedberg

Interior and Cover Design: Donna Davis

Print Buyer: Randy Hurst

Art Editors: Marta Kongsle and Roberta Broyer

Permissions Editors: Robert M. Kauser and Cathy Aydelott

Page Makeup: Al Burkhardt

Technical Illustrators: Barbara Barnett, Darwen and Vally
Hennings, Carlyn Iverson, Jeanne Koelling, Alex Teshin
Associates, John and Judy Waller

Copy Editor: Betty Duncan-Todd

Compositor: Jonathan Peck Typographers, Santa Cruz

Signing Representative: Charles Delmar

Printed in the United States of America   34

1 2 3 4 5 6 7 8 9 10—94 93 92 91 90

Library of Congress Cataloging-in-Publication Data

Graham, Robert B., 1934–
    Physiological psychology / Robert B. Graham.
        p.   cm.
    Includes bibliographical references.
    ISBN 0-534-10104-6
    1. Psychophysiology.   I. Title.
QP360.G675   1990
152—dc20   89-70599
                                              CIP

Brief Contents

Detailed Contents

6 Vision 197

7 Auditory and Chemical Senses 253

17 Brain Dysfunction 649

18 Neuropsychology of Cortical Function 691

Preface

Textbooks sometimes resemble mere catalogs of experiments and conflicting theories with little integration or synthesis. This book is an attempt to make a good "story" out of what we know about the nervous system. Thus, my motivation was to find the best interpretation of the research in any area of knowledge, or to create one if none existed. Wherever possible, I piece together conflicting theories into a coherent Gestalt by showing how one subsumes the other or how one applies under condition A, the other under condition B. Care is taken to let the reader discriminate the research evidence from my own interpretations.

In keeping with my goal of avoiding a catalog of concepts and findings, there is more emphasis on general principles and interpretation and less discussion of individual experiments. I explain concepts at greater length than is usual in a text of this sort. Instead of simply presenting more research on the same topic, I offer examples that tie the concepts to everyday life or to other ideas in the text. My hope is that students will complete their course in physiological psychology with a new, introspective view of their own minds rather than just a memorized list of brain parts and functions.

Illustrations

The illustrations have been prepared with great care and are employed extensively in the exposition of the ideas because I am convinced that it is much easier to retain concepts about a brain structure when one can visualize it. For example, it is much easier to remember the research on hippocampal function if those results can be associated with an image of the hippocampus.

With well over 400 figures, this book may be the most completely illustrated physiological psychology text available. Wadsworth selected a group of highly motivated artists to do the renderings, many of whom committed a number of hours to library research before even beginning the rough drafts of their drawings. Even so, the quest for anatomical accuracy and clarity of exposition frequently necessitated multiple drafts of the more complex pictures. I am convinced that the dedication of the artists and art staff and their patience with my continuous requests for somewhat "picky" changes will pay off for the students.

Locating Ideas

I have tried to make it as easy as possible to find the locations of concepts rapidly and effortlessly. The outline at the beginning of each chapter lists all major concepts and the sections in which they are found boldfaced. Further, the glossary at the end of each chapter shows the page where the concept first appears. This should make test construction easier and might also aid in answering student questions about particular points in the discussion. The chapter summaries are longer than those in most texts, and while this adds to the overall length of the book, it does not add to the student's burden. The summaries represent useful redundancy, restating ideas in somewhat different wording so that the reader has another chance to obtain the clearest understanding of difficult concepts. That same principle of useful redundancy is also evident in the figure captions. I tried to write them in such a way that the illustrated idea could be learned from the caption alone.

■ For Those Who Find Ideas Exciting . . .

Very few psychologists have time to keep up with recent developments in every one of the diverse areas of neuroscience research. Exciting new theoretical ideas are generated almost monthly, and it is possible that some of these may have escaped your attention so far. I have made it a chief concern to bring this text as close as possible to the cutting edge of current theory in every topic area, and I hope to provide you with a few delightful surprises as you read the chapters. For example, did you realize that the outer hair cells of the cochlea may be more motor than sensory? Did you know that it is now possible to tie the retinal X and Y ganglion cells into two separate pathways and trace those paths all the way through LGN, through areas 17, 18, and 19, and into parietal and temporal visual cortex? Many empirical findings that had to be offered to students without explanation can now be understood in terms of a focal vision path and an ambient vision path.

The hippocampus has become such a research "hot spot" (especially with regard to LTP, NMDA receptors, and evoked potentials) that the hippocampal portion of the memory "story" had to be assigned a separate chapter of its own (Chapter 15). Did you know that O'Keefe and Nadel's famous place units are now being reinterpreted as coding for something more general than environmental locations—a finding that suggests an event memory role for that structure? The fields of clinical neuropsychology and cognitive neuropsychology have burgeoned during

the last decade; Chapter 18 is devoted to their contributions, but their immense impact on modern memory theory shows up in the hippocampus chapter. With the distinctions between procedural and declarative memory, and between working and reference memory, we can finally understand memory sparing in amnesics.

Among the physiological psychologists whom I know personally, the motor system is regarded as somewhat less interesting than a 1949 report on farm futures. In the past, the motor parts of the brain (which constitute about one-half of that organ) have been the province of neurologists. In 1990, however, they are simply too interesting to leave out of a psychology course. I am sure you are aware that the basal ganglia are the focus of the neural tissue transplant experiments. Less pressworthy but just as fascinating are the new organizing concepts of *central pattern generator* and *fractionation*, which tie the whole motor hierarchy from M1 cortex to ventral horn motor neuron into an organized theory. The motor system has finally become fun to teach!

As you can see from the last few paragraphs, my chief focus has been to collect the best set of current *explanations* of brain function. I have tried to avoid the presentation of research results that cannot yet tie into some reasonable theory. For most of my students, it is in these explanatory concepts that one finds the real excitement of neuroscience.

■ Acknowledgments

Although this book bears my name, it is actually a team effort. I would like to thank the following reviewers for their helpful comments: Shirley Barker, Los Angeles City College; R. Bowen, Loyola University; Thomas Breen, California State University, Fresno; Rebecca Chesire, University of Hawaii, Manoa; Richard Ehmer, University of Bridgeport; Edna Fiedler, St. Mary's University; Judith L. Gibbons, St. Louis University; Barry Haimson, Southeastern Massachusetts University; Wayne Hren, L.A. Pierce College; W. Lloyd Kelly, San Diego Mesa College; Kenneth Kleinman, Southern Illinois University,

Edwardsville; Jim H. Patton, Baylor University; Thomas B. Posey, Murray State University; Richard L. Russell, Santa Monica College; and Paul Watson, University of Tennessee, Chattanooga. In particular I would like to thank Marie Banich, University of Illinois, Urbana–Champaign; Leslie Fisher, Cleveland State University; and Mary Arbogast for their valuable comments and suggestions. My special thanks to the excellent (and long-suffering) Wadsworth staff who guided the book to completion: Vicki Friedberg, Marta Kongsle, Bobbie Broyer, Donna Davis, and Bob Kauser. I am deeply grateful to the people who made this project possible: Ken King, whose idea it was; Fred King and John Munson, who provided the education; and Wilbur Castellow, who gave me the time to work on it.

ROBERT B. GRAHAM

Sampling Physiological Psychology: A Preview

T he field of knowledge you are about to explore has its roots in the earliest history of psychology. In the mid-1800s, before psychology existed as a discipline, some scientists, trained as physiologists or physicists, had already become interested in how the human mind sensed, perceived, thought, and remembered. They wanted to know how the brain functioned to give us our senses and perceptions. A few of these researchers began calling themselves psychologists and established the brand new field of science by opening laboratories or establishing chairs of psychology at universities.

■ The Basic Viewpoint

A chief goal of those early labs was to explore the connections between mental events and the physiological functions of the nervous system. By the beginning of the 20th century, it had become evident to scientists that the mind was located in the brain—a fact that had not been clear to many philosophers of the Middle Ages. Today, this link between the mind and the brain has been established through brain-stimulation experiments and other methods that we will examine in Chapter 5. For example, stimulation at various brain sites can cause the person to feel angry or to have an experience resembling a vivid memory. But how should the link between mind and brain be viewed? Is the electrically elicited brain activity *causing* mental experiences in the mind, or are the patterns of neural activity and the mental experiences just two aspects of the same thing? Philosophers have named the first interpretation dualism and the second monism.

Dualism holds that the mind and body are two different phenomena. The body is a biological mechanism that obeys physical laws, but the mind is the nonphysical, spiritual soul. Mind and brain could be viewed as completely independent of one another but acting simultaneously on the same stimuli and responses—a position called parallelism—or could be coordinating their actions because each can influence the other. Parallelism made sense to prescientific thinkers of the early Renaissance but is sharply refuted in modern times by the knowledge that manipulations of the brain can alter the mind. Remove one part of the brain, and the person can no longer understand printed words on the page; damage another part, and the left side of the person's body vanishes from conscious experience ("left-side neglect" to the clinician). Altering the brain also affects the mind, so modern dualists propose that the brain can cause changes in the mind and vice versa—a position called **interactional dualism**. A few neuroscientists have espoused such a dualistic position (Popper & Eccles, 1977), but most seem to be more comfortable with **monism**, the view that the mind and brain are one—that the mind is simply the *functioning* of the brain. Monism is the viewpoint from which this text was written.

In her discussion of dualism, the philosopher Patricia Churchland (1988) points out that there is a complete lack of objective empirical evidence for a purely mental, nonphysical substance that could influence physical matter. In her opinion, the dualism–monism argument is now unimportant compared to the question of reductionism.

Reductionism is a strategy for developing explanations of phenomena by analyzing them into components at a more molecular level. **Molar** refers to the whole and **molecular** to the parts. A molecular, or reductionistic, explanation analyzes the wholes into their parts to see how the parts interact. A molar explanation of car trouble might state that the car stopped running because the engine couldn't get enough gas. A more molecular explanation states that the problem was a clog in the fuel line between the gas tank and the carburetor. Note that both explanations would be correct but at different levels of analysis. In psychology, the fact that an animal eats might be explained on a molar level by saying that eating occurs whenever the hunger drive is aroused. A molecular approach seeks to identify the "hunger areas" of the brain and discover the way in which those parts interact to determine when the animal

will eat. Thus, a molecular approach tries to explain a phenomenon by reducing it to its underlying parts—that is, hunger reduced to the actions of particular brain circuits.

Reductionism is endless. It explains the mind by reducing it to the interactions between neural circuits, which in turn can be understood as a collection of cell membranes that generate ionic currents. The membranes and currents are explained by the laws of chemistry, which govern how molecules and parts of molecules interact. The behavior of molecules in turn can be understood through the laws of physics, which specify how electrons, protons, and neutrons interact. Reductionism implies that, once we have learned enough, we should be able to explain the mind in terms of the interactions between subatomic particles. For practical reasons, however, we are usually satisfied with reducing to the next level below the phenomenon under study; this approach has been highly successful in psychology.

For the psychologist, the problem implicit in reductionism is, Can a molar science of the mind and behavior continue to exist, or are psychological concepts like ego, short-term memory, and anxiety just temporary explanations awaiting a more complete understanding through reduction to the underlying brain processes? Will psychology be replaced by neuroscience? Molar theory has its defenders (Churchland, 1988); some argue that molar concepts like anxiety and cognitive dissonance can never be understood through reductionism—that the whole is always greater than the sum of its parts. Reductionists argue back that an understanding of all parts plus how they *interact* with one another always explains all data.

Perhaps the most fruitful way to advance our science is to assume that all phenomena, at any level of explanation (psychological, biological, or chemical), could be explained by reducing them to components at a more molecular level but that such reductionism is not always the most useful approach. If a social worker must understand why a man beats his wife every Saturday night, an explanation employing the molar idea of drunkenness is far more useful than a full reductionistic explanation of the effects of alcohol and its metabolites on circuits in the limbic system and hypothalamus of the brain. Truth exists at both levels, however, and the relatively fuzzy, molar concept of drunkenness is of little help when we want a complete, precise understanding of the principles relating aggression to alcohol intoxication. In that case, a molecular, reductionistic explanation is the best. In a pragmatic approach then, both molar and molecular explanations are required, and which is chosen in any circumstance depends on the needs of the knowledge user. The corollary of this idea is that cognitive psychologists and physiological psychologists should work together to create molar and molecular explanations that agree with one another, rather than operating in private domains of knowledge that generate competing, conflicting understandings of the human mind.

What will the reductionistic orientation of this book mean to you, the student? Other courses in psychology—such as those on learning, sensation, perception, or thinking—present the basic laws governing a particular set of functions. In a course on learning, for example, you discover the rules of reinforcement and how they determine behavior. You learn how learning occurs, how to alter its rate, how to measure it, what the various types of learning are and how they differ; but you never get to grapple with the most fundamental question: What exactly *is* learning? What is happening in your head when you create a new memory? Physiological psychology is the only field that comes to grips with the most basic questions: What is emotion? What is memory, thinking, learning? What does it *mean* to see, to hear, or to feel pain? Physiological psychology attempts to search out the foundations of what it means to be a conscious, thinking human being.

■ Origins

Some basic ideas that we use to understand brain function originated in the 18th century. From experiments on muscle contraction in 1791, Luigi Galvani (1737–1798) proposed the idea of animal electricity, which led eventually to the insight that the nervous system accomplishes its tasks with electric currents (Brazier, 1959). Anatomists like Santiago Ramón y Cajal (1852–1934) learned how to reveal the microscopic structure of the brain, and his work supported the **neuron doctrine** advanced by Waldeyer (1836–1921). This doctrine proposed that the brain was composed of individual cells that Waldeyer called **neurons** (also termed **nerve cells**). In 1868, Bernstein described how neurons can generate the electric currents we call **nerve impulses**. Thus, by the late 19th century, the brain was thought of as generating mental events through patterns of nerve impulses in neurons. Johannes Müller (1801–1858) wondered how visual stimuli could be distinguished from auditory stimuli. Were impulses leaving the eye different from those leaving the ear? No, he concluded in his **doctrine of specific nerve energies**; all nerve impulses are qualitatively the same. The impulses in the visual neurons give us visual, not auditory, sensations because they travel to the visual parts of the brain. Hypothetically, if we could route them to the auditory parts, we could hear light.

The neuron doctrine was extended by Sir Charles Sherrington (1857–1952) in 1897 when he declared that neurons communicate with one another at contact points he called **synapses** (Eccles, 1982). In 1950 Eccles and others established that this communication was achieved by passing chemicals called neurotransmitters from one cell to the other (Kandel, 1982). This achievement provided the foundation for our current understanding of how drugs affect the mind. Sherrington also showed how neurons can combine into circuits called **reflex arcs** that link stimuli with responses.

Although these scientists provided foundations for modern brain research, none was a psychologist. Before the 1950s, physiological psychology was a thinly populated discipline, which had advanced relatively slowly. In 1949, however, Donald Hebb published his ground-breaking book, *The Organization of the Brain,* which revealed to many people for the first time how concepts like learning, perception, memory, and intelligence might be reduced to interactions between neurons. As a scientific theory, it has long been surpassed, but there probably has never been a single, more powerful source of influence on psychology majors considering a career in physiological psychology. Throughout the 1960s, the discipline experienced a flood of new PhDs and with them a flood of research results.

In the 1970s, biologists became more interested in how the brain produces behavior (essentially, a psychological concern), and more physiological psychologists pursued reductionistic explanations of psychological phenomena down into the levels of biology and chemistry. The disciplines were flowing together into a new amalgam that combined the efforts of psychology, biology, and chemistry. It was formally anointed as the field of **neuroscience** by the formation of the International Society for Neuroscience in 1969.

In the 1970s and 1980s, a dozen or more universities opened departments of neuroscience to which more and more physiological psychologists are now migrating. Does this mean that in the years to come physiological psychology will be completely absorbed into neuroscience? Probably not. Already clinical psychology has given birth to a branch called **neuropsychology**, which examines the effects of brain damage on patient behavior (see Chapter 18). Other psychologists have joined forces with mathematicians and computer-oriented scientists to proclaim the advent of **cognitive neuroscience**, a discipline that uses the information-processing ideas of the computer world to understand the relation between brain events, thinking, and language. Although some people leave for the field of neuroscience, the interest in brain function among psychologists grows yearly. The spawning of the new disciplines is simply an indication of an unprecedented wave of interest in learning how the human mind relates to the workings of the brain.

■ Understanding the Human Mind Requires . . .

It is impossible to explain how your behavior and conscious experience depend on brain parts and functions until you have some basic knowledge of the brain as an organ. In other words, you must know something about brain anatomy and neurophysiology before we can discuss the physiology of sleep, learning, and emotion. Here, we will glance briefly

at three areas of knowledge—anatomy, transmitter systems, and brain physiology—and look at specific examples of the fascinating kind of understanding available to anyone who becomes acquainted with the brain as an organ. First, we will see that understanding brain dysfunctions depends on knowing what the various parts of the brain are and what they do—that is, a knowledge of brain anatomy. Then, we will find that understanding the actions of mind-affecting drugs depends on our knowledge of how nerve cells (neurons) transmit information to one another. Last, we will find out how important it is to understand the physiology of the brain by reviewing the specific case of brain-tissue transplants.

■ Understanding Brain Anatomy: Tourette Syndrome

Many symptoms of brain dysfunction masquerade as emotional problems or poor upbringing. A man riding on the subway who suddenly bursts out swearing at nothing in particular, for example, would be viewed as vulgar or "crazy," not brain-damaged. But such involuntary behavior is a standard symptom of the brain disorder called **Tourette syndrome**, named after the French physician Georges Gilles de la Tourette (1857–1904), who first described it in 1885. Even the patient may not realize that a physical disease is involved and sometimes suffers from the affliction for a decade or more before it is recognized for what it is.

The Symptoms

The basic symptom in Tourette syndrome is the **tic**, an involuntary muscle contraction or behavior. When the disease first begins to show itself (usually between the ages of 7 and 11), the problem may be only a single tic, such as an exaggerated eye blink. Soon, however, other parts of the body exhibit twitches, jerks, and spasms. Socially, the worst tics are the vocal ones. While talking to someone, the patient may find himself echoing what was just said or aping the person's gestures. In some cases, the tic takes the form of a compulsion to utter obscenities or vulgar phrases, a symptom termed **coprolalia**. Frequently, the words are shouted with considerable force and emotion, despite the patient's attempts to inhibit them.

Victims of Tourette syndrome try to suppress their symptoms in the presence of others, but the effort is extremely tiring. On the other hand, the constant movement and violent jerking of unsuppressed tics means chronically aching muscles. One patient described his life as follows:

> I feel like you would if there were a powerful man who had you by the throat and just kept tightening his grip. I end my days exhausted because of the energy I expend both ticquing and warding off the tics. In school, taking a test was utterly draining. I had to coordinate my muscles so I could write, and at the same time I had to think carefully to answer the questions. And that effort seemed to make the ticquing worse. (Garelik, 1986)

Tourette syndrome is quite rare (there are only about 750 recorded cases), so not all physicians are aware of its existence. Many cases go undiagnosed for years, during which the victim may lose friends and even family support. One man went through Navy boot camp with some officers believing that he was an incorrigible goof-off, whereas others were sure that he was suffering drug-withdrawal symptoms.

Aid from Haloperidol

What hope does a Tourette patient have for relief from symptoms? At this time, the best therapy is far from ideal. The drug **haloperidol** helps reduce the frequency of symptoms in the majority of cases, but there is no hope for a cure until the origins of the disorder are understood (Bonnet, 1982). Haloperidol is one of a class of drugs called **antipsychotics**, used chiefly to treat schizophrenia. Antipsychotics affect the activity level of a system of nerve cells within the brain that are stimulated by the chemical **dopamine**. Neurons (nerve cells) excite one another by means of chemicals called **neurotransmitters**, and dopamine is the neurotransmitter employed by a set of nerve cells that may be involved with producing patterns of movements.

Perhaps Tourette patients have nerve cells that are too sensitive to dopamine. Haloperidol does decrease the sensitivity of cells to dopamine (Lohr & Wisniewski, 1987), but other drugs that decrease sensitivity fail to bring relief from tics. This suggests that dopamine is not the only chemical involved in the disorder. In fact, an unusual number of Tourette patients appear to react abnormally to the slight amounts of copper found in their diets (Robertson et al., 1987). Slowly accruing damage to the nervous system by minute quantities of copper over years and years might eventually turn out to be a major factor in causing the syndrome; at the present time, however, this is just one possible hypothesis. In Chapter 17, you will learn more about the drugs used to treat psychoses like schizophrenia and more about the role of neurotransmitters in that disorder.

Is the Cingulate Cortex Involved?

The first major step in understanding the cause of Tourette syndrome or any other brain disorder is to find the location of the dysfunction in the brain. Which brain structures are damaged or are malfunctioning? A group of French neurosurgeons has elicited tics in non-Tourette patients during neurosurgery by electrically stimulating a part of the brain called the **cingulate cortex** (Figure 1.1). Because the brain contains no pain receptors, patients undergoing brain surgery are frequently kept conscious during the operation (with local anesthetics for scalp pain). Consequently it was possible to ask these people to try suppressing the tics elicited by the electric current. Just as in Tourette syndrome, some suppression was possible. Furthermore, Tourette-like vocalizations were elicited by the stimulation. In some species of monkeys, electrical stimulation to the cingulate cortex elicits basic communication calls signaling food, aggression, or sexual desire. These built-in vocalizations are simple grunts and vowel sounds that resemble Tourette vocal tics (Bonnet, 1982). Do humans have a similar set of "hard-wired" vocalizations tied to basic emotions and drives?

Many tics of Tourette syndrome have a quality of compulsive repetition that is found in **obsessive–compulsive disorder (OCD)**, a psychiatric syn-

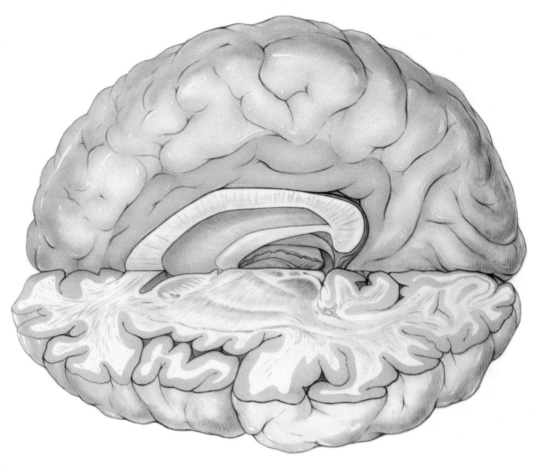

Figure 1.1 Cutaway view of the human brain showing the cingulate cortex (shaded).

drome in which the person feels compelled to perform meaningless acts like repeatedly raising an arm
or touching each corner of a chair before sitting.
Before drugs became available for treating OCD, one
therapy involved cutting the nerve connections into
and out of the cingulate cortex.

Evidence that the cingulate cortex may be
involved in Tourette syndrome probably has little
meaning for you at this time. However, as you
become familiar with the anatomy of the brain, facts
such as these will take on much greater significance.
In the coming chapters, for example, you will learn
that the cingulate cortex is a part of the emotion
system of the brain—an idea that seems to fit neatly

with the emotional quality of the vocal tics. The more
anatomy you know, the more sense you can make
out of any new fact about a brain disorder or normal
brain process. For this reason, Chapter 3 gives you
an anatomical overview of the nervous system.

■ Understanding Transmitter Systems: Obsessive–Compulsive Disorder

A knowledge of brain anatomy is vital if you want to
understand the neural origins of normal or abnormal
behavior, but it is not enough. The nervous system

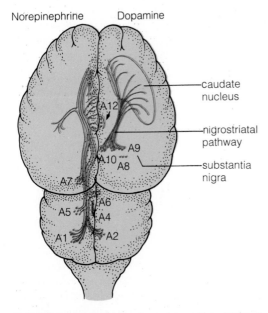

Norepinephrine   Dopamine

caudate
nucleus

nigrostriatal
pathway

substantia
nigra

A12
A9
A10
A8
A7
A6
A5
A4
A1
A2

Figure 1.2 Cat brain seen from above with locations of two neurotransmitter systems indicated. The norepinephrine system is shown only in the left hemisphere and the dopamine system only in the right. The areas labeled A1–A12 are zones containing neurons that use either norepinephrine or dopamine as a transmitter. (Adapted from Ungerstedt, 1971)

is not only organized into anatomical structures, it is also organized chemically into functional systems that cut across the boundaries of those structures.

Neurotransmitters

All behavior is produced by circuits of nerve cells in the nervous system. These circuits are created by linking nerve cells at connecting points called synapses. The first cell in the circuit can excite the second cell at a synapse between the two by secreting a neurotransmitter such as dopamine. A group of cells all using the same neurotransmitter is called a **neurotransmitter system** (Figure 1.2).

Different systems in the brain have different functions. The transmitter dopamine, for example, seems to be involved in the process of reinforcement dur-

ing learning (discussed in Chapter 14). Glutamate is the transmitter in a major memory circuit (see Chapter 15). Such neurotransmitter systems extend through the brain and spinal cord over considerable distances, with links and branches in numerous anatomical structures. Some brain processes can be studied extensively by concentrating on one anatomical structure. Such is the case with the language areas (Chapter 18), which occupy the central region of the cortex in the left hemisphere. Other processes such as reinforcement can only be understood through chemical systems like the dopamine system (Chapter 14), which runs from the top of the brain stem up into the core of the brain. As you can see, understanding how the brain works means first learning a little anatomy and something about neurotransmitters.

The system of neurons that uses **serotonin** as a neurotransmitter has functions at which we are still guessing. Among other things, it may be involved in producing or maintaining the state of sleep (discussed in Chapter 10). When it malfunctions, the result may be OCD.

The Symptoms

Obsessions are "recurrent, persistent ideas, thoughts, images, or impulses" that the person does not wish to experience (American Psychiatric Association, 1987). They usually make no sense and invade the mind no matter how fervently the person wants to avoid them. Typical obsessions involve thoughts of killing someone, worries about being contaminated by coming into contact with people or objects carrying disease, and recurrent doubts such as wondering if you remembered to lock your door before leaving home. **Compulsions** are "repetitive, purposeful and intentional behaviors that are performed in response to an obsession, or according to certain rules or in a stereotyped fashion" (American Psychiatric Association, 1987). Typical compulsions include repetitive handwashing, counting, and checking and touching objects. A businessperson who cannot begin the work day without counting every paper clip and recording the number on a pad suffers from a compulsion. Realizing that the activity is purposeless and preferring to avoid doing it, this person feels increasing tension the longer the behavior is delayed.

Obsessive–Compulsive Disorder and Serotonin

Psychiatrists have tried with little success to trace the causes of OCD to early childhood experiences. Recently, the growing conviction is that the disorder stems from a problem in one of the neurotransmitter systems rather than solely from the person's past experiences. A clue to which transmitter might be involved came from the study of a different disorder—depression. Many patients with severe depression have a defect in the brain mechanism that controls the endocrine gland system. They fail to react to **dexamethasone**, a drug that turns off the endocrine response to stress in normal people. Some patients with OCD also show this failure to suppress their glandular stress response. (We will explore the nature and implications of the stress response in Chapter 13.) Is there some relation between depressive disorder (which seems to have a basis in brain physiology) and OCD?

Zohar and Insel (1987) tried an antidepressant drug on their OCD patients. Several antidepressants had no effect on the symptoms, but one drug, clomipramine, significantly reduced the number of obsessional thoughts. What was distinctive about clomipramine? Among the various antidepressants tried, it appears to have the most effect on the neurons that use serotonin as a transmitter. This finding suggested a second experiment. Zohar and Insel (1987) reasoned that if OCD was partly the result of some fault in the serotonin system, then further disabling that system of nerve cells should intensify the symptoms. They accomplished this with a drug that blocks the action of serotonin at the synapses. Such blocking drugs are called **neurotransmitter antagonists**. As predicted, when patients were given a serotonin antagonist, their obsessions and compulsions increased in strength and frequency. (In Chapter 4, we will see other examples of how drugs can affect the synapse.)

Other researchers are currently studying the function of the serotonergic system and how the neurons affect the flow of information in the brain.

With that basic knowledge, we might be able to devise drugs to change how the system works. If obsessions and compulsions do originate from a neurotransmitter problem in the brain, then such a drug might provide a cure for OCD. The possibility also exists that increased knowledge of other transmitter systems may yield drugs to solve the problems of schizophrenia, depression, and a host of other disorders.

■ Understanding Brain Physiology: Tissue Transplants

When an adult human suffers brain damage through disease or accident, the nerve cells that die can never be replaced. By the time you are 2 years old, you have all the nerve cells you will ever have; from then on, the number most probably decreases every year from minor problems. During infancy many cells die as a natural part of development, but in adulthood cell loss is probably due to damage. A large loss of brain tissue from an accident.can leave a person still alive but paralyzed, blind, amnesic, or unable to speak or comprehend language. If replacement brain tissue could be grafted into a damaged brain in such a way that the transplanted nerve cells lived and functioned normally, we would have achieved one of the most important advances in the history of medicine. It is small wonder, then, that so much excitement has been generated by the recent experiments suggesting that such therapy might eventually be possible. However, realizing this goal is complicated by immense physiological problems. As you learn about neurophysiology in this text, you will become more and more sensitive to the difficulties faced by transplant researchers.

Problems in Replacing Lost Brain Tissue

If you have kept up with recent news about tissue transplants, you already know that the human immune system (the parts of the body that fight infections) attacks and kills the transplanted tissue. This tissue rejection occurs unless the new organ is made of the same individualized types of protein that the recipient's own body creates. Thus, a piece of your own skin can be removed from one area of your body and grafted to another, as is often done in the treatment of large burns. Sometimes, the proteins manufactured by a close relative are similar enough to your own that your body would not reject a transplant from that person. Tissue donations from genetic strangers, however, are promptly and completely rejected unless the recipient is heavily dosed with dangerous drugs designed to suppress immune system activity.

Fortunately, the brain and spinal cord are apparently exempt from the immune process (Fine, 1986). Tissue transplanted into the brain from a genetically unrelated person will not be attacked and killed. Rejection, then, is not the real problem in grafting brain tissue.

Nonscientists find it difficult to understand just how completely and totally impossible brain-tissue grafting seems to the neuroscientist. Having heard about heart and kidney transplants, the nonscientist probably imagines that if those organs can be transplanted then why not brain tissue? The difference, of course, is in the physiology of the organs. In relative complexity, the kidneys bear the same resemblance to the brain that a tricycle does to a fully computerized F111 jet interceptor. Normal brain function depends on the connections between nerve cells. Grafted nerve tissue is useless to the recipient unless the replacement tissue can form the billions of highly specific connections to make it functional. Simply inserting a tissue transplant into an area of brain damage and expecting it to replace lost functions would be like repairing your TV by opening up the back and tossing in a boxful of electronic chips.

Early Research: Parkinson's Disease

Surprisingly, one of the first brain-tissue transplant experiments was performed as early as 1903 (Fine, 1986). Elizabeth Dunn transplanted small bits of tissue from brains of donor rats into brains of recipient rats. After 3 months, she removed the brains of the recipients and examined them to see whether any transplanted tissue had survived. In 10 percent of the animals, she found some nerve cells from the grafts still alive. Although limited these results were cause for great optimism, but they were so astounding that researchers largely ignored them. Yet, even if they had not been ignored, little immediate good would have come of it. At the beginning of the century, very few research techniques were available for studying the nervous system. As we will see in Chapter 5, it is the availability of techniques and methods that allows great discoveries to be made. In 1903 there really was no way to follow up on the initial experiment. Elizabeth Dunn was born 70 years too soon.

Symptoms of Parkinson's Disease Serious interest in brain-tissue transplants finally awakened during the 1970s as a remotely possible way of treating an incurable brain disorder called **Parkinson's disease** (which we will examine further in Chapter 9). Slowly over decades, Parkinson's disease erodes a person's ability to control voluntary muscles. Starting as stiffness and trembling, it progresses until the person is completely unable to walk, move the arms, manipulate objects with the hands, or even hold up the head.

The immediate cause of the motor problems is the loss of nerve cells from an area of the upper brain stem called the **substantia nigra**. Most nerve cells have long extensions called **axons**, which carry information to other nerve cells. Cells of the substantia nigra extend their axons several inches up into the brain to a structure called the **striatum**, where they make connections (synapses) with striatum cells (Figure 1.3). Because these cells connect the substantia nigra to the striatum, we call them **nigrostriatal neurons**. The neurotransmitter employed at the synapses between the axons and the cells of the striatum is the chemical dopamine. Thus, one source of stimulation for the nerve cells of the striatum is dopamine from the axons of the nigrostriatal neurons.

Symptoms of Parkinson's disease appear when there are no longer enough dopamine-secreting axons entering the striatum to stimulate the cells there. The standard therapy is to stimulate the remaining nigrostriatal cell axons to secrete more dopamine. This only treats the symptoms, however.

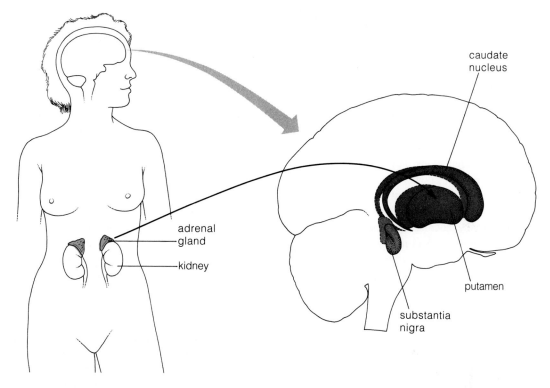

Figure 1.3 The cause of Parkinson's disease is death of neurons in a pair of brain-stem areas called the substantia nigra that normally supply the striatum (putamen and caudate nucleus) with the transmitter dopamine. One form of therapy for Parkinson's disease involves the transplantation of some of the dopamine-secreting cells of the adrenal gland into the striatum. (Adapted from Kiester, 1986)

Cells of the substantia nigra continue to die, leaving fewer and fewer axons to secrete dopamine. Thus, the therapy gradually becomes ineffective.

Transplants for Parkinson's Disease In an effort to find a real cure for Parkinson's disease, as opposed to a treatment for symptoms, some researchers have tried transplanting neural tissue into the damaged brain to replace the lost nigrostriatal neurons. In the United States, this technique must first be tested on animals before it can be applied to humans. This presents a problem because animals do not seem to contract Parkinson's disease naturally. To work with a rat that has lost substantia nigra cells, the experi-

menter first must find a way to kill some of those neurons selectively. Several **neurotoxins** (nerve poisons) have been available, but it is doubtful that any of them are as selective as the disease itself in killing nigrostriatal nerve cells. The drug **6-hydroxydopamine**, for example, kills dopamine neurons, but the brain has three major dopamine systems, only one of which consists of nigrostriatal cells. Thus, this neurotoxin does not create a perfect mimic for Parkinson's disease, but it does give us a crude substitute with which to experiment. Many transplant studies on rats have used this technique to produce the damage that tissue transplantation will try to correct (Perlow et al., 1979).

An even better solution to the problem of producing Parkinson's disease in the laboratory has recently been discovered by accident and with the help of some unwitting human "guinea pigs." In California a few years ago, legal authorities became aware that unknown chemists had been manufacturing and selling newly designed synthetic types of heroin. These "designer drugs" were not illegal because they were entirely new molecules with no legislation or regulations directed at them. Like almost any street drug, however, they contained contaminants. In this case, unlucky users not only got a heroin high but also contracted Parkinson's disease. The contaminating chemical, present in only the tiniest amounts, was **MPTP** (1-methyl-4-phenyl-1,2,3,6-tetrahydropyridine); MPTP turned out to be exactly what researchers needed. Apparently, the cell loss it causes in substantia nigra (Mytilineou & Cohen, 1984) mimics the destruction of Parkinson's disease almost perfectly, producing a syndrome in humans that can barely be discriminated from the real disease (Langston, 1985). The drug is now being used in studies with primates to produce the first real "animal model" of Parkinson's disease. The result of this discovery will almost surely be a tremendous surge of discoveries regarding Parkinson's disease in this decade. Perhaps the unfortunate heroin users who made this discovery possible will not have thrown away their lives for nothing.

Once the researcher has a group of animals with damaged substantiae nigrae, the next problem is the best way to keep transplanted tissue alive in the host brain. In the simplest method (Figure 1.4), a tiny sliver of tissue from the donor is inserted into a cut in the host brain. However, few donor cells remain alive after a few weeks (Björklund & Stenevi, 1984). One trouble is that the new tissue never receives a sufficient blood supply. This defect led to the development of a second technique (Figure 1.4b) in which a small cavity is made, the wound closed, and the brain allowed a 4-week recovery period before the transplant is made. During this time, blood vessels have grown into the walls of the cavity, and the new tissue finds a much more hospitable environment in which to survive. This technique has significantly improved survival rates (Björklund & Stenevi, 1984). Perhaps the least damaging method of transplantation begins by using a chemical called an enzyme to break down the donor tissue into its individual cells so that they can be injected directly into the host brain through a syringe (Figure 1.4c).

Problems for Transplant Therapy One enormous problem with brain-tissue transplants is to find a source of donors. A decade of research has shown very clearly that transplanted tissue from adult brains fails to thrive in the host brain. Very few, if any, neurons survive more than a few weeks. The only really successful transplants so far have used embryonic or fetal tissues (Björklund & Stenevi, 1979, 1984). If this technique were applied in humans, the donor tissue would have to come from aborted fetuses. However, in 1988 the federal government banned the National Institutes of Health from using fetal tissue in transplants (Lewin, 1988).

Because they anticipated social and legal problems with using fetal tissues, some experimenters tried transplanting tissue from the animal's own adrenal gland (Freed et al., 1981). Along with hormones such as adrenalin, these glands produce some dopamine, which is the transmitter missing in Parkinson's disease. Using adrenal tissue is a very clever idea, but it has drawbacks. Dopamine-producing nerve cells of the substantia nigra can withhold their dopamine until it is needed; adrenal cells release dopamine continuously. Also, the dopamine secreted by adrenal-cell transplants is released between the neurons and circulated widely to areas of the brain where it should not be found, whereas transplanted fetal tissue appears to establish synaptic connections that may limit release to specific zones (Freund et al., 1985). Furthermore, adrenal-tissue grafts in the brain may be guilty of breaking down the barrier between the bloodstream and the brain tissue so that nerve cells are exposed to a variety of chemicals that may be toxic to them (Rosenstein, 1987). The best donor tissues still seem to be those of aborted human fetuses (Fine, 1986).

Even if nerve cells are used in the transplant, there is no guarantee that they will function normally, however. As we pointed out earlier, one end of a substantia nigra cell is located far down in the brain stem; its axon extends several inches up into the striatum at the core of the brain. If cells are implanted

Figure 1.4 Three methods of transplanting brain tissue. (**a**) The simplest is to make a slit in the host's brain and slip in a small piece of donor tissue. The results are usually poor, with the donor tissue dying within days. (**b**) Better results can be obtained when a greater blood supply is available for the transplanted tissue. In the first stage of this technique, a cavity is made in the host brain, and the animal is allowed to recuperate for a number of days. When the time arrives for reopening the skull and inserting the donor tissue, the walls of the cavity are covered with new blood vessels that will then provide a ready supply for the transplant. (**c**) The least injurious technique involves separating the donor cells from one another with an enzyme solution and then injecting them into the correct brain area through a fine tube. (Adapted from Fine, 1986)

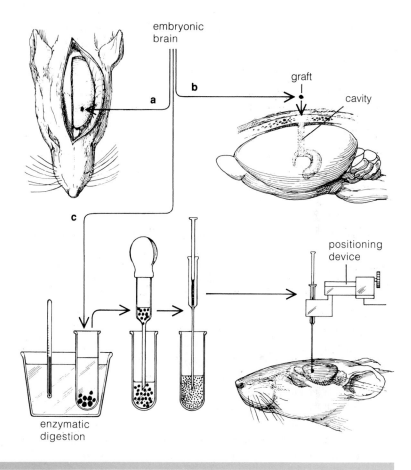

directly into the striatum, dopamine will be secreted at the proper place, but the timing of its release will be uncontrolled because correct timing depends on the connections that normal substantia nigra cells have with the rest of the brain stem. If one takes the other strategy and transplants the tissue into its normal site in the brain stem, there is no guarantee that cells can then grow the enormously long axons needed to reach the striatum. If axons do grow, will they grow randomly or in the proper direction? To make connections in the striatum, these axons would have to penetrate several inches of adult brain tissue, twisting their way between millions of other nerve cells without connecting prematurely with these

intervening neurons. When the axons have reached their destination, they would have to send out thousands of tiny synaptic shoots that would bypass all the incorrect striatum cells, while somehow mysteriously selecting only the correct ones with which to form new synaptic connections. This is a very large order! Does this mean that real, functional connections between the nerve cells of the host and those of the transplant are simply out of the question?

There is some cause for limited optimism. A number of studies have shown that the transplanted neurons can grow axons into the host brain tissue and, almost miraculously, thread their way through a maze of other neurons to find their way to neurons that normally receive their kind of transmitter (Björk-lund & Stenevi, 1984; Fine, 1986). However, no one has yet been able to get axons to regrow all the way from the brain stem to the striatum.

Researchers interested in memory rather than Parkinson's disease have also been testing tissue transplants into damaged memory-related brain structures such as the hippocampus. (We will talk about memory and the hippocampus in Chapter 15.) They have found that rats perform significantly better on learning and memory tasks following transplants (Woodruff et al., 1987). Their results suggest that a therapy to help control the terrible loss of memory and intellect characteristic of Alzheimer's disease may be possible (Chapter 17). The ability to learn avoidance of noxious stimuli also declines in old age, and transplants of neurons from the norepinephrine system have reversed this decline in older rats (Collier et al., 1988).

During the last decade, several dozen exploratory experiments demonstrated that brain-tissue transplantation was a reasonable procedure warranting systematic exploration. Now comes the hard part. The next decade will be dominated by research identifying all problems that have lain hidden so far. A few have already begun to surface. The parts of neurons called **dendrites**, on which the synaptic connections between cells are formed, do not seem to be normal in the transplanted cells (Zemanick et al., 1987). Furthermore, when striatal neurons were transplanted into the striatums of normal host rats, the recipients' brains appeared to shrink over a period of weeks. This strongly suggests that the graft resulted in the death of millions of neurons. As this was happening, the rats gradually became more and more hyperactive at night, even to the point of losing body weight (Hagenmeyer-Houser & Sanberg, 1987). We probably have many such problems to examine before we can know whether tissue transplantation will ever become a form of therapy.

Human Experiments

Unfortunately, people suffering from brain-consuming diseases cannot afford to wait for the development of rational therapies to save their failing abilities. They are willing to offer themselves as guinea pigs for half-thought-out ideas that have little chance of working but that at least offer some tiny hope. During the 1990s, we may see many hopes raised and dashed. The first attempts at therapy have already begun, some 10 years sooner than American scientists anticipated.

In 1982 two Swedish researchers, Olson and Seiger, took the drastic step of transplanting adrenal tissue into the brain of a Parkinson's disease patient. The first patient chosen was so severely affected that he was described as "truly burned out"; but within days of the surgery, the man had regained some mobility of his arms. Measurements of his cerebrospinal fluid revealed higher levels of dopamine by-products, an indicator of increased dopamine secretion. The period of improvement was short-lived, but at least further deterioration seemed to have been halted for a few years (Kiester, 1986). A second patient also showed immediate but temporary improvement followed by apparent stabilization of the symptoms.

In 1986 a Mexican team of researchers tested an improved version of the adrenal-tissue transplant that placed the tissue near rather than in the striatum. Their first 40 patients "enjoyed dramatic and continued improvement, with the abolition of tremors, speech impairments, and movement disorders" (Lewin, 1987). However, these results seem entirely too good to be real. Although the operation placed tissue only into one side of the brain, patients supposedly recovered on both sides. So far, no believable explanation has been offered.

American surgeons are now responding to the growing pressure from their patients with transplant attempts of their own, but early results have failed to live up to the hopes. Although there has been some relief of symptoms in many of the 85 American patients, not one has been cured, and drug therapy must be continued in all cases (Lewin, 1988). American researchers suggest that the improvements seen in the Mexican patients may have come as much from placebo effects and changes in drug doses as from the transplant. They suggest that we simply do not yet know enough to use transplants therapeutically (Sladek & Shoulson, 1988).

Summing Up

Now that you have a taste of the knowledge being generated by the brain sciences, it should be apparent that this chapter simply skimmed along the surface. In the next four chapters, you will discover the basic concepts of physiology, anatomy, and synapse function. With that knowledge in hand, you will be able to delve into the questions of what it means to see, hear, and smell; where and how experience is stored in the brain; how male and female brains differ; and what it means to be awake or asleep. Last, we will see how brains can be damaged and what the results are for the brain-damaged person.

■ Summary

1. Physiological psychology has its roots in the work done in the earliest laboratories of psychology during the late 19th century.

2. Philosophers disagree over how the mind relates to the brain. Some choose a dualistic approach in which the mind is seen as spiritual, the brain as physical. The two might either operate independently (parallelism) or cause changes in one another (interactional dualism). Most scientists studying the brain take a monistic viewpoint, which holds that the mind is simply the functioning of the brain.

3. Physiological psychology offers reductionistic explanations of mental and behavioral events, but the more molar explanations offered by social and cognitive psychology are equally important.

4. The science of the nervous system began with discoveries of animal electricity by Galvani in the 18th century, the neuron doctrine of Waldeyer, the postulation of nerve impulses by Bernstein, and the doctrine of specific nerve energies by Müller. Sherrington contributed the ideas of the reflex arc and synapse, and Eccles showed that most synapses were chemical.

5. To understand how your brain produces your behavior and conscious mind, you must understand something about brain anatomy, physiology, and the functioning of neurotransmitter systems.

6. Tourette syndrome provides an example of the need to understand anatomy. The basic symptom of Tourette syndrome is an involuntary muscle contraction or behavior stemming from some sort of brain dysfunction. Tics vary from muscle twitches to involuntary vocalizations including vulgar words and phrases. The drug haloperidol helps to reduce the frequency of tics.

7. The brain area that may be malfunctioning to produce Tourette syndrome is the cingulate cortex. Electrical stimulation of this area during surgery produces vocalizations resembling vocal tics. Furthermore, tics have much in common with compulsions, and one of the therapies used for compulsive behaviors is the cutting of connections between the cingulate cortex and the rest of the brain.

8. Obsessive–compulsive disorder (OCD) provides an example of the need to understand transmitter systems. Nerve cells connect with one another at points called synapses. The neuron on one side of a synapse can excite the cell on the other side by secreting a chemical called a neurotransmitter. Large collections of neurons, all of which use the same neurotransmitter, form transmitter systems. There is some evidence that in OCD the serotonin transmitter system is faulty.

9. The symptoms of OCD include obsessions (undesired, irrational, and persistent thoughts, images, and impulses) and compulsions (repetitive, stereotyped behaviors over which the person seems to have little control).

10. OCD may be related to depressive disorder, which has been linked to a malfunction in one or more of the brain's transmitter systems. Like depressed patients, OCD patients fail to respond normally to the dexamethasone test and do respond to antidepressant drugs, especially the ones that most strongly affect the serotonin systems of the brain. Furthermore, OCD symptoms can be increased experimentally by administering drugs that block serotonin's action at synapses.

11. The possibility that Parkinson's disease patients might be treated by grafting tissue into their brains

provides an example of the need to understand brain physiology. Parkinson's disease is a movement disorder characterized by tremors and difficulty in initiating muscle contractions. It results from loss of neurons in the substantia nigra that make connections between that brain area and another called the striatum. These neurons, called nigrostriatal neurons, secrete dopamine as their neurotransmitter.

12. Various transplant techniques can be tested in animals given artificial Parkinson's disease through chemical destruction of nigrostriatal neurons. In some techniques, a percentage of the transplanted neurons can survive for weeks and even form some useful connections with the cells of the striatum. Behavioral tests show that some of the disease symptoms are relieved. It has been impossible,

however, to implant nigral neurons into their proper place in the brain (at some distance from the striatum) and have them grow the lengthy fibers that would normally connect them to the cells of the striatum.

13. Because of the legal problems in applying fetal-tissue technique to humans, some researchers have tried implanting cells from the patient's own adrenal gland. These cells are not neurons, but they do make the chemical dopamine as a step in the process of creating their hormone adrenalin. This therapy seems to have provided some temporary relief to patients in Sweden and Mexico, but no lasting changes have yet been reported. Although brain-tissue transplantation as a therapy is still in its infancy, its enormously exciting possibilities are attracting more researchers every year.

Glossary

antipsychotics A class of drugs used to treat schizophrenia. (6)

axons The long, fibrous extensions of neurons that carry nerve impulses to other nerve cells. (10)

cingulate cortex A part of the brain related to emotions that may be malfunctioning in Tourette syndrome. (6)

cognitive neuroscience A discipline that uses the information-processing ideas of computer science to understand the relation between brain events, thinking, and language. (5)

compulsions Repetitive, purposeful, and intentional behaviors that are performed in response to an obsession, in accordance with certain rules, or in a stereotyped fashion. (8)

coprolalia A tic, characteristic of Tourette syndrome, that takes the form of a compulsion to utter obscenities or vulgar phrases. (6)

dendrites Long, branchlike extensions from the center of a neuron on which the synaptic connections are formed. (14)

dexamethasone A drug that turns off the glandular response to stress in normal people but not in some

patients who suffer from depression or obsessive–compulsive disorder. (9)

doctrine of specific nerve energies Müller's insight that all nerve impulses are qualitatively the same regardless of the type of information they carry (e.g., visual, auditory). (4)

dopamine A neurotransmitter employed by a system of nerve cells involved with producing patterns of movements. (6)

dualism A philosophical position that views the body as a biological mechanism that obeys physical laws and the mind as a separate, spiritual soul. (2)

haloperidol One of the antipsychotic drugs. (6)

interactional dualism Holds that the brain can cause changes in the mind and vice versa. (3)

molar Refers to the holistic view of a phenomenon, which avoids reductionism. (3)

molecular Refers to explanations that are reductionistic, i.e., that analyze wholes into their parts to see how the parts interact. (3)

monism The view that the mind and brain are one—that the mind is simply the *functioning* of the brain. (3)

MPTP A chemical contaminant of "street" drugs that brings about the death of nigrostriatal neurons. (12)

nerve cell One of the cells of which the nervous system is composed; a neuron. (4)

nerve impulse Electrical events occurring in neurons when they are active. (4)

neuron One of the cells of which the nervous system is composed; a nerve cell. (4)

neuron doctrine Proposal that the nervous system is composed of separate, individual cells called neurons, or nerve cells. (4)

neuropsychology A branch of psychology that examines the effects of brain damage on patients' behavior. (5)

neuroscience A new science that combines our knowledge of the biology, psychology, and chemistry of the nervous system. (5)

neurotoxins Nerve poisons. (11)

neurotransmitter A chemical secreted by a neuron at its synapses to excite the neurons it contacts. (6)

neurotransmitter antagonist A drug that blocks the action of a neurotransmitter at synapses. (9)

neurotransmitter system A group of nerve cells all using the same neurotransmitter and usually all having the same function. (8)

nigrostriatal neurons The cells that connect the substantia nigra with the striatum. (10)

obsessions Recurrent, persistent ideas, thoughts, images, or impulses that the person does not wish to experience. (8)

obsessive–compulsive disorder See *compulsions* and *obsessions.*

Parkinson's disease An incurable brain disorder that slowly erodes a person's ability to control the voluntary muscles. (10)

reductionism A strategy for developing explanations of phenomena by analyzing them into components at a more molecular level. (3)

reflex arc A circuit composed of neurons that connects a receptor organ with muscles to produce an automatic response to a stimulus. (4)

serotonin A sleep-related neurotransmitter that may also be involved in obsessive–compulsive disorder. (8)

6-hydroxydopamine A neurotoxin that can kill cells using dopamine as a neurotransmitter. (11)

striatum Part of the brain that normally receives impulses from the substantia nigra; the striatum malfunctions in patients with Parkinson's disease. (10)

substantia nigra An area of the upper brain stem that is important to muscle control. This area is damaged in patients with Parkinson's disease. (10)

synapse The point at which one neuron contacts and communicates with another. (4)

tic An involuntary muscle contraction or behavior. (5)

Tourette syndrome A collection of brain-damage symptoms, the most outstanding of which is tics. (5)

The Cells of the Nervous System

Physiological psychology, as a science, is driven by an intense human need to understand the origins of mind and behavior. What are emotions, motives, memories? Why do we sleep, experience pain, see color? How can people lose the capacity to speak, move, or comprehend what they see? What has gone wrong in those suffering from depression or schizophrenia? As we search for the answers to those questions by examining the function of the brain, we discover repeatedly that much of the understanding can be found only within the workings of that basic unit of life, the cell.

Animals and plants are made up of various **organs**, each designed to perform some vital service to the whole animal. Your heart, lungs, muscles, blood vessels, and brain are all examples of organs. Because the complete animal is essentially a collection of organs, it is called an **organism**. If we analyze the organs into the building blocks from which they are formed, we find that the basic unit is the **cell**. Cells with similar functions combine into groups called **tissues**, and several types of tissue organized to do a particular job make up an organ. To understand how an organ works then, one must examine its cells.

■ Cell Structures and Processes

Your body contains hundreds of different types of cells with different shapes and functions. Cells are as different in their appearances and behaviors as different breeds of dogs, yet all human cells do have certain basic features and tasks in common. So we begin our examination of cells by looking at the characteristics of a hypothetical, generalized cell from which we can glean the most general principles of cellular organization.

The Parts of a Cell

The generalized cell in Figure 2.1 can be thought of as possessing three divisions: bilayer membrane,

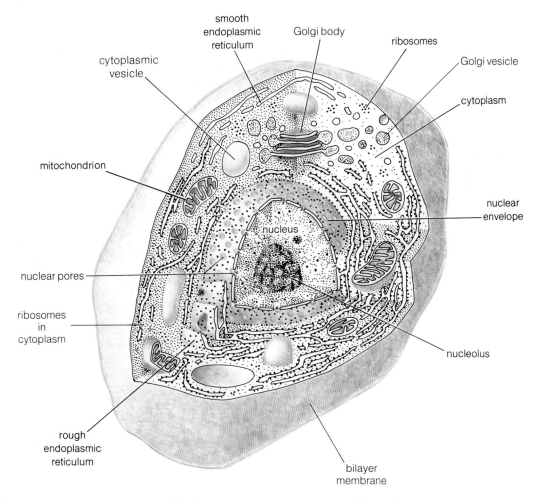

cytoplasmic vesicle

smooth endoplasmic reticulum

Golgi body

ribosomes

Golgi vesicle

cytoplasm

mitochondrion

nuclear envelope

nucleus

nuclear pores

ribosomes in cytoplasm

nucleolus

rough endoplasmic reticulum

bilayer membrane

Figure 2.1 A generalized cell showing features common to most cells, including those of the nervous system. (Adapted from Wolfe, 1983)

nucleus, and cytoplasm. Each consists of several parts, which we examine in some detail.

The Membrane Because the inside of a cell is filled with fluid, you might expect it to have a thick, tough, protective "skin." Amazingly, the **cell membrane** is only two molecules thick, with little or no structural rigidity. Essentially, it is two layers of **phospholipid**

(FOSS-foe-LIP-id) molecules oriented in opposite directions (Figure 2.2). The phospho "head" end of each molecule is attracted to water, whereas the lipid "tail" end is attracted to fats (lipids) and repellent to water. With the lipid "tails" of the molecules turned inward toward each other, the membrane becomes a chemical barrier to water and yet attracts to its surface the needed chemicals floating in the water

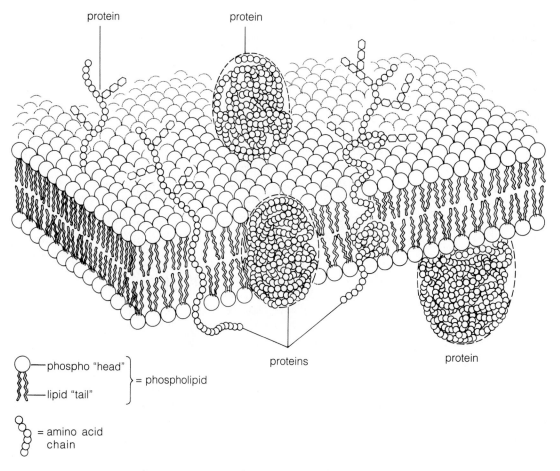

protein   protein

phospho "head"
lipid "tail"   } = phospholipid

= amino acid chain

Figure 2.2 Model of cell membrane as a phospholipid bilayer with proteins embedded. In the outer layer, the phospho "heads" are turned toward the extracellular fluid that surrounds the cell. In the inner layer, the heads are turned inward toward the intracellular fluid. The heads have an affinity for the water of the intra- or extracellular fluid, whereas the lipid "tails" are attracted to fats and repel water. This creates a membrane that is a watertight barrier. The embedded proteins are involved in tasks such as enabling needed molecules to enter the cell. (Adapted from Fowler, 1984)

within or between the cells. This is a part of the arrangement that allows the cell to pick and choose which waterborne molecules will be allowed to enter or exit the cell.

The most astounding thing about this lipid bilayer membrane, which surrounds the contents of every cell in your body, is that it is a fluid (Becker, 1986).

In the **fluid bilayer membrane**, the phospholipid molecules slip and slide against each other, remaining loosely together but not rigidly attached. In fact, the whole membrane has the consistency of a film of light oil (Becker, 1986). Interestingly, one of the lipids involved is cholesterol, the fat that many people try to eliminate from their diets; the more cholesterol there is in the membrane, the more viscous and stable the film becomes.

Piercing the membrane at various points are large protein molecules, some with hollow tubular shapes that form channels connecting the intracellular fluid with the extracellular environment. These proteins enable many vital cell functions to occur, such as the nerve impulse of the neuron. Protein molecules tend to float through the membrane more or less like dumplings in gravy unless they are anchored to one spot by chemical attractions to other molecules. We will return to these proteins in later chapters when we discuss conduction in the axon and the synaptic changes that produce memory.

The Nucleus The **nucleus** (NEW-klee-us) of a cell is analogous to the brain of an organism; it is the control center, issuing orders about all the various cellular functions. During the course of a person's physical development from embryo to adult, the nuclei of cells control what proteins will be manufactured by each cell. The type of protein determines the structure of the cell and what its function will be. In the adult animal, the nucleus continues to exert this same type of control over what proteins will be manufactured to maintain the cell in a healthy condition.

Control is exerted by allowing particular chemical reactions to proceed and disallowing others. The instructions for what reactions to allow are coded into immensely long molecules of the chemical **deoxyribonucleic acid** (dee-OX-ee-RYE-bo-new-KLEE-ik), a form of nucleic acid; this **DNA** is stored in a web-work of strands within the nucleus called **chromatin** (KROME-uh-tin). When a human cell is about to replicate itself by splitting into two daughter cells, the chromatin condenses into 23 pairs of DNA strands called **chromosomes** (KROME-uh-somes). (However, chromosomes would not normally be observed in the neurons of mature adults because replication of neurons ceases early in infancy.) DNA molecules consist of long strings of smaller units called **genes**, and each gene contains the plans for manufacturing a particular type of protein.

To initiate the manufacture of a needed protein, DNA must create another kind of molecule, **ribonucleic acid (RNA)**, which can carry the plans for

the protein molecule out of the nucleus. DNA itself never leaves its station inside the nucleus. RNA first goes to the **nucleolus** (new-KLEE-uh-lus), a special area of the nucleus in which the RNA is combined with proteins to form tiny structures called **ribosomes** (RYE-buh-somes). (See Figure 2.1 for a picture of the nucleolus.) Ribosomes leave the nucleus through the many pores that puncture the membrane, separating it from the cytoplasm. Protein formation is vital to our understanding of learning, memory, and hormone function; thus, we will trace the process step by step. But first you will need to be familiar with several other features of cells.

The Cytoplasm Surrounding the nucleus and enclosed by the cell membrane is a fluid, the **cytoplasm** (SITE-oh-plaz-um), which is made thick by the various amino acids, proteins, and other chemicals suspended or dissolved in it. Scattered throughout this mixture, like vegetable chunks in a bowl of soup, are a variety of inclusions such as endoplasmic reticulum, mitochondria, filaments, and microtubules, some of which are pictured in Figure 2.1. Mitochondria and endoplasmic reticulum can be thought of as microscopic organs of the cell and so are called **organelles**.

At the physiological level, life is a dance of protein molecules. Like sidewalk crowds in a busy city, clusters of protein molecules are constantly moving through the cytoplasm from one place to another. Wear and tear throughout the cell makes continual replacement of parts necessary, and protein molecules are the construction materials. Other proteins are specialized for speeding the construction of chemicals needed by the cell and float around combining smaller molecules into larger ones. All this hustle and bustle of proteins begins at their point of manufacture in the **endoplasmic reticulum** (END-oh-PLAZ-mick reh-TICK-you-lum). The word *reticulum* means a loose network, and *endoplasmic* indicates that this network is within (*endo*) the cytoplasm (*plasmic*). Endoplasmic reticulum comes in two varieties—rough and smooth—but only the former is important to us. The **rough ER** (Figure 2.3) is the site of protein formation. It looks rough through the microscope because it is heavily dotted with ribosomes. The reticulum is the destination of the ribo-

smooth ER

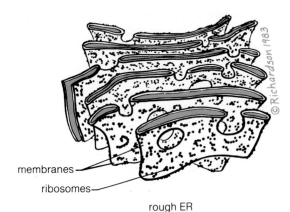

membranes
ribosomes

rough ER

Figure 2.3 The endoplasmic reticulum. Rough ER consists of many folds of membranes dotted with ribosomes, which give it a rough appearance in electron micrographs. The rough ER is the site of protein assembly in the cell. (From Fowler, 1984)

somes that emerge from the nucleus of the cell with their cargo of RNA specifications for the construction of new molecules.

Another cell organelle is the **Golgi complex** (GOAL-jee), which performs different functions in different cells. Of greatest interest to us is the type found in glandular cells. The Golgi complex (Figure 2.4) is a network (reticulum) of pancake-flat, hollow

storage vessels, formed from lipid bilayer membrane, which grows continually, shedding portions of itself in the form of little spheres called **secretion vesicles**. Each vesicle is just a "skin" of bilayer membrane enclosing a tiny packet of chemicals (e.g., hormone molecules) that will be secreted by the glandular cell.

Glance back at Figure 2.1 and locate the mitochondria (pictured at a higher magnification in Figure 2.5). **Mitochondria** (MITE-oh-KAHN-dree-yuh) are the energy factories of the cell. The more of these you see in any part of the cell, the higher the energy demand there.

A mitochondrion has a double membrane around it and contains a few strands of its own, unique DNA. It even has a few ribosomes. In fact, it has the appearance of a primitive cell. These features have led to the hypothesis that mitochondria were originally a separate form of microbial life that gradually evolved into a symbiotic existence with some of our ancestors when they were still just single-celled creatures living in the seas. In a symbiotic relation (*bio* = life; *sym* = together), each partner contributes to the welfare of the other. The symbiosis in this case gave the mitochondrion a source of free food in return for sharing some of its energy. It is strange to think that humans, in a certain sense, may have cells that contain another animal.

The membrane of a cell, being only two molecules thick, has no structural rigidity and little strength. It has evolved to be a barrier to molecules, holding in those that the cell needs and excluding those not required. Yet, cells have shapes, and they hold these shapes despite the lack of a solid shell. What little rigidity they possess is contributed by the **cytoskeleton** (SIGH-toe-SKEL-leh-ton), a network of proteins running through the cytoplasm like the system of braces and guy wires holding up a circus tent (Figure 2.6). If a cell is chemically treated to dissolve its cytoskeleton, it immediately collapses into a perfect sphere like a drop of water (Porter et al., 1979). Two structural elements make up the cytoskeleton: **filaments**, which are strands of proteins, and **microtubules**, which constitute the "plumbing and pipes" of the cell (Porter et al., 1979). Whenever molecules must be transported over relatively long distances

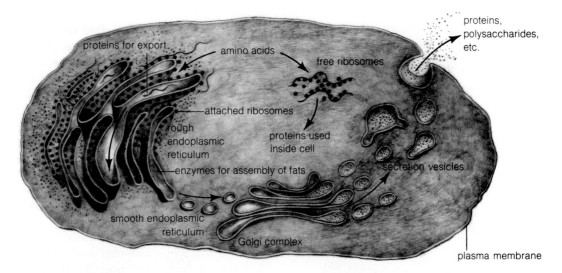

Figure 2.4 The Golgi complex. This cytoplasmic organelle consists of membranes folded into sacs that collect proteins or hormones. In an endocrine gland cell, portions of the Golgi bodies break away continually to form "packages" of hormones called secretion vesicles. These granules migrate to the cell membrane where they release the hormone molecules into adjacent blood vessels. (Adapted from Fowler, 1984)

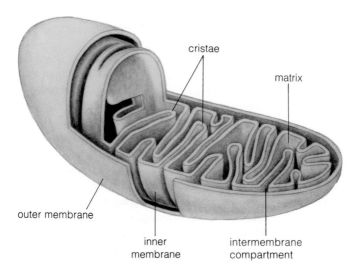

Figure 2.5 A mitochondrion. This cytoplasmic organelle is the place where oxygen and glucose (blood sugar) are converted into energy stored in the form of ATP molecules. (From Wolfe, 1983)

Figure 2.6 A cross section of a cell showing the microtubules of the cytoskeleton within the cytoplasm. (Adapted from Starr & Taggart, 1987)

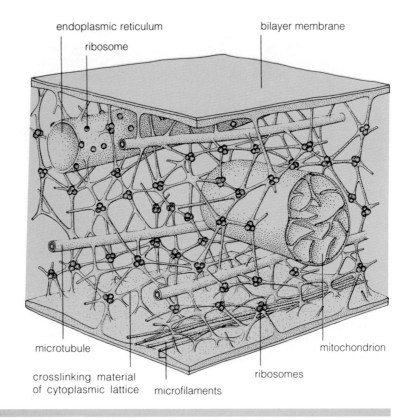

endoplasmic reticulum

ribosome

bilayer membrane

microtubule

crosslinking material of cytoplasmic lattice

microfilaments

ribosomes

mitochondrion

within a cell (e.g., down the length of a nerve cell axon), they are piped through the microtubules.

Cell Processes

As we noted earlier, many interesting features of brain function, such as the creation of memories and the control of hunger and body weight, can be thoroughly understood only at the molecular event level within cells. This makes it imperative that we understand at least the basic rudiments of metabolism. **Metabolism** is the collection of chemical reactions that make up our physiological life processes. **Anabolism** is the series of constructive reactions that build chemicals needed by the body; **catabolism** is the collection of destructive reactions that destroy chemicals in order to extract energy.

Energy Anabolism All cell processes are chemical reactions in which one chemical (i.e., type of molecule) is changed into another, either releasing or absorbing energy in the process. One of the most basic anabolic sequences our bodies possess is a chain of reactions using oxygen and **glucose** (blood sugar) to create the chemical **adenosine triphosphate** (ah-DEEN-uh-sin try-FOSS-fate), usually known by its abbreviation **ATP**. The energy stored in glucose is transferred to the ATP in the form of chemical bonds between the atoms of the molecule. Whenever the cell needs energy to trigger a set of chemical reactions, energy is readily available in ATP molecules floating in the cytoplasm. So, one reason that you eat and breathe is to make ATP. Without it your life processes very quickly come to a halt. For good reason, ATP has often been thought of as "money" or "energy currency" of the cell.

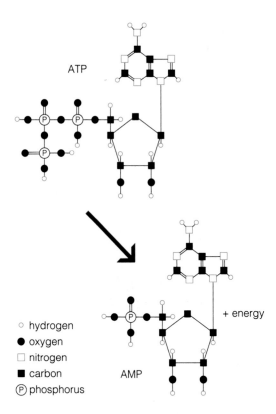

ATP

○ hydrogen
● oxygen
□ nitrogen
■ carbon
ⓟ phosphorus

AMP

+ energy

Figure 2.7 Adenosine triphosphate (ATP), with its three phosphate groups (phosphorus plus oxygen). Energy is required to attach the phosphates, and this energy can later be released to power other chemical reactions in the cell. ATP gives away the energy stored in its molecular bonds by giving up one or more of its phosphate groups. In this diagram, it has lost two phosphates to become adenosine monophosphate (AMP).

Most cells of the body have the ability to "open a savings account" for their energy supply by storing glucose in a slightly altered form called **glycogen**, but nerve cells lack this ability and quickly develop a glucose shortage if their blood supply is cut off. Without a steady supply of glucose and oxygen, they run low on ATP and stop functioning. This is why a person loses consciousness within seconds when the blood supply is interrupted. Anabolic metabolism can continue to produce very small amounts of ATP from glucose even in the absence of oxygen, but the

brain uses large quantities of ATP. Without a continuing supply of glucose and oxygen, metabolism comes to a halt (Shepherd, 1983).

The ATP model in Figure 2.7 shows why the molecule has triphosphate in its name. A phosphate group consists of one atom of phosphorus combined with three of oxygen, and ATP has three phosphate groups attached to a molecular fragment called adenosine. In anabolic metabolism, ATP is built up by attaching two phosphate groups to a molecule of AMP (adenosine monophosphate) or one phosphate to a molecule of ADP (adenosine diphosphate). In catabolic metabolism, in which the cell "spends" this energy, ATP gives up one or two of the phosphates to some other molecule. The energy from the bonds holding the phosphate can then be used to power cell functions.

Most ATP molecules are created within the mitochondria on the multiple folds of membranes called **cristae** (KRIS-tee) (see Figure 2.5). Mitochondria command the lion's share of ATP production because they contain the chemicals necessary for the job. Most chemical reactions in the body proceed automatically if you bring the ingredients together at body temperature, but the rate at which the reactions occur is so slow as to be biologically useless. Speeding the reactions enough to produce useful amounts of a chemical like ATP requires specialized protein molecules called **enzymes**. Some enzymes make it easier for two molecules to join to create a larger one; others help molecules split into smaller chemicals. The secret of the mitochondria's success at manufacturing ATP lies in having all the needed enzymes. In Chapters 14 and 16, we will see how ATP plays a role in the communication between nerve cells.

Protein Anabolism Proteins are the "bricks" out of which your body is built. Approximately three-quarters of the dry weight of your body consists of proteins (Blout, 1967). Proteins come in an astounding variety of coiled, crinkled, and folded shapes, but if you uncoil them you find that all are built of the same components. Each protein consists of a long string of smaller units called **amino acids**. There are only 20 common amino acids (Figure 2.8), but they

Amino Acids

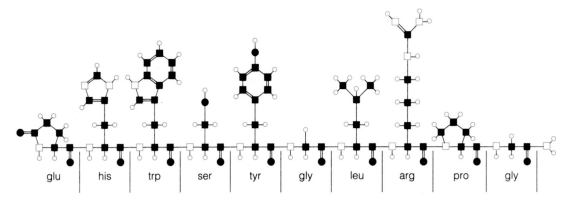

○ hydrogen
● oxygen
□ nitrogen
■ carbon

ala	alanine	gly	glycine	pro	proline
arg	arginine	his	histidine	ser	serine
asn	asparagine	ile	isoleucine	thr	threonine
asp	aspartic acid	leu	leucine	trp	tryptophan
cys	cysteine	lys	lysine	tyr	tyrosine
glu	glutamic acid	met	methionine	val	valine
gln	glutamine	phe	phenylalanine		

glu · his · trp · ser · tyr · gly · leu · arg · pro · gly

Figure 2.8 The structural formula for luteinizing hormone–releasing factor. This chemical is secreted by a part of the brain that controls endocrine glands. It consists of a string of amino acids assembled on a ribosome. Listed above the molecule are the 20 amino acids. Notice that each acid can be used more than once in a protein molecule. In this molecule, for example, glycine appears at both the sixth and the tenth positions.

can be strung together into thousands upon thousands of different protein combinations, just as the 26 letters of our alphabet can be used to create more than 200,000 words.

Proteins are put together by the cell to form components of the organelles and many other features of the cytoplasm, like the microtubules and filaments. Different proteins have different shapes; when they are combined, the shape and function of the resulting organelle largely depends on what proteins have been used. Thus, a nerve cell in your brain produces certain proteins, whereas a liver cell produces different ones. Because the type of protein produced determines the structure and function of the cell, the complete set of plans for constructing the human body can be reduced to a list of required proteins. Indeed, DNA is exactly such a list, but it is also a mechanism for executing the plans.

DNA has the surprising ability to make copies of itself, an ability that is the basis of life. From what we know about biochemistry and the geology of the earth several billion years ago, life must have begun with a chance chemical reaction that produced the first self-replicating molecule. There was nothing new about the elements that went into this hypothetical ancestral molecule, just the same carbon, oxygen, nitrogen, and hydrogen that made up hundreds of already existing chemical compounds floating in lifeless seas. It was the structure, the pattern of atoms, that was unique. Like many chemicals, this molecule would react with other molecules that bumped into it, providing they fit into its structure.

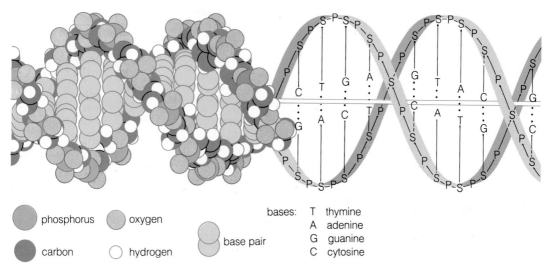

phosphorus   oxygen

carbon   hydrogen

base pair

bases: T thymine
        A adenine
        G guanine
        C cytosine

Figure 2.9 A short section of a DNA molecule. The "solid" portion of the model at the left portrays the atoms as balls. S = sugar and P = phosphate. A DNA molecule is composed of two ribbons of sugar phosphate molecules, twined around each other to form a double helix. Connecting the two strands like rungs of a ladder are four types of bases (thymine, guanine, cytosine, and adenine). It is the bases that form the codons of the genes. (From Fowler, 1984)

Gradually acquiring smaller fragments from the chemical "soup" around it and "pasting" them on where they fit, the molecule grew. The peculiarity of this molecule's structure was that it could assemble these fragments into a precise, mirror-image copy of the original molecule. Then, the copy could split off from the original, leaving both itself and the original free to collect more molecular fragments and turn those into still more copies. From this tiny chemical event would arise all of life. Essentially, every animal and plant on earth is simply a set of chemical structures that can reproduce itself.

The first molecule to twin itself may have been simpler than DNA, our modern molecule of life. As a human, you represent the eventual result of millions of years of that evolutionary process, and within each cell you carry a tiny bit of the primeval ocean from which life arose. The fluids of your cytoplasm possess a chemistry nearly that of seawater.

In structure DNA is reminiscent of a long twisting ladder. The sides are twin strands of **sugar phosphate** groups, and the rungs are formed by pairs of four **bases**—adenine, cytosine, thymine, and guanine (Figure 2.9). Now think of the ladder being split down the middle, lengthwise. Each half consists of a sugar phosphate backbone with attached bases. The sequence of bases along the backbone make up the genetic code. Normally, the two backbones are joined together into a full ladder because each base has a strong affinity for one of the others and can link to it. The adenine of one half links to the thymine of the other, and guanine links only to cytosine (Figure 2.10). Each backbone is twisted into a spiral shape called a helix; when the two helixes are joined by their bases, a double helix is formed.

When a DNA molecule replicates, it first splits lengthwise between the pairs of bases. Each half then is free to attract a new base molecule to match each base on its string. Adenine always reacts with thymine and guanine with cytosine (Figure 2.10). Each new

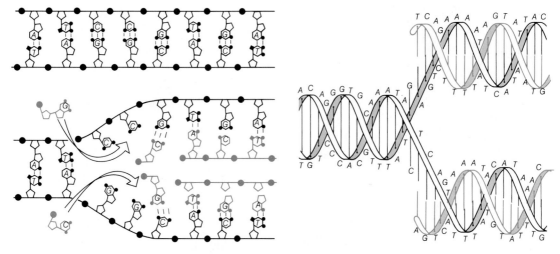

Figure 2.10 DNA replication. At left, the molecule has been straightened out and flattened to show the bonding between the base pairs. These bonds are broken when the molecule unzips into two complementary strands. To replicate itself, each strand gradually collects new base molecules from the surrounding fluid until two complete double helixes have been formed. Each new base molecule brings its own sugar phosphate molecule with it. (From Jensen et al., 1979)

base that attaches to the DNA half-molecule brings along a sugar phosphate group to act as its part of the backbone for the new half being constructed. As the original double helix unwinds, each half grows a replacement "twin." When the original molecule has unzipped end to end, two DNA molecules exist where before there was only one (Figure 2.10).

DNA replication occurs when a cell is about to split into two daughter cells and assures that each new cell will have a full copy of all the genes possessed by the parent. The chromatin is normally spread out through the protoplasm of the nucleus, but during replication it gathers together into the pairs of well-defined rodlike structures we call chromosomes. All normal human cells (except for ova and sperm) have 23 pairs of chromosomes. Taken together, these 23 pairs contain roughly 100,000 genes. A typical gene is a segment of about 10,000 base pairs on one DNA molecule, and the total of all of a person's DNA (with genes plus nongene base

pairs) contains about 3 billion base pairs (White & Lalouel, 1988).

A DNA molecule can create either a duplicate of itself or the near duplicate RNA. In RNA the thymine is replaced by uracil; otherwise the molecule is the same as a single strand of its parent DNA. Because the creation of RNA can be thought of as copying information from one recording to another, the process is called **transcription**. The information being transcribed is the set of instructions for what amino acids should be assembled into proteins. In the DNA molecule, a particular sequence of three consecutive bases, called a triplet, is required to specify each amino acid. Glycine, for example, is specified by the sequence guanine-guanine-guanine, whereas the code for histidine is cytosine-adenine-thymine. In the RNA molecule, these triplets are called **codons**.

An RNA molecule, then, can be thought of as a long chain of codons. The pattern contained in this sequence of codons determines what protein will

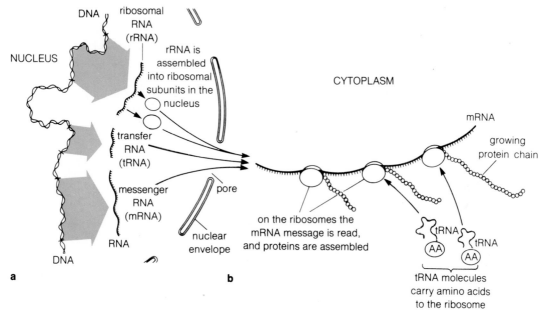

Figure 2.11 Protein manufacture. (**a**) In the transcription process, RNA molecules are assembled along a single strand of DNA. Ribosomal RNA is combined with proteins to create ribosomes, which leave the nucleus with mRNA and tRNA. Their destination is the rough ER where the second step, translation, occurs. (**b**) In translation, free-floating amino acids are captured by molecules of tRNA and brought to the appropriate codon site on the mRNA. There the ribosome locks each together with its neighboring amino acid, thus extending the growing chain of acids that makes up the protein molecule. (From Fowler, 1984)

be created by any particular stretch of RNA. Genes, the units of heredity, are sequences of codons that specify a protein or series of proteins.

To make a protein, DNA must first create a stretch of RNA with the correct codon sequence. This molecule is called **messenger RNA (mRNA)** because it carries the code out of the nucleus to the rough ER, where the assembly of amino acids takes place (Figure 2.11). The messenger RNA attaches to a ribosome and then settles on the rough ER to serve as an assembly template. Amino acids are brought to the ribosome by tiny scraps of nucleic acid called **transfer RNA (tRNA)**, specialized for this task. Each molecule of tRNA has one end shaped to react only with one particular amino acid, which it encounters

as it floats randomly through the cytoplasm. The other end of the tRNA molecule is specialized for reacting with the codon that matches the amino acid being transferred (Figure 2.11). After picking up its amino acid, tRNA floats until it encounters a ribosome–mRNA combination having the correct codon. The tRNA then links to the mRNA, and the amino acid reacts with the adjoining amino acid. When all the codon "slots" on the mRNA have been filled, a chain of amino acids has been created. This process of converting the genetic code into amino acid chains is called **translation**. The structural information in the gene (the codon sequence) has been translated from one form to another.

The completed chain of amino acids breaks off

from the ribosome, leaving the mRNA molecules behind. It then may join other such amino acid strands to become even longer. Finally, crumpling into a structure of many loops and folds, the amino acid becomes a complete protein molecule. The folds and loops are not random; they are determined by the sequence of amino acids and are critical to the functioning of the protein molecule. Its shape determines whether it can serve, for example, as an enzyme, a structural protein, or a messenger from one cell to another. Sometimes, when atoms or electrons are added to or removed from a protein, the shape of the molecule changes. This new shape often has different chemical properties, which the body takes advantage of. For example, there are protein molecules embedded in the membrane of a neuron that can briefly change their shape to create channels through which particles can pass in and out of the cell. This channel property allows the neuron to generate its nerve impulses.

Nervous System Tissue

Very little DNA in any cell actually gets used. A nerve cell, for example, does not need the same set of proteins required by a liver cell, so the "liver" por-

tions of the genetic code are not read out into the mRNA of a neuron. Cells are specialized for particular functions and give up the ability to perform other functions that lie latent within their DNA.

A group of cells all specialized for the same function is called a tissue. The cells of a tissue are linked together by junctions of various sorts that allow them to cling to one another and to communicate by exchanging chemicals. Over most of their surfaces, the membranes of neighboring cells do not quite touch one another. In between cells runs a tiny (20-μm), fluid-filled crack known as the **intercellular space.**

The two most important cell types in the tissue of the nervous system are neurons and glial cells.

Neurons

Your perception of this page; your understanding of the words printed on it; your fantasies during lapses of attention; your anticipations of tests, grades, degrees, vocations; and all your future hopes and present wishes are literally activity patterns in large collections of neurons within your brain. In the last analysis, your entire conscious mind and personality exist only in those patterns. Once their electrical activity ceases, so does your mind and self. Mechanical respirators can substitute for the normal con-

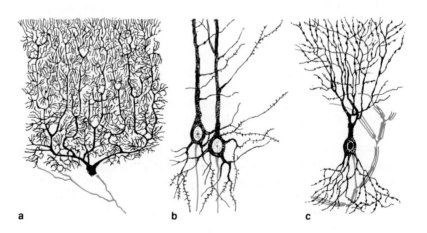

Figure 2.12 Some types of neurons from different parts of the nervous system, showing how different functions call for different shapes. (From Starr & Taggart, 1987)

a   b   c

tractions of the diaphragm in breathing, and the heart can be made to beat with a careful patterning of electrical stimulation, but without neural activity in the brain, the body lives on like an empty house. The mechanical systems are functioning, but the inhabitant has left.

Neurons (or **nerve cells**) come in numerous sizes and shapes (Figure 2.12), but many of the different types share common features. The neuron in Figure 2.13 possesses a **cell body** (or **soma**), which houses the cell nucleus with its allotment of DNA. Extending in all directions from the soma are branchlike processes involved in making connections with other nerve cells. Most of these extensions are **dendrites**, relatively short processes (less than 1 mm) designed as receiving areas for messages from other neurons. Many neurons also have one extremely long process called an **axon**, which carries information from the cell into other areas of the nervous system.

At its far end, the axon divides repeatedly, forming a treelike structure of tiny branches called **telodendria** (*telo* = far; *dendron* = tree) (Figures 2.13 and 2.14). Each telodendron (TELL-uh-DEN-dron) ends in a swelling known as a **terminal**, which is a point of contact between cells. Such junctions between two neurons are known as **synapses**. Because neurons tend to have hundreds of telodendria and terminals, they usually form hundreds of synapses on other cells. Some nerve cells contact as many as 1,000 other neurons, and many neurons receive terminals of other neurons in profusion all over their somas as well as dendrites. With the thousands of dendritic branches and telodendria all tangled together, neural tissue often resembles a thicket of cell fibers in which the neuron somas are embedded like raisins in a fruitcake. The tangle of fibers is called the **neuropil**.

The dimensions of neurons are astounding. Many axons seem enormously long to be growing out of somas the size of pinpoints. For example, motor neurons that contract the muscles of your foot have their invisibly small cell bodies in the spinal cord about one third of the way up your back; this means that their axons, which reach all the way down your leg, are well over 3 feet in length. The tiny speck of a soma, which controls the chemistry of the entire cell, must manufacture all molecules needed by that

whole length of axon and then send them floating slowly down to their distant destinations. Not all neurons have lengthy axons, however. So far we have been discussing **Golgi type I** neurons, which must have long axons because they provide the connections between areas within the central nervous system or between cord and muscle. **Golgi type II** cells (also called **interneurons**) have axons that are usually less than 1 mm long and are meant for connecting the neurons *within* a particular limited area of the brain or spinal cord. One reason why one part of the brain performs one function while another does something quite different is that each part has its own unique pattern of connections between Golgi II neurons.

Notice that the axon in Figure 2.13 is encased in a series of wrappings that are not a part of the neuron. This casing is created by a type of glial cell.

Glial Cells

It has been estimated that the brain contains over 10 billion neurons, yet this enormous collection of densely packed nerve cells represents only around one half of the cells that make up your brain. The nonneural cells in the nervous system are called **neuroglia** (ner-RAHG-lee-uh), or simply **glia** (GLEE-uh) after the Latin word for glue because it was originally thought that they served solely to "stick the neurons together" and create a tissue with some amount of structural strength. Some of the glial cells do indeed serve this function, but even with their help, nerve tissue is still very soft and rather sloppy. In fact, surgical removal of brain tissue is usually accomplished with a very fine-tipped, glass tube attached to a suction hose rather than with a scalpel.

There are five types of glial cells: Schwann cells, astrocytes, ependymal cells, microglia, and oligodendroglia. Schwann cells exist only in the nerves of the peripheral nervous system; the last four are found in the brain and spinal cord.

Neuroglia of the Peripheral Nervous System The peripheral nervous system consists of all nerves leaving and entering the brain and spinal cord. The nerves consist of bundles of neuron axons. Glial cells called **Schwann cells** support these axons in

Figure 2.13 A common type of nerve cell. A number of processes branch out from the soma (cell body). One of these processes is the axon; the rest are dendrites. The axon is too long to be pictured in its entirety; only its beginning and end are shown. It is covered with a myelin sheath composed of a chain of glial cells. At its end, the axon branches into telodendria, which end in terminals. The terminals occur where the telodendria contact the dendrites or soma of another neuron. Notice that another neuron, out of the picture at the top, sends its telodendria to make contact with the cell in view. The enlarged picture of a terminal at the right shows what a synapse looks like. The vesicles hold a chemical that is released into the synaptic gap to stimulate the postsynaptic neuron.

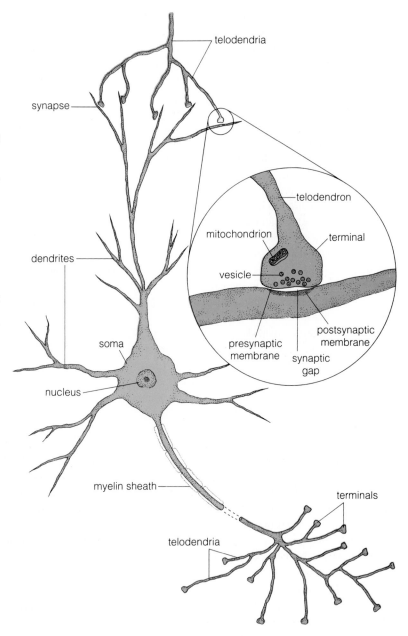

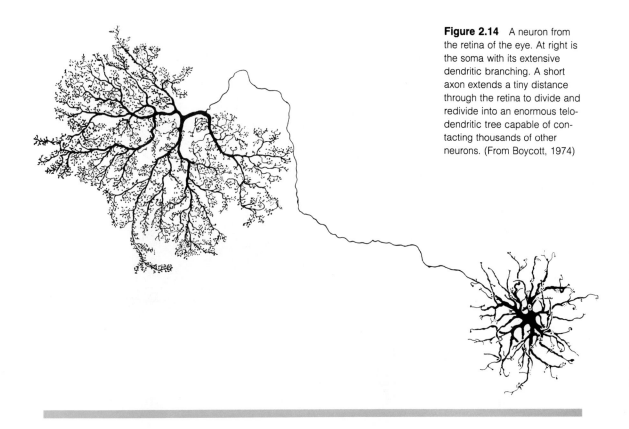

Figure 2.14 A neuron from the retina of the eye. At right is the soma with its extensive dendritic branching. A short axon extends a tiny distance through the retina to divide and redivide into an enormous telo-dendritic tree capable of contacting thousands of other neurons. (From Boycott, 1974)

a number of important ways, including the provision of each axon with a wrapping called a **myelin sheath** (see Figure 2.15).

Schwann cells grow around axons as the nervous system develops before birth, wrapping themselves as many as 10 times around an axon so tightly that cytoplasm is squeezed out and only their cell membranes and nuclei remain (Figure 2.15). Early in the history of neuroanatomy, this many-layered axon wrapping was identified and named **myelin**, as though it were a separate tissue. It was only with improved microscopy that myelin was revealed to be the membranes of the Schwann cell. A chief lipid in the Schwann cell membrane is cholesterol, the fat that gives the myelin sheath a white appearance. The sheath provides a type of electrical insulation for the axon that is important for the conduction of its nerve impulses. An axon together with its sheath of Schwann cells is called a **nerve fiber**. The myelin

sheath around a fiber is not continuous from one end of the axon to the other; rather, it is formed by many individual Schwann cells. In Chapter 3, we will see how Schwann cells enable a damaged axon to regenerate correctly.

Neuroglia of the Brain and Spinal Cord Many axons within the brain and cord also have myelin sheaths, although the glial cells that form the coverings are a different type. The four types of brain glia are pictured in Figure 2.16.

Astrocytes (ASS-tro-sites) are named for their starlike shape (astro = star). Their many branches spread out to form an intertwining mesh that isolates the neurons from one another as well as providing the structural support mentioned earlier. They are sometimes called the "skeletal" neuroglia for their structural role (Bodian, 1967).

Astrocytes seem to afford some protection from

Figure 2.15 (**a–c**) A cross section of a nerve fiber showing myelination of a peripheral nerve axon during fetal and infantile development. The glial Schwann cell slowly grows around the axon, wrapping it in a sheath composed mainly of myelin. (**d**) Photomicrograph of myelinated axon (courtesy of Art Nitz). (From Fowler, 1984)

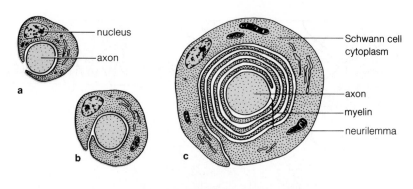

nucleus

axon

a

b

Schwann cell cytoplasm

axon

myelin

neurilemma

c

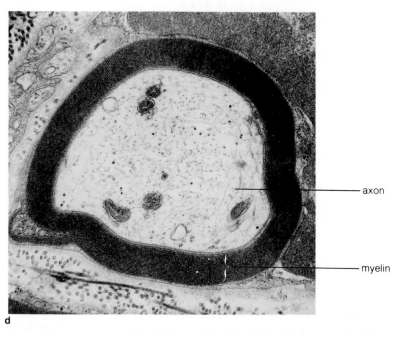

axon

myelin

d

---

anoxia (an-NOX-ee-uh), the lack of oxygen that can lead to neuron death within minutes. Further, they store glycogen, which presumably is converted to glucose and passed along to nerve cells that run short. Finally, astrocytes take up excess potassium released by active neurons that might incorrectly trigger activity in neighboring nerve cells (Vibulsreth et al., 1987). Without astrocytes to help maintain a favorable chemical environment, we might suffer far greater neuronal loss or temporary malfunction than is now typical.

Microglia (my-KRAHG-lee-uh) are very small cells that apparently lie dormant until damage occurs in the nervous system. Then, they transform themselves into much larger cells that move through the brain searching for and cleaning up the debris left by dead neurons and glia. The clean-up is accomplished by **phagocytosis** (FAG-uh-sigh-TOE-sis), a mechanism in which the microglial cell (now called a phagocyte) engulfs and digests bits of dead material (*phag* = to eat).

Oligodendroglia (AH-lig-go-den-DRAHG-lee-uh)

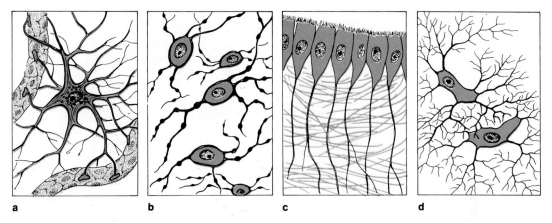

Figure 2.16 Various forms of glial cells. (**a**) Astrocytes. (**b**) Oligodendrocytes. (**c**) Ependymal cells. (**d**) Microglia. (From Fowler, 1984)

probably help the astrocytes maintain chemical balance in the environment of the nerve cells, but they also have a unique function. **Oligodendrocytes** (AH-lig-go-DEN-drah-sites), as the single cells are called, provide myelin sheaths for axons within the brain and spinal cord. The processes extending from the soma of the oligodendrocyte in Figure 2.17 have grown into sheaths for three axons.

Brain neurons, then, are among the most pampered cells in the body. They have oligodendrocytes to insulate their axons, astrocytes for physical–chemical support, and microglia to repair damage to their environment. One other type of glial cell, the **ependymal cells**, form the lining of the fluid-filled cavities of the brain.

The Blood–Brain Barrier

Astrocytes also aid in maintaining the chemical stability of the brain by participating in a mechanism called the **blood–brain barrier.** Concentrations of vital chemicals like sodium, calcium, and potassium must be maintained at very precise levels in the intercellular fluids between nerve cells. The brain cannot tolerate the relatively extreme concentration fluctuations found in the bloodstream, so the blood–brain barrier acts as a gateway regulating the passage

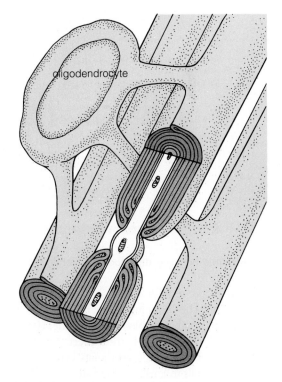

Figure 2.17 An oligodendrocyte provides myelin sheaths for several axons. The cutaway portion shows the wrapping layers around the axon in the center. (Adapted from Bunge, 1968)

Figure 2.18 The blood–brain barrier. (**a**) An astrocyte forming part of the barrier between the nerve cells and the blood vessels. (**b**) A cross section of the same tissue as in **a**. The major portion of the blood–brain barrier is formed by the tight junctions that permit no leakage where the endothelial cells of the blood vessels contact each other. (Adapted from Kuffler & Nicholls, 1976)

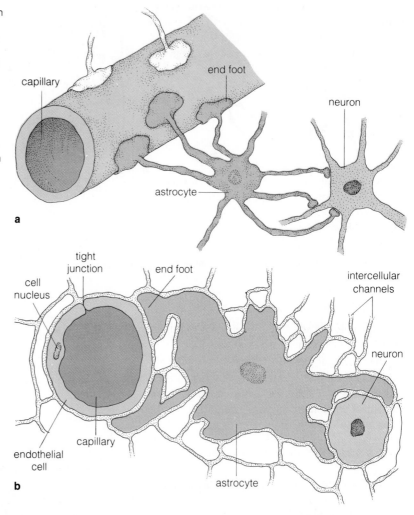

of chemicals between the blood and brain fluids (Davson, 1978).

Every blood vessel in the brain is covered with astrocyte branches, forming a thin membrane that apparently is a part of the blood–brain barrier (Bradbury, 1979). The major barrier effect, however, comes from the unusually tight joints between the **endothelial cells** that make up the walls of the blood vessels (Figure 2.18). Outside of the brain, these junctions are looser and allow useful leakage from the vessels (Feldman & Quenzer, 1984). Many large molecules, which might be harmful to neurons, find it hard to leave the blood through the membranes

of the endothelial cells, whose semipermeability allows them to act as a filter. The filter allows needed chemicals to diffuse through the fluid of the intercellular space until they are absorbed by a cell (Kuffler et al., 1984).

There are a few places in the brain where the blood–brain barrier is leaky. One of these, the **area postrema** (below the cerebellum), is next to the cells in the brain stem that control vomiting. Poisons carried from the intestines are able to leave the blood at this point and trigger activity in the vomit center (Feldman & Quenzer, 1984).

The blood–brain barrier plays an important role

in the therapeutic use of drugs because many chemicals that would alter neuron function if placed directly on nerve cells have no effect when injected into the bloodstream. They are excluded from the brain by the action of the barrier.

Viewing Neurons

Our understanding of how neurons and glia look has not been easy to come by. A simple concept, the idea of the synapse, which you can read and absorb in 30 seconds, can take years of lab time to establish. Such knowledge is difficult to obtain, partly because neurons are so difficult to see.

The light microscope (Figure 2.19) can magnify images up to 1,200 times their size. That is enough to let us see whole Golgi II cells but not enough to study small areas of a dendrite or other cellular features. For an examination of the cell membrane and synapses, we need the much higher resolving power of the electron microscope. Let's examine the nerve cell on both of these levels.

The Whole Neuron: Light Microscopy

"It's easy to see tiny objects," you say, "just use a microscope." Well, it isn't quite that simple.

Tissue Preparation A standard light-transmission microscope shines light up through the tissue being examined, through the lens system, and into the eye of the observer (Figure 2.19). If you simply place a brain on the stage of the microscope, you will see nothing; individual cells are nearly transparent, but a sizable chunk of brain tissue is not. One must examine a brain one slice at a time. Such slices, called **sections**, are normally so thin that a stack of 20 would stand only 1 mm tall. Brain tissue in its natural state is too soft and mushy to slice that thin. Consequently, the first step in the process of viewing neurons is to **fix** the brain (soak it in a chemical called formalin, to stop all deterioration and begin a hardening process). Then the tissue is frozen or **embedded** in a substance like paraffin. The fixed, embedded (or frozen) brain is then ready to section

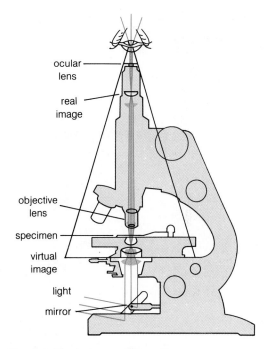

Figure 2.19 A standard light microscope. (From Starr & Taggart, 1987)

on a machine that can make the world's thinnest slices—a **microtome** (*tom* = cut).

Staining Everyone knows that neurons are too small to be seen with the naked eye, but few people realize that even if we could magically expand them to elephantine proportions, neurons would still be difficult to see. They are transparent. Viewing them in their natural state is like trying to perceive the shapes of clear-glass structures embedded in larger, clear-glass structures behind bent and twisted glass walls. The problem of visualizing neurons, then, is twofold: small size and transparency. Microscopes have solved the size problem, and tissue staining allows us to make the transparent visible.

Over the last 100 years, various staining techniques have been discovered, and each technique reveals something different about the neural tissue. Nissl stains, for example, reveal cell bodies but not

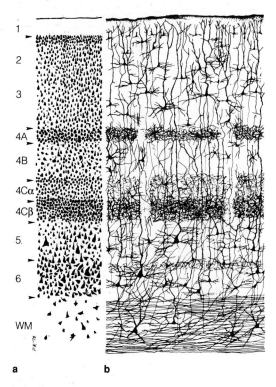

1
2
3
4A
4B
4Cα
4Cβ
5.
6
WM

a   b

Figure 2.20 Cross sections of cerebral cortex of the brain stained two different ways. (**a**) Nissl stain, which reveals cell bodies. (**b**) Golgi–Cox stain, which shows both somas and dendrites as well as some axons. The numbers along the left side indicate the six layers of the cortex. (From Rakic, 1979)

it contacts. Thus, the open network of cells in Figure 2.20b is deceptive; most of the neurons in that area simply didn't stain. You must imagine, then, that the blank areas between the stained neurons are crammed with an army of invisible nerve cells sandwiched between an even greater number of glial cells. The distances between these cells are so small that the gaps cannot be seen with an ordinary light microscope. Neurons, glial cells, and neuropil are sardine-packed, shoulder-to-shoulder, with no nook or cranny unfilled. This fact, however, is not evident in **photomicrographs** (photographs made through a microscope) and is only truly revealed by the most sensitive of all magnifying instruments, the electron microscope.

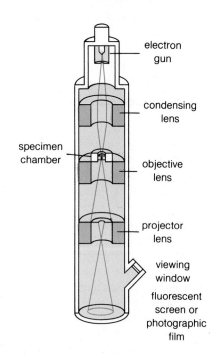

Figure 2.21 An electron microscope. The specimen to be viewed is placed in a vacuum chamber because air molecules would interfere with the electron beams. The beams must be focused with large magnets acting as lenses. (From Starr & Taggart, 1987)

dendrites or axons (Figure 2.20a). This makes them excellent for differentiating gray matter from white matter and can also help in discriminating one nucleus from another within the gray matter. Myelin stains reveal white matter areas, and membrane stains like the **Golgi–Cox method** (Figure 2.20b) color both somas and dendrites. Such selective staining, which colors only a small proportion of structures, is more valuable than a nonselective stain that colors everything. The latter would produce a solid mat of colors in which most individual structures would be hidden.

The Golgi–Cox method is particularly selective in that it stains only a small percentage of the neurons

Spines, Synapses, and Neuropil: Electron Micrography

Some of the objects scientists wish to see are smaller than light waves, and this makes it impossible to form light images of them. Electrons, however, vibrate at faster rates than do the photons that make up visible light. Hence, electrons have shorter wavelengths and can resolve finer details. An electron microscope is capable of magnifications of 1 million times.

Transmission electron microscopes (Figure 2.21) use basically the same principles as the light microscope. A beam of electrons is projected through an ultrathin slice of nerve tissue stained with a metal such as lead. The beam of electrons, just like the beam of light in a light microscope, must be brought to a focus. Because optical lenses cannot do this, magnetic fields are used instead. The variations of light and dark that make up an image occur because some parts of tissue stained with heavy metals absorb electrons better than do others, leaving dark areas in the beam as it emerges. Cell membranes, mitochondria, and nuclei, for example, absorb electrons better than does cytoplasm, so they appear darker in a photograph made with the microscope. (Such a photograph is called an electron micrograph.)

With a light microscope, you can see the image

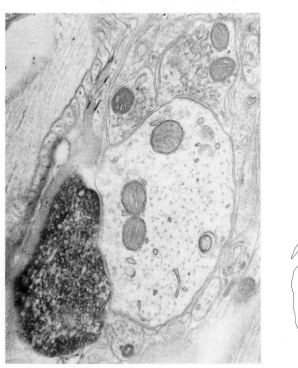

a

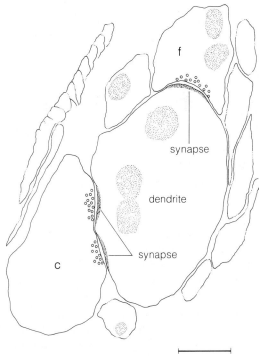

b

Figure 2.22 (**a**) Transmission electron micrograph of a small section of olfactory cortex. (**b**) Diagram of the same section of tissue shown in the micrograph. Three synapses are visible on the dendrite at the center. The terminal labeled c is stained with horseradish peroxidase; the terminal labeled f is unstained. The calibration bar at the bottom right = 2 μm. (Adapted from Renehan et al., 1988)

Figure 2.23 Two types of synapses—one on a spine, the other on the dendrite itself. Only the electron microscope can yield magnifications of this size (around 24,000×).

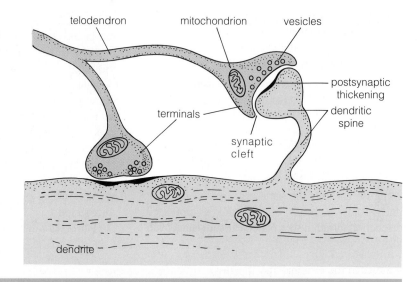

telodendron   mitochondrion   vesicles

postsynaptic thickening

terminals

dendritic spine

synaptic cleft

dendrite

Figure 2.24 Transmission electron micrograph of terminals surrounding a dendrite. The terminals can be identified by the multiplicity of transmitter vesicles they contain. Each vesicle looks like a small, slightly irregular circle. Do not confuse the vesicles with the cross sections of microtubules inside the dendrite (at the center of the picture). Microtubules appear to be black dots strewn at random throughout the dendrite. The five larger circular objects within the dendrite are mitochondria. A number of synapses are visible between the terminals and the dendrite. They appear as darker strips along the borders of the two cells. One clearly defined example of a synapse can be found in the terminal at the middle right, which contains a single visible mitochondrion. The synapse with the dendrite is the dark, thickened area in the middle of the portion of the membrane adjacent to the dendrite. The magnification in this micrograph is ×25,000. (From Heimer, 1971)

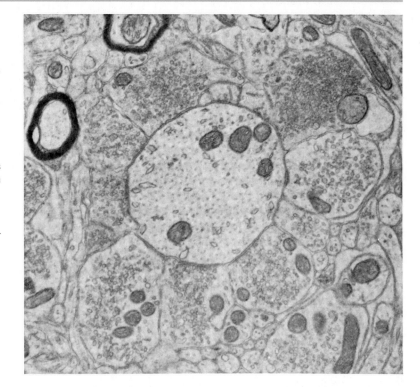

directly by letting the light beam enter your eye. This direct observation is not possible with an electron microscope because the eye is not constructed for perceiving images from electron arrays. The electron beam carrying the image from the tissue must be directed at some substitute for the human retina, such as a cathode ray screen (similar to the one in your television set).

An advantage of electron micrography is that electron-absorbing stains allow all cells to be seen rather than just a selected few. The electron micrograph in Figure 2.22 gives you a good idea of the packing density in the neuropil. No somas are in view; at this magnification, a single-cell body would fill dozens of these pictures. With electron micrography, synapses can be identified by three features: **synaptic vesicles** in the terminal, the widening of the intercellular space into what is called the **synaptic cleft**, and a darker area of the membrane on the dendritic side of the synapse called the **postsynaptic thickening** (Figure 2.23). The synaptic vesicles contain neurotransmitter chemicals like those discussed in Chapter 1. In the upper center of Figure 2.22, you can see a synapse formed between a terminal of one cell and a dendrite of another. In Figures 2.22 and 2.24, see if you can identify the synapses by their vesicles, clefts, and thickenings.

The invention of the electron microscope also allowed us to see that some of the synapses in certain brain areas are formed on extensions of dendrites called **dendritic spines**. Scientists had known about dendritic spines through light micrography, but their real shapes and function had not been discovered. They simply appeared as rough bumps on the dendrites. In Chapter 16, we will find that dendritic spines are probably an important part of the brain's memory mechanism.

Scanning Electron Micrography

Figure 2.25 is an electron micrograph of a neuron soma and one dendrite, but you will notice that it differs in appearance from the micrographs you have just viewed. Rather than looking somewhat like an abstract pattern for kitchen linoleum, it shows a solid-looking object standing out from its background. This three-dimensional effect can only be

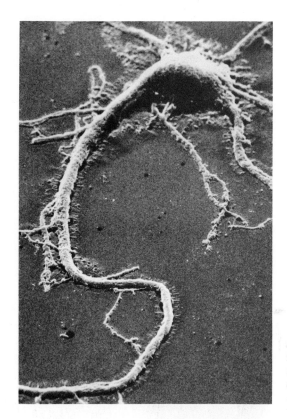

Figure 2.25 Scanning electron micrograph of a neuron soma and one large dendrite. This cell is whole, not sectioned into slices as it would be for a transmission electron micrograph. (From Gore, 1971)

achieved with a special type of electron microscope called a **scanning electron microscope**.

The neuron looks three dimensional because it did not have to be thin-sectioned before being photographed. It could be photographed whole because the microscope does not transmit electrons through the material. It shoots a stream of electrons at the surface of the object to be pictured. This focused stream of electrons starts at one side of the tissue sample, sweeps across it, then moves down the sample, a notch at the end of each full sweep. In this manner, the pinpoint electron beam gradually scans, line by line, the entire sample.

When high-energy electrons penetrate the sample, they excite electrons within the nerve tissue,

Figure 2.26 The basic elements in a scanning electron microscope. The magnetic lenses shape the cloud of electrons into a beam and focus it. The scanning circuit moves the beam back and forth across the sample in synchrony with the sweep of the electron beam within the cathode ray tube (television monitor). Each sweep across the sample is at a level below the previous one, so that after a number of sweeps the entire surface of the sample has been crossed by the beam. Detectors collect the electrons that boil out of the sample when they are hit by the beam and register them in the detector as a small voltage. The voltage is amplified and sent to the monitor, where it appears as a spot of light on the screen. Many electrons make a bright spot; a few electrons make a darker spot. All spots of varying brightness, when seen together, make a picture of the sample. (From Starr & Taggart, 1987)

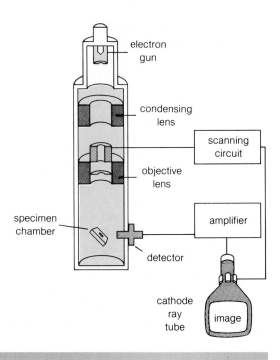

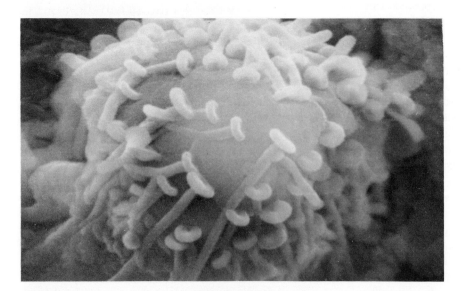

Figure 2.27 Scanning electron micrograph of terminals covering the surface of a cell body. Each terminal has a short length of telodendron still attached to it. Some terminals appear to have fallen away from the area of the synapse on the neuron soma. This sample is magnified 11,000 times and comes from the marine snail *Aplysia*. (From Lewis et al., 1969)

which fly out into the surrounding vacuum of the microscope chamber where they are attracted to a detector (Figure 2.26). The number of electrons hitting the detector at any moment determines the brightness of one spot in the image that is building up line by line on the monitor screen. The three-dimensional effect occurs because the beam excites more electrons from the tissue when it hits a slanting surface than when it strikes a surface head on. For example, the terminals in Figure 2.27 look rounded rather than flat because of the shading from light to dark on each curved surface. The less the surface curves away from the beam, the fewer electrons it contributes and the darker that area is in the picture. The result is a remarkable illusion of depth and solidity.

In Chapter 3, we will make use of the knowledge afforded us by the anatomist's microscopy techniques to survey the most important structures of the nervous system.

■ Summary

1. Animals and plants are made up of basic units called cells. A collection of cells having the same function make a tissue, and tissues with various functions are combined into organs. An animal (an organism) can be thought of as a collection of organs.

2. A cell has three basic divisions: membrane, nucleus, and cytoplasm. The membrane is a fluid bilayer made of phospholipid molecules oriented with the water-attracting phospho "heads" pointed out and the lipid "tails" pointed inward toward each other to make a watertight barrier.

3. The nucleus is the control center of the cell. It contains the genetic plans for cellular structures coded into DNA molecules and a nucleolus in which RNA is combined with proteins to form ribosomes.

4. The cytoplasm is a thick fluid in which float organelles such as rough endoplasmic reticulum (ER), mitochondria, and Golgi bodies. Rough ER is the site of protein formation. Golgi complexes package chemicals such as hormones. Mitochondria produce energy for the cell. Cytoplasm also contains microtubules and filaments that make up the cytoskeleton.

5. The set of chemical reactions that constitute the living processes of the cell is called metabolism. Anabolism is the series of constructive metabolic reactions that build chemicals needed by the body; catabolism is a collection of destructive reactions that destroy chemicals to extract energy. In anabolism, ATP is produced in the mitochondria using the energy stored in glucose and oxygen.

6. Another part of anabolism is the construction of proteins from their constituent amino acids. Fabrication of proteins begins in the nucleus when an RNA molecule is constructed from a section of DNA that constitutes the gene for a particular protein. This "readout" of the genetic code into a molecule of mRNA is called transcription. After being inserted into a ribosome, the mRNA leaves the nucleus for the rough ER where the process of translation (converting the genetic code into a sequence of amino acids) takes place. Molecules of tRNA, each bearing the codon for a single amino acid, find their amino acids in the cytoplasm and bring them to the ribosome where they can be linked together. Once the long chain of amino acids that forms the protein molecule is complete, it breaks free of the ribosome and crumples into the shape that will determine its function.

7. Brain tissue consists of neurons and neuroglia (glial cells). Most neurons (nerve cells) possess a cell body (soma) with a number of short processes called dendrites and one long process called an axon. The soma contains the nucleus. At its far end, the axon branches into a number of telodendria that end in swellings called terminals. The terminals lie next to the dendrites or soma of another neuron and create synaptic contact points between the two cells.

8. Nerve cells designed to send messages over long distances in the nervous system have long axons for that purpose and are called Golgi type I neurons. Golgi type II cells (interneurons) have either very short axons or none at all. Their task is to form microcircuits within the various areas of the brain and spinal cord.

9. There are five types of neuroglia: Schwann cells, astrocytes, ependymal cells, oligodendroglia, and

microglia. The last four are found in the brain and spinal cord.

10. Schwann cells are found in the nerves outside the brain and spinal cord. A nerve is a bundle of axons connecting the neuron cell bodies within the spinal cord to distant muscles or receptors in the body. Each axon within the nerve is wrapped in a myelin sheath composed of the cell membranes of many Schwann cells. The sheath provides insulation from neighboring axons. An axon plus its sheath cells is called a nerve fiber.

11. Astrocytes provide structural support for nerve cells, aid in establishing the blood–brain barrier, and afford some protection against anoxia. Microglia clean up an area of tissue that has suffered damage. Oligodendroglia aid neurons in maintaining chemical balance and provide myelin sheaths for CNS axons.

12. The blood–brain barrier protects nerve cells from potentially harmful molecules in the bloodstream and from extreme fluctuations in the concentrations of needed chemicals. It is formed by astrocytes and endothelial cells that line the blood vessels.

13. To study neural tissue, one must fix, embed, section, and stain it. Different stains reveal different cell features. The Golgi–Cox method stains somas and dendrites. Other stains show only myelin or chemicals within the cell bodies.

14. Electron microscopes achieve much greater magnification than light microscopes. Transmission electron microscopes project a beam of electrons through the sample tissue; scanning electron microscopes send a beam back and forth across the surface of a whole (unsectioned) sample. The electron microscope has allowed the study of the fine features of synapses such as dendritic spines.

Glossary

adenosine triphosphate (ATP) A chemical that transfers energy to wherever it is needed in the cell. (26)

amino acids Chemicals out of which proteins are built. (27)

anabolism The series of constructive metabolic reactions that builds chemicals needed by the body. (26)

anoxia Loss of oxygen supply to the cells. (36)

area postrema An area of the brain below the cerebellum in which the blood–brain barrier is relatively leaky. Location of the vomit center. (38)

astrocytes Glial cells with a starlike shape that help provide structure to brain tissue plus some protection against anoxia. (35)

axon A single, relatively long process that carries information from the soma to some distant destination. (33)

bases Chemicals that react with acids to form salts. (29)

blood–brain barrier An endothelial cell lining of blood vessels that prevents many large-molecule chemicals from leaking out of the vessels into the intercellular space where they might harm nerve cells. (37)

catabolism The collection of destructive reactions that destroy chemicals in order to extract energy. (26)

cell The basic unit from which the tissues of organs are formed. (20)

cell body (soma) "Center" of the neuron where the nucleus is located. (33)

cell membrane The double layer of phospholipid molecules in which proteins are embedded. It forms the "skin" of a cell. (21)

chromatin A webwork of strands within the nucleus consisting of DNA. (23)

chromosome A single DNA molecule. (23)

codons Triplets of adjacent base pairs in a DNA or RNA molecule. Each triplet is the code for an amino acid. (30)

cristae A folded membrane within the mitochondrion on which ATP molecules are formed. (27)

cytoplasm The contents of a cell between the membrane and the nucleus. (23)

cytoskeleton A network of filaments and microtubules running through the cytoplasm that imparts structure to the cell. (24)

dendrites Relatively short, heavily branched processes extending out from the soma. (33)

dendritic spine Minute bump or knob on a dendrite that forms the site for synapses. (43)

deoxyribonucleic acid (DNA) A double-stranded, helical molecule that contains the genes. (23)

embedding Preparing a piece of tissue for microtome sectioning by covering it with some material, such as paraffin, that hardens around it. (39)

endoplasmic reticulum An organelle in the cytoplasm formed of many folds of membrane. (23)

endothelial cells Those that provide linings of structures such as blood vessels. (38)

enzyme A biochemical, made by the cell, that speeds a reaction between two other chemicals. (27)

ependymal cells Type of glial cell that forms the lining of the fluid-filled cavities of the brain. (37)

filaments Strands of protein in the cytoplasm that make up part of the cytoskeleton. (24)

fixation Preventing decay in tissue by soaking it in some chemical such as formalin. (39)

fluid bilayer membrane See *cell membrane*.

gene The basic unit of heredity consisting of a sequence of base pairs along a stretch of DNA. (23)

glia See *neuroglia*.

glucose Blood sugar. (26)

glycogen A stored form of glucose. (27)

Golgi complex A network (reticulum) of pancake-flat, hollow storage vessels for the cells' secretions, formed from lipid bilayer membrane. (24)

Golgi–Cox method A method for staining tissue that colors the membranes, especially revealing somas and dendrites. (40)

Golgi type I neurons Long-axoned nerve cells that provide the connections between areas within the CNS or between cord and muscle. (33)

Golgi type II neurons (interneurons) Short-axoned nerve cells that provide the connections within limited areas of brain or spinal cord. (33)

intercellular space Tiny, fluid-filled crack between the membranes of adjacent cells. (32)

interneurons Short-axoned nerve cells that provide the connections within limited areas of brain or spinal cord. (33)

messenger RNA (mRNA) Carries the code out of the nucleus to the rough endoplasmic reticulum where the assembly of the amino acids will take place. (31)

metabolism The collection of chemical reactions that make up our physiological life processes. (26)

microglia Dormant glia that respond to brain damage by growing into active phagocytes. (36)

microtome An instrument for making slices only fractions of a millimeter thick. (39)

microtubules Microscopic tubes running through the cytoplasm as a part of the cytoskeleton. (24)

mitochondria Organelles responsible for energy metabolism in the cell. (24)

myelin Layers of high-cholesterol Schwann cell membrane. (35)

myelin sheath Insulating multilayer of myelin wrapped around an axon. (35)

nerve fiber Peripheral axon together with its myelin sheath. (35)

neuroglia (glia) Support cells of the nervous system that provide myelin sheaths and chemical support and that participate in the blood–brain barrier. (33)

neuron One of the cells of which the nervous system is composed; a nerve cell. (33)

neuropil The tangle of dendrite branches, telodendria, and glial branches in which neuron somas are embedded. (33)

nucleolus A special area of the nucleus in which the RNA is combined with proteins to form ribosomes. (23)

nucleus Part of the cell that contains the DNA and controls the life of the cell. (23)

oligodendrocyte One of the oligodendroglia, a type of glial cell that provides myelin sheaths for axons within the brain and spinal cord. (37)

oligodendroglia See *oligodendrocyte*.

organ A collection of tissues that performs some function for the organism. (20)

organelles Specialized structures within the cytoplasm. (23)

organism An animal seen as a collection of organs. (20)

phagocytosis Process in which a "clean-up" cell called a phagocyte engulfs bits of dead material and digests them. (36)

phospholipid The type of molecule that makes up the basic structure of the cell membrane. (21)

photomicrograph Photograph made through a microscope. (40)

postsynaptic thickening A darker area of the dendritic membrane at a synapse that reveals the presence of transmitter receptors. (43)

ribonucleic acid (RNA) A molecule formed from DNA that carries the genetic code out of the nucleus. (23)

ribosome A tiny structure composed of RNA and protein that manufactures new protein molecules. Found in the rough ER. (23)

rough endoplasmic reticulum Site of protein formation. (23)

scanning electron microscope A microscope that forms its images by capturing electrons emitted by a chunk of tissue being bombarded by an electron beam. The image has a three-dimensional quality. (43)

Schwann cells Glial cells of the peripheral nervous system that provide myelin sheaths. (33)

secretion vesicle A sphere of bilayer membrane containing a chemical manufactured by the cell. (24)

sections Ultrathin slices of tissue prepared for microscopy. (39)

soma (cell body) "Center" of the neuron where the nucleus is located. (33)

sugar phosphate group Molecular fragment from the backbone of a DNA molecule. (29)

synapse Junction between two neurons. (33)

synaptic cleft Widening of the intercellular space at a synapse. (43)

synaptic vesicles Bubblelike spheres of cell membrane enclosing a small amount of neurotransmitter that are found on the presynaptic side of a synapse. (43)

telodendria A treelike structure of tiny branches at the end of an axon. (33)

terminal The swelling at the end of a telodendron that forms the point of contact with another neuron. The location of synapses. (33)

tissue A group of cells with similar structure and function. (20)

transcription Creating an RNA molecule from one of DNA. (30)

transfer RNA (tRNA) Brings amino acids to the ribosome for assembly into proteins. (31)

translation The ribosomal conversion of genetic code into amino acid chains. (31)

transmission electron microscope Microscope that forms an image by sending a beam of electrons through a tissue section. The image results from the different electron absorption capacities of the various cell parts. (41)

3

Basic Plan of the Nervous System

Organization of the Nervous System
Concepts: anterior, posterior, rostral, caudal, lateral, medial, superior, inferior, central, peripheral, dorsal, ventral, central nervous system (CNS)

PERIPHERAL NERVOUS SYSTEM
Concepts: nerves, peripheral nervous system

Nerves
Concepts: tracts, fibers, sensory (afferent) fiber, motor (efferent) fiber, cranial nerves, spinal nerves

Somatic Versus Autonomic Fibers
Concepts: autonomic fibers, somatic fibers, viscera, smooth muscles, striate muscles

Injured Nerves
Concepts: degeneration, regeneration, neuroma

ORGANIZATIONAL PRINCIPLES
Concepts: gray matter, white matter, nucleus (nuclei), ganglion, cerebral cortex

Structures of the Central Nervous System

SPINAL CORD
Concepts: reflex, reflex arcs

Cord Anatomy
Concepts: vertebra, roots, dorsal root, ventral root, primary afferent neurons, dorsal root ganglion, dorsal horn, ventral horn, interneurons (association neurons)

Autonomic Nervous System
Concepts: autonomic nervous system (ANS), sympathetic chain ganglia, preganglionic fibers, postganglionic fibers, sympathetic nervous system, parasympathetic nervous system

BRAIN STEM
Concept: brain stem

Medulla Oblongata
Concepts: medulla oblongata, vagus nerve, nucleus of tractus solitarius (NTS)

Pontine Region
Concepts: pontine region, cerebellum, pons, cerebellar hemispheres

Midbrain
Concepts: midbrain, colliculi, superior colliculi, inferior colliculi, reticular formation

VENTRICLES AND CEREBROSPINAL FLUID
Concepts: ventricles, cerebrospinal fluid (CSF), lateral ventricles, third ventricle, septum, fourth ventricle, cerebral aqueduct, dura mater

THALAMUS
Concepts: thalamus, sensory projection system

HYPOTHALAMUS: CONTROL OF THE INTERNAL ENVIRONMENT
Concept: hypothalamus

Control Through the Nervous System
Control Through the Endocrine System
Concepts: endocrine system, hormones, exocrine glands, endocrine glands, pituitary, gonads, pancreas, adrenal glands, adrenal medulla, adrenalin, noradrenalin, adrenal cortex, mineralocorticoids, glucocorticoids, thyroid gland, congenital hypothyroidism, posterior pituitary, anterior pituitary

CORPUS STRIATUM: MOTOR HABITS
Concepts: corpus striatum, caudate nucleus, putamen, globus pallidus, striatum

This chapter provides a guide to the nervous system, first in the form of a broad, overall view and then a closer look at some of the parts. Finally, we consider an hypothesis of how the nervous system evolved these various parts at different times during the history of our prehuman ancestors.

■ Organization of the Nervous System

There are two ways to consider the map of the nervous system to be revealed here: First, we name and locate the anatomical parts and subparts of the nervous system; second, we look at the whole system again in terms of how those parts function.

In discussing the anatomy of the nervous system, we must define a few directional terms. **Anterior** means toward the front end, **posterior** toward the rear (Figure 3.1). These are terms frequently used in speaking of the brain, whereas rostral and caudal are usually used in reference to the body or the whole nervous system. **Rostral** means toward the head end (*rostrum* = head), **caudal** toward the tail end (*caudum* = tail). **Lateral** indicates toward the side, **medial** toward the middle. **Superior** is toward the top, **inferior** toward the bottom. **Central** refers to the core of the nervous system, along which one finds the brain and spinal cord, whereas **peripheral** refers to the direction away from this central axis. The spinal cord, for example, is central, whereas the receptors out in the skin are peripheral. **Dorsal** (on the back side) and **ventral** (on the belly side) might be a little confusing at first. The superior surface of the brain is also termed dorsal even though it is not really toward the back in the human brain. This stems from the fact that the superior surface is on the back of any four-footed animal, including our distant ancestors. Only creatures that walk on two legs bend their heads forward so that the top of the brain is no longer on the back side (Figure 3.2).

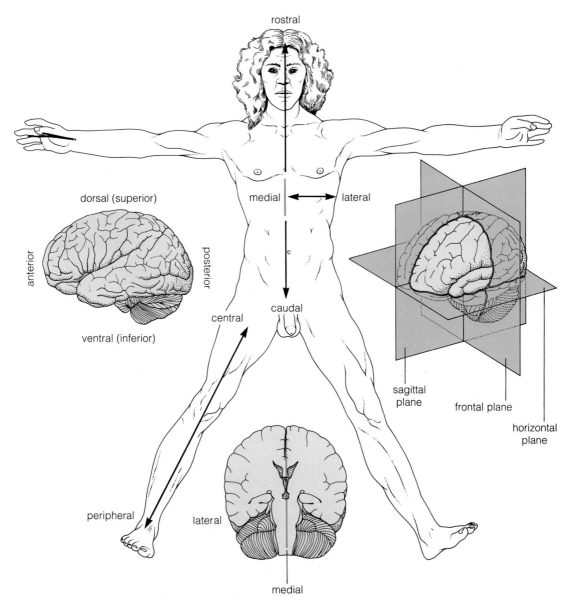

Figure 3.1 Directional terms and planes of section. *Anterior* means "toward the front"; *posterior* is "toward the back." *Rostral* means "toward the head end"; *caudal* "toward the tail." Note that the feet are no farther caudal than are the hips. The *dorsal* side is the back, and the *ventral* is the belly side. *Lateral* means "toward the side"; *medial* "toward the middle." In the brain, *superior* is synonymous with *dorsal*, *inferior* with *ventral*. The continuum from the central axis of the body to the fingers and toes is the *proximal–distal* dimension. The three planes show the different directions in which the brain can be sliced to reveal its interior. A frontal section is shown below the figure of the man.

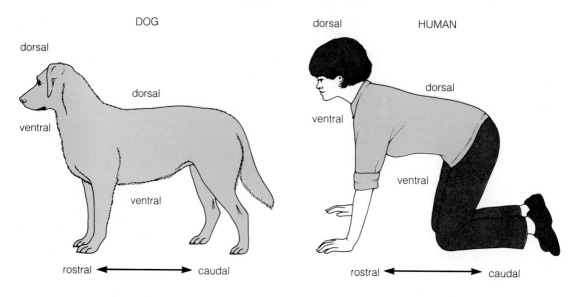

Figure 3.2 Directional terms for the head and body. *Rostral* means "toward the head end"; *caudal* means "toward the tail end." The feet are no farther caudal than are the hips. *Dorsal* means "toward the back"; *ventral* means "toward the belly side." Because of the unique upright posture taken by humans, the ventral side of the brain is toward the ground (as in a four-footed animal), but the ventral side of the body points forward. To reduce confusion about these terms that often arises when discussing both human and animal brains, the human is shown here in a four-footed posture.

The nervous system extends into all areas of the human body (Figure 3.3). Its two basic divisions are the central and peripheral nervous systems (Figure 3.4). The **central nervous system (CNS)**, consisting of the brain and spinal cord, is the control mechanism for everything that goes on in an animal. Hence, it must be connected to all body parts. The CNS uses the information coming into it from sensory receptors in order to decide what commands to send out to the muscles and glands.

Peripheral Nervous System

The sensory information and muscle commands are sent along a system of communication "cables" called **nerves**. It is nerves that make up the **peripheral nervous system**.

Nerves It is important to distinguish between *nerve cells* and *nerves*. As you learned in Chapter 2, most nerve cells have three parts: a soma, dendrites, and an axon. A nerve, however, is made up of axons; it contains no somas or dendrites. Furthermore, nerves (unlike neurons) are only found outside of the CNS. (Bundles of axons *inside* the CNS are termed **tracts**.) Figure 3.5 shows what a nerve looks like in cross section. The axons are grouped into small bundles wrapped in a sheet of connective tissue. Associated with them are small blood vessels that must be close by to supply oxygen and fuel. Nerve cells are more sensitive to oxygen deficiency than are any other cells of the body and are among the first to die if the blood supply is interrupted. If you could look beneath your skin, nerves would appear as small, whitish threads running across the surface of your

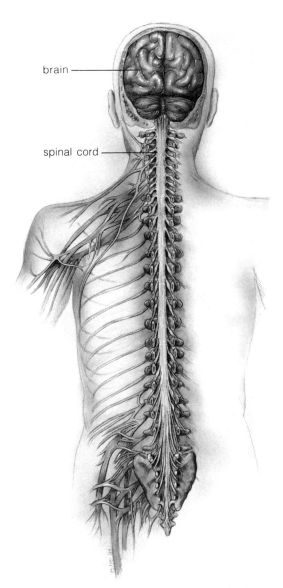

brain

spinal cord

Figure 3.3 The human nervous system consists of brain, spinal cord, and nerves. (From Starr & Taggart, 1987)

muscles. Each nerve contains hundreds, if not thousands, of axons, each sprouting from its own soma. Their somas may be far away inside the brain or spinal cord, or they may be in one of the clusters of somas that are scattered throughout the body.

Nerves contain two types of fibers: **sensory (afferent)**, which conduct impulses from receptor organs to the CNS, and **motor (efferent)**, which conduct impulses from the CNS to muscles and glands.

There are two kinds of nerves: spinal and cranial. **Cranial nerves** emerge from the brain, and **spinal nerves** emerge from the spinal cord. Figure 3.3 shows that spinal nerves emerge in pairs along the spinal cord, one pair between each set of ribs. There are 12 pairs of cranial nerves (Figure 3.6), numbered in Roman numerals from the most anterior (cranial nerve I) to the most posterior (cranial nerve XII). Some cranial nerves, like I (olfactory) and II (optic), contain axons only of sensory neurons (those that conduct information from receptors to the CNS), whereas others are made up of motor neurons (those that conduct information from the CNS out to the muscles). Cranial nerves V, VII, IX, X, and XI are mixed nerves that contain sensory and motor fibers. Spinal nerves are all mixed.

Somatic Versus Autonomic Fibers The sensory–motor categorization of nerve fibers distinguishes them according to the direction in which they conduct their impulses—toward or away from the CNS. Another way of dividing up fibers depends on the type of organs they serve. **Autonomic fibers** connect the CNS to visceral organs, and **somatic fibers** serve the rest of the body. The term **viscera** refers to all internal organs, from heart, stomach, and lungs to tear ducts, glands, and blood vessels (Figure 3.7). Thus, autonomic sensory fibers carry information about the state of visceral organs, and somatic sensory fibers conduct information from receptors in skin, joints, and tendons.

Autonomic motor neurons serve the flat, white sheets of muscle, called **smooth muscles**, in the viscera. Much of the body's smooth muscle is in the stomach and intestines, where it acts to move the food along. Walls of arteries are also smooth muscle, and contraction and relaxation of these muscles can expand or narrow the diameter of the vessel to increase or decrease the blood supply within an organ. Red-colored **striate muscles** (also called striped muscles) are stimulated by somatic motor fibers. These muscles of the arms, legs, trunk, and

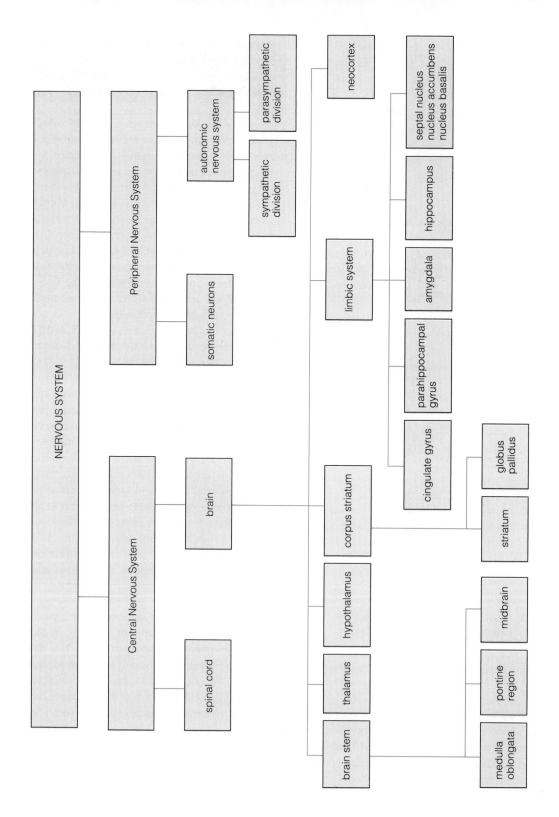

head are called voluntary muscles because they are under your conscious control. Smooth muscles, in contrast, are almost all contracted reflexively.

Injured Nerves The peripheral nervous system has an interesting property that the CNS probably does not possess. It can often repair damage to itself and restore lost function after injury. Imagine an automobile accident in which you suffered a deep gash in your right upper arm. The cut severed a major nerve branch running down the arm to your right hand. Thus, many sensory receptors in that hand and in the arm below the injury are now cut off from the spinal cord, as are muscles served by motor neurons in that particular nerve. Consequently, your lower arm and hand seem numb in places, and some muscles either feel weak or are completely paralyzed, depending on how many axons were damaged.

Severed nerve fibers no longer receive a steady supply of nutrients from their cell bodies in the spinal cord; thus, the nerve fibers begin to die (Figure 3.8). Within 3 or 4 days, each neuron has lost its axon segments peripheral to the cut. Furthermore, some of each axon between the cut and the spinal cord has died, although it is still attached to the soma. Both parts of the axon leave behind an empty tunnel of myelin sheath. Because they are independent cells, there is no reason for the Schwann cells that make up the sheath to die. They do eventually break apart from each other and pull their membranes back into a more normal cellular shape (Figure 3.8). But aside from the few directly within the zone of the injury, Schwann cells remain alive and in location, waiting for the return of their axon. This sequence of changes in the axon and glia is known as **degeneration.**

As soon as the axon has died and the dead bits and pieces are scavenged by clean-up cells called microglia, new growth begins from the soma. Millimeter by millimeter, a creeping tendril of new axon grows out from the soma toward its original termination point. This regrowth process, called **regeneration,** is apparently guided by Schwann cells left

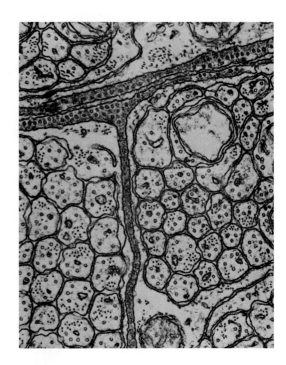

Figure 3.5 A cross section of a nerve showing how the individual axons are "packaged" into bundles by membranes of connective tissue. The connective tissue is the heavy, dark T-shaped membrane that cuts across the picture from left to right and drops down to the bottom, dividing the picture into three parts. Axons in this nerve section have lost their roundness because of dehydration during the fixation process that prepares the tissue for slicing and photographing. The magnification in this picture is ×80,000. (Micrograph by Alexander von Muralt; from Keynes, 1979)

behind from the axon's first life. As the axon grows between these living guideposts, they once more enfold it in a sheath of myelin insulation. All goes well until the axon grows into the zone of greatest injury where the myelin path has been disrupted. Regeneration continues, however, sheath or no, and the growing axon may eventually find its way into some sheath on the opposite side of the wound. Because a nerve of any size contains hundreds to thousands of axons, the chances that an axon will find the correct sheath and regrow to exactly the same termination point in skin or muscle would

Figure 3.4 The major divisions of the human nervous system (opposite page).

Figure 3.6 The cranial nerves seen as they emerge from the ventral side of the brain. The 12 nerves are numbered in the order from most rostral to most caudal. I—olfactory nerve (smell), II—optic nerve (vision), III—oculomotor (control of eye muscles), IV—trochlear (eye muscles), V—trigeminal (skin and muscles of head), VI—abducens (eye muscles), VII—facial (skin and muscles of head, taste sensitivity), VIII—vestibulocochlear (hearing and balance), IX—glossopharyngeal (taste, glandular, and muscle control), X—vagus (parasympathetic fibers to viscera), XI—spinal accessory (neck muscles), XII—hypoglossal (tongue muscles). (From Creager, 1983)

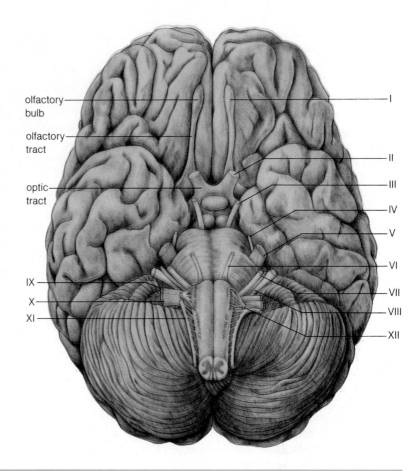

seem exceedingly slim. A good surgeon can help nature by carefully realigning the severed ends of a nerve in hopes of placing the sheaths reasonably close to their old locations. However, the larger the gap between the nerve ends, the greater the chance that the regenerating axons will tangle together and enter the wrong sheaths on the peripheral side of the cut.

Figure 3.9 shows a severed nerve (in a rat) that tried to regenerate across a wide gap within the zone of injury. Because most of the axons had no sheath to follow as they grew through that area, they twisted and twined around each other as though searching for the correct path. The result was a tangled ball of axon tendrils called a **neuroma**, which might have acted as a source of chronic pain for months to come if the rat had lived. A surgeon tries to prevent such

Figure 3.7 The viscera and autonomic nervous system. The sympathetic division is in black, parasympathetic in color. Cell bodies of most autonomic neurons are in the brain stem or spinal cord. Their axons run out through a nerve to synapse on autonomic neurons within a ganglion. These preganglionic fibers are shown as solid lines. Nerve fibers from the sympathetic ganglia run to one of the visceral organs either directly or indirectly by way of another ganglion. These postganglionic fibers are shown as dashed lines. Because each ganglion is linked to the one above it and the one below by fibers running between them, the whole assemblage is called the sympathetic chain, and the ganglia sometimes are called chain ganglia. (The somas of the neurons in the chain ganglia are not shown.) Parasympathetic fibers emerge from the brain stem in the vagus nerve or from the bottom of the spinal cord in some of the lower spinal nerves. (Adapted from Creager, 1983)

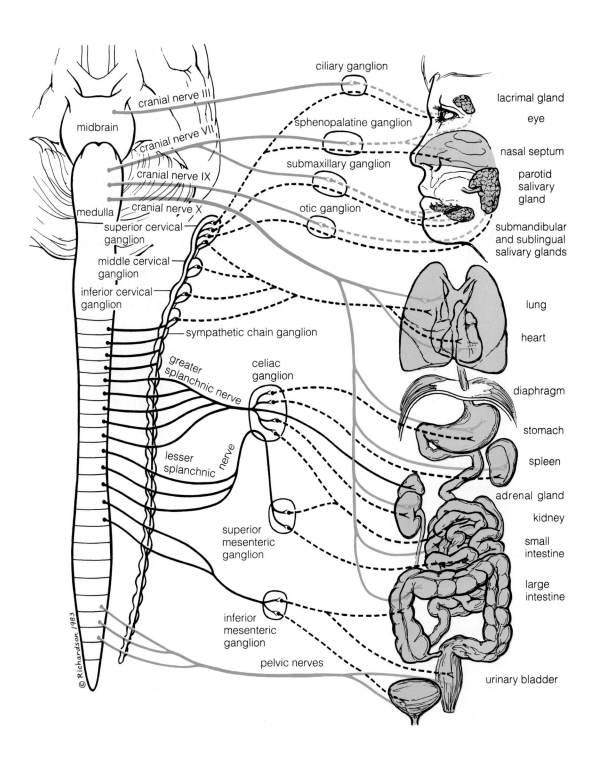

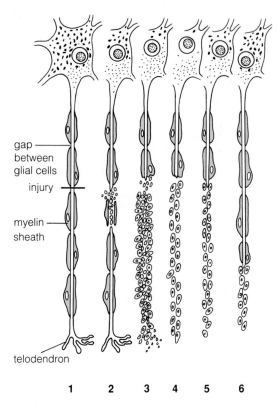

gap between glial cells

injury

myelin sheath

telodendron

1   2   3   4   5   6

Figure 3.8   Six stages of degeneration and regeneration in an injured axon. The myelin sheath (**1**) is shown as a string of Schwann cells wrapping the axon. The point of injury is marked. Within hours (**2**) the axon peripheral to the cut begins to degenerate and be scavenged by phagocytes. Several days later (**3**), the axon is nearly gone, and Schwann cells have shrunk and lost their myelin but are still maintaining their position. The axon remnants are gone (**4**), and only a trail of Schwann cells is left. Some degeneration has also occurred in the fiber central to the cut. The axon begins to regenerate (**5**) its growing tip, following the path of glial cells, and the myelin sheath begins to grow again around some of the regenerated axon (**6**). (Adapted from Gardner, 1975)

aberrant regeneration, but there is no way to pair all sheaths on one side of the cut with their correct mates on the other. When axons regrow through the damaged area, their choice of sheaths will have been randomly determined, and their final destinations in skin or muscle are unlikely to be the same as before

the accident. Because of these complications of regeneration, recovery of function after nerve injury is rarely perfect. Motor control in the affected body part will probably never be quite as fine, and some sensory capacity will be lost; with good surgical care, however, the amount of function recovered is truly gratifying.

In a few, unusual circumstances, motor control suffers greatly. Usually when a motor neuron regenerates through a randomly selected sheath, little harm is done because all motor axons in most peripheral nerves go to the same muscle. However, if the nerve that is regenerating carries axons for several different muscles, then results can be catastrophic. The unfortunate individual in Figure 3.10 suffered damage to the left side, cranial nerve III, a pathway for motor axons innervating muscles of the left eyelid, pupil, and muscles that pull the left eye up, down, or toward the nose. The regenerated left-side connections are so scrambled that a command from the brain that should rotate the left eye upward instead causes the left eyelid to close. An attempt to look to the right side produces a downward deflection of the affected eye. No surgical treatment exists for this condition. A surgeon simply cannot recognize each individual microscopic axon and realign its cut end with the proper pathway on the other side of the injury.

Organizational Principles

When you look at a cross section of a brain (Figure 3.11), especially one that has been fixed in formalin, one feature stands out right away: some parts look gray, whereas others have a whitish cast. The white coloration derives from the fatty substance called myelin. Recall that myelin sheaths are only found around axons, never around dendrites or somas. In a fixed brain, normally transparent cell bodies and dendrites appear grayish. So, when you see **gray matter**, you are viewing somas and dendrites; when it is **white matter**, you are looking at bundles of axons. This distinction has considerable functional importance.

Gray matter areas conduct the real business of the nervous system. Here, cell bodies and dendrites

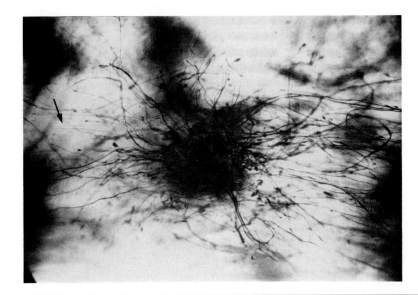

Figure 3.9 Unsuccessful nerve regeneration across a gap of 1 mm. The end of the cut nerve, at the left, is mostly out of focus (arrow). Some regenerating fibers can be seen growing out of the end and forming a neuroma in the center of the view. The remains of the peripheral part of the nerve are at the right. Very few fibers were able to grow straight across the cut and successfully pick up the glial trail again on the other side. (From Pollock & Harris, 1981)

process incoming information by means of millions of synaptic connections with the telodendria of incoming axons. Once processed, the information may be sent, in the form of nerve impulse patterns, to other processors elsewhere in the nervous system. When neurons fire, their nerve impulses leave the gray matter to travel in millions of axons within the white matter, toward dozens of locations elsewhere in the nervous system. Thus, when you look at white matter, you are viewing the long-distance communication system of the brain. No neuron somas exist there—only "telephone line" axons whose job it is to link one area of gray matter with another.

The basic organizational plan of the brain and spinal cord, then, is a network of cell-body clusters (gray matter areas) interconnected via cablelike bundles of axons (white matter). Each cluster of cells can make a particular type of decision according to what inputs it receives and how synapses are arranged. One cluster might decide that the stimulus being viewed is red rather than blue; another might send the message to other clusters that this red object is food. Still another might fire off a pattern of impulses to motor neurons of the spinal cord, commanding the arm to reach for the object.

A large group of cell bodies within the CNS, usually containing a number of different cell clusters with related functions, is called a **nucleus** (plural, **nuclei**) (NEW-klee-us; NEW-klee-eye). Such a group of cell bodies located outside of the CNS is termed a **ganglion** (GANG-glee-on). Look at Figure 3.11 and find the gray matter area labeled the *thalamus*. This area, near the center of the brain on either side of the midline, is composed of more than a dozen nuclei, each with a different set of functions. Just below the thalamus is the hypothalamus. Another 10 or so nuclei are contained within the hypothalamus (anatomists have yet to agree on the exact count), and dozens more are found in the brain stem. However, not all somas and dendrites are found in nuclei. Billions of them are arranged in the form of a wrinkled sheet of gray matter, called the **cerebral cortex**, that covers the rest of the brain (Figure 3.11).

Notice that the word *nucleus* has a new meaning in this chapter. When we are discussing single cells, a nucleus is that part of each cell that contains DNA. For the nervous system as a whole, a nucleus is a collection of neurons (each of which contains its own cell nucleus). Like many other words, the meaning shifts with the context.

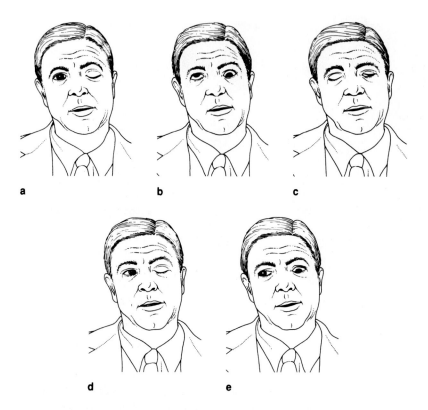

Figure 3.10 A case of regeneration in a nerve that supplies several muscles. Some of the regrowing motor axons have slipped into the wrong glial paths at the place where the nerve was cut and have regrown to the wrong muscles. Because the connections between the parts of the brain that instigate voluntary eye movements and the motor neurons that produce contractions of the eye muscles are genetically determined rather than learned, this accident victim has no hope of correcting his defect of regeneration through relearning.

In each picture, the intended movement is indicated by the position of the man's right eye. (**a**) At rest the upper left lid relaxes completely instead of staying half open. (**b**) When the patient attempts to look upward, the left eye looks down instead, and the upper left lid is raised. (**c**) When the intention is to close the left eye, the upper lid is again raised. (**d**) A leftward look closes the left lid completely. (**e**) An attempt to look right raises the left lid and points the left eye downward. (Adapted from Pollock & Harris, 1981)

Axons connecting various nuclei with the cortex and with each other are clustered into tracts. So, information is processed in the nuclei or cortical gray matter and then transmitted from one processor to another by way of white matter tracts. For example, the axon of a neuron in the cortex might extend out of the cortex as a part of a tract and connect that cell to other neurons in subcortical gray matter areas such as the thalamus and hypothalamus. That axon plus millions of others like it make up the white matter zone beneath the cortex that is visible in Figure 3.11. The same arrangement is found in the peripheral nervous system, but there ganglia (rather than nuclei) are connected to one another by nerves (rather than tracts).

With these organizational principles in mind, we are ready to survey the structures of the CNS to find out what each contributes to your existence.

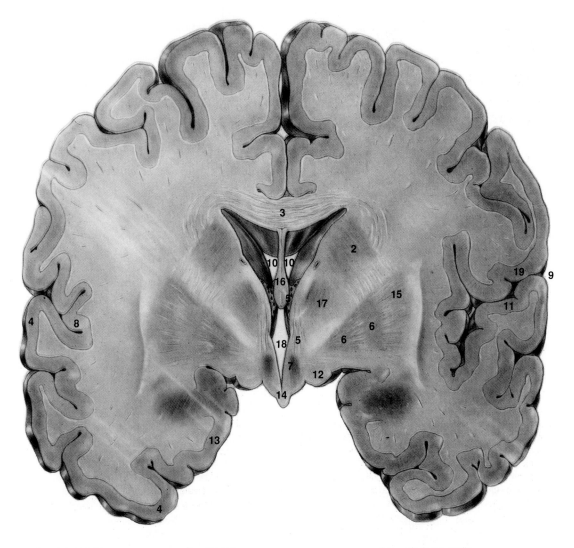

Figure 3.11 A frontal cross section of the human brain. The cut was made through the hypothalamus. (Adapted from Nieuwenhuys et al., 1981)

1. amygdala	8. insula	14. pituitary stalk
2. caudate nucleus	9. lateral fissure	15. putamen
3. corpus callosum	10. lateral ventricle	16. septum
4. cortex	11. lower bank of lateral fissure	17. thalamus
5. fornix	12. optic tract	18. third ventricle
6. globus pallidus	13. parahippocampal gyrus	19. upper bank of lateral fissure
7. hypothalamus		

Structures of the Central Nervous System

Our plan is to start with the parts controlling the simplest behaviors and work up to those that determine the most complex. By a simple behavior we mean a reflex, such as the one that causes you to withdraw from a painful stimulus. Complex behaviors are those such as problem solving and language.

Spinal Cord

Toiling away at the lowest levels of the nervous system, reflexes are the sensory–motor slaves of the nervous system. Their lowly but vital duties include digestive contractions, breathing, swallowing, speeding and slowing heartbeat, dilation and constriction of the pupils of the eyes, and convergence of the eyes on the visual target. Reflexes are also responsible for a host of less pleasant but usually beneficial behaviors such as choking, gagging, vomiting, sneezing, and coughing. This is but a small sample of the dozens and dozens of reflexes that enable your body to adjust to a multitude of internal and external changes occurring every moment. Just sitting still in a chair requires an entire collection of reflex circuits in your spinal cord, adjusting the tone of postural muscles in your neck, trunk, and legs. Without a certain level of tension in those muscles, you would go completely limp and slowly slide out of the chair onto the floor.

We tend to take our reflexes completely for granted. Perhaps this is because most reflex circuits reside within the spinal cord, a part of the nervous system probably not involved in consciousness. All reflex responses are automatic and unconscious. They are involuntary, initiated by external and internal stimuli rather than by voluntary processes. Shine light in your eye, and your pupil contracts; no thinking is required. Reflexes are involuntary because the circuits that produce them are relatively simple pathways connecting sensory neurons with motor neurons. These pathways were determined by your genes (i.e., inherited) rather than being established by learning experiences. We define a **reflex**, then, as a single, simple, unlearned response consisting of a fairly fixed pattern of muscle contractions that is automatically elicited by a particular kind of stimulus because of the existence of genetically determined connections within the nervous system. Circuits that produce reflexes are called **reflex arcs.** To trace some of these pathways, we must first learn our way around the spinal cord.

Cord Anatomy The cord floats in a tough, membranous sac within the column of bones that make up the spine. Each bone in the spinal column is called a **vertebra.** A pair of spinal nerves emerges between each vertebra and its neighbor. (The horizontal cross section in Figure 3.12 is cut to show this.) In Figure 3.13, note that a spinal nerve carries both afferent (sensory) and efferent (motor) fibers; just outside the cord, these two types separate into bundles called **roots.** The **dorsal root** (which connects with the dorsal, or back, side of the cord) contains the afferents from skin, muscle, and joints; the **ventral root** (which connects with the ventral, or belly, side of the cord) contains the efferent fibers.

Primary afferent neurons are sensory cells with receptor endings in skin, muscles, joints, or internal organs. They have a peculiar and distinctive shape with one long fiber that functions as both axon and dendrites (see Chapter 2). Their cell bodies are located in a swelling on the dorsal root called the **dorsal root ganglion** (Figures 3.12 and 3.13). Each soma has only one process, a short stalk that connects it to its fiber; there are no dendrites. The fiber (axon) begins in the sensory endings within skin, joints, or muscles; runs toward the spinal cord in a spinal nerve; enters a dorsal root; extends past the soma in the dorsal root ganglion; and terminates in the gray matter of the cord. On entering the cord, the afferent fiber spreads its terminal branches through much of the gray matter area called the **dorsal horn** (Figure 3.13).

Ventral roots of spinal nerves have no cluster of cell bodies comparable to the dorsal root ganglia; cell bodies of the efferent fibers are located within the gray matter of the spinal cord in an area known as the **ventral horn** (Figure 3.13). Each ventral horn cell sends its axon to a particular bundle of fibers in a striate muscle. Striate muscle contractions occur

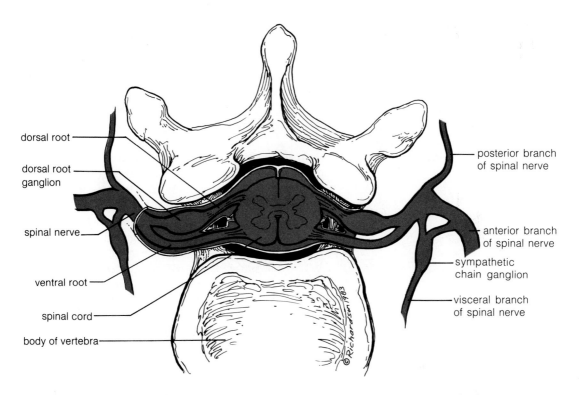

Figure 3.12 A cross section of spinal cord within the vertebral column. The cord floats in cerebrospinal fluid enclosed within a membrane. Dorsal is toward the top of the picture, ventral toward the bottom. Each spinal nerve splits into dorsal and ventral roots. The dorsal root ganglion contains somas of the primary afferents; cell bodies of the motor neurons are in the gray matter of the cord. The posterior branch of each spinal nerve serves the back of the body, the anterior branch serves the front, and the visceral branch carries autonomic fibers to the viscera. (From Creager, 1983)

only when ventral horn cells fire. Ventral horn cells, then, are motor (efferent) neurons.

Figure 3.13 also illustrates two reflex arcs. The one on the left consists of only two varieties of neurons, afferents and efferents. To keep the diagram simple, only one of each was drawn, but any real reflex arc would probably employ dozens of sensory and motor cells. Most reflex arcs are like the one on the right, which contains **interneurons** (also called **association neurons**), connecting the afferents with the efferents. The arc is a self-contained stimulus–response unit; that is, it can function without any help from higher levels of the nervous system. Any

stimulus to the primary afferents that is strong enough will excite the interneuron, triggering the motor neuron to contract muscles. Higher brain areas do become involved with reflex arcs, however, when we must stop the behavior from occurring (e.g., stifling a cough or sneeze). Many reflexes are compelling, and learning to inhibit them may be no easy matter. Children may require many months to learn to inhibit their bowel and bladder reflexes, for example. Inhibitory control is exerted by way of axons descending in ventral white matter tracts of the cord. Figure 3.13 shows one such axon descending from the brain to make an inhibitory connection

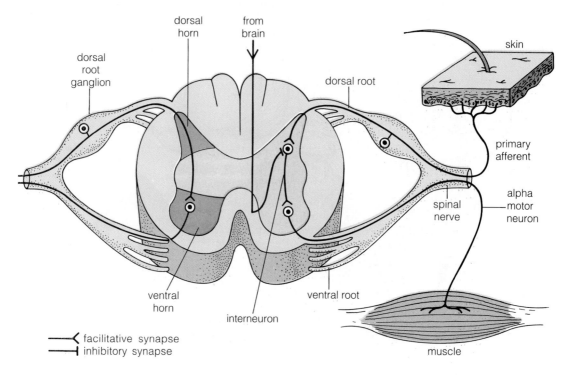

Figure 3.13 A cross section of spinal cord showing horns of gray matter and a reflex arc. An arc begins with a primary afferent that has its sensory endings in the skin or internal organs and its soma in the ganglion of the dorsal root. The cell body has only one process, a short stalk that connects it to its fiber (axon). There are no dendrites. The axon begins at the sensory endings, joins with other fibers to make a nerve, enters the dorsal root, passes by the stalk of the soma, and terminates within the dorsal horn of the gray matter, where it synapses with an interneuron. The interneuron's very short axon extends only to the ventral horn, where it synapses with an alpha motor neuron. The motor fiber leaves the cord by way of the ventral root and travels through a spinal nerve to its destination in a muscle. Thus a stimulus that excites a set of primary afferents may elicit the contraction of some muscle or set of muscles.

with the interneuron of the reflex arc. Stopping the interneuron from responding to the sensory neuron prevents the reflex action. Inhibition will be discussed more completely in Chapter 4.

The sensory information coming into the nervous system along the primary afferents is needed in the higher levels of the nervous system as well as in the reflex arcs. Thus, some afferents have axon branches that enter the dorsal white matter, join an ascending tract, and proceed up into the brain. We will track

their course later in the chapter when we discuss sensory projection systems.

Autonomic Nervous System The sensory and motor autonomic neurons that we discussed earlier and the ganglia housing some of their somas are organized into a coordinated network, the **autonomic nervous system (ANS)** (Figure 3.7). The ANS is not really an anatomical entity; it is a functional organization of neurons serving the viscera. Some

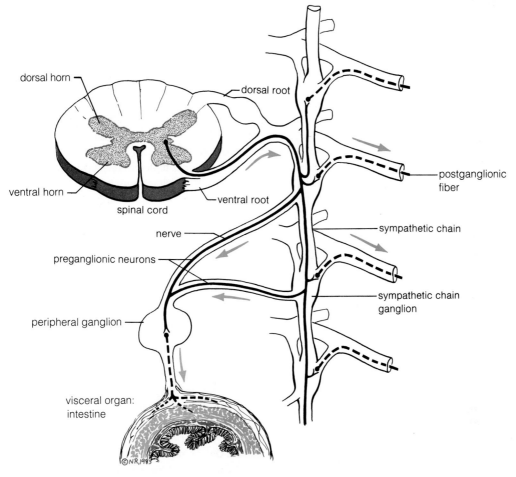

dorsal horn

ventral horn

spinal cord

dorsal root

ventral root

nerve

preganglionic neurons

peripheral ganglion

visceral organ:
intestine

postganglionic
fiber

sympathetic chain

sympathetic chain
ganglion

Figure 3.14   The preganglionic neurons of the sympathetic nervous system have their cell bodies in the gray matter between the dorsal and ventral horns. The axons leave the cord by the ventral root, travel in a spinal nerve for about 1 cm, and then leave the nerve to enter one of the sympathetic chain ganglia. Some axons synapse on postganglionic neurons within the ganglion, whereas others simply pass through, enter a nerve, and travel to synapses in a peripheral ganglion close to one of the visceral organs. Many preganglionic fibers send branches up and/or down to ganglia at other levels, thus providing the basis for coordinating all levels of the cord into "sympathetic" action. The neuron pictured is a composite of all types described. (Adapted from Creager, 1983)

of its cell bodies are within the CNS, some within the peripheral nervous system.

Just outside the spinal column lies a string of interconnected ganglia belonging to the sympathetic nervous system (Figure 3.14). These are the **sympathetic chain ganglia** and contain the cell bodies of neurons whose axons join spinal nerves. Axons connect chain ganglia to visceral organs controlled by the sympathetic nervous system (Figure 3.7). A

cell in a chain ganglion receives input from a sympathetic neuron located in the spinal cord (Figure 3.14). Sympathetic axons whose cell bodies are located in the gray matter of the cord, in a small area between the dorsal and ventral horns, are the **preganglionic fibers**. Axons of neurons whose cell bodies are located within the chain ganglia are **postganglionic fibers**. Figure 3.14 shows that preganglionic fibers may send branches up to higher sympathetic ganglia in the chain or down to lower ones. This coordination between levels makes the sympathetic nervous system tend to act as a whole. Thus, it is difficult to elicit one sympathetic response (e.g., heart-rate increase) without eliciting most of the others as well (such as secretion of adrenalin, release of glucose from the liver, increased respiration, sweating, etc.). The preganglionic and postganglionic fibers of the sympathetic nervous system are parts of reflex arcs controlling visceral reflexes.

The ANS is the Jekyll and Hyde of the body. At one moment, the ANS activates the whole body by speeding the heart rate, moving fuel to be burned into the cells, and shifting blood out of the intestines and into the muscles and brain where it is needed for fast, powerful reactions. At another time, the ANS slows the heart, acts to store fuel, and shifts blood out of the brain and muscles into the intestines and stomach. This latter action causes you to feel sluggish and sleepy after a full meal. The ANS has two such opposite "faces" because it consists of two diametrically opposed systems: the sympathetic and the parasympathetic. The **sympathetic nervous system** is the division that activates when you need to be quick and alert. During such times of arousal (e.g., playing tennis), you burn energy like a spendthrift and wear down your muscles as your whole body becomes adjusted temporarily for maximum effort, concentration, and powerful movements. The sympathetic division also dominates when you take a test. Then, you can feel its effects not only on your heart but also on your sweat glands when you notice how wet your palms are.

At some time during each day, you must pay back your organs for all the wear and tear from a period of sympathetic dominance. At that time, your **parasympathetic nervous system** takes over and begins replacing the resources you have used up. Neurons of the parasympathetic division send their axons to the same visceral organs as does the sympathetic division but have exactly the opposite effect. For example, where the sympathetic division inhibits the digestive organs, the parasympathetic speeds those smooth muscles. During parasympathetic dominance, you may feel lazy and lethargic, but visceral organs that process food for fuel replacement are tuning up for their greatest work output.

You are far more conscious of the actions of voluntary muscles than of those controlled by the ANS. Smooth muscles are controlled by a collection of unconscious autonomic reflexes that are reminiscent of the controls that automatically move your washing machine through its cycles or the thermostat that turns your heating system on and off. Hence, even though you are completely relaxed in front of the television, not "moving a muscle," your visceral muscles actually may be working at full speed.

All spinal cord circuits produce reflexes; none are for more complex behaviors. By contrast, the brain stem contains not only reflex circuits but more complicated circuits as well.

Brain Stem

The **brain stem** is the region between the top of the spinal cord and the most inferior (bottom) part of the brain itself (Figures 3.15 and 3.16). We divide it into three parts: the medulla oblongata positioned just superior to the spinal cord, the pontine region just above the medulla, and the midbrain at the very top of the stem (Figure 3.4).

Medulla Oblongata Like the rest of the nervous system, the **medulla oblongata** (med-DULL-la OB-long-GOT-ta) contains both white and gray matter. White matter of this brain stem region consists of axons of spinal cord neurons carrying information up into the brain and axons coursing in the opposite direction, from brain to cord. Gray matter is mostly organized into nuclei, each specialized to control some basic bodily function such as respiration or blood pressure. Nerve cells whose somas make up the nuclei are interneurons in reflex arcs. Because they are located in the brain stem rather than in the cord, most primary afferents of these reflex arcs travel in cranial nerves rather than spinal nerves. An example is the vagus nerve.

Cranial nerve X, the **vagus nerve** (VAY-guss), follows a twisting, winding path through the trunk (*vagus* = wanderer) to reach most visceral organs (Figure 3.6). Its efferent fibers form a large part of the parasympathetic nervous system; its afferents feed visceral sensory information into a region of the medulla, the **nucleus of tractus solitarius**

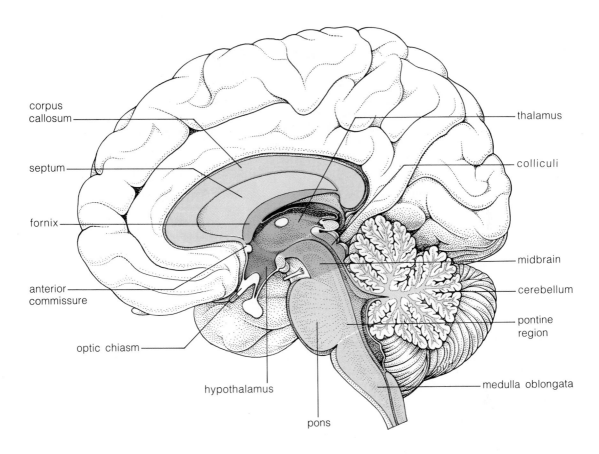

Figure 3.15 Midsagittal view of the right hemisphere of the human brain. Note in particular the boundaries of major structures (such as thalamus, midbrain, and pontine region), as indicated in color. (Adapted from Nieuwenhuys et al., 1981)

(NTS) (TRACT-tuss soll-ih-TAIR-ee-us). Because NTS receives information about nutrients passing through the liver and information from the tongue about the intensity of sweet and fat flavors from a particular food, it is in a good position to make associations that help influence how much hunger is experienced (see Chapter 11).

The nucleus also controls heartbeat and respiration. Your heart can beat on its own, but its pace must be adjusted for the current behavior level by reflexes of the medulla. When you exercise, you need a faster heart rate, higher blood pressure, and a more powerful contraction of heart muscles. With-

out these changes, your muscles use up too great a proportion of the available fuel and oxygen carried by the blood and leave the brain with a short supply. You feel such a shortage as fatigue and dizziness. If it becomes severe enough to shut down a lot of neurons, you lose consciousness (faint). You may experience a little of this despite the functioning of your reflexes whenever you stand up too quickly from a squatting position, especially if you are quite warm. Blood pressure is lowered under such circumstances, and the reflex changes needed for standing cannot always be made quickly enough to prevent a moment of dizziness.

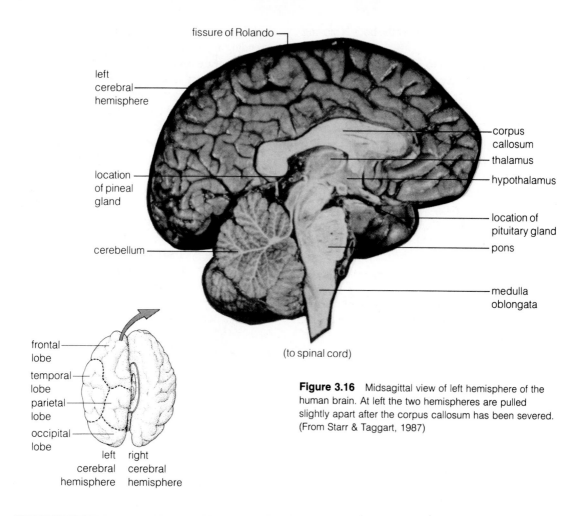

fissure of Rolando

left cerebral hemisphere

location of pineal gland

cerebellum

corpus callosum

thalamus

hypothalamus

location of pituitary gland

pons

medulla oblongata

frontal lobe

temporal lobe

parietal lobe

occipital lobe

left cerebral hemisphere

right cerebral hemisphere

(to spinal cord)

Figure 3.16 Midsagittal view of left hemisphere of the human brain. At left the two hemispheres are pulled slightly apart after the corpus callosum has been severed. (From Starr & Taggart, 1987)

Because vital functions are controlled by the medulla oblongata, it is one of the most critical regions in the brain for life. A human can lose nearly half of the brain and still survive if higher, more recently evolved regions are the ones destroyed. But if as little as 1 cc of medulla is damaged by a tumor, life may be extinguished.

Pontine Region The **pontine region** (PON-teen) (Figure 3.15), between medulla and midbrain, is composed of the pons, cerebellum, and a variety of smaller structures.

The **cerebellum** (SAIR-uh-BELL-um), a motor

structure on the dorsal side of the pontine region, consists of a cortex of gray matter and several nuclei embedded in the underlying white matter. The cerebellum functions to smooth and coordinate complex movements. Several senses feed information into this structure. It collects information from sensory receptors in skin, muscles, and joints and combines the information with visual images to coordinate body movements that are guided by the eyes. Also vital to coordination and balance are sensory messages coming into the cerebellum from vestibular receptors in the inner ear. This source of information informs the cerebellum about the direction of up and down and whether the body is moving through space.

All this input is used to calculate the timing and force of movements that were chosen by other parts of the brain. The cerebellum smooths movements, giving them precisely the correct amount of force and determining exactly when muscle contractions should cease in order to obtain the greatest accuracy. The intricate, highly controlled patterns of movement exhibited by a human gymnast would not be possible without a brain structure like the cerebellum, devoted to integrating the rotations about the various joints into smooth, coordinated whole-body motions. The cerebellum is to the body as a conductor is to the orchestra; without the cerebellum, various muscle groups would all be playing at a different tempo. Such subtle aspects of movement are not determined reflexively; they are learned. It is most likely that pathways through the cerebellum are set up through the process of learning rather than by genes. However, cerebellar circuits are below the brain structures that give us consciousness and do their job best when your conscious mind is attending to something other than the movement itself. If you are worried about getting the movement precisely correct, motor areas of the cortex apparently take over, imposing their influence and sometimes seeming to override cerebellar commands. The result is frequently a loss of smoothness and coordination of the sort seen when an Olympic ice skater bungles a movement by concentrating on it too intensely.

In Figure 3.15, find the pontine region and note the large, egg-shaped area on the ventral side of the brain stem. This is what the pons looks like in cross section. The word *pons* is Latin for *bridge,* and the **pons** of the brain stem is a huge bridge of nerve cell fibers that emerges from one half of the cerebellum, swings down around the ventral side of the brain stem like a sling (Figures 3.17 and 3.18), and runs back up to the opposite side of the cerebellum. Thus, it is the main connecting link between the two mirror-image **cerebellar hemispheres** (halves) of the cerebellum.

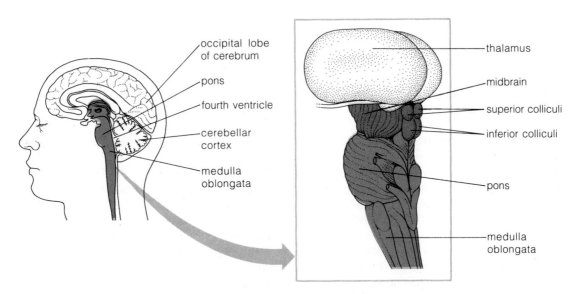

Figure 3.17 Lateral view of brain stem and thalamus. The medulla oblongata occupies the area from the base of the pons down to the first spinal nerve root. The midbrain extends upward from the top of the pons to the thalamus. (Adapted from Creager, 1983)

Structures of the Central Nervous System ■ **69**

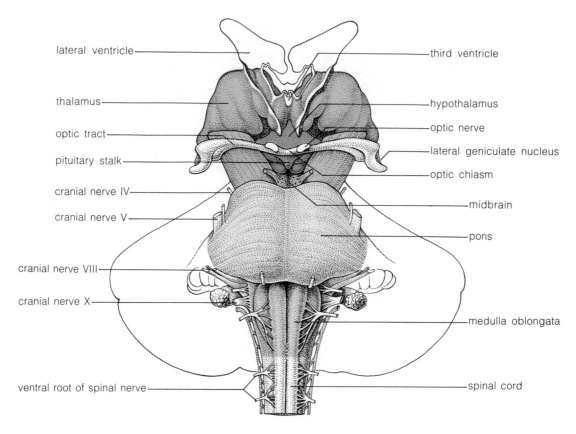

Figure 3.18 Ventral view of the brain stem, thalamus, and hypothalamus. The medulla oblongata is at the bottom of the picture, beginning just above the last pair of spinal nerve roots. Above it is the pons, the large tract connecting the two hemispheres of the cerebellum (pictured here just with the suggestion of an outline) on the dorsal side of the stem. The area between the pons and the optic chiasm (and tracts) is mostly the base of the hypothalamus. The midbrain is largely hidden by the bulge of the pons, but some is visible between the pons and the stalk of the pituitary. The tracts connecting the brain with the cord and stem have been cut just above the optic tracts to reveal more of the thalami. (Adapted from Nieuwenhuys et al., 1981)

The area of the pontine brain stem dorsal to the pons and ventral to the cerebellum contains various circuits that are important in moving the body around in space (walking, running, crawling, etc.), in controlling eye muscles, and in localizing the direction from which sounds are coming. Also, the entire region is heavily involved in dream sleep. We will come back to the pontine region repeatedly in subsequent chapters and fill in more of its structures and functions as we discuss learning, movement, sensory processes, and sleep.

Midbrain The most complex functions of the brain stem are found in the **midbrain**, the uppermost level of the stem (Figures 3.15 and 3.17). In lower vertebrates like cats and rats, the neural circuits for a long list of basic, unlearned behaviors are located in this region (Clemente & Chase, 1973; Grillner & Wallén, 1985). For example, the feline behavior of raising one forepaw to strike is organized by the midbrain. Cells in that region produce the sequence of movements by exciting the correct pattern of cord reflexes. The forepaw lashes out to land at exactly

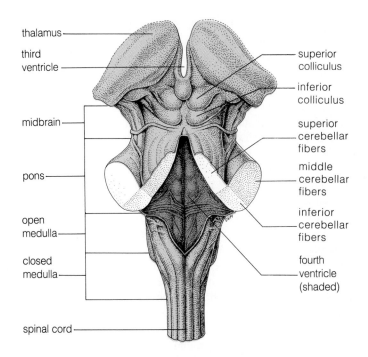

thalamus

third
ventricle

midbrain

pons

open
medulla

closed
medulla

spinal cord

superior
colliculus

inferior
colliculus

superior
cerebellar
fibers

middle
cerebellar
fibers

inferior
cerebellar
fibers

fourth
ventricle
(shaded)

Figure 3.19 Dorsal view of the brain stem and thalamus. The cerebellum has been cut away on the left to reveal the floor of the fourth ventricle and the fibers emerging from the cerebellar hemisphere, which swing around the ventral side of the brain stem to form the pons. Visible are the superior colliculi and inferior colliculi of the midbrain and the floor of the fourth ventricle in the pontine region. (Adapted from Fowler, 1984)

the correct point in space with a force that is adjusted to the size of the prey. To accomplish this, the brain stem must locate the target in space, calculate the trajectory of the paw, and then translate that intended movement into the correct pattern of muscle contractions. Trajectory calculations are probably done in the pontine region (especially within cerebellar circuits), but the location of the prey in space is most likely accomplished in an area of the midbrain called the superior colliculus.

The midsagittal view in Figure 3.15 shows two "bumps," named **colliculi** (kuh-LICK-you-lie), on the dorsal side of the midbrain. The top pair of colliculi (there is one colliculus on either side of the midline) are the **superior colliculi**, and the bottom pair are the **inferior colliculi**. The function of these two nuclei is to localize visual and auditory stimuli with respect to the body. Compare Figure 3.15 with Figures 3.17 and 3.19 to see what the colliculi look like.

Each superior colliculus contains a layer of cells receiving information from the retinas of the eyes, and this information is distributed across the visual layers of the colliculus so that it forms a map of visual space around the animal. If the neural activity focuses at one point in this map, the stimulus being viewed might be located, for example, far away and to the left; activity at a different point on the map might indicate that the stimulus was near and to the right—and so forth. Another layer of the superior colliculus beneath the visual layer contains a somatic map representing the body surface and receiving information from skin receptors. This map is lined up in correspondence with the visual map, thus suggesting that the two work together to produce behaviors such as reflexively looking down at a body part that has just been stimulated.

A third map in still another layer of the superior colliculus receives auditory information from the inferior colliculus that locates the source of a sound. Again, this map is aligned with the other two maps (Middlebrooks & Knudsen, 1984) so that a sound anywhere in your auditory environment reflexively prompts the motor circuits of your brain stem to turn your head and eyes toward the sound source.

If you are busy paying attention to some stimulus of importance to you, this reflexive orienting of visual receptors is inhibited; but if your mind is just wandering, the response occurs automatically without any prompting from your conscious self. So, the superior colliculus is a miniature biological computer that works out the locations of visual, auditory, and somatic stimuli and then computes the movement of head and eyes needed to view these stimuli (Middlebrooks & Knudsen, 1984).

Running through the core of the midbrain, pons, medulla, and spinal cord is a column of neurons that controls the intensity of responses and adjusts the amount of impact that any stimulus input will have on the rest of the brain. This structure is the **reticular formation,** and we will see (in Chapter 10) how the portion lying within the midbrain controls the arousal of the entire nervous system. This ability to determine the organism's arousal level makes the reticular formation of the midbrain a key to understanding attention and sleep.

Ventricles and Cerebrospinal Fluid

Return to Figure 3.11 for a moment. Directly in the center of that frontal section, you can see a thin hole in the brain that lies right on the midline between the two hemispheres. This cavity and three others in the brain are called **ventricles** (VEN-tri-culs). They serve as storage containers and circulation "pipes" for the fluid that bathes nerve cells, the **cerebrospinal fluid (CSF)**, which was discussed in Chapter 2.

The two **lateral ventricles,** one for each hemisphere, are shaped roughly like Cs with tails. The **third ventricle** lies in the cavity of the C at the center of the brain. In Figure 3.20 you can see through a transparent cortex to view the lateral ventricle of the left hemisphere. The lateral ventricle appears to be in the same plane as the third ventricle, but this is deceptive. The lateral ventricle is much closer to you, whereas the third ventricle lies along the midline and helps divide the brain into two hemispheres. The view of the ventricles from above clarifies this. The third ventricle and lateral ventricle are also flatter than you might judge when looking at the top picture in Figure 3.20. In Figure 3.11, you can find

the third ventricle and both lateral ventricles. (You won't find the temporal horn of the lateral ventricle because this section is too far anterior, but the frontal horn is clear.) Notice that the medial wall of each lateral ventricle is formed by a thin sheet of tissue, the **septum.** (At the bottom of its anterior end, the septum thickens into the septal nucleus—a structure we discuss in "Limbic System: Emotions and Motivation.") Also check Figure 3.15 and find the septum. Recall that immediately behind it is the lateral ventricle. The **fourth ventricle** lies in the pontine region of the brain stem and is connected to the third by a thin tube, the **cerebral aqueduct** (Figure 3.20). The floor of the fourth ventricle can be seen in Figure 3.19.

CSF is generated in the ventricles and circulates from them to the space around the brain. A tough, heavy membranous sac, the **dura mater** (DUR-uh MAY-tur), separates the brain from the inside of the skull and holds in the CSF. Thus, the brain floats in a bath of fluid within the dura. The CSF not only acts as a circulatory fluid for the nervous system but also cushions the brain against being bumped against the skull as you move your head suddenly.

Thalamus

Return again to Figure 3.11 and locate the third ventricle. The structure on its left and right that forms part of the walls of this ventricle is a collection of nuclei, the **thalamus**. Now examine Figure 3.15. The cut that sliced the brain in half for this picture ran right through the third ventricle so that the wall of the thalamus is visible just under the tract called the fornix and just above the midbrain. The bulk of the thalamus is hidden behind the plane of the picture. We can see more of it in Figures 3.17 and 3.19 where the cortex and some of the subcortical nuclei have been removed, leaving the thalamus as the highest structure remaining.

The location of the thalamus at almost the exact center of the brain seems well suited for its role as a central distributor of information. With the single exception of smell, all sensory information from all senses must pass through the thalamus on its way to the processing circuits in the cortex. Furthermore, various regions of the cerebral cortex can commu-

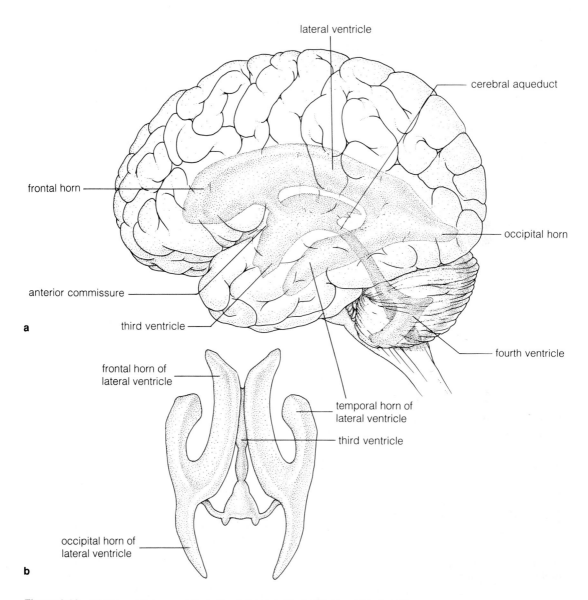

lateral ventricle

cerebral aqueduct

frontal horn

occipital horn

anterior commissure

third ventricle

fourth ventricle

a

frontal horn of
lateral ventricle

temporal horn of
lateral ventricle

third ventricle

occipital horn of
lateral ventricle

b

Figure 3.20 (**a**) The ventricles seen through a transparent brain. The two lateral ventricles, one in each hemisphere, extend from the frontal lobes (frontal horn) back to the parietal lobes where they curve around into the temporal lobes (temporal horn). At the place where they bend down into the temporal lobes, each extends a "finger" into its occipital lobe (occipital horn). The third ventricle separates the right-hemisphere thalamus and hypothalamus from the left-hemisphere thalamus and hypothalamus. It connects with the fourth ventricle of the pontine region by way of a thin tube called the cerebral aqueduct. (**b**) The ventricles as seen from above. (Adapted from Nauta & Fiertag, 1986)

nicate with one another by way of connections in and out of the thalamus. Some research suggests that certain thalamic nuclei are critical to your ability to choose a focus of attention. When you shift your attention from a visual to a sound stimulus, it may be neurons in the thalamus that allow the auditory input to take command away from the visual input.

Brain-stem circuits are capable of making reflex responses to sensory inputs, but conscious perception of stimuli completely depends on neurons in the thalamus and cortex. Each sense therefore has a neural route reaching from receptors that take in the stimulus through the nervous system to the cerebral cortex where conscious perception can take place. This route from receptors to cortex is called a **sensory projection system**.

For example, the projection system for taste begins in the mouth and ends in the cortex. The projection systems for vision, audition, taste, skin senses, and muscle sense all make synaptic connections through the thalamus. Each has its own nucleus where the incoming axons synapse with thalamic neurons. Axons of these thalamic neurons carry the information up to the area of cortex reserved for the particular sense. Visual information goes from the eye to a visual nucleus in the thalamus, whereas auditory input travels from the ear, up the brain stem to an auditory nucleus. Neurons in the visual nucleus send their axons to the visual projection area of the cortex at the back of the brain. When we study the cortex, we will locate the cortical projection areas for all senses.

Hypothalamus: Control of the Internal Environment

Just ventral to the thalamus lies a group of nuclei that control the internal environment of the body. Collectively, they are the **hypothalamus** (Figures 3.15 and 3.21). The hypothalamus in those figures is not a cut section. The viewpoint is from within the third ventricle, and you are seeing the side of the hypothalamus as it forms the wall of this cavity.

Biologically, the phenomenon called life consists of an enormously complex web of thousands of interacting chemical reactions. Human death, whether from disease, accident, or old age, usually

is the result of an interruption of one or more of these reactions. To provide the chemical conditions necessary for these reactions, there must be a mechanism to control such things as ion concentrations and the availability of glucose to fuel the reactions and hormones to turn them on and off. Neural control mechanisms for this huge mass of chemistry reside in the circuits of the hypothalamus. Some of its nuclei regulate the rate at which fuel is burned (and thus how warm you feel), whereas others take part in determining the rate at which fuel is taken into the body (hunger). Still other hypothalamic cells monitor the amount of water in cells and blood and work to keep that amount reasonably constant (through water conservation in the kidneys and the thirst drive), with the secondary effect of keeping blood pressure constant. The heart and all other visceral organs are controlled by the hypothalamus. Because it receives input from the parts of the brain in which your thoughts and emotions occur, the hypothalamus is the link between your conscious mind and the chemical functioning of your body. It is through this part of the brain that your emotions can affect your health (something we will learn more of in the chapter on stress and emotions).

The hypothalamus can exert its influence over the internal environment of your body through two avenues: the nervous system (controlling viscera) and the endocrine system (controlling body chemistry).

Control Through the Nervous System Nerve fibers leading out to visceral organs belong to the ANS, a part of the nervous system that has its origins in the brain stem and spinal cord. Those autonomic neurons in turn are controlled by fibers projecting down into the cord and stem from the hypothalamus. Within the hypothalamus, anterior nuclei have stronger connections to the parasympathetic branch, the posterior nuclei with the sympathetic branch. Most information about conditions in visceral organs reaches the hypothalamus by way of its connections with the NTS in the medulla.

The link from the hypothalamus to the ANS exists chiefly to regulate visceral organs. The sympathetic branch speeds heart rate, increases the volume of blood moved per beat, slows digestion in the intes-

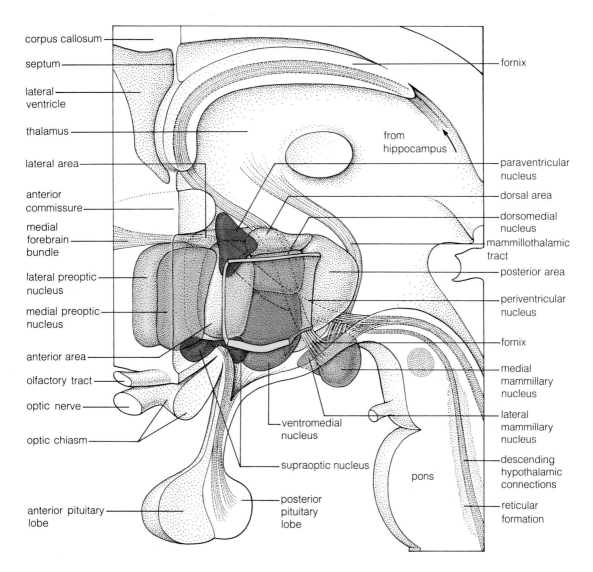

Figure 3.21 The major nuclei of the hypothalamus. Note the position of this brain area, immediately below the thalamus and anterior commissure (a tract connecting the two hemispheres) and above the pituitary and optic chiasm. The fibers of the fornix are shown looping over the dorsal side of the thalamus and then dropping down through the hypothalamus to their destination in the mammillary nucleus on the ventral side of the hypothalamus. Another such tract, the medial forebrain bundle, is shown running up from the brain stem through the nuclei of the hypothalamus and continuing forward toward the limbic areas just anterior to the hypothalamus. The thin, membranelike periventricular nucleus forms the wall of the third ventricle. (Adapted from Netter, 1962)

Figure 3.22 Location of endocrine glands in the body. (From Creager, 1983)

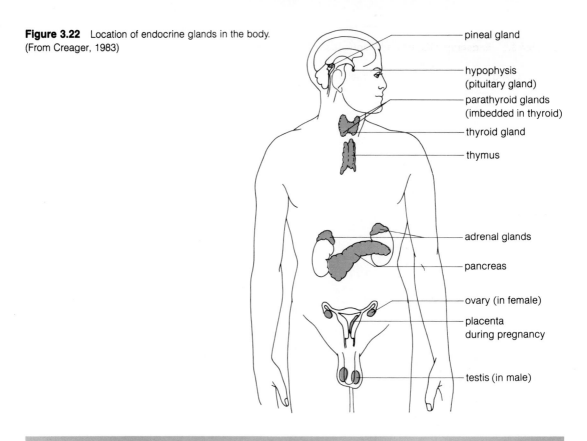

pineal gland

hypophysis (pituitary gland)

parathyroid glands (imbedded in thyroid)

thyroid gland

thymus

adrenal glands

pancreas

ovary (in female)

placenta during pregnancy

testis (in male)

tines, constricts certain blood vessels and opens others to move more blood into the brain and muscles, dilates the pupils of the eyes, and dilates the airways leading down to the lungs. The parasympathetic branch exerts the opposite effects.

The total effect of sympathetic influence on viscera is to produce a state that we term *arousal* or *activation,* and the level of arousal is an important component of most emotions. Anger and fear, for example, are states characterized by high arousal, whereas depression, sadness, and gloom are identified, in part, by their very low arousal levels. What this means is that the hypothalamus with its controlling circuits for the sympathetic nervous system has much of the responsibility for emotional arousal. Experimenters have demonstrated this repeatedly through experiments in which emotional responses were elicited in animals by way of electrical stimulation of the hypothalamus (see Chapter 13).

Control Through the Endocrine System The second aspect of internal environment, body chemistry, is controlled by the hypothalamus through the endocrine system. The **endocrine system** is a group of glands (Figure 3.22) that secrete chemicals called **hormones**. Glands can be grouped into **exocrine glands** (such as salivary glands), which deliver their secretions directly to the point where they are used, and **endocrine glands**, which secrete their chemicals into the bloodstream to be carried to their point of use. Endocrine gland secretions are regulated by a master gland, the **pituitary**, located just below the hypothalamus. The control route from hypothalamus to pituitary to endocrine glands to cells of the body will be central to our later discussions of hunger, thirst, reproductive behavior, and stress. Table 3.1 lists most of the endocrine glands, their hormones, and effects on the body.

Figure 3.22 shows the locations of the various

Table 3.1 Endocrine Glands and Hormones

Gland	Hormone	Effect
Adrenal cortex	Mineralocorticoids Glucocorticoids	Regulate concentrations of ions such as sodium Help body respond to stressors
Adrenal medulla	Adrenalin/noradrenalin	Mimic actions of the sympathetic nervous system
Gonads	Estrogens Progesterone Testosterone	Create female secondary sex characteristics Prepares uterus for pregnancy Creates male secondary sex characteristics
Pancreas	Insulin	Enables glucose and fats to enter cells
Parathyroid	Parathyroid hormone	Regulates blood calcium concentration
Thyroid	Thyroxin	Regulates metabolic rate, protein synthesis
Anterior pituitary	GH ACTH TSH FSH LH	Regulates growth of all body tissues Stimulates adrenal cortex Stimulates thyroid to secrete thyroxin Stimulates gonads to develop ovum or sperm Controls development in gonads
Posterior pituitary	Oxytocin Vasopressin	Stimulates release of milk from breast Helps maintain blood pressure

endocrine glands. All are pictured, but some such as the parathyroid are not of great importance to the psychologist so we will not discuss them. The **gonads** secrete the reproductive hormones estrogen (ESS-tro-gen), progesterone (pro-JEST-er-own), and testosterone (tes-TAHS-ter-own), which are responsible for creating secondary sex characteristics, masculinizing or feminizing the brain, and controlling the sequence of events in pregnancy. The **pancreas** secretes the hormone insulin, which enables two of the body's major fuels (glucose and fats) to get into cells where they can be used. The **adrenal glands**, sitting atop the kidneys, are really two glands in one. The central core, the **adrenal medulla**, secretes the hormones **adrenalin** and **noradrenalin**, which act on visceral organs in the same way as the sympathetic neurons. They speed heart rate, shift glucose into the blood, shift more blood to the brain, and so forth. The outer portion of the adrenal is the **adrenal cortex**, which produces **mineralocorticoids** (MIN-er-RAL-oh-KOR-tih-KOIDS) and **glucocorticoids** (GLUE-ko-KOR-tih-KOIDS). The major mineralocorticoid acts on the kidneys to conserve salt and water by returning them to the blood during urine formation. Glucocorticoids are secreted during stressful experiences like disease or injury and are important to the process of recovery. They act everywhere throughout the body. The **thyroid gland** secretes the hormone thyroxine, which sets the base level for metabolism (i.e., the rate at which cells throughout the body burn glucose and synthesize proteins). A person deprived of thyroxine feels sluggish and tired. If the thyroid is malfunctioning before birth, the fetus cannot develop properly. Muscles, bone, and nervous tissue all fail to grow, leaving the child with a dwarflike appearance. Typically, the hands, feet, and legs are short and stubby and the skin is dry and scaly. The large, thick, protruding tongue makes it difficult for the child to keep the mouth closed. Unless there is immediate medical treatment, the child is mentally deficient (Lemeshow, 1982). The condition is known as **congenital hypothyroidism** (or, in older terminology, cretinism).

Like the adrenal, the pituitary is also two glands

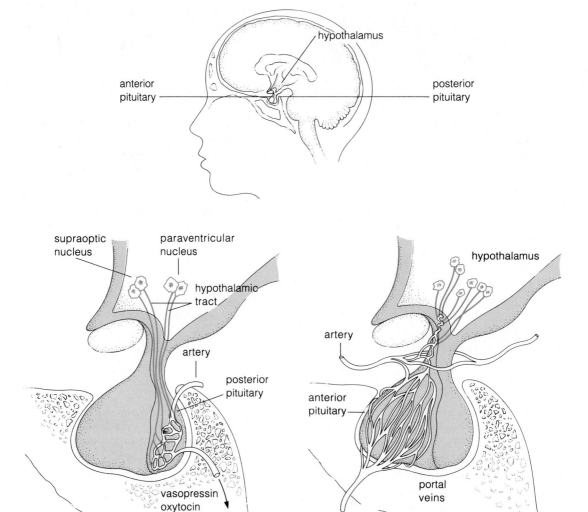

Figure 3.23   Connections between the hypothalamus and the pituitary glands. (**a**) Two hypothalamic nuclei, the paraventricular and supraoptic, control secretion of hormones from the posterior pituitary by way of axons running down the pituitary stalk. (**b**) Cells in other hypothalamic nuclei control anterior pituitary secretion by secreting releasing factors (hypothalamic hormones), which are sent to the pituitary by way of portal veins. The abbreviations at the bottom of the picture refer to the hormones secreted by the anterior pituitary. The anterior pituitary secretes andrenocorticotrophic hormone (ACTH), thyroid-stimulating hormone (TSH), luteinizing hormone (LH), follicle-stimulating hormone (FSH), and growth hormone (GH).

in one. Figure 3.21 shows the location of the pituitary at the base of the brain just inferior to the hypothalamus and posterior to the optic chiasm. Figure 3.23 shows how the double gland is provided with the extra-security shelter of a bony socket in the skull. This positioning is not accidental. You can afford to lose many ounces of brain tissue, but the loss of the pituitary means the complete disruption of the entire chemical system of the body, with death the inevitable result.

Cells of the **posterior pituitary** release their hormones into blood vessels that so richly supply the gland. One hormone of the posterior pituitary, oxytocin (ox-EE-toe-sin), acts on the uterus to initiate the contractions of labor and to stimulate the mammary glands to release the milk stored there. Another hormone of the posterior pituitary is vasopressin, which is important in maintaining blood pressure. Neither hormone is manufactured within the gland. The posterior pituitary differs from the anterior pituitary in that it receives nerve fibers from several of the hypothalamic nuclei (Figure 3.23). Surprisingly, it is these hypothalamic neurons, not the pituitary, that actually make oxytocin and vasopressin. The hormones are transported through the microtubules of neuron axons from the somas in the hypothalamus to the terminals in the pituitary and released like neurotransmitters. In fact, they are also found in various areas of the brain where they are suspected of serving as neurotransmitters rather than hormones.

As you can see, it is sometimes difficult to tell the difference between transmitters and hormones, neurons and endocrine cells. Very likely the two types of cells evolved from the same ancestor. The major difference seems to be that most neurons are specialized to form synaptic zones into which they secrete their chemicals, whereas endocrine cells pour theirs into the bloodstream. Some hypothalamic cells seem to be both neural and endocrine.

The **anterior pituitary** is a completely different gland than the posterior. Its cells manufacture the hormones it secretes, and the hypothalamic control over their release into the bloodstream is comparatively indirect. Figure 3.23 shows cells in the posterior hypothalamus that secrete chemicals called releasing factors. These hormonelike hypothalamic chemicals are carried to the anterior pituitary by a set of blood vessels called portal veins. Each type of releasing factor induces pituitary cells to release a different anterior pituitary hormone into the bloodstream. For example, gonadotropin-releasing factor (GRF) induces the release of two anterior pituitary hormones that stimulate the gonads. The gonads respond by increasing the output of their hormones, which circulate through the blood to all cells of the body. Thus, there is a clear, chemical chain of command by which the hypothalamus controls the body's basic chemistry within each cell.

Corpus Striatum: Motor Habits

Between the cortex, covering the outside of the brain, and the thalamus at its center lies a group of three very large nuclei called the **corpus striatum.** Look at these structures in Figure 3.24 and imagine that you are looking through a transparent brain at an opaque corpus striatum within. Now look at Figure 3.25 and see how these structures would appear if the surrounding brain were peeled off. The largest of the group of three, a **C**-shaped nucleus that curls around the dorsal side of the thalamus, is the **caudate nucleus.** At its anterior end, it blends into a flat, egg-shaped nucleus, the **putamen,** which is partially cut away in Figure 3.25 to reveal the thalamus at the center of the brain. The cutaway shows that the putamen is between you and the thalamus. It also reveals the third nucleus, the **globus pallidus,** which in Figure 3.24 remains completely hidden behind the putamen. Now go back to the frontal section in Figure 3.11 and find these same three nuclei. Note that the caudate forms the lateral wall of the lateral ventricle. The thalamus looks small in Figure 3.11 because this frontal section was made toward the front of the brain and the slice caught only the anterior nucleus. The tracts running between the thalamus and cortex cut the caudate nucleus off from the putamen and give the illusion that these are separate nuclei. Actually, they function as a unit and are frequently referred to as the neostriatum or, simply, **striatum.**

Injuries to the corpus striatum have given us some hypotheses concerning its role in brain function. Symptoms most typically associated with destruction of these parts center on the ability to move. Appar-

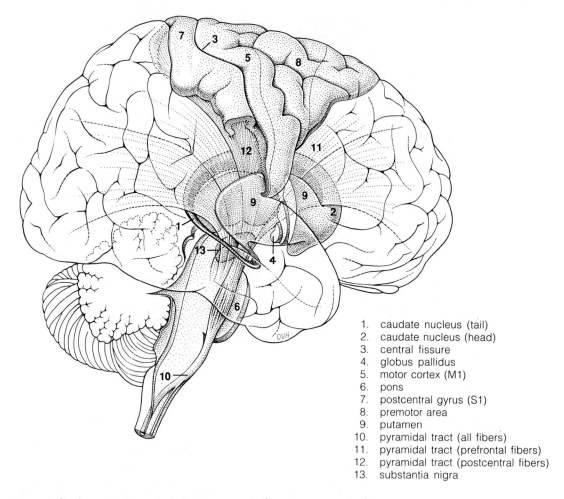

1. caudate nucleus (tail)
2. caudate nucleus (head)
3. central fissure
4. globus pallidus
5. motor cortex (M1)
6. pons
7. postcentral gyrus (S1)
8. premotor area
9. putamen
10. pyramidal tract (all fibers)
11. pyramidal tract (prefrontal fibers)
12. pyramidal tract (postcentral fibers)
13. substantia nigra

Figure 3.24 Transparent brain showing the position of the corpus striatum within. The putamen and globus pallidus have been partly cut away to reveal their three-layered arrangement. Compare this figure with Figure 3.25 to get a clearer idea of their shapes. The corpus striatum works in close association with the M1 motor cortex and the premotor area of the frontal lobe. Also shown in this picture is a major pathway, the pyramidal tract, which connects the cortical motor neurons with the spinal cord. The figure shows its route through the brain stem. A portion of the pyramidal tract originates in S1, the postcentral gyrus. (Adapted from Nieuwenhuys et al., 1981)

ently, the structures of the corpus striatum are important parts of the motor system, but what is it that they contribute? We know that reflex movements are controlled by circuits in the cord and brain stem; is it possible that the corpus striatum contains the circuits for voluntary, conscious movements? The answer seems to be clearly, No. Those circuits run from the motor parts of the cerebral cortex (which we will discuss soon) to the brain stem and cord.

Brooks (1986) suggests that the striatal structures help the corticocerebellar circuits in their attempts to produce needed movements. Muscle contractions do not occur in a vacuum; there is always a context of ongoing movement and existing posture that must

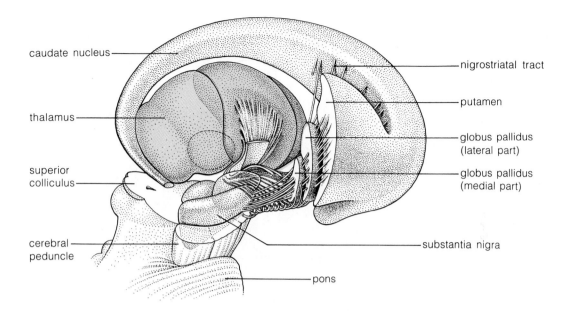

caudate nucleus
nigrostriatal tract
thalamus
putamen
globus pallidus
(lateral part)
superior
colliculus
globus pallidus
(medial part)
cerebral
peduncle
substantia nigra
pons

Figure 3.25 The position of the corpus striatum in relation to the thalamus and midbrain.
The brain stem has been sliced at the level of the superior colliculus and a section
removed. This leaves the thalamus and corpus striatum "floating" above the lower midbrain.
The red nucleus and substantia nigra, however, have not been cut through, and their whole
forms can be seen in three dimensions. Fibers of the nigrostriatal tract can be seen arising
from the substantia nigra, where the cell bodies are located, and running up into the striatum, where they terminate. The other tract pictured is one that connects the striatum with
the thalamus. (Adapted from Nieuwenhuys et al., 1981)

be taken into account. For example, the sequence of muscle contractions that you use to sign your name on a paper lying atop the desk at which you are sitting is quite different from that needed to sign your name on that paper when you are standing. Try the two postures and feel the difference. The actual muscle contractions commanded by the motor plans stored in the cortical circuits must be modified and interpreted to fit into the context of your current posture. Most of your voluntary acts can be accomplished from a great variety of starting positions (postures), each therefore calling for a different set of contractions. Imagine how many ways you can grip a door handle when you turn it or how much variation there is to the movements in walking as you change your gait or move from a smooth to a bumpy surface. Each variation on the basic theme must be worked out by some brain structure.

Most of what the corpus striatum does, it does at an unconscious level, which allows you to perform the very complex series of movements and delicate shifts in balance needed to climb a set of stairs while controlling the more than 20 speech muscles needed to carry on a conversation (or simply, walking while talking). In fact, most of your behavior occupies two levels: a conscious set of movements controlled by the cortex and a half-conscious set controlled by the striatum, which allows you to do some simple, routine tasks simultaneously. It has been suggested that the motor cortex learns its movements (i.e., assembles its control circuits) through the process of insight, whereas the corpus striatum learns through rote memorization (Brooks, 1986). Thus, teaching the corpus striatum to ride a bike or shift gears or walk is a matter of practicing the movements over and over.

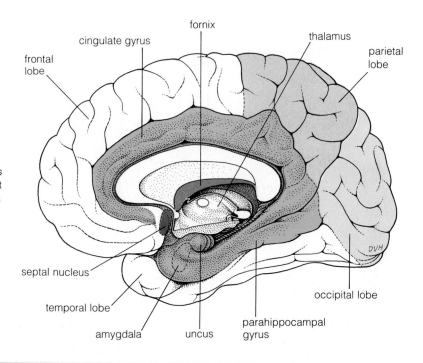

Figure 3.26 Midsagittal view of brain with brain stem cut away to show the ring of limbic structures around the central core of the brain. The septal nucleus is showing through the transparent structures covering it. Not visible are the nucleus accumbens and nucleus basalis, which are hidden behind the septal nucleus. The uncus of the medial temporal lobe has also been rendered transparent in order to reveal the amygdala within it. The hippocampus is buried within the parahippocampal gyrus. Compare this picture with Figure 3.27.

In summary, nuclei of the corpus striatum do not store the plans for movements. Instead, they aid the cortical circuits (where the plans are apparently stored) by selecting the proper variation of each voluntary movement that best fits the momentary context of posture and ongoing behavior. These nuclei also rote memorize simple, routine movement sequences that can be performed simultaneously with the conscious movements as a part of their context.

Limbic System: Emotions and Motivation

Near the midline of the brain is a system of interconnected structures that form a ring around the central core (Figure 3.26). The major parts of this **limbic system** are the cingulate gyrus, septal area, nucleus accumbens, nucleus basalis, parahippocampal gyrus, amygdala, and hippocampus. Figure 3.27 illustrates these structures as solid, three-dimensional shapes showing through a transparent brain.

If you think of the cerebral cortex, that wrinkled mass of gray matter that covers all other structures of the brain, as rolling over the top of each hemisphere and down into the deep fissure separating them, you can see that its boundaries are fringed by limbic structures. In fact, the word *limbus* is Latin for *edge* or *border*.

MacLean (1949), who gave these parts of the brain the name *limbic system,* also refers to them as the *visceral brain.* Electrical stimulation of limbic areas frequently results in visceral responses such as changes in blood pressure, sweating, and respiration. Furthermore, the limbic system has very strong connections with the hypothalamus, the part of the brain most involved with events in the viscera. Sensory information coming into the brain from receptors throughout the internal organs pours into the NTS. From this nucleus, the information goes to the hypothalamus and from there to many of the limbic areas (Nauta & Fiertag, 1986). Thus, we can expect the limbic system to be involved in many of the same

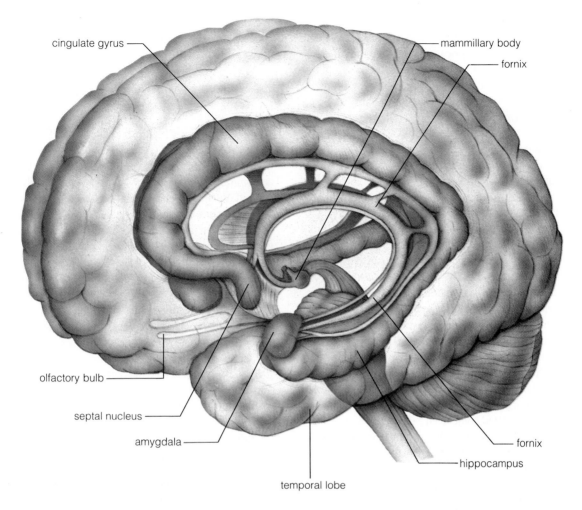

cingulate gyrus

mammillary body

fornix

olfactory bulb

septal nucleus

amygdala

fornix

hippocampus

temporal lobe

Figure 3.27 Transparent brain with limbic structures showing through. Notice that they form a ring around the central core of the cerebrum. The empty spaces just below the cingulate gyrus are normally filled by the corpus callosum. (Adapted from Snyder, 1977)

functions as the hypothalamus—that is, physiological motivations and emotional responses. That leads immediately to a puzzle. If the hypothalamus is already in charge of emotional responses, food and water intake, temperature regulation, and reproductive functions, why are the limbic areas needed for those same things? There doesn't seem to be much doubt about its involvement. For example, stimulating or removing the amygdala in animals can alter emotional responses in social situations and modify food preferences. Electrical stimulation of the human amygdala produces feelings of fear or anger sometimes accompanied by visceral sensations such as "churning stomach" (Nauta & Fiertag, 1986). Septal nucleus lesions (damage) can turn a tame animal into a vicious one, and amygdalar destruction can tame a wild animal. So, we must try to discover what contribution the limbic system is making to emotional and motivational functions.

A second puzzle is the large body of evidence

implicating some of the limbic system in the creation of memories. As we will see in Chapter 16, bilateral removal of the **hippocampus** makes it very difficult for a person to form new long-term memories of the events in his or her life. The **amygdala** (ah-MIGG-dah-la) also seems to be vital for the acquisition of certain types of memory, especially those dealing with whether a stimulus should be approached or avoided.

Fortunately, we can now see a way to meld these different ideas into a single explanation of what most limbic structures are doing. The hypothalamus and brain stem apparently contain circuits that direct visceral organs to do something (secrete a chemical, speed or slow a movement, etc.). Internal responses that are a part of emotion seem to originate from those two areas. Limbic structures have a higher-level task; they store your experiences and use those memories to decide when you should be motivated or emotional. For example, it is probably the amygdala that decides whether you should treat a particular food as edible or not. It collects past experiences, such as memories of what you ate all through childhood, and uses those to judge that you should treat a hamburger as food but not fried grasshoppers (or vice versa if you come from a different background). Monkeys with large limbic system lesions involving the amygdala have been observed putting nuts and bolts into their mouths as though they were food (Klüver & Bucy, 1938).

The **septal nucleus** may be a repository of memories concerning the appropriate emotional levels to display in any situation. (We will examine the evidence in Chapter 13.) The other nuclei at the anterior end of the limbic ring, the nucleus accumbens and nucleus basalis, also seem involved with memory, but we do not yet know enough about their function to say in exactly what way they are involved. The posterior portion of the **cingulate gyrus** and the **parahippocampal gyrus** (PAIR-uh-HIP-oh-CAM-pull) collect somatosensory, visual, and auditory information from bordering areas of the cerebral cortex and funnel it down into the hippocampus (Van Hoesen, 1982) where presumably it constructs your memories of events (discussed in Chapter 15). The anterior cingulate, however, remains a mystery.

In general, the limbic system stores motivational and emotional memories as well as memories for events. Table 3.2 gives a summary of functions for individual structures.

Neocortex

When you examine a human brain, most of what you see is cerebral cortex. The word *cortex* is a general term for any outside covering (literally, bark) of an anatomical structure, and you may recall that the cerebellum and adrenal glands both have cortexes. The **cerebrum** is all of the brain above the level of the brain stem, and the cerebral cortex is the gray matter covering of the cerebrum.

An immediately striking peculiarity of the cortex is its "wrinkles." Technically, they are called **convolutions**, and they represent a way of squeezing more cortex into roughly the same-sized skull. The cortex is a six-layered sheet of cells averaging about 2.5 mm in thickness. About two thirds of the cortex lies hidden within the folds of the convolutions (Shepherd, 1979). If one could spread the cortex out flat, it could be seen as a sheet of gray matter measuring about 4,000 cm^2 (Mountcastle, 1979), or 6.25 sq ft. That is an immense amount of brain tissue, and it has been estimated that this mammoth structure may hold as many as 13,653,000,000 neurons (Crosby et al., 1962).

Some parts of the limbic ring are cortex (cingulate, parahippocampal, etc.). Limbic cortex, however, has a different microscopic structure from the rest of the cortex and reached its full development earlier in the course of evolution. The majority of cerebral cortex has a six-layered structure and is called **neocortex** (*neo* = new) in reference to its later evolutionary development. There seem to be only about 30 types of cells in the neocortex; within any microscopic area, these types are organized into a set of circuits that performs some function. Each set of circuits, called a **module** or **minicolumn**, occupies a tiny vertical cross section of cortex, stretching across the six layers from its outside surface to the underlying white matter below and usually containing about 110 neurons (Mountcastle, 1979). Next to this module is an identical one and next to that another. Indeed, the entire sheet of gray matter consists of nothing more than several million

Table 3.2   Structures of the Limbic System

Name	Pronunciation	Location in Limbic Ring	Proposed Function
Cingulate gyrus	SING-you-let JYE-russ	Between septal nucleus and occipital lobe	Connects motivational circuits of limbic with motor cortex(?)
Hippocampal gyrus	HIP-oh-CAM-pul	Between occipital lobe and septal nucleus	Funnels all sensory input into hippocampus
Hippocampus	HIP-oh-CAM-puss	Immediately beneath the hippocampal gyrus	Stores memories for events
Amygdala	ah-MIGG-duh-la	Beneath hippocampal gyrus anterior to hippocampus	Stores memories for what to approach and avoid
Septal nucleus	SEP-tul NEW-klee-us	Between hippocampal gyrus and anterior cingulate gyrus	Decides emotional intensities
Nucleus accumbens	ah-KUM-bens	Just lateral to the septal nucleus	Is part of the reinforcement system
Nucleus basalis	bay-ZAL-iss	Lateral and ventral to nucleus accumbens	Has unknown memory function

replications of this one fundamental set of circuits (Mountcastle, 1979).

It is fascinating that the cortex is able to perform functions as different as fine control of finger movements and perception of visual depth with nearly equivalent circuits. The most important characteristic in creating the functional differences between, for example, the speech area and the auditory area is that each zone of the cortex has a unique set of inputs and outputs. An area that takes in only visual information, for example, would almost be forced by that fact alone to function as a visual processor rather than a motor or speech area. Thus, it is not that the visual area contains visual circuits whereas the speech area contains speech circuits. They all have the same sort of modules but with different inputs and outputs.

Anatomy of the Neocortex   On discovering a new territory, an explorer's first instinct, it seems, is to name every feature in sight. Early anatomists, looking at the outside of the brain, named every wrinkle they could find, even though many of the minor convolutions fail to appear in every brain. Human brains are just as individual in appearance as human faces, and what appears to be a clear landmark in one may be barely discernible in another. However, just as every normal face has one nose, two eyes, and so on, the surface of the cortex has some landmarks that are relatively easy to find in every brain.

To begin with, the "hill" portion of each convolution is called a **gyrus** (JYE-russ), the plural being gyri (JYE-rye). A "crack" separating one gyrus from another is a **sulcus** (SULL-kuss), and the plural is sulci (SULL-sye). Very large, deep sulci are **fissures** and are used by anatomists as boundaries between large segments of cortex called lobes. In Figure 3.28 find the **central fissure**. Just anterior to this fissure is the **frontal lobe**, and just posterior is the **parietal lobe** (puh-RYE-eh-tul). Running up the lateral surface of each hemisphere is the **lateral fissure**. It gives us a boundary for separating off the **temporal lobe**,

Figure 3.28 The human brain showing the lobes of the cerebral cortex: (**a**) lateral view; (**b**) dorsal view. (From Creager, 1983)

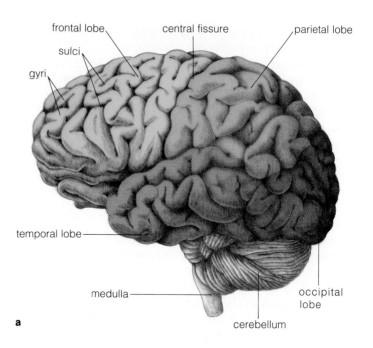

frontal lobe

central fissure

parietal lobe

sulci

gyri

temporal lobe

medulla

occipital lobe

cerebellum

a

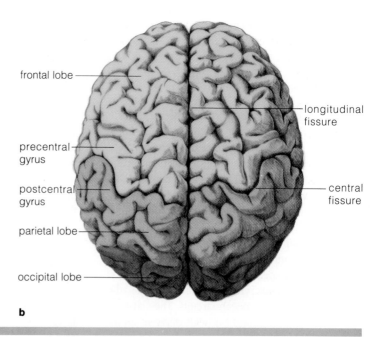

frontal lobe

longitudinal fissure

precentral gyrus

postcentral gyrus

central fissure

parietal lobe

occipital lobe

b

which is all the cortex inferior to the lateral fissure. The posterior end of the cortex is the **occipital lobe** (ahk-SIPP-it-uhl); unfortunately, there are no clear, easy landmarks to serve as boundaries for it.

The largest fissure of the entire brain is the **longitudinal fissure** (LAWN-jih-TUDE-in-nul), so called because it runs the length of the cortex from anterior to posterior (longitudinally). The longitudinal fissure separates the brain into right and left **cerebral hemispheres** (half-spheres). Notice in Figure 3.26 that the frontal, parietal, and occipital lobes curl over into the longitudinal fissure and form its banks down to the level of the limbic cortex of the cingulate gyrus. If you cut a real brain in two, this fissure is so deep that you could not cut actual brain tissue until you reached the core of the brain. Specifically, the **corpus callosum** (kuh-LOHS-um) is the first structure to be severed as you pull the hemispheres apart from the top (Figures 3.11 and 3.15). The callosum is a giant fiber tract composed of axons of cortical neurons. It is the major communication link between the two hemispheres at the cortical level.

It is important to remember that sulci and fissures are not true functional boundaries. As you can see from Figure 3.11, cortex is one continuous sheet of tissue and curves right around the bottom of every sulcus. This means that there is a certain artificiality about the "places" we have named in the cortex. Why, for example, should we decide that the upper dorsolateral surface of the cortex should be divided into two lobes—frontal and parietal—rather than being treated just as one? The cortex does not stop at the central fissure and take up again on the other side. Microscopic examination of the cortex on the two sides shows that the frontal cortex has a slightly different balance of neurons in the various layers than does the parietal cortex, but both are made of the same modules and presumably function identically. Most of our anatomical names for cortical features are largely arbitrary and mostly for convenience in communication.

Be sure to note the large areas of cortex that lie hidden in the banks of fissures. For example, in Figure 3.11 find the lateral fissure and see how it contains a large, hidden zone of cortex called the insula. Figure 3.29 shows another way to reveal this buried cortex.

Sensory–Perceptual Areas of the Neocortex The cortex can be roughly divided into a frontal half that deals with action and response and a back half handling sensory–perceptual functions. Sensory information reaches the cortex by way of the sensory projection systems. Each projection system terminates in a zone of cortex reserved for that particular sense, called a **sensory projection area**. Except for the sense of smell, all these systems have a synapse in the thalamus where each sense has its own nucleus. The visual projection system carries information from the eyes through the thalamus to the cortex. The **visual sensory projection area** (or, in more modern terminology, **V1**) is in the occipital lobes, which are entirely devoted to visual processing. Visual perception apparently can be analyzed into dozens of individual functions (form, color, location, movement, depth, etc.), and each one requires at least one cortical **processor area**. As indicated in Figure 3.30, the region of the cortex devoted to visual functions extends into the posterior parietal lobe and inferior portion of the temporal lobe. Visual information enters this system of visual processors by way of V1 at the posterior end of the occipital lobe. From V1, visual information spreads across the occipital lobe, being processed a little further at each synapse in each processor area. In V1 it likely represents nothing more than an unrelated collection of lines, colors, locations, and distances. By the time this flow of information reaches the inferior temporal lobe areas, contributions of all processors have been combined into the perception of an object against a visual background (e.g., an image of your automobile parked in the driveway). Of all cortical analyzer areas in the visual cortex, V1 is the most critical. The great majority of visual information arriving in the cortex must pass through this set of analyzers; if an accident destroys that part of your brain, you will be blind even if your eyes and optic nerve are perfect. We will examine cortical blindness in Chapter 18.

Look at the temporal lobe in Figure 3.30 and find the projection area for **audition**. Most of this zone is hidden within the lateral fissure where it forms part of the lower side. Figure 3.29 reveals its full extent by opening up the lateral fissure to show its sides. Without this projection area, you would prob-

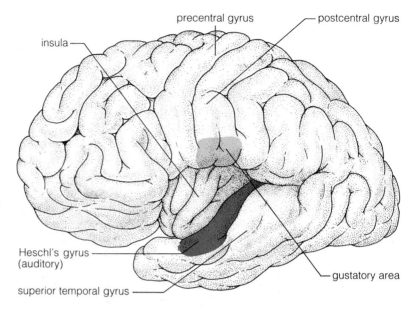

Figure 3.29 Lateral view of the human brain with the superior temporal gyrus pulled downward to reveal the insula, an area of neocortex buried in the depths of the lateral fissure. This view shows the parts of the cortex normally hidden within the lateral fissure. Heschl's gyrus, the primary auditory projection area, forms part of the lower bank of the lateral fissure, whereas the gustatory area of the postcentral gyrus constitutes part of the upper bank. The lateral fissure, in cross section, is T-shaped, and the insula forms the cap of the T. Compare this figure with Figure 3.30. (Adapted from Geschwind, 1972)

ably be unable to recognize sequences of sounds, although you might still be able to judge the loudness or pitch of a sound. Without recognition for sequences, music would be just a series of meaningless noises, as would speech. Neurons of the auditory projection area are a first stage of sound processing in the cortex. They pass on their results to other groups of neurons in the surrounding temporal cortex, and eventually the information finds its way into the parahippocampal gyrus and hippocampus where it is integrated into your memories of what you saw and heard during the day. We will look at the auditory projection system in Chapter 7.

The upper bank of the lateral fissure contains the projection area for **gustation**—the sense of taste. Because it is within the lateral fissure, most of this area is hidden in a normal lateral view of the brain (Figure 3.30). Only a small part of it rolls up over the lip of the fissure and appears at the bottom of the parietal lobe. (See Figure 3.29 for a view of the entire area.) The taste receptors are, in one sense of the term, skin receptors located in the "skin" inside the mouth. It is not surprising, then, to find the projection area for the rest of the skin receptors located just superior to the taste area in the parietal lobe in

the gyrus just posterior to the central fissure (Figure 3.30). This gyrus is very logically named the **postcentral gyrus** (its anatomical name) and **S1** (its functional name). The *S* in S1 stands for **somatosensory** (*somato* = body), an adjective that refers to the somatic senses. There are three somatic senses (those having their receptors in skin and internal organs): mechanoreception, thermoreception, and nociception. **Mechanoreception** includes pressure, touch, pulling, twisting, stretching, and so on. **Thermoreception** is the sense of warmth and cold, whereas **nociception** is the sense of pain. All these somatic senses have a common projection area (S1) in the postcentral gyrus.

S1 is also the projection area for still another related sense called **kinesthesia**. Whenever you move a part of your body, receptors in your muscles and joints give the CNS information that can be used to keep track of where all body parts are located in space at any one moment. This kinesthetic information is extremely important for your ability to move about because the brain cannot produce an accurate movement signal to the muscles unless it knows what the starting position of the body part will be. Getting up from a chair requires one set of

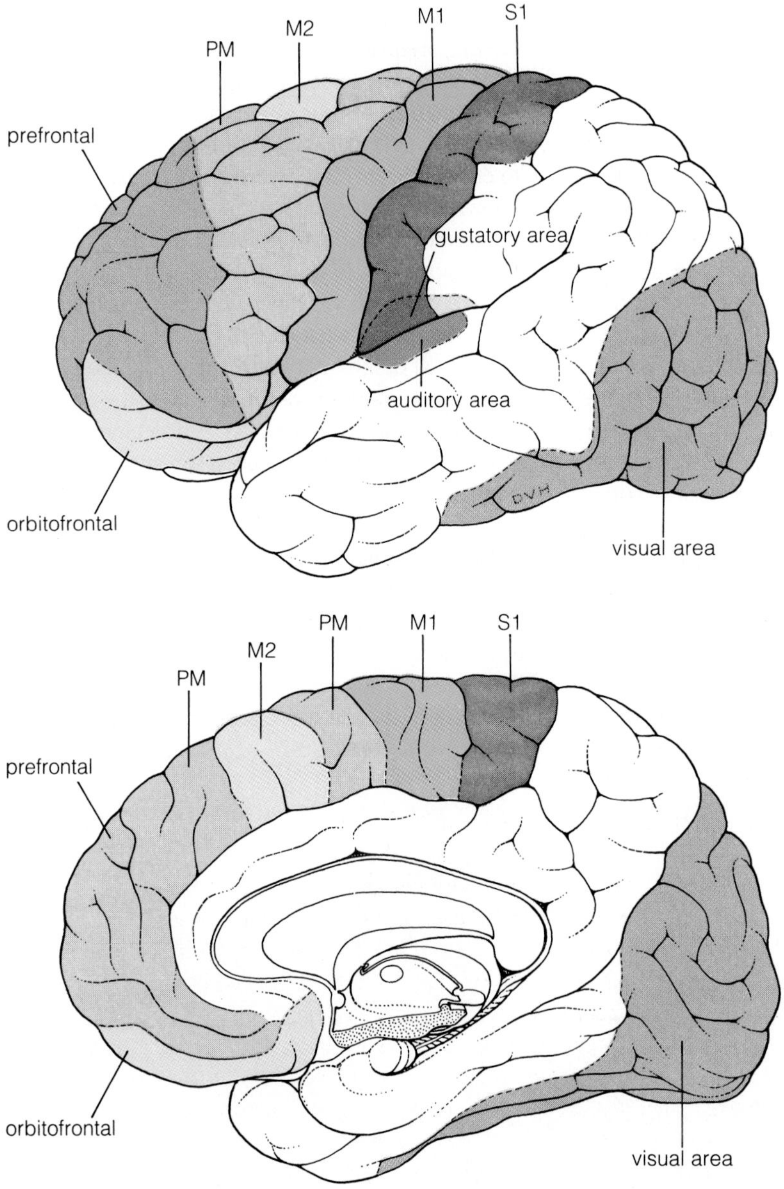

Figure 3.30 Some functional areas of the cerebral cortex. See Figure 3.29 for more complete views of the gustatory and auditory areas.

contractions; getting up from the floor requires quite a different set. All this kinesthetic information must be blended with somatic information to give the brain the complete picture, and that is why it all ends up mixed together in S1.

The postcentral gyrus contains groups of cells specific to the face, another for the hands, and still others for the arms, trunk, and so forth. In fact, these groups are arranged into a sort of map of the body. The right-hemisphere S1 contains the map for the left side of the body, and the left S1 contains the map for the right side. It has been suggested that this map is the source of your mental "image" of your body—the image that gives you the continual knowledge of where all your body parts are at any moment. If you lose part of the postcentral gyrus in an accident, you lose much of the conscious somatic–kinesthetic experience from a particular part of the body. For example, if enough cells are lost from the left-hemisphere hand area, your right hand no longer provides much information about the things that you touch. You probably would still feel an object that you pick up, but you could not identify its shape without looking at it. You could tell if it were icy cold or burning hot; however, in between those extremes, it would be hard to specify the temperature of the object.

Somatosensory–kinesthetic information travels to neuron groups posterior to S1 in the parietal lobe for further analysis. Here, the body map expands to a cognitive map of surrounding space that locates your body parts with reference not to one another but to objects outside the body—the chair on which

you are sitting, the table in front of you, and so forth. Herein originate the concepts of "in front of me" and "under me" and all other ideas that make up the cognitive map of your immediate environment. Farther back in the parietal lobes, this mapping extends to environments remembered but not present. Your knowledge of how to get from your desk to the refrigerator or from your 9:00 class to your 11:00 class apparently is stored here. Loss of the middle parietal cortex leaves a person confused about how to get around in what should be familiar surroundings. Much of the information needed to build such mapping memories is visual, and it is in the posterior half of the parietal lobes that visual input coming from the occipital regions meets somatic information coming from S1.

Language Areas In most people, language functions are mainly found in the left hemisphere. They occupy a wide zone reaching from the frontal lobe to the occipital (Figure 3.31). The anterior parts of this zone deal more with the expression of language (speaking), whereas the posterior portions give you

Figure 3.31 The language zone of the left hemisphere. The more anterior areas of this zone tend to have greater involvement with the production of language (speech), whereas the posterior areas handle language comprehension.

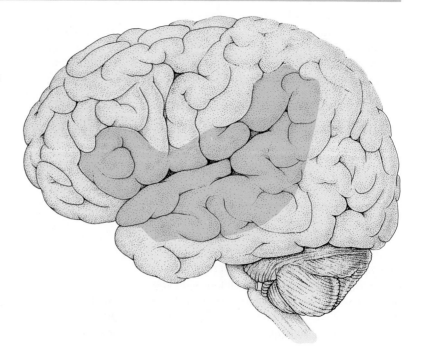

the receptive aspects (language comprehension). A person suffering brain damage within this zone might be unable to speak or understand what others are saying, depending on the location of the damage.

Motor–Action Areas The language areas duplicate on a small scale the overall division of the cortex into action functions toward the anterior end and sensory functions toward the posterior. The entire frontal lobe is devoted to creating action sequences. **M1**, also known as the primary motor area, has the task of creating the finest, precision movements, usually in the muscles of the face and hands. It has this role because of its very close relations with S1 from which it gets the sensory information that makes fine control possible. M1 occupies all of the **precentral gyrus** (Figure 3.30) and contains a map of half of the body, similar to that of S1. The right-hemisphere M1 controls muscles of the left side and vice versa. Damage to M1 leaves the patient with weakness or paralysis of the affected muscles.

Directly anterior to M1 is the **premotor area (PM)**. This appears to control sequences of movements, as opposed to the single movements produced by M1. It probably does this by way of commanding individual movements from M1, triggering them in the correct order according to visual and auditory information coming into it from occipital and temporal lobes. For example, when you cut an 8-ounce sirloin at the local steak house, the individual movements of your knife hand, which delicately adjust the pressure and direction of the blade to every nuance of resistance to the cut, are decided by M1 acting on sensory information from S1, interpreted in terms of the "toughness" of the meat. Each cutting movement is decided in terms of the visual stimuli also. It is probably the premotor area that adjusts the position of your arm so that each succeeding cut moves across the meat to a portion yet to be severed, and it makes this adjustment according to the information delivered by the visual system. The individual cuts are directed by M1, but it is the premotor area that organizes the sequence of cuts. Further, the premotor area working with the striatum adjusts other muscles of the body, including those of the arm and hand holding the fork, so that they

support the action of the cutting hand. That is, you adjust your sitting posture so that your cutting arm is free to move through its arc and your shoulders so that your cutting hand is up, above the plate. Thus, the premotor area deals more with entire acts, whereas M1 is specialized for single, precision movements.

M2, often called the supplementary motor area, seems to be strongly related to the cingulate cortex immediately inferior to it on the medial surface of the hemisphere (Figure 3.30). If M2 is lesioned, the patient loses the desire to move or speak. This part of your brain seems to be associated with your intentions to act rather than with the actions themselves. An EEG electrode placed over M2 can detect a large potential just prior to any voluntary action. This electrical wave occurs even when a subject is instructed merely to imagine doing something. It is conceivable that every bit of your voluntary behavior begins in the circuits of M2. Why that is so, we have yet to discover.

We have seen that the premotor area controls short sequences of behavior, but what about longer sequences such as driving your car to the laundromat or going to all of your Monday classes? This seems to be the province of the **prefrontal** and **orbito-frontal areas**. Because of their ability to set up extended behavior sequences spanning days, weeks, and even years (like the complex sequence involved in getting a BA degree), these areas also are responsible for your ability to plan for the future. Memories of lengthy behavior sequences are apparently stored in the prefrontal cortex and connected to motivations by way of the orbitofrontal area. The prefrontal cortex and language areas are two parts of the brain that set us apart from lower animals more than any other brain differences. Because of the prefrontal area, humans can imagine future possibilities and plan ahead further than any other species. Other mammalian species have this part of the cortex but in such small amounts that their abilities are tiny compared to ours.

Puzzling Features of the Human Brain

Did you notice, when viewing brain diagrams, how many parts of the brain seem to curve around at the posterior end and run forward into the temporal lobes? Glance again at Figures 3.20 and 3.24 and notice that the curve of the lateral ventricles matches that of the caudate nucleus. Locate the hippocampus in the temporal lobes and see how the major tract emerging from it, the fornix, curves up and around under the parietal lobes, around the top of the thalamus, and down into the hypothalamus (Figure 3.27). Notice how close the anterior tip of the hippocampus is to the hypothalamus. Despite this proximity, the hippocampus sends messages to the hypothalamus by way of the long, roundabout route through the fornix. If you had to design a brain, is this the way you would do it? There are a number of peculiarities of anatomy like this, and there is a good reason for all of them as we will see in the next section.

There is also the puzzle of apparent redundancy; many structures seem to overlap in function, apparently performing similar duties. Why, for example, does the premotor area of the cortex contain a region that controls eye movements when that function is already assigned to the superior colliculi? Why is the auditory cortex involved in pitch perception when pitches can be discriminated at the brain-stem level? And there are other questions about the nature of the brain that are less apparent unless you really loosen up your thinking and stop taking familiar things for granted. For example, why is your brain in your head rather than in your chest? Why is the whole nervous system divided into two mirror-image halves? Not all animals are organized this way. Starfish and many other species have nervous systems built on a radial plan in which the parts radiate out from the center, like spokes on a wheel.

The organization of the human brain may appear peculiar and at times unnecessarily redundant unless you understand how the various structures came to exist. The whole plan only makes sense when you realize that the brain is a collection of parts that were added one by one over a period of roughly 400 million years. The nature of our brain was determined by the history of vertebrate evolution. Let us see how our knowledge of evolution can provide some possible answers to the questions we have just asked.

■ Evolution of the Vertebrate Nervous System

The way to understand the history of vertebrate evolution is to first get some idea of how species of animals are categorized. Then, we can trace the presumed course of evolution and see how it affected the brain.

Phylogeny: A Glimpse at Evolution

As the oceans slowly filled with life 350 million years ago, the competition between species for food and living space must have become a major factor in survival. Prey organisms could evade predators better if they evolved camouflage or the ability to make escape maneuvers. Predators could better survive if they in turn evolved better sense systems for detecting elusive quarry and superior motor mechanisms for pursuit. Other survival tricks involved improvements in body chemistry that allowed new substances to be used as food and familiar food to be used more efficiently.

Some species adapted to their environments with near perfection; in a few of these cases, their environments remained so stable that hardly any changes occurred even over millions of years. Modern horseshoe crabs, for example, are remarkably similar to their ancestors of 400 million years ago. Sharks have changed little in the last 60 million years. By studying these living examples of primitive species, we can get a glimpse of what the evolutionary process might have looked like if we had been there to observe it through the eons.

All existing species can be categorized into large groupings called **phyla** (FY-la). There are about 20 of these phyla (more or fewer, depending on whose

Figure 3.32 Phylum Chordata. Primitive urochordates and cephalochordates have a spinal cord but no backbone. Subphylum Vertebrata (chordates with backbones) is represented by the six dashed lines at the right and shows the five vertebrate classes: fish (cartilaginous and bony), amphibians, reptiles, birds, and mammals. (From Starr & Taggart, 1987)

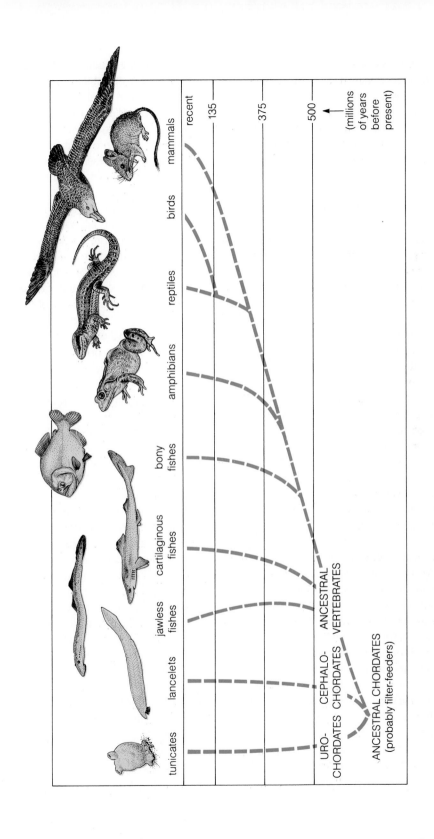

tunicates lancelets jawless cartilaginous bony amphibians reptiles birds mammals
fishes   fishes   fishes

URO-   CEPHALO-   ANCESTRAL
CHORDATES CHORDATES   VERTEBRATES

ANCESTRAL CHORDATES
(probably filter-feeders)

recent
135
375
500

(millions
of years
before
present)

system you adopt) ranging from single-celled animals up to chordates (Figure 3.32). They are ordered from lowest to highest according to how evolved they are. The single-celled organisms at the bottom of the hierarchy never even reached the evolutionary point of combining into multicelled organisms; the chordates at the top have evolved to the point where some of them have brains capable of reading this book.

Humans belong to the **phylum Chordata**, which gathers together all animals that have a nerve cord running down their backs. There are 44,794 different species in our phylum Chordata; although an impressive number of relatives, it is a drop in the bucket compared to the number of species of arthropods (insects, arachnids, crustaceans, etc.), mollusks (seashell organisms), and worms. The earliest chordates seem to have originated about 425 million years ago as a set of improvements on marine worms. As you can see from the example of a primitive chordate (lancelet) in Figure 3.32, these animals still had a somewhat wormlike appearance despite their relatively sophisticated nervous system. About 400 million years ago, some chordate species began to develop a set of bones called **vertebrae** (VERT-uh-bray), which surrounded their delicate nerve cord, protecting it from damage and providing a foundation on which to hang powerful trunk muscles. These chordates now form a subphylum called **Vertebrata** (animals with spinal columns).

Vertebrates: Fish to Birds The subphylum Vertebrata consists of subdivisions called **classes**, and most of the 43,000 species of vertebrates belong to five of these classes: fish, amphibians, reptiles, birds, and mammals. The earliest vertebrates were primitive fish, some of which were our ancestors. Modern fish have evolved quite a way from these early forms, so none of our far-distant relatives resemble a modern perch or salmon. Our progenitors trace back to species of fish that lived in very difficult, demanding fringe conditions, probably in freshwater lakes or rivers that went dry periodically. Some powerful environmental pressure (such as the need to escape drying ponds to find fresh water or the need to escape predators) selected the members of these species that had fins strong enough to propel them

on land for short distances. (A modern example of a species with this ability is the Florida "walking" catfish, which can travel for short distances over land to reach a better pond.) The real trick to surviving in this water–land fringe environment, however, was the ability to obtain oxygen from the air as well as the water. A fish possessing not only gills but also the primitive beginnings of lung tissue would have a marked advantage during the dry season. Such creatures did evolve (Figure 3.33), and one species did so well with this adaptation that its modern descendant, the lungfish, has hardly changed over the millennia. Several million years of natural selection eventually produced legs from fins and lungs from gills: amphibians emerged to take advantage of an enormous untapped reservoir of food that awaited them on dry land. All modern land vertebrates owe their existence to those earliest amphibian ancestors.

The amphibians of 360 million years ago, like today's more highly evolved amphibians, were not really land animals. They hunted on land but reproduced in their native element, the water. Amphibians still must fertilize their eggs in the water, and the eggs must hatch there because the young are fishlike and spend their early lives swimming after their food in close imitation of their ancestors. The adult frog is well adapted to land, but as a tadpole it would die out of water.

Roughly 300 million years ago, this one-foot-in-the-water adjustment was finally abandoned by one group of animals as it evolved a key characteristic that became the final step in the great emergence onto land. When the hard-shelled, amniotic egg appeared, reptiles were born. Reptiles spend their "tadpole time" inside the hard casing of their eggs, emerging only after legs have grown and lungs have replaced gills. The newly hatched reptile is equivalent in a way to the adult amphibian. In mammals like ourselves, a faint reflection of the steps of evolution occurs within the womb. A human fetus for a while resembles its marine ancestors, growing a suggestion of gill slits and showing finlike limb buds (see Figure 3.34 for a comparison with other animals).

For a while, amphibians and reptiles more or less had the land environment to themselves, although they had been preceded by plants and insects and

Figure 3.33 Larva of the tiger salamander, an amphibian whose external gills suggest that it represents a transitional stage in the evolution between fish and amphibians.

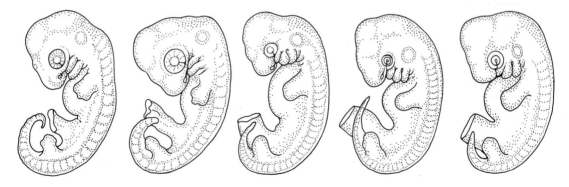

Figure 3.34 From left to right, embryos of a reptile (tortoise), bird, pig, rabbit, and human. (Adapted from Hotton, 1968)

so had plenty to eat. However, about 250 million years ago in a period before the great dinosaur reptiles emerged, a group of small, light-boned, tree-dwelling reptiles found a survival trick that worked so well that a whole new class of vertebrates emerged from it. From the fossil record and other evidence, we can guess that the trick was to evade predators by soaring from tree to tree on membranous webbing that stretched between their elongated toes. Such behavior would have made these sometime reptiles very difficult to prey on and given them a distinct survival advantage. Scales evolved into feathers to aid gliding, and strong trunk muscles made true flight possible as membranes became wings.

Mammals Sixty or 70 million years after this emergence of birds, at the height of the dinosaur age, another astounding set of changes began to take place in a line of small, inconspicuous reptiles called therapsids. Rather than watching over their eggs until hatching and then simply abandoning the offspring to fend for themselves, these newer animals fed their young from body secretions generated especially for that purpose. Named after the gland from which they nursed their offspring, they are called mammals. Their most important contribution to evolution, however, lay not in their mammary glands but in the fact that they were the first vertebrates not to lay eggs. Most mammals give birth to their young.

There is one species of primitive mammal still alive that lays eggs (the duck-billed platypus) and several that give birth to what amount to fetuses (kangaroos and opossums); however, most mammals belong to a subclass that developed a way to nurture the young inside their bodies for weeks or even months. The organ that makes possible this dramatic improvement is the placenta. The umbilical cord from the growing fetus leads to this broad, flat, blood vessel–filled structure that grows into the wall of the uterus and connects the circulatory system of the fetus to that of the mother, thus making possible continuous exchange of nutrients and removal of waste. The weeks of protected development inside the uterus make possible the lengthy assembly of an organism far more complex in structure and chemical organization than any reptile that ever hatched.

The organ that benefits the most from this added development time is the brain.

The **mammalian class** divides into 14 groups called **orders**, ranging from the more primitive insectivores (shrews, moles, etc.) through rodents, artiodactyles (camels, giraffes, etc.), and lagomorphs (rabbits) to carnivores (lions, dogs, etc.), cetaceans (whales, dolphins, etc.) to primates. As mammals developed, they spread to dominate the earth and take the place of the great reptiles, nearly all of which became extinct within a short period about 63 million years ago. The herbivores (grazing animals) took over the grassland ecological niche, rodents evolved as consumers of smaller plants and insects, carnivores ate everyone else, cetaceans returned to the sea as imitation fish, and primates were left in command of the treetops.

Primates Our ancestors did quite well in the branches, climbing out of the reach of predators and gobbling insects. There are five major groups of primates: prosimians, New World monkeys, Old World monkeys, apes, and humans. The closest modern approximation to these ancestral primates would be our era's prosimians: the tree shrews, tarsiers, lorises, and galogos. As these first primates evolved further, their paws became more handlike, and their brains developed to give them greater manipulative ability. Early on, vision became the most important sense, and excellent stereoscopic (depth) vision developed to enable rapid travel through the treetops. New World varieties like the modern squirrel monkey were daytime foragers whose diet now went far beyond insects. Later-developing, Old World monkeys (macaques, baboons, etc.) had more highly developed brains and superior learning skills. Learning ability was becoming a chief survival trait within the primate order. Apes evolved about 18 million years ago out of a preape that was our ancestor as well. Some preapes went on to evolve into humankind, while others evolved into chimps, gorillas, orangutans, and gibbons. Chimps and orangutans appear to be the most intelligent primates aside from humans, with the former showing some possible signs of language-learning ability of a primitive sort.

Now that we have had a brief look at the course

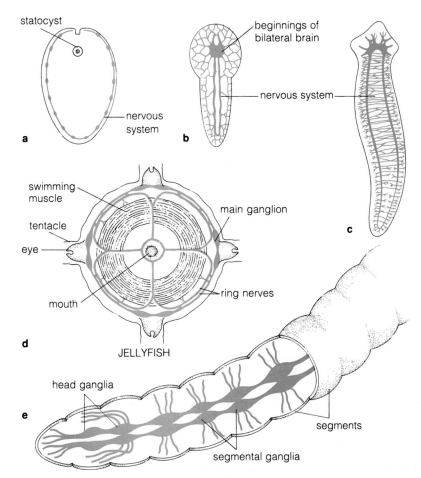

statocyst

nervous system

a

beginnings of bilateral brain

nervous system

b

c

swimming muscle

tentacle

eye

mouth

d

main ganglion

ring nerves

JELLYFISH

head ganglia

e

segments

segmental ganglia

Figure 3.35 Primitive nervous systems. (**a**) Early flatworm with a nervous system, that is, a network of neurons spread throughout the skin and underlying muscle. The chief sense organ is the statocyst. (**b**) More highly evolved flatworm with the beginnings of a bilateral brain evolving around the statocyst. (**c**) Later flatworm with definite bilateral brain. The nervous system has lost its original network arrangement and now clearly possesses a head and a tail end, with the brain giving the head end dominance over the animal. (Adapted from Hodgson, 1977) (**d**) The jellyfish has a radially organized nervous system as opposed to one with head-to-tail organization. (Adapted from Mackie, 1980) (**e**) Worms developed a structure called segmentation in which each section of the body is controlled by its own nerves emerging from its own segmental ganglia, with the first few segments dominating the rest.

of vertebrate evolution, we are ready to make some intelligent guesses concerning the way in which the vertebrate brain changed over the millennia.

Some Possible Answers to the Puzzles

The human nervous system was created bit by bit over hundreds of millions of years of evolution. Beneath our mammalian cortex lies older reptilian additions, and beneath that is the original fish–amphibian brain stem. To find the origins of our lower brain stem and spinal cord, we would probably have to go back even beyond the first chordate.

Encephalization and Bilateral Symmetry Long before fish appeared in the oceans, worms were busy

making a living by scouring the bottom mud for decaying plant and animal matter. It is presumed that the earliest versions of this very simple type of animal had a nervous system like the one shown in Figure 3.35a. Judging from existing primitive species, nerve cells must have been linked together into a loose network that connected skin receptors to muscles. Because these ancestors of ours spent their days burrowing through mud, their muscle contractions were controlled by two types of receptors: those in the skin, which could signal contact or loss of contact with mud, and the **statocyst** (STAT-oh-sist), which detected the pull of gravity and provided the sense of up and down. Fossil remains of ancient worm burrows reveal a twisting, turning, looping pathway that stayed within the narrow layer of organic-rich mud at the top of the sediment. Skin receptors could probably help detect the difference between mud and seawater or rock. Central neurons between the statocyst and muscles could program the worm to burrow down for a while and then reverse direction and head up once more.

To the casual observer, worms may not seem any more closely related to humans than are other simple oceanic organisms like jellyfish and starfish, but appearances are deceptive. Unlike jellyfish and many other species, worms orient their bodies in a particular direction when they travel, and this gives them something important that a jellyfish never had—namely, a front end (Figure 3.35d). Without a head–tail difference in body parts, there would have been no need for a central neural controller at the front end of the animal, and the brain as we know it would probably never have evolved. Because one end of the worm always came into contact with the new environment before any other part of the body, this end became the best place for the entrance to the digestive tract—the mouth. By contrast, the mouth of a starfish, jellyfish, or octopus is located right at the center of the organism. The front end also became the logical spot for a number of special sense organs like the chemical detectors used in locating food and discriminating food objects from nonfood objects. The cluster of nerve cells at the anterior end also developed there to serve the statocyst (Hodgson, 1977). Concentrating the receptors at one end of the body gave the ganglia located there a far more important role in determining the behavior of the whole organism. More and more, it was the ganglia in the "head" that controlled all muscles. This process of centralizing the control over the segments in one head ganglion is called **encephalization** (en-SEFF-uh-lih-ZAY-shun).

These detectors stayed at their anterior location throughout the course of evolution and gradually developed into our sense organs for taste and smell. The statocyst also stayed at the head end and evolved into our inner-ear receptors, which allow us to sense the direction of gravity and the acceleration of our bodies when we are riding.

The result of this concentration of nerve cells in the front end was that the nervous system gradually lost its netlike arrangement and began to look like

the one in Figure 3.35c. This arrangement apparently proved to be highly beneficial to survival and was kept throughout the long road from worm to human. If this theory is true, then we have very distant ancestors to thank for the fact that our brains are in our heads rather than in some other part of the body.

The more sophisticated nervous system shown in Figure 3.35c also displayed another characteristic that would be handed down to future species: each side was a mirror image of the other. This mirror arrangement, called **bilateral symmetry**, persisted through the evolution of our fish ancestors who passed it on to amphibians and reptiles who gave it to us mammals. Thus, humans have a nervous system divided into two mirror-image halves from the spinal cord up to the two hemispheres of the cerebrum.

As worms developed in complexity, some evolved a body pattern called **segmentation** in which the same pairs of muscles and nerve cells were repeated in each unit all along the length of the worm (Figure 3.35e). This resulted in a ladderlike nervous system formed of the pairs of segmental ganglia (clusters of control neurons) and their interconnections. A good guess is that this ladder arrangement was the origin of the spinal cord now possessed by all vertebrates. As the ganglia grew in size and complexity, they fused into the solid cable of nerve cells and connections that is the spinal cord. The basic segmentation still remained, however, and is even evident in the human cord. At some point in the evolutionary line we are tracing, our worm ancestors (Figure 3.36a) left the mud and adapted to a free-swimming life in the ocean itself. The worm mouth (Figure 3.36b and d) developed a hinged jaw (Figure 3.36c and e), enabling it to prey more easily on smaller marine life. Segmentation was maintained as the basic body plan, the first five segments specializing as a head with brain (Jollie, 1977). Each of the remaining body segments was controlled by its section of spinal cord. The first chordate had evolved. The animal in Figure 3.36 is a protochordate (*proto* = early or first) but not yet a vertebrate. It not only lacked a backbone but had no bones at all. Its nervous system was mostly nerve cord (the predecessor of our spinal cord) with just the bare beginnings of a brain in the first few segments. However, in the protochordate you can see the same basic pattern that would persist across

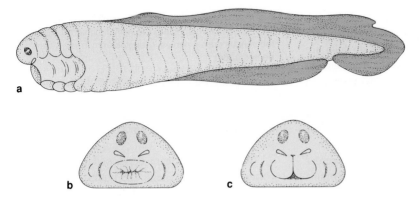

Figure 3.36 Protochordate. When our ancestor worms evolved into free-swimming species, they presumably looked like the creature in **a, b,** and **d.** The next step in evolution produced the protochordate with hinged jaw shown in **c** and **e. D** and **e** show that brain growth occurred mostly within the first two segments. (Adapted from Jollie, 1977)

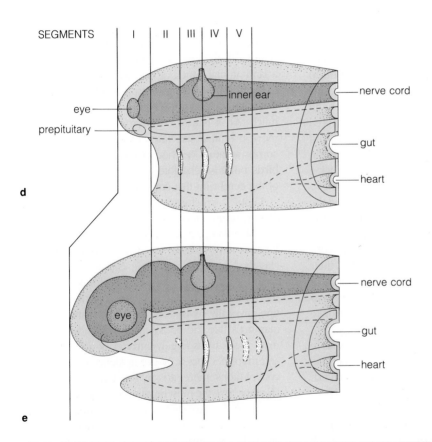

millions of years of evolution to eventually form the overall plan for the human nervous system. All up and down our cord, spinal nerves emerge in pairs, one pair to each "segment." These nerves contain sensory neurons carrying information to the cord from receptors in organs and skin as well as motor nerve cells carrying messages out from the cord to the muscles.

Evolution of the Human Brain When you read earlier in this chapter about the medulla oblongata of the brain stem, you might have been struck by the idea that a person can lose an entire cerebral hemisphere and still live but that death occurs immediately if a few cubic centimeters of medulla are damaged. The reason is that the medulla contains all the circuitry for the most basic life processes such as heartbeat, blood pressure, and respiration. But why should these vital functions reside at the lowest level of the brain? Again, we look to evolution for an answer.

Basic processes like heart rate had to be present in even the most primitive vertebrates, and the brains of those animals were roughly the equivalent of our brain stem. As evolution produced amphibians from fish and reptiles from amphibians, new parts were added to allow for improved sensory analysis, motor control, and learning ability. For example, the visual sense in fish is severely limited in comparison to primate vision because fish have no cerebral cortex to process input from the eye and must rely on brain stem visual areas (colliculi). Fish are not bothered by this because other senses serve them quite well in a murky-water environment where good vision might frequently be wasted. Land animals, receiving images through the relatively clear air, were able to use vision to a much greater extent and evolved the thalamic and cortical areas to take advantage of the situation. Land animals also needed many more motor control circuits because they had far more joints to move (in arms, digits, and legs) and their movements over the uneven and varying surfaces of land called for a far more sophisticated type of control. These new circuits are found in structures like the corpus striatum.

The phylogenetic sequence of modern species in Figure 3.37 gives us some idea of how the vertebrate brain must have been altered by evolution from fish to human. The fish has all 12 cranial nerves, and note that they are the same 12 cranial nerves that we humans have. You may not recognize the cerebellum of a codfish because it is shaped differently, but it provides the same functions in fish as it does in humans and marks the pontine region of the stem in both species. The fish brain essentially consists of a rough equivalent of our brain stem and hypothalamus plus a small anterior nucleus called a cerebrum. The cerebrum of the fish is not differentiated into the nuclei and cortex of the human cerebrum,

Figure 3.37 A vertebrate family tree with the brains of six representative species. The Roman numerals indicate the various cranial nerves. (Adapted from Truex & Carpenter, 1964)

and one finds only vague hints of thalamus and corpus striatum.

The thalamus is clearly developed in the frog, but cortex is still nonexistent. The bump labeled *optic lobe* in Figure 3.37 is the major visual processing area for the fish and amphibian. It is in the midbrain and is the equivalent of the human superior colliculus. Reptilian brains show the enormous development of the cerebrum that one would expect of a land animal. Much of this mass of tissue belongs to the rapidly expanding corpus striatum. The goose brain shows that the cerebrum has expanded so much that it is now covering many of the deeper, more primitive structures of the brain stem. The corpus striatum reached high-level development in birds, but it is debatable whether they have any area of the cerebrum that could be called true cortex.

Limbic structures showed themselves most clearly for the first time in reptiles, the direct ancestors of both birds and mammals (Northcutt, 1981). Reptiles have areas of the cerebrum that could be classified as primitive limbic cortex. Neocortex is almost certainly an evolutionary product of mammals; no other vertebrates have any tissue that is unequivocally six-layered. Evolution from primitive mammals like the opossum to highly evolved primate species was largely a matter of growing more and more neocortex. Notice in Figure 3.37 how few convolutions there are in the cortex of the cat. Humans have the most heavily convoluted neocortex of any species except for whales and dolphins.

Each addition to the evolving vertebrate brain yielded new capacities. Vision, for example, was vastly improved in mammals to enable many of those species to have extraordinary acuity, depth perception, and visual memory. Most of these improvements were the result of adding cortical areas. Herein lies the source of the apparent redundancy between different brain parts that was mentioned in the last section. One visual area in the cortex, for example,

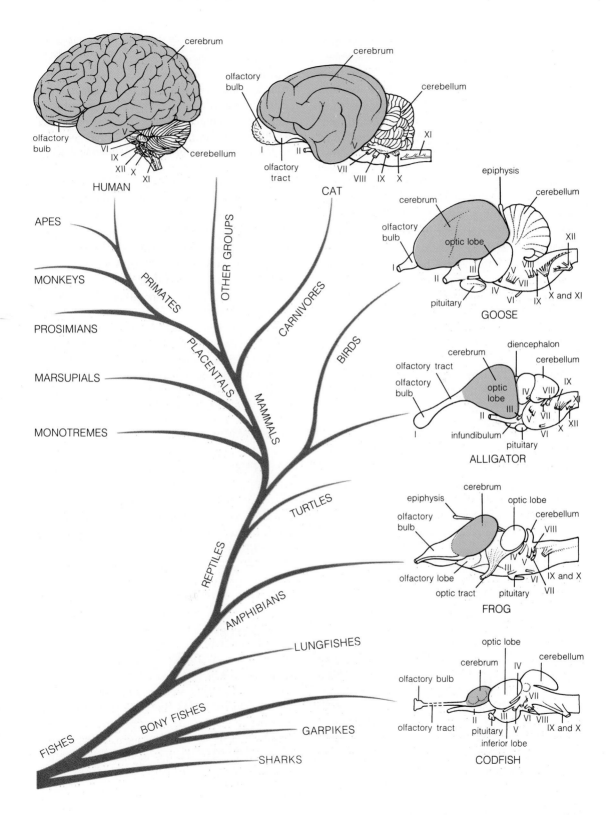

HUMAN

cerebrum

olfactory
bulb

cerebellum

V
VI
IX
XII X
XI

CAT

cerebrum

olfactory
bulb

cerebellum

olfactory
tract

I
II
V
VII
VIII IX X
XI

APES

MONKEYS

PROSIMIANS

MARSUPIALS

MONOTREMES

PRIMATES

OTHER GROUPS

CARNIVORES

BIRDS

PLACENTALS

MAMMALS

TURTLES

REPTILES

AMPHIBIANS

LUNGFISHES

GARPIKES

SHARKS

BONY FISHES

FISHES

GOOSE

epiphysis

cerebrum

cerebellum

olfactory
bulb

optic lobe

XII

I

II

III

pituitary

IV

V
VI
VII
IX

X and XI

ALLIGATOR

diencephalon

cerebrum

cerebellum

olfactory tract

olfactory
bulb

optic
lobe

IV
VIII
IX

XI

III

V
VII

X
XII

II

I

infundibulum

VI

pituitary

FROG

epiphysis

cerebrum

optic lobe

olfactory
bulb

cerebellum

VIII

IV
V

olfactory lobe

III

optic tract

pituitary

VI
VII

IX and X

CODFISH

optic lobe

cerebrum

IV

cerebellum

olfactory bulb

VII

II
III

olfactory tract

pituitary

VI VIII
V

IX and X

inferior lobe

localizes a visual object in the perceptual space around you. It gives you the ability to know where things are in relation to your body. This might seem redundant because the superior colliculus also locates visual stimuli. This has led some researchers to suggest that the more recently evolved higher structures have taken over the function of the lower ones to eliminate duplication of function. A closer inspection of the function of the higher and lower areas, however, casts doubt on this interpretation. For example, the cortical area devoted to visual localization connects directly to motor areas of the cortex, whereas the superior colliculus is limited to influencing only the kinds of behavior commanded by the brain stem, that is, eye movements and other orienting responses. Outputs of the cortical area and colliculus are used in two different ways. This is why the cortex has not taken over the colliculus or rendered it obsolete. The redundancy, then, is more apparent than real.

Origin of the Temporal Lobes One last peculiarity mentioned in the previous section was the odd

arrangement of the tract that links the hippocampus with the hypothalamus—the fornix. The mystery was why the hippocampus should send axons of its neurons looping around the top of the thalamus in a 270° arc just to get to the hypothalamus, which is only a few centimeters away. The reason for this peculiarity lies in the expansion of the neocortex during evolution. In primitive mammals like the rat, which have a smooth, unconvoluted cortex (top drawing in Figure 3.38), the hippocampus is located near the dorsal surface. As the frontal cortex underwent its dramatic expansion, however, the posterior cortex was pushed down and around to where it was migrating forward in the skull (see the third step in Figure 3.38). It was this folding forward of what had been the posterior end of the cortex that created the lateral fissure and the temporal lobe. The last step in Figure 3.38 shows that this folding also accounts for the buried cortex within the lateral fissure—the insula (Figure 3.29). The hippocampus was carried along with this posterior migration and wound up "turning the corner" into the temporal lobe. The fornix connection with the hypothalamus (the arrow

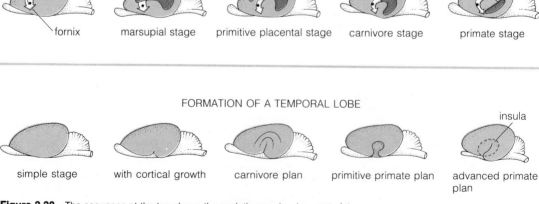

Figure 3.38 The sequence at the top shows the evolutionary development of the corpus callosum with resulting displacement of the hippocampus. At the bottom is the evolution of the temporal lobe. Both sequences are displayed on a generalized mammalian brain. (Adapted from Isaacson et al., 1971)

in Figure 3.38) had originally taken the shortest, most direct path to the hypothalamus; but with the migration of the hippocampus, it became more and more stretched. Because it couldn't be given up, it became the peculiarly circuitous route seen in the human brain. The folding that created the temporal lobes also explains why the striatum and lateral ventricles curve around in a **C** shape. Many of the evolutionary events presented here are fairly speculative; we have very little simple, direct evidence out of which to create our history of brain evolution. Fortunately, we do know enough to be able to answer some questions about the peculiarities of our brain's shape and function and to make reasonable hypotheses for others.

■ Summary

1. The central nervous system (CNS) consists of brain and spinal cord. The peripheral nervous system is made up of cranial (emerging from the brain) and spinal (emerging from the spinal cord) nerves. A nerve is a bundle of axons outside the CNS. Inside the CNS, such a bundle is termed a tract. Nerves can carry both sensory fibers and motor fibers.

2. Axons of a cut nerve can regenerate, after first dying back to the somas, and restore some function lost to the damage. If regeneration is incomplete, there is a permanent loss of some sensation from the affected area and/or muscle weakness. Severing all motor fibers to a particular muscle leaves it completely paralyzed.

3. The peripheral nervous system consists of somatic and autonomic subdivisions. The somatic division contains most of the sensory fibers and all motor fibers serving the striate muscles. The autonomic division is made up mostly of motor axons going to the smooth muscles of the viscera and a few afferents from internal organs.

4. The sympathetic branch of the autonomic nervous system (ANS) controls the same visceral organs served by the other branch, the parasympathetic, but the two branches have opposite effects on these organs. The sympathetic nervous system allows the organism to expend energy in fast, high-performance behavior, whereas the parasympathetic nervous system replaces energy reserves and repairs the effects of organ wear from periods of sympathetic nervous system dominance.

5. Two types of tissue are visible to the naked eye in the CNS: white matter and gray matter. The former is made up of axons and gains its coloration from the myelin of the axon sheaths. The latter consists of cells, somas, and dendrites. The basic work of the nervous system, the processing of information, takes place in gray matter. Axons of white matter simply carry messages from one gray matter area to another. Some gray matter in the brain consists of soma clusters termed nuclei; the rest is organized into layers and is called cortex. Each nucleus or separate area of cortex has a different set of inputs and outputs from any other gray matter area, and it is this uniqueness that decides the function of each area.

6. Gray matter of the cord is organized into a column that runs through the central core from one end to the other. Within it are the synaptic connections that create reflex arcs, the circuits that produce reflex responses. A reflex arc consists of sensory (primary afferent) neurons synapsing in the dorsal horn with short interneurons that connect with the motor neurons of the ventral horn. This yields a straight pathway from sensory receptors to muscles. Sympathetic reflex arcs often involve an additional synapse in one of the sympathetic chain ganglia just outside the cord.

7. The brain stem, from lowest zone to highest, consists of the medulla oblongata, pontine region, and midbrain. The medulla contains circuits for basic life functions such as heartbeat and respiration. Also found there is the nucleus of tractus solitarius (NTS), which receives visceral sensory information entering the brain from the vagus nerve.

8. The pontine region contains the cerebellum (whose function is to smooth and coordinate movements through proper timing of muscle contractions), the pons (a tract connecting the two cerebellar hemispheres), and various nuclei concerned with sleep, eye movements, and other functions.

9. The inferior and superior colliculi, primitive auditory and visual centers, are found in the midbrain.

The superior colliculus provides the ability to orient to visual, auditory, and somatic stimuli. The midbrain portion of the reticular formation, a column of gray matter that forms the core of the brain stem, projects to the entire cortex and provides the arousal that makes the difference between sleeping and waking.

10. The cavities within the brain are called ventricles. Their function is to store and circulate cerebrospinal fluid (CSF), which protects the neurons from direct contact with blood. The lateral ventricles are found within the lobes of the cerebrum; the third ventricle separates the two thalami and the two hypothalami. The fourth ventricle is at the core of the pontine brain stem.

11. The neural route from receptors to any sensory area of the cortex is called a sensory projection system. With the sole exception of the olfactory sense, all senses include the thalamus in their projection systems as the last synapse prior to the cortex. There is a separate thalamic nucleus for each sense.

12. Ventral to the thalamus lies a group of nuclei concerned with regulating the internal environment, the hypothalamus. This structure exerts its control over the rest of the body through two avenues: a neural route and a chemical route. The former involves tracts leading from the hypothalamus to the sympathetic neurons in the spinal cord and the NTS. Thus, the hypothalamus commands visceral organs by way of the sympathetic and parasympathetic nervous systems.

13. The hypothalamus exerts chemical control over internal environment by way of endocrine glands. It controls the secretion of hormones from the posterior pituitary gland through a neural connection with that gland, and it commands the release of anterior pituitary hormones by way of hypothalamic hormones called releasing factors.

14. Between the thalamus and cortex is a cluster of three large nuclei called the corpus striatum, consisting of the caudate, putamen, and globus pallidus. The caudate and putamen function together and are called the neostriatum, or striatum. The corpus striatum is the part of the motor system of the brain that furnishes the proper unconscious background muscle contractions that provide the postural context for any conscious voluntary movement.

15. Structures of the limbic system include the hippocampus, cingulate gyrus, parahippocampal gyrus, amygdala, septal nucleus, nucleus accumbens, and nucleus basalis. These gray matter areas are found in a ring around the central core of the brain. They provide event memories and memories related to emotions and motivations.

16. Completely covering the hemispheres of the cerebrum is a six-layered gray matter structure called the neocortex. It is convoluted into "bumps" (gyri) separated by "cracks" (sulci). Deep sulci are termed fissures. The central fissure separates the frontal lobe from the parietal lobe. The lateral fissure separates frontal and temporal lobes. The most posterior portion of the cortex is the occipital lobe. The longitudinal fissure separates the two hemispheres down to the level of the corpus callosum, the largest tract connecting the hemispheres.

17. Occipital lobes are made up of many separate visual areas, each of which gives us some different visual capacity. The visual projection system terminates in an area called V1 at the very back of the occipital lobes. Visual areas are also found on the inferior surface of the temporal lobes. The auditory projection system terminates in the uppermost gyrus of the temporal lobe. Just above it, at the base of the postcentral gyrus of the parietal lobe, is the projection area for gustation. The remainder of the postcentral gyrus is S1, the projection area for somatic senses.

18. The business of frontal lobes is to create and store memories of actions. These range from the short, single voluntary movements produced by the M1 cortex of the precentral gyrus through more complex sequences of movements in the premotor area to the complex, long-term future plans of the prefrontal cortex. The language cortex includes parts of frontal, temporal, and parietal lobes. The more anterior parts of this large zone in the left hemisphere provide speech functions, whereas the posterior portions underlie language-comprehension abilities.

19. A number of puzzling features of the brain can be best explained with hypotheses based on evolutionary principles. Humans belong to the group of animals called phylum Chordata, subphylum Vertebrata, class Mammalia, order Primate. Fish were

the first vertebrates to evolve. They spawned the amphibians, which gave rise to reptiles. Both birds and mammals evolved from reptiles. The primate order of the class Mammalia can be divided into the following major groups: prosimians, New World monkeys, Old World monkeys, apes, and humans.

20. Some features of our primate nervous system originated even before vertebrates had evolved. Early protochordates were wormlike ocean-bottom dwellers. From them we inherited our bilateral symmetry and encephalization. The earliest version of our brain stem and hypothalamus seems to have

originated in fish. The thalamus became distinct with amphibians. Reptiles added the corpus striatum and the beginnings of the limbic system. Mammals contributed the neocortex.

21. Because the plan for our primate brain was constructed over millions of years of evolution, adding new features to the already existing parts created hierarchies of structures that seem to duplicate each other's functions. This redundancy is more apparent than real, however, because each level of the nervous system controls behavior at a different level of complexity.

Glossary

adrenal cortex Endocrine gland that secretes glucocorticoids and mineralocorticoids. (77)

adrenal gland Endocrine gland capping the kidney; consists of an outer layer (cortex) around an inner core (medulla). (77)

adrenalin Hormone secreted by the adrenal medulla and neurotransmitter released by adrenergic neurons. (77)

adrenal medulla Endocrine gland that secretes adrenalin (epinephrine) and noradrenalin (norepinephrine). (77)

amygdala A cluster of nuclei in the anterior temporal lobe vital for the acquisition of certain types of memory, especially those dealing with whether a stimulus should be approached or avoided; part of the limbic system. (84)

anterior Toward the front end. (50)

anterior pituitary The "master" endocrine gland; secretes ACTH, TSH, gonadotropin, and growth hormone. (79)

association neurons Small, short-axoned cells in gray matter areas, some of which provide connecting links between afferents and efferents of reflex arcs; interneurons. (63)

audition The sense of hearing. (87)

autonomic fibers Afferent and efferent axons serving the smooth muscles and visceral organs; belong to either the sympathetic branch or the parasympathetic branch. (53)

autonomic nervous system (ANS) The part of the peripheral nervous system that serves the viscera. (64)

bilateral symmetry Being the same on both sides of the midline. (98)

brain stem Lowest (most caudal) portions of brain; consists of medulla oblongata, pontine region, and midbrain. (66)

caudal Toward the tail end. (50)

caudate nucleus Structure lying between the thalamus and cortex that is a part of the striatum. (79)

central Refers to the core of the nervous system (brain and spinal cord). (50)

central fissure Separates the frontal lobe from the parietal; extends from the midline down the lateral surface of the cerebrum to the lateral fissure. (85)

central nervous system (CNS) Brain and spinal cord. (52)

cerebellar hemispheres The halves of the cerebellum. (69)

cerebellum A motor structure on the dorsal side of the pontine region; consists of a cortex of gray matter with underlying white matter containing several nuclei. (68)

cerebral aqueduct Thin tube at the midline of the brain stem that connects the third and fourth ventricles. (72)

cerebral cortex Wrinkled sheet of gray matter that covers the cerebrum. (59)

cerebral hemispheres The halves of the cerebrum. (87)

cerebrospinal fluid (CSF) Special circulatory fluid adjusted chemically by the body to fit the needs of neural tissue; found in the ventricles. (72)

cerebrum All of the brain above the level of the brain stem. (84)

cingulate gyrus Limbic cortex lying immediately dorsal to the corpus callosum. (84)

classes Subdivisions of phyla or subphyla; humans belong to the mammalian class. (94)

colliculi Nuclei on the dorsal surface of the midbrain. (71)

congenital hypothyroidism A set of birth defects and growth deficiencies resulting from lack of thyroxin. (77)

convolutions The gyri and sulci of the cortex. (84)

corpus callosum Large tract connecting the neocortex of the two hemispheres. (87)

corpus striatum Motor structure consisting of the striatum and globus pallidus. (79)

cranial nerves Those nerves that emerge from the brain. (53)

degeneration Sequence of changes following damage in which an axon breaks up and disappears. (55)

dorsal On the back side. (50)

dorsal horn Area of gray matter toward the back of the spinal cord where many afferent neurons terminate. (62)

dorsal root Bundle of sensory fibers that splits off from a spinal nerve to enter the spinal cord. (62)

dorsal root ganglion A swelling on the dorsal root containing the cell bodies of the primary afferent neurons. (62)

dura mater Tough, membranous sac inside which the brain floats in CSF. (72)

encephalization The tendency in evolution for the anterior end of the nervous system to acquire the bulk of the control over the body and the rest of the nervous system. (98)

endocrine glands Glands that secrete their hormones into the bloodstream to be carried to their point of use. (76)

endocrine system A group of glands that secretes chemicals called hormones. (76)

exocrine glands Glands that deliver their secretions directly to the point where they are used, usually through a duct. (76)

fiber Axon and its myelin sheath. (53)

fissure A very deep sulcus. (85)

fourth ventricle Most caudal ventricle; located at midline in the pontine region. (72)

frontal lobe Portion of neocortex anterior to the central fissure. (85)

ganglion Cluster of neuron somas in the peripheral nervous system. (59)

globus pallidus Motor structure medial to the putamen; together with the striatum it makes up the corpus striatum. (79)

glucocorticoids Hormones secreted during stressful experiences like disease or injury that are important to the process of recovery. (77)

gonads Endocrine glands that secrete reproductive hormones; they also contain tissue that generates ova and sperm. (77)

gray matter Aggregation of cell bodies and dendrites. (58)

gustation The sense of taste. (88)

gyrus One of the "ridges" of the cerebral cortex. (85)

hippocampus Limbic structure lying just under the medial surface of the temporal lobe; involved in storing long-term memories. (84)

hormones Chemicals secreted by one type of cell (usually in a gland or the brain) that travel some distance in the body (often through the bloodstream) to affect the function of another type of cell. (76)

hypothalamus Set of nuclei at the base of the brain that controls the body's internal organs and biochemistry. (74)

inferior Toward the bottom, underneath. (50)

inferior colliculi A pair of midbrain nuclei important in the localization of sound sources. (71)

interneurons Small, short-axoned cells in gray matter areas, some of which provide connecting links between afferents and efferents of reflex arcs; association neurons. (63)

kinesthesia The sense of body movement. (88)

lateral Toward the side. (50)

lateral fissure Separates the temporal lobe from the frontal and parietal lobes. (85)

lateral ventricles The two largest cavities in the brain; there is one in each hemisphere. (72)

limbic system A system of interconnected structures that forms a ring around the central core of the brain; related to motivation and emotion. (82)

longitudinal fissure Separates the cerebrum into two hemispheres at the midline of the brain. (87)

M1 The primary motor cortex; the precentral gyrus. (91)

M2 Small motor area extending from the cingulate gyrus up over the lip of the longitudinal fissure and a short distance across the dorsal surface of the frontal lobe; also known as the supplementary motor area. (91)

mammalian class A subdivision of subphylum Vertebrata. (96)

mechanoreception The somatic sense for mechanical types of stimulation; includes pressure, touch, pulling, twisting, stretching, and so on. (88)

medial The middle. (50)

medulla oblongata The most caudal portion of the brain stem, located just above the spinal cord. (66)

midbrain Uppermost level of the brain stem; located above the pontine region and below the thalamus. (70)

mineralocorticoids Hormones with many functions, one of which is to conserve salt and water by returning them to the blood during urine formation. (77)

minicolumn See *module*.

module (cortical) Minicolumn of the interconnected cells cutting across the six layers of cerebral cortex. (84)

motor (efferent) fiber Axon carrying impulses from CNS to muscle or gland; efferent fiber. (53)

neocortex The more recently evolved, six-layer cortex that makes up the lobes of the cerebrum. (84)

nerve Bundle of axons in the peripheral nervous system. (52)

neuroma A tangle of neuron filaments formed during unsuccessful regeneration of a nerve. (56)

nociception The sense of pain. (88)

noradrenalin Hormone secreted by the adrenal medulla and neurotransmitter released by adrenergic neurons. (77)

nucleus Cluster of cell bodies within the CNS. (59)

nucleus of tractus solitarius (NTS) Area in the medulla that receives visceral sensory information. (66)

occipital lobe The neocortex posterior to the parietal and temporal lobes. (87)

orbitofrontal area Portion of the frontal lobe immediately ventral to the prefrontal cortex; mostly on the ventral surface. (91)

order Subdivision of a class; humans belong to the primate order. (96)

pancreas The endocrine gland that secretes insulin. (77)

parahippocampal gyrus Limbic cortex wrapped around the outside of the hippocampus and visible on the medial surface of the temporal lobe. (84)

parasympathetic nervous system Division of the autonomic nervous system responsible for helping to restore resources following a period of arousal. (66)

parietal lobe Portion of neocortex lying between the occipital lobe posteriorly and the frontal lobe anteriorly. (85)

peripheral Away from the central axis. (50)

peripheral nervous system The spinal and cranial nerves with their ganglia. (52)

phyla The primary divisions of the animal kingdom; singular is *phylum*. (92)

phylum Chordata The chordates, a group of animals having a nerve cord down their backs. (94)

pituitary An endocrine gland located at the base of the brain; it provides the hormones by which the hypothalamus controls body chemistry. (76)

pons Large tract connecting the two cerebellar hemispheres. (69)

pontine region Pons, cerebellum, and a variety of smaller structures; located between medulla and midbrain. (68)

postcentral gyrus The gyrus immediately posterior to the central fissure; contains S1. (88)

posterior Toward the rear. (50)

posterior pituitary Releases the hormones oxytocin and vasopressin. (79)

postganglionic fibers Axons of sympathetic neurons whose cell bodies are located within the chain ganglia. (65)

precentral gyrus The gyrus immediately anterior to the central fissure; it extends from the longitudinal fissure to the lateral fissure. (91)

prefrontal area Portion of the frontal lobe anterior to the premotor cortex and dorsal to the orbitofrontal. (91)

preganglionic fibers Sympathetic axons whose cell bodies are located in the gray matter of the cord, in the small area between the dorsal and ventral horns. (65)

premotor area (PM) Portion of the frontal lobe anterior to M1 and posterior to the prefrontal area. (91)

primary afferent neurons Sensory cells with receptor endings in the skin, muscles, joints, or internal organs. (62)

processor area (cortical) Small region of cortex containing the modules devoted to one particular function (for example, perceiving visual movement in depth). (87)

putamen Motor nucleus lying between the cerebral cortex and thalamus; together with the caudate nucleus it makes up the striatum. (79)

reflex An unlearned, automatic response. (62)

reflex arc Circuit that produces a reflex. (62)

regeneration Regrowth of a fiber following degeneration. (55)

reticular formation A column of neurons at the core of the midbrain, pons, medulla, and spinal cord that controls the intensity of responses and adjusts the amount of impact that any stimulus input will have on the rest of the brain. (72)

root See *dorsal root* and *ventral root*.

rostral Toward the head end. (50)

S1 The somatosensory and kinesthetic projection area; located in the postcentral gyrus. (88)

segmentation Division of an animal into a series of similar parts in which the same structures are repeated in each part. (98)

sensory (afferent) fiber Axon carrying impulses from sense organ to CNS; afferent fiber. (53)

sensory projection area A zone of neocortex in which a sensory projection system terminates; there is a separate one for each major sense. (87)

sensory projection system A neural route for each sense that extends from its receptors through the nervous system to the area of cerebral cortex serving that sense. (74)

septal nucleus A limbic structure at the midline of the brain; sets appropriate levels of emotion to display in any situation. (84)

septum Thin membrane separating the third ventricle from the lateral ventricles; merges ventrally into the septal nucleus. (72)

smooth muscle White muscle found in the viscera; used in reflex responses only. (53)

somatic fibers Afferent and efferent axons serving the sense organs and striate muscles. (53)

somatosensory Pertaining to the somatic senses: mechanoreception, thermoreception, and nociception. (88)

spinal nerves Those nerves that emerge from the spinal cord. (53)

statocyst Sense organ found in lower animals that detects the direction of gravity. (97)

striate muscle Red muscle found in head, trunk, and limbs; used in voluntary and reflex movements. (53)

striatum Motor structure consisting of the caudate nucleus and putamen. (79)

sulcus A "crack" separating one gyrus from another. (85)

superior Toward the top. (50)

superior colliculi A pair of midbrain nuclei important to the localization of visual stimuli and control of eye movements. (71)

sympathetic chain ganglia A string of interconnected ganglia belonging to the sympathetic nervous system and lying just outside the spinal column. (65)

sympathetic nervous system Division of the autonomic nervous system that produces arousal of body. (66)

temporal lobe All the neocortex inferior to the lateral fissure. (85)

thalamus Collection of nuclei at the center of the brain; serves as the main connecting link between the cerebral cortex and the rest of the brain. (72)

thermoreception The sense of warmth and cold. (88)

third ventricle The CSF-filled cavity separating the left and right thalami and hypothalami. (72)

thyroid gland Endocrine gland that secretes the hormone thyroxine, which sets the base level for metabolism. (77)

tract Bundle of axons within the CNS. (52)

vagus nerve Cranial nerve X; constitutes most of the parasympathetic nervous system. (66)

ventral The belly side. (50)

ventral horn Area of gray matter toward the front of the cord that contains the cell bodies of motor neurons. (62)

ventral root Bundle of motor fibers emerging from the spinal cord; joins dorsal root to make a spinal nerve. (62)

ventricles Four cavities within the brain that contain cerebrospinal fluid. (72)

vertebrae Bones in the spinal column. (62)

Vertebrata A subphylum within the phylum Chordata; animals with backbones and spinal cords. (94)

viscera The internal organs. (53)

visual sensory projection area (V1) The area of occipital cortex in which the visual projection system terminates. (87)

white matter Aggregation of myelinated axons. (58)

How Neurons Carry and Transmit Information

N erve cells are specialized for generating and moving information around in the nervous system. These two simple functions are the origin of all your conscious experience and responses. Information generated by the soma and dendrites is carried by the axon to some other place in the nervous system, coded into patterns of nerve impulses.

The Nerve Impulse: An Introduction

The brain, the prime control center of the body, crouches within the bony shelter of the skull, resembling in a way the underground war room beneath the Pentagon. Messages pour in from data-collecting outposts in eyes, ears, skin, and elsewhere, and commands are sent out to response units—muscles and glands. The brain, like the commander in the windowless war room, has no direct connection with the outside world. By itself the brain is blind and deaf—totally insensitive. For knowledge of the environment, it is wholly dependent on messages in the form of nerve impulse patterns coming in along the nerves. Every stimulus to which the nervous system can react is first changed by a sense receptor into the only "language" the brain can understand, nerve impulse patterns. Music, lemon juice on the tongue, a blast of icy air on the skin, even the sight of a friend's face are all reduced to patterns of nerve impulses with a slightly different pattern for each variation in the stimulus. Inside the brain itself, messages are sent from place to place as patterns of impulses in axons. The nerve impulse is a fundamental component of your hearing, thinking, feeling, loving, hating, and hurting. It underlies every conscious experience. As students of the mind, we must understand what the impulse is and how it works.

The Nature of Nerve Impulses

First, the nerve impulse is an electrical event within the axon of the nerve cell. It is a traveling event, starting at the cell-body end of an axon and running down to the telodendria at the other end. Under normal conditions then, a nerve impulse is only conducted in a particular direction, toward the telodendria. This is the principle of **one-way conduction**.

A second important principle of conduction is the all-or-none law. When you walk into a dark room and turn on the light, nerve messages tell your brain that the light-intensity level has increased. How is this information about intensity conveyed? Does a more intense light create bigger nerve impulses? The answer to that question is to be found in the **all-or-none law** that states that if an axon fires at all, it will fire at full strength. Each axon has only one size of nerve impulse, and stronger stimuli simply produce more frequent impulses.

To understand this principle more fully, picture an experiment in which a nerve fiber (axon) in one of the peripheral nerves of a rat has been isolated from surrounding fibers. A fine wire called an **electrode** is gently lowered to make contact with the axon, which responds to the pressure initially by firing a few times before it "settles down." Next, a very low-level stimulating current is sent through the electrode. The researcher watches the instruments, but nothing happens. Apparently, the stimulus was too weak; the experimenter now increases the current level. The axon now begins to fire at a slow, steady rate. Another twist of the dial further increases the stimulus level, and now the firing rate picks up to a lively pace. Each increase in the current causes the axon to fire faster. The neuron is "coding" stimulus intensity into frequency of impulses. The researcher's instruments indicate that each impulse is still the same size as the first one elicited by the weakest stimulus. The all-or-none law dictates that each axon has just one size of impulse; thus, the only way for a fiber to code information is with patterns of impulses, and the simplest pattern is the rate at which impulses occur.

The brain cannot react to a stimulus until the pattern of impulses reaches it. The decision about what response to make requires the conduction of millions of impulses back and forth within the brain from one area to another. The reaction itself depends on new patterns being sent out along nerves to set muscles into motion. The response of pulling your hand back from a hot stove might take about 500 milliseconds (ms) (500/1,000 of a second), and some of this delay is due to the time it takes for nerve impulses to travel along axons. When you flip on a light switch, the light bulb reacts almost instantaneously. The electric current travels from switch to light bulb at nearly the speed of light. A nerve impulse is also an electrical event, but compared to the current in house wiring, it travels at the speed of a tired turtle. The fastest impulse ambles down the length of its axon at the "leisurely" pace of about 100 meters per second (m/s), while the slowest—at about 3 m/s—would be no match for you in a footrace. The fast impulses are found in the largest axons. In general, the smaller the diameter of the axon, the slower is its impulse, and even the fastest impulse is hundreds of times slower than the electric current in a wire. The reason for this difference in speed lies in the type of electric current involved.

Bioelectricity

The nerve impulse involves a different kind of current than the one traveling in a length of lamp cord. A **current** is a flow of charged particles, and that definition holds no matter where the current is found. However, the *particles* that make up the current in a nerve impulse are quite different from those in a house wire. Before you can learn about the specific particles involved, you need a little background information.

Solid matter of the sort with which humans are most familiar is composed of particles called **molecules**, which in turn are made up of **atoms**. A molecule of table salt, for example, is composed of a sodium atom (symbolized as **Na**) and a chlorine atom (**Cl**) and is called sodium chloride (NaCl). Atoms themselves consist of two parts: solid centers called **nuclei** (composed of protons and neutrons) and orbiting particles called electrons. Atomic nuclei carry a positive charge, and electrons carry a negative charge. A basic law of physics states that positively charged particles are attracted to negatively charged

Figure 4.1 A water-filled glass with dissolved salt. (**a**) The separation of the positive (+) and negative (−) ions by the barrier creates a potential (voltage) across the partition. (**b**) A hole punched in the barrier creates an electric current by allowing the charged particles to move toward each other. The potential is gradually lost as opposite charges mix and cancel each other's charges.

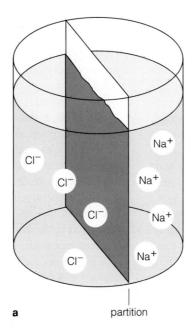

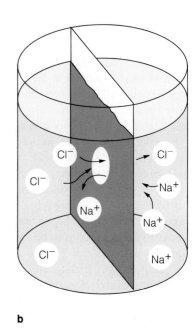

a   partition   b

particles and that this attraction of unlike charges holds together the two parts of the atom. Because the negatively charged electrons cancel the positive charges on the nucleus, the atom as a whole is neutral—all positive charges within the atom are balanced by negative charges. In some situations, however, the balance is lost when an atom acquires or loses one or more electrons. In either case, the resulting unbalanced (charged) particle is called an **ion**. An ion has a positive charge when it has too few electrons and a negative charge when it has too many electrons. When table salt (NaCl) is dissolved in water, the molecules break apart into ions. Each chlorine atom carries off one of the electrons belonging to a sodium atom, thus leaving the chlorine negatively charged and the sodium positively charged. The negative chloride ion (Cl^-) is continually attracted to the positive sodium ion (Na^+) and vice versa. The two ions move toward each other in a solution of water, but other forces balance this attraction and keep them from recombining into a molecule of NaCl.

Earlier we said that currents in the nerve impulse were different from those in a wire. Now we can find out why that is so. The current in a house wire is the flow of *electrons* jumping between the metal atoms that make up the wire; nerve impulses, on the other hand, involve currents in which the charged particles are *ions* flowing through fluid. Two types of ion that flow in your brain whenever you think, act, feel, or see are sodium ions and chloride ions. You eat salt because it tastes good, but the reason that it tastes good is that your whole conscious existence depends on it. Tasting "good" means that your brain contains circuits whose vital function is to make you find and consume salt. Other ions are also involved in the currents that make up the nerve impulse, but the basics of bioelectricity can be illustrated with sodium and chloride.

The Resting Potential

Let's conduct an imaginary experiment. Figure 4.1 shows a glass of water divided into two separate compartments by a partition running across the center. We put sodium ions in one of the compartments and chloride ions in the other. The ions are strongly attracted to one another (mutual attraction of oppo-

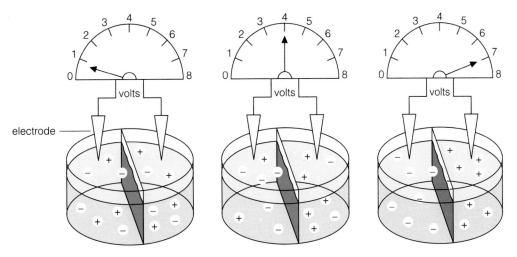

Figure 4.2 Greater separation of charges means higher potential (voltage).

site charges) but are held apart by the dividing wall. Now if a hole is created in the partition, the mutual attraction produces a flow of sodium ions into the chloride side and vice versa. This flow of charged particles is an electric current and continues until every positive ion is closely associated with a negative ion. We have demonstrated that one can generate an ionic current if the opposite charges are first separated and then allowed to flow back together.

At the end of the first step in this procedure, when all sodium ions have been separated into one compartment and chloride ions into the other, the current has not yet occurred—the partition has not yet been punctured—but the potential for a current flow is there. **Potential** is a technical term here and refers to the separation of charges between two places; the positive charges are in one place and the negatives in another. For that reason, a potential can never be located at one point; it must exist between two places. One can speak of the potential *between* the two compartments in the water glass or *across* the barrier.

The greater the initial potential, the stronger the current will be when it is released. That is, if all of the sodium ions and chloride ions are mixed

together on both sides, there is no potential (no difference between them), and no current will flow. If 10 percent of the sodium ions in such a homogeneous mixture are removed from one side and taken to the other side, then a small potential is created; this small difference in charge between the two sides produces a brief current when the partition is punctured. On the other hand, if great quantities of ions are involved and the separation is 100 percent, then the potential across the divider is great, and a large current can flow for a long time (Figure 4.2). The size of the potential created is measured in units called **volts (V)**. So, if all other factors are held constant, a greater voltage should cause a larger current.

The partitioned water glass is a very basic, primitive **battery** (technically called a wet cell) because it stores electricity in the form of positive and negative ions waiting for the chance to flow together. The battery that powers a transistor radio probably has a potential of 9 V between its two sides and does not leak its electrons through a hole in the partition. The battery is designed so that the electrons race from one side of the partition to the other through an external wire or, more precisely, through the wires of the radio circuits. Just press your thumb on

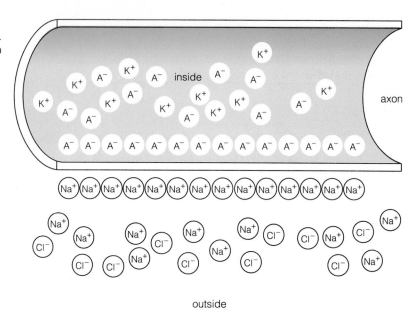

Figure 4.3 Intracellular vs. extracellular distribution of ions. An excess of positive ions is on the outside, and an excess of negatives is on the inside. This unequal distribution of charges produces a voltage of 70 mV between the inside and outside, called the resting potential.

the electrode at the top of the battery (which connects to one compartment inside) and your finger on the metal at the bottom of the battery (which connects to the other compartment), and a few electrons flow through your hand from one compartment to the other, canceling out some of the potential when they arrive. The resistance of your skin to currents is very high, however, and the very few electrons that struggle through to the other side of the battery are not detected by the receptors in your hand. To get a current strong enough to feel, you would probably have to use a potential of around 40 V. This is a large contrast to the voltages within the nervous system where we will be dealing with fractions of a volt. The potential between the inside of an axon and its outside is a mere 70 millivolts (mV)—that is, 70/1,000 of a volt.

Figure 4.3 illustrates a section of axon slit lengthwise so that we can see the inside and outside. One glance at the diagram may be enough to show that axons function like biological batteries. Note that the cell membrane acts just like the partition in our water glass; it keeps the positives on one side from reaching the negatives on the other. However, unlike charges provide enough attraction to keep the ions

lined up along the inside and outside of the membrane. The diagram shows several types of negative and positive ions: sodium ions (Na^+), chloride ions (Cl^-), **potassium ions** (K^+), and **protein anions** (AN-eye-uns) (A^-). Also note in the drawing that there is only a small separation of charges; many positive ions remain inside and many negatives on the outside. The separation is strong enough, however, to create the measurable potential of 70 mV mentioned earlier. This 70 mV is present across the membrane (i.e., between the inside of the axon and the outside) whenever the cell is at rest (i.e., not conducting an impulse). For this reason, it is called the **resting potential** of the axon.

Creating the Resting Potential

Creating a voltage (potential) across the cell membrane seems at first to be a simple thing; all that is needed is more positive ions on one side than on the other. However, there are at least four factors that have a say in how ions will be distributed between the inside and outside of a neuron: (1) semipermeability, (2) sodium/potassium pump, (3) diffusion pressure, and (4) electrostatic repulsion/

attraction. As we examine these four factors, keep in mind that each small area of axon membrane contains a perfect balance of ions. There are just enough positives to balance the negatives, just enough sodium ions to go with all the chloride ions, and exactly enough potassium ions to match the protein anions. Establishing a potential is a matter of disrupting these perfect balances so that one side of the membrane has too many positives and the other has too many negatives.

Diffusion Pressure It is easier to understand how the four forces work if we imagine a hypothetical set of circumstances in which each force can occur by itself. We will begin with diffusion pressure alone and then add in the other three, one at a time. **Diffusion** is the tendency for identical particles in solution (like ions) to move apart from one another so that they fill all the available space with the greatest possible distance between each other. You have seen the principle of diffusion at work if you have ever watched the particles in a drop of ink disperse throughout a glass of water. So, if no other force were present, the mechanism of diffusion would move enough ions through the membrane for there to be equal numbers of each on both sides (Figure 4.4a).

Semipermeability Semipermeable membranes like those of neurons allow some ions to diffuse through readily but not others. Potassium (K^+) and chloride (Cl^-) are able to diffuse through easily, but sodium moves through only with difficulty (until a nerve impulse begins). The protein anion is too big to fit through the membrane and is permanently trapped inside the cell (Figure 4.4b). The ions that can move through the membrane do so by way of large, cylindrical protein molecules called **ion channels**, which create tubelike openings through the membrane at frequent intervals.

Electrostatic Forces The inability of the protein anions to diffuse out of the axon creates a large electrostatic repulsion between them and the chloride ions. **Electrostatic repulsion** is the tendency for particles with identical charges to repel one another. The repulsion pushes most of the chloride

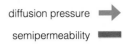

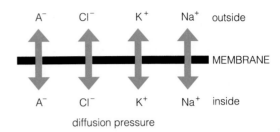

diffusion pressure

a

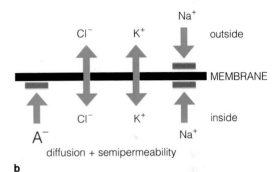

diffusion + semipermeability

b

Figure 4.4 Hypothetical distributions of ions across the neuron membrane that would hold true if it were possible to combine the four forces one at a time. (**a**) With only diffusion at work, ions distribute themselves evenly across the membrane. (**b**) When semipermeability is added, protein anions are confined entirely to the inside of the cell where they are made. Cl^- and K^+ can still diffuse freely, but Na^+ is constrained. Given enough time, sufficient Na^+ gradually leaks through to balance the concentration on both sides of the membrane, but within any brief time frame, the membrane is as good as impermeable to the ion.

ions out of the axon. A few chloride ions remain inside because the electrostatic repulsion is countered in part by the diffusion pressure pushing the chloride ions inward. This leaves the inside of the axon with slightly more negative ions than there are on the outside (Figure 4.5a).

The greater number of negative ions on the inside than on the outside establishes a potential across the

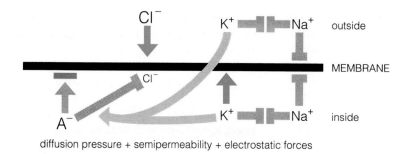

Figure 4.5 The four forces that create the resting potential. The relative sizes of the arrows and symbols indicate the relative sizes of the forces and concentrations. (**a**) In a hypothetical axon experiencing only diffusion pressure, semipermeability, and electrostatic forces, all A^- would be found inside, as would most Cl^-. Na^+ would be in equal concentrations inside and out. There would be slightly more K^+ inside because of semipermeability plus electrostatic attraction from the excess of negative ions inside. Electrostatic repulsions between the positive ions have been shown, although they would not contribute to a difference across the membrane at this stage in our example. (**b**) When the sodium–potassium ion pump is added to the other three forces, the resting potential is completed. Most Na^+ is transported outward, the K^+ inward; this creates large Na^+ and K^+ diffusion pressures. However, inward Na^+ diffusion is blocked by semipermeability. Outward K^+ diffusion is blocked by the electrostatic repulsion from all the Na^+ trapped on the outside and by the potassium pump. K^+ are also held inside in part by electrostatic attraction to the excess of negative ions there. To keep the picture simpler, the less important electrostatic attractions are omitted.

membrane and would appear to explain how the resting potential comes about. But we still have not explained the distribution of potassium and sodium ions. The force of electrostatic repulsion is matched by **electrostatic attraction;** unlike charges attract one another. This attraction pulls a few extra potassium ions inward but not enough of them to cancel the negativity there. The rest are held back by the strong diffusion pressure from the inside potassium

ions (Figure 4.5a). This pressure builds as more potassium ions are attracted inward, and finally a point is reached at which the inward electrostatic attraction is balanced by the outward diffusion pressure. This is called an **equilibrium point**, and it is reached before many potassium ions have entered. The sodium ions remain equally distributed across the membrane until we introduce the last of the four forces.

The Ion Pump So far, our explanation has accounted for (1) the fact that all the protein anions are inside, (2) the excess of chloride ions on the outside, and (3) some excess of potassium ions inside. The only remaining differences between our hypothetical axon and a real one (as in Figure 4.3) are the equal distribution of sodium ions across the membrane and the size of the difference in potassium ion distribution. Diffusion pressure and electrostatic force, have had a negligible effect on the sodium ions because the membrane is nearly impermeable to their passage. However, a set of chemical reactions, the **sodium–potassium pump**, works continually through the day to move sodium ions to the outside of the membrane and the potassium ions to the inside. It must draw on the chemical energy supply of the neuron to do this because it must transport the sodium ions against the forces of diffusion and electrostatic repulsion. Once some of the sodium ions have been moved to the outside, an equilibrium between all the opposing forces is reached (Figure 4.5b). It is this combination of forces that is responsible for the resting potential.

To summarize: The resting potential develops because the protein anions are all held inside by the membrane, and when some chloride ions are forced in by diffusion, the inside turns slightly negative. The sodium ions are unable to cancel out this resting potential because of the ion pump and membrane impermeability; there aren't enough potassium ions inside to do the job because of the outward diffusion pressure. So, in its resting state, the cell membrane stays negative on the inside and positive on the outside.

Movement of Ions During the Nerve Impulse

With a resting potential established, a nerve impulse becomes possible. As soon as the gates on the sodium channels open, the membrane becomes completely permeable to sodium ions, and they flow inward, creating an electric current by their movement. It has been estimated that each channel opening allows the passage of about 100 ions (Keynes, 1979). They are *attracted* inward by the excess of negative charges there, and they are also *pushed* inward by the diffusion pressure from overcrowding

outside the axon. If sodium ions moved inward only because they were electrostatically attracted to the excess of negative ions there, the flow of sodium ions would stop as soon as all the negative charges had been balanced. Instead, the flow continues until the inside of the axon reaches a charge of +30 mV.

It is the diffusion pressure of all the sodium ions on the outside that pushes the extra ions into the cell. As the extra sodium ions enter, however, they produce an overall positive charge inside the cell, which creates electrostatic repulsion for the sodium ions that are still on the outside. The more extra sodium ions that enter the cell, the more the ones still outside are repelled by the growing positive charge in there. The entrance of extra sodium ions has left the outside of the cell with a slight excess of negative charges, which attracts the remaining sodium ions. So, as more and more sodium ions enter the axon, the electrostatic forces that resist this flow become greater and greater. Finally a point is reached where the electrostatic forces that resist the entrance of sodium are strong enough to balance the diffusion pressure that is sending them inward. The flow stops. The two forces have reached an equilibrium, and the voltage at this equilibrium point is +30 mV in the axons of a mammal (Dudel, 1976). Thus, a potential of +30 mV on the inside of the membrane is called the **sodium equilibrium potential** (Figure 4.6). It is the equilibrium that determines when the inward flow of sodium ions will be cut off. As the sodium current ends, the membrane once more becomes impermeable to sodium ions.

At this point in the process, the axon is like a gun that has been fired; in order to get it to fire again it must be reloaded. In other words, the neuron must reestablish its resting potential if there is to be another current flow. The problem is solved by an outward flow of potassium ions that begins just as the sodium current is slacking off. The potassium current continues until the negative charge on the outside of the membrane has been neutralized, and then, just as with the sodium current, it continues beyond that point to establish a positive charge outside the membrane. The force that pushes out these extra potassium ions is diffusion pressure (just as in the case of the sodium current). The overcrowding of potassium ions inside the cell is overcoming the

Figure 4.6 The role of diffusion pressure and electrostatic repulsion in the action potential. (**a**) At the resting potential of −70 mV, prior to the action potential, both forces are working to push sodium, and both are very strong. (**b**) At this point, Na⁺ channels have opened, and the voltage has fallen to zero. Much of the Na⁺ diffusion pressure has been relieved, and an electrostatic balance has been achieved. For the moment, electrostatic repulsion is not a factor. (**c**) As more sodium ions are driven in by diffusion pressure, the excess of sodium ions inside the membrane begins to build electrostatic repulsion inside the membrane, which grows until it exactly equals the inward-driving diffusion pressure at +30 mV. At that point, the two forces are in balance, and the flow of sodium stops. The equilibrium potential has been reached.

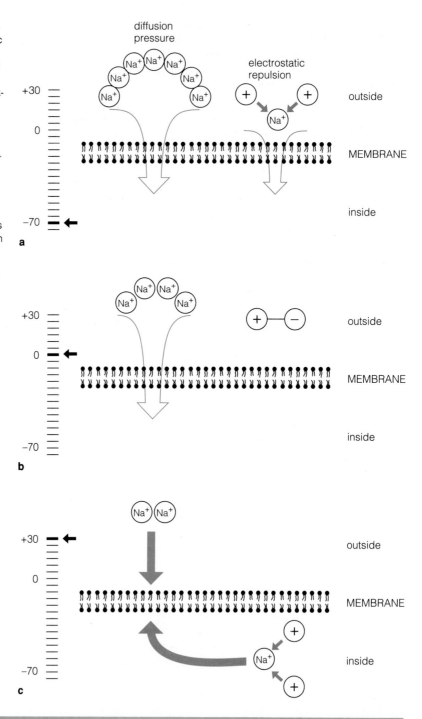

electrostatic repulsion of positive ions flowing into an area that already has a positive charge on it. But, once more, as more positive ions flow out, the electrostatic force resisting that flow automatically becomes greater. Finally, at +70 mV the force of electrostatic repulsion is strong enough to balance the diffusion pressure, and the outward flow of potassium ions stops. The **potassium equilibrium potential** has been reached. This voltage is also the resting potential, which has now been reestablished. The axon is once more "loaded" and ready to be "fired" again.

One problem remains. Every impulse draws more sodium inward and more potassium outward. However, the sodium–potassium pump works day and night to restore the ions to their starting points. Although it moves ions much more slowly than does the sudden opening of membrane channels, the pump continues to work even during slack periods when the axon is conducting few impulses. Not even the busiest axon ever seems to "get ahead" of its ion pump.

The exchange of sodium and potassium across the membrane is the **action potential** of the axon. Action potentials consist of two **transmembrane currents**, one flowing inward (Na^+) and the other flowing outward (K^+) at one point on the membrane. (*Transmembrane* means *through the membrane*.) The **nerve impulse** consists of a sequence of such transmembrane currents progressing down the length of the axon from soma to telodendria. Next we must find out how such a sequence of transmembrane currents can come about.

Conduction of the Impulse

Figure 4.7 shows you the point on the neuron where the axon emerges from the cell body. This area is

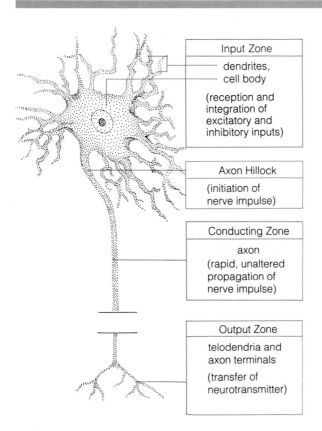

Input Zone
dendrites,
cell body
(reception and integration of excitatory and inhibitory inputs)

Axon Hillock
(initiation of nerve impulse)

Conducting Zone
axon
(rapid, unaltered propagation of nerve impulse)

Output Zone
telodendria and axon terminals
(transfer of neurotransmitter)

Figure 4.7 Axon hillock and three functional zones of the neuron. (From Starr & Taggart, 1987)

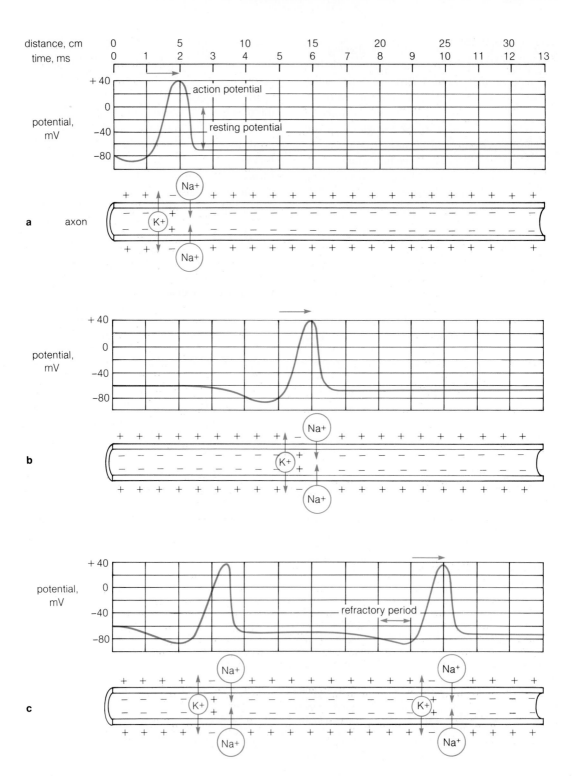

called the **axon hillock** or **initial segment**, and it is in this initial segment that impulses are born. Currents from the cell body (which will be discussed in a later section) disturb the membrane of the hillock and cause the channels in that area to open. Sodium ions rush inward, drawn by the presence of the negative ions within the axon. The flow of ions through the membrane constitutes an electric current, and the presence of this current disturbs the neighboring membrane next door to the initial segment. Consequently, channels in the neighboring membrane open and allow a current to flow there also. This current, in turn, disturbs the next area of membrane a bit farther down the axon, which responds by opening its channels—and so on, down the entire length of the axon. Once this chain reaction is triggered by the current in the cell body it then proceeds from cell body to telodendria as automatically as knocking over a row of dominoes; disturbance occurs, channels open, current flows (producing another disturbance), neighboring channels open, current flows there, and so on. This traveling wave of disturbances and transmembrane currents is the nerve impulse (Figure 4.8).

Electrotonic Currents The "disturbance" that opens the ion channels is a drop in the voltage across the membrane. Current from a stimulating electrode can be used to decrease the voltage across the membrane: This is why an experimenter is able to artificially trigger an action potential with a small electric shock. The current in a stimulating electrode is a flow of negatively charged electrons rather than ions. If the electrode is on the outside of the membrane

and the electrons are flowing *off* of it, then their negative charges will begin canceling out the positive charge on that side of the membrane. In other words, the flow of electrons will lower the positive–negative difference (voltage) between the outside and inside of the cell. The membrane could also be stimulated by inserting an electrode into the cell and causing the current to run in the opposite direction so that negatively charged electrons would leave their ions to flow into the electrode and be removed from the interior of the cell. Again, this would result in reducing the voltage between the outside and inside of the cell, thus opening the gates on the ion channels and allowing the transmembrane currents to flow.

What causes a voltage drop in the parts of the membrane not stimulated directly by the electrode? The answer is a process called an **electrotonic current**. This is a type of current that consists of a flow of *electrons*, jumping from one ion to the next in much the same way that electrons in an electrical wire move from one molecule of copper to the next (Stein, 1982). Whenever an ionic transmembrane current flows it generates an accompanying electrotonic current that spreads out along the axon membrane in both directions (Figure 4.9). This current decreases the voltage in the regions adjacent to the area of membrane occupied by the transmembrane currents. The voltage drop opens the ion channels, thus triggering a sodium current in the new region. The new transmembrane current also generates electrotonic currents that spread to unstimulated regions of axon, decreasing the voltage there and triggering ionic currents. Thus, the original transmembrane current started by the electrode spreads

Figure 4.8 Propagation of the nerve impulse along the axon. The impulse (action potential) is moving from left to right in this diagram. (**a**) The rising side of the action potential reflects the transmembrane Na^+ current that flows inward. The K^+ transmembrane current flows outward, creating the back side of the potential. (**b**) The impulse moves from its point of origin when sodium currents disturb the resting potential on the neighboring area of membrane, opening the ion channels there and triggering more Na^+ currents. At this point (6 ms after the impulse began), channels in the first few centimeters of the axon have closed again, cutting off the transmembrane currents and allowing the resting potential to be reestablished at that point. (**c**) Once the resting potential has been recovered, a second action potential can be triggered. (From Jensen et al., 1979)

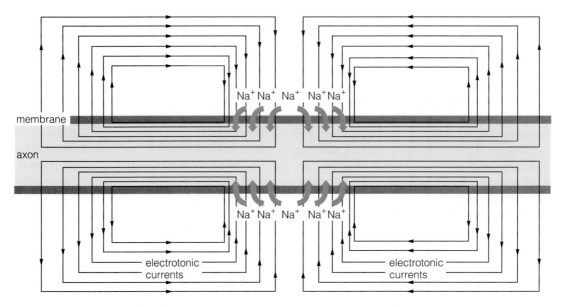

Figure 4.9 Electrotonic currents spreading down the axon in both directions from their origin in the transmembrane sodium current. The currents spread out along the inside of the membrane and return along the outside.

down the entire length of the axon as each region of membrane stimulates its neighbor with electrotonic currents.

Another way of describing the nerve impulse is to say that an action potential at one end of the axon will set off a wave of action potentials along the whole axon. Because the impulse at one point on the membrane triggers the impulse at the next point, nerve impulses are said to be self-propagating. One result of **self-propagation** is that the strength of the nerve impulse does not weaken as it progresses down the axon. The size of the action potential in each segment of axon is determined by the diameter of the segment rather than by how far the impulse has already traveled. This characteristic of the impulse is frequently called **nondecremental conduction;** that is, the impulse shows no decrement (does not decrease) as it travels. The nondecremental conduction of impulses stands in sharp contrast to electrotonic currents, which lose strength as the distance from their source increases. When we discuss transmission, we shall see that the soma and dendrites are characterized by *decremental* conduction, whereas nondecremental conduction is the rule in the axon.

Saltatory Conduction Fast-conducting axons are vital for responses requiring short reaction times. In the myelin sheath of the axon, evolution has provided vertebrates with a device for enhancing speed of conduction. The myelin (see Chapter 2) provides an insulation for each axon that minimizes the degree to which electrotonic currents can reach the ion gates in the membrane. Figure 4.10 shows a stretch of vertebrate nerve fiber with its myelin sheath. Note that the glial cells that constitute the sheath do not cover the entire axon. In between glial cells there are breaks in the myelin sheath where bare axon is revealed. These bare spots between glial cells are the **nodes of Ranvier** (rhawn-vee-ay), and they are the only places on a myelinated fiber where transmembrane currents can be elicited. The nodes are located just close enough to one another that the electrotonic currents from the action potential at one

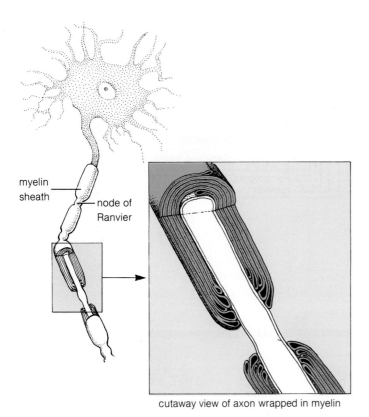

myelin
sheath

node of
Ranvier

Figure 4.10 A node of Ranvier. The Schwann cell wrappings have been partly cut away to reveal the axon underneath. The node itself is the short segment of bare axon between the two Schwann cells. (Adapted from Starr & Taggart, 1987)

cutaway view of axon wrapped in myelin

node can reach and stimulate the membrane at the next node. The nerve impulse in a myelinated axon, then, uses only the nodes; those are the only points where transmembrane currents flow. This restriction of transmembrane currents to nodes of Ranvier is called **saltatory conduction.**

In saltatory conduction, a transmembrane current occurring in the first segment of axon spreads its electrotonic currents along the intervening myelin. When these currents reach the bare membrane at the first node of Ranvier, they open the ion gates there, triggering another action potential. The sodium current at the first node evokes electrotonic currents that flash down the axon to the second node and initiate an action potential there before the original transmembrane currents in the initial segment have had a chance to die away. Almost immediately, the electrotonic currents generated by the action

potential at the second node are stimulating the membrane at the third node, and so on, down the entire length of the axon (Figure 4.11). In myelinated axons the nerve impulse jumps from one node of Ranvier to the next like a stone skipping over the water.

Measuring Action Potentials

At this point in our discussion it may seem somewhat magical that scientists can describe the flow of invisibly small particles across microscopic membranes of nerve cells. How is it possible to study phenomena that are not only too small for the eye to see but also as invisible as electricity itself? In this section, we look at some methods of measuring membrane currents and discover some of the laws governing nerve impulses.

Figure 4.11 Saltatory conduction. Two nodes of Ranvier are shown on the cross section of an axon. A nerve impulse is traveling from right to left. Na$^+$ channels have opened at the right-hand node, and the ionic currents there (arrows) are creating electrotonic currents (field lines with arrows showing current direction). Electrotonic currents are depolarizing the exposed membrane of the node at the left, which soon leads to the opening of ion channels there. Because no channels open in the length of membrane intervening between the two nodes, the impulse essentially "skips" from one node to the next in a very rapid form of conduction.

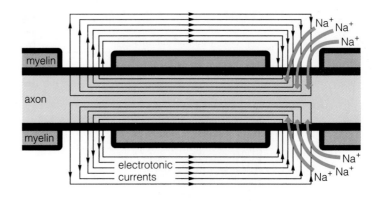

The Oscilloscope Nerve impulses are not only invisible but also begin and end in less time than it takes to think "nerve impulse." The key to obtaining a physical recording of such a short event is the instrument called the **oscilloscope**. With a "scope," one can record voltage changes that occur in less than 1 ms (1/1,000 of a second).

An oscilloscope has a lot in common with a television receiver. The screen of an oscilloscope or television is the face of a large glass tube containing a partial vacuum, called a **cathode ray tube (CRT)**. The inside of the CRT's screen is coated with a phosphorus compound that glows brightly for a moment wherever it is struck by a stream of electrons. The electron stream is emitted by an electron "gun" at the back of the tube (Figure 4.12). When you switch on the oscilloscope, you see the beam, end on, as a bright point of light at the center of the screen.

The reason for using an electron beam is that it can be moved across the screen fast enough to show the extremely rapid voltage changes of the nerve impulse. As the voltage increases, the beam is pulled upward; as it decreases, the beam drops. As the nerve impulse passes the two recording electrodes on the axon, voltage changes between them pull the beam

sharply up and then down, almost too fast for your eye to follow. The result, persisting on the scope face for a second or two, is an electronic "snapshot" of the whole sequence of negative–positive–negative voltage changes. Because this trace fades within seconds, you must photograph it or record it in computer memory if you wish a permanent record of the impulse.

The Nerve Impulse of the Squid Let's look into a neurophysiology lab where membrane potentials are being measured. To one side of the researcher is a rack of electronic gear, which includes a **stimulator** to generate an electrical current carefully shaped to fit the needs of the experiment, an amplifier to boost tiny voltages to a size big enough to be recordable, and an oscilloscope to view changes in voltage. On a table in front of the experimenter is a long plastic tray containing a biological solution in which lies an 8-cm length of axon. The threadlike axon had been patiently teased out of the body of a squid (Figure 4.13) and then cut free of the cell body and telodendria. It has the enormous diameter of 1 mm (the same size as the wire in a paper clip) and is probably one of the largest nerve fibers anywhere

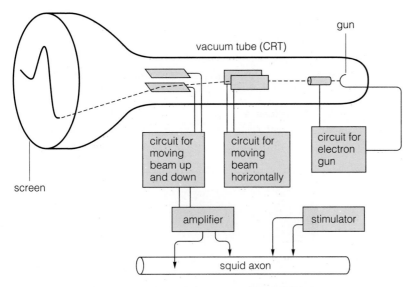

Figure 4.12 Arrangement for displaying a nerve impulse from a squid axon on an oscilloscope. Only the CRT and selected circuits from the oscilloscope are depicted (front panel is not shown). The two arrows pointing to the left end of the axon represent the recording electrodes, one inside the axon and the other outside.

in nature. Hundreds of human axons could be stored within this huge tunnel of a fiber. Why is it so unusually large?

The giant axon belongs to the part of the squid's nervous system that produces instant defense reactions. Impulses racing down the length of this titanic tube contract the muscles that propel the squid away from danger and stimulate the glands to eject a murky, black "ink" into the water behind the fleeing animal. In other words, slow impulses in this particular fiber would be a disaster for the species; there would soon be very few squid and a lot of fat sharks. A basic principle of neurophysiology is that larger axons have faster impulses. Modern-day squid have huge axons in their defense systems because small-axoned squid in previous generations rarely lived long enough to pass along their genes for small axons. But, whatever the reason for the axon, its size is gratefully exploited by neurophysiologists, who usually get to meet axons only distantly as dead, stained, blurry streaks eyed with difficulty through multiple lenses of a microscope. Instead, here in the tray in front of our researcher lies the still-living strand of visible, touchable nerve tissue to which electrodes can be applied and whose "behavior" can be recorded with a minimum of effort.

Figure 4.12 shows the arrangement of the experiment. A brief pulse of current from the stimulator provides the initial "disturbance" that opens channels in the axon's membrane and triggers a *transmembrane* current of ions flowing between the inside and outside of the axon. Two electrodes leading to the amplifier sense the electrical difference (the voltage) between the inside and outside of the axon. The sodium and potassium currents that constitute the impulse create moment-to-moment changes in this voltage, which are boosted in size by the amplifier and displayed visually by the oscilloscope. Thus, our experimenter can watch the progress of currents indirectly by looking at voltage changes that accompany them. Now let's see what this experimental arrangement can reveal about transmembrane currents.

Depolarization and Excitability Look at the voltage graph at the top of Figure 4.14. The resting potential for this particular nerve fiber (axon) is shown as −70 mV. That this potential is negative means that we are looking at it from the perspective of *inside* the cell rather than from outside. This is merely a convention. We could just as easily have used the outside electrode as our reference and shown a

Figure 4.13 (**a**) The giant axon used in the study of the nerve impulse is one of the fibers of the squid's stellate nerve serving the mantle. (**b**) Photomicrograph shows the electrode tip inside the axon. (**c**) Before the axon is stimulated, the oscilloscope screen shows a flat, horizontal trace indicating no change in voltage between the inside and outside of the axon. (**d**) The delivery of a shock triggers an action potential, which shows its waveform on the screen. (From Starr & Taggart, 1987)

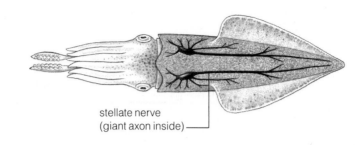

stellate nerve
(giant axon inside)

a

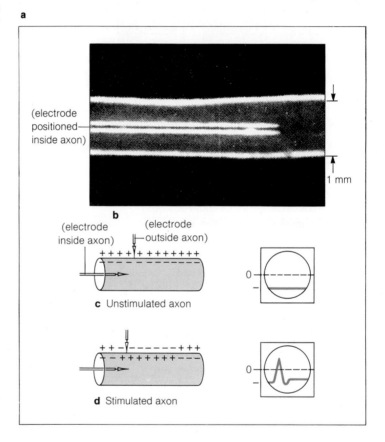

(electrode positioned inside axon)

1 mm

b

(electrode inside axon)

(electrode outside axon)

c Unstimulated axon

d Stimulated axon

+70-mV difference. It's just like viewing a hill from the top and talking about a 45-degree drop versus viewing it from the bottom and calling it a 45-degree rise. It's still the same slope whether viewed from the top or from the bottom. By general agreement, we usually take the inside electrode as our reference point.

In discussing nerve impulses, several concepts are almost always used. For example, a membrane with a resting potential across it is said to be **polarized**. This simply means that there is some separation of charges so that more positives are on one side and more negatives on the other. The greater the separation of charges, the more the membrane is polarized. **Depolarization** would, of course, be a decrease in polarization either through the removal

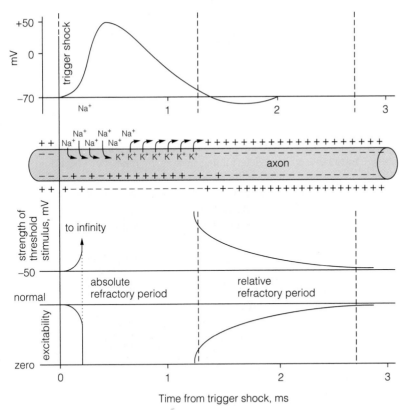

Figure 4.14 The action potential. The top graph shows voltage changes that define the action potential. Under that are shown the ion movements that create these voltage changes. The bottom graph shows how the threshold of excitation and its reciprocal, excitability, fluctuate during the course of the potential. The vertical dashed line just after the 1-ms mark indicates the approximate end of the absolute refractory phase; the second vertical dashed line shows the end of the relative refractory period.

of charges from the situation or by the coming together of unlike charges to cancel out one another. Polarization can be in either the positive or negative direction. Moving away from zero voltage in either the positive or negative direction increases the polarization; moving back toward zero decreases it.

The **action potential** (sometimes, **spike potential**) shown in Figure 4.14 is the sequence of voltage changes seen at any one point on a neuron membrane when a nerve impulse passes through. The action potential could be described as a shift from polarization (at −70 mV) through depolarization (−70 to 0 mV) to repolarization (0 to +30 mV). Notice in Figure 4.14 that the curve representing voltage starts upward as the inside of the membrane depolarizes from negative to zero and then continues upward as the inside repolarizes from zero to positive. The downward shift of the curve that forms

the back side of the action potential occurs as the inside of the axon depolarizes to zero and then repolarizes to its starting point, −70 mV.

Let's imagine that our experimenter has decided to measure the excitability of the squid axon—that is, to find the threshold for firing it. The **axon threshold** is the least amount of electrical stimulation (in millivolts) required to trigger an action potential. **Excitability** is the opposite of threshold. An axon with a *high* threshold is hard to excite (i.e., has a *low* excitability) and vice versa. As excitability increases, threshold decreases; more excitable cells have lower thresholds. The experimenter is interested specifically in how excitability fluctuates during a nerve impulse, so the stimulator is set to deliver two shocks in quick succession. The first shock is to elicit a nerve impulse, during which excitability can be measured, and the second shock is for measuring the excitability. By varying the voltage of the second shock, one can see how readily the axon produces a second impulse while the first one is still in progress. If it requires less-than-normal voltage to trigger the second impulse, then the threshold has dropped; if a greater-than-normal voltage is required, excitability has decreased (the threshold has risen). The results of these measurements show that a second nerve impulse can indeed be triggered before the first one is over but that more voltage must be used to overcome decreased excitability.

The researcher can also vary the amount of time between the two stimulation pulses. By trying test shocks at many different voltages at different times following the first shock, one can generate the excitability curves shown in the lower part of Figure 4.14. When looking at these graphs, remember that excitability is the reciprocal (mirror image) of the threshold voltage.

Refractory Periods   Figure 4.14 shows that if the test shock comes during the sodium current (in the early part of the action potential), then the excitability is at its lowest. In fact, for about 1 ms, excitability drops completely off the graph while the voltage required to reach threshold goes to infinity. In other words, during that fraction of a second, absolutely no amount of voltage would reexcite the membrane. This short period of nonexcitability is called the **absolute refractory period**. At the ionic level, this simply means that the first impulse already has the membrane channels open; the stimulus cannot reopen something that is already open.

Immediately following the absolute refractory period comes the **relative refractory period**, during which it again becomes possible to obtain a nerve impulse with the test shock. At this time then, a second shock produces a second action potential before the axon has completely recovered from the first. The axon does not have to repolarize all the way to −70 mV for depolarization to be initiated. Because few ions actually flow through the membrane in each action potential, the second impulse shows no decrease in strength from the first, despite being triggered before repolarization was complete. Its size is limited by the same sodium equilibrium potential that set the limit for the first. Because this

potential remains constant even as the axon fires hundreds of times in quick succession, the size of nerve impulses in any axon always remains the same. You met this idea earlier in the chapter as the all-or-none law.

Thus, an axon cannot fire again if it is still in its absolute refractory phase, but once it enters the relative refractory phase, it becomes progressively easier to reexcite. These facts are quite important for determining how many times per second an axon can be fired. Consider the case of a sensory neuron that provides an area of skin with pressure receptor endings. Imagine a stimulus pressing against the skin for 10 seconds or so and the axon responding repeatedly to this continuing pressure, signaling to the brain that the stimulus is still there. Can this axon signal the *intensity* of the pressure, or can it only react the same to all degrees of stimulation? If the pressure increases, the axon cannot make larger nerve impulses to represent that increase; the all-or-none law prevents that. Then how does the brain discover that the pressure has increased? The answer to this dilemma lies in the nature of the relative refractory phase.

Early in the relative refractory period, the threshold is still high, and it takes a strong stimulus to refire the axon. Weaker stimuli must wait further into the relative refractory phase until the threshold has dropped to a lower level before they can refire the cell. So, a strong stimulus can fire the axon again very quickly after the first action potential, whereas a lesser stimulus must wait longer. The stronger the stimulus, the faster the axon fires. In other words, the brain knows how intense the stimulus is by listening to the rate at which the receptor cells fire. Stimulus intensity is "coded" into frequency of firing.

There is a limit to the rate at which an axon can be fired, and this rate is set by the duration of the absolute refractory phase. If a stimulus increases in strength, it fires the neuron earlier and earlier in the relative refractory phase. Eventually, however, it reaches the beginning of that period, and further increases can do nothing to make the cell fire faster. Because the absolute period is longer in some neurons than in others, some cells are capable of much faster rates of firing than are others. The record speed is about 1,000 impulses per second, but a more typical rate is around 500 per second. If you do a moment's worth of simple arithmetic, you will see that these more typical cells must have absolute refractory periods that last about 2 ms.

Transmission of Information Between Neurons

Axons are like telephone lines in that they simply carry messages from one place to another. They take no part in the creation of the conversation at one end of the line or in the comprehension of the information at the other end. Cell bodies are analogous to humans at the two ends of the line. The processes within the soma and dendrites create the information to be transmitted along the axon in nerve impulse code. You have now learned enough about neurons that we can begin to describe some of the simpler features of how neurons receive and generate information. The process begins with the transmission of information from one neuron to another at synapses.

First, let's understand some basic terms. The neuron labeled *cell B* in Figure 4.15 receives impulses from cell A and sends impulses to cell C. Points of contact between the cells are synapses (see Chapter 2), and three of these connections are pictured between A and B, two between B and C. If we are discussing one of the synapses between A and B, then A is referred to as the **presynaptic** cell, and B is the **postsynaptic** cell. However, if one of the synapses between B and C is under discussion, cell B becomes the *pre*synaptic element and cell C is the *post*synaptic one. Our discussion begins on the presynaptic side.

Presynaptic Events in Transmission

Imagine a nerve impulse in the axon of cell A in Figure 4.15. On reaching the telodendria (only three of which are pictured), the single impulse becomes many impulses, one for each telodendron. Thus, picture a nerve impulse racing down each of the three telodendria, heading for the **terminal (end bulb)** at its tip. When the impulse reaches the terminal, it will run out of membrane to depolarize and flicker

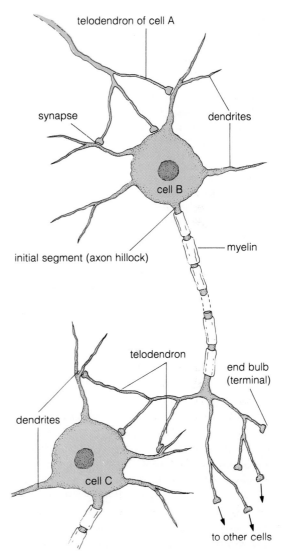

Figure 4.15 Illustration of the terms *presynaptic* and *postsynaptic*. If a synapse between A and B is the focus of attention, then cell A is presynaptic and cell B is postsynaptic. If attention shifts to a synapse on cell C, then B is presynaptic.

out of existence. As it depolarizes the membrane of the terminal, however, it triggers the next step in the process of passing information to the postsynaptic cell.

Figure 4.16 shows a terminal with synapse. At the top of the picture we see the last few microns of

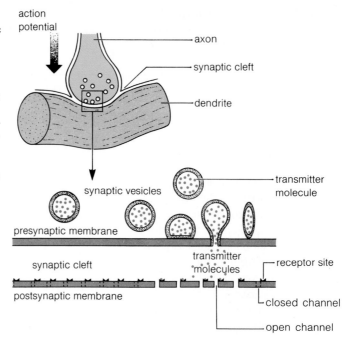

Figure 4.16 A synapse consists of a section of presynaptic membrane, the synaptic cleft (gap), and a section of postsynaptic membrane. At the top is a terminal with transmitter-filled vesicles nearly touching a dendrite. The enlargement at the bottom shows synaptic vesicles grouping near the presynaptic membrane, merging with the membrane, and emptying the transmitter into the synaptic cleft. Transmitter molecules diffuse through the fluid of the cleft until they reach the postsynaptic membrane at the other side of the synapse where they bind with receptor sites to open ion channels. (From Jensen et al., 1979)

telodendron just before it broadens into its end bulb. The term **synapse** refers to an area that includes parts of the two connecting cells plus the gap between them. The part of the synapse called the **synaptic gap** (or **cleft**) is the fluid-filled space between cells. Despite the fact that the distance between neighboring cells is greater at the synapse than anywhere else, the gap is hardly more than a few molecules wide. Just above the synaptic cleft in Figure 4.16, we can see the **presynaptic membrane**, the part of the end bulb closest to the gap. Below the gap is the **postsynaptic membrane**, which is a part of either a dendrite or a soma of the postsynaptic neuron. These three components—presynaptic membrane, synaptic cleft, and postsynaptic membrane—make up the synapse.

When neuroanatomists look for synapses in nerve tissue by searching photomicrographs (see Chapter 2), one outstanding synaptic feature that helps them find what they are looking for is the cluster of tiny, bubblelike **vesicles** that are always present in the terminal. The vesicles are storage "bottles" for chemicals called **neurotransmitters**. The picture of the

terminal in Figure 4.16 shows that these transmitter-filled vesicles cluster near the presynaptic membrane, and in some cases, they even meld with the membrane and spill their contents into the synaptic gap. Transmitter molecules diffuse across the gap and trigger activity in the postsynaptic neuron.

Secretion of neurotransmitter from the presynaptic terminal must be carefully controlled because it is the carrier of information. The postsynaptic neuron should be stimulated by transmitter only when the presynaptic cell has fired. Any transmitter released between impulses is unrelated to true information and resembles the static that interferes with the reception of AM radio stations. Furthermore, if two impulses arrive at the terminal in quick succession, then twice as much neurotransmitter should be secreted. Let's examine the mechanism for controlling the release of transmitter.

The arrival of an impulse in the terminal opens not only the sodium gates in the membrane but gates on **calcium channels** as well (Schmidt, 1976). Calcium ions (Ca^+) act as a go-between, allowing vesicles to bind themselves to the inside of the presynaptic membrane preparatory to opening into the gap (Stein, 1982). If the vesicle membrane cannot fuse into the neuron membrane, it has no way to get its molecules of transmitter into the synaptic gap. The closer a vesicle is to a group of calcium channels, the more likely the vesicle is to release its transmitter (Atwood & Lnenicka, 1986). Figure 4.17 shows calcium ions flowing into the terminal to do their job of linking vesicle to membrane. Each impulse allows more calcium to flow in, and the more of these ions there are, the more vesicles can release transmitter. In other words, if two impulses arrive in quick succession, twice as much calcium will be admitted, and the amount of transmitter released is doubled.

To summarize, a single impulse in a presynaptic axon becomes many impulses as the axon branches into telodendria. Each impulse dies as it runs out of membrane at the telodendron terminal, but as it depolarizes the membrane of the end bulb, calcium channels are opened. Calcium ions rush into the terminal and react with both the membrane of a nearby vesicle and the presynaptic membrane of the neuron itself, binding the two together so that the vesicle can open and release its molecules of neurotransmitter into the synaptic gap. Each vesicle releases about 10,000 molecules of transmitter (Stevens, 1979).

It is at this level of molecular events wherein lies a real understanding of how the human brain works. For example, when we look at the physiological basis of memory in a later chapter, we will see that being able to remember something is a matter of the strengthening of particular synaptic connections and that calcium may be involved in the early stages of memory formation. One way to strengthen a synapse could be to increase the amount of transmitter released per impulse. This would increase the influence of the presynaptic neuron over the postsynaptic. In some cases, creating a memory is a matter of guaranteeing more calcium per impulse.

Postsynaptic Potentials

Once released from vesicles, neurotransmitter molecules quickly diffuse into the fluid and reach the postsynaptic membrane of soma or dendrite. Figure 4.18 pictures a fragment of postsynaptic membrane

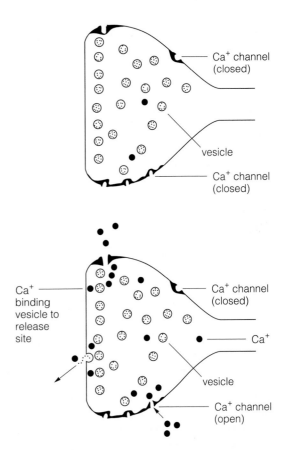

Figure 4.17 Ca$^+$ control of neurotransmitter release. The terminal at the top contains vesicles but is discharging none of its transmitter into the synaptic gap because the vesicles have not been bound to the membrane. In the bottom terminal, a nerve impulse has just arrived, opening the Ca$^+$ gates and allowing calcium into the terminal. Some of the calcium ions have already encountered vesicles and have bound them to the membrane. One vesicle has proceeded to the next step of merging with the presynaptic membrane and has discharged its contents into the gap.

pierced by large protein molecules forming ion channels. Each channel is formed by one immensely long protein molecule that twists and turns, curling into complex helixes and twining back through itself to create, in outline, the "solid" shape seen in Figure 4.18 (Miller, 1983). The portion of the molecule on the outside of the membrane, poking into the syn-

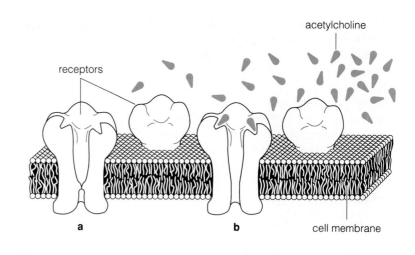

Figure 4.18 Ion-channel protein molecules embedded in a section of postsynaptic membrane. Two molecules are shown in cross section so that the ion channel at the center is visible in each. In the molecule at (**a**), the channel is closed. At (**b**), however, acetylcholine (Ach) molecules have bound to the receptor sites in the channel molecule, which has changed its shape so that the channel is now open. The shapes shown in this diagram are as close as possible to the actual overall forms of the molecules. In reality, of course, each channel molecule is not a solid form but a tangled mesh of atoms. (Adapted from *The Salk Institute Newsletter*, 1983)

aptic gap, has three cusps in which the twists of the molecule have created shaped depressions. These "sockets" are called **receptor sites** because their shape matches that of a neurotransmitter molecule. These particular sites are designed by genes to receive molecules of the neurotransmitter **acetylcholine (Ach)** (ass-SET-uhl-KO-leen). Each type of neurotransmitter in the nervous system has a different shape to its molecule and requires a differently shaped receptor site molecule to receive it.

A close look at Figure 4.18a reveals that the channel molecule has empty receptor sites and its ion channel is closed, preventing the flow of sodium ions. In Figure 4.18b, Ach molecules have drifted across the synaptic gap and into the receptor sites where they react with the channel protein. The chemical reaction, called **binding**, twists the protein molecule a little further, opening up the ion channel through its center and allowing sodium ions to flow inward. This is the nature of the gates to which we referred in our discussion of the nerve impulse. Conceptually, they act like gates, but in reality they might better be likened to throats that can open and close.

Figure 4.19 is an electron micrograph of a frag-ment of postsynaptic membrane showing how closely clustered receptor molecules look from the viewpoint of transmitter molecules approaching them through the fluid of the synaptic cleft. This gives you some idea of how transmitter molecules can find their receptor sites. The "finding," of course, is done strictly by chance as the molecules float about, bouncing off each other or off nonreceptive parts of the membrane. But, the distances are unimaginably small and the channels so closely packed that the whole trip from release to binding takes some molecules less than 1 ms. The 10,000 molecules from one vesicle open about 2,000 channels (Stevens, 1979).

As soon as channels begin to open, sodium molecules flow inward, creating a transmembrane current. This current has a very short life (about 15 ms) because transmitter molecules that initiated it remain in the receptor sites for only a brief moment. Their binding is easily reversed (Nathanson & Greengard, 1977), freeing them to float away and, perhaps, bind to another channel. As soon as a receptor is empty once more, the channel it controls closes immediately, thus shutting off the current. Because these

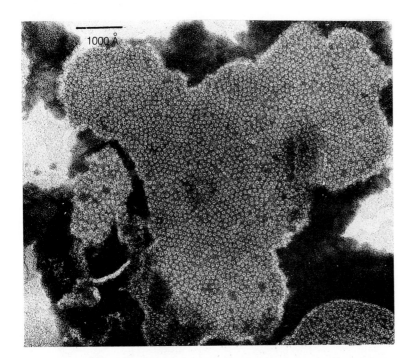

Figure 4.19 Photomicrograph of a dissected section of postsynaptic membrane showing hundreds of channel proteins (viewed end-on), with the ion channel visible at the center of each. The resolution is not great enough to reveal the receptor sites. (Electron micrograph by R. M. Stroud)

small transmembrane currents tend to excite the neuron, they are called excitatory postsynaptic potentials (EPSPs).

Excitatory Postsynaptic Potentials Versus Nerve Impulses

The last paragraph did not tell you that the neurotransmitter set off a *nerve impulse* in the postsynaptic cell. It is an EPSP that occurs when ion channels open, not an impulse, and there is a great difference between nerve impulses and EPSPs.

The **excitatory postsynaptic potential (EPSP)** is a small transmembrane current of inward-flowing sodium ions and outward-flowing potassium ions that occurs at the postsynaptic membrane. Just like the transmembrane currents that make up the nerve impulse, it is accompanied by electrotonic currents that spread across the surrounding cell membrane. These electrotonic currents can spread all the way from the tip of a dendrite branch through the soma to the axon hillock (initial segment). If it is strong enough to depolarize the initial segment, the sodium gates there open, initiating a nerve impulse. So, EPSPs are the triggers for nerve impulses (Figure 4.20).

The major difference between EPSPs and impulses lies in the nature of the channels through which they flow. Gates on the sodium channels of the axon are held closed by a voltage between the inside and outside of the membrane; when depolarization occurs, gates open and transmembrane currents flow. Thus, channels used by the nerve impulse are **voltage-regulated**. Ion channels in the membrane of the dendrites and soma, however, are opened not by a voltage drop but by a neurotransmitter. Thus, the channels responsible for EPSPs are **transmitter-regulated**.

This difference in channel-gate regulation creates another important difference between EPSPs and impulses. When a transmembrane current flows through the membrane of the *axon*, its accompanying electrotonic currents depolarize the adjoining membrane and open the channels there to produce

Figure 4.20 An EPSP triggering a nerve impulse. An impulse has just arrived at the presynaptic terminal, shown at the bottom, and transmitter is being released. The enlarged view of the synaptic zone (inset) shows transmitter molecules binding with receptors on ion channels in the postsynaptic membrane and opening the channels to a flow of ions. These ion currents have already initiated electrotonic currents, which have spread to the axon hillock and depolarized the membrane there, triggering nerve impulses in the postsynaptic axon. The EPSP consists of the ion flow through the membrane plus the electrotonic currents that accompany the ion flow.

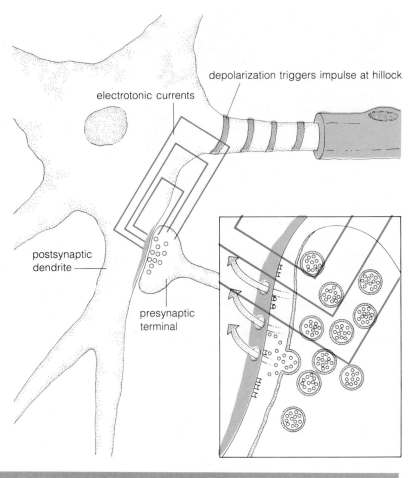

depolarization triggers impulse at hillock

electrotonic currents

postsynaptic dendrite

presynaptic terminal

another set of transmembrane currents. The impulse is self-propagating. It keeps re-creating itself, and this is why it flows down the length of the axon. If you pause and think about it a moment, you will see that EPSPs cannot propagate themselves. As transmembrane currents flow, the accompanying electrotonic currents depolarize the neighboring area of dendrite but with no effect. The channels of dendritic and somatic membrane can only be opened with a transmitter. Consequently, an EPSP flowing at a synapse influences the distant axon hillock only with the spread of its electrotonic currents, and these grow weaker the farther they spread. Sometimes this spread of electrotonic current is spoken of as a form of conduction, but in acknowledging the fact

that it decreases in strength as it travels, it is called **decremental conduction**. In contrast, the succession of equal-strength currents that make up the nerve impulse is referred to as nondecremental conduction.

Triggering Nerve Impulses

Functionally, most large nerve cells are split into two parts, and each part performs a different task. The axon and telodendria constitute the communications unit. Their job is to carry information from the part of the nervous system in which the soma is located to some distant part where postsynaptic cells use the information. For example, cell B in Figure 4.15 might have its soma located in the thalamus, and its axon might extend out of the thalamus to make contact with cell C whose soma lies several inches away in the cerebral cortex. The axon is like a telephone line connecting two computers. It delivers the computations (the output) of the first computer to the second computer, which will use this information in its own computations. Without stretching the analogy too far, the brain can probably be thought of as a highly interconnected collection of biological computers, each with a particular function. Some of these brain structures process data coming directly from sense organs, but most of them process input that is the output from other such computing devices elsewhere in the brain.

If communication is the function of the axon of the neuron, then computing is the job of the other unit, the cell body and dendrites. Each soma–dendrite unit receives inputs from thousands of terminals scattered over most of its surface. These terminals come from hundreds of presynaptic cells, each of whose soma could be located in any one of a dozen or more places around the nervous system. Every second, a veritable flood of information arrives at each postsynaptic cell in the form of a continually changing pattern of presynaptic impulses.

If one could capture this pattern photographically, it might resemble a thousand twinkling lights playing over the surface of the dendrites and soma. The pattern would be continually in flux, changing from one millisecond to the next and, perhaps, never exactly repeating itself within the lifetime of the neuron. Everywhere across the busy surface of the cell, vesicles would be spilling transmitter into clefts, and ion channels would be opening and closing. Dozens of EPSPs would "flash" into existence every moment, spreading their effects across the membrane and reaching toward the axon hillock.

It is at the hillock that our microscopic "biological computer" does its most important adding and subtracting. Because each individual EPSP is too tiny to reach the axon threshold and trigger a nerve impulse by itself, the generation of an impulse has to await that moment when a number of EPSPs all arise more or less simultaneously. Electrotonic currents from different EPSPs can add together in a process called **summation**. If there is sufficient summation, the

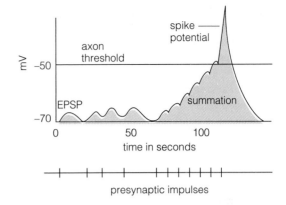

Figure 4.21 Voltage changes in the initial segment showing EPSPs and action potential. Each vertical slash underneath the graph indicates the arrival time of one presynaptic nerve impulse at one of the synapses on this neuron. The resting potential is at −70 mV.

axon threshold is reached, and the sodium gates there open to initiate a nerve impulse.

Figure 4.21 is a graph of this summation process. Voltage levels are shown along the vertical axis, time along the horizontal. The vertical hatch marks at various points along the time line indicate the arrival of presynaptic impulses at synapses on the postsynaptic neuron. The first presynaptic impulse produces a small "hump" on the graph, indicating a miniature, short-lived change in voltage. This hump is one EPSP. Notice that it is much too small to reach the threshold for triggering a nerve impulse in the axon of the postsynaptic cell. Furthermore, it appears and disappears very rapidly, the whole process lasting a mere 15/1,000 of a second. The next EPSP, however, is followed rapidly by a third that arrives in time to build on top of (summate with) the dying potential. Still a fourth impulse arrives, but the spacing is too far apart for it to sum with the previous ones. The graph shows that a short period then follows in which no impulses arrive and the voltage drops back to the resting level. (Notice that this drop actually is a shift toward a higher negative voltage.)

The next event on the graph is the arrival of six presynaptic impulses that are spaced so closely together that the summated potential is decreased all the way to the threshold level. The result is a nerve impulse (shown on the graph as a tall *spike potential*). EPSPs shift the membrane potential away from its resting level of −70 mV toward a lower, less negative voltage. In other words, the term *summation of EPSPs* refers to a shift of the membrane potential toward zero.

Note that the timing of the arrival of presynaptic impulses at the synapse is crucial to the summation. In the example illustrated in Figure 4.21, a 30-ms delay in the arrival of the 10th impulse would have allowed the previous EPSPs to dissipate to the point where the summated potential would still have been below threshold. As you can see, the temporal (time) pattern is very important in determining how big the summated potential will be. This means that when an impulse does finally occur in the axon of the postsynaptic cell it is a signal that the soma has received a particular *pattern* of presynaptic impulses. It is into patterns of this sort that information is coded in the nervous system. Thoughts, percepts, and emotions are apparently all patterns of nerve impulses in the 10 billion or so neurons of the nervous system.

When a nerve impulse arrives at a synapse, one of two things can happen. This impulse may simply add its EPSP to the existing summated potential without providing enough additional voltage to push the axon over its threshold (a condition called **facilitation**), or the impulse may be the last one needed to boost the summated potential above threshold and fire the axon (a condition called **excitation**). Thus, facilitation is the act of simply providing the postsynaptic cell with one more EPSP, whereas excitation refers to firing its axon. The word *facilitate* means "to make easier," and you can see how the addition of another EPSP to the summated potential would make it easier for any subsequent impulses to fire the axon. It is possible that certain structures of the brain, such as the midbrain reticular formation, may achieve their results strictly by providing facilitation to neurons in other parts of the brain. That is, reticular cells may never fire the cortical neurons on which they synapse but simply provide facilitation that summates with input from thalamic neurons. This reticular facilitation would enable the thalamic neurons to decide when a cortical cell will fire.

Types of Receptors

Now that you have a general idea of how postsynaptic potentials originate and how they relate to nerve impulses, let's examine a variety of receptor types and their differing effects on the neuron. So far, you have learned only about receptors that trigger EPSPs, but there are others that induce an inhibitory current. Further, we have covered only the simplest type of receptor—the one that is directly attached to the ion channel it opens. A more complex type involves a second-messenger system.

Second-Messenger Systems Some neurotransmitters such as dopamine and norepinephrine bind to receptor sites that are not attached to ion-channel proteins. Instead, the binding of the transmitter activates an enzyme that triggers a series (or cascade) of chemical reactions terminating in the opening of a channel that may be relatively distant from the receptor. The best-studied case is that of the **cyclic AMP cascade** illustrated in Figure 4.22. The enzyme activated by the binding of the transmitter converts a molecule of adenosine triphosphate (ATP) to cyclic AMP (cAMP). The cAMP floats in the intercellular fluid until it randomly contacts a segment of the membrane containing an ion channel and a molecule of **protein kinase (PKC)**. The kinase normally holds the ion channel in its closed position, but when cAMP bonds to PKC, the channel is allowed to open. Thus, when the transmitter binds to its receptor site, cAMP carries the message of its arrival to the ion channel. If one thinks of the neurotransmitter as a messenger sent from the presynaptic neuron to open channels in the postsynaptic cell, then cAMP is a **second messenger** that completes the journey. When we discuss memory in Chapter 16, we will discover that this second-messenger system forms a part of the basis for one type of memory.

Inhibitory Receptors Not all receptors open sodium channels and produce the EPSPs associated with facilitation; some types create an **inhibitory postsynaptic potential (IPSP)**. For example, at neuron junctions with striate muscles, acetylcholine opens sodium channels and creates an excitatory

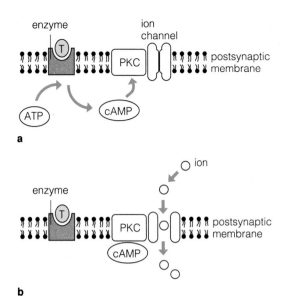

a

b

Figure 4.22 The cyclic AMP second-messenger system. Some transmitter receptors are not connected directly to ion channels. (**a**) The transmitter molecule (T) binds with the receptor site, activating an enzyme. The activated enzyme picks up an ATP molecule from the intracellular fluid and converts it to cyclic AMP (cAMP), which floats until encountering a molecule of protein kinase (PKC) embedded in the membrane. (**b**) When cAMP binds to it, the kinase can open the associated Na⁺ channel, thus initiating an EPSP.

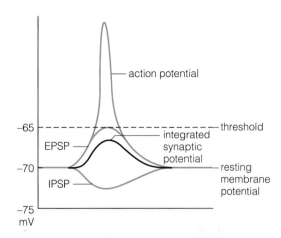

Figure 4.23 The relation between EPSPs, IPSPs, and action potentials. An EPSP depolarizes the membrane (*decreases* the voltage in either the positive or negative direction), and an IPSP polarizes it. Here, the EPSP has lowered the potential from −70 mV to −65 mV. Had it gone a fraction farther, the EPSP would have crossed the axon's threshold and induced an action potential. The IPSP *increased* the polarization by raising the voltage to −72 mV. (From Starr & Taggart, 1987)

potential; but in heart muscle, Ach binds with a receptor type that controls potassium channels, and the result is inhibition (Kuffler et al., 1984). If potassium channels are opened, some of the potassium that has been pushed into the cell by the sodium–potassium pump will be able to flow out. Adding these positive ions to the excess already outside increases the polarization of the membrane, making it harder than normal to depolarize the initial segment and fire the axon. This increase in polarization (usually to about 10 mV above the resting potential) is called **hyperpolarization**, and this is the basis of inhibition.

Now put this together with what you have learned about EPSPs. In facilitation the summated potential

at the initial segment gets closer to the threshold of the axon with each presynaptic impulse. In other words, each EPSP adds further depolarization. In **inhibition** the summated potential gets *farther* from the axon threshold (−65 mV). This is because the potential created by the transmitter binding to an inhibitory receptor site *increases* the polarization across the membrane, driving it toward −75 mV (Figure 4.23).

Inhibition is a widely employed mechanism, involving perhaps as many as half of the synapses in the nervous system. Most neurons are specialized to either inhibit or facilitate their postsynaptic cells, but this is not always the case. A few neurons can facilitate through one synapse while inhibiting through a different one (Kandel, 1976).

Some neurotransmitters seem to "specialize" for inhibition. The transmitters GABA and dopamine, for instance, usually produce IPSPs rather than EPSPs. **Gamma-aminobutyric acid (GABA)** (GAM-uh-uh-

MEEN-oh-byu-TIR-ik) binds with two types of receptors, both of which produce IPSPs. One type, the **GABA$_A$ receptor**, is connected directly with a chloride channel (Bormann, 1988). If the neuron is at its resting potential of -70 mV, Cl$^-$ ions have already reached their equilibrium, and opening channels for them won't make them cross the membrane. If, however, the membrane has been partially depolarized by a preceding EPSP, there will be enough positive ions (Na$^+$) inside the cell to pull the chloride ions in with electrostatic attraction. The inhibitory chloride current has the effect of canceling out some of the preceding sodium current.

A second type of molecule to which GABA can bind is the **GABA$_B$ receptor** that opens potassium channels (Bormann, 1988). This receptor is either directly coupled to the ion channel or communicates with it indirectly by a second messenger and protein kinase (Levitan, 1988).

Summation

IPSPs spread to the initial segment and interact with EPSPs by subtracting from them. Figure 4.23 shows us two summating potentials: an EPSP just below the threshold for a spike potential and an IPSP, which is reducing it. The product of these two conflicting potentials is the **summated potential** seen between the EPSP and IPSP records. The IPSP reduced the EPSP by about 1.5 mV. A typical neuron receives many inputs each second, some facilitative and some inhibitory, so (theoretically) there could be a fine "balance point" where the IPSPs just equal the EPSPs and the summated potential stays right at the resting level of -70 mV. This may lead you to wonder what the value of inhibition is. We address that question in the next section.

■ The Soma as a Decision Mechanism

Transmission between neurons may seem unnecessarily complicated. Why should one synapse cancel out the excitatory efforts of another? When the neurotransmitter opens the ion channels in the postsyn-

aptic membrane, why doesn't it just trigger a nerve impulse? Why did nature complicate matters by having the transmitter set off EPSPs, which then conduct to the initial segment where they may or may not summate sufficiently to produce a nerve impulse? If the point of the whole matter is to have an impulse in the presynaptic cell trigger an impulse in the postsynaptic cell, then why not just do it in a dendrite and get it over with? The answer is that we do *not* want a system in which a nerve impulse in a presynaptic neuron can reliably trigger a nerve impulse in each postsynaptic neuron. Let's first see why that is a terrible design for a nervous system, and then we will go on to see what good the EPSP device is.

The Simple, Unworkable Human

Let's do a little "thought experiment." Picture a nervous system like yours and mine, except that every neuron can generate and conduct nerve impulses in its dendrites and soma just as easily as it does in its axon. No EPSPs are generated. Whenever an impulse arrives at a synapse and transmitter is released, its molecules cross the gap and (*always*, without fail) set off an impulse in the dendrite or soma of the postsynaptic cell. How well would such a system work when actually put to the test?

Let's begin our experiment by touching the skin of one finger of our mythical person. This action evokes a few impulses in a few dozen sensory cells. Each impulse then travels down its axon to the hundreds of synapses at the ends of the telodendria where the action at each synapse triggers an impulse in every postsynaptic neuron. Hundreds of neurons are now conducting impulses toward their telodendria where hundreds will become tens of thousands. At the next set of synapses, tens of thousands become hundreds of thousands or even millions.

Given the extreme interconnectivity of the nervous system, only a few seconds should suffice to arrive at the point where every neuron is swept up into the hurricane of neural activity. When this tidal wave of impulses arrives at the motor neurons of the spinal cord, all muscles attempt to contract simultaneously. The muscles of the diaphragm receive a continual stream of impulses, contracting convulsively to expel one last breath. Our "simplified" nervous system seems to be a prescription for a "terminal" human.

However, it is doubtful that the EPSP mechanism evolved to solve this sort of theoretical problem. There are many positive reasons for its existence, as we will now see.

The Value of Postsynaptic Potentials

The beauty of spinal reflexes is that they require no conscious thought. That not only frees your cortex for other jobs but also produces faster reaction time. If your hand accidentally comes to rest on a very hot surface on your kitchen range, you react by withdrawing the overheated skin even before you are aware of the danger. For you to consciously experience the fact that your hand is too hot, nerve impulses must carry information up the cord to the thalamus, the thalamic neurons must be fired, and impulses in their axons must rush to the cortex where the "thermal" neurons are located that can produce the feeling of heat. The frontal cortex must be notified, make a decision that the hand should be moved, and notify the motor system to send a movement pattern down to the spinal cord. This process could take as long as 500 ms. Fortunately, the hand will already be in motion long before the completion of this activity, thanks to the simple, straight-through, sensory-to-motor reflex connections in the cord.

There is no doubt that this automatic, "mindless," reflex mechanism has saved many a human from serious injury, but there is another side to the coin. Sometimes, we would rather take the injury than the consequences of making a reflex response. Your guest is sitting at the candle-lit table, sipping wine, and you are pulling that absolutely perfect casserole of veal scaloppini from the oven. What you haven't realized yet is that one of the hotpads you are using has a thin spot in it that leaks heat like a sieve. As your hand begins to burn, an entire afternoon's worth of gourmet cooking is threatened with being dumped on the floor as the hand reflexively withdraws from the potentially harmful stimulus. Miraculously, you retain your grip and gracefully deliver the dish to the center of the table with only a passing grimace. When reflexes are unwanted, they can be

turned off. How can that be accomplished? Let's speculate a bit, drawing on our general knowledge of the nervous system.

You want your formal dinner to be perfect, with no embarrassing mishaps. This attitude probably consists of activity in cortical circuits. It includes the idea that you should not make any gross, clumsy movements or movements with unpredictable outcomes, like certain reflex responses. This "ban" probably consists of IPSPs in the motor neurons of the spinal cord—including the ones that produce the reflexive opening of the burnt fingers. The IPSPs undoubtedly come from impulses in descending axons coming from neurons in the cortex (Figure 4.24). So, a "set" toward making only dignified movements probably consists of activity in circuits in the cortex. When these cells are active, cord reflexes are "damped down" or inhibited altogether. The focus of our present interest, of course, is in axons of those spinal motor neurons that failed to fire despite the considerable facilitation from incoming sensory impulses from the hand. Apparently, impulses descending from the brain produce enough IPSPs in their somas to overwhelm the EPSPs from the afferent neurons.

The mechanism just described probably is the most important reason why the nervous system is divided into separate neurons connected by synapses. The EPSP–IPSP mechanism allows the organism to exercise *decisions* or *choice*. Without that mechanism, you would be a primitive robot, completely at the mercy of your stimulus–response circuits. It seems reasonable to assume that each cell body, anywhere in the nervous system, is a choice mechanism, toting up the information coming in from different sources (in the form of EPSPs and IPSPs) and producing a sequence of impulses in its axon that represents all these sources rather than just one. To cite one example from thousands, neurons within the temporal lobe have been found that respond selectively to the color green, but only when that color is being used as a signal that food can be obtained (Fuster & Jervey, 1981). These neurons then could be the basis for the brain's ability to *choose* whether to respond—to *decide* whether to react.

A last but most important reason for EPSPs is that this mechanism allows synapses to vary in strength.

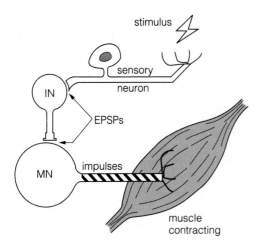

a Cord reflex working

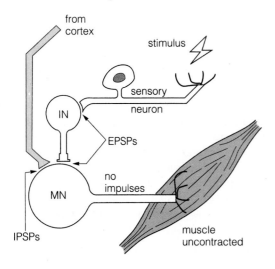

b Reflex inhibited

Figure 4.24 This example of inhibition shows how the postsynaptic potential mechanism of the cell gives us the ability to decide whether to allow a reflex response to take place. (**a**) A reflex circuit responding automatically to the stimulus, as you would expect. (**b**) The same circuit failing to respond because of the overriding influence of the processes in the cortex, representing thoughts about preventing clumsy actions. Cortical circuits have their influence in this hypothetical model by way of descending neurons that trigger IPSPs in the motor neurons of the reflex arc. The IPSPs are enough, in this case, to cancel the EPSPs (IN = interneuron; MN = motor neuron).

A synapse might produce large EPSPs that come close to firing the axon all by themselves or very small EPSPs that contribute only in a minor way. As we will see in later chapters, it is the strengthening of synapses that probably underlies the process of learning. Creating a memory of a new acquaintance's face may be simply a matter of ensuring larger EPSPs at certain synapses so that particular presynaptic cells have better control over certain postsynaptic cells.

■ Transmitters, Drugs, and Neurotoxins

Throughout this book, we will use the knowledge you have just acquired about the workings of synapses. All brain capabilities—learning, seeing, feeling, commanding movement, and so on—are products of synaptic events. It will require the rest of the text to explain what we know about those topics, but we do not have to wait to apply your knowledge about synapses. Many drugs and poisons have their effects through alterations of synaptic function, and we can look at a few examples right now.

There are numerous ways in which drugs can affect the nervous system through action at synapses. We examine five of these mechanisms: receptor blocking, release blocking, transmitter depletion, enzyme deactivation, and reuptake blocking.

Receptor Blocking

It is near noon in the upper Amazon basin, and the endless tropical rain forest sweats and steams in the sun. A troop of chattering, arguing squirrel monkeys flits noisily through the upper branches of tall ironwoods. In the shadows of the forest floor one hundred feet below, a tribesman lifts his blowgun and sends a tiny dart streaking silently upward. Only minutes later, his reward falls at his feet—a paralyzed, soon-lifeless monkey for his family's cookpot. The deadly dart, hardly big enough to wound a baby monkey seriously let alone a full grown adult, had achieved its purpose thanks to its poisonous tip. The missile carried a few milligrams of curare, a nerve toxin obtainable from the tuber of a common amazonian plant.

Curare is a paralytic drug because of its action at synapses that connect motor neurons of the peripheral nervous system to muscle fibers they control. These nerve–muscle synapses are called **neuromuscular junctions**. Striate muscles cannot contract without a stimulus from the motor neurons. If this stimulus is lost because of damage to a peripheral nerve, then the muscle stays completely limp all the time—a condition known as **flaccid paralysis**. However, it is possible for flaccid paralysis to occur even when the motor neuron is alive, healthy, and conducting impulses, providing that no transmission occurs at the neuromuscular junction. The transmitter at this junction is acetylcholine (Ach), and any chemical that interferes with Ach can cut off the muscle from its source of stimulation and produce paralysis.

Let's see how curare interferes with Ach transmission at the neuromuscular junction. Ach excites the muscle fiber by fitting into receptor sites in the muscle membrane and opening ion gates to trigger an action potential. Acting much like a nerve impulse, this muscle potential sweeps down the length of the muscle fiber causing it to contract. Curare contains a substance (*d*-turbocurarine) whose molecules are coincidentally shaped so that they can bind with the Ach receptor sites. Curare fits into the sites well enough to keep the Ach out but not well enough to open the ion channels. If enough sites are occupied by the toxin, then it won't matter how desperately the motor neurons are firing or how much Ach is flooding the junctions, the muscles still hang limp and slack. When paralysis reaches the respiratory muscles of the diaphragm, breathing stops.

Curare is an important research tool for many neuroscientists. It paralyzes striate muscles (all of which use Ach) but leaves smooth and cardiac (heart) muscle alone. Thus, an experimenter using curare to paralyze an animal has little trouble maintaining the heartbeat of the subject but must provide artificial respiration to compensate for the paralysis of the diaphragm muscles. With extraneous muscle contraction eliminated by the drug, much more precise data can be collected on skin and muscle sense systems.

Curare is not the only substance whose effect depends on the principle of **receptor blocking**. A number of therapeutic drugs have their action by blocking receptor sites in both the peripheral and central nervous systems. Blood pressure is controlled by drugs that block receptor sites for the transmitter norepinephrine. Some relief from schizophrenic symptoms can be obtained with **chlorpromazine** (klor-PRO-mah-zeen), a drug that presumably blocks receptor sites for the transmitter **dopamine** (DOPE-uh-meen). Some drugs that do not bind to receptors can achieve the same effect by binding to the inside wall of the receptor's ion channel and plugging it up so that an EPSP is prevented (Adams, 1978).

Release Blocking

For David S. Cohen, a 32-year-old furniture-company executive in Knoxville, Tennessee, last October 5 began, like many other Saturdays, with a quiet family breakfast. There was for Mr. Cohen no warning that it would be his last—that he would be the victim of an accident of chemistry that would spread fear through the entire nation.

Like millions of other Americans, the Cohens liked smoked herring, or chubs as they are sometimes called. They had them often for breakfast. On this day Cohen's daughter, Amy Beth, 10, joined her father in eating the juicy, golden fish. Her sister, Lisa Merle, seven, put a serving on her plate, but—she would recall later—didn't eat any. Mrs. Cohen took none.

That afternoon, at a football game, David Cohen thought at times he was seeing double. When he got home, he felt ill, but simply blamed it on eyestrain. Then Amy complained that she was sick too. At 4:30 the following morning both were awakened by severe nausea. When it continued, David Cohen was taken to Fort Sanders Presbyterian Hospital. Amy followed in a few hours.

The condition of father and daughter grew rapidly worse. Paralysis crept over their limbs. Their vision dimmed. Their tongues refused to move. Swallowing became difficult. Soon all muscle coordination was lost, and they could neither sit nor stand. By eight o'clock Monday morning both were dead. (Berland, 1964)

The Cohens were victims of a chemical secreted by *Clostridium botulinum*, a bacterium that can grow in an airless environment. The fish eaten by the Cohens had been smoked and then vacuum packed but never cooked. Inside the lethal packages, the microbes flourished, dining on fish and exuding one of the deadliest toxins on this planet. Theoretical calculations indicate that only 1 milligram (mg) of botulinus toxin is a lethal dose for 1 million grams of living tissue and that 100 grams (about 3.5 oz) is sufficient to wipe out the entire human population of the world (Van Heyningen, 1965). Botulism poisoning is usually the result of incorrect canning procedures in which the canned food is not heated sufficiently to kill bacterial spores. The toxin is odorless and tasteless, so your best clue to watch for is a can top that bulges and can be depressed with a pop. When the can is opened, one can hear pressure being released.

Botulinus toxin has its effect at the neuromuscular junction where it blocks the release of Ach from motor neuron terminals, thus producing flaccid paralysis. The result—although slower in arriving—is much the same as that of curare. Cutting off the release of Ach yields the same effects as blocking the Ach receptor sites. In either case, striate muscles are cut off from their source of nerve impulse stimulation. When botulinus toxin finds the presynaptic membrane, it binds permanently. The only way to recover from such poisoning is to grow new synapses (Cotman & Nieto-Sampedro, 1982).

Transmitter Depletion

Strangely enough, the release-blocking action of botulinus toxin can be countered by another toxin. Black widow and brown spider venom also acts on the neuromuscular junction, but the effect is the opposite. Rather than blocking release, these venoms speed the release to such a point that the current supplies of the transmitter are soon exhausted. Before this point is reached, however, a veritable flood of transmitter is disgorged into the synaptic gaps. In a laboratory nerve–muscle preparation, an application of spider venom can reverse the effects of botulinus toxin. In the intact human, however, this

thoroughly nasty sounding antidote wouldn't necessarily work and isn't used therapeutically.

Transmitter depletion also occurs at synapses within the brain, and certain therapeutic drugs are designed to take advantage of this. There is a class of transmitters called **monoamines** (MON-oh-am-EENS), which includes **serotonin** (SAIR-uh-TOE-nin) and the **catecholamines: epinephrine, norepinephrine**, and dopamine. Monoamine synapses seem to be the site of action for certain antipsychotic drugs such as **reserpine**. Vesicles that store the monoamine transmitters are made unstable by reserpine; often after a few daily doses, most of the transmitter has leaked out and been lost. This state of depletion continues as long as the daily dose is maintained. Cutting down the amount of dopamine transmission by interfering with its release helps prevent the hallucinations and delusions of schizophrenia.

Enzyme Deactivation

Once a neurotransmitter has crossed the synaptic gap and triggered a potential in the postsynaptic cell, it has served its purpose and must be disposed of. A nervous system can't afford to leave "trash" transmitter molecules lying around in the synaptic cleft. As long as those molecules are available, they will find receptor sites and trip EPSPs. The problem with this is that each EPSP is supposed to represent another, separate nerve impulse in the presynaptic neuron. If a single nerve impulse can leave a transmitter "residue" after it is gone, the pattern of impulses that carries the information will be lost, just like losing a radio station signal in static. What the brain needs is some sort of disposal system to get rid of transmitter molecules immediately after they have served their purpose. This problem has been solved in a number of ways.

At **monoaminergic synapses** (those employing one of the monoamine transmitters), transmitter molecules are brought back into the terminal through a process called **reuptake**. Some of these find their way into new vesicles that are being formed, but most come into contact with an enzyme called **monoamine oxidase (MAO)**, which destroys the molecules by breaking them down into basic molecular components.

At least one of the monoamines, norepinephrine, is a transmitter in the neural pathways that produce activation and arousal. Further, the neural problem of patients suffering from psychiatric depression may turn out to be a deficiency of arousal. Therefore, it seems reasonable to guess that depressed patients might be lacking norepinephrine. Is there a way to supply them with more of this transmitter? There is

no good way to do this directly, but it can be done indirectly by slowing the destruction of norepinephrine by MAO. This allows more of the transmitter to be recycled after reuptake, thereby increasing the supply. One can accomplish this with one of a class of antidepressant drugs called **MAO inhibitors**.

Not all transmitters need to be returned to the terminal for deactivation by an enzyme. At **cholin-**

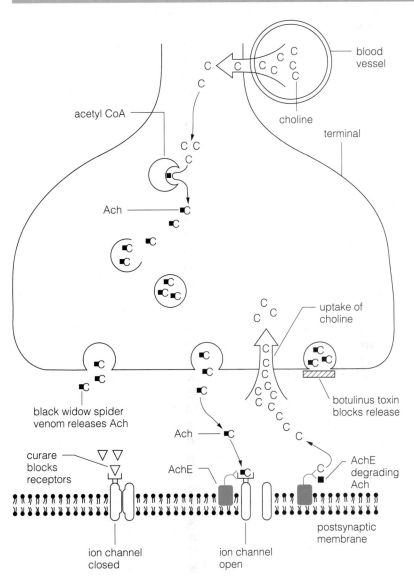

Figure 4.25 Neurochemistry of the acetylcholine synapse. On entering the neuron terminal, choline (C) is converted to acetylcholine (Ach) by acetyl coenzyme A (acetyl CoA) and placed in vesicles. After being released into the synaptic gap and binding with a postsynaptic receptor, Ach is degraded into choline and acetyl by the enzyme acetylcholinesterase (AchE). Choline is taken back up into the terminal to be recycled. Black widow spider venom speeds the release of Ach, quickly exhausting the supply in the terminal. Botulinus toxin blocks the release of Ach. Curare paralyzes muscles by preventing their stimulation by Ach.

blood vessel

acetyl CoA

choline

terminal

Ach

uptake of choline

black widow spider venom releases Ach

botulinus toxin blocks release

Ach

curare blocks receptors

AchE

AchE degrading Ach

postsynaptic membrane

ion channel closed

ion channel open

Figure 4.26 Neurochemistry of the norepinephrine synapse. The manufacture of norepinephrine (NE) begins when tyrosine (T) is taken into the terminal from the blood. This amino acid is first converted to I-DOPA, then to dopamine, and finally to NE. After being released into the synaptic gap and binding momentarily with the receptor site, NE is taken back up into the terminal and destroyed by the enzyme MAO. Some antidepressants work by blocking the action of MAO, thus providing more NE for release with the next nerve impulse. Reserpine inhibits transmission at noradrenergic synapses by allowing NE to leak from the protective vesicles so that it can be destroyed by MAO. Cocaine amplifies the transmission at the synapse by blocking reuptake of NE, thus providing the postsynaptic cell with constant stimulation. NE opens the sodium channels in the postsynaptic neuron by way of a second messenger, cyclic AMP.

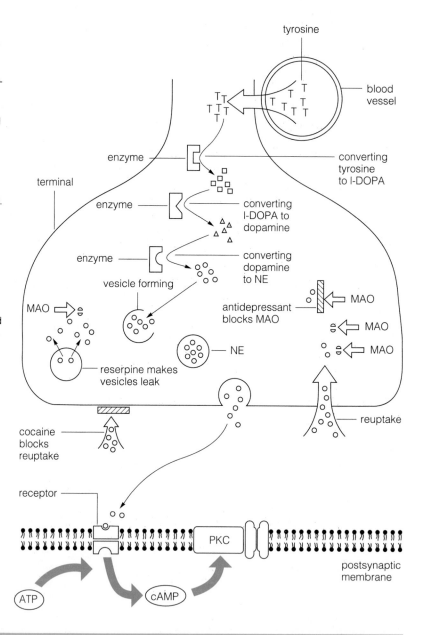

ergic synapses (those employing Ach), the destruction of the transmitter is accomplished in the synaptic cleft by the enzyme **acetylcholinesterase (AchE)** (as-SET-uhl-KO-lin-ES-ter-ase). Without AchE, neuromuscular junctions would be rapidly swamped with Ach. The enzyme can destroy 25,000 molecules of Ach per second (Iversen, 1979). An abnormal, continual abundance of Ach at the junction would give the muscles no rest from stimulation, and they would respond with a strong, continuous contraction. You would have no ability to stop this abnormal contraction, and if it took over the diaphragm muscles, respiration would cease. This is exactly the fate in store for victims of nerve gases developed by military research. Many nerve gases are chemicals that inhibit AchE and thereby remove the "brake" on runaway muscle contraction. The organophosphore insecticides (such as malathion and parathion) are also AchE inhibitors and (in larger doses) can kill mammals as well as insects.

Reuptake Blocking

Halting the enzymatic destruction of monoamines apparently makes more monoamine-transmitter molecules available for release into the synapse, thereby indirectly increasing the firing rate in the postsynaptic neurons that receive the extra transmitter. Another way to enable such postsynaptic cells to fire faster is to keep the transmitter in the synapse longer after each impulse. Drugs such as **amphetamines** and **cocaine** serve as stimulants because they block the reuptake of norepinephrine (Feldman & Quenzer, 1984). Long before cocaine became a street drug, it was used by Bolivian natives living at high altitudes in the Andes. To ingest the drug, they chewed coca leaves, which helped them resist the fatigue born of working in a cold, low-oxygen environment.

Making and Using Transmitters

Acetylcholine is synthesized in the neuron from **choline** and **acetyl coenzyme A (acetyl CoA)** (Figure 4.25). Choline is a common organic substance found in vegetables, egg yolk, seeds, and legumes; acetyl CoA is manufactured in the mitochondria. After Ach is released from the presynaptic terminal and binds to a postsynaptic receptor, it is degraded by the enzyme AchE. Some choline released in that reaction is recovered by the presynaptic neuron to be reused.

Catecholamine transmitters are manufactured from the amino acid tyrosine, which is converted by various enzymes first to **l-DOPA**, then to dopamine. Dopamine can then be altered by another enzyme to norepinephrine, which can be converted to epinephrine. Figure 4.26 summarizes these steps and the actions of some drugs.

■ Summary

1. Nerve impulses occur in the axon of the neuron and normally are conducted from the axon hillock to the telodendria. Impulses follow the all-or-none law; a stimulus either elicits a full-sized impulse or none at all. Impulses consist of a succession of transmembrane currents, which flow when ion channels in the membrane are open.

2. An electric current is a flow of charged particles. In a house wire, it is the flow of electrons; in the neuron, it is a flow of ions. Ions are charged fragments of molecules.

3. A current cannot flow between two points until a potential has been established between them. This is done by separating charges so that one of the two locations has more positively charged particles; the other has more negatively charged particles. The greater the separation, the greater the potential. This potential can be thought of as electrical "pressure," and it is measured in units called volts. Once a potential has been established between two locations, a current can flow.

4. The membrane of the neuron is semipermeable; that is, it will allow some ions to pass through it with greater ease than others. Chloride and potassium ions pass through readily, whereas sodium can do so only during an impulse. The large protein anions cannot pass through at all.

5. Diffusion is the tendency for ions to move apart from one another so that they fill all available space with the greatest possible distance between each particle.

6. Negatively charged protein anions are trapped inside the axon, and their presence in large numbers there keeps most of the negative chloride ions outside by means of electrostatic repulsion. Because there are not enough positives inside to balance the protein anions plus the few chloride ions pushed back in by diffusion pressure, the inside of the axon keeps a slightly negative charge.

7. The positively charged sodium ions are actively transported through the membrane by a mechanism called the sodium–potassium pump, which does not depend on membrane permeability. The pump pushes enough sodium ions out of the axon to create an excess of positive ions there. Thus, the

inside of the axon has become negatively charged, and the outside has become positively charged. This positive–negative difference across the membrane is called the resting potential.

8. A nerve impulse begins when sodium channels in the axon membrane open. Sodium ions are pushed inward until the electrostatic force inside the axon becomes strong enough to stop the sodium flow (at +30 mV). This +30-mV point is called the sodium equilibrium potential.

9. The resting potential is reestablished by the opening of the potassium channels. Potassium ions flow outward until the repulsion from the growing positive charge on the outside balances the diffusion pressure from inside. The point of balance is called the potassium equilibrium potential.

10. Transmembrane currents that make up the nerve impulse are initiated by a drop in membrane voltage (depolarization). Transmembrane currents flowing in one segment of the axon produce electrotonic currents that spread down the axon and depolarize neighboring segments, initiating new action potentials. Thus, the nerve impulse propagates itself down the axon by means of the electrotonic currents. These currents consist of electron flows rather than ion flows and become weaker the farther they spread. The nerve impulse, then, can be defined as a succession of transmembrane currents, each triggered in a new segment of axon by electrotonic currents spreading from the preceding segment.

11. In saltatory conduction, transmembrane currents are prevented except at the nodes of Ranvier. A nerve impulse can propagate between nodes because the electrotonic currents can spread from one node to the next. This makes the impulse much faster than if it had to be elicited in every segment.

12. Impulses are visualized and measured by means of an instrument called an oscilloscope. Electrodes are placed on the axon (one inside and one outside), and the voltage changes that occur during the current flows are displayed on the screen of the oscilloscope.

13. The voltage swing from −70 mV to +30 mV and back, which are seen on the oscilloscope as the nerve impulse sweeps past the electrodes, is called

the action potential (or spike potential). The resting potential can be thought of as a state of polarization (separation of unlike charges); during the first part of the impulse, the membrane undergoes depolarization because of the influx of sodium. In the return from +30 mV to −70 mV, the membrane is being repolarized by the outflow of potassium.

14. The axon threshold is the amount of stimulation (in volts) required to trigger an action potential. Threshold and excitability curves can be generated by repeatedly giving the axon a trigger shock (to elicit an impulse), followed by a test shock (to see if a second impulse can be elicited).

15. The excitability measurements show that there is a period of about 1 or 2 ms following the trigger shock when no amount of test-shock strength is sufficient to start a second impulse. This time is called the absolute refractory period. It is followed by a short period known as the relative refractory phase, during which the axon can once again be fired but only by a stronger-than-normal test shock.

16. A synapse consists of the presynaptic membrane of the axon terminal, the gap (cleft) between the two cells, and the postsynaptic membrane of the dendrite or soma. The terminal contains vesicles that encapsulate the neurotransmitter. When a nerve impulse reaches the terminal, calcium is admitted into the cell where it enables vesicles to fuse with the membrane and eject the neurotransmitter into the cleft.

17. After diffusing across the synaptic gap, transmitter molecules bind with receptor sites in the postsynaptic membrane, thereby opening sodium channels and triggering a transmembrane current. This current is called an excitatory postsynaptic potential (EPSP). Each EPSP generates electrotonic currents that spread out across the dendrites and soma, reaching all the way to the axon hillock and depolarizing the membrane there. It is this depolarization that triggers a nerve impulse.

18. EPSPs do not self-propagate like an impulse because they occur in the membrane of the dendrites and soma rather than in the axon. Ion channels in the axon open when the voltage across the membrane is decreased, but the channels in the dendrites and soma are insensitive to voltages and

are opened only by transmitter binding. Axon channels are said to be voltage-regulated, whereas soma–dendrite channels are transmitter-regulated.

19. Because of decremental conduction, an EPSP may be very weak when it reaches the axon hillock—too weak to reach the threshold of the axon. However, several EPSPs can summate to fire the axon. When a presynaptic neuron stimulates a postsynaptic cell at a synapse, an EPSP is produced. This is called facilitation. If this EPSP is the last one needed in the summation process to depolarize the membrane of the axon hillock and fire the axon, then the word *excitation* is used.

20. Acetylcholine (Ach) receptors are attached to sodium channels and open them directly. Other transmitters may bind with receptors not associated with ion channels. These require a second messenger to reach the channel and open it. The best-known second-messenger system uses cyclic AMP (cAMP) and protein kinase (PKC).

21. Some types of transmitter (such as GABA and dopamine) usually act to produce inhibitory postsynaptic potentials (IPSPs) rather than facilitating the postsynaptic neuron because they bind with receptors that open either chloride or potassium channels. IPSPs increase the membrane potential, hyperpolarizing instead of depolarizing.

22. Postsynaptic potentials (inhibitory and facilitative) enable the nervous system to exhibit choice and decision making by spreading the control of each postsynaptic cell over a number of presynaptic cells.

23. Drugs can affect the nervous system through their actions at synapses. Curare, for example, causes flaccid paralysis of muscles by blocking Ach receptors at neuromuscular junctions. Chlorpromazine helps relieve the symptoms of schizophrenia by blocking receptors on neurons sensitive to dopamine.

24. Another way to prevent transmission at a synapse is through release blocking. Botulinus toxin blocks the release of Ach at the neuromuscular junction and kills by paralyzing respiratory muscles.

25. Reserpine relieves psychotic symptoms by depleting the store of monoamine transmitters (norepinephrine, dopamine, and serotonin) in the terminals. After monoamine transmitters are removed from the synaptic gap by reuptake, they are either recycled into vesicles or destroyed by the enzyme monoamine oxidase (MAO). Because clinical depression involves a lack of monoamine transmitters, some antidepressant drugs have their effect by inhibiting MAO, thereby making more of these transmitters available within the terminals. Other transmitters are cleared from the synapse by different means. Ach is destroyed in the cleft by the enzyme acetylcholinesterase (AchE). Cocaine and amphetamines act by blocking the reuptake of catecholamines.

Glossary

absolute refractory period Period of time during the action potential in which no amount of depolarization will trigger another impulse. (128)

acetylcholine (Ach) Neurotransmitter used at the neuromyal junction and at some synapses between neurons. (132)

acetylcholinesterase (AchE) An enzyme that destroys Ach. (144)

acetyl coenzyme A (acetyl CoA) One of the substances from which Ach is made. (145)

action potential The exchange of sodium and potassium across the membrane during a nerve impulse and the accompanying change in inside voltage from -70 mV to $+30$ mV to -70 mV. (119)

all-or-none law Rule that in any one axon each impulse is always the same size. (111)

amphetamines A group of drugs that serve as stimulants because they block the reuptake of norepinephrine. (145)

atomic nuclei Collections of protons and neutrons. (111)

atoms Particles composed of neutrons, protons, and electrons; they combine to create molecules or ions. (111)

axon hillock See initial segment. (121)

axon threshold The least amount of electrical stimulation (in millivolts) required to trigger an action potential. (127)

battery Device for storing oppositely charged particles in isolated compartments until a current is needed. (113)

binding Chemical reaction in which one molecule attaches to another. (132)

calcium channel Hole in postsynaptic membrane formed by protein molecules; can open to allow calcium ions to enter cell. (130)

catecholamines A group of monoaminergic neurotransmitters that includes dopamine, epinephrine, and norepinephrine. (142)

cathode ray tube (CRT) Vacuum tube similar to the picture tube of a television set. (124)

chlorpromazine A drug useful in treating schizophrenia; it presumably blocks dopamine receptor sites. (141)

choline One of the substances from which Ach is made. (145)

cholinergic synapse One that employs Ach. (143–144)

cocaine A stimulant drug that acts on catecholaminergic synapses. (145)

curare A drug that paralyzes by blocking receptor sites at the neuromuscular junction. (141)

current A flow of charged particles. (111)

cyclic AMP cascade A second messenger system involving adenylate cyclase, cyclic AMP, and protein kinase. (136)

decremental conduction A decrease in amplitude of a current as it flows away from its source; the electrotonic currents of EPSPs conduct decrementally. (134)

depolarization A decrease in the voltage across the membrane. (126)

diffusion The tendency for identical particles in solution to move apart from one another so that they fill all the available space with the greatest possible distance between each other. (115)

dopamine One of the catecholaminergic neurotransmitters. (141)

electrode A conductor that is designed to carry an electric current to or away from some part of the body. (111)

electrostatic attraction The tendency for unlike charges to attract one another. (116)

electrostatic repulsion The tendency for particles with identical charges to repel one another. (115)

electrotonic current A flow of *electrons* that jumps from one ion to the next any time an ionic transmembrane current flows; it spreads out along the axon membrane in both directions from the ionic current, depolarizing it. (121)

end bulb See *terminal*. (129)

epinephrine A catecholaminergic transmitter and adrenal hormone. (142)

equilibrium point The point at which two opposing forces are in balance. (116)

excitability The reciprocal of the threshold voltage. (127)

excitation Elicitation of a nerve impulse ("firing" the axon). (136)

excitatory postsynaptic potential (EPSP) Depolarizing flow of sodium ions into the cell that does not self-propagate along membrane. (133)

facilitation Summation insufficient to reach the threshold of the axon. (136)

flaccid paralysis Condition in which the muscles cannot be contracted and have no tone. (141)

GABA A neurotransmitter that usually produces IPSPs. (137)

$GABA_A$ receptor The type of GABA receptor that is connected to a chloride channel. (138)

$GABA_B$ receptor The type of GABA receptor that is connected to a potassium channel. (138)

hyperpolarization An increase in the potential across the membrane beyond the normal resting level. (137)

inhibition The occurrence of IPSPs at the initial segment. (137)

inhibitory postsynaptic potential (IPSP) A hyperpolarizing current; one that flows in the direction opposite that of the EPSP. (136)

initial segment The segment of axon closest to the cell body; also called the axon hillock. (121)

ion A charged particle consisting of a fragment of a molecule or atom. (112)

ion channels Tubelike openings in the membrane through which ions can pass. (115)

l-DOPA Chemical from which dopamine is made. (145)

MAO inhibitor Any chemical that blocks the action of MAO. (143)

molecules Particles of matter made of atoms. (111)

monoamine oxydase (MAO) An enzyme that destroys monoamine transmitters. (142)

monoaminergic synapses Those employing one of the monoamine transmitters. (142)

monoamines A group of neurotransmitters including serotonin and the catecholamines. (142)

nerve impulse A sequence of transmembrane currents progressing down the length of the axon from soma to telodendria. (119)

neuromuscular junctions The synapses between motor neurons and their muscle fibers. (141)

neurotransmitter Chemical released by presynaptic neuron to stimulate postsynaptic cell. (130)

nodes of Ranvier Short unmyelinated sections of axon between the ends of Schwann cells. (122)

nondecremental conduction Movement of the impulse along the axon membrane without any decrease in the size of the transmembrane or electrotonic currents. (122)

norepinephrine A catecholaminergic transmitter and adrenal hormone. (142)

nuclei See *atomic nuclei*.

one-way conduction Rule that the nerve impulse normally travels toward the telodendria. (111)

oscilloscope Electronic instrument for displaying voltage changes on a cathode ray tube screen. (124)

polarization Existence of a potential (voltage) across the membrane so that one side is positive, the other negative. (126)

postsynaptic cell The cell at a synapse that receives the neurotransmitter. (129)

postsynaptic membrane Portion of the soma or dendritic membrane bordering a synaptic gap; location of receptor sites. (130)

potassium equilibrium potential Point in the nerve impulse where the outward flow of K^+ stops because electrostatic repulsion of postive charges outside the membrane is strong enough to balance the diffusion pressure of the K^+ ions inside; $+70$ mV. (119)

potassium ion (K^+) A potassium atom that has lost one electron and thus carries a positive charge. (114)

potential A separation of charges between two places. (113)

presynaptic cell The cell at a synapse that releases neurotransmitter. (129)

presynaptic membrane The portion of the membrane of a terminal that borders the synaptic gap; site of transmitter release. (130)

protein anion (A^-) Protein molecule that has gained an extra electron and, thus, has a negative charge. (114)

protein kinase (PKC) An enzyme that can open an ion channel when activated by $_cAMP$. (136)

receptor site A place on an ion channel protein molecule where a neurotransmitter molecule can bind. (132)

relative refractory period Period of time during the action potential in which a larger than normal voltage charge will trigger a second action potential on top of the first. (128)

reserpine A drug that depletes monoaminergic transmitters and provides some relief from symptoms of schizophrenia. (142)

resting potential The voltage across a cell membrane; the outside is slightly positive with respect to the inside. (114)

reuptake A process in which neurotransmitter molecules are brought back into the terminal from which they were released. (142)

saltatory conduction Restriction of transmembrane currents to nodes of Ranvier. (123)

second messenger systems Chemicals within the postsynaptic cell that carry information about the occurrence of an impulse in the presynaptic cell; they provide a link between the receptors and ion channels. (136)

self-propagation The ability of transmembrane currents at one point on the membrane to trigger similar currents farther along the axon; responsible for nondecremental conduction. (122)

semipermeability Ability of a membrane to act as a selective filter, allowing some molecules to pass through it while denying passage to others. (115)

serotonin See *monoamines*.

sodium equilibrium potential The point in the nerve impulse at which the diffusion pressure forcing Na^+ into the cell is balanced by the electrostatic forces pushing it out; $+30$ mV in mammalian axons. (117)

sodium–potassium pump A set of chemical reactions that moves Na^+ to the outside of the membrane and K^+ to the inside. (117)

spike potential The sequence of voltage changes seen at any one point on an axon membrane when a nerve impulse passes through. (127)

summated potential The sum of all the EPSPs and IPSPs occurring at any moment in the initial segment. (138)

summation The adding together of electrotonic currents from EPSPs and IPSPs (the latter subtracted from the former). (135)

synapse The area of contact between presynaptic and postsynaptic neurons; consists of presynaptic membrane, synaptic gap, and postsynaptic membrane. (130)

synaptic cleft See *synaptic gap*. (130)

synaptic gap The fluid-filled space between the presynaptic and postsynaptic cells into which the presynaptic terminal discharges the transmitter. (130)

terminal The ending of a telodendron where a synapse is formed with a postsynaptic cell; also called an end bulb. (129)

transmembrane currents Currents created as Na^+ and K^+ flow through the membrane. (119)

transmitter See *neurotransmitter*.

transmitter-regulated channels Ion channels that are opened by the binding of a transmitter molecule to a receptor site. (133)

vesicles Tiny, bubblelike spheres containing neurotransmitter; found in terminals. (130)

volt Unit in which potentials are measured. (113)

voltage-regulated channel Ion channels that are opened by depolarization of the membrane (a change in voltage). (133)

Exploring the Nervous System Through Science

You happen to be obtaining your college education in the midst of what may one day be called the "Golden Age of Neuroscience Research." The last two decades have produced as much new knowledge about the nervous system as was gathered in the previous 200 years. More than 50 neuroscience journals print the enormous volume of experimental data pouring out of laboratories; one of these, *Brain Research*, alone publishes about 10,000 pages a year of experimental reports.

The most important limit on the growth of knowledge within a science is the availability of new methods, and recent years have given us a sudden cornucopia of techniques such as nuclear magnetic resonance imaging, axial tomography, and immunofluorescence and radioactive labeling. Each new method immediately opens up an entire field of research and impels excited researchers into their labs in pursuit of a host of fresh insights.

Consider the impact of one method born in the 1930s. Almost nothing of any value was learned about sleep until the electronic amplifier was invented. Once scientists were able to amplify the extremely tiny voltages at the scalp produced by the brain, the whole field of electroencephalography was born. It was out of electroencephalography that the field of sleep research grew. We know a great deal about some aspects of the nervous system thanks to the availability of methods like electroencephalography, and we know very little about other aspects because no one has yet invented a really good technique for gathering the needed data. One could argue that the heart of any science is its methods and techniques.

In this chapter, we look at some of the original methods that built the foundations of the field and then move on to the more recent additions of our repertoire, some of which are so startling in their abilities as to resemble science fiction.

Beginnings

In the first half of this century, three basic strategies were available to brain researchers: they could stimulate the brain electrically to see what behaviors resulted; they could record the electrical activity of the nervous system, looking for changes that correlate with behaviors or states of minds; and they could examine behavioral changes that appeared when a part of the brain was lost to disease or surgery.

Clinical Observation

Much of our data about human brain function comes to us from **clinical observation** of people with damage to one part or another of their brains. This technique dates back to the ancient Greeks. In modern science, it is the **neuropsychologist** who gathers together all clinical observations and attempts to derive from them an explanation of function. An early example of clinical observation occurred in 1861 when Paul Broca announced to his scientific and medical colleagues that language is localized to a fairly small area within the cerebral cortex of the left frontal lobe. Broca drew this conclusion from observing the behaviors of several brain-damaged patients and then examining their brains at autopsy.

Broca's conclusion was only partly correct, which illustrates one problem with clinical observation; the data are usually less reliable than those from true experiments. Neuropsychologists have to wait for "nature" to provide the experiment by damaging someone's brain through disease or accident. Further, no two patients have exactly the same damage nor the same life history prior to the damage, both of which may influence the resulting behavior. Thus, many neuropsychological data are somewhat less trustworthy than the experimental data neuroscientists collect from animals reared under identical conditions and given nearly identical areas of brain damage. Furthermore, in an animal experiment, each subject can be *randomly assigned* to either an experimental or control group. Random assignment minimizes the risk that a difference between experimental and control data could be the result of individual differences between subjects rather than the result of the brain damage. When you compare a group of human brain-damage patients with a group of normal humans, random assignment is impossible. This means that any difference you find may have already existed prior to the brain damage and cannot reveal anything about the function of the missing brain parts. Ultimately, however, we are much more interested in understanding human brains than animal brains, so we must examine clinical observations despite their relative unreliability and try to fit them together with data from experiments.

Figure 5.1 illustrates a typical example of a clinical observation. The patient was a 22-year-old college student with a temporal lobe tumor. After surgery she complained of memory problems and was given a series of tests to assess her remaining memory abilities. Her scores on verbal memory were normal, but the test for visual memory revealed that she was unable to retain information about visual shapes (Kolb & Whishaw, 1985). If these observations are put together with the surgeon's estimate of the area of damage in the temporal lobe, the function of visual memory can tentatively be associated with a particular area of temporal cortex.

Unfortunately, exact boundaries of a lesion can only be guessed at unless the patient dies and the brain tissue can be examined microscopically. Even such autopsy data would still be only one observation, and the chances that a second patient will be found with exactly the same lesion are almost nil. A theory of cortical localization based exclusively on human data would take a long while to reach a serviceable level of validity and precision. Fortunately, the process of understanding localization has been immensely speeded for most functions by combining the human clinical observations with data from clear, well-controlled animal lesion experiments.

Surgical Lesions

A great deal has been learned from the conceptually simple technique of removing part of the brain and then finding out how the loss of that part affects behavior. The area of damage is termed a **lesion** and

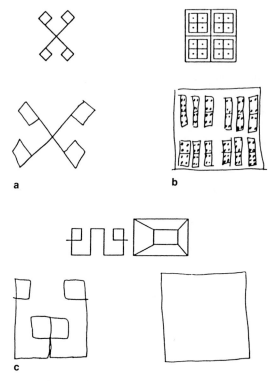

a   b

c

Figure 5.1 Responses of a patient, following temporal lobe surgery. In each case (**a, b,** and **c**), the bottom drawing is the patient's attempt to draw the top (stimulus) figure from memory, immediately after having viewed it for 10 seconds. Figure **c** especially reveals the memory problem. Ten minutes after stimuli were presented, the patient was unable to recall even the simplest figure. (Adapted from Kolb & Whishaw, 1985)

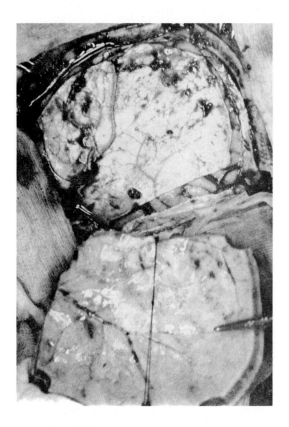

Figure 5.2 Human neurosurgery. A large flap of skull has been folded back at the bottom of the photo. The exposed cortex, still covered with dura, is seen at the top. Drill holes can be seen at the corners of the bone flap. (From Penfield & Roberts, 1959)

the method, **lesioning**. If a very large area is removed, such as an entire lobe of the cortex, the technique is called **ablation**.

Creating brain lesions in monkeys involves many of the same techniques as in human neurosurgery. Because monkeys, like humans, are primates, they are fairly susceptible to human diseases and require sterile surgical conditions. After the monkey is fully anesthetized, its head is shaved and scrubbed with an antiseptic solution, and a sterile sheet is spread. The surgeon opens the scalp and carefully detaches the scalp muscles, revealing the skull beneath. Typ-

ically, several circular holes are bored through the skull, one at each corner of the bone area to be removed. These openings allow the insertion of skull scissors that will cut between the holes. Once the skull fragment has been removed, the outer covering of the brain (the dura) is revealed. The surgeon must snip through this with fine scissors, avoiding as many large blood vessels as possible while creating a flap that can be pulled back out of the way (Figure 5.2). The second membrane enclosing the brain (pia mater) is gossamer thin and can be penetrated with an extremely narrow-bladed scalpel. Bleeding can usually be stopped with mild pressure or a chemical that promotes coagulation.

The cortex itself is now exposed. Even in the human brain, this layer of gray matter is only ¼ to ½ inch in thickness, so if the lesion is to be limited to the cortex, a scalpel is not a delicate enough tool. Instead, a technique called **aspiration** is used. A small length of glass tubing, drawn to a very fine point, is attached to a suction hose. The finely polished tip of the tube is inserted into the hole in the pia, and the gelatinous cortical tissue is sucked out of the brain. The surgeon continues the aspiration until there is a change in color, indicating that the white matter has been reached and the lesion is deep enough.

With the lesion made, the surgeon can close the wound in layers. After the wound is packed with Gelfoam to inhibit bleeding, the dura is folded into place, the cut edges are sutured (sewn) together, and then the scalp is sutured. The animal is watched carefully through recovery and given a special diet and antibiotics. In conformity to the ethical codes of either the Society for Neuroscience or the American Psychological Association, considerable care is taken in the treatment of the animal to minimize pain and discomfort. Laboratory inspectors, acting under federal law, frequently review the animal care in every lab to see if it meets the standards set by the U.S. Congress.

Lesion research was extremely important in the 1930s–1950s, giving us a comparatively easy way to discover the broad outlines of functional location within the brain. For example, it helped us establish the location of the cortical motor and sensory areas and the function of the cerebellum, colliculi, and frontal lobes.

Electrical Stimulation of the Cerebral Cortex

Soon after the phenomenon of electricity was discovered, biologists realized that events within the brain might be electrical. There was no way to know for sure, however, until 1827 when Leopoldo Nobili constructed a galvanometer (a device for measuring electrical currents) with which he clearly demonstrated that animals actually do generate electrical currents in nerves and muscles (Valenstein, 1973a).

We are now reasonably sure that every thought that passes through your mind does so as a series of electric currents in thousands of neurons, and we know with a certainty that muscle cells only contract at the command of electric currents (action potentials) coursing along their lengths.

Before 1870 finding where a particular function resided in the brain depended on examining humans with brain damage or deliberately ablating areas of animal brains and noting what functions were lost. A somewhat grisly source of information was provided by the Prussian–Danish War of 1864.

Dr. Eduard Hitzig, a military surgeon, noted that touching the surface of the exposed cortex provoked movements (twitches) on the opposite side of the body. After the war, he collaborated with anatomist Gustav Fritsch in a series of experiments on dogs involving electrical stimulation of the cortex. The complete lack of laboratory facilities failed to impede the investigators; they simply conducted the experiments on the dressing table in Hitzig's home. As they shifted their stimulating electrode across the surface of the animal's cortex, stimulating first here and then there, different muscle systems contracted to move one body part and then another. They had located the primary motor cortex of the cerebrum (Boring, 1950) and opened up a whole new vista of discoveries using the technique of brain stimulation.

Given this exciting finding, it was inevitable that someone would snatch the opportunity to stimulate the human cortex electrically. In 1874 the occasion occurred when Mary Rafferty, a 30-year-old "feebleminded" woman became the patient of Dr. Roberts Bartholow of Cincinnati (Valenstein, 1973a). Mary had an advanced case of cancer that had produced a 2-inch ulcerative hole in her skull through which the brain coverings could be seen. It was a fairly simple matter for Dr. Bartholow to insert needle electrodes that were insulated up to the tip so that the current could be confined to a small area of brain tissue. He had, however, no good way to control the size of the current nor any knowledge about an appropriate current strength to use. Bartholow observed a brief hand movement (apparently elicited by the stimulation) followed by a seizure and convulsion (usually the sign of overstimulation). Mary recovered from the seizure but later died, probably of the cancer, and Dr. Bartholow conducted an autopsy. Not much was learned from this experience other than the fact that such experiments are not viewed sympathetically by the general public. Dr. Bartholow was forced to leave town by irate citizens (Valenstein, 1973b). Indeed, today his "experiment" would be viewed as the most grievous breech of ethics (and probably morality) because his patient was not intelligent enough to give consent to the procedure after being told of its risks. Nowadays, much important information is collected by means of brain stimulation during neurosurgery but only under conditions that minimize the risk to the patient and only after the patient has been thoroughly acquainted with the intended procedure and understands it well enough to agree to its use.

Some cases of epilepsy are caused by small areas of damage within the cortex, which can be surgically removed. By the 1930s, it was known that the speech areas of the cortex were located in the left hemisphere, but their precise boundaries were unknown. This left neurosurgeons in a quandary; should left-hemisphere epilepsy be treated by surgery when the result might deprive the person of speech? Wilder Penfield, a Montreal neurosurgeon, developed a method, which made use of electrical brain stimulation, to circumvent this problem. Because the electrode introduced an artificial current to the cortex, Penfield reasoned that stimulated neurons should fire in unnatural patterns, disrupting the function of the affected area. Thus, if the speech cortex were stimulated, one should *not* expect the patient to be forced into saying something; rather, speech should be prevented. Could he verify this principle and use it to locate the elusive speech areas so that they could be avoided when the surgeon began to remove cortex?

For this scheme to work, Penfield needed his patients awake during much of the surgical process. Fortunately, there are no pain receptors within the cortex, so a local anesthetic around the scalp and skull openings is all that is needed. Penfield's technique involved laying a silver-ball electrode on the area of cortex to be tested and then stimulating while the patient was speaking. If the patient's speech became slurred, garbled, or just suddenly stopped, the area was tagged as a speech zone. To mark each

spot, a numbered tag of sterile paper was dropped onto the cortex as the electrode was moved (Figure 5.3).

Because a wide zone of cortex had to be explored, Penfield's data provided us with a map of the motor and somatic areas of the cortex as well as the speech cortex itself. In Figure 5.3, for example, one of the tags indicates part of the motor area for moving the jaw, and another shows the zone that provides the sense of touch for the outside of the lower lip. Since the time of these early explorations, hundreds of neurosurgeons have used Penfield's stimulation technique and have provided us with a wealth of information about localization of functional zones within the cerebral cortex.

Recording the Brain's Electrical Activity

It was much easier for early investigators to stimulate the brain electrically than to record that organ's own electrical activity. Hans Berger, a German psychiatrist, began his attempts to capture a "picture" of brain activity as early as 1902, but it was not until 1929 that his findings were announced to the scientific world. His new technique of electroencephalography quickly became an important research tool; in 1935 with the discovery of electroencephalographic patterns characteristic of epilepsy, it became established in the clinic setting as well.

The word **electroencephalograph (EEG)** is a combination of three smaller word parts: *electro-* because it is the electrical activity of the brain that is being examined; *encephalo* (en-SEFF-uh-low) referring to the head and brain; and *graph*, because the machine is a recording instrument. So, the EEG (electroencephalograph) is a device for recording the electrical activity of the brain (Figure 5.4).

Figure 5.5 shows the major elements of an EEG-recording system. Functionally, an EEG resembles an old record stereo system: it amplifies very weak voltage changes and turns them into something you can see or hear. In a home sound system, a needle is vibrated back and forth by the grooves in the record, and these vibrations generate tiny voltage changes that mimic those produced by the original sound waves from the musicians. The amplifier makes these voltage variations large enough to push the speaker cone in and out, thus regenerating the same sound waves. The only differences between such a sound system and the EEG are that the voltage shifts are being produced by the brain instead of a phonograph needle, and we choose to *look* at these variations rather than to hear them. Indeed, if we choose to listen to them, we could run the wire from the EEG amplifier to a loudspeaker and hear someone's brain working away. However, millions of tiny EPSPs and nerve impulses all combining in seemingly random patterns yield nothing but "static." Only when microelectrodes are being used to record from single neurons does a researcher use a loudspeaker because it is then possible to listen to individual nerve impulses and hear their pattern.

In an EEG, the wire from the amplifier carries the voltage changes, now thousands of times larger than they were at the scalp of the subject, to a motor that drives an ink pen back and forth across a moving strip of paper. When the voltage increases, the pen moves up; a decrease moves it down. This back-and-forth movement of the pen shows up on the moving strip of paper as waves, hence the name "brain waves." Note that the brain does *not* broadcast electrical waves as some devotees of ESP assume. There are waves in this process only because we choose to move the paper under the pen. If the paper remained still, we would still see an accurate picture of moment-to-moment voltage fluctuations in the brain as we watched the pen jiggle back and forth, but the resulting record would not show how those fluctuations spread out through time. Brain "waves" are a recording phenomenon, not a brain phenomenon.

What brain processes produce the up and down fluctuations in voltages at the scalp? Each minuscule electrical current within the nerve cells of the brain produces a surrounding electrical field that decreases in strength (voltage) with distance from the current. These tiny electrical fields extend out through the coverings of the cortex, through the cerebrospinal fluid (CSF) surrounding the brain, and through the skull to the scalp where they can be sensed by EEG electrodes. By the time they reach the electrodes, they are enormously weakened and require amplification sometimes as high as 1 million times. The currents that generate these penetrating

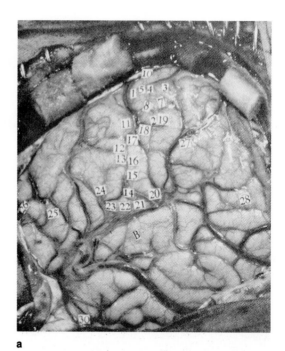

a

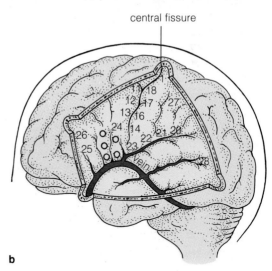

b

Figure 5.3 Penfield's use of cortical stimulation in human neurosurgery. (**a**) This is the same patient as in Figure 5.2, but the dura has now been pulled back to reveal the cortex. Each numbered tag marks a spot where electrical stimulation was tried. (From Penfield & Roberts, 1959) Figure **b** shows some features more clearly. Compare with **a**. (Adapted from Penfield & Roberts, 1959)

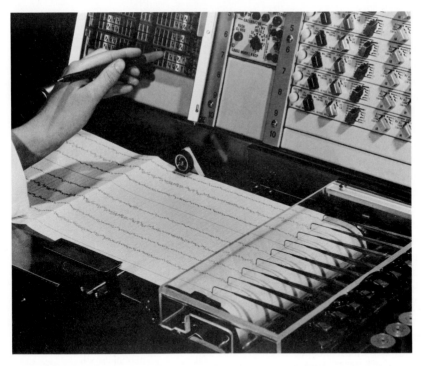

Figure 5.4 An electroencephalograph. The recording pens are visible beneath the Plexiglas cover. The paper rolls off to the left. The amplifiers can be seen in the rack above the paper drive, one for each recording pen and pair of electrodes. (Courtesy Grass Instrument)

electrical fields are spike potentials (action potentials), EPSPs, and IPSPs of neurons. Most of each wave must be contributed by postsynaptic potentials, which are much more numerous than action potentials.

The wave recorded by the EEG pen represents an increase and decrease of voltage at one point on the scalp that is the algebraic summation of current fields from literally millions of individual neurons. These current fields are the electrotonic currents from EPSPs, IPSPs, and nerve impulses (see Chapter 4), some of which are positive, some negative. If the positives momentarily outweigh the negatives, the pen moves in one direction; when the negatives outnumber the positives, it goes in the opposite direction, thus creating "waves." Neurons close to the electrode make the strongest contribution to these waves because electrotonic currents weaken as they spread, but the total wave does include the minor influences of more distant cells as well.

EEG waves vary along two dimensions: amplitude and frequency. **Amplitude** is the height of the wave and represents the amount of energy involved; **frequency** is the number of repetitions of the wave in 1 second. **Wavelength** is systematically related to frequency under most circumstances because waves get shorter as frequency increases, longer as frequency decreases (Figure 5.6). Faster frequencies and lower amplitudes indicate that the subject is more aroused and alert, whereas low-frequency, high-amplitude waves are associated with the deepest levels of sleep. The EEG gave us our first objective means for deciding when the subject is truly asleep. The entire field of sleep research was built on this one methodology.

The EEG is also important in the clinic. Insomnia

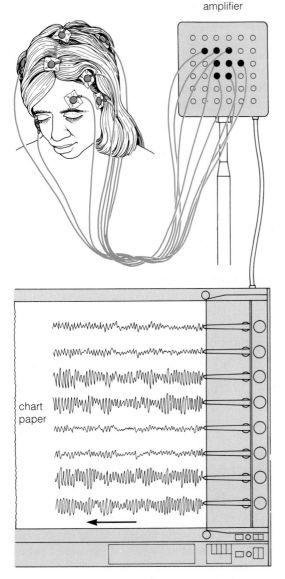

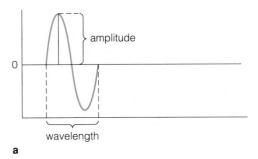

Figure 5.5 The major elements in EEG recording. The human head at the top has eight silver-cup electrodes, filled with conductive paste, attached. Each electrode is connected by a wire leading to the amplifier. The amplified signals (voltage changes) are sent to pen motors that drive a recording pen upward across the paper as the voltage increases, downward as it decreases. The paper rolls under the pens and off to the left. There is usually one pen (channel) for each pair of electrodes.

Figure 5.6 Amplitude differences vs. frequency differences. (**a**) One cycle of an EEG wave illustrates the ideas of amplitude and wavelength. The amplitude is the height of the wave from the zero baseline; length is the distance from the beginning of the cycle to the end. (**b**) Four cycles of an EEG wave in which each successive cycle has a lower amplitude than the preceding one. Because all four cycles have the same wavelength, the frequency is the same throughout. (**c**) Five cycles of an EEG wave in which the amplitude remains constant but the frequency increases (i.e., the wavelengths get shorter).

and other sleep problems are now being vigorously attacked from the basis of objective data. Some insomniacs are surprised to find out that they sleep much more than they had thought; others find that the drugs they believed were giving them more sleep are actually disturbing the "architecture" of their sleep. The EEG is a significant tool in the diagnosis and treatment of epilepsy, a disorder in which the chief symptom is recurring electrical seizures that produce highly distorted EEG waves (see Chapter 17).

Basic electroencephalography has not changed much in the last 30 years, yet it remains a "workhorse" technique basic to many modern experiments and clinical diagnoses. From it have sprung the more modern techniques of depth recording and neural signal averaging, which we look at in the next section.

Probing the Brain's Interior

After the initial successes with lesions, cortical stimulation, and electrical recording from the cortex, researchers began looking for ways to explore subcortical regions of the brain. Was there a way to selectively lesion a tiny subcortical nucleus without first having to strip away masses of cortical tissue in order to reach the area of interest? Could an EEG be recorded from such deep regions as the thalamus and hypothalamus? During the 1950s, some answers to these problems were beginning to emerge.

Implanted Electrodes

One way of examining the workings of neural circuits is to trigger firing in their neurons and record the result. Neurons can be fired with tiny electric currents delivered through wire electrodes inserted into the brain. The wires are insulated down to their tips so that only 1 mm or less of metal is exposed. This starts the current at one small location. Limiting the area stimulated is critical, especially in a rat brain where many structures are less than 1 mm in breadth. Current only flows if there is some destination for it; thus, electrodes are frequently made in pairs with the two wires being twisted or glued together. The majority of the current takes the path of least resistance from one electrode tip to the other. However, current always spreads as it flows along this path, and the stronger the current, the greater the spread. Conversely, the weaker the current, the more easily it is confined to the zone between the electrode tips.

Placing subcortical electrodes into the brain involves calculations, good technique, a bit of artistry, and heavy finger crossing. You cannot open up the brain and visually find the area to be stimulated because small nuclei are usually not discernible until the tissue has been stained. Furthermore, the amount of damage created by such exploratory surgery would be a tremendous drawback. Instead, a small hole is drilled through the skull, the dura is punctured, and the electrode pair gently driven down into the brain with no direct visual check on where it is going. The secret of success is the use of two items: a stereotaxic brain atlas and a stereotaxic instrument.

A **stereotaxic brain atlas** shows an average-sized brain as a series of frontal sections separated by 0.5 mm. On each section, it labels all known structures and shows their boundaries. Along the side and bottom of each brain section are millimeter rulers that show where each point in the brain can be located (Figure 5.7). For example, to place our electrode tips within the substantia nigra, we find the section in the atlas that shows that structure and then read the rulers to discover how many millimeters our target is from the midline and how many from the top of the skull.

To make these measurements meaningful, the anesthetized animal's head must be placed into exactly the same position as the brain in the atlas. This can be accomplished with a **stereotaxic instrument** (Figure 5.8), which holds the head very firmly in a fixed position. A rat's head, for example, is positioned by being clamped at three points: bars that fit into the ear canals keep the nose pointed straight ahead, and a bar just behind the two top incisor teeth tilts the rat's head to the same angle as the head in the atlas (Figure 5.8). The scalp then is opened, and a hole is drilled for the electrodes. Each electrode pair is clamped into a metal arm called an electrode carrier that can be fixed into position over the rat's head at a particular anterior–posterior position. A millimeter scale on the carrier arm holding the electrode allows the electrode to be moved the desired number of millimeters out from the midline. A vertical scale on the carrier makes it possible to lower the tip of the electrode the number of millimeters prescribed by the atlas. To move the electrode down into the brain, the experimenter slowly turns a knob

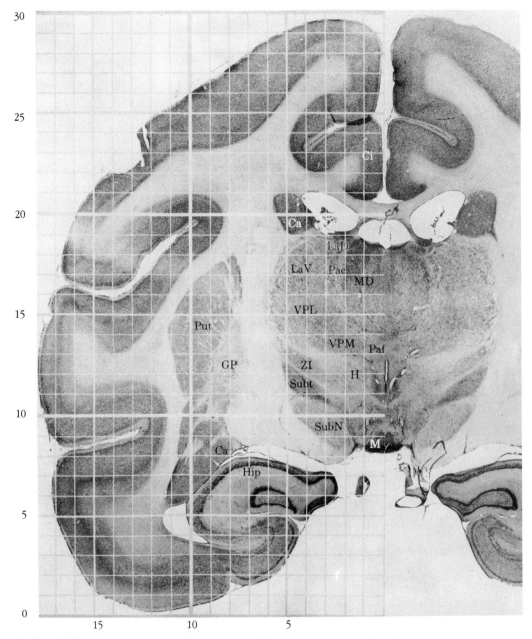

Figure 5.7 One page from a stereotaxic brain atlas of the squirrel monkey. A grid with 1-mm separation between lines is laid over the brain slice to make it easier to find the coordinates for any structure. This section is a frontal plane (Ca = caudate nucleus; Ci = cingulate gyrus; GP = globus pallidus; Hip = hippocampus; LaD = dorsolateral nucleus of thalamus; M = mammillary body; Put = putamen; SubN = substantia nigra; Subt = subthalamus; VPL = ventroposterolateral nucleus of thalamus). (From Gergen & MacLean, 1962)

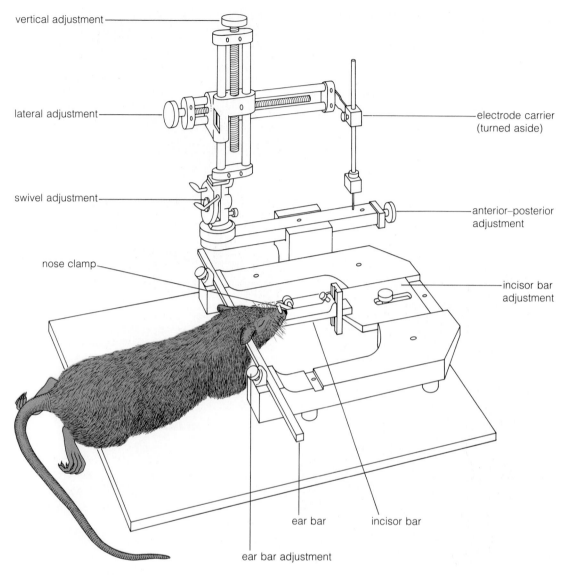

vertical adjustment

lateral adjustment

swivel adjustment

nose clamp

electrode carrier
(turned aside)

anterior–posterior
adjustment

incisor bar
adjustment

ear bar   incisor bar

ear bar adjustment

Figure 5.8 A rat positioned in a stereotaxic instrument. To align the rat's head in the position of the brain in the stereotaxic atlas, the skull is pinned between the two ear bars and clamped at the nose to a thin bar running just under the incisors. (Adapted from Hart, 1969)

on the electrode carrier, which is geared to move the electrode in fractions of a millimeter. The wires do some damage as they penetrate the brain tissue, but if they are very fine wires arranged side by side, the damage is so small that there is rarely any behavioral result.

When the electrode tips reach their destination, the experimenter plugs the hole in the skull, leaving the tops of the wires protruding, and then attaches them to a socket that the rat will wear atop its head. The socket is affixed to the skull with dental cement, and the scalp is drawn up tight around the plug. In the case of rats (which are quite resistant to disease), an antibiotic should be enough to prevent infection. After a few days to recover from surgery, the rat can be plugged into a cable through which a stimulating current can be delivered (Figure 5.9). The wires from the cable fit into the plug on the rat's head; they do not penetrate the skull as some laypeople imagine when they read about this technique. The carefully implanted electrodes within the brain are never allowed to move even a fraction of a millimeter after their positioning. They are held rigidly in place by the plug and cement and, in some cases, skull screws (Figure 5.10). After a few hours, the rat rarely gives

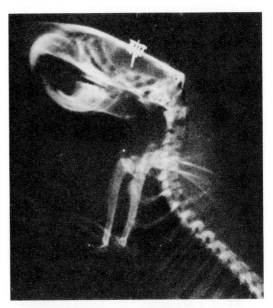

Figure 5.10 An X-ray photo of a rat skull showing an electrode implanted deep in the brain. The wires are embedded in a plastic socket (invisible to X rays), which has been attached to the skull with four screws. The free ends of the electrode wires (above the socket) can be connected to a stimulator circuit. (From Olds, 1956)

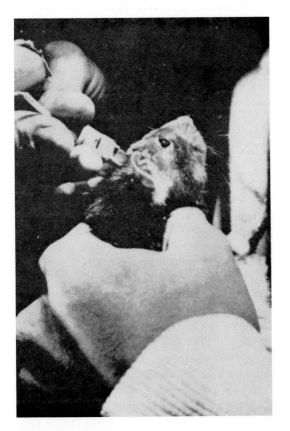

Figure 5.9 An experimenter connects a cord from the stimulator to the electrode socket on the rat's head. This procedure does not move the wires implanted in the brain and is not painful. (From Olds, 1956)

any sign that it remembers their existence, let alone that it is bothered by them. Once the electrodes are implanted, they can be used in a number of ways. EEG recordings can be made through them, or they can carry stimulating pulses of current to evoke firing and perhaps elicit behavior.

Deep electrodes are now used in a few cases of human medical treatment. In Figure 5.11a, surgeons are adjusting the angle of the electrode carrier while it is affixed to a "dummy" stereotaxic device, prior to transferring it to the actual stereotaxic instrument now clamped to the patient's skull. In Figure 5.11b, correct angles are set, the carrier is transferred to the patient's instrument, and electrodes are inserted into the brain (Figure 5.12). Recordings through these electrodes can reveal an abnormal EEG, indicative of brain dysfunction that is completely disguised in a normal surface EEG from the scalp (Figure 5.13).

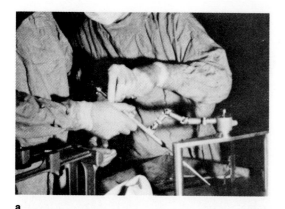

a

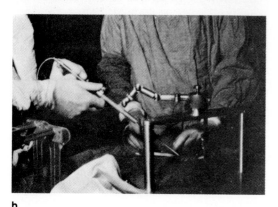

b

Figure 5.11 Human stereotaxic surgery. (**a**) Surgeons use a "dummy" head frame to set the angles of the stereotaxic electrode holder. (**b**) The holder is transferred to a real stereotaxic frame, which has been positioned exactly and clamped on the patient's head. The fine-wire electrodes are housed in the long tube extending down to the patient's skull. After the dura has been opened, the electrodes will be pushed through the tube and into the brain. (From Mark & Ervin, 1970)

Implanted electrodes also solve the immense problem of creating small, selective lesions deep within the brain without disturbing the overlying tissue (Figure 5.14). A current between electrodes heats and eventually destroys the tissue through which it passes. This damage is termed an **electrolytic lesion** (*electro* = electrically; *lytic* = disruptive). The size of an electrolytic lesion can be gauged fairly well by multiplying the current strength by the length of time the current is flowing. Figure 5.15 shows a rat brain in which the mammillothalamic tract (connecting the mammillary bodies of the hypothalamus with the thalamus) was destroyed on both sides with electrolytic lesions. Cutting this tract with a scalpel would have been nearly impossible without doing immense damage to the rest of the brain.

Increasing Precision with Chemical Lesions

The basic logic of a lesion experiment is to discover what behavioral function is lost when the brain area is removed and then to reason that the missing area must have governed that function. This strategy works to a limited extent some of the time. A host of complications prevent it from being the clear, simple cause and effect that it seems when first considered. For example, removing the primary visual cortex at the back of the occipital lobe obviously deprives the brain of all neurons that had their somas in that region. What is not so obvious is that this lesion also killed millions of cells in the thalamus, even though it came nowhere near the boundaries of that structure. Neurons of the lateral geniculate nucleus (the visual portion) of the thalamus send their axons up into the primary visual cortex. Because these geniculate neurons lose the ends of their axons when the cortex is removed, the entire cell usually dies. Because of such complications, it is nearly impossible to remove a brain area and confine the damage to that area alone. Thus, interpreting behavioral loss becomes quite difficult. For example, what if an area of the hypothalamus is removed and the animal quits eating? Did the behavioral change occur because the missing area normally produced eating, or did it result from damage to neurons whose axons pass through or end in the hypothalamus?

It was not until the mid-1970s that a way was found to kill the cell bodies within a region without harming the axons entering or passing through. The answer was a group of chemicals called **neurotoxins**

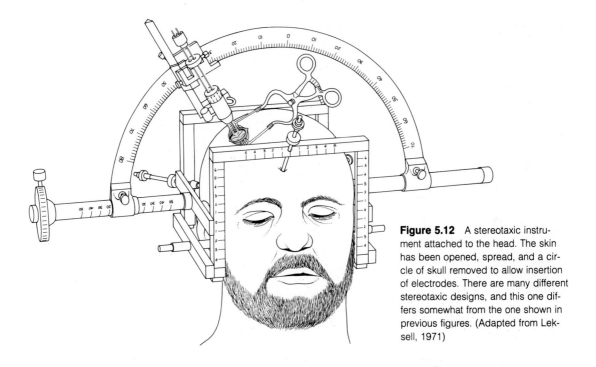

Figure 5.12 A stereotaxic instrument attached to the head. The skin has been opened, spread, and a circle of skull removed to allow insertion of electrodes. There are many different stereotaxic designs, and this one differs somewhat from the one shown in previous figures. (Adapted from Leksell, 1971)

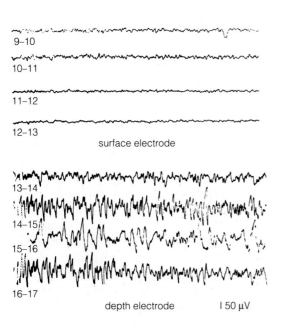

9–10

10–11

11–12

12–13

surface electrode

13–14

14–15

15–16

16–17

depth electrode   I 50 μV

Figure 5.13 The top four lines of the EEG record were from electrodes laid on the surface of the brain; the bottom four lines were from depth electrodes implanted in the brain of the same human patient. The surface recordings appear normal and reveal none of the abnormal activity causing the patient's symptoms. The depth recordings, however, show high-voltage, seizurelike activity. (Adapted from Mark & Ervin, 1970)

electrode carrier
hemostatic forceps
nose clamp

electrode   cut edge of skin   ear bar

Figure 5.14 To create an electrolytic lesion, the animal is first positioned carefully in the stereotaxic apparatus so that the brain is aligned with the sections in the stereotaxic atlas. Then, the scalp is opened and retracted, holes are drilled through the skull, electrodes are inserted and moved to the correct depth, and a lesion is made by passing current between the two tips for a measured amount of time. After all lesions have been made, the holes are filled, and the scalp is sutured. (Adapted from Hart, 1969)

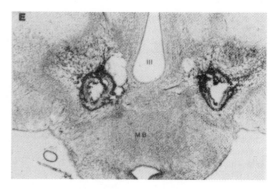

Figure 5.15 The frontal section of the base of a rat's brain showing two lesions, one in the mammillothalamic tract in each hemisphere. The third ventricle is marked with Roman numeral III. Each lesion shows a hole in the center, surrounded by a blackened ring of tissue, which contains some living cells among the dead ones. (From Thomas & Gash, 1985)

(nerve poisons). These toxins are each relatively specific to a particular type of neuron and do not harm other types. The neurotoxin most widely used so far is **6-hydroxydopamine** (high-DROCK-see-DOPE-uh-mean), or simply **6-OHDA**, which is used to selectively destroy catecholaminergic neurons (ones that secrete one of the catecholamine neurotransmitters. **Catecholamines** are a group of transmitters built around or from a basic molecule called DOPA. The simplest is dopamine, which can be converted to norepinephrine and then to epinephrine. Catecholamine transmitters are removed from the synaptic gap through the process of reuptake (see Chapter 4), and this process is selective for catecholamine molecules; any other transmitter molecules present are refused entry into the neuron. This selectivity of catecholaminergic neurons for their own transmitter makes the 6-OHDA technique a very powerful tool. Molecules of this neurotoxin so strongly resemble dopamine (DA) and other catecholamines that catecholaminergic cells take them back up as though they were neurotransmitters (Jonsson, 1980). Once inside, 6-OHDA immediately begins to decompose, producing hydrogen peroxide that attacks the molecules of the cell. It is probably the peroxide that destroys the cell (Coyle, 1978), killing it usually within a few hours (Jonsson, 1980).

A neurotoxin like 6-OHDA cannot be employed by simply injecting it into the bloodstream of an animal. Some neurotoxins cannot cross the blood–brain barrier; even if they could, the result would be the widespread, meaningless death of the particular neuron type throughout the nervous system rather than a select set within a particular structure.

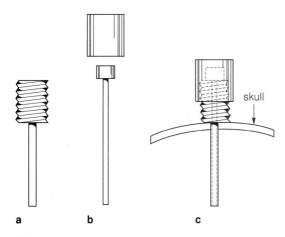

Figure 5.16 Cannula used for delivering chemical solutions or crystals directly into the brain. (**a**) The outer barrel, which is implanted stereotaxically into the brain and is fixed to the skull. It serves as a guide for the inner barrel (**b**) through which the chemicals pass. A protective cap (**c**) fits over the opening at the top except during injections. (Adapted from Valenstein, 1973a)

a   b   c

skull

Consequently, the toxin is injected directly into the brain, usually through an implanted cannula. A **cannula** is a hollow needle that can be inserted stereotaxically into a deep structure of the brain just like an electrode (Figure 5.16). At the proper point in the experiment (perhaps after the animal has been trained on some task), microquantities of the toxin can be injected through the cannula, directly into the group of neurons to be removed (Figure 5.17). Any axons entering or passing through the tissue, as well as any neurons using a different transmitter, are left undamaged. If the animal is then found to have lost some behavioral function (e.g., memory), one can infer that the missing neurons probably provided that function.

Glutaminergic neurons (those releasing the transmitter glutamate) have been the target of a considerable amount of research with neurotoxins. **Glutamate** is the most likely candidate for a transmitter in a number of places in the nervous system, such as the hippocampus—a part of the temporal lobe apparently vital to memory. Although it may be a natural neurotransmitter in microquantities, in larger doses glutamate is a powerful neurotoxin. Olney (cited in Coyle, 1978) injected newborn mice with monosodium glutamate (the MSG that seasons so much Chinese restaurant food) and found that large areas of the retinas as well as parts of the hypothalamus degenerated. One explanation of glutamate's neurotoxicity holds that the excessive quantities of the chemical around an injection site subject the surrounding neurons to prolonged overstimulation; that is, the neurons are literally "excited to death" (Jonsson, 1980).

Several neurotoxins related to glutamate are used to kill glutaminergic neurons. Among them are **ibotenic acid** (found in mushrooms) and **kainic acid** (kah-in-ik) (extracted from seaweed). The latter has been used for years in Japan to kill harmful soil worms and is called the "ghost from the sea" (Ottersen & Storm-Mathisen, 1979). Both are **excitotoxins** because they excite neurons in many areas of the nervous system, probably because they fit into glutamate receptor sites. Kainic acid selectively lesions the cell bodies within the injected region while leaving alone the axons and telodendria. This selectivity is not perfect, of course. The toxin does kill some axons, and it tends to diffuse away from the injection site rather easily, but it is an immense improvement on electrolytic lesions.

One of the most exciting uses of neurotoxins arises from the fact that they can in some respects imitate natural disease lesions. This enables researchers to reproduce in experimental animals the type of brain damage generated by the disease. The result is what clinical researchers call an **animal model** of the disease and is usually the first step toward a real understanding of the disease process. For example, Huntington's chorea (which we will examine in detail in Chapter 9) stems from the death of a certain type of neuron in the striatum. This loss produces a continuous flow of jumpy, jerky partial movements of the hands, arms, and face, which interrupt whatever behavior the person is trying to execute. There still is no cure or even any therapy to halt the cell death. The symptoms progress inevitably to death. Excitotoxins offer the first hope of producing an animal model that may eventually bring an understanding of the circuits involved and a rational therapy.

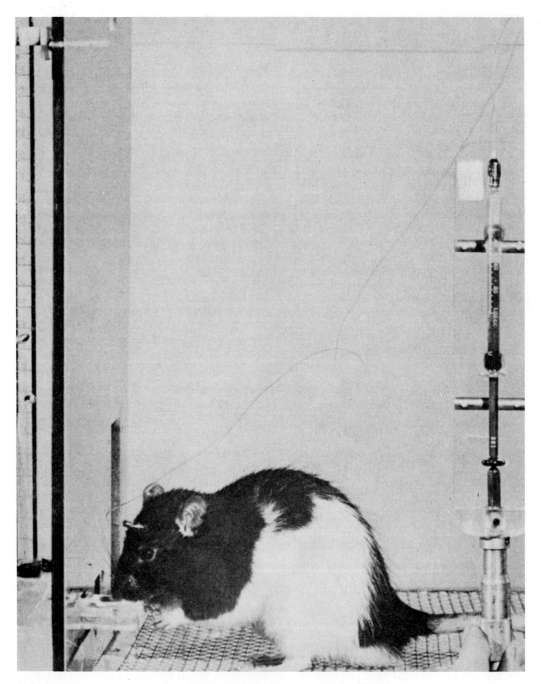

Figure 5.17 A rat in a bar-press box wearing an implanted drug-injection system. The experimenter operates a microinjector, which sends a tiny, carefully measured dose of drug through the thin plastic tube and implanted cannula, directly into the rat's brain. The experimenter then observes any changes that might occur in bar pressing. (From Fisher, 1964)

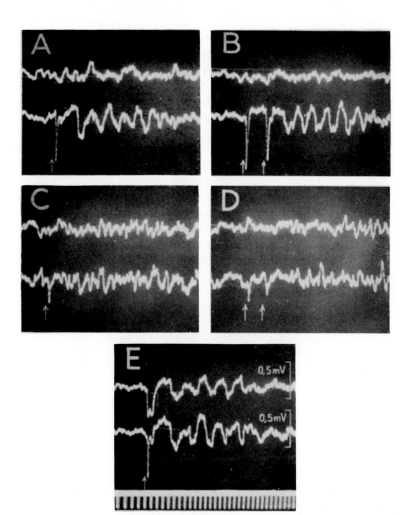

Figure 5.18 Evoked potentials from the auditory cortex of a cat. Each picture is about two-thirds of a second's worth of an EEG record showing brain waves recorded from two different electrodes resting directly on the cat's brain. The marker below the record shows 20-ms intervals. The small arrows mark the click stimulus, and the sharp downward spike following each arrow is the auditory evoked potential. (From Bremer, 1954)

Probing Deep with Surface Electrodes

Most of the techniques we have discussed cannot be used with human research subjects. Except for unusual clinical cases in which neurosurgery is required as a part of treatment, lesioning the human brain is out of the question. Depth EEG is likewise permissible only as a side feature to a few forms of treatment. However, an extremely clever extension of the EEG method allows us to obtain records from structures far below the brain's surface without even penetrating the scalp.

If an EEG electrode is placed on the skull over the auditory cortex and a click is played into the subject's ear, a wave occurs in the EEG record that is distinguishable by being a little larger than the surrounding waves and by appearing just after the click sounds (Figure 5.18). This large wave, an **auditory evoked potential**, represents the voltage changes occurring in the cortex as the burst of impulses enters it from the auditory nucleus of the thalamus. A similar voltage wave is created by each nucleus in the auditory pathway to the cortex as the signal from the click stimulus sweeps upward through the nervous system. These other evoked potentials, however, are weaker and remain hidden in the tangle of neural signals reaching the electrode from all brain areas simultaneously active. Furthermore, the potentials evoked in the lower levels of the brain stem are so far from the recording electrode on the skull that they are almost impossibly small by the time they reach it. They are theoretically present in the EEG record, but seeing them is like trying to pick out a friend's face 300 rows away in the Rose Bowl. Finding a way to record these "needles in the haystack" of ongoing brain activity was one of the most spectacular achievements of electrophysiology in the last half century.

In attacking this problem, electrophysiologists reasoned that at the moment the click sounded there would be numerous other potentials in the brain related to all other ongoing events in the various systems but that these were only *randomly* related to the click. That is, if the click were sounded repeat-

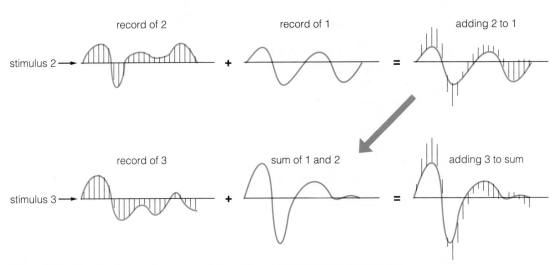

Figure 5.19 The signal-averaging process that creates averaged evoked potentials. The first record is the sequence of EEG waves immediately following stimulus 1. The computer divides it into equal units of time and measures the voltage within each unit. Each voltage is positive if above the zero line, negative if below. Stimulus 2 evokes a second EEG fragment with waves somewhat different from those of the first record. The computer also divides this second record into units of time and then adds together the two records. If the voltage in any particular unit of time is positive in both records, the computer stacks the second voltage on top of the first (summation). If they are both negative, the second is "hung" under the first. When the voltages have opposite signs, the second is subtracted from the first. Notice that the first two waves of each record are related to the stimulus and thus are consistent from one stimulus occurrence to the next. As a result, the first and second waves get steadily larger with each new record. The third and fourth waves are unrelated to the stimulus, and their randomness from one signal to the next keeps them from growing very large.

edly, any one of the other potentials might just happen to occur right after *one* of the clicks but could not occur after *every* click because only the auditory potentials are directly related to that particular stimulus. In other words, if you compared 100 records of the time immediately following 100 separate clicks and looked at the waves unrelated to each click, you should find that chance has made half of them negative and half positive. Only the click-evoked potentials are all in one direction. If these 100 records are combined, the random activity cancels out, leaving the click potential all by itself. (See Figure 5.19 for a simplified representation of the process.) This technique is called **signal averaging**, and the recordings themselves are termed **averaged evoked potentials.** The process that combines the various records is called averaging, even though it really consists of simply adding the voltages together algebraically.

To perform the calculations involved in the averaging, a computer was built that would take all EEG waves that occurred within a certain time following a click (e.g., 500 ms) and store all those voltage changes in the computer memory. With each succeeding click, new potentials were taken in by the computer and added to the previous voltages. This was usually done millisecond by millisecond so that the final composite record for 500 ms of EEG consisted of 500 dots, each representing the total of all voltages that occurred during that particular millisecond of time following the click. At any one point in time (let's say 200 ms after the click), the voltage might have been highly positive following some of the 100 clicks but strongly negative following the others. Such random events would simply cancel out one another, and the line would fail to grow at the 200-ms point. However, some points during that 500 ms will be relevant to the click. For example, at some point within a few milliseconds of the click, impulses in the VIIIth nerve reach the cochlear nuclei and fire the cells there. This event should happen consistently following *every* click. Other consistent events occur when the signal enters the superior olivary nucleus or when output from the cochlear nuclei reaches the inferior colliculus. Each of these events should create a particular change in voltage that should *consistently* be either positive or negative with roughly the same amplitude and

should occur almost exactly at the same point in time. In other words, events in the auditory system should be the same with every click, and all other brain events should be random with regard to the click. Because the consistent events are always either positive or negative, the record at those points either gets higher and higher with each click or lower and lower. The random events, on the other hand, are positive about half the time and negative the other half so that their points fail to grow with each click.

It is fascinating to watch the recording of averaged evoked potentials. The "averaged" potential is displayed on the computer screen and changes a little with each succeeding click (Figure 5.20). Out of a seemingly random line of squiggles (which researchers nickname "grass" because that's what it looks like), there suddenly appears a peak or two and then a valley. These features grow and take on more definite shape with each click until, after 50 or more stimuli, the small but reliable evoked potential emerges from the background of random waves.

A sensory evoked potential consists of a series of waves. Each wave derives from the EPSPs and IPSPs generated within a different part of the sensory pathway from receptor to cortex. The earliest waves come from subcortical nuclei that are the first brain structures to receive input from receptors. It takes 15–20 ms for the information to pass through all subcortical processors and reach the cortex; thus, the later waves in the evoked potential show the functioning of various cortical areas. The averaged potentials in Figure 5.21 cover a span of 900 ms (almost 1 second) following a visual stimulus and were gathered from the scalp over the occipital lobes. The potentials generated by subcortical stages in the visual path are all within the first 50 ms; everything that follows them presumably represents the actions of visual processing areas in the cortex and their interactions with other brain areas. As of yet, however, very few correspondences have been worked out between particular waves and the parts of the brain that produced them.

The potentials in Figure 5.21 were evoked by flashing a letter on a screen in front of the subject. In this case, the subject was a child with dyslexia, a serious reading disability that prevented him from understanding the words his eyes were taking in. He

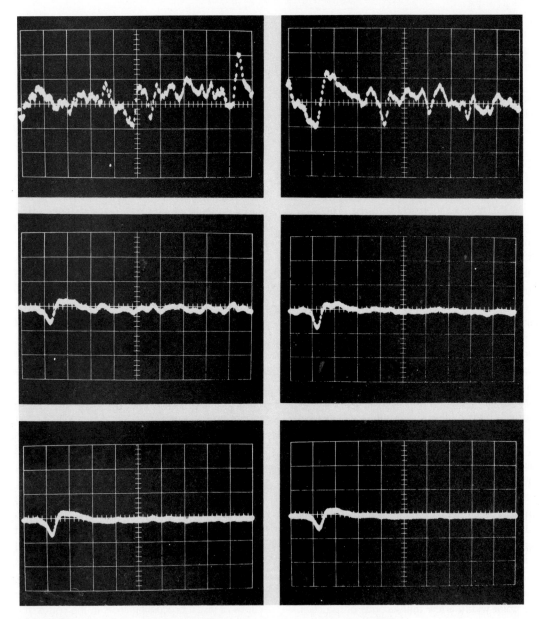

Figure 5.20 Averaged brain wave records (oscilloscope traces) showing response to a series of clicks. Following the first click (top left), the response to the stimulus is completely lost in the random jumble of EEG events from other brain areas. The second record (top right) (the combined traces from the first two click responses) shows a downward wave just at the place where the response will eventually show itself, but this is probably coincidental. By the time 32 traces (third record) are averaged together, much of the random "noise" has canceled itself out, and the response to the click shows clearly. As more and more traces are averaged, the noise level decreases, leaving a flat line except where the auditory evoked potential occurred. (Adapted from Brazier, 1962; records from Nelson Kiang)

.... first letter
———— third letter

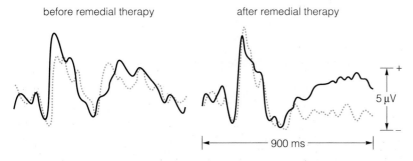

before remedial therapy   after remedial therapy

+

5 μV

–

|←————— 900 ms —————→|

Figure 5.21 Visual averaged evoked potentials from a dyslexic child at two different times during remedial reading training. Potentials were evoked by letters flashed on a screen. Each series of three letters might or might not spell out a word. The child's task was to determine whether they did make a word. Thus, the last letter in each series—the one that determines whether the letters make a word—should evoke a different sort of potential, reflecting the word–no word decision process in the brain. Before therapy the dyslexic child lacks this decision process. Thus, a difference between the first letter and last letter potentials is present only after 1 year of training. The dotted lines are the potentials from 200 first letters; the solid lines are from 200 last letters. (Adapted from Shelburne, 1978)

was shown a series of three letters in quick succession (each flash evoking a visual potential). The child's task was to tell whether the three letters made a real word or just a nonsense syllable. In the figure, the dotted lines represent the potential averaged from 200 first letters, and the solid lines come from the last letters on those 200 trials. For a normal reader, the first-letter averaged potential looks different from the last-letter potential. Apparently, the mental act of identifying the letters as either a word or nonword shows up in the averaged evoked potential, and this effect cannot appear, of course, until the last letter has been flashed on the screen. The dyslexic child showed no significant difference between first and last potentials, suggesting that the word-identification process had not taken place. After a year of remedial therapy, the third-letter potential showed a normal swing toward positivity in the region from 450 ms to 900 ms (Shelburne, 1978). This change together with the patient's improved reading performance suggests that some mental process, acquired during the year of special training, was critical to the comprehension of words

and that this process shows up in the EEG record. The fact that it appears after 450 ms strongly suggests that his dyslexia had nothing to do with the initial steps of visual information processing either at subcortical levels or within the cortex. Perhaps that portion of the potential represents a stage of processing in which the results of processing earlier stimuli (the first two letters) are being retrieved from memory, combined with the third letter, and compared with word memories from the language cortex. Although the use of averaged evoked potentials is in its infancy, some exciting discoveries have already been made with this sophisticated method of analyzing EEG data.

Probing Single Neurons

Electroencephalography and averaged evoked potentials are valuable techniques for examining the broad, overall functioning of a brain region, but some experimental questions can only be answered by seeing how individual neurons react. Over the last two decades, the technique of recording electrical events from single cells has been developed to an art and has produced some of the greatest insights yet achieved into sensory and cortical function.

To record from single neurons, researchers use exceptionally thin electrodes. These **microelectrodes** either are glass tubes filled with a conductive solution of ions and drawn to a microscopic tip or are a very fine tungsten wire insulated down to the tip.

A microscope is of no use in locating single cells within the cerebral cortex because the neurons are usually buried anywhere from 0.5 to 4.0 mm beneath the cortical surface. Instead, they are found electrically with the help of loudspeakers and an oscilloscope. If the oscilloscope is wired to the microelectrode, then any nerve impulse in the vicinity of the electrode shows up on the screen as a sudden up-and-down sweep of the oscilloscope beam. Outside of any neuron, the electrode picks up weak potentials from many nearby cells, and the oscilloscope trace is a clutter of different-sized spikes. However, once the electrode penetrates a neuron, the trace flattens out except for occasional, large, clear potentials that represent the cell's own impulses. At that point, the experimenter stops the micromanipulator that has been slowly driving the electrode down through the layers of the cortex, micron by micron. The neuron's reactions to various stimuli can now be tested using this **intracellular microelectrode technique**.

Another way to locate a neuron is to listen to its amplified signal through a loudspeaker. Whenever the electrode picks up a nerve impulse, you then hear it as a small "popping" sound of the sort that sometimes occurs in radio static.

Only neuron somas can be penetrated by an electrode; mammalian axons are usually too small. To record from axons, the experimenter positions the electrode tip as close as possible to the fiber but leaves it on the outside of the membrane. This same **extracellular microelectrode technique** is used with cell bodies when a longer recording session is needed from a soma because it leaves the cell undamaged. The intracellular technique eventually kills the cell.

In the next chapter, we will see how the micro-electrode recording has enabled us to understand the contributions of single types of neurons to the process of analyzing visual stimuli.

■ Mapping the Brain

The brain has been studied by scientists from many disciplines ranging from physiological psychologists (looking for the origins of behavior) to neuroanatomists (interested only in the structure of the organ) to neurochemists (concerned chiefly with neurotransmitters). When we attempt to integrate all this diverse knowledge, we realize that the brain is organized in different ways at different levels. At the level of gross anatomical structures, there is the division between gray matter areas (nuclei and cortex), in which information processing takes place, and white matter zones consisting of axon tracts that interconnect parts of gray matter. Anatomists have worked for decades to find techniques that would reveal axon connections between various nuclei and cortical areas. This basic "road map" of the brain cannot be seen under the microscope, and anatomists have had to be exceedingly clever to find these invisible paths.

At a second level of organization, neurochemists have discovered that the whole brain can be divided into "systems" of neurons using the same transmitter and that these systems cut across anatomical boundaries to create pathways with chemically determined functions. Finally, a variety of chemical and radiological methods have allowed us to map functional areas of the cerebral cortex, an organization that again cuts across the boundaries of other (anatomical and chemical) levels. Let's examine the ways in which these levels of organization were revealed to researchers by looking first at methods for tracing internal connections and then by examining the most modern techniques for discovering functional zones of the cortex.

Tracing Internal Connections

The function of any single neuron in the brain is determined by which axons connect to it and where it sends its own axon branches. The most basic organization is at the level of the anatomical connections between brain areas. Cutting across that is the chemical organization of axons using the same transmitter. We start at the anatomical level.

Following Axons The inability to recognize each individual axon is a problem that plagues researchers. Imagine yourself as a neuroscientist trying to find out whether a nucleus of cells in the midbrain connects with a particular nucleus in the pontine brain stem. If you section the brain stem in just the right plane, the cut passes through both nuclei. You peer through your microscope at one of the stained sections and focus up and down until one neuron in the midbrain nucleus stands out sharply. You carefully move the slide across the microscope stage, millimeter by millimeter, following the progress of the hair-thin axon down the brain stem. But the tract you are following, just like all tracts in the CNS, dips and bends, snaking between other nuclei along a trajectory with enough wobbles to make a drunkard blush. Your axon suddenly disappears from view, having turned out of the plane of the section. You realize that there is no way to find it on the next slide, as it would look just like hundreds of its neighbors. If you try to solve this problem by cutting the section thick enough to catch all bends and twists, you find yourself looking at a dense thicket of fibers in which your axon has become the proverbial needle in a haystack. Either way you lose. Tracing the paths of single axons over any sizable distance in adult vertebrate nervous systems seems nearly impossible.

But unless we can trace pathways from one gray matter area to another, we cannot discover the basic wiring diagram of the nervous system, and complete understanding of brain function will be impossible. The first big step toward solving this problem was the development of a tissue-staining technique by Walle Nauta and Paul Gygax in 1954. The effort cost Nauta 6 long, frustrating years of trying and rejecting hundreds of variations before he and Gygax finally achieved their goal (Nauta, 1979). The **Nauta–Gygax method** employs a silver salt to selectively stain degenerating axons. To employ this method in our hypothetical example of tracing a path in the

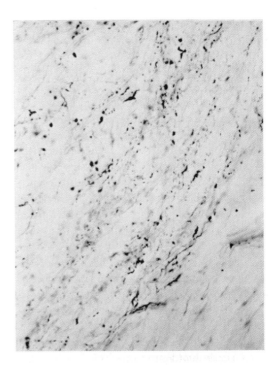

Figure 5.22 A section of the thalamus stained using the Nauta–Gygax method. The hundreds of degenerating axons in this view are marked by the dots and globs of silver that clearly reveal a path between the part of the thalamus in the upper right of the picture and the tissue in the lower left. The magnification is too great to see beyond the boundaries of the thalamus. (From Ebbesson & Rubison, 1969)

brain stem, you would first lesion a tiny area of the midbrain nucleus, thus killing some of its cell bodies. During the next few days, axons of these cells would begin to degenerate into broken lines of bits and pieces. You then must kill the test animal, remove and fix the brain, section it, and stain the sections in Nauta–Gygax solution. In the staining process, the majority of the stain is taken up by the remaining bits and pieces of degenerating axons. If you have adjusted your solutions just right (and this is really an art!), degenerating axons take up more silver than do the undamaged ones, and the pathway from the point of your lesion stands out as scattered lines of tiny black dots and blobs (Figure 5.22) that lead like a trail of Hansel and Gretel bread crumbs to their destination in the pontine nucleus. You may not be able to trace individual fibers, but the total pathway between any two nuclei in the brain is made reasonably clear, and a major research problem has been solved.

In recent years, more reliable pathway-tracing techniques have been discovered that provide more information (Jones & Hartman, 1978). In the **autoradiographic method**, some chemical essential to neurons (such as an amino acid or sugar) is made radioactive so that it can be located after being incorporated into brain tissue. Because most brain molecules incorporate at least one atom of hydrogen, tritium (an unstable form of hydrogen that decays rapidly into normal hydrogen by emitting radiation) is commonly used. A **tritiated molecule** (one having tritium substituted for its hydrogen atoms) constantly emits radiation. Such a chemical is said to be **labeled**.

The labeled chemical is injected into gray matter where it is taken up into cell bodies. The experimenter waits long enough for the labeled molecules to be used in the construction of cellular constituents (like protein molecules), which are transported down the axon to the telodendria. The animal is then killed and the brain fixed and sectioned. To find where injected neurons sent their axons, the experimenter doesn't have to follow fibers down their entire lengths but merely looks for brain nuclei containing telodendria with labeled molecules. How do these molecules reveal themselves? The radiation they emit is really the same thing as light but at a much shorter wavelength. Consequently, like light it can expose photographic film. If brain sections are coated with photographic emulsion and placed in a lighttight compartment for a week or so, the tagged telodendria gradually take a picture of themselves, thus revealing their location in the brain. *Autoradiography*, then, refers to a picture (*graph*), made from radiation (*radio*), coming from oneself (*auto*).

A second modern method of tracing connections that does not rely on degeneration of axons is the **horseradish peroxidase (HRP)** technique. HRP is an enzyme (a chemical that triggers or enables reactions between other chemicals). If you inject it into an area of gray matter, terminals and telodendria entering that area take it up. HRP finds its way into the **microtubules**, which carry chemicals from one end of the axons to the other, and arrives at the somas about 24 hours later (in rats). If the experimenter removes and sections the brain at this time and then bathes the sections in one of the chemicals that react with HRP, the cells containing the enzyme stain brown or blue and stand out against their background (Olsson & Malmgren, 1978; Towns, 1984). Again, we have a technique that shows which nuclei or gray matter areas interconnect with one another. Because the chemical is transported from telodendria to soma (rather than vice versa), the method is called **retrograde tracing** (*retro* = backward). By contrast, the autoradiographic technique described in the previous paragraph relies on the cell to transport the radioactive-labeling molecules from the soma out to the ends of the axons; hence, it is called **anterograde tracing** (*antero* = forward).

HRP is now the most important and widely used tracing technique. All of the thousands of potential pathways in the brain must be checked in this manner, but we have had retrograde-tracing methodology only since 1971 (Kristensson & Olsson, 1971). Obviously, our knowledge of brain anatomy is still in its childhood. Interestingly, HRP and autoradiography methods cannot be applied to the human brain, but the older Nauta–Gygax technique can. Christiana Leonard has discovered that when a person suffers a brain lesion and axons of dead cells degenerate the bits and pieces of axon are not scavenged by the body's phagocytic cells as they are in other animals. She has succeeded in staining tracts within the human brain even when the brain damage had nothing to do with the person's death and had occurred 12 years earlier (Leonard, 1979). Thus, if enough people who have suffered small, discrete brain lesions leave their brains to science, neuroscientists will be able to discover whether the pathways they have traced in lower-primate brains are identical to those in the human brain.

Invisible Organization: Tracking Chemical Systems of the Brain The brain has more than 20 established or suspected neurotransmitters, and each establishes what might be called a *system* of neurons. For example, neurons that secrete serotonin as a transmitter are not sprinkled haphazardly throughout the nervous system; their somas are grouped into distinct clusters called raphe nuclei, which lie along the midline of the brain stem. Serotonergic axons gather together into definite bundles to run toward particular terminal sites in the brain. Regularities of this sort suggest strongly that not only can neurons be grouped by what transmitter they use but also that cells employing different transmitters have different functions. Thus, it becomes very important for neuroscientists to be able to disentangle these various systems and trace them from their origins to their destinations.

How is it possible to tell whether a particular neuron is dopaminergic (i.e., uses dopamine as a transmitter) or cholinergic, GABAergic, or glutaminergic? We will look at four of the more widely used methods for solving that problem: histofluorescence, reuptake radiography, receptor labeling, and immunohistochemical labeling.

The first solution arrived in the early 1960s through the development of a new research tool called **histofluorescence**. *Histo* refers to cells, and *fluorescence* is the property of giving off light when stimulated by ultraviolet light or some other form of radiation. If brain slices are exposed to formaldehyde or glyoxylic acid, monoamine neurotransmitters are converted into fluorescing compounds, thereby revealing their location in brain tissue with a ghostly yellow–green glow (Steinbusch et al., 1986). Because norepinephrine (a monoamine) is made in cell bodies and transported down the length of the axon to the terminals, anatomists have been able to visualize the entire norepinephrine system from one end to the other, a rare accomplishment. The various monoamines can be distinguished by their fluorescent color: serotonin fluoresces yellow–green, norepinephrine is more of a greenish yellow, dopamine is green, and epinephrine fluoresces only faintly.

Because histofluorescence works only with monoaminergic neurons, the search for ways to identify and visualize transmitter systems continued. Researchers soon discovered that the cellular mechanism of reuptake could be used to identify terminals. (You will recall from Chapter 4 that some neurotransmitters are taken back up into the terminals that released them.) In **reuptake autoradiography**, radioactive molecules of neurotransmitter are injected into an area of gray matter so that they will be taken up by any terminals in that area that use the particular transmitter. After waiting for the CSF to wash out any labeled transmitter remaining outside of the neurons, the experimenter removes the brain, freezes and sections it, and coats the sections with photographic emulsion. Any terminals that took up the labeled transmitter molecules photograph themselves, revealing the location of that transmitter system in the brain. The major limitation of the technique is that many terminals (e.g., cholinergic) do not use the reuptake mechanism to clear out the synapse. However, reuptake autoradiography does work for all monoamine transmitters plus glutamate and GABA (Jones & Hartman, 1978).

Another form of autoradiography with even wider applicability is **receptor labeling**, which involves marking receptor sites with radioactive molecules. Once the radioactive molecules have bound with the receptor sites, the pattern of radioactivity in brain tissue then reveals every location in which the transmitter is used. A problem with the receptor-labeling method is that some chemicals cannot be used because they do not cross the blood–brain barrier. They can only be used when the brain is no longer in the animal. Kuhar (1981) has developed an **in vitro autoradiographic** technique in which slices of brain tissue are exposed to the labeled chemical. *In vitro* means that the experiment is conducted on tissue removed from the body. This method also provides much more control of chemical concentrations than does the **in vivo** technique (in which the tissue remains within the living animal).

The most promising, most widely applicable cell-marking technique of the 1980s is the **immunohistochemical method**, which can potentially label almost any part of any neuron anywhere in the nervous system. It comes to us from immunology, the study of the body's immune system. The **immune system** is a set of chemical reactions and specialized cells that are designed to fight off infections and tumors (see Chapter 13 for more details). All viruses and microorganisms have protein molecules called **antigens** on their surfaces that our immune systems use to recognize and destroy them. The recognition is done at a basic chemical level. Your body manufactures proteins called **antibodies**, each of which is designed to bind with a specific antigen. An organism carrying that antigen is marked by the antibody for destruction by cells of the immune system. Antibodies also are responsible for the problem of tissue rejection in human organ transplant surgery. Different individuals use slightly different proteins in building the same organs, and the recipient's immune system attacks the "foreign" protein of the transplanted organ just as though it were a bacterium or virus. The closer the relation between the donor and recipient, the fewer the protein differences and the weaker the immune response to the transplanted tissue. The weakest immune response would presumably be between identical twins, and the greatest would be between animals of two different species.

Neurochemists realized that any protein can be an antigen for some antibody, even if the antibody has to be created in the laboratory. Furthermore, such "designer" antibodies could enable scientists to label just about any structure they wanted. Once injected into the blood, antibodies would circulate until they encountered the antigen (the protein to which they were designed to react) and then bind to it, thus tagging the antigen for the researcher to find. The first step in immunohistochemical labeling is to create an antibody that has been combined chemically with either a fluorescing dye or with HRP prior to the binding (Jones & Hartman, 1978). Either of these stains would allow the anatomist to see the places where binding occurs. Next, brain tissue is exposed to the antibody long enough for it to bind to the chemical being located (e.g., glutamate receptors). Any area of fluorescence or HRP stain then indicates where the antigens are in the brain. For example, if dopamine receptors were chosen as the antigens and fluorescing antibodies were injected, then areas containing dopamine receptors (like substantia nigra, striatum, and parts of the limbic and neocortex) would show fluorescence.

Antibodies have now become available for marking many of the enzymes that create transmitters; proteins that form parts of the cytoskeleton, receptor sites, and synaptic vesicles (Reichardt & Matthew, 1982); Schwann cells; and two types of glial cells (Mirsky, 1980). Through a clever adaptation of the technique, Geffard and colleagues were able to form antibodies against Ach. Now for the first time in the long history of research on this very important neurotransmitter, we can state with certainty exactly where it is used in the nervous system (Geffard et al., 1985).

This review of pathway-tracing methods is far from complete; dozens of variations exist for the techniques discussed. Fortunately for knowledge, our stock of neurochemical methods has more than doubled in the last decade. Now that we can begin to see the brain as a collection of chemical systems, we have reached the point where an understanding of neural circuits seems possible in the near future.

Mapping Cortical Functions

All mapping techniques discussed so far in this section provide information only on anatomy; none of these methods is able to make the link between a brain area and the behavioral function of that area. We now look at three new techniques that can make just such a link: regional cerebral blood flow technique, 2-deoxyglucose autoradiography, and voltage-sensitive dye technique.

Regional cerebral blood flow technique ($_rCBF$) is a method that can reveal the activity levels in various parts of the human brain during the execution of behavioral tasks, without invading the skull. When a part of the brain stops "idling" and begins to process information, the flow of blood to that region increases. The increase in nerve impulse production by millions of nerve cells devours oxygen and glucose at an enormous rate, and the resting blood flow simply isn't sufficient to support normal amounts of working activity, so the blood vessels in the active region must dilate to increase flow.

If we had a way to measure the changes in blood flow into specific areas of the brain, we could present the subject with a task and then see which brain area became the most active. This can be done with radioactive isotopes whose radiation readily penetrates the skull and can be detected with radiation counters. In one variation of $_rCBF$, the subject breathes a small amount of the radioactive gas ^{133}Xenon, which is carried in the bloodstream to the brain. As the gas circulates, it gives off a small but measurable amount of radiation that is picked up by radiation counters. Figure 5.23a shows an array of 254 such detectors

Figure 5.23 System for recording rCBF. (**a**) A detector array designed to fit against the human head. Each of the 254 black dots is a radiation detector. (**b**) The patient lies with head against the radiation detectors. Signals from the detectors are counted by the computer at the right and translated into colors on the monitor. (From Lassen et al., 1978)

a

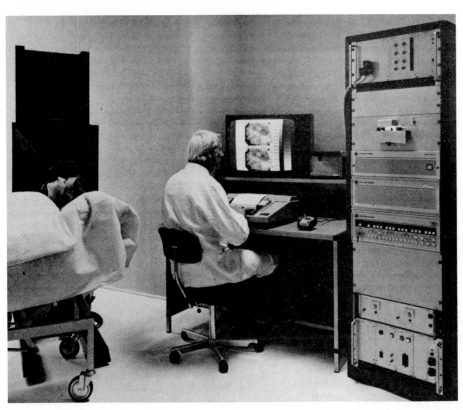

b

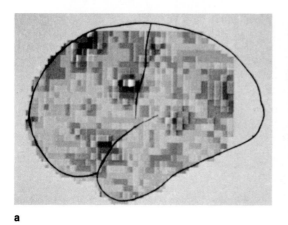
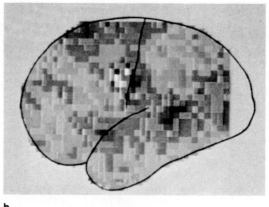

a   b

Figure 5.24 Computer pictures of ₍CBF under two conditions. (**a**) The patient is reading silently and (**b**) reading aloud. (From Lassen et al., 1978)

mounted in a head rest. Figure 5.23b shows a patient, with her head against the array, being monitored as ^{133}Xenon courses through her cerebral circulation. Whichever areas of her brain are most active at the moment will have the greatest blood flow and therefore the highest radiation count. A computer collects all 254 counts and displays the radiation levels as different colors with each colored square representing the flow rate in 1 cm² of cortex. In Figure 5.24, the darkest squares show the highest counts.

The data in Figure 5.24 were recorded while the subject was reading. Silent reading (Figure 5.24a) activates the language area of the frontal lobe, an association area at the posterior tip of the lateral fissure, the frontal eye fields of the frontal lobes just anterior to the central fissure, and the supplementary motor area on the superior surface of the frontal lobe. Each zone must play a part in the act of reading, but we have yet to discover the nature of those roles. When the same subject is reading aloud (Figure 5.24b), several more zones become active because the function of speech is added to the performance. For example, the mouth area of the primary motor cortex just forward of the central fissure is added together with the mouth area of the somatosensory cortex just posterior to the central fissure, plus a large area of auditory cortex in the upper temporal lobe. That these three zones should become active

makes considerable sense because reading aloud usually involves moving the mouth muscles, sensing those movements, and hearing what one is saying.

The ₍CBF technique has been used extensively to find which cortical areas are involved in different aspects of language function, a type of research that can only be done with humans.

Another way to reveal what parts of the brain have been functioning in any specific task is **2-deoxyglucose (2-DG) autoradiography**. Because the brain must be removed, this method can only be used with animals. The subject is given a task or exposed to a stimulus immediately following an injection of the chemical. As the animal works on the task, the relevant parts of the brain increase their use of glucose. If this glucose could be made radioactive, then autoradiography could be used to find out what parts of the brain were involved in working on the task. It is easy enough to make glucose radioactive by substituting an unstable atom of carbon-14 (^{14}C) for the normal carbon in the glucose molecule, but the resulting chemical is difficult to use because the animal uses up glucose molecules at such a high rate. What is needed is a molecule that will stay in the cell long enough for the procedure to be accomplished. The answer to the experimenter's prayers is a close relative of glucose called 2-DG, which is readily admitted into the neurons but cannot be used

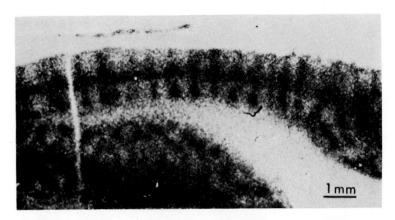

Figure 5.25 A cross section of primary visual cortex from the brain of a monkey. The animal received an injection of radioactive 2-DG as it viewed a pattern of vertical black stripes. The visual stimulus activated the vertical line-detecting cells in the visual cortex, which then took up more of the 2-DG than did the neurons around them, thus becoming radioactive. The radioactivity was used to expose a photographic film, revealing that the vertical-line detectors were grouped into columns (the black vertical bands in the picture). (From Hubel et al., 1978)

metabolically. Once inside of the cell, it stays there long enough for the experimenter to complete the experiment and extract the brain for the radiography (Sokoloff, 1978).

The 2-DG method can show functional location in the brain in much finer detail than is possible for the $_r$CBF technique. For example, when vision scientists needed to find the locations in the visual cortex of neurons that react to vertical lines, they injected radioactive 2-DG, exposed a monkey to a field of vertical lines, and then removed the brain to make the autoradiographs seen in Figure 5.25. The dark stripes are columns of cortical neurons emitting radiation because of the 2-DG they took up during the stimulus-exposure time. The lighter columns in between are neurons that respond to horizontal (and other) line orientations not present in the stimulus (Hubel et al., 1978). This research verified an earlier suspicion from microelectrode studies that cells of the visual cortex are arranged into columns and that each column performs a different task. For people trying to understand the circuitry of the visual cortex, this provided an absolutely essential bit of information.

No method is perfect. The amount of radiation revealed in the various brain areas by 2-DG may not be exactly the same as that which should result from similar measurements using glucose itself (Cunningham & Cremer, 1985). As with any method, the results must be interpreted with caution, and especially they must be verified with similar findings using different techniques.

A third and very recent method of revealing the function of various cortical areas is amazingly direct. The experimenter places a pool of **voltage-sensitive dye** on the general area of cortex that should be involved and then presents a stimulus. The dye fluoresces when the action potentials and postsynaptic potentials of the neurons pass through it (Orbach et al., 1985), revealing which specific zones process that particular form of stimulation. Wherever neurons are active, the dye either fluoresces or changes color; the more neural activity there is, the more the dye changes.

Blasdel and Salama (1986) studied the visual cortex of the monkey using voltage-sensitive dyes. The visual cortex not only contains horizontal and vertical line detector cells, it also has neurons sensitive to all degrees of slant in between (see Chapter 6). With this in mind, the experimenters exposed a

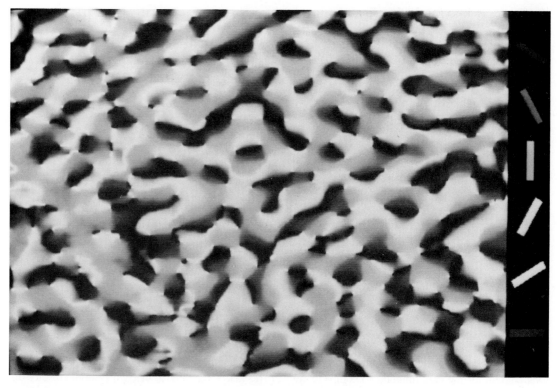

Figure 5.26 A composite map of stimulus orientation preferences for one 8-mm-wide patch of visual cortex. Each shade represents a different degree of slant. (From Blasdel, 1986)

bit of the monkey's visual cortex to a dye and then showed the animal a series of visual stimuli, each a set of lines slanted at a different angle. For example, when they showed horizontal lines for a few minutes and recorded the color patterns from the cortex, the dye would reveal where the "horizontal" cells were located. Then they repeated the procedure through a number of angles. A computer used the video recordings to generate a composite picture of the cortical activity, which is shown in Figure 5.26.

This dye technique is too new for us to know how valuable it will prove to be, but it does have an obvious advantage over the 2-DG method; the brain does not have to be removed to obtain the data. This means that several different functions can be examined, one after the other in the same subject. To duplicate Blasdel's (1986) line-slant experiment using 2-DG, a new set of animals would have to be used for each of the line slants, and the composite picture would have to be constructed from the brains of different animals rather than from just one, despite the fact that individual brains may differ considerably with regard to the placement of each slant zone. Furthermore, the dye technique may possibly be adapted for use in neurosurgery for easier identification of areas (such as the speech cortex) that the surgeon wishes to avoid damaging.

Windows into the Living Brain

Most neuroscience methodology has been created by biologists, psychologists, and chemists, but it is physics that has produced some of the most exciting recent advances.

Radiological Techniques

Psychiatrists have long wished for a way to peer inside the living brain of a psychotic patient to check it for neuropathology and observe the metabolic responses of its various parts. Amazingly enough, it is now possible to do that. In the last two decades, the field of medical radiology has undergone a revolution with an impact comparable to that of the introduction of the first clinical X-ray device. This upheaval centers around two new radiological techniques: computerized axial tomography and positron-emission tomography.

Computerized Axial Tomography (CT)   When a physician makes an X-ray picture of your leg to see if it is broken, a piece of photographic film is placed on one side of the leg, and an X-ray source is placed on the other. **X rays** are a form of electromagnetic radiation just like light rays but much shorter in wavelength; hence, they are not visible. Short wavelengths can penetrate living tissue fairly readily but not completely. They are attenuated (absorbed) more by bone than by muscle; thus, the X-ray picture of your leg shows each bone as a patch of white, indicating that few X rays were able to reach the film at that point to expose it and turn it black.

Making a useful X-ray picture of the brain is quite difficult because it is surrounded by bone. If the rays are intense enough, they can penetrate the two layers of skull, but will they provide any information? Brain tissue absorbs X rays better than does CSF, so if the radiation exposure is adjusted correctly, there ought to be more rays reaching the part of the film that is located behind the ventricles (containing the CSF). The ventricles ought to show as darker areas in the picture, but—thanks to the interference from two layers of skull—the contrast is very poor. It is also true that white matter attenuates X rays better than

does gray matter (Mastaglia & Cala, 1980), but the difference is too slight to have any impact on an ordinary X-ray picture.

The major problem with head X-ray pictures is the missing third dimension. If the X-ray source is on one side of the head and the film on the other side, the light–dark variations represent tissue-density differences anywhere along the path of the rays as they travel through the brain. A dark spot on the picture might represent an object lying just under the right side of the skull only inches from the X-ray machine, an object at the midline of the brain, or an object way over on the left side of the brain close to the film. I suspect that neurosurgeons must have interpreted such pictures with their fingers crossed.

What radiology needed rather desperately was a way to take a three-dimensional picture of the inside of the body—a rather large order. Despite the apparent impossibility of ever finding a solution to this problem, the answer arrived on the medical scene in 1973 in the form of computerized axial tomography. **Computerized axial tomography** involves taking dozens of separate X-ray pictures through the head at dozens of different angles (Figure 5.27) and then combining the results with a computer to create a CT scan. The term *axial* refers to the procedure of rotating the X-ray source and the radiation detectors around an imaginary axis running through the patient's head. The detectors stop every few degrees and take a reading, which is passed on to the computer. The computer program, consisting of dozens of mathematical manipulations, takes this series of intensity readings from the radiation detectors and blends them together into a three-dimensional model of the contents of the skull. Now the dark spot produced by a left-hemisphere, temporal lobe tumor (for example), which cannot be located in the left hemisphere in a side shot, becomes distinctly left-hemisphere in a top view. The top view cannot tell you whether the tumor is in the temporal lobe or in the overlying frontal lobe, but the side shot can. Putting together views from many angles allows for an exact three-dimensional location of each feature.

The combining form *tom* refers to a cut or slice;

Figure 5.27 In a CT scan, the radiation source rotates around the patient's head, taking a new X-ray picture every few degrees (3° in this example). These individual images are blended together by the computer to derive a three-dimensional representation, which can be displayed slice-by-slice on the computer screen. (Adapted from Mastaglia & Cala, 1980)

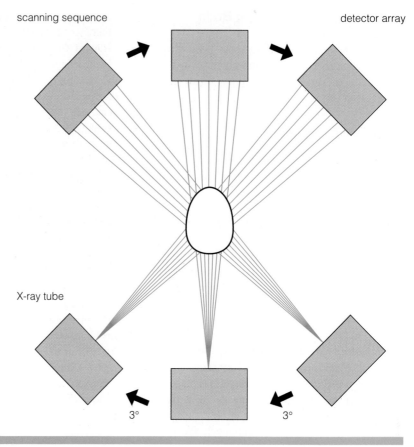

scanning sequence

detector array

X-ray tube

3°   3°

thus, the term *tomography* means creating a pictorial representation (graph) slice by slice. Once the computer has assembled all the separate X-ray pictures into a three-dimensional composite, it can compute what each slice of the brain should look like from the top down to the bottom, from one side to the other, or from front to back. Figure 5.28 is a horizontal cut near the top of the brain and reveals a large tumor in the right frontal lobe. Dark areas of the lateral ventricles appear at either side of the midline. Bulging into the ventricles from their lateral sides near their anterior ends are the two caudate nuclei. Toward the posterior, the ventricles curve around the bulges of the right and left thalami. It is evident from this that CT scans can be used in diagnosing brain damage. They allow neurosurgeons to see whether major brain areas have been distorted

by damage or have shrunk. Some disorders that lead to a slow deterioration of memory and judgment result from the gradual loss of neurons in a particular cortical lobe or throughout the brain. This lost brain tissue shows up in a CT scan as enlarged ventricles.

Positron-Emission Tomography (PET) The newest development in radiology is **positron-emission tomography**. In a **PET scan**, just as in a CT scan, radiation detectors collect rays from all points of the compass around the patient's head, and the computer uses these dozens of separate pictures to build up a composite three-dimensional model of the person's brain. The difference is that the radiation is not being pushed through the patient's brain by a machine; it is coming from the brain itself because the brain has been made momentarily radioactive.

PET scanning is based on the fact that neural tissue must continually take in supplies of oxygen, carbon, and other elements needed for the production of energy and the manufacture of its structural proteins, enzymes, and other chemicals. Many elements come in a variety of forms called **isotopes**, each of which has a different number of neutrons and protons in the nuclei of its atoms. Some isotopes have an unstable balance of protons and neutrons that leads to their eventual disintegration. When unstable atoms disintegrate, they emit radiation, hence the term **radioactive isotope**. The radioactive isotope oxygen-15 (^{15}O) can be combined with other chemicals to produce some raw-material molecule that the brain will take up and use, such as glucose, and then this compound can be injected into the bloodstream. Within minutes it will be incorporated into the metabolic processes of the brain where it can then be used in the PET scan (Raichle, 1983).

The radioactive isotope ^{15}O begins to decay as soon as it is formed; within 2.05 minutes, half of the atoms have disintegrated into a stable, nonradioactive isotope. (None of the radioactive isotopes used in PET scanning last long enough to create a radiation hazard for the patient.) When an ^{15}O atom decays, it emits a **positron**, a particle like an electron but with a positive charge that is pushed through the brain tissue by the force of the atom's disintegration. Positrons move only a short distance through the tissue before colliding with other atoms and producing particles of electromagnetic radiation called **photons**. Because these particular photons penetrate tissue so easily, they leave the brain and are picked up by the radiation detectors circling the head.

Relative intensities of photons tell us the density of the tissue through which they had to pass before reaching the detectors. Thus, intensity differences create the image, just as differences in light intensity create a regular photograph. Using our knowledge of tissue density, the computer applies formulas that calculate the probable origin in the brain of every recorded photon and, from such calculations, constructs its three-dimensional model.

The resolving power (clarity of focus) of PET is not as great as that of CT. Currently, PET scanners have a resolution of about 1 cm (Raichle, 1983), and that means that the images are fuzzy, with structural

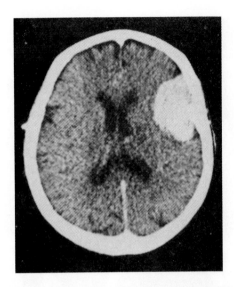

Figure 5.28 A CT scan of the human brain. The front of the brain is at the top of the picture. The lateral ventricles show as black areas on either side of the midline. The right frontal lobe has been massively invaded by a tumor, which shows on the scan as an oval white area between the skull and the ventricle. (Fred J. Hodges, III, of Johns Hopkins School of Medicine; from Kety, 1979)

differences less than 1 cm lost entirely. Figure 5.29 shows three methods of viewing the same brain. The top two sections are photographs of the actual brain at autopsy; the middle two images are CT scans; and the bottom pair are PET scans. A comparison of the CT and PET images shows clearly the resolution problem with the PET technique.

Nevertheless, everyone puts up with the problem because a PET image can yield information that is obtainable in no other way. Look at Figure 5.29c and notice the three black arrows pointing to the unnaturally light areas in the left frontal lobes. When this patient was injected with radioactive glucose, a PET scan showed that the left frontal region had a 21 percent lower glucose use than did the right frontal. This deficit surely must have been related to the dementia from which the patient suffered. Note that this "functional lesion" is visible only in the PET scan. PET may be crude in portraying the outlines of struc-

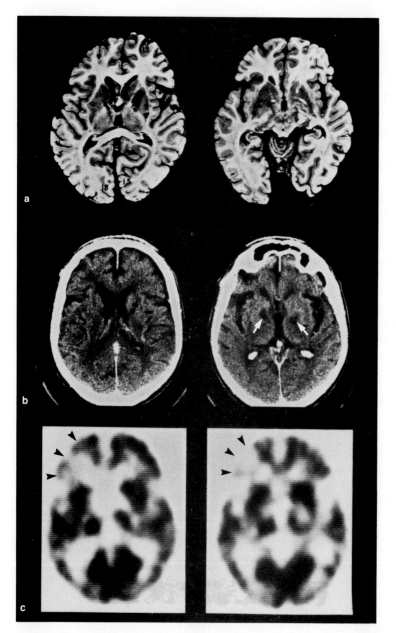

Figure 5.29 Comparing PET scanning with other imaging techniques in a human brain sectioned at two different levels. Before this patient died, a CT scan (**b**) and a PET scan (**c**) were taken in an attempt to find why memory and judgment had been lost. (**a**) Photographs of the actual brain from autopsy. The white arrows on the right CT scan (**b**) indicate areas of damage resulting from stroke. The black arrows on the PET scans (**c**) indicate areas of the left frontal cortex exhibiting lower than normal use of glucose. These areas appeared normal in the CT scan and actual brain section; only the PET scan revealed the loss of frontal lobe function. (From Phelps & Mazziotta, 1985)

tures, but it alone can reach deep into the living brain and reveal which parts are functioning chemically and which are quiet.

Nuclear Magnetic Resonance

The amazing views in Figure 5.30 are not X-ray photos. Even the best CT scans come nowhere near producing an image so closely resembling a photograph made at autopsy. The images in Figure 5.30 were created with the **nuclear magnetic resonance (NMR)** method on a living patient, and it was done with less danger to the person than is involved in any of the radiological techniques.

NMR makes use of the fact that some types of atomic nuclei act like miniature magnets with north and south poles. If a patient is placed within a strong magnetic field (Figure 5.31), all magnetizable nuclei will orient in the same direction. A radio antenna then broadcasts radio waves through the body. When the nuclei absorb the energy of the radio waves (a phenomenon called *resonance*), they are knocked out of alignment with the magnetic field. The radio wave pulse only lasts a moment; when it is over, the atoms "relax" back to their previous alignments with the magnetic field by shedding the energy they absorbed from the radio waves. The energy is emitted as radiation that can be used to generate the NMR picture. NMR can be used to produce an image of the tissue inside the body because of differences in the way that various kinds of tissue affect the speed with which the relaxation occurs. A more viscous part of the brain, for example, shows up as a difference in the emitted radio waves because the less viscous tissue around it sheds its radio energy at a different rate (Gademann, 1984).

NMR is providing medicine with very clear images of the insides of living brains and is used in diagnosing brain defects and detecting brain damage after accidents. It is also being used in basic research on normal tissue function. Each type of atom has its own resonant frequency, so by varying the frequency of the radio waves sent into the brain and noting which ones evoke resonance, the researcher can determine what chemicals are present in tissue (Prichard & Shulman, 1986). In one recent application

of this idea, clinicians examined the brain chemistry of newborn infants who had suffered brain damage during birth.

■ The Use of Animals in Neuroscience

In recent years, many Americans have become concerned about the welfare of animal subjects in scientific research. Most research on the nervous system inevitably demands the death of the animal at some point in the experiment. In many cases, the subject must undergo loss of an organ or some neural tissue. Experiments on pain must, by definition, subject the animals to painful experiences. The beneficiaries of the knowledge thus generated are humans suffering from disease, nervous system damage, or chronic pain that can be helped because of new therapies growing out of the basic knowledge. But, is this knowledge being achieved at too high a cost in animal suffering? Can researchers perform any procedure they wish on their subjects, or are they limited by ethical and legal constraints?

The Society for Neuroscience, an international organization of approximately 8,000 scientists involved in nervous system research, has established a set of ethical guidelines that its membership is expected to follow whenever animals are used in research. The guidelines stipulate what sort of procedures should or should not be used to minimize pain and discomfort and promote humane methods of animal care, housing, and postsurgical care. These guidelines are reprinted in the appendix at the end of this chapter.

The federal government has also issued a set of guidelines for animal research, and it is very similar to the ethical guidelines established by neuroscientists themselves. These federal regulations are based on the **Animal Welfare Act** (as amended in 1976; Public Law 94–279), a law inspired by the lobbying of various animal welfare groups. Several sections of the regulations are reprinted as follows:

IV. Proper use of animals, including the avoidance or minimization of discomfort, distress, and pain when consistent with sound scientific practices,

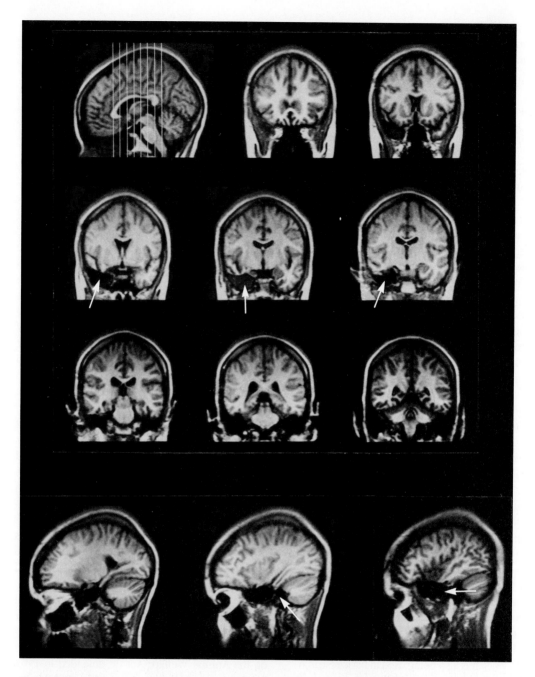

Figure 5.30 NMR scans of patient with right temporal lobectomy. The midsagittal view at top left shows the anterior–posterior location of each of the eight frontal sections in rows 1, 2, and 3. In the bottom row are three sagittal sections with the most medial at the left, lateral at the right. The arrows indicate the cavity left by the removal of the lobe. (Courtesy of Dr. Antonio Damasio; from Damasio & van Hoesen, 1983)

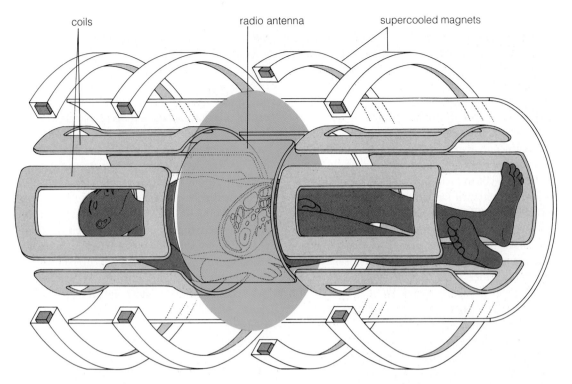

coils   radio antenna   supercooled magnets

Figure 5.31 Scanning and imaging in the NMR method. (Adapted from Sochurek & Miller, 1987)

is imperative. Unless the contrary is established, investigators should consider that procedures that cause pain or distress in human beings may cause pain or distress in other animals.

V. Procedures with animals that may cause more than momentary or slight pain or distress should be performed with appropriate sedation, analgesia, or anesthesia. Surgical or other painful procedures should not be performed on unanesthetized animals paralyzed by chemical agents.

The regulations also cover housing and veterinary care. One of their most important provisions is the mechanism for enforcing these rules. Each research institution is required to establish an **animal care and use program** that follows the explicit and detailed instructions found in the 83-page U.S. government publication, *Guide for the Care and Use of Laboratory Animals* (Committee on Care and Use of Laboratory Animals, 1985), and to appoint an **animal care and use committee** to oversee all projects using animals. This committee must include one scientist from the institution who is involved in animal research, a doctor of veterinary medicine, and one person who is not affiliated with the institution. This last post could be filled by some member of the community interested in animal welfare.

Among the many duties of the animal care and use committee of a university is to decide whether to allow certain experimental procedures. When an experiment is aimed at understanding how the pain systems of the nervous system function, for example, using anesthesia would defeat its purpose. If the animal's pain system has been rendered inoperative by a pain-killing drug, then there is no point to conducting the experiment. You cannot find out how a part of the nervous system works if you start by disabling its normal function. In cases such as these, the committee must decide whether to make an exception to the rules and allow the researcher to inflict pain. The committee is also charged with inspecting facilities to ensure that animals have a clean, comfortable environment and are given adequate medical care after surgery (Committee on Care and Use of Laboratory Animals, 1985).

In recent years, some animal rights advocates have chosen to disregard the democratic process in favor of a militant approach to their goals. In 1981 a Maryland group sought out the local police and accused Dr. Edward Taub of the Institute for Behavioral Research (IBR) of breaking state animal cruelty laws. Without consulting Taub or any of the administrators of IBR, the police, accompanied by the activists, mounted a raid on the labs and seized 17 monkeys. Rather than keeping the animals in a municipal facility or arranging for their care by a veterinarian, the police simply handed over all monkeys to the animal rights activists.

When IBR went to court and obtained an order for the return of the animals, they mysteriously disappeared from the private home where the group was trying to house them. After threat of court action, the monkeys were finally returned. Taub was tried and convicted in a hearing without benefit of jury (Ad Hoc Committee on Animals in Research, 1983). An appeal to a higher court was heard by a jury that acquitted Taub on five of the six counts. In a further appeal, the last count was also overturned, and Taub's name was cleared. After hearing the case, the judge ruled that Taub's work had not inflicted "unnecessary or unjustifiable" pain or suffering. The affair had produced the publicity desired by the activists, however, and Taub lost his grant, his research project, and his job (Ad Hoc Committee on Animals in Research, 1984).

Taub's research involved learning about the changes that take place when a person (or monkey) suffers nerve damage that leaves a limb "deafferented" (lacking sensory nerves). One result is that the skin becomes easily infected. The veterinarian at IBR advised against bandaging the skin sores because bacteria breed easily in bandages. The animal activists did not understand this and thought that the monkeys were simply being neglected. When the medical explanation was given them, they chose not to believe it.

Since the Taub case, animal rights advocates have become more militant and destructive. For example, in a break-in at the University of California at Riverside, pigeons, rabbits, and other animals were stolen from 20 labs. Data that took months to collect were destroyed. Computers were smashed and graffiti was scrawled on the walls in spray paint. The floors were littered with broken equipment, data sheets, and gobs of paint.

In 1984 the University of Pennsylvania neurosurgery labs were broken into, and research videotapes of head injury experiments were stolen. Later, television audiences saw 5-second clips from these tapes of monkeys receiving skull-crushing head injuries. News commentators did not point out that the largest cause of brain injury to young adults is from head injuries received in automobile accidents. No one pointed out that neurosurgeons trying to mend the crushed skulls of humans brought into the emergency wards from such crashes are no better than the knowledge they have gleaned from the research reported in the scientific literature. The Pennsylvania case has provided animal rights advocates with so much emotionalized publicity that the possibility of quietly working out the best compromise between human and animal needs is seriously in danger. If we leave decisions about research animals exclusively in the hands of animal rights lobbyists, we run the risk of losing future medical knowledge that could make the difference between a normal life following nervous system trauma versus a life of crippled debility.

You and other American voters have the unquestionable right to decide through the democratic process whether you wish this sort of knowledge to be generated. What one must realize, however, is that medical science *cannot* progress in certain areas without experiments using animal subjects. There is a price to pay for this knowledge, and our society must decide where the balance will fall between protecting animals and protecting people.

■ Summary

1. The earliest way of obtaining information about brain function was through clinical observation of brain-damage victims. Data from such observations are less valid and reliable than data from experiments because subjects cannot be randomly assigned to conditions and because the extent and placement of the damage cannot be controlled. The surgical ablation or lesioning of animal brain tissue has provided most of our useful experimental results.

2. Another important early method was electrical stimulation of the cortex. Fritsch and Hitzig established the existence and location of the motor cortex in the dog's brain with their experiments in the 1870s. Modern neurosurgery has provided much of our information about localization of various functions in the cerebral cortex because the surgeon must often stimulate the cortex in order to establish the location of speech areas.

3. The development of modern electronic amplifiers made possible the electroencephalograph (EEG). Brain waves recorded on the EEG are voltage variations between pairs of electrodes, which reveal the algebraically summated influence of millions of EPSPs, IPSPs, and action potentials within the vicinity of the electrodes. The EEG waves vary in frequency and amplitude; from changes in these two variables, the organism's state of arousal can be judged.

4. Brain structures underlying the cortex can be stimulated using implanted electrodes. To position electrodes with a stereotaxic instrument, researchers use the coordinates found in a stereotaxic atlas. In some experiments, electrodes are implanted in two brain locations so that one location can be stimulated and the results of this stimulus recorded at the second location. The wave picked up by the recording electrode is called an evoked potential.

5. Implanted electrodes can also be used to make small, discrete lesions deep within the brain, something that is not possible surgically. One problem with these electrolytic lesions is that the current not only destroys the cells in the affected region but also kills axons entering or passing through the zone of destruction. The result may be the unin-

tended death of cell bodies in regions far removed from the lesion site. Chemical lesions created by the injection of neurotoxins such as 6-OHDA or one of the excitotoxins can be confined to the cell bodies within the lesion area and are thus considerably more precise.

6. Evoked potentials have been used extensively, especially to study the brain's sensory systems. An evoked potential is an EEG wave produced either through direct electrical stimulation of a part of the nervous system or through stimulation of a sense organ. When the recording electrode is far from the site of the potential, a special technique called signal averaging must be used to extract the evoked potential from the background of irrelevant potentials from other brain regions.

7. The behavior of single neurons can be studied with either intracellular or extracellular microelectrodes.

8. The brain can be mapped in three different ways: anatomically, chemically, and functionally. Anatomical connections between gray matter areas can be mapped with the Nauta–Gygax, autoradiographic, or horseradish peroxidase (HRP) techniques.

9. The chemical mapping of neurotransmitter systems can be accomplished with histofluorescence, reuptake autoradiography, or receptor-labeling methods. The immunohistochemical method employs "designer" antibodies to label nearly any part of any cell in the nervous system. It is the most sophisticated method of chemical mapping.

10. Mapping the brain to locate various functions can be accomplished with the regional cerebral blood flow ($_rCBF$), 2-deoxyglucose (2-DG), or voltage-sensitive dye techniques.

11. Older X-ray techniques for obtaining an image of a living brain are being supplanted by the far more useful methods of computerized axial tomography (CT scans), positron-emission tomography (PET scans), and nuclear magnetic resonance (NMR) imaging.

12. There are ethical guidelines for animal care published by research organizations and federal laws aimed at animal protection. Most experiments in neuroscience cannot be carried out in any form without using animals as subjects.

Introduction

Research in the neurosciences contributes to the quality of life by expanding knowledge about living organisms. This improvement in quality of life stems in part from progress toward ameliorating human disease and disability, in part from advances in animal welfare and veterinary medicine, and in part from the steady increase in knowledge of the abilities and potentialities of human and animal life. Continued progress in many areas of biomedical research requires the use of living animals in order to investigate complex systems and functions because, in such cases, no adequate alternatives exist. Progress in both basic and clinical research in such areas cannot continue without the use of living animals as experimental subjects. The use of living animals in properly designed scientific research is therefore both ethical and appropriate. Nevertheless, our concern for the humane treatment of animals dictates that we weigh carefully the benefits to human knowledge and welfare whenever animal research is undertaken. The investigator using research animals assumes responsibility for proper experimental design, including ethical as well as scientific aspects.

The scientific community shares the concern of society at large that the use of animals in research should conform to standards that are consonant with those applied to other uses of animals by humans. While it is unlikely that any particular set of standards will satisfy everyone, it is appropriate for scientific societies to formulate guidelines that apply to the humane use of laboratory animals in particular areas of research. Ideally, such guidelines should also be acceptable to society at large as reasonable and prudent.

Most of the more specific sections of this document were formulated with respect to research using warm-blooded vertebrates. As a general principle, however, ethical issues involved in the use of any species, whether vertebrate or invertebrate, are best considered in relation to the complexity of that species' nervous system and its apparent awareness of the environment, rather than physical appearance or evolutionary proximity to humans.

Factors That Relate to the Design of Experiments

The primary factor used to evaluate humane treatment in animal research is degree of distress or discomfort assessed by anthropomorphic judgments made by reasonable and prudent human observers. *The fundamental principle of ethical animal research is that experimental animals must not be subjected to avoidable distress or discomfort.* This principle must be observed when designing any experiment that uses living animals.

Although most animal research involves minimal distress or discomfort, certain valid scientific questions may require experimental designs that inevitably produce these effects. Such situations, while uncommon, are extremely diverse and must be evaluated individually. It is critical that distress and discomfort be minimized by careful experimental design. It is also important to recognize that there is no difference between distress and discomfort that may be inherent in a valid experimental design and that which may occur as an unintended side effect. It is therefore incumbent on the investigator to recognize and to eliminate all *avoidable* sources of distress and discomfort in animal subjects. This goal often requires attention to specifics of animal husbandry as well as to experimental design.

Invasive procedures and paralytic drugs should

never be employed without benefit of anesthetic agents unless there is a very strong scientific justification and careful consideration is given to possible alternatives. Advances in experimental techniques, such as the use of devices chronically implanted under anesthesia, can offer alternative approaches. If these are not feasible, it is essential to monitor nociceptive responses (for example, recordings of EEG, blood pressure, and pupillary responses) that may indicate distress in the animal subject, and to use these as signals of the need to alleviate pain, to modify the experimental design, or to terminate the experiment.

When designing research projects, investigators should carefully consider the species and numbers of animals necessary to provide valid information, as well as the question whether living subjects are required to answer the scientific question. As a general rule, experiments should be designed so as to minimize the number of animals used and to avoid the depletion of endangered species. Advances in experimental methods, more efficient use of animals, within-subject designs, and modern statistical techniques all provide possible ways to minimize the numbers of animals used in research. This goal is completely consistent with the critical importance of replication and validation of results to true progress in science.

Factors That Relate to the Conduct of Experiments

Research animals must be acquired and cared for in accordance with the guidelines published in the *NIH Guide for the Care and Use of Laboratory Animals* (National Institutes of Health Publications, No. 85-23, Revised 1985). Investigators must also be aware of the relevant local, state, and federal laws. The quality of research data depends in no small measure on health and general condition of the animals used, as well as on the specifics of experimental design. Thus, proper animal husbandry is integral to the success of any research effort using living animal subjects. General standards for animal husbandry (housing, food quality, ventilation, etc.) are detailed in the *NIH Guide*. The experienced investigator can contribute additional specifics for optimum care for particular experimental situations, or for species not commonly encountered in laboratory settings.

Surgery performed with the intent that the animal will survive (for example, on animals intended for chronic study) should be carried out, or directly supervised, by persons with appropriate levels of experience and training, and with attention to asepsis and prevention of infection. Major surgical procedures should be done using an appropriate method of anesthesia to render the animal insensitive to pain. Muscle relaxants and paralytics have no anesthetic action and should not be used alone for surgical restraint. Postoperative care must include attention to minimize discomfort and the risk of infection.

Many experimental designs call for surgical preparation under anesthetic agents with no intent that the animal should survive. In such cases, the animals ordinarily should be maintained unconscious for the duration of the experiment. At the conclusion of the experiment, the animal should be killed without regaining consciousness and death endured before final disposition.

Certain experiments may require physical restraint, and/or withholding of food or water, as methodological procedures rather than experimental paradigms. In such cases, careful attention must be paid to minimize discomfort or distress and to ensure that general health is maintained. Immobilization or restraint to which the animals cannot be readily adapted should not be imposed when alternative procedures are practical. Reasonable periods of rest and readjustment should be included in the experimental schedule unless these would be absolutely inconsistent with valid scientific objectives.

When distress and discomfort are unavoidable attributes of a valid experimental design, it is mandatory to conduct such experiments so as to minimize these effects, to minimize the duration of the procedure, and to minimize the numbers of animals used, consistent with the scientific objectives of the study.

Glossary

ablation Removal of a part. (154)

amplitude (EEG waves) The height of a wave. (158)

animal model An experimentally induced disease condition in an animal that mimics a natural human disorder. (167)

anterograde tracing Method for discovering a tract by injecting a chemical label into the somas and discovering where the axons carry it. (176)

antibodies Immune-system proteins designed to bind with antigens; a part of the immune response that kills bacteria, virus, and tumors. (177)

antigens Natural cell-surface proteins that serve as distinctive markers. (177)

aspiration Ablation of a brain area by means of suction. (155)

auditory evoked potential EEG record of the voltage changes in the CNS elicited by a single, discrete sound (such as a click). (169)

autoradiographic method Method that can reveal which brain area was active when a radioactive tracer chemical was taken up by the cells; also can be used to trace connections between gray matter areas. (176)

averaged evoked potential A neural response to a stimulus that has been made visible in the EEG record by adding many records together. (171)

cannula A hollow needle that can be inserted stereotaxically into a deep structure of the brain just like an electrode. (167)

catecholamines A group of monoamine neurotransmitters (such as dopamine) built around or from a basic molecule called DOPA. (166)

computerized axial tomography Computerized technique for constructing a three-dimensional image of a body part such as the brain from a series of X-ray photographs. (183)

CT scan Image created by computerized axial tomography. (183)

electroencephalograph (EEG) Electronic instrument for recording voltage changes ("waves") from the brain. (156)

electrolytic lesion Area of damage created by passing a current through the tissue. (164)

excitotoxin A neurotoxin that can trigger EPSPs in the neurons it kills. (167)

extracellular microelectrode technique The process of using a microelectrode to locate single neurons and record voltage changes from outside of them. (174)

frequency (EEG waves) The number of waves per second. (158)

glutamate A neurotransmitter found in many brain areas. (167)

histofluorescence Method of revealing the locations of monoaminergic cells by treating them with chemicals that convert their neurotransmitters into fluorescent compounds. (177)

horseradish peroxidase (HRP) An enzyme easily taken up by the terminals and transported down the axon to the cell body; used to trace tracts. (176)

ibotenic acid An excitotoxin used by researchers to kill glutaminergic neurons. (167)

immune system The body's defense system against infections and tumors. (177)

immunohistochemical method Method of revealing the locations of particular cells by injecting antigens that will serve to mark them. (177)

intracellular microelectrode technique The process of using a microelectrode to locate single neurons and record voltage changes from within them. (174)

in vitro autoradiography Method of locating particular cell types by treating brain slices with labeled molecules. (177)

in vivo autoradiography The use of labeled molecules to locate particular cell types in the living brain. (177)

isotope One of several forms that an element can take. (185)

kainic acid An excitotoxin used by researchers to kill glutaminergic neurons; selectively kills somas. (167)

labeled molecule A radioactive molecule that can be used as a tracer in autoradiography. (176)

lesion An area of damage. (153)

microelectrodes The fine wires or glass pipettes drawn to a microscopic point; used for recording from a single neuron. (174)

Nauta–Gygax method A method for staining degenerating axons with a silver compound. (175)

neuropsychologist A clinical psychologist specializing in brain dysfunction. (153)

neurotoxins Nerve poisons. (164)

nuclear magnetic resonance (NMR) A method of

creating images of the living brain based on radio waves emitted from brain tissue subject to a strong magnetic field. (187)

PET scan Image created by positron emission tomography. (184)

photon A discrete packet of electromagnetic energy; the smallest divisible amount of light. (185)

positron Particle like an electron but with a positive charge. (185)

positron-emission tomography Computerized technique for constructing a three-dimensional image of a body part (such as the brain) from a series of records of radiation emitted from labeled molecules being used by a body organ. (184)

radioactive isotope An unstable form of an element that emits radiation as it transforms into a different element. (185)

receptor labeling Locating particular types of receptors in the brain by injecting the appropriate labeled transmitter and then reading the patterns of radiation. (177)

regional cerebral blood flow technique (ᵣCBF) A method that can reveal the activity levels in various parts of the human brain by monitoring radiation emissions from blood vessels. (178)

retrograde tracing Method for discovering a tract by first injecting a labeled chemical at the terminals that will be transported to the somas and then recording where it appears in the brain. (176)

reuptake autoradiography The use of labeled transmitter molecules to reveal the presence of terminals that secrete monoaminergic transmitters. (177)

signal averaging The technique of adding evoked potentials together to bring a tiny, stimulus-related voltage change out of the random fluctuations that are hiding it. (171)

6-hydroxydopamine (6-OHDA) A neurotoxin that selectively destroys catecholaminergic neurons; used as a lesion-making research tool. (166)

stereotaxic brain atlas A collection of photographs of brain sections on grids that show the vertical, horizontal, and anterior–posterior distance to any location in the brain. (160)

stereotaxic instrument A device that can move an electrode tip to an exact location anywhere in the brain. (160)

tritiated molecule One having tritium substituted for its hydrogen atoms; used as a radioactive tracer. (176)

2-deoxyglucose (2-DG) autoradiography Method for establishing which brain area was active during a task by injecting labeled glucose and observing where in the brain the radiation occurred. (180)

voltage-sensitive dye A dye that fluoresces when brain potentials pass through it, thus revealing what brain areas were activated by the stimulus. (181)

X rays A form of electromagnetic radiation that penetrates tissue. (183)

6

Vision

Y ou may have read somewhere in a popular magazine or in a high school science text that the eye is like a camera, but—aside from the fact that both eye and camera focus light on a light-sensitive surface—there is hardly any resemblance at all between the two. Another idea often expressed is that the visual system of the brain carries an image to the cortex, where perception takes place. This is also a distortion of the facts. Still another misconception may come from your own general experience. You may think, as you look at the scene in front of you, that you are seeing the world as it really is. This is a delusion born of never having been able to see it with any other sensory equipment than your own. As we explore the nature of light, we will find out that there is much more that our species might have been capable of seeing had our ancestors' environments been different.

The first concept you must understand about vision is the interaction between light and the environment. An object in your visual field becomes visible if light strikes its surface and is partially absorbed, leaving a remainder to reflect back into your eye. If the object were able to absorb all the light, its surface would be perfectly pitch black, and all you would see would be an outline. If, on the other hand, the object perfectly reflected all the light striking it, all you would see would be a mirror surface reflecting the image of the light source. So, the fact that only part of the light hitting a surface is reflected back into your eye becomes critical in determining how you see an object. Parts of objects that absorb more light appear darker than other parts because they reflect back less light to your eye. It is the patterns of light and dark in the image that reveal the shapes and surfaces of objects.

The color of an object is largely determined by which wavelengths of light it absorbs or reflects. The factor of wavelength turns out to be very important to understanding the whole process of vision and a key to understanding how incomplete and uniquely human our visual images of our environment really are. Before we can understand vision then, we must understand light itself a little better.

The Nature of Light

Light is just one of the many forms of a type of energy called **electromagnetic radiation**. It can be thought of as waves of varying lengths or as small, discrete packets called photons. A **photon** is the smallest quantity of light possible. You possess receptors, located in your eyes and skin, that are sensitive to electromagnetic radiation. The ones in your skin, however, react to slightly different wavelengths than do the ones in your eyes. Look closely at Figure 6.1, a diagram of the **electromagnetic spectrum**. The spectrum is an ordered arrangement of all known forms of electromagnetic radiation, showing that the only difference between one type of radiation and another is the lengths of their waves. For example, radio waves, bearing their daily burden of "Top 40" rock hits, differ from the deadly, killing gamma rays (spawn of hydrogen bomb explosions) only because gamma waves are shorter than radio waves. Very short electromagnetic waves can readily penetrate living tissue, leaving behind them a trail of broken DNA molecules and disrupted chemical reactions. The long-wavelength radio waves, on the other hand (lethal only to folks over 40) are too long to penetrate and are instead absorbed by the skin's surface or reflected from it.

Look again at the electromagnetic spectrum (Figure 6.1) and see how many familiar names you find there: microwaves (used in radar and cooking appliances), infrared, ultraviolet, and X rays; all are forms of radiation that differ only in their wavelengths. Now take special notice of that diminutive sliver of spectrum sandwiched between the two much larger areas of ultraviolet and infrared. That somewhat-less-than-impressive zone of wavelengths known as the **visible spectrum** contains all wavelengths of the rainbow—from violet at the short end to red at the long—and constitutes the only fragment of electromagnetic radiation that your eyes are capable of sensing.

So there you sit with radio waves flooding the air about you and microwaves leaking out of your oven door or coming through the window from the traffic light control at the corner. Ultraviolet waves swarm

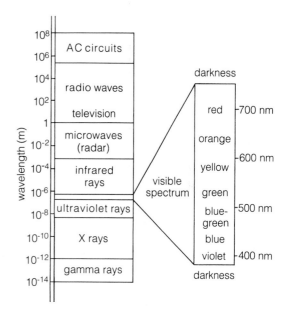

Figure 6.1 The electromagnetic radiation spectrum from the longer wavelengths at the top to the shorter at the bottom. At the right, the visible part of the spectrum has been extracted and magnified. The unit *nm* (for *nanometer*) is equal to 1 billionth of a meter. (Adapted from Hartmann, 1987)

through the unshaded window to wreak havoc in your skin cells; occasional gamma rays whiz through your body, having been flung from the colossal hydrogen furnace of the sun a few moments before. As a matter of fact, the sun itself bombards you with all of these various wavelengths. They are all there, continually present in your normal everyday environment; so, the natural question is, Why does the human nervous system let all that stimulation go to waste? If the objects around us are reflecting ultraviolet, infrared, and microwaves into our eyes, then why aren't our eyes capable of perceiving those stimuli? Then too, if we are insensitive to so many of these other wavelengths, we are forced to revise our whole appreciation of what it means to see the world around us. Our vision certainly does not seem to be capturing a true picture of the environment—not when our nervous system apparently misses 80 percent or more of what is really out there. Instead of a real image of the world, we are obtaining a uniquely human picture, highly selective and designed expressly to enable our species to survive in the existing conditions.

Our prehuman ancestors evolved the senses that we now enjoy; if we lack some potential perceptual ability, it is probably because the possession of such an ability was not critical to survival in the environment experienced by those ancestors. For example, we cannot sense gamma radiation with our eyes because our predecessors were never pressed to detect gamma radiation. But what if our world had been just a little different? What if there had been numerous large deposits of highly concentrated radioactive minerals close to the surface when our prehuman forefathers roamed the planet? Creatures that blundered into these "hot" zones and stayed too long would have died of radiation poisoning. Who would have survived? Only those with some beginnings of an ability to detect the deadly rays and associate periods of radiation sickness with the memory of those sensations. It is they who would have learned to avoid the dangerous areas, thus giving their genes a much greater chance of being passed on. Eventually, we would have been the recipients of those genes and would have had the ability to sense gamma radiation.

You have the senses that you possess not by chance but because each capability meant the difference between surviving and not surviving at some time in our evolutionary past. Each sense was forced on our ancestors as a vital solution to a nearly fatal problem. Regardless of the esthetic heights to which artists and musicians have raised vision and hearing, we humans carry no spare perceptual luggage in our armory of stimulus-detection devices.

Not all of the nonvisible spectrum is lost to us through the lack of receptors, however. Some wavelengths are deliberately discarded by the nervous system. Our visual receptors are sensitive to a fair portion of the ultraviolet spectrum, but several parts of the eye are colored yellow and thus filter out ultraviolet waves. Very short wavelengths (like ultraviolet ones) are very difficult for our eye to focus,

and if we allowed them to reach the light-sensitive surface inside the eye, a blurred image would result. The coating on a camera lens achieves the same result for the same reason.

Infrared radiation presents a still different problem. We do have the ability to sense these relatively long wavelengths, but the receptors are in our skin rather than in our eyes. Infrared is the same thing as radiant heat, and it is given off by any warm object. Consider that it might be quite nice to walk down a dark street on a moonless night and still clearly see approaching people and even vegetation. To see like that at night would surely have made survival easier. Why, then, didn't our predecessors evolve the ability to sense infrared wavelengths?

The variations in intensity between one area of the image and another constitute the boundaries of the objects you are viewing. A face, for example, emits much infrared, and its features and outline would represent an area of relatively intense rays within the overall image, whereas a person's clothing emits less heat and would appear in the image as darker zones. The differences between lighter (more intense) areas and those that are darker (less intense) reveal the shape. But this infrared image with its tiny but important variations in intensity has competition when it arrives at the receptors. The source of infrared radiation (heat) nearest your eye is your own eye. All living cells generate heat. The tissue surrounding the receptors, as well as blood vessels serving this tissue, also contributes infrared. The rays coming in from the outside world would probably be masked by more intense rays from internal metabolic sources. Consequently, your vision would be blurred and hazy, and objects would be as difficult to sense accurately. There is a distinct survival advantage in *not* seeing infrared wavelengths.

■ The Receptor Organ

The eyeball is enclosed in a tough, membranous sac called the **sclera**. Light waves reflected from objects in the environment enter your eye through the **cornea**, the transparent, anterior portion of the sclera (Figure 6.2). The rest of the sclera is translucent. The

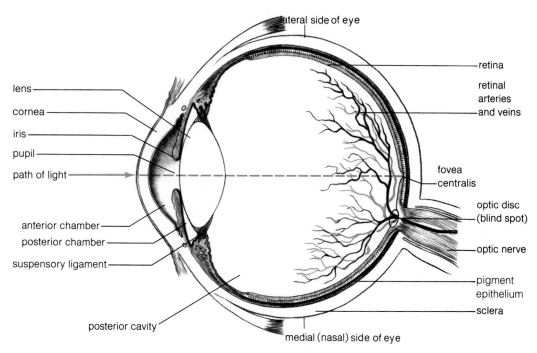

lateral side of eye

lens

cornea

iris

pupil

path of light

anterior chamber

posterior chamber

suspensory ligament

posterior cavity

medial (nasal) side of eye

retina

retinal arteries and veins

fovea centralis

optic disc (blind spot)

optic nerve

pigment epithelium

sclera

Figure 6.2 A cross section of the eye. The chambers in front of and behind the lens are filled with a fluid called a humor. The fovea is the tiny region at the center of the retina, which shows in the diagram as a depression. (Adapted from Fowler, 1984)

rounded shape of the cornea focuses the light rays as they pass through it into the fluid-filled chamber just behind.

To reach the light-receptive cells, the light must pass through a hole formed by a ring of muscles called the **iris**. By contracting or relaxing, the iris can increase or decrease the size of the hole (the **pupil**) to allow more or less light into the inner chamber of the eye. The iris reflexively opens the pupil if you move from higher to lower illumination, thus aiding the process of adapting to the dark. Another reflex, the orienting reaction, opens the pupil wide whenever a novel stimulus occurs that needs to be categorized by the nervous system as important or unimportant. This means that if you see a person's pupil dilate (open wider) and there has been no decrease in illumination, then it is likely that something has just occurred to which the person

is orienting. If dilation continues, it usually indicates interest and attention on the part of the person. It is very likely that this pupillary dilation is what novelists are really thinking of when they talk about a person's eyes "sparkling with interest."

Further focusing of light rays is accomplished by the **lens**, a transparent crystalline structure. Muscles around the borders of the lens can change its shape to allow for focusing on near versus far objects—an adjustment termed **accommodation**. If the cornea, lens, and eyeball are shaped correctly, light rays should come to a perfect, focused image on the inside surface of the eyeball where the receptors are. In some people, however, the eyeball grows too long, and the focus always falls short of the receptors, causing a blurred image (Figure 6.3). This so-called near-sightedness, technically named **myopia** (my-OPE-ee-uh), can be corrected with an additional lens.

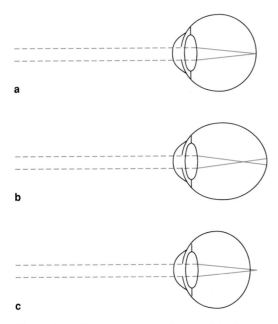

Figure 6.3 Effect of incorrect eyeball growth on image focusing. (**a**) Eyeball of the correct length allows image to focus exactly on retina. (**b**) If the eyeball grows too long, the image focuses in front of the retina, producing a condition called myopia. (**c**) If the eyeball is too short, the image can focus only at an imaginary point in back of the retina, and this produces the condition called hyperopia.

In **hyperopia** (HIGH-per-OPE-ee-uh), the eyeball is too short, and image blurring occurs because the focal point is behind the receptors (farsightedness). In some eyes, focus is impaired even before the light reaches the lens. Tiny flat places on the cornea produce small blurred areas, a condition called **astigmatism** (as-STIG-ma-tiz-um).

■ The Retina

Light receptors are one part of a complex receptor–processor organ called the **retina**, which covers the inside of the eyeball like a cup. Figure 6.4 shows what the physician sees when viewing the inside of the eye through a fundascope. You can see the extensive network of blood vessels branching and re-branching all over the surface of the retina. To reach receptors, light must pass between or through these blood vessels, thus making it inevitable that some of the fine information in the light image is lost before reaching receptors. This loss constitutes a form of "noise," but it is a very small problem compared to the "noise" you would have experienced if you had been born with receptors that could react to all the infrared emitted from that lacework of vessels. The loss is minimized still further for a tiny area right at the center of the retina, called the **fovea**, where the network of vessels parts to allow light an unimpeded path to receptors. The fovea is the center of the retina and receives light from the object directly in front of the eye—from the object at which you are looking.

Figure 6.4 shows that all surface blood vessels of the retina gather together at one point where they penetrate the eyeball. This point, the **optic disc** (Figure 6.2), has no receptors and so constitutes a region of blindness in your retina that produces a blind spot in the visual field of each eye. (See Figure 6.4 for instructions about how to locate your blind spots.)

The retina is the first of many processors that make up the visual system of the brain. Its initial task is to convert light energy into electrochemical energy, and this is accomplished by two receptor cell types, **rods** and **cones** (Figure 6.5). The process of converting from one energy form to another is termed **transduction**. Because patterns in the light image contain information about objects in the outside world, we can think of this light-to-electrochemical conversion as also being a translation of the image information into the "language" of the nervous system—patterns of electrical activity.

Receptors themselves can only react to the presence of light rays, but other layers of cells in the retina are connected to receptors in such ways as to make their responses specific to patterns of light. Later in this section, we will see how this is done. Rods and cones are connected synaptically to **bipolar cells** and **horizontal cells** that in turn synapse on **amacrine cells** and **ganglion cells** (Figure 6.6). Of these types, only the ganglion cells use nerve impulses. Receptors, bipolars, and horizontals employ **local currents**, which are similar to EPSPs in that they are not all-or-none and become weaker as they are conducted away from the source.

Note in Figure 6.6 that for incoming light to reach rods and cones it must first pass through a layer of

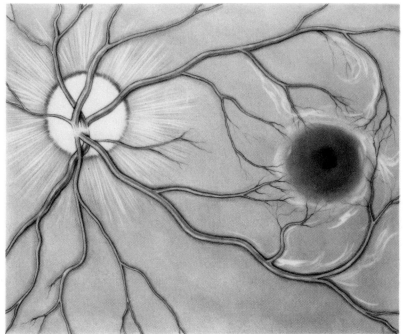

Figure 6.4 This is what the physician sees when peering through a fundascope at the retina of your left eye. At the right is the fovea. At the left is the optic disc, from which emerge the blood vessels that branch out in all directions across the surface of the retina. Because there is no room for receptors at the optic disc, it constitutes a blind spot. You can locate the blind spot by closing your right eye and fixating on the **X** while holding this page about 12 inches from your face. The circle on the left should disappear. You can move it in and out of the blind spot by moving the page closer to or farther from your face (but stay within a range of about 6 inches of the original location). For the right eye blind spot, fixate the circle and watch the **X** disappear. (From Kaufman, 1974)

ganglion and amacrine cells and then a layer of horizontal and bipolar cells. The neurons are quite transparent, thus little information is lost in the light image as it makes this passage. Intuitively, one would expect to find receptors out at the surface of the retina, the first cells to meet the light, but hardly anything about vision conforms to our intuitive assumptions.

More primitive retinas in less-evolved species have their receptor cells "out front" where the light reaches them first, but there is a disadvantage to this. Receptors are metabolically very active and require an immense blood supply. At the back of the retina next to the sclera is a dark layer called the **pigment epithelium** that has a very rich blood supply, which serves the adjacent rods and cones. If receptors were placed on the inside of the retina where light could reach them first, all this blood supply would have to grow through the retina or across its surface to reach

them. Either scheme would absorb part of the incoming light and increase the "noise" level in the pattern reaching the receptors.

Nerve impulses are scarce in the retina. All receptors, bipolars, horizontals, and amacrines produce **graded potentials** rather than all-or-none action potentials. Although the term is not frequently used by retinal researchers, graded potentials are essentially EPSPs and IPSPs of various types. The only retinal neurons that emit nerve impulses are the ganglion cells. They must translate the information into patterns of nerve impulses in their axons because only a self-regenerating impulse could carry the pattern along the entire length of the ganglion-cell axon; EPSPs would dwindle to nothing before the next synapse was reached. Ganglion cells are the **output neurons** of the retina. It is their axons that gather together from all points in the retina and form the optic nerve.

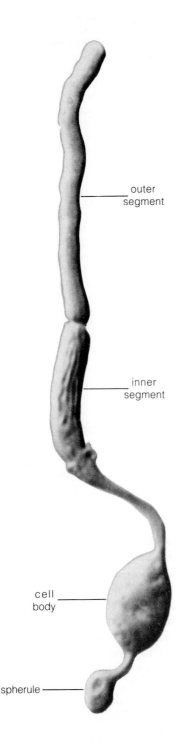

outer
segment

inner
segment

cell
body

spherule

Figure 6.5 A single rod isolated from a rabbit retina. The outer segment contains the rhodopsin. The spherule is the synaptic zone where the cell is contacted by bipolar and horizontal cells. Magnification is ×3,500. (From Townes-Anderson et al., 1988)

So, the surface of the retina is covered with ganglion cell axons streaming toward the optic disc where they exit the eyeball together with blood vessels. At the optic disc, they penetrate the retina and the eyeball as the **optic nerve**—their destination, the thalamus and superior colliculi.

Transduction

Rods and cones are light receptors because they are capable of converting light energy into electrical responses. This transduction is made possible by **photochemicals** contained in the **outer segments** of receptors (Figure 6.7). **Rhodopsin** is the photochemical in rods, and it is so sensitive to electromagnetic radiation that a single photon (the smallest quantity of light possible) is enough to trigger the release of its energy (Schwartz, 1985).

Can a few photons release enough energy to transmit the information through synapses to the horizontal and bipolar cells? If the energy were used to set off an EPSP, the resulting current would probably be too weak to release sufficient transmitter at the rod–bipolar synapse. Instead, the energy provided when a photon strikes a molecule of rhodopsin is used to trigger a chain of chemical reactions that results in the *closing* of sodium channels in the rod cell membrane (Hagins, 1979); this is also true of cones. In either receptor, the transduction process stops a current rather than starting one. Oddly enough, this is exactly what happens. A receptor cell is constantly *depolarized* in the dark with a strong sodium current, called the **dark current**, flowing into its outer segment. Because this is a depolarizing current, its flow results in the release of transmitter at its synapses with bipolars and horizontals. When light strikes the rod, rhodopsin molecules are broken apart, releasing energy for reactions that close ion gates and stop the dark current (Schwartz, 1985). Although this mechanism may seem backward, it

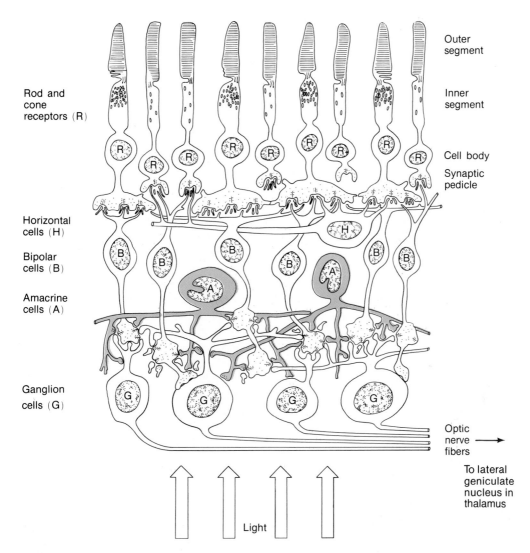

Rod and cone receptors (R)

Outer segment

Inner segment

Cell body
Synaptic pedicle

Horizontal cells (H)

Bipolar cells (B)

Amacrine cells (A)

Ganglion cells (G)

Optic nerve fibers

To lateral geniculate nucleus in thalamus

Light

Figure 6.6 A cross section of primate retina. Incoming light must first pass through layers of ganglion, amacrine, bipolar, and horizontal cells before reaching receptors at the back of the retina. This is a very thin cross section; thus, some axons and terminals leave this plane of section or enter this one from another. Synaptic end feet (terminals) of several rods, together with their synapses, are not in this plane of section; that is why they seem to have smaller end feet than some of the others that are more completely in the picture plane. (Adapted from Dowling & Boycott, 1966, in Goldstein, 1989)

apparently has a strong advantage over something more straightforward. When a current is already flowing in the receptor cell, a very small stimulus (e.g., a few photons) can produce a very considerable change in transmitter release—more of a change than would be produced by *starting* the depolarization of a completely polarized cell (Dowling, 1979).

You may be wondering what bipolar and horizontal cells do in the dark if rods and cones are busy

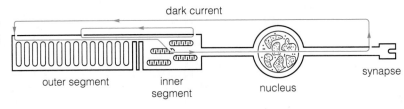

Figure 6.7 Diagram of a generalized vertebrate receptor (rod or cone), showing the dark current. Photopigments are in the outer segment of the cell. When these pigments absorb photons of light, the dark current is decreased. (Adapted from Hagins, 1979)

dark current

outer segment

inner segment

nucleus

synapse

feeding them transmitter molecules at that time. The answer is that the horizontals and some of the bipolars are activated by the transmitter (Werblin, 1979) and thus may be more active in the dark than in the light. Again, however, this is not a drawback. A cell suddenly stopping its activity conveys just as much information to "downstream" neurons as does the starting of activity. However, there are two types of bipolars: those that respond when light strikes their area of retina (ON-bipolars) and those that turn off in the light (OFF-bipolars). OFF-types must be connected to their receptors with an excitatory synapse. In the dark, the receptor stimulates the bipolar; but when light strikes the receptor, it ceases the stimulation, and the bipolar falls silent. ON-types must be wired with an inhibitory synapse because they have the opposite response. They start up a current when light hits their receptors. Therefore, receptors must have been inhibiting them until the light appeared. So, although all rods are turned off by light, some bipolars turn on while others turn off (Dowling, 1979).

Transduction in cones is a little more complicated than in rods because cones are the receptors most important for color vision. Color perception is something you have probably taken for granted all of your life. It is a rare person who asks what color is—what it means to perceive colors. Few people realize that colors are all inside of their heads or that light has no color, only different wavelengths. Color is the nervous system's response to differences in wavelengths. Figure 6.1 shows the visible part of the electromagnetic spectrum, magnified so that we can see the effects of varying wavelength. Note that the shortest wavelengths produce a sensation of violet and

blue, while the longest are seen as orange and red.

When light strikes a surface, some of the light energy is absorbed, and the rest is reflected back. A colored surface absorbs more of some wavelengths than do others. Although the light striking the cover of a book may contain all wavelengths, the cover may extract most of the short ones and reflect back mostly long ones. Such a book would look orange or red. Another book might absorb mostly long wavelengths and appear blue or violet. If your eye contained only rods, these two books might appear identical—the same shade of gray. Obviously, a rod-only eye misses a lot of the information contained in a light image. Our distant vertebrate ancestors in the ocean evolved color vision, and the reason for the appearance of this ability was that fish needed to be able to discriminate between objects with roughly the same shape that differed mainly in the wavelengths their surfaces absorbed. Color differences help a fish tell male from female and friend from foe. Without it survival would be much chancier.

Color perception is the ability to discriminate between wavelengths. How do cones give us this discrimination ability? Rather than containing rhodopsin in their outer segments, each cone contains one of three separate types of **opsin**, and each opsin, is sensitive to a different part of the spectrum. Thus, some cones are good at absorbing light from the long end of the spectrum, others are good at medium wavelengths, and still others are best with the short lengths (Figure 6.8). Wavelength is measured in units called **nanometers** (NAN-uh-meet-urs), which are 1 billionth of a meter. The longest visible wavelengths are about 760 nanometers (nm), and the shortest are about 380 nm.

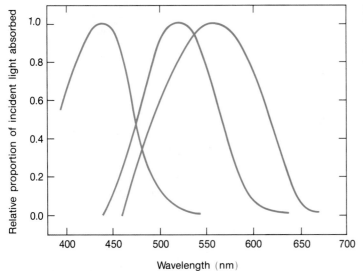

Figure 6.8 Absorption curves for human short-, medium-, and long-wavelength cones. Each curve shows the degree to which the opsin of that cone reacts to the indicated range of wavelengths. (Adapted from Wald & Brown, 1965, in Goldstein, 1989)

Because humans can discriminate so many different colors, you would think that just three cone types would be inadequate to explain the full range of color perception, but a clever set of ideas called the **Young–Helmholtz theory** shows that three cone types may be quite enough. First, we assume that the more light a cone absorbs, the greater the effect on its dark current, thus the greater the change in transmitter released at its synapses. Now look at Figure 6.8 and find one wavelength such as 480 nm. (Light with a 480-nm wavelength gives us the sensation of blue–green.) Now, trace straight upward from the approximate position of 480 nm until you intersect with a curve. Note that at 480 nm, the long- and short-wavelength cones absorb equal amounts of light, and the midrange cone is absorbing more than either of the other two. Now, shift down the scale to 450 nm and see how the absorption pattern changes. At 450 nm, the long-wavelength cone drops out of the picture altogether. There is little change in its dark current even though light is shining directly on it. The opsin it contains simply isn't sensitive to this wavelength. Note also that the short-wavelength cone is absorbing much more light at 450 nm than it was at 480 nm, so much so that it

now surpasses the midrange cone that has decreased sensitivity for this kind of light. At 480 nm the *pattern* of absorption in the three cones is very different from the pattern at 450 nm. In fact, every wavelength yields a different activity pattern in the three cone types. Each wavelength produces a different facilitation pattern at the synapses with bipolars and horizontals. Each separate absorption pattern, then, yields a different excitation pattern in the brain, and that means each is experienced differently in the conscious mind. Only three kinds of cone are needed to provide every color available in the entire spectrum.

The Retina as a Double-Function System

When you begin to pay attention to one particular object in your visual field, reflexes automatically move your eyes to center the light from the object on your foveas. The fovea is the center of each visual field. Surrounding the fovea is a transition area of indefinite size that separates the fovea from the **peripheral retina**, which receives light from objects around the borders of your visual field. Because foveal vision and peripheral vision are different in many important ways, we can think of the retina as a dual-function system. This duality enables the retina to solve two major visual problems: acuity and sensitivity.

Acuity Besides their different roles in color perception, rods and cones also differ in their ability to handle information about visual shapes. Being able to discriminate one visual form from another has been one cornerstone of survival among primates for millions of years, and good form vision is impossible without clarity and sharpness—in other words, without **acuity**. Poor acuity is similar to viewing the world slightly out of focus so that edges, boundaries, and outlines are fuzzy and indefinite. If you project the image of a line on a screen but throw the image out of focus, the line looks fuzzy because light rays from the line are being spread over a wide area rather than all being brought sharply to one place. The resulting image is indefinite; it fails to clearly indicate exactly where within the fuzzy zone the real line should be located. Place three or four such fuzzy images close together and they spread into one another so badly that you may not be able to see the original lines at all—just a surface with areas of lighter and darker gray. Poor acuity then results in the loss of visual detail—individual lines and edges—and this fact dictates the usual methods of testing for degree of acuity in a human (Figure 6.9).

Whereas rods are specialized for discriminating brightness and for operating under the lowest levels of illumination, cones and the system of retinal circuits they hook into are specialized for acuity and the detection of forms. Because the density of cones is greatest in the fovea, acuity is also greatest there. The farther away from the fovea the image falls, the less the clarity and sharpness of the perception despite the fact that the image is focused just as well on the peripheral retina as it is centrally. Why are cone circuits so much better at producing acuity than are rod circuits? The answer depends on the concept of receptive field.

The **receptive field (RF)** of any neuron in the visual system is the area of retina within which light triggers activity in that neuron. The RF of a bipolar is usually larger than the field of a receptor because most bipolars collect from a number of rods and cones rather than from a single receptor. Further-

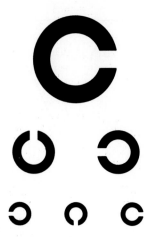

Figure 6.9 Landolt rings for measuring visual acuity. Pictured here are the top three lines of a chart that extends down several more levels to smaller and smaller rings. The subject's task is to say whether the break in the ring is at the right, left, top, or bottom. Correct placement of the break indicates the subject's ability to perceive it, and the breaks become smaller and smaller from the top of the chart to the bottom. When the subject can no longer locate the breaks, the threshold of acuity has been reached. (From Riggs, 1965, in Goldstein, 1989)

more, it is typical for a ganglion cell to be influenced by a still larger area of retina because it collects from several bipolars rather than just one.

The visual parts of the brain (where conscious visual experiences apparently take place) have no direct connection to the optical image on the retina; they know only what retinal ganglion cells tell them. The acuity of the entire visual system is going to depend on the degree of detail contained in the information coming to the brain along axons of retinal ganglion cells. If the pattern of activity in the optic nerve fails to convey fine details of the visual image then, for the visual cortex, those details might just as well never have existed. For example, a high-acuity system can look at two very small dots laid very close together and tell that there are indeed two dots rather than one. A low-acuity system would blur the two together into a fuzzy perception of a single wide dot. How can the pattern of activity in the optic nerve signal the existence of two dots rather than one? The simplest answer would be that impulses in one nerve axon would signal an image at one point on the retina, whereas impulses in two axons would indicate that two different locations on the retina have been stimulated. If the brain receives "dot" information from two separate nerve fibers then, it should be able to decide that there are two dots in the image rather than just one. But if two dots in the image stimulate only one ganglion cell and all information goes to the brain along one optic nerve fiber, then the two dots should look like one dot.

But why would two separate dots, side by side, stimulate the same ganglion cell? They easily could if they were close enough together to both be within the RF of that cell. Thus, it is logical to assume that large RFs that would "funnel" lots of visual detail into the same ganglion cell would produce poor acuity. Any pattern of stimulation falling within a large RF would all be reduced to one set of nerve impulses in a single axon of the optic nerve. Small RFs, on the other hand, could capture small details because each part of the pattern would have its own small RF, its own ganglion cell, and thus its own private line into the brain (Figure 6.10).

At last we can answer the question asked at the beginning of this section: Why are cone circuits of the fovea so much better at producing acuity than are rod circuits of the peripheral retina? The answer is that RF size tends to increase as you go from the fovea toward the peripheral retina. Where peripheral ganglion cells may have RFs that cover as many as 1,000 rods, each cone of the fovea seems to have its own ganglion cell (Shepherd, 1979).

Sensitivity   Rods and cones also differ in their sensitivity to light. **Sensitivity** is the ability to respond to weak stimuli, and it is usually described in terms of **absolute threshold**, the *least* amount of a stimulus needed to obtain a response from a cell. Sensitivity and threshold are reciprocally related; as the threshold rises, sensitivity decreases and vice versa. Rods have a lower threshold for stimulation than do cones; that is, they are more sensitive to light. In a situation where the illumination level is steadily decreasing, a point is finally reached at which only rods can continue to function. The light becomes too weak to stimulate cones, and they simply cease to respond.

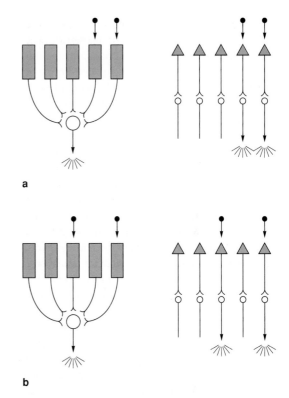

a

b

Figure 6.10   Neural circuits for the rods (left) and cones (right). Receptors are being stimulated by two spots of light (**a**) close together and (**b**) farther apart. (From Goldstein, 1989)

With them goes color vision. On a moonlit night, all colors disappear into shades of gray and black; all reflecting surfaces become **achromatic** (lacking in color).

As you know from personal experience, your night vision improves as you remain in the dark. This gradual increase in sensitivity produced by lowering the illumination level is called **dark adaptation**. Much adaptation occurs within the first few minutes in the dark, and the process is nearly complete after about 30 minutes. When you return to the light, you go through a reverse process called **light adaptation**, which is a rapid decrease in sensitivity. With these two opposing processes, the human eye can operate over an enormous range of light intensities. Rods are so sensitive that a completely dark-adapted person with good night vision can see (on a clear, dark night) the flame of a candle 30 miles away (Galanter, 1962). Yet that same eye that saw the candle flame must also be able to operate in the full, brilliant, noonday sun without going blind. From one end of this range to the other is a change in intensity of *100 billion to 1* (Dowling, 1967).

Rods and cones are distributed differently across the retina, with cones the exclusive receptors in the fovea and rods having the extreme peripheral retina all to themselves. Between the fovea and the far periphery, both types mix. If you move outward from the fovea to the borders of the retina, cones gradually thin out, and rods increase in density. This distribution has important implications for night vision. When you see something "out of the corner of your eye," the image falls on your peripheral retina; even on a dark night, some rods there will respond. But when you turn your eye to look directly at the object, you place the image on your fovea where there are no rods. The perceptual result is that the object "disappears." On a dark night, the entire fovea is a blind spot squarely in the center of your visual field. This is fertile soil for a superstitious mind. Imagine such a person passing a graveyard on a moonlit night where tree branches are swaying in the breeze. The movement so easily caught by the peripheral retina vanishes like a ghost as the eyes turn toward it! The military takes foveal night vision very seriously, teaching soldiers to fire in the dark by looking to one side of the target, thus throwing the image onto an area of the retina containing rods.

One surmise that could be drawn from this discussion is that the human retina is a compromise between two important survival needs: we must be able to resolve tiny visual detail (acuity) but still see well enough to get around on a dark night (sensitivity), and these two functions are to some extent mutually incompatible. Nature's compromise was to place the acuity function in the area in and around the fovea and give over the peripheral retina to sensitivity. In effect, we have two eyes in one.

Extracting Information from the Image

The retina does more than just transduce light into nerve impulses. Information carried by patterns of intensity and wavelength variations in the optical image must be extracted by the collection of analyzers that makes up the visual system. The first few analyzers are in the retina.

Analyzers The term **analyzer**, as it is being used here, refers to a set of synaptic connections between a group of input neurons and a group of output neurons. These connections are arranged so that the output cells fire only if one particular pattern of inputs occurs. This being the case, the firing of the output neurons becomes a signal that some particular event is occurring in the environment. For example, if the set of connections is a color analyzer for the color red, then the output cells fire only when something red is being viewed. Movement is detected in the visual image by another set of connections designed to make particular output cells respond to moving boundaries but not to stationary ones. Each visual capacity you possess—color, form, movement, location, depth, texture, and so forth— is available to you only because, somewhere in your visual system, the information flows through a set of synapses designed to filter out and recognize that particular aspect of visual experience.

How do you recognize the book in front of you as being a book? Its rectangular outside boundaries (edges) give it the general shape of a book, and the tiny, black-on-white contours filling the pages produce the shapes of the letters. The essence of form perception is the ability to detect boundaries and contours, making it no surprise that contour detection begins as early in the visual system as the retina. The first step in perceiving a boundary or contour is to detect the presence of a change in illumination between adjacent regions of the optical image—a lighter area next to a darker area. So, edges and contours in the environment are represented in the light image as sudden changes in illumination. A light area next to a darker one constitutes **contrast**, and the greater the difference between the two regions, the greater the contrast. Because contrasts in the image come from edges and boundaries of objects in the visual field, the act of perceiving forms, patterns, and figures is a matter of detecting areas of contrast; this contrast analysis is the major function

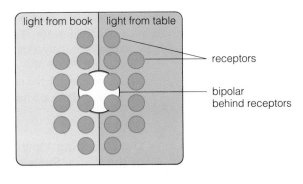

BACK VIEW
(looking straight
into receptors)

light from book | light from table

receptors

bipolar
behind receptors

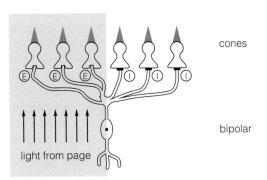

SIDE VIEW

cones

bipolar

light from page

Figure 6.11 The side view is a retinal cross section showing how a bipolar could have excitatory (E) connections to some cones (as on the left) and inhibitory (I) connections to others (on the right) so that no response is possible to whole-field illumination. In this example, light from the page of the book is striking the cones on the left but not the ones on the right because they are receiving the image of the dark table. The edge of the paper is a strong stimulus for this bipolar because it falls exactly along the boundary between the bipolar's excitatory and inhibitory connections.

of the retina. Let us see how a set of synapses might be arranged so that the output cell becomes a contrast detector.

The Circuitry of Contrast Detection   Figure 6.11 pictures a hypothetical edge detector. Notice that the inhibitory synapses are arranged so that they perfectly balance the facilitative synapses. This means that if all receptors are stimulated simultaneously by uniform illumination of the bipolar's entire receptive field, the bipolar does not respond. The inputs are generating as many IPSPs as EPSPs, and the opposing currents cancel out one another. So, this particular bipolar, wired the way it is to the receptors, totally ignores uniform illumination of the sort you would get from a blank white wall. The mere presence of light on its receptive field accomplishes nothing because to stimulate this bipolar the light must contain a pattern. Because this ON-bipolar is a simple edge detector, the pattern is the most basic one imaginable—just a shift from a light area to a dark area such as would come from the cover of a light-colored

book against a dark desk top. The shift from dark to light gives you the edge, or contour, of the book. If the light–dark shift falls at the right place in the receptive field of the bipolar, the cell fires, indicating the presence of a boundary (edge) in the visual field.

Now that you have the idea of how edge information can be detected in the optical image, let's modify our analyzer so that it more closely resembles ones that actually exist in the primate retina. In Figure 6.11 the edge of the book is detected because several rows of receptors are connected to one bipolar with positive connections on one side and negative on the other. Figure 6.12 shows a more realistic model in which the RF is arranged concentrically so that one of the two areas is a circle at the center of the field, and the other is a ring completely surrounding the circle (Dowling, 1979; Grüsser, 1979). This configuration is called a **center–surround receptive field**.

The center–surround organization enables the bipolar to detect (analyze for) regions of contrast in the light falling on the retina. We call the bipolar

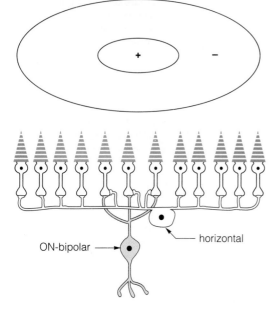

Figure 6.12 ON-bipolar receptive field. The field (seen here from above and at a slant) has the shape of two concentric circles with the center being excitatory (i.e., light on the surround polarizes the bipolar). Under the field is a two-dimensional, schematic view of the cells that create it. The cones in the field's center connect to the bipolar. When they are polarized by light, the bipolar responds (depolarizes). The cones of the surround synapse with the horizontal cell, which depolarizes the center cones, thus inhibiting the bipolar.

neuron in Figure 6.12 a contrast analyzer because it responds only when the light falling on its RF contains areas of contrast. When there is no area of contrast, the cell remains quiet because *all* the receptors have been stimulated, thus activating both facilitative and inhibitory connections. Presumably, the bipolar cell is arranged so that the inhibitory inputs coming from the surround just exactly balance the facilitative inputs of the center bipolars. However, a high-contrast edge (like the edge of a piece of white paper on a dark background) falling in the field so that the center and only part of the surround is illuminated produces a balance favoring facilitation, and the cell fires. Although this concentric shape doesn't seem to be well designed geometrically for fitting straight edges, several rows of such tiny, circular

receptive fields could be wired to another cell to serve as an edge detector. However, we will see that edge analyzers are too complex for the retina and first appear at the level of the cortex. The task of the retina is to analyze for the raw, optical material out of which visual edges are formed, namely, contrast.

■ Our Changing View of the Visual System

Research often runs well ahead of textbooks, and in the case of the visual system, the gap is something in the neighborhood of 15 years. At the end of the 1960s, visual researchers had already begun to upset the classic understanding of the visual brain and to substitute an expanded model that incorporated important brain areas omitted from the previous model. In the 1980s, we have had a veritable eruption of research on the visual cortex from which a third viewpoint is just beginning to emerge. Because most introductory psychology texts still teach the classic visual system of the pre-1970 era, this text presents the up-to-date model only after a brief review of the two older positions.

The Classic Model

Visual research up to 1950 gave us the viewpoint that *the* visual system consisted of the retina and its pathway through the optic nerve, optic chiasm, optic tract, lateral geniculate nucleus (thalamus), and striate cortex (**area 17**) in the occipital lobes (Figure 6.13). It

Figure 6.13 The classic visual system, consisting of retinas, optic nerves, optic chiasm, optic tracts, lateral geniculates, optic radiations (axons of lateral geniculate nucleus neurons), and occipital lobe visual areas. The term *optic nerve* denotes the portion of ganglion cell axons between the retina and chiasm, and the term *optic tract* is given to the parts of those same axons lying between the chiasm and the lateral geniculate nucleus of the thalamus. There is no synapse in the chiasm; it is merely a point at which some axons from each eye cross to the opposite side of the brain. The first synapse outside the retina is in lateral geniculate nucleus, and the next is in striate cortex. (Adapted from Netter, 1962)

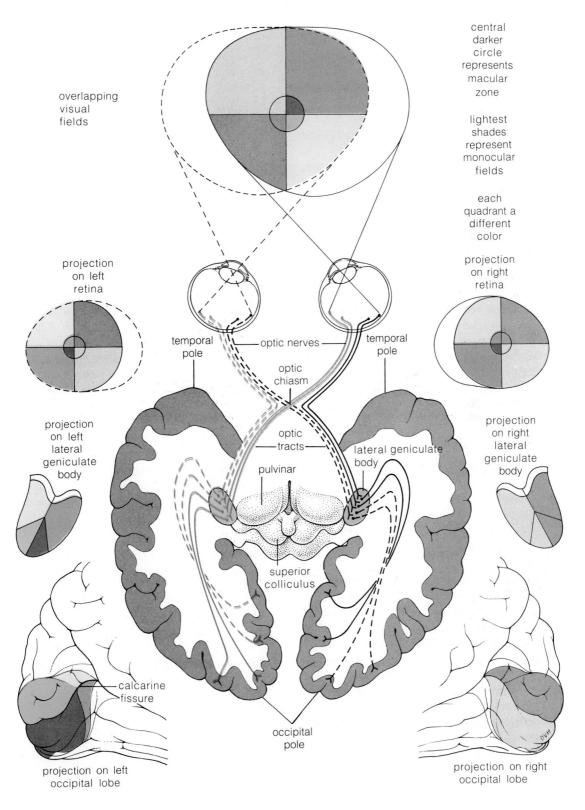

central
darker
circle
represents
macular
zone

lightest
shades
represent
monocular
fields

each
quadrant a
different
color

overlapping
visual
fields

projection
on right
retina

projection
on left
retina

temporal
pole

optic nerves

temporal
pole

optic
chiasm

projection
on left
lateral
geniculate
body

projection
on right
lateral
geniculate
body

optic
tracts

lateral geniculate
body

pulvinar

superior
colliculus

calcarine
fissure

occipital
pole

projection on left
occipital lobe

projection on right
occipital lobe

was known that the retina also sent some optic nerve fibers into the superior colliculus and other brainstem areas but these projections were almost totally ignored by psychologists and regarded as important only for visual reflexes. Conscious perception of the visual world, it was assumed, was entirely a function of the pathway from retina through area 17—the **visual projection system**.

Because clinical reports stated that loss of an area of striate cortex produced a blind spot in the visual field and that complete loss of area 17 in both hemispheres resulted in total blindness, it was generally accepted that conscious visual sensation began in the occipital lobe. Anatomists had found that the striate cortex (area 17) contained a complete representation of the retina such that any two points lying side by side on the retina had two adjacent zones in the cortex. This is because the optic nerve fibers maintain positions relative to one another that mimic the positions of their cell bodies (ganglion cells) in the retina. Thus, neighboring neurons remain grouped together through the thalamus and into the cortex, forming a "map" of the retina in area 17. This point-for-point correspondence between retina and cortex led people to surmise that the function of the retina was to translate the optical (light wave) image into a nerve impulse "image" that the projection system took to the striate cortex to be interpreted as a conscious image of the outside world. This view treated the complex circuitry of the retina as though it didn't exist and relegated the **lateral geniculate nucleus (LGN)** of the thalamus to the role of a relay station that merely passes the image on to the cortex unaltered.

Clinical reports also made note of a peculiar phenomenon called **visual agnosia** that occurred when areas of the occipital cortex just outside of area 17 were damaged. Agnosia victims could see objects and had no trouble with eye–hand coordination, but they often failed to identify or distinguish between various common items. For example, a patient might fail to identify a pair of scissors until they were placed in the hand where they could be perceived by touch. The defect seemed to be less a matter of blindness than of failure to understand what was being sensed. The damage that produces agnosia is in the zones

classified by Brodmann as **area 18** and **area 19** (Figure 6.14). Some psychologists drew the conclusion that area 17 provided raw visual sensations (unidentified color and form), which it then passed on to areas 18 and 19 for the addition of meaning. In other words, whereas area 17 merely sensed, areas 18 and 19 perceived. Where 17 sensed only a collection of colored geometric shapes, 18 and 19 perceived a chair or a face. Anatomists established that areas 18 and 19 (also termed **peristriate cortex**) did indeed receive axons from the striate cortex. Thus, the classic visual system was extended into the forward part of the occipital lobe.

A further development in the 1950s was the discovery that the peristriate cortex projected, in turn, down into the lower portion of the temporal lobe, an area termed the **inferotemporal (IT) cortex** (Figure 6.14). The posterior inferotemporal (PIT) cortex was shown to be important for the ability to discriminate between objects on the basis of some visual dimension such as pattern, shape, size, brightness, and color (Gross et al., 1981). The PIT projects into the anterior inferotemporal (AIT) cortex, which apparently is the last stage of visual processing. For years, the IT area was treated like a sort of appendix to the visual system. Textbooks maintained that visual cortex was in the occipital lobes but added the temporal area as an afterthought. There are still texts that fail to recognize that vision occupies large areas of both parietal and temporal lobes, as well as the entirety of the occipital lobes.

The 1970s Model

During the 1960s, research produced a fundamental remodeling of our understanding of the visual system. By the mid-1970s, everyone knew that the route

Figure 6.14 Cortical areas of the visual system as they were known in 1970. The numbers are for areas proposed decades ago by Brodmann from his study of variations in the six layers of the cortex. The inferotemporal cortex roughly encompasses area 20 and part of area 37. (Adapted from Nieuwenhuys et al., 1981)

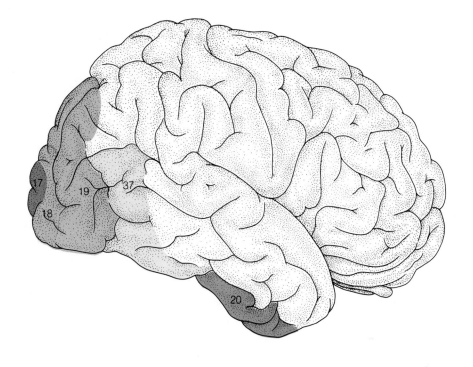

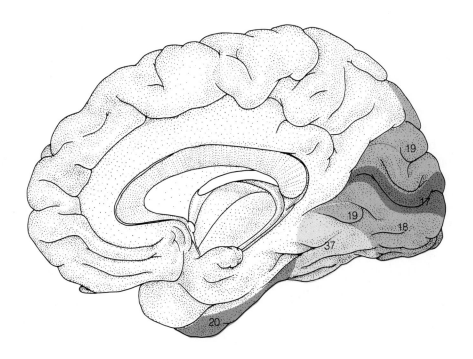

from the retina through LGN to area 17 was not the only visual projection. Most people now pictured the visual system as a dual projection from the retina.

A few researchers became interested in the superior colliculus of the midbrain in the 1960s. Schneider (1967), for example, ran hamsters through a classic series of experiments aimed at finding out more about this neglected part of the brain. After the hamsters had recovered from surgery in which they lost the superior colliculus on both sides, Schneider tested them for vision by holding sunflower seeds an inch or so away at various positions in their visual fields. A normal hamster would immediately approach and take the seed in its mouth; the lesioned hamsters made no response at all unless the seed was held so close that it actually touched one of their whiskers. They appeared to be blind, but were they? The superior colliculus does not lie along the visual projection system from retina to cortex, so that pathway was intact.

To learn more about this, Schneider tested his hamsters in a two-choice visual discrimination apparatus (Figure 6.15) in which the animal had to choose the correct door and push through it to get to a water reinforcer. The only way to tell the correct door was that it had vertical black-and-white stripes on it instead of horizontal stripes—a strictly visual cue. The "blind" hamsters solved the problem with no trouble at all. How could they appear to be blind in the seed test and sighted in the visual discrimination test? Schneider collected a new group of hamsters and removed the visual cortex from each of their brains. He then tested this second group in the same way he had tested the first one and found completely opposite results. The cortex group had no trouble at all in seeing the seeds but found the visual discrimination task nearly impossible.

Schneider interpreted his results to mean that both groups of animals were simultaneously blind and sighted but in different ways. The cortical ablation group were no longer able to identify visual patterns and so could not tell vertical from horizontal stripes, but they still could *locate* objects visually and so were able to orient properly toward the seeds (which they probably knew were present because of odor). The collicular ablation group had lost the brain area devoted to locating objects visually, so

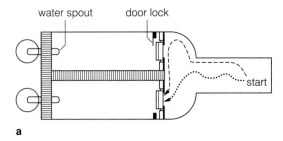

a

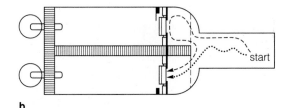

b

Figure 6.15 Two-choice, visual discrimination apparatus used by Schneider in assessing the effects of lesions to the superior colliculus. (**a**) The dotted line indicates the path of a normal hamster who approaches the two doors and then correctly chooses the one with vertical black-and-white stripes (on the animal's left). The hamster with both superior colliculi missing habitually followed a path indicated by the dashed line, always going to the incorrect (locked) door first. This remained the case even after a partition was added to increase the effort required to correct a wrong choice (**b**). (Adapted from Schneider, 1967)

even though they probably could see that sunflower seeds were somewhere nearby, they were unable to tell where and then to turn their heads in that direction. Schneider gave us the first experimental evidence that the superior colliculus operates to locate objects in visual space and to orient the eyes and head toward those objects. The really startling revelation, however, was that two visual processes that seem inextricably tied together could be physically separated within the brain. The colliculus can tell us *where* an object is but not *what* it is, whereas the visual cortex tells us what it is but cannot locate it in space with respect to the body. This was the first hint that the unified visual perception of our environment that we hold in our brains may not be unified at any one place within the brain. Instead, our perception of the visual world may be the product of visual areas scattered throughout the brain. But before we explore that possibility, let's examine a theory that sprang from Schneider's experiment and dozens of others like it.

Trevarthan (1968) proposed the idea of a **dual visual projection system** to take the place of the now-inadequate classic viewpoint. This theory proposes that two pathways simultaneously process the retinal output in parallel with one another: the **geniculostriate path**, specialized for pattern and color vision, and the **retinotectal path**, which has the task of locating objects in visual space and orienting the body toward them. The form and color functions of the geniculostriate path give us the capacity to identify and discriminate between objects; thus it is not surprising that when the pathway is severed we feel that we cannot see anything at all. Theoretically, a person with a cranial gunshot wound who has lost area 17 (but who still has the colliculus) might still retain the capacity to locate objects visually despite a complete lack of conscious form perception.

The clinical literature does have notes in it about occipital patients who seem to be able to detect sudden shifts in illumination or pure movement in the visual field (Weiskrantz, 1975). Furthermore, Weiskrantz removed the striate cortex of monkeys and showed that they were still able to reach for objects in their visual fields, just as Schneider's hamsters did. Pasik and Pasik (1971) produced data that suggest that even form perception of some sort may still be available to monkeys deprived of the striate cortex. All these results imply that people who have been "blinded" by loss of their striate cortex may actually have some visual capability left, which they have not learned how to use. This prompted Poeppel to explore the possibility of training humans with missing striate cortex to locate visually objects that they "couldn't see" (cited in Perenin & Jeannerod, 1979). He found that these subjects were able to reach in the direction of the visual target on enough of the trials that the results could not be explained by chance. Weiskrantz calls this peculiar ability to see without seeing, "blindsight." Although the accuracy of the reaching, with the amount of practice afforded by the experiment, was far from perfect, the patients

definitely showed that their subjective sensation of blindness is not an accurate guide to how much visual capability remains after damage to a part of the visual system.

Why do patients with striate cortex damage claim to be blind when they are still able to visually locate objects in their environment? Perhaps it is because almost all of what we think of as visual experience concerns just two facets of visual function, the shape of objects and their colors. Both shape and color are analyzed by the geniculostriate system, not the retinotectal. Thus, the only conscious visual experience remaining for the patient with no striate cortex would apparently be a colorless, formless "feeling" of where something might be. The patient might easily regard such a peculiar sensory experience as too vague and indefinable to be a real sensation and so just ignore it. Having to rely on this type information gives one the feeling of guessing rather than the sense of certain knowledge.

This "guessing" explanation, however, is probably only part of the story. We must also explain why the patients failed to perform with perfect accuracy. If blindsight is the product of an undamaged retinotectal system, then the imperfect pointing suggests that the superior colliculus, while unharmed, is not functioning perfectly. This indeed should be the case because the colliculus normally receives an important input from the occipital lobes; in patients without area 17, this source of information is missing (Perenin & Jeannerod, 1979).

Blindsight is a phenomenon that would have been a mystery within the framework of the classic view of the visual system but is explainable in terms of Trevarthan's dual-projection theory. That theory also proposes that we possess two types of vision that work in parallel with one another because we have a dual-function retina and a dual-projection system. Recall from our earlier discussion of the retina that the greatest concentration of cones (which are associated with visual acuity and form vision) is in the fovea. Outside of the fovea, rods are mixed in with cones in increasing numbers as one moves toward the periphery of the retina. This change is associated with a decrease in ability of ganglion cells of the region to resolve small spatial details (acuity). The best form vision is available only from the very small central area that is the fovea. In the geniculostriate path, axons from foveal ganglion cells each synapse with many LGN neurons, thus spreading the influence of each ganglion cell over a wide area. This expansion of foveal influence is so great at the level of the striate cortex that each tiny point on the fovea is represented by an entire cortical area. Thus, the geniculostriate system acts like a magnifier for foveal vision.

With these things in mind, Trevarthan postulated two parallel forms of vision: **focal vision**, aimed at the analysis of fine spatial detail in small areas of the visual field, and **ambient vision**, for perceiving "space at large around the body" (Trevarthan, 1968). Focal vision is dependent chiefly on the geniculostriate path, ambient on the retinotectal. When reading the words on this page, you are using focal vision; as long as your attention is focused on the print, your foveal retina and geniculostriate path dominate the processing in your visual system. But, should a friend walk up to your desk, you detect his approach "out of the corner of your eye" with ambient vision from the peripheral retina and retinotectal path. The perception produced by ambient vision may not be precise enough to identify the person because facial recognition is just another form of pattern or form perception, and that is the function of focal vision. The solution to this identification problem is so unconscious and reflexive that you are only vaguely aware that it occurs. The retinotectal projection informs the colliculus that a new object has entered your visual field from the side, and the task of the colliculus then is to provide directional information to the eye- and head-movement circuits so that you can look up at your friend's face. The purpose of looking up, of course, is to shift from ambient vision to focal vision. Spread across the surface of the colliculus is a functional "map" of the retina that is used to calculate exactly what eye and head movements are required to bring the image of your friend's face directly onto the foveas of your retinas. The task of ambient vision then is to maintain a low-level "background" awareness of the world around the point in space to which you are directing the bulk of your attention. Whenever something of interest occurs outside of foveal vision, the ambient system can repo-

sition the foveas for a fine-grain analysis of this new phenomenon.

The dual-projection model of the visual system gave us a much more complete and sophisticated understanding of how the brain produces our visual, perceptual world, but it was only another step along the road toward a final, complete theory of vision. There were still many visual areas of the brain not encompassed by Trevarthan's theory, and its view of the geniculostriate path treated that route as a single system, an idea that fails to explain more recent findings. An extension of Trevarthan's model could now be made in which the visual system is viewed as a multiple set of parallel processing pathways.

■ The Visual System in the 1980s: Parallel Processing Pathways

Trevarthan never claimed that focal vision was *exclusively* the function of the geniculostriate path while the retinotectal handled *only* ambient vision. The research of the 1970s failed to find any such easily understood division of labor. Instead, both pathways seem to be composed of a collection of subpathways, each of which processes the output of retinal ganglion cells in a somewhat different fashion in order to extract different kinds of information. Besides its main role in detecting patterns, the geniculostriate seems capable of a limited sort of spatial–ambient type of analysis; the retinotectal path, chiefly a spatial location specialist, may also have a crude capability for extracting information about form and shape. These parallel processing paths within each major pathway were discovered through careful study of retinal ganglion cells.

Parallel Paths Within the Geniculostriate System

Two different types of retinal ganglion cells, **Y cells** and **X cells**, have been definitely defined in the retina of the cat. Y cells have larger RFs, and X cells have smaller RFs. Y-cell RFs are located away from the center of the retina, with the largest fields being in the extreme periphery. X-cell fields are concentrated toward the center. Apparently, X cells are the ones sensitive to the fine-pattern details of the visual image (Ikeda, 1979), and this idea goes together with their central location and small fields. Y cells, on the other hand, are best equipped to respond to the larger, broader outlines of forms (Sherman, 1979). In the primate retina there are ganglion cells that have much in common with the X and Y cells of the cat. Sherman and co-workers (1976) present data supporting the generalization of the division to primates, and we will adopt their viewpoint. As you read this print, you probably are depending on mainly X cells in and around your fovea. When your attention broadens out from that narrow focus to take in the shape of the whole page and other objects on your desk, then Y cells are dominant.

The X–Y division does not stop at the retina but continues right on up through the LGN, where the two cell types are organized into separate layers (Friedlander & Sherman, 1981) and on into the striate cortex (Weller & Kaas, 1981). Thus, there are at least two parallel processing paths within the geniculostriate system—an X-cell path that is apparently the basis of focal vision and a Y-cell path that is designed more for ambient vision. The retinotectal path also contains X and Y axons, but as you might suspect, there are far more Y cells in this pathway. Correspondingly, more retinal X cells project into the geniculate (Stone, 1983). Judging from this, the geniculostriate path should be more important to focal vision and the retinotectal more important to ambient vision, just as Trevarthan's theory suggests. Data on ganglion cell types seem to agree with the behavioral work of Schneider described earlier.

The focal–ambient division appears to be represented in geniculate anatomy. The primate LGN is divided into layers of cells. The more dorsal layers contain small neurons and are termed **parvocellular,** whereas the large-celled ventral layers are called **magnocellular** (Shapley & Lennie, 1985). Y cells terminate in the magnocellular layers, X cells in the parvocellular. We will put this distinction to work when we discuss the visual cortex.

Parallel Paths Outside the Geniculostriate System

The dual-projection theory concentrates its attention on pathways that end in the cerebral cortex and ignores the fact that much important visual processing takes place at a subcortical level.

The superior colliculus projects to the thalamus and thus indirectly to the visual parts of the cortex. This means that there are two pathways from the retina to the visual cortex, each delivering a different type of visual information. The key structure in the collicular path is the thalamic nucleus called the **pulvinar**. From the pulvinar, visual location information is sent to the frontal eye fields of the frontal lobes, to the IT cortex, and to areas 17 and 18 (see the flowchart of the visual system in Figure 6.16). The **frontal eye fields (FEF)** direct eye movements, just as do the brain stem visual nuclei. However, this is not a duplication of function because it allows the higher cognitive functions of the cortex to have a say in choosing the objects at which we direct our gaze. Without FEF all our eye movements would be controlled reflexively. Researchers have become quite interested in the projection from colliculus to cortex by way of the pulvinar. To recognize this bit of progress, let us rename the retinotectal path, the **tectopulvinar pathway**. Now you can begin to see how limited was the understanding of vision based on the classic view, which entirely failed to recognize the existence of a second major projection from the retina to the cortex, equal in importance to the originally known geniculostriate path. Even Trevarthan's dual-projection theory ignores the multiplicity of subcortical visual pathways, each using visual input to achieve some different, limited goal. The geniculostriate system itself can now be thought of as a collection of parallel processing paths (X, Y, and others) rather than a single path. It is clear that we need to revise our model of the visual system to see it as a collection of **multiple parallel processing pathways**.

Why So Many Parallel Pathways?

No one can be sure about the origins of vision in the course of evolution, but the study of today's more

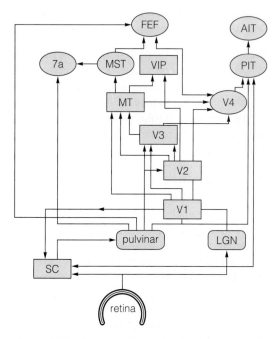

Figure 6.16 Flowchart of the major structures and cortical analyzer areas of the primate visual system. Rectangles represent clearly identified areas with established borders; ovals indicate less well-established areas. (AIT = anterior inferotemporal, FEF = frontal eye fields, LGN = lateral geniculate nucleus, MST = medial superior temporal, MT = middle temporal, PIT = posterior inferotemporal, VIP = ventral inferior parietal.) (Adapted from Van Essen, 1985)

primitive animals suggests that the whole elaborate collection of abilities began millions of years ago in some simple marine animal as a patch of light-sensitive cells that provided only a light versus dark discrimination. This newfound sensory capacity must have proved very handy for animals that needed to be in one ocean depth during the day and another at night (as is the case with some marine species in our age). Later, connections must have grown from sensors to avoidance circuits so that the shadow of a large predator approaching from above would trigger an escape response. Presumably, abilities such as these were gradually added one by one over the eons, eventually producing the huge "grab bag" of visual analyzers that we find in the primate nervous

system. Perhaps the most realistic model of the visual system might be that of a network of analyzers ranging from those in the retina that extract simple boundary information up to those in the cortex that can recognize faces.

Cortical Analyzers of the Primate Visual System

In primates the visual sense has evolved to such a high degree that most visual processors are located in the cortex. In humans cortical visual analysis occupies the occipital lobes, some of the posterior parietal cortex, and much of the IT cortex. We have only just begun to map this region in monkeys and have already located at least 15 separate analyzers (Figure 6.16). The labels for various areas have changed in recent years. Area 17 goes by the name **V1**, area 18 is **V2**, and area 19 is **V3** and **V4**. Be sure that you trace out the classic geniculostriate path from the retina through the LGN to area 17 (V1) in Figure 6.16 and note what a tiny portion of the whole system it represents. In the 1950s, that path plus V2 and V3 were considered to be the entire visual system. Also note that the tectopulvinar route projects to the frontal, parietal, and temporal lobes. The fact that a route exists between pulvinar and V1 suggests that the superior colliculus plays a part in determining the RFs and response characteristics of the neurons there, but what its effect might be remains to be discovered.

V1 appears to be the first processor in a whole chain of cortical visual areas, with each one extracting one or two more bits of visual information to add to the stream that is passed on to the next analyzer (summarized in Ashford & Fuster, 1985). Each analyzer represents another fragmental visual ability in that immense collection of abilities that we term *vision*. Information tends to flow through this network in a direction that is away from the earliest and simplest levels of processing in the occipital lobe and toward the later, more sophisticated levels in parietal and temporal lobes.

Mishkin, a leading theorist, proposes that there are two major pathways that relate to two important

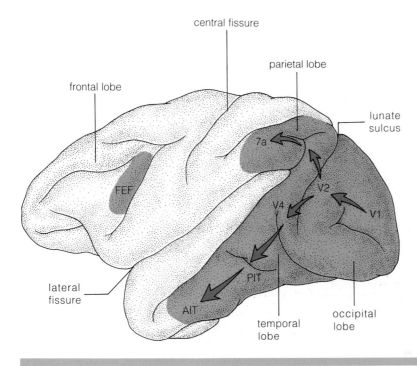

Figure 6.17 Diagram of macaque monkey brain showing the object and spatial vision paths. Shaded parts are primarily visual. Area V3 is hidden inside the lunate sulcus. (AIT = anterior inferotemporal cortex, PIT = posterior inferotemporal cortex, FEF = frontal eye fields.) (Adapted from Mishkin et al., 1983)

aspects of visual experience (Mishkin et al., 1983; Ungerleider & Mishkin, 1982). The first path leads from the LGN through V1, V2, V3, V4, PIT to the AIT (Figure 6.17). Because this series of analyzers extracts information about color and form, Mishkin calls this the **object vision pathway**. Another route ends instead in the parietal lobe and analyzes for the location of the stimulus in space and its movements through space. Mishkin refers to this route as the **spatial vision pathway**. Although Mishkin has accumulated some evidence to the contrary (Mishkin & Ungerleider, 1982), it still seems likely from an evolutionary standpoint that this path should begin in the superior colliculus, which unquestionably is the oldest structure having to do with locating objects in space around the body. The main route would be superior colliculus through pulvinar to V2 and V3, MT, MST, and 7a, but the cortical areas would undoubtedly also use information from V1, as Mishkin suggests in his theory.

Although Mishkin did not explicitly propose the idea, his object vision route appears to be a contin-

uation of the focal vision pathway that begins with the X cells of the retina and continues through the parvocellular layers of LGN to V1. The spatial vision route continues the ambient vision pathway from the retinal Y cells through the magnocellular LGN layers to V1. We will now trace these two chains of analyzers, starting with the object vision pathway.

The Object Vision Pathway

Analyzers of the object vision pathway extract chiefly three types of information: shape, depth, and color. These are the factors that allow us to *recognize* the objects we view (as opposed to perceiving their location).

The Pioneering Work: Hubel and Wiesel In 1981 the Nobel Prize in physiology went to David Hubel and Torsten Wiesel, a pair of researchers whose pioneering efforts led to the idea of neural analyzers. Their experiments in the 1960s were among the first microelectrode studies of cortical neurons, and they

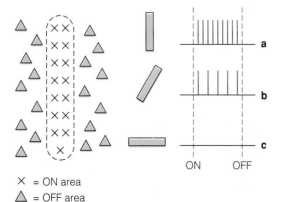

X = ON area

△ = OFF area

Figure 6.18 The receptive field (left) and the response characteristics (right) of one type of V1 simple cell (line-orientation detector). Triangles denote areas of the receptive field in which a spot of light produced an inhibitory response (reduced firing); ×'s mark positive responses (increased firing). The letters **a**, **b**, and **c** each indicate the number of impulses (vertical lines) induced by the presentation of a bar of light in one of three orientations. (Adapted from Hubel & Wiesel, 1959, in Goldstein, 1989)

completely overturned several earlier assumptions about the visual cortex. In a typical experiment, the subject (usually a cat) was anesthetized and arranged in a headholder so that the eyes were pointed toward a stimulus screen. Patterns would be moved across the screen at various rates and in different directions while the experimenters listened for any change in activity in the neuron at the electrode tip. After discovering what stimulus would evoke activity in the cell, the electrode would be pushed farther into the cortex until a new nerve cell was contacted; then the testing process would be repeated.

Figure 6.18 shows the sort of data obtained by Hubel and Wiesel in their early experiments. One of the first things that they established was that visual cortex neurons, like retinal and geniculate cells, have RFs on the retina. Recall that no matter where in the brain the neuron is located, its RF is the area of retina (or visual image) within which it can be fired by an appropriate stimulus light. In the left column of Figure 6.18, the results of 33 separate stimulations with spots of light are displayed. X's mark the places in

the field where light increased the firing of the neuron, and triangles denote inhibition of base-level firing by the stimulus. Just as in the retina and LGN, the RF is divided into an excitatory zone and one or more inhibitory zones. However, rather than a center–surround organization, these V1 cells have an excitatory zone shaped to detect a straight line of light. If a spot is enlarged until it entirely fills the field, it produces no response at all.

Some of these cells had inhibitory center strips with excitatory zones on either side and seemed to be detectors of dark lines. When Hubel and Wiesel shifted to using lines and edges as stimuli, they found that the cell would respond maximally only when a line of light was oriented at the certain angle on the retina so that it fell within the excitatory zone (Figure 6.18). When the bar was rotated to any other angle, much of it fell outside of the excitatory zone, and the firing rate declined. The neuron in Figure 6.18 is set to detect vertical lines and ignore any orientation that doesn't at least approximate this ideal. Other cells react best to other orientations. In fact, every possible bar position through 180° of rotation is represented by a cortical cell "tuned" to that orientation. Apparently, area 17 contains analyzers for linear edges at particular orientations. The concentric, center–surround RFs of the retina and geniculate have somehow been combined into elongated fields of cells that might be called line detectors, or **line-orientation analyzers.**

In 1962, the fact that neurons could possess such selectivity came as an astounding revelation. The classic view of the visual system still prevailed, and most neuroscientists assumed that the retina passed the visual image on to the cortex in the form of a picture composed of nerve impulse "dots" separated by "white spaces" where there were no active neurons. All neurons in area 17 were thought to be functionally the same—one homogeneous mass of cells waiting for the impulse "image" to be impressed on them. Now Hubel and Wiesel had found that each visual cortex neuron "looked" at its own particular area of the visual field (its RF) and responded only to a particular stimulus (either an edge, a light bar, or a dark bar), which had to be in a particular orientation (Barlow, 1982). Several theories of visual perception that treated all area 17 neurons as having

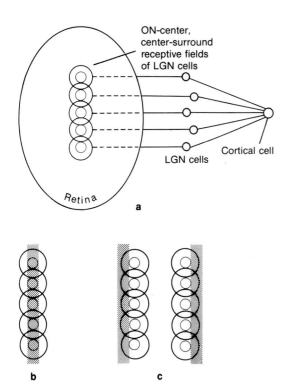

ON-center, center-surround receptive fields of LGN cells

LGN cells

Cortical cell

Retina

a

b

c

Figure 6.19 Possible "wiring diagram" for a V1 simple cell. (**a**) Five ganglion cells with ON-centers arranged in a straight-line connection through LGN to a single cortical neuron. (**b**) Because of these connections, the simple cell fires when a bar falls across the ON-centers of ganglion cell RFs. Light from the bar also falls on portions of the inhibitory surrounds but fails to produce enough inhibition in ganglion cells to overcome the excitation from the centers. (**c**) If the bar is positioned to one side or the other, only inhibitory areas are stimulated, and the V1 cell remains unstimulated. Thus, it is set to detect a bar of light in a particular orientation at a particular place on the retina. (From Hubel & Wiesel, 1962, in Goldstein, 1984)

identical properties died overnight. (In fact, I was new to teaching physiological psychology when their first article appeared and had to tear up 3 hours worth of brand new lecture notes and write completely new ones.)

What sort of "wiring diagram" might produce these area 17, line-orientation analyzers? Figure 6.19 reveals one possible arrangement that could explain both the shape of the effective stimulus (a line versus

a spot) and the orientation selectivity. Notice that the particular ganglion cells that synapse with the pictured cortical neuron have neighboring RFs that fall along a straight line on the retina. Thus, if a line of light were oriented at the correct angle on the retina and moved so that it fell on all the ON-centers of these ganglion cells, the cortical neuron would receive the maximal possible input. Presumably, if the stimulus shifted to the right or left so that it no longer fell on the centers of these fields, it would instead fall on the centers of another string of ganglion-cell RFs that feed a different cortical neuron. Thus, area 17 can not only detect an edge in the visual field but also can tell where the edge is by which cortical cells respond. As a line is moved across the retina, activity in the cortex shifts from cell to cell. Hubel and Wiesel named this type of cell the **simple cortical neuron**. In summary, it detects entire edges or lines (rather than just spots of contrast) in particular orientations at particular places within the visual field.

Although it is important to have cells that signal where the edge is located in the visual field, there is a price to pay for this bit of information. Consider the problem of visually identifying some shape such as the letter **A**. Obviously, at least three types of simple cells will be needed for the perception of this stimulus: one for the horizontal line and one each for the two angled arms of the **A**. This pattern of simple-cell activity could only be evoked by this particular stimulus; thus, it comes to represent that stimulus. Presumably, it is the neural representation, the engram, of the letter. Recognition occurs whenever that pattern becomes active again. In other words, if you are exposed to a stimulus at some later time that evokes activity in those three cells, then you will say, "I recognize that letter. It's an **A**."

The problem with this notion is that to evoke activity in exactly those three cells and no others the stimulus **A** must be positioned exactly within their RFs. The moment you move your eyes even a fraction of a millimeter, the image shifts on the retina, and the edges of the **A** fall within the RFs of different cortical simple cells. It would seem that an engram constructed of simple cells is not such a good idea because what we need is a group of cells (a pattern of firing) that responds to the **A** no matter where it is placed in the visual field. This is the problem of **transposition**. We need to be able to transpose the stimulus from one place to another within the field and still be able to recognize it. Fortunately, there is another type of neuron within area 17 that meets this requirement admirably. Hubel and Wiesel called it the **complex cortical neuron.**

If one moves an edge into the RF of a complex cell, it begins to respond and keeps right on firing no matter where the edge is shifted, so long as it stays within the RF and maintains the particular angle of orientation to which this cell is tuned. As with simple cells, there are complex cells for every possible angle of orientation from 0° to 180° (Hubel & Wiesel, 1962). Area 17, then, contains output cells for at least two different visual analyzers. Complex cells can form the part of the engram that represents a stimulus no matter where it is in a large area of the visual field, and simple cells can probably locate the stimulus with respect to neighboring stimulus patterns. Each analyzer has something to contribute to the overall pattern of information that the nervous system is generating from the visual image. This is the way our visual system "sees" the outside world. It is definitely not like "taking a picture" of a scene. Instead, it is a matter of multiple analyzers extracting dozens of bits and pieces of visual information (edge, angle of edge, location, degree of contrast, color, etc.) and assembling them into a perception that is uniquely human.

You may be wondering what method complex cells use to overcome the problem of transposition; what is their "wiring diagram"? Figure 6.20 illustrates the scheme proposed by Hubel and Wiesel to explain this property (Hubel, 1963). If each complex cell receives input from a whole row of simple cells, then its RF is the sum of all their RFs, and it can respond to a properly oriented edge anywhere within that field. This idea also explains the fact that complex-cell RFs are considerably larger than simple-cell fields.

Form Analysis The edge analyzers of V1 (simple and complex) form the basis for the perception of shapes and forms. It is well established that these cells pass their output to V2, which extracts more information and passes that onto V3. Few data are

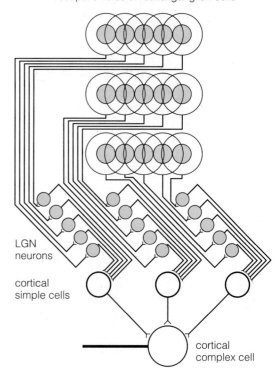

receptive fields of retinal ganglion cells

LGN neurons

cortical simple cells

cortical complex cell

Figure 6.20 "Wiring diagram" for a cortical complex cell. Ganglion cells are represented by their RFs. All ganglion cells with RFs in a row project through LGN to the same cortical simple cell. Because all three simple cells project to the same complex cell, a line of light that is correctly oriented for one simple cell can be moved over to the field of the next simple cell, and the same complex cell will still be activated. In other words, the image can be transposed across the retina.

yet available on exactly what V2 and V3 do with their input, although we know that it has something to do with obtaining more information about form, color, depth, and, perhaps, motion (Van Essen, 1985). One thing that is certain is that V2 cells (at least, in the cat) are more specific than V1 cells in that they won't respond to just any properly oriented edge. Instead, the edge must end at some particular point (Hubel & Wiesel, 1965a). This could be the basis for perceiving corners. This doesn't seem like much of a gain over the output of V1, but corners are a vital part of perceiving the world truthfully.

Consider for a moment what this implies. There is an enormous number of such stimulus dimensions present in the scene that you are now viewing—angles, edges, corners, curves, line orientations, depth, color, and more—and consider that each perception has been obtained for your use by the laborious process of evolving a separate set of cortical neurons with just the right set of input connections to give you that tiny, additional bit of visual information. If this line of thinking is correct, we must then have hundreds of separate visual analyzers. It is easy to see why these analyzers occupy the entire posterior end of the cerebrum and why it required millions of years of evolution to assemble this phenomenal biological computer.

As you can see from the flowchart in Figure 6.16, V3 passes its analysis on to V4, and V4 feeds the IT cortex. We have known since the 1950s that the IT cortex was involved in the ability to discriminate between different shapes visually (Mishkin, 1966). Apparently, by the time the processing reaches this very high level in the visual hierarchy, enough bits of information have been extracted that whole forms can now be identified and discriminated from one another.

Iwai and Mishkin (1968) realized that this zone was really too large to be involved in just one stage of visual processing and set out to see if they couldn't find more than one function located there. A series of ablation experiments in monkeys revealed that the PIT cortex was involved more with the perception of forms (lesions there hurt the learning of visual discriminations), while the AIT cortex seemed to be more related to visual memory. A typical visual memory test would be the **delayed match-to-nonsample task** in which the monkey first views an object for a few seconds, waits through a short delay, and is then shown two objects, each of which covers a shallow hole. One of the two objects is new, and the other is the original one. The monkey's task is to choose the new object by moving it off the hole and removing the food placed there. This is an easy task if there is no delay between the experience of viewing the original object and the choice situation with the two objects. Adding a few seconds of delay makes it much more difficult. Monkeys with AIT lesions can visually discriminate between the two choice objects by

using the intact PIT cortex, but they have trouble with remembering which of the two choice objects they saw before if the delay is even as short as one minute.

Using the microelectrode technique in the IT cortex has provided us with a more detailed idea of how those analyzers function. As you might expect from neurons receiving input from so many downstream visual analyzers, these cells often have very sophisticated properties. For example, Fuster and Jervey (1981) found some IT neurons that would respond selectively to the color green, but only after green had been used for a number of trials as a cue that food would appear if a particular response were made. On trials requiring a different response, IT cells ignored the green stimulus. Now that is a fairly "smart" neuron!

After Hubel and Wiesel's discoveries, some people began to reason that if each step of the visual hierarchy of analyzers added another feature or two and then passed its information on to the next highest level, then the IT cortex might be the end of the sequence—the place where each cell received enough highly processed input to enable it to respond selectively to an entire shape or object. Scientists joked about no one yet having discovered a "grandmother cell," the hypothetical neuron that would fire only when exposed to the sight of your grandmother's face. Is this, indeed, the way in which the visual system works? Are we able to recognize all objects with which we have had past experience because the learned connections created a specific cell for each object?

Desimone and colleagues (1984) went searching for stimuli that would excite neurons in the IT area. Because they were using macaque monkeys as subjects, they chose a number of three-dimensional plastic objects, most of which might have special significance to a monkey: a fur-covered monkey doll, a red apple, a yellow banana, a human head and hand, a coiled black snake, a yellow flower, a large black spider, and a variety of colored brushes. Many cells would respond energetically to a stimulus such as the apple only to disappoint the experimenters by responding just as well to the snake, hand, flower, and scrub brushes. In other words, although the cells seemed to be tuned to objects in general, they cer-

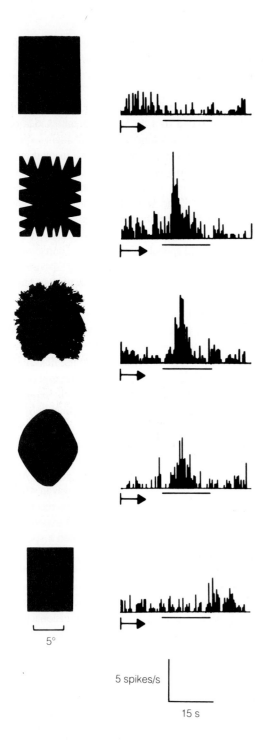

Figure 6.21 Response histograms for one neuron of the IT cortex. The stimuli to which it was exposed are shown down the left side of the figure, and its rate of firing is indicated to the right. Each of the five histograms has time along the horizontal axis and number of impulses per time segment along the vertical. Segments were slightly less than 1 second each. Under each histogram is a time line showing when the stimulus was present. The calibration lines at the bottom of the figure indicate that each stimulus was present for more than 15 seconds. (Adapted from Desimone et al., 1984)

tainly weren't designed to identify particular objects. Desimone reasoned that they must be responding to some stimulus characteristic present in most of the stimulus objects, and a variety of two-dimensional patterns were tried in an effort to discover the feature that the cell was detecting. Little came of this, however, except to find that some cells did have a slight preference for irregular edges or boundaries with particular irregularities.

Figure 6.21 shows the behavior of one of these cells. Notice that this particular neuron seems to be a bit inhibited by a black rectangle but responds beautifully to the same shape with ragged edges. It does just as well to the silhouette of a brush but "loses interest" when the irregular edges are smoothed off. It seems to be broadly tuned for irregular edges, but how this might fit into the overall scheme for producing a complete perception is not readily apparent.

Desimone concluded from the survey of 151 neurons that the IT cortex was not organized to produce object-specific neurons ("grandmother cells") and that the complete perception of a visual scene must be the product of simultaneous activity in a great many cells in most of the analyzer areas of the visual system. Presumably then, a visual object is recognized when a specific *pattern* of neurons, as opposed to a single cell, becomes active. This pattern would constitute the engram (memory) of that object.

There was, however, one other finding from that same study that constituted a dramatic exception to the rest of the valuable but unexciting revelations. A small area within the superior temporal sulcus was located in which were found a special class of neu-

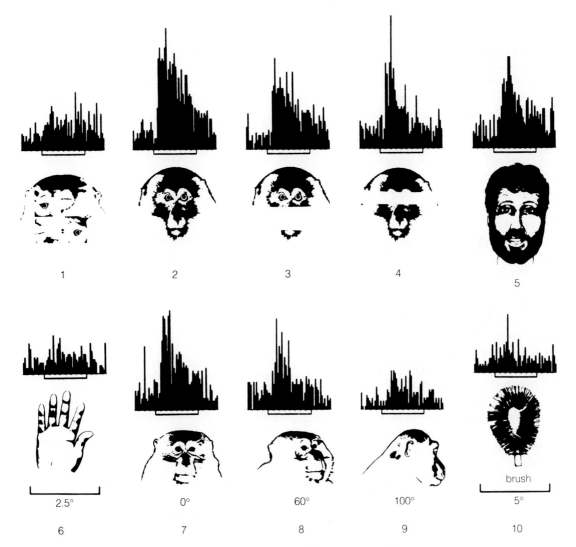

Figure 6.22 Responses of single IT neurons to pictures of faces. Ten stimuli are shown, and above each is a response histogram that shows the number of impulses the cell emitted before, during, and after the stimulus was presented. The horizontal bar under each histogram indicates the 2.5 seconds during which the stimulus was available. Each vertical bar in the histogram shows the number of impulses for one fraction of a second. The cell responded poorly to a "face" with scrambled features. Omission of eyes or mouth weakened but did not eliminate the response. A human face received a moderate response, but the cell largely ignored nonface stimuli. This was a full-front face neuron (0°) because it responded well to a frontal view, weakly to a 60° view, and poorly to a 100° view. (Adapted from Desimone et al., 1984)

rons that did indeed possess the sought-for object specificity. Figure 6.22 shows the response histograms for a neuron that was selectively sensitive to faces. When a picture of a macaque is moved across

the receptive field of the neuron, it responds very well. As a control test, the picture was cut up and reassembled in such a way that the general outline remained the same but the internal contours of eyes, mouth, and nose were scrambled. As you can see in the first two histograms, the neuron could tell a real face from a scrambled one. Removing parts of the face removed some of the firing, and no particular part of the face seemed to be any more important than any other. This neuron also seems to be specific to a full-face, frontal view so that when the stimulus head is rotated to a side view, the cell gradually loses its responsiveness. The most fascinating aspect of its behavior, however, is that the cell responds so well to a human face. Compare the picture of the human face with that of the macaque, and try to view them as an artist would—as a collection of objective lines and shadows. The overall shape is different, the eyes have very little in common as geometric forms, and the noses are so different that the only thing they have in common is their central location. This cell seems not to be responding to the actual geometric lines, curves, and angles but rather to eyes and face as *concepts*. These **face cells** seem to be able to generalize their responding to a wide variety of different stimulus shapes as long as all of them are very specifically faces.

Desimone and colleagues (1984) also found one other type of object-specific cell, a **hand cell**. This gives rise to an inevitable question. Why should hands and face, as visual objects, be exceptions to the apparent rule of organization in the visual brain that requires whole assemblages of neurons to recognize objects? Why should it take a collection of many neurons to recognize a house or car when only a single cell is needed to detect a face? Desimone reasons that hands and faces are unique stimulus objects to primates and that their immense importance in communication (perhaps, especially between mother and infant) has led to a genetic predisposition to develop these particular synaptic connections.

Binocularity and Stereopsis You have two eyes but only one perceptual world in your mind. Somewhere in your visual system the outputs from the two retinas must be melded. V1 seems to be that place; there is no interaction between the streams of information from the two eyes until those streams reach the cortex. Hubel and Wiesel (1965b) used microelectrode recordings to find out whether single visual cortex neurons received input from one

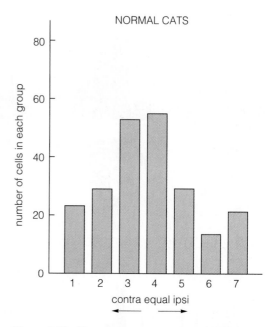

Figure 6.23 Histogram showing Hubel and Wiesel's seven categories of ocular dominance and the proportion of V1 cells found in each category. A score of 1 indicates strong dominance by the contralateral (opposite side) eye; 7 means the cell is controlled by the ipsilateral (same side) eye. Many cells have degrees of dominance between these two extremes. For example, a cell scoring 2 would show a strong response to the contralateral eye and a weak but measurable response to the ipsilateral. A 4 indicates equal responsiveness to either eye (no dominance). (Adapted from Barlow, 1982)

eye or both eyes. They discovered that a small percentage is dominated exclusively by either right or left eye but that most are **binocular** (i.e., receive from both eyes). Some binocular cells are equally responsive to stimuli in both eyes, but most seem to be more strongly connected to one or the other eye—an arrangement that Hubel and Wiesel term **ocular dominance**. This creates a whole spectrum of cell types, based on how much they are dominated by a particular eye, which Hubel and Wiesel divide into seven categories (Figure 6.23).

Among binocular cells, most have the same type of RF in both eyes (i.e., responds to the same type of edge in the same orientation). Furthermore, the right-eye RFs are in roughly the same part of the

a

b

Figure 6.24 Your two eyes capture slightly different images from the same scene because of the distance between them. (**a**) This picture shows what the left eye sees; (**b**) this picture shows the right-eye image. Notice the difference in the distance between the bottles. (Adapted from Sekuler & Blake, 1985)

visual field as the left-eye RFs. These facts hint that these neurons are a part of the analyzer for stereopsis, one of the most important visual capacities possessed by primates.

Primates, unlike many other animals such as rabbits and birds, have both eyes set relatively close together in the front of their heads. This arrangement sacrifices a survival ability of great importance to many species—a wide field of view. The rabbit has a field of view extending nearly 300° around its head. It can crouch in the grass and scan its entire environment for minutes with only the smallest of head movements. By contrast, we primates have only about 180° in our visual fields. Different survival needs produce different sensory abilities, and the rabbit's constant need to watch for predators accounts for its eye placement. Primates, on the other hand, originated in the trees and prospered by traveling from branch to branch high above the most dangerous of their enemies. Yet a wide field of vision

would be a very handy thing to have, even in the trees. Why did primates fail to evolve this capacity?

This question might almost answer itself if we turned it around. Could a rabbit, suitably equipped with monkey arms, hands, and tail, prosper in the tree tops, safely out of reach of its predators? Emphatically, no. The first time such a "tree rabbit" leaped out to grab the next branch it would find itself plunging ignobly to the forest floor. Our remodeled rabbit would still lack a visual ability vital to survival when swinging hand-over-hand through the trees. It wouldn't have stereoscopic depth perception—something that is available only if the eyes are positioned at the front of the head so that the two visual fields have almost complete overlap.

Stereoscopic depth perception (usually called **stereopsis**) refers to three-dimensional (*stereo*) vision (*opsis*), and it arises because the two retinal images aren't exactly alike. Each eye sees the same view from a slightly different angle (Figure 6.24).

This leads to a question that you should consider for a moment: Do you often experience "double vision"? That is, do you frequently see two images of objects within your field of view? If you have normal vision the answer is, Yes, almost all the time. When we noted earlier that you have a single perceptual view despite having two eyes, we weren't quite telling the truth. Your two eyes do give you a single image of whatever you are fixating on, but many other objects outside the area of fixation come out as double images. You tend not to notice this unless your attention is called to it because you automatically fixate on whatever is commanding your attention, and whatever is fixated produces only a single image. Why is this the case?

Take a moment from your reading to try this demonstration. Hold your finger up at arm's length from your eyes and fixate on it. Then slowly move the finger closer to your nose, while maintaining your fixation on it. Notice that your eyes must rotate toward one another to keep the fixation, a movement called **convergence**. Move your finger away from your face while fixating on it, and you get the opposite set of eye movements, divergence. When you look at something at least 30 feet distant, your eyes have diverged so much that their lines of sight are parallel with one another, and the two retinal images are essentially identical. There is no stereopsis beyond 30 feet. Now look at Figure 6.25. In **a** the two eyes are converging on a cup, which means that

Figure 6.25 Binocular disparity produces double images. (**a**) The eyes are fixated on the cup so its image falls on the fovea (f) of each eye. The two circles with cups represent the retinal images, and the oval indicates the conscious experience. The two cup images fuse because they come from corresponding places on the retina. (**b**) Convergence is again centered on the cup so the light from the bottle must fall on noncorresponding retinal points. Point X in the right retina corresponds to point X in the left retina. The same is true of the two Y points. The bottle image falls on Y in the left eye and X in the right. Thus, in the left-eye image, the bottle is to the right of the cup, but in the right-eye image it is to the left. This produces a double image in conscious experience.

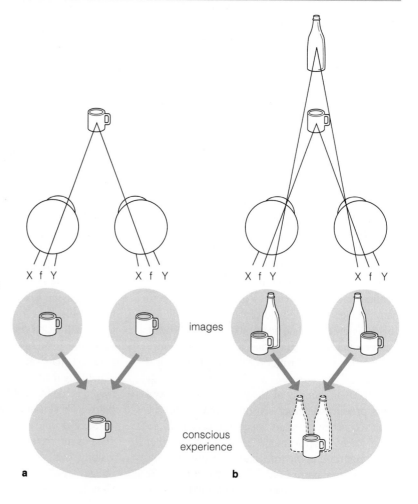

the image of the cup will be centered on the fovea of each eye. Two other reference points are marked in each retina. Point X in the left eye corresponds exactly to point X in the right eye, and the same is true for the two Y points. The two foveas, of course, are also corresponding points on the two retinas. To get just one conscious image of an object, the light image must fall on corresponding points. Because the cup falls on the foveas, there will be only one conscious image of it, but what about the bottle behind it on the table? In **b** it is evident that as long as the cup is fixated, light rays coming from the bottle will fall on *noncorresponding* points on the retina. In the left eye, the bottle's image falls on point Y, in the right eye it falls on X. This difference in the location of the image (in this example, the distance from point X to point Y) is called **retinal disparity**, and it is disparity that the brain uses to calculate the distance from the eye to the object. Before we see how disparity is used to produce stereopsis, however, let's look at what disparity does to retinal and conscious images.

Figure 6.25 shows you that the image of the cup is located on corresponding points on the retina (the fovea in this case) so that the right-eye image fuses with the left-eye image and in conscious experience you see only one cup. Because the bottle falls on noncorresponding points and produces images at two different locations, you consciously experience two images of the bottle—double vision! To demonstrate this for yourself, hold the index finger of each hand up in front of your face with the right hand about 1 foot in front of your nose and the left hand right behind the right but about 1 foot farther out. Now fixate on the nearer finger. As your eyes converge on the near finger, note that you now see two images of the far finger.

Now let's take the idea of disparity one step further. Shift your fixation from the near to the far finger and see what happens to the image of the near finger. Again, you get double images. Figure 6.26 shows that exactly the same rules apply. The only difference is that double images come out on opposite sides from our first example because, in this case, the bottle is on the near side of the cup, whereas in the first example it was on the far side of the cup. Hence, we have two kinds of disparity: **near disparity** and **far**

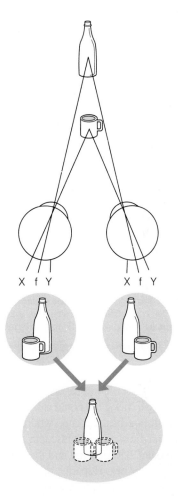

Figure 6.26 An example of near disparity. Because the eyes are focused on the bottle, light from the cup falls on noncorresponding points on the retina, thus producing a double image of the cup. This is near disparity rather than far disparity because the object yielding the disparate images is nearer to the eye than the fixation point.

disparity. What this means is that you see a double image of every object in your visual field except for the few that fall on corresponding points of the retina.

Now to return to stereopsis. If the bottle is behind the cup, there is a certain amount of disparity between its two image locations on the two retinas. If the bottle is brought forward, closer to the cup, the two images slide across the retinas closer to the

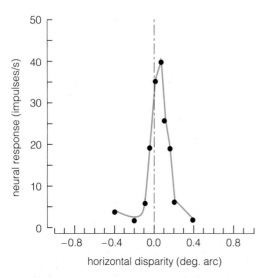

Figure 6.27 Responses of a tuned disparity neuron from the visual cortex. This neuron is connected to the retina in such a way that it is maximally sensitive to 1° of retinal disparity. (Adapted from Poggio & Poggio, 1984)

foveas, and the amount of far disparity decreases. If you continue to bring the bottle closer on the table, it eventually reaches the cup (where there is no disparity and the two images fuse into one) and then passes to come between you and the cup. Now it is in the region of near disparity; the closer it comes to your eyes, the more the near disparity increases. So what we have is a gradient of disparity between double images that can tell us exactly how far away any object is. Are there any neurons that respond to different degrees of disparity?

It is now well established that V1 and V2 contain many binocular neurons that act as disparity detectors. Poggio and Fischer (1977) describe **tuned disparity neurons**, which are maximally stimulated by a particular amount of either near or far disparity (Figure 6.27). In some fashion yet to be discovered, such cells combine their outputs to translate the disparity stimulus into our conscious experience of depth (stereopsis). This system may still be evolving, and not every human may yet have the genes for all of these cell types. A few individuals exhibit a defect called **stereo blindness**, which is an inability to construct a three-dimensional (stereo) image of their

visual world. They are not altogether without depth perception because that total ability depends on so many different binocular and monocular stimuli, but they do show peculiarities of stereopsis. Some of them have trouble telling how far apart two objects are if both objects are distant from their eyes. Apparently, they lack the reciprocal far cells that would provide the analysis of far disparity (Poggio & Poggio, 1984). Others have the opposite problem—an inability to appreciate near disparity and are probably lacking reciprocal near cells. In between the extremes of distance, these people have quite normal stereopsis (Jones, 1977).

Color When you read the section on color earlier in this chapter, you may have thought that color perception was completely explained by the Young–Helmholtz trichromatic (three-color) theory. Recall that this idea proposes three types of cones (red, green, and blue) and suggests that any color can be represented by the correct combination of activity levels in these three. Strangely enough, the nervous system abandons this trichromatic representation before the information leaves the retina. Neural connections of the retina recode the color information into a set of three **opponent processes**, each represented by a separate type of ganglion cell. One opponent-process ganglion cell reacts to red light on the center of its RF by increasing its rate of firing over the steady baseline level. It reacts to green light on its RF surround by decreasing its firing below baseline. A lower-than-normal number of impulses in this neuron means that you are viewing something green, whereas a higher-than-normal rate means something red. For this cell, red and green are opponents (Lennie, 1984). Other red–green types have a reversed center–surround arrangement with a green center and red surround. A second type of ganglion cell opposes blue and yellow. Some of these have "centers" with no surrounds; for example, a blue light anywhere in the RF turns the neuron on, whereas a yellow light anywhere in its field turns it off (or vice versa for the yellow-ON/blue-OFF variety). The third type of ganglion cell seems to be achromatic (not involved in color) and comes in two varieties: center-ON/surround-OFF or the opposite. Because it responds to a wide range of wavelengths rather than being tuned to a particular region of the spectrum, it is called a **broad-band cell**. Both **red–green** and **blue–yellow ganglion cell** types are X cells, whereas broad-band types are Y cells (Stone, 1983). At the level of ganglion cells then, every conceivable color is translated into some unique pattern of firing levels in these three neuron types. Because broad-band cells are tuned to simple light–dark differences rather than to colors, they apparently take care of the brightness differences that distinguish light colors from dark colors.

How is the translation made between the trichromatic cones and the opponent-process ganglion cells? No one has deciphered the precise neural connections, but one possible general "wiring diagram" is shown in Figure 6.28. The broad-band cell would have to receive from all three cone types in order to be receptive across the entire spectrum. It would achieve sensitivity to a band of short wavelengths through its connections with the blue cones and to midrange and long wavelengths through connections to green and red cones. The red–green cell obviously must be connected to both red and green cones. Only the blue–yellow cell may seem a little mysterious. When you mix blue light with green light, the result is a color that lies midway between blue and green on the spectrum, namely, blue–green. When you mix red and green, you also get a color that lies midway between red and green on the spectrum, namely, yellow. The color yellow, it turns out, is really a reddish green. (Keep in mind that this is a *light mixture*; mixing red paint with green paint will not give you yellow because paints do not have the spectral purity of lights.) As you can see from Figure 6.28, the yellow part of a blue–yellow RF must receive from both red cones and green cones.

The neurons in the LGN adopt the characteristics of the retinal ganglion cells feeding into them, so the same cell types are also present in the thalamus. In the cortex, however, V1 neurons receive a more complex set of connections and are more complex in the way they respond. Livingstone and Hubel (1984a) did find broad-band (achromatic) cells; red–green, center-only, opponent-process cells; and center–surround, opponent-process neurons as in the LGN (Figure 6.29); but many of the cortical cells were

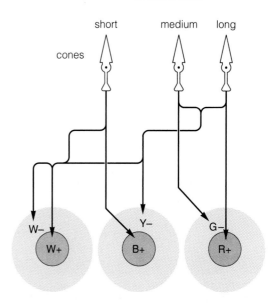

WAVELENGTH

Figure 6.28 Conceptual scheme showing the information combinations needed in the conversion from the trichromatic coding in the cones to the opponent-process representations of color in ganglion cells of the retina. Long wavelengths produce a sensation of red, medium lengths produce green, and short yield blue. Yellow is a blend of long and medium wavelengths; white is a blend of all three. (W = white, R = red, B = blue, Y = yellow, G = green. + means ON [an increase in firing]; − means OFF [a decrease in firing].)

a new type with a center–surround, double-opponent RF. A double-opponent cell of the sort shown in Figure 6.29 would respond to a spot of red light located on its center by increasing its rate of firing and to a green light by decreasing the rate. If the spot is placed on the surround instead, the opposite occurs; red depresses the rate, and green increases it. A spot of white light anywhere in the entire RF produces little, if any, response. More interestingly, a large red spot covering the entire field also elicits very little activity (Livingstone and Hubel, 1984a) because the inhibitory effect of the red on the surround cancels its facilitative effect on the center.

Perhaps it is double-opponent cells of V1 that feed into the color-contrast neurons that Zeki (1980)

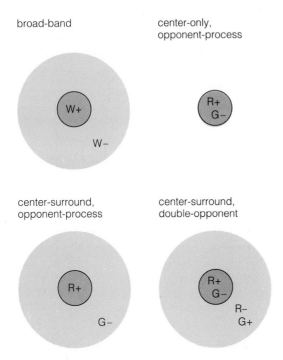

broad-band

center-only,
opponent-process

W+

W−

R+
G−

center-surround,
opponent-process

center-surround,
double-opponent

R+

G−

R+
G−

R−
G+

Figure 6.29 Types of color cells found in V1 by Livingstone and Hubel, represented here by their RF properties. (W = white, R = red, G = green. + means ON [an increase in firing]; − means OFF [a decrease in firing].) (Adapted from Livingstone & Hubel, 1984a)

than red, this phenomenon is called **color constancy.** We do not know exactly how the visual system is able to tell that this is not really the red that the stimulus wavelengths are telling you it is, but the ability to partly ignore these wavelengths may arise in the wiring between V1 and V4. Microelectrode studies show that V4 neurons that respond to a red patch under normal illumination ignore the same wavelengths coming from a piece of white paper under red illumination despite identical wavelengths. Zeki believes that V4 gives us many of our color-perception abilities.

Architecture of V1 Before going on to discuss visual areas farther up the hierarchy, some mention should be made of how the cortex of V1 is organized structurally. It has been known for decades that neocortex consists of six layers and that these same six layers are present throughout the entire cortex in all four lobes, so some degree of organization exists. Until 1960 it was thought that within these layers the cells were jumbled randomly and that the input connec-

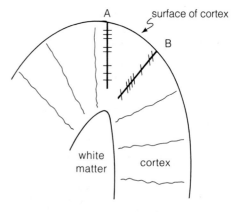

Figure 6.30 A cross section of V1 cortex with two electrode tracts (labeled A and B). Each short line crossing a tract indicates the point at which a cell was recorded, and the angle of the line shows the orientation of a stimulus bar preferred by that cell. If the electrode penetrates the cortex perpendicular to its surface and proceeds straight through to the white matter, all cells along any one tract have the same orientation, which is different from the orientation for neighboring tracts. (Adapted from Goldstein, 1984)

discovered in V4. These neurons respond not to wavelengths reflected off a surface but to a comparison of those wavelengths with wavelengths from surrounding areas of the image. When you look at a piece of paper that reflects only long wavelengths into your eye, you see a red paper. If that sample is placed on a white background (one that reflects all wavelengths), you still see a red sample on a white background. But if we now take away the normal full-spectrum light that has been shining on the paper and illuminate that whole scene with red light, both the sample and the background reflect long (red) wavelengths into your eye. Yet, surprisingly, you do not see the "white" background as red even though it is now giving you the same wavelengths that originally came from the sample red paper. Because you still see the background as more whitish

tions from the LGN were also random. Hubel and Wiesel's discovery that each cell has a preference for stimuli oriented at a particular angle, however, suggests that input connections must be highly organized rather than random. Unless each LGN neuron links up with a particular set of cortical cells, it is quite difficult to explain the origin of the orientation preference. This was the first hint of the vastly detailed structure that is now gradually being revealed.

As Hubel and Wiesel sought out the simple and complex cells of V1 with their microelectrodes, it quickly became apparent to them that the six-layered cortex was also organized vertically into what are now called **orientation columns**. Their recording technique called for gently pushing the microelectrode down through the cortex until they encountered the kind of shift in potential that indicated the penetration of a neuron membrane. Then they would stop and explore the stimulus preferences of the cell, categorizing its orientation and classifying it as simple or complex. Having finished with the first cell, they would continue to drive the microelectrode down into the cortex, seeking another neuron. You can see from Figure 6.30 that a great many cells are explored with each penetration and that, if the electrode is angled so that it is perpendicular to the surface of the cortex, all cells found have the same orientation. However, if the electrode is angled, it cuts across several columns, finding a different orientation preference in each. So all cells within any one column (both simple and complex) have the same orientation, but there are enough columns in a 0.6-mm length of cortex to detect every possible line orientation (Barlow, 1982).

Even more structure emerged as neurons were studied for the degree to which they were dominated by one eye or the other. Hubel and colleagues (1974) discovered a way to reveal the ocular dominance of all cells in V1 in one picture. They injected the radioactive chemical [³H]**proline** (read "tritiated proline") into one eye of a monkey and then waited for the molecules to be absorbed into ganglion cells and transported up their axons to the LGN in the thalamus. Strangely enough, [³H]proline crosses the synapse in the LGN and continues to be transported all the way up LGN axons into V1 cortex. The monkey is put to sleep, the brain is removed, and the visual cortex is placed against a piece of photographic film that is exposed by [³H]proline's radioactivity. The developed film clearly shows which areas of the cortex contain neurons receiving connections from the injected eye (Figure 6.31). Neurons dominated by one eye are arranged in stripes that alternate with stripes for the other eye in a zebralike pattern across V1. These stripes are called **ocular dominance**

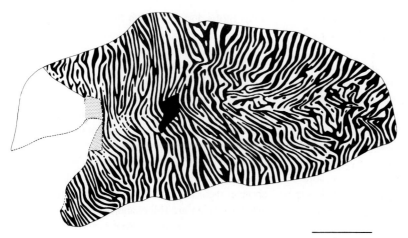

Figure 6.31 Drawing of the complete striate cortex as it would look after being stained for ocular dominance bands and then spread out flat. (LeVay et al., 1985)

1 cm

Figure 6.32 Tangential section through the border between V1 and V2 cortex of a squirrel monkey. The section has been stained with cytochrome oxidase to reveal the blobs in V1. This procedure also brings out a pattern of stripes in V2. The pattern is an alternation of thick stripes and thin stripes with lightly stained interstripe zones separating them. (Adapted from Hubel & Livingstone, 1987)

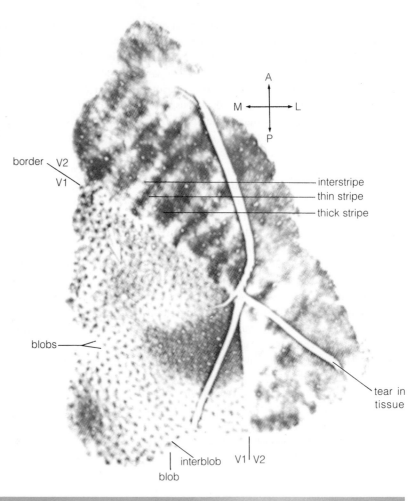

bands, and they have been shown to be as deep as the cortex, running all the way from the surface to the white matter (LeVay et al., 1985).

By the end of the 1970s, the visual cortex had lost its reputation as a random, jumbled collection of neurons and was now perceived as a network of ocular dominance bands crosscut by orientation columns. By 1980 Wong-Riley (1979), Hubel, and others had discovered still another organizational feature in V1. They found a way to stain a neuronal enzyme called **cytochrome oxidase,** which is most abundant in cells that are more active. When V1 was stained for cytochrome oxidase, islands of darker, more heavily stained cells dotted the cortex (Figure 6.32). Hubel and Livingstone (1983) call these dark areas **blobs** and found that they were arranged in rows that ran along the centers of the ocular dominance bands (Hendrickson, 1985). Neurons within the blobs are quite different in function from neurons outside (Livingstone & Hubel, 1984b). Blob cells are dominated by one eye or the other (as you would expect from their position at the centers of the bands). They prefer color stimuli and are not responsive to angle of orientation. Cells outside of the blobs within the **interblobs** are responsive to stimuli in either eye (little or no ocular dominance), show no color preference, and have orientation selectivity. They are Hubel and Wiesel's original simple and complex neurons. So it would seem that the blob areas of V1 are for color processing, and the interblob areas are for stereopsis and edge and orientation detection. But matters may not turn out to be that simple. There are a few questions left to be answered that don't seem to fit this model (Hendrickson, 1985). For example, if the blobs are color-analyzer zones, why don't rodents that have retinas containing many cones (such as ground squirrels) have them? On the other hand, why does a nocturnal primate like the owl monkey, who has hardly any cones, have cortical blobs? However, in the face of mounting positive evidence, these remain minor questions, and researchers have incorporated blobs into their overall picture of cortical architecture.

Hubel and Livingstone (1983) point out that each point in the visual field (or on the retina) is represented by an area of V1 cortex measuring 2 × 2 mm (at the surface) and that this area of 4 mm² must contain one entire set of analyzers for every function located in V1. In other words, it must contain every type of color cell plus a column for each possible line orientation, and these must be repeated for both eyes. If any are missing in any area of V1, then you would be blind to some particular color combination, to some angle of orientation, or to some combination of retinal disparities at one point in your visual field. (Fortunately, this sort of defect does not seem to occur.) The visual cortex, then, is organized as a sheet of six-layered, 2-mm × 2-mm "cubes" set side by side. Each is identical to all the others in terms of input and output connections as well as function, and each represents a single point in your visual field. Hubel calls this concept of cortical architecture the **ice-cube model** (Figure 6.33).

As the word *cube* implies, we need to extend our two-dimensional thinking about blobs and ocular dominance bands into the third dimension; blobs really are columns that extend from layer 1 to layer 4 (with a disconnected portion in layers 5 and 6). Because dominance bands extend down through all layers, they really should be called *ocular dominance slabs* (but no one has yet adopted that term). Orientation "columns" are not cylindrical but extend across the width of a dominance band and probably also should be called slabs for that reason. Notice that the artist has labeled each of the orientation columns (slabs) in the dominance band for the left eye with the particular angle of orientation that it is

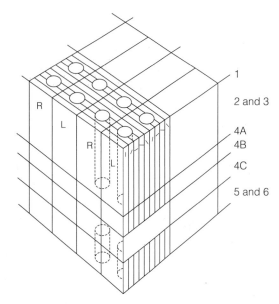

Figure 6.33 Hubel and Livingstone's ice-cube model of the structural organization in the striate cortex. Layer 1 is at the surface of the cortex, and layer 6 is at the bottom next to the white matter. The short lines on the orientation columns indicate their preferred angles of orientation (R = right eye, L = left eye). The picture reveals that blobs are really circular columns that extend down through layer 3, skip layer 4, and reappear in layers 5 and 6. The dominance bands cut across the orientation columns. (Adapted from Hubel & Livingstone, 1983)

set to detect. Layer 4, with its various subdivisions, has a different organization than the rest of the layers because that is the initial "receiving" area into which input arrives from the LGN. Layers 5 and 6 contain major output neurons whose axons travel to the LGN and other cortical areas. Layers 2 and 3 are mostly involved in processing the input from layer 4 and sending it to the bottom output layers.

Layer 4 apparently does do some processing, but it works with a different type of information than that entering other layers. Earlier you learned that X cells, the foveal ganglion cells that give us focal vision, project to the parvocellular layers of the LGN. Retinal Y cells, hypothetically responsible for ambient vision, project to the magnocellular layers. The information carried by the X cell–parvocellular path is processed

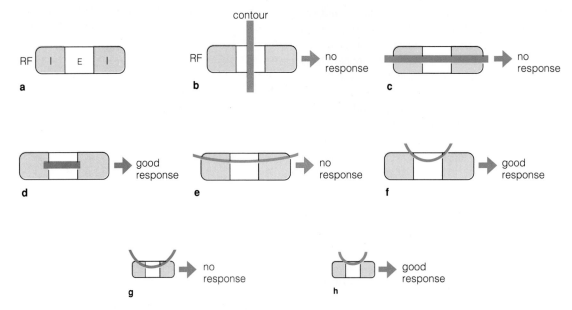

Figure 6.34 Curvature selectivity in end-stopped V2 neurons. (**a**) Shape of the RF of an end-stopped neuron. A central excitatory area (E) is bordered by two inhibitory zones (I). (**b**) A contour crossing the excitatory zone in the wrong orientation elicits no response. The contour must be oriented parallel to the long axis of the RF. (**c**) A correctly oriented contour still elicits no response if it overlaps too much into the I zones. (**d**) When a contour is correctly oriented and covers much more E than I, the cell responds with a high rate of firing. (**e**) A curve that invades the inhibitory zones gets no response. (**f**) A curve that doesn't invade the I zones elicits a good response. (**g**) The same curve as in (**f**) gets no response from this smaller RF because it invades the I areas. (**h**) Smaller curves, however, can elicit a response. So, smaller RFs are selective for smaller degrees of curvature.

further by blob and interblob neurons of V1 with their color and orientation detectors. The information from the Y cell–magnocellular path passes through V1 layer 4 and is sent to V2. Let us further trace these two information paths, the first dealing with the identification of visual details and the second with the positions of objects with respect to each other.

Architecture of V2   From V1, information flows into V2. When Hubel and Livingstone (1987) applied the cytochrome oxidase technique to the V2 cortex of squirrel monkeys, they again found that some areas stained more heavily than others. A pattern of alternating thick and thin stripes stained dark by the cytochrome oxidase emerged and were separated from

one another by very lightly stained interstripe zones. This sequence of thick stripe–interstripe–thin stripe–interstripe was repeated a number of times across the cortical surface (Figure 6.32). Another outstanding feature of V2 was the great number of end-stopped cells found there. **End-stopped cells** have elongated RFs with an excitatory area in the middle and inhibitory zones at both ends. They are located mostly within the interstripe. These cells do not respond to a contour that runs across their RF in the wrong direction; they are orientation-selective (Figure 6.34). This selectivity probably means that end-stopped cells get their input from V1 interblob simple cells. However, end-stopped cells get their name because a contour oriented correctly across their RF gets no response if it crosses much of either inhibitory zone. The contour's ends need to stop before extending very far into the inhibitory areas.

End-stopped cells answer a question that has long puzzled us. How can the orientation-specific contour-detector cells give us our perception of forms when they all seem to be set for straight lines? Hubel and Livingstone (1987) now propose that the end-stopped cells are quite adequate for detecting different degrees of curvature. A long curve that crosses into the inhibitory parts of the field would get a poor response, whereas a shorter curve limited to the excitatory portion would trigger many nerve impulses (Figure 6.34). Smaller curves would fire only cells with smaller RFs.

The V1 interblob regions apparently project to the end-stopped cells in the interstripe zones of V2. The blob regions project into the thin stripes. Thus, cells in the **thin stripes** are analyzing for color, those in the **interstripe** cells, for shape (Livingstone & Hubel, 1987b). The **thick stripes** receive from the layer 4 cells of V1 (Livingstone & Hubel, 1987a), which are orientation selective, sensitive to motion, and selective for different degrees of retinal disparity (Figure 6.35). The focal–object vision path maintains its separation from the ambient–spatial vision path through V2.

The Spatial Vision Pathway

Spatial vision involves knowing where an object is in relation to your own body and knowing its direction of motion relative to yourself if either you or the object is moving. The motion aspects of this sort of knowledge are analyzed by the middle temporal (**MT**) and medial superior temporal (**MST**) areas (Newsome et al., 1985; Tanaka et al., 1986).

Perceiving Movement   Neurons in MT (Figure 6.36) respond to moving stimuli but not stationary ones, and many of them are selective for a particular direction of movement. There is probably a column arrangement for direction of movement in MT similar to the orientation columns of V1 because microelectrode recordings show that the preferred direction of the sampled neurons changes systematically as the electrode moves across an area of cortex (Tanaka et al., 1986). Each column would rep-

resent a different direction. Saito and colleagues refer to these directionally selective motion-detector neurons as **D cells** (Tanaka et al., 1986).

Motion is a very complicated idea. Sometimes the motion of a part of the image across the retinas means that a part of the real world is moving, but at other times the motion occurs because our eyes are moving. Furthermore, a figure that remains at exactly the same spot in our retinal image may come from an object in the real world that is actually in motion. It may seem a simple matter to perceive the motion of your roommate walking across the room toward the door, but remember that neurons of your cortex cannot directly see your roommate; they receive input only from your retinas. If you are staring at a picture on the wall as your roomy crosses your line of vision, then her image does progress across your motionless retinas. But if you are fixating on her with your eyes moving as fast as she does, her image is actually frozen on your foveas. Your brain must be able to perceive motion of an object even when its figure in the image does not move across the retina. Further, as your eyes track your roommate's movement, your eyes are sweeping across the room; accordingly, the image of the room *is* moving across your retinas. So at times a stationary image must be interpreted to be in motion, and a moving image must be seen as stationary.

Thus, motion perception depends as much on knowing when your eyes are moving as it does on any movement within the retinal image. The visual system can take information about the speed and direction of your eye movements and combine it with the motion in the visual image when your eyes follow your roommate and "deduce" that the motionless figure in the image is actually moving.

When you watch your roommate cross the room, your perceptual processes divide the image into two parts: a figure moving across a ground. The **figure** is the object on which you are fixating and to which your attention is directed. The **ground** is the rest of the scene, the part to which you are not attending. Employing this distinction, Saito and colleagues (Tanaka et al., 1986) arranged for monkeys to watch a black bar (figure) on a field of dots (ground) while recording from cells in MT. Some of the D cells sampled seemed to be very simple, unsophisticated

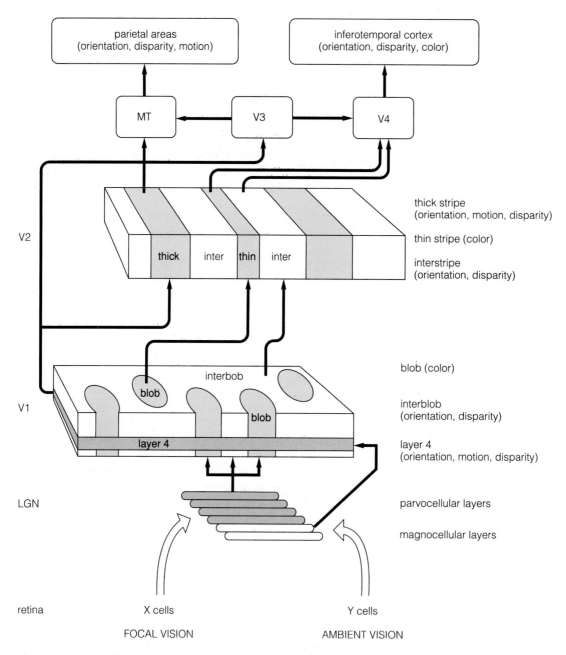

Figure 6.35 Two major information flow paths through the visual system. The focal vision path starts in the X cells of the foveal retina and proceeds through the parvocellular layers of LGN to the blob and interblob regions of V1, thin-stripe and interstripe regions of V2, V4, and the IT cortex. The ambient vision path starts in the nonfoveal retina and proceeds to the magnocellular layers of LGN and layer 4 of V1. From there it flows to V3 and to the thick stripes of V2. From the thick stripes, the information goes to MT and then to the visual areas of the parietal lobe. The blob–interblob route extracts information about color and form of objects, and the layer 4/thick-stripe route is concerned with spatial location.

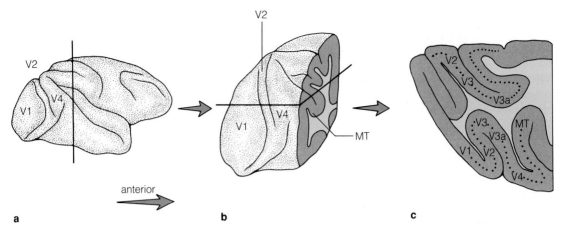

Figure 6.36 Locations of cortical visual areas hidden within sulci. (**a**) A lateral view of a macaque monkey brain showing V1 and V2 in the occipital lobes and V4 in the parietal. The sulcus that separates V2 from V4 is called the lunate sulcus, and the next one anterior to it is the superior temporal sulcus (which extends up into the parietal region). The vertical line indicates where the brain will be cut for **b**. (**b**) This is the back portion of the brain shown in **a**, and the cut has revealed area MT lying within the superior temporal sulcus and forming one of its banks. The horizontal line across the brain shows where it will be cut to make **c**. (**c**) The top of the brain portion seen in **b** has been removed and the remainder has been tilted so that you are now viewing it from above rather than from the side. (The longitudinal fissure is at the top of this drawing.) MT is visible again from a different perspective. V2, V3, and V3a are also visible within the lunate sulcus and again within another sulcus on the medial side of the hemisphere. They are arranged as long strips that curl over the top of the brain and down the medial wall. (Adapted from Van Essen, 1979)

motion detectors; they might respond either to movement of the figure or ground. They liked anything that moved in any fashion. It seems reasonable to guess that these might be providing input to the more selective D-cell types such as **figure neurons**. The latter responded only to the bar (the figure) and only under certain circumstances. If both bar and dot background were moving in the same direction at the same rate of speed, the figure neuron failed to respond. If the background was in motion, the figure neuron would respond only if the bar was moving in the opposite direction—in other words, only if there was a *relative* motion between figure and ground.

Can you see how useful such a cell might be? For example, if your eyes sweep across a room to fixate on a new object of attention, a veritable cascade of images flows across your retinas. Most likely, the simple motion-detector D cells would respond

wildly to this bonanza of meaningless movement, a reaction that amounts to getting all excited over nothing. The figure neurons, however (sophisticates that they are), calmly ignore this deluge of input because all possible figures in the flow of images are moving across the retina at exactly the same speed and in the same direction as the ground. Figure neurons can tell the difference, in a case like this, between real motion and motion of the image generated by simply moving the eyes.

Some figure neurons are also found in another area, MST, together with a variety of a D cell that is found only in that area. This new D cell, the **field neuron**, usually ignores figures (like the dark bar Saito used as a stimulus) but responds nicely to a background (Saito's field of dots). These neurons may be especially helpful in separating real motion generated by eye movements. Whenever you turn your head toward a new fixation point, your eyes are drawn across the visual field, and a succession of images flows across your retina. This motion should not be interpreted as environmental movement, yet exactly the same visual image flow could indeed represent real movement if you were standing close to a railroad track and watching a train go by. How can you tell the two situations apart when the stimulus is the same? What you need in that case is a little help from the vestibular senses. When you turn your head, the semicircular canals in your inner ear produce a "head-in-motion" output that could be used to interpret the ambiguous visual stimulus. If the canals are not signaling that your head or eyes are moving, then your visual system can read the image flow on the retina as representing real movement of the environment (boxcars rolling by). For the inner ear sensations to be used in interpreting visual information, the two senses must come together somewhere in the nervous system. Saito reports that both vestibular and eye-movement information (probably from FEF) arrive in the parietal cortex, and this is one of the cortical zones to which MST sends its output (Tanaka et al., 1986).

Still more analyzers have been discovered in MST (more than can be discussed in this chapter). Among them are neurons that react to the expanding motion of an object's image that occurs when the object gets closer to the eye and cells that detect rotary motion around an axis (Saito et al., 1986). We have just barely begun to discover how wealthy the visual system is in terms of analyzer types and how long it must have taken the evolutionary process to generate this vast, interlocked system.

Spatial Vision and Visual Attention   Where in the brain does the visual system end? There appears to be no precise boundaries to it. The top end of the hierarchy of visual analyzers just gradually blends into other functions, becoming less and less visual and more and more something else. In the temporal lobes, the transition from the PIT to the AIT is a shift away from pure visual discrimination to memory of visual discrimination to pure memory. In the parietal lobe (our interest at this point), the shift is from purely visual analysis to **polysensory analysis**—that is, to analyzers that receive input from more than one sense system and that act to integrate the two

streams of information. **Area 7a** and the **VIP** (ventral inferior parietal) **area** (Figure 6.16) make up a polysensory zone called the posterior parietal region, which receives input from the V1–V4 route, the MT–MST route, the collicular–pulvinar route, and the somatosensory cortex. In other words, it receives information about the form of the figure, its movements, and its location in space with reference to the body.

Inputs to the posterior parietal region suggest that one function of this area might be to somehow relate the body to visual space. For example, what does it mean to you to "know where your arm is located" when you raise it to a particular position with your eyes closed? It means that you not only can *feel* it in that position but you also expect to *see* it in a particular region of visual space. That expectation is really a visual prediction based on somatosensory information. ("If my arm feels this way, then I know what the visual scene should look like when I open my eyes.") In other words, the task of the posterior parietal area may be more related to ambient vision than to focal vision. This notion is supported by the existence of the input from the tectopulvinar pathway and because many neurons in this region react nicely to stimulus patterns presented in the peripheral visual field but fail to respond to foveal stimuli (Motter & Mountcastle, 1981).

Because area 7a receives from MST, you would expect to find neurons there that respond to movement, and this is the case. Among the various types of motion detectors discovered in 7a by Motter and Mountcastle were two they named **opponent vector cells**. Figure 6.37 indicates the type of stimulus to which these respond. The best response for one type of opponent vector neuron (the expansion type) occurs when contours in the image move outward from the fovea toward the periphery, whereas the best response for the other (the contraction type) is the opposite direction of movement. A vector is a direction of movement, and the word *opponent* refers to the fact that the motion on one side of the image must be in the opposite direction to the motion on the other for the cell to be excited.

Motter and Mountcastle suggest that these neurons might possibly be involved in perceiving depth. If you are looking straight ahead as you walk or run,

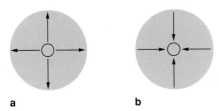

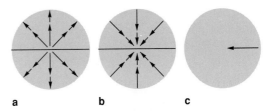

Figure 6.37 Appropriate forms of motion stimuli for opponent vector cells. (**a**) Expansion type responds to motion of image elements outward from the center of the field. (**b**) Contraction type responds to inward motion.

Figure 6.38 (**a**) Expansion of elements outward across the visual field that occurs in the retinal image when you look straight forward at a point on the horizon toward which you are moving. The horizontal line represents the horizon. (**b**) Directions of movement of image elements from a scene as you move away from it. (**c**) Movement of the retinal image of an object approaching you from one side. Some contraction-type opponent vector cells can respond to this stimulus.

the elements of the visual image on your retina move out from the central fixation point (usually the horizon) toward the peripheral retina (Figure 6.38). This is precisely the pattern of stimulation that the expansion type of opponent vector neurons require. The contraction type would be excited when you look back over your shoulder at the environment you are leaving.

The authors suggest another, possibly more important, function for the contraction type. Many of these cells would respond to an inward-moving stimulus even if it was just on one side of the field (Figure 6.38c). Such a stimulus would be produced by an object approaching you from one side and headed into your path of travel. It would also be produced by your own hand if you picked something from the table at your side and brought it around in front of you. In either case, the object probably should command your attention because it is moving from ambient vision into focal, thus, it is possible that the output of these neurons link into the attention mechanism of the brain.

There are several ways in which the firing of these neurons might produce the phenomenon we call attention. Their axons may lead back to visual analyzers lower in the hierarchy (MT, V4, and so on) where the pattern of their firing might aid in determining which neurons should respond to the sensory input from still lower areas. There is no doubt about the existence of connections backward through the hierarchy; nearly every pair of areas that are connected in an "upward" direction has also been shown to be connected in the "downward" direction (Van Essen, 1985).

Another part of paying attention to a stimulus involves orienting one's receptors to it. Midway forward in the frontal lobes there is a small zone called the frontal eye fields (FEF) that appears to have originated to allow the cortical visual areas some control over the eye-movement mechanisms of the brain stem (Figure 6.17). The posterior parietal zone connects indirectly with the FEF by way of MST, and neurons in 7a have been found to fire just before an eye movement to a new fixation point (Wurtz et al., 1982). With such connections, opponent vector cells would be ideal for the task of eye–hand coordination. Perhaps they could react to hand movements by directing the eyes to the same point in space occupied by the hand. Wurtz and colleagues (1982) trained monkeys to fixate straight ahead while waiting for a cue to press a lighted panel that was located off to one side. The monkey had to wait for the panel to dim before reaching over to touch it and collect the reward. Through a microelectrode, Wurtz was watching the activity of a type of 7a neuron that responds to stationary stimuli. Wurtz was trying to see if these cells were just involved in eye movements or whether their function was more one of "paying attention"; he arranged that the monkey would be reinforced for pressing the panel when the light dimmed but only if it didn't allow its eyes to leave the central fixation point. The 7a neurons

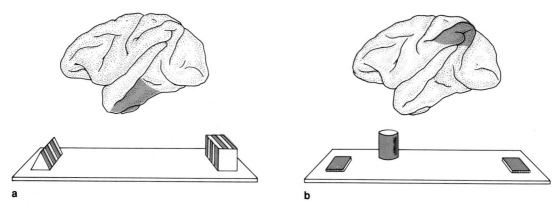

Figure 6.39 Object vs. spatial vision. (**a**) A typical stimulus arrangement for one trial in a visual discrimination task for a macaque monkey. Each stimulus object covers a food well, but only the well under the correct object is baited. An IT lesion eliminates or weakens this type of learning. (**b**) The arrangement for spatial learning, landmark task in which the objects covering the wells provide no information as to which one is baited. The monkey must choose on the basis of which well is closest to the landmark object—a cylinder in this example. The landmark task is not affected by IT lesions but cannot be learned following lesions of area 7a (posterior parietal). Parietal lesions have no effect on visual discrimination learning. Thus, object vision is apparently handled by the route through IT cortex, spatial vision by the route through 7a. (From Mishkin et al., 1983)

began firing the moment the panel dimmed, even though there was no eye movement, but this response occurred only in trials when the monkey responded to the cue by reaching for the panel. Because it is obvious from their location in posterior parietal lobes that these cells have nothing to do with initiating the hand movement itself, a good explanation for the activity just prior to the movement is that these cells are a part of the **spatial attention mechanism** that makes possible such abilities as eye–hand coordination.

What happens to a monkey with lesions in 7a on both sides of its brain? Pohl (1973) sought to answer this question by employing an experimental task he called the **landmark discrimination**. In this task, the monkey could find a piece of food under one of two blocks if it chose correctly. The two blocks were identical, and the block that was to be correct on any one trial was selected at random. The only cue (S$^+$) available to the subject was an object on the board between the two blocks that was always placed closer to the correct block (as a landmark). Two

groups of monkeys were tested: one with IT lesions and one with posterior parietal (7a) lesions (Figure 6.39). Both groups were given the landmark task plus a visual form-discrimination task. The IT group was unable to learn the form discrimination but had no trouble at all with the landmark task. The posterior parietal group, however, could not solve the landmark task but did quite well with form discrimination. Apparently, monkeys with IT lesions noticed where objects were but failed to note what they looked like, whereas the parietal-lesioned subjects could perceive the differences between objects but disregarded their positions. Without the posterior parietal cortex, the ability to attend to where objects are located is lost.

Humans suffering from a lesion to one or the other parietal lobe frequently reveal this loss of attentive ability by forgetting to deal with objects on the side of their bodies contralateral to the side of the lesion. This is a symptom called unilateral neglect, which we will discuss in some detail in the chapter on neuropsychology.

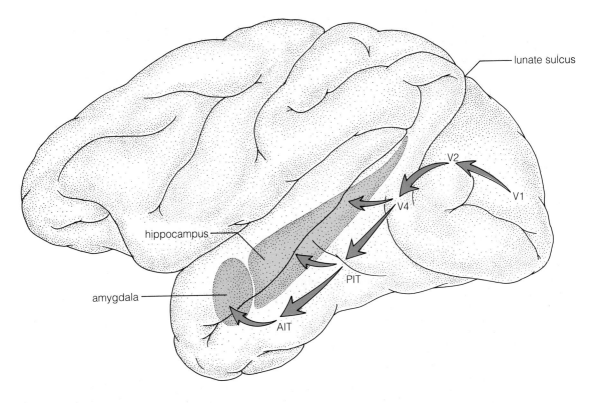

Figure 6.40 Lateral view of macaque monkey brain showing general direction of information flow through the visual system and on into the memory system of the medial temporal lobe. (AIT = anterior inferotemporal area, PIT = posterior inferotemporal area.) (Adapted from Mishkin et al., 1983)

The Visual System in the 1990s

In this chapter we have seen how the application of the scientific process has steadily broadened our understanding of the visual system from our original narrow idea that all visual processes lay within the geniculostriate path to the view that there existed two projection systems (geniculostriate and tectopulvinar) and, finally, to the notion that those two paths actually contained multiple pathways (X- and Y-cell paths, a form–color path, a spatial location path, and perhaps others). In my opinion, however, the experimental work of the 1980s has rendered even the multiple-pathways view obsolescent. We now can pick out some 17 separate analyzer areas in the cortex, each of which undoubtedly contains several different analyzers, and more are being delimited every year. The problem with the pathway idea is that anatomists have now clearly shown that these areas are not arranged in simple upward hierarchical routes (Van Essen, 1985). Instead, each one connects to at least three others, and many of the connections are down to "lower" areas. This anatomy is best described as a **network of interconnected analyzers** rather than as parallel pathways. Information flows "upward" in this system, for example, when IT neurons collect color information from analyzers in V1 (and perhaps, V2, V3, and V4 analyzers) and blend it with orientation information from V1 and V2 to get a whole visual shape. Yet it can also flow downward when you examine a shape more carefully, paying attention to fine details rather than the entire form taken as a whole (Mishkin, personal communication). Each analyzer contributes one tiny scrap of information to the construction of your visual world, and most of the ones in the cortex depend for their analysis on the information coming from several other analyzers.

There does, however, seem to be a shift from fine, detailed information in the occipital lobes to more and more holistic information as you move forward through the temporal lobes. The final destination of all this information is the memory mechanism of the medial temporal lobes—the hippocampus and amygdala. Figure 6.40 shows how each set of analyzers from anterior occipital to anterior temporal sends output to the episodic memory system. At that juncture we have finally found the last step in the long, elaborate process of primate visual processing.

■ Summary

1. Visible light is only one form of electromagnetic radiation. Other forms include infrared, microwaves, radio waves, ultraviolet, X rays, and gamma rays. Our visual receptors are insensitive to all of these except visible wavelengths and ultraviolet (which the eye filters out before it reaches the retina).

2. Light enters the eye through a transparent portion of the sclera called the cornea. The pupil, an opening in a ring of muscles called the iris, admits light to the lens, which focuses it on the light-sensitive inner surface of the eyeball, the retina.

3. The fovea is the center of the retina. It receives the light coming from the object at which you are directing your eye. Near the fovea is the optic disc, a blind spot devoid of receptors because of the passage there of the optic nerve and blood vessels.

4. Light passes through the ganglion-cell layer, then the bipolar layer, then through the receptors, and finally is absorbed by the dark pigment epithelium just in back of the retina.

5. Visual transduction, the process of converting light energy into graded neuron potentials, is accomplished by the receptors, the rods, and cones. Infor-

mation from receptors passes to the bipolar and horizontal cells, which in turn pass information to amacrine cells and output cells of the retina, the ganglion cells. Axons of ganglion cells form the optic nerve.

6. Transduction is accomplished by photochemicals contained in the outer segments of receptors, rhodopsin in rods, and various opsins in cones. A receptor is depolarized in the dark, with a sodium current (called the dark current) flowing into its outer segments. Light diminishes the dark current; that is, light tends to polarize the cell. During depolarization, receptors secrete transmitter that stimulates some types of bipolar cells but inhibits others.

7. Color perception is the ability to tell one wavelength from another, and it is entirely dependent on the cones. There are three types of cones, each with a different kind of opsin that gives the cell a sensitivity to a particular range of wavelengths. We have long-, medium-, and short-wavelength cones whose absorption areas overlap. Each wavelength of light is absorbed to a different degree by one or more of the cone types so that the pattern of activity in the cones is different for each color of the spectrum. Thus, only three types of cones are required to code every possible color. This idea is the Young–Helmholtz theory.

8. Acuity is the degree of clarity in the person's perceived image and determines how small visual details can become before they are no longer visible to the viewer. The cone system is specialized to produce high acuity. Cone ganglion cells of the fovea have smaller receptive fields (RFs) than do peripheral ganglion cells, and that arrangement gives the cone area of the central retina more separate data lines (axons) per square millimeter to carry information to the brain than are possessed by peripheral cells. Thus, where two separate lines of light lying very close together might excite two separate foveal ganglion cells, they would only excite one peripheral ganglion cell. The RF of a cell is the area of retina or portion of the optical image to which it responds.

9. Sensitivity refers to the ability of the system to respond to weak stimuli, and the most common measure of sensitivity, the absolute threshold, is the least amount of light needed to produce sensation.

Rods have a lower absolute threshold than do cones. Because of this, sensitivity is greatest in the peripheral retina. Dark adaptation lowers the threshold, and light adaptation raises it.

10. A neural analyzer is a neuron with a set of connections that allow it to detect the existence of a certain set of conditions (usually stimuli) by responding selectively only when those conditions are present. The most basic type of visual analyzer is the contrast detector of the retina that ignores a uniformly illuminated field and responds only to a contrast between parts of its field. Bipolar and ganglion cells have concentric, center–surround receptive fields in which light hitting the center excites the neuron, whereas light on the surround inhibits it, or vice versa.

11. In the classic model of the visual system, the retina simply converted an optical image consisting of points of light having different brightnesses and colors into a nerve-impulse image that was carried point for point by the visual projection system through the lateral geniculate nucleus of the thalamus (LGN) to the visual cortex for interpretation. Area 17 converted the image into objects, and occipital areas 18 and 19 contained the memories of what these objects were. Although the anatomical facts are correct, the classic model either misinterprets or oversimplifies the way in which the parts function. As the first step in its modification, researchers found that the occipital visual areas projected into a farther visual zone, the inferotemporal (IT) area, which served visual discrimination.

12. In the 1970s, this model was converted to a dual-projection system in recognition of the work on the superior colliculus that showed that the route through the colliculus extracted different information than did the route through the LGN. The geniculostriate route was specialized for handling form vision (or, as Trevarthan's theory claims, focal vision); the retinotectal route established where these forms were located in the space around the organism (ambient vision).

13. The viewpoint of the 1980s considers the visual system to be a collection of processing pathways running in parallel from the retina through the cortex. The separation of these paths begins with the difference between the X and Y cells in the retina. X cells are more involved in focal vision and Y in ambient vision. The X path projects through the parvocellular layers of the LGN to V1, whereas the Y path reaches V1 through the magnocellular layers of the LGN. Other paths take retinal output to many brain-stem nuclei. The superior colliculus projects into many areas of the visual cortex (including the frontal eye fields—FEF) by way of the pulvinar nucleus of the thalamus.

14. Mishkin proposed that the cortical visual analyzers are roughly organized into an object vision pathway that flows from V1 through the anterior inferotemporal (AIT) cortex and a spatial vision path from V1 through area 7a in the parietal lobe. The pioneering work in finding visual cortex analyzers was done by Hubel and Wiesel. They found striate cortex cells that acted as line-orientation analyzers. Rather than having concentric RFs, these cells have straight-line boundaries between the areas of contrast.

15. Simple cells are orientation detectors with ON and OFF RF areas at fixed locations on the retina, whereas complex cells are orientation detectors that react to a boundary at many places within its RF. It is hypothesized that the former is wired to a single line of concentric LGN RFs, whereas the latter derives its characteristics from being wired to a set of simple cortical cells. The complex cell solves the problem of retinal transposition.

16. Perception of shapes is built up piece by piece as V1 analyzers (simple and complex cells) pass their analysis to V2 cells. From there the information is developed by V3, V4, the posterior inferotemporal (PIT) cortex, and AIT. The PIT area is involved in the ability to visually discriminate between different forms, and the AIT area is devoted to memory of such shapes.

17. A few cells in the region around PIT are detectors for specific shapes, namely, hands or faces. Most IT cells prefer more complex shapes over less complex but are not committed to any one shape. A shape such as a table or tree is apparently represented in the IT cortex as a pattern of activity in a particular group of cells.

18. Most simple cells in V1 receive inputs from both eyes. A few are totally dominated by one or the other eye, but most fall somewhere along a continuum between being equally responsive to both eyes and being completely dominated by one. This continuum is called the degree of ocular dominance.

19. Stereoscopic depth perception (stereopsis) is three-dimensional vision that depends on the fact that the two retinal images are not exactly alike because of the physical separation between the eyes. The more the eyes converge, as the fixated object gets closer, the greater the difference (disparity) between the images. Thus, the degree of disparity indicates the distance or depth. V1 and V2 contain detectors tuned for different degrees of disparity as well as cells that analyze for near disparity and far disparity.

20. Color perception begins as a trichromatic process in the receptors, so called because the whole spectrum is sensed by only three cone types: short-, medium-, and long-wavelength cones. Within the retina, however, this three-way code is converted into an opponent-process code yielding three basic ganglion cell types with opposing center–surround RFs: a red versus green cell (either red-ON/green-OFF or vice versa), a blue–yellow cell, and a broad-spectrum (white) cell.

21. The architecture of V1 is currently best described by Hubel and Livingstone's ice-cube model, which specifies that color cells are found in columns called blobs, occurring at intervals along vertical slabs of cells all having the same orientation (orientation columns). There is a separate orientation column for each possible angle of line. Further, this set of columns is duplicated for each eye with all columns for one eye being grouped together into an ocular dominance band.

22. V2 is divided into stripes. Thick-stripe cells process the ambient vision information from retinal Y cells, LGN magnocellular layers, and layer 4 of V1. Thin-stripe cells process color. Interstripe cells handle the shape information of focal vision coming from the retinal X cells, LGN parvocellular layers, and V1 interblob regions.

23. Along the spatial vision path are found areas MT and MST, which contain motion analyzers called D cells. One type of D cell is the figure neuron, which responds to a figure that is moving relative to the ground. The field type of D cell ignores figures and responds to ground movement.

24. Area 7a and VIP are polysensory. Opponent vector cells that respond to an expansion motion of image elements outward from the fovea or the opposite, a contraction of the elements inward toward the fovea, have been discovered in area 7a. The latter type may be important in attention because it would signal the appearance of objects moving into one's path of movement from the side. These cortical areas are connected to the FEF, apparently so that a shift in conscious attention can direct eye movements to the new focus of attention. Damage to this posterior parietal region leaves a monkey with normal visual discrimination ability but unable to solve the landmark problem, which involves attention to spatial relations.

25. I propose that the viewpoint of the 1990s will shift from seeing the visual system as a collection of parallel processing pathways in favor of viewing it as a network of analyzers, thus emphasizing the importance of downward and same-level connections between cortical areas that the pathway view overlooks.

Glossary

absolute threshold The least amount of a stimulus needed to obtain a response from a cell. (209)

accommodation A change in the shape of the lens to allow for focusing on near or far objects. (201)

achromatic Lacking in color. (209)

acuity The degree of sharpness or clarity in vision. (208)

amacrine cells Retinal cells that interconnect bipolars and ganglion cells. (202)

ambient vision The part of vision concerned with the positions of objects in space around the body. (218)

analyzer A set of synaptic connections between a group of input neurons and a group of output neurons that is arranged to detect a particular feature in a stimulus input; same as processor. (210)

area 7a Posterior parietal lobe area involved in visual-spatial perception. (242)

area 17 Occipital cortical area in which axons of LGN output cells terminate; also called V1. (212)

area 18 Cortical visual area just anterior to V1 in the occipital lobes; also called V2. (214)

area 19 Cortical visual area anterior to area 18; equivalent to V3 plus V4. (214)

astigmatism Small areas of blur in the image caused by irregularities on the surface of the cornea. (202)

bipolar cells Retinal neurons that connect receptors to ganglion cells. (202)

blobs Circular areas of V1 cortex within ocular dominance bands; contain cells that detect color but not line orientation. (236)

broad-band cell A type of Y ganglion cell that responds to a wide range of wavelengths rather than being tuned to a particular region of the spectrum. (233)

center–surround receptive field RF consisting of two concentric circles, one with a facilitative effect on the cell, the other with an inhibitory effect. (211)

color constancy The ability to perceive a stimulus object as having an unchanging color despite changes in the intensity and wavelength of the stimulating light. (234)

color perception The ability to discriminate between wavelengths. (206)

complex cortical neuron V1 cell with connections from thalamus and simple cells that enable it to detect a particular line orientation regardless of where the simulus is on the retina. (224)

cones Photoreceptors associated with color perception. (202)

contrast A light area next to a darker one. (210)

convergence The inward or outward rotation of the eyes as they track an object moving closer to or farther away from you. (230)

cornea The transparent, anterior portion of the sclera. (200)

cytochrome oxidase A neuronal enzyme present in greatest abundance when the cell is active; used experimentally as a way of labeling active neurons. (236)

dark adaptation A gradual increase in visual sensitivity produced by lowering the level of illumination. (209)

dark current The current present spontaneously in a photoreceptor cell until light strikes it. (204)

D cell Directionally selective motion detector neuron found in MT. (239)

delayed match-to-nonsample task Discrimination learning problem in which the stimulus not previously presented must be chosen for reinforcement to occur. (225)

dual visual projection system Viewpoint that sees the visual system as divided between the geniculostriate path and the retinotectal path. (217)

electromagnetic radiation A form of wave energy. (199)

electromagnetic spectrum An ordered arrangement of all of the known forms of electromagnetic radiation from the shortest to longest wavelengths. (199)

end-stopped cell V2 neuron having an elongated receptive field with an excitatory area in the middle and inhibitory zones at both ends; may detect different degrees of curvature. (238)

face cell Type of neuron in IT cortex that is selective for faces. (228)

far disparity Objects more distant than the visual fixation point fall on noncorresponding areas of retina and create double images. (231)

field neuron Type of D cell that responds to the motion of the ground instead of the figure; found in MST. (241)

figure The object on which you are fixating and to which your attention is directed. (239)

figure neurons Cells in MT that respond to the motion of a figure relative to ground. (241)

focal vision The part of vision concerned with the analysis of fine spatial detail in small areas of the visual field. (218)

fovea A tiny area right at the center of the retina that provides the greatest acuity. (202)

frontal eye fields (FEF) Portion of the frontal cortex that exerts some control over eye movements. (219)

ganglion cells Retinal cells whose axons form the optic nerve. (202)

geniculostriate path The part of the visual projection system that runs from the retina through LGN to V1. (217)

graded potentials See *local currents*. (203)

ground The part of the visual scene outside of the figure; the unattended part. (239)

hand cell Type of neuron in IT cortex that is selective for hands. (228)

horizontal cells Retinal cells that interconnect rods, cones, and bipolar cells. (202)

[^{3}H]proline Tritiated proline; a radioactive chemical used in anterograde tracing of pathways. (235)

hyperopia Blurred image that occurs because the lens focuses the light at a point behind the retina rather than on it; farsightedness. (202)

ice-cube model Hubel and Wiesel's early theory of how the blobs, ocular dominance columns, and layers of V1 are arranged. (237)

inferotemporal (IT) cortex Region of visual cortex on inferior surface of temporal lobe. (214)

interblobs V1 areas within ocular dominance columns but outside of blobs; contain cells that are selective for particular line orientations but not for color. (236)

interstripes Areas between stripes in V2 that contain cells selective for orientation and disparity; part of the object vision pathway. (239)

iris A ring of muscles located behind the cornea; the colored part of the eye. (201)

landmark discrimination A learning task in which a monkey must choose a stimulus closest to a "landmark" object; tests for spatial vision. (244)

lateral geniculate nucleus (LGN) The thalamic nucleus in which the optic tract terminates. (214)

lens Transparent crystalline structure just behind the iris that focuses light. (201)

light adaptation A rapid decrease in visual sensitivity in response to increased illumination. (209)

line-orientation analyzers Neural connections in V1 that respond selectively to a line oriented at a particular angle. (222)

local currents Currents similar to EPSPs that are found in receptor cells and retinal bipolars; same as graded potentials. (202)

magnocellular layers Ventral layers of LGN; termination point for Y cells. (219)

MST Medial superior temporal area containing analyzers for visual perception of motion. (239)

MT Middle temporal area of cortex at the parietal–occipital boundary containing analyzers for motion. (239)

multiple parallel processing pathways The idea that the visual system consists of a collection of pathways from the retina, each leading through a different chain of processors set to detect different features. (219)

myopia Blurred image that occurs because the lens focuses the light at a point in front of the retina rather than on it; nearsightedness. (201)

nanometer One billionth of a meter. (206)

near disparity Objects closer than the visual fixation point fall on noncorresponding areas of retina and create double images. (231)

object vision pathway Part of the cortical visual system that extracts information about color and form; ends in IT cortex. (221)

ocular dominance The principle that some cortical visual neurons are more strongly connected to one eye than to the other. (228)

ocular dominance bands Areas of V1, each of which is dominated by one eye. (235–236)

opponent processes Neural processing in which one stimulus increases the firing rate of the neuron, whereas the opposite stimulus decreases it. (232)

opponent vector cells Motion detector cells sensitive either to movement toward the center of the visual field or movement out from the center of the visual field. (242)

opsin Photochemical found in the cones. (206)

optic disc Area of the retina void of receptors; exit point of optic nerve and blood vessels. (202)

optic nerve The axon bundle connecting the retina to the rest of the brain; cranial nerve II. (204)

orientation columns An area of V1 cortex that cuts across the layers from white matter to cortical surface; each column contains only those simple cortical cells having one particular orientation preference. (235)

outer segment (of a receptor) The portion of a receptor containing photochemicals. (204)

output neurons The type of neuron in a neural structure such as the retina whose axons carry the processed information to other structures of the nervous system. (203)

parvocellular layers The most dorsal layers of LGN; termination point of X cells. (219)

peripheral retina The portion of retina around the edges that receives light from objects around the borders of the visual field. (207)

peristriate cortex Areas 18 and 19. (214)

photochemicals Chemicals that react to light. (204)

photon A discrete packet of electromagnetic energy; the smallest quantity of light. (199)

pigment epithelium A layer of dark cells at the back of the retina between the receptors and the sclera. (203)

polysensory analysis Predominantly visual analysis involving not only inputs from visual analyzers but also inputs from analyzers for other senses. (242)

pulvinar A thalamic nucleus with visual functions. (219)

pupil The hole formed by the iris through which light passes to reach the retina. (201)

receptive field (RF) The area of receptor surface (such as the retina) within which the cell in question can be stimulated. (208)

retina The cup-shaped triple layer of neurons on the inside of the eyeball that contains the receptors for light. (202)

retinal disparity The fact that corresponding points of

light in the two retinal images fall on noncorresponding areas of the two retinas; basis for stereoscopic depth perception. (231)

retinotectal path The part of the visual projection system that extends from the retina to the superior colliculus. (217)

rhodopsin The photochemical contained in the rods. (204)

rods Photoreceptors associated with perception of varying brightnesses. (202)

sclera A tough, membranous sac that forms the eyeball. (200)

sensitivity The ability to respond to weak stimuli. (209)

simple cortical neuron V1 cell with a set of connections to the thalamus that makes it a line-orientation analyzer. (223)

spatial attention mechanism The ability to direct visual analyzer activity to focus on one or another part of the visual field. (244)

spatial vision pathway Part of cortical visual system that extracts information about spatial location; ends in parietal cortex. (221)

stereo blindness An inability to perceive a three-dimensional (stereo) image; that is, to see depth. (232)

stereopsis Stereoscopic depth perception. (229)

tectopulvinar pathway The path from the superior colliculus neurons to the pulvinar. (219)

thick stripes Areas of V2 containing neurons selective for line orientation, motion, and retinal disparity; part of the spatial vision pathway. (239)

thin stripes Areas of V2 containing neurons selective for color; part of the object vision pathway. (239)

transduction The process of converting information from one energy form to another. (202)

transposition The visual capability to recognize a stimulus no matter where it occurs on the retina. (224)

tuned disparity neuron Visual cortex neuron with connections that enable it to respond selectively to a particular amount of near or far disparity; part of the analyzers for depth. (232)

V1 Occipital cortical area in which axons of LGN output cells terminate; also called area 17. (220)

V2 Area 18; part of the peristriate visual cortex in the occipital lobe. (220)

V3 Part of area 19 in the visual cortex. (220)

V4 Part of area 19 in the visual cortex. (220)

VIP area Ventral inferior parietal area; together with area 7a makes up a polysensory analyzer area. (242)

visible spectrum The part of the electromagnetic spectrum capable of stimulating the eyes. (199)

visual agnosia Symptom of brain damage in which objects can be seen but not understood. (214)

visual projection system The route that visual information takes from the retina to the visual cortex. (214)

X cells Retinal ganglion cells with relatively small receptive fields concentrated around the fovea; may be most sensitive to fine visual patterns. (218)

Y cells Retinal ganglion cells with relatively large receptive fields; probably involved in the perception of the overall outlines and positions of objects. (218)

Young–Helmholtz theory Explanation of the role of short-, medium-, and long-wavelength cones in color perception. (207)

Auditory and Chemical Senses

Olfaction

Summary

I n this chapter, we look at the oldest senses and the youngest one. The chemical senses probably date back to when our ancestors were single-celled creatures. As cell colonies evolved into integrated organisms, the original generalized chemical sense of the single cell began to differentiate into a set of more specialized mechanisms, leading eventually to the variety of chemical sensors possessed by primates. Humans have sense receptors in their blood vessels for detecting changes in blood gases (especially carbon dioxide); receptors throughout the mucous tissues of the nose, mouth, and throat for sensing potentially harmful chemicals (such as capsaicin in chili peppers); receptors on the tongue and in the lining of the mouth that are involved in the sense of taste; receptors in the nose for the sense of smell; and possible receptors in the liver and digestive tract (yet to be verified) for sensing ingested nutrients. Because most of what we know revolves around the taste and smell systems, those two chemical senses are discussed here.

Two of the senses covered in this chapter are "air" senses that became much more important after vertebrates emerged from the oceans and became land creatures. Both hearing and smell depend on the atmosphere around us to carry the information about distant objects to our waiting receptors. Although the chemical senses still play a very important role even in primates such as ourselves, the sense of hearing has assumed a pivotal position in the affairs of humans because it forms the basis of our language ability. We discuss it first.

■ Audition

If humans didn't possess **audition** (the sense of hearing), you might not be reading this book right now. In fact, there might not be any books at all because our written language is an outgrowth of spoken language. Perhaps a human race without audition could have evolved manual sign language, but it is doubtful that such communication could duplicate the subtleties and fine discriminations available in communication through sound. To understand audition, we must first find out a little about the nature of sound and sound waves.

Detecting Sound Waves

Human language is a wondrous thing, but it does have its drawbacks. People often use its ambiguities to make problems for themselves. For example, you may have heard the ancient paradox: If a tree falls in a forest in which there is no one to hear it, does it make a noise? Actually, this is not a paradox; it is simply an illustration of ambiguity. The word *sound* is used in everyday discourse to refer both to the physical stimulus created by the falling tree and to the psychological experience within a listening nervous system. If we separate these two and name them differently, the "paradox" is eliminated. Let us call the physical stimulus for audition sound waves, and the psychological **sensation**—the event within the nervous system of a listener—we will call **sound**. Now it is obvious that the tree creates sound waves when it falls, but without a listener, it makes no sound.

The Nature of Sound Waves   Unfortunately, the term **sound wave** is misleading for some people. It evokes an image of something moving up and down through the air like an ocean wave. A better term would have been *pressure cycle*, for that is exactly what a sound wave really is. Figure 7.1 shows the cross section of a drumhead that is vibrating back and forth after having been struck. In Figure 7.1a the drumhead pushes out against the surrounding air, compressing the air molecules in its path into a band of higher pressure. The drumhead then starts to snap back in the other direction, but the molecules it has pushed continue to move out in the same direction they were headed. Thus, a zone is created between the drumhead and the pressure ridge in which there are fewer than normal air molecules—in other words, a low-pressure area. The molecules originally contacted by the drumhead actually do not get very far before they bump into other air molecules. (There are about 400 billion, billion molecules of

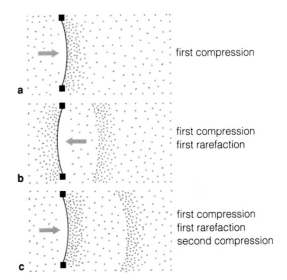

Figure 7.1   A drumhead seen in cross section at three successive moments. (**a**) The head has just been struck and is moving out against the surrounding air molecules (shown as black dots). As it moves, it gathers them into a ridge of compressed air. (**b**) The elasticity of the drumhead snaps it back in the opposite direction, leaving a zone behind it in which there are fewer than normal air molecules (rarefaction). (**c**) Elasticity again reverses the membrane's direction of travel, thus starting the whole cycle over again (second sound wave). The first wave continues to travel outward as the second is being generated.

air per cubic inch.) This contact slows or stops the progress of the first set of molecules and imparts movement to the molecules contacted. This second set of molecules immediately bumps into a third set, again passing on the movement. The overall picture then is of a bump that rapidly travels through the air, passed from one molecule to another. It is this bump, rather than the original air molecules, that travels from the drum to your ear. This bump or pressure ridge is, of course, a sound wave.

But there is more to a sound wave than just a traveling ridge of increased pressure. A sound wave has a **compression** phase (which we have just discussed) and a **rarefaction** phase. In Figure 7.1b, you

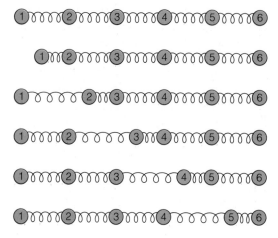

Figure 7.2 The movement of individual air molecules in a sound wave. The top line shows that before a sound wave arrives the molecules are evenly spaced. The second line represents the next moment as the compression phase of the first wave arrives at this point in space. Molecule 1 is pushed toward 2. The bump from 1 sends 2 speeding toward 3 in the third moment, while 1 is sucked back toward its original position. The molecules act as though they were connected with springs, thus affecting each other but never moving outside the confines of one tiny little area of space. (Adapted from Denes & Pinson, 1973)

see the drumhead snapping back and producing low pressure (rarefaction) in a zone just back of the compression zone, which is moving out toward your ear. Because this low-pressure area is a partial vacuum, it tends to suck the original air molecules back toward the drumhead. So, when the first set of molecules slam into the second set, they don't just stop and stay in a new location. Instead, they immediately begin to move back in the direction of their original location near the drum. Figure 7.1c shows the next moment. The drumhead snaps forward once more and again bumps the same air molecules as they are returning to their original locations. Again, the molecules move out from the drum, contact other molecules, and impart their energy to this second set, which in turn bumps a third set and so forth. Because the drumhead can vibrate back and forth several hundred times per second, the end result is a whole series of pressure ridges alternating with zones of

low pressure, all moving out, away from the drum in all directions. Figure 7.2 shows the back-and-forth motion of the individual molecules in a sound wave.

Now let's look at a graph of the whole process. Figure 7.3 shows air pressure on the vertical axis and time along the horizontal axis. If we record the air pressure at a particular point in space between the drum and your ear, we see the pressure first increase above normal and then dip below normal. This represents one cycle of a sound wave, and you can see now why these cycles are called waves. When graphed in this manner they do indeed look like waves.

Sound waves can vary along two major dimensions: frequency and amplitude. **Frequency** refers to the number of waves generated per second, and it is measured in units called **hertz** (**Hz**) (pronounced, HAIRTS). So, a 100-Hz tone, for example, would be one having a frequency of 100 cycles of compression and rarefaction per second. **Amplitude** is the amount of pressure change between the point of greatest compression and the point of greatest rarefaction; in the graphic representation, amplitude is shown by the height of the wave. When we are talking about sound waves as psychological stimuli, the term **intensity** is often substituted for amplitude.

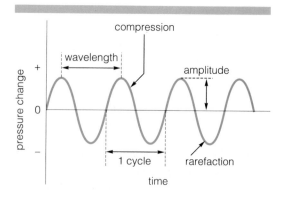

Figure 7.3 Graphic representation of cycles of compression and rarefaction that make up a sound wave. Time increases along the horizontal axis, pressure along the vertical. The zero pressure change level would be whatever air pressure is normal for the altitude of the subject's environment (14 lb/sq in. at sea level). (Adapted from Schiffman, 1976)

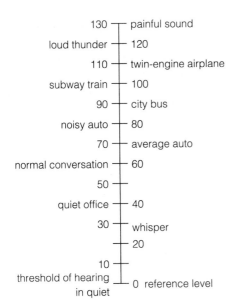

130	painful sound
loud thunder — 120	
110	twin-engine airplane
subway train — 100	
90	city bus
noisy auto — 80	
70	average auto
normal conversation — 60	
50	
quiet office — 40	
30	whisper
	20
10	
threshold of hearing	0 reference level
in quiet	

Figure 7.4 Intensities of some common sound sources expressed in decibel units. (Adapted from Stevens & Davis, 1938)

Frequency and amplitude are *stimulus* dimensions. What are the dimensions of sensation? The psychological dimension that correlates best with frequency is **pitch**. Higher frequencies give higher sounding tones. Young humans with excellent hearing can detect frequencies all the way from 20 Hz (which produces such a low pitch that it tends to be experienced more as a huge vibration than as a tone) up to 20,000 Hz (a thin, ultrahigh whistle that is way off of any musical scale). The best psychological correlate of wave amplitude (intensity) is **loudness**. Amplitude is usually measured on the **decibel** scale, and Figure 7.4 gives you some idea of the degree of loudness associated with various decibel levels.

Anatomy of the Ear   What we usually refer to as our "ears" are just a minor part of those very complex organs and go by the technical name of **auricles** (OR-ic-ulls). The whole organ can be divided into three parts: outer, middle, and inner. In Figure 7.5, locate the auricle and the external auditory canal, the two parts of the **outer ear**. The auricle is built to collect sound waves and the canal to funnel them inward

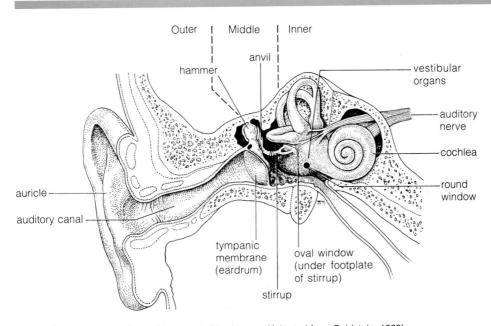

Figure 7.5   Outer, middle, and inner ear of the human. (Adapted from Goldstein, 1989)

toward the eardrum, or **tympanic membrane**, which is the dividing line between the outer ear and the **middle ear**. The compression phase of a sound wave pushes the tympanic membrane inward, while the rarefaction phase pulls it back out. So, if you are listening to a flute playing middle C, your eardrum is vibrating back and forth 256 times each second, and with each of those vibrations, it moves the three tiny bones of the middle ear—the **hammer, anvil,** and **stirrup**—which carry the vibrations to the inner ear. The third bone in the chain, the stirrup, is attached to a flexible membrane called the **oval window**, which is the entrance to the inner ear. The middle ear is an air-filled cavity, but the inner ear is filled with lymphatic fluid containing many of the ingredients of seawater. Notice in Figure 7.5 that the **inner ear** is a complex collection of chambers and tunnels through the bone of the skull. The three looping tunnels (the semicircular canals) and the chambers with which they connect are the **vestibular organs** (containing receptors for the vestibular senses), whereas the object that looks like a snail shell is the **cochlea** (containing receptors for audition). Vestibular senses inform the brain of the direction of gravity and of the direction of its own movement (discussed in Chapter 9).

The Middle Ear   The middle ear has several functions, but the most important one is to act as an amplifier that can partially compensate for the fact that sound waves in air are such weak stimuli. Consider the rather amazing fact that you can stand at one end of a large classroom and hear a person speaking to you from the opposite end. For that to be accomplished, the speaker must force a column of air out of her lungs, set it to vibrating between high- and low-pressure zones (sound waves), and shape it with tongue, lips, and teeth. Those sound waves must then travel 50 feet through the air and still have enough energy left at the end of this trip to move your tympanic membrane in and out. The movement of the eardrum is so slight in some cases that it is only the width of a few air molecules. Then consider that the speaker can raise her voice a little and be heard out in the hall even if the classroom door is shut. This means that she imparted enough energy to the waves that they actually set the door

and wall into microscopic vibrations. In other words, the solid structure of the building carried the waves and, on the hall side, acted just like a drumhead by setting air molecules there into motion at the same frequencies. Not only has the speaker directly moved a portion of every listener's body but she has also literally shaken the building itself.

In reality, of course, the human voice carries extremely little energy. The people to whom you are speaking cannot feel your sound waves colliding with their skin. (If you are close enough, they can feel your breath, but this is not sound waves. Remember that unlike the case of wind or a puff of air the molecules in sound waves do not travel more than a fraction of a millimeter.) That a listener in the hall can hear a speaker behind a closed door is a testament to the extreme sensitivity of the human ear rather than to the power of the human voice. Let's see how the bones of the middle ear contribute to this sensitivity.

Sound waves enter the receptor organ of the inner ear by moving the oval window in and out (Figure 7.6a). The oval window is moved by the stirrup, which is moved by the anvil and hammer and, ultimately, by the tympanic membrane. The eardrum is considerably larger in diameter than the oval window, and it is this size difference that allows an amplification effect to occur at this site. Figure 7.6b shows that when a large collection of weak forces (individual air molecules) pushes on a relatively large area (the tympanic membrane) and all these little forces are "funneled down" into a narrow area (the oval window), the amount of force per unit area will be increased. A weak force over a large area has been converted into a strong force over a little area. This effect is especially important because there is fluid, rather than air, behind the oval window and the resistance of the oval window to being moved inward is much greater than the resistance of the eardrum. The action of the middle-ear bones increases the force of the waves at the oval window by 90 times over what they are at the eardrum.

The Inner Ear and the Reception Process   The cochlea consists of a triple set of tunnels ("canals") that wind all the way from the oval window up to the point at the top, like compartments in a snail's shell

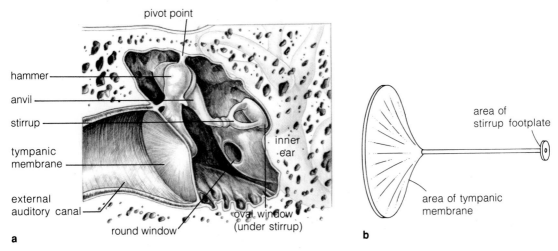

Figure 7.6 Amplification of sound waves in the middle ear. (**a**) When the tympanic membrane is pushed in by the compression phase of the sound wave, it carries with it the attached hammer and anvil. The tip of the anvil rotates toward the stirrup, thus pushing the latter toward the oval window. This action flexes the oval window inward during compression and pulls it back out during rarefaction. (**b**) A weak force over a large area (eardrum) equals a strong force over a small area (oval window). The oval window is only 1/25 the area of the eardrum. (**a** Adapted from Fowler, 1984; **b** adapted from Goldstein, 1989)

(Figures 7.7 and 7.8). At the tip of the cochlea, two of these canals (**vestibular canal** and **tympanic canal**) join together through an opening called the **helicotrema** (HEL-ih-COT-rem-uh). Sandwiched between them runs a third canal (the **cochlear duct**), which contains receptor cells (Figure 7.7). The base of the cochlear duct is formed by a piece of elastic tissue named the **basilar membrane**, on which one finds the **organ of Corti**. This organ contains the **hair cells** in which the actual conversion of sound waves to electrical currents takes place. Synapsing with each hair cell is an **auditory nerve fiber** whose cell body can be found in the spiral ganglion at the center of the cochlea.

Now let's see what happens when a sound wave enters this complex receptor organ. The compression phase of the wave pushes in the tympanic membrane, and this push is carried through the bones of the middle ear to be exerted against the oval window. As this membrane moves inward, it displaces fluid that exerts pressure up the length of the vestibular

canal and downward against the wall of the cochlear duct (**Reissner's membrane**). Because the base of the cochlear duct (basilar membrane) is flexible, the pressure wave can depress the whole duct (Figure 7.8). As the basilar membrane is pushed down into the tympanic canal, the fluid there (which is not compressible) must move out of the way. It is shoved down the tympanic canal toward the **round window**, which then bulges out into the air of the middle ear to make room. In the rarefaction phase of the sound wave, the whole process reverses with the oval window being pulled back out by the stirrup, which sucks the cochlear duct upward, which eventually pulls the round window inward.

Transduction takes place when the sound wave pushes and pulls the basilar membrane up and down. The hairlike **stereocilia** protruding from the tops of hair cells are the triggers that initiate electrical activity. When they are bent over, the receptor cell responds by generating electrical currents that then excite the terminal of the auditory nerve fiber, which

Figure 7.7 Anatomy of the cochlea. (**a**) Cross section through one turn of the cochlear spiral. (**b**) Enlarged cross section of the organ of Corti. (**a** Adapted from Goldstein, 1989; **b** adapted from Gulick, 1971, in Goldstein, 1989)

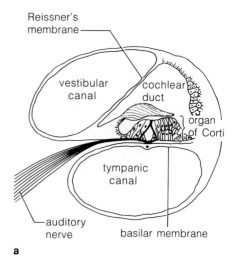

a

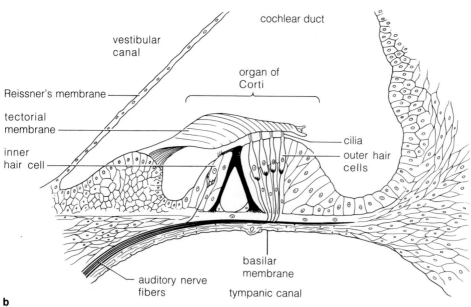

b

contacts the receptor. How then are stereocilia bent by the sound wave? Many of the cilia are attached at their tops to the **tectorial membrane** (Figure 7.7b), and this membrane is anchored to the wall of the cochlea at the narrow side of the cochlear duct. When a sound wave depresses Reissner's membrane and the organ of Corti, receptor cells are not only carried downward but are also carried slightly to one side in what is termed a **shearing action** (Durrant & Lovrinic, 1977). During this sideways shearing movement, the tectorial membrane moves in one direction, the organ of Corti (with cell bodies of the hair cells) goes the opposite way, and stereocilia, which are attached to both structures, are caught in the middle (Figure 7.9). Because it only takes a microscopic shearing action to strongly bend stereocilia,

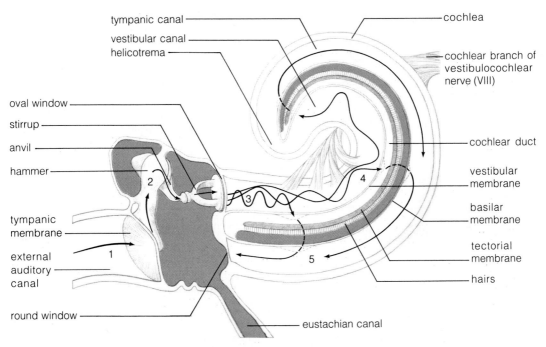

Figure 7.8 Transmission of sound waves through the ear. (1) Sound waves move the tympanic membrane and (2) attached bones of middle ear. (3) In-and-out movements of the oval window push on fluid of the inner ear (cochlea). (4) The pressure on the fluid of the vestibular canal is relieved by the cochlear duct bending downward into the tympanic canal. (5) The resulting pressure on the fluid of the tympanic canal is relieved when the round window bulges out into the middle-ear cavity. Three sound waves are shown entering the cochlea. The highest-frequency wave displaces the cochlear duct close to the oval window, whereas the lowest-frequency wave exerts its maximum pressure near the helicotrema. Displacement of the cochlear duct by sound waves stimulates the hair cells of the organ of Corti, thus producing nerve impulses in the VIIIth nerve. (Adapted from Fowler, 1984)

Figure 7.9 A schematic diagram showing how sound wave pressure is translated into shearing action. (**a**) The cochlea is at rest. One hair cell with three stereocilia is shown to illustrate the point. Notice that both the basilar membrane carrying the organ of Corti and the tectorial membrane above are suspended from the wall of the cochlea at the left and that there is a gap between these two structures across which the stereocilia protrude. (**b**) A sound wave is deforming the structures, and because of the way they are attached to the wall of the cochlea, the tectorial membrane tends to slip to one side while the organ of Corti goes in the other, thus producing the shearing action indicated by the arrows. This shear is a force far more powerful than the downward pressure of the wave itself and represents an amplification effect. To make conceptualization easier, the amount of shear is exaggerated in the diagram.

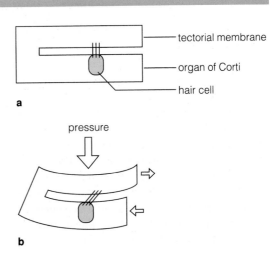

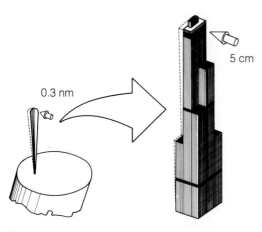

Figure 7.10 Least amount of cilium deflection needed to produce a response in the human auditory system. At the left, a hair cell and single cilium indicate that a threshold-level stimulus (one that is just barely audible) deflects the cilium only 0.3 nm at its tip. If the cilium were as tall as the Sears Tower, the equivalent tip movement would be 5 cm. (Adapted from Dallos, 1988)

the hair cells are sensitive to exquisitely tiny deflections of the basilar membrane and organ of Corti. At the threshold of human hearing, the sound wave produces a hair cell response despite a basilar membrane movement that is only one-tenth the diameter of a hydrogen atom (Uttal, 1973). At this sound level, the tip of each stereocilium moves back and forth only 0.3 nm. Or, in more familiar terms, if the stereocilium were as tall as the Sears Tower in Chicago, its tip would be swaying only 5 cm—about 2 inches (Figure 7.10). You depend on movements of this size to hear the quietest sounds.

No one is certain yet why bending stereocilia should trigger a current in the hair cell, although there are several theories about how this might occur (Hudspeth, 1982, 1985). By one means or another, the bending of cilia opens the potassium gates in the membrane of the hair cell, and the resulting potassium current depolarizes the membrane enough to release neurotransmitter at the synapse with the cochlear nerve fiber, (Sellick, 1979). The neurotransmitter initiates nerve impulses in the nerve fiber, and the pattern of these impulses carries information

about the sound wave. The way in which different information is coded into different patterns has been a question of great interest to researchers, as we will see next.

Neural Correlates of Sensation

One thing that helps you tell female from male voices is the average pitch the person is emitting. Furthermore, you can tell when a person is asking a question rather than making a statement because the pitch of the speaker's voice rises rather than falls at the end of a sentence. (You may not be aware that you vary your pitch as you speak. Try saying "yes" as a statement and then as a question and listen for the difference in the pitch at the end of the word.) In some languages, like Chinese, several words can have the same phonemes (pronunciation sounds), and they are distinguishable from one another only by differences in pitch. An overall shift in the pitch of a person's voice can signal a change in emotional state. Generally, when a person's pitch rises in a conversation, it indicates growing excitement, fear, or anger; lower pitches suggest calmness or boredom. It is obvious then that pitch perception has been of great use to the human race because much of our survival ability has depended on our skill at interacting with each other through oral communication. What then is the neural basis for our ability to hear pitch?

The ability to hear pitches, like the ability to see colors, is really a matter of being able to discriminate between stimuli. In the case of color, it is a discrimination between wavelengths of light; with pitch it is a discrimination between frequencies of sound waves. How is the brain able to tell one sound wave frequency from another? Two major ideas have been proposed to explain this capability—frequency theory and place theory—and we will see that both concepts are needed for a complete explanation.

Frequency Theory This set of ideas is the simplest, most direct explanation of how frequency might be coded into a pattern of nerve activity. It suggests that nerve cells carry sound wave–frequency information through the nervous system in the form of nerve impulse frequency. In the cochlea, as the compression phase of each sound wave moves the basilar membrane, hair cells respond with an impulse or two and then fall silent during the rarefaction phase. Thus, there is one burst per wave. A low, 100-Hz tone fires the cochlear nerve 100 times per second, whereas a midrange tone of 300 Hz fires the cells 300 times per second. This is often called **frequency following** because the frequency of nerve firing follows the frequency of the sound wave.

If the frequency of firing represents (codes for) the frequency of the sound wave, then how is the intensity (amplitude) of the wave represented neurally? In other words, what is the neural code for loudness? Apparently, as the intensity of the wave increases, more and more hair cells respond; thus, the code for amplitude is the number of neurons active at any one moment.

A problem with the frequency theory arises immediately. How do we perceive high pitches produced by frequencies in the thousands of cycles per second? There is a limit to how many times per second a neuron can fire. If you recall from Chapter 4, axons have an absolute refractory period of about 1 ms between impulses. Theoretically then, some axons might fire as many as 1,000 times per second, but this leaves frequency coding above 1,000 Hz unexplained. In fact, there is evidence that the cochlear nerve, taken as a whole, can follow frequencies at least up to 3,000 Hz, even if its individual nerve fibers cannot (Geldard, 1972).

Wever (1949) devised an explanation of this seeming paradox and called his idea the **volley principle**. Not all fibers must fire with each sound wave; some can be recovering while others work (Figure 7.11). Wever's use of the term *volley* came from a trick used by the infantry in the 18th century. Reloading a musket took so long that a charging enemy could be on top of a line of defenders before the next shot was rammed home. The army solved this problem by arranging troops in three rows facing the enemy. The first row would fire and drop to one knee to reload as the second row fired. As the second row dropped, the third would fire, and as soon as they began to reload, the first row would be ready to stand and fire their second round. In this way the three lines could sustain continuous firing. The whole process was, of course, called *volleying*.

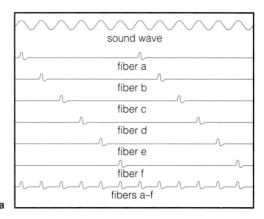

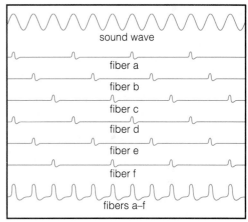

Figure 7.11 The volley theory of frequency following in the auditory nerve. (**a**) Time lines are shown for six individual fibers and the bundle of fibers as a unit. Blips on the time lines show when an impulse occurred. The sound wave is shown at the top. The first fiber fires on the first wave and is recovered sufficiently to fire again on the seventh. The second fiber fires on the second wave and is recovered in time to fire again on the eighth, and so forth. Thus, a fiber bundle as a whole responds to every wave despite the inability of any one of its fibers to respond that frequently. (**b**) A higher-amplitude sound wave can fire axons more frequently because of the relationship between stimulus intensity and the relative refractory phase of the fiber (see Chapter 4). The result is that two fibers fire on each wave rather than one. Thus, intensity is coded into number of fibers firing on each wave. (Adapted from Wever, 1949)

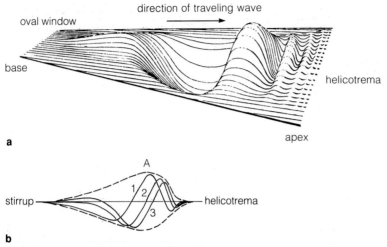

a

b

Figure 7.12 (**a**) Traveling wave on the basilar membrane. Note that the basilar membrane is wider at the top of the cochlea (apex) than at the bottom, near the oval window. The height of the wave is grossly exaggerated with respect to the size of the basilar membrane in order to make the shape of the wave easier to see. The actual height is a distance smaller than the diameter of some molecules. (**b**) A traveling wave caught at three successive moments. The wave envelope (indicated by dashed lines) is the boundary within which crests and troughs fit. It shows where on the membrane the greatest deflections occur. In this example, the peak of the wave (indicated by A) came about 28 mm from the oval window. (**a** Adapted from Tonndorf, 1960, in Goldstein, 1989; **b** adapted from von Békésy, 1960, in Goldstein, 1989)

Thanks to volleying, the cochlear nerve can follow frequencies up to about 3,000 Hz, but that still leaves the range from 3,000 to 20,000 Hz unexplained. For that we will need place theory.

Place Theory   The **place theory** of frequency coding is best represented by von Békésy's interpretation of basilar membrane mechanics. The basic idea is that each frequency is represented in the nervous system by the firing of a different set of neurons. The ability of the cochlea to assign different cells to different sound wave frequencies depends on the fact that each different sound wave frequency flexes the basilar membrane maximally at a different *place* along its length. Thus, different hair cells respond to different frequencies. Now we must ask how the basilar membrane is able to change its place of maximal flexion as the frequency changes. The answer is found in von Békésy's idea of a **traveling wave**.

When the oval window pushes in and out on the cochlear fluid and flexes the basilar membrane up and down, each in-and-out push creates a ripple in the membrane that starts at the oval window and moves up the cochlea toward the helicotrema at the top (Figure 7.12a and b). Imagine you and a friend holding a long sheet stretched between you. The friend gives his end a snap, and you see a ripple rush across the sheet to your end. You have created a traveling wave similar to the one that the stirrup creates as it pushes the oval window in and out.

Each wave that travels up the basilar membrane grows taller as it travels until it reaches a maximum height at some point along the way. The wave in Figure 7.12a was caught near the moment when it was at its highest point. As we noted earlier, the place at which this maximum deflection occurs is determined by the frequency of the sound wave. Figure 7.13 shows the heights of two traveling waves of

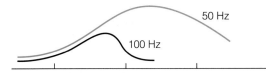

Figure 7.13 Envelopes of a 50- and 100-Hz wave. The higher-frequency traveling wave is confined to the lower part of the basilar membrane near the oval window, while the lower-frequency wave deflects the membrane along most of its length. Note that the higher-frequency wave peaks at a fairly specific place on the membrane, while the lower-frequency wave is spread out with no clear place of maximal stimulation. (Keep in mind as you look at this that these curves are envelopes and that they do not show the shape of the traveling wave—only its height at each point along the membrane.) (From Tonndorf, 1962)

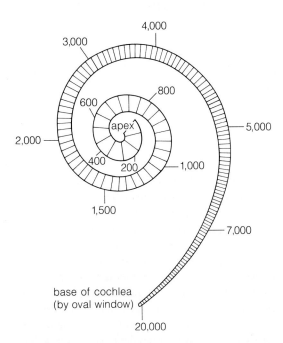

Figure 7.14 Locations along the organ of Corti showing how waves of different frequencies have their maximum effects at different places. The numbers refer to hertz. What is not shown here is that the places are very specific for the high frequencies but broaden from sharp points into fuzzy regions for the low frequencies. Thus, below 1,000 Hz the specific locations are not as meaningful. (From Creager, 1983)

different frequencies, showing that the place of maximum movement is closer to the oval window for higher frequencies and closer to the helicotrema for lower frequencies. This correlation between frequency and place of maximum movement is the result of several factors, the most important of which is the stiffness of the vibrating membrane. The basilar membrane becomes less elastic toward the oval window, and a less elastic membrane vibrates more readily at higher frequencies. Thus, there is a gradual loss of stiffness as one moves from the oval window to the apex (helicotrema), with the result that obtaining maximum displacement requires a lower and lower frequency. So, near the oval window we have a stiff membrane that vibrates nicely at the highest frequencies, while at the other end of the cochlea, the apex, we have a looser, more elastic membrane that reacts best to the lowest frequencies.

Now all our theory needs is one last assumption: The greater the up-and-down displacement of the basilar membrane, the more the hair cells will be stimulated. For each different frequency, there will be a small area in which the hair cells are more completely depolarized because they are located at the place of maximal basilar membrane movement (Figure 7.14). The activity of those particular receptors leads to the conscious experience of a particular pitch.

One concern with the place theory is that the traveling wave stimulates a great number of neurons as it moves up the cochlea and that the area of maximal deflection may be a fairly broad zone of hair cells. How then can our nervous systems ever achieve acute frequency discrimination? This question has inspired researchers to discover how broad a band of cells an individual wave does stimulate. Measurements of the height of the traveling wave as it moves up the basilar membrane show that low-frequency waves peak over a very broad area, whereas higher-frequency waves have their maximum deflection at a fairly definite point in the cochlea (Figure 7.13). That should mean that a high-frequency wave maximally stimulates only a few select hair cells, whereas a low-frequency wave stimulates cells along a great stretch of membrane. Evidence for this difference in selectivity is seen in the results of a study with anesthetized guinea pigs subjected

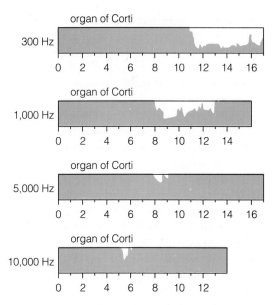

Figure 7.15 Diagrams of the extent of damage to the organ of Corti and the place of damage. The white areas are the zones of damage, and their height indicates the amount. These results could be predicted from our knowledge of traveling waves because lower frequencies (300 and 1,000 Hz) have broader areas of damage than do higher frequencies (5,000 and 10,000 Hz), and, as the frequency rises, the area of damage shifts toward the oval window. (From Smith, 1947; Smith & Wever, 1949; in Goldstein, 1989)

to destructively intense pure tones (Smith, 1947). Figure 7.15 shows what was found when their cochleas were examined for areas of damage. Each black bar indicates the unrolled organ of Corti stretched out from the stirrup end at the left of the figure to the helicotrema end at the right. The white areas indicate where dead hair cells were found, and the depth of the white shows the extent of the damage. As you can see, low-frequency (300 Hz) waves killed receptors over a great length of the cochlea near its peak at the helicotrema. A midrange (1,000 Hz) tone did about half the damage over a smaller distance closer to the oval window. The two high-frequency tones (5,000 Hz and 10,000 Hz) selectively killed cells only in very narrow bands, thus confirming the difference in selectivity between high and low frequencies and showing that the place theory would work well for high tones but not so well for low tones.

Electrical recording data from single cochlear nerve fibers tends to support this conclusion. If traveling waves (at least those from high-frequency waves) maximally stimulate only a small, specific area of basilar membrane, then cells in that area should respond best to that particular frequency. Furthermore, nerve fibers serving those hair cells should also be fairly specific to that particular frequency. Figure 7.16 shows the **tuning curves** for four cochlear nerve fibers, each presumably serving a different area of the organ of Corti. To generate a tuning curve, the experimenter locates a nerve fiber with an electrode tip and then begins presenting pure tones to the animal's ear and recording how intense the tone must be in order to evoke a response from the fiber. This threshold amount of intensity differs for different frequencies, and as you can see from Figure 7.16, each cell has a "favorite" frequency at which its threshold is lowest. Thus, in the figure, the cell at the left is labeled a *2,000-Hz* tone because, when the intensity is turned down to 100 dB below the standard, the cell no longer responds to any frequency other than 2,000 Hz. That frequency is its point of greatest sensitivity; it seems to be "tuned" to that frequency. This is a fairly broadly tuned cell, however, because it loses much of its frequency specificity as the intensity is raised closer to the standard. Fibers with best frequencies above 2,000 Hz have narrower tuning curves. In other words, as the frequency of the sound wave is raised, the fibers that respond are more and more selective (have smaller and smaller tuning curves). It is evident from Figure 7.16 that a moderately intense stimulus of 2,000 Hz would trigger impulses in not only the 2,000-Hz fiber but also in the 2,600-Hz and 3,700-Hz fibers. However, when the frequency is as high as 17,000 Hz, the tuning curves are so narrow that the cells that respond to that frequency hardly respond to any other frequencies at all; they are very frequency-specific.

The place theory, of course, needs frequency-specific neurons. For the idea to work, a particular frequency should stimulate a specific place on the basilar membrane, thus exciting a select group of

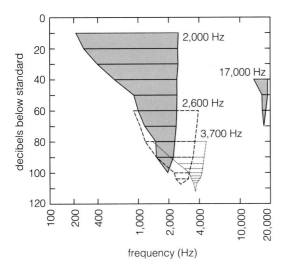

Figure 7.16 Tuning curves for four auditory nerve fibers. The vertical axis of the graph shows how weak the stimulus can be and still get a response from the fiber. The horizontal axis shows how this threshold point changes with different frequencies. For example, the 2,000-Hz fiber can just barely respond to a tone 100 dB below the standard if the tone is at 2,000 Hz. It will respond to a 1,000-Hz tone, but as you can see from the graph, the tone has to be much stronger (only 60 dB below standard). It is important to note that the width of the response area for each fiber (the number of different frequencies to which it will respond) is generally predictable from our knowledge of traveling waves. That is, the fiber that is "tuned" to a lower frequency (2,000 Hz) has the broadest response area, while the fiber tuned to the highest frequency (17,000 Hz) has the narrowest. The width of the fiber's response area reflects the sharpness of the traveling wave's peak. (Adapted from Galambos & Davis, 1943)

cells that represent that frequency and only that frequency. As you can tell from the data on traveling waves and tuning curves, frequency specificity is found only in the higher ranges. Our conclusion must be that place theory works nicely for high frequencies, and frequency theory works well for low frequencies. And that, believe it or not, seems to be exactly the way that our hearing is arranged. Pitch perception depends on frequency following between 20 Hz and about 100 Hz. Above 100 Hz, place detection begins to be useful but only in a crude way; so between 100 Hz and about 4,000 Hz, place

and frequency following work together to determine what pitch you will hear. Beyond 4,000 Hz, even volleying cannot produce frequency following; thus, pitch perception throughout the high end of the range depends exclusively on place of stimulation.

Tuning the Basilar Membrane The place theory then seems to work nicely for the higher frequencies and moderately well for the midrange. It is a puzzling fact, however, that the midrange tuning is sharper than one would predict from von Békésy's data on the traveling wave. He found it to have a fairly broad hump in the midrange rather than a sharp peak at a particular place. Von Békésy worked on cochleas from cadavers, and more recent research with living ears has shown more sharply peaked traveling waves for most frequencies (Lippe, 1986). What is there about living cochleas that allows the place mechanism to work better? A clue can be found in the phenomenon of cochlear emissions.

Kemp (1978) sealed a very small microphone and speaker into the external ear canal of a subject; a series of clicks was sent through the speaker. A recording made through the microphone revealed that each click was followed by a sound that did not originate from the loudspeaker. The click had stimulated the cochlea to create a tiny sound of its own (usually less than 10 ms in duration) that traveled back through the middle ear and tympanic membrane. Such sounds are now called **cochlear emissions** and are thought to be generated by the same process that enables living ears to sharpen the traveling waves of the basilar membrane (Pickles, 1985). They reveal that the basilar membrane is not just a passive sheet of tissue that allows itself to be vibrated by incoming sound waves. Rather, it seems to be an active organ that can vibrate itself. This suggests that it may be able to alter some of its characteristics (such as the gradient of stiffness from oval window to apex) in such a way as to actively increase the sharpness of the traveling wave peak. The sharper the peak, the smaller the area of hair cells stimulated and the better the nervous system can tell one frequency from another. How does the basilar membrane actively alter its own properties? The answer seems to depend on the outer hair cells.

Outer hair cells (Figure 7.17) may not be the

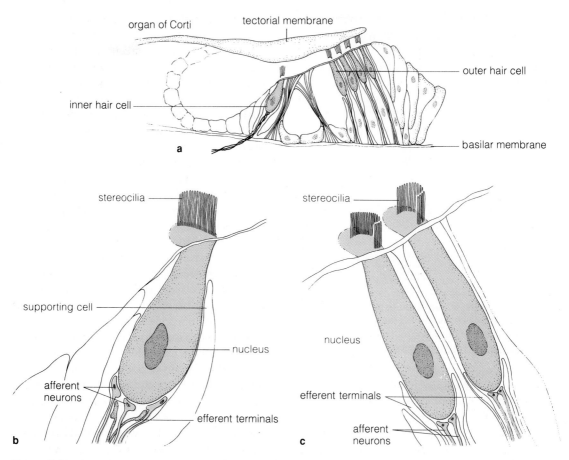

organ of Corti   tectorial membrane

outer hair cell

inner hair cell

basilar membrane

a

stereocilia   stereocilia

supporting cell

nucleus

nucleus

afferent
neurons

efferent terminals

efferent terminals

afferent
neurons

b   c

Figure 7.17 The inner and outer hair cells of the organ of Corti. (**a**) Inner hair cell embedded between its supporting cells. (**b**) Outer hair cell. Note the half-circle of stereocilia ("hairs") protruding from its top. (Adapted from Pickles, 1985)

sensory receptors they appear to be. Only 5 percent of the afferent fibers of the cochlear nerve synapse with outer hair cells; the rest go to inner hair cells. Some fibers in the cochlear nerve are motor rather than sensory, and it is these efferents that contact outer hair cells (Lippe, 1986). Moreover, outer hair cells contain the same sort of contractile proteins found in muscle fibers, and when stimulated electrically, they elongate or contract (Brownell et al., 1985). Elongation would make the basilar membrane stiffer at that point, and contraction would make it more compliant (Brownell et al., 1985). Such changes occurring within a narrow region of the

cochlea might have the effect of tuning that region to resonate at a particular frequency. Further research will tell us whether this is the origin of the active process that sharpens the traveling wave and improves the place mechanism of pitch discrimination.

What about the 5 percent of the afferent cochlear nerve fibers that do synapse on outer hair cells? Dallos (1985) suggests that the little bit of information entering the cochlear nerve directly from outer hair cells may concern the state of the organ of Corti rather than the sound stimulus. Such information might allow the brain to adjust the tension of the basilar membrane to bias it in favor of different frequencies at different times, as when you shift your attention from a male voice (lower frequencies) to a female voice (higher frequencies). If this speculation proves to be the case, then the mechanism by which we shift our attention from one auditory stimulus to another may extend all the way down the hierarchy to the receptor organ itself.

Summary Frequency discrimination seems to depend both on the ability of auditory neurons to match their firing frequency with the sound wave frequency (for low and midrange tones) and on the traveling wave to stimulate the basilar membrane at different places for different sound wave frequencies (for midrange and high tones). The selectivity with which a particular frequency can stimulate a specific area of hair cells is apparently achieved only because outer hair cells adjust the tension of the basilar membrane to "focus" the peak of the traveling wave to a narrow zone. Without this active response of the basilar membrane, the region of hair cells stimulated by midrange frequencies would probably be too broad to serve as a useful place mechanism.

The intensity of a sound wave must also be coded into nerve impulse patterns if we are to hear some sounds as louder than others. Intensity information is apparently carried as the number of nerve fibers responding. Thus, an intense 200-Hz tone would fire many neurons 200 times per second, whereas a soft 200-Hz tone would fire only a few neurons 200 times per second.

Auditory Projection System

The raw frequency and intensity information generated by the cochlea is carried by the cochlear nerve bundle of **cranial nerve VIII** (the vestibulocochlear nerve) into the brain where it is used to make decisions about alerting, attention, orienting, approaching, or avoiding. In humans much of this input also contains language information. The brain-stem auditory analyzers extract very basic forms of information from this input, probably in much the same way that they did in our prehuman mammalian ancestors; the cortex analyzes both the frequency–intensity input together with the outputs from the lower analyzers and extracts highly sophisticated information about the very brief, complex sounds that are the components of vocal communication. Let's see what is known about each step of analysis from the most primitive brain-stem mechanism to the most highly evolved cortical analyzer. The whole hierarchy of analyzers from cochlea to cortex is termed the **auditory projection system** (Figure 7.18).

Brain-Stem Analyzers: Localization Auditory fibers of the VIIIth nerve synapse in the **cochlear nuclei** of the medulla near the border of the pontine region of the brain stem. Very little is known about how these neurons enter into decision making at lower levels.

Cochlear nuclei send the results of their analysis upward to the inferior colliculus and across the brain stem to a collection of nuclei at the medulla–pontine border called the **superior olivary complex** (usually referred to simply as the *superior olive*). It contains two parts: **medial superior olive** and **lateral superior olive**. This analyzer is cleverly arranged to extract a type of information from the auditory input that is still just as vital to a human being at a cocktail party as it was 10 million years ago to a mammal listening for the movements of a predator in the surrounding jungle. The olive is the primary step in the mechanism for detecting the location of a sound source in the space around the listener. It works like this.

Sound waves coming to you from a source on your right side strike the right ear before they arrive at your left ear. That means that when the compression phase of the first wave finally reaches the far ear, the rarefaction phase of the wave is already at the right ear. The oval window in the right cochlea is already moving back out into the middle ear as the oval window in the left cochlea finally begins to move inward. In other words, because of the distance between your two ears, the sound waves at your right ear are out of phase with those at your left ear. (The **phase** of a wave is the stage of its cycle in which it is at any given moment.) Since a phase difference arises because the waves take a little longer to get to the far ear, the difference is often referred to as the **interaural time difference** (*interaural* = between ears). For a typical size human head, the

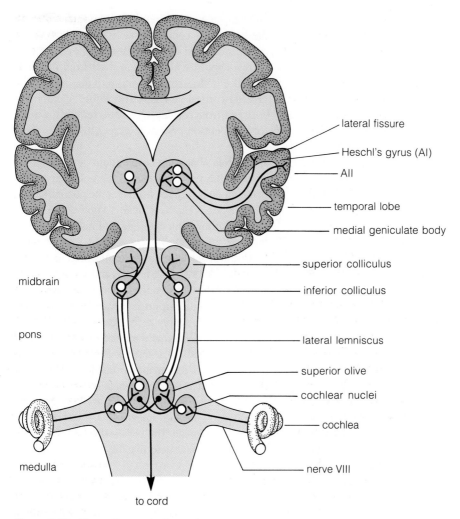

lateral fissure

Heschl's gyrus (AI)

AII

temporal lobe

medial geniculate body

superior colliculus

inferior colliculus

lateral lemniscus

superior olive

cochlear nuclei

cochlea

nerve VIII

midbrain

pons

medulla

to cord

Figure 7.18 The auditory projection system.

arrival time difference between the two ears is less than 1/10 of a second, but it contains important information about the location of the sound source. If the source is directly opposite either ear (at a 90° angle to your direction of gaze), the phase difference will be at its greatest. As you turn your head toward the sound or as it moves around to the front of you, the interaural time difference gets less and less. If the source is directly in front of you, the waves should arrive at the two ears at exactly the same moment

with no phase difference. So phase difference translates directly into degrees away from the midline. Evidence suggests that neurons within the medial superior olive are set to detect the amount of phase difference (Aitkin, 1986).

Unfortunately, the phase-difference cue only works for low-frequency sound waves because they are the longest ones. If the sound wave is short enough (high enough frequency), then the first wave arriving at your left ear from a source on your right

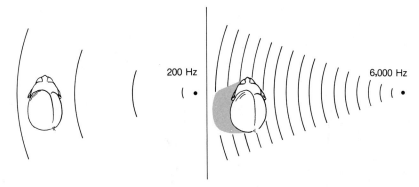

Figure 7.19 The head produces a sound shadow for waves at the higher frequencies. Low-frequency waves have no shadow because they are longer and can spread around the head. (From Goldstein, 1989)

200 Hz

6,000 Hz

side could be in its compression phase at the same moment the compression phase of the second wave hits your right ear. The nervous system can detect what phase any wave is in, but it cannot tell the first wave from the second. The brain would read this circumstance as a no-phase-difference situation and conclude that the source was in front of you when actually it was next to your right ear. Recall that this problem only arises with higher frequencies; thus, the nervous system can make good use of the phase-difference cue at low frequencies.

There is another feature of the stimulus that the brain can employ with higher frequencies, and that is an **interaural intensity difference**. Sound waves grow weaker as they move through the air, and there is actually a noticeable difference in strength between the waves at the ear near the source and the ear farther from it. This difference is increased because the head blocks direct reception of sound waves arriving from the side of the head opposite to the ear; thus, each ear is located in a **sound shadow** for such stimuli (Figure 7.19). The ear in the shadow gets the waves "second hand" as they hit some surface and are reflected back to it. Thus, there is an appreciable weakening of the waves when they reach the shadowed ear, and the nervous system can use this difference in strength to calculate where the sound source is located.

Each cell in the *lateral* superior olive receives input from both ears. Remember that sound intensity is coded into the number of impulses per second.

When a sound source is directly in front of you so that there is no intensity difference at the two ears, cells of the lateral superior olive get the same number of impulses from both inputs. Input from the cochlear nucleus on the same side as a particular lateral olivary cell tends to excite that cell, whereas input from the opposite side inhibits it. When the sound intensities are the same, the two inputs to the olivary cell are the same in terms of impulses per second (there are just as many excitatory impulses as inhibitory), and the two cancel out. Thus, when the sound source is directly in front of you, your superior olive does nothing (Harrison, 1978). When the source moves around to your left side, the waves at the left ear are more intense than at the right ear, and that means that the olive on the left side is getting more excitation than inhibition. It starts firing. (The right olive receives more inhibition than excitation and remains silent.) As the sound source moves farther to the left of the midline, the intensity difference at the two ears becomes greater, and the balance of inputs at the left olive swings toward more and more excitation with less and less inhibition. The farther the sound source moves away from the midline and toward your left ear, the harder the left lateral olive fires. If the source moves toward your right ear, the right olive starts firing while the left becomes inhibited (Aitkin, 1986). Working together the two superior olives would seem to provide near-perfect analysis of sound localization. However, notice in Figure 7.19 that low frequencies can spread around the head and directly stimulate the ear "behind the head"; the sound shadow really only exists for high-frequency tones. This means that the lateral superior olive is only working with midrange to high frequencies.

For the localization mechanism of the superior olive to work correctly, inputs from the two ears must be balanced. That is, when the sound source is directly in front of you, each olive should be receiving the same number of impulses per second (or, at least, some balance that produces a zero firing level). What happens then to a person who suffers a hearing loss in one ear so that a sound source directly ahead produces a significantly lower level of activity in one VIIIth nerve than it does in the other? When tested in the laboratory, these people show that sound sources directly in front of them were perceived as off to the side. To get a perception of "directly ahead" from these hearing-impaired subjects, the experimenter had to adjust the intensities of the sound waves in each earphone so that the bad ear got a higher intensity, and it had to be enough stronger than the wave to the good ear to balance out the hearing deficit (Knudsen, 1984).

In everyday situations, hearing-impaired people compensate for this problem by relying on visual cues to locate the sound source. As Knudsen (1984) points out, the visual system is so proficient and accurate at localizing stimuli in space that it tends to overwhelm data from other senses. (This is the basis for ventriloquism.) Where there is disagreement between visual and auditory localization of a probable sound source (as in the case of hearing defect), then the visual is probably going to win out. For example, if a hearing-impaired person is talking to a group of five people and needs to localize the sound of the voice to know who is talking, her ears will give her the wrong location, but she can correct for that by seeing whose lips are moving.

With a hearing impairment, localizing male voices is probably a bit easier than localizing female voices. Males use a lower-frequency range, and with low frequencies, localization can be accomplished with a cue unaffected by most hearing deficits, namely, phase differences. Many victims of hearing impairment are not even aware that they have a localization problem.

Brain-Stem Analyzers: Orienting Figure 7.18 indicates that the next analyzer in the auditory projection system is near the top of the brain stem in the midbrain, the **inferior colliculus**. Microelectrode research has shown that the nucleus collects frequency information from the cochlear nuclei and spatial localization information from the superior olive (Pickles, 1982). Apparently, collicular neurons combine the frequency information with the time- and intensity-difference information coming from medial and lateral superior olives to produce a spatial map that gives each frequency in the sound stimulus a spatial location. Thus, the inferior colliculi allow us to recognize the location of the sound source we are hearing (Knudsen et al., 1987).

The output of the inferior colliculus is passed up to the thalamus and *superior* colliculus. That means that the inferior colliculus must be informing the superior colliculus about the nature and location of some sound source, probably identified by its pattern of frequencies. The superior colliculus contains the connections that transform sound-location information into movements that produce body and receptor orientation toward the correct spatial location (Knudsen et al., 1987). The superior colliculus comes into play when a person off to one side says your name and you reflexively turn your eyes toward that sound source as a part of the act of shifting your attention to that new stimulus. Thus, the connection from inferior to superior colliculus is a higher-level portion of the alerting–attention mechanism whose foundation is the startle response. The superior colliculus connects with the brain-stem reticular formation and motor circuits and can use auditory input to control those pathways to enable you to orient toward sounds.

In species such as the barn owl that locate sound sources (e.g., prey) much more by sounds alone than by a combination of sight and sound, the inferior colliculus assumes a more important role (Aitkin, 1986). The owl's inferior colliculus contains a spatial map of its environment that apparently tells the neck muscles how to point the head precisely in the direction of a sound source (such as a mouse fleeing in the dark) (Knudsen & Konishi, 1977). There is some evidence for a similar map in the inferior colliculus of the cat (Aitkin, 1986), which like the owl also hunts in the dark. However, in a visually oriented, daylight creature such as a primate, it is doubtful that the localization information coming into the inferior colliculus does more than feed through to the spatial map within the superior colliculus where it can be correlated with visual input.

Thalamus and Auditory Cortex Above the brainstem level, the auditory projection pathways feed into the **medial geniculate body (MGB)** of the **thalamus**, and the neurons in the MGB project upward to the various parts of the **auditory cortex** in the temporal lobe. Apparently, the thalamus functions as a traffic director for the cortex. A part of the attention mechanism resides in the reticular formation of the thalamus and acts as a gateway to the cortex, regulating what information the cortex should spend its time with. When you are attending a lecture and are busily taking notes as fast as you can, it is probably your thalamus that rejects all the irrelevant nerve impulse patterns coming in along the VIIIth nerve—such as those carrying information about feet shuffling, papers turning, coughs and sneezes, whispers from some conversation two rows back, and people passing in the hall.

The highest levels of auditory analysis are in the temporal lobes of the cortex. Notice in Figure 7.18 that the fibers running up from the MGB to the cortex terminate in a part of the temporal lobe that is hidden down inside the lateral fissure. That fissure has a "ceiling" and a "floor" of cortex, and the thalamic axons are synapsing in the "floor." The anterior end of this floor is called **Heschl's gyrus**, and because it is the primary area for receiving auditory information from the thalamus, it is also referred to as **area AI** (Figure 7.20). Its key position in the primate auditory system is demonstrated by the large hearing loss that occurs when it is lesioned bilaterally (Heffner & Heffner, 1986).

Lateral to area AI, out on the lip of the lateral fissure, is a secondary auditory zone called **area AII** that receives auditory information from a different portion of the MGB. Beyond that, on the lateral surface of the temporal lobe in the uppermost temporal gyrus, are other auditory zones (which we can call secondary auditory cortex) that not only receive output from the thalamus but also from areas AI and AII. We know too little about these various regions to specify the precise function of each at this time, but some general facts can be noted about all of these plus AI and AII, taken as a group (which will be referred to as the *auditory cortex*).

None of the cortical analyzers seems to have anything to do with pitch or loudness perception, all of which seems to be adequately accomplished in the cochlea and lower brain stem. One can remove the entire auditory cortex of a cat, and the animal will still learn with ease any frequency-discrimination or intensity-discrimination problem you present (Ravizza & Belmore, 1978). This is not to say, however, that pitch information is absent in the cortex. Stimulation with a variety of pure tones while recording from Heschl's gyrus reveals that AI has a **tonotopic arrangement**. That is, the frequency continuum is laid out across AI, with the high frequencies at the posterior end and the low at the anterior end (Brugge, 1975). Apparently, the cortex makes use of frequency information in its analyses—hence, the tonotopic arrangement.

Diamond and Neff (1957) were the first to gain some insight into the nature of the analyzers in auditory cortex. They discovered that cats without auditory cortex could recognize different tones individually but could not tell one *sequence* of tones from another. High–low–high would be the same to the cats as low–high–low. Furthermore, cats had trouble discriminating between tones of long and short duration. These results led Neff (1961) to conclude that loss of auditory cortex produces an auditory short-term memory deficit.

As research continued, experimenters became more sensitive to the importance of the stimulus duration. Lesioned cats could solve a localization problem if the sound remained on, and they were able to scan by moving their heads back and forth, but they were completely unable to localize brief sounds (Ravizza & Belmore, 1978). The idea that at least one of the cortical auditory processors might have evolved in order to analyze very brief sounds fits very nicely with the fact that the left-hemisphere communication area in primates would have to handle exactly that sort of stimulus. Many human speech sounds are extremely brief, especially the quick frequency shifts that create the consonant sounds. Mon-

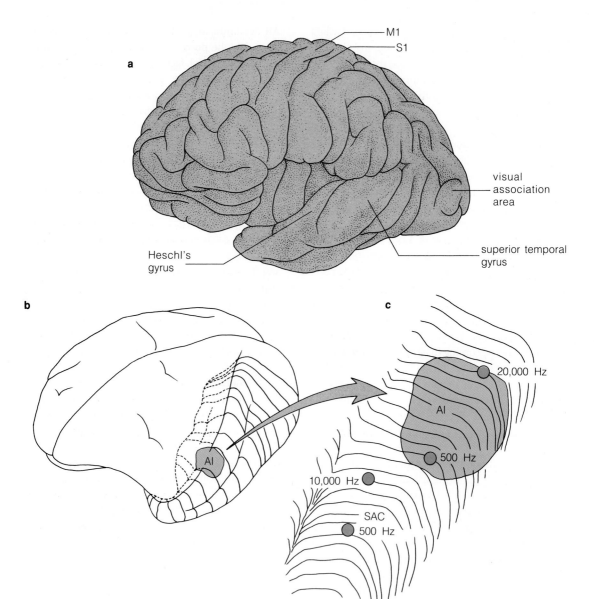

Figure 7.20 Location of area AI in the human and monkey. (**a**) Human brain with the lateral fissure pulled open to reveal the cortex inside. The primary auditory projection area (AI) is located in Heschl's gyrus found in the part of the temporal lobe that forms the lower wall of the lateral fissure. (**b**) Monkey brain showing location of area AI within lateral fissure (boundary indicated by dotted line). (**c**) In the monkey brain, both AI and the secondary auditory cortex (SAC) have been found to have a tonotopic organization. The lines running across the cortex are frequency lines, along which all cells respond best to the same frequency. The lowest best frequency is along the most anterior line of each area, highest along the most posterior. (**a** Adapted from Geschwind, 1972; **b** and **c** adapted from Brugge, 1975)

keys deprived of auditory cortex could no longer discriminate the various communication calls of their species, despite having no trouble with frequency discrimination. They also lost the ability to discriminate human speech sounds (Ravizza & Belmore, 1978). Single-cell studies show that some auditory cortex neurons respond only to communication sounds, and many are adjusted to respond only to rising frequencies or falling frequencies (Evans, 1975). These quick frequency changes are the building blocks of human speech.

Clinical data from humans who have lost their auditory cortex on both sides (a very rare disorder!) revealed that hearing was still possible in some limited fashion without the cortical analyzers, but the detection of brief sounds was badly hurt. Furthermore, the ability to perceptually separate two brief sounds that occurred close together in time was decreased. Such sounds tended to fuse together into something different (Ravizza & Belmore, 1978). This sort of failure made language comprehension either difficult or impossible.

Difficulties in Hearing

Loss of hearing usually has far worse consequences for a person's adjustment than does loss of sight. Total loss of hearing not only makes it nearly impossible to understand what other people are saying, it also hampers the person's voice control and thereby undermines the ability to speak with normal intonation. Let's look at a variety of types of hearing problems and then see what can be done to help a person with hearing impairment.

Hearing Impairment The word *deaf* is rarely used by professionals who work with hearing-impaired people because the word is so ambiguous. It is really an absolute idea denoting a condition in which there is a total loss of auditory sensitivity. Complete absence of hearing, however, is a rare condition; most people with nonnormal hearing have some amount of hearing ability remaining. Furthermore, not all hearing impairments involve a loss of sensitivity. A person may have normal thresholds for hearing pure tones but still cannot understand what you are saying.

In many cases of sensitivity loss, the problem can be traced to middle-ear damage and is referred to as a **conductive loss**. A common source of such damage in middle age is a calcification of the oval window with complete elimination of stirrup movement—a condition called **otosclerosis** (OH-toe-sklair-OH-sis).

If the damage is in the cochlea or nervous system, the defect is called a **sensorineural loss** and can arise from disease or from overstimulation by intense sounds. Recall that hearing is accomplished when cilia of cochlear hair cells are bent in a shearing action by the sound waves. Stereocilia are straight and stiff and can shatter when excessively stressed (Hudspeth, 1983). Sensitivity loss is quite possibly in your own future because it is so widespread in our culture. The curves in Figure 7.21 show the extent of average normal hearing loss with age for both men and women. Each curve shows the threshold increase above the 25-year-old level. There are separate curves for different frequencies because most of the loss is usually in the high frequencies. For example (the worst case), 80-year-old men show almost a 75-dB increase in threshold (decrease in sensitivity) over the 25-year-old level at 8,000 Hz. Other data indicate that in the higher-frequency region of the cochlea, the average 65-year-old male has already lost most of his outer hair cells (Dallos, 1988). One conclusion that can be drawn from these data is that middle-aged men are probably wasting their money if they buy a really high-fidelity sound system for their recordings because much of the fidelity paid for is in the accurate reproduction of higher frequencies.

Why do males seem to incur more loss in sensitivity than do females? There are probably some biological reasons for this yet to be discovered, but one cultural explanation lies in the fact that more males have jobs with high noise levels. It is interesting to compare hearing loss in U.S. males with loss in Sudanese males who live in a very quiet environment (Figure 7.22). Notice that with every age group, from the 10- to 19-year-olds up to the 70- to 74-year-olds, the losses increase as you go up the frequency scale, but also note the tremendous difference in the amount of loss between the two cultures. There are many possible explanations for

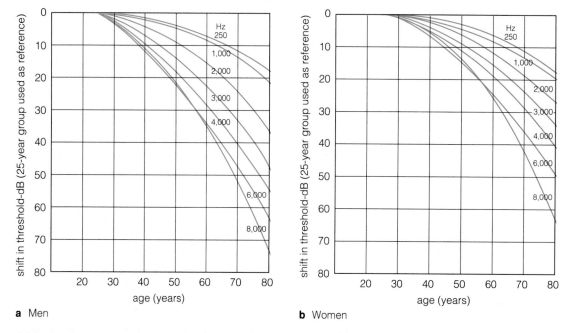

a Men **b** Women

Figure 7.21 Graphs showing how pure-tone thresholds for people with "normal" hearing shift with age. Seven different pure tones (from 250 to 8,000 Hz) were used in the test, and there is a separate curve for each. If you compare the two graphs, you can see that sensitivity drops off more sharply with age for men (**a**) than for women (**b**), and the loss is much worse for high frequencies than for low. (Adapted from Spoor, 1967)

Figure 7.22 Hearing loss curves for (**a**) Sudanese males (Mabaan tribe) and (**b**) American males. Sound wave frequency is shown on the horizontal axis. (Adapted from Rosen et al., 1962)

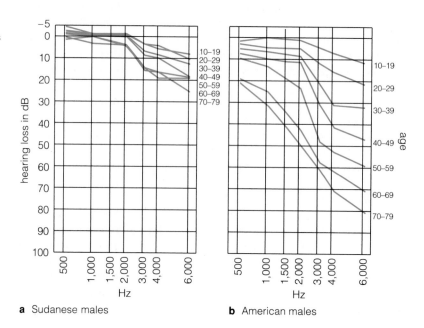

a Sudanese males **b** American males

these differences, of course. The Sudanese may be genetically disposed toward better retention of their hearing as they age. The American diet might be involved with the greater impairment in some way. But, the only factual difference that stands out at this time is the amount of exposure to high levels of noise.

There is no doubt that our culture is an extremely noisy one, and the noises are frequently the right sort to produce the most cochlear damage. Inside your middle ear is a tiny muscle called the tensor tympani, which attaches to the tympanic membrane. When it contracts, it tightens the eardrum so that the membrane cannot be vibrated as far in either direction. This may be a protective device against overly intense sound waves. When the intensity gets into the high decibel range, the muscle contracts, thereby damping the motions of the eardrum and lowering the intensity of the vibrations reaching the cochlea. There is, however, a certain amount of reaction time involved in this response (10 ms), and noises that rise to a peak in a fraction of a second get ahead of the reflex (Durrant & Lovrinic, 1977). Examples of fast-rise-time noises that reach dangerous levels over 100 dB are target pistol and rifle shots; lawnmower, chain saw, and motorcycle noises; and amplified musical instruments such as drumbeats and sudden chord "attacks" on an electric guitar.

Rock musicians can experience a hearing loss during a concert, part of which is called a **temporary threshold shift** because it is recovered within a day, but they may also fail to recover a part of the loss each time. Usually the permanent loss is too subtle for the person to notice the change following any single exposure; thus, permanent debilitating hearing impairment creeps up on a person over many years of exposure. The temporary shift, however, can be dramatically noticeable. The person who stood too close to the speakers at a rock concert or in a night club may complain at the end of the evening of ringing in the ears (a phenomenon called **tinnitus**) and a muffled quality to voices as though the ear canals were stuffed with cotton (Davis & Silverman, 1978).

There is a lengthy list of diseases ranging from infections to tumors that cause hearing impairment by attacking tissue from the cochlea to the cortex.

There are even medications (such as antibiotics like streptomycin) that can cause damage to the auditory system and over-the-counter drugs like aspirin that can cause temporary threshold shifts (Bergstrom & Thompson, 1976). Is there any way in which victims of hearing impairment can have any of their lost ability restored?

Measuring Hearing Loss The first step in helping someone who suspects a hearing loss is to get an accurate measurement of the present ability. For accuracy this should be done by a professional audiologist using a variety of tests. Impairment in the middle ear and cochlea are usually assessed with an instrument called an **audiometer**, which presents pure tones at graded intensities up and down the frequency scale. To uncover damage to the auditory projection system, it is usually necessary to use a speech-discrimination test because damage at those levels may not affect pure-tone thresholds. Another way to measure hearing loss employs evoked potentials. (See section on signal averaging in Chapter 5.)

Auditory evoked potentials, recorded from the top of the skull, occur in the EEG record whenever a sound is played into the patient's ear. Each wave in the evoked potential represents the voltage changes occurring in an auditory analyzer as the signal from the click stimulus sweeps upward through the auditory projection system (Figure 7.23). After 100 or more auditory stimuli (typically, clicks) have been played into the ear and the resulting average computed, a clear, detailed picture emerges of the entire sequence of potentials evoked as the "click" travels up the auditory pathway from lower centers to higher.

The averaged evoked response has a common shape from moment to moment and from person to person. Each of the major waves has been named (N1, P2, N2, P2, etc.) all the way from the click to a point 500 ms following the click. Figure 7.24 is a record showing a stack of eight averaged potentials, each covering the 10 ms after the click. Within that time, the information from the click would have reached the inferior colliculus, so these little 10-ms snapshots show the events in all brain-stem analyzers. These eight records came from one patient.

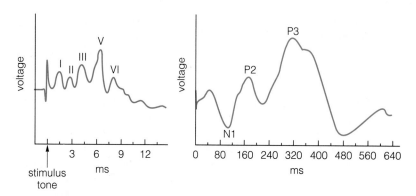

Figure 7.23 Two idealized averaged evoked potentials recorded from scalp electrodes on a human subject. The individual waves are named for the time at which they occur following the tone stimulus. Wave II is probably from the auditory nerve, and wave III is the response of the cochlear nucleus. Wave V is the superior olive, and wave VI is the inferior colliculus. A more compressed time scale is needed to display the late waves. The negative N1 wave at about 100 ms and the positive P2 at about 200 ms are from the cortex. The P3 wave is not often seen because it is associated with unexpected events. It can be evoked by *omitting* one of the tone stimuli now and then at random intervals. Each of the above potentials illustrates how the waves look after averaging 200–400 individual evoked potentials.

Notice that the top four are from the right ear, the bottom four from the left ear. See how much clearer the waves are in the left-ear records; something is definitely wrong with the auditory projection system on the right. The eventual diagnosis for this patient was a right-side tumor of the cerebellum. Although the tumor itself was outside of the auditory system, it could easily have been squeezing the brain stem directly beneath it. Evoked potential averaging is rather good at spotting tumors and can roughly localize their sites to brain versus cochlea and upper versus lower stem (Musiek, 1983).

Relieving Hearing Loss Our technology for measuring hearing impairment and locating the site of malfunction is far in advance of our ability to improve the lot of the patient. Conductive loss from middle-ear problems can sometimes be dealt with by surgeons because the problems concern bone and membrane tissues, but there is nothing that surgeons can do to repair neural tissue. Sensorineural losses in the cochlea, VIIIth nerve, or brain are permanent. If the damage is in the middle ear, cochlea, or nerve,

amplification may help. Hearing aids are especially helpful in the case of middle-ear conductive loss because the bones of the skull conduct sound waves, and this fact can be used to bypass the damaged middle ear. A hearing aid consists of a microphone, amplification circuits like the ones in your "stereo" system, and a tiny (and tinny!) loudspeaker pressed into the ear canal. If the amplifier boosts the sound waves sufficiently, the skull conducts them straight into the cochlea without any help from the bones of the middle ear. It is this bone conduction through the skull that normally stimulates your cochlea when you are speaking. You hear your own voice in two ways simultaneously: the obvious way through the ear canal and the less obvious way directly from the throat through the jaw bone to the temporal bone of the skull, which contains the cochlea (von Békésy, 1967). The latter route carries low frequencies better than high and gives you a different perception of your own voice than any of your listeners get. If you want to know how your voice sounds to other people, you have to listen to a recording of it. Most people find this experience somewhat disillusioning

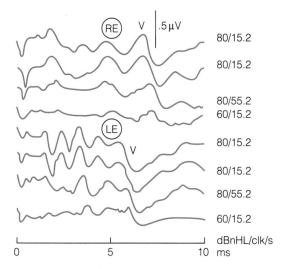

V | .5 μV

RE

80/15.2

80/15.2

80/55.2
60/15.2

LE

V

80/15.2

80/15.2

80/55.2

60/15.2

0   5   10   ms

dBnHL/clk/s

Figure 7.24 Auditory averaged evoked potentials from a neurological patient. The top four averages are from the right ear, bottom four from the left. The numbers down the right side refer to decibel level and number of clicks per second used in the averaging. Note the time scale at the bottom. These records cover only the first 10 ms after click onset so only brain-stem analyzers are represented. The difference between right and left sides reveals the loss of the auditory projection system on the right. (Adapted from Musiek, 1983)

because the voice without bone conduction contains far more high frequencies and tends to sound thin and reedy.

Hearing aids, unfortunately, can never restore realistic hearing. They are manufactured more with cosmetic requirements in mind than auditory ones. To be as inconspicuous as possible, the size has been reduced to the point where there isn't enough room for adequate electronics, and the small size of the speaker guarantees that the reproduction of low frequencies will be severely distorted. If people were not concerned with disguising the fact that they wear an aid, the device could probably be made to reproduce sounds with considerably more fidelity.

The most ambitious attempt to overcome hearing impairment is the very recent effort to develop a **hearing prosthesis** for patients with complete hearing loss due to cochlear damage. A prosthesis is an artificial part added to compensate for the loss of an organ or its function. An artificial leg would be an example. In the case of hearing, the prosthesis must include a microphone, electronics for amplification and selection of wanted parts of the signal, a power supply, and electrodes to carry the processed signal to the cochlea or VIIIth nerve. The sound waves are converted by the microphone into electrical signals, which are then used to stimulate what remains of the devastated cochlea or nerve. Eight laboratories are currently conducting research on auditory prostheses, four of these in the United States (Millar et al., 1984). The motivation for this effort is to afford these patients some amount of speech perception; no attempt is made to work with people who were deaf from birth and thus never had a chance to learn speech. Most of the current versions of auditory prostheses make an attempt to include electronic circuits that will do some of the frequency processing that the missing organ of Corti was doing before it was lost, but at this time there has not been enough basic research on audition to allow us to make a real substitute for the cochlea. So far the results with the prosthesis have been good with a few patients. The best that can be expected by any patient at this time is for the prosthesis to provide additional auditory information to aid the usual technique of understanding speech through lip reading (Moore, 1984). Considering the risks of the surgery involved in the implant procedure and the problems of containing a foreign object within the body for years at a time, the benefits outweigh the problems for only a handful of carefully selected victims of extreme hearing impairment. The research data that these patients provide in the course of trying to use the prosthesis, however, may be of great value to our theoretical understanding of the hearing process and thus provide a foundation from which future efforts can produce true cochlear substitutes.

■ Taste

Taste and smell are the two major chemical senses. The taste sense reports to the rest of the nervous system on what chemicals have entered the mouth,

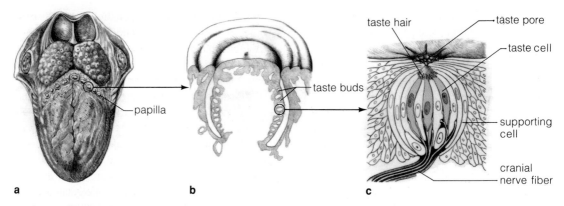

Figure 7.25 Taste receptors. (**a**) The human tongue showing papillae. (**b**) Cross section of a papilla. (**c**) Cross section of a taste bud on wall of papilla. (Adapted from Creager, 1983)

whereas the sense of smell samples and categorizes the molecules that float through the air. The two senses meet two very different survival needs. Taste informs the brain only of stimuli immediately present and about to be ingested, whereas smell can detect the molecules from an object before it arrives in our presence and even after it has left. In the history of mammalian evolution, taste probably evolved as a way of evaluating food, while smell became the key to finding a mate, identifying others of the species, finding food, and avoiding the fate of becoming food.

Millions of years ago, our ancestors (who were fish at the time) had only one undifferentiated chemical sense rather than two specialized ones. Because fish literally swim through everything they taste, it is advantageous for them to have chemical receptors not only in their mouths but also all over their skins to better catch the drifting molecules that signal dinner or danger. Taste and smell differentiated when animal life spread out of the sea onto the land. Chemical receptors from the inside of the fish's mouth were very handy for food identification and classification; thus, they persisted throughout the course of mammalian, primate, and human evolution. Chemical sensors on the skin, however, were not located strategically for the reception of airborne molecules. To interact with receptors, stimulus mol-

ecules must be suspended in liquid (mucus), and such a medium is difficult to maintain outside the body. The ideal solution was to gather all these receptors together into a tissue that could be kept moist while being continually exposed to air taken into the lungs. Thus, land animals gradually developed two separate sets of chemical receptors: one for air sampling and one to keep track of what was taken into the mouth. In mammals that have returned to the sea (porpoises), the separate sense of smell has been lost (Wenzel, 1973).

Processing Taste Information in the Nervous System

Most of our taste receptors are on the tongue. Figure 7.25 shows the human tongue to be a rather unlovely organ covered with wartlike bumps. These bumps, technically termed **papillae** (pap-PILL-eye; singular is papilla), are the site of taste reception. In Figure 7.25 one can see from the cross section of a papilla that receptor cells (**taste cells**) are arranged in small clusters called **taste buds**, which line the vertical sides of papillae. So, for you to taste your food, molecules of the substance must wash down into the cracks between papillae, enter the pore of a taste bud, and stimulate a taste cell.

A human infant is born with about 9,000–10,000 taste buds, each having roughly 30 taste cells, but the adult has far fewer because these receptors are among the shortest-lived cells in the human body. Considering that a typical life span for a taste cell is only 10 days, you might wonder that a human has any taste receptors left at all by adulthood. Fortunately, new taste cells are constantly forming to replace many of the aged ones (Beidler, 1978). Despite this replacement, aging does seem to impair the sense of taste. Elderly people cannot discriminate between tastes as well as younger people and complain that food often seems tasteless (Schiffman et al., 1979).

Taste cells look more like skin cells than parts of the nervous system. They have no axon or dendrites; all they do is produce voltage patterns that contain information about chemicals. Each taste cell is contacted by a fiber of a neuron running in one of three cranial nerves (VII, IX, or X), and this fiber conveys the information into the CNS. All three cranial nerves that carry taste information synapse in the **nucleus of tractus solitarius (NTS)**, a cluster of cells found in the medulla and pons of the brain stem (Figure 7.26). The NTS also receives input from the liver and digestive tract, and it is quite likely that the processing task of the NTS is to combine the two types of information for the higher levels of the brain. This kind of sensory input about the nature of the food that has just gone past your receptors and is now stimulating the stomach and intestine could perhaps be used by the brain to determine how much of each needed nutrient has been ingested and when it is safe to stop eating. The response of neurons in the NTS to taste stimuli is influenced by how full the stomach is and by the level of blood sugar (Travers et al., 1987). In the chapter on hunger, we will learn that electrical stimulation of certain areas of the hypothalamus induces eating in a satiated animal. It is interesting that this same stimulation also changes the firing rates of taste cells in the NTS, and the change is in the same direction (increase or decrease) as produced by taste stimuli on the tongue (Murzi et al., 1986).

Many decisions that affect the internal environment of the body depend on the actions of cells in the hypothalamus, so it is not surprising that the output of NTS cells winds up in the lateral hypothalamus (after a relay in the pons). Taste information may participate directly in the rather automatic, low-level circuits that are the basic controls over hunger and eating, but it also has a role in higher processes. The pontine taste cells (which receive from the NTS) send their output not only to the hypothalamus but also to the cortex by way of the thalamus. The **gustatory** (taste) **cortex** is a part of the face area of the parietal somatosensory cortex that forms the "ceiling" of the lateral fissure (Figure 7.26). This group of cells is probably necessary for your conscious experience of tastes. In the more primitive limbic system, the amygdala processes information sent from the pontine taste area and produces decisions about whether the tasted substance should be avoided as dangerous or sought after as "good tasting" (Lasiter & Glanzman, 1985).

Coding Taste Quality

Psychologists investigating taste are faced with two major theoretical questions: How does the nervous system tell one chemical from another, and how does it code that information into nerve impulses? The problem of how the taste system tells one chemical from another has proved a tough nut to crack. In 1916 Henning proposed a theory that stated that there are only four **primary taste qualities**—sweet, sour, salty, and bitter—and that all other tastes are combinations of these primaries. Since then, scientists have searched for common factors between all chemicals that taste salty, all that are sweet, and so forth, but only a few clear facts have been turned up. Saltiness seems to be associated with compounds that ionize (i.e., break into charged particles) but that do not produce hydrogen or hydroxyl ions. Sour taste seems definitely linked to acids, and that should mean that the stimulus for sour is always a hydrogen ion. But there are some acids that taste sweet! Sweetness depends on organic compounds (those built from carbon combined with other elements), but there are thousands of organic compounds that do not taste sweet. Bitter taste is frequently produced by alkaline compounds, but recent psychological research strongly suggests that there is a fifth primary that tastes "alkaline" rather than bitter (Schiffman &

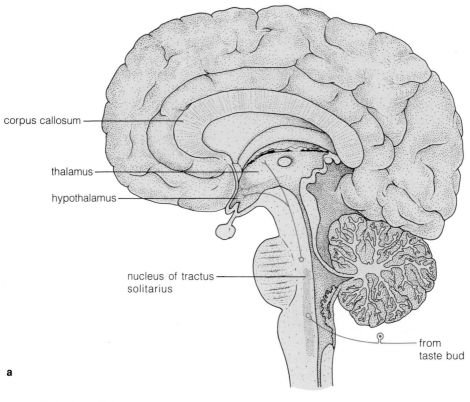

corpus callosum

thalamus

hypothalamus

nucleus of tractus
solitarius

from
taste bud

a

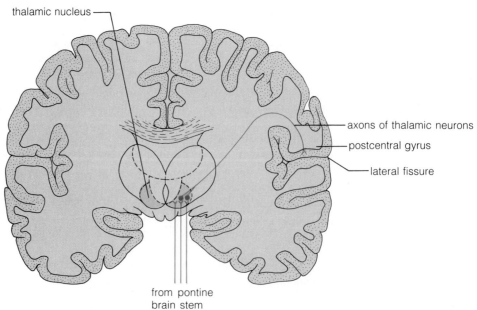

thalamic nucleus

axons of thalamic neurons

postcentral gyrus

lateral fissure

b

from pontine
brain stem

Erickson, 1971). There is even some evidence for primary tastes of sulfurous and fatty (Schiffman & Dackis, 1975).

To some theorists like Schiffman, this inability to establish a small number of clearly primary tastes and to discover the appropriate stimulus for each suggests that the idea of primaries may not be very useful in our attempts to understand the sense of taste. Schiffman's interpretation centers around the problem of how taste information is coded into nerve impulses.

Theories of Taste Coding

Two possible coding tactics have been suggested for the taste system: labeled-line theory and across–fiber pattern theory. The **labeled-line theory** proposes that there are four primary tastes, each with its own type of receptor taste cell and cranial nerve fiber. The theory could easily be expanded to include more than four primaries should the evidence for other primaries ever grow sufficient to convince the critics. The essence of the theory is that each receptor type has its own "line" to the taste centers of the brain and that the brain can tell what chemicals are stimulating the tongue by which lines are active.

The **across-fiber pattern theory** holds that there are no primaries and that each separate chemical stimulus is coded into a different pattern of active fibers. This idea arose from experiments in which electrical recordings were made from cranial nerve axons (fibers) while the tongue was being laved with various chemicals. Fortunately for taste researchers, one branch of the VIIth nerve carrying taste fibers, the **chorda tympani,** runs right across the face of the tympanic membrane, thus making it relatively easy to position electrodes. Figure 7.27 shows the response pattern of each of nine axons (fibers) to five different chemical stimuli (Erickson, 1963).

Notice that fiber 9 responded very well to the third stimulus (HCl, hydrochloric acid), which would suggest that it might be one of the lines labeled "sour." But if that is the case, why is it also responding to the first stimulus (salty) and the fourth (bitter)? Fiber 4 gives a magnificent response to the NaCl (sodium chloride) but does just about as well with the acid. Is it a "salt–sour" line? This does not fit the labeled-line theory in its simplest, clearest form.

How then is the presence of salt signaled to the brain, according to the *pattern* theorist? As the name of the theory tells us, we must look at the pattern across neurons. Thus, the brain would know that salt was present in the mouth when fibers 1, 2, 3, and 9 responded moderately; fibers 4, 5, 6, and 7 responded strongly; and fiber 8 showed only a weak response. Among this particular set of fibers, this would be the "salt" pattern. You can see that there is a distinctly different pattern for each stimulus chemical.

The data from the fiber-recording experiments can be interpreted in several ways, however. Notice that most of the neurons in Figure 7.27 respond best to only one type of chemical. Perhaps these neurons really are labeled lines. Cells within the brain may adjust to "listen" to each nerve fiber only when it is firing near maximum; lower levels of firing would be ignored. In Figure 7.27, you can see that taking the near maximum firing and ignoring all else would mean that each nerve fiber is allowed to report the existence of only one type of chemical, that is, the one to which it responds most strongly. This would create labeled-line fibers out of cells that actually respond to a broader range of stimuli.

The existence of labeled lines would help explain why the tongue varies in its sensitivity to the primaries as you move across its surface. Figure 7.28 shows that sweet is best sensed near the tip, bitter toward the back, and so forth. The pattern theorist,

---

Figure 7.26 (**a**) Midsagittal view of the brain showing the taste projection system from receptor to thalamus. (**b**) Frontal section of the brain showing taste cells in the thalamus projecting to the cortical taste area in the ceiling of the lateral fissure at the base of the somesthetic area in the parietal lobe.

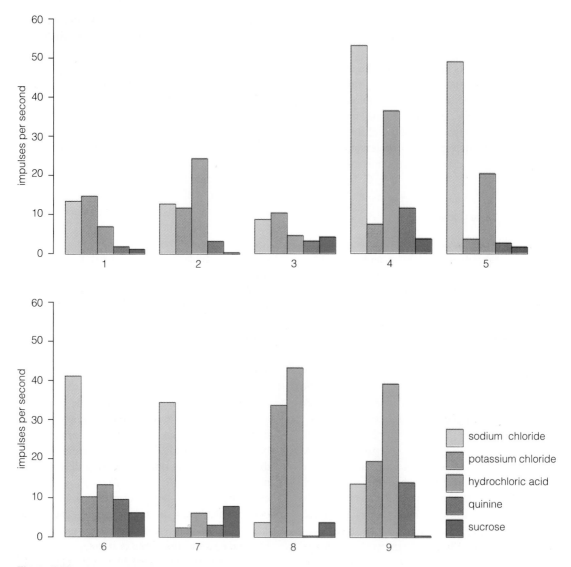

Figure 7.27 Responses of nine nerve fibers in the chorda tympani nerve to five different taste stimuli. (Adapted from Erickson, 1963)

Figure 7.28 Taste sensitivity varies in strength across different regions of the tongue. For example, although sweet can be detected on most of the tongue, the greatest sensitivity for this flavor is at the tip. (From Creager, 1983)

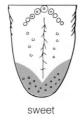
sweet

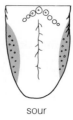
sour

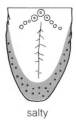
salty

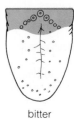
bitter

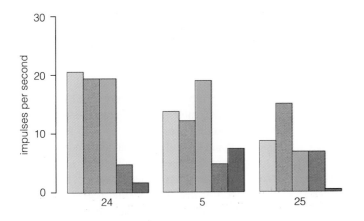

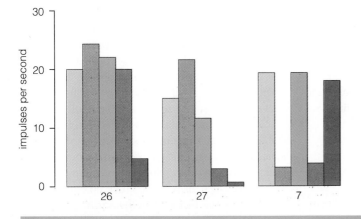

Figure 7.29 Responses from a sample of six neurons in the NTS to five different taste stimuli. The number of impulses per second is shown on the vertical axis. The number under each graph indicates the neuron from which the data were collected. (Adapted from Erickson, 1963)

sodium chloride

potassium chloride

hydrochloric acid

quinine

sucrose

however, would point out that the sensitivity variation across the surface of the tongue is sizable only for sweet and bitter. Furthermore, the idea that cells within the brain may respond to firing in nerve fibers only when the rate is near maximum runs into trouble from single-cell records from the NTS (Erickson, 1963). If that idea were correct, one would expect each NTS cell to respond just to one primary and not to any others. Figure 7.29 shows that NTS cells are even less specific to one primary taste than are nerve fibers. Pattern theory, on the other hand, has a hard time explaining why taste-suppressant substances seem to eliminate a single primary taste rather than affecting a whole group of tastes. Potassium gymnemate, for example, suppresses sweetness. If you chew a few leaves from the Indian plant

Gymnesma sylvestre, sugar becomes as tasteless as sand (Bartoshuk et al., 1969).

It is, of course, possible that some taste areas of the brain might need labeled-line type of coding, while others might require an across-fiber pattern. Keverne (1978) suggests a **dual-processing theory** in which the subcortical areas of pons, hypothalamus, and amygdala use the input as labeled lines, the neocortex as across-fiber patterns. This would allow the lower parts of the brain to make primitive approach–avoidance decisions on the basis of very simple sensory analysis—for example, if it's bitter, spit it out; if it's sweet, find more of it—whereas the cortex could perform a more refined analysis of the patterns to create more complex but more adaptive decisions (e.g., the first human to ever sample a roasted coffee bean might have thought: "This is slightly bitter, slightly sour. I like the flavor, but the bitter makes me hesitate, so I think I will try just a nibble more"). Avoidance of bitter flavors may be an inherited survival device built into lower brain centers because bitterness is so frequently associated with poisonous substances. There may also be an inherited approach tendency to sweet substances mediated by lower centers because sweet is strongly associated with nutrients.

Keverne's idea is interesting but research data are not in total agreement yet about the role of the neocortex in taste. Keverne cites research showing that a rat with neocortex totally removed can still learn to avoid dangerous tastes (Keverne, 1978). Other researchers (Kiefer et al., 1982) found that a rat's memory for a learned taste aversion was lost after damage to the taste area of the neocortex. If future studies can resolve such discrepancies, Keverne's hypothesis that the brain uses both labeled-line input and patterned input might provide a firm foundation for the true understanding of our taste abilities.

◼ Olfaction

The senses of taste and smell (**olfaction**) are occasions for some of your most intimate interactions with the environment. Both chemical senses involve actually taking molecules of the environment into your own body in order to identify the chemical or the object that produced them. This is a pleasant thought when the objects are food, drink, or one's lover, but in the case of less desirable sources of molecules, we try to avoid the conscious realization that we are coming into direct contact with something we would rather avoid. To be an **olfactory stimulus** (i.e., to be smellable), a substance must be **volatile**. That is, it must be able to release some of its surface molecules into the air. Substances like gasoline, perfumes, and onion oil are highly volatile and make good **odorants** (olfactory stimuli). Others like steel, concrete, and wood contain very few volatile chemicals and are weak odorants. Some substances such as water release molecules from their surfaces very readily but are not odorants for

humans. Being volatile is not enough; the nervous system must be sensitive to the molecules as well. Carbon dioxide (CO_2) is completely odorless to a human (which is a good thing, because we manufacture so much of it and pour it out of our noses, past olfactory receptors with every breath), but to a mosquito, CO_2 must be a very attractive odor. The female mosquito uses this gas to zero in on you, tracking your CO_2 trail upwind to its unlucky source.

With most people, olfaction is an underrated sense. One listens to gourmet cooks extol the virtues of this food or that, all the while referring to how excellent it *tastes*, rarely dwelling on its odor. Yet, it turns out that the majority of stimulation from most food is in terms of smell rather than taste. **Flavor** is a compound stimulus consisting of both tastes and odors (Coburn et al., 1984), and the extent to which this is true becomes appallingly apparent whenever you get a bad head cold and lose your sense of smell. It becomes difficult to distinguish one food from another except by its feel, and most of the pleasure of eating is lost. The reason that the smell of food is so often confused with taste is that much of the smelling occurs *after* one puts food into the mouth. The nasal cavity opens into the back of the mouth to allow air down into the windpipe; thus, when you chew, the odor-laden air is pushed back up into the nasal cavity and into contact with the organs of smell.

Receiving and Identifying Odorants

The sense organ for smell is the **olfactory epithelium** (ol-FAC-tor-ee EPP-i-THEE-lee-um) (Figure 7.30). This patch of specialized skin in the back of the olfactory cavity contains receptor cells and mucous cells. The latter keep the surface of the olfactory epithelium covered with a mucous layer in which the odorant molecules can dissolve on arrival. As the dissolved molecules float through this mucous layer, they eventually come into contact with the little hairlike cilia that project from the bottom of each receptor cell, and apparently these cilia are the site of reception. The receptors respond to the odorant molecules by firing their axons, and the resulting pattern of nerve impulses carries the information up into the brain by way of the olfactory nerve. Cranial nerve I, the **olfactory nerve**, is extremely short and

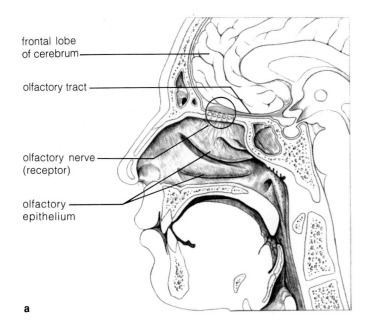

frontal lobe
of cerebrum

olfactory tract

olfactory nerve
(receptor)

olfactory
epithelium

a

Figure 7.30 The human olfactory system. (**a**) Olfactory bulb and nerve of the right hemisphere. (**b**) The olfactory epithelium (mucosa) is shown in cross section. (Adapted from Creager, 1983)

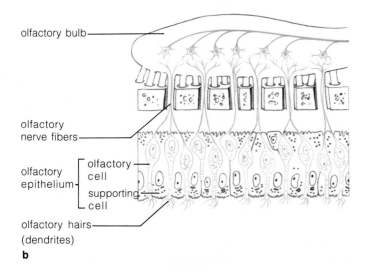

olfactory bulb

olfactory
nerve fibers

olfactory
epithelium

olfactory
cell

supporting
cell

olfactory hairs
(dendrites)

b

spread out. It is made up of axons of olfactory receptor cells, all of which thread their way through holes in the bottom of the skull and enter the **olfactory bulb,** where they synapse.

Wine tasters and gourmets are making the most of a sensory capability that seems to be less important to modern humans than it must have been to our prehuman ancestors. The proportion of cerebral cortex given over to olfactory analysis has apparently not increased during the course of primate evolution, whereas visual analysis has grown to cover more than a quarter of the hemispheres. Evolution apparently has economized more and more on human olfactory sensitivity as the sense of smell became less and less important to our ancestors' chances of survival. By contrast an excellent olfactory sensitivity always remained a necessity for the wild dog ancestors of our current pets because they used it to track game, to distinguish one dog from another, and to tell willing females from those not in heat. It is not surprising to find that even the domesticated German shepherd has something like 224 million olfactory receptor cells, whereas humans have only about 10 million (Wenzel, 1973). Each human receptor cell extends 6–8 cilia into the mucous layer to pick up odorant molecules; a dog's receptors possess 100–150 cilia (Brown, 1975). (Apparently, the bloodhound's ability to find the scent of a human from the imprint of a shoe in the earth may be explainable just on the basis of more receptive capacity.)

However, do not despair for our species. Human thresholds, although not as low as a dog's, still indicate a spectacular degree of sensitivity. One single molecule of the chemical mercaptan mixed with *50 trillion* molecules of air is still detectable by the human nose (Geldard, 1972). A person with normal olfactory ability can detect 1 mg of skatol (a chemical that smells like feces) spread throughout a large room 500 m long, 100 m wide, and 50 m high (Moncrieff, 1951). So although our species may not list among the world's greatest sniffers, when it comes to smelling, we can still stick our noses proudly in the air.

The question of how **olfactory transduction** (the conversion of chemical information into nerve impulse patterns) takes place continues to interest researchers. The most plausible interpretation (in my opinion) is the **lock-and-key theory**, which is based on the rules of cell membrane chemistry with which you are already familiar (see Chapter 2). In this view, the odorant molecule is similar to a neurotransmitter molecule in that it stimulates the cilium of a receptor cell by fitting into a receptor site. Presumably, this reaction between the odorant molecule (the key) and the receptor site molecule (the lock) triggers reactions in the cell that open ion channel gates and initiate an EPSP. EPSPs then sum to trigger an impulse in the axon of the cell, just as in a typical CNS neuron (Lancet, 1984). There may be a difference between odorant receptor sites and neurotransmitter receptor sites, however. It is possible that some odorant molecules may bind much more permanently to their sites than transmitters do to theirs. If this is the case, then olfactory receptor cells might "wear out" as its receptor sites are used up. This could explain why olfactory receptor cells are continually dying and being replaced throughout our lifetimes (Easter, 1984).

How would lock-and-key theory explain our ability to tell one odor from another? A beginning toward answering this question was made by Amoore and colleagues (1964) who proposed that there are only a handful of different receptor site types but that each molecule would fit best into just one type of site (Figure 7.31). This would produce a set of olfactory "primaries" equivalent to the primaries red, green,

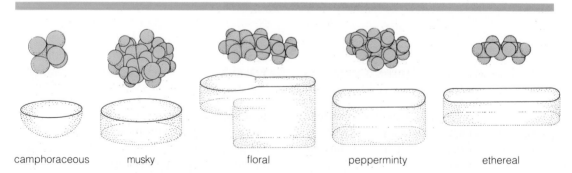

| camphoraceous | musky | floral | pepperminty | ethereal |

Figure 7.31 Five of Amoore's proposed olfactory receptor site shapes and examples of molecules that would fit into each. (Adapted from Amoore et al., 1964)

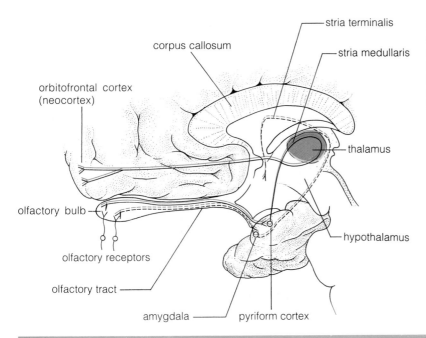

Figure 7.32 Cortical levels of the human olfactory system showing connections into the orbitofrontal cortex, which seems to be the primary cortical area for smell. (Adapted from Keverne, 1978)

stria terminalis

stria medullaris

corpus callosum

orbitofrontal cortex (neocortex)

thalamus

olfactory bulb

olfactory receptors

hypothalamus

olfactory tract

amygdala

pyriform cortex

and blue in vision. All odors would be either primaries or combinations of primaries. Amoore attempted to identify these proposed primaries as "minty," "fruity," "musky," and so on, but recent research has not been able to verify this set or even back up the idea of olfactory primaries (Schiffman, 1974a, b). One problem with such a labeled-line theory of olfaction is that it would demand a different receptor type for each basic odor. Not only is there no evidence for this but even the evidence for specialized receptor cells is shaky. Recent research has shown that the supporting cells that pack around the olfactory receptor neurons react just as strongly to the odorants used in experiments as do the receptors themselves (Dionne, 1988). They receive the odorant stimuli but cannot be considered receptors simply because they have no synapses with olfactory bulb neurons.

How the Brain Uses Olfactory Input

Neurons in the olfactory bulb send their axons out through the **olfactory tract** to synapse in a number of areas including the **amygdala** and **pyriform cor-**tex (Figure 7.32). From the amygdala, a path runs to the hypothalamus. Another pathway runs from the pyriform cortex through the thalamus and forward to the **orbitofrontal cortex** (*orbito* means in the vicinity of the eyes, the orbs). The orbitofrontal cortex may be the area best designated as the *olfactory cortex* (Figures 7.32 and 7.33). Takagi (1979) reports lesion and stimulation experiments that show the lateral area to be important for olfactory discrimination in monkeys.

Despite the fact that a number of areas in our brains are involved in processing olfactory information, evolution has shrunk the number of processors rather than expanding it. This is in dramatic contrast to the situation with vision, where evolution has produced a whole network of cortical areas and has given up none of the subcortical ones held over from previous species. What exactly is it that primate brains lost and that most other vertebrate brains still possess and find so vital to existence? For an answer, look at Figure 7.34. The **vomeronasal organ** (VOM-er-oh-NAY-zul) is an olfactory epithelium similar to but separate from the main olfactory epithelium. It also possesses receptor cells, and these receptors

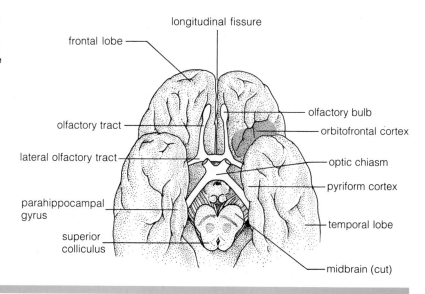

Figure 7.33 Ventral view of the human brain showing the position of the olfactory bulbs and tracts. The location of the orbitofrontal cortex is only approximate.

longitudinal fissure

frontal lobe

olfactory tract

lateral olfactory tract

parahippocampal gyrus

superior colliculus

olfactory bulb

orbitofrontal cortex

optic chiasm

pyriform cortex

temporal lobe

midbrain (cut)

fire into the **accessory olfactory bulb,** which projects to the rest of the brain through the **accessory olfactory system.** Without this additional olfactory system, the snake cannot find food or a mate. It is a veritable linchpin of species survival for this reptilian animal. Human beings (as the old movie line goes) may "speak with forked tongue," but snakes actually *smell* with theirs. The two tongue tips are arranged so that when they withdraw back into the mouth, they come into direct contact with the opening to the tubes containing the vomeronasal organ on each side. As the snake slithers along the ground seeking the odor trail of some prey animal (like an earth-

worm), it constantly flicks its tongue out onto the ground and then back into the mouth, taking a small chemical sample of the environment with it. For this kind of smelling, the odorant doesn't even have to be volatile; it is as though the snake were tasting with its nose. In this same manner, a male garter snake finds and identifies a female garter snake, guided by the sexual attractant pheromones she secretes.

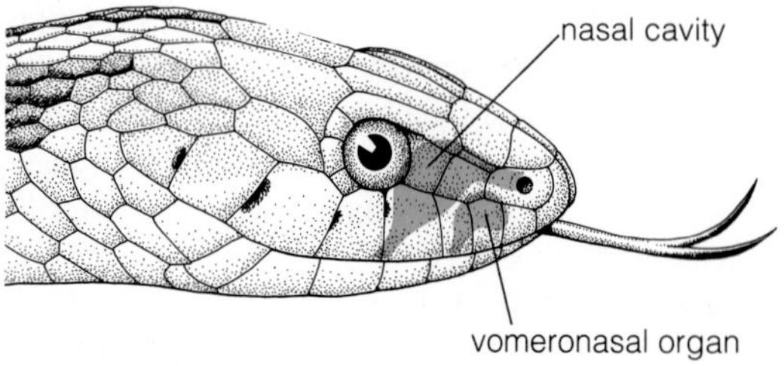

Pheromones Pheromones (FAIR-uh-moans) are chemicals secreted by organisms for the purpose of communication with other members of the species. There are two types: **attractants** and **primers.** Attractants are usually secreted by the female for the purpose of luring and guiding the male. Primer pheromones are more subtle and complex. They produce changes in the recipient animal's endocrine gland system, changes that can profoundly affect the functioning of the animal's body.

Are you feeling sexy? Do you feel your period coming on? Are you pregnant? If you were a rodent, the answers to these questions would probably be determined by what you had been sniffing lately. Immature female mice will begin puberty earlier if they are exposed to the odor of male urine. Adult female urine, on the other hand, delays the onset of puberty (Keverne, 1983). There are primer phero-

nasal cavity

vomeronasal organ

Figure 7.34 Location of vomeronasal organ in the garter snake. (Adapted from Halpern & Kubie, 1984)

mones in those excretions, which are picked up by an immature female as she snuffles and sniffs about the floor of her cage, and those pheromones signal the hypothalamus of her brain by way of the vomeronasal organ. The hypothalamus in turn signals the pituitary gland to alter its hormone output, and the changes that lead to sexual maturity either speed or slow. If a group of adult female rodents are housed together, they eventually synchronize their sexual cycles so that they all come into estrus simultaneously. Again the coordinator of this change is a primer pheromone in the urine. Perhaps the most startling example of this type of chemical control through smell is the **pregnancy block**. If a female rat is impregnated and then exposed to a new male rat of a different strain, pheromones from the male act on her hypothalamus to prevent implantation of the fertilized egg in her womb. The pregnancy has been canceled simply because the female sniffed a particular odor. This does not happen if the second male is of the same strain as the first or if the second male has been castrated (Keverne, 1983). Apparently, this mechanism evolved as a way of conserving the reproductive resources of the female by allowing pregnancy only when there is a good chance of pup survival.

Olfaction is the primary sense used by many mammals to recognize their sexual partner, their mother, their offspring, and their home. Nursing kittens even come to be able to discriminate a favorite teat on their mother by smell and soon show a strong preference for feeding at that location (Rosenblatt, 1983). This reduces competition and aggression between littermates and increases chances of survival. But much of this use of odorant stimuli depends on the main olfactory system rather than the vomeronasal. In mammals many infant behaviors, like the huddling together of littermates, are more than reflexive; they involve learning (Rosenblatt, 1983). In the first few days of life, kittens huddle for warmth by simply staying in contact with another kitten after accidental contact has been made. Within a few days after birth, however, kittens can recognize each other's odors, and those smells have become **incentives** (stimuli that have acquired positive motivational properties). Now the kittens move toward each other deliberately rather than accidentally and

remain in contact not only for the warmth but also for the odor. Because it depends on sensory discriminations between similar stimuli, this sort of learning is probably on a higher level than the basic approach–avoidance conditioning of the amygdala and hypothalamus. It is a reasonable hypothesis that learning of this sort depends to some extent on the olfactory cortex and the main olfactory system. In rodents the main olfactory system also seems to be involved in the recognition of the opposite sex (Johnson & Rasmussen, 1984).

Keverne (1978) tried to analyze the difference between the contribution of the primitive vomeronasal system and the more recently evolved main olfactory system. In the case of procreation in rodents (Figure 7.35), he found that the main system is most important at the outset of mating probably because of its involvement in sexual arousal—that is, for identifying a female and finding her sexually receptive. After the male has mounted the female, the accessory system (vomeronasal) takes over. As the male nuzzles and licks the female, he apparently picks up primer pheromones that act through his vomeronasal and endocrine systems to help prime the brain and cord for the sensory stimuli that will reflexively produce ejaculation. Keverne points out that the second phase of mating can be quite mechanical and therefore can be handled at the level of hypothalamus and cord, but the early attraction and arousal phase needs to be processed at a higher (cortical) level. For example, the learned experiences stored by the cortex can override the arousal process when a predator or boss male is nearby. Lower centers of the brain are not capable of deciding when arousal is appropriate and when it is not. Thus, the mechanism of sexual arousal by attractant pheromones may, at an early stage in evolution of mammals, have resided at the level of the limbic system and hypothalamus but then shifted to the more versatile, less mechanical level of the cerebral cortex as evolution progressed.

Pheromones in Human Physiology   In primates the vomeronasal system has been lost entirely during the course of evolution. However, olfactory connections into the amygdala and hypothalamus are still present in the human. Do humans show any hints

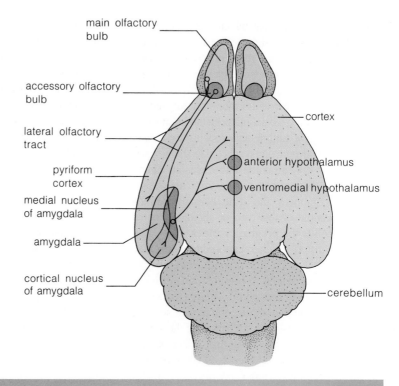

Figure 7.35 Horizontal cross section of a rat brain showing main olfactory and accessory olfactory systems. In the rat brain (which does not have a temporal lobe), the amygdala and pyriform cortex are much closer to the back than in the human brain. (Adapted from Keverne, 1983)

main olfactory bulb

accessory olfactory bulb

lateral olfactory tract

pyriform cortex

medial nucleus of amygdala

amygdala

cortical nucleus of amygdala

cortex

anterior hypothalamus

ventromedial hypothalamus

cerebellum

of retaining some of the basic mammalian sensitivity to pheromones and other odor cues? Some interesting research has begun on the olfactory interactions between human mothers and their infants, which remind one of the sort of incentive learning found in kittens. For example, infants apparently can distinguish between and show a preference for breast pads worn by their mothers versus pads worn by strangers. Further, mothers can distinguish garments worn by their own infant by smell alone (Porter & Cernoch, 1983). However, we cannot be sure that this chemical sensing involved pheromones. More convincing evidence for human pheromones is found in connection with sexuality.

McClintock (1971), in a classic study, found that close friends at an all-female college gradually shifted their menstrual cycles until—after seven cycles—they were nearly in synchrony with one another. This is very reminiscent of the rodent studies showing the synchronizing of estrous cycles in females housed together. Is it possible that humans

might produce and be sensitive to sexual pheromones? A follow-up study showed that a woman would begin to synchronize her menstrual cycle with that of a second woman if she were exposed daily to the underarm perspiration of the second woman (Russell et al., 1980). A chemical called copulin has been isolated from human vaginal secretions, and the concentrations of this substance increase to a peak at the time of ovulation. This timing would suggest that copulin might act as an attractant pheromone to induce mating at the time of greatest fertility. When copulin was smeared on the sex skin of female rhesus monkeys, male monkeys were sexually stimulated (Michael, 1972).

Vieth and co-workers (1983) reasoned that males might also emit pheromones and that these might be primers that influence the fertility of females. They studied undergraduate college women over a period of 40 days, measuring the rate of ovulation (egg production) by means of careful body-temperature records. They found that women who spent at least 2 nights in a man's bed during the 40-day period showed a significantly higher rate of ovulation than did women who were not thus exposed to male pheromones. Their data showed that the frequency of actual intercourse had nothing to do with this increase. As a whole, these studies suggest the presence of both attractant and primer pheromones acting in humans. At this point in the history of such research, however, it is too early to be sure that human pheromones do exist and, if they do, the extent to which they can influence our biology and behavior.

Summary

1. Sound waves are the physical stimulus for the psychological set of sensations called sound. A sound wave is a series of regular pressure changes alternating between a compression phase and a rarefaction phase. A cycle equals one compression and one rarefaction. Sound waves can vary in frequency (number of cycles per second) and amplitude (degree of compression and rarefaction). The psychological correlate of frequency is pitch, and the correlate of amplitude is loudness. Amplitude is measured on the decibel scale, frequency on the hertz scale.

2. There are three parts to the ear: outer, middle, and inner. The outer consists of an auricle and external auditory canal and terminates at the tympanic membrane. The middle ear is an air-filled cavity between the tympanic membrane and the inner ear, which contains three bones: the hammer, anvil, and stirrup. As sound waves vibrate the tympanic membrane back and forth, the chain of bones is also moved. The last bone in this chain, the stirrup, is attached to the oval window of the inner ear, and its motion during a sound wave is like a piston pushing in and out against that membrane. Auditory receptors are in the inner ear. The inner ear, a fluid-filled cavity in the skull, contains the cochlea (housing the auditory receptors) and the vestibular organs.

3. The middle ear acts as an amplifier by using lever action to increase the force of the stirrup against the oval window and by condensing a large area of weak force at the eardrum down into a small area of strong force at the smaller oval window.

4. When the compression phase of a sound wave pushes the oval window inward, the pressure is carried through the fluid of the vestibular canal to the cochlear duct. The pressure pushes the whole cochlear duct downward so that it bulges slightly into the tympanic canal. The base of the cochlear duct is the basilar membrane; riding on this membrane is the organ of Corti, which contains receptor cells.

5. Receptors are called hair cells because each has a bundle of hairlike stereocilia protruding from its top. These stereocilia are attached at their tips to the tectorial membrane, which overhangs the organ of Corti. Whenever a sound wave moves the organ of Corti, hair cells are displaced slightly to one side, and stereocilia are caught in a shearing motion, which bends them. The bending triggers currents in hair cells, which release transmitter at the synapse between the hair cell and its auditory nerve fiber.

6. Two major ideas have been advanced to explain how we hear differences in pitch: frequency theory and place theory. The main task for a theory of pitch perception is to propose how sound wave frequencies are coded into patterns of neural activity. The frequency-following theory states that hair cells respond at the peak of each sound wave so that there is one impulse per wave. The number of impulses per second equals the number of waves per second. The problem with this simple coding scheme is that neurons cannot fire faster than 1,000 times per second, thus leaving the coding of frequencies above 1,000 Hz unexplained. The volley principle takes care of frequencies up to about 3,000 Hz but does not handle the range from 3,000–20,000 Hz.

7. Place theory can explain the coding of high frequencies. Each sound wave causes a traveling wave to move up the basilar membrane from the oval window to the helicotrema, stimulating hair cells as it goes. Sound waves of different frequencies make traveling waves that have different places of maximal stimulation along the basilar membrane and thus are represented by different hair cells.

8. Traveling waves from high frequencies peak at very specific points on the basilar membrane, but waves from low frequencies peak broadly over half the length of the membrane. Thus, low frequencies do not have the places of maximal stimulation called for by the place theory. The theory works for higher frequencies, however, and is supported by the fact that many auditory nerve fibers show that they are "tuned" to specific frequencies. Inner hair cells may also be tuned by mechanical action of outer hair cells, thus improving the place mechanism.

9. Apparently, both the place theory and the frequency-following theories are partly correct. Pitch perception depends on frequency following from 20 Hz to about 100 Hz. Between 100 and 4,000 Hz, both frequency following and place seem to act together; above 4,000 Hz, place alone codes for sound wave frequency.

10. The cochlea is connected to the brain stem by way of the cochlear bundle of the VIIIth nerve. The cochlea, VIIIth nerve and nuclei, tracts, and cortex within the brain that handle auditory input are collectively known as the auditory projection system.

11. The auditory fibers of the VIIIth nerve synapse in the cochlear nuclei of the medulla. The superior olivary complex of the upper medulla receives inputs from the cochlear nuclei, and these connections are arranged so that the particular olivary cells activated by a sound indicate the direction of the sound source. The olive uses both the phase difference between the waves at the two ears and the time difference to calculate the location of the sound source.

12. Another analyzer for audition is the inferior colliculus of the midbrain. Its output to the superior colliculus suggests that it provides the superior colliculus with information about the localization of sound sources toward which the superior colliculus orients the eyes and skin receptors.

13. Above the brain-stem level, the auditory projection pathways feed into the medial geniculate body (MGB) of the thalamus, whose neurons in turn project to the auditory cortex in the temporal lobe. The MGB probably acts as a gateway to the auditory cortex, allowing relevant information into the cortex and excluding irrelevant information. Thus, its main function would be that of directing attention.

14. Fibers from the MGB terminate in the primary auditory cortex, Heschl's gyrus, which forms part of the floor of the lateral fissure. This gyrus is frequently designated as area AI; the adjacent cortex just over the lip of the lateral fissure into the superior temporal gyrus is termed area AII. Neither area has anything to do with basic pitch or loudness perception but rather seems to be important for remembering sound sequences and for localizing sounds that are too brief for the olive to handle. The importance of brief sounds is that all fundamental sounds of speech fit into this category.

15. Loss of hearing sensitivity can result from a conductive loss in the middle ear or a sensorineural loss in cochlea or nervous system, resulting from aging, disease, or exposure to damaging sound levels. Hearing sensitivity for pure tones is measured with an instrument called an audiometer. Damage in the auditory projection pathway can frequently be detected by averaging auditory evoked potentials. Averaged evoked potentials are also useful in assessing the hearing of infants and other patients incapable of language.

16. Hearing aids are useful in cases of conduction loss because bone conduction carries amplified waves through the skull to the oval window, bypassing the damaged middle ear. They also have some use in sensorineural loss from damage in the cochlea or nerve but are of no value in cases of lesions to the pathways within the CNS. The development of an electronic hearing prosthesis to replace a nonfunctional cochlea was begun recently. So far, it has been somewhat of an aid to lip reading in selected patients.

17. Taste and smell are the two major chemical senses. Smell seems to have evolved out of taste to meet the need of land animals to sense airborne molecules.

18. Receptors for taste are the taste cells, which cluster in taste buds located on the surfaces of the papillae of the tongue and mouth lining. Like hair cells of the cochlea, taste cells have no axon or dendrites. A nerve fiber from one of three cranial nerves (VII, IX, or X) makes contact with each taste cell and carries the taste information to a cluster of cells in the medulla of the brain stem, called the nucleus of tractus solitarius (NTS). Cells in this nucleus project to the pontine taste area, and the pontine neu-

rons connect through the thalamus with the gustatory area of the cortex at the bottom of the somatosensory zone in the parietal lobe.

19. In the past, it was thought that there were only four primary taste qualities (sweet, sour, salty, and bitter) and that there were probably only four types of taste cells to match these primaries, but recent research suggests that more primaries may exist.

20. The labeled-line theory of taste coding states that there is a limited number of receptor cell types and that each type has its own "line" to the cortex so that the brain knows what chemical is on the tongue by which line is active. That theory has been challenged by the across–fiber pattern theory that holds that there are no primaries and that each separate chemical stimulus is coded into a different pattern of active fibers. Keverne suggests a dual-processing theory in which the subcortical parts of the brain use the taste input as though it came from a labeled-line system, while the cortex uses it as across–fiber pattern input.

21. Olfaction (the sense of smell) is closely related to taste, and the flavor of a food is really as much odor as it is taste.

22. The sense organ for smell is the olfactory epithelium of the nose. It contains receptor cells with their cilia projecting into a mucous coating. The olfactory nerve (cranial nerve I) connects the receptors to the olfactory bulb at the base of the frontal lobes of the brain.

23. The lock-and-key theory of transduction suggests that receptor cell cilia have receptor sites on their surfaces into which a wide variety of molecules can fit. One version of this theory holds that there is a limited number of receptor site types and that each type represents one olfactory primary (such as "fruity," minty," and so forth), but there is not much evidence for this.

24. Neurons in the olfactory bulb connect by way of the olfactory tract with the amygdala and pyriform cortex of the medial temporal lobe. Cells in those areas project forward into the orbitofrontal cortex near the olfactory bulbs. This seems to be the olfactory cortex.

25. Nonprimate mammals all have a second olfactory system called the accessory olfactory system. Its receptor is the vomeronasal organ located near the olfactory epithelium in the nose. Whereas the main olfactory system is involved with the discrimination of one odor from another and learning about the significance of various odors, the vomeronasal organ functions mainly to receive pheromones, chemicals that act as communication signals. There are attractant pheromones, which are usually secreted by females for the purpose of luring males, and primers, which directly produce changes in the recipient animal's endocrine glands.

26. Pheromones may exist in human interactions. Research has shown that mothers can identify their infants by smell and that women living together gradually synchronize their menstrual cycles, probably through contact with each other's sexual primers.

Glossary

A1 An area of auditory cortex within which the medial geniculate neurons terminate. (273)

AII An area of auditory cortex that receives input from the medial geniculate and A1. (273)

accessory olfactory bulb Part of the accessory olfactory system that receives input from the vomeronasal organ. (290)

accessory olfactory system A second olfactory system present in many nonhuman mammals. (290)

across-fiber pattern theory Theory of taste coding that postulates a different pattern of active fibers to represent each separate chemical stimulus. (283)

amplitude The amount of pressure change between the point of greatest compression and the point of greatest rarefaction. (256)

amygdala Group of nuclei under the cortex of the temporal pole; major destination for information from the olfactory bulb. (289)

anvil Middle-ear bone that connects the hammer to the stirrup. (258)

attractant A type of pheromone usually secreted by a female for the purpose of luring and guiding a male. (290)

audiometer An instrument used for measuring hearing thresholds. (277)

audition The sense of hearing. (254)

auditory cortex Portions of temporal cortex devoted to analyzing auditory input. (273)

auditory evoked potential A series of EEG waves triggered by a sound stimulus. (277)

auditory nerve fiber Axon of cranial nerve VIII; synapses with hair cells of cochlea and carries auditory information to the cochlear nuclei in the medulla. (259)

auditory projection system The route taken by auditory information as it travels from the cochlea to the auditory cortex. (269)

auricles The part of the outer ears visible on the outside of the head. (257)

basilar membrane The membrane forming one wall of the cochlear duct and the base of the organ of Corti. (259)

chorda tympani One branch of the VIIth nerve that carries taste fibers. (283)

cochlea The auditory receptor organ. (258)

cochlear duct The coiled tube of the cochlea that is situated between the vestibular and tympanic canals; contains the organ of Corti. (259)

cochlear emission A sound stimulus "echo" emitted by the ear. (267)

cochlear nuclei The neurons in the medulla of the brain stem upon which the auditory neurons of the VIIIth nerve terminate. (269)

compression phase The part of the cycle of the sound wave in which air molecules are pushed together. (255)

conductive loss Hearing loss resulting from problems in the middle ear. (275)

cranial nerve VIII The vestibulocochlear nerve; usually called the VIIIth nerve. (269)

decibel Unit of soundwave intensity adjusted to match human hearing. (257)

dual-processing theory Theory of taste that postulates that subcortical areas use taste input as labeled lines whereas the neocortex uses it as across-fiber patterns. (285)

flavor A compound stimulus consisting of both taste and odor. (286)

frequency The number of waves per second. (256)

frequency following The principle that the frequency of firing in the VIIIth nerve is determined by the frequency of the sound wave. (263)

gustatory cortex Area in parietal lobe that processes taste information. (281)

hair cells The receptor cells of the cochlea; *inner* hair cells are located in the portion of the organ of Corti closest to the center of the cochlea. (259)

hammer Bone attached to the tympanic membrane. (258)

hearing prosthesis Implanted electronic device for artificially transducing sound waves into patterns of impulses in the VIIIth nerve. (279)

helicotrema The opening at the apex of the cochlea; connects the vestibular canal to the tympanic canal. (259)

hertz (pronounced HAIRTS) The unit of wave frequency; cycles per second. (256)

Heschl's gyrus Temporal lobe gyrus on the lower bank of the lateral fissure; location of A1. (273)

incentive A stimulus that has acquired positive motivational properties. (291)

inferior colliculus Midbrain nucleus involved in localizing sound stimulus sources. (272)

inner ear Collection of fluid-filled cavities in the skull that contain the receptor organs for audition and the vestibular senses. (258)

intensity Wave amplitude. (256)

interaural intensity difference Difference in strength between the waves at the ear near the source and the ear farther from it. (271)

interaural time difference A difference in arrival time of the same sound wave at the two ears. (269)

labeled-line theory Theory of taste coding that postulates four primary tastes, each with its own type of receptor cell and nerve fiber. (283)

lateral superior olive Nucleus containing analyzer for interaural intensity differences. (269)

lock-and-key theory Theory of olfactory reception in which olfactory receptors are seen as genetically prepared to react to specific odorants by having membrane receptors for those molecules. (288)

loudness Aspect of sensation most related to amplitude. (257)

medial geniculate body (MGB) Thalamic nucleus in the auditory projection system. (273)

medial superior olive Nucleus containing analyzer for interaural phase differences. (269)

middle ear Air-filled cavity with tympanic membrane on one side and the oval window on the other. (258)

nucleus of tractus solitarius (NTS) A cluster of cells

found in the medulla and pons of the brain stem; it receives sensory information from the viscera through the Xth nerve. (281)

odorant See *olfactory stimulus*. (286)

olfaction The sense of smell. (286)

olfactory bulb The first analyzer in the olfactory system; termination point for the olfactory nerve. (287)

olfactory epithelium Patch of specialized skin in the back of the olfactory cavity that contains mucous cells and receptor cells for olfaction. (286)

olfactory nerve Cranial nerve I; it contains the olfactory receptors to the olfactory bulb. (286)

olfactory stimulus (odorant) A chemical that elicits a sensation of odor. (286)

olfactory tract Axons of the olfactory bulb output neurons. (289)

olfactory transduction The conversion of airborne chemical information into nerve impulse patterns in the olfactory nerve. (288)

orbitofrontal cortex Ventral portion of the frontal lobes that receives olfactory information from the pyriform cortex and the amygdala. (289)

organ of Corti Cochlear structure that contains the receptor cells for audition. (259)

otosclerosis Damping of stirrup movement caused by bony growth over the oval window. (275)

outer ear Portion of ear that includes the auricle and external ear canal; ends at eardrum. (257)

outer hair cells The hair cells located in the portion of the organ of Corti farthest from the center of the cochlea; may serve a motor function. (267)

oval window Membrane through which sound waves gain access to the inner ear. (258)

papillae Small protrusions on the surface of the tongue that contain taste buds. (280)

phase (of a wave) The stage of its cycle in which it is at any given moment. (269)

pheromone A chemical secreted by an organism for the purpose of communication with other members of the species. (290)

pitch Aspect of sensation most related to wave frequency. (257)

place theory Explanation of how higher frequencies are coded by the organ of Corti. (264)

pregnancy block Circumstance in which an inhaled pheromone prevents implantation of a fertilized egg. (291)

primary taste qualities Sensations that cannot be divided into more fundamental tastes. (281)

primer Type of pheromone that produces changes in the recipient animal's endocrine system. (290)

pyriform cortex One destination for information from the olfactory bulb. (289)

rarefaction phase The part of the cycle of the sound wave in which air molecules are pulled apart from one another. (255)

Reissner's membrane Separates the vestibular canal from the cochlear duct. (259)

round window Membrane separating the middle ear from the tympanic canal. (259)

sensation The conscious, psychological event elicited by a stimulus. (255)

sensorineural loss Hearing loss caused by damage to the cochlea or auditory projection system. (275)

shearing action The sideways force exerted on the stereocilia by the slippage of the tectorial membrane over the organ of Corti. (260)

sound The sensation produced when sound waves stimulate a nervous system. (255)

sound shadow Volume of space within which an ear cannot receive sound waves directly from a source because the source is on the opposite side of the head. (271)

sound wave Cycle of rarefaction and compression of air (or vibration in a solid medium). (255)

stereocilia The hairlike extensions protruding from the tops of the cochlear hair cells. (259)

stirrup Middle-ear bone that is attached to the oval window. (258)

superior olivary complex Set of brain-stem nuclei containing analyzers for direction of the sound source. (269)

taste buds Clusters of cells on the sides of the papillae; they contain the taste receptor cells. (280)

taste cells The receptor cells that transduce chemical stimulation into neural activity in the taste system. (280)

tectorial membrane Membrane to which the tops of the stereocilia are attached. (260)

temporary threshold shift Partial hearing loss which will disappear after a few hours in a quiet environment; usually accompanied by a smaller permanent hearing loss. (277)

thalamus Group of nuclei at the center of the brain that provides connections in and out of the cerebral cortex. (273)

tinnitus "Ringing" in the ears; continuing high pitched pure tone not caused by sound waves. (277)

tonotopic arrangement Organization of the geniculate inputs to A1 in which low frequencies are represented at one end of a strip of cortex and high frequencies at the other. (273)

traveling wave Flexion of basilar membrane created by each in-and-out movement of the stirrup; it starts at the oval window and travels up the basilar membrane to the helicotrema. (264)

tuning curve Graph showing how much wave energy is required to fire an VIIIth nerve axon at each of a series frequencies; represents the receptive field of the neuron. (266)

tympanic canal The coiled tube of the cochlea that has the round window at one end and the helicotrema at the other. (259)

tympanic membrane Membrane separating the outer ear from the inner; ear drum. (258)

vestibular canal The coiled tube of the cochlea that has the oval window at one end and the helicotrema at the other. (259)

vestibular organs Receptors that detect the direction of gravity, rotary acceleration, and linear acceleration; saccule, utricle, and semicircular canals. (258)

volatile Able to release molecules into the air. (286)

volley principle Individual fibers in the VIIIth nerve take turns at responding to sound wave peaks; enables nerve as a whole to fire with a frequency beyond the capability of any single fiber. (263)

vomeronasal organ Receptor organ (olfactory epithelium) for the accessory olfactory system. (289)

8

Somatic Senses

Quick! In no more than 5 seconds, can you name the body's largest sense organ—that magnificent piece of biological equipment that not only gives us three sense modalities but also is vital to temperature control, acts as a barrier to ultraviolet radiation, and keeps our body fluids from leaking out? What is it? The skin, of course.

For a normal-weight male of 6-foot height, there is an enormous 3,000 square inches of skin, all of it loaded with somatic receptors (Figure 8.1). The three sense modalities supplied by these receptors are mechanoreception, thermoreception, and nociception. These three, plus the kinesthetic sense discussed in Chapter 9, make up the **somatic senses**.

The Nature of Somatic Sensitivity

Mechanoreceptors (meh-CAN-oh-re-SEP-tors) translate mechanical forms of energy like pressure, twisting, bending, and pulling into patterns of nerve impulses that the brain combines and interprets as sensations of touch, pressure, and sometimes vibration. **Thermoreceptors** (THER-mo-re-SEP-tors) react to thermal (temperature) changes and give us our sense of warmth and cold. **Nociceptors** (NO-sis-SEP-tors) provide the brain with part of the information needed to create pain sensations. Most stimuli contacting the skin evoke responses in all three somatic modalities simultaneously so that the sensory experience is that of a blend rather than a feeling of pure touch or pain or warmth. For example, if you put your hand into a bucket of ice water, you not only experience the sensation of cold but also pain and pressure (the latter especially around the wrist where the change from water to air occurs).

Throughout our discussion of the somatic senses, it is important to remember the difference between a **stimulus** (some energy change outside of the nervous system) and a **sensation** (the resulting pattern of activity within the nervous system and its accompanying conscious experience). Touch, for example, is a sensation, not a stimulus. It is an event inside

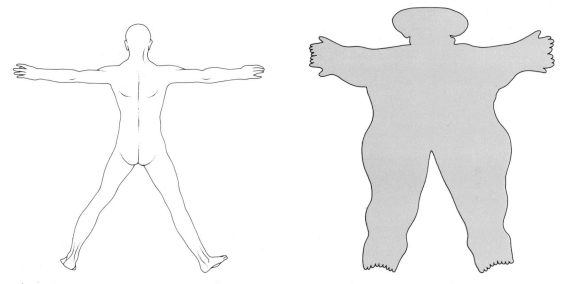

Figure 8.1 If the whole human skin were laid out flat, this is how big it would look. (Adapted from Montagna, 1965)

your head rather than out there in an arm or leg.

An important characteristic of the relation between stimulus and sensation is that a sensation is more likely to result from a change in energy rather than from energy at a continuous level. For example, to effectively stimulate mechanoreceptors, the stimulus must deform the skin (i.e., bend or stretch it), but constant pressure over the skin surface, although it keeps the skin deformed, may produce little or no sensation.

The skin is not the sole source of somatic stimulation: a number of somatic receptors can be found inside the body. Both blood vessels and sheets of connective tissue that support the intestines contain nociceptors. The former seem to be involved in headaches, whereas the latter react to distention of the intestines by producing the pains of gas cramps. We can keep these separate from somatic skin receptors by calling them **deep somatic receptors**. These deep receptors also include the kinesthetic receptors in muscles, joints, and tendons that are discussed in

Chapter 9. Skin receptors (our major concentration in this chapter) can be called **cutaneous receptors** to distinguish them from deep receptors.

Cutaneous Somatic Mechanoreceptors

Women have smooth, hairless skin, whereas men are hairy all over, right? . . . Wrong! On the average, women have just as much body and facial hair as do men. Their hairs are usually much finer and lighter in color so that they are much less visible at a distance, but they are there. Why is that so? As a matter of fact, why is it that humans still have this thin covering of hair over most of the skin surface even after all these thousands of years of evolving away from their hairy ancestors? Could it be that body hairs, those supposedly useless appendages, still serve some important function in human survival?

Figure 8.2 A section of human skin showing its three layers and six types of somatic receptors. (Adapted from Gardner, 1975)

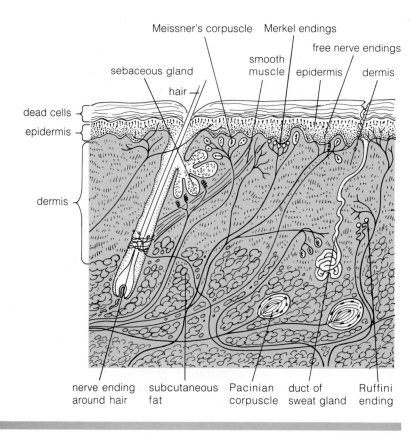

Meissner's corpuscle   Merkel endings

free nerve endings

smooth muscle   epidermis   dermis

sebaceous gland

hair

dead cells

epidermis

dermis

nerve ending around hair   subcutaneous fat   Pacinian corpuscle   duct of sweat gland   Ruffini ending

Figure 8.2 provides an answer to this puzzle. As the picture indicates, each hair grows out of a bottlelike hole in the skin known as a **hair follicle** (FAH-lick-cul), which is contacted by terminals of a sensory neuron. These endings generate nerve impulses in the sensory fiber when stimulated mechanically by pressure. In other words, the hair follicle ending is one form of mechanoreceptor. The mechanical pressure that triggers these receptors is applied by the hair itself. Outside the skin, some stimulus (such as a breeze or clothing rubbing against the skin) pushes against the hair. Pivoting in its follicle, the hair presses its root against the neuron endings and sends a train of nerve impulses off to the CNS, signaling contact at that point on the body.

Other receptors are visible in Figure 8.2. Note that the skin has three layers: on top, a thin layer of dead cells, which forms an outside protective coating; below that, the epidermis into which a few nerve cell endings penetrate; and finally, at the deepest level, the dermis itself containing most of the various skin organs. Most sensory neurons terminate in a treelike set of branches called **free nerve endings**, but some end in specialized structures. The picture shows four of these specialized endings: **Meissner's corpuscles**, **Merkel endings**, **Ruffini endings**, and **Pacinian corpuscles**. At one time, it was hoped that cold sensations could be associated with one type of ending, warmth with another, light touch with another, and so on.

A major problem encountered in linking sensations with particular receptors is that neuron endings are impossible to see in living skin. Experimenters have gone so far as to stimulate a patch of their own skin, note the sensations, and then cut off that area for examination under the microscope. But even that kind of dedicated observation has problems. How can you be sure which of the tiny endings in your microscope picture were the ones responding to the stimulus when a dozen or more might have been under the point of stimulation?

Unfortunately, no solid evidence has ever been found to link pain, warmth, or cold with any type of receptor ending (Sinclair, 1981). Possibly each of these receptor types may be involved in several modalities. That is, a single ending may be serving as both a mechanoreceptor and a thermoreceptor. Others might combine thermoreception with nociception. Pattern theory holds that we distinguish cold from touch from pain because each has its own pattern of active nerve endings. Any one of the receptors might become active as the part of several different patterns, and none by itself yields a specific type of sensation. Specificity theory, on the other hand, postulates that each receptor is dedicated to either nociception, mechanoreception, or thermoreception. If pattern theory is correct, then we should stop hunting for "pain receptors" and "cold receptors" because no such structure exists. In some of the deep tissues and organs as well as in the cornea of the eye, the only receptors appear to be free nerve endings, yet these tissues are sensitive to pressure, temperature, and pain (Tanelian & Beuerman, 1984). This means that the so-called free nerve endings must be capable of serving as mechanoreceptors, thermoreceptors, and nociceptors (Sinclair, 1981). Pattern theorists would explain the ability of a single type of neuron to evoke a variety of sensations by postulating a different pattern of impulses in the neuron for each type of stimulus. However, the idea that there are such things as free nerve endings comes from the earlier research using light microscopes. Modern researchers with electron microscopes are not sure they have found any terminals that could truly be called free endings (Iggo & Andres, 1982). We have much yet to learn about the nature of somatic receptors.

Enough data exist on both sides of this pattern–versus–specificity argument to suggest that some afferent neurons are strictly mechanoreceptors and a few may be specialized as nociceptors (Burgess & Perl, 1973) but that most are involved in several types of sensation. In the rest of this section we will treat Meissner's corpuscles, Merkel endings, Ruffini endings, and Pacinian corpuscles as though they were related only to mechanoreception; however, keep in mind that this may not be true for every type of stimulus.

The Human Hand

The hairless skin on the palmar side of the hand is a superb sense organ. It contains about 17,000 mechanoreceptors altogether, with about 100 of them per square centimeter in the fingertips where they reach their highest density (Johansson & Vallbo, 1983). These receptors, like all skin receptors, are the terminals of nerve fiber branches. Thousands of such fibers, called **primary afferents**, come together into great bundles called nerves. Nerves run up the arm across the trunk and into the spinal column. Primary afferent fibers synapse inside the gray matter of the spinal cord.

On their way up the arm, some of these nerves lie rather close to the surface of the skin, and this relative accessibility inspired a series of very important experiments. The subject (often one of the team of experimenters) allows a very fine wire electrode to be pushed through his skin and into the nerve where it can make contact with one of the primary afferent fibers. With this "wiretap" in place, the experimenters can now stimulate the subject's hand and listen in on the resulting nerve impulse messages as they flash past on their way to the spinal cord. The pattern of nerve impulses produced by each stimulus event can tell us a great deal about what kind of information the brain gets from the skin.

One of the first things discovered in such nerve fiber research was that all the fibers responding to mechanical types of stimulation fell into two general categories: **fast adapters (FA)** and **slow adapters (SA)**. Figure 8.3 shows a recording of nerve impulses from several primary afferent fibers. Note how the FA fiber fires very rapidly when the stimulus is first applied and then stops firing after the stimulus pressure is continued for a few moments. This loss of response from a receptor, despite continuing stimulation, is called **adaptation**. At first glance, adaptation seems to be simply a matter of fatigue, but this is not the case. The bottom record in Figure 8.3

Figure 8.3 Patterns of nerve impulses in FA and SA fibers. Each short vertical line represents one nerve impulse occurring at that point on the time line. The long vertical lines indicate when the stimulus probe contacts the skin and when it is lifted off the skin. The picture at the top shows the contrast between slow and fast adapters. The bottom picture shows how the FAs respond to both the application and removal of a stimulus.

Notice that the FA fiber soon stops firing, even though the point is still depressing the skin—that is, the fiber *adapts* quickly to the stimulus. The SA, on the other hand, keeps on firing throughout the stimulus contact time, but its rate grows steadily slower. If the stimulus continues long enough, the SA eventually adapts just like the FA.

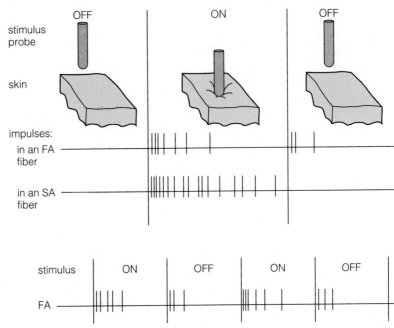

shows that the fiber can continue to fire over and over as long as the stimulus is removed and reapplied repeatedly. The receptor can sense the change in pressure that occurs as the stimulus is applied (or removed) but rapidly becomes "blind" to a steady, unchanging pressure stimulus.

In Figure 8.3, both the FA and SA fibers show adaptation, but only FA fibers were able to adapt completely in the short time allotted. Notice that the FA fiber fires again when it is restimulated by the removal of the stimulus object. No one is certain exactly how this adaptation works, but its importance to human perception has become clear, as we will see shortly.

Mechanoreceptors can also be grouped according to the nature of their receptive fields. Each fiber branches out into a limited area of skin, and it can only be fired from a stimulus applied to this limited zone. The patch of skin within which one can trigger impulses in the primary afferent fiber is called the **receptive field (RF)** of that fiber. RFs of some neurons are much larger than those of others. Figure 8.4 shows RFs from a sample of two kinds of fibers: I's and II's. **FA I**'s and **SA I**'s can only be triggered from a tiny area covering about 4–10 fingerprint ridges, whereas the fields of **FA II**'s and **SA II**'s can be as large as an entire finger. You can trigger an impulse with equal ease from anywhere within the small field of a I, but within the II field, sensitivity decreases steadily the farther you go in any direction from a small, central area of good sensitivity (Johansson & Vallbo, 1983).

Based on the characteristics of the RF and the rate of adaptation, we now have four distinct types of primary afferent, mechanoreceptive fibers: FA I's, SA I's, FA II's, and SA II's. Is it possible that each of these fiber types might have a separate type of receptive ending that helps create its distinctive field and adaptation properties? Years of research on this question have produced some reasonably firm conclusions (Iggo & Andres, 1982). FA I's apparently end in Meissner's corpuscles, FA II's in Pacinian corpuscles, SA I's in Merkel endings, and SA II's in Ruffini endings.

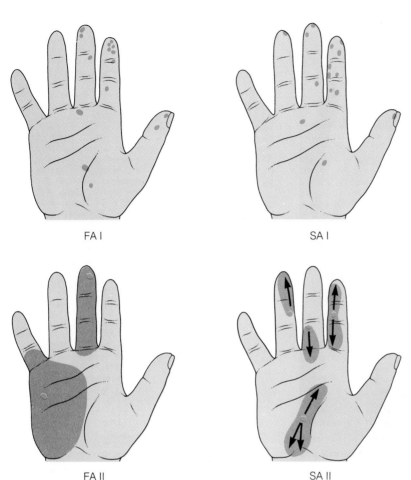

FA I

SA I

FA II

SA II

Figure 8.4 Typical RFs of the FA and SA I and II fibers from the hand. Type I fibers have very small RFs with relatively uniform sensitivity throughout. There are thousands of these fibers for each hand, and the few shown in the top two illustrations (as color spots) are just the particular sample studied by Johansson and Vallbo. FA II RFs each have a small central spot of maximal sensitivity surrounded by a very large area (shaded) in which sensitivity grows weaker with distance from the center spot. The arrows on the SA II RFs indicate the directions in which the skin must be stretched to stimulate the four SA II receptors studied in this experiment. (Adapted from Johansson & Vallbo, 1983)

What Each Receptor Contributes

How do the specialized endings participate in creating the wealth of sensory experience available to you through your skin?

Mechanoreceptive Threshold The smallest amount of mechanical stimulation (e.g., pressure against the skin) that produces a conscious sensation is called the **mechanoreceptive threshold**. The threshold for touch is lower than most people imagine. Galanter has taken the abstract physical measures that describe the threshold and translated them into a rather poetic description: the least amount of pressure that the human skin is capable of sensing is equal to the impact on your cheek of a bee's wing falling from a height of 1 cm (Galanter, 1962). This spectacular sensitivity is probably due more to Meissner's corpuscles and Merkel endings than to any other receptor types.

FA I fibers with their Meissner's corpuscles (Figure 8.5) seem to be the part of the somatic sensory system designed to catch the tiniest mechanical stimuli. In most of the sensory systems (visual, auditory, etc.), it is doubtful that a single impulse in a single afferent axon could produce a sensation all by itself; it would be like a single brush stroke in a large painting. In the somatic senses, however, a single nerve impulse in just one SA I fiber is enough to stimulate neurons all the way up to the brain and

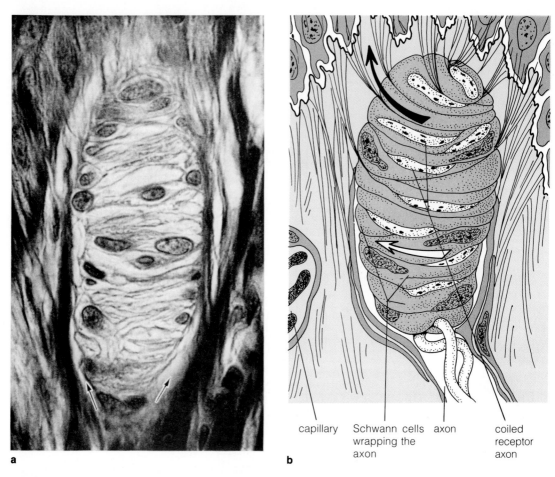

capillary   Schwann cells   axon   coiled
             wrapping the   receptor
             axon   axon

a   b

Figure 8.5 (**a**) Photomicrograph of Meissner's corpuscle from palmar skin (magnification ×1,800). (**b**) Drawing of same corpuscle with parts labeled. Above the corpuscle are skin cells. The fine lines are protein fibers connecting skin cells to the corpuscle. When the skin is deformed by pressure, a pull is exerted through the fibers that twists the top coils of the corpuscle in the direction of the black arrow. This twist is relieved a moment later as the bottom coils move (in the direction of the white arrow) to "catch up" with the top. The tension on the nerve fiber exerted by the twist at the top fires the axon. The firing stops a moment later as the tension is relieved. Thus, the ability of the bottom coils to relieve the tension on the nerve fiber gives the Meissner's corpuscle the ability to adapt rapidly to pressure. (Adapted from Andres & von Düring, 1973)

produce a conscious experience of light touch (Johansson & Vallbo, 1983; Vallbo et al., 1984). A clever experiment has given us direct confirmation of this point. After using a recording electrode to find a single SA I fiber in a nerve of a human volunteer, the experimenters converted the electrode for stimulation and turned on the current. The sensation produced by this single-fiber stimulation was that of an object pressing gently against the skin. Some subjects described the feeling as "a faint and uniform pressure like that of a leaf held against the skin" (Vallbo et al., 1984). The intensity of the experience would, of course, have been different with greater amplitudes of stimulation. Notice also that the report from the subject described the sensation as a continuing pressure rather than a tap or blow, as you would expect from an FA I. Only an SA fiber can transmit information about continuing pressure.

Localization We learned earlier that FA I afferents with their Meissner's endings have very small RFs. Is there any value to a small versus a large field? Consider the fact that your brain knows only what the receptors tell it. If each of your hands had just one FA I with an RF that covered the whole hand, then a stimulus anywhere on that hand would excite exactly the same route to the brain. The brain would get the same message (impulses in the single FA I) no matter where on the hand you were touched. There would be no way for you to know where the stimulus was except by looking. If you had two receptors, one for the fingers and one for the palm, you would be able to **localize** the stimulus as either on the palm or on the fingers. Three receptors would give you still greater localization, and so on. Obviously, many tiny receptive fields give you a much better ability to localize than would a few big ones.

Localization in turn is critical to **shape recognition**, the ability to perceive the form of an object held in the hand. How would you be able to detect an object's shape if you couldn't tell where its corners and edges were? The finer your localization ability, the better your shape recognition. FA I fibers with their very small RFs seem to be designed so you can localize stimuli and determine the shapes of objects.

Spatial Acuity SA I's with their Merkel endings (Figure 8.6) also have small RFs and probably also participate in shape recognition. Both types of I's are constructed to enable you to feel various parts of the stimulus object as separate and distinct, even when they are very close to one another on the skin. This ability is called **spatial acuity** and can be measured using a test for two-point threshold. In the two-point test, a drafting compass is lowered smoothly onto the skin so that both of its points make contact at the same instant. The subject, who is blindfolded, must decide whether there are one or two points.

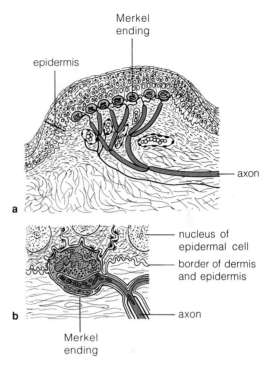

Figure 8.6 (**a**) Cluster of Merkel endings in hairy skin, one at the end of each branch of the primary afferent axon seen entering from the right, deep in the dermis. (**b**) A single Merkel ending in its typical location at the border of the dermis and epidermis. (Adapted from Gardner, 1975)

If the points are very close together, both fall within the same RF and stimulate only one afferent fiber. The brain is mistakenly informed of only one stimulus. If, however, the points are far enough apart so that each one contacts a different RF, then two neurons report to the brain and two points are perceived. The least amount of distance between the two points of the stimulator that can still be sensed as two points rather than just one is called the **two-point threshold**.

As you might expect, the smallest two-point thresholds are found in the fingertips where receptor density is greatest (Johansson & Vallbo, 1983). It is precisely for this reason that blind readers use their fingertips to read Braille rather than using some other area of skin. In the **Braille system**, each letter is represented by a different pattern of one to six dots arranged close together in three columns. Each dot stands out from the paper by only 1 mm (the distance across the shaft of a pin) and is separated from its neighbors by as little as 2.3 mm. On most areas of skin, two points that close together would fall below the two-point threshold and be perceived as one point.

Texture Perception   One kind of input that your brain must receive from the skin in order to avoid clumsiness in handling objects is information about textures—that is, how rough or smooth a surface is. Slick objects must be picked up more carefully than rough objects because they afford less friction between fingers and object to help you maintain your grasp. FA I's and SA I's with their Meissner's corpuscles and Merkel endings are probably the most important neurons involved in discriminating texture differences.

Texture perception depends on active rather than passive sensing; it is a matter of touching as opposed to being touched. To obtain a good feel of a texture, you must actively move your fingers over the surface. Imagine yourself feeling the textures of silk versus woolen tweed or a varnished board versus an unfinished plank. You don't press your fingers against the surface to see how rough it is; you run them back and forth across the object. Braille reading really is just a specialized case of detecting texture patterns. For a Braille reader, "seeing" a certain letter more clearly does not mean pressing the fingers down harder on the dot pattern. Instead, it refers to brushing fingertips across the difficult letter. If a finger were pressed down steadily on a letter and held there, the feel of the dot pattern would quickly fade, and reading would become very difficult (Kenshalo, 1978). As always, the best stimulus is an energy change rather than continuous energy at one level.

The perceiving of texture appears to depend on a combination of the impulse patterns in the slow adapters with patterns in the fast adapters (Darien-Smith, 1982). As your skin moves across a rough surface (one full of many microscopic bumps), the FA I's are stimulated repeatedly and become very active (Figure 8.7). As each microbump momentarily depresses your skin, the FA I fires once or twice. If

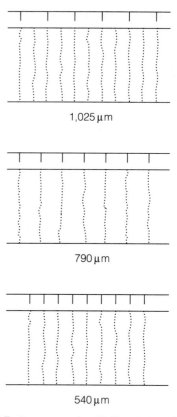

1,025 µm

790 µm

540 µm

Figure 8.7   Responses of an FA fiber to three different surfaces of varying roughness. The surfaces were the rims of wheels having raised ridges of uniform height at regular intervals. These wheels were rolled across the skin of the subject (a monkey) at a fixed rate of speed (66 mm/second) so that frequency with which the ridges contacted the skin could be calculated. The top record in this figure is from a surface with ridges set 1,025 µm apart, the second has them set at 790 µm, and the third at 540 µm. Thus, the top record is from the roughest surface, the bottom from the smoothest. The stimulus surface contacted 25 mm² of skin on the pad of the index finger with a force of 60 g. On each record, the horizontal line at the top is a time line, and the short vertical bars indicate the moment at which a ridge contacted the skin. Below this time line are rows of dots, read from left to right, from the top row to the bottom. Each dot indicates the occurrence of a nerve impulse in the fiber. The data indicate that this fiber fired twice for each ridge when the bumps were spaced at 1,025 µm but only once per ridge when they were closer together. At the closer spacings, the fiber's frequency of firing matches the frequency of stimulation. Thus (within a certain range), faster frequencies signal finer textures. (Adapted from Darien-Smith, 1982)

the bumps are farther apart, the fiber reacts to each with two impulses, but if the spacing is closer, there is only one impulse for each. The closer together the bumps, the faster the neuron fires so that the frequency of microvariations in the surface is matched by the frequency of firing in the afferent fiber. This is called **frequency matching**, and it is the way in which roughness information is carried in the somatic system.

It is possible that SA I's make their greatest contribution when the stimulus is a smooth surface. The microscopic bumps on a smooth surface are very small and infrequent so that the stimulus is more continuous than ON–OFF. Under such nearly continuous stimulation, FA I's should quickly adapt and quit firing, while SA I's should keep right on working.

Vibration The endings of the II fibers (Pacinian corpuscles and Ruffini endings) lie deeper in the skin than do the endings of the I's. This means that a stronger stimulus is required to trigger their activity and that they do not participate as much in shape discriminations. The Pacinian corpuscle, however, is ideally arranged to detect vibrations and to help in discriminating between different frequencies of vibration. Figure 8.2 shows that a Pacinian corpuscle consists of many layers of tissue arranged like an onion around the end of the FA II fiber. If the skin above a Pacinian corpuscle is pressed down slowly enough, the onionlike layers can absorb most of the pressure and prevent the stimulus from affecting the FA II ending. Thus, if you slowly press the point of your pencil into your hand and hold it there for a second or two, Pacinian corpuscles in that area remain silent. They are blind to that kind of stimulus (Burgess, 1973). However, if you then tap the pencil point on your skin three or four times, you get a burst of activity in the FA II's. The layers of the Pacinian corpuscle are unable to shield the ending from fast pressure changes. Because the FA II can be stimulated many times in quick succession, it becomes the perfect receptor for rapid, ON–OFF shifts in pressure—that is, for vibrations.

Grip Control When you hold a glass of water, you squeeze the glass hard enough to prevent gravity from pulling it out of your hand, yet your grip is fairly relaxed, even gentle. It is a long way from your strongest grip. The job of holding the glass safely is being accomplished at minimum effort. How does your brain know exactly how hard the glass must be gripped? The information needed by the brain to make this judgment concerns the amount to which the skin in contact with the glass is being stretched by the downward pull of the object. The heavier the glass, the more the skin will be pulled down (stretched) by the weight. So a skin receptor that is selectively sensitive to skin stretch could provide exactly the information that the brain needs to control muscle contractions in the hand. The Ruffini ending of the SA II fiber has the needed capability of sensing skin stretch (Figure 8.8). Thanks to SA II primary afferents, you can pick up an egg between thumb and fingers without dropping it and without reducing it to an eggshell omelet.

Table 8.1 contains a summary of all features of the four major types of mechanoreceptors. Now that we have surveyed some of our knowledge of mechanoreceptors, let's find out what happens to this information as it enters the CNS and proceeds to the cortex.

Mechanoreception in the Central Nervous System

If we are to follow the sensory information into the brain, we must trace the path of the **somatosensory projection system**, the route from receptors to the sensory area of the cortex. Figures 8.9 and 8.10 show the somatic and kinesthetic projection systems, both of which share the same route to the cortex. Because the kinesthetic sense is such a vital part of the process of body movement, we will save our discussion of it for Chapter 9.

All mechanoreceptors, thermoreceptors, and nociceptors translate stimuli into patterns of nerve impulses that are carried to the spinal cord by the primary afferent fibers. On leaving the skin, these fibers group themselves together into nerves, each of which may contain thousands of afferents traveling toward the spinal cord. Just outside the cord, each nerve splits into a **dorsal root**, which contains all of the afferents from the nerve, and a **ventral root**, which contains all of the efferents. Thus, the dorsal

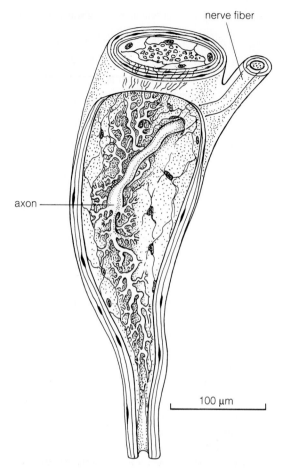

nerve fiber

axon

100 μm

Figure 8.8 Ruffini corpuscle from skin of the cat. The axon enters the capsule at the right (labeled *nerve fiber*), loses its myelin sheath, and begins to branch (just below the axon) into many fiber endings. (Adapted from Chambers et al., 1972)

root is strictly sensory; the ventral root is strictly motor. The dorsal root contains a swelling called the **dorsal root ganglion** in which one finds the cell bodies of the primary afferents. Each cell body is attached to its fiber by way of a short stalk. The fiber itself extends on past this stalk and into the portion of the spinal cord gray matter called the **dorsal horn**. As you can see from Figure 8.9, some afferents end in the dorsal horn, whereas others turn and run up the cord to the medulla of the brain stem where they

synapse. In either case, they make synaptic connections with secondary afferents called **transmission cells (T cells)**. Note from the picture that these T cells send their axons across the midline to run upward on the opposite side of the nervous system. This means that sensory information from the right side of the body is handled largely by the left side of the brain and vice versa. All T cells, from those with somas at the very bottom of the cord to those at the top, send their axons up into the thalamus where they synapse within either the **ventroposterior nuclei** or **posterior thalamic complex** (Figure 8.10). Information can be sent from the thalamus to many other brain areas, and it is quite possible that much of our conscious experience of somatic stimulation resides in these connections. However, the projection system we have been tracing includes only thalamic cells whose axons carry the information up into the postcentral gyrus of the parietal lobes. Thus, the entire somatic projection route employs just three sets of neurons: (1) primary afferents with their receptor endings, (2) T cells of the cord, and (3) thalamic neurons with their cell bodies in the ventroposterior nuclei and their axon terminals in S1 or S2 areas of the parietal lobes.

Somatic Cortex

The postcentral gyrus contains the two areas of cortex that receive somatic messages arriving from the projection system. These two **somatic projection areas** (regions that receive somatic thalamic projections) are called **S1** and **S2**. Input from the left side of the body goes to areas S1 and S2 in the right parietal lobe and vice versa.

S1 is the larger of the two projection areas and takes up most of the postcentral gyrus. A microscopic examination of S1 reveals the same six-layered organization found in all neocortex (see Chapter 3). The fifth and sixth layers are specialized for output; that is, they contain the large Golgi I neurons with long axons that carry the "message" generated within an area of cortex to its destinations. The fourth layer is specialized for receiving input, and it is in this layer that the axons of thalamocortical cells of the ventroposterior nuclei terminate.

When S1 is electrically stimulated in the waking

Table 8.1 Types of Cutaneous Afferents

Characteristics of four primary afferent nerve fibers innervating the hairless skin of the human hand.

	FA I	FA II	SA I	SA II
Adaptation	Fast	Fast	Slow	Slow
Receptive field	Small and uniformly sensitive	Large with graded sensitivity	Small and uniformly sensitive	Large with graded sensitivity
Receptor	Meissner's corpuscle	Pacinian corpuscle	Merkel endings	Rufinni endings
Receptor depth	Shallow (dermis)	Deep (dermis and subdermis)	Shallow (epidermis)	Deep (dermis)
Probable functions	Shape identification	Vibration perception	Shape identification	Skin stretch detection and grip control

From Johansson & Vallbo, 1983.

human, as is often necessary during the surgical relief of epilepsy, a wide variety of conscious somatic experiences are reported by the patient: throbbing, flutter, pushing, vibration, warmth, cold, touch, tapping, water running over the skin, talcum powder being sprinkled onto the skin, sensation of hand moving, or feelings of movement inside the body (Libet, 1973).

One might expect that damage to S1 would produce complete anesthesia (lack of sensation) in some part of the body comparable to the loss of vision with damage to primary visual cortex. Instead, there is a more subtle loss of somatic sensitivity. Without S1 it becomes quite difficult to localize a stimulus on the body surface or to tell one point of stimulation from two points (Semmes, 1973; Sinclair, 1981). It also becomes more difficult to detect light touch or small changes in temperature. The S1 somatosensory cortex seems to be much more important in the analysis of mechanical stimulation than in thermoreception or nociception. Apparently, a good deal of ability to perceive warmth, cold, and damage still persists after loss of the postcentral gyrus (Ruch & Patton, 1965). Even studies finding permanent deficits in touch perception and shape perception never claim that the deficit is complete even with the entire

area destroyed (Darien-Smith, 1982). Therefore, it has long been assumed that much of our conscious experience of temperature and pain, as well as some of our more primitive touch perception, depends on the thalamus (Ruch & Patton, 1965), and if this is true, it would explain the inability to destroy sensation by removing the cortex.

Figure 8.10 indicates the approximate extent of cortex devoted to each region of the body. As you can see, skin zones containing the largest number of receptors command the greatest portions of the S1 projection area. Neurons for the face are grouped together in one place, those for the hand in another, and so on; this is probably not accidental. This map-like arrangement may help the brain localize stimuli on the body surface. There are at least four of these "maps" of the body in S1 (Kaas et al., 1979) and probably another in S2, each one serving a different function.

We have already noted that the ability to localize is partly lost when the postcentral gyrus is damaged and that two-point threshold is increased (i.e., made poorer). When the hand area is damaged, there may also be impairment of **stereognosis**, the ability to perceive the shapes of solid objects with your hands. In part this loss of stereognosis would result from

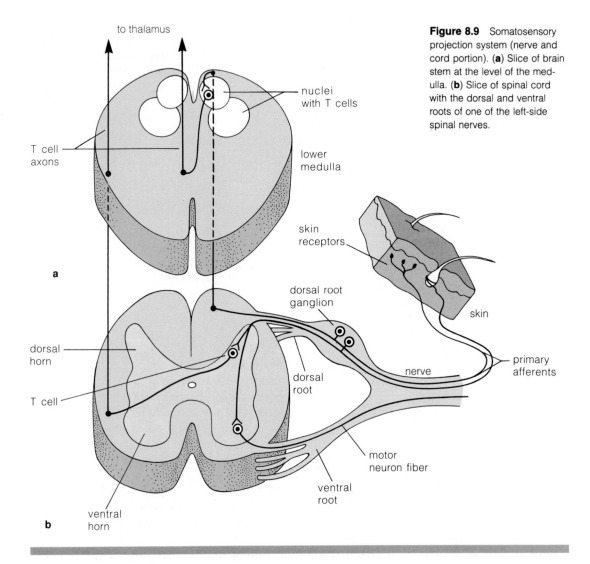

to thalamus

Figure 8.9 Somatosensory projection system (nerve and cord portion). (**a**) Slice of brain stem at the level of the medulla. (**b**) Slice of spinal cord with the dorsal and ventral roots of one of the left-side spinal nerves.

nuclei with T cells

T cell axons

lower medulla

skin receptors

dorsal root ganglion

skin

dorsal horn

dorsal root

nerve

primary afferents

T cell

motor neuron fiber

ventral root

ventral horn

damage to the kinesthetic parts of the hand area in S1, but also contributing would be the impaired ability to sense pressures on the skin and inability to know exactly where on your hand you are being touched (Corkin, 1978). Your perception of shapes depends on exact localization of all points on the skin being stimulated by the object you are holding, so with loss of S1 you would find it very difficult to identify the size or shape of an object by touch and would probably not be able to name it until you looked at it.

The orientation of the stimulus on the skin is also important in perceiving objects; thus it is interesting that neurons have been identified in S1 that are orientation-specific (Hyvärinen & Poranen, 1978) (Figure 8.11).

The S2 projection area lies farther down the post central gyrus and is mostly hidden from view inside the lateral fissure. Microelectrode recordings from cells in S2 show that some of these neurons will not respond at all to an object pressing against the skin. They respond vigorously, however, when the subject

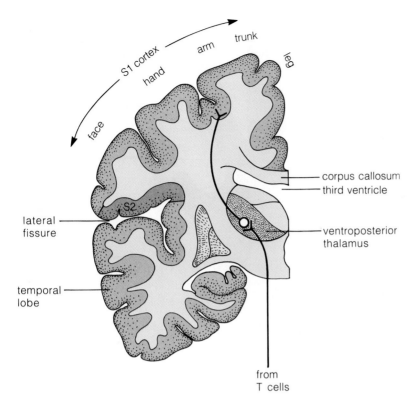

Figure 8.10 Somatosensory projection system (thalamocortical portion) shown on a frontal section of one hemisphere. Impulses coming up the brain stem in axons of T cells reach synapses in one of the thalamic nuclei (ventroposterior is shown). Ventroposterior thalamic cells relay information to the S1 somatosensory cortex, and cells in the posterior thalamic complex send information to the S2 cortex buried within the lateral fissure.

actively touches and manipulates the stimulus object rather than being passively stimulated by it (Darien-Smith, 1982)

Columns and Barrels Neurons of the S1 cortex are also organized into columns that cut through all six layers from the top of the cortex to the underlying white matter—an arrangement reminiscent of the V1 cortex in the occipital lobes. Much of what we know about these columns comes from work on the rodents (Woolsey & Van der Loos, 1970). Rats and mice have a set of specialized hairs on their snouts called **vibrissae** (vih-BRISS-eye; singular, vibrissa) that are much longer and thicker than any in the rest of the animal's fur. They serve to extend the area around the animal's head in which tactile sensing can warn of contacts with other objects. This is extremely useful for nocturnal animals that must rely much of the time on senses other than vision. Given the importance of these specialized sensory hairs, it

is not surprising to find fairly large areas of S1 devoted to processing their input. Figure 8.12 shows the five lines of vibrissae on the snout of a rat pup and the corresponding areas of S1 that serve each of them. Each little circle in the diagram represents a group of cells in layer 4 of S1 cortex, and every cell in a group receives from the same vibrissa. These layer-4 groups are called **barrels** because of their shape (Figure 8.12). Seen from the top, each barrel is a ring of neurons that send their dendrites into a central "core" area in layer 4 where they collect inputs from telodendria arriving from the ventroposterior thalamus (Kaas et al., 1983). According to Favorov and Whitsel (1988a), each barrel is anatomically a part of an entire cortical column extending through all six layers, and it is likely that all cells within the entire column serve the same input source (in this case, a single hair).

The same column arrangement has now also been found for mechanoreceptive neurons in the

Figure 8.11 RF and recorded responses of an orientation-selective neuron in area 2 of the S1 cortex of a monkey. (**a**) The neuron responded to pressure of an edge anywhere within the skin of the upper palm just beneath the base of the index and middle fingers. Five different orientations of the stimulus edge are shown with the nerve impulse records they produced. This particular neuron happens to be selective for edges oriented perpendicular to the edges of the hand. This selectivity is evident because the perpendicular orientation produced the highest rate and longest burst of firing. (**b**) If the stimulus is kept at the optimal orientation and moved to different positions in the RF, the boundaries of the field can be located. (Notice the absence of impulses in some of the records.) (Adapted from Hyvärinen & Poranen, 1978)

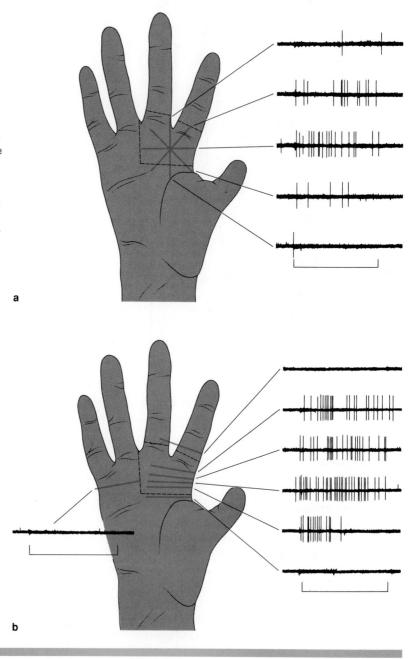

a

b

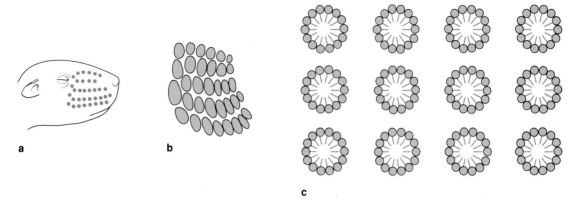

Figure 8.12 (**a**) Organization of vibrissae representation in the S1 cortex of the rat pup. The rat has five rows of long, sensory facial hairs called vibrissae (whiskers). In the S1 cortex, each hair is represented by a cylindrical area, called a barrel, that extends through layer 4. In a cross section of layer 4, these regions would appear roughly circular (**b**), and they are arranged in five rows. (**c**) A schematic diagram of a row of four barrels. Each is composed of a ring of cortical neurons with their major dendrites pointing inward to collect from a common group of thalamic input axons at the center. (Adapted from Kaas et al., 1983)

monkey brain, thus making it the likely arrangement for the human S1 cortex (Favorov & Whitsel, 1988a,b).

Altering Cortical Body Maps At the bottom of the spinal cord lie the somas of the T cells receiving input from the feet. Just above that level of the cord, primary afferents from the legs enter and connect with "leg" T cells. Axons of "leg" T cells ascend in the white matter of the cord right next to axons of "foot" T cells. At a still higher level of the cord, axons for the trunk are added next to those for the legs and then "arm" cells next to "trunk" cells. This orderly layering of T cells creates a map of the body within the tracts of the somatosensory system, which is maintained all the way up through S1 and S2 in the cortex. Thus, all area S1 cells receiving input from the right index finger are found in one small region of S1, rather than scattered at random throughout the whole zone. Cortical body maps seem to have been determined and inexorably fixed for the life of the organism by the genetically controlled growth processes that created the nervous system during embryonic development. That is, they seem to have been determined in this fashion, and until the 1980s, no one had the least doubt that this was true.

In a series of experiments in the early 1980s, Merzenich and Kaas upset our preconceptions by showing that cortical body maps in adult brains can reorganize themselves whenever their inputs change. Figure 8.13 shows how the fingers of the right hand are represented in the body maps found in subareas 3b and 1 in the S1 cortex of the owl monkey. Also shown are the results of cutting the right median nerve so that the cortical areas representing the palmar surfaces of digits 1, 2, and part of 3 were cut off from their skin input. Cells in this area of "deprived" cortex remained healthy but with no job to do. The now-severed median nerve was their only connection to receptors in the skin. However, when the monkey's brain was examined with recording electrodes several months after the nerve section, it was discovered that all neurons in the "deprived" zone once more possessed RFs. They had become parts of the areas representing the dorsal

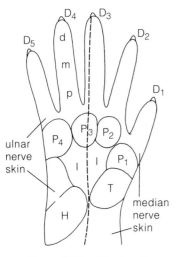

a Nerve fields of the hand

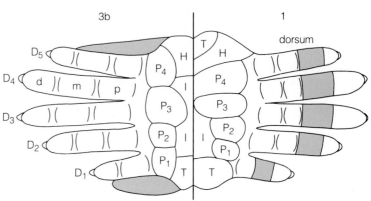

b Topographic pattern of hand representations

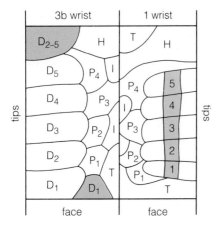

c Normal hand representation

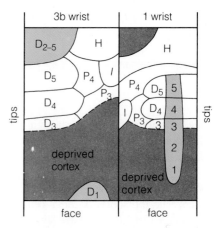

d Cortex deprived by median nerve section

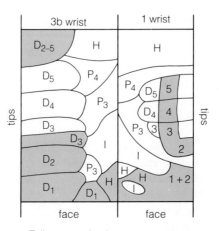

e Fully reorganized cortex

Figure 8.13 Reorganization of body map in S1 after cutting off input from the zone of the right hand served by the median nerve. (**a**) Monkey hand showing median nerve zone (d = distal; m = middle; p = proximal; P = palmar pad; H = hypothenar pad; T = thenar pad; I = insular pad). (**b**) How the hand is represented in S1 subareas 3b and 1. The cortical zones in color represent the dorsal (back) side of the hand. The rest of the representation is palmar. (**c**) A more precise map of the hand in subareas 3b and 1. Note that this area borders on the wrist area on one side and the face area on the other. (**d**) After the median nerve has been cut, much of the hand area of the cortex (in gray) is deprived of its normal input from receptors. (**e**) This same area of cortex after 2 months of deprivation. Many neurons that responded to stimulation on the palmar side of digits 1 and 2 now respond to the dorsal side instead. This reorganization is not due to the growth of ulnar and other nerves into the field of the median nerve; it is a brain alteration. (Adapted from Merzenich & Kaas, 1982)

surfaces of the digits, which are served by a different nerve (Merzenich & Kaas, 1982). If instead of cutting off input to the cortex by severing a nerve an entire finger is removed (Figure 8.14), the areas representing the adjacent fingers spread until they incorporate the idle neurons (Fox, 1984).

Apparently, cortical neurons are never allowed to "retire" when deprived of proper input. Instead, the cortical map is readjusted so that they now become responsive to some other unaffected input. The RF of a cortical neuron, then, is not something that is fixed at birth. It seems that a number of inputs are available to the cell and that somehow a choice is made as to which input the cell will dedicate itself. If that chosen input disappears, then the cell can become responsive to a second choice. Merzenich

Figure 8.14 Reorganization of the S1 cortex in an owl monkey, following loss of sensory input due to amputation. (**a**) Numbers refer to locations of digit representations in the hand part of the body map prior to amputation. (**b**) The same area of cortex several weeks after amputation. Cells that previously served the third digit now respond to receptors on digits 2 and 4. (Adapted from Fox, 1984)

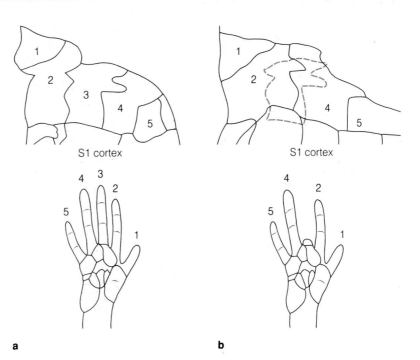

a

b

and Kaas suggest that the inputs compete with one another to command the cortical neuron and the strongest input wins (Kaas, 1987; Kaas et al., 1983). Because output cells of S1 can inhibit one another, this idea of competition and "winning" would probably be a matter of which cells could send the strongest inhibition to their neighbors.

You might wonder what effect the addition of extra cortical neurons might have on the function of the cortical areas for the remaining fingers. There is some evidence that sensory abilities are improved for the fingers that inherit the additional cortical territory (Fox, 1984). Kaas speculates that any activity that increases the amount of input coming from a particular body part should increase the size of the cortical representation at the expense of its less active neighbors (Merzenich & Kaas, 1982). Thus, a typist or a concert pianist might have unusually large areas for the fingers. However, some data suggest that there are limits to this plasticity; in one study, the face area, which lies adjacent to that of the hand, failed to expand into the deprived zone when all input from the hand was removed (Kaas et al., 1983).

■ Cutaneous Thermoreception

If you are headed for a career in neuroscience research and you would like to make a name for yourself immediately, try the area of thermoreception. You can have it almost to yourself. The volume of thermoreception research compared to that of vision is a contrast between a gnat and a whale. Here we are in the 1990s, a century after the initiation of research into human thermal sensitivity, and (comparatively speaking) we hardly know more than when we started.

One of the first discoveries in experiments on human subjects was that somatic sensitivity does not seem to be uniformly distributed over the surface of the skin. Warmth and cold seem to be sensed in discrete spots, and strangely enough, cold can be sensed in far more places than can warmth (Figure 8.15). However, the ratio of warmth to cold spots varies with the region of the body. The finger has

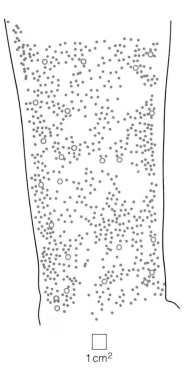

Figure 8.15 Map of cold spots (dots) and warmth spots (circles) on the human dorsal forearm. The whole area represented is about 1 cm². There were 24 warmth spots recorded and about 700 cold spots, a ratio of about 1:29. (Adapted from Stevens & Green, 1978)

nine times more warmth spots than the dorsal side of the upper arm (Stevens & Green, 1978). Some regions have so few warmth spots that the region seems to be completely insensitive to temperature increases. However, the spot data in these experiments are collected by pressing a heated or cooled point against the skin, and this metal point measures about 1–2 square millimeters at its tip. If a larger tip is used (1 cm²), then areas in the "insensitive" skin can be found in which the stimulus does produce a sensation of warmth. A mechanism of **thermal summation** is at work here. The larger the area stimulated, the warmer the stimulus appears to be (Kenshalo, 1978).

When sensitivity spots were first discovered, it was hoped that they would reveal the locations of

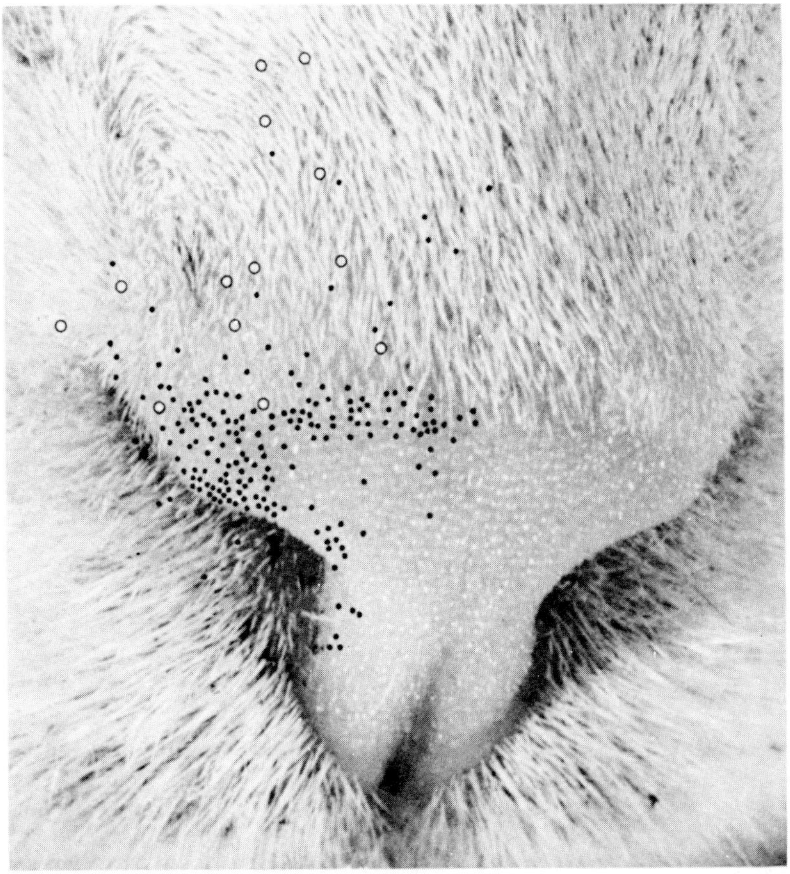

Figure 8.16 RFs of cold fibers (dots) and warmth fibers (circles) on the nose of a cat. (From Hensel, 1973)

thermal receptors, but searches found no specialized endings of nerve fibers that were clearly and consistently associated with cold or warmth spots (Hensel, 1973). Furthermore, data from large-tip stimulators were difficult to explain. Yet another complication arose when it was discovered that a tip heated to a temperature a little below that required to elicit pain (about 45°C) produced a sensation of cold when applied to a previously mapped cold spot. The phenomenon is called **paradoxical cold**. We still have no theory that does a good job of explaining these facts.

Thermoreceptor research was greatly aided by the advent of microelectrode-recording techniques that allow us to see what type of stimulus will excite a particular, identified neuron. Some small, lightly myelinated fibers were found that respond to cooling the skin and others that respond to warming. The latter, however, are not specific to temperature sensing. They turned out to be mechanoreceptors that also are sensitive to skin warming (Hensel, 1973). Most of these data come from cats (see Figure 8.16), and so far no warmth fibers have been found in humans (Hensel, 1973).

Microelectrode recording not only allows us to distinguish cold and warmth fibers but also enables us to map the RF of a fiber. Once the area of skin has been identified, the skin can be removed and

Figure 8.17 Nerve fiber ending underlying a cold spot in the nose skin of a cat. A Schwann cell wraps the branches of the axon all the way up to their ends. Only the tips, at the base of the epidermal layer of the skin, are exposed. However, the Schwann cell loses its myelin wrap near the bottom of the dermal layer. (Adapted from Hensel, 1973)

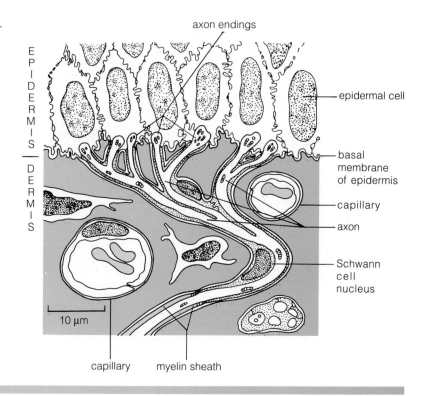

examined microscopically. Figure 8.17 shows a set of terminals from a fiber that was identified in this way as a cold receptor.

Thermoreceptors, like mechanoreceptors, adapt to a continuing stimulus. The adaptation is slow, requiring up to half an hour; however, for some temperatures, it is so complete that the warm or cool stimulus can disappear from consciousness altogether (Kenshalo, 1978). But complete adaptation can only occur within a narrow range of temperatures, namely, 30–36°C. Below or above that range, the stimulus persists in feeling cold or warm no matter how long it is applied to the skin (Figure 8.18). If this fact does not seem to correspond to your everyday experience with warm and cold objects, keep in mind that the results come from carefully controlled tests in which skin temperature is maintained at some measured amount throughout the adaptation period. If you simply heat an object to a certain temperature and then hold it against your skin, the object is cooled by the skin and surrounding air. The skin temperature then drops, invalidating the test.

The 30–36°C range in which you can obtain complete adaptation is the normal range for skin temperatures and is called **physiological zero**. Within this temperature zone, a stimulus applied constantly to the skin (such as an infrared beam) can be changed without eliciting any sensation at all if the rate of change is slower than the adaptation rate of the nerve cells (Kenshalo, 1978). If the stimulus temperature is increased or decreased rapidly, however, a warming or cooling is sensed.

The phenomenon of adaptation makes it difficult to describe the threshold point at which a stimulus is felt as warm or cool. An examination of Figure 8.19 shows that the threshold is not a single temperature; it changes as the adapted temperature of the skin changes. The vertical axis shows the number of degrees that a stimulus must be above or below

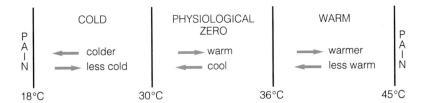

Figure 8.18 Cold, warmth, and pain thresholds for temperature stimuli on the skin. The arrows show what sensory experience occurs as the result of temperature changes in the indicated directions. For example, between 30 and 36°C all stimuli feel neutral after a period of adaptation, but if the stimulus increases in temperature, it is felt as warm. If the increased temperature is still below 36°C, adaptation again occurs, and the warmth fades to neutral. (Adapted from Kenshalo, 1978)

Figure 8.19 Graph showing how much the temperature of a stimulus at a point on the skin must be changed for it to be felt as noticeably cooler or warmer. The size of this just-noticeable difference changes according to the adapting temperature (i.e., how warm the skin is initially). The horizontal axis shows how warm the skin is at the start, and the vertical axis shows the number of degrees that the skin is warmed or cooled. The open dots indicate how big the change must be at a particular adapting temperature to obtain a just-noticeable difference (as between cool and cooler). The solid dots show how great a change is required to shift the sensation from neutral to warm or neutral to cool (i.e., the threshold point). The range of adapting temperatures between the two vertical dotted lines is physiological zero. So, for example, if you wish to know how much you would have to increase the temperature to get a sensation of warmth when the skin area was adapted to 34°C, find 34 on the horizontal axis and read up to the upper curve that separates neutral sensations from feelings of warmth and then read across to the vertical axis. You would have to increase the stimulus about 0.3°C (i.e., to 34.3°C) in order to experience the stimulus as warm rather than neutral. (Adapted from Kenshalo, 1972)

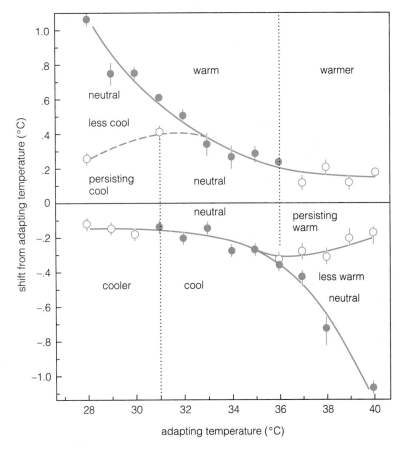

the skin temperature in order to be felt as cool or warm rather than neutral. The dots on the graph represent actual measurements, and the lines show the theoretical boundaries along which all points probably would have fallen if all experimental error could have been eliminated. The lower curve is the boundary between cool and neutral, the upper curve the boundary between neutral and warm. If you read the numbers along the horizontal axis, you can find the range of physiological zero (30–36°C); note a vertical line above each of these numbers. The area between the two curves and between the two vertical lines is the neutral zone representing all the possible increments or decrements in temperature that are not felt. So, for example, if you would like to know how cool an object would have to be to be felt as cool when your skin had been adapted to a temperature of 35°C, read up from 35 until you hit the bottom curve. It tells you that the stimulus must be about 0.3°C cooler than your skin (i.e., 34.7°C). Any stimulus between that temperature and 35.3°C (approximately) is not experienced as either warm or cool—providing that your skin was adapted to 35°C. If you had been lying out on a hot beach and your skin was adapted to 38°C, then an object would have to be a little bit cooler (0.7°C cooler) to be felt as cool. Verify this by finding 38°C on the horizontal axis and then read up to the bottom curve and across to the vertical axis.

Pain

Mary whisked into the examination room and started taking her clothes off the moment the nurse closed the door. She quickly tied on the examination gown with fingers that had become skilled with much practice. This would be the 10th physician in the 14 months since her severe back pains had begun, and Mary gloomily predicted to herself that this diagnosis wouldn't do her any more good than any of the previous ones. No one seemed capable of finding the source of the pains that were making it more and more difficult to stand or move about. Mary had begun to picture herself spending the rest of her life sitting in a wheelchair. Last week she had reluctantly

quit her job ("Where is next month's rent going to come from?"). Fortunately, the children were both in high school and able to take care of themselves to a great extent. She looked at her 45-year-old visage in the mirror. ("The children are too old to need me now, anyway. And, I don't think Fred really cares much about me anymore. When was the last time he pawed me?") Mary grimaced a little at the thought of having sex, but the feeling of revulsion was quickly replaced by worry. She touched the hardening lines around her eyes. ("Crow's feet! I used to be so pretty. The first five years we were married, Fred couldn't keep his hands off of me. Now I'm used up.") Mary reached around to massage the ache in the small of her back. ("I took care of that man, bore his children, and put up with his lust for 25 years, and now he barely looks at me.") A stabbing pain through her spine made her wince. ("And these stupid, stupid doctors who keep telling me that there isn't anything wrong with my back. All they do is prescribe pills that don't work. Why did I bother to try another doctor? It'll just be the same thing all over again.") The examination room door opened.

"Good morning, Mrs. McCarthy. What seems to be the trouble?"

The Nature of Pain

Mary McCarthy is a fictional composite of the majority of psychiatric patients complaining of chronic pain who were treated by J. Mersky (1975). They complain of severe, even debilitating pain that seems to have no organic origin. Mary McCarthy's problem is not in her back. The origins of her "pain" lie in her feeling of frustration with the way her life is turning out. She is suffering from **conversion reaction**; her emotional problems are being converted into a physical problem. Some physicians would probably suggest that Mary's back pain is "all in her mind" because it is easily established that it cannot originate in her back. But, what does "all in the mind" mean? Does it mean that Mary is not really experiencing pain, or that she is experiencing "fake pain," or that she imagines that she is experiencing pain?

A great deal of effort has gone into attempts at answering questions such as these. As a somatic sense, pain is unique in two ways. Unlike mechanoreception and thermoreception, nociception has inspired enormous amounts of medically oriented research, and a large part of our knowledge centers around the question of how to eliminate the sensory experience. Its other source of uniqueness lies in its relations to the motivational parts of the brain. Much of what we call pain seems to be not a sensory experience at all but rather an emotional response to sensations. This has made pain difficult to understand and has led to the sorts of questions we asked about the Mary McCarthy case. Before we try to answer those questions, however, we need to consider several additional problems.

Problems in Understanding Pain The pain experienced while recovering from surgery can be quite severe, and morphine is often administered to control it. In some clinical tests, however, patients were given a placebo rather than morphine. A **placebo** (pluh-SEE-bo) is a pretended, rather than real, treatment. The patients, of course, were not told whether they were receiving the placebo or morphine. The results of studies like these show that about 35 percent of the patients receiving the placebo experienced relief of the sort one would expect from morphine (Melzack, 1972). There is no question about the reality of postsurgical pain, yet discomfort apparently disappeared when the patients received an injection of a totally inert salt solution. Does this mean that the pain was real, but the relief was "all in their minds"?

When you cut your finger, where is the pain itself located? If you think that the pain experience is in your finger, then consider the victim of amputation who knows that she has lost her entire right leg below the knee but still feels that leg. Pains run up her shin—the shin that isn't there. Her right foot itches until she swears she would sell her soul to be able to scratch that foot. She is suffering from the phenomenon called **phantom limb**. The existence of such "phantoms" as a commonplace result of amputations leads us to ask, If the pain is truly out there in the skin and muscles of the leg, then why doesn't it disappear along with the limb?

Placebos, neurotic pain, and phantom limbs present a problem for those who must understand pain, but we now realize that much of that problem arises from ambiguities in some of the words we use in discussing painful circumstances. Clarity will begin to emerge if we first agree that the word *pain* only refers to a conscious experience, a neural–psychological event occurring within the nervous system. Wounds, burns, disease, damage, and so on are pain-causing stimuli; that is, they are events outside the nervous system. The brain's conscious response to any stimulus is called a sensation. So pain is a sensation, not a stimulus. It is the way in which we are conscious of the firing of a particular set of neurons somewhere within the brain. Where, exactly, might those neurons be located?

The Pain-Projection System Let's trace the neural activity arising from the application of a harmful stimulus. A wound in the skin stimulates receptor endings of nociceptors. Axons of these sensory cells then carry the resulting pattern of nerve impulses from the site of damage into the spinal cord. Within the cord, sensory cells synapse with T cells, which convey the information to the brain. Figure 8.20 indicates that some T cells carry information to the ventroposterior thalamus, whereas others take their input to the posterior thalamic complex, **medial thalamic nucleus**, or **intralaminar nucleus**. The route shown on the right in Figure 8.20 runs through the ventroposterior nucleus to the S1 cortex and is the pathway previously described in the discussion of the somatosensory projection system. It seems to carry mechanoreceptive information and, perhaps, some thermoreceptive, but there is little solid evidence that it has anything to do with nociception. For example, the S1 cortex can be electrically stimulated without causing pain (Casey, 1978). The cells that respond to noxious stimulation are the ones that make up the routes from the spinal cord through the thalamus to the S2 cortex and from the cord through the reticular formation and thalamus to the limbic system (Casey, 1978, 1982; Melzack & Wall, 1965) (see Figure 8.20).

Which brain areas are most closely connected with the conscious experience of pain? The spinal cord does not seem to be involved directly in conscious experience, so the firing of T cells probably precedes the experiencing of pain from a stimulus. Conscious experience is most closely associated with activity in the cortex and thalamus, and because pain

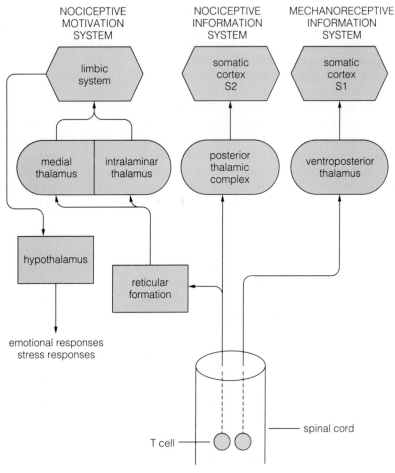

Figure 8.20 Three routes for somatosensory information. The one on the right may also handle thermoreceptive information but probably has little to do with nociception. The middle route (to the S2 cortex) seems to be involved with all three types of somatosensory information. The route to the limbic system and hypothalamus (left) is probably exclusively nociceptive.

NOCICEPTIVE MOTIVATION SYSTEM

NOCICEPTIVE INFORMATION SYSTEM

MECHANORECEPTIVE INFORMATION SYSTEM

limbic system

somatic cortex S2

somatic cortex S1

medial thalamus

intralaminar thalamus

posterior thalamic complex

ventroposterior thalamus

hypothalamus

reticular formation

emotional responses stress responses

spinal cord

T cell

information appears to be sent to S2 cortex (Chudler et al., 1986), that area might be critical to pain experience. Surprisingly, that does not seem to be the case; even losing the entire cortex does not prevent the consciousness of pain (Casey, 1978). What might be lost with such a lesion is the ability to localize any pains that are experienced.

Casey (1978) suggests that pain has two aspects: first, an objective, informational aspect dealing simply with the detection of the kind of stimulus pattern that signals something is going wrong and the localizing of these patterns in the body; second, a motivational–emotional part around which our conscious experience centers. Our ability to decide

where the pain-producing stimulus is located on (or in) our bodies may depend on the posterior thalamus–S2 cortex pathway, whereas the motivational part—the feeling of hurting and needing to do something about it—depends on the route through the medial and intralaminar thalamic nuclei to the limbic system and hypothalamus.

There is fairly good evidence for the involvement of the medial and intralaminar thalamic nuclei with suffering. It is in these nuclei that pain-relieving neurosurgery often produces the best results (Casey, 1982; Mark et al., 1963). Cells in the intralaminar nuclei increased their rate of firing when an animal was given aversive brain stimulation (i.e., stimulation in the midbrain reticular formation). The same neurons decreased their activity when the reward–pleasure system was stimulated (cited in Casey, 1978). The medial and intralaminar nuclei of the thalamus appear to be the connecting point between the informational and motivational pain systems. It is not surprising that it is the brain area that we so far have found to be most strongly associated with conscious pain experience.

Some Tentative Explanations We cannot be sure that the pain experience is located in these thalamic nuclei, but it is fairly safe to conclude that pain is the activity of neurons somewhere within the brain. Once this is understood, then it is easy to see that anything capable of eliciting activity in those brain cells will produce pain. For example, thalamic pain cells are normally fired by some environmental stimulus acting through pathways coming up the spinal cord, but there are many other influences available. Thalamic pain areas receive inputs from a great variety of other points within the CNS, such as thalamic nuclei, globus pallidus, and limbic system (Crosby et al., 1962). All these brain areas have the potential of collaborating in the task of exciting the pain cells into activity.

Could these other inputs be the source of neurotic pain? Behavioral data show that anxiety increases pain (Livingston, 1943), and it is a widely accepted clinical assumption that anxiety is generated by circuits within the limbic system. It is possible that under certain circumstances the limbic input to the thalamus might be enough to trigger firing even in the absence of any significant input from a noxious stimulus. So, perhaps when Mary McCarthy bends over a little way, thus randomly stimulating a few nociceptors in her back, this tiny input (normally below threshold) now gets enough help from the limbic circuits to actually fire thalamic cells and produce conscious sensations of pain. This proposed interpretation of pain shows us how we might go about answering the questions asked at the beginning of this section:

Is neurotic pain real?

If our assumption is correct that pain is the activity in certain neurons of the thalamus and other brain areas, then it doesn't matter if these cells are being fired by the normal sensory input from nociceptors or by the emotion circuits of the limbic system. It is the fact that they become active that counts rather than the source of that activity.

If a placebo can relieve a pain, does that mean that the pain wasn't real?

If the activity of neurons in pain areas was triggered mostly by input from anxiety circuits, then any procedure that relieves anxiety should turn off the pain. A placebo in which the patient firmly believes should reduce anxiety about experiencing further pain.

Why Do We Experience Pain?

Among the various sense modalities, pain is unique in the degree to which it ties in with the person's motivational system. There is survival value in having a sense of pain that carries motive force. But just how important to survival is the pain system? Could a human exist without a sense of pain, or must our pain sense constantly prod us into lifesaving behaviors? A confident answer to that question would be hard to obtain were it not that very occasionally a person is born with a total insensitivity to noxious stimulation—that is, without a sense of pain.

The best documented of all cases of congenital insensitivity to pain is Miss C., a young Canadian girl who was a student at McGill University in Montreal. Her father, a physician in western Canada, was fully aware of her problem and alerted his colleagues in Montreal to examine her. The young lady was highly intelligent and seemed normal in every way except that she had never felt pain. As a child, she had bitten off the tip of her tongue while chewing food, and had suffered third-degree burns after kneeling on a hot radiator to look out the window. When examined by a psychologist . . . she reported that she did not feel pain when noxious stimuli were presented. She felt no pain when parts of her body were subjected to strong electric shock, to hot water at temperatures that usually produce reports of burning pain, or to a prolonged ice-bath. Equally astonishing was the fact that she showed no changes in blood pressure, heart rate, or respiration when these stimuli were presented. Furthermore, she could not remember ever sneezing or coughing, the gag reflex could be elicited only with great difficulty, and corneal reflexes (to protect the eyes) were absent. A variety of other stimuli, such as inserting a stick up through the nostrils, pinching tendons, or injections of histamine under the skin—which are normally considered as forms of torture—also failed to produce pain.

Miss C. had severe medical problems. She exhibited pathological changes in her knees, hip and spine, and underwent several orthopaedic operations. Her surgeon attributed these changes to the lack of protection to joints usually given by pain sensation. She apparently failed to shift her weight when standing, to turn over in her sleep, or to avoid certain postures, which normally prevent inflammation of the joints.

Miss C. died at the age of twenty-nine of massive infections that could not be brought under control. During her last month, she complained of discomfort, tenderness and pain in the left hip. The pain was relieved by analgesic tablets. There is little doubt that her inability to feel pain until the final month of her life led to the extensive skin and bone trauma that contributed in a direct fashion to her death. (From a case reported by Baxter & Olszewski, as described in Melzack, 1973)

Chronic Pain

Normal pain arises from harmful circumstances outside the nervous system and is an adaptive response to environmental threat. It subsides when treated with **analgesics** (an-al-GEE-zicks), pain-killing drugs. When the threatening stimulus is removed, normal pain disappears. **Chronic pain**, on the other hand, is not normal and does not have the characteristics listed above. Chronic pain is defined as pain that persists for months or years, often without any identifiable cause, and does not respond well to mild analgesics like aspirin or even, in some cases, to those as strong as morphine. It usually follows the occurrence of a CNS infection, surgery, trauma to the peripheral nervous system or diseases such as cancer, arthritis, and herpes infection. Most typically, it seems to arise from direct injury to the nervous system itself. (Phantom limb is an example of chronic

pain.) Because it usually appears after the victim has recovered completely from the infection or injury, one interpretation of chronic pain is that it represents the malfunctioning of a nervous system that has sustained irreparable damage.

Controlling Chronic Pain   Until just recently there were only two medical approaches to control of chronic pain: drugs and surgery. Because drugs are either inadequate for many cases or addictive, the surgeon has often attempted a rather desperate brand of "cure" involving destruction of some part of the nervous system. For example, if the intractable (untreatable) pain is felt in the arm, one or more of the nerves coming from that limb can be severed or the dorsal root that serves that area of the body is cut. If that fails, a horizontal cut can be made across a whole area of spinal cord above the level at which the arm fibers enter in hopes of stopping the pain by preventing the impulses in T cells from reaching the thalamus. Often the relief from these extreme measures is temporary or even totally lacking.

Fortunately, drugs and surgery are no longer the only alternatives for treating chronic pain. One new technique that seems promising involves the permanent implantation of electrodes into the spinal cord or brain. Hosubuchi and colleagues (1979) have reported a number of successes with electrodes placed in an area of the midbrain and pons called the **periaqueductal gray (PAG)** (PAIR-ee-AK-qwuh-DUCK-tull) (Figure 8.21). Once the PAG electrode has been inserted and tested to see if stimulation relieves the pain, the top of the electrode is connected to a fine, supple wire that is run beneath the scalp and under the skin of the neck and chest. This wire connects to a silver dollar–sized receiving antenna implanted just beneath the skin of the chest. Whenever pain relief is needed, the patient picks up a box about the size and shape of a cigarette package and holds it just over the buried receiver. The box is a stimulator device that induces an electric current in the wire going to the patient's PAG. Usually about 15–30 minutes of stimulation is needed for relief, but the pain may not recur for several hours or even days.

No system of this sort is perfect of course, and defects are bound to develop. It doesn't work for

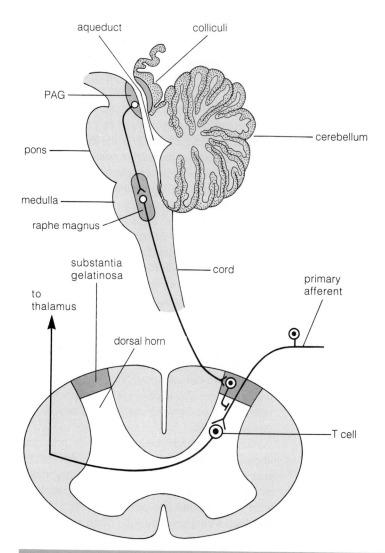

aqueduct colliculi

PAG

cerebellum

pons

medulla

raphe magnus

substantia gelatinosa

cord

to thalamus

primary afferent

dorsal horn

T cell

Figure 8.21 The descending pain-suppression pathway. The view of the brain stem shows the origin of this path in the PAG of the midbrain. PAG cells send their axons down to synapse on cells in the raphe magnus nucleus of the medulla, and raphe cells connect with the substantia gelatinosa (SG) cells in the dorsal horn. SG cells inhibit T cells by diminishing the size of the sensory impulses in the primary afferents. The gelatinosa is the outermost portion of each dorsal horn. One of the SG cells is shown in the right dorsal horn.

every patient, and it may not be a permanent solution for any person. The major problem mentioned by Hosubuchi is that of tolerance. If more than one or two stimulation periods are attempted per day, then the strength of the analgesic effect begins to diminish unless the stimulation level is increased. It is quite interesting that this loss of effect strongly resembles the tolerance that develops for morphine and heroin. As we will see shortly, the resemblance may not be coincidental.

Opiate Analgesia Opiates are frequently used on a short-term basis for handling severe pain. Because all are addictive, long-term use is severely limited. The three basic opiates are **opium**, a resinous substance that exudes from the bud of the poppy flower; **morphine**, the active ingredient in opium; and **heroin**, a chemically altered version of morphine that works faster than morphine because it is able to cross the blood–brain barrier more readily. Psychopharmacology laboratories have produced scores of other opiates over the years, a few that are used medically (e.g., codeine) and some that are much stronger than heroin.

All these opiates have two major effects on the user: **analgesia** (relief from pain) and **euphoria** (a state in which one feels especially good, relaxed, happy, and carefree). It is a reasonable guess that analgesia involves the suppression of the objective informational aspect of pain, whereas euphoria is the opposite of the emotional, suffering aspect. Recall that information about noxious stimuli is probably extracted by the posterior thalamic complex and the S2 cortex. A drug that affects these brain structures or hinders the flow of information coming up the cord to them should be able to produce analgesia. The emotional aspect of pain, which forms one end of a suffering–euphoria continuum, is probably the product of limbic system circuits. In other words, an opiate probably produces analgesia by way of its action on the pain route to the thalamus, while its euphoric effect probably is accomplished through changes in the limbic system. If this turns out to be a true distinction, then the strange fact that limbic lesions (like prefrontal lobotomy) can relieve the hurt of chronic pain without stopping the pain sensation (Vogt et al., 1979) would be understandable. Such lesions apparently leave the informational part of pain intact while removing the emotional aspect.

The Descending Pain-Control System

Opiates do not relieve all types of chronic pain; they work best on pains of peripheral origin resulting from nerve damage and work poorly on pain of central origin in which the damage is in the brain itself. Interestingly, the same is true of PAG stimulation (Hosubuchi et al., 1979). Could it be that these two very different sources of pain relief are related? Recent research has suggested an explanation for how PAG stimulation might produce analgesia.

Anatomy of the Pain-Control System We know that PAG neurons send their axons down the brain stem to synapse on cells in the **nucleus raphe magnus** of the medulla and that axons of the raphe magnus neurons descend into the spinal cord to make synapses on neurons lying in an outer column of the

dorsal horn called the **substantia gelatinosa** (see Figure 8.21) (Kerr & Wilson, 1978; Yingling, 1978). PAG neurons excite raphe cells, which in turn stimulate substantia gelatinosa (SG) neurons in the dorsal horn (Basbaum & Fields, 1984). SG cells inhibit T cells of the dorsal horn, thus canceling out some of the excitation of these cells by the primary afferent pain fibers. Thus, the route from the PAG to the spinal cord constitutes a descending pain-control system that would appear to have the task of "turning down the volume" on pain input from nociceptors.

One might ask why a system should exist to suppress or modulate pain input when pain information is so vital to survival. Perhaps the answer lies in the idea of attention. It has frequently been suggested that one way in which the brain "pays attention" to one particular sensory input channel (e.g., vision) is to suppress input in all the other sensory channels (audition, smell, taste, etc.). Could our proposed descending pain-modulation system be just one part of a suppression mechanism involving all sense systems and operating to produce a part of the phenomenon we call *attention*? Should this suggestion prove valid, we also need to ask what survival advantage there is in directing our attention away from a painful stimulus.

Consider the survival needs of our prehuman ancestors who were evolving the brain we now possess. Pain must have been valuable to such a primate as a warning that a wound had been sustained. But what if the wound had been earned in a fight to the death with a large animal? During such a battle, pain would act as a potentially fatal distraction rather than a source of important information. Thus, pain suppression could have been a survival device (Bolles & Fanselow, 1982). One scrap of evidence that fits with this line of thinking comes from the work of Duggan (1982) who found that electrical stimulation of the PAG not only produces pain suppression but also increases the volume of blood pumped by the heart and improves blood flow into muscles. Perhaps pain suppression is just one of many ways in which the PAG functions to aid the organism in a combat situation.

If the pain-suppression pathway is a part of the attention circuitry of the brain stem, as our hypothesis suggests, then more than just pain may be involved. All somatic senses—mechanoreception, thermoreception, and nociception—are regulated by attention. Does the descending control system also affect somatic senses other than nociception?

There is evidence that stimulation of the PAG affects mechanoreception. When rats were given PAG stimulation sufficient to inhibit pain (hypoalgesia), their performance with an ongoing tactile-discrimination task was noticeably poorer, thus indicating possible inhibition of mechanoreceptive input (Frommer, 1985). Tentatively, we can hypothesize that the pain-suppression path is just one portion of a general sensory input–regulation mechanism that underlies our ability to attend or ignore selected stimuli. Other experiments lead to the idea that this part of the attention mechanism employs a synaptic mechanism called presynaptic inhibition.

Physiological evidence exists for the idea that most primary afferent fibers are subject to continual inhibitory control from some source. In many electrical recording experiments, nerve impulses in primary afferent fibers suddenly lose strength just as they reach the terminals. The result of this apparent inhibition is that a much smaller amount of transmitter is released from the terminals of the afferents and only weak EPSPs are generated in postsynaptic T cells (Schmidt, 1973). The inhibition involved in this regulation of incoming sensory information is called **presynaptic inhibition**. It is the work of terminals that synapse on the terminals of primary afferents rather than on dendrites of T cells (Figure 8.21). All types of primary afferents seem to be subject to presynaptic inhibition of their terminals, even those involved in kinesthesis, but the mechanism may have its greatest influence on the small, lightly myelinated fibers that are most heavily involved in carrying pain information (Schmidt, 1973).

Opiates, Transmitters, and the Pain-Control Pathway
It is unlikely that many morphine or heroin addicts die of old age. A much more common route to "terminal analgesia" is by way of an overdose of opiate. There is usually no way for an addict to know the exact strength of the heroin he is shooting into his vascular system, and misjudgments are many. Many hospital emergency rooms are now familiar with the signs of opiate overdose and are equipped to pull

the addict back from the brink of death. The heart of the emergency treatment is an injection of a substance called an **opiate antagonist** (synonym, **opiate blocker**). In a matter of just minutes from injection, the drug coma is dispelled, the heart rate is normalized, and respiration is stable.

Naloxone is one of these lifesaving opiate antagonists. For us, the importance of naloxone lies in what it can tell us about how opiates affect the brain. Opiate blockers like naloxone can stop the effects of opiates because they find and occupy the neuron receptor sites into which the opiate molecules fit. Recall for a moment what you learned about receptor sites: neurons communicate with one another at synapses when the presynaptic cell secretes neurotransmitter molecules that cross the synaptic gap and fit into protein molecules (receptor sites) in the postsynaptic membrane. When the transmitter molecules momentarily bind to (attach to) receptor sites, a reaction is initiated that opens ion channels allowing sodium and potassium ions to cross the membrane. In other words, transmitter molecules set off EPSPs in the postsynaptic cells by binding to receptor sites. But what if another molecule is already occupying the site? In that case, the neurotransmitter is blocked; it cannot affect the postsynaptic cell. A molecule that fits into a receptor site in such a way that it prevents the intended transmitter from binding, but not in such a way as to open the ion channel, is called an **antagonist** or **blocker**.

When neurochemists sought to find the mechanism by which opiate antagonists like naloxone had their blocking action, they first established that the naloxone did indeed bind to receptor sites in postsynaptic membranes. Now consider the implications of that finding: if naloxone blocks morphine by filling up morphine's receptor sites, then morphine must have its effects on the nervous system by acting just like a neurotransmitter. Morphine and heroin must fire nerve cells (or inhibit them) by binding to receptor sites and creating EPSPs (or IPSPs).

This little bit of logic created a veritable tidal wave of excitement in neurochemistry labs. The human brain has receptor sites built for the shape of the morphine molecule. How can that be? Are humans so perverse that they have evolved receptor sites specially designed for an illicit drug? Obviously, the sites were really "designed" by nature for a normal neurotransmitter secreted by presynaptic terminals in various regions of the brain. The physical resemblance to a normal transmitter that allowed the opiates to fit into these sites might simply be a blind accident—a freak of nature. The chemical for which the sites were meant would be the transmitter involved in those parts of the brain whose activity could produce euphoria and analgesia. What had neurochemists so excited was the fact that no such transmitter had ever been identified or even suspected!

For a few months, there was a scramble of research—a frenzied race to be the first to find the brain's own "natural opiate." The result of all this frantic science was the discovery of a whole class of substances called **endogenous opioids** (en-DODGE-en-us OH-pee-oyds). *Endogenous* means from within, and *opioid* means a substance that resembles an opiate. These opioids break down into two major categories: the **endorphins** (en-DOR-fins) and the **enkephalins** (en-KEFF-uh-lins). Both types of opioid apparently have receptor sites prepared for them on various neurons within the CNS, and it is these receptor sites that morphine molecules are accidentally shaped to fit.

Now consider another implication. Morphine stops pain by fitting into receptor sites designed for enkephalin or endorphin or both. That means that neurons bearing those receptor sites must be part of a pain-suppression system within the CNS. Could this be the same pain-suppression system that runs from the PAG to the substantia gelatinosa? That does indeed seem to be the case. Synapses using enkephalin as a transmitter have now been identified in the substantia gelatinosa, and it seems that cells within the PAG may use both enkephalin and endorphin (Basbaum & Fields, 1984; Casey, 1982; Moss & Basbaum, 1983).

Acupuncture Analgesia

Use of **acupuncture** as an anesthetic has caught on slowly in the United States, and only a few dentists make use of it, but it has been used successfully for years in Europe (Nathan, 1978). The procedure involves inserting needles into the skin and then twirling them for 20–30 minutes. It originated in China, the earliest record of use being from the sixth century BC (Barend ter Haar, 1978). Despite acupuncture's 2,500-year history in China, American physicians have really only become aware of its value in the last two decades. The idea of relieving pain by sticking needles into the person seemed outrageously nonsensical to the average Westerner, and it took quite a bit of exposure to the idea before anyone began serious tests of its effectiveness. There is now sufficient research available to definitely establish that acupuncture is not the tool of quacks; it really does produce some pain suppression in many situations.

Chinese surgeons employ acupuncture regularly as a substitute for general anesthesia. This is a very practical thing to do when possible because the level of anesthesia used in surgery severely depresses the activity in the brain stem where the circuits for respiration and heart-rate control are found. It is only the constant monitoring of vital signs by an anesthesiologist that gives the patient a higher probability of reviving than dying from the anesthetic. Acupuncture presents no such risks.

Does Acupuncture Work Through Suggestion?

The amount of anxiety a person has about the source of pain is an important factor in determining how much pain the person will experience. In the use of acupuncture as dental or surgical anesthetic, care is taken to relax the patient and build confidence that the procedure will indeed work. It is amazing how little pain arises from an injury when the person is confident that all is well and that the discomfort will not be intolerable. It is possible that some of the pain relief or prevention attributed to the needles is actually the result of belief that something positive is being done that will prevent pain.

However, recent research suggests that there is something more to acupuncture analgesia than just anxiety relief. If the technique depended entirely on relaxing the patient and creating a belief that the pain stimulus did not really represent harm, then acupuncture should not work with animals. Nathan (1978) tested this idea with cats. He measured the degree of pain indirectly with a nociceptive response called the **viscerosomatic reflex**, a sudden contraction of the abdominal wall in response to a painful stimulus in the abdominal region. Nathan found that the viscerosomatic reflex was harder to elicit if the cat had been given acupuncture in either a hindlimb or forelimb previous to the painful stimulus. Pain suppression by acupuncture has also been demonstrated in mice and rats (Hamba & Toda, 1985). Apparently, acupuncture provides analgesia just as well in lower animals as in humans.

Acupuncture and the Pain-Suppression System
Nathan also found that the analgesia could not be produced any longer in a cat whose spinal cord had been cut at its very top. Cuts at several other levels revealed that acupuncture would only work if the level of the brain stem containing the PAG was still connected to the spinal cord. This suggests that acupuncture works through the descending pain-suppression pathway.

Recall that there are several synapses in the pain-suppression path (i.e., in the PAG and substantia gelatinosa) that employ the endogenous opioids as transmitters. If acupuncture depends on this pathway, then it should also depend on the opioids. There is now some evidence that acupuncture may indeed obtain at least some of its analgesic effect by way of endogenous opioids (Yingling, 1978). Subjects in several experiments have undergone electrical stimulation of their teeth in order to stimulate pain fibers within the pulp. The amount of pain generated is carefully measured on a rating scale, and then an acupuncture procedure is begun. Generally, needles are twirled in the subject's skin for about one-half hour in order to reach a maximum level of analgesia, and then the sensitivity to tooth pulp stimulation is measured once more. The drop in sensitivity (rated intensity of the pain) following acupuncture is recorded. At this point in the experiment, the evidence collected shows that acupuncture definitely has reduced the pain but does not reveal how that analgesia was produced.

In the next phase of the experiment, naloxone is injected into the subject, and a third pain rating is taken during pulp stimulation. Because naloxone is an opiate antagonist, its presence in the nervous system should block transmission at the synapses in the PAG and substantia gelatinosa; the pain-suppression path should stop functioning. As expected, the third pain measurement showed a loss of the acupuncture analgesia; pain sensitivity had been restored to its normal level. These data fit perfectly with the idea that acupuncture produces analgesia by way of the pain-suppression path.

One point should be clarified at this time. Neither acupuncture nor the pain-suppression path really produces analgesia—that is, a complete suppression of pain. What you get is partial suppression. A better term for this reduction in pain intensity is **hypoalgesia** (HIGH-po-al-GEE-zee-uh), and this is the term we will use in the rest of the chapter.

Does Pain Reduce Pain?

One facet of acupuncture that we have not yet considered in this discussion is that inserting needles into the skin and twirling them does cause pain even while it is inducing hypoalgesia for other pains. Strangely enough, a painful electric shock also produces a degree of analgesia (Lewis et al., 1980). One can demonstrate this by counting the seconds that it takes for a rat in a restraint tube to decide to flick its tail from under a spot of hot, focused light. This **tail-flick latency** gives us a measure of how painful the heat was. When the heat intensity is only mildly burning, the number of seconds from the onset of the light to the tail flick (the latency) is greater than when the light intensity is turned up, so the latency presumably reflects the amount of pain felt. Now, if the rat has received a series of painful electric shocks to its feet just prior to the tail-flick test, the response latency is increased; that is, the rat is significantly slower in responding to the heat. The shock seems to have caused a reduction in the pain.

Has pain-induced hypoalgesia ever been demonstrated in humans? Research by Roby-Brami and colleagues (1987) suggests that the concept does apply to humans. To measure the amount of pain, these researchers found the level of shock to the skin of the lower leg sufficient to elicit a nociceptive flexion reflex in the leg (i.e., a muscle twitch). This stimulus was described by the subjects as resembling a slightly painful pinprick. While continually shocking the leg and recording the size of the reflex twitch induced by the shock, they then delivered 2 minutes

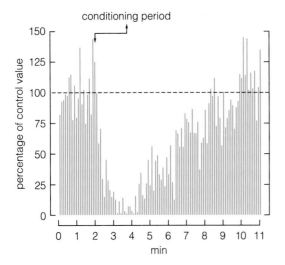

Figure 8.22 Shock-induced hypoalgesia in the human. The graph shows the changes in the size of a nociceptive reflex in a leg muscle as pain was experienced elsewhere in the body. (This nociceptive reflex consisted of a twitch in the muscle each time the leg was shocked, and it is the size of the twitch that is displayed.) About 10 reflex responses were elicited every minute for 11 minutes. During the second minute, a 2-minute series of shocks to the hand was begun (see the horizontal arrow at the top labeled *conditioning period*). The result of the hand shocks was a large suppression of the nociceptive reflex to the continuing leg shocks. (Adapted from Roby-Brami et al., 1987)

of shocks to the fingers of one hand. The nociceptive reflex immediately dropped in size by almost 100 percent and then slowly recovered during the 8 minutes following the end of the finger shocks (Figure 8.22). Apparently, hypoalgesia was induced by the finger shocks and it even lasted well beyond their termination.

Did the hypoalgesia demonstrated by Roby-Brami depend on the pain-suppression system of the brain stem? The entire experiment was repeated on a group of five quadriplegic patients, and quite different results were found. In quadriplegia the spinal cord has been severed just below the medulla so that all connections between the cord and brain have been destroyed. This means that the part of the suppression system running from the raphe magnus

down to the substantia gelatinosa is no longer functional. Thus, one would predict that in these patients the nociceptive reflex should not be affected by the finger shock despite the fact that the finger areas of the cord and the leg areas are still in communication with one another. In fact, the results of the experiment were that the nociceptive reflex showed no suppression by the finger shock at all (Roby-Brami et al., 1987). It is unlikely then that the pain suppression in normal subjects was simply some interaction of reflexes within the spinal cord; it clearly originated in the brain itself, and the likeliest place would be the PAG.

The Analgesia of Avoidable and Unavoidable Pain
We asked earlier why such an important mechanism as pain should ever be deliberately suppressed by the nervous system, and our answer was that survival in some situations may depend on diverting the attention to other stimuli. That explanation, however, may not help us understand why pain should be suppressed by painful stimuli. Perhaps there are situations in which pain is unavoidable, and experiencing it serves no purpose. Consider the pain of childbirth, for example, or the prolonged pain during the recovery from serious injury. Could one of the functions of the pain-suppression system be to reduce the stress of pain when the pain is inescapable? Recent research with rats has found that forceful stimulation of the cervix (the entrance to the uterus) produces a profound state of hypoalgesia (Komisaruk, 1980). Thus, when the cervix dilates during labor and the vaginal tissues are stretched by many times their normal size, some relief from the possibly excruciating pain may be afforded the mother by a protective pain-suppression response from the PAG. Further, it has been shown that there are higher levels of endorphins in women undergoing labor, and this is what one might expect if the descending pain-control path was heavily in use (Akil et al., 1984).

Unavoidable pain was examined in rats by comparing a group that was given an opportunity to learn to avoid shocks with a group given no such opportunity. We have known for some time that an animal with repeated experience of unavoidable shock appears to "give up" and fails to learn an avoidance when the opportunity is later presented. This phenomenon has been termed **learned helplessness.** Jackson and colleagues (1979) discovered that learned helplessness is accompanied by hypoalgesia. No similar pain suppression was discovered in animals given the opportunity to learn an avoidance response. Does this mean that pain suppression only occurs after a lengthy experience with unavoidable shock when the animal has given up hope of avoidance?

Analgesia from Brief Versus Prolonged Pain Further research quickly showed that there was more to this story. It was found that rats developed hypoalgesia from only a very brief series of inescapable shocks—a series too brief for the development of learned helplessness (Grau, 1987; Terman et al., 1984). Earlier work by Lewis and colleagues (1980) suggested that there might be a quick-starting, nonopioid form of hypoalgesia as well as a slow-starting, opioid form of the sort involved in learned helplessness. This was confirmed by Drugan and colleagues (1982) who tested rats for hypoalgesia after 20 shocks ("brief" condition) and again after 80 shocks ("prolonged" condition) and found that pain suppression was reversed by an opiate blocker only in the 80-shock condition. This opiate-blocker effect appeared in the prolonged-pain condition only when the shock was unavoidable (Drugan et al., 1985). Thus, in brief pain or prolonged avoidable pain, the suppression system may be turned on via routes

other than through the PAG, and these alternate routes may use a nonopioid transmitter. Figure 8.23 indicates that some of the synapses in the substantia gelatinosa may be nonopioid. Some evidence suggests that the pain-suppression system contains noradrenergic synapses (Basbaum & Fields, 1984).

There may be some inconsistencies between experiments from various laboratories. Grau (1987) reports finding an opioid form of hypoalgesia from only two or three shocks, too few for learned helplessness or even for the rat to discover whether the shocks were avoidable or not. In response to this, Drugan suggests that there may be another pain-suppression mechanism that acts very early in a pain episode (i.e., after only one or two shocks) but that quickly adapts out as the nociceptive stimuli continue, leaving only the nonopioid paths working (Drugan et al., 1985). Then, if the nociceptive stimulus still persists and proves to be unavoidable, a second, slow-starting opioid system is activated. The best overall summary of these results appears to be that the brain stem contains a complex set of pain-suppression pathways involving both opioid and nonopioid transmitters and having at least three different times of action. Table 8.2 summarizes all these interpretations.

One other factor makes the slow-starting opioid system unique. It is the only one that appears to rely on the pituitary gland (see Chapter 3). The pituitary releases endorphin along with its stress-related hormone ACTH (Akil et al., 1984), and if it is removed,

Table 8.2	Forms of Hypoalgesia Elicited by Shock	
Duration of Shock Stimulus	Escapable Shock	Inescapable Shock
Initial (1–3 Shocks)	Opioid neural	Opioid neural
Brief (20 Shocks)	Nonopioid	Nonopioid
Prolonged (80 Shocks)	Nonopioid	Opioid neural with hormone amplification

Figure 8.23 Basbaum and Fields's summary of known and presumed circuitry within the descending pain-control system. Each nerve cell symbol represents a single member of a type of neuron. Wherever possible the type of transmitter employed is shown next to the synapse or cell body. (5HT = serotonin; GABA = gamma aminobutyric acid; NE = norepinephrine; SG = substantia gelatinosa cells.) There are two areas of importance in the rostral medulla, the nucleus raphe magnus (NRM) and the nuclei reticularis magnocellularis and reticularis gigantocellularis (represented by one cell labeled NR). Not all suspected neuron types are shown (e.g., the enkephalinergic cell in the dorsal horn is missing). (Adapted from Basbaum & Fields, 1984)

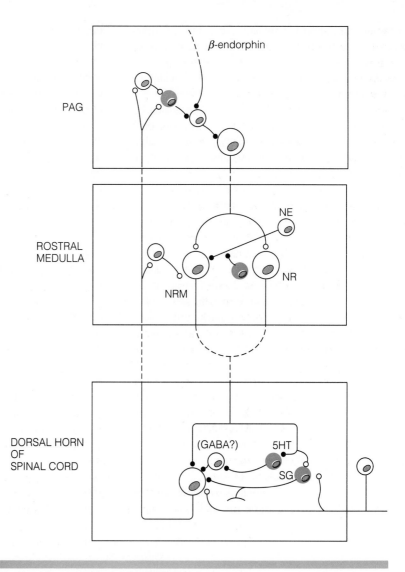

much of the hypoalgesic effect is lost. Grau (1987) thinks that the bloodborne endorphin may have an important effect in the PAG and cord. He proposes that during a long exposure to a nociceptive stimulus, the pain-suppression system develops tolerance to its transmitters, and its response begins to weaken. The extra endorphin from the pituitary could serve to counteract this growing tolerance by summating with the transmitter secreted by neuron terminals.

Fear and Stress There is little doubt that shocks provoke hypoalgesia and apparently accomplish this through the pain-suppression system. But is it the pain that triggers the system, or is it some other aspect of the shock situation such as fear? If, on a number of occasions, a rat experiences a neutral stimulus such as a tone while being shocked, the previously neutral stimulus acquires the ability to elicit hypoalgesia. This is obviously a case of classic conditioning with the tone serving as a conditioned stimulus (CS), which gradually acquires the ability to elicit hypoalgesia through being paired with shock. Bolles and Fanselow (1982) propose a theory in which fear plays a pivotal role. The **Bolles–Fanselow theory** posits that shock elicits fear, which turns on the pain-suppression system. A tone (or any other neutral stimulus) associated long enough with the shock also acquires the ability to elicit fear and therefore pain suppression. Bolles and Fanselow point out that the survival utility of hypoalgesia in normal circumstances would be to free the person from concerns over injury during a dangerous situation in which concentration must be focused on fighting or some other defensive behavior, in other words, a fear situation. It makes little sense to them that pain should act to suppress pain, but it seems very reasonable that fear should do this.

Much of the social communication between rats is accomplished through odors, and one study reported by Bolles and Fanselow (1982) found that odors left behind by rats that had undergone stress were sufficient to elicit hypoalgesia in other rats sniffing the odors. In another study that involved no pain experience at all, rats were exposed to a cat for a few minutes and then tested for pain threshold. The fear experience was enough to produce hypoalgesia (Lester & Fanselow, 1985).

The Bolles–Fanselow theory has even been tested in the psychological clinic setting. A now-classic treatment for phobias is a process called systematic desensitization in which the patient is led through a number of levels of fear. The first level involves a very mild fear, and the patient easily learns to overcome it. The next step is to a stronger fear, which can then be overcome thanks to the experience with the more minor fear. The process continues through greater and greater levels of fear, with the patient gradually learning to overcome each. The process depends completely on evoking the fear during therapy so that coping can be learned. In a recent study, the therapists reasoned that because endorphins appear to be a part of the fear mechanism of the brain, naloxone given to the patients prior to therapy should block fear and render the therapy unworkable. This proved to be the case (Hunt et al., 1988).

It seems reasonable that the fear circuitry of the limbic system (which has strong anatomical connections to the PAG) should be able to command the pain-suppression pathway in certain circumstances (Basbaum & Fields, 1984), but the Bolles–Fanselow theory seems to argue that no pain suppression at all occurs outside of fear situations and that fear always leads to hypoalgesia. Both restrictions are questionable. Whether fear leads to hypoalgesia seems to depend on the specific situation. For example, when you are fearful during a battle, the fear directs your attention away from pain toward stimuli more important for immediate survival. When you accidentally cut yourself with a knife in your own kitchen, however, the anxiety you experience concerns the extent and seriousness of the injury, and the pain in that circumstance is amplified rather than suppressed. Thus, the factor of attention may be the key to whether the Bolles–Fanselow theory applies or fails to apply to any particular situation. Personal introspections of the above sort, however, are not data, and until the theory is examined experimentally in this light, we will not know if the attention factor is important or not.

Bolles and Fanselow's other idea, that fear is required to produce hypoalgesia, fails to consider the anatomy of the pain-control system (Figure 8.23), which clearly is that of a loop between dorsal horn and brain stem. Reticular neurons in the medulla that send their axons into the dorsal horn to inhibit nociceptive input receive input from branches of T-cell axons climbing the brain stem on their way to the thalamus. In other words, one of the most reliable sources of stimulation for pain-suppression neurons is input from neurons bringing pain information to the brain (Basbaum & Fields, 1984). This argues for the idea that pain may produce hypoalgesia without any intervention from higher processes such as fear. Evidence for this comes from an experiment in which shock-induced hypoalgesia was demonstrated in rats that had their brain stems completely cut at the level of the midbrain (Klein et al., 1983). Thus, with all limbic connections cut and no chance for fear to influence the descending path, hypoalgesia still occurred. Such findings do not mean that fear never reduces pain intensity. Instead, we are able to see that fear is simply one more of the many factors that induce hypoalgesia.

If we broaden the Bolles–Fanselow theory to

allow multiple causes for hypoalgesia, then several other sources of pain suppression can be better understood. For example, rats forced to swim in cold water develop hypoalgesia, as do rats that have been food-deprived. Even sexual behavior can lead to reduced pain (Akil et al., 1984). Most of these examples are situations that produce some amount of stress. Recall that the pituitary gland reacts to stressful stimuli by secreting both ACTH, a hormone that stimulates the adrenal gland, and endorphin. The endorphin may have its effects by amplifying transmission in the PAG. The increased activity in the descending system may serve to block incoming sensory information about cold and discomfort in the swimming rat and allow it to concentrate on swimming or block useless hunger pangs in a starving rat during inescapable deprivation. However, this analysis suggests that even with stress situations, the key factor that decides whether the descending system will become active may be that of attention. It is possible that all other factors that produce hypoalgesia (fear, pain, stress, and conditioning) are merely parts of the overall mechanism that determines what stimuli are going to be attended to and which are to be inhibited.

■ Summary

1. The three somatic senses are mechanoreception, thermoreception, and nociception. Stimuli (such as skin deformation, heating, and damage) are events outside the nervous system, whereas sensations are the resulting patterns of activity within the nervous system and their accompanying conscious experience. Somatic receptors are found in the skin (cutaneous receptors) and in viscera, muscles, joints, and tendons (deep somatic receptors).

2. Cutaneous somatic receptors include free nerve endings (involved in nociception and thermoreception) and a variety of mechanoreceptors with specialized endings: hair follicle ending, Meissner's corpuscle, Pacinian corpuscle, Ruffini ending, and Merkel ending.

3. All cutaneous mechanoreceptors in hairless skin can be classified as either fast-adapting (FA) or slow-adapting (SA). (Adaptation is the gradual loss of responding despite continuing stimulation.) They can also be classified as type I or type II according to the nature of their receptive field (the area of skin within which a stimulus can fire the fiber).

4. Meissner's corpuscles appear to be the endings of FA I fibers, Pacinian corpuscles of FA II's, Merkel endings of SA I's, and Ruffini's of SA II's. FA I's and SA I's appear to be specialized for sensitivity and acuity. They participate in localization, shape recognition, spatial acuity, and texture perception. FA II's are ideal for vibration discrimination, whereas SA II's seem well adapted for providing the motor system with the input needed for handgrip control.

5. A sensory projection system is the chain of neurons connecting receptors with their sensory area in the cortex. Primary afferents are the first link of this chain. They carry the nerve impulse patterns from receptors to transmission cells (T cells) that lie either in the dorsal horn of the cord or in the medulla of the brain stem. These T cells send their axons across the midline and then up to the thalamus on the opposite side of the nervous system. The thalamic cells (in the ventroposterior nuclei) relay the information to the somatic cortex.

6. The postcentral gyrus of the parietal lobe is the primary somatic cortex (S1). A secondary somatic projection area (S2) lies mostly buried within the lateral fissure immediately posterior to S1. Stimulation of S1 produces a wide variety of conscious somatic experiences such as flutter, pushing, and warmth. Damage to S1 impairs tactile sensitivity, thermal sensitivity, and the ability to localize stimuli accurately on the skin. S2 cortex may be involved in stereognosis.

7. S1 cortex is organized into cylindrical vertical columns that extend from layer 1 through layer 6. Each column appears to receive its input from a group of primary afferents with overlapping RFs within the same general region of skin. In the rat, each vibrissa has its own column, called a barrel.

8. Merzenich and Kaas have shown that the body maps in S1 are not permanent. They change if part of their input is removed (as in an amputation). It is also possible that the area for any body part may expand if that part is used more than others.

9. The skin can be mapped into a mosaic of spots in which warmth or cold or both are perceivable.

These spots do not seem to represent single-receptor endings, as was first thought. Warmth and cold are sensed by bare nerve endings with no apparent specialization, some of which are also mechanoreceptive. Thermoreceptors can adapt completely to temperature shifts within the range 30–36°C (a zone known as physiological zero) and less completely outside of that range.

10. The phenomena of conversion reaction, phantom limb pains, and placebos lead to basic questions about the uniqueness of pain as a sense that can only be answered from an examination of the anatomy of the pain-projection system. T cells carrying nociceptive information up the spinal cord synapse in several areas of the thalamus, including medial and intralaminar nuclei. Some information reaches the S2 cortex, and the rest is sent into the limbic system. The former route probably handles the objective, informational aspect of pain, whereas the route into the limbic system is presumably responsible for the motivational–emotional (suffering) aspect. Pain is a sensation, not a stimulus, and the most likely site in the nervous system for this type of conscious experience is in the medial and intralaminar nuclei of the thalamus. Thus, neurotic pain may be the result of thalamic neurons being fired by events in the limbic system without accompanying input from any somatic receptors. A placebo might act by relieving anxiety, thus removing the limbic stimulation of thalamic cells.

11. Chronic pain persists for weeks or months and responds only poorly to analgesics such as aspirin. It usually seems to be the product of damage somewhere in the nervous system. It has been treated with opiate drugs and surgery. Recently, surgeons have tried relieving chronic pain through stimulation of brain areas by implanted electrodes. Such analgesia can be induced by stimulation of the periaqueductal gray (PAG) of the midbrain. Cells there project to the nucleus raphe magnus of the medulla, and those neurons send their axons down the cord to the substantia gelatinosa where inhibitory connections are made to the primary nociceptive afferents. This route is called the pain-suppression system.

12. Naloxone is an opiate blocker that can stop the action of morphine by blocking receptor sites for endogenous opioids (endorphins and enkephalins). Endogenous opioids are transmitters in the pain-suppression system. Thus, morphine has its analgesic effect by exciting the pain-suppression system.

13. Acupuncture is a procedure that involves inserting needles into the skin and then twirling them to reduce pain somewhere else in the body. It works as well in animals as in humans. Acupuncture seems to depend in part on the opioid parts of the descending pain-suppression path because some types of acupuncture analgesia can be blocked by naloxone.

14. A series of mild electric shocks can produce reduction of pain (hypoalgesia), and this effect depends on both opioid and nonopioid parts of the pain-suppression system. According to current theory, two or three shocks elicit hypoalgesia of short duration that employs the opioid path. A series of 20 shocks induces hypoalgesia by way of a nonopioid path, and a prolonged series of shocks (e.g., 80) works by way of nonopioid paths if the shock is escapable but induces a long-lasting hypoalgesia through opioid paths if the shock is unavoidable. This latter circumstance is the condition for learned helplessness, and it also stimulates the pituitary to release systemic endorphin that amplifies hypoalgesia.

15. Bolles and Fanselow's suggestion that pain elicits hypoalgesia by way of fear could be broadened by substituting the concept of stress for that of fear.

Glossary

acupuncture Chinese medical practice employing the use of needles to relieve pain. (330)

adaptation The loss of response from a receptor despite continuing stimulation. (303)

analgesia Relief from pain. (328)

analgesics Pain-reducing drugs. (326)

antagonist (blocker) A chemical that prevents a neurotransmitter from binding with its receptor site. (329)

barrel A group of cells in layer IV of S1, all receiving from the same vibrissa. (313)

blocker See *antagonist*. (329)

Bolles–Fanselow theory An explanation of shock-induced analgesia in which the pain suppression system is turned on by fear. (335)

Braille system A system for translating the letters of the alphabet into raised bumps on a page; used by blind readers. (307)

chronic pain Abnormal pain that continues for weeks or months and usually signals dysfunction in the nervous system. (326)

conversion reaction The unconscious generation of a physical symptom such as paralysis or blindness to adjust to an emotional conflict. (322)

cutaneous receptors Somatic receptors found in skin. (301)

deep somatic receptors Somatic receptors found in tissues under the skin. (301)

dorsal horn The dorsal portion of the gray matter within the spinal cord. (310)

dorsal root The branch of the spinal nerve that contains the afferent fibers. (309)

dorsal root ganglion Cluster of somas of the afferent fibers of a spinal nerve; located just outside of the cord on the dorsal root. (310)

endogenous opioids Opiatelike chemicals produced naturally in the brain. (330)

endorphins A class of endogenous opioids. (330)

enkephalins A class of endogenous opioids. (330)

euphoria A state in which one feels especially good, relaxed, happy, and carefree. (328)

FA I Afferent fiber that adapts rapidly and has a small RF. (304)

FA II Afferent fiber that adapts rapidly and has a large RF. (304)

fast adapting fiber (FA) Mechanoreceptor that responds only to the first moments of a continuing stimulus. (303)

free nerve ending Sensory fiber terminations that act as somatic receptors but have no specialized structure. (302)

frequency matching The nervous system's method for coding of texture by having the stimulated afferent fiber fire once as each microbump in the felt surface is contacted by the finger moving across it. (309)

hair follicle A bottlelike hole in skin containing the root of a hair and the sensory nerve ending that contacts it. (302)

heroin A chemically altered version of morphine that works faster than morphine. (327)

hypoalgesia A diminished sensitivity to pain stimuli. (331)

intralaminar nucleus A group of thalamic neurons connected to the thalamic reticular formation and receiving input from the pain system. (323)

learned helplessness Inability to learn avoidance responses after prolonged experience with an unavoidable aversive stimulus. (333)

localization of stimulus Sensing where the stimulation is occurring on or in the body. (307)

mechanoreceptive threshold The smallest amount of mechanical stimulation that will produce a conscious sensation. (305)

mechanoreceptors Transduce mechanical stimuli into nerve impulse patterns. (300)

medial thalamic nucleus Portion of thalamus involved to some extent in the transmission of pain information. (323)

Meissner's corpuscle Somatic receptor of an FA I fiber; specializes in localization and shape recognition. (302)

Merkel ending Somatic receptor of an S1 fiber; specializes in spatial acuity. (302)

morphine An opiate drug; the active ingredient in opium. (327)

naloxone An opiate antagonist. (329)

nociceptors Transduce damaging or potentially damaging mechanical or thermal stimuli into nerve impulses. (300)

nucleus raphe magnus A midline group of serotonergic cells in the reticular formation of the medulla. (328)

opiate A drug derived from opium. (327)

opiate antagonist A drug that blocks the action of an opiate at synapses; also, opiate blocker. (329)

opiate blocker See *opiate antagonist*. (329)

opium A resinous substance that exudes from the bud of the opium poppy flower. (327)

Pacinian corpuscle Somatic receptor of an FA II fiber; specializes in vibration sensing. (302)

pain suppression pathway Route from PAG to substantia nigra that reduces pain intensity by inhibiting transmission in the dorsal horn. (328)

paradoxical cold Sensation of cold from a stimulus heated to 45°. (319)

periaqueductal gray (PAG) Central gray matter of the midbrain that surrounds the cerebral aqueduct. (326)

phantom limb Common sequel of amputation in which pains and other somatic sensations are experienced as originating in the missing body part. (323)

physiological zero The normal 30–36° skin-temperature range. (320)

placebo A pretended, rather than real, medical treatment. (323)

posterior thalamic complex Group of small thalamic nuclei at the rear of the thalamus, medial to the medial geniculate and posterior to the ventroposterior nuclei; related to pain sensitivity, these cells project to S II cortex and insula. (310)

presynaptic inhibition Inhibition of a terminal's transmitter release by another neuron. (329)

primary afferent A sensory neuron with receptor endings in the skin and terminals in the dorsal horn of spinal cord. (303)

receptive field The area of skin or body within which a stimulus will trigger impulses in the neuron; each afferent fiber has its own receptive field. (304)

Ruffini ending Somatic receptor of an S II fiber; specializes in sensing stretch. (302)

S1 The primary somatosensory and kinesthetic projection area; located in the postcentral gyrus. (310)

S2 The secondary somatosensory and kinesthetic projection area; located posterior to S1 and within the lateral fissure. (310)

SA I Afferent fiber that adapts slowly and has a small RF. (304)

SA II Afferent fiber that adapts slowly and has a large RF. (304)

sensation Stimulus-produced pattern of activity within the nervous system and its accompanying conscious experience. (300)

shape recognition The ability to perceive the form of an object held in the hand. (307)

slow adapting fibers (SA) Mechanoreceptors that maintain their response to a continuing stimulus. (303)

somatic projection areas Regions of the cerebral cortex devoted to the somatic senses. (310)

somatic senses Kinesthesis, mechanoreception, thermoreception, and nociception. (300)

somatosensory projection system The neural route extending from the receptors to the projection areas in the cortex. (309)

spatial acuity The ability to feel various parts of the stimulus object as separate and distinct even when they are very close to one another on the skin. (307)

stereognosis The ability to perceive the shapes of solid objects with your hands. (311)

stimulus Some energy change outside of the nervous system. (300)

substantia gelatinosa A column of neurons at the edge of the dorsal horn of the cord near the entrance of the dorsal root. (328)

tail-flick latency Amount of time a rat takes to remove its tail from a hot plate. (331)

texture perception The sensing of size and frequency of irregularities in a surface. (308)

thermal summation Characteristic of the thermoreception system that makes a thermal stimulus appear warmer if the area of stimulation is greater. (318)

thermoreceptors Transduce thermal stimuli (temperature changes) into nerve impulse patterns. (300)

transmission cells (T cells) Cord neurons receiving input from primary afferents. (310)

two-point threshold The least amount of distance between the two points of the stimulator that can still be sensed as two points rather than just one. (307)

ventral root Branch of a spinal nerve that contains the efferent (motor) fibers. (309)

ventroposterior nuclei Two thalamic nuclei (lateral and medial) serving the somatic senses; their cells project to S1 cortex. (310)

vibrissae Specialized snout hairs that detect the presence of objects in the immediate vicinity of the rodent's face. (313)

viscerosomatic reflex A sudden contraction of the abdominal wall in response to a painful stimulus in the abdominal region. (330)

The Production and Sensing of Movement

Muscles
Concepts: striate muscles, smooth muscles, peristalsis, muscle fibers, neuromyal junction, acetylcholine (Ach)

NEURAL CONTROL OF MUSCLES
Concept: motor unit

REFLEX ARCS
Concepts: disynaptic arc, monosynaptic arc, multisynaptic arc, Renshaw cell, recurrent collateral, isometric contraction, isotonic contraction, posture

Sensory Control of Movement and Posture

KINESTHESIS
Concepts: kinesthesis, muscle spindles, tendon, Golgi tendon organ

STRETCH REFLEX
Concept: stretch reflex

Mechanics of the Stretch Reflex
Concepts: load, extensor muscle, flexor muscle, patella, patellar tendon reflex

Tuning the Stretch Reflex with the Gamma Efferent
Concepts: servomechanism, set point, gamma efferent, alpha motor neuron, muscle tone

VESTIBULAR SENSES

Gravity and Linear Acceleration
Concepts: gravitational sense, saccule, utricle, macula, stereocilia, otoliths, linear acceleration, inertia

Rotary Acceleration
Concepts: rotary acceleration, semicircular canals, ampulla, cupula, vestibular nuclei

Cerebellum
Concept: cerebellum

SYMPTOMS OF CEREBELLAR INJURY
Concepts: ataxia, decomposition of movements, dysmetria, tremor

CEREBELLAR FUNCTION
Concepts: coordination, agonists, antagonists, biceps, triceps, reciprocal inhibition, intention tremor

Locomotion

THE ROOTS OF WALKING
Concepts: extensor thrust reflex, stepping reflex, deafferentiation, electromyogram (EMG)

CENTRAL PATTERN GENERATORS
Concepts: central pattern generators (CPGs), synergists, program, subroutine, mesencephalic locomotor region

Corpus Striatum

ANATOMY OF THE CORPUS STRIATUM
Concepts: caudate nucleus, putamen, internal capsule, striatum, globus pallidus, substantia nigra

SYMPTOMS OF DAMAGE TO THE CORPUS STRIATUM

Huntington's Disease
Concepts: chorea, autoimmune disease

Parkinson's Disease
Concepts: bradykinesia, rigidity, tremor at rest, nigrostriatal pathway, precursor, l-DOPA

A s psychologists our chief desire in studying the nervous system is to understand how behavior originates. Behavioral psychologists have discovered that their understanding of how reinforcement selects certain responses over others is improved when they pay attention to the fine details of behavior. For example, in training a retarded child to pull on her pants, the reinforcement must be delivered at precisely the right time for the correct response to be learned. The more we learn about analyzing complex acts (e.g., putting on pants) into the component parts (individual movements), the more potential we have for understanding the learning process and controlling it. It is important then that we discover how movements and postures are generated by the motor system of the brain and how they are regulated and directed by the kinesthetic and vestibular senses.

■ Muscles

It is interesting how much of our own bodies we have little or no conscious control over. We all have two general categories of muscle (striate and smooth), and our voluntary control extends to only one of these. **Striate muscles** (also called striped, or skeletal) are the ones that are attached to bones and move the parts of our bodies around or hold them in fixed positions (postures). These are the ones we are used to thinking of as muscles, and they are red in color with faint striations (stripes). We have some voluntary control over them in most situations because they are controlled by the CNS. The **smooth muscles** are whitish and show no striations. They are found in the esophagus, stomach, intestines, bladder, heart, and the walls of blood vessels. (Smooth muscles of the heart are often called *cardiac muscles*.) Most of their contractions are involuntary (reflexive) and are controlled through the autonomic nervous system (ANS) rather than directly by the CNS. Smooth muscle can contract all by itself with no need for an outside stimulus. The intestines, for example, maintain a 24-hour state of continuous rippling contractions that start at the upper end of an intestinal segment and slowly migrate to the other end, moving the intestinal contents along as they go—an action called **peristalsis**. The *rate* of smooth muscle movements, however, can be regulated reflexively by the ANS. For example, the heart speeds during exercise and slows during rest.

A striate muscle (Figure 9.1) is composed of a number of fascicles, each of which is composed of a bundle of **muscle fibers**. An axon of a motor neuron of the peripheral somatic nervous system makes contact with each muscle fiber, forming a synapse called a **neuromyal junction** (Figure 9.2). (The combining form *myal* refers to muscle.) A striate muscle does not normally contract without being stimulated to do so by a motor neuron. When the nerve impulse in the nerve fiber reaches the neuromyal junction, a neurotransmitter called **acetylcholine (Ach)** (as-SET-tul-KO-leen) is released from presynaptic vesicles and diffuses across the gap to receptor sites in the muscle fiber. The muscle fiber responds to Ach by generating an action potential that courses down its whole length, producing contraction as it goes. This remarkable similarity of mechanisms in nerve and muscle fibers leads one to speculate that these two types of tissue might have a common evolutionary origin.

Neural Control of Muscles

During the course of human prenatal development, each motor neuron axon grows out to the muscle it will serve and finds a group of muscle fibers with which to synapse. Each nerve fiber stays with this same group of muscle fibers throughout life, and this permanent combination works together as a unit. A motor neuron together with the muscle fibers with which it connects is called a **motor unit**. After birth you grow no new motor neurons and no more muscle cells. Your early childhood was spent in developing brain circuits to improve control over a fixed number of motor units, each of which produces

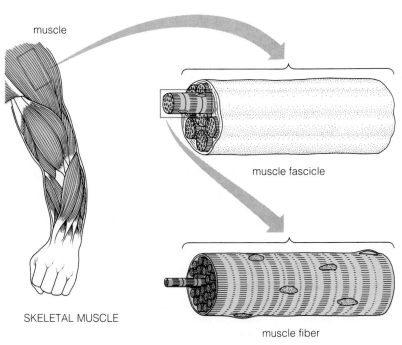

muscle

SKELETAL MUSCLE

muscle fascicle

muscle fiber

Figure 9.1 A muscle is composed of a number of fascicles, each of which is a bundle of muscle fibers. (Adapted from Bloom & Fawcett, 1975)

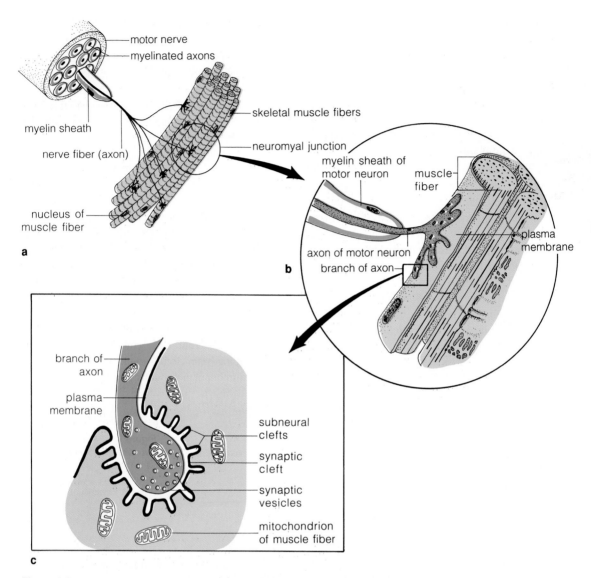

motor nerve
myelinated axons
myelin sheath
nerve fiber (axon)
skeletal muscle fibers
nucleus of muscle fiber
neuromyal junction
myelin sheath of motor neuron
muscle fiber
axon of motor neuron
branch of axon
plasma membrane

a

b

branch of axon
plasma membrane
subneural clefts
synaptic cleft
synaptic vesicles
mitochondrion of muscle fiber

c

Figure 9.2 The neuromyal junction. (**a**) In a motor unit, an axon of a motor neuron branches to several muscle fibers. (**b**) Each branch of the axon forms a neuromyal junction. (**c**) The branch of the axon rests in a groove in the muscle fiber, the motor end plate. (Adapted from Creager, 1983)

a fixed, known amount of contraction to each nerve impulse. If you started generating new muscle cells at this time in your life, they would change the contraction characteristics of the motor units they became a part of, and that would render all those hard-won brain connections obsolete. In other words, if your legs were to grow new muscle cells throughout your life, you would probably spend most of your time relearning how to walk —a daunting prospect to some of us who feel that we may have just barely succeeded the first time.

When a muscle works, not all motor units may

be active at once. Simply raising your arm without lifting anything, for example, requires only a small proportion of the units to participate at any one moment; thus, to prevent muscle fatigue, the units rotate the work between them, some resting while others maintain the contraction. However, if a load has to be lifted, the rest periods (which are actually only fractions of a second) become shorter, with the result that more motor units are working during any one moment of the muscle contraction. So, the way in which you exert more force is to excite more units simultaneously. Now let's say that you have just lifted a book from the desk and you are holding it out to a friend. The movement has been completed, and your arm is no longer moving. Does that mean that muscles are no longer contracting? Obviously not. If they stopped their action, your arm would fall, and your friend would have to pick the book off the floor. The upraised arm is held there by continuing contractions, but the rate at which motor units are becoming active again has dropped to the point where the muscle is just able to resist gravity but not able to raise the arm any further. Somewhere in the neural control mechanism for this muscle, a very fine balance has been struck. Some of the spinal cord circuitry controlling this balance between gravity and muscle contraction has been worked out. Reflex arcs (Chapter 3) make up the bulk of these circuits.

Reflex Arcs

Each arc starts with a primary afferent bringing sensory information from somesthetic or kinesthetic receptors (Figure 9.3). This afferent enters the cord through the dorsal root and synapses either with an interneuron in a **disynaptic arc** (DIE-sin-AP-tic) or directly with a motor neuron in the ventral horn as a **monosynaptic arc** (i.e., one synapse). Axons of motor neurons exit the cord through the ventral roots and make their way out to muscles by way of a nerve. **Multisynaptic arcs** with more than one interneuron also exist. Disynaptic and multisynaptic reflex arcs are the rule in the nervous system; we only encounter one type of monosynaptic arc.

Reflex arcs are the most primitive mechanisms the nervous system has for responding to the outside world. Through them an outside stimulus can trigger a particular response, the nature of which is entirely determined by which motor neurons are connected to the primary afferents. An example would be the defensive reflex in which the stimulus is something noxious (like a burning hot surface contacting the fingers), and the response is a rapid withdrawal of the hand. No higher centers are needed for this mechanism to work; the reflex arc is a self-contained circuit.

Reflexes are described as involuntary because the higher parts of the brain involved in conscious processes (like the cortical circuits) are not responsible for their initiation. On the other hand, reflexes can be controlled to some extent by higher centers. Figure 9.3 shows a descending axon coming down the cord from a cell body somewhere in the brain and making an inhibitory connection with the interneuron in one of the arcs. When this axon fires, it creates IPSPs in the interneuron, and these currents can counteract to some extent the EPSPs triggered by impulses from the sensory neuron. Thus, the descending axon can adjust the degree to which the interneuron responds to the sensory neuron and thereby determines the degree to which the outside stimulus controls the response. In an emergency, you can deliberately grab something that is burning hot because your cortex is able to override the basic defensive mechanism in the cord. One of the major trends in vertebrate evolution is to provide the nervous system with more and more higher centers that can override the machinelike lower mechanisms and make them adapt to situations too complex for their simple-minded, stimulus–response circuitry.

Some primary afferent fibers entering the cord synapse with a type of interneuron called a **Renshaw cell**, whose function is to produce those rest periods in motor neuron activity mentioned earlier (Figure 9.3). The input to the Renshaw cell comes from an axon branch of the motor neuron called a **recurrent collateral**. Every time the motor neuron fires, its impulse not only commands muscle fibers to contract but also stimulates the Renshaw cell. The axon of the Renshaw cell leads right back to the original motor neuron where it makes an inhibitory synapse. Thus, every time the motor neuron fires a burst of impulses, it inhibits itself by way of the Renshaw cell. This inhibition can last as long as half a second,

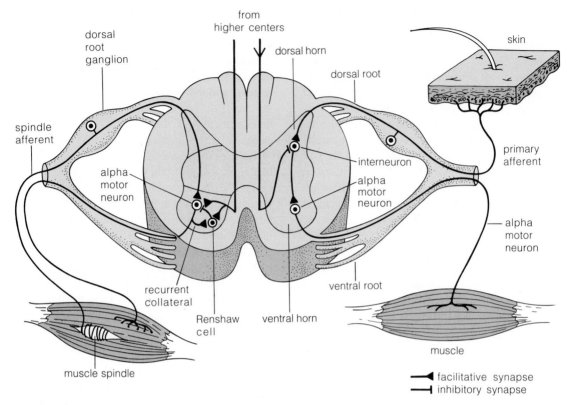

Figure 9.3 Section of spinal cord illustrating a variety of reflex arcs. In the disynaptic reflex arc shown on the right side of the cord, a primary afferent synapses with an interneuron, which synapses with an alpha motor neuron whose axon leads to a muscle. On the left, a monosynaptic arc is illustrated together with a Renshaw cell, which can inhibit the motor neuron for brief periods. By means of a recurrent collateral axon branch, the Renshaw cell is stimulated by the same motor neuron it inhibits. Higher centers can either facilitate (on left) or inhibit (right) reflex arcs. The motor neuron can recover sooner and fire faster when higher centers inhibit its Renshaw cell. The monosynaptic arc on the left recontracts a muscle when the muscle spindle receptor reports relaxation. This recontraction is called the stretch reflex.

during which the muscle fibers are getting a rest period. Different motor neurons are inhibited at different times so that some fraction of the motor units of a working muscle are always contracting.

A few paragraphs back, you learned that your muscle can contract more intensely if the rest periods shorten so that more motor units are active at the same moment. How might this shortening come about? If the contraction is intensifying because you are consciously exerting more effort, then the shortening must be the result of cortical activity. Many descending pathways connect cortex to cord directly and by way of other processors; it is possible that one or more of these routes may send an axon to the Renshaw cell to inhibit it. The less the Renshaw cell can fire, the less the motor neuron is inhibited and the harder the muscle works. The nervous system frequently employs this sort of "double-negative" system of accomplishing something by inhibiting an inhibitory neuron.

Another way in which higher levels of the nervous system could have an effect on contraction strength in a muscle is by way of connections with the motor neuron itself (Figure 9.3). For example, an axon of a reticular formation neuron might make a facilitative synapse with the ventral horn cell, providing it with EPSPs to counteract some of the IPSPs from the Renshaw cell. With this help, the motor neuron recovers sooner, and the motor unit is active more of the time. In ways like this, the higher motor centers can "play tunes" on the ventral horn motor units. For example, higher centers might first bring enough of them into action to make the muscle raise an arm and then diminish facilitation to the point where there is only enough contraction to hold the arm in the air but not enough to raise it further. Thus, a movement is changed into a posture.

The balanced condition of contraction without movement has a name: **isometric contraction** (*iso* = same; *metric* = length). There is contraction without any shortening of the muscle. Usually, we think of muscle contractions pulling parts of the body around (e.g., the biceps muscle flexing the forearm, or the triceps extending it away from the body). Contractions that move body parts are termed **isotonic contractions.** So, lifting a book into the air requires an isotonic contraction, whereas holding it there involves isometric contraction. We tend to forget or ignore isometric contractions (probably because they are so much less obvious), but most of us with desk jobs very likely expend more energy daily in isometric contractions than in isotonic. It is isometrics that produce **posture**—the maintenance of body parts in certain relatively fixed positions. A person sitting very still is contracting neck muscles that hold the head upright and trunk muscles that prevent the body from slumping over onto the floor. When you realize that this sort of isometric contraction must continue for hour after hour, it is obvious that there is more physical work to sitting behind a desk than there might appear at first. People whose job requires them to stand all day discover that, although their feet may be sore at the end of the day as expected, the real fatigue is in the back muscles that worked all that time at keeping the trunk upright.

■ Sensory Control of Movement and Posture

Some of the earliest senses to evolve were undoubtedly those related to movement and balance. The primitive gravity sensor that guided our protochordate ancestors as they burrowed up and down through the mud of the ocean bottom was the probable predecessor of the vestibular apparatus of fish. That organ gave birth to our inner ear, site of the cochlea and vestibular organs. It is your vestibular senses that control the automatic postural adjustments that allow you to sit, stand, walk, and (if you *really* trust your vestibular senses) walk across Niagara Falls on a tightrope. Vestibular senses work closely with kinesthesis (the muscle–joint sense) to run dozens of basic reflexes, all at an unconscious level.

Kinesthesis

If anyone ever asks you if you have a "sixth sense" tell them, certainly! If you have been counting as you read through the last three chapters, you must realize at this point that we have already discussed five senses and indeed are now taking up a sixth. The old saw about humans having only five senses began with the ancient Greeks and has, in our own culture, been promulgated by grammar school teachers despite all the facts to the contrary.

Kinesthesis is the sense that you use to tell where your body parts are in relation to one another and to tell where they are moving, at what speed, and with what force. Its receptors are found in muscles, joints, skin, and tendons (Figure 9.4). Many of your conscious sensations of body position and movement are produced by a blend of kinesthetic and somesthetic input, and these two senses are represented in the same area of cortex (the postcentral gyrus of the parietal lobe).

A common neurological test for trouble in the kinesthetic system is to have the patient close his eyes, extend his arm out to one side level with the ground, and then—bending his arm at the elbow— bring his index finger around to where it touches the tip of his nose. The eyes are closed, thus pro-

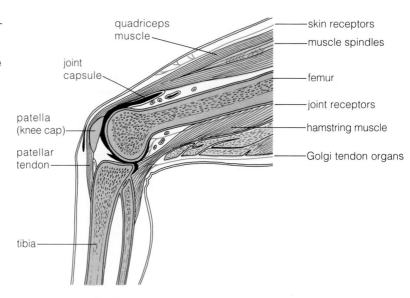

Figure 9.4 Kinesthetic receptors include muscle spindles, joint receptors, and Golgi tendon organs. Joint receptors are stimulated when the bones rotate at a joint. Muscle spindles, like the one pictured in the quadriceps muscle, respond when the muscle lengthens (is stretched). Tendon receptors are sensitive to tension exerted on the tendon as it is stretched by muscle contraction. (Adapted from Shepherd, 1983)

quadriceps muscle

joint capsule

patella (knee cap)

patellar tendon

tibia

skin receptors

muscle spindles

femur

joint receptors

hamstring muscle

Golgi tendon organs

viding no visual guidance for this movement. Skin receptors can help a little as the arm bends at the elbow, but the brunt of the sensing must fall on receptors in the elbow joint and in muscles of the arm that keep track of exactly how far the forearm has rotated and whether the arm is still horizontal at the level of the nose. This is really quite a show of sensory ability when you think about it, but it by no means tests the limits of your kinesthetic abilities. Imagine yourself picking up a single sheet of paper off of a stack. The sheet you pick up feels too thick, and you realize that it actually is two sheets rather than one. How did you sense that? At least part of this judgment is probably based on joint-rotation information from the knuckles of your index finger and the joint where the base of your thumb connects to the wrist. This kinesthetic information tells you how far apart the tips of your thumb and index finger are spaced. These joints are among the most sensitive to rotation in your whole body, the threshold in each being less than 0.5° of movement (Geldard, 1953).

Joints, however, yield only part of the information in kinesthesia; muscle receptors also provide significant input. Every muscle contains a sprinkling of special fibers that contribute nothing to the contraction of that muscle. These special fibers, called **muscle spindles**, are receptors that tell the nervous

system whether the muscle is contracting or relaxing. Several sensory nerve endings are arranged along each spindle, and the whole mechanism is structured so that when the muscle lengthens (stretches), the receptors fire (Figure 9.5). If the muscle contracts, the spindle afferents fall silent. At the end of each muscle, fibers join together and fuse into a band of exceptionally tough connective tissue, known as a **tendon**, which connects muscle to bone. Attached to each tendon is a sensory ending called a **Golgi tendon organ**, which responds to the tension on the tendon (Figure 9.5).

Muscle spindles and tendon organs probably contribute more to our conscious knowledge of body position than do joint receptors. This would explain why orthopedic patients who have had to have a joint removed surgically and replaced by a metal prosthesis can still feel where their limbs are in relation to the rest of the body (Tracey, 1978). Missing joint receptors may be important to the basic reflexes involved in movement but may not enter into conscious perception until the joint is fully flexed or extended. The range in between these two extremes is handled by muscle and tendon receptors with occasional help from skin receptors (McCloskey, 1980). In fact, you can have a strange illusion of limb movement if a vibrator is put on the tendon of a

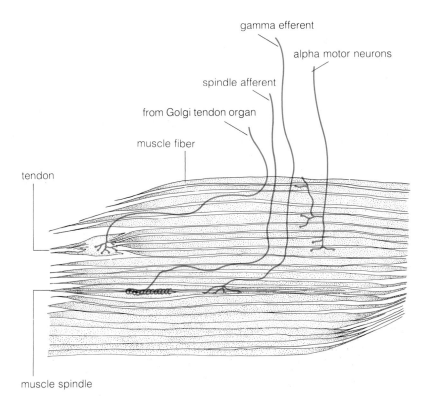

gamma efferent

alpha motor neurons

spindle afferent

from Golgi tendon organ

muscle fiber

tendon

muscle spindle

Figure 9.5 Muscle fascicle with Golgi tendon organ and muscle spindle. Two afferents are shown leaving the muscle, the primary afferent fiber from the spindle and one from the tendon organ. Three motor fibers are entering the muscle, two alphas and one gamma efferent for the muscle spindle. (Adapted from Fulton, 1943)

major muscle. The vibrations stimulate the Golgi tendon organs and muscle spindles without affecting joint receptors, and the feeling that arises is that your limb is moving around that particular joint. If the vibration is sufficiently intense, you can even experience the feeling that the limb is bent back beyond where it is capable of going naturally (Tracey, 1978).

The conscious levels of the motor system, however, are just the tip of the iceberg. The greatest use of muscle spindle input is down at the level of the spinal cord, particularly in a reflex circuit known as the stretch reflex.

Stretch Reflex

One of the most important uses the nervous system has for the input from muscle spindles is in maintenance of postures. Your conscious mind really has very little direct control over your muscles. If you were cursed with full and complete conscious con-

trol over every muscle contraction, you would indeed have a lot on your mind. Sitting in a chair would involve constantly reminding your trunk muscles to tense so that you wouldn't slump over, plus telling your neck muscles to maintain enough tension to keep your head from falling to one side. You wouldn't have a lot of spare time to think about this page because maintaining postures is a full-time job except when you are lying down with all parts of your body completely supported. Postures also underlie all conscious movements. You only swing a baseball bat while standing up—in other words, while maintaining a particular posture that involves contraction of leg, hip, and trunk muscles—yet it is the swing itself that is the focus of your consciousness, not the posture. Many of those automatic muscle adjustments that produce posture are made for you by a spinal cord mechanism called the stretch reflex. The **stretch reflex** is the automatic contraction of a muscle that is either lengthening when it shouldn't be or not contracting fast enough. To understand how it works, we first need a few basic concepts.

Mechanics of the Stretch Reflex   The afferent (sensory neuron) for the stretch reflex is the muscle spindle receptor, and the efferent (motor neuron) connects back to the same muscle that contains that receptor (Figure 9.3). Thus, the stretch reflex allows a muscle to stimulate itself. The sequence in Figure 9.6 shows what happens when a weight is placed in your hand and your intention is to hold your hand steady. In technical terms, when the weight hits your hand, the load on the biceps muscle is increased. The **load** is the amount of force acting against the muscle. Before the weight is added, the load on the biceps is just the weight of the forearm itself, but afterward it becomes the arm plus the metal weight. The biceps had been contracting isometrically just enough to compensate for the drag of gravity against the arm and hold it there in a fixed position—a posture. That amount of contraction is insufficient to counteract the increased load so the hand drops a bit. Notice that when the hand drops, the biceps is automatically *stretched*. The stretch is sensed by the spindles in the biceps. When the spindle is stimulated, afferent impulses rush into the cord (along some of the fastest fibers we possess), motor neurons are fired, and the muscle is immediately stimulated to recontract, bringing the forearm back up to the desired posture. So, the term *stretch reflex* comes from the stimulus that triggers the arc rather than from the response produced. The reflex response is a *contraction* of a muscle that is being stretched.

The sequence of events in the stretch reflex can be seen in Figure 9.7. When the muscle is being stretched by the increase in load, the spindle is stretched along with it, and this fires the afferent. The efferent responds to the afferent by producing a contraction of the muscle that shortens its length, thus making the spindle go slack and removing the stimulus to the afferent ending. All this takes only a fraction of a second, and it happens continuously as you hold your arm raised. As soon as the biceps has recontracted and taken the stretch off the spindle, the afferent stops facilitating the motor neuron through the reflex arc. When the motor neuron

responds to this decrease in EPSPs by slowing its firing, the biceps loses some of its contraction force and begins to lengthen once more. This new stretch is immediately sensed by the spindle, and the afferent once more increases its rate of firing. Cycle after cycle of this repetitive process occurs as you hold your arm "steady." In other words, the isometric contraction that creates a posture is really a series of microrelaxations (stretches) and contractions rather than a perfectly steady state. When you have given your muscles a really hard workout so that they are fatigued and slower to respond to nerve impulse commands, this cycle of stretch–contract is slowed and exaggerated enough that you can feel it as a tiny tremor in arms or legs—a feeling of shakiness.

The normal working of stretch reflexes is one of the signs of good health that a physician examines when you undergo a "physical checkup." An easy place to test the stretch reflex is in the quadriceps muscle of the leg. The quadriceps is an **extensor muscle**, which means that it moves a limb out, away from the body (extends it). It is arranged so that its bottom tendon attaches to the bone of the lower leg (Figure 9.8). Thus, when it contracts, the lower leg swings out. The semitendinosus, on the other hand, is slung on the back of the thigh so that when it contracts, the lower leg is drawn back in. For that reason, the semitendinosus is called a **flexor muscle**. Flexors and extensors oppose one another, the one extending the leg and the other flexing it. The physician tests the stretch reflex of the extensor by hitting its tendon with a hammer. The tendon of the quadriceps actually attaches directly to the **patella**, a small, circular piece of bone that forms your "knee-cap"; the tendon from the patella attaches to the bone of the lower leg, but the parts act as if they were all one tendon. When this tendon is struck by the hammer, the lower leg swings up and out in a movement called the **patellar tendon reflex**. This is really a quadriceps stretch reflex in disguise. Hitting the tendon stretches it and pulls on the quadriceps, stretching it in turn. This action stimulates the spindle afferents within the muscle, and their connections with the motor neurons of the quadriceps immediately recontract that muscle. If the lower leg is free to swing, the contraction is seen as a slight extension of the limb.

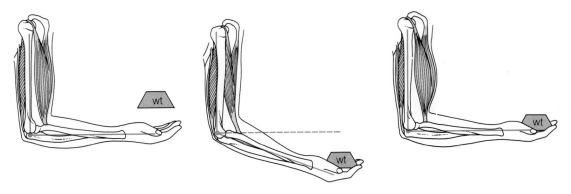

Figure 9.6 The stretch reflex is a mechanism for recontracting a muscle stretched by the application of a load. (Adapted from Carlson, 1981)

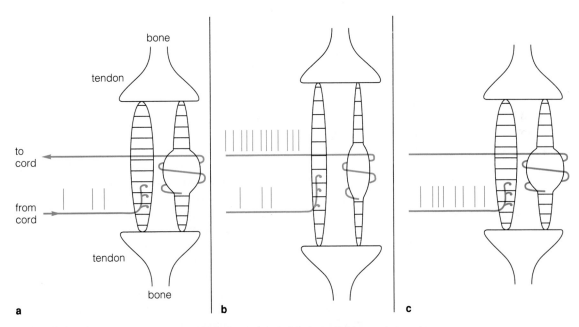

a   b   c

Figure 9.7 The action of the muscle spindle in passive stretch. In each frame, only two of the muscle's fibers are shown: a muscle fiber on the left and a spindle on the right. The primary afferent is wrapped around the receptor part of the spindle fiber, and the neuron fires when this central portion is stretched. (**a**) The muscle is slightly contracted by a few impulses in the motor fiber. The spindle is slack (unstretched) and unstimulated. (**b**) The muscle is stretched by the addition of a load or by the contraction of its antagonist. The spindle responds with a train of impulses that excite the motor neuron in the cord. (**c**) The motor neuron responds with a train of impulses that recontract the muscle and quiet the spindle. The short vertical lines over the nerve fibers represent the pattern of nerve impulses in each active fiber.

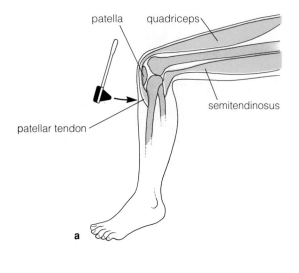

patella quadriceps

semitendinosus

patellar tendon

a

Figure 9.8 The patellar tendon reflex. (**a**) To elicit the reflex, the physician taps the tendon connecting the patella (kneecap) to the bone of the lower leg. (**b**) This stretches the quadriceps, eliciting its stretch reflex. (**c**) The sudden recontraction of the quadriceps against no load other than the leg itself makes the lower leg swing out.

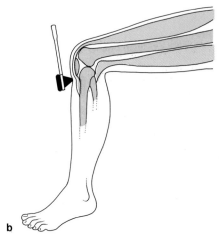

b

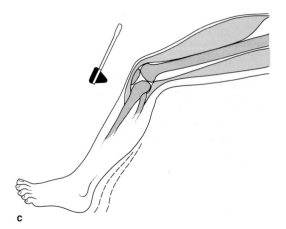

c

Tuning the Stretch Reflex with the Gamma Efferent
Engineers often make use of devices called **servo-mechanisms**, which respond to environmental changes (sensory feedback) by making adjustments designed to counteract some unwanted system change. A house thermostat, for example, turns the furnace on when the temperature drops to a specified level. Although the room temperature does have to drop a little below the thermostat setting to trip the switch, the fluctuation is minimal. You can see that the stretch reflex works in exactly the same way; a spindle replaces the thermometer, and stretch is sensed rather than temperature. The wiring of the thermostat turns on the furnace, whereas the cord circuit of the stretch reflex "turns on the muscle."

The stretch reflex fits the definition of a servo-mechanism in one other important respect. It is not very convenient to have a thermostat regulate your house temperature unless you can choose the temperature at which the furnace will turn on and be able to change this **set point** whenever the house needs to be warmer or cooler. The stretch reflex is equipped with a variable set point that increases or decreases the amount of stretch needed to trigger the reflex. The key element is a little motor neuron with its cell body in the ventral horn alongside the somas of the regular motor neurons. Its axon runs out the ventral root and goes to the same muscle as its neighbors, but its endings are not on a muscle fiber. Instead, it synapses with a muscle spindle fiber. It is called the **gamma efferent**. To distinguish which kind of motor neuron we are discussing, from now on the regular motor neurons will be called **alpha motor neurons**.

When the gamma efferent fires, the muscle spindle contracts, and this shorter length means that it will take less stretch to trigger the spindle afferent

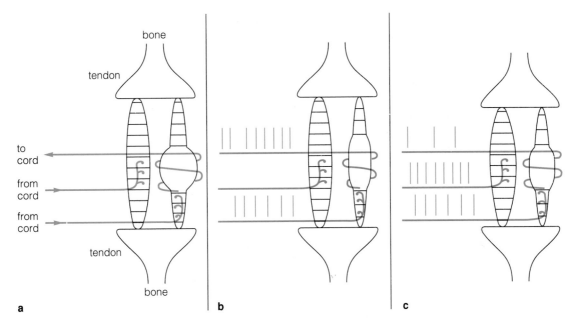

to cord

from cord

from cord

bone

tendon

tendon

bone

a   b   c

Figure 9.9 Control of spindle sensitivity by the gamma efferent. The nerve fiber at the top in each frame is the afferent from the muscle spindle; the middle fiber is the alpha motor neuron; and the bottom fiber is the gamma efferent, which connects with the muscle portions of the spindle. (**a**) The muscle is slightly stretched, but there is little tension on the spindle and the primary afferent is quiet. (**b**) The gamma efferent becomes active, increasing the sensitivity of the spindle by contracting its muscular ends. This stretches the sensory middle portion of the spindle and fires the afferent. Nerve impulses are indicated by short vertical lines over the appropriate nerve fiber. (**c**) The activity in the afferent has facilitated the alpha motor neuron in the cord (stretch reflex), and the alpha is now sending a train of impulses to the muscle fibers that contract them. Notice that this shortening takes some of the stretch off of the sensory part of the spindle and reduces the firing rate of the spindle afferent. The result of increasing the sensitivity of the spindle (by way of the gamma efferent) is to keep the muscle more strongly contracted.

(Figure 9.9). If this seems a bit confusing, keep in mind that the stimulus that triggers the spindle afferent is the stretching of the area of the muscle spindle that lies under the afferent endings rather than the stretch of the whole muscle spindle. This receptor area can be stretched in two different ways: by the lengthening of the entire muscle with the resulting stretch of the whole muscle spindle (Figure 9.7) or by the contraction of the muscular ends of the spindle fiber itself so that the shortening at both ends puts tension on the receptor area at the middle (Figure 9.9).

With the spindle fiber partly contracted, the muscle is allowed less stretch before the reflex circuit fires and commands it to recontract. It is just like changing the set point on the thermostat. If the gamma is firing at a very low rate, the spindle shortens just a little and remains relatively less sensitive to the stretch of its muscle. If the gamma is very active, the spindle is strongly contracted, and very little stretch is required to fire the spindle afferent and trigger the reflex.

Steady isometric contraction is termed **muscle tone**, or tension. Your muscle tone varies from one situation to another. When you are anxious, your muscles are quite tense (a high level of isometric contraction); when you are relaxed, the muscles are stretched out and slack. Could it be that higher brain centers may be changing the set point on your stretch reflexes by stimulating or inhibiting the gamma efferents? It is reasonably certain that the reticular formation adjusts muscle tone when commanded by the limbic system and other brain areas. It is probably the limbic system and reticular formation that induce tension headaches by keeping neck muscles at too high a level of musle tone for long periods. However, we are not quite sure that the reticular formation controls tone through the gamma efferent (Burke, 1978). Reticular facilitation may go straight to the alpha motor neurons instead. Another decade of research will probably be needed to sort this out.

Vestibular Senses

If you are going to do any moving around in your environment, you had better be able to tell what direction you are moving, how fast you are getting there, and which way is up. Vision helps supply some of this knowledge—especially to the conscious decision makers of the cortex—but the unconscious, automatic circuits of the motor system depend much more on information coming to the brain stem from the vestibular organs of the inner ear.

There are three vestibular capabilities: the sensing of gravity, linear acceleration, and rotary acceleration.

Gravity and Linear Acceleration Knowing up from down is basically a matter of being able to sense the direction of gravity. Out in space, away from the planetary source of gravity, there is no up or down. Through our lives, we learn to associate many visual stimuli with the pull of gravity, and eventually most of us come to mistakenly assume that up and down are visual experiences. But sky is up only because it is consistently associated with the direction away from gravity, and ground is down because it is in the direction of gravity. Here is a sensory capacity basic to our ability to orient ourselves in our physical world and to be able to maintain our balance while moving about; yet our classic (and erroneous!) view

that there are only five senses doesn't even mention a **gravitational sense**. Let's see how this obscure but vital sense works.

Vestibular organs are a collection of caves and tunnels running through the bone of the skull. The two largest globular cavities are the **saccule** and **utricle** (Figure 9.10), both of which contain a patch of receptor cells called the **macula** (Figure 9.11). The receptors of the macula are hair cells similar to those in the cochlea. Their **stereocilia** (hairs) protrude out of their top surface into a mass of jellylike substance, which is capped with tiny fragments of bone called **otoliths**. Neural currents are started in hair cells when stereocilia are bent, and otoliths have a hand in the bending. When you tilt your head to one side, you also tilt the macula. The relatively heavy otoliths are pulled by gravity so that the gelatinous mass capping the macula slumps downward, bending the stereocilia in the process. The cilia are arranged so that bending them in one direction triggers an excitatory current in the hair cell and increases its rate of spontaneous firing. Bending them in the opposite direction inhibits the cell and decreases its spontaneous rate. Thus, you are able to tell not only that you are bending your head but also to which side.

This same mechanism also gives us our ability to sense **linear acceleration**. As your car moves away from a stoplight, gathering speed, your saccule and utricle in each ear are giving your brain stem a constant update on your rate of acceleration. The maculas can sense acceleration because of the principle of inertia. The idea of **inertia** is that all objects tend to continue in their present state. If they are at rest, they resist being moved; if they are moving, they resist stopping. If you throw a ball across your yard, its motion is stopped by friction with the air and by the drag of gravity; but if you were to throw it in outer space, it would demonstrate its inertia very clearly by traveling on forever. When your car moves forward from the stoplight, it carries your body with it, but it does not carry all parts at an equal rate. Otoliths are denser than the jelly on which they sit and therefore have more inertia. The base of the macula with the hair cells is firmly attached to the skull and goes along with the car instantly, but the jelly allows the otoliths to lag behind a little. This

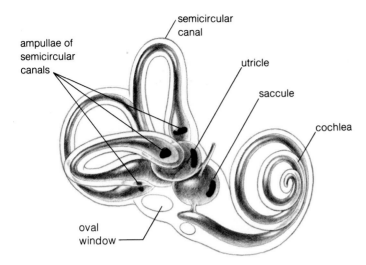

ampullae of
semicircular
canals

semicircular
canal

utricle

saccule

cochlea

oval
window

a

Figure 9.10 The vestibular organs of the inner ear. (**a**) The organs consist of three semicircular canals, the saccule, and the utricle. The dark patches within these cavities are where the receptors are found. (**b**) Each semicircular canal is arranged to detect rotation in a different plane. The three planes are at 90° from one another so that all three dimensions are covered. (Adapted from Creager, 1983)

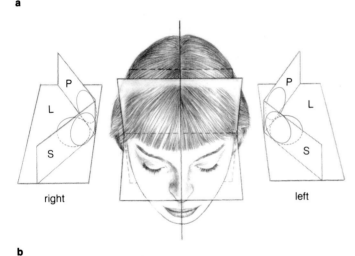

right

left

b

lag bends the stereocilia and stimulates the hair cells. The faster you accelerate, the more the otoliths get "left behind," and the more the cilia are bent. Greater bending produces greater stimulation, and the brain can tell slow acceleration from fast. If you stop accelerating at 35 mph and hold a steady speed, the otoliths finally have a chance to catch up with the rest of the macula, and the mass of jelly levels back up to its normal position on top. This stops the bending, and the hair cells stop responding. The macula cannot sense constant motion, only acceleration or deceleration.

When you put your foot on the brake, your skull decelerates right along with the car; but otoliths, sitting on their mass of jelly, obey the law of inertia by continuing their forward motion as long as they are able. They slide forward, bending the cilia as they go, and only ease back into their normal position when the car has come to a complete stop.

During acceleration (or deceleration) the macula is stimulated in the same way it is when you tilt your head. The brain must use past knowledge and visual stimulation to categorize this stimulation as movement rather than the pull of gravity. In some circum-

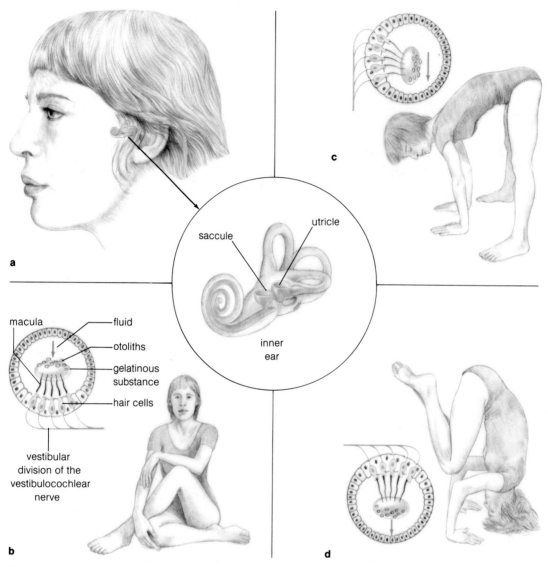

Figure 9.11 The saccule and utricle. (**a**) Position of the vestibular organs in the head. (**b**) The macula is a receptor organ found in the saccule and utricle. It consists of hair cells with stereocilia projecting into a gelatinous substance capped by otoliths. The cavities of saccule, utricle, and canals are filled with a fluid. (**c**) The weight of the otoliths pulls the cap of the macula in the direction of gravity, thus bending the stereocilia and starting a current in the receptor (hair) cells. (**d**) Position of macula when head is upside down. (Adapted from Creager, 1983)

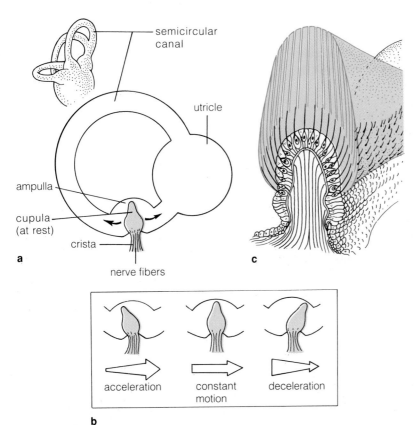

semicircular canal

utricle

ampulla

cupula (at rest)

crista

nerve fibers

a

b

c

acceleration

constant motion

deceleration

Figure 9.12 (**a**) A semicircular canal is filled with fluid. Near its base there is a swelling called the ampulla in which the receptor organ, the crista, is found. The cupula (cap) of the crista is gelatinous and can be deflected to either side by fluid flowing past it. Deflection bends the cilia embedded in it, and this action fires the hair cells of the crista. (**b**) As the head begins to rotate in the direction of the arrow, the crista is forced to plow through the standing fluid. This deflects the cupula in the direction opposite to rotation. When the head stops rotating, the cupula is again deflected by the fluid, which, although it lagged, did start to move along with the head. Because the fluid was moving in the same direction as the head rotation, the cupula is deflected in the direction of movement. (**c**) Structure of the crista. (**a** Adapted from Schiffman, 1976; **c** adapted from Wersäll & Bagger-Sjöbäck, 1974)

stances, however, there would be no difference. If you were on a spaceship moving at a constant speed, your body would be moving through space at the same speed as the ship, and you would float weightless with no feeling of up or down. When the ship started to accelerate, however, your inertia would cause your body to lag behind the ship's motion until the back wall of the cabin arrived at your position in space and started pushing you. From your perspective, the acceleration would be felt as gravity, and as you "fell" toward it, the back wall of the cabin would feel as though it had become the floor. In other words, if you are removed from your normal world where you have learned to interpret some macular signals as representing gravity and others as meaning acceleration, the difference is lost, and acceleration feels just like gravity.

Rotary Acceleration The word *linear* means along a line, and *rotary* refers to rotation. The sense of **rotary acceleration** comes into play most often as you turn your head. The vestibular organ for this sense is the **semicircular canals**, which are pictured in Figures 9.10 and 9.12. There is one canal in each ear for each of the three dimensions: up–down, front–back, and right–left. No matter what head motion you make, at least one of the canals senses it and responds. Thanks to this input (plus kinesthetic information from the neck muscles,) the brain knows the exact position of the head at every moment.

At the base of each canal is a swelling called the **ampulla** (Figures 9.10 and 9.12) in which the receptors are located. As with all inner-ear receptors, these are hair cells, and as in the macula, these cells have their stereocilia embedded in a gelatinous mass (the cupula). As you can see in Figure 9.12a, the cupula fills the ampulla so that there can be little flow of fluid past it. When you turn your head, the cupula turns immediately because it is attached to the skull, but the inertia of the fluid in the canal cannot be overcome so easily. In Figure 9.12b, the ampulla is moving to the right, and the fluid is resisting the push of the cupula, resulting in a deflection of the cupula to the left. This deflection only lasts as long as the head is accelerating because the inertia of the fluid is quickly overcome and, with the fluid moving the same speed as the skull, the pressure is taken off the cupula. The last step in Figure 9.12b shows that when the head comes to a stop, the whole process is repeated in reverse. The ampulla stops moving the moment the skull does, but the fluid continues its motion a moment longer (because of inertia); this means that the cupula is deflected in the direction of the movement.

Each time the cupula is pushed over to one side, the stereocilia embedded within it are bent and the hair cells stimulated. Hair cells trigger impulses in the vestibular branch of the VIIIth nerve, and the brain is appraised of the acceleration and deceleration of the head. Acceleration can be distinguished from deceleration because of the resting discharge of the hair cells. When nothing is stimulating them, the hair cells release transmitter periodically at a moderate rate. If the cilia are bent in one direction, the rate of discharge increases; bending in the opposite direction decreases it.

Nerve impulses from vestibular receptors go to the **vestibular nuclei** of the brain stem where connections are made to a wide variety of reflex arcs and to tracts leading up to the thalamus and cortex. Many of these reflex arcs are involved in postural reflexes such as the ones that occur as you turn to look at something behind you. When you turn, you cannot stand with equal weight on both legs. One leg must move forward a bit while the other takes all the weight and becomes a pivot point for the body. If you rotate to the left, then your weight shifts to your left leg, and the extensor muscles there must increase their level of isometric contraction to take on the extra load. If they don't do this, your leg buckles and you fall to one side. Stretch reflexes

help produce this leg muscle contraction but only after the shift in posture has already begun. The vestibular information from the semicircular canals can get extensor reflexes going even before the body has started to turn, thus eliminating any possible loss of balance.

There is one peculiar situation in which this set of postural reflexes is tricked into incorrectly contracting the wrong muscles with a resulting loss of equilibrium. Let's say you are on a ride at a theme park in which you spend several minutes being spun in the same direction. As you start to spin to the left, the cupula in one of your semicircular canals on each side is pushed over to the right by the inertia of the fluid in the canal. This sends a signal to the extensor muscles in your left leg, stiffening it to bear the expected load increase. The nervous system has misinterpreted the signal from the semicircular canals. Normally, a signal of such strength would only occur with a head turn of many degrees—one that would ordinarily have to be accompanied by a turn of the body in the same direction. It is quite an unusual circumstance for the whole body to be turned passively as is happening in the carnival ride. During the ride you probably do not notice at all that one leg is stiffened more than the other, but when the ride is over you certainly notice the aftereffects of the spin. When you step out of your seat and try to walk away, you find that you are dizzy and that you have to keep fighting a strong tendency to fall over to the left. What is the origin of this dizziness and loss of balance?

If you have been spinning for more than a few seconds, the fluid in your canals has caught up with your head and is moving at the same speed. Inertia keeps the fluid moving even when you have stopped. Because the cupula is attached to your skull, it stops its movement the moment the ride comes to a halt. This means that the still-moving fluid bends the cupula over as it passes by, thus firing the hair cells. Figure 9.12b shows that the cupula is bent in the opposite direction from that during acceleration. During acceleration the left leg reflexively stiffens, so with this opposite deflection, the right leg stiffens. As you walk away from the ride, then, your reflexes tend to push you over to the left because the right

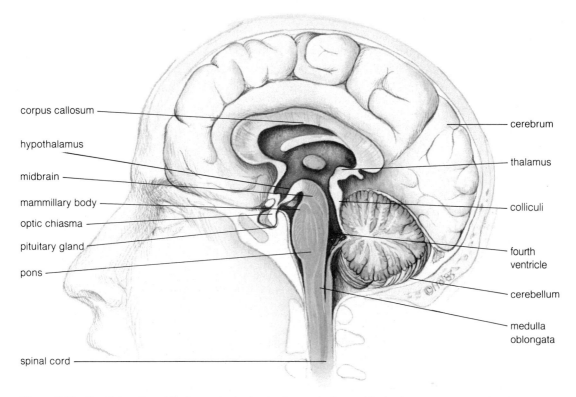

Figure 9.13 Saggital section of the human brain showing the cerebellum and brain stem. (Adapted from Fowler, 1984)

leg is more extended than it should be. The signals coming out of the semicircular canals at this time would, in more normal circumstances, indicate that you are rotating to the right, so they elicit a reflex extension in your right leg. The brain stem continues to compensate for nonexistent rotation until the fluid in the semicircular canals finally stops circulating. The fluid motion itself probably lasts only seconds, but the aftereffects of rotation may last a minute or more because the vestibular system adapted to the rotation and now must readapt to the lack of it (Schiffman, 1976). One of the charms of carnival rides, then, is that they are designed (unknowingly) to take advantage of some postural reflex connections that perform incorrectly under circumstances that never (or very rarely) occurred during the course of their evolution.

◼ Cerebellum

Halfway up the brain stem on its dorsal side lies a mystery. Its name, **cerebellum**, means "little brain," and a glance at its internal structure shows why (Figure 9.13). Just like the cerebrum, it consists of a cortex wrapped and folded around a set of deep-lying nuclei. It possesses two hemispheres connected by a large tract of fibers, the pons, that drops out of one side of the cerebellum and loops around the ventral side of the brain stem to reach the other side.

A great deal of research has been done on the cerebellum, and we now know its circuitry intimately, yet we are still baffled about the function of these circuits. In humans the structure makes up a fairly large proportion of the total brain, and a good guess would predict a terrible effect on behavior should it be lost. For that reason, it is more than a little disturbing to find that an animal deprived of its cerebellum can get around quite nicely, apparently still in possession of its entire repertoire of normal behaviors. The existence of this large, seemingly motor-related structure is apparently not vital to any kind of movement (Arshavsky et al., 1983).

Symptoms of Cerebellar Injury

Even after heavy cerebellar damage, a human can walk, talk, throw balls, drive a car, and eat. However, such an individual could definitely never be an athlete or a musician. The person's movements eventually get the job done, but they are slow and clumsy with much faltering and tremor in the hands. Walking is an unsteady business requiring the patient's concentration on every step. Clinicians term this disturbance of gait, **ataxia**. Extreme forms of ataxia are found in certain strains of laboratory mice bred especially for genetic defects that produce misgrowth in portions of their cerebellums (Caviness & Rakic, 1978). The various strains, each named for its major behavioral problem, are called leaners, lurchers, reelers, staggerers, and weavers, and each strain has its own form of scrambled cerebellar circuitry (Figure 9.14).

Besides the ataxia, there seems to be a **decomposition of movements** into the various individual muscle contractions of which movements are composed. Patients report that reaching for an object now requires thinking out the movements at each joint, one-by-one ("raise the arm," "now extend it," "now open the hand," "now close the fingers") (Eccles, 1977). This loss of automatic coordination between the individual circuits in the brain stem and cord could easily explain much of the observed clumsiness and ataxia. The need of the patient to concentrate on each part of the movement suggests that the motor cortex of the cerebrum is now being used to accomplish tasks usually handled by the cerebellum.

Soldiers who suffered gunshot wounds to the head in World War I have provided us with more insight into cerebellar function. Several of these patients had one cerebellar hemisphere destroyed with little or no damage to the other. Thus, in the

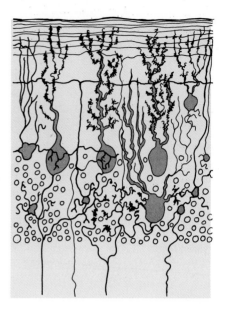

a

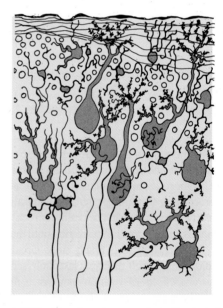

b

Figure 9.14 Diagrams of nerve cell arrangements in the cerebelli of two strains of mice: (**a**) normal and (**b**) reeler. (Adapted from Caviness & Rakic, 1978)

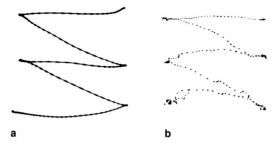

Figure 9.15 Records of hand movements of a war veteran with unilateral cerebellar damage. The records were made by attaching a light to the subject's finger and photographing him in a dark room as he pointed in sequence to each of six lights. (**a**) Record of the hand still served by an intact cerebellar hemisphere. (**b**) Record of hand served by damaged cerebellar hemisphere. (Adapted from Holmes, 1939)

study of their disability, they became their own controls (cited in Eccles, 1977). A light was attached to the finger of one such patient, and movies were made of his arm movements as he performed the task of pointing in sequence to each of six lights arranged in two columns. Figure 9.15a shows his performance with the hand being helped by the intact cerebellar hemisphere; Figure 9.15b is a record of the opposite hand, working without a cerebellar hemisphere. The second record reveals two common symptoms of cerebellar damage: the wobbly, jerky path of the arm's trajectory (**dysmetria**) and the tiny, back-and-forth oscillations of the finger at the end of each movement (**tremor**). Let's see how well modern theory of cerebellar function can explain symptoms of this sort.

Cerebellar Function

Because cord, brain stem, and cerebellar functions apparently play no part in conscious experience, most of us are entirely unaware of the dozens of tiny adjustments required just to move an arm from one position to another. Some of these adjustments involve altering the timing of contractions in the various muscles that produce the movement in such

a way that they do not conflict with one another. We know for sure that this sort of **coordination** is the work of the cerebellum, but we are not exactly sure how it goes about achieving this end. One really promising hypothesis revolves around the coordination of agonist and antagonist muscles.

Muscles whose contractions propel the body part in the direction of the intended movement are called **agonists** (AG-on-ists), whereas muscles pulling in the opposite direction are **antagonists** (an-TAG-on-ists). Extensors and flexors are antagonistic to one another. For example, let's say you want to bring your hand up to scratch your forehead—a movement that involves flexing your arm. The flexor that is slung between your shoulder and elbow, whose job it is to pull the forearm in toward the body, is the **biceps**. On the other side of your upper arm is the **triceps**, the extensor that pulls the forearm out, away from the body. If these two muscles pull against each other with equal force, your arm becomes rigid and goes nowhere. So, when you want to scratch your forehead, not only must the flexor be activated but the extensor must also be inhibited.

Figure 9.16 reveals some of how the nervous system accomplishes this task. As you start to scratch your forehead, alpha motor neurons for the biceps (flexor) are strongly facilitated by the motor cortex. They begin to contract the biceps. Simultaneously, gamma efferents for the biceps are facilitated so that muscle spindles also contract. As long as the spindle contraction keeps a little bit ahead of the muscle contraction, spindle afferents continue to fire, eliciting the stretch reflex in the biceps, thus aiding the contraction of the muscle. If you trace the fibers in Figure 9.16, you will see that spindle afferents in the biceps not only connect with alpha motor neurons for that muscle but also synapse with tiny interneurons that can inhibit alpha motor neurons of the antagonist muscle, the triceps. This suggests that when the biceps contracts, it automatically inhibits the triceps. Why should this happen? Does this mean that without the inhibitory control the triceps would contract and interfere with the movement?

Although the fact is not pictured in Figure 9.16, the triceps also has muscle spindles that react to muscle stretch. When the biceps contracts, the triceps must be passively stretched if the arm is to

Figure 9.16 Inhibition of an antagonist muscle by a spindle afferent of an agonist. One branch of the afferent stimulates the motor neuron controlling the biceps, while the other branch fires an internuncial that inhibits the triceps motor neuron. In this example, the biceps is pictured as the agonist and the triceps as the antagonist, but in other situations their roles are reversed. The triceps also has muscle spindles that connect with cord interneurons, some of which can inhibit the biceps motor neurons. (Adapted from Fowler, 1984)

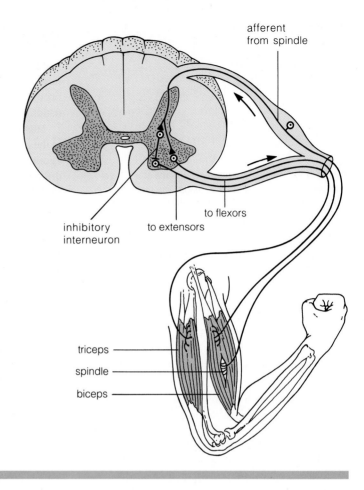

afferent from spindle

to flexors

inhibitory interneuron

to extensors

triceps

spindle

biceps

move. But this stretch is the perfect stimulus for triceps stretch reflexes, which immediately act to recontract the triceps and stop the movement as soon as it has begun. If something doesn't counteract the triceps stretch reflex, you are never going to get your hand up to your forehead. The answer, of course, is the inhibition of triceps motor neurons by spindle afferents from the biceps.

Notice that this is a two-way system; both biceps and triceps are capable of inhibiting each other through their stretch reflexes—an arrangement called **reciprocal inhibition**. How is it decided which muscle will contract and which will be inhibited when the circuits are set up so that each muscle can inhibit the other? It seems to be strictly a matter

of timing; the muscle that responds first gets the edge. Because the biceps starts its contraction before the triceps stretch reflex can start up, the triceps is inhibited before it can inhibit the biceps.

Sometimes, timing problems of this sort cannot be solved by the circuits within the cord and brain stem, and it is in these cases that help is obtained from an expert on timing—the cerebellum. Now you can understand more specifically what is meant when we say that the job of the cerebellum is coordination. At least in some cases, coordination refers to slowing the contraction of one muscle and/or speeding the contraction of another so that they cooperate, rather than conflict, with one another. The cerebellum accomplishes its task by taking in kinesthetic and vestibular data and using them to compute correction factors that slow a contraction here or speed one there. Notice that it has no direct control over the muscles themselves; it works exclusively as a "coordination consultant" to the reflex arcs, making slight but critical adjustments in the number of impulses per second by applying a few EPSPs or IPSPs at the right moments.

When disease or accident results in the loss of the cerebellum, essential timing adjustments are lost, and the other parts of the motor system begin to "step on each other's toes." The symptom of **intention tremor** is an example. Oddly enough, tremor resulting from cerebellar damage is never present when the patient is at rest or starting a movement. It only appears as the movement is nearing completion and is especially evident when the body part must arrive at a fairly precise location. For example, recall the movements of the war veteran (Figure 9.15) who was required to point first at one light, then another. The movements usually started off well enough, but midway through, the finger would often begin to move in the wrong direction, then return. At the very end of each movement, this wavering became so rapid that it could be called tremor. Flament and colleagues (1984) have given us an explanation of this phenomenon.

Tremor occurs because of a tendency to overshoot at the end of a movement. A moving limb gathers inertia as it accelerates. It does not stop its movement automatically when the muscle finishes contracting; it must be actively stopped at the correct point. This braking at the end of a movement is accomplished by the antagonist. The biceps contracts to move your hand toward your forehead, and midway through this movement the triceps begins to contract to brake the movement. If the antagonist muscle begins to contract at exactly the right moment, the limb stops exactly on target; too soon or too late produces under- or overshoot. Using kinesthetic information from the shoulder and elbow joints plus spindle input from the biceps, the cerebellum calculates the exact moment to begin braking.

With the cerebellum missing, braking eventually occurs anyway, probably because the increasing stretch of the triceps produces a greater and greater output from its spindles, which eventually overwhelms the inhibition from the biceps. But this activation of the triceps by its stretch reflex obviously comes too late and overshoot occurs, allowing the hand to come up too far. The more the hand is pulled in toward the body by the biceps, the more the triceps is stretched. When the triceps is finally freed from inhibition, it has built up so much facilitation from its muscle spindle that, instead of just pulling the arm to a clean stop, the triceps actually reverses the direction of motion and starts the hand moving back away from the body. Sensing the error, the cortex activates biceps spindles that then recontract the biceps to stop this backward movement; but again there is overshoot, and the whole process repeats itself (Flament et al., 1984). Left to themselves, antagonistic stretch reflexes are never able to balance against one another to bring the hand to a steady, pointing position; the best the patient can produce is a series of miniature back-and-forth movements in the vicinity of the target. If the cerebellum were available to briefly inhibit one of these two competing arcs, the tremor would disappear.

The correct timing of the braking signal from the cerebellum is different for different loads and different body parts. It is specific to each separate movement of each body part. This means that there are thousands and thousands of different combinations of movement, body part, and load, and each combination requires a different braking signal from the cerebellum. Could all those combinations possibly be prewired into the cerebellum by the genes? That is very doubtful. The alternate hypothesis, that the cerebellum learns each combination through experience, has been incorporated into several modern theories of cerebellar function (Ito, 1974). This sort of memorization of the hundreds of thousands of combinations of movement, force, and direction sounds exactly like the sort of thing that might be occurring in the brain of a musician or gymnast as the correct moves are practiced repeatedly. Perhaps, those of us who have limited athletic skills, or no ability with a musical instrument despite lessons, have only mediocre cerebellums and benefit less from practicing movements. A normal but poorly functioning cerebellum might produce difficulty in thousands of everyday experiences like putting a key into the lock on first try, climbing the stairs without stumbling, reaching for and grasping a glass of water without spilling it, and so forth. Only a few experiments have been done on the possibility of cerebellar learning (see, for example, Andersen, 1982), but interest is growing, and the next decade should decide whether the concept is a reality.

■ Locomotion

The neuron networks that enable us to move about in our environment extend from the most primitive parts of the nervous system up to the most advanced levels. They have inspired more research than any other aspect of motor organization and have been studied in creatures as diverse as cats, crayfish, worms, fish, sea snails, and humans. Further, the general principles discovered are probably not limited to locomotion but apply to all aspects of motor control.

The Roots of Walking

A newborn human infant can "walk" if you help her. A day-old baby, supported under the arms with feet just touching a solid surface, shows clear stepping motions, alternating one leg, then the other, in a preview of behavior yet to come. Why does this strange capacity exist? These stepping motions reveal the existence of genetically determined motor circuits that provide the "building blocks" from which behaviors like walking will be constructed as the nervous system matures. Two of these motor organizations laid out by the genes are the **extensor thrust reflex** and the **stepping reflex**, and it has been suggested that they are the basic units out of which the behavior of walking is put together.

When pressure is applied to the sole of the foot, the leg stiffens into a column that resists the push—the extensor thrust reflex. Its purpose is to support the weight of the body when the center of gravity is shifted over that leg. The stepping reflex is the flexion counterpart of the extensor thrust. When pressure stimulation is *removed* from the sole of the foot, the leg tends to flex so that the foot is raised into a

stepping position. It is easier to elicit these two reflexes in the newborn if you rock the baby slightly from side to side so that the center of gravity shifts from one leg to another, alternately applying pressure to the sole of each foot and then removing it.

What is it, then, that the infant is learning when he learns to walk? First, learning may be necessary to weld the two reflexes together into a unit that automatically lifts one foot and then the other in a steady cycle. Second, to shift from one foot to another, you must shift your center of gravity from one side to another while also shifting it forward a little to give you forward propulsion. It has often been said that, in humans, walking is a series of arrested falls. One clinician who treats patients with corpus striatum damage has suggested that these large motor structures above the brain stem play a part in the appropriate shifts in center of gravity. Some of his patients with damage to the corpus striatum of one hemisphere get "stuck" when they try to start walking and simply cannot seem to get their legs to go. However, when they carry some heavy weight (like a chair) on their bad side, they are able to walk. Apparently, the remaining corpus striatum on the undamaged side can shift the weight in one direction but not back in the other—the weight of the chair must do that. One of the things the infant must learn, then, is to be able to shift the center of gravity around so that the appropriate reflexes are elicited. Put in another way, the baby must first learn to use vestibular input to control the extensor thrust reflexes in both legs well enough to maintain balance while standing. Then the child must learn how to override the vestibular influence enough to shift all weight to one leg at a time—a much more difficult balancing act. After that comes all the learning about walking on the slant, on different surfaces, and around obstacles.

The idea that learning to walk is a matter of learning to organize reflexes into a sequence is appealing, but as an explanation, it falls short because it cannot account for all research data. A great deal of work has been done with cats in recent years that suggests that reflex arcs are not the only type of circuits to be found in the spinal cord. A decorticate cat is placed in a support harness on a treadmill where it proceeds to walk while records are made of the activity of muscles and cord neurons (Grillner & Zangger, 1984). Lacking a cortex, the cat has no voluntary movements; the walking is elicited strictly by the motion of the treadmill. The reflex explanation of this walking would say that correct reflex is triggered when the treadmill moves a leg backward, but it is a little difficult to see how this simple backward motion of all paws simultaneously could trigger the alternating, right–left sequence of walking.

More trouble for the reflex explanation is produced by a further step in this experiment. The cat now undergoes spinal cord surgery in which the dorsal roots serving its legs are cut. If you recall the anatomy of the spinal cord, this operation severs only the sensory fibers because the motor fibers are almost all in the ventral root. The process is termed **deafferentation** (DEE-AFF-er-en-TA-shun). This procedure allowed the very important discovery that deafferented cats walked on the treadmill nearly as well as they did before they lost the sensory halves of their reflex arcs (Grillner & Wallén, 1985).

To obtain an objective record of how well the deafferented cat could walk, electrodes were pasted on the legs to record the electrical potentials produced by the muscles as they contracted. A recording of this sort is called an **electromyogram (EMG)** (ee-LEK-tro-MY-o-gram). Figure 9.17a and b show the EMG typical of cats with and without sensory input from their limbs as they walked on the treadmill. Notice that the sequence of hip–toe–ankle–knee is relatively undisturbed by the loss of the reflex arcs (Grillner & Wallén, 1985). (However, these particular record samples do show the knee muscles starting earlier in the deafferentation data.) Figure 9.17c shows the rotations of the various limb parts around their joints during a single step. You can see the sequence of hip–toe–ankle–knee movements in the first four frames that show up on the EMG record. (Remember that cats walk on their toes; the joint halfway up the picture of the leg is the ankle.) The data do not show reflexes to be entirely irrelevant to locomotion. In the deafferented cat, the pattern would often break down after a minute or two, the legs getting in each other's way and failing to coordinate, but some basic circuit obviously was present in the cord that could organize the correct sequence of muscle contractions even without sensory input.

It did not take long for researchers to postulate the existence of such circuits and to name them central pattern generators.

Central Pattern Generators

Central pattern generators (CPGs) are networks of interconnected neurons that collectively control a set of muscles needed to produce a movement or sequence of movements. The term *central* refers to the idea that the pattern of contractions can be generated from within the nervous system itself without need of sensory input. CPGs have been studied mostly in reference to cyclic behaviors like swimming (fish), walking, and scratching (cat). Much of the work has been done with very simple nervous systems like those of insects and crayfish because it is so much easier to work out the circuitry in those species. In fact, in some simple animals like worms and sea snails, individual neurons are actually recognizable from one animal to the next, enabling the same cell to be studied in a whole group of subjects. The crayfish, for instance, has so few neurons that most of them have been named and studied individually. An example would be cell C109, which has been found to be a sensory neuron that responds to eyestalk movement. C109 is found in the same place doing the same job in every crayfish studied (Horridge, 1968). In mammals not only are the nervous systems more complex by many orders of magnitude but also the behaviors themselves are far more complex in terms of number of muscles involved and the number of different possible combinations of contractions. It is impossible to know if a particular cell under study has exactly the same input and output connections as an analogous cell in the nervous system of another subject, thus mapping the circuitry of mammalian CPGs has yet to be accomplished. At this time, we are getting more of the basic concepts of how CPGs operate from our study of insects than from mammals. When you get down to the level of nerve cells, it's hard to tell an insect from a human!

We do have some fairly secure notions about CPGs in mammals, however. Most of the cells of a CPG involved in walking would be within the spinal cord gray matter. They are the tiny interneurons found between the dorsal and ventral horns. To pro-

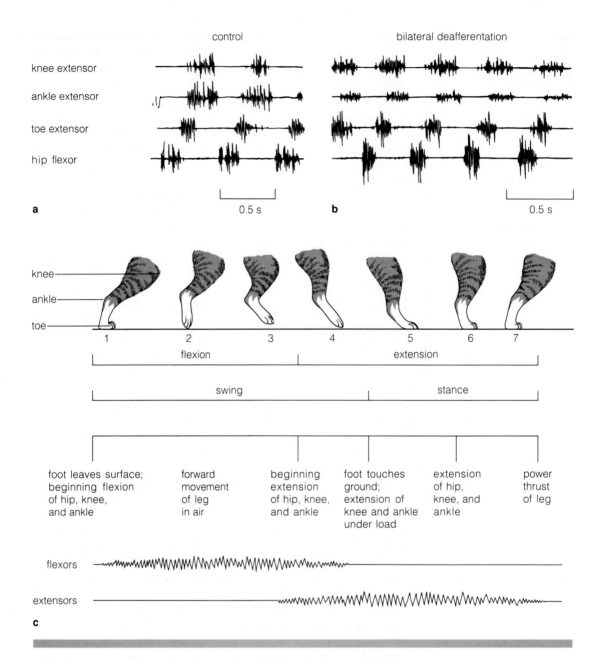

control

knee extensor

ankle extensor

toe extensor

hip flexor

a

0.5 s

bilateral deafferentation

b

0.5 s

knee
ankle
toe

1   2   3   4   5   6   7

flexion   extension

swing   stance

foot leaves surface;
beginning flexion
of hip, knee,
and ankle

forward
movement
of leg
in air

beginning
extension
of hip, knee,
and ankle

foot touches
ground;
extension of
knee and ankle
under load

extension
of hip,
knee, and
ankle

power
thrust
of leg

flexors

extensors

c

duce a movement in a structure as complex as a mammalian leg, with its many joints and scores of muscles, the CPG must be able to influence the motor neurons controlling agonists, antagonists, and synergists.

Synergists are muscles whose contractions aid the agonist muscle by pulling a body part in the same direction. For example, when you flex your index finger, most of the movement is produced by the long flexor muscle, but near the point of extreme flexion as the fingertip nears the palm, another muscle—the interosseous—begins to add its contrac-

Figure 9.17 EMGs (records of the electrical activity in contracting muscles) made from a cat as it walked. (**a**) Before deafferentation; and (**b**) after deafferentation. The time marker below the record indicates how long 0.5 second is on each record. The four EMGs are from a knee extensor, an ankle extensor, a toe extensor, and a hip flexor—all in one leg. Record **b** covers four steps. The pattern of contractions persists even after removal of stimulus input. In **c** the flexions and extensions that produced the EMGs are shown. The first EMG burst in the control record **a** comes from the hip flexors, and the resulting movement is shown in frames 1 and 2 in **c**. The next EMG burst is generated by the toe extensors, and the movement can be seen by comparing the toe position in frames 2 and 3. The knee and ankle extensors begin firing simultaneously in the control record. The movement they produce is seen in frame 4. (**a** and **b** Adapted from Grillner & Zangger, 1984; **c** adapted from Shepherd, 1983 and Wetzel & Stuart, 1976)

tion. The main job of the interosseous is to move the index finger away from the middle finger (Figure 9.18), but in the case of full flexion of the index finger (a completely different movement), it acts as a synergistic muscle. Thus, a single muscle can be both an agonist and a synergist. Many muscles can also participate as antagonists, having three different roles depending on what movement is being performed.

So, when you flex your index finger enough to touch the palm with the fingertip, your brain is presumably activating a CPG somewhere in the upper levels of your spinal cord, and this network of interneurons has connections to motor neurons for both the long flexor muscle and the interosseous. Furthermore, neurons within the CPG are organized so that the ones that facilitate the long flexor motor cells fire first, while those controlling the interosseous motor neurons wait until the movement is almost complete. In other words, the CPG can produce a temporal pattern of facilitation, hence the name central *pattern* generator.

When a whole limb is moved, many CPGs have to act in coordination with one another. For a cat to walk, the CPGs for each limb have to be organized into a temporal pattern of activation (Figure 9.19). Note how the pattern changes as the cat goes from walking to trotting. An increase in speed, then, involves much more than just harder muscle contractions. It calls for a reorganization of the timing of CPG elicitation. Possibly, each pattern (walk, trot, pace, gallop) has its own CPG in the brain stem that controls lower-level CPGs in the cord. As you can

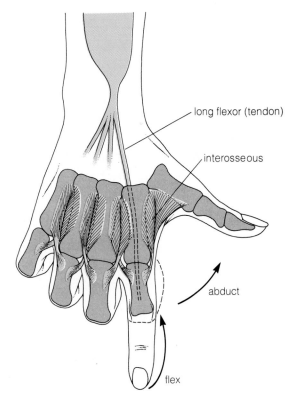

long flexor (tendon)

interosseous

abduct

flex

Figure 9.18 Example of synergy between two muscles, the long flexor and the interosseous. The main job of the interosseous is to abduct the index finger, but it also helps the long flexor in the final stage of flexing the index finger into the palm. (Adapted from Desmedt, 1980)

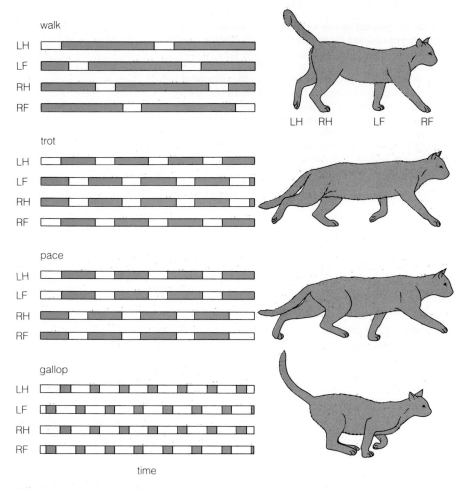

walk

LH
LF
RH
RF

LH RH   LF   RF

trot

LH
LF
RH
RF

pace

LH
LF
RH
RF

gallop

LH
LF
RH
RF

time

Figure 9.19 Four mammalian gaits. As the cat speeds up from a walk to a trot to a pace to a gallop, it must alter the pattern with which it moves its legs. This pattern is called a *gait*. Each gait must have its own separate neural organization in the nervous system. (Adapted from Pearson, 1976)

see, it takes an enormous organizational effort just to walk a few steps. It is small wonder that roughly half of your nervous system is related directly to generating or controlling movements.

If locomotion is to be explained with the functioning of central pattern generators, then what happens to the reflex explanation based on the extensor thrust and stepping reflex? When the act of walking is examined in the detail needed to describe Grillner's CPGs, it becomes obvious that a combi-

nation of two simple reflexes is too simplistic a theory. One way out of this dilemma is to propose that most reflex arcs are much more complicated than we ever thought. Perhaps, instead of connecting into one or two interneurons, the sensory neuron feeds its signal into a collection of CPGs. The decision as to which CPG will respond to the afferent input would be made by higher centers in the cortex, corpus striatum, and brain stem. So the old idea of cord circuits consisting of afferent neurons connecting with interneurons that connect with motor neurons (reflex arcs) may be supplanted with the idea that afferents connect with CPGs that connect with motor neurons. Thus, we would have a continuum of sensory–motor connections ranging from the ultra-simplicity of the stretch reflex with its two-neuron arc through arcs having CPGs as their central element to arcs containing all the CPGs for a limb.

If this line of thinking has any truth to it, the so-called extensor thrust reflex (when we understand its circuitry) will probably turn out to be the extensor half of the CPG working under the control of external stimuli (i.e., the pressure to the sole of the foot). In other words, the reflex explanation was not really wrong; it was just an oversimplified early version of our current understanding in which we recognize that leg extension is generated by an independent cord circuit but that this CPG still needs to be controlled by stimulus input (Delcomyn, 1980). There is evidence for the notion that CPGs respond to stimulus input and use it to modify their timing. A dogfish shark deprived of its forebrain can still swim; apparently, the movements are produced by an organization of CPGs in the cord. Delcomyn (1980) tells us that if you grab the shark's tail and start to move it back and forth at a faster speed (anything for science!), the nervous system begins to pick up the new rhythm and shift to it. The timing of CPG actions is apparently modified to some extent by stimulus input.

The deafferentation experiments showed that CPGs were capable of producing walking all on their own, but that does not mean that they would produce serviceable walking if they were all you had. The stimulus input must still be used to alter the timing of the CPG output to take into account the variations of the real terrain over which you must walk. Your walking CPGs might take you down a smooth-floored hallway quite nicely, but when you arrive at the stairs and your foot goes down into blank space, all internal timing must be altered. As the right foot comes down on empty air, pressure receptors in the right foot fail to send in their sensory message signaling contact with firm ground. This signal could be used to temporarily delay the shift to the next phase of the cycle when the flexors take over in the left leg and the extensors in the right leg (Grillner, 1981). A "phase-

delay" circuit of this sort has been shown to exist in the cat (Stein, 1978). When you step off with your right foot, your left leg is still supporting all your weight; if it began its flexion phase before your right foot found the stair step, you would lose your balance and probably find yourself at the bottom of the stairs sooner than anticipated.

The idea that sensory input is necessary to time the initiation of activity in each CPG fits precisely with what we know about programming computers to make robots move. A great deal of cross-fertilization goes on between computer science and neuroscience, and some of it can be seen in Figure 9.20, which shows a flowchart for a motor program designed to produce stepping.

A **program** is the sequence of steps needed to bring about some specific result. This particular program raises and lowers a foot. Trace it through from beginning to end, and you will see that it is a cyclic process that can repeat any number of times. Not only does the program loop back on itself, it also is constructed of a series of smaller loops. For example, the loop "start flexion → is leg off the ground?" continues to cycle endlessly until the sensory feedback indicates that the leg is off the ground. Then the program can proceed to its next phase. The question *"Is leg off the ground?"* represents a matching process between a desired input pattern and the actual sensory pattern. The comparison between the stored pattern and the current sensory pattern of impulses would probably occur in the dorsal horn of the cord. A match between the two patterns would be needed to inhibit the ongoing CPG and allow the next one in the sequence to take over. Thus, when the sensory endings in the foot indicate that pressure has been removed from the sole and kinesthetic receptors in the knee indicate a flexion (together with a number of other sensory inputs also signaling that the foot is off the ground), then the program proceeds to the next loop—that is, to the next CPG. There is a great advantage in thinking about the motor system in this computer-program framework. It tends to clarify the logic of how the system must be organized to achieve its ends. Before we leave this set of ideas, let's see how the stepping program fits into the larger context.

At the top of Figure 9.20, there is an arrow coming

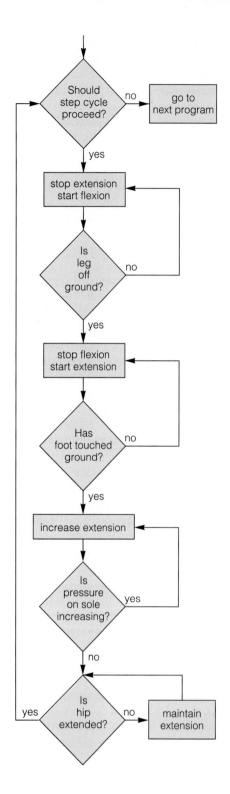

Figure 9.20 A flowchart for a motor program designed to produce stepping. (Adapted from MacKay, 1980)

into this program from a program that immediately preceded it (perhaps one for standing, running, or turning) and an outgoing arrow to the program that will run off next. A program like this one for stepping is organized by the genes, by learning, or by both and then called up whenever that particular behavior is needed. In computer language, such a standard sequence that fits as a unit into a great number of larger programs is called a **subroutine**. CPGs are subroutines.

We have seen that CPGs probably act like loops in a computer program and are thus switched on and off by sensory input. But sensory input is not the only source of control over CPGs. How does the cerebellum exert its smoothing influence over behavior? Perhaps part of this influence is achieved through coordinating the timing of the activity in the CPGs. Without the cerebellum, walking can still occur, but the limbs tend to bump into one another and the feet are frequently placed poorly (Grillner & Wallén, 1985). The brain stem undoubtedly also exerts considerable influence over CPGs, especially from an area of reticular formation located at the pontine–midbrain border called the **mesencephalic locomotor region**. If this region in cats or primates is stimulated electrically, walking is produced; if the current is increased, the pace speeds (Grillner & Wallén, 1985).

Above the brain stem are two major structures that influence movement, probably through their connections with cord CPGs: the corpus striatum and the motor cortex. These parts of the brain are our focus in the next two sections.

■ Corpus Striatum

Between the cortex and the thalamus is a group of large nuclei called the **corpus striatum**. In the brain of the reptile and bird, these nuclei plus a bit of primitive limbic cortex are the highest-level processors. Mammals went on to evolve the neocortex, thereby relegating their corpus striatum to a subordinate position. Normal functioning of these nuclei, however, seems to be just as important to the mammal as it is to the bird. Damage to the corpus striatum produces grievous symptoms, as we will see.

Anatomy of the Corpus Striatum

The corpus striatum consists of caudate nucleus, putamen, and globus pallidus. The **caudate nucleus** is the largest nucleus of the corpus striatum, with a head lying beneath the cortex of the frontal lobe and a tail (*caudate* = having a tail) that extends posteriorly toward the occipital lobe and then swings down and forward into the temporal lobe (Figure 9.21). The head forms a wall of the anterior end of the lateral ventricle.

The **putamen** (Figure 9.21) is split off from the caudate by a band of white matter called the **internal capsule**. Recall that white matter consists of axons of cell bodies found in gray matter. Many of the axons that make up the portion of the internal capsule between the caudate and putamen come from cell bodies within those two structures and the overlying cortex. Simply because axons happen to exit the structures at that point doesn't mean that this is a true boundary for either the caudate or the putamen. Indeed, they may be two portions of the same structure artificially divided by the internal capsule. Because they do seem to share some common functions, the caudate and putamen are frequently spoken of as a unit and called the **striatum** (stry-A-tum).

The **globus pallidus** is the light-colored gray matter (*pallidus* = pale) lying just medial to the putamen. In Figure 9.21 get your bearings by tracing this sequence from lateral to medial: putamen, globus pallidus, internal capsule, thalamus, and third ventricle. Next look at Figure 9.22, a frontal section cut through the frontal lobes and tips of the temporal lobes. Find the corpus callosum with the lateral ventricles right underneath. The lateral wall of each ventricle is formed by the caudate nucleus. Then look across the internal capsule and find the putamen and globus pallidus, which lie more ventrally. In a frontal section, those two structures form a wedge shape split into three parts by bands of white matter. The

outermost portion is the putamen, and the smaller, inner two parts form the globus pallidus. The medial tip of the globus pallidus nearly contacts the fibers of the optic tract at the base of the brain.

Just below the frontal section of Figure 9.22 is a cross section of the midbrain from near the top of the brain stem. On that section is the **substantia nigra** (sub-STAN-she-uh NIG-rah), a nucleus whose dark coloration earned it the Latin name for *black substance*. Although the substantia nigra is not a part of the corpus striatum, it works in such a close relation with that structure that it must be discussed here.

Symptoms of Damage to the Corpus Striatum

One of the greatest mysteries of the nervous system is the function of the corpus striatum. The majority of opinion holds that it is a group of strictly motor structures (see, for example, Marsden, 1980), whereas others point to its strong connections with sensory and planning (prefrontal) areas of the cortex and suggest that it has a cognitive function (Cools et al., 1981; Öberg & Divac, 1981) of the reasons for the persisting controversy and mystery is the fact that comparatively little pure, basic research has been done on the corpus striatum. Much of the current theorizing about the functions of this set of structures has come from observations of clinical symptoms exhibited by victims of corpus striatum disease and from research directed at trying first to understand the diseases; basic research has been scarce. In fact, the whole research approach to the study of this set of structures has been dominated by two, incurable, terminal diseases of the brain: Huntington's disease and Parkinson's disease.

Huntington's Disease The central symptom of this disorder is **chorea**, the presence of continual, involuntary jerky movements of the face, tongue, extremities, and, occasionally, the trunk and respiratory muscles (*choreia* is Greek for dance). The twitches and jerks are especially apparent when the patient is trying to hold a posture or make a voluntary movement. The usual age of onset is between 35 and 45, and the symptoms steadily worsen over a course of roughly 15 years until the person dies (often from pneumonia). If the disease appears during child-

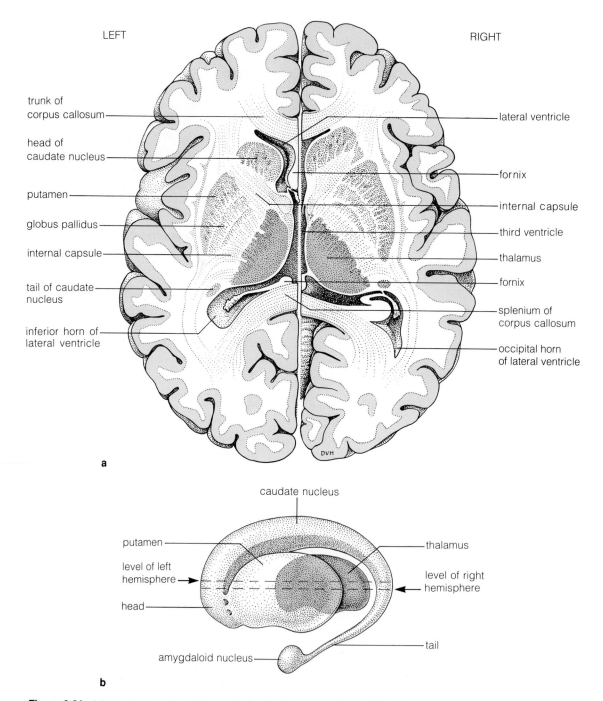

LEFT   RIGHT

trunk of
corpus callosum ——————————   —————— lateral ventricle

head of
caudate nucleus ——————————   —————— fornix

putamen ——————————   —————— internal capsule

globus pallidus ——————————   —————— third ventricle

internal capsule ——————————   —————— thalamus

tail of caudate ——————————   —————— fornix
nucleus

inferior horn of ——————————   —————— splenium of
lateral ventricle   corpus callosum

                                              —————— occipital horn
                                                       of lateral ventricle

a

                            caudate nucleus

putamen ——————————   —————— thalamus

level of left
hemisphere ————→   ←———— level of right
                                                       hemisphere

head ——————————

amygdaloid nucleus ——————————   —————— tail

b

Figure 9.21 (**a**) Horizontal sections of the brain showing the corpus striatum. The right hemisphere is cut at a lower level than the left. (**b**) Schematic illustration showing the interrelationship of the caudate nucleus, the thalamus, the putamen, and the amygdaloid nucleus. (Adapted from Netter, 1962)

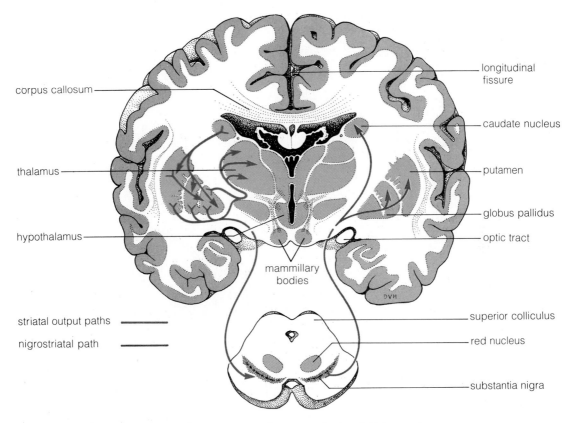

corpus callosum

longitudinal fissure

caudate nucleus

thalamus

putamen

globus pallidus

hypothalamus

optic tract

mammillary bodies

striatal output paths

nigrostriatal path

superior colliculus

red nucleus

substantia nigra

Figure 9.22 A frontal section of the human brain cut near the anterior tips of the temporal lobes to show the corpus striatum. Because the entire brain stem is posterior to this section, the cross section of midbrain had to be added separately at the bottom to show the substantia nigra. The nigrostriatal pathway is shown on the right, the outputs from the corpus striatum to thalamus and substantia nigra on the left. (Adapted from Duvoisin, 1976)

hood, death occurs in only a few years; late onset of the disease, in the 60s or 70s, leads to such a prolonged deterioration that death is usually from some completely unrelated source (Bird, 1978).

A loss of nerve cells throughout the brain is the cause of symptoms in Huntington's disease, with the most significant loss occurring within the corpus striatum. Specifically, it seems to be the neurons that project back down to the substantia nigra that die. These cells use GABA as their transmitter and act to inhibit nigral cells (Bird, 1978). The transmitter dopamine also is involved because drugs that raise dopamine levels in the brain intensify the chorea, whereas those that lower dopamine levels (e.g.,

reserpine or chlorpromazine) decrease the symptoms (Pincus & Tucker, 1978). This may give us an important clue to the function of the corpus striatum. If you trace the connections in Figure 9.22, you will see that the striatum (caudate plus putamen) projects to the substantia nigra, which projects back up to both parts of the striatum. The nigrostriatal projection (substantia nigra to striatum) consists of cells that use dopamine as their transmitter. Therefore, it looks as though the loss of the striatal neurons with their inhibitory transmitter (GABA) releases the nigrostriatal cells from control, and their resulting overactivity produces the choreic movements (Mann et al., 1980).

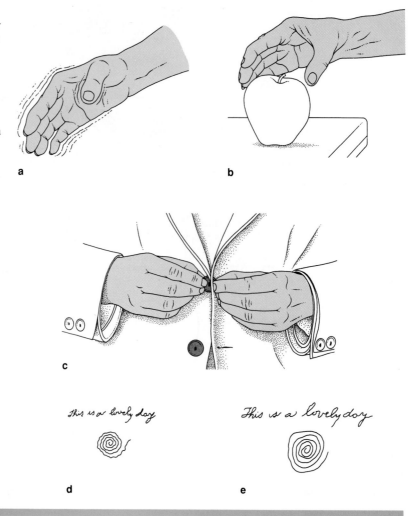

Figure 9.23 Symptoms of Parkinson's disease: (**a**) tremor of one hand is a frequent early manifestation of parkinsonism; (**b**) tremor often improves or disappears with purposeful function; (**c**) difficulty in performing simple manual functions may be initial symptom; (**d**) writing shows micrographia and effects of tremor; (**e**) improvement after I-DOPA therapy. (Adapted from paintings by Frank Netter in Duvoisin, 1976)

a

b

c

This is a lovely day

This is a lovely day

d

e

The origin of the disease, the gradual death of cells in the corpus striatum, is not well understood. We know that it is the result of some sort of genetic error because it is clear that Huntington's disease is inherited, but the specific mechanism remains obscure. One hypothesis is that the body may begin mistakenly forming antibodies against a particular protein that is fairly specific to striatal neurons and thus bring about its own destruction in what is termed an **autoimmune disease** (Bird, 1978).

Parkinson's Disease   Usually appearing about age 50, Parkinson's disease progresses for 15–20 years,

gradually bringing the patient into a condition of complete invalidism. There is no cure. In the first stages, a slight tremor begins in one hand, and the patient finds increasing difficulty in performing everyday tasks like buttoning clothes. As the disease progresses, spontaneous involuntary movements like swinging the arms during walking, blinking the eyes, altering facial expression, and gesturing with the hands tend to decrease and finally disappear altogether. Voluntary movements become very slow, deliberate, and difficult to initiate. The posture becomes bent forward, and walking is accomplished with small, shuffling steps while the hands tremble

Figure 9.24 Stages in the development of parkinsonian symptoms. (**a**) Stage 1: unilateral involvement; blank facies; affected arm in semiflexed position with tremor; patient leans to unaffected side. (**b**) Stage 2: bilateral involvement with early postural changes; slow, shuffling gait with decreased excursion of legs. (**c**) Stage 3: pronounced gait disturbances and moderate generalized disability; postural instability with tendency to fall. (**d**) Stage 4: significant disability; limited ambulation with assistance. (**e**) Stage 5: complete invalidism; patient confined to bed or chair; cannot stand or walk even with assistance. (Adapted from paintings by Frank Netter in Duvoisin, 1976)

(Figures 9.23 and 9.24). This is the movie caricature of a person in old age, but these are not normal aging symptoms. They are definitely the result of corpus striatum dysfunction. The chief symptoms of Parkinson's disease then are **bradykinesia** (slowness and deliberateness of movement), **rigidity** (stiff limbs and postures with little spontaneous movement), and **tremor at rest** (trembling of hands that diminishes during voluntary hand movement) (Larsen & Calne, 1982).

In the final stages of Parkinson's disease, the person suffers loss of balance and falls too frequently to permit walking. This does not seem to be a vestibular defect; rather it appears to be an inability to maintain the continual extensor contractions that maintain upright posture. Little voluntary movement is left, and the victim simply sits or lies throughout the day. Eventually, even with excellent nursing care, the patient usually dies of an infection such as pneumonia (Duvoisin, 1976).

The cause of parkinsonian symptoms is the death of dopaminergic neurons that form the **nigrostriatal pathway**. Nigrostriatal neurons have their cell bodies in the substantia nigra and extend their axons forward through the hypothalamus and up into the corpus striatum where they synapse (Figure 9.22). There does not seem to be a good theory of what starts the cell death in the substantia nigra, but the list of possibilities includes viral infection and exposure to toxic substances in the environment. One study, for example, showed a high correlation (0.967) between the incidence of Parkinson's disease in a geographic area and the level of pesticide use in that region (Lewin, 1985). Inheritance does not seem to be a factor (Larsen & Calne, 1982).

Finding the ultimate cause in any one case of Parkinson's disease may be made especially difficult by the fact that symptoms may not really begin to manifest themselves until years after the initial damage to the brain. For example, if a young person is exposed to some toxic pollutant that kills many of the nigrostriatal neurons, there may be only a brief period of a few weeks during which this injury shows itself in symptoms. The brain is amazingly adept at adjusting to loss, and the most likely response is for axons of the remaining nigrostriatal neurons to sprout new axon branches that then make connections with striatal cells that have lost their input from the substantia nigra. This form of compensation may not produce perfect function, but it seems to be enough to mask the loss of neurons. Compensation has been shown to occur in rats receiving lesions to the nigrostriatal pathway when young. The initial symptoms from the injury diminished greatly in the first 20 days after surgery and remained difficult to detect throughout the rat's "middle-age" period but then began to show up again in old age (Schallert,

1983). The continual loss of neurons that seems to occur with normal aging would explain the eventual reappearance of the symptoms and would explain why, in humans, Parkinson's disease is diagnosed so late in life. When the nigrostriatal cell population has already been severely depleted by some accident or disease early in life, there aren't enough cells left to allow for the normal attrition to be expected from 50 years of life. If this hypothesis is true, then the steady deterioration of the parkinsonian patient is not the result of some ongoing, current disease process but rather reflects normal cell death from aging adding to an earlier injury that it is much too late to do anything about. It has been observed that patients only begin to show the first mild symptoms of Parkinson's disease when about 80 percent of the cells in the substantia nigra have been lost (Langston, 1985).

Fortunately, it is possible to slow the process of deterioration with drugs like bromocriptine and lergotrile. These chemicals substitute for the dopamine that would have been secreted as transmitter by the missing nigrostriatal neurons. Both drugs have problems, however, because lergotrile creates liver damage and bromocriptine causes nausea, dizziness, and occasional hallucinations (as well as costing $15 a day). By far the most effective treatment devised for the symptoms of Parkinson's disease is to increase the availability of the natural transmitter dopamine. This is not as easy as it might sound. If dopamine were given orally, the stomach would simply digest it. If given intravenously, little would reach the brain because of the blood–brain barrier (see Chapter 2). The answer to this problem is to use what is called a **precursor**, a substance from which the chemical of interest is made. The precursor for dopamine is l-DOPA, a molecule that has little trouble slipping out of the bloodstream and into nerve tissue. When first given, the effect of l-DOPA is often dramatic, with rapid loosening of rigid limbs, cessation of trembling, and a return of voluntary control over movement.

After about 3 years of l-DOPA therapy, the drug begins to lose its hold on parkinsonian symptoms, and there are periods when the drug seems to fluctuate on and off—suppressing symptoms for a few hours and then losing all effect for another few hours

(Marx, 1979). Abnormal movements begin to appear that are similar to chorea, and the patient may suffer hallucinations. These very likely are side effects of the drug rather than a product of Parkinson's disease. It is not surprising to see chorea appear if you recall that these random, jerky movements are a symptom of Huntington's disease, which involves loss of cells from the corpus striatum. These striatal cells normally control the dopamine-secreting cells of the substantia nigra, and when they are lost, nigral cells are free to secrete too much dopamine. If too much dopamine in some way produces chorea, then the tie with l-DOPA seems, on the surface, to be obvious. Prolonged l-DOPA therapy (intended to increase the level of dopamine in the striatum) has resulted in surges of excess dopamine. Unfortunately, this easy explanation ignores a wealth of complexity gradually being revealed by continuing research and probably will not stand the test of time. A possible alternative is that dopamine receptor sites are fluctuating in sensitivity or densities.

As researchers struggle to understand the influence of the nigrostriatal neurons on the corpus striatum, clinical experimenters are busy pursuing a possible new therapy for Parkinson's disease. As we saw in Chapter 1, the transplantation of dopamine-producing cells, either from the patient's adrenal medulla or from the substantia nigra of an aborted fetus, may become the preferred therapy of the 1990s.

Functions of the Corpus Striatum

Evolution seems to have given vertebrates a **hierarchical motor system**. A hierarchy is a vertical organization in which the units are arranged so that those at each level command the units at lower levels and are commanded by those at higher levels. In such a system, motor units of the spinal cord represent the fundamental "workers" on the bottom rung of the ladder, and the corpus striatum is in an executive position at the top. Cord CPGs, once the highest level of organization, were reduced to the rank of "crew bosses" by the evolution of higher centers. A CPG coordinates the efforts of a set of motor units to accomplish a particular movement or set of movements. Farther up the hierarchy, in areas like the mesencephalic locomotor region of the brain stem reticular formation, "middle management" organizes larger chunks of behavior by calling on sets of CPGs. An example would be the organization of all CPGs for both legs that are involved in the act of walking. Larger motor patterns called **species-typical behaviors**, which probably organize whole sequences of CPGs, reside in the reticular formation of the midbrain (specifically in the PAG). An example would be the stalking behavior with which all cats are born.

The "executive" corpus striatum neurons presumably evolved to organize sets of brain stem and cord CPGs into complex subroutines (Figure 9.25). Apparently, a single command from a set of corpus striatum neurons can trigger several entire subroutines from lower levels. For example, in a hungry animal searching for food, it would be the corpus striatum neurons that elicit the locomotor routine and maintain it until food is reached, then elicit the inspection subroutine, the picking-up subroutine, and finally, the biting, chewing, and swallowing routines.

Thus, the rule of this hierarchical organization in the motor system is that each newly evolved level would presumably handle larger and larger sequences of behavior in a single command. We do not know that this analysis is completely correct, but it does make good sense in terms of present knowledge.

Because it is a relatively recent addition to the vertebrate brain, the corpus striatum is more involved in constructing motor sequences from experience than are the brain stem and cord. It is likely that the primitive corpus striatum of ancient reptiles received sensory input from parts of the thalamus that existed at that time and used that information to adjust species-typical behaviors to changes in the environment. This learning ability of the corpus striatum enabled the animal to inhibit its built-in behavior patterns and release them at the most appropriate times, based on past experience. A blackbird, for example, has specific food behaviors that could be triggered whenever the animal lands, but it is capable of withholding these responses until it has hopped into a patch of shade where its prey (worms) are more likely to be found (Kamil & Roitblat, 1985).

Figure 9.25 Hierarchical structure proposed as the plan for the precortical motor system. In the cord, the neurons at the right (MN) are motor neurons projecting to muscles. A single motor cell may participate in a number of different CPGs. Circuits in the reticular formation and PAG of the brain stem organize spinal CPGs into higher-level CPGs and STBs (species-typical behaviors). Command circuits in the basal ganglia organize CPGs and STBs into larger units of behavior.

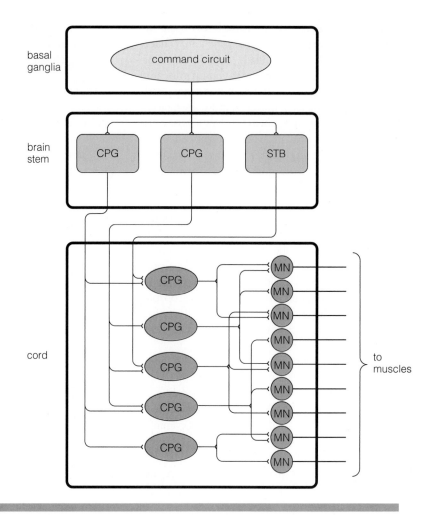

Neurons whose firing patterns are related to the memory of when to make a response have been located and studied in the corpus striatum and substantia nigra. Evarts and colleagues (1984) found neurons in the substantia nigra that respond to a target light flash toward which the monkey is supposed to direct its gaze. To get reinforcement, however, the response had to be withheld until the end of a brief waiting period, and it was during the wait rather than during the response that the neuron response appeared (Evarts et al., 1984). Neurons in the corpus striatum also respond to memory aspects of stimuli. In one study, neurons that made no

response at all when the monkey was gazing at unobtainable food and failed to respond at the sight of the experimenter's hand suddenly came alive when that same hand was seen moving food toward the animal (Marsden, 1980). This sort of "intelligent" response supports the idea that the corpus striatum is a place where sensory input can be associated with available motor routines. In the corpus striatum, we can see the evolutionary tendency toward greater and greater reliance on learning as a survival mechanism.

Even though it works hand-in-hand with the cortex, the corpus striatum appears to have nothing to do with consciousness. Loss of tissue does not leave a "hole" in conscious experience as happens, for example, with loss of visual cortex (blindness) or somatosensory cortex (unawareness of pressure and temperature differences). Consequently, Marsden (1980) concludes that the corpus striatum is responsible for *subconscious* motor routines. If so, that would still give it a place of some prominence in the nervous system because a high percentage of our daily behavior is not at a conscious level. As you walk to class with a friend, for example, you are conscious of your conversation, your direction of travel, and some of the people and objects you encounter, but you probably have little, if any, awareness of the walking behaviors, including stepping on and off curbs and climbing stairs (unless you feel the extra effort involved). You probably are unconscious entirely of the lip-and-tongue movements that create your speech sounds and may be only vaguely aware of the complex muscle contraction patterns that produce your constantly changing facial expressions. Each one of these movements is probably run from a lower-level CPG that may be a part of a sequence organized by the corpus striatum. In performing its task in the human brain, the corpus striatum probably takes orders from the prefrontal cortex where long-term plans and goals appear to be stored. Your conscious mind (cortical function) remains aware of your goals but is not aware of the motor sequences used in reaching them (corpus striatum function).

Any conscious, voluntary response superimposed on the automatic behavior (such as reaching for an object being handed to you as you walk) is controlled by the motor cortex, but the selection of the particular response may be up to the striatum. Usually there is a large variety of muscle contraction possibilities for creating any response (like picking up a book), but the best possible choice for any situation depends on what other movements you are making simultaneously. Think for a moment how different are the arm and shoulder movements needed to toss a basketball through the hoop from a standing position versus those from a dead run toward the basket. Both posture and ongoing movement provide a context that must modify and shape the primary conscious movement if it is to succeed. According to

Brooks (1986), the corpus striatum handles the coordination of the conscious primary movement (controlled by the motor cortex) with the context of ongoing postural adjustments.

Interpreting Symptoms of Damage

Penny and Young (1983) propose a theory of motor system function that contains an explanation of symptoms seen in Huntington's and Parkinson's diseases.

Chorea The jerky, spasmodic involuntary movements of chorea have given some clinicians the impression that they are observing a whole series of related but incomplete movements. It is as though each movement is interrupted just as it gets started, and then a moment later, the interrupting movement is itself interrupted by a third movement. Such a sequence would produce an impression of jerkiness as each new movement suddenly changes the direction in which the body part was headed. As you recall from the section on Huntington's disease, chorea is linked to the death of cells throughout the brain, but especially within the corpus striatum.

In a normally functioning brain, the substantia nigra can command the corpus striatum to interrupt an ongoing behavior, and it is the malfunctioning of this **interrupt signal** that may be the cause of chorea (Penny & Young, 1983). Normally, any response requires at least a few seconds to complete, and during this time, the motor cortex must continue to facilitate motor neurons of the spinal cord so that muscle contraction is maintained. A path from the substantia nigra through the corpus striatum to the cortex seems to play a strong role in stopping (interrupting) this maintained muscle contraction once the movement has been completed. For example, when you get up from a chair, the movement must be halted by the substantia nigra–corpus striatum at the moment you attain an upright posture or you might fall forward. So, in the Penny–Young theory, the motor cortex starts each response and maintains it, whereas the substantia nigra, working through the corpus striatum, interrupts the response circuit when the response is complete. In a brain with corpus striatum damage, the interrupt signal may occur erratically during movements rather than at their completion points. Thus, a new response is allowed to begin before the ongoing one is complete. The result is chorea.

Bradykinesia One of the major symptoms of Parkinson's disease is a slowing of behavior and difficulty in initiating responses—bradykinesia. In a recent study (Bloxham et al., 1984) parkinsonian patients were compared with normal controls on a pursuit-tracking task in which the subject had to keep a pointer on a moving target on a screen. In previous research with a tracking task, the parkinsonian patients had scored more poorly than normals, but in this study, they performed just as well. For some reason, their bradykinesia failed to hinder their performance. The difference, apparently, was the pattern of movement followed by the target. In the previous study, the target kept reversing its direction; in this experiment, the movement was circular. Bloxham and colleagues argue that parkinsonian patients are not really slower than normal once a movement has been started; the slowness comes in beginning new movements. Thus, they should get poorer scores at a tracking task that involves many reversals when it is compared with one that involves none because the former requires the subject to initiate a new response for each reversal, whereas the latter task involves only one response initiation with the rest of the time spent in a continuous circular motion. They tested this interpretation with a reaction-time task (which is essentially all start-up) and found that parkinsonian patients did score more poorly than normals, as predicted. Thus, bradykinesia may be a matter of slow reaction time in initiating each new movement in a behavior sequence rather than slowness of the movement itself.

Penny and Young (1983) are able to explain bradykinesia if it is viewed as a difficulty in response initiation. To begin a new movement, the ongoing behavior must be stopped or interrupted. Thus, a problem in response initiation turns out to involve the same interrupt mechanism that was misbehaving in chorea. In Parkinson's disease, however, it is the substantia nigra neurons forming the nigrostriatal pathway that have been seriously damaged and are functioning at a very low level. This means that ongoing behaviors are very difficult to interrupt so that new ones can start.

It is commonly observed that parkinsonian patients have a hard time stopping a movement (Pincus & Tucker, 1978). Observations of animals whose nigrostriatal projection is unable to function fully because of a shortage of the transmitter dopamine show a reduction in the variety of responses (Cools et al., 1981), which could mean that many of the motor routines normally available to the animal are now too difficult to halt. Also in support of the Penny–Young theory is that parkinsonian patients find it difficult to get up from a sitting position or to start walking from a standing position. By this point in this chapter, you know enough about the motor system's involvement with postures and their maintenance to realize that a particular posture (sitting, standing, etc.) is really a response as far as the nervous system is concerned. One does not stand still because the motor system is turned off and nothing is happening. One stands only if the correct postural motor routines are available and "running." Thus, starting to walk is difficult for the parkinsonian patient because it is so difficult to stop standing!

■ Motor Cortex

Within the cortex is a sensory-to-motor continuum of functions from the back of the brain to the front. Motor functions are confined mainly to the frontal lobes. If you start at the central fissure and move forward, you encounter another continuum; one based on the number of synapses between the cells in question and the motor neurons in the ventral horns of the cord. In the **precentral gyrus**, lying just anterior to the central fissure (Figure 9.26), is an area called **M1** (the primary motor cortex), whose output neurons send their axons down into the cord to synapse with the motor neurons (Figure 9.27). Thus, M1 is only one synapse away from the muscles themselves (or two synapses if, as some people assert, M1 axons synapse with cord interneurons that synapse with motor neurons). So, at the posterior end of the continuum, there is close proximity to the ventral horn cells. As you move forward along

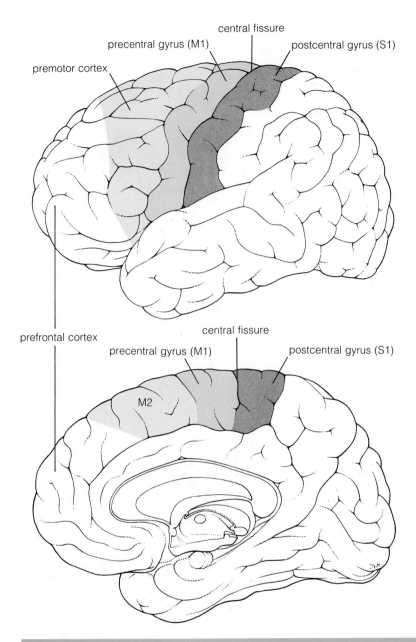

Figure 9.26 Motor areas of the cerebral cortex. M1 is the primary motor cortex; S1 is the primary somatosensory (somesthetic) cortex. The prefrontal areas are not motor.

the surface of the frontal lobe, you enter the **premotor cortex (PM)** containing cells that send their axons across into M1 and also down into the reticular formation of the brain stem. Reticular cells connect with ventral horn cells by way of the **reticulospinal tract.** Thus, cells in the premotor cortex are at least one more synapse removed from ventral horn cells.

Anterior to the PM lies the prefrontal cortex that connects with the motor areas but that is usually regarded as nonmotor. Prefrontal areas are involved in the planning of behavior rather than its execution. Close analysis, however, reveals that it is difficult to

Figure 9.27 Diagram of corticospinal system from M1 to the motor neurons of the ventral horn. (Adapted from Fowler, 1984)

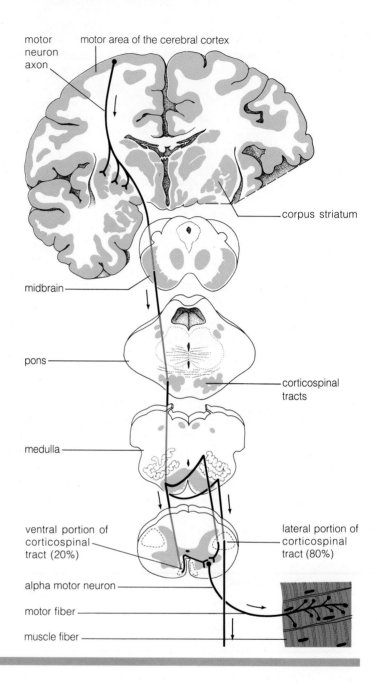

motor neuron axon

motor area of the cerebral cortex

corpus striatum

midbrain

pons

corticospinal tracts

medulla

ventral portion of corticospinal tract (20%)

lateral portion of corticospinal tract (80%)

alpha motor neuron

motor fiber

muscle fiber

draw a sharp line between the cognitive function of planning and the motoric business of producing movements. As you raise your arm, you are executing a movement that could be part of a plan called "turn-ing the door knob," which is a series of movements embedded within a larger plan called "opening the door of the classroom," which in turn belongs to the larger plan called "going to class," which is a part of "passing the course," which is a part of "getting an education," which is a part of . . . There seems to be a continuum within the frontal lobes then, with the smallest, most motoric units of planning at the back of the lobe and the largest, most cognitive chunks of planning (like "getting an education") nearer the front. We have, perhaps arbitrarily, drawn a line between the prefrontal areas and the PM, attributing cognitive functions to the one and motor to the other.

Over on the medial surface of the frontal lobe is another motor zone, **M2** or **supplementary motor cortex** (SMA), which may be a part of the PM but has characteristics that give it somewhat different functions. The three areas (M1, PM, and SMA) taken together make up the **motor cortex**.

M1: Primary Motor Cortex

One of the first scientific discoveries about brain function was made during the 1870s when it was observed that electrical stimulation of the precentral gyrus (the gyrus just anterior to the central fissure) would elicit involuntary movements in animals. Anatomists found that axons of cells in the precentral gyrus formed a prominent pathway (the **corticospinal tract**) that terminated in the ventral horns of the spinal cord (Figure 9.27). That particular cortical area possessed a direct connection to the motor cells controlling the muscles. It seemed obvious to early neuroscientists that the precentral gyrus was the area of the brain from which all voluntary movement originated, and this idea gained even more acceptance when the gyrus was mapped carefully with low-voltage electrode stimulation that would affect small, discrete zones. This work showed that a representation of the body was laid out along the gyrus so that specific areas controlled movement in specific body parts (Figure 9.28). Thus, the precentral gyrus came to be called the motor cortex.

As research continued, it became clear that other areas of the frontal lobe were also involved in movement, so what had been called "the motor cortex" now had to be termed the "primary" motor cortex. This designation is still in use to some extent despite the fact that we now view the function of the precentral gyrus in a completely different light. The term widely employed by researchers is M1.

Effects of Destruction Early experiments indicated that damage to M1 produces **flaccid paralysis** in which the muscles remain limp and voluntary control of contraction is lost. If the damage is only on one side, then the paralysis is limited to the muscles on the opposite side of the body, a result of the fact that the corticospinal tract crosses to the other side of the brain on its way through the brain stem. Paralysis on only one side is far more common than on both and is usually referred to as **hemiplegia**. The muscles of the trunk are much less affected by hemiplegia than are those in the arms, hands, and face. In fact, more recent lesion studies with monkeys, in which the damage could be carefully limited to just M1, fail to show the dramatic paralysis that one would expect to see if M1 lived up to its original designation as the sole source of all voluntary movements. After removal of M1 from both hemispheres, monkeys are still capable of a wide variety of postures and movements such as walking and manipulating food (Brobeck, 1973). Their limb control is awkward and limited, with little involvement of fine finger movements. The larger, grosser movements like the rotation of the upper arm around the shoulder joint are the most typical. However, there certainly is not the total paralysis that the older view led us to expect. Human patients often report a weakness in many of the affected muscles rather than a total paralysis, and this partial condition is known as **paresis**. In fact, an important early neurological theorist, Hughlings Jackson, suggested that the result of losing the corticospinal input to the cord is not actually paralysis at all but rather the loss of the full use of certain muscles in certain kinds of movements (Evarts, 1979). For example, spinal cord circuits are adequate to run the respiratory muscles if mere breathing is the goal, but if the brain needs to take over control of these muscles for use in speech modulation (e.g., talking vs. shouting), then M1 and its major pathway—the corticospinal tract—must be functioning. Jackson's insight is truly an important one because it anticipated the modern view of M1 function, as we will see later when we discuss the concept of fractionation.

Relation to S1 A problem for those theorists who clung to the idea that all voluntary movement origi-

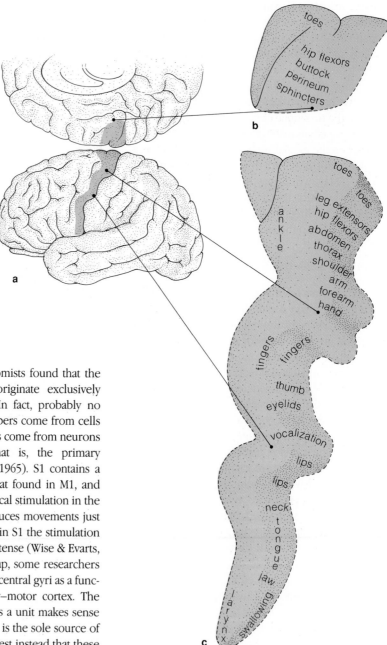

Figure 9.28 Human brain showing M1 areas of the left hemisphere. Pairs of dots connected by lines show identical points on **a** and **b** and on **a** and **c**. Note that **c** allows you to see the cortex of the anterior wall of the central fissure—cortex that is normally hidden from view. Also note that **b**, the medial portion of M1, is drawn with its most dorsal part up and ventral down. That is its normal position in the brain. In **b** the medial cortex is shown upside down. (Adapted from Krieg, 1966)

nated in M1 arose when anatomists found that the corticospinal tract did not originate exclusively within the precentral gyrus. In fact, probably no more than 31 percent of the fibers come from cells in M1, while many of the others come from neurons in the *post*central gyrus—that is, the primary somesthetic cortex S1 (Ruch, 1965). S1 contains a map of the body similar to that found in M1, and Woolsey discovered that electrical stimulation in the various areas of this map produces movements just as in M1; the difference is that in S1 the stimulation has to be considerably more intense (Wise & Evarts, 1981). As a result of this overlap, some researchers refer to the precentral and postcentral gyri as a functional unit, called the sensory–motor cortex. The idea that S1 and M1 function as a unit makes sense if we drop the old idea that M1 is the sole source of voluntary movements and suggest instead that these two cortical areas evolved to provide finer sensory (somesthetic) feedback control over movement.

Wondering what would happen to movement control if somesthetic input were lost, Mott and Sherrington deafferented monkeys in one upper limb (by cutting the dorsal roots) and observed that the ani-

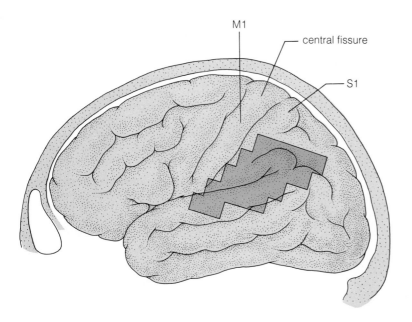
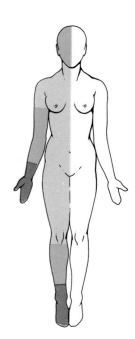

Figure 9.29 An area of cortex damaged in Jeannerod's patient. The loss of most of S1 accounts for the complete anesthesia in the right hand and foot and partial anesthesia (indicated in color) in the rest of the right side of the body surface. (Adapted from Jeannerod et al., 1984)

mals stopped using that arm unless forced to and that movements of the affected hand were awkward and difficult. None of the motor system had been destroyed; only sensory feedback was missing (see Jeannerod et al., 1984). A human patient was found who had a cortical lesion limited to S1 in the left hemisphere (Figure 9.29). She was unable to feel anything with her right hand or forearm, yet her manipulative ability was not seriously harmed as long as she could keep track of the right hand visually. For example, without looking at her hand, she was unable to touch her thumb with her forefinger, although she had no trouble moving either digit. In Figure 9.30, the patient was asked to crumple a sheet of paper with each hand simultaneously while watching. The left hand had the task completed in 7–12 seconds, whereas the right hand required 20 seconds, fumbling and contorting the fingers as it worked. Visually guiding five fingers all at once is not an easy business. Apparently, the somatosensory

cortex works very closely with M1 to enable movements, especially of the hands. Although all body areas are represented in M1, the muscles of the hands and face have the greatest number of neurons there.

The Motor Hierarchy and Fractionation So far in our discussion of M1, we have established that it is not (as originally thought) *the* motor cortex but simply one of many areas involved in voluntary movement, and we have also seen that it seems linked especially strongly to the somatosensory cortex. How then can we characterize M1's place in the overall motor system?

In discussing the corpus striatum, it was suggested that evolution has continually added higher-level structures to the motor system hierarchy with the most recent addition always exerting its influence by commanding the cells at the next lower level. However, this thinking leads to a seeming inconsistency. The next step in evolution beyond the corpus

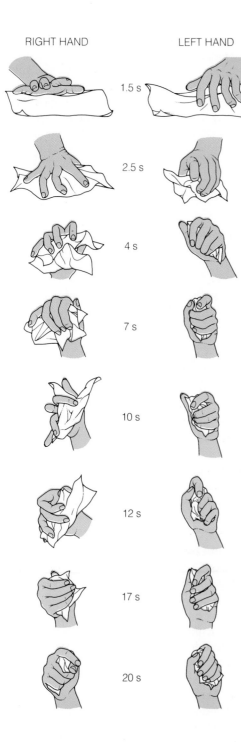

1.5 s

2.5 s

4 s

7 s

10 s

12 s

17 s

20 s

Figure 9.30 Performance of Jeannerod's patient during a paper-crumpling task. The pictures are redrawn from a motion picture, and the amount of elapsed time in seconds is shown beside each frame. Note that the left hand (controlled by the intact right hemisphere) completes the task in 7–12 seconds, whereas the right hand (guided by the injured left hemisphere) requires 20 seconds and exhibits poor control and bizarre finger postures. M1 was intact in both hemispheres; thus, the movement impairment is apparently due to the loss of S1 on the left side. (Adapted from Jeannerod et al., 1984)

striatum was the neocortex, and our hierarchical scheme would call for the motor cortex to oversee the entire motor system by telling the corpus striatum what behaviors should be elicited from the brain stem and cord. But M1 does not send its major output down to the corpus striatum. Instead, the corticospinal tract descends through the brain stem, ignoring in its passing not only the corpus striatum but the midbrain and pontine reticular formation as well, and terminates on or near the alpha motor neurons themselves. It's as though, when some job needed doing, the president of the firm ignored all vice-presidents, section heads, and supervisors and went down to the factory floor to talk directly to the machine operators themselves. This may be a very democratic sounding idea, but it usually works poorly in practice. What exactly is going on in the motor system to produce such a seeming inconsistency?

The answer to this puzzle according to Evarts (Wise & Evarts, 1981) and Grillner and Wallén (1985) is the idea of fractionation. To understand what fractionation is, first think of the kinds of behaviors available to our precortical ancestors, the reptiles. When a reptile moves a leg, that limb is treated almost as though it were a solid object—or at least it would seem so in comparison to a primate. How much rotation does a reptile show around the elbow and wrist? How many reptiles have you seen flexing each digit independently? The movements available to the paw of an alligator are so limited in comparison to a primate paw that it makes the former seem like a stick. Not that the alligator cares, of course. The CPGs in its cord have organized the paw to act as a unit because that suits reptilian needs. But that organization was determined by genes—genes that we may well have inherited ourselves from our protoreptilian ancestors. Indeed, we can use our hands as units—as when we hit someone with a fist or push against a closed door—and at those times our hierarchical motor system may be calling on spinal CPGs as ancient as the early reptiles.

With the evolution of primate digits, which were better physically separated, and more important, with the appearance of the sensory cortex came the opportunity for really fine control over hand movements. But to get the fingers to move separately and the wrist to flex into all manner of elegant postures, it was necessary to either throw out the old CPGs or somehow override their influence whenever a finer movement was demanded. Because evolution rarely ever seems to throw out much of the nervous system but rather is content to simply paste a new mechanism on top of the existing heap, the motor cortex was born. It evolved not as a superexecutive directing the most global aspects of the behavior stream from a lofty perch overlooking the many lower levels but rather as simply a new component that would plug into the rest of the system and add a new feature—sort of like adding a tape deck to your existing stereo system. Its specialty is the ability to use the output of the cortical somatosensory analyzers to produce *fine* control over any muscle system. It is relatively unimportant when gross crude movements will do (walking, running, swinging a stick, hoeing weeds, etc.). It is the fine tuner that rotates the trunk in fractions of a degree (should you ever need to do that) or, more likely, rotates an index fingertip through a fraction of a degree of arc (which you probably need to do quite often). Some reptiles (lizards, for example) have fingerlike toes that look as though they might act like fingers, but imagine such an animal trying to pick up one piece of paper from a stack of papers. The shape of the paw is no great hindrance, but the lack of single-digit control dooms the effort to failure. Most of M1's area is devoted to the hands and face because these are the two zones within which most of the fine, somesthetically controlled movements are needed, but the other body parts are represented to some extent, and this fact is occasionally useful.

For somatosensory information (especially kin-esthetic) to be useful in controlling individual muscles, the ancient motor hierarchy had to be bypassed. The single-muscle commands had to go straight to the cord itself, and even there, the CPGs may have to be circumvented. The term for this sort of direct control over the smallest units of motor organization is **fractionation**, the idea being that M1 deals with fractions of CPGs. It is interesting in a philosophical way that the motor cortex, that pinnacle of evolution, represents a return to the primitive roots of the motor system.

Supplementary Motor Cortex (M2)

Most of M2 is hidden down inside the longitudinal fissure on the medial surface of the cortex (Figure 9.26). It wasn't well-named originally; it was called the supplementary motor cortex because M2 was discovered after M1, during the time when everyone thought M1 was the entire motor cortex. The more modern designation M2 is more objective.

The study of M2 anatomy shows that this area projects to M1 and into the cord by way of the corticospinal system. M2 is not just a duplicate of M1; the major inputs are not the same, and the cells behave differently. Whereas M1 gets its sensory information mainly from S1, M2 receives little somatosensory input and a great deal of visual–auditory information in its place. Many M2 neurons fail completely to respond during movement but fire bursts of impulses whenever a visual cue for movement appears (Wise & Strick, 1984). Others are sensitive to auditory cues for the same response (Tanji, 1984).

When the M2 areas in both hemispheres are lost or heavily damaged (usually along with a bit of the cingulate cortex just ventral to M2), the result is **akinesia**, a severe difficulty in the initiation of movements of any kind, and **mutism**, the absence of speech (Freund, 1984). Lighter damage decreases verbal output, facial expressions, and gestures (Stuss & Benson, 1984).

M2 and Preparatory Set Electrodes placed on the top of the skull at the midline (a point called the vertex) reveal a **vertex readiness potential**. This is an EEG wave that always occurs just before a movement and seems to be associated with the intention

Figure 9.31 Summary of the stimulus conditions and results in the experiment by Tanji and Kurata (1985). Two sets of M2 neurons were found. One type fired during the time the 300-Hz tone was present, and the other fired during the 100-Hz tone. When the M2 cells sensitive to 300 Hz fired, M1 neurons would respond to a tone by producing the conditioned response. When the 100-Hz M2 cells fired, M1 neurons would respond only to a vibratory stimulus. M2 apparently produced a response set.

STIMULUS CONDITIONS

NEURON RESPONSE IN M2

if 300 Hz

| then | S⁺ was a 1,000-Hz tone | M2 300-Hz cells fired, and M1 cells responded to the tone but ignored the vibration |
| | S⁻ was a vibration | |

if 100 Hz

| then | S⁺ was a vibration | M2 100-Hz cells fired, and M1 cells responded to the vibration but ignored the 1,000-Hz tone |
| | S⁻ was a 1,000-Hz tone | |

to move or a readiness to make the response rather than with the response itself. The vertex is located right over the M2 areas of both hemispheres, and chances are good that the vertex readiness potential reflects the functioning of M2 (Freund, 1984).

Tanji and Kurata (1985) have studied neurons in M2 whose activity may be responsible for the readiness potential. They taught monkeys to discriminate between S⁺ (a 1,000-Hz tone) and S⁻ (a vibration on the hand). In other words, the monkeys learned to make a response (a key press) when they heard a tone but not when they felt the vibration. Then the procedure was reversed—with the vibration becoming S⁺ and the tone serving as the S⁻. Neurons in M1 reacted to this situation just as the whole organism did; that is, they began responding when S⁺ appeared but did not respond to S⁻. Then an initial cue was added. Prior to the appearance of each S⁺ or S⁻, another tone sounded. If the tone was 300 Hz, then the S⁺ would be a 1,000-Hz tone and the S⁻ a vibration; if this initial cue was a 100-Hz tone, then the vibration was the S⁺ and the 1,000-Hz tone the S⁻. In other words, changing the initial tone reversed the S⁺ and S⁻. A 100-Hz tone meant "get set to respond to the vibration and ignore the tone," whereas a 300-Hz tone dictated the opposite (Figure 9.31). Thus, the initial tones established a **preparatory set** or readiness for making a particular response to a particular stimulus.

Fifty percent of the M2 cells sampled responded to the initial cues, most of these showing continuous activity from the time the initial cue began to the moment the S⁺ appeared. Many of the neurons that fired throughout the period when the initial cue was present were specific to either the 100-Hz or the 300-Hz tone (Tanji & Kurata, 1985). The obvious interpretation is that the activity of these neurons constitutes the preparatory set that allows the monkey to choose the correct discrimination. The learning of the set probably occurs as the formation of new connections between M2 and M1 neurons. Also, it may be M2 cells that produce the vertex readiness potential when they become active.

Studying M2 Functions with Regional Cerebral Blood Flow Measurement Further support for the hypothesis that M2 produces preparatory sets comes from the research technique, regional cerebral blood flow ($_r$CBF) measurement (see Chapter 5). By presenting the subject with a task and then measuring the changes in blood flow into specific areas of the brain, we can see which brain areas become the most active. In Figure 9.32a, the subject was making continuous movements of the fingers of the right hand. The recording shows higher activity in the hand area of M1 and the adjacent hand area of S1 across the central fissure. Notice that the dorsal portion of the PM plus M2 is active. Could this mean that a motor

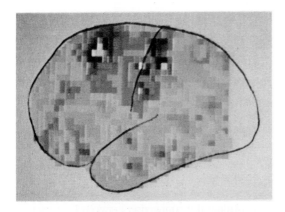

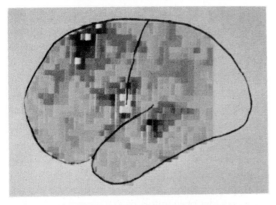

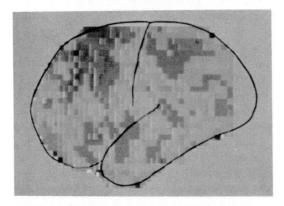

Figure 9.32 Regional cerebral blood flow records taken during various tasks. White and lightest grays indicate higher than average blood flow, medium gray is average, and dark grays are below average for this particular moment in this patient. (**a**) This recording was made while the patient was moving the fingers of the right hand, (**b**) counting aloud to 20, (**c**) counting silently to 20. (Adapted from Lassen et al., 1978)

preparatory set is in effect? That is indeed the case. The subject was instructed to make continuous finger movements during the recording so that while one finger began its motion the subject had a set that held the next finger's movement in readiness until the appropriate moment. If the experimenter says, "wiggle your fingers until I tell you to stop," then the subject must keep prepared for finger movements until verbal cue for stopping comes. In Figure 9.32b, a preparatory set was again given, but this time it was for oral behavior; the subject was told to count aloud from 1–20 repeatedly. The result was an activation of the PM and M2, together with the face and mouth areas in M1 and S1 plus the auditory area (because one listens to what one says out loud). In Figure 9.32c, the instructions were again to count from 1 to 20 but to do it silently. Thus, there is no activity in the auditory area, S1, or M1, but PM and M2 are active. Thinking about counting is the same thing as a preparatory set for counting.

One patient was asked to compress a spring between thumb and forefinger and hold that position. The $_r$CBF to M1 increased more than 30 percent during the time the spring was being held, but no change at all occurred in M2. In another task, the patient was asked to make a particular hand movement over and over but to vary the rate when asked by the experimenter. In this case, both M1 and M2 experienced increases in flow. The rate-change instructions were to be given vocally. Thus, the subject's task was to maintain a motor preparatory set until the occurrence of a particular auditory cue, just as in the monkey experiment. In the case of the human subject, however, the auditory cue was not a tone but the instruction spoken by the experimenter. The clearest demonstration of M2's involvement in preparatory set came when the patient was required to imagine making a particular movement but to withhold the actual movement until cued to start it. During this preparatory period before the response, the flow in M2 increased by 23 percent, and this increase occurred only in M2 (Reivich, 1982).

Clearly, one of the most important functions of M2 is to prepare the brain for a movement to be made on the arrival of some event in the environment. Bilateral lesions of M2 would do away with this preparatory set and produce the akinesia described earlier. In this interpretation, akinesia is not a form of paralysis (reflex movements are still working), but rather a loss of the ability to get ready to move at a particular time (Freund, 1984).

M2 and Hemispheric Coordination Unilateral lesions of M2 (i.e., lesions only in one hemisphere) rarely leave a lasting deficit that can be detected with existing tests (Freund, 1984). Moreover, ,CBF studies have shown that M2s in both hemispheres are always simultaneously active despite the fact that the movement may be occurring only on one side of the body and is therefore controlled only by the M1 on the contralateral side (Roland, 1984). These two facts imply that the two M2 areas must work together to accomplish some task, and the most obvious possibility is the task of dividing the labor between the two hemispheres. In other words, it may be the two M2 areas that decide what role each hand should play in any job. For example, when you open a soft-drink can, you grab the pull tab with the index finger of your preferred hand (right hand for most people), while holding the can with the nonpreferred hand. The nonpreferred always takes the supporting role with a completely different set of movements or postures. Somewhere in the nervous system this division of labor must be decided, and M2 may be that place.

In a study by Brinkman (1984), monkeys were given an opportunity to retrieve bits of food from finger-sized slots in a board. Normal monkeys can learn to do this by poking the food through the hole with the preferred hand and catching it in the non-preferred hand, which was held open and cupped beneath the slot—an excellent example of bilateral division of labor. Monkeys with just one M2 area removed, however, lost this ability. Rather than taking different roles, both hands tried to poke the food out. Brinkman suggested that it looked as though the remaining M2 was setting up the motor program for the preferred hand in both hemispheres rather than just the "dominant" hemisphere. A right-handed monkey behaved as though it had two right hands! This result was most pronounced when the M2 for the nonpreferred side was removed, leaving the dominant M2 in place. Of course, the M2 of the left hemisphere could only influence the right-hemisphere M1 by way of connections through the corpus

callosum. When Brinkman cut the callosum, the strange "double right-handedness" disappeared. Thus, a second function of M2 appears to be to divide the labor between the two sides of the body.

Premotor Cortex

The premotor cortex (PM) is sandwiched between the prefrontal areas, purportedly the site of planning and intentions, and the primary motor cortex, the site of fine motor control (Figure 9.26). This location suggests that PM mediates between those two areas by providing the connection between broad intentions and actual motor programs designed to reach those goals. Perhaps PM can translate the idea "I think I'll walk to the door" into the sequence of movements that will realize that intention. Stimulation of PM rarely evokes movements, and this observation fits with the idea that PM contains no motor subroutines itself but helps in some way to organize patterns of movements whose subroutines are found in other motor areas like M1.

Three major hypotheses of PM function have been proposed: It acts to provide sensory guidance for movements, it integrates movements into sequences, or it provides preparatory sets (Weinrich et al., 1984).

Sensory Guidance Anatomical evidence exists for a connection from the visual and auditory areas of the cortex into PM (Wise, 1985) and another connection from PM to M1 (Freund, 1984). Thus, visual information might have an influence on fine movements by way of PM. When recordings are made from single cells within PM, it is found that visual stimuli are highly effective at evoking responses (Weinrich & Wise, 1982), as are auditory stimuli (Wise & Strick, 1984). It is doubtful, however, that this means that PM is engaged in sensory analysis. When the neurons respond to an auditory or visual signal, that stimulus is always being used by the experimenter as an S^+ or S^-, and it is this property of acting as a behavior cue that elicits the response. However, PM function is certainly not simply and directly related to the mere production of movements. In one study (Weinrich et al., 1984), many of these PM cells began responding at the onset of an S^+ or S^- but terminated their activity at the onset of the response regardless of whether the stimulus continued. This is not exactly what one would expect of a simple motor system neuron. Thus, good evidence exists for the idea that PM functions in the sensory guidance of movement. However, this does not seem to be the entire story.

Movement Sequencing In early experiments, observations of monkeys with PM damage led to the conclusion that the animals had lost the ability to put movements together into sequences (reviewed in Weinrich et al., 1984). Recent research qualified this finding when it was shown that monkeys with PM ablations were still able to perform sequences of movements, but only if these sequences were routine and not guided by visual cues. It should be noted that this sequencing hypothesis of PM function does not disagree with the sensory guidance theory but rather incorporates it. When analyzed carefully, the term *sensory guidance* is seen to refer to the use of a stimulus as an S^+ or S^-, and a behavior sequence would then consist of S_1^+–R_1, ... , S_2^+–R_2, ... , S_3^+–R_3, ... , and so on. For example, if you decide to take a drink from a glass, you first locate the glass visually. The sight of the glass (S_1^+) triggers the first response, an arm movement (R_1). Seeing the movement of the hand toward the glass (S_2^+) triggers an opening of the fingers (R_2), and contact of the fingers with the glass (S_3^+) produces a contraction of the hand around the glass (R_3). The occurrence of each movement within the sequence is determined by its own stimulus cue. Discriminative stimuli (S^+s and S^-s) are the "glue" that holds the sequence together.

Preparation for Movement Weinrich and colleagues (1984) taught monkeys to hold a light at a particular position and wait until a cue for a second response occurred. They discovered neurons in PM that began firing at a high rate at the beginning of the waiting period and continued until the appearance of the cue for the second response. In other words, the cells were active all during the time that the monkey was set to respond. The premotor cortex, then, shares with M2 a sensitivity to visual and auditory stimuli and neurons that are involved in specific preparatory sets for specific movements.

If M2 and PM both provide preparatory sets using the same types of stimulus inputs, is it really correct to regard them as two functionally separate areas? An answer may possibly be obtained from human patients with PM damage. A unilateral lesion produces mostly a weakness in the shoulder and hip muscles on the opposite side of the body plus some loss of coordination between the limbs (Freund, 1984). The weakness in the shoulder muscles makes arm movements quite difficult. The hands, however, are affected only very minimally, which is quite a contrast to the paresis following M1 damage. There is no trouble with getting the two hands to work together, as would be expected after a lesion to M2, nor is there any akinesia or mutism. Bilateral damage produces more severe symptoms such as problems with postures in stance and gait.

After reviewing these symptoms, Freund (1984) drew the conclusion that PM normally exerts control of grosser, postural contractions involved in the preparation for impending movements. He also notes that PM cannot join M1 and M2 in their control of fine movements because it does not project into the cord by way of the corticospinal tract. Instead, its output neurons gather their axons into the **corticoreticulospinal tract**, which, as the name tells you, runs from the cortex down to the reticular system and then into the spinal cord. PM cells, however, reach no farther than the brain stem, where they synapse on reticular neurons (Figure 9.33). Thus, they produce their effect on a higher level of the motor hierarchy rather than helping in the fractionation of the lower-level CPGs. Recall from the earlier discussion that reticular neurons seem to organize collections of spinal CPGs to produce whole postures and behaviors rather than single, discrete rotations around a joint.

The production of supporting postures is vital to movement. Many movements cannot be made at all except from a fairly specific starting posture, and usually the accuracy of a movement depends on arriving at a particular final posture. In other words, a preparatory set would usually involve arranging your body into some particular posture from which it is easy to make the anticipated movement. There seems to be very little conscious awareness of these preparatory postural adjustments, much to the disgruntlement of offensive football linemen who frequently give away the upcoming play to the

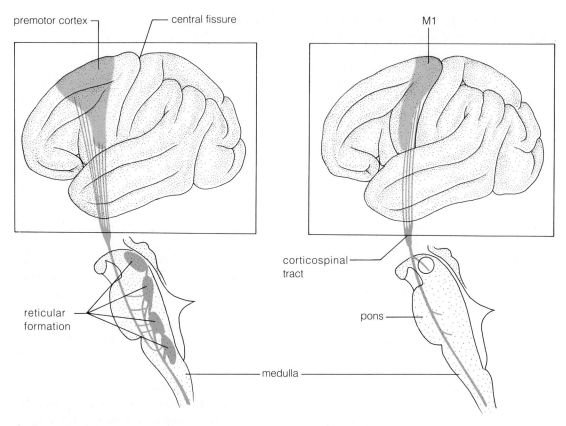

premotor cortex — — central fissure   M1

corticospinal tract

reticular formation

pons

medulla

Figure 9.33 Comparison of PM area and M1 projections into the cord. M1 projects directly into the ventral horn of the cord by way of the corticospinal tract, whereas PM influences the cord only indirectly by way of its projection to the reticular formation and the reticular projection to the cord. These latter two projections make up the two stages of the corticoreticulospinal pathway. Because reticular cells project to combinations of cord motor neurons (CPGs) rather than to individual cord neurons, PM cannot fractionate to the degree available to M1. (Adapted from Freund, 1984)

opposition when the other team is smart enough to read their slight changes in posture just before the ball is put into play.

To get a feel for the importance of supporting postures, sit squarely in your chair, leaning slightly forward with your feet on the floor, and rest your forearm on the table in front of you with the surface supporting the weight of the arm. Now raise your arm an inch off of the table. You can, of course, feel your shoulder and arm muscles contract to raise the arm, but if you try the move several times, relaxing completely in between each trial, you will become aware of the fact that your leg and lower trunk muscles also contract as the arm rises. If you have a hard time feeling this increase in muscle tension, try leaning forward farther and make sure that you start with the table fully supporting the weight of the arm. The reason for the activity in the leg muscles is that raising the arm throws your center of gravity forward. Without increased isometric contraction in the trunk and legs that are supporting your body posture, the weight of your arm would actually pull your upper torso forward until the forearm was resting on the table again. Many postural adjustments of this sort are not really movements. They are isometric rather than isotonic contractions, and that is why they are so much less conscious and so easily overlooked despite the impossibility of having normal movements without them.

Summary and Comparisons

M1 and M2 control finer movements because of their ability to fractionate the more primitive CPG circuits of the cord and gain direct control over the individual motor units. PM neurons, on the other hand, trigger CPGs or organizations of CPGs rather than separate motor units; thus lesions of PM affect grosser movements and postures more than fine movement.

Except for their outputs, M2 and PM seem to be organized nearly the same. Whereas M1 cells fire when movements are in progress and stop when the movement stops, many neurons in PM and M2 fire prior to the intended movement, bridging the gap between the S^+ for the movement and the actual start of the contractions. For this reason, both M2 and PM are thought to be involved in the organization of sequences and the production of motor sets—M1 for fine movements and PM for grosser movements and postural adjustments.

M1 works very closely with the somatosensory cortex (S1) to guide fine movements with sensory feedback. It apparently receives very little, if any, direct input from any other sense analyzers. M2 and PM, however, show little responsiveness to somatosensory input but are heavily involved in the use of visual and auditory stimuli.

A final distinction is that both M1 and PM seem to exert their effects on the contralateral side of the body from their hemisphere and work independently from their counterparts in the opposite hemisphere, whereas M2 has strong interhemispheric connections and works closely with its mate on the other side—especially in the coordination of the two hands.

Summary

1. Striate muscles are directly controlled by the CNS and are responsible for voluntary movements; smooth muscles are controlled through the ANS and produce reflexive responses in the internal organs. Striate muscles are composed of many muscle fibers, each controlled by a motor nerve fiber. The motor neuron contacts the muscle cell at a specialized type of synapse called a neuromyal junction and uses the transmitter acetylcholine (Ach) to trigger an action potential in the muscle.

2. A motor neuron together with the several muscle fibers it serves is called a motor unit. During a contraction, some motor units are resting while others work. The nervous system increases the strength of contraction in a muscle by calling more motor units into action. Motor neurons can inhibit themselves through an interneuron called a Renshaw cell, thus providing their muscle fibers with a short rest period. Higher centers can control the duration of these rest periods and thereby control the strength of muscle contraction.

3. Isotonic contraction involves shortening of the muscle and is the basis for moving body parts; isometric contraction does not change the length of the muscle and is used in maintaining body parts in particular positions (postures) despite the pull of gravity or other forces.

4. Kinesthesis is the sense that tells you where your body parts are in relation to one another, as well as how fast and hard they are moving. Kinesthetic receptors in a muscle are found on specialized fibers called muscle spindles, which are sensitive to stretch. Most of your conscious perception of where your body parts are in space comes from Golgi tendon organs and muscle spindles. Joint receptors are important for reflexes.

5. Much of the business of the motor system involves the maintenance of posture, and one of the primary mechanisms of posture control is the monosynaptic stretch reflex arc. The load is the amount of force against which the muscle must contract. If the load is increased, the muscle stretches. This stretch is sensed by its muscle spindles, and the stretch reflex is elicited. When motor neurons of the stretch reflex

fire, the muscle contracts, thus removing the stretch from the spindles and quieting the stretch reflex. The stretch reflex enables you to hold a posture by keeping muscles at some constant length.

6. The sensitivity of the stretch reflex can be adjusted by the gamma efferent neuron when it contracts the spindle fiber. The more contracted the spindle fiber, the less muscle stretch is needed to fire the spindle afferent.

7. A major source of sensory input for many reflexes is the vestibular system. There are three vestibular senses: the sense of gravity, linear acceleration, and rotary acceleration. Receptors for these senses are the saccule, utricle, and semicircular canals.

8. The saccule and utricle are fluid-filled cavities in the skull, which are located within the inner ear next to the cochlea. Both contain a patch of receptor cells called the macula. Stereocilia of macular hair cells are bent when the head tilts, thus signaling the direction of gravity. Maculas of the saccule and utricle also respond to linear acceleration (an increase in rate of forward motion). Rotary acceleration depends on the receptors found in the semicircular canals, which are three other vestibular cavities of the skull connecting with the saccule and utricle.

9. The cerebellum is a structure composed of nuclei and cortex attached to the dorsal side of the brain stem at the pontine level. Symptoms of cerebellar injury are ataxia, slowness and difficulty in walking; decomposition of movements, in which each separate movement must be thought out consciously; dysmetria, inability to create smooth, straight-line movements; and tremor, a shaking of the hand as it approaches a target. The job of the cerebellum is to improve the smoothness, speed, and accuracy of movements by coordinating muscle contractions in all agonist and antagonist muscles involved in the movement.

10. Intention tremor occurs in cases of cerebellar damage because, without cerebellar input to the cord reflex arcs, antagonistic stretch reflexes produce a series of overshoot contractions rather than contractions that would be just sufficient for braking at the end of the movement. If learning does take place within the cerebellum, it would involve memories of how to use various kinesthetic and vestibu-

lar input patterns to produce the most successful combinations of movement force, direction, and timing.

11. There are two reflexes involved in walking. In the extensor thrust reflex, pressure to the sole of the foot contracts extensor muscles of the leg, converting it into a pillar that can hold the weight of the body. Removing the weight from the sole of the foot elicits the stepping reflex, a contraction of flexor muscles that bend the leg at the knee and raise the foot from the ground. Learning to walk involves combining these two reflexes into a sequence.

12. Walking cannot be completely explained as a sequence of reflexes because deafferented cats can still walk, although not very well. These results led to the idea of central pattern generators (CPGs)—networks of interconnected neurons that collectively control a set of muscles needed to produce a movement or sequence of movements.

13. The corpus striatum includes the caudate, the putamen (grouped together as the striatum), and the globus pallidus. The substantia nigra works together with these structures.

14. Huntington's disease is a syndrome resulting from loss of cells within the corpus striatum. The major symptom is chorea, a condition characterized by continual, involuntary jerky movements of the face, tongue, and extremities. Parkinson's disease, another corpus striatum syndrome, is characterized by bradykinesia, slowness and deliberateness of movement; rigidity, a stiffness in the limbs and difficulty in shifting posture; and tremor at rest, a trembling of the hands that diminishes during voluntary movement. This syndrome results from loss of cells in the substantia nigra, a midbrain nucleus that projects into the corpus striatum and forms inhibitory dopamine synapses there. Replacing the missing dopamine can offer some symptom relief.

15. The corpus striatum probably evolved to enable learning to have more control over motor routines. Apparently, the corpus striatum organizes sequences of behaviors that are well learned and runs them off at a subconscious level. Walking over broken ground, swimming, riding a bike, shifting gears in a car, and eating with knife and fork are all examples of this type of behavior sequence.

16. The Penny–Young theory explains chorea as a chronic tendency for the motor system to interrupt behavior loops before the movement has been completed. The problem lies in the loss of striatal neurons. Penny and Young interpret bradykinesia (slowness and difficulty in movement) as an inability to turn off the cells commanding a prior posture so that a new posture or movement can take place. The "interrupt" signal carried by the nigrostriatal path is weak or absent because of cell death in the substantia nigra; without this command signal to the corpus striatum, the motor cortex tends to prolong any ongoing behavior or posture.

17. The motor cortex includes M1, the primary motor area located in the precentral gyrus and having direct connections to the ventral horn cells; premotor area (PM) lying just anterior to M1 and connecting with the motor neurons of the ventral horn only indirectly by way of both M1 and a path through the brain stem reticular formation and the reticulospinal path; and M2 (supplementary motor area), located anterior to M1 on the medial surface of the frontal lobes just above the cingulate gyrus and having direct connections to the cord through the corticospinal tract.

18. Each part of M1 controls a different part of the body, and the parts are laid out along the precentral gyrus roughly in the order from toe to head. M1 connects to the motor neurons of the cord by way of the corticospinal tract. Damage to M1 can produce flaccid paralysis, but usually the result of the damage is paresis. M1 and S1 function as a unit rather than as separate sensory and motor areas, apparently to enable finer somatosensory control over precise, detailed movements, most of which occur in the hands and face.

19. M1 and the corticospinal tract evolved to gain direct control over parts of CPGs, thus making fractionation possible.

20. M2 is similar to M1 in that it projects directly to the motor neurons of the cord by way of the corticospinal path; but instead of somatosensory input, M2 receives information from the visual and auditory areas of the cortex. Damage to M2 produces akinesia and mutism. M2 appears to prepare the other motor areas of the brain to make a particular response when the correct stimulus occurs. It is also involved with division of labor between the hemispheres.

21. The premotor cortex (PM) receives visual and auditory input like M2 and also seems to take part in preparatory sets, but unlike M2, some of its output goes to the brain stem reticular formation rather than directly into the cord. Thus, PM is probably more involved with preparatory postural sets and gross body adjustments that accompany the finer movements dictated by M2 and M1.

Glossary

acetylcholine (Ach) The neurotransmitter secreted at the neuromyal junction. (343)

agonists Muscles whose contractions propel the body part in the direction of the intended movement. (361)

akinesia A severe difficulty in the initiation of movements of any kind. (387)

alpha motor neuron A motor neuron (ventral horn cell) that innervates a muscle fiber. (352)

ampulla A swelling at the base of each semicircular canal in which is found the cupula. (357)

antagonists Muscles whose contractions work in opposition to the intended movement. (361)

ataxia Failure of muscle coordination; symptom of cerebellar damage. (360)

autoimmune disease A disorder in which the body self-destructively forms antibodies against its own tissues. (374)

biceps The flexor that is slung between your shoulder and elbow, whose job it is to pull the forearm in toward the body. (361)

bradykinesia Slowness and deliberateness of movement. (375)

caudate nucleus Largest structure in the corpus striatum. (371)

central pattern generators (CPGs) Networks of

interconnected neurons that collectively control a set of muscles needed to produce a movement or sequence of movements. (365)

cerebellum Pontine brain-stem structure composed of nuclei overlaid with convoluted cortex; serves to time and coordinate muscle contractions. (359)

chorea Continual, involuntary jerky movements of the face, tongue, extremities, and, occasionally, trunk and respiratory muscles. (371)

coordination Timing the facilitation of synergistic muscles and inhibition of antagonistic muscles so that their actions are not in conflict with one another. (361)

corpus striatum A group of large motor nuclei lying between the cerebral cortex and the core of the cerebrum. (370)

corticoreticulospinal tract A pathway that runs from the cerebral cortex, through the reticular formation, into the spinal cord. (391)

corticospinal tract A large fiber bundle connecting the more anterior regions of the cerebral cortex with the spinal cord. (383)

cupula the gelatinous mass that contains the hair cells of the ampulla. (358)

deafferentation Cutting off the sensory input from a segment of the body. (365)

decomposition of movements Cerebellar damage syndrome in which the person must consciously think out each movement in order for it to occur. (360)

disynaptic arc Reflex arc having a set of interneurons interposed between the afferents and motor neurons; thus, having two sets of synapses. (345)

dysmetria Symptom of cerebellar injury in which the trajectories of movements are wobbly and jerky. (361)

electromyogram (EMG) Recording the electrical activity generated when muscle fibers fire. (365)

extensor muscle A muscle that extends a limb away from the body. (350)

extensor thrust reflex Reflex that extends the leg into a rigid pillar in response to pressure on the sole of the foot. (364)

flaccid paralysis A loss of control over muscle contraction and loss of tone (muscles are limp). (383)

flexor muscle A muscle that pulls a limb toward the body. (350)

fractionation Breaking into CPG circuits to command fractional parts of these groupings; this allows cortical control over individual movements. (387)

gamma efferent A motor neuron that innervates the muscle spindle fiber. (352)

globus pallidus A nucleus lying just medial to the putamen that makes up part of the corpus stratum. (371)

Golgi tendon organ Kinesthetic receptor on tendon. (348)

gravitational sense Ability to sense the direction of gravity; one of the vestibular senses. (354)

hemiplegia Paralysis on one side only. (383)

hierarchical motor system Arrangement in which the parts of the motor system at each level command the units at lower levels and are commanded by those at higher levels. (377)

Huntington's disease Fatal brain disease involving loss of cells in the striatum with accompanying motor problems such as chorea. (371)

inertia Tendency for objects to remain in motion once started or to remain still once stopped. (354)

intention tremor Oscillation of the hand that increases as the hand nears the target of an arm movement. (363)

internal capsule A collection of tracts that cuts through the striatum, separating it into caudate and putamen. (371)

interrupt signal Theoretical signal from substantia nigra to striatum that stops ongoing behavior in order for a new behavior to start. (379)

isometric contraction Contraction that does not shorten the muscle. (347)

isotonic contraction Contraction that shortens the muscle. (347)

kinesthesis The muscle, skin, tendon, and joint sense that tells you where your body parts are relative to one another. (347)

l-DOPA The precursor for dopamine. (376)

linear acceleration sense Sense mode that enables you to feel yourself being moved through space at an increasing or decreasing speed. (354)

load The amount of force acting against the muscle. (350)

M1 The primary motor cortex; located in the precentral gyrus. (380)

M2 The supplementary motor cortex; located in the medial surface of the frontal lobe anterior to M1. (383)

macula A patch of receptor cells found in both the saccule and the utricle; receptor for the gravitational and linear acceleration senses. (354)

mesencephalic locomotor region A midbrain area

containing control circuits for walking and related behaviors. (370)

monosynaptic arc Reflex arc having only afferents connecting directly to efferents, thus having one set of synapses. (345)

motor cortex The region of the frontal lobe that includes M1, M2, and the premotor area. (383)

motor unit A motor neuron together with the muscle fibers with which it connects. (343)

multisynaptic arc Reflex arc having one or more sets of interneurons interposed between the afferents and efferents, thus having more than one set of synapses. (345)

muscle fiber A muscle cell. (343)

muscle spindle Muscle fibers specialized as sensory receptors that detect degree of contraction. (348)

muscle tone The level of steady, isometric contraction in the muscle. (353)

mutism The absence of speech. (387)

neuromyal junction The synapse between a motor neuron and a muscle fiber. (343)

nigrostriatal pathway The axons of substantia nigra neurons that project to the striatum. (376)

otoliths Tiny bone fragments that weight the top of the maculas in the saccule and utricle. (354)

paresis A partial paralysis that is seen as a muscle weakness. (383)

Parkinson's disease Incurable brain disorder with loss of neurons in the substantia nigra; symptoms are tremor, rigidity, and bradykinesia. (374)

patella A small, circular piece of bone that forms your "knee cap." (350)

patellar tendon reflex A rapid contraction of the quadriceps when it is stretched with a blow to the patellar tendon. (350)

peristalsis Slow, rhythmic movements of the esophagus, stomach, and intestine. (343)

postures Relatively static positions of body parts produced by patterns of isometric contraction. (347)

precentral gyrus Area of frontal lobe just anterior to the central fissure. (380)

precursor A substance from which the chemical of interest is made. (376)

premotor cortex (PM) Region of frontal lobe between M1 and the prefrontal cortex. (381)

preparatory set A readiness for making a particular response to a particular stimulus. (388)

program A sequence of steps needed to bring about some specific result. (369)

putamen One of the nuclei of the corpus striatum; it lies just lateral to the internal capsule. (371)

reciprocal inhibition Arrangement between some pairs of reflex circuits that allows each circuit to inhibit the other. (362)

recurrent collateral An axon branch that returns to the region of the cell body; for example, motor neurons send recurrent collaterals to Renshaw cells. (345)

Renshaw cell A type of ventral horn interneuron that can induce the motor neuron to rest by inhibiting it. (345)

reticulospinal tract Pathway connecting the brainstem reticular formation with the gray matter of the spinal cord. (381)

rigidity Stiff limbs and postures with little spontaneous movement. (375)

rotary acceleration sense Sense mode that enables you to feel increases or decreases in the speed with which your head is being rotated. (357)

S⁺ A stimulus that signals that a particular response will now be reinforced. (388)

S⁻ A stimulus that signals that no reinforcement will follow the response. (388)

saccule One of the cavities of the inner ear containing receptors for the vestibular senses. (354)

semicircular canals Sense organs of the inner ear responsible for the rotary acceleration sense. (357)

servomechanism A device that uses feedback to keep a system functioning within prescribed limits. (352)

set point The target point for the servomechanism; the desired state that it is set to maintain. (352)

smooth muscles Found in the viscera; they are whitish with no striations. (342)

species-typical behavior Large, genetically determined motor pattern that integrates many reflexes and CPGs into a goal-oriented act; for example, nest building. (377)

stepping reflex Flexion of the leg in response to removal of pressure on the sole of the foot. (364)

stereocilia Hairlike protrusions on the receptor cells of the macula and cupula. (354)

stretch reflex The recontraction of a muscle triggered by stretch or relaxation of that muscle. (349)

striate muscles The muscles that are attached to bones and that move the parts of our bodies around or hold them in fixed positions; also called striped, or skeletal. (342)

striatum The caudate nucleus and putamen taken together. (371)

subroutine A sequence of commands that can be used as a part of several larger programs. (370)

substantia nigra A midbrain motor nucleus that appears to supply an "interrupt signal" to the circuits between the motor cortex and striatum. (371)

supplementary motor cortex Area on the medial surface of the frontal lobe just anterior to M1; also called M2. (383)

synergists Muscles whose contractions aid the agonist muscle by pulling a body part in the same direction. (366)

tendon Connective tissue that attaches a muscle to a bone. (348)

tremor Small, back-and-forth oscillations of a limb, especially the hand; cerebellar symptom. (361)

tremor at rest Trembling of hands that diminishes during voluntary hand movement; symptom of Parkinson's disease. (375)

triceps The extensor that pulls the forearm out, away from the body. (361)

utricle One of the cavities of the inner ear containing receptors for the vestibular senses. (354)

vertex readiness potential An EEG wave that always occurs just before a movement and seems to be associated with the intention to move or a readiness to make the response rather than with the response itself. (387)

vestibular nuclei Brain-stem areas containing the first set of synapses in the vestibular projection system. (358)

Sleep and Attention

Sleep-Associated Disorders

INSOMNIA
Concept: insomnia

Acute Versus Chronic Insomnia

Drug Treatment of Insomnia
Concepts: barbiturate, flurazepam, benzodiazepine

NARCOLEPSY
Concepts: narcolepsy, cataplexy, waking nightmares, automatic behavior episodes

Summary

I f you are a typical person, you spend between a quarter and a third of your life lying down doing nothing. That sounds like it just might be the greatest waste of time that nature ever invented. If you weren't sleeping during all those hours, you could be partying, studying, working at a part-time job, or enjoying yourself in innumerable other ways. Sleep seems to be an absolute necessity, but why? It's true that the body needs rest and relaxation from time to time, but the need for rest can't be the reason for sleep. If it were, you could relieve the feeling of sleepiness just by lying down and taking it easy for a while. Perhaps it is the brain more than the body that really needs the time out. The fatigue dispelled by sleep may be mental rather than physical. This is an appealing explanation at first glance, but it too has a problem; the brain never rests. Even during the deepest sleep, nerve cells throughout the nervous system are firing repeatedly, working hard at their jobs. So, if the brain needs time out, we must ask, time out from what?

Arousal is an important aspect of sleep. One of the major differences between sleeping and waking is the level of arousal in the nervous system. Attention improves as you go up the sleeping–waking continuum and gets worse as you go down the continuum into lower levels of arousal. Brain-stem structures such as the raphe nuclei that are involved in altering the waking brain's responsiveness to stimuli (Chapter 8) are also involved in sleep. Attention, sleep, and arousal are all so interrelated that it is difficult to discuss one without the others. In fact, it could be that the process of attending is the key to understanding the need for sleep.

■ Arousal, Brain Waves, and Attention

The study of sleep, arousal, and brain correlates of attention had to await the electronic age. Before electronic amplifiers became available, there was no way to record the one type of data that is absolutely indispensable if we are to see objectively a subject's arousal level, namely, brain waves. Without the electroencephalograph we have no way of knowing whether a person is awake or asleep. Because the following discussions assume that you have a basic understanding of an EEG recording, it would be a good idea to glance back at the explanation of the EEG in Chapter 5 before you read further.

The Meaning of Brain Waves

The voltage changes pictured in the EEG record are the algebraic summations of millions of EPSPs, IPSPs, and nerve impulses occurring within the general vicinity of the electrode (Brazier, 1962). Each of these types of current generates a field that spreads out, weakening as it goes (see Chapter 4). Overlapping fields combine in complex fashions, sometimes adding to each other, sometimes subtracting. Presumably, the greater the number of impulses occurring together at one time, the greater is this summation and the larger the resultant voltage shift (Verzeano, 1977). In other words, the more the impulses are synchronized with one another, the larger the EEG wave (Figure 10.1). Thus, in the language of EEG researchers, **synchrony** refers to the clustering of electrical events as opposed to **desynchrony**, the condition in which they spread out randomly in time. Synchrony produces large, slow waves; desynchrony yields small, high-frequency waves. Note that the size of an EEG wave is not necessarily a reflection of the number of active neurons near the electrode but rather the degree to which cells are synchronizing their impulses. So, the largest EEG waves in a normal brain occur in the highly synchronous state of deep sleep in which the *fewest* cells are active.

When you first look at an EEG record, it may seem like a line of meaningless squiggles. The more you look at such records, however, the more you begin to see regularities. For example, Figure 10.2 shows that there are certain sections of the record in which there is greater synchrony than at other times. **Alpha waves**, the easiest ones to spot, are moderately synchronous and occur at the rate of about 8–12 per second (8–12 Hertz). **Beta waves** are quite small (highly desynchronized), and the variations are very rapid—about 30–45 Hz (Figure 10.2). Alpha waves are generated by the thalamus and seem to represent

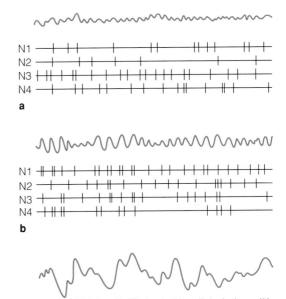

Figure 10.1 Three samples of a fictitious EEG record showing varying degrees of synchrony. N1–N4 are four cortical neurons. The short vertical lines crossing the time lines under the EEG record represent the nerve impulses that contributed to the brain waves shown. (**a**) A desynchronized rhythm. (**b**) The impulses begin to cluster, and synchrony appears in the record as alpha rhythm. This synchrony builds to the level of delta rhythm in **c**. The clustering of the nerve impulses during synchrony would have been more obvious if the firing of several hundred neurons could have been depicted rather than just four.

an "idling rhythm" that occurs when the visual parts of the cortex are not particularly busy. It is the random appearing desynchronous beta waves that are best correlated with thinking, perceiving, and decision making.

EEG waves can vary in two ways: amplitude (height) and frequency (cycles per second). Alpha waves have moderate amplitude and frequency, and beta waves have low amplitude and high frequency. At the opposite extreme from beta waves are **delta**

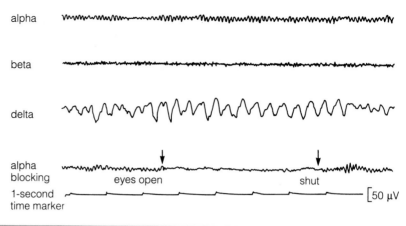

Figure 10.2 EEG records showing alpha waves (rhythm), beta waves, delta waves, alpha blocking, and a 1-second time marker. Alpha blocking refers to the replacement of alpha with beta rhythm when the eyes are opened. The sizes of the potentials are indicated by the 50 μV marker at the bottom. (Adapted from Cooper et al., 1980)

waves (Figure 10.2) with high amplitude (extreme synchrony) and very low frequency (about 1–4 per second). The strong synchrony of delta waves may mean that giant groups of neurons are being driven to fire roughly in step with one another rather than being allowed to participate in the small but meaningful networks assumed to underlie individual thoughts. If this is true, then it is not surprising that delta waves only appear when a person is unconscious, either asleep or in a coma. Without thoughts or percepts, the conscious mind does not exist.

Arousal and Habituation

The subject whose EEG record is pictured in Figure 10.2 is demonstrating a very interesting effect. When the subject's eyes are closed, alpha rhythm shows up strongly, but as soon as the eyes open, it disappears and is replaced with low-voltage, fast rhythms near the beta range of 30 cycles per second. This sudden replacement of alpha rhythm with beta rhythm is called **alpha blocking** and isn't necessarily linked just to vision. For example, if a subject is asked to mentally multiply 19 × 3 (with eyes closed), the same alpha blocking occurs; beta replaces alpha while the subject is concentrating on the problem. Concentration involves arousal, and arousal produces desynchrony in the EEG. The shift from the synchrony of alpha to the desynchrony of beta suggests that the cortex has stopped "idling" and begun processing input. In the case of the math problem,

the input originated in some area of the brain, but in the case of opening the eyes, the input came up the visual system from the retinas. Cortical desynchrony (alpha blocking) is now a standard, accepted way of assessing a subject's state of arousal and attention.

Figure 10.3 shows the desynchronization of a dog's EEG by a loud whistle. The large, synchronized slow waves at the beginning of the record indicate that the dog is sleeping at that time. The whistle arouses the nervous system, and the EEG reveals this change with a shift toward lower-voltage, fast rhythms. Notice, though, that the whistle also elicited behavioral responses from the dog; the head came up, the eyes opened, and the ears and head turned toward the direction of the sound. These changes and the desynchronization are parts of a pattern called the orienting reaction.

The Orienting Reaction In the evolutionary development of the attention–concentration mechanisms of the brain, it is likely that the starting point was the appearance of some primitive form of orienting reaction. One basic survival capacity needed by even primitive organisms is the ability to classify any novel stimulus (i.e., one never experienced before) as either dangerous, food-related, relevant to mating, or just unimportant. This cannot be accomplished in a slow, careful study of the novel stimulus; it must be done in a second or less. If not, the prey will escape, or the predator will strike. What was desperately needed for survival was a reflexlike response pattern, involving the entire body and brain, that would completely interrupt ongoing behavior in favor of immediately collecting all possible information about the stimulus to be classified. The **orienting reaction**, then, involves a whole list of components, some of which include pupillary dilation for better vision; temporary decrease in auditory threshold (about 4–10 dB in humans); cortical desynchronization; striate muscle responses that orient receptors toward the stimulus; rise in muscle tone for faster-responding, blood vessel dilation in brain and constriction in gut and skin; increased respiration; temporary slowing of heart rate; and a sudden drop in the electrical resistance of the skin associated with activation of the sweat glands.

The orienting response (OR) may have had its origins in life-and-death survival situations, but it certainly does not wait for a crisis before it appears. It is the novelty of the stimulus that is important; the greater the novelty, the more strongly the stimulus elicits the OR. Slightly novel stimuli get a small but measurable OR; a sudden, unexpected intense stimulus such as you experience when the wind slams a door behind your back brings out the entire pattern in full strength. If you are beginning to lose interest in this explanation of the OR, your EEG is probably beginning to show more and more synchrony in the form of increased alpha rhythm, your respiration is slowing, and your muscle tone is decreasing. But if something is said in the next sentence that is a new and unexpected idea, your EEG shifts back toward desynchrony, your skin resistance decreases, respiration increases, and so on. In other words, you experience a mild orienting reaction to the novel idea. If you are studying in a very quiet room and someone opens the door and enters, you must actively inhibit your natural orienting response to this novel stimulus if you do not wish to interrupt your studying. Your day is full of orienting responses of varying intensity. Orienting is the most basic process in attention.

Arousal and the Reticular Formation   So far we have used the word *arousal* in an everyday sense simply to designate a state of increased awareness, but now it is time to become more precise. There are at least three aspects to **arousal**: experientially, it is an alteration of consciousness in the direction of becoming more alert with increased concentration on selected stimuli; behaviorally, it is an orienting reaction; in terms of brain waves, it is desynchronization. The part of the brain that is responsible for arousal is the reticular formation of the brain stem.

The **reticular formation** (Figure 10.4) is a long column of gray matter that starts at the bottom end of the spinal cord and runs up through the brain stem into the thalamus (Brodal, 1957). Because of its central location, it is often described as the core of those structures. The brain-stem portions of this system are the zones most intimately connected with arousal.

Figure 10.5 is drawn from a remarkable microscope slide of an entire rat brain stem and shows a single reticular neuron with its cell body and dendrites in the pontine reticular formation and axon branches running down into the cord and up into thalamus and hypothalamus. Each of the little side branches coming off of the main axon is carrying that cell's nerve impulses to a different part of the nervous system. If you count these side branches, you can see that this one cell is spreading its influence to more than 25 different areas, each with its own function. What a contrast there is between this reticular cell and (for example) a neuron in one of the sensory projection systems that typically sends its axon to two or three nuclei at best. This generalized projection of pontine reticular cells implies that they are doing something very basic that is needed by almost the entire brain stem. The regulation of arousal levels to determine sleeping and waking would be that sort of basic, general effect. In fact, the portion of the reticular formation in the pons seems to be heavily involved in sleep, as we will see.

The high levels of arousal that characterize the waking state are heavily dependent on the part of the reticular formation just above the pontine level, the **midbrain reticular formation (MBRF)** (Steriade et al., 1980). Axons of these cells travel upward (Figure 10.4), some of them synapsing on reticular neurons in the thalamus and others traveling through the hypothalamus to reach the cortex (Scheibel & Scheibel, 1970). The lower route through the hypothalamus is most likely involved in producing the generalized kind of arousal that makes the difference between sleeping and waking, while the connections into the reticular nuclei of the thalamus are probably involved in the short bursts of arousal that are such an important part of attention and the orienting response (Jasper, 1954; Scheibel, 1980).

It is the neurons of the MBRF, then, that desynchronize the cortical EEG record during arousal. What is it that triggers these neurons to produce this state of arousal? The visual, auditory, and somatic–kinesthetic projection systems (Chapters 6–8) all send axon branches into the reticular system, and

reticular neurons spread their dendrites across all of these input channels like a spider's web, catching every sensory message the receptors emit. Each neuron collects from at least several senses; thus summating EPSPs in those cells are not specific to any one piece of sensory information. All sensory messages are thrown together into a general "mish mash" that apparently no longer contains any specific information; just the fact that "something is happening out there in the outside world that must be dealt with." That appears to be the message these cells send to the rest of the brain, and this lack of specificity is one of the reasons for calling this source of

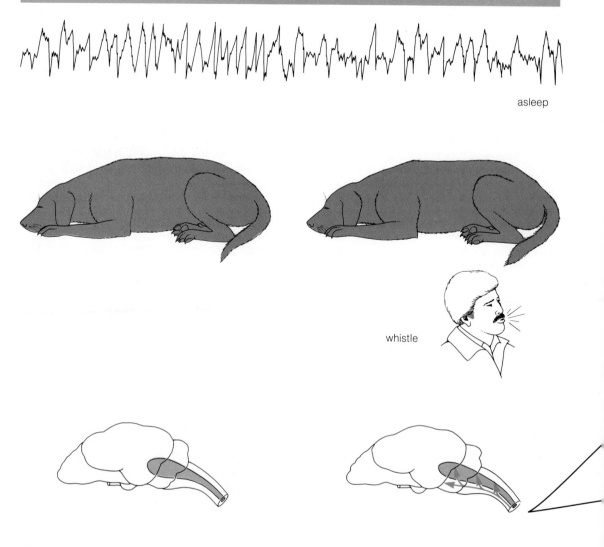

asleep

whistle

facilitation, **nonspecific**. So, it is sensory messages in the projection systems that trigger activity in the MBRF. This is illustrated in Figure 10.3, which shows the auditory system arousing the MBRF, which in turn arouses thalamic reticular formation and cortex.

Sensory input is not the only source of excitation for reticular neurons. The cortex also sends axons into the MBRF. If you have developed the bad habit of thinking about your next day's problems after you have gone to bed and are trying to go to sleep, your insomnia may well be the result of this link from the cortex. Through it the thought processes in the cortex are probably able to stimulate the reticular formation, which in turn would stimulate the cortex. This additional cortical arousal would make it even easier to think about the next day's problems and

Figure 10.3 Orienting reaction in a sleeping dog. Large, slow delta waves characterize the EEG before arousal from sleep. The brain pictures show the auditory activity from the whistle stimulating the dog's brain-stem reticular formation, which in turn arouses the cortex. The lower row of brain diagrams shows that the auditory information about the whistle is being routed up to the audi-

tory areas in the cortex, but a response cannot be generated until the cortex has been aroused by the reticular formation. The EEG record here looks a bit different than in previous figures because the EEG paper was moving at a lower speed, thus compressing the waves. (Adapted from French, 1957)

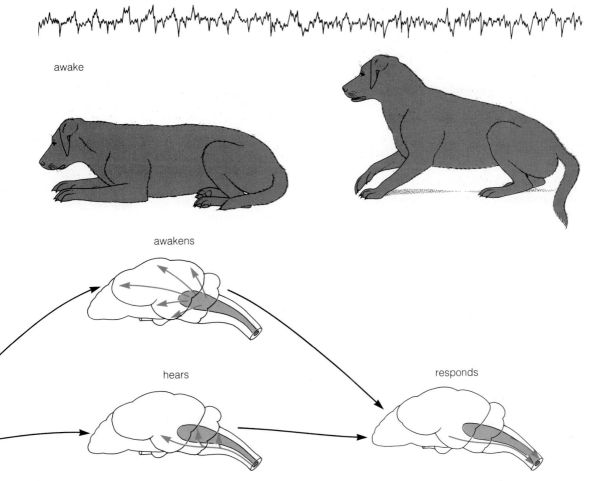

awake

awakens

hears

responds

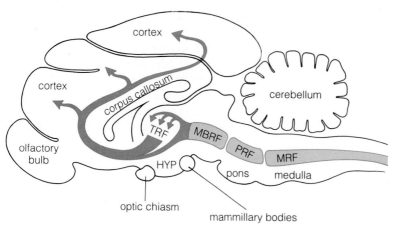

Figure 10.4 Midsagittal view of a cat brain with a schematic diagram of the reticular formation. Reticular cells are found all the way from the spinal cord up through the thalamus. (MBRF = midbrain reticular formation; MRF = medullary reticular formation; PRF = pontine reticular formation; TRF = thalamic reticular formation; HYP = hypothalamus.) Pathways taken by the axons of the MBRF are shown in blue. Some axon branches swing in a dorsal direction from the MBRF to synapse within the TRF, whereas other branches grow in a ventral direction through the hypothalamus. (The hypothalamus is the area from the mammillary bodies forward to just anterior of the optic chiasm.) In the vicinity of the hypothalamus, MBRF axons are joined by TRF axons, and both course forward into the cortex.

much harder to go to sleep. Arousal is an important aspect of the emotional state we call anxiety.

The thalamus contains several nuclei (reticular and intralaminar) that seem to be a branch of the reticular formation specialized for attention. When the MBRF is activated, the entire cortex is aroused as a unit; but when thalamic reticular cells are fired, localized areas of facilitation appear in the cortex, and their location depends on which reticular cells are active (Jasper, 1954; Lynn, 1966). Recall from Chapter 8 that the reticular and intralaminar nuclei were discussed in connection with the process of attending to pain sensations. Apparently, information coming into the cortex along the sensory projection systems has relatively little effect on the cortex unless the thalamic reticular formation is helping out. If you flash a light in the eyes of a cat made completely unconscious by anesthesia, you can still see a wave of activity in the EEG that indicates that the information arrived in the cortex; but without reticular arousal, the cat fails to respond. The reason can be seen in the experiment shown in Figure 10.6. The two records are evoked potentials (see Chapter 5) recorded in the visual cortex following stimulation of the visual fibers of the optic chiasm. In comparing the two potentials, you can see that the cortex barely responds to the visual input unless the reticular formation is also active (Singer, 1979).

So, the MBRF and the thalamic reticular formation both facilitate cortical neurons; in the case of the MBRF, however, this help has nothing to do with paying attention to a specific stimulus. Thus, the help from the MBRF is called nonspecific facilitation, whereas the thalamic variety, which is directed only at the particular area of cortex needed at the moment, could be called specific facilitation. So, there are two reasons for calling the facilitation from the MBRF "nonspecific." It is nonspecific in the sense that the specific sensory information has been lost and it also lacks a specific destination in the cortex. It is my hypothesis that both specific and nonspecific facilitation occur as a part of the orienting reflex.

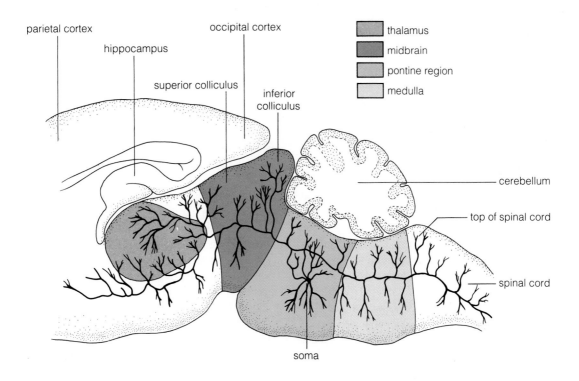

parietal cortex

occipital cortex

hippocampus

superior colliculus

inferior colliculus

	thalamus
	midbrain
	pontine region
	medulla

cerebellum

top of spinal cord

spinal cord

soma

Figure 10.5 Midsagittal section of a rat brain showing the soma, dendrites, and most of the axon of one pontine reticular formation neuron. The soma and dendrites are located in the pontine brain stem, but the long, multibranched axon sends one arm down through the medulla into the spinal cord and the other up through the midbrain into the thalamus and on into the limbic system. The cerebellum lies between the inferior colliculus and the top of the spinal cord. The occipital cortex lies immediately above the superior and inferior colliculi of the midbrain in this picture. Between the parietal cortex and thalamus lies the hippocampus, which in the rat is much more dorsal than in the human. (Adapted from Scheibel & Scheibel, 1967)

Figure 10.6 Two short segments of an EEG record showing cortical evoked potentials. The segments are "magnified" in time with each being only about 35 ms long. (**a**) A shock to the optic chiasm (indicated by the first arrow) produces an evoked potential in the visual cortex consisting of four successive waves, two of which are in the positive direction, two in the negative. (**b**) The potential is greatly enhanced, especially in waves 3 and 4. The difference is that in **b** the reticular system was stimulated along with the optic chiasm, thus strongly facilitating the cortical neurons. (Adapted from Singer, 1979)

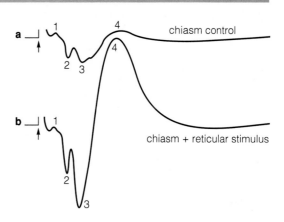

a

chiasm control

b

chiasm + reticular stimulus

Habituation An organism can't spend the entire day orienting to every stimulus that appears. Most daily stimuli are unimportant events that have no bearing on the life of the animal. Consider a rabbit munching foliage in a meadow. A breeze is rippling the tops of the plants around it, creating constant movement. Birds are singing, dogs are barking in the far distance, and cars are passing along the road 100 yards away. None of this stirs the rabbit because none of these stimuli are novel. The animal has oriented to all of them repeatedly in the past, and they have gradually lost their ability to evoke the OR. This loss of the OR is a very basic form of learning called **habituation**.

Sokolov (1963), in his classic studies of the OR, would fasten a dog in a harness on a table (just as Pavlov had done earlier) and present stimuli such as a 60-Hz tone sounding for 2 seconds. At first the tone produced an excellent OR, but as it was repeated at fairly regular intervals over the next 10 minutes, the response gradually habituated. Some part of the dog's nervous system had constructed a memory of the tone and was using that memory to recognize each subsequent presentation. Another part of the brain had classified the stimulus as unimportant. The result was a decrease in the ability of the tone to arouse the dog's cortex.

Now, Sokolov raised the pitch of the tone to 120 Hz and continued to present tone after tone. At the first presentation of the higher pitch, the OR was back again, showing that this stimulus was now different enough that it did not fit the memory the dog had constructed. You can only habituate to a stimulus you have memorized. However, in a few more trials with the 120-Hz tone, habituation had returned. If the process were repeated with 500-Hz, 600-Hz, 700-Hz, and 800-Hz tones, each new frequency would probably elicit the OR, but habituation would become faster and faster. This decrease in habituation time is called **generalization of habituation** (Lynn, 1966), and we will meet it again later when we try to explain why sleep occurs.

Not every stimulus habituates. If you sound the tone every day just before you feed the dog, the stimulus takes on meaning through classical conditioning. Any stimulus associated with a motivation such as hunger, thirst, sex, or emotion like fear or anger does not habituate. It has become a cue that other, more meaningful stimuli are about to appear. There are probably thousands of house cats in the United States that give magnificent ORs to the sound of a can opener. It is rumored that male sophomores rarely show habituation to a stimulus resembling the noise of a pop-top parting from a beer can.

At first glance, one might suspect that habituation occurred not because of any stimulus learning but simply because the repetitive stimulus fatigues neurons in the sensory paths. Fatiguing a neuron, however, is a very difficult thing to do. Most neurons can fire hundreds of times a second for scores of seconds without dropping their rate. But the real evidence against a fatigue theory is the fact that an OR can occur to an absent stimulus (Sokolov, 1963). For example, if the dog in the harness has listened to 50 tones presented at regular 20-second intervals and has completely habituated to the sound, a beautiful OR can be obtained by simply omitting a tone when the time comes for it to be presented. The omission is just as novel as the tone was the first time it occurred. In a conditioning experiment, the non-occurrence of an expected reward elicits a strong OR (Grastyan, 1959). We can speculate that in habituation a neural network is first constructed to represent the stimulus (i.e., the stimulus is learned), and then this neuron network inhibits the OR to that stimulus whenever it recurs (Lynn, 1966). The site of the habituation process in the brain appears to be the reticular formation.

■ The Nature of Sleep

We noted at the beginning of this chapter that the brain does not "turn off" when a person goes to sleep. It remains as busy as during relaxed wakefulness. However, its whole pattern of activity reorganizes, and the result of this radical shift is that the person stops responding to or paying attention to the environment. Attention may exist during some parts of sleep, but if so, it seems to be directed inward to the brain's own processes. Thought processes of various sorts occur during sleep, but some of them are radically different from waking cognitions; the

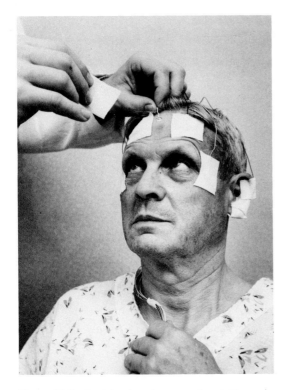

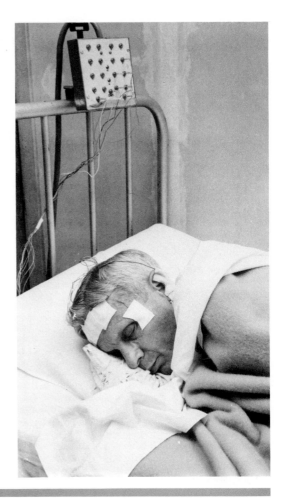

Figure 10.7 A subject in a sleep experiment. Electrodes are fixed on the scalp with conductive paste. The wires from the electrodes run to a connector box on the bed, and the cable from the connector runs through the wall to EEG amplifiers in the next room. (From Kleitman, 1960)

type of mental process experienced at any time depends on the level of arousal. Just as in the waking state, we can follow the changes in a person's arousal level during sleep by watching the changes in EEG waves (Figure 10.7).

Arousal Levels and Sleep

We have seen that EEG desynchronization, a shift from lower to higher frequencies, indicates arousal in the nervous system and accompanies an increase in attention. We now want to see what happens to conscious experience when the EEG shifts toward synchrony. The entire continuum of arousal from highest to lowest is described in Table 10.1. Note

that as you drop down the continuum from the highest level, the EEG shifts from low-voltage, fast-frequency waves to high-voltage, slow waves. In other words, synchrony increases in the sleep regions of the continuum, with the very low-frequency delta waves at the very bottom. The division of sleep into four stages according to the EEG pattern is now universally accepted in clinics and research labs.

EEG Identification of Sleep Stages During stage 1 sleep, low-voltage, high-frequency waves dominate the EEG record. Sleep stage 2 EEG is characterized by alphalike, synchronized waves of about 10–16 Hz that first increase in amplitude and then decrease.

Table 10.1 The Arousal Continuum from Highest to Lowest Levels

Level	EEG Description	Characteristic Waveform
Excitement–emotion	Low voltage, high frequency (30–45 Hz)	Beta
Alert–attentive	Low voltage, fairly fast (15–30 Hz)	—
Relaxed–wakeful	Moderate amplitude, moderate frequency (8–12 Hz and some faster)	Alpha mixed with faster
Drowsy	Moderate amplitude and frequency	Mostly alpha
Sleep Stage 1	Low-voltage fast rhythms similar to alert state	—
Stage 2	Moderate amplitude with short bursts of 10–16 Hz waves and K complexes	Sleep spindles
Stage 3	Transition zone: contains some spindles and some slow waves	Delta
Stage 4	More than 50% high-voltage slow waves	Delta

Based on Lindsley, 1957, and Webb, 1975.

This waxing and waning gives them a spindle shape and earns them the name **sleep spindles**. Also apparent is the **K-complex**, a combination of a few high-voltage slow waves followed by about 1 second of 14-Hz waves. As a sleeper drops down into stage 3, delta waves begin to appear, and stage 4 is almost entirely high-amplitude delta waves (Figure 10.8).

Our rule that the frequency decreases as arousal decreases holds nicely with one exception: stage 1 sleep. As a subject becomes drowsy, the record shows more and more synchrony in the form of alpha and from the frequency rule, you would expect this to increase gradually into delta waves. What happens instead is that sleep onset (stage 1) wipes out alpha rhythm and replaces it with beta rhythm—an event termed **desynchronization**. This is so unexpected

at this level of activation that one researcher was led to call stage 1, "paradoxical sleep" (Jouvet, 1967a).

The Architecture of Typical Sleep The average sleeper on a typical night drops from the waking, drowsy level of arousal down into stage 1, then 2, 3, and 4. After about 20–30 minutes in stage 4, arousal begins to increase again, with the cycle being completed as the sleeper emerges through stages 3 and 2 into stage 1 again (Figure 10.9). At this point, we must make an important distinction between the type of stage 1 that is entered from the drowsy condition (called **initial stage 1**) and the type entered from stage 2 (called **emergent stage 1**). The most obvious difference between the two is that during emergent

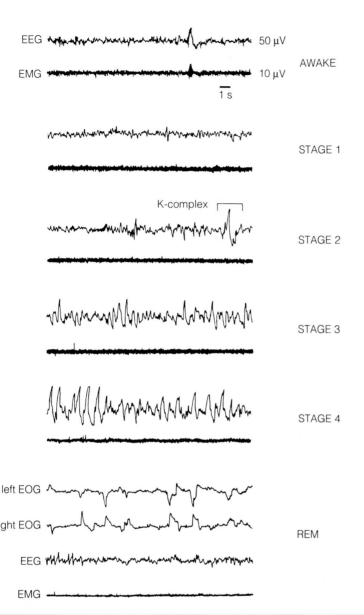

EEG   50 μV

EMG   10 μV

AWAKE

1 s

STAGE 1

K-complex

STAGE 2

STAGE 3

STAGE 4

left EOG

right EOG

EEG

EMG

REM

Figure 10.8 EEG, EMG, and EOG records from different points on the sleep–wake continuum. Both initial stage 1 and emergent stage 1 (REM) are similar to the waking state when EEG is considered, but note the difference in EMG between the two. The stage 2 record shown here contains one K-complex but no clear spindles. (Rechtschaffen & Kales, 1968)

stage 1, the eyes show peculiar bursts of movement beneath the closed lids. For this reason, this sleep state is often called **rapid eye movement sleep**, or **REM sleep**. The rest of sleep (stages 2, 3, and 4 plus initial stage 1) is collectively called **NREM sleep**. Notice that the normal route to REM sleep is via NREM sleep. As we will see later, this separation of the waking state from the REM state may be a vital protection against a serious neurological problem. However, the separation is missing in healthy, newborn infants without ill effects (Schultz et al., 1983). Humans start their lives having many waking–to–REM transitions along with the waking–to–NREM transitions that are normal for adults, but they gradually lose direct shifts to REM as they mature (McGinty, 1979).

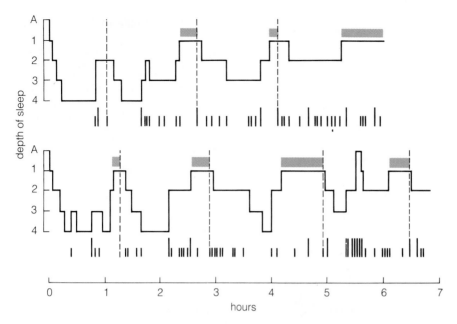

Figure 10.9 Sleep records from two subjects, each record covering an entire night of sleep (A = awake; 1–4 = the four stages of sleep). The continuous black line indicates the level of sleep; the dotted vertical lines show the end of one sleep cycle and the start of the next. Thick horizontal bars show the duration of each REM episode (emergent stage 1). Each vertical line below the record indicates a body movement, with the short lines for minor movements and the longer lines for major movements. (Adapted from Dement & Kleitman, 1957)

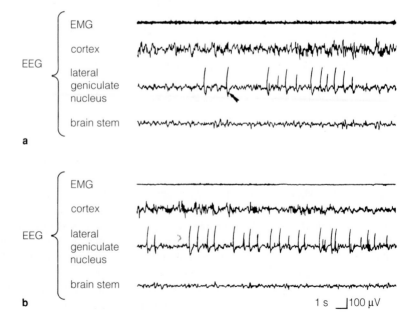

Figure 10.10 EEG and EMG records from a cat during the transition from NREM to REM sleep. The **b** segment follows the **a** segment immediately in time. As the transition is made, the EMG amplitude dwindles to near zero, indicating atonia. At the same time, PGO waves (indicated by arrow), another phenomenon of REM sleep, appear in the geniculate channel. (Adapted from Brooks, 1967)

After spending only 5 or 6 minutes in the first REM episode, the sleeper again drops down through stages 2 and 3 into stage 4 and then back up to REM sleep. A typical night includes at least three of these cycles, each of which is about 90 minutes long. In general, NREM periods get shorter as the night progresses, while REM periods become longer. Dreaming occurs whenever REM sleep is entered. Dreaming is a type of mental activity, or **mentation** in the terminology of dream researchers, and NREM sleep also has a type of mentation. Although the distinction is far from perfect, REM mentation is usually dreamlike in that there tends to be more images and bizarre, illogical events. NREM mentation resembles the drifting, loose associations of the drowsy state in which one mulls over real events from the previous day or anticipates coming events (Webb, 1978). This type of mentation is also occasionally reported by subjects who are awakened from REM sleep, just as dreams sometimes seem to occur in NREM sleep. The distinction between the two is far from precise. In light sleepers (those easily aroused by an external stimulus), the difference becomes even more blurred because they report a dream nearly three quarters of the time when awakened during NREM sleep, as opposed to less than one quarter for deep sleepers. Despite the indefiniteness of the line between REM and NREM mentation, there is a strong tendency for REM-state mental activity to be the most unusual sort of mental process that one will experience during any 24-hour period. We will probably only begin to understand REM mentation and its differences from waking thought after we have come to comprehend the reorganization of brain function that occurs during REM sleep.

Characteristics of REM Sleep

Discoveries about what happens in the nervous system during sleep come from experiments in which the subjects are not people but cats. A typical cat falls asleep 5–15 minutes after being placed on a soft cushion in a large, dark box; cats are exceptionally willing sleepers. Using cats also allows an investigator to permanently implant fine-wire electrodes into structures deep within the brain rather than being forced to record EEG from the scalp.

EEG records from a number of brain structures are usually supplemented by eye-movement and muscle recordings. One channel of the recorder is used for an **electro-oculogram (EOG)** (ee-LEK-tro-AHK-you-low-gram), which displays the voltage shifts generated by the eyes as they move. An electrode pair on both sides of one eye picks up these changes, and the EOG that results is a line that can move away from center in either direction according to the direction of the eye movement. Another channel displays an **electromyogram (EMG)** (ee-LEK-tro-MY-oh-gram), a record of the electrical activity of a muscle. The EMG is usually recorded from the neck muscles because they are especially good at revealing sleep states. Figure 10.10 shows three EEG channels and one EMG. The bottom four lines came right after the top four in the course of time. They are read as one continuous record from top left to top right to bottom left to bottom right. The entire sequence represents about 63 seconds and shows a typical transition from NREM to REM sleep.

Look first at the cortex channel. Notice the strongly synchronized, high-voltage slow waves at the beginning of the period, indicating NREM sleep. Now follow that channel through the lower half of the record and see how the amplitude of the waves gets smaller and smaller. If the record had been made at a slower paper speed so that the individual waves were more spread out, you could see clearly that as the waves get smaller they are also occurring more frequently. In other words, the cortical EEG is desynchronizing as the brain shifts from NREM to REM.

EMG voltage changes produced by the action potentials in the neck muscles occur so rapidly that, at this slow paper speed, the waves all run together into a fuzzy dark line (Figure 10.10), but notice the amplitude decreasing throughout this transition period. At the end of this section of record, with REM sleep fully in progress, the EMG record is almost nonexistent. The muscles have practically ceased to contract at all—that is, muscle tone has almost disappeared. This is a very unusual condition for cats or humans. Even when you are sitting perfectly relaxed in your most comfortable, overstuffed recliner chair, your muscles maintain considerable tone. They stay partly contracted in readiness to respond instantly to the call for the next movement. Even in NREM sleep, they maintain a minimal level of tone so that they can answer to your need to move into a new position. Only in the peculiar condition of REM sleep is muscle tone completely lost. This state of near paralysis is called **atonia**, and it is one of the best indicators that the sleeper has entered REM sleep.

REM-Sleep Atonia If you get a chance to observe a cat sleeping, note that the animal has two basic postures: a flattened crouch with its legs beneath the body and a sprawl on one side in which all body parts are completely supported by the surface on which the animal lies. In the crouch, the cat may give the illusion of being supported by the surface, but it is really holding its body in that posture with muscle contractions in trunk and leg muscles. The nose is held up off the surface, an impossible feat without a good deal of neck muscle tone. This is the same muscle tone that you see disappear from the EMG record in Figure 10.10 as the cat slips into REM sleep. So, if you see the cat suddenly flop over onto one side, it is likely that a REM sleep episode has begun.

Why does this atonia occur in the REM state, and what part of the nervous system is responsible for it? Muscle tone is a state of partial contraction that is produced by a mechanism, called the **stretch reflex**, found at all levels of the spinal cord (see Chapter 9). Receptors for this reflex are in the muscles themselves and respond to the stretching of the muscle. When a muscle is working, it is contracted, not stretched. When it stops working and relaxes, it stretches out. As soon as the muscle begins to relax (stretch), the receptors fire impulses back to motor neurons in the spinal cord, which respond by recontracting the muscle, thus maintaining muscle tone.

Higher centers in the brain can regulate the degree of tone. They do this by facilitating or inhibiting the motor neuron in the stretch reflex arc. In REM sleep, the stretch reflex is under intense inhibition, apparently from the reticular formation of the medulla (Pompeiano, 1970). This fact immediately provokes the question of why the entire striate muscle system should have to be actively inhibited during REM sleep. The answer to this may be clear

if you reflect for a moment. During REM sleep, the brain is at an arousal level similar to that of the waking state during active movement. Could it be that muscles are being inhibited to prevent movement? Perhaps the cat (or human) would be standing up and literally acting out a dream were it not for this state of near paralysis.

While making lesions in the dorsomedial part of the pontine brain stem, Jouvet discovered that some lesions seemed to remove the REM atonia (Morrison, 1979). When a cat with such a lesion enters REM sleep, it suddenly raises its head and appears to be watching something, yet its pupils are in the tightly contracted condition typical of sleep (Figure 10.11). Furthermore, the nictitating membrane (the translucent inner eyelid) is partly closed over the eye so that normal vision is not possible. All other signs of REM sleep are evident, yet the cat may now stand up and begin to move about. The species-typical predatory attack movements of stalking and cuffing with forepaw may occur, but they are directed at some point in midair. Is the cat stalking a dream mouse? Jouvet believes the movements are definitely the product of dream imagery because they are not well coordinated with the actual environment (Jouvet, 1979).

Atonia is not produced by a single mechanism. Morrison (1979) made tiny pinhead lesions scattered throughout the dorsomedial pontine reticular formation with different lesion sites in different cats and found that in each cat different muscle groups would be released from inhibition during REM sleep. Some animals could only get up on their forelegs, whereas others could actually walk. Some could follow a moving stimulus with their eyes in a crude sort of way, but others seemed completely unaware of visual stimuli. Predatory attack occurred with some lesions, head and eye orienting with others. Which behavior was released depended on which cells were lesioned (Hendricks et al., 1982). Apparently, the pontine region of the brain stem is full of motor control circuits for the reflexes that produce specific inborn behaviors, and these circuits seem to control the inhibitory neurons in the medulla. Surgically removing some of the neurons from the pons releases selected cord reflex circuits from control during the arousal of REM sleep (Figure 10.12).

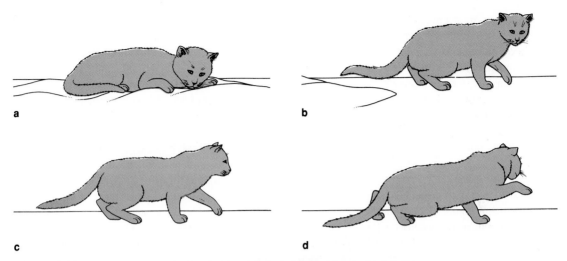

a

b

c

d

Figure 10.11 Cat with brain stem lesions that have eliminated REM-sleep atonia. In **a**, the REM episode begins, and the cat starts to get up. Note the tightly contracted pupils (showing that the cat is still sound asleep) and the peculiar half-erect posture in **b**. In **d**, pawing movements resembling attack are made, suggesting a reaction to some dream stimulus. (Adapted from Hendricks et al., 1982)

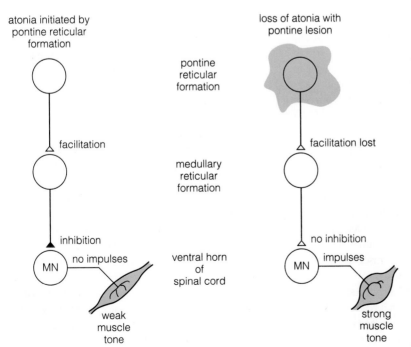

atonia initiated by pontine reticular formation

loss of atonia with pontine lesion

pontine reticular formation

facilitation

facilitation lost

medullary reticular formation

inhibition

no inhibition

MN   no impulses

MN   impulses

ventral horn of spinal cord

weak muscle tone

strong muscle tone

Figure 10.12 In the normal cat, cells in the pontine reticular formation command medullary neurons to inhibit motor paths to muscles, thus producing REM-sleep atonia. When pontine neurons have been killed, the inhibition is lost, and motor cells (MN) are free to contract muscles during sleep.

Could human sleepwalking or speaking during sleep be related to these phenomena? Some speech and body movements short of walking may occur for a moment right at the very end of a REM episode, but the majority of sleep movement and talking and all sleepwalking occurs in NREM sleep (Schwartz et al., 1978; Weitzman, 1981). Apparently, these phenomena do not indicate that something is going wrong in the pontine reticular formation.

PGO Waves A flat EMG record (indicating atonia) is not the only way to detect REM sleep. Look at the EEG record in Figure 10.10 from the electrode in the lateral geniculate nucleus (LGN) and note the high-voltage, spiked waves that occur every few seconds. These typically begin at the end of a NREM sleep episode just as the shift to REM is starting, and they continue on throughout the REM episode. They are called **PGO waves** because they are found in the pons (P), geniculate (G), and occipital lobe cortex (O) (Brooks, 1967). Apparently, they indicate a chain of activity that begins in the pontine reticular formation and sweeps up through the MBRF, the lateral geniculate, and finally the visual areas of the cortex (Munson & Graham, 1971). This means that they are found in all major visual areas of the brain from the eye-movement circuits of the brain stem to the pattern detectors of the cortex. It is a good guess that they have something to do with vision.

However, PGO waves do not relate exclusively to vision. If you have ever watched a cat or dog in sleep, you may have seen the animal occasionally twitch its tail or one leg. Whiskers vibrate momentarily, facial muscles jerk, and there are even minor spasms of the whole body. Body twitches are just as characteristic of REM sleep as are rapid eye movements. The best guess about their origin is that the firing in the pontine reticular formation that is seen in an EEG record as a PGO wave momentarily inhibits reticular cells in the medulla. These lower reticular neurons inhibit stretch reflexes in the cord, and when inhibitors of muscle contraction are themselves inhibited, the result is muscle contractions.

Do PGO waves themselves produce the eye movements of REM sleep as some researchers have suggested? No. The eye movements *precede* the PGO wave by about 20 ms (Jouvet, 1979), so if there is a cause-and-effect relationship, the eye movement would have to cause the PGO wave. This leads to an interesting theory that REMs cause dreaming (Jouvet, 1979). If each REM triggered a PGO wave from the pontine reticular formation that swept through the visual system, everywhere exciting neurons, the expected result would be some sort of visual experience. Because this experience originates in the physiology of the brain stem rather than from sensory inputs or memories, it should be rather illogical and should shift from one visual scene to another in a more or less random fashion.

What if some error were to occur in the brain-stem circuitry such that PGO waves were unleashed during the waking state? How would a person experience the sudden intrusion of irrelevant visual images on the normal thought processes? There would be no way for the person to judge that these images originated in a neural accident and are completely fictitious. They should appear just as real as any other pattern of activity in the visual system. The problem for such a person would be that no one else present at the time would share these visual experiences. In other words, they would be called hallucinations. The victim of waking PGOs would be regarded as psychotic (Jouvet, 1979).

It is possible to elicit PGO waves during the waking state by altering brain-stem function with a drug. Dement and colleagues (1969) used the drug PCPA, and others (Munson & Graham, 1973) used the tranquilizer reserpine. Dement's cats seemed to react to invisible objects during the drugged state, batting at points in thin air as though warding off another cat or striking at prey. Both PCPA and reserpine act on a group of midline brain-stem cell clusters called the **raphe nuclei** (rah-fay), which are the only cells in the nervous system that use **serotonin** as their transmitter. The drugs prevent the manufacture of the transmitter; after a number of hours, the drugged brain runs out of serotonin, and raphe cells lose their control over the rest of the brain. When control over the pontine reticular formation is lost, that area of the brain is allowed to produce PGO waves. The evidence for this comes from single cell–recording studies that show raphe cells stop firing during REM sleep (McGinty & Siegel, 1977). Jacobs and Trulson (1979) think that dreams and psychotic hallucinations are both the result of losing the effects of raphe neuron activity and believe that the hallucinatory drug LSD interferes with serotonin.

There are problems with this idea, however. Munson (personal communication) found that LSD did not produce PGO waves. Furthermore, a reduced form of PGO wave was found accompanying eye movements in the waking state in normal cats (Munson & Graham, 1971). Munson and Schwartz (1972) discovered that these waves occurred together with all kinds of eye movements and were timed to occur with the fixation at the end of the movement. This suggests that the PGO wave might be a reticular system arousal signal (sort of a mini-orienting reaction) to help the visual system react to the new visual image that has just stabilized on the retina following the eye movement. Ultimately, however, we may find that this interpretation of PGOs is not really in conflict with that of Jacobs and Trulson.

The Search for a Brain-Stem Sleep Center

Sleep is not an event that occurs because brain cells fatigue and quit working. It is an active process of temporarily shutting down the organism's behavior while the neurons remain quite busy. Thus, it must be a brain event that is organized and triggered by some group or groups of neurons somewhere in the nervous system.

Transecting the Brain Stem   The search for a sleep center began decades ago with some rather crude lesion experiments. In one of these, Bremer (1937) severed a cat's brain stem at the midbrain level between the inferior and superior colliculi (Figure 10.13). This cut off the brain from most of the midbrain reticular formation (MBRF), although in 1937 no one realized the significance of such a disconnection. The cat had permanent synchrony on the EEG and never showed any behavioral signs of waking. Bremer tried another cut farther down between the medulla and the cord and found that the cat, although paralyzed, showed normal sleep–wake cycles. He concluded that there was a sleep–wake center lying somewhere within the brain stem.

Later, Batini and colleagues (1958) severed the brain stem at the midpontine level (Figure 10.13) and produced cats with insomnia. Their subjects

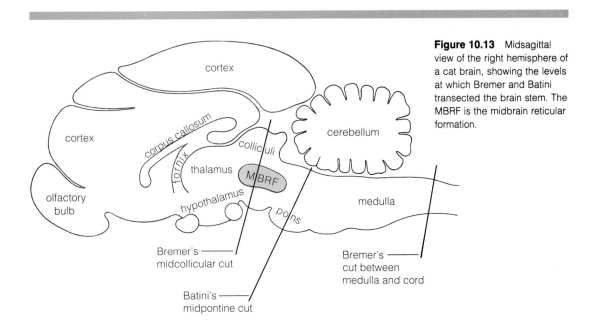

Figure 10.13   Midsagittal view of the right hemisphere of a cat brain, showing the levels at which Bremer and Batini transected the brain stem. The MBRF is the midbrain reticular formation.

went from a normal waking time of about 35 percent of each 24 hours before the operation to roughly 80 percent afterward. One way to interpret all these results is to hypothesize that the upper pons and midbrain produce the waking state and that some area within the medulla or lower pons may be important for initiating sleep. How has this interpretation fared?

The idea of a waking (or arousal) mechanism within the midbrain has stood the test of time; the MBRF fills that role. The importance of the MBRF in explaining Bremer's findings was not realized until 1949 when Morruzzi and Magoun placed electrodes in the midbrain of a cat and found that electrical stimulation to that area would waken the animal from sleep and produce cortical desynchronization. Steriade and co-workers (1980) showed that the MBRF is involved in the desynchrony of REM sleep as well as that of waking.

The idea of a sleep-inducing center in the medulla or lower pons, on the other hand, has not fared as well. Experiments like Batini's in which the entire stem is severed are just too crude to use as tools in analyzing brain-stem functions. You can see why by examining Figure 10.5, which shows that axons of pontine reticular cells extend down into the cord and up through motor nuclei, into the thalamus, and on into the limbic system. When Batini cut through the brain stem at the pontine level and produced insomnia, the sleeplessness may not have meant that the brain had been cut off from a sleep-inducing mechanism lying below the cut. It may simply have meant that a lot of pontine reticular cells *above* the cut were no longer functioning properly because the descending branch of their axons had been killed. The sleep-inducing mechanism could lie above Batini's cut rather than below.

Jouvet and the REM–NREM Cycle   More recent evidence points strongly to the importance of the rostral pontine region in controlling sleep, and this area, of course, lies above Batini's cut. Jouvet (1967b) was the first to propose a theory of REM–NREM cycling in which REM sleep was initiated by the locus coeruleus and NREM by the dorsal raphe nucleus (Figure 10.14).

The raphe nuclei make up a system of cells lying along the midline of the brain stem and extending from the medulla up through the pontine area. All employ the transmitter serotonin and are referred to as **serotonergic neurons**. Like reticular cells, they have long axons that project down into the cord and

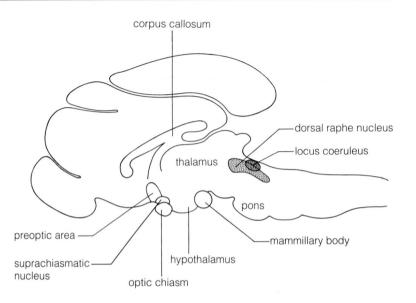

Figure 10.14 Midsagittal view of a cat brain showing location of brain stem and hypothalamic structures.

corpus callosum

dorsal raphe nucleus

locus coeruleus

thalamus

pons

preoptic area

mammillary body

suprachiasmatic nucleus

hypothalamus

optic chiasm

up through the hypothalamus into the limbic system. Such wide dispersion puts the raphe system in a good position to exert some sort of basic influence over the entire brain. Jouvet, however, ignored the raphe's contacts with the higher parts of the brain and suggested that the job of the raphe nuclei was to induce NREM sleep by inhibiting the MBRF.

Balanced against the raphe nuclei in Jouvet's theory was the **locus coeruleus (LC)** (LOW-kuss suh-RULE-ee-us). This small cluster of cells in the dorsal brain stem at the pontine–midbrain border (Figure 10.14) has a peculiar color—a sort of coerulean blue—that makes it easy to see. Its cells use norepinephrine as a transmitter and, like raphe nuclei neurons, send their axons spreading throughout the nervous system. Again, Jouvet ignored these brainwide connections and proposed that activity could slowly build up in the locus coeruleus (LC) to a point where it could inhibit the raphe nuclei. This change would trigger REM sleep. Cortical arousal would occur in REM sleep because of the loss of inhibitory control that raphe cells were exerting over the MBRF during NREM sleep. The two systems would alternate back and forth like this throughout the night. When dorsal raphe cells were active, the MBRF would be inhibited, thus damping arousal and producing NREM sleep. When the LC became active, it would stop dorsal raphe from inhibiting the MBRF, cortical arousal would resume, and the brain would shift from NREM to REM sleep.

Jouvet's idea of two brain-stem areas that were connected together in such a way that they had to alternate in their control made a great deal of intuitive sense and outlasted the theory itself. Some of the other concepts in the theory, however, did not fare as well. Jouvet's theory predicted that REM sleep could not occur without the locus coeruleus, yet lesions that destroyed that structure failed to alter sleep cycling (Jones et al., 1977). Recordings from single cells within the dorsal raphe nucleus showed that they were most active during waking, rather than NREM sleep as the theory would predict (McGinty & Siegel, 1977). Their activity declined in NREM and decreased even further in REM sleep. Other experiments confirmed these findings (Fornal et al., 1985) and also noted that dorsal raphe cells had higher firing rates in an active waking condition than in

quiet waking (Trulson & Jacobs, 1979b). This suggests that raphe cells are important to some waking functions and irrelevant to sleep. However, we will see below that there is other evidence that raphe cells do play some role in sleep.

The Hobson–McCarley Theory   A completely different role for the locus coeruleus was suggested by Hobson and McCarley (Hobson et al., 1975) based on their microelectrode recordings from that structure and from an area of the pontine reticular formation called the **gigantocellular tegmental field (FTG)** (Figure 10.15). They discovered that LC cells that were active in the waking state and NREM sleep fell silent in REM sleep, whereas neurons in FTG did exactly the opposite (Figure 10.16). From these and other data, they devised the **reciprocal interaction model** of sleep-cycle control. During the waking state, FTG neurons are inhibited by LC cells, which are quite active at that time. Some of this inhibition is lost during NREM when LC cells slow their rate of firing and the loss allows a low level of activity in FTG. This activity seems to promote itself (perhaps through FTG neurons stimulating one another), and the rate of firing increases throughout NREM until it seems to overwhelm the inhibition from LC. At that point, REM sleep begins, during much of which LC remains quiet. Eventually, however, the arousal released by FTG stimulates LC back into activity; when the rate of firing rises to a high enough level to once more inhibit FTG, the REM period is over (Figure 10.17). Thus, Hobson and McCarley explain the cycling between REM and NREM with Jouvet's idea of two competing brain-stem areas, but the specific areas are different. The theory also explains why cats with unilateral lesions of the caudal portions of LC show an increase in the amount of time in REM (Caballero & DeAndrés, 1986). The loss of many LC neurons removes much of the inhibition to the FTG neurons that (theoretically) ends the REM period.

Hobson and McCarley's reciprocal interaction model has no special place for the raphe nuclei, but they are not necessarily excluded from playing a part. Earlier experiments had shown that completely destroying the raphe nuclei or preventing the synthesis of serotonin, their transmitter, would leave the cat in a state of continual insomnia (reviewed in

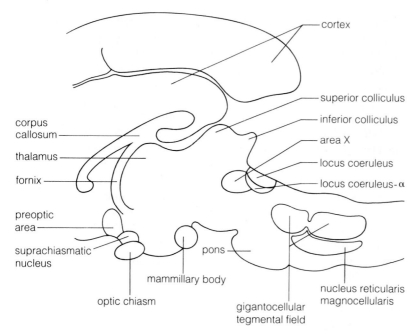

Figure 10.15 Sagittal section of a cat brain stem near midline. This section is too lateral to show the raphe nuclei, which are directly on the midline, but it does show five reticular areas important to sleep: the gigantocellular field, locus coeruleus, nucleus reticularis magnocellularis, area X, and locus coeruleus α.

Figure 10.16 Single-cell recordings from the brain stem reveal that the firing rate of FTG neurons rises in REM sleep (labeled D for desynchronous), while the rate in LC neurons drops. The opposite is true of the waking state (W). NREM sleep (labeled S for synchronous) represents an intermediate state between those two extremes. (Adapted from Hobson et al., 1975)

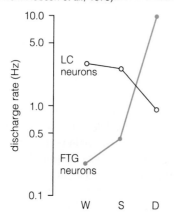

Sallanon et al., 1985). This suggests that raphe cells must have more to do with NREM sleep than with REM because going to sleep is always (in the normal brain) a matter of shifting from waking into NREM. Hobson and McCarley propose that the raphe nuclei may aid LC in suppressing FTG activity during waking and NREM. Indeed, response rates of raphe and LC neurons are very similar (Table 10.2). Furthermore, anatomical studies have shown that FTG cells receive input from the dorsal raphe nucleus and locus coeruleus—connections that could carry the proposed inhibitory influence.

Several problems have arisen for the reciprocal interaction model. FTG neurons have been found to be active in short bursts in waking animals, whereas the theory calls for them to be inhibited at this time. If they truly function as maintainers of the REM-sleep state, then they should be *continuously* active throughout each REM episode; however, Sakai

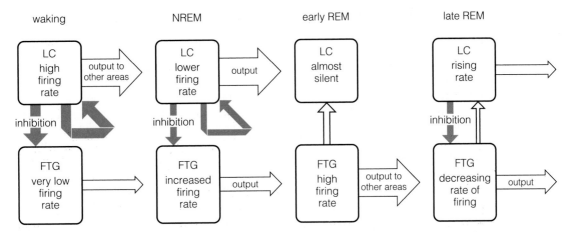

waking   NREM   early REM   late REM

Figure 10.17 Reciprocal relation between locus coeruleus (LC) and the gigantocellular tegmental field (FTG) as postulated by the Hobson–McCarley theory. During waking, LC neurons are very active, and among other things, they inhibit FTG cells. They also direct some of their inhibitory output back onto themselves, thus gradually reducing their rate of firing. When NREM sleep starts, LC neurons have a severely reduced rate, and FTG cells have been able to increase their output because of the reduction of inhibition from the less active LC cells. By REM onset, LC cells are almost silent, and FTG neurons (being uninhibited) have reached their highest firing rate. Some of their facilitation is directed back at LC. This latter effect raises the firing rate in LC once more so that, by late in the REM episode, LC neurons are once more able to send inhibition to FTG, thus beginning a second episode of NREM sleep.

Table 10.2 Response Rates of Neurons in Three Brain-Stem Areas

	Waking	NREM	REM
LC	Slow, steady (about 3/second)	Decreased	Nearly zero
DRN	Slow, steady (about 3/second)	Decreased	Nearly zero
FTG	Very slow (about 0.2/second)	Increased	Fast (about 10/second)

(1985a) claims that they are not. In addition, lesions of the FTG area fail to prevent REM sleep (Sakai, 1985a). Even though the FTG seems to participate in bringing on REM sleep, the data imply that it is not solely responsible for inducing that state. It appears to be quite difficult to pinpoint a single part of the brain to which we can assign the entire responsibility for initiating REM sleep. Several researchers have now concluded that we may never find such "executive" cells because they are not needed (Parmeggiani et al., 1985). They have given up the search for a REM-sleep center and have concentrated on trying to locate the origins of individual REM-sleep phenomena.

Locating the Generators of REM-Sleep Phenomena

PGO waves apparently originate in the reticular formation in the region of the pontine–midbrain border (Sakai, 1984). Two reticular subdivisions that seem especially important in this respect are the **X area** anterior to LC and **locus coeruleus-α (LC-α)**, a group of cells just ventral and lateral to LC (Figure 10.15). They contain cholinergic neurons (those employing Ach as a transmitter) and receive input from both the dorsal raphe nucleus and locus coeruleus itself. Lesions of area X and adjacent area result in REM sleep without PGO waves.

Jouvet's research group hypothesizes that LC-α and the adjacent region contain cells that initiate the postural atonia of REM sleep (Sakai, 1985b). Axons from LC-α cells descend to a part of the reticular formation in the medulla called the **nucleus reticularis magnocellularis (NRMC)**, and it is these medullary neurons that actually produce the atonia (Figure 10.15). Their axons run down into the spinal cord to make inhibitory synapses with the motor neurons there.

The desynchrony of REM sleep may arise both from the MBRF, which is active in both waking and REM episodes, and from the NRMC, which sends axons up to higher levels in addition to its projection to the cord. NRMC neurons seem especially important because they become active continuously during REM but not during the waking state (Sakai, 1984). If a cut is made across the brain stem at the level of the pons, EEG records from the cortex show desynchronization during waking periods but not during sleep. However, even though the desynchrony of REM sleep is missing, PGOs still appear, coupled with large, high-voltage waves characteristic of NREM sleep (Siegel, 1985). We can explain this if we assume that NRMC is responsible for the fast waves of REM periods. In the cat with the midpontine transection, the PGO generator is above the level of the cut and can still produce its waves, but the apparent instigator of REM desynchrony, the NRMC, is below the cut and can no longer exert any influence on higher brain structures.

Summary We have seen that each specific aspect of REM sleep is controlled by a different group of cells that seems capable of acting independently of the others in damaged brains. PGOs, for example, can be obtained without desynchrony, and both PGOs and desynchrony can occur without atonia. These facts, however, have not stopped researchers from seeking a REM-sleep "center." The role of this center has simply been altered to that of an executive that coordinates the activities of LC, FTG, NRMC, and raphe nuclei during sleep. The problem with this approach is that so far negative evidence has been found against every area proposed for such an executive center.

McGinty solves this problem to his satisfaction by proposing that all or most of the neurons in the core of the brain stem have built-in physiological mechanisms that create alternating periods of high and low activity, and it is these mechanisms that cause the REM–NREM cycle. (Later in this chapter, we will return to this idea and propose a specific physiological mechanism.) The role of FTG, LC, NRMC, and the raphe nuclei is to speed or slow this intrinsic cycling so that all neurons are coordinated and have their cycles adjusted to meet the needs of the various brain-stem circuits involved in respiration, heart rate, and higher functions (McGinty, 1985). Perhaps, REM-sleep periods begin not because a few executive cells somewhere in the brain stem begin to fire but because several different interconnected neuron groups finally chance to reach critical levels of activity simultaneously. In other words, the switch from one conscious state to the other may be a "committee," rather than an "executive," decision. This would explain why lesion experiments show that several scattered areas within the brain stem are involved in producing REM sleep, yet none of these areas alone seems to be critical for it.

Is There a Sleep Center Above the Brain Stem?

A number of experimenters have claimed to have found a sleep center above the brain stem after observing their animals go to sleep during electrical stimulation of the region in question. Unfortunately, the subjects were usually cats, and the amount of stimulation prior to sleep onset was usually at least several minutes. Because it is not in the least uncommon for a normal cat to drop off to sleep in 1 or 2 minutes without any help at all, we should remain quite skeptical of most of those results. One exception to this problem is the work on the **preoptic area (POA)** of the hypothalamus (Figure 10.15), a zone at the very base of the brain just above and forward of the optic chiasm. Stimulation of these cells produces cortical synchrony typical of NREM sleep within only 30 seconds (Sterman & Clemente, 1962). Kaitin (1984) found neurons in the POA that fired during NREM sleep but not during waking or REM sleep; Nauta (1946) established that when POA is lesioned in rats, the result is total insomnia. Thus, it is possible that POA is an initiator of NREM sleep. It could accomplish this function by way of inhibitory connections to the MBRF.

The idea that POA might be able to inhibit MBRF is supported by one of Bremer's studies of the orienting response (1970), which focused on how MBRF desynchronized the cortex in response to each novel stimulus. Bremer discovered that if the POA was stimulated right after the novel stimulus, the cortex would go back to a synchronized rhythm. The synchrony, of course, indicates loss of arousal—it is the first step toward sleep—and POA apparently induced the synchrony.

■ Why Do We Sleep?

To some people, sleep seems close to death. This fear might not seem completely irrational when one considers the peculiar state of the ANS during REM sleep. Irregular heart rhythms are frequent at that time, and electrical heart attacks may be triggered if the heart is diseased. Death rates are higher at night than in the day (Dement, 1979). Sudden infant death syndrome, in which perfectly healthy babies are found dead in their cribs, is a sleep-related phenomenon. According to Dement, victims of sleep apnea (difficulty with breathing during sleep) would be better off if they never slept at all.

Not only does sleep contain a certain element of danger, it often seems like a great waste of time. Rechtschaffen (1971) notes that, for our ancestors, sleep interfered with hunting for food, eating, and procreation. He adds, "If sleep does not serve an absolutely vital function, then it is the biggest mistake

the evolutionary process ever made." Dement (1979), who views sleep from the standpoint of a clinician who treats sleep-related problems, states that if we ever find a way to make sleep unnecessary then we should hasten to do away with it at the earliest opportunity.

However, there is much to suggest that sleep does have vital functions, and it is unlikely that we will ever be able to free ourselves of it. In this section, we will look at a number of theories that attempt to explain the existence of sleep. First, however, we ought to be clear on just how many states of consciousness we are trying to explain. Is sleep one condition or several?

Everything we have discussed in the last three sections of this chapter points to the idea that there are two kinds of sleep. For clinical purposes, sleep is divided into four stages based on the EEG record, but the distinctions between stages 2, 3, and 4 seem trivial compared to the split between emergent stage 1 (REM) and the rest of sleep (NREM). We have seen that the arousal level of the cortex in NREM sleep is depressed, showing EEG synchrony; in REM sleep, it shows the desynchrony of arousal. Behaviorally, NREM involves considerable movement (postural adjustments to ease stiffness), whereas in REM movement ceases completely until the transition to waking or NREM. Eye movements and PGO waves are characteristic of REM but not NREM, and dreaming is more characteristic of REM. NREM sleep seems to originate in the hypothalamus, whereas REM is controlled by the brain stem. The safest conclusion is that we should not speak of waking versus sleeping, but rather waking versus REM sleep versus NREM sleep. So, rather than explaining the existence of sleep, we will need separate explanations for its two forms. Let's start with NREM.

The Role of NREM Sleep

If we examine the course of evolution by comparing present-day species, it would seem that a general sort of sleep state appeared long before REM and NREM sleep. Fish and amphibians sleep, as do their more advanced cousins, the reptiles. EEG data from turtles and lizards suggest a primitive sleep state that has not yet differentiated into a clear-cut division between REM and NREM (Rojas-Ramirez & Drucker-Colin, 1977). Birds and mammals, those two off-spring of reptiles, both show a division of sleep into REM and NREM. Later in this section, we will see that there is good reason to believe that REM sleep is related to learning, and this idea may help explain its appearance in birds and mammals—animals that depend more heavily on learned behaviors for survival. If this line of reasoning is correct, then it would seem that REM is the more highly specialized form of sleep and that our own modern NREM is more like the original, primitive sleep. REM sleep may have evolved out of NREM sleep. This suggests that NREM must have a function rooted deep within animal physiology.

The Restorative Theory   To most people, the reason for sleep seems obvious. If you stay awake long enough, you get tired and must sleep to relieve the fatigue. So, waking activity puts some sort of wear on the body, which sleep repairs. There may be something to this "everyday" interpretation of sleep. Several experiments have shown that exercise has some effect on NREM sleep, although the relation is complex. For example, exercise just before bed reduces the amount of time it takes to get to sleep by as much as 50 percent if the exercise is of a static sort, such as lifting and holding heavy objects or doing push-ups (Browman, 1980). Furthermore, the length of the early NREM periods is increased by this form of exercise. Dynamic, aerobic exercises like running, walking, and bicycling, however, tend to make it more difficult to get to sleep. Both types of exercise may produce considerable fatigue, but the dynamic sort also stimulates the reticular formation and generates an arousal state that takes some time to dissipate. The physical condition of the person is also a factor (Buguet et al., 1980). Physically fit subjects tend to react to exercise by getting more NREM sleep, but subjects in poor physical condition are apparently stressed by the effort, hence experiencing more arousal and finding it more difficult to get to sleep. So, following exercise NREM onset is decreased and duration increased if these effects are not masked by exercise-induced arousal.

Not everyone in the field of sleep research agrees that the body must have actual sleep for recuperation; rest might do just as well. In a survey Webb (1981) found that many people sleep less than 7 hours a night and show no difference from 8-hour sleepers in terms of their health, intelligence, or temperament. Older people tend to sleep less, and Webb's survey also found one group of 70-year-olds in good health that averaged only 5 hours per night. Two Australian men turned up who need less than 3 hours, and the stay-awake champion of them all was a 70-year-old woman who exists on 1 hour a night. Although Webb does not suggest that we only need 1 hour of sleep each night, he does feel that many people sleep more than is really needed and that waking rest periods could substitute for much of the sleep time.

In contrast to Webb, Moruzzi emphasizes that the need for sleep is more than just the need for rest, and he is very critical of the idea that it is the body that has the sleep need (cited in Webb, 1979). For Moruzzi, sleep evolved as brains reached a certain level of complexity and serves to restore function in the synapses involved in learning. He is not very clear on why such synapses should need any kind of recuperation, but we will see that other theorists took up this idea and added more detail.

If sleep is meant for the brain, then sleep deprivation should have an adverse effect on brain function. Such an effect does indeed show up although it is more subtle than you might expect. Normally, people in sleep-deprivation experiments do not become psychotic, exhibiting hallucinations and delusions. Such symptoms seem to appear only in subjects with atypical emotional histories (Webb, 1981). In fact, most subjects who went without sleep for 2 or 3 days showed that they could perform accurately on many tasks such as repeating digits backward and memorizing nonsense syllables (Webb, 1981). A number of experiments had to be conducted before the real difference between normal and sleep-deprived subjects could be found. The latter group could perform quite adequately for short bursts, but if they were called on to maintain attention to an unchanging task for more than 5 or 10 minutes, lapses of attention began to show. As the degree of deprivation increased, the lapses became more frequent. The attention mechanism of the brain was apparently the major victim of the sleeplessness. The subjects found it more and more difficult to maintain orientation to a specific stimulus.

Oswald (1966) studied these momentary lapses and decided that they were extremely short episodes of sleep. He applied the term *microsleeps* and stated the principle that total sleep deprivation is impossible. After 2 or 3 days, the number of microsleeps begins to increase to the point where the subject is obtaining a measurable amount of sleep whether or not it is desired. Oswald went to great lengths to keep his subjects awake, constantly changing their activities and never letting them stay with a situation long enough to encourage habituation to it. Even postural changes had to be continually suggested, such as "Why don't we walk a bit now?" or "Why don't you cross your legs the other way for a while?" (Oswald, 1966). Unless a stimulus has considerable personal meaning to an individual, it must be novel to activate the reticular formation and provide arousal. Apparently, in a sleep-deprived condition, it becomes harder and harder to find ordinary, everyday stimuli with arousal ability. Oswald even found that his subjects could drift into sleep while walking down the street.

When Oswald's subjects were finally allowed to sleep (after 108 waking hours), they spent far more than the normal amount of time in NREM sleep. Apparently, there is a rebound effect of deprivation that gives NREM priority over REM when sleep is being made up. (REM sleep also shows a rebound effect that is evident when the subject has selectively lost only REM sleep.) This fits with the idea that NREM sleep acts as a restorative. Others have also found this NREM rebound and have discovered that people who sleep less than 8 hours spend a higher proportion of that sleep time in NREM than do people who sleep 8 or more hours per night (Cohen, 1979). All this suggests that NREM sleep is more basic to the survival of the organism than is REM sleep, as would be expected if NREM sleep does indeed act to restore normal function in the brain and/or body.

If NREM sleep does act as a restorative, then the proportion of NREM in a night's sleep should be related to the quality of the sleep—how restful it

seemed. What has happened to a person who "gets up on the wrong side of the bed"? Why do some nights leave you grouchy and irritable in the morning with feelings of fatigue despite adequate sleep time? Could the problem be a poor balance between REM and NREM with too much of the former and not enough of the latter? In one study, subjects were awakened by a loud buzzer either as they entered REM or stage 4 of NREM sleep. The subjects thus deprived of stage 4 NREM were irritable and tired the next morning and complained of aches and pains; the REM-deprived subjects had no complaints (Moldofsky & Scarisbrick, 1976). The pains were of particular importance to Moldofsky because of his interest in a syndrome called **fibrositis**, in which the patient complains of chronic fatigue, stiffness, muscle pain, and irritability. Moldofsky decided that fibrositis might be a sleep problem involving a balance favoring too much REM sleep. EEG records from fibrositis patients confirmed that they had too little delta wave time in NREM sleep, much of the delta waves having been replaced with alpha waves (Moldofsky & Lue, 1980). Researchers in another lab (Goetz et al., 1983) found that sleep spindles (10–16 Hz) may be related to the feeling of not having slept well. In both studies then, very slow EEG rhythms (delta) were associated with refreshing sleep, while faster rhythms (alpha, spindling, and the fast rhythms of REM sleep) were linked with the subject's judgment of poor-quality sleep. The symptoms of fibrositis can be relieved by the drug chlorpromazine, which restores the needed stage 4 portion of NREM sleep.

One of the outstanding symptoms of clinical depression is fatigue, sleep loss, and irritability, so some researchers proposed that depression might also be the result of a REM–NREM imbalance. This led to an interesting substitute for the usual therapy with antidepressant drugs. It was reasoned that the suspected imbalance could be corrected with a certain amount of REM-sleep deprivation. Studies with depressed patients have consistently shown that total sleep deprivation for one or two nights does decrease symptoms of depression, but the improvement is lost with the first subsequent night of sleep (van den Hoofdakker & Beersma, 1984). Although sleep deprivation will never be useful as a therapy, deprivation research has led to the potentially important idea that REM-sleep abnormalities are the cause of depression and that antidepressant drugs have their effects by way of decreasing the proportion of time spent in REM sleep (Chase, 1982).

Altogether, then, the literature of sleep research is full of hints that point to NREM sleep as a restorative process. We are not sure whether it is both the brain and the body being restored or just the brain. Sleep-deprivation studies suggest that the ability to pay attention must be restored through sleep and that the refreshed feeling that most of us seek from a night's sleep stems more from NREM than REM sleep. However, it may be the balance between the two that turns out to be critical. In any case, the restorative interpretation seems to be a theory with a strong future.

The Habituation Hypothesis   It is possible, of course, that there may be several reasons for the existence of sleep and several different ways in which it can be initiated. Most students who have endured a semester under the tutelage of a boring, droning lecturer will find some merit in the idea that sleep is related to boredom. But what, exactly, is boredom? It seems to represent a gradual loss of arousal in the absence of any stimulus that the organism considers as interesting. In other words, boredom seems to be another term for habituation.

Sokolov (1963) found that the habituation of the orienting reaction occurred in several stages. For example, a light flash might elicit the full OR, with desynchronization over the whole cortex for the first 10–15 presentations, then fade to partial desynchronization over just the visual area, and then finally cease altogether. We can presume that in the first stage the whole reticular arousal system was reacting to the stimulus but that the MBRF gradually habituated, leaving the thalamic reticular formation to play its part alone for a while longer. Apparently, as it nears the last stage of habituation, the brain is still keeping track of the stimulus but only at a very reduced level of attention. The interesting thing for us is that the last stage, total habituation, is followed by the subject dropping off to sleep. This suggests that sleep may be the result of habituation.

When a dog has learned everything it can about its environment—that is, when it has habituated to all of its stimuli—then there is nothing left to provide arousal by stimulating the reticular formation. Sleep is almost inevitable because the reticular system does not seem capable of arousing itself (Gastaut & Roger, 1960).

Throughout the day, you are bombarded with stimuli, many of which your brain dutifully records. But all birds sound quite a bit alike, as do all cars. All trees have much in common and so do all books. Gradually, you habituate to more and more stimuli and generalize the habituation to members of a stimulus class that you haven't experienced yet. For example, you begin your studying by reading your psychology text but become bored with it after about an hour. Each page has new sentences and new ideas, but they all belong to the general stimulus class of "words about the brain" and you are gradually habituating to this class of stimuli. So you shift to your history text. The change of topic provides enough novelty to keep your reticular formation going for, perhaps, another 30 minutes. But the visual stimulus involved in reading history is still words on a page, so you begin to yawn. You shift to sociology, but after 10 minutes, your head is nodding. Even though you had never seen those pages in your sociology text before, they had already lost much of their novelty because of generalized habituation from the previous texts.

If the habituation hypothesis is correct, one wonders why a person ever wakes up again. After dropping off to sleep because of total and complete loss of interest in every aspect of your environment, how can that same environment look so fresh and inviting once more in the morning? Sleep must act not only to restore the body to its previous state of well-being, according to the habituation hypothesis, but it must also restore the brain. Somehow during sleep most of the previous day's habituation must be undone and the brain readied for another day of similar stimuli. Moruzzi proposed an idea of this sort and considered the elimination of this "brain fatigue" more important than the elimination of body fatigue as a reason for sleep (cited in Webb, 1979). Such thinking has a definite intuitive appeal, but little research has yet to focus on it.

Sleep as a Part of the Brain's Circadian Rhythm

Both the restorative and habituation hypotheses have merit, but there may be still one other fundamental factor in the control of sleep. The sleep–wake cycle happens to be just one of many dozens of daily cycles found in living tissues (plants as well as animals). Cycles that are approximately 24 hours in length are called **circadian rhythms** (sir-KADE-ee-un) from the Latin *circa* (around, nearly) and *dies* (day). Your body physiology operates on circadian rhythms; for example, the number of white blood cells you have and the concentration of adrenal hormones in your blood vary with the time of day (Luce, 1970). Plasma concentrations of amino acids and the rate at which they are converted into protein are both tied to circadian rhythms. The basic energy-carrying molecule of the body, ATP, is manufactured faster and is more available during one part of the 24-hour cycle than another. Body temperature varies in a cyclic manner, being low for most people around dawn and rising during the day. Good sleepers experience a fast rise near time of waking, but poor sleepers experience a slow rise that stretches throughout the morning (Luce, 1970).

Not all rhythms are circadian. Their durations range from those that are seasonal in length (mating and reproduction in many species, hibernation in others), to the circadian rhythms already mentioned, to the very short rhythms of the respiration and heartbeat cycles. Many such rhythms do not seem to stem from or depend on the brain. Rather, the brain acts to regulate and coordinate the rhythm that is already natural to the tissue. For example, heart muscle fibers grown artificially in a lab dish develop rhythmic contractions. As they grow and come in contact with one another, their various individual rhythms begin to synchronize into a common group rhythm. Every human heart has a cluster of specialized cells called the A–V node that sends electrical signals to all heart cells in order to synchronize their contractions into a coordinated heartbeat. The control function of the brain is to speed this natural heart rhythm when faster circulation is needed (as in exercise or emotional arousal) or slow it during relaxation. The rhythm itself is in the tissue. Recent research has shown that longer rhythms of circadian length can also be built into tissue (Jacklet, 1978),

with even single cells changing their function according to the time of day (Strumwasser, 1967).

The importance of all this is that the sleep–wake cycle may also be based on some sort of rhythm born into single cells and the task of the brain may simply be to coordinate that rhythm with the earth's rotation and with behavior. But what rhythm intrinsic to individual cells could possibly be related to sleep? The answer is in the chemistry of protein manufacture.

The structure of a cell is created out of a multitude of different proteins. The enzymes that control the rates of all chemical reactions making up the life of the cell are proteins. One of the most important functions any cell has is to continually synthesize new protein for enzymes and to replace worn-out structures. This protein synthesis occurs very slowly during the waking state and far more rapidly during sleep; it is following a circadian rhythm. The interesting thing is that this rhythm does not seem to be imposed by the brain on the process of protein manufacture. It seems to stem from the synthesis process itself. One theory holds that the rate of synthesis is controlled by negative feedback. That is, the synthesis mechanism works faster with fewer proteins around. The manufactured proteins inhibit the synthesis of more proteins. After their manufacture, protein molecules are gradually assimilated into the structure of the cell or used to make enzymes, transmitters, or hormones. Eventually, the protein level is too low to inhibit the synthesis mechanism, and it once more starts to function. Jacklet (1978) provided some indirect evidence for these ideas by establishing that circadian rhythms in certain tissues can be slowed or speeded by inhibiting protein synthesis.

Because protein synthesis starts with the manufacture of RNA from DNA and includes several steps prior to the synthesis of protein itself, there may be quite a lag between the beginning of this sequence and actual appearance of the first protein molecules. The negative-feedback idea suggests that the whole cycle takes roughly 24 hours. This timing may not be an accident. It is likely that on this particular planet organisms whose protein cycles were in the neighborhood of 24 hours had a better chance of surviving. Sunlight is the fundamental energy source

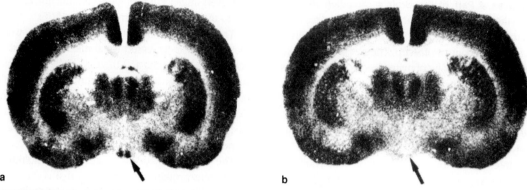

Figure 10.18 Frontal sections of whole brains from rats injected with deoxyglucose. The dark **C**-shaped structure on the outside of each hemisphere is the cortex. The white sliver beneath the cortex is white matter. Just beneath the white matter is the dark, bean-shaped basal ganglia, and at the center is the dark area of the thalamus. The deoxyglucose technique makes the more active areas of the brain show up dark in these radiographs and the less active areas as white. At the base of the brain is an arrow pointing to the SCN, which appears quite active in the photo taken during the day (**a**) and inactive in the photo taken at night (**b**). (From Schwartz & Gainer, 1977)

for all life on earth; thus, it is quite handy for a creature to have basic life processes that stay in step with the light–dark cycles. Although evolution, working through genetic selection, could produce protein-synthesis cycles approximating the earth's light–dark rhythm, it is the task of the brain to fine-tune this relationship by slowing or speeding synthesis to exactly match the day–night cycle. This matching is called **entrainment**.

If circadian rhythms grow out of basic chemical rhythms, then we should expect the entrainment mechanism to be found in the part of the brain devoted to regulating body chemistry—the hypothalamus. Figure 10.18 shows two slices of rat brain, one cut from the brain of a rat killed during the day, the other from a rat whose brain chemistry was stopped during the night. Both rats had been injected with radioactive **deoxyglucose** (see Chapter 5). The neurons admit this altered glucose but cannot metabolize or dispose of it. Because active cells take up nutrients faster than do cells in less active brain regions, the radioactivity becomes highest in the brain areas that were most active just before the rat died and reveals what parts of the brain the rat was

using (Jones & Hartman, 1978). Variations in the level of radioactivity revealed in the brain slices of Figure 10.18 make it clear that one area of the hypothalamus, the **suprachiasmatic nucleus (SCN)** (SOUP-rah-KY-as-MAT-ik), was more active during daylight than in the dark (Schwartz & Gainer, 1977).

Considerable evidence now agrees that the SCN (Figure 10.15) is the entrainment center for the rat brain (Rusak & Groos, 1982) and probably for the human. The word *suprachiasmatic* means "just above the optic chiasm," and this placement is not accidental. Some of the optic nerve fibers coming from the retina terminate in the SCN, and it is a safe bet that it is these neurons that inform the SCN of the state of night or day (Brainard et al., 1988). As you can tell from Figure 10.15, the SCN is close to the POA, which we have already seen is linked to the initiation of NREM sleep. A good hypothesis would be that the SCN can act on POA to hurry or delay the onset of NREM sleep in order to coordinate sleep periods with dark periods.

So, we have found that the sleep–wake cycle may be simply one more circadian rhythm in a whole collection of such rhythms that grew out of a basic cycle of protein synthesis. In the next section, we will explore the relevance of this idea to REM sleep and learning.

The Role of REM Sleep

You can change the pattern of sleep in a rat simply by teaching it something. Train the animal on some complex learning task and you will find that the amount of REM sleep in the next sleep period increases over the usual amount (Fishbein et al., 1974; Lucero, 1970). If you separate a group of rats into fast learners and poor learners, the poor ones show less REM sleep after training than do the good ones (Stern & Morgane, 1977). Something must be happening during REM sleep that is related to learning. Kesner (1977) thinks that the learning experiences of the day are being reviewed as dreams and that this is important for the subsequent memory of the experiences. A related but more specific interpretation depends on the idea of consolidation (see Chapter 16).

Consolidation Theory Just after an event is experienced the memory of it is in short-term memory (STM), a very brief, temporary storage mechanism. New information is continually coming into STM, and the capacity of this storage mechanism is limited. It appears to be capable of holding only about seven items at once, so as new items are added old ones must be lost. The only way to save a memory is to transfer it to long-term memory (LTM), a storage device that is at least semipermanent. The transfer of information from STM to LTM is called **consolidation**. The extent to which a STM is consolidated usually depends heavily on the amount of practice, that is, on how many times the learning experience has occurred. Because STM lasts only seconds, consolidation must be initiated immediately after the experience or the opportunity to form a LTM will be lost. Yet animal studies with electroconvulsive shock suggest that consolidation may not be complete for minutes or hours (see Chapter 16), and some theorists believe that consolidation requires years for completion in humans (Squire, 1982). The fact that the memory must continue in some sort of form during this lengthy consolidation time has led to the proposal that there exists a second temporary storage mechanism ("intermediate-term"?) that is triggered by STM and that carries the memory trace until the LTM has been constructed. If there is an intermediate-term memory that could hold information for 18 hours or more, then it becomes plausible to suggest that most consolidation might take place during a special part of the circadian cycle designed especially for that process. This special time would, of course, be the REM-sleep period. Such an interpretation would explain the increase in REM sleep after a learning experience.

If this version of consolidation theory is correct, then depriving an animal of REM sleep should hinder consolidation and prevent good recall later. REM deprivation is easily accomplished in the cat or rat. Because rodents can maintain enough muscle tone during NREM to sleep in a crouched posture, the experimenter simply places the rat on an upside-down flower pot in a large pool of water and leaves it there for half a day. The rat cannot escape from the pool by swimming and thus must crouch on its tiny island with its tail sticking over one edge and its nose over the other. NREM sleep produces no problems for the rat, and it can get as much of this sleep as can any rat still comfortably at ease back in the cage room, but REM sleep is a different matter. As soon as the atonia of REM sleep begins, the rat's neck muscles go limp, and the animal's nose dunks into the water. The result is immediate arousal. What we learn from such experiments is that a rat that has undergone training during the hours previous to REM deprivation is prevented from fully consolidating the memory of this training. Thanks to REM deprivation, next-day retention is poorer than that of the controls (Kesner, 1977).

The flower-pot technique causes some amount of stress, of course, and some investigators suggested that this, rather than consolidation failure, might explain the poor retention. To test this hypothesis, Pearlman (1982) injected the drug imipramine, which diminishes REM sleep without disturbing NREM or producing stress. The rats REM-deprived with imipramine acted just like the rats in the flower-pot technique; they had poor recall the next day. Imprinting is a basic form of learning, and in the sleep episodes following an imprinting session, chicks showed increased REM time and more REM episodes (Solodkin et al., 1985). Not all studies show this kind of correlation between REM sleep and learning (e.g., van Hulzen & Coenen, 1982), but all things considered, consolidation failure still seems to be the best explanation for cases where retention is decreased. REM sleep probably exists to aid the consolidation process.

If REM sleep does aid consolidation, how does it accomplish this task? One major difference between the waking state and both sleep states is that very little sensory input occurs during sleep. It could be that REM sleep offers the brain its only arousal period in which it has a "time out" from new information input. NREM could not serve this function because of the low arousal levels at that time. During REM sleep, the rate of firing in cortical neurons is nearly that of the waking state, with both being significantly higher than the rate in NREM (Evarts, 1967). So, in REM sleep the cortex appears to have the benefits of both arousal and limited sensory input. It is unlikely, however, that this is the whole explanation, since the fact that two major contributors to cortical function, the locus coeruleus and raphe system, are both strangely quiet during REM sleep remains to be explained (McGinty & Siegel, 1977).

Protein Synthesis In Chapter 16, we will examine the idea that consolidation involves the construction of new tissue in the brain (e.g., receptor sites, terminals, etc.). New tissue is built of protein; hence, brain protein synthesis would appear to be a crucial part of the learning process.

Earlier in this chapter, we saw that our circadian rhythms may have grown out of a basic chemical cycle of protein synthesis and use. This would explain why amino acid levels in the blood also have a circadian rhythm. One amino acid, tyrosine (out of which dopamine, norepinephrine, and epinephrine are made), has its highest level around 10 A.M. and lowest between 2 and 4 A.M. (Luce, 1970). You might think that these low levels occur simply because 2 A.M. is a long way from the last meal, but experiments in which very large, high-protein meals were consumed showed that alterations in eating failed to affect the rhythm (Luce, 1970). Men who

were eating 500 g of liver at 8 P.M. had the same blood amino acid levels at night as did men who were fasting. Apparently, sleep is a time when body cells strip the bloodstream of all available amino acids and start manufacturing proteins. In fact, sleep onset can be speeded by adding extra amino acids to the blood. Eating a large meal with a high-protein content tends to induce a drowsy condition.

The height of protein synthesis seems to occur during REM sleep (Drucker-Colin, 1979). It is interesting that human newborn infants spend half their sleep time (about 8 hours a day) in REM as opposed to 15 percent of sleep time in REM for adults (Roffwarg et al., 1966). By the time the child is 2, her REM time is almost down to the adult level. Human brains have not completed their development at birth. Most of the long-axoned cells that connect one area with another are in place (these are the ones heavily determined by the genes), but the tiny short-axoned cells that make connections within structures have much growth yet to accomplish and most of it happens in the first 2 years. With so much brain growth going on, large amounts of REM time should be needed if REM sleep does indeed specialize as a time for brain protein synthesis. Guinea pigs are further along in development than humans when they are born, so it is interesting that the amount of REM sleep in these animals does not change during development (Jouvet-Mounier et al., 1970).

Protein synthesis, whether it is in the body or brain, is a basic biochemical process and as such comes under the control of that overseer of all body chemistry, the hypothalamus. Regulation is accomplished with a pituitary secretion called **growth hormone (GH)**, which is released from the anterior pituitary following a command from the hypothalamus. GH helps amino acids enter cells and apparently also aids protein synthesis (Sassin, 1977). Most of the GH secreted during a 24-hour period is produced during NREM sleep (Takahashi, 1979). Because NREM sleep always precedes REM sleep and REM is a period of protein synthesis, perhaps GH triggers onset of REM sleep. Cats injected with GH showed significantly more REM sleep during the subsequent 7 hours than did the control cats (Stern & Morgane, 1977).

Synthesis

The basic idea of the restorative theory is that sleep is a time for the body to repair and refurbish. That viewpoint does not seem to be in conflict with the protein-synthesis theory; rather the two ideas seem to complement one another. To make repairs, the body must have a period of little or no movement in which protein synthesis in the muscles and other organs can proceed at a faster pace than protein destruction. This is NREM sleep. As for REM sleep, the "repair" in this case may be the removal of a day's worth of habituation learning. Additionally, REM appears to provide a time of insulation from new stimulus input in which the memories from the previous day can be consolidated.

The reason why most mammals sleep at night and are active in the day (or vice versa) is that there is survival value to this arrangement for each species. For day creatures like our ancestors, it would have been metabolically inefficient to be awake at night when hunting and gathering would be so much more difficult. They would have been burning precious fuel without obtaining any replacement. For night foragers, daytime waking would be inefficient (because their prey is also nocturnal), so sleep is an adaptive survival device for them also. Because the body already had need for a circadian rhythm of activity and rest based on protein-synthesis rhythms, it simply remained for evolution to entrain these rhythms to the light–dark cycles.

Thus, circadian rhythms, body restoration, protein synthesis, consolidation, and removal of habituation all seem to fit together in a general way. From this perspective, none of the sleep theories discussed here seem in conflict with any of the others. Each may have a piece of the truth.

■ Sleep-Associated Disorders

Millions of people have trouble getting to sleep at night, staying asleep, or staying awake during the day. Only in the last decade has our society begun to generate a real understanding of their problems and find some tentative solutions. A number of sleep clinics have opened, mostly in association with large universities such as Stanford. With treatment facilities becoming more widespread every year and new therapies being devised, there is finally some hope for solving a variety of human problems that have in the past evoked more amusement than sympathy.

Insomnia

The word **insomnia** is usually understood to mean a failure to obtain enough sleep, but we will see that the actual condition is not that easy to describe. Some people with insomnia find it difficult to initiate sleep, whereas others complain of being unable to sleep past 3 or 4 A.M. Many insomniacs log 7 or 8 hours of sleep a night but complain that they "hardly slept a wink." The crux of the problem really doesn't seem to be how much sleep time shows up in objective measurements like EEG records. Rather, it lies in the degree of emotional comfort or discomfort that the person feels during the sleep period and/or during the next day. People who take their insomnia to a physician typically complain of being continually restless during the night and of feeling tired, uninterested, and "washed out" during the next day (Weitzman, 1981).

Acute Versus Chronic Insomnia Investigators have begun to sort out cases of insomnia into meaningful categories, each of which has a different set of causes. Many short-term sleep problems are associated with emotional crises or times of acute stress. This sort of insomnia is the kind in which the sleeper's anxieties maintain reticular activity for minutes or hours after the person retires for the night. Such crises rarely last long enough to produce serious impairment of the person's faculties through sleep loss. If such an individual comes to a physician seeking "sleeping pills," it is probably relief from the anxieties rather than from the sleeplessness that is most important to the person in the long run. There is considerable doubt in some minds that drugs are the best answer to a problem that seems really to call for supportive psychotherapy.

Chronic insomnia is a more common complaint

and is more likely to be a symptom of neurochemical problems. Many cases are associated with clinical depression, technically known as *mood disorder* Some people with mood disorder have a greatly shortened first NREM period and are missing normal amounts of stages 3 and 4 throughout the rest of the night. They wake repeatedly and finally, in the early hours of the morning, give up altogether their attempts to go back to sleep. Other people with mood disorder not only manage to get quite a bit of sleep at night but also nap excessively in the afternoons. Yet they feel unrefreshed and in constant need of obtaining a more satisfactory sort of sleep. EEG records show that they are not just imagining their problem; their sleep contains far too small a proportion of NREM time (Weitzman, 1981).

People with emotional problems often have difficulties with insomnia and display unusual EEG patterns. Alpha rhythm may superimpose itself on NREM EEG activity, suggesting that the thalamic reticular formation is being partially activated. Sleep spindles may appear together with the eye movements of REM sleep so that the boundaries of REM and NREM sleep become blurred. Patients with such symptoms regularly obtain 6–7 hours of sleep according to EEG records yet insist that they obtained only a few hours or no sleep at all. Perhaps they had enough arousal from their thalamic reticular formations to produce almost continuous NREM mentation, with frequent wakings and good recall of their thoughts. Such a combination would leave a person completely convinced that sleep had never occurred the whole night. In fact, one study (Knab & Engel, 1988) showed that insomniacs fail to perceive awakenings during the night and are thus unable to realize that they have been asleep. Have people with this condition really slept as well as anyone else, or is there something they are missing that is vital to their body chemistry? The hypothesis that disturbed sleep results from disturbed biochemistry has supported a widespread prescription of drugs for relief from insomnia.

Drug Treatment of Insomnia When the Institute of Medicine reviewed the data on sleep drug prescriptions in 1979, they found that 25 million such prescriptions had been written that year in the United States alone. About 47 percent of these were for **barbiturates** (bar-BICH-your-ruts), the original "sleeping pills." The remaining 53 percent was for the drug of choice against insomnia for the last decade, **flurazepam** (flur-AZ-uh-pam), which is best known by its trade name, Dalmane. Flurazepam is one of a class of drugs called the **benzodiazepines** (BEN-zo-die-AZ-uh-peens), which are sometimes called the "minor tranquilizers" and which include Valium and Librium.

Physicians receive very little information about sleep in the course of their formal education (Smith, 1979). It is likely that many undergraduate psychology majors have read more about sleep research than most physicians who are licensed to prescribe drugs for insomnia. Drugs may be the crudest form of insomnia therapy available, but drugs are a familiar tactic to every physician, and new drugs are brought to their doorstep every week by sales representatives pushing their products. Is there any evidence that drugs help with sleep problems? Let's look first at the case history of one of Dement's patients, Mr. B. (Libassi, 1975).

Mr. B. was the victim of short-term, crisis insomnia. In the course of studying for several weeks to pass a civil service exam that would qualify or disqualify him for employment in the federal government, he became anxious enough to have trouble getting to sleep at night. Not sleeping left him groggy the next day, making studying more difficult and increasing his anxiety. He knew of no solution for this problem except to visit his physician and request "something to help him sleep." His physician (probably also ignorant of any alternative solution) prescribed sodium amytal, one of the barbiturates. The drug seemed to be effective for several nights, but then the insomnia returned. Mr. B. did what millions of others would do in that situation. Rather than look for a different way to get to sleep, he increased the dose of amytal. That was his first step toward barbiturate addiction. As the days went by, Mr. B.'s tolerance to the drug continued to increase, and he continued to react to that with heavier doses. By the night before the test, he was taking four times the prescribed dose.

After the test was over, Mr. B. assumed that his insomnia would end automatically. For the first time in several weeks, he went to bed without taking amytal. Sleep did not come. After tossing and turning for hours, he finally dropped off, only to be awakened shortly by a terrible nightmare. He managed to get to sleep again, but the nightmare returned. Finally he went to the medicine cabinet and took out the amytal. Perhaps his physician had not known enough to warn him that barbiturates heavily suppress REM sleep and dropping the drug would produce a strong case of REM rebound with attendant nightmares (Hinman & Okamoto, 1984a).

By the time Mr. B. saw Dement at the Stanford Sleep Disorders Clinic, he was taking 1,000 mg of amytal every night, and his sleep was more disturbed than ever. He had never had any sleep difficulties before this incident. The EEG records taken at the clinic showed that his sleep contained hardly any delta time at all. Almost his entire night was spent in stages 1 and 2.

Dalmane and barbiturates (such as amytal) are addictive. To keep achieving the drug effect, you must take a heavier and heavier dose each time to compensate for the fact that your body is adjusting to them. When you stop the drug, your body is left in a maladjusted condition. Barbiturate-withdrawal symptoms include anxiety, involuntary muscle twitches, tremor, weakness, dizziness, nausea, vomiting, weight loss, low blood pressure, and, of course, insomnia. In the worst cases, there are generalized convulsions and delirium (Hinman & Okamoto, 1984b). Neither drug ever completely leaves the system of a person who doses nightly. Twenty-four hours is too short a time for the liver to destroy all the barbiturate in one normal nightly dose, and Dalmane is converted by liver enzymes into a long persistence metabolite with strong brain effects (Smith, 1979). Tolerance develops rapidly to these drugs. Recent data on Dalmane suggest that effectiveness begins to drop after 7 days and is completely gone in 2 weeks. In other words, if you keep on taking Dalmane after 2 weeks of steady use, you will not experience any help from the drug. You will, however, experience some side effects brought about by the build-up of the metabolite in your system. A week of Dalmane dosings leaves most people with diminished alertness and poor eye–hand coordination. It gives one pause to think that each morning there are about 2 million people out there in the automobile traffic who took Dalmane the previous night.

Why are physicians writing 25 million prescriptions a year for anti-insomnia drugs if the medication has so little benefit and produces such risk? The problem is that physicians, just like nonmedical people, mistake unconsciousness for sleep. If you think back over what you have learned about the complexities of the two types of sleep and their pattern of interweaving through a normal night, you will see that what insomniacs should be seeking and physicians trying to reproduce is a highly complex phenomenon far too intricate to replicate by the simple expedient of pouring one chemical into the bloodstream.

Narcolepsy

While some people have trouble obtaining enough sleep, others have sleep forced on them by mysterious neural defects that we have only begun to explore. The word **narcolepsy** (NARK-oh-LEP-see) comes from the Greek *narke* (numbness) and *lepsis* (seizure), and it designates a disorder in which the dominant symptom is an overwhelming desire to sleep. Besides the sleep attacks, three other symptoms make up the syndrome: cataplexy, waking nightmares, and automatic behavior episodes (Dement, 1972).

Much of a narcoleptic's waking day is spent in a drowsy, half-alert condition, and on occasion the person succumbs to an irresistible temptation to drift into sleep even if it happens to be in the middle of a business meeting. These involuntary sleep episodes last only 2–5 minutes and usually occur in a fairly monotonous environment. **Cataplexy** is a sudden attack of atonia that frequently strikes the neck muscles (resulting in a sudden drop of the chin onto the chest) but can appear in any muscle group or even involve the entire body. It seems often to be triggered by an emotion like surprise, anger, excitement, sadness, or laughter. Oswald (1966) describes one victim of this symptom who crumples over in paralysis whenever she laughs and another who loves card games but whose jaw muscles go slack whenever she draws a winning hand.

During the cataplectic attack (which usually lasts less than a minute), the person seems to be in a condition similar to the atonia of REM sleep. Furthermore, narcoleptics tend to go directly into REM sleep at night without passing through initial stage 1 (Dement, 1972). It looks very much as though narcolepsy involves an intrusion of REM sleep on the waking state In most people, this is prevented by the necessity of going through NREM sleep in order to get to REM, but in narcolepsy this buffer is apparently missing. This explanation would also account for the **waking nightmares** of narcolepsy. The person frequently experiences vivid, frightening, sensory images especially just before sleep or just after waking. These "hallucinations" are probably dreams emerging into the waking state (Jacobs & Trulson, 1979).

The strangest symptom of narcolepsy is the occurrence of **automatic behavior episodes**. These generally begin with a feeling of drowsiness that the person tries to fight off with an increase in stimulation (changing position, opening a window, turning up the radio, etc.), but the feeling usually grows stronger anyway. Gradually, awareness of self and much of the environment is lost. Only automatic behavior persists. Simple, unskilled behaviors are performed adequately, but anything involving thought and reflection proves too much for the person in this state. During this period of altered consciousness, which seems to be neither sleep nor waking, there is apparently no recording into long-term memory; after the episode, the patient is always amnesic for the events that transpired.

The symptoms of narcolepsy strongly suggest that some of the phenomena of REM sleep (especially atonia and involuntary sensory imagery) are occurring outside their normal context. Research on narcolepsy and other sleep-related disorders may eventually give us some of our best leads to understanding the complex, interwoven control mechanisms that produce normal sleep.

■ Summary

1. Sleep and attention are related in that both involve changes in activation level (arousal). Levels of arousal can be measured with the EEG, a device that records brain waves. Each brain wave represents the algebraic summation of hundreds of thousands of EPSPs, IPSPs, and nerve impulses. When these events are grouped together into clusters occurring roughly at the same time (synchrony), large waves are created; but if they are spread out through time (desynchrony), the result is small (low-voltage) waves.

2. Alpha waves are those with a frequency of 8–12 Hz and moderate voltage. Beta waves are a fast (35–45 Hz), low-voltage, desynchronized rhythm associated with attention and alertness. Alpha rhythm is characteristic of a relaxed, wakeful state, whereas delta rhythm (2–4 Hz, high-voltage) appears during deep sleep.

3. Alpha blocking (the replacement of alpha waves by beta waves) occurs whenever the nervous system experiences a stimulus that is novel. It is one component of the orienting reaction. Loss of the orienting reaction following repeated presentation of the same stimulus is called habituation.

4. The reticular formation consists of the column of gray matter at the center of the spinal cord and brain stem plus certain nuclei within the thalamus. The midbrain portion is the structure that provides the rest of the CNS with nonspecific arousal. At the cellular level, arousal is probably the provision of EPSPs in the aroused neurons.

5. In the EEG record, arousal can be seen as a shift from lower to higher frequencies and from higher to lower voltages. The lowest level of sleep, stage 4, is characterized by delta waves, whereas the highest level, stage 1, exhibits low-voltage, fast rhythms resembling slow beta.

6. When stage 1 is entered from the drowsy, waking state, it is called "initial stage 1"; if it is entered from sleep, it is called "emergent stage 1." Because rapid eye movements (REMs) occur only during emergent stage 1, another name for this state is REM sleep. All other stages taken together are called NREM sleep.

7. A normal night's sleep involves several cycles of alternating NREM and REM sleep. The night always begins with a NREM episode.

8. When studying the nervous system in sleep, researchers typically record EEG, EMG, and EOG. REM sleep is characterized by a flat EMG record, indicating atonia, and eye movements in the EOG record. Area X and locus coeruleus-α (LC-α) contain circuits that control the atonia of REM sleep, and lesions to these areas can release motor neurons from inhibition, allowing the sleeping cat to move about during REM. Another characteristic of REM sleep is the production of PGO waves by reticular cells around locus coeruleus (area X and LC-α).

9. If the brain stem is cut so that the MBRF is disconnected from the higher parts of the brain, the cat will never again show signs of waking, either behaviorally or by EEG desynchronization. If the stem is cut in the lower medulla, the sleep–wake cycle remains normal. The regions for producing REM sleep appear to be in the pontine brain stem, but it has proved to be impossible to find a "sleep center" that is responsible for initiating either REM or NREM sleep. REM sleep seems to start when the various areas involved (FTG, area X, LC-α, and NRMC) all arrive simultaneously at some sort of critical condition, which we have yet to understand precisely.

10. Although it does not seem to be in sole control of NREM sleep, the preoptic area (POA) of the hypothalamus is capable of advancing the onset of that state.

11. Lower vertebrates may have just one generalized sleep state that evolution of the mammalian brain differentiated into the two specialized sleep states: REM and NREM.

12. The restorative theory of sleep suggests that the reason we sleep is to provide the body with a time of low activity to allow for repair of wear and tear. The habituation hypothesis proposes that during the waking day the brain gradually habituates to a wide variety of stimuli and generalizes this habituation to the point where no possible stimulus is novel and arousing. The inevitable result is a drift into lower and lower arousal levels until sleep is reached. Sleep would be a condition of brain organization designed to undo the habituation of the last waking period and allow the brain to once more react to stimuli.

13. Circadian rhythms are related to sleep, and a third theory of sleep proposes that this state evolved from the rhythm of protein synthesis intrinsic to all cells of the body. Protein synthesis increases during sleep and decreases during the waking day. The suprachiasmatic nucleus (SCN) of the hypothalamus appears to have the task of entraining our sleep–wake cycle to the light–dark cycle of the planet. It connects to the POA, which is suspected of initiating the secretion of growth hormone (GH) from the pituitary. It is GH that controls protein synthesis throughout the body.

14. It has been suggested that it is the rise of GH levels during the first half of the night that predisposes the pontine brain stem toward more and more REM episodes during the latter portion of sleep. The importance of increasing protein manufacture during REM sleep would lie in the possibility that REM sleep exists as a state especially designed for the consolidation of memories—a process involving the construction of new synaptic structures out of protein.

15. Chronic insomnia may be the result of neurochemical problems and is often a symptom of depression. In depression there is too little NREM sleep and, what there is of it, includes too much stage 2 with not enough stage 4. The two major types of "sleeping pills" have been the barbiturate drugs and the benzodiazepines (especially flurazepam). Both types are addictive and have insomnia as the chief withdrawal symptom.

16. Narcolepsy is a syndrome that includes sleep attacks, cataplexy, waking nightmares, and automatic behavior episodes. Narcoleptics seem to lack the protection of a mandatory NREM episode between waking and the first REM period. Features of REM sleep (especially dreams and atonia) are able to intrude into the waking state.

Glossary

alpha blocking The replacement of alpha rhythm by beta in response to a focusing of attention. (402)

alpha waves Moderately synchronous EEG waves that occur at the rate of about 8–12 Hz. (401)

arousal A condition of increased alertness, focused attention, and bodily activation. (403)

atonia Complete lack of muscle tone. (414)

automatic behavior episodes Narcoleptic condition in which the person is incapable of any acts other than simple, unskilled behaviors that require a minimum of conscious attention. (434)

barbiturates A category of drugs that depresses central nervous system function. (432)

benzodiazepines A family of drugs used as minor tranquilizers and sleeping pills. (432)

beta waves Small, highly desynchronized EEG waves that occur at a rate of about 30–45 Hz. (401)

cataplexy A sudden attack of atonia; symptom of narcolepsy. (433)

circadian rhythm A near-24-hour cycle in any physiological or behavioral variable. (427)

consolidation The theoretical process whereby memories are strengthened by physiological changes; REM sleep may have originated to allow this process to take place. (429)

delta waves High amplitude, highly synchronized EEG waves that occur at a rate of about 1–4 Hz. (401–402)

deoxyglucose An altered form of glucose that can be taken up by brain cells but not metabolized; used to map active brain areas. (428)

desynchronization The appearance of desynchronous EEG waves during sleep; indicative of stage 1. (410)

desynchrony The condition in which nerve impulses and postsynaptic potentials occur randomly through time. (401)

electromyogram (EMG) Record of muscle action potentials; indicates degree of muscle contraction. (413)

electro-oculogram (EOG) Record of the changes in electrical potential from a series of eye movements. (413)

emergent stage 1 The type of stage 1 sleep entered from stage 2; REM sleep. (410)

entrainment Matching circadian rhythms to the light–dark cycle of the planet. (428)

fibrositis A syndrome characterized by chronic fatigue, stiffness, muscle pain, and irritability; may be the result of too high a ratio of REM to NREM sleep. (425)

flurazepam A drug in the benzodiazepine family used against insomnia. (432)

FTG (gigantocellular tegmental field) An area of the pontine reticular formation that may be involved in triggering REM sleep by inhibiting locus coeruleus. (419)

generalization of habituation A decrease in the number of repetitions required for habituation to a stimulus when it resembles another stimulus to which habituation has already occurred. (408)

gigantocellular tegmental field See *FTG*. (419)

growth hormone (GH) A pituitary secretion that promotes growth in tissue; it may also play a part in initiating REM sleep. (430)

habituation Loss of the orienting response to a particular stimulus when that stimulus occurs repeatedly within a short time and signals nothing of significance in the organism. (408)

habituation hypothesis Idea that sleep occurs because of pervasive generalized habituation that dissipates during sleep. (426)

Hobson–McCarley theory Explains alternation of REM and NREM sleep through actions of circuits in the pontine brain stem; also called the reciprocal interaction model. (419)

initial stage 1 The type of stage 1 sleep entered from the waking condition. (410)

insomnia Perceived difficulty in initiating or maintaining a sleep state. (431)

K-complex An EEG event that consists of a few high-voltage slow waves followed by about 1 second of 14-Hz waves; characteristic of stage 2 sleep. (410)

locus coeruleus (LC) Small cluster of adrenergic cells in the dorsal brain stem at the pontine–midbrain border; part of the reticular formation. (419)

locus coeruleus–α (LC–α) Group of cells just ventral and lateral to LC; one of the cell groups that appears to be responsible for PGO waves. (422)

mentation Mental activity. (413)

midbrain reticular formation (MBRF) The portion of the reticular formation that arouses the cerebral cortex. (403)

narcolepsy A disorder in which the dominant symptom is an overwhelming desire to sleep. (433)

nonspecific facilitation Stimulation of cortical neurons by patterns of nerve impulses that carry no specific sensory information. (405)

NREM sleep Sleep stages 2, 3, and 4, collectively. (411)

nucleus reticularis magnocellularis (NRMC) Medullary reticular neurons that project into the spinal cord to produce the atonia of REM sleep. (422)

orienting reaction A reflexlike response pattern involving the entire body and brain that is designed to collect immediately all possible information about some novel stimulus. (403)

PGO waves Brief, high-voltage EEG waves characteristic of REM sleep. (416)

preoptic area (POA) Zone at the very base of the brain just above and forward of the optic chiasm that may help to initiate NREM sleep. (423)

raphe nuclei Brain-stem reticular formation nuclei lying at the midline; the neurons are serotonergic. (416)

rapid eye movement (REM) sleep Emergent stage 1 sleep. (411)

reciprocal interaction model Hobson and McCarley's idea that reciprocal inhibition between FTG and LC underlies the alternation between REM and NREM sleep. (419)

restorative theory of sleep Explains existence of sleep as a state designed to allow the body to recuperate from a day's activities. (424)

reticular formation A long column of gray matter that starts at the bottom end of the spinal cord and runs up through the brain stem into the thalamus; responsible for inducing arousal. (403)

serotonergic neurons Neurons that use serotonin as a transmitter. (418)

serotonin The neurotransmitter used by the cells of the raphe nuclei. (416)

sleep spindles A pattern of alphalike, synchronized EEG waves of about 10–16 Hz that first increase in amplitude and then decrease; characteristic of stage 2 sleep. (410)

stretch reflex Recontraction of a stretched or relaxed muscle; basis of muscle tone. (414)

suprachiasmatic nucleus (SCN) Portion of the hypothalamus lying just above the optic chiasm; responsible for entrainment. (428)

synchrony The condition in which nerve impulses and postsynaptic potentials cluster together through time. (401)

waking nightmares Vivid, frightening sensory images especially just before sleep or just after waking; symptom of narcolepsy. (434)

X area A region of the reticular formation at the pontine–midbrain border; one of the cell groups that appears to be responsible for PGO waves. (422)

The Control of Ingestion

Summary

Ingestion is the process of taking into the body certain substances needed for life, such as water and nutrients. Psychologists have dominated the research on neural ingestive mechanisms despite the heavy involvement of chemical and physiological concepts. The original research question was simply to discover the parts of the brain that created hunger and thirst and find out how they worked; but as our knowledge base grew, we found that one could not understand hunger or thirst without studying how the body uses and stores fuels and water. In other words, our interest broadened to encompass all of nutrient and water homeostasis.

Homeostasis is the state of remaining nearly the same (static) from one time to another. The body strives to maintain the concentrations of many chemicals (such as sodium, potassium, and glucose) at nearly the same level from moment to moment; in other words, the body attempts to maintain homeostasis. The neural circuits and hormonal secretions employed to this end are called **homeostatic mechanisms.** If the concentration of a needed chemical in the blood is below the desired level, called the **set point**, the homeostatic mechanism drives it back up; if it is above the set point, the concentration is lowered. Water levels above the set point can be lowered by excretion, and excess blood nutrients can be stored. When concentrations fall *below* the set point, the brain may be called on to solve the problem by means of behavior, that is, food- or water-seeking and ingestion. However, the brain also acts to conserve water and fuel when concentrations are too low as well as drawing on stored supplies (in the case of nutrients). Eating and drinking then are really just two fragments of an enormous homeostatic system having many alternate ways of trying to reestablish proper concentrations. Hunger and thirst cannot be understood until we grasp the workings of this entire system. Already we understand enough, for example, to explain to the frustrated dieter why fat can continue to accumulate even while the number of ingested calories has been cut.

In this chapter then, our primary interest is in hunger and thirst, but we start each section with a review of what we now know about the entire homeostatic system of which each is a minor part.

■ Hunger

Many kinds of nutrients are needed to maintain homeostasis, but not all are connected to the neural homeostatic mechanisms that produce eating. Just because your body needs some substance doesn't necessarily mean that you will feel that lack or have a desire to find the substance and ingest it. For example, during the great age of exploration in the 16th and 17th centuries, sailors had to live on salt pork and ship's biscuits for months at a time. Under such dietary conditions, men found that their gums started bleeding, their teeth came loose in their sockets and fell out, their skin developed open sores, and eventually they died. The body simply cannot function without vitamin C, and the diet on some voyages contained almost none of that substance. Yet during all of their weeks of sickness and steady decline, not one of those unfortunates ever complained of a craving for some missing chemical. They did not feel their body's need for the vitamin. They simply felt sick and had no idea what was happening. Eventually, some intelligent captain made the shrewd guess that the disease had something to do with diet and started stocking limes and other citrus. The correct remedy (consuming vitamin C) was finally found through associative learning, not through the automatic action of a homeostatic mechanism commanding behavior.

The human body needs vitamins, minerals, and certain trace elements, but these are so often automatically present in most diets that vertebrates apparently never needed to evolve a hunger for any of them (with the possible exception of salt). Instead, hunger seems to center on fats, carbohydrates, and, perhaps, proteins. Let's see how each of these is used.

Use and Storage of Fuels

The body treats nutrients differently according to whether the concentrations are above or below the set point. Just after a meal, you enter the **absorptive phase** of your eating cycle in which concentrations are high. As nutrients are gradually disposed and concentrations fall below the set point, you enter the **fasting phase** of the cycle. Each phase has its own

mechanisms. We can start with the absorptive phase.

All foods, even that glorious 14-topping garbage pizza you had last week, are essentially collections of fats, carbohydrates, and proteins put together in various proportions with a wide assortment of organic and inorganic molecules tossed in for flavor. As you eat, all these ingredients slide down your esophagus (the tube connecting your throat to your stomach) and spend a while being mixed with acid and digestive enzymes in your stomach. **Enzymes** are chemicals that assemble molecules out of smaller parts or break down molecules into their constituents. Some digestive enzymes break down starch and other carbohydrates into simple sugars like **glucose**, while others disassemble protein molecules into their original **amino acids**. (See Chapter 2 for amino acids.) Fats are broken down into **free fatty acids** and **glycerol**.

The stomach churns the food, mixing it with hydrochloric acid to break it down into small pieces from which the nutrients can be more efficiently extracted. Now and then, a small quantity is released from the stomach through the **pyloric sphincter**, the ring of muscles that closes the outlet from the stomach, into the **duodenum**, the initial 12-inch length of small intestine in which most of the digestion by enzymes occurs. The duodenum also contains receptors that can detect the presence of sugars, fats, and proteins (Thompson, 1979). The remainder of the small intestine (about 20 feet in length) has the task of absorbing food into the blood vessels embedded in its walls. Figure 11.1 illustrates the digestive system.

In the absorptive phase, glucose and fats are removed from the blood by body cells to be burned as fuel. Figure 11.2, which illustrates absorption, shows neurons separated from the rest of the body cells because they normally burn only glucose. During starvation when glucose is unavailable, the neurons fall back on a set of chemicals manufactured by the liver from fats called **ketones**. Excess glucose can be stored by the muscles and liver, after being converted to a different form called **glycogen**, and by **lipocytes** (fat cells), after conversion to a type of fat called **triglyceride**. Glycogen stores are a short-term energy supply and are used up in minutes,

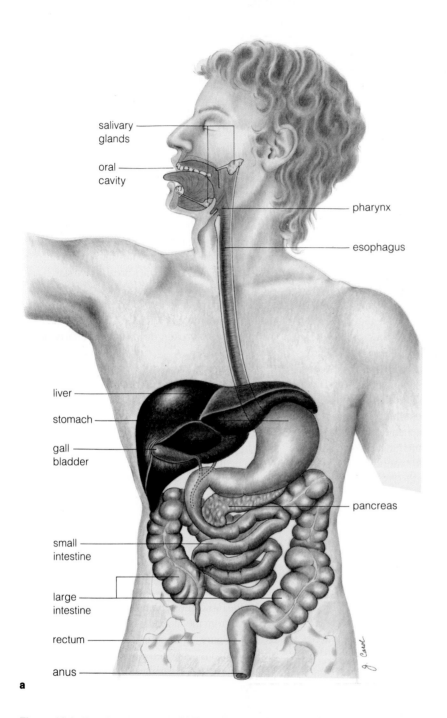

salivary
glands

oral
cavity

pharynx

esophagus

liver

stomach

gall
bladder

pancreas

small
intestine

large
intestine

rectum

anus

a

Figure 11.1 The digestive system. (**a**) The major digestive organs. (**b**) View of the stomach showing the pyloric sphincter and first segment of the small intestine, the duodenum (see opposite page). (From Fowler, 1984)

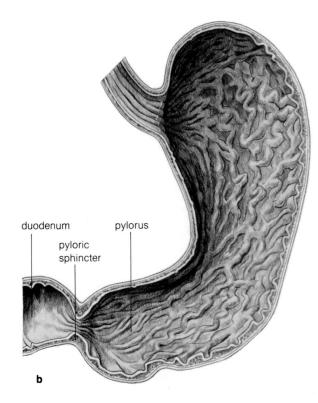

duodenum

pyloric
sphincter

pylorus

b

whereas fat stores are designed for hoarding fuels for weeks and months. Amino acids are used by all body cells as the basis for cellular structure and as the material out of which enzymes are made. Amino acids can also be converted to glucose by the liver. (Dieters take note. A protein diet still creates fat when glucose from extra amino acids is converted to fat by lipocytes.)

The fasting phase of the eating cycle begins when most of the nutrients have been absorbed and disposed of by the cells of the body. The **pancreas** (Figure 11.1), a small organ located near the base of the stomach and beginning of the small intestine, reacts to this shift by secreting the hormone **glucagon**, which enables the liver and muscles to convert glycogen to glucose. Lipocytes convert triglycerides back to free fatty acids and glycerol, which can circulate in the blood. The liver can change free fatty acids to ketones that can be used by most of the body cells as fuel. When muscle cells run out of glycogen, they may start converting their protein back to amino acids, which are then converted to glucose by the liver (Figure 11.3).

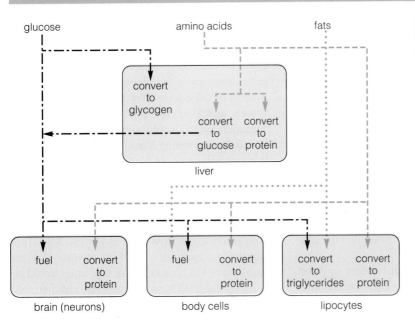

Figure 11.2 Disposition of nutrients during the absorptive phase.

Figure 11.3 Disposition of nutrients during the fasting phase.

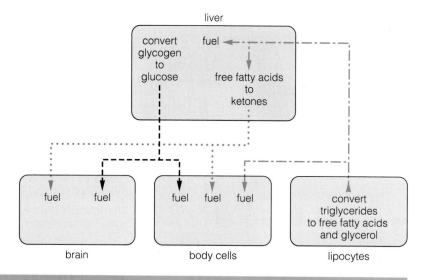

Turning Hunger On

We have seen that the body apparently has no way of linking the need for substances like vitamins to the act of ingestion. If we define hunger as the set of brain processes that produces eating and gives us the conscious desire for food, then it follows that we do not get hungry for vitamins. However, a link may exist for carbohydrates, fats, and proteins. Let's explore the possibility that hunger may be a felt desire to ingest these substances.

Glucostatic Theory The first researcher to propose a possible homeostatic mechanism by which the brain could sense a carbohydrate need was Carlson (1916). In his hypothesis, hunger started when blood glucose levels fell below a certain point and stopped when blood glucose again rose to normal levels following a meal. Presumably, a drop in blood sugar stimulates certain neurons in the brain, and activity in these cells constitutes hunger. The activity of eating, then, could be thought of as a way of keeping blood glucose levels relatively constant, that is, relatively static. Thus, this hypothesis is called the **glucostatic theory** of hunger.

An early test of the glucostatic theory involved injecting rats with insulin to see if they would then eat more than noninjected rats (Wagner & Scow, 1957). **Insulin** is a hormone secreted by the pancreas that enables glucose to enter the body cells where it can be used. The more insulin available, the faster glucose is drawn from the blood and used. Thus, according to the glucostatic theory, an insulin injection should lower blood sugar levels and trigger hunger. The experiment was successful; injected rats did indeed eat more than rats not receiving insulin.

However, a problem arose for the glucostatic theory that centered around a disease called **diabetes mellitus**, a disorder characterized by inadequate production of insulin. In diabetes the body cells slowly starve for glucose while plentiful supplies of blood glucose flow past them in the blood vessels, unable to cross the cell membrane barrier. Treatment usually involves regular insulin injections. For us the interesting feature of diabetes is the fact that a diabetic—whose blood contains so much glucose that the kidneys treat it as waste—can still become hungry!

Mayer (1952) saw a way out of this dilemma. He proposed that hunger was triggered not by low glucose levels but by low rates of glucose use. Thus, people who have not eaten for a number of hours would have less glucose to use (the brain would be using up the small supply in the liver) and therefore a lower rate of use. The low rate would make them hungry. Diabetics, on the other hand, would have low use-rates (and become hungry) because of the inability to use the sugar. Even this clever idea has many problems (most of which are reviewed by Friedman & Stricker, 1976), and the fate of the glucostatic theory remains uncertain. The best guess at this time seems to be that a part, but not all, of hunger may involve a glucose-sensing mechanism in the nervous system.

Aminostatic Hypothesis A second possible source of hunger would derive from the homeostatic regulation of amino acids and proteins. An **aminostatic hypothesis** would postulate the same kind of mechanism as the glucostatic hypothesis but substitute protein for glucose. However, no compelling data exist to suggest that protein deficit can act as a hunger trigger. Rats seem to tolerate considerable protein deprivation without significantly altering their eating habits (Rogers & Leung, 1977). Moreover, if they are maintained for a number of days on a heavily imbalanced diet containing 50 percent protein, they begin eating less; if given a choice between that diet and one containing 25 percent protein, they avoid the 50 percent diet. They also avoid food that has an excess of one amino acid and will even reject that diet in favor of one with no protein at all (Rogers & Leung, 1977). Amino acids are absolutely vital to the animal, but for them to be used, they must be ingested in the proper relative quantities. Molecules tend to compete for places on the chemical transport mechanism that carries them through the blood vessel and somatic cell membranes. If there is a shortage of one particular amino acid, cells may actually receive more of it from a low-protein diet than from one high in competing acids.

Apparently, this fact is important enough that the brain has evolved receptors to monitor the amino acid balance of the blood coursing through it. In one experiment (described in Rogers & Leung, 1977), rats maintained on a diet deficient in the amino acid isoleucine refused food high in other amino acids until a trace of isoleucine was injected into an artery leading to the brain. Injections of isoleucine into a vein leading away from the brain had no effect on ingestion. At this time, it appears that the brain monitors amino acids not for the purpose of triggering eating when amino acid levels are low but rather for biasing the selection of what will be eaten.

Lipostatic Theory The third group of nutrients, fats (technically termed **lipids**), show more promise as a source of hunger. The **lipostatic theory** (Kennedy, 1953) states that the body tries to hold the size of its fat (lipid) deposits static. If you eat less than normal for a few meals and use up some of your fat deposits, your body acts to restore them. This tendency toward a set point also works in the opposite direction. If rats are forced to overeat until they are obese and then returned to a schedule of voluntary eating, their food intake drops until they lose the extra weight.

To see if this decreased eating truly represented the operation of a lipostat, Carpenter and Grossman (1982) manipulated the levels of fat breakdown products in the bloodstream of rats and found that when such products as free fatty acids increase, food intake decreases. Thus, free fatty acids could constitute a signal to the brain about the amount of stored lipids.

Turning Hunger Off

Hunger apparently begins when our glucose use-rate and blood lipid levels fall too low, but what is it that causes our hunger to cease? In technical terms, we want to know what produces **satiety**, the state of feeling "full" and no longer hungry. The most obvious guess is that hunger stops when glucose and lipid levels have been restored to normal, but there is a problem with that hypothesis. Digestion takes time. Food is held in the stomach for awhile to give the stomach time to break it up and is then released into the intestine in small packets. Digested nutrients are slowly absorbed into the blood as the food travels down the intestine. A few foods are rapidly absorbed, but most require at least tens of minutes. Only a very unusual meal would elevate the glucose and fat levels back to normal within a half-hour. If satiety depended on restoration of normal nutrient levels, you might sometimes go on eating for as much as an

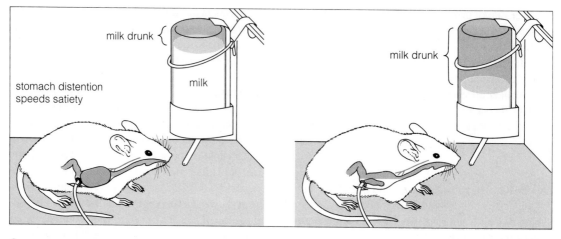

a

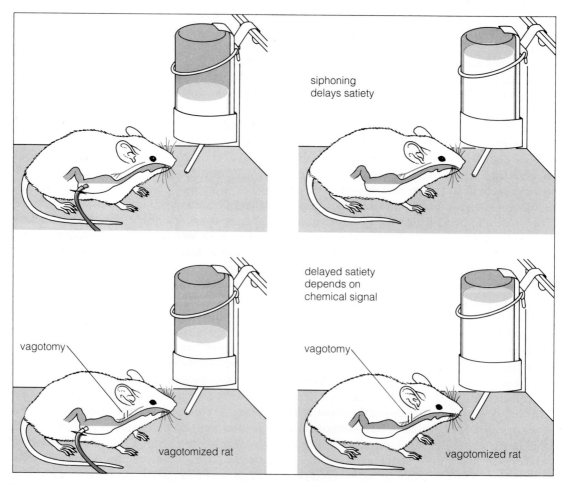

b

Figure 11.4 Experiments identifying satiety signals. Levels of milk in bottles show how much milk was drunk to reach satiety. (**a**) Increasing stomach distention with an inflated balloon speeds satiety. Control rats with uninflated balloons drink more before stopping. (**b**) Siphoning food from the stomach as it is drunk retards satiety (the rat with the siphon drinks longer). This effect persists even when the vagus nerve is cut. This lack of difference between normal and vagotomized rats indicates that satiety depends on a chemical signal because no stomach distention information was available after vagotomy.

hour and a half, and such unrestrained eating could have unwanted repercussions. The stomach is a very stretchable organ, but when filled to a certain point, it suddenly ceases its normal churning contractions and simply empties its undigested contents into the intestine. This is called "dumping" and represents very inefficient use of fuels because much of the food will simply be excreted. Efficient eating demands a neural control mechanism that will produce satiety long before the circulating nutrients have reached normal levels.

A common satiety experience is the sensation of an overly full stomach one gets from a large meal. Perhaps distention of the stomach is the factor that shuts off eating. Is there any way for the brain to know about what condition the stomach is in? Afferent nerve fibers in the vagus nerve connect the brain stem to the visceral organs (Crosby et al., 1962), and some of the afferents might be carrying messages from the stomach to the brain, so the potential connections do exist.

To test the effects of distention, Geliebter and colleagues (1987) inflated balloons in the stomachs of their rats and found that food consumption was lower than when the balloons were in place but uninflated (Figure 11.4). The animal seemed to be cutting down the size of each meal because of the added stomach distention, and this effect was strong enough over days to lead to a significant weight loss. Would satiety occur if distention were prevented? Rats implanted with tubes into their stomachs had some of the food siphoned back out as they ate. The result was that satiety was significantly delayed, even though more than enough food had been swallowed for one meal (Deutsch et al., 1978).

However, there appears to be more than one satiety signal sent from the stomach to the brain. When rats were fed with diluted canned milk, siphoning out food delayed satiety just as much in the rats with severed vagus nerves as it did in normals (Gonzalez & Deutsch, 1981). The implication is that there may be a chemical signal carried from the stomach to the brain by way of the blood (Figure 11.4).

The chemical most often suggested as a bloodborne satiety signal is **cholecystokinin (CCK)** (KOLE-leh-SIS-toe-KIN-in). CCK is secreted by intestinal cells when food enters the duodenum (Zhang et al., 1986) and appears to have a hand in stimulating the secretion of digestive enzymes from the pancreas. When CCK is injected into hungry animals, they stop eating (Whalen & Simon, 1984), and humans who have been given the hormone also decrease their food intake (Kissileff et al., 1981). In a group of obese men (average weight 209 pounds), six out of eight reduced their meal sizes in amounts from 977 to 852 g following CCK injections.

However, although we know that CCK is secreted in the duodenum, we have no direct evidence that it is secreted by the stomach. Furthermore, it is possible that CCK has its effects entirely within the gastrointestinal tract. It is well established that food entering the duodenum acts somehow to close the pyloric sphincter so that stomach contents are retained longer before being released to the intestine (Thompson, 1979). There is evidence that CCK may be the mediator of this effect (Miceli, 1985), which would mean that at least some of its satiety effect might be achieved by way of creating gastric distention. This would explain the greater satiety effect of CCK in monkeys whose stomachs are first loaded with saline (reported in Miceli, 1985) and the loss of the CCK-satiety effect in animals with severed vagus nerves (Smith et al., 1981). CCK also seems to amplify the sensations of gastric distention by increasing the sensitivity of stretch receptors in the stomach wall (Raybould et al., 1988).

Stomach distention cannot explain all of CCK's effects, however. When the pyloric sphincter is disabled, thus preventing CCK from helping produce stomach distention, the chemical still has some amount of satiety effect (Miceli, 1985). Moreover,

CCK can be found in the brain itself, and its concentration increases following a meal (McLaughlin et al., 1985), just as one would expect if the chemical had traveled there from the digestive tract. Its target in the brain may be the medial areas of the hypothalamus that border the third ventricle because satiety can also be produced by directly injecting CCK into the ventricles (Della-Fera & Baile, 1979). One possible problem with this idea is that CCK appears to have difficulty in crossing the blood–brain barrier (Zhang et al., 1986); thus, it is uncertain whether the brain CCK came from the stomach or was generated in the brain as a neurotransmitter (McLaughlin et al., 1986).

Another interpretation of CCK's ability to induce satiety is the possibility that it inhibits eating by producing nausea (Verbalis et al., 1986). However, CCK does not seem to produce the same sensations in rats as is produced by lithium chloride, a chemical known to induce nausea and vomiting (Davidson et al., 1988). Furthermore, although CCK will inhibit the eating of lab chow, it fails to stop rats from consuming a highly palatable mixture of saccharin and glucose (cited in Whalen & Simon, 1984). It seems possible that CCK turns on a brain system that places a negative interpretation on the stimuli associated with eating and that the higher the concentration, the stronger becomes this negative response. High concentrations of CCK, as were used in the Verballis study, might elicit a strong enough response to turn on the nausea–vomiting circuitry.

In summary, eating appears to frequently stop before blood nutrient levels have risen, and this implies the existence of a satiety mechanism. A part of this mechanism seems to depend on vagus nerve input to the brain that signals a full stomach, while another part is chemical. CCK enhances the stomach-distention signal by slowing stomach emptying and sensitizing receptors, but it may also travel directly to the brain via the blood. Satiety probably depends on a chemical signal, except when stomach distention becomes severe.

The Hypothalamus and Hunger

The idea that hunger might be the action of a particular area of the brain was best expressed by Stellar (1954) who proposed a pair of opposing centers somewhere in the brain: an excitatory "hunger center" and an inhibitory "satiety center." The excitatory center would consist of neurons that could control food-seeking behavior and eating and whose activity would be felt in conscious experience as hunger. The inhibitory center would measure food intake and would inhibit further eating once enough nutrients had been ingested. Activity in these inhibitory neurons would be experienced as a feeling of satiation and a desire to avoid food. The hypothalamus seemed the most likely place to look for the hunger centers because neurologists and neurosurgeons treating patients with tumors and other brain diseases had found that hypothalamic damage seemed to be associated with eating disorders. The case described by Celesia and colleagues (1981) is typical:

> The patient, a 28-year-old male, had been admitted to the hospital with complaints of a growing weakness in the muscles of his left arm and a sudden voracious appetite. He had begun eating five to six meals a day and would eat even when his stomach was uncomfortably full. Tests revealed a tumor in the right basal ganglia and the hypothalamus on both sides. Despite radiation treatment, tumor continued to grow, and seven months later, the patient died. During the course of the disease he had gained 16 kilograms (over 35 pounds) in 60 days.

The **hypothalamus** (see Chapter 3) is a small area below the thalamus, just at the base of the brain, that forms part of the walls of the third ventricle (Figures 11.5 and 11.6). The patient described above had several areas damaged in each hypothalamus with the worst destruction in a nucleus called the **ventromedial hypothalamus (VMH)** (ven-tro-ME-dee-uhl). In a famous experiment by Brobeck and coworkers (1943), rats were given bilateral ventromedial hypothalamic lesions (that is, their VMH was destroyed on both sides), and then their eating behavior was observed. Almost immediately the VMH-lesioned rats began to overeat and gain weight. Soon they had acquired two or three times the weight of a normal rat, and some were so obese that they must have experienced great difficulty in simply moving about (Figure 11.7). Brobeck called this unnatural overeating **hypothalamic hyperphagia**

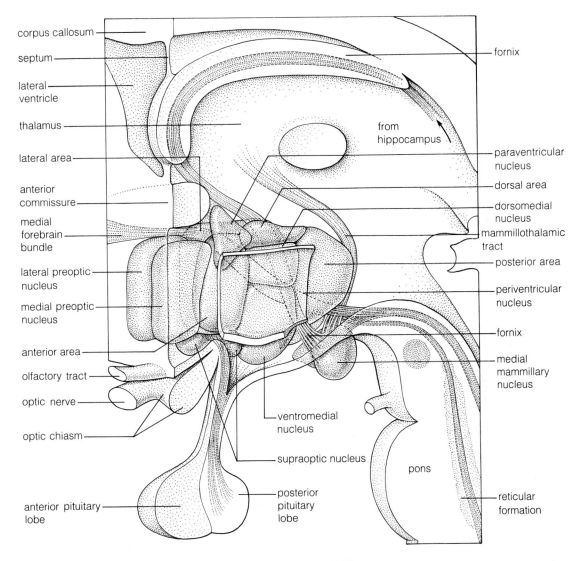

Figure 11.5 The nuclei of the hypothalamus. (Adapted from Netter, 1962)

(HIGH-per-FAY-gee-uh), and the proposal was advanced that such hyperphagia occurred because the missing ventromedial nucleus was a satiety center. Lesioned rats still had their excitatory hunger centers to start them eating but no inhibitory centers to stop them.

Other research (e.g., Anand & Brobeck, 1951) revealed that **aphagia** (complete noninterest in eating) could be induced in rats by lesioning the **lateral hypothalamic nucleus** bilaterally. These animals would starve to death with food directly in front of them. Electrical stimulation of the lateral hypothalamus (LH) in unlesioned rats would induce eating (Hoebel & Teitelbaum, 1962) and, if given daily, would eventually produce obesity (Morgane, 1961). Such results seemed to indicate that the lateral hypothalamus was the excitatory hunger center of the brain.

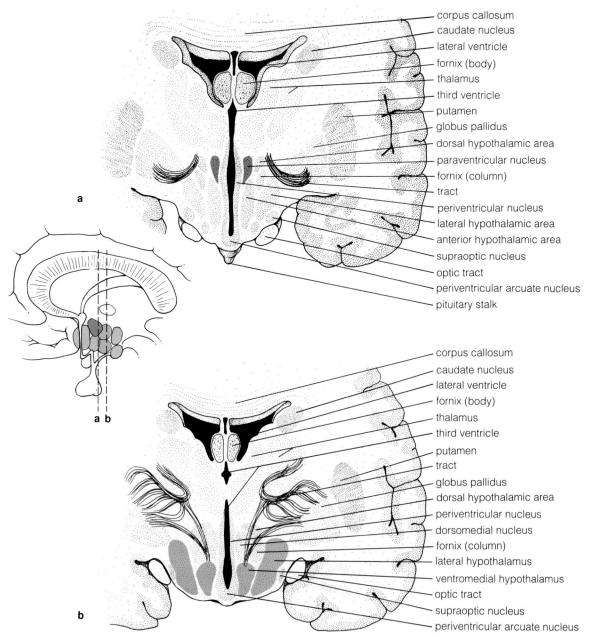

corpus callosum
caudate nucleus
lateral ventricle
fornix (body)
thalamus
third ventricle
putamen
globus pallidus
dorsal hypothalamic area
paraventricular nucleus
fornix (column)
tract
periventricular nucleus
lateral hypothalamic area
anterior hypothalamic area
supraoptic nucleus
optic tract
periventricular arcuate nucleus
pituitary stalk

a

a b

corpus callosum
caudate nucleus
lateral ventricle
fornix (body)
thalamus
third ventricle
putamen
tract
globus pallidus
dorsal hypothalamic area
periventricular nucleus
dorsomedial nucleus
fornix (column)
lateral hypothalamus
ventromedial hypothalamus
optic tract
supraoptic nucleus
periventricular arcuate nucleus

b

Figure 11.6   Frontal sections of the human brain at the level of the hypothalamus showing many of the nuclei involved in ingestion. The inset at the left shows the planes of section for **a** and **b**. (Adapted from Netter, 1962)

Figure 11.7 Hyperphagic rat. The scale reads 80 g.

Lateral Hypothalamus as a Hunger Center: Problems The hypothalamic theory of hunger had a great appeal, but results that the theory could not handle began to appear in the literature. Teitelbaum and Epstein (1962) discovered that rats with LH lesions did not permanently lose their appetites after all. If the animals were nursed through the first few weeks after surgery and then given especially palatable foods, they began to eat on their own. Although recovery was never so complete that the animals would maintain their body weights on food of low palatability or eat when low on glucose, the question remained of why the rats returned to eating at all when their hunger center had supposedly been destroyed.

Other problems also emerged. Anatomists showed that the hypothalamic nuclei are much more than just clusters of cell bodies. Axons running between the brain stem and areas in the cortex and limbic system coursed like superhighways through the hypothalamic nuclei, carrying information vital to sensing, movement, and perception. The possibility existed that aphagia resulting from a lesion to the lateral hypothalamus was caused not by the loss of hypothalamic cells but rather by the interruption of one or more of these tracts—especially those in the medial forebrain bundle.

The large collection of axons called the **medial forebrain bundle (MFB)** (Figures 11.5 and 11.8) contains a group of tracts connecting the higher centers with the brain stem (and vice versa). The two tracts most relevant to aphagia are the nigrostriatal and mesolimbic. The **nigrostriatal tract** (NIG-row-stry-ATE-ul) begins in a midbrain nucleus called the **substantia nigra** (see Chapter 1) and terminates in the **corpus striatum** (Chapters 3 and 9). If this set of connections is damaged, the person has difficulty starting and stopping movements. Could it be that LH lesions result in aphagia simply because the rat finds it difficult to orient toward food, approach it, pick it up, and chew it? Morgane (1961) was able to make rats aphagic with lesions limited to the **globus pallidus** (GLOW-buss PAL-id-us), one of the nuclei in the corpus striatum. In other studies, aphagia was produced by lesioning the nigrostriatal path outside of the lateral hypothalamus and by depleting dopamine, the transmitter used by the nigrostriatal neurons (Zigmond & Stricker, 1972). Such results led a few researchers to ascribe all of LH aphagia to motor problems with eating.

The **mesolimbic system** is also interrupted by LH lesions. These axons have their cell bodies in a midbrain nucleus called the **ventrotegmental area (VTA)**, which lies next to the substantia nigra (Figure 11.8). The axons terminate in limbic areas such as the amygdala, nucleus accumbens, and septal area. The tract is a central portion of the hypothesized reinforcement system of the brain (Chapter 14), and electrical stimulation of the fibers apparently induces a state of pleasure. As the mesolimbic fibers course through lateral hypothalamus, they send off branches to make synapses with hypothalamic neurons. The tract also picks up axons of LH cells traveling to midbrain and limbic structures. All this suggests that LH lesions might severely disrupt the reinforcement system with the result that food and eating-related stimuli (sweet flavors, etc.) might lose their rein-

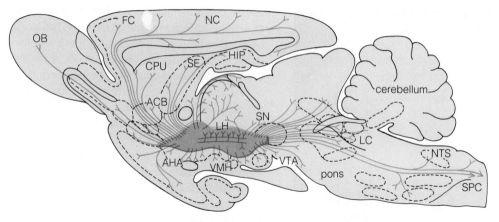

Figure 11.8 Midsagittal section of rat brain showing structures in which fibers of the medial forebrain bundle terminate. For ease of illustration, the segment of the bundle in the hypothalamus is depicted as a solid mass. On either end of the hypothalamus the bundle fans out into a wider array of smaller tracts. Abbreviations: ACB = nucleus accumbens, AHA = anterior hypothalamic area, LH = lateral hypothalamus, OB = olfactory bulb, CPU = caudate and putamen, FC = frontal cortex, HIP = hippocampus, LC = locus coeruleus, NC = neocortex, NTS = nucleus of tractus solitarius, SE = septal nucleus, SN = substantia nigra, SPC = spinal cord, VMH = ventromedial hypothalamus, VTA = ventrotegmental area. (Adapted from Nieuwenhuys et al., 1982)

forcing qualities. The aphagic rat might be ignoring food because food has become "tasteless" (in the sense that the pleasure it used to evoke is absent).

If the LH-lesioned rat has a hard time making the movements involved in eating and cannot enjoy the once pleasurable stimuli associated with the act, the aphagia it suffers might well be explained without hypothesizing any hunger-initiating ability for the lateral hypothalamus. But other data strongly suggest that LH cells are related to the regulation of nutrient supplies. Microelectrode studies of single LH neurons in normal monkeys performing a bar-press for food show that some cells begin responding at the start of the press and continue until the food has been delivered (Nishino et al., 1987). Some fire in relation to the cue stimuli that indicate to the trained animal that a food-related response is now possible; other neurons wait to become active only as the food reinforcement itself appears. During satiety these responses are lost even though the same stimuli and movements occur. The cells only become active when training has produced an association between outside stimuli and food as a reinforcer.

Microelectrode data are important, but it would be helpful to also have data from lesion studies. Is it possible to separate the effects of removing LH cells from the effects of damaging the MFB tracts? Fortunately, **kainic acid** (kye-in-ik), a chemical related to one of the chief transmitters of the nervous system, glutamate, is poisonous to cell bodies. Injected into LH it selectively kills the neurons there without damaging the axons passing through. The result of this sort of lesion is a temporary period of aphagia without any of the motor symptoms or insensitivity to stimuli displayed after electrode lesions (Grossman et al., 1978). Apparently, a lesion that affects only the cell bodies in the lateral hypothalamus does still reduce eating, but not as much as one that also injures motor and reinforcement systems.

Chemicals can also solve another problem. Electrical stimulation of LH induced eating, but the results were ambiguous. Did the eating occur because LH cells can turn on hunger or because firing the MFB activates motor and reinforcement pathways? Grossman (1960) implanted tiny glass tubes called **cannulas** into the brains of rats and injected a chemical that stimulates neurons receptive to nor-adrenaline without affecting nearby axons. The result was an increase in eating, and it must have originated in the lateral hypothalamus itself.

In summary, much of the aphagia seen after electrode lesions can be traced to disturbances in the functions of the motor and reinforcement systems, but not all of it. Chemical stimulation and lesion techniques show that the lateral hypothalamus does seem to have a role in the initiation of eating. We can now investigate what that role might be.

The Role of Lateral Hypothalamus in Hunger There is nothing intrinsically reinforcing about food, as anyone knows when thoroughly satiated from a large meal. Food only acquires its reinforcement value during hunger. Somewhere in the nervous system, a link must exist to give food stimuli a positive reward quality when, and only when, hunger exists (Grossman, 1979). The intimate connections between LH and the mesolimbic system suggest that the connection between reinforcement and hunger might lie within this part of the hypothalamus. If an electrode is implanted into LH and hooked to a stimulator, the rat can be trained to press a lever to deliver tiny shocks to its own brain. In other words, it treats LH stimulation as though it were a reinforcer. Nakamura and Taketoshi (1986) discovered cells in LH that would respond to this self-stimulation and to a glucose drink. When a tone was used during bar-pressing to signal the rat that either glucose or LH stimulation was about to occur, LH cells gradually began to respond to the tone. When the tone no longer was associated with these events (extinction procedure), LH neurons no longer fired as the tone sounded. In monkeys, LH cells have been found that respond to the sight of food (but not to nonfood objects) and do so only during hunger (in Rolls et al., 1976). This suggests that it may be activity in certain LH cells that ties food and food-related stimuli to the reinforcement system, thus giving them reward value.

LH may also play another role in hunger that relates more directly to the initiation of hunger. A small percentage of neurons in LH alter their firing in response to a dose of glucose applied directly to the hypothalamic tissue (Nishino et al., 1987; Rolls,

1978). It is possible that they act the part of a glucostat by monitoring the blood for glucose levels and becoming active when the glucose use-rate falls. They may serve to facilitate the eating and food-seeking circuits by way of their connections into the brain stem. Axons of LH neurons connect with an area of the medulla called the **nucleus of tractus solitarius (NTS)**, which receives input from taste receptors and is apparently involved in eating. LH also connects to the corpus striatum by way of the MFB and thus has the anatomical possibility of facilitating some of the motor circuits of eating. Other connections to the cerebral cortex suggest the possibility of triggering the circuits that control the voluntary aspects of eating (Rolls et al., 1976).

However, it is possible that LH cells get their information about glucose levels indirectly from another source rather than directly monitoring the blood. Friedman and Stricker (1976) suggest that the levels of circulating fats and glucose are measured not in the lateral hypothalamus but in the blood vessels of the liver, and evidence does exist for liver glucose receptors (Russek, 1970). Nutrient-level information could be conveyed into NTS by way of the vagus nerve and from there probably to hypothalamus and, perhaps, VMH.

A third way in which LH may be involved in hunger involves insulin. Stimulating the lateral hypothalamus either electrically or chemically increases the level of circulating insulin (Steffens et al., 1972). LH connects with the **motor nucleus of the vagus** (cranial nerve X), which contains the somas of many of the fibers of the vagus nerve, some of which go to the pancreas. It is by this route that LH can stimulate the pancreas to release insulin (Figure 11.9). Apparently, LH has the role of matching the amount of insulin with the current levels of glucose. If there is not enough insulin, glucose cannot get into the somatic cells to be used and is wasted by being filtered into the urine. If there is too much insulin, glucose is used too rapidly and can lead to a deficiency great enough to starve the brain into a state of coma.

In summary then, lateral hypothalamus may have at least three roles in hunger: acting as a glucostat to initiate hunger when glucose use-rate becomes too low, providing associative connections between

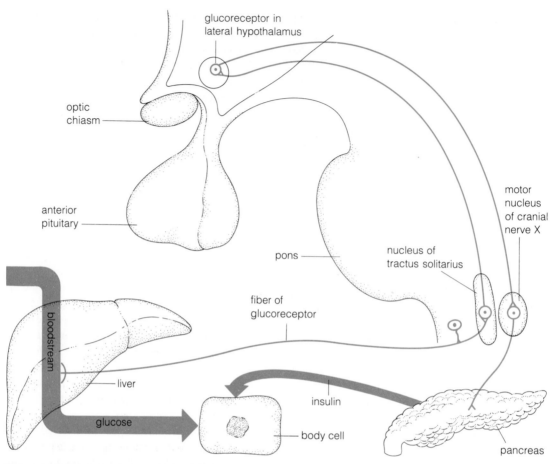

Figure 11.9 Possible role for the lateral hypothalamus. Glucoreceptors in LH stimulate the pancreas (by way of the motor nucleus of the vagus) to secrete insulin. Additional insulin makes it easier for glucose to enter cells and thus raises glucose use-rate. Additional information from liver receptors about blood glucose levels may reach LH via the vagus nerve and the NTS.

food-related stimuli and the reinforcement mechanism, and coordinating the secretion of insulin with glucose levels. Loss of the first two could explain why LH lesions lead to aphagia even without damage to the MFB.

The Hypothalamus and Hyperphagia

The idea of an inhibitory (satiety) center in the ventromedial hypothalamus has not fared well. The fact that removal of VMH produces severe overeating (hyperphagia) suggests that VMH normally acts to stop eating when enough calories have been ingested or when stomach distention occurs. However, several lines of research reveal circumstances in which the VMH-lesioned rat appears to experience satiety despite the loss of its hypothesized satiety center.

Evidence Against a Satiety Center Brobeck and colleagues (1943) found that the initial phase of hyperphagia (the **dynamic phase**) in which the animal eats voraciously and gains weight very rapidly is followed in most rats by a **static phase** in which just enough is eaten to maintain the new body weight. However, if the satiety center has been removed and there is nothing to stop the rat from eating continually, how can a rat in the static phase limit its intake to just enough for maintenance of body weight?

Another problem for the idea of a satiety center in VMH arises from a study by Hoebel and Teitelbaum (1966) in which rats were fattened up prior to having VMH lesions. These already obese rats reacted quite differently to the loss of their hypothalamic nuclei; they failed to become hyperphagic and ate only enough to maintain their obesity. These researchers also found that a rat made hyperphagic and obese by a VMH lesion, then force-fed to become still more obese, would stop being hyperphagic. That is, when the forced feeding was discontinued and the rat was allowed to eat only as much as it wanted, it would sharply curtail its intake until it had lost the fat put on during forced feeding. It would then maintain the level of obesity produced by the VMH lesion. In both of these studies then, rats that supposedly no longer had satiety centers were showing what looks like satiety behavior. Obviously, the VMH is not acting as a simple satiety center.

In the original theory, the job of the VMH was to inhibit the hunger center in the LH as soon as enough food had been eaten. Without this satiation, the rat would be left with an uninhibited hunger drive. So, one would expect a VMH-lesioned rat to eat everything in sight with gusto and abandon. But again, the data surprise us. The VMH animal is picky and finicky, turning up its nose at tasteless lab chow and completely refusing bitter-flavored food even to the point of losing all the weight put on after the lesion when it is offered no other choices (Ferguson & Keesey, 1975). Once these rats diet down to a normal body weight, however, they begin to eat the bitter food and maintain their weight as a normal animal would. Were they too fat to experience normal hunger until they lost their excess weight?

Hyperphagic rats also show a disregard for food when they have to do much work to obtain it (Graff & Stellar, 1962). Effortful work, such as 50 bar-presses to obtain one piece of food, appears to be particularly aversive to VMH-lesioned rats. However, if they were given extensive bar-press training before their VMH lesions, to desensitize them to the effort involved, they would then work as hard as a normal rat to obtain food.

To summarize the objections to the VMH as a satiety center: How can hyperphagic rats control their eating during the static phase when they have lost the control device—the satiety center? How can they stop overeating when released from forced feeding if they have no satiety center? How can they be finicky eaters and unwilling to work for food when they are supposedly in a chronic state of uncontrolled hunger?

Set-Point Theory: Defending a Body Weight In an attempt to explain these problems, it was proposed that body weight was regulated homeostatically and must therefore have a set point toward which the system strives (Keesey & Powley, 1986; Nisbett, 1972). This point could be considered the body's "true" weight to be defended against deviations upward or downward. Thus, rats that had been given short rations for several days would compensate by eating more when food became available again, and rats that had been force-fed to a higher body weight would cut their daily consumption until they had slimmed down to their set point.

Applying this idea to the behavior of hyperphagic rats led to the conclusion that VMH lesions must have given the rats a new, higher set point. During the dynamic phase, the animals overate enough to bring their body weight up to the new standard, but on reaching that point they had to diminish their eating in order not to go beyond the set point, thus displaying the behavior of the static phase. Animals force-fed before receiving VMH lesions failed to exhibit hyperphagia because they were already at their new set point, and those that were force-fed following lesioning and hyperphagia had to "diet" off some of their fat in order to reach their set point.

Unfortunately, the theory never provided any good reason why VMH lesions should shift the set point upward. Furthermore, evidence shows that hyperphagic rats do not always show a static phase (Hallonquist & Brandes, 1981), with some evidence that continuing hyperphagia may depend on the availability of highly palatable food (Cox & Smith,

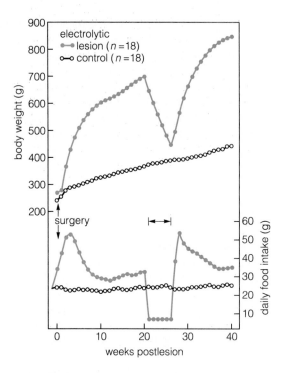

Figure 11.10 Evidence for a sliding set point. Rats in the lesioned group were given bilateral VMH lesions; controls were not. Food intake (lower curves) and body weight (upper curves) were measured over 40 weeks. Between weeks 20 and 26, the lesioned group was restricted to 5 g of food daily. At all other times, all rats were allowed to eat as much as they wanted. Advocates of set-point theory hold that the much faster rate of weight gain following the period of deprivation is explained by a sliding set point. That is, in the postdeprivation period, the rats were starting further below the set point than they had been at the beginning of the experiment and thus put on weight faster. (Adapted from Hallonquist & Brandes, 1984)

1986). This continued overeating seems to contradict the idea that VMH lesions simply shift the set point to a higher level. The animals behave as though they have no set point at all. Yet some strong advocates of set-point theory have interpreted this continued hyperphagia to mean that the animal's set point was continually shifting upward. This smacks of double-talk, but the researchers point to data, such as in Figure 11.10, in which VMH-lesioned rats were

allowed their hyperphagia but then put on restricted diet for 7 weeks. When food again became plentiful, the rats once more were able to overeat and rapidly made up their weight losses. The important point is that they regained at a much faster rate than they had been gaining prior to the period of starvation (Hallonquist & Brandes, 1984). Thus, they may have been attempting to regain a sliding set point. However, we will see that there is another way to explain these data. Set-point theory also has no explicit explanation for the finickiness displayed by hyperphagic rats after the first few weeks.

Last and most important, the idea that body weight should be important to the maintenance of normal body function and needs to be regulated seems dubious at best. What exactly is the survival value of a weight set point? The authors of the theory suggest that a lighter animal has more maneuverability (Keesey & Powley, 1986), but this would not be important for finding food because an obese animal could easily live off its own fat until it is thin enough to hunt once more. Mating behaviors might be hampered, but most young animals in reproductive prime would not have had enough time to become obese.

Do We Defend Body Weight or Nutrient Availability? Friedman and Stricker (1976) are convinced that hunger is determined by the availability of nutrients in the bloodstream—not by body weight. Hunger is turned on by low levels of fats and glucose and turned off by high levels, regardless of weight loss or gain. Unlike body weight, blood nutrient levels are something that can be directly sensed by the nervous system and therefore controlled.

There is an abundance of evidence that hunger correlates with levels of bloodborne chemicals. Carpenter and Grossman (1982) have manipulated the levels of fat breakdown products in the bloodstreams of rats and found that, when products such as free fatty acids increase, food intake decreases. In the **parabiotic-twins technique**, two rats are surgically joined together like "Siamese" twins so that they share the same circulation. If one of the members of the pair is made obese with prolonged stimulation of the lateral hypothalamus or with medial hypothalamic lesions, the other member develops an active aversion to food, eats less than normal, and loses weight (Hervey, 1959; Mrosovsky, 1986). Thus, the parabiotic twin fails to defend a body weight but does seem to react to some chemicals in the bloodstream. However, it remains to be seen whether those chemicals are nutrients or something like CCK.

The strongest link between the availability of nutrients in the blood and hunger is the actions of the hormone insulin. If the vagus nerve is severed in a hyperphagic VMH rat, the rat stops overeating (Powley, 1977). The vagus nerve carries instructions from the motor nucleus concerning how much insulin the pancreas should secrete. Insulin helps both glucose and lipids through the membrane of adipocytes (fat cells). Thus, the more insulin there is in the bloodstream, the easier it is for glucose, free fatty acids, and glycerol to be converted into triglycerides for storage. In other words, the more insulin you have, the faster you build fat deposits. This is relevant because hyperphagic rats have unusually high levels of insulin in their blood whether or not they have overeaten (Bernardis & Frohman, 1970). Perhaps loss of the VMH removed an important control mechanism for limiting insulin secretion. Because of the overabundance of insulin, the lipocytes are able to rapidly absorb most of the glucose and lipids circulating in the blood and convert them into fat. The bloodstream is depleted of nutrients too rapidly, and hunger arises again sooner than it should. Thus, the rat with a VMH lesion must eat continually to keep nutrients available in circulation. Interestingly enough, the animal stays hungry because it is getting fat rather than vice versa.

Can the insulin hypothesis explain the same data that were handled by the set-point theory? The key feature of the insulin hypothesis is that the animal's food intake is regulated by the abundance of nutrients immediately available to it in the bloodstream rather than by its body weight. In the first few weeks following the VMH lesion, the bloodstream remains stripped of nutrients by the high rate at which they are absorbed into fat cells because of insulin levels. As time goes by, however, insulin begins to lose its effect. A negative-feedback mechanism called **receptor down-regulation** senses that there is too much insulin activity and slows the crea-

tion of insulin receptor sites on cell membranes (Flier, 1983). That makes it difficult for insulin to help nutrients into lipocytes despite the high levels of the hormone. As down-regulation continues, lipocytes absorb less and less of the available, circulating nutrients, leaving more for the other body cells. Higher levels of nutrients mean less chance of hunger being triggered and a lessening of hyperphagia. This would explain the "static phase." It has been established that obese humans are relatively insensitive to insulin (Flier, 1983), which suggests that their obesity may in part be the result of too much insulin.

Another explanation for the static phase that does not depend on body-weight set point focuses on the fact that the static phase often occurs only when the rats are fed plain lab chow. VMH-lesioned rats on high-fat diets continue to be hyperphagic (Cox & Smith, 1986). The ability to reduce consumption of plain lab chow may stem from a partially restored responsiveness to the satiety effect of CCK. An injection of CCK stops the VMH-lesioned rat from eating more lab chow but has no effect on such a rat offered a high-fat food (Krinsky et al., 1979). Maggio and colleagues (1988) suggest that the hypersensitivity of the VMH-lesioned rat to the sensory qualities of highly palatable food allows its reward value to overcome the satiety effects of CCK.

Why would a VMH-lesioned rat that had grown obese and then made still fatter through forced feeding begin to "diet" when forced feeding stopped? The answer is that this rat got a double dose of insulin. The taste of food in the mouth is enough to release insulin (Powley, 1977), so a rat forced to feed during its "static" phase still gains weight because of the extra insulin, which compensates for the scarcity of receptor sites. When the forcing stops, the insulin level decreases with the result that nutrients remain longer in the bloodstream, inhibiting the onset of hunger. The higher insulin levels induced by forced feeding would also increase receptor down-regulation. So, when released from forced feeding, the rat has too few receptors to allow its lipocytes to grow. They now release fats faster than taking them up, with a resulting loss in body weight.

The insulin hypothesis does a better job than set-point theory of explaining the finickiness displayed by hyperphagic rats. Hyperphagia tends to appear only when the food available tastes good. Taste is usually improved by adding carbohydrates or fats, which strongly stimulate insulin release. Thus, the rat given such a diet should get hungry sooner than does the rat on a less palatable diet because it is secreting more insulin and transferring nutrients into the lipocytes at a faster rate. The low-carbohydrate diet elicits less insulin, and thus the nutrients last longer in circulation, inhibiting hunger. For this reason, VMH-lesioned rats eat less often when given less palatable foods and thus appear to be finicky.

As we learn more about what controls the storage and release of fat from lipocytes, the relatively vague set-point concept that is currently so popular in obesity clinics may give way to more specific biochemical explanations centering around the availability of enzymes, insulin, and receptors.

Hyperphagia and Satiety: VMH or PVN? The idea that the ventromedial hypothalamus (VMH) is a satiety center no longer seems as obvious as it once did. It had always been observed that the largest "VMH" lesions yielded the greatest hyperphagia, and some of those large lesions extended laterally beyond the boundaries of the nucleus. Sclafani (1971) examined the possibility that the tissue just lateral to VMH might be involved in hyperphagia by making tiny, discreet knife cuts just outside of VMH. Although VMH remained unharmed, the rats became hyperphagic. Gold (1973) compared such cuts to very carefully placed electrode lesions of VMH that remained within the boundaries of the nucleus. The damage to VMH resulted in no hyperphagia, whereas the cuts outside produced the syndrome. Both Sclafani and Gold conclude that hyperphagia was the result of damage to fibers passing through and just lateral to VMH rather than to the cells within the nucleus. What fibers were these?

Gold (1973) suggested that the most potent knife cuts had severed a portion of the axons in the **ventral noradrenergic bundle** that is bringing input from the brain-stem reticular formation. Many noradrenergic axons originate in the medullary reticular formation in the general vicinity of the nucleus of tractus solitarius (NTS) (Feldman & Quenzer, 1984). The bundle terminates in a variety of places including

the paraventricular nucleus. The **paraventricular nucleus (PVN)** (PAIR-uh-ven-TRICK-you-lar) of the hypothalamus lies near the midline of the brain and forms a wall of the third ventricle (Figures 11.5 and 11.6). Aravich and Sclafani (1983) compared lesions in PVN with knife cuts lateral to VMH and found that both produced hyperphagia, although the effect was smaller with PVN lesions. Apparently, much of the so-called VMH hyperphagia can really be attributed to removing some of the brain-stem input to the PVN. VMH lesions may have also cut many of the output fibers from PVN to the brain stem (Kirchgessner & Sclafani, 1988).

Does this mean that VMH is in no way involved in satiety? That conclusion would be unwarranted because of microelectrode studies of ventromedial neurons. Anand and Pillai (1967) found that VMH cells fired more slowly than do LH neurons during the fasting phase. This would agree with the idea that increased activity of LH cells is involved in hunger and that neurons that produce satiety should be inactive in that state. They also found that the firing rates in VMH cells increased as a balloon was inflated in the stomach to produce distention. In other studies, glucose-sensitive cells were found in VMH, and firing rates were found to increase with food consumption (cited in McGinty & Szymusiak, 1988). This fits the idea that satiety neurons might receive information about blood levels of nutrients and become more active as those levels rise. Glucose infused into the third ventricle inhibits eating (Kurata et al., 1986), and it could have had this effect by diffusing into the cells of VMH, which lie next to the ventricle. Furthermore, CCK concentrations rose in VMH after the animal had been fed or injected with CCK (McLaughlin et al., 1985, 1986). (Apparently, it may be possible for CCK to cross the blood–brain barrier in some small quantities.) Thus, several lines of research in various labs suggest a role for VMH in satiety despite the results of PVN studies.

Does the hyperphagia that follows destruction of PVN or its input indicate that this nucleus is a satiety center? Perhaps not, for there is an alternative way of explaining the effect. Figure 11.11 shows that PVN sends axons to the motor nucleus of cranial nerve X, which contains somas of the vagus nerve motor neurons that stimulate insulin secretion from the

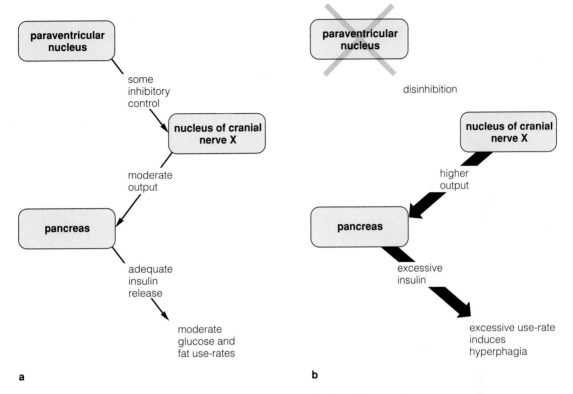

Figure 11.11 The paraventricular nucleus (PVN) influences ingestion through its control over insulin secretion. (**a**) PVN prevents overactivity in NTS through continuous partial inhibition. The NTS is only able to stimulate the pancreas to release moderate levels of insulin—enough to allow fats and glucose to be used at a relatively slow pace. (**b**) PVN has been lesioned, thus disinhibiting NTS. The resulting high insulin levels in the blood use up nutrients very rapidly, leading to immediate and continuing hunger.

pancreas (Luiten et al., 1986). As we have seen, insulin speeds the entry of glucose and fats into cells where they can be used or stored, and too much insulin can produce hyperphagia. Thus, hyperphagia can still be explained with the insulin hypothesis. We can extend the idea by hypothesizing that PVN controls insulin production through inhibition of the motor nucleus. Lesioning PVN removes the brake on the motor nucleus with resulting hyperphagia and obesity (Figure 11.11). The production of an effect through removal of an inhibitor is called disinhibition, so we can say that the motor nucleus was disinhibited by the PVN lesion. The experiments of Leibowitz and colleagues show that the motor

nucleus can be disinhibited naturally by activity in the fibers of the ventral noradrenergic bundle that enter PVN from the brain stem. Drugs that stimulated noradrenergic receptors on PVN neurons, as well as noradrenalin injected into PVN, induced rats to eat more than normal (cited in Chafetz et al., 1986; Shor-Posner et al., 1985), which would occur if PVN were inhibited, thus disinhibiting the motor nucleus.

However, removing or inhibiting PVN fails to induce eating if the pituitary gland has been removed (Leibowitz et al., 1984), and it is this fact that may lead us to an understanding of PVN's role in nutrient control. The anterior pituitary gland (Chapter 3) secretes the hormone ACTH during any stress situa-

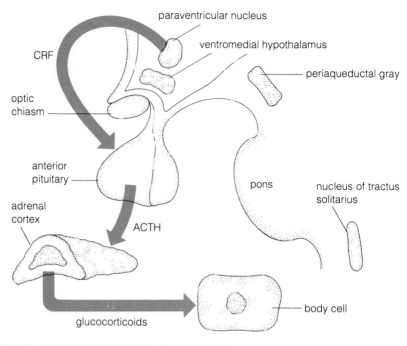

Figure 11.12 Hormonal route through which the paraventricular nucleus prepares the body's cells against stress. The PVN secretes corticotropin-releasing factor (CRF), which circulates through the blood to the anterior pituitary where it stimulates the release of adrenocorticotropic hormone (ACTH). ACTH stimulates the production of glucocorticoids from the adrenal cortex, and these hormones provide the body cells with stress resistance.

tion, but it does so as a response to the hormone **corticotropin-releasing factor (CRF)**, which is secreted by certain cells within the paraventricular nucleus of the hypothalamus (Swanson & Sawchenko, 1983). ACTH circulates through the bloodstream to the cortex of the adrenal gland, where it provokes the secretion of a class of adrenal hormones called **glucocorticoids**. These have a variety of effects on many tissues throughout the body, all related to stress resistance (Figure 11.12).

So now we must ask, Why should PVN have two completely unrelated jobs: regulating insulin levels and ordering the secretion of glucocorticoids to combat stress? Bear in mind that PVN's control over insulin only seems to be there when glucocorticoid levels have risen (Leibowitz et al., 1984), that is, in a stress situation. Also consider that insulin levels are already regulated by the lateral hypothalamus (why have two regulators?) and that PVN receives input through the ventral adrenergic bundle from the reticular formation—a structure one would expect to be active in the arousal produced by stress. Further consider that PVN receives input indirectly

from VMH, which also projects into the PAG (periaqueductal gray), a part of the midbrain from which one can electrically elicit species-specific defense behaviors like the ones involved in fighting (Chapter 13). This whole system concerns high-activity stress situations like fighting or fleeing, which require rapid expenditures of large quantities of glucose. To provide this fuel, the "hormonal" cells of PVN secrete CRF to raise the levels of circulating glucocorticoids, which help mobilize glucose from the liver. The ventromedial hypothalamus can order the pancreas to secrete glucagon, which will release more glucose from the liver. Finally, PVN neurons that project to the motor nucleus of X can allow those cells to release more insulin so that all the added glucose can actually be used by the body's cells (Figure 11.13).

Now we can see why both PVN and LH regulate insulin levels. LH is concerned with providing enough insulin to handle the glucose that is being added to the blood by digestion. This makes it a part of the hunger mechanism of the brain. PVN, on the other hand, regulates insulin only as one part of a

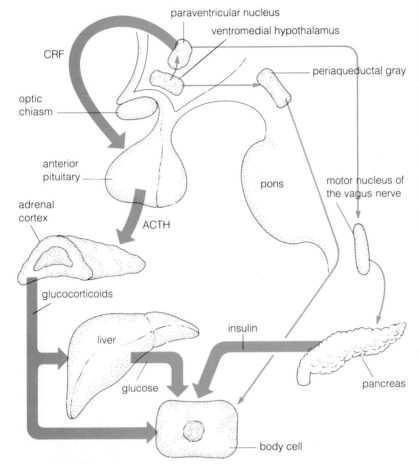

Figure 11.13 Summary of nutrient regulation in stress situations. The ventromedial hypothalamus can stimulate the periaqueductal gray to release species-specific defense behaviors that require high-energy expenditure. It also connects to PVN and so presumably can signal the need of more nutrients and stress hormones. PVN can respond by stimulating the anterior pituitary with CRF, inducing the release of ACTH. That hormone acts on the adrenal cortex to increase the secretion of glucocorticoids. The corticoids stimulate glucose release from the liver and aid body cells in stress resistance. Through a neural path, PVN also disinhibits the motor nucleus of the vagus nerve, thus increasing the secretion of insulin from the pancreas. The insulin acts at cell membranes to allow more glucose into body cells (especially muscle cells).

total "stress-resistance package." The fact that lesioning PVN creates hyperphagia, then, probably has nothing to do with damaging a satiety center. The lesion simply releases the motor nucleus of X from PVN's control and allows it to produce so much insulin that hyperphagia results. If there is a group of cells involved in satiety, they are probably found in ventromedial hypothalamus where they were originally thought to be.

Weight Control in Humans

If this year is like previous years, Americans will spend over $5 million on diet foods, diet drugs, and diet literature. In 1983 1 billion tablets of phenyl-propanolamine, an appetite suppressant, were purchased at a cost of $4.5 million (Kolata, 1985). The need to understand the factors that control food ingestion is becoming more important as more Americans become overweight. Data from the National Center for Health Statistics show an increase in childhood obesity of 54 percent for 6- to 11-year-olds (Kolata, 1986), and overweight children do not seem to lose their excess fat as they reach adulthood. Obesity (having too much fat) is regarded as a health risk by many physicians and even as a disease by some (Kolata, 1985), but ridding oneself of fat can sometimes seem to be almost impossible.

Types of Obesity There is a great deal of confusion in the popular press concerning the causes of obesity and what to do about the condition. One of the reasons for this is the failure to recognize that obesity has many origins and, for this reason, no weight control scheme can work equally well with all people. The main types of obesity are genetic, pathological, and functional obesity.

Genetic obesity occurs when the individual's genes program an excessive number of lipocytes in relation to the number of muscle cells. Each lipocyte has the ability to absorb glucose and fats and to convert them into triglycerides; thus, the more lipocytes the body has, the more nutrients will be taken from the blood and converted to fat. Nisbett (1972) suggests that lipocytes must be kept filled or hunger will be triggered; thus, the more lipocytes one has, the harder it is to keep them all filled and the easier it is to get hungry. If Nisbett is correct, then genetically obese people can never reach a point in dieting where their body adjusts to a lower weight. They will always be hungry unless they are obese. If this is true, it would help explain why the weights of adopted children correlate better with the weights of their biological parents than with those of the parents who are feeding them (Kolata, 1986). The experimental support for the idea that too many fat cells lead to obesity has not been strong, and a better explanation might be found in a genetic predisposition to manufacture too much lipoprotein lipase.

Lipoprotein lipase (LPL) is the most important enzyme for converting circulating fats into stored triglycerides (Hamilton et al., 1984). The more LPL you have, the more readily you store fats rather than burning them. There is greater LPL activity per fat cell in obese humans than in those of normal weight (cited in McMinn, 1984). When a normal-weight person goes on a low-calorie diet, LPL levels drop so that consumed lipids can be used rather than stored, but this was not true of previously obese men who dieted (cited in McMinn, 1984). Their LPL levels remained high even 28 months after a loss of 10–28 percent of body weight, thus giving credence to the frequent claim of obese dieters that despite their best efforts the fat won't stay off. A genetic predisposition toward high LPL levels would appear to mean that the dieter could lose weight and maintain that loss only at the expense of being permanently hungry.

Cases of **pathological obesity** include patients suffering from endocrine gland disorders and VMH tumors. Such medical problems are rare, and very few overweight individuals in the United States fall into this category.

In **functional obesity**, the problem stems more from habits acquired through experience. This category includes most of the people who "worry about" their weight. After Hirsh and Knittle (1970) discovered that some obese people have an unusually large number of fat cells, a number of articles appeared in popular magazines that suggested that all obese people were victims of excessive lipocytes, even those who only became obese during middle age. Did their overeating create more fat cells that then had to be kept filled to minimize hunger? Sims and colleagues (1968) showed, by overfeeding prison volunteers, that adults do not add fat cells as they become obese. Instead, the existing lipocytes simply become larger.

Other research (Knittle & Hirsh, 1968) suggested that overfeeding during infancy might produce more fat cells than are called for by the genes, and it was speculated that mothers were responsible for obesity. Data from rats failed to support this claim, however. Hausberger and Volz (1984) were unable to create obese adult rats by overfeeding them during infancy but had no trouble making adult rats obese by offering a high-fat diet. Furthermore, human studies showed that obesity of overweight infants could readily be explained by their lower activity levels (Hausberger & Volz 1984). The total amount of body fat and the number of lipocytes do not seem to be very strongly related to one another. For example, there is a strain of pigs that is comparatively lean but that has no fewer lipocytes than does a fatter strain (cited in Hausberger & Volz, 1984). Although we cannot discard the hypothesis that excessive eating creates more lipocytes, the evidence for it is not strong at this time.

Extreme Solutions Many people have tried dieting as a means of weight control and found that it was not successful for them. Consequently, some people have tried extreme measures such as drugs, surgery, and fasting.

Of those three, the most commonly used are appetite-suppressant drugs. These usually contain some amount of one or more of the CNS stimulants called **amphetamines** (am-FET-ah-meens), which increase "nervous energy" and decrease appetite. Amphetamines also have serious side effects and are strongly addictive if taken in sufficient quantities over a period of time. The final outcome of constant usage is amphetamine psychosis. Leon (1976), in a review of various treatments for obesity, concluded that the long-term outcome of weight-control programs using drugs was uniformly poor.

Even more dangerous than drugs is a surgical technique called **intestinal bypass** (technically, jejunoileal bypass), in which a shortcut connection is made that routes food past most of the small intestine. Because the patient is left with a bare minimum of intestine with which to absorb nutrients, much of the food eaten is simply excreted rather than used. Presurgery weights of patients typically have been in the range of 350–500 pounds, and postsurgical weight loss has averaged about 10.5 pounds per 6 months. Generally, weight loss slows with time and stabilizes after about 2 or 3 years. Serious medical complications are common, including chronic diarrhea, sodium and potassium imbalance, liver changes, abdominal bloating, impaired vitamin-B_{12} absorption, and hair loss. Mortality rate in one study was 6 percent (Leon, 1976). Bypass surgery is not to be taken lightly. A much more popular form of "fat cure" is **fasting**, which involves taking absolutely no food of any form for days or weeks at a time. Some people are able to accomplish this feat of abstinence without artificial aids, whereas others have a dentist wire their jaws shut. In either case, initial results are often gratifying to the faster because there typically is a measurable weight loss in just a day or two. Unhappily, however, most of the poundage shed is the result of water loss rather than fat reduction. Our bodies are the genetic heritage of millions of years during which survival was so difficult that only a few accomplished it. For our distant ancestors, a few days without food might be the prelude to famine. Because we are built from the genes of the survivors, we have all sorts of automatic reactions to food shortages that tend to protect reserve nutrient supplies in our fat tissue. Accordingly, our bodies do not react to fasting by making the energy from that carefully hoarded triglyceride easily available. Instead, metabolism slows down, and body temperature falls. Dieters tend to feel tired, weak, and chilly.

The needs of the brain come first. That organ requires between 400 and 600 calories daily, and normally it burns only glucose. When the liver's supply of glucose has run short, your system must go hunting for a new source. The most readily available substance is protein, of which there is a good supply in the form of muscles.

So when you fast, you are losing not only fat but also muscle. And for every gram of protein stolen from the muscles and burned for fuel, 3 g of water are also lost. Such dehydration quickly shows up as an appreciable weight loss and gives the dieter an illusion of "fat melting away." With the 3 g of water also goes a sizable portion of sodium and potassium ions that will have to be replaced if the body is to function normally. But during fasting, the person is usually not taking in needed ions, only water.

Most people are somewhat confused about what they are trying to accomplish when they fast or go on a diet. They talk about losing weight when actually they want to selectively lose fat while keeping water balance and muscles intact. Unfortunately, it is much more difficult to measure fat deposits than overall weight. As a result, dieters fool themselves by treating every drop in weight as though it were a loss of fat. Only after several days of fasting is there any appreciable loss of fat (Mayer, 1977), and one study showed that the average protein loss during a month of fasting was 14 pounds. Muscle is a great deal harder to replace than is fat and requires exercise to stimulate the process. An overweight person who goes on periodic bouts of severe dieting with minimal exercise in between may lose a little more protein during each diet period than is replaced between diets. The lean-to-fat ratio in that person's body would then gradually shift toward a greater and greater proportion of fat, even when there is no long-term gain in body weight. Ideally, we should quit measuring weight and start measuring our ratio of lean-to-fat. Unfortunately, the equipment to do that is quite large and expensive and requires you to fully immerse your body in a tank of water to get the measurement. A crude but very cheap substitute is the "pinch" test. Take a pinch of your skin between thumb and forefinger and note the thickness. Because many fat deposits are just beneath the skin, it generally works out that bigger pinches mean more fat.

Dieting Dieting, the most popular of all weight-loss schemes, might be thought of as "semifasting." If the diet severely restricts food intake, then many of the same biochemical events as in fasting will occur in the first few days. There should be a sharp drop in weight because of water loss (and intestinal emptying), but in this case the ions lost with the water will probably be replaced through food intake. As in fasting, there is the possible drawback of having to convert muscle into glucose for the brain. (If the diet continues for any length of time, the brain begins to fall back on a second metabolic line of defense in which it uses lipid breakdown products called ketones, but this does not prevent the continuing conversion of proteins into glucose.) Again, the body treats a low-calorie diet like a partial famine by slowing the dieter's basal metabolism (which accounts for 70 percent of the calories burned daily). It may also take other steps to conserve fuel, such as stimulating the intestine to increase the amount of nutrient absorbed from the food and to store a greater percentage of it as fat (Lima et al., 1982). Thus, a "quick-weight-loss" diet is not an efficient way to control the size of fat tissue.

Because insulin is so important in determining how much of our food will be converted into stored triglycerides, we should be interested in what factors control the amount of insulin secreted. Woods and colleagues (1974) cite three circumstances that could lead to oversecretion of insulin: constant exposure to a high-carbohydrate diet, poor meal distribution, and classical conditioning of insulin secretion.

Most Americans take in too many carbohydrates. The diet of the stereotypical, beer-drinking, "meat-and-potatoes man" includes a high proportion of carbohydrates and thus high blood insulin levels. The more insulin he generates, the greater the percentage of fuels his body will use for creating fat. In other words, if all other factors are held constant, a person who takes in half of a 3,000-calories-per-day diet in carbohydrates will get fatter than a person who takes in only one third of those same 3,000 calories in carbohydrates.

The distribution of meals during the day is also important in determining the amount of insulin secreted. Many small meals seems to produce less insulin than do a few big meals. A comparison of rats who nibbled throughout each day whenever they got hungry with rats who had to eat one large meal a day (because food was only available for a short time) showed that the one-meal rats became significantly more obese than the nibblers (cited in Woods et al., 1974). A parallel study compared three groups of children, one that ate three meals a day, another that had five meals, and a last that ate seven meals. Despite the fact that the three-meal children took in exactly the same number of calories in their big meals as did the seven-meal children with their smaller ones, the children with only three meals were the ones that became significantly fatter (cited in Woods et al., 1974). Snacking throughout the day apparently can help you stay thinner, as long as you don't eat any meals in addition to the snacks! However, we need to find out more about how the factor of food-type interacts with meal size. When natural "gorgers" (rats that voluntarily ate fewer but larger meals) were compared with natural "nibblers," no significant difference was found in weight gains on regular lab chow. On being switched to a high-carbohydrate, high-fat diet, however, the gorgers immediately began gaining weight faster than did the nibblers (Drewnowski et al., 1984).

Of the three insulin factors we are discussing, conditioned secretion has the most potential for making mischief with a diet. To understand this, first recall what you learned earlier about Pavlov and classical conditioning. Pavlov discovered that any reflex response could be transferred to a neutral stimulus—the conditioned stimulus (CS)—if it were paired often enough with the stimulus that automatically elicited the reflex—the unconditioned stimulus (UCS). To a dog, the sound of a bell is a neutral stimulus until it has been paired with the stimulus for the salivating reflex—namely, food in the mouth. When the bell (the CS) and the food (the UCS) have been paired numerous times, the bell alone is sufficient to produce salivating.

This sort of primitive learning occurs quite readily in many reflexes involved with eating or digestion, including the secretion of insulin. The UCS for insulin secretion is probably the stimulation of liver receptors for glucose and fat by circulating nutrients. Any neutral stimulus that is present over and over again with food intake should become a CS and eventually be able to elicit insulin secretion without any help from food. Do you always eat at exactly the same time of day? The hour could become a CS, and at that hour your pancreas would dutifully secrete a jolt of insulin even if there were no food in sight.

Do most of your meals contain something with a sweet taste? The sweet flavor could easily become a CS for insulin secretion (Lucas et al., 1987), a fact that has some nasty implications. Let's say that for years you have been eating anything you wanted whenever you wanted, which in American culture means a high-carbohydrate diet. Every meal is washed down with a soft drink. Suddenly the day arrives when your image in the mirror no longer fits between the sides of the frame, and you decide to diet. As a part of this effort, you switch to diet drinks. But will that help keep the fat from going on? Thanks to the high proportion of carbohydrates in your pre-

vious diet, you have for years been pairing food with sweet taste. Your digestive system is conditioned; it secretes insulin just as easily in response to non-nutritive diet drinks as it does to the ones made with sugar. So even if you eat nothing for lunch but the diet drink, you will still get fatter. This results from insulin taking the few nutrients that are still circulating in your blood, plus glucose drawn from your liver stores, and moving them into the cells (Storlien et al., 1985). The muscles will absorb only a few calories, because you are not exercising at the moment, but the fat cells stand ready to absorb all the rest. Thus, the extent to which you have been conditioned to secrete insulin may have been an important factor in determining how fat you now are. Overweight humans in one study showed a surge of insulin secretion about 7 minutes following the beginning of a meal, which was not present in lean subjects (Simon et al., 1986), a difference probably traceable to past conditioning (Figure 11.14).

Have you become overweight by eating large meals? If you have, don't expect your body to adjust its insulin levels immediately to smaller meals. Those big meals included many neutral stimuli (sight and

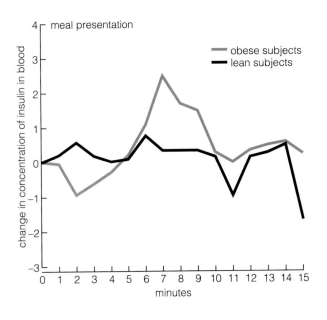

Figure 11.14 The stimulus effect of food on insulin secretion in lean and obese subjects. Obese eaters experienced a surge of insulin secretion beginning about 7 minutes after the start of a meal. No surge was found in lean subjects. A possible explanation is that obese subjects had developed a stronger conditioned insulin-secretion response to food CS's. (Adapted from Simon et al., 1986)

smell of food, table, silverware, etc.) that may have become CS's for insulin secretion, and those same stimuli may be there during your smaller meals. Extra insulin will remove the nutrients from your blood faster, burning them or allowing more of them to be converted to fat. It might be days or weeks before your body stops storing excessive amounts of the food you give it, and every extra calorie it converts to triglycerides is denied to the rest of your body to use as fuel. This might explain why cutting food intake makes some people feel much more desperately hungry than they had expected to feel.

So, is dieting the best way to lose fat? When people tell you that they are "going on a diet," it usually means that they are going to temporarily interrupt their normal life-style in order to restructure their appearance. They don't have a permanent change in life-style in mind, yet they expect the weight loss to be permanent. Dieting almost has to be a temporary thing because normally it is too painful to continue for very long. Now that you know about a few of the complex changes that are forced on your body by dieting, can you really expect any short-term, temporary effort to produce a permanent result? Perhaps a functionally obese person should forget about dieting and make some permanent changes in the types of food eaten (low-fat and low-carbohydrate), have a lot of very small meals each day rather than a few big ones, start a regular exercise program to increase calorie use and rebuild lean tissue, and start seeking new sources of pleasure that have nothing to do with food or eating.

Thirst

Psychologists began their quest to understand thirst by trying to answer a seemingly simple question: What is the stimulus that leads to thirst? Negative evidence was quickly found for such simple suggestions as "a dry mouth," and investigators soon became aware that thirst and drinking could not be understood apart from the entire homeostatic mechanism for regulating water, salt concentration, and blood pressure. The desire to drink stems from the complex interplay between kidneys, heart, blood vessels, adrenal cortex, and brain. To find the triggers for thirst, we must understand how water moves across cell membranes, how water is conserved by the kidneys, and why salt homeostasis is a part of the same mechanism that makes us drink. A good place to start is to see how water is distributed and conserved.

Anatomy of Body Water

In terms of water, the body can be divided into two compartments: **intracellular space** (inside the cell) and **extracellular space** (between cells). Most of the contents of a body cell is water. As a matter of fact, you are about 66 percent water by weight, and about two thirds of that water is found inside your cells. If one traces the evolution of the human species back many millions of years, one finds that our distant ancestors were sea-dwelling animals. It comes as little surprise to find that our body cells contain a fluid strongly resembling seawater, with most of the salts and minerals that one finds in the ocean.

We divide the extracellular space into two parts: the space between cells and the volume within the blood vessels. The latter is termed **vascular space** after the vascular system, which includes the heart, blood vessels, and lymph ducts. Both of these extracellular spaces are water-filled; the gaps between cells contain about 23 percent of your body's water and the vascular system about 10 percent.

Intracellular space is separated from extracellular space by the membrane of the cell. The membrane is porous and allows water molecules to pass through it along with certain ions such as sodium and chloride. There is a natural tendency for ions to distribute themselves evenly throughout any space; if there are more sodium ions on one side of the membrane than on the other, the ions on the high-concentration side will try to slip through the membrane to get to the low-concentration side. The force that pushes them through the membrane is called **osmotic pressure** (ahhz-MOT-ik).

As the ions shift through the membrane and the concentration on one side comes closer and closer to matching the concentration on the other, the

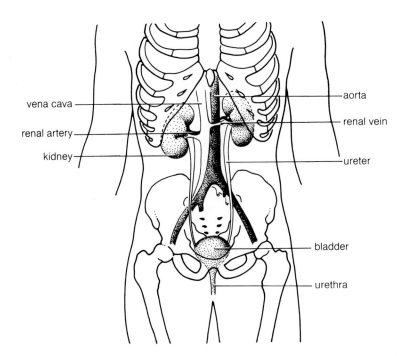

Figure 11.15 Kidneys and bladder. The ureter is a tube that connects the kidney to the bladder. The vena cava is a vein returning blood to the heart, and the aorta is an artery bringing blood from the heart. (From Jensen et al., 1979)

vena cava

renal artery

kidney

aorta

renal vein

ureter

bladder

urethra

osmotic pressure grows weaker and weaker. But what if the ions cannot squeeze through the membrane? Recall from Chapter 4 that nerve cells actively pump sodium out of themselves, thus creating a considerable difference in concentration between the inside and the outside of the cell. When the ions cannot cross the membrane, osmotic pressure simply pulls water from the low ion–concentration side to the high-concentration side. Thus, the side with few ions sees its concentration increase because the number of ions stays the same while the water holding them decreases. Conversely, the side with the greater number of ions sees its concentration decrease as water moves across to provide more and more elbow room for the same number of particles. Eventually, the concentration on one side equals the concentration on the other. So if the ions can't cross the membrane, the water will. This is a very important fact to keep in mind if you enjoy playing sports in hot weather. Why? Well, it has to do with what

you need to drink to satisfy your thirst after sweating a lot, which in turn has to do with the way your kidneys operate.

Conserving Water and Maintaining Blood Pressure

The body cannot build reserves of water like it stores excess glucose and lipids. Water must be recycled, and the kidneys (Figure 11.15) are the focus of this conservation effort. We will see how they work, how neural mechanisms enable them to work more efficiently during high water-loss activities like athletics, and how all this interacts with blood pressure.

Kidney Function Blood not only carries fuel and oxygen around to the cells of the body but also is the major trash collector, picking up metabolic by-products from cells and transporting them to the "dump." Within the kidneys (Figure 11.16), the blood

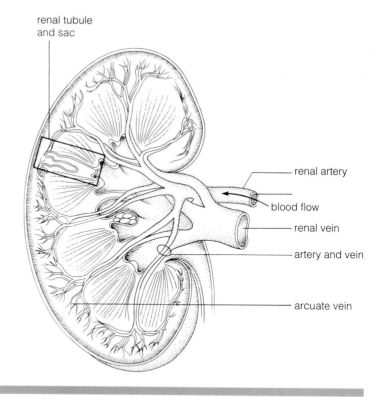

Figure 11.16 Section through the kidney. One of the thousands of renal tubules with its collecting sac is shown outlined within the kidney. (Adapted from Perry & Morton, 1989)

renal tubule and sac

renal artery

blood flow

renal vein

artery and vein

arcuate vein

vessels branch repeatedly into fine networks of tiny vessels called **capillaries** (CAP-ul-AIR-ees) that line the insides of a series of collecting sacs. Water diffuses through the capillary membrane and then through the membrane of each sac. Osmotic pressure forces glucose, salt, and metabolic by-products through the membranes along with water because the concentrations are lower in the sacs than in the blood. The fluid now contained in the sacs is called urine and will be piped down to the bladder for holding.

Notice that as the blood dumps its load of "trash" into the sacs, it also loses a good deal of water. In fact, your kidneys draw about 45 gallons of water a day from the bloodstream. Forty-five gallons! This is possible because the kidney not only filters out the waste but also reabsorbs about 99 percent of that 45 gallons for recycling. Before it leaves the kidney, the newly created urine enters one of many **renal tubules** (REE-nul TUBE-yules), each of which snakes around through a thicket of capillaries before finally

emptying into a main collecting duct heading for the bladder. This tangle produces a large area of contact between the tubules and capillaries along which the water in the tubules can osmose back from the thinly concentrated urine to the more concentrated blood. Thus, thinned once more to normal concentration, the blood leaves the kidneys to recirculate through the body. It carries with it most of the glucose that it brought into the kidneys and most of the sodium, both of which were reabsorbed from the tubules.

Sodium is vital to your ability to move and think. Without sodium to create membrane potentials, muscles couldn't contract, and neurons couldn't produce impulses. The kidneys guard your supply of sodium by reabsorbing most of what might be lost in the urine. But what about those hot, sweaty summer softball games when you lose so much salt by perspiring? Can the kidneys be encouraged to conserve yet more sodium to compensate in part for its loss through the skin? Yes, the **adrenal cortex** (the outside portion of the adrenal gland) secretes a hor-

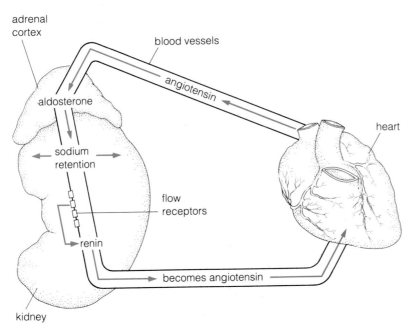

Figure 11.17 One portion of the water-conservation system of the body. When blood volume is decreased by dehydration, flow receptors in blood vessels of the kidney respond by triggering the production of renin. When renin is released into the blood, it is converted to angiotensin, a chemical that can stimulate the adrenal cortex to release the hormone aldosterone. The blood carries aldosterone to the kidney where it increases the retention of sodium. As sodium is reclaimed from the urine, it draws water along with it osmotically.

mone called **aldosterone** (al-DAH-steer-own), which reaches the kidneys by way of the blood and increases the rate of sodium reabsorption.

Water and Salt Conservation When you sweat, you not only lose sodium but water as well. Some of this fluid is lost from the vascular system, and the decrease in blood flow can be sensed by receptors in the blood vessels of the kidneys. When these receptors are stimulated by a low blood volume, the kidney responds by secreting a chemical called **renin**. After being poured into the bloodstream, renin is altered to **angiotensin** (AN-geo-TEN-sin), a substance that is capable of stimulating the cells in the adrenal cortex. Can you put two-and-two together and guess what the adrenal cortex secretes in response to angiotensin? Recall that the cortex produces a hormone called aldosterone, which acts on the kidneys to increase the retention of sodium. So, the sequence of events is: a low volume of blood flow stimulates kidney receptors that makes the kidneys produce renin that is converted to angiotensin that acts on the adrenal cortex to obtain aldosterone

that produces better sodium retention in the kidneys (Figure 11.17). But what does better sodium retention have to do with conserving water?

The gallons of water that are reabsorbed daily from the urine in the kidney tubules are not actively pumped back into the capillaries. It is sodium that is actively reclaimed, and water molecules simply tag along to rebalance osmotic pressures. Without sodium reabsorption, there would be very little water reabsorbed. Thus, if low blood pressure can get the adrenals to secrete aldosterone, more salt will be recaptured, and the vessels will once more swell up with the accompanying water.

So what sort of liquid should you drink to satisfy your thirst when you are sweating heavily? The more you perspire, the more salt you lose, and the less sodium there is in the tubules. The lower the concentration of salt there is in the kidney tubules, the smaller the quantity of water that can be reabsorbed. If you drink straight water throughout your softball game, more and more of it will be passed straight through as urine, less and less will stay in your body. To keep the water you drink, you need to take salt

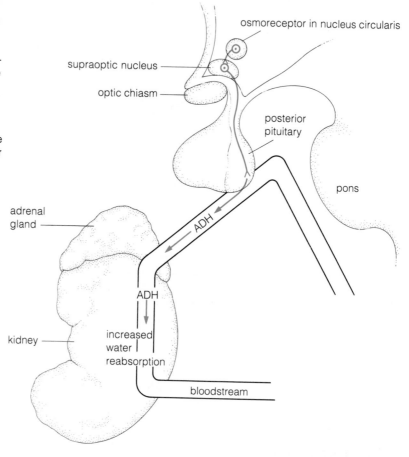

Figure 11.18 A second water-conservation mechanism depends on osmoreceptors in the nucleus circularis of the hypothalamus that detect cellular dehydration. Their response stimulates the supraoptic nucleus to secrete ADH, which is sent to the posterior pituitary to be released into the bloodstream. When ADH reaches the kidney, it acts to increase water reabsorption.

along with it, either straight out of the shaker or mixed in one of the "sports drinks" now on the market.

There is also a second way in which the body can increase the amount of water reclaimed by the kidneys. Verney's research (see Swanson & Sawchenko, 1983, p. 305) suggested to him that specialized hypothalamic cells existed that were sensitive to stretch. Hypothetically, such cells would fire when dehydrated but stop firing as they swelled up with water and the receptor elements attached to the membrane were stretched. If neurons like that do exist, they would function as a sensing mechanism to detect loss of fluid from the cells and would be appropriately called **osmoreceptors**. Neurons in the **nucleus**

circularis of the hypothalamus (Figure 11.18) seem to qualify as osmoreceptors. Hatton (1976) found evidence that circularis neurons are sensitive to the change in osmotic pressure that occurs as extracellular water is lost. Circularis neurons connect with the cells of the **supraoptic nucleus** (SOUP-rah-OP-tic) of the hypothalamus that manufacture **antidiuretic hormone (ADH)** (AN-tye-DIE-your-RET-ik). ADH is transported through the axons of the supraoptic neurons into the posterior pituitary where it is stored or released directly into the bloodstream. Circulating to the kidneys, ADH acts on the renal tubules to increase their reabsorption of water from the urine (Figure 11.18).

Problems can occur with the brain mechanisms

that regulate water balance. For example, one of the many toxic effects of alcohol is its interference with ADH. If you have ever found yourself to be extra thirsty despite drinking several pints of beer, it is because the alcohol has lowered your ADH levels and you are losing water faster than the beer can replace it. In the illness **diabetes insipidus**, the **posterior pituitary** fails to secrete enough ADH, and water retention becomes so poor that the victim may excrete as much as 22 liters of urine a day. Needless to say, this disorder produces considerable thirst. Certain cases of brain damage (probably involving the supraoptic nucleus) result in **hypodipsia** (inadequate water intake) together with too little ADH secretion (Andersson & Rundgren, 1982). If these two symptoms continue for any length of time, fatal dehydration can occur.

Maintaining Blood Pressure Perhaps the most immediate problem that arises when the body loses water is the maintenance of blood pressure. If much of the fluid volume of the blood is lost, there won't be enough left to quite fill up the blood vessels. Much of the force of your heartbeat would then be absorbed just by stretching slack blood vessel walls, and as a result, your blood pressure would drop. If you have ever gotten up from a sitting position too fast, the resulting dizziness is a good clue about what low blood pressure does to the brain. Neurons are more demanding of a constant supply of oxygen and glucose than is any other body tissue, and it takes a good-sized push to get that blood uphill as far as the head. The body must defend against dangerously low levels of blood pressure, and that can only be done by defending its water content.

With this in mind, it is not surprising that ADH secretion can be triggered by a second set of receptors within the heart itself. These are called **baroreceptors** because they can sense low pressure (*baro-* as in barometer, a pressure meter). Their input apparently travels through the vagus nerve to NTS and from there to the supraoptic nucleus where ADH is manufactured (Figure 11.19). ADH helps raise blood pressure by increasing the amount of water reabsorbed into the blood.

High blood pressure (**hypertension**) is just as bad (if not worse) than low blood pressure. It is associated with "hardening" of the arteries and heart failure. You are probably aware of the fact that physicians put hypertensive patients on low-salt diets. Now you can see why. There is some evidence that people diagnosed as hypertensive have a tendency to retain sodium, and it is quite possible that this trait was inherited (Light et al., 1983). No one is sure whether increased sodium retention is the sole cause of hypertension, but it would certainly add to the problem. Furthermore, there are hints throughout the medical literature that chronic stress may contribute to vascular disease (heart trouble and stroke), perhaps because stress produces hypertension. Light and co-workers (1983) discovered that young men with parents suffering from hypertension would begin to retain sodium and water when subjected to a stressful mental task. Notice that it took two factors working together to produce this effect. Not only was each person subjected to stress, but he also had a good probability of having inherited a tendency toward hypertension.

We have seen that the body makes strenuous efforts to conserve water, but inevitably some water must be lost. Some urine must be excreted, water must evaporate off the skin for cooling, and a good deal of moisture leaves the lungs as vapor whenever you exhale. Conservation is not enough; the body must also have a mechanism for replacing water, and this is where the nervous system and thirst enter the picture.

Role of the Nervous System in Thirst

Thirst is the conscious experience accompanying neural activity in those parts of the brain that initiate water-seeking and drinking. The stimuli for thirst are intracellular dehydration and low blood pressure. We examine intracellular dehydration first.

Osmotic (Intracellular) Thirst Drinking in goats was induced by Andersson and McCann (1955) by injecting tiny amounts of salt solution into the hypothalamus. They concluded that some of the cells in the stimulated area of the hypothalamus must be sensitive to dehydration and are set to react to it by triggering the circuits that control drinking. But how

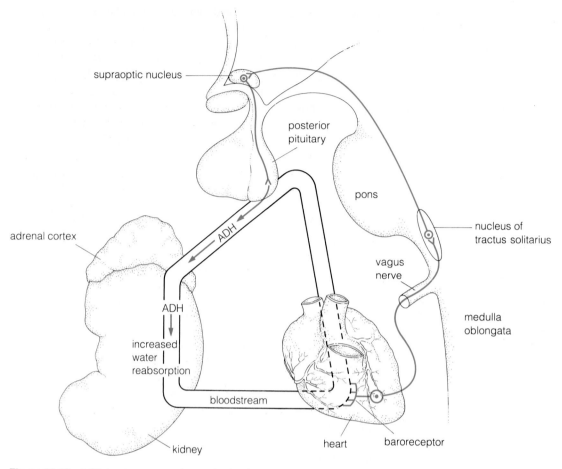

Figure 11.19 A third water-conservation mechanism involves baroreceptors located in the heart that sense low blood pressure. Their input is relayed to the supraoptic nucleus by way of the vagus nerve and nucleus of tractus solitarius. The nucleus responds by secreting ADH, which increases water reabsorption.

could a salt solution dehydrate these cells? The answer is osmotic pressure. The sodium concentrations inside and outside the cell cannot be equalized by shifting salt inward because the sodium pump constantly pushes sodium out; thus, the concentrations must be equalized by drawing water out of the cell to dilute the extracellular salt solution. Thus, when Andersson and McCann injected the salt solution, they were dehydrating the intracellular space in that area of the hypothalamus and firing the dehy-

dration-sensitive osmoreceptor cells located there. These osmoreceptors are apparently linked to the drinking circuits that are probably located in the brain stem.

Some evidence now exists for osmoreceptors in the **medial** and **lateral preoptic areas** of the hypothalamus, a zone at the anterior tip of the third ventricle (Hatton & Armstrong, 1981). The medial preoptic area (MPOA) probably connects directly with the drinking circuits lying within the **mesen-**

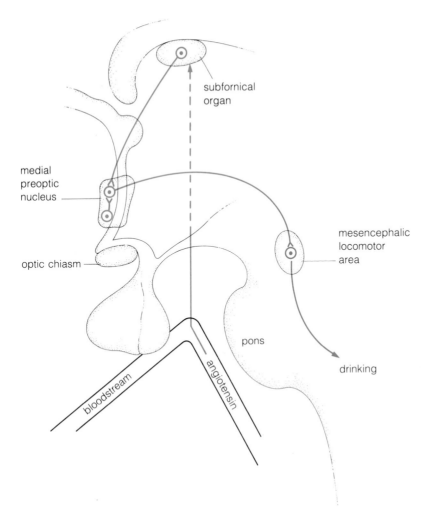

Figure 11.20 Drinking behaviors are organized in the mesencephalic motor area of the midbrain. Activity in these circuits is triggered by cells in the MPOA, which are responding to input from nearby osmoreceptors and/or input from the subfornical organ. The subfornical organ is stimulated by bloodborne angiotensin from the kidneys. Thus, thirst can be triggered either osmotically by receptors in the MPOA or hypovolemically by flow receptors in the kidneys and angiotensin.

cephalic locomotor area (Swanson et al., 1987). So, the route for osmotic thirst seems to be dehydration → osmoreceptors in MPO area → brain stem → behavior (Figure 11.20).

LH lesions that produce aphagia also stop an animal from drinking, a condition known as **adipsia** (a-DIP-see-uh). If the lesion is in the anterior hypothalamus, forward of LH, the adipsia is probably the result of removing osmoreceptors or their connections to the pituitary gland. Adipsia from damage to

LH itself, however, is a different matter. Neurons in MPOA send axons down to the drinking circuits in the brain stem, and along the way they must pass through or near the lateral hypothalamus. It is possible that LH lesions cut the thirst-drive mechanism right in half, isolating the need-sensing part in the anterior hypothalamus from the behavioral part in the brain stem. Perhaps an animal with LH lesions remains thirsty all the time but fails to drink because it no longer associates drinking with thirst.

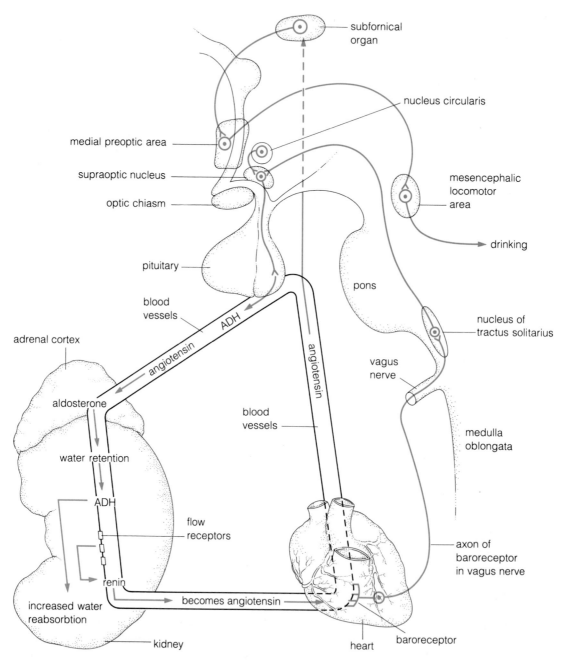

Figure 11.21 Summary of water-conservation and thirst mechanisms.

Hypovolemic (Extracellular) Thirst The prefix *hypo* means below normal, and the suffix *volemic* refers to the volume of fluid in the extracellular compartment. Recall that kidney receptors react to this condition by secreting renin, which becomes angiotensin. In its role as a part of the conservation mechanism, angiotensin stimulates the adrenal cortex; but as a thirst stimulus, it also goes to a part of the brain called the **subfornical organ (SFO)** (so named for its position below the fornix). SFO neurons then stimulate cells in a part of the MPOA, which connects to the drinking circuitry (Figure 11.20). Figure 11.21 summarizes the conservation and thirst mechanisms.

Satiation of Thirst

Water—good, clean, unpolluted water—is the one substance that is absolutely safe and can be consumed in any quantity you want . . . Correct? Or, can even water be harmful in excess?

A researcher working with rats can measure precisely how much water the animals have lost over several hours of deprivation and then measure how much they drink when water is once more available. When Stricker (1969) did this, he discovered that rats stopped drinking before the deficit had been made up. Later periods of extra drinking were required to finally replace all the water lost. When rats stopped drinking the first time, the hypothalamus was presumably still getting signals from baroreceptors, osmoreceptors, and circulating angiotensin, all indicating that there was still a water shortage. So why did the drinking stop? Is there some sort of inhibitory mechanism in the brain that deliberately cuts off drinking before the body is rehydrated?

The **septal nucleus** might function as an inhibitor of drinking. It is a midline structure right in front of the anterior hypothalamus, and it has strong connections with the hypothalamus and brain stem. When Harvey and Hunt (1965) destroyed the septal nucleus on both sides of the brain, they discovered that their rats immediately began overdrinking—a behavior technically known as **hyperdipsia**. It was as if a brake had been removed from the thirst drive.

But why should mammals have evolved a mechanism to actively turn off the thirst drive when it is so much simpler to just drink as long as the dehydration signals are triggering thirst? The answer lies in the timing of absorption. When water reaches the stomach, it is held there for awhile and slowly let out into the small intestine in limited quantities. Even after reaching the small intestine, there is still quite a bit of time involved before any rehydration occurs, however, because most water absorption is accomplished in the large intestine, several yards down the line. By the time the first "new" water enters the blood and is delivered to the waiting cells, enough time has passed for a really rapid drinker to have consumed many pints—even quarts. (According to Rolls et al., 1980, about 7.5–12.5 minutes must pass between the first swallow and complete rehydration of the cells.)

And too much water, it turns out, actually can be dangerous. While it's in you and your kidneys are striving to unload the excess, all your body fluids have weaker concentrations. The symptoms of water intoxication include confusion and poor motor control and occur when sodium concentration reaches a dangerously low level. Occasionally, seizures can result (Zubenko, 1987). Recall that it is the critical adjustment of sodium-ion concentrations inside and outside the cells that enables neurons to generate nerve impulses. There is at least one report in the medical literature of compulsive water drinking severe enough to cause death (Rendell et al., 1978).

But water intoxication can be prevented if your brain has a mechanism that inhibits drinking even while the cells are still signaling a deficit. When this mechanism goes into action, the conscious experience would presumably be the familiar feeling of fullness that we call satiation. How might such a satiety mechanism work? Blass and Hall (1976) found that satiation involves at least two factors, one oral and the other gastric. The gastric factor seems to be simply sensations of discomfort when the stomach gets too full of water. The oral factor probably depends on signals from receptors in membranes of the mouth and throat. At this point in the research on oral factors, we can only speculate about the details, but it is possible that the amount of water drunk is totaled up somewhere in the brain (the septal area?), and when the tally reaches a certain level, an inhibitory signal goes out to the drinking circuits. Because a deprived animal that drinks fairly rapidly (like most humans) will stop drinking before making up its deficit and then return repeatedly for short bursts of additional drinking, the inhibitory signal must decrease as time from the last swallow increases. In other words, the inhibition (satiety) builds up as drinking proceeds, reaches a point where it temporarily stops the drinking, and then slowly dissipates to a level low enough to allow another burst of drinking. Presumably, all during this time, stretch receptors are signaling that the deficit has not yet been made up and that drinking should continue. Only after the cells are completely rehydrated again do the bursts of drinking finally stop. Note that all of this applies to fast drinkers like dogs and humans. Some species such as rats are slow drinkers and apparently do not need a strong satiety mechanism to prevent hyperhydration.

■ Summary

1. Ingestion is the process of taking into the body certain substances needed for life, such as water and nutrients in an attempt to maintain homeostasis, the state of remaining nearly the same (static) from one time to another.

2. Hunger is a part of the homeostatic mechanisms for maintaining availability of glucose, fats, and proteins. In the absorptive phase of the eating cycle, carbohydrates are converted to glucose, which is used as fuel or stored as glycogen or fats. Proteins are broken down into amino acids, and fats are either used as fuel or stored. In the fasting phase, fuel is obtained when glycogen is converted to glucose, fats are released from storage, and proteins converted to glucose.

3. The glucostatic theory seeks to explain how the need for glucose homeostasis is linked to the desire to eat. In the fasting phase, the scarcity of glucose decreases its use-rate to a level low enough to stimulate receptors located (probably) in the lateral hypothalamus and these neurons stimulate the feeding circuitry in the brain stem. There is little evidence for an aminostatic mechanism to link protein need to hunger. Lipostatic theory suggests that there is a homeostatic mechanism for maintaining the size of the body's fat deposits.

4. Satiety occurs during the absorptive phase sooner than could be expected if it depended on the return of nutrients to homeostatic levels in the blood. Instead, it seems to depend on two signals from the viscera: distention of the stomach signaled by the vagus nerve and some chemical secreted by the stomach or duodenum. The chemical might be cholecystokinin (CCK), a duodenal hormone.

5. In early experiments on the hypothalamus and hunger, it was found that lesions of LH produced aphagia. This suggested that LH was a hunger center responsible for the desire to eat. Problems with this interpretation were that lesioned rats would begin eating once more if they were nursed through the initial stages of aphagia and if the food were highly palatable; LH lesions interrupted the medial forebrain bundle (MFB), which connects motor parts of the feeding system; and interruption of the MFB also disconnects parts of the reinforcement system and probably removes the rewarding aspects of eating. However, chemical lesions that kill cells in LH without damaging fibers passing through still affect eating. LH does seem to be involved in instigating hunger as well as connecting food with reinforcement and ensuring that the amount of insulin secreted matches blood glucose levels.

6. Early experiments that made rats hyperphagic by lesioning the ventromedial hypothalamus (VMH) suggested that this part of the hypothalamus was a satiety center. Problems for this interpretation include the loss of hyperphagia during the static phase and the hypophagia seen in forced-feeding studies. The set-point theory (a form of lipostatic theory) interprets the evidence to mean that VMH lesions disrupt the homeostatic mechanism in the brain for regulating fat supplies and allow the set point to rise to a level that would result in obesity. Friedman and Stricker argue that the set point is not for a certain body weight but for a particular level of circulating nutrients (especially fats). Hyperphagia occurs because the hypothalamic lesion releases the pancreas from control and allows it to oversecrete insulin, a hormone that raises the use of glucose by allowing it into cells. Insulin clears the blood of circulating nutrients too

fast, triggering hunger again too soon after the previous meal. All these hypotheses are superior to the original idea that VMH lesions simply prevented satiety.

7. The early hyperphagia experiments were also incorrect about the area of the hypothalamus most affected by the damage. "VMH" lesions actually produce hyperphagia by damaging the fibers passing through from the paraventricular nucleus (PVN) to the motor nucleus of the vagus nerve. The cells in the motor nucleus stimulate the pancreas to secrete insulin, and the fibers from the PVN inhibit this action. The PVN controls secretion of stress hormones from the anterior pituitary and adrenal cortex. Its control of insulin secretion via the motor nucleus can be explained by the need to raise the rate of glucose use during stressful conditions.

8. Human obesity can be classified as either genetic (possibly too many fat cells), pathological (the result of a metabolic defect), or functional (acquired through experience). The number of calories consumed per day is not the sole determinant of whether a person will acquire functional obesity. The more carbohydrates there are in the daily calories, the more insulin is secreted and the greater the proportion of nutrients stored as fat rather than burned. Smaller meals produce less insulin than do large meals and thus lead to less fat storage. Past experience with high-carbohydrate diets means that insulin secretion has been classically conditioned to such stimuli as sweet flavors.

9. Water homeostasis depends on water-conservation mechanisms and thirst. Water conservation occurs in the kidneys where it first carries waste out of the blood into the urine, and then draws sodium and water back into the blood.

10. When the volume of water drops in the bloodstream, flow receptors in the kidneys sense the change and induce kidney cells to secrete renin. Once in the blood, renin is converted into angiotensin, a chemical that stimulates the adrenal cortex to secrete aldosterone. The hormone aldosterone acts on the kidneys to increase the amount of sodium reclaimed from the urine. Higher levels of sodium in the blood draw water back into it from the urine.

11. Decrease in water volume is also sensed by osmoreceptors in the nucleus circularis of the hypothalamus. These cells induce the supraoptic nucleus to secrete antidiuretic hormone (ADH), which is transported to the posterior pituitary and released into the blood as needed. ADH travels to the kidneys where it increases water retention.

12. The maintenance of blood pressure depends on keeping the proper water volume in the blood. Thus, the heart contains baroreceptors that react to a decrease in blood pressure by signaling the brain by way of the vagus nerve and nucleus of the tractus solitarius (NTS). That nucleus stimulates the supraoptic to secrete ADH.

13. Conservation cannot recycle all the body's water. To compensate for loss, there must be a mechanism for inducing drinking—that is, thirst. Osmotic thirst occurs when water lost from the cells. This osmosis of water from the cells is sensed by osmoreceptors probably located in the medial and lateral preoptic nuclei. The medial preoptic area (MPOA) connects with the drinking circuitry in the mesencephalic locomotor area of the midbrain. Hypovolemic thirst occurs because of loss of extracellular water. The angiotensin produced in response to low blood volume can enter the brain through the subfornical organ (SFO) and trigger a neural response that stimulates the mesencephalic drinking circuits by way of the MPOA.

14. A satiety mechanism is needed to cut off drinking before too much water has been consumed. Satiety appears to be triggered by receptors in the mouth and stomach, perhaps working through the septal area.

Glossary

absorptive phase The portion of the eating cycle starting just after a meal and lasting until the nutrients are absorbed into the bloodstream. (441)

adipsia Cessation of drinking despite need for water. (473)

adrenal cortex The outside portion of the adrenal gland. (468)

aldosterone A hormone that increases the rate of sodium reabsorption in the kidneys. (469)

amino acids Chemicals out of which proteins are made. (441)

aminostatic hypothesis The idea that hunger is initiated by low blood levels of amino acids; there is no firm evidence for this. (445)

amphetamines Stimulant drugs that decrease appetite. (463)

angiotensin A substance that stimulates cells in the adrenal cortex to secrete aldosterone. (469)

antidiuretic hormone (ADH) A posterior pituitary hormone that acts on the renal tubules to increase their reabsorption of water from the urine. (470)

aphagia Complete lack of interest in food or eating. (449)

baroreceptor Receptor sensitive to changes in pressure. (471)

cannula A tiny tube that can be implanted into the brain for delivery of chemicals directly into brain tissue. (452)

capillaries Tiny blood vessels that are the final branchings of arteries and the beginning of the venous system. (468)

cholecystokinin (CCK) A chemical secreted by intestinal cells when food enters the duodenum. (447)

corpus striatum Motor nuclei between the thalamus and the cortex. (451)

corticotropin-releasing factor (CRF) A hypothalamic hormone secreted by the paraventricular nucleus to release ACTH from the anterior pituitary. (460)

diabetes insipidus A disease in which water retention is inadequate because the posterior pituitary fails to secrete enough ADH. (471)

diabetes mellitus A disease in which the cells cannot obtain enough glucose; one frequent cause is the underproduction of insulin. (444)

duodenum The initial 12-inch length of small intestine in which most of the digestion by enzymes occurs. (441)

dynamic phase Initial stage of hyperphagia in which the animal eats voraciously and gains weight very rapidly. (454)

enzymes Chemicals that assemble molecules out of smaller parts or break molecules down into their constituents. (441)

extracellular space Space between cells. (466)

fasting Taking absolutely no food of any form for days or weeks at a time. (463)

fasting phase The portion of the eating cycle lasting from the end of the absorptive phase until the next meal. (441)

free fatty acids Soluble lipids that can circulate in the bloodstream. (441)

functional obesity An overweight condition of psychological origin. (462)

genetic obesity A condition in which the individual's genes program an excessive number of lipocytes in relation to the number of muscle cells. (462)

globus pallidus One of the nuclei in the corpus striatum. (451)

glucagon A pancreatic hormone that enables the liver and muscles to convert glycogen to glucose. (443)

glucocorticoids Hormones of the adrenal cortex that have a variety of effects on many tissues throughout the body, all related to stress resistance. (460)

glucose Blood sugar. (441)

glucostatic theory A theory that proposes that hunger is initiated by a drop in glucose use-rate. (444)

glycerol A soluble lipid that can circulate in the bloodstream. (441)

glycogen A form of glucose that can be stored in the liver or muscles. (441)

homeostasis The state of remaining nearly the same (static) from one time to another. (440)

homeostatic mechanism A neural circuit or hormonal secretion employed in achieving homeostasis. (440)

hyperdipsia Excessive drinking. (475)

hypertension Dangerously elevated blood pressure. (471)

hypodipsia Inadequate water intake. (471)

hypothalamic hyperphagia Overeating that results from damage to either the ventromedial nucleus or a tract from the paraventricular nucleus of the hypothalamus. (448)

hypothalamus Region of the diencephalon ventral to the thalamus at the base of the brain; control center for body chemistry. (448)

hypovolemic (extracellular) thirst Thirst that originates from lack of fluid volume in the extracellular space (especially the blood vessels); hence, extracellular thirst. (475)

insulin A pancreatic hormone that enables glucose and fats to enter the body cells. (444)

intestinal bypass Surgical procedure that rearranges the alimentary canal to route food past most of the small intestine. (463)

intracellular space Space inside the cell. (466)

kainic acid A chemical that can kill cell bodies in a nucleus without damaging the axons passing through. (452)

ketones A set of chemicals manufactured from fats by the liver. (441)

lateral hypothalamic nucleus Contains cells that sense glucose use-rate and may help to initiate eating and adjust insulin levels. (449)

lateral preoptic area The brain area immediately anterior to the hypothalamus that contains osmoreceptors. (472)

lipids Fats. (445)

lipocytes Fat cells. (441)

lipoprotein lipase (LPL) The most important enzyme for converting circulating fats into stored triglycerides. (462)

lipostatic theory States that the body tries to hold the size of its fat deposits static by adjusting the level of hunger. (445)

medial forebrain bundle (MFB) Large bundle of tracts coursing through LH that connects the brain stem with parts of the limbic system and corpus striatum; site of self-stimulation reinforcement effect. (451)

medial preoptic area (MPOA) The hypothalamic zone that contains osmoreceptors and connects to drinking circuits. (472)

mesencephalic locomotor area A central region of the midbrain containing programs for many routine behavior patterns such as walking and drinking. (472–473)

mesolimbic system A group of tracts in the medial forebrain bundle that connect the ventrotegmental area with the limbic. (451)

motor nucleus of the vagus Area of the medulla that contains the somas of many Xth nerve motor neurons, including those that run to the pancreas. (453)

nigrostriatal tract Connects the substantia nigra to the corpus striatum by way of the medial forebrain bundle. (451)

nucleus circularis Hypothalamic nucleus containing osmoreceptor cells. (470)

nucleus of tractus solitarius (NTS) An area of the medulla that receives input from taste receptors and is apparently involved in eating. (453)

osmoreceptor Neuron that can detect loss of fluid by reacting to a change in osmotic pressure. (470)

osmotic pressure The force that pushes chemicals through the cell membrane. (466)

osmotic (intracellular) thirst Thirst that originates from lack of fluid within the cells; hence, intracellular thirst. (471)

pancreas An endocrine gland located near the base of the stomach and beginning of the small intestine that secretes glucagon and insulin. (443)

parabiotic-twins technique Method in which two rats are surgically joined together like "Siamese" twins so that they share the same circulation. (456)

paraventricular nucleus (PVN) Hypothalamic cell group that lies near the midline of the brain and forms a wall of the third ventricle near the anterior end of the hypothalamus. (458)

pathological obesity Obesity that results from some disease process like a tumor or endocrine defect. (462)

posterior pituitary The posterior lobe of the gland that obtains its hormones from hypothalamic cells. (471)

pyloric sphincter The ring of muscles that closes the outlet from the stomach into the duodenum. (441)

receptor down-regulation Homeostatic cell mechanism that decreases the number of available receptor sites when there is too much agonist available, thereby decreasing its effect. (457)

renal tubules Ducts that contact the capillaries of the kidney to allow some of the water in the urine to osmose back into the blood. (468)

renin A kidney secretion that is altered in the bloodstream to angiotensin. (469)

satiety The state of feeling "full" and no longer hungry. (445)

septal nucleus A midline structure in front of the anterior hypothalamus that has strong connections with the hypothalamus and brain stem; might function as an inhibitor of drinking. (475)

set point The desired level toward which a homeostatic mechanism drives the factor it controls. (440)

static phase Stage of hyperphagia in which just enough is eaten to maintain the new body weight. (455)

subfornical organ (SFO) Brain structure just under the fornix that reacts to angiotensin in the blood by stimulating the thirst-drinking circuits of MPOA. (475)

substantia nigra Motor nucleus at the rostral end of the midbrain. (451)

supraoptic nucleus Hypothalamic nucleus dorsal to the optic chiasm that manufactures ADH for release by the posterior pituitary gland. (470)

triglycerides A storable form of fat found in lipocytes. (441)

vascular space Space within the blood vessels and heart. (466)

ventral noradrenergic bundle Tract connecting the brain-stem reticular formation with areas such as PVN. (458)

ventromedial hypothalamus (VMH) A nucleus located at midline of the brain bordering the third ventricle in the most ventral portion of the hypothalamus. (448)

ventrotegmental area (VTA) Region of the rostral midbrain related to reinforcement. (451)

12

Sexuality and Reproduction

Development of Sexual Dimorphism and Gender
Concepts: gonad, hermaphroditic, morphology, dimorphism

CHROMOSOMAL FACTOR
Concepts: genes, chromosomes, X chromosome, Y chromosome, embryo, testes, testosterone, ovaries, estrogens

ROLE OF HORMONES
Concepts: androgens, cholesterol
Prenatal Development
Concepts: Müllerian duct, Wolffian duct, seminal vesicles, vas deferens, Sertoli cells, Müllerian-inhibiting factor (MIF), uterus, fallopian tubes
Postnatal Development
Concepts: puberty, preoptic area (POA), gonadotropin-releasing factor (GRF), anterior pituitary gland, gonadotropic hormones, follicle-stimulating hormone (FSH), luteinizing hormone (LH), secondary sex characteristics, menstrual cycle, follicles, ovulation, corpus luteum, progesterone, estrus

PROBLEMS IN DETERMINING GENDER
Concepts: gender identity, gender assignment
Androgen-Insensitivity Syndrome
Concept: intersexuality
Female Hermaphroditism Syndromes
Concepts: progestin-induced hermaphroditism, androgen-induced hermaphroditism, adrenogenital syndrome, 21-hydroxylase
5α-Reductase Syndrome
Concepts: dihydrotestosterone (DHT), 5α-reductase

Six Determinants of Gender
Concepts: genetic factor, prenatal hormonal balance, internal genitalia, external genitalia, gender assignment, socialization

BRAIN DIFFERENTIATION
Concept: brain differentiation
Masculinizing the Prenatal Brain
Concepts: organizational effect, masculinization, activational effect, critical period, alpha feto-protein
Organizing Mammalian Reproductive Behavior
Concepts: spinal nucleus of the bulbocavernosus, bulbocavernosus muscle, levator ani muscle, secondary impotence, anterior hypothalamus, medial preoptic area (MPOA), mounting, lordosis, ventromedial nucleus, medial forebrain bundle (MFB), ventrotegmental area (VTA), feminized, masculinized

Do Gonadal Hormones Influence Adult Human Behavior?

DO HORMONE LEVELS DETERMINE SEXUAL MOTIVATION?

DOES TESTOSTERONE DETERMINE AGGRESSIVENESS?

IS HOMOSEXUALITY THE RESULT OF HORMONAL ERROR? ELLIS AND AMES
Concept: sexual orientation
Animal Evidence
Concept: sexual inversion
Human Evidence
Concept: LH surge

Summary

You have probably had a great number of questions about sex since you were old enough to start wondering about such things, but here is one you may never have thought to ask: Why does nature bother with two sexes? Many species get along quite nicely with just one sex and skip the whole business of mating, but most of these animals are single-celled or very simple multicelled organisms. As creatures evolved into complex forms with many intricate internal systems (muscular, vascular, respiratory, etc.), sexual reproduction seemed to become the norm. Apparently, the chances of survival are considerably increased if the offspring can sample from the gene collection of two parents rather than just one. In fact, as one ascends the phylogenetic scale to the level of the fishes, sexual reproduction becomes so important that some potential parents will even go so far as to switch their sex in order to assure the possibility of mating.

The marine fish *Anthium squamipinnis* lives normally in small groups containing both males and females, and mating is no problem for it. On occasion, however, a group may lose some of its males, a fact that apparently threatens the group with partial reproductive failure. *Anthias*, however, is a hermaphroditic species, and the loss of some of the males simply acts as a stimulus for one or more of the females to switch gender. Within 3–7 days, new males begin to appear, taking the place of the missing ones, and this switch is no mere superficial thing limited to external appearance. It is an actual change in the **gonads** (reproductive glands); the ovaries of the female are altered into testes, the male glands (Shapiro, 1980). The term **hermaphroditic** (her-MAFF-row-DIT-ik) means "having both sexes in one body." In Greek mythology, Hermaphrodite, son of Hermes and Aphrodite, had his body invaded by a water nymph and was doomed to live thereafter as both male and female. *Anthias* can only assume one sex at a time, so it is not completely hermaphroditic, but its gender-switching ability is still strange and startling to most of us.

People tend to view gender as a far simpler and much more rigidly fixed condition than it really is. We will see that clearly defining a person as either male or female may be quite difficult in some cases and perhaps unrealistic. The **morphology** of the body (its shape, structure, or appearance) may be hard to classify, or the person may have female genes and male morphology. Sexual morphology focuses on the body parts that are associated with being male or female. Let's examine several factors that produce **dimorphism** (body differences) between the sexes.

Development of Sexual Dimorphism and Gender

A commonly held but false idea about sexual dimorphism is that a baby's sex and therefore its later gender identity are inherited. In reality dimorphism is the product of genes plus hormones, whereas gender is the result of at least six equally important factors: chromosomes (genes), hormones, internal genitalia, external genitalia, gender assignment, and socialization.

Chromosomal Factor

The complete set of building plans for an entire human body are laid out in the thousands of individual segments of DNA, called **genes**. The genes are arranged into 23 pairs of groupings called **chromosomes**. One of the 23 pairs contains all the genes that help create sexual dimorphism. To make a female, you need a pair of **X chromosomes**; for a male, a **Y chromosome** must be paired with an X. Surprisingly, few adult sexual dimorphic characteristics are specified by these two chromosome combinations. Each baby is born with genes for both penis and female genitalia (labia, vagina, and clitoris). Each has the plans for a male brain and a female brain, fine body hair and coarse, broad shoulders and narrow, high-pitched voice and low-pitched, and so forth. At the moment of conception, the newly fertilized egg is hermaphroditic in that it contains all the plans for female and male morphology.

Eventual dimorphism for this new human hangs by the narrow thread of one developmental difference: the type of gonads that the baby grows. For the first 6 weeks, the cluster of cells in the uterus of the mother show no sex differences at all. The first 2 weeks of life are spent as a simple globe of primal cells that attach themselves to the mother's uterine wall and begin to divide and redivide. During the period from week 3 through week 12, the baby is called an **embryo**, and it is during this embryonic period that gonads first form. At first they are as undifferentiated and hermaphroditic as those of the fish *Anthias*. They contain a core that could mature to make sperm and male sex hormones and an outside that could mature to make ova (eggs) and female sex hormones. However, if the cells of the embryonic gonad contain XY pairs of chromosomes, then week 6 of development brings a growth of the male core and a withering away of the female outside portion. The gonads now become **testes** (male gonads) and begin to secrete the male sexual hormone **testosterone** (tess-TAH-ster-own). If the gonads contain XX chromosome pairs, they differentiate into **ovaries** (female gonads) and secrete the female sex hormones, the **estrogens** (ESS-tro-gens). No one yet knows how the genes manage this differentiation (Kolata, 1986). Once the gonad has developed, testosterone or estrogen pours into the bloodstream of the developing embryo, and this hormonal influence directs all the rest of the prenatal steps of sexual differentiation. The genes have no further influence on the process (Adkins-Regan, 1985; Wilson et al., 1981).

Role of Hormones

Because all of the difference between becoming female versus becoming male depends on which sex hormone is present in the embryo, one would imagine that testosterone would be chemically very different from estrogen. It is astonishing to discover that such an important set of physical differences could be produced by two molecules that look almost alike. Actually, testosterone is just one of a family of chemicals called **androgens** that the body derives from **cholesterol**, a type of fat (Figure 12.1).

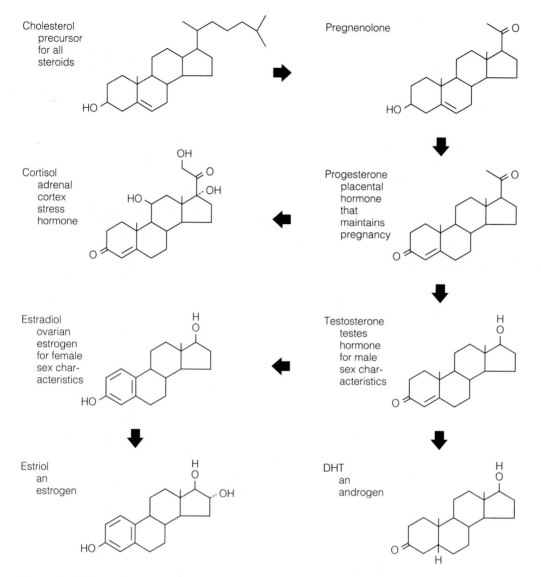

Cholesterol
  precursor
  for all
  steroids

Pregnenolone

Cortisol
  adrenal
  cortex
  stress
  hormone

Progesterone
  placental
  hormone
  that
  maintains
  pregnancy

Estradiol
  ovarian
  estrogen
  for female
  sex char-
  acteristics

Testosterone
  testes
  hormone
  for male
  sex char-
  acteristics

Estriol
  an
  estrogen

DHT
  an
  androgen

Figure 12.1 Metabolic pathways for the creation of sex and stress steroids from cholesterol. Each hormone contains the basic "three-and-a-half-hexagon" shape of the original
cholesterol molecule. Each hexagon represents the joining of six carbon atoms (one at
each corner). The differences between the various hormones all depend on which atoms
are attached to the basic carbon frame. H = hydrogen; O = oxygen; OH = a hydroxyl ion.
A protruding line with no atom at the end indicates another carbon atom.

From several of these androgens, the body can manufacture a group of closely related hormones, the estrogens. It is somewhat misleading to speak of androgens as "male hormones" because even testosterone is made in the female body as a step in the production of estrogens. Conversely, males turn some androgen molecules into estrogens that the male system uses for various purposes. The determining factor at many points in the process by which the body differentiates into male or female is not the mere presence of one or the other of estrogens versus androgens but rather the relative concentrations of the two types of hormones. Let's trace this hormone-directed growth.

Prenatal Development By week 7 of uterine development, the embryo has differentiated its gonads into either testes or ovaries, but the rest of its sexual apparatus is still not specifically male or female. As you can see from Figure 12.2, each embryo contains two temporary structures—a female **Müllerian duct** and a male **Wolffian duct**. If the embryo has developed testes, so that it is manufacturing more testosterone than estrogen, the Wolffian duct grows into a set of structures designed to release sperm during mating. These structures include the **seminal vesicles** (the sacs that hold sperm until they are ejaculated) and the **vas deferens** (the tubes that carry sperm from the testes to the seminal vesicles). As the Wolffian ducts are differentiating into these various male tissues, the Müllerian ducts must be suppressed so that female organs will not develop alongside the male. The Y chromosome handles this problem by generating **Sertoli cells** that secrete a chemical to accomplish the suppression. Sertoli cells secrete **Müllerian-inhibiting factor (MIF)**, a defeminizing hormone that prevents the development of the Müllerian duct (Kahn & Cataio, 1984).

On the other hand, if the embryo has developed its gonads into ovaries, the Wolffian ducts are the ones to degenerate, and the Müllerian ducts develop instead. Out of these ducts emerge the female reproductive organs: the **uterus** (YOU-ter-us), in which fertilized eggs will mature into fetuses, and **fallopian tubes** (fal-OPE-ee-un), which transport the ova (eggs) from the ovaries to the uterus.

During week 9 of development, the external genitalia begin to differentiate. One area of tissue becomes either the female labia or the male scrotum and penis shaft, while another area develops into either a clitoris or glans (tip) of the penis (Figure 12.3). The internal and external male genitalia will fail to develop unless the testes have begun to secrete testosterone, but in the female the internal and external genitalia will develop to some extent whether the ovaries are functioning or not. When in doubt, nature makes a female.

Postnatal Development By the time the fetus is ready to be born, the initial period of sexual differentiation has ended. The subsequent growth and physical development of infancy and childhood contributes very little toward making the genders more distinct. The final burst of physical gender development occurs at **puberty**, the period that begins adolescence and during which a person acquires the ability to reproduce. Sometime around the age of 11 (for girls) or 13 (for boys), a biological clock, whose mechanism still remains a mystery, triggers the changes in the brain that propel the body into adulthood. The area of the hypothalamus near the stalk of the pituitary gland seems to be the critical part of the brain. In the rat, a portion of this brain region called the **preoptic area (POA)** contains groups of cells responsible for sexual behaviors (Figure 12.4). It also releases a chemical called **gonadotropin-releasing factor (GRF)**, which provides the link between the nervous system and the chemical environment of the body. The chemical is called a releasing factor because it stimulates the **anterior pituitary gland** to release **gonadotropic hormones** (chemicals that stimulate the gonads).

The pituitary—the master endocrine gland that controls all other glands in the endocrine system—is divided into anterior and posterior parts (Figure 12.4) that secrete quite different hormones (see Chapter 3). As puberty begins, the anterior pituitary releases **follicle-stimulating hormone (FSH)** and **luteinizing hormone (LH)** into the blood. These two gonadotropic hormones awaken the testes and ovaries from the dormancy of childhood and set off a tremendous increase in secretion of testosterone

MALE AND FEMALE IDENTICAL

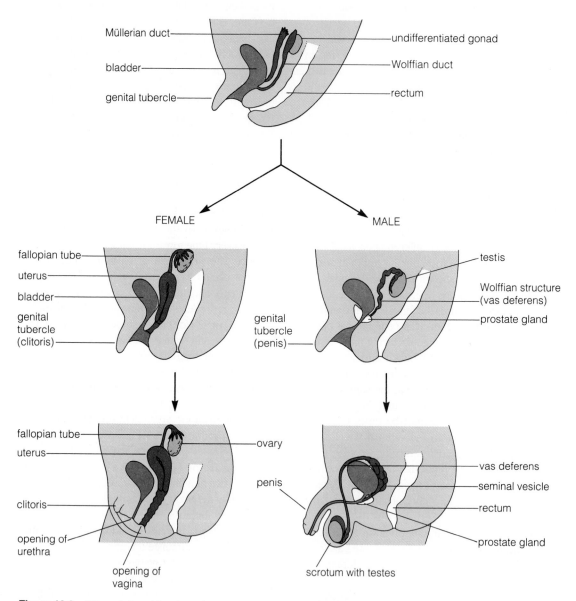

Figure 12.2   Differentiation of female and male genitalia in the human fetus. (Adapted from Money, 1987)

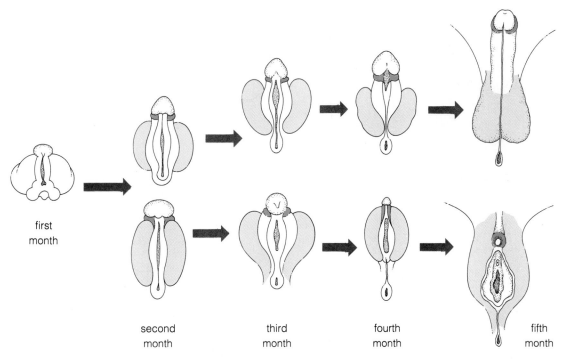

first
month

second
month

third
month

fourth
month

fifth
month

Figure 12.3 Embryonic and fetal differentiation of external genitalia. (Adapted from Silber, 1981)

and estrogen. It is these last two hormones that direct the body changes that convert the child to an adult.

The whole body reacts to the sudden increase in gonadal hormones. These chemicals bring about not only the primary changes within the reproductive organs that initiate the menstrual cycle in the female and sperm production in the male but also a whole list of **secondary sex characteristics**, which begin to appear as a result of hormonal action. Estrogen begins the development of the breasts, the growth and darkening of pubic hair, and the shaping of fat tissue around the hips. Testosterone begins adding mass to the muscles, coarsening and thickening the body; stimulating growth of pubic and facial hair; enlarging the voice box; and increasing the size of the penis.

Because estrogens are manufactured from androgens, it is not surprising that the ovaries secrete both

"male" and "female" hormones. The testes likewise secrete both testosterone and estrogens. During childhood both sexes have nearly equal, low levels of the two types of hormones, and during puberty the levels of both chemicals rise in both sexes. The bloodstream of a woman, however, contains only about one tenth the testosterone found in a male. It is the relative balance of the two hormones, not their absolute presence in the blood, that produces the secondary sex characteristics of one gender rather than the other.

LH and FSH, the initiators of puberty, remain vital all the way through the reproductive life of the individual. In the human female, LH and FSH levels increase periodically (roughly every 28 days) and produce the **menstrual cycle**. The cycle begins as hypothalamic cells (probably within the POA) increase their output of luteinizing hormone–releas-

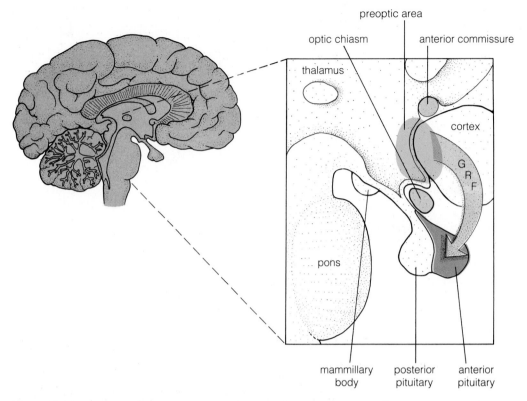

Figure 12.4 The hypothalamic region of the human brain. The preoptic region is just behind the plane of this midsagittal picture and is shown as a shaded "phantom" lying just above the optic chiasm and below the anterior commissure. The preoptic region contains cells that secrete gonadotropin-releasing factor (GRF), which is sent to the anterior lobe of the pituitary gland to stimulate the secretion of LH and FSH. This then is the route by which the hypothalamus controls the menstrual cycle and other reproductive functions.

ing factor (LH–RF) and follicle stimulating hormone–releasing factor (FSH–RF).

These chemicals command the anterior pituitary to secrete first FSH and then LH. The FSH does just what its name suggests; it stimulates one of the small pockets of cells within the ovaries (called **follicles**) to mature the ovum (egg) within it. An upsurge in LH secretion a few days later bursts the follicle and releases the ovum to begin its journey down the fallopian tube to the uterus. The release of the ovum is called **ovulation**, and the event represents the start of a critical time during which conception can take place. In some species such as the rat, the gonado-

tropic hormones LH and FSH increase the chances of conception through their effects on behavior. The increase in circulating amounts of LH and FSH creates a brief increase in estrogen, and this gonadal hormone sensitizes the brain circuits involved in sexual receptivity (Nordeen & Yahr, 1983). The female rat becomes maximally receptive to sexual advances from the male just at the time when sperm have the best chance of finding a waiting ovum.

Meanwhile, the ruptured follicle, having released the ovum, converts itself into an endocrine gland called the **corpus luteum** and begins to secrete another important hormone in the female repro-

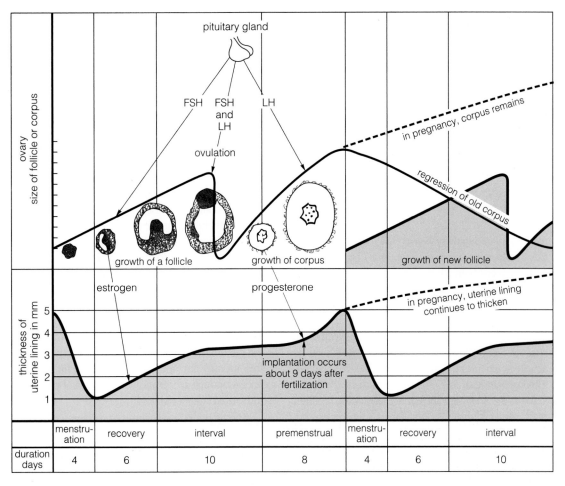

Figure 12.5 The human menstrual cycle is triggered by the secretion of follicle-stimulating hormone (FSH) from the anterior pituitary. FSH stimulates the growth of a follicle in the uterus. At maturity a few days later, the follicle is ruptured by luteinizing hormone (LH), and the egg is released. During the period when the egg was maturing, the follicle secreted estrogen to stimulate growth of the uteral lining in preparation for pregnancy. After releasing the egg, the follicle converts itself into the corpus luteum and begins to make progesterone, a hormone that further prepares the uterus. If the ovum goes unfertilized, the secretion of progesterone declines, and the uterine lining deteriorates and sloughs off, creating the discharge called menstruation. (Adapted from Gardner & Osburn, 1968)

ductive cycle, **progesterone** (Figure 12.5). Besides preparing the uterus for the implantation of the ovum, progesterone seems to have an inhibitory effect on female receptivity (Zucker, 1968). In the rat, the estrogen-produced rise in receptivity and the progesterone-linked fall, occurring about 16 hours later, mark the period of **estrus**.

Problems in Determining Gender

The sex that any person considers herself or himself to have is called that person's **gender identity**. Most of us had so little trouble achieving a gender identity that we tend to think of our femininity or masculinity as an absolute physical attribute rather than a relative abstract idea. Some physicians, however, know first-hand just how relative gender can be. Your gender identity traces back to the moment when the physician who delivered you held up your squalling form and pronounced you to be either a girl or a boy. This is the **gender assignment** that appears on the birth certificate, and it is not necessarily correct. Physicians can sometimes find it difficult to guess whether the baby is XX or XY just from looking at external genitalia. There are at least a half-dozen endocrine problems that are guaranteed to confuse gender assignment.

Androgen-Insensitivity Syndrome A person with this syndrome (group of symptoms) begins life as an embryo with an XY-chromosome combination—a condition that should produce a male. The gonads begin to differentiate into testes and to secrete androgens. The concentration of testosterone in the blood builds up to normal levels and circulates to the tissues of the Wolffian duct where it should have its action. At that point, however, the sequence is halted. Through some unknown flaw, the tissues are insensitive to the hormone and cannot use it. The Wolffian duct remains undeveloped. The Y chromosome, however, has generated Sertoli cells, and the MIF from these has begun to inhibit the development of the Müllerian duct. Under these circumstances, neither set of genitalia can develop.

At birth, the child has a partial uterus and incompletely formed testes that will produce no sperm. Instead of descending into the scrotum, the testes may remain in the abdomen as though they were ovaries. Because the penis does not form properly and the urinary opening is placed below it (as in the female), it is usually not possible to distinguish the penis from the clitoris of a baby who is genetically female. The slit is not closed to form a scrotum, and the tissue to either side looks more like female labia. It is easy for the physician delivering the baby to assign a female gender without realizing that the child has male genes.

The initial assignment of gender sets off a whole pattern of child-rearing practices, most of which are so taken for granted that they are nearly unconscious. These aspects of child rearing are all aimed at emphasizing gender differences and building a strong gender identity. If the child with male chromosomes is believed to be a girl, then clothing differs sharply from clothing of children regarded as male. Toys have a female slant and, most important, the parents subtly adjust their behavior toward the child according to their expectancies for a girl. Rough-and-tumble play is fine for boys, but most parents find that the same amount of such behavior in their little girl is a trifle disconcerting, and they may suggest to the child that some other way of playing is better. "That's too rough for a little girl. You might get hurt." Girls, of course, are not physically weaker or smaller on the average than boys and, at certain ages, are physically larger and more mature. A parental warning about the possibility of getting hurt promotes the cultural gender idea that females are the "weaker sex" and need to be protected. It is a web of a thousand little incidents of this sort out of which is constructed, thread by thread, the elaborate and extensive gender identity within which the core of the person exists. By the time a child reaches puberty, this identity includes many separate little experiences, enough to constitute a large, vital part of the individual's personality.

The victim of androgen-insensitivity syndrome is typically raised as a girl, and there may be no trouble with this gender role until puberty when the anticipated menstruation fails to occur. Breasts do appear however, and the overall morphology is persuasively female (Figure 12.6). Most important, the person is 100 percent sure that she is female despite the sudden news from her physician that she has male genes. Puberty is really too late for a person to discover painlessly that the identity given her could have been different—that her gender is not a definite, unequivocal female but an ambiguous, relative sort of thing. Her rearing has given her an entirely female gender identity, and her body has been responding to the low but adequate levels of estrogen produced by her testes. The enormously greater amounts of testosterone also being produced by her gonads, of course, have been totally ignored by her cells. They are unable to use any androgen. Except for the inability to produce ova and support a fetus, she does quite well at being a female. With adequate counseling, the person can be helped to get through the crisis of

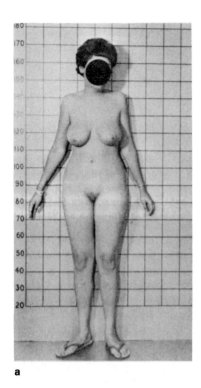

a

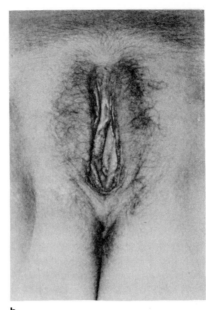

b

Figure 12.6 (a) A patient with androgen-insensitivity syndrome. Genetically, this person is a male. The female secondary sex characteristics appeared at puberty because of the small amounts of estrogen normally secreted by the testes. (b) External genitalia of the same patient. She was assigned and raised as female and is adjusted sexually to that gender. (From Money & Ehrhardt, 1972)

discovering her incompletely established gender and can usually go on to be happily married and become a mother by adoption.

Androgen-insensitivity syndrome shows us that the difference between male and female is not as clear-cut as it seems on the surface. A person's gender is not decided by genes alone. There are at least six factors that work together to determine gender identity: genes, hormones, internal genitalia, external genitalia, gender assignment, and socialization (which includes rearing). If the entire developmental sequence proceeds normally, the person achieves a gender identity that agrees with all six criteria. The person insensitive to androgen is male in terms of genes and prenatal hormones (more androgens than estrogens) but is neuter with regard to internal genitalia (undeveloped Wolffian structures and undescended testicles) and external genitalia and is female in terms of gender assignment and socialization. When such conflicts arise between the six factors determining gender identity, the person is termed **intersexual**.

Female Hermaphroditism Syndromes This type of disorder is not named with a great degree of accuracy because the word *hermaphroditism* entails the ability to take part in reproduction as either male or female. No human has ever been a true hermaphrodite. In all of these female "hermaphroditism" syndromes, an XX embryo is masculinized, and the result is a person who is intersexual, not truly hermaphroditic. However, we will conform to the current usage.

In the 1940s, a synthetic steroid drug (progestin) was introduced with the claim that it would help prevent miscarriages. Not only did this hope fail to materialize but also the drug had the side effect of creating a number of intersexual children. The external genitalia were masculinized enough to make gender assignment difficult, but most of the infants were correctly assigned as genetic females and were given corrective surgery. The enlarged clitoris could be reduced in size, and labia that had begun to fuse into a scrotum could be separated. This syndrome is usually termed **progestin-induced hermaphroditism** (Figure 12.7).

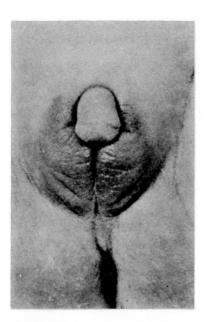

Figure 12.7 Masculinization of the external genitalia of a genetic female whose mother received a synthetic progesterone to prevent miscarriage. (From Money & Ehrhardt, 1972)

In some rare cases, a pregnant woman carrying an XX fetus will develop a tumor in the ovaries or adrenal cortex that results in an excess of androgens. Recall from our earlier discussion of steroid hormones that this disorder could occur simply through failure to produce the enzymes that convert androgens to estrogens and other hormones. For some reason, the tumor only begins to secrete abnormal levels of androgens after the embryo has already begun to develop the Müllerian duct. Therefore the excess androgen has no effect on the internal genitalia but does masculinize the external genitalia. This syndrome, **androgen-induced hermaphroditism**, produces an infant that may be assigned a male gender. There have been two cases with this gender assignment who underwent surgery during infancy to further masculinize the external genitalia and were given hormone therapy (testosterone injections) during adolescence to suppress the development of breasts and menstruation (through

the penis). They were raised as boys, were successful as husbands in their marriages, and were accepted by their male peers as normal men. However, if the original gender assignments had been female rather than male, corrective surgery and hormone therapy could have produced successful women capable of bearing children (Money, 1987).

The **adrenogenital syndrome** is very similar to androgen-induced hermaphroditism in that it is caused by overproduction of androgens by the child's own adrenal cortex. Through the inheritance of two particular recessive genes, the fetus is missing the enzyme **21-hydroxylase**, which normally converts some of the progesterone to cortisol, a hormone involved in resisting stress. If you glance back at Figure 12.1, you can see that progesterone can be changed into either cortisol or testosterone, and in the absence of 21-hydroxylase, all of it goes into testosterone production. The fetus suffers the same sort of masculinization of the external genitalia seen in the two hermaphroditism syndromes. However, after a few weeks there is usually no doubt as to the infant's genetic sex because the adrenogenital syndrome includes a nonsexual dysfunction stemming from the lack of 21-hydroxylase. The inability to produce cortisol means that the baby also cannot manufacture the derived hormone, a mineralocorticoid, which is vital to maintaining a proper salt balance (see Chapter 11). When the baby becomes sick and the underlying problem is discovered, the infant is frequently reassigned from male to female with corrective surgery recommended. In the cases that are not severe enough to trigger medical attention, the continuous outpouring of testosterone induces early puberty, sometimes even as early as 18 months (Money, 1987).

5α-Reductase Syndrome In Figure 12.1, it is evident that testosterone can be converted into another androgen, **dihydrotestosterone (DHT)**, and it is actually DHT rather than its precursor, testosterone, that encourages the development of the external male genitalia. Without the enzyme, **5α-reductase**, DHT cannot be made, and without DHT male genitalia cannot develop (Ellis & Ames, 1987). Infants lacking this enzyme are often assigned as females. Internal genitalia, however, do not depend on DHT;

hence, testes develop and secrete testosterone. Thanks to the testosterone, the Wolffian duct develops into male organs. At puberty some secondary male sex characteristics may appear, possibly through the direct influence of the testosterone. However, with a clitoral penis, labia that have not fused into a scrotum, and undescended testicles (they are still in the abdominal cavity), the person has more of a female than male appearance. As we will see in a later part of this chapter, much speculation about the origins of homosexuality has originated from cases such as these.

Six Determinants of Gender   The cases of intersexuality we have reviewed lead to an appreciation of how complex gender identity is. It appears that there are at least six factors that go into its determination. The **genetic factor** (an XX pair of chromosomes versus an XY pair) is simply the first step in a lengthy process of gender differentiation. Genes only set the stage for the embryo to develop a **prenatal hormonal balance** that favors either estrogens or androgens. It is largely this balance that instigates the third factor, the type of **internal genitalia** the child develops. The person suffering from adrenogenital syndrome is female gender according to the genetic factor and internal genitalia but male gender according to the prenatal hormonal balance. In the case of androgen insensitivity, the first two factors dictate a male gender while the other four predispose a female. The 5α-reductase syndrome gives the person a male gender on three of the factors (genetic, prenatal hormonal balance, and internal genitalia) but results in a female gender for the fourth factor, **external genitalia**. Because the fifth factor, the original **gender assignment**, is based largely on external genitalia, it too comes out female. The female gender assignment determines that the sixth factor, **socialization**, which includes interactions with parents (rearing) and with peers, is also female-oriented. Considering the complexities of the chemical processes involved in development (with more than 16 sex hormones, each with its own enzyme), it is a wonder that the vast majority of humans have been lucky enough to have all six factors consistent with one or the other gender and to have a clear-cut gender identity.

Brain Differentiation

Evolution has endowed mammals with many genetically determined response patterns, but none are more fundamentally tied to the survival of a species than are the reproductive behaviors. Because the male must have a different set of behaviors for the mating situation than those for the female, male and female brains in most species must have built-in circuits that are different for the two sexes. The male rat must mount the female while she crouches in a receptive posture called lordosis. For mating to be successful, the male rat must have circuits in his motor system that produce mounting behaviors, not lordosis. Male and female brains need to be built differently. The developmental processes that lead to sex-specific brain circuits are called **brain differentiation**.

Masculinizing the Prenatal Brain   Birds, especially canaries and finches (Figure 12.8), make good subjects for experiments studying the sexual differentiation of the brain. Bird songs generally fall into two classes: male calls designed to attract females and male territorial calls sung to warn away competing males. Females of many species never sing at all; it would serve no function. Because bird song is a complex behavior needing special circuits within the brain, investigators hoped to find areas of male finch brains that were distinctly different from the corresponding areas in female brains. There was also the possibility that sex hormones might play a part in creating these proposed male–female brain differences. Consistent with this idea was the discovery that young male finches learn their songs by imitating their fathers, but the amount of singing they do depends heavily on the level of testosterone in their blood. If that hormone is injected, their singing rate increases; if they are castrated, their songs become infrequent (Arnold & Gorski, 1984). Apparently, the male behavior of singing is induced by testosterone. Could a female finch be made to sing by simply injecting her with the hormone? When this was tried in adult birds, it was found not to work, but if newly hatched females were injected with testosterone, they would sing like males when again given the hormone as adults (Nordeen et al., 1986).

Figure 12.8 Zebra finches: female on the left, male on the right. (Adapted from Konishi & Gurney, 1982)

Phoenix and co-workers (1959) provided us with an explanation of these hormonal influences on behavior. They proposed that testosterone has a different effect on the adult brain than on the prenatal. Before birth (or around the time of hatching), the hormone has an **organizational effect**. It determines that male circuitry will be established in the new brain, a process called **masculinization**. (Left to itself, the brain becomes feminized.) Simply having a masculinized brain, however, does not guarantee a high rate of male behavior in the adult. The masculine circuitry of the adult seems to function better in the presence of testosterone secreted by the gonads. This is called an **activational effect**. The fact that androgens have no effect on normal adult females means that their brains can no longer be organized by the hormones. There seems to be a **critical period** around the time of hatching in which the organizational effect can occur (Arnold & Gorski, 1984).

It seems reasonable that giving testosterone to a neonatal female finch could masculinize its brain, but injections of estrogen also produce the same result. The reason is that estrogen is made from androgens. Apparently, when the circulating testosterone enters the brain cells of the neonatal finch, it is metabolized to estrogen, which is responsible for the actual masculinization of the brain (Arnold & Gorski, 1984). If this is true, we seem to have a

paradox; if neonatal female finch brains can be masculinized by estrogen, then what protects their brains from the estrogen secreted by their own ovaries? The answer, in part, lies in a chemical called **alpha feto-protein** that circulates in the blood of neonates and binds estrogen so that it cannot cross the blood–brain barrier and affect the nervous system (MacLusky & Naftolin, 1981). Testosterone, however, can cross the barrier and be metabolized into estrogen in the nerve cells (Figure 12.9). Thus, males can be masculinized by estrogen converted from testosterone. The alpha feto-protein disappears from the blood after about 28 days in the rat (Greenstein, 1978). This enables gonadal estrogen to affect the brain after the critical period for brain differentiation is over.

As we noted earlier in the chapter, it is somewhat misleading to speak of estrogen as a female hormone and testosterone as a male hormone. Such a perspective leaves one with philosophical quandaries, notes Greenstein, such as wondering why "the male brain should convert the male sex hormone into a female sex hormone in order to turn a female type brain into a male type brain" (Greenstein, 1978).

What exactly is it that occurs in the developing brain during the process of masculinizing? Thanks to the pioneering work of Nottebohm (1981), researchers interested in masculinization knew just where to look in the brain of the finch for the circuits

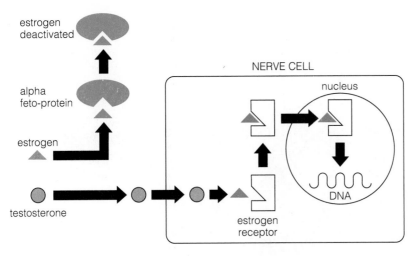

Figure 12.9 Male brain differentiation is produced by testosterone circulating in the blood. When the testosterone enters a nerve cell, it is converted to estrogen. It is the estrogen that actually reacts with a receptor and is carried to the nucleus to trigger the DNA sequences controlling the growth of the neuron. Any estrogen entering the cell from the blood could have exactly the same effect of masculinizing the neuron, but males have very little circulating estrogen. Females are protected during the critical period against the masculinizing effects of estrogen on the brain by the presence of alpha feto-protein, a substance that reacts with the estrogen in their blood to deactivate it.

controlling song. They discovered that the nuclei responsible for singing were visibly larger in the male than in the female, with larger neurons and a larger number of cells in each nucleus (Arnold & Gorski, 1984). It was also found that the increase in cell size was accomplished by estrogen, but that the greater number of neurons was the result of a different metabolite of testosterone, namely, DHT. Some of the testosterone entering the neurons is converted to estrogen to produce larger somas and more extensive dendrites (Figure 12.10), whereas the rest must be metabolized to DHT that apparently, in some way, allows the DNA in the nucleus to initiate cell replication.

Now another question arises. If the male brain is organized for singing by testosterone during some critical period around the time of hatching, then why is testosterone also needed later in the adult for activation? What exactly is activation? Some startling answers have arisen from work on a relative of the zebra finch. The canary, like many other birds, is

a seasonal singer. The song is needed only at that time of the year when mating is taking place and a food-gathering territory around the nest must be defended. When the molting period begins in mid-August, singing stops. When singing begins again after molt, it is tentative and not uniform from day to day. As the new season progresses, the male seems to imitate other males, and his song becomes stabilized and more uniform. Each year, then, the canary develops a new song repertoire specialized for that particular year (Hammer, 1982). Nottebohm's amazing discovery was that several of the song nuclei of a canary shrink during molting and regrow to male size during the breeding season (Nottebohm, 1981). Much of the change in size is the result of adding dendritic branches—exactly the sort of change that underlies the process of learning new stimuli and responses (see Chapter 16). It seems that the male has larger song nuclei than does the female because the circuits set up during the process of learning the songs require new connections

Figure 12.10 Sexual dimorphism at the level of the neuron. Shown at the same scale are a male and a female neuron from the same area of the finch brain, the area that controls vocalization. The scale bar indicates 100 μm (millionths of a meter). Not only do male finches possess larger vocalization areas in the brain, they also have larger neurons in those areas. (From Konishi & Gurney, 1982)

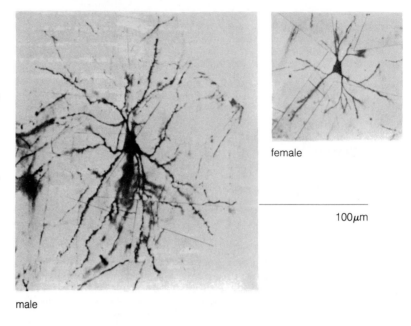

female

100μm

male

between neurons and even the creation of new cells. It is these changes that apparently constitute the activation effect in songbirds. They do not occur, and singing is not learned without the secretion of testosterone.

We have much yet to learn about this amazing process that simply erases neural circuits when they are not needed and then reestablishes them later when they are. If you had suggested such an idea to a neuroanatomist 20 years ago, you would have been treated as simpleminded. Until just recently, such changes in the brain were inconceivable. Note that this kind of hormone-dependent neural organization in the adult brain is very similar to the organizational effect of the prenatal period but has the impermanence of an activational effect. Thus, it blurs the distinction between the two concepts. Perhaps a third category of "adult reorganizational effect" will have to be adopted. Probably we will never find such an extreme reorganizational effect in mammalian brains, but the songbird research has alerted us to recognize one if it appears in the data.

Organizing Mammalian Reproductive Behavior Sexual differentiation is astonishingly clear in the avian (bird) brain, but humans are mammalian, not avian. Although mammals and birds share a common reptilian ancestor millions of years ago, the course of evolution has seen birds evolve in one direction, while mammals have taken an entirely different path. Thanks to their shared reptilian ancestry, both mammals and birds have the same brain-stem structures, thalamus, hypothalamus, and basal ganglia, but it has never been established that birds have a true cerebral cortex. Is there any evidence of sex differentiation within the mammalian nervous system?

In the lower regions of the spinal cord of the rat is a cluster of neurons called the **spinal nucleus of the bulbocavernosus.** Presumably, the same cluster exists in the human spinal cord. These are motor neurons whose axons reach out to two muscles: the **bulbocavernosus** and **levator ani** (Figure 12.11). These are predominantly male muscles. In the human, the comparable muscles (bulbospongiosus, ischiocavernosus, and levator ani) are significantly

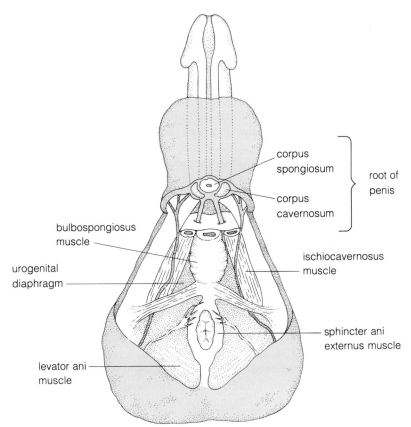

Figure 12.11 Dissection of the human male genitoanal region revealing the bulbospongiosus and ischiocavernosus muscles (combined in the rat as the bulbocavernosus muscle) and the levator ani muscle. (Adapted from Gardner & Osburn, 1968)

corpus
spongiosum

corpus
cavernosum

root of
penis

bulbospongiosus
muscle

ischiocavernosus
muscle

urogenital
diaphragm

sphincter ani
externus muscle

levator ani
muscle

smaller in the female than in the male. In the male, they aid in the ejaculation of sperm and in the maintenance of an erection; in the female, their contraction seems to have little effect. These muscles do not exist at all in the female rat, despite their importance in the male of that species.

In keeping with this muscular difference between male and female rats, sexual differentiation of the spinal cord gives the male a spinal nucleus of the bulbocavernosus that is 300 percent larger than that of the female and contains neurons that are twice as large (Arnold & Gorski, 1984). The availability of androgens in the rat fetus organize not only the growth of the spinal nucleus but also the development of the muscles they serve. In the adult rat, maintenance of this organization is to some extent dependent on the continued secretion of testosterone. Without the hormone, both muscles and spinal nucleus shrink in size (Arnold & Gorski, 1984). It is not yet known if the human system is as dependent on the secretion of androgens in adulthood.

The autonomic nervous system (ANS) is also involved in penile erection. It is a reflexive response that begins with the stimulation of the penis or surrounding skin and the flow of impulses from the nerve endings along the afferent fibers and into the spinal cord. Within the gray matter of the cord, synapses are made with the autonomic neurons that control the blood flow into and out of the sinuses (cavities) of the penis. This reflex arc, like all reflexes, works quite automatically. The proper skin stimulation increases the blood volume within the penis, thus creating the stiff, swollen condition of erection. Higher centers in the brain are not needed for this to happen, and indeed an erection can occur when the lower part of the spinal cord containing the reflex connections has been completely cut off from the brain by injury (Hart, 1974). Ejaculation of semen and the rhythmic pelvic movements accompanying it also seem to be produced by cord reflexes.

But the cord is rarely allowed to function on its own in the normal, intact nervous system. Instead, higher centers like the limbic system usually make connections into the reflex arcs at their synapses within the cord and the reflexive autonomic response to the correct stimulus then fails to occur unless the higher centers allow it. Limbic areas have their influence over the cord by way of the hypothalamus, which in turn controls the ANS.

One expression of this higher control involves the ability of the sympathetic branch of the ANS to constrict the arteries of the penis. Such constriction decreases blood flow to the sinuses and diminishes the erection. Because the sympathetic nervous system (SNS) is dominant over the parasympathetic nervous system (PNS) during such emotional states as anxiety, one can see the neural basis for some forms of male sexual problems like **secondary impotence** in which anxiety renders the person incapable of having or keeping an erection during intercourse.

Posterior portions of the hypothalamus control the sympathetic branch of the ANS, and the anterior hypothalamic areas control the PNS. Shunting the necessary blood into the sinuses of the penis is accomplished by dilating its arteries, and arterial dilation is typically a PNS job. This means that we should expect the hypothalamic neurons, which regulate the erection reflex, to connect with the PNS, rather than the SNS and, accordingly, be found in the anterior hypothalamus rather than posterior. This turns out to be the case. The zones researchers have discovered in the rat brain so far are the **anterior hypothalamus** and, forward of that near the septal region, the **medial preoptic area (MPOA)** (Zuckerman, 1971) (Figure 12.12).

Both anterior and posterior hypothalamus have strong connections with the rest of the limbic system, and this probably explains why electrical stimulation at many limbic sites in the primate brain can elicit the erection response (MacLean, 1965). It is probably these higher areas in the limbic system that are active when a human male elicits his erection response by simply thinking about intercourse.

In the hypothalamus, circuits mediating one function are intertwined closely with those handling other functions, and separating them conveniently into handy areas of specialized cells is almost impossible. The small piece of territory including the anterior hypothalamus and medial portions of the preoptic nuclei have been shown to be important for male sexual behavior. Male rats given lesions in the region of the MPOA generally lose permanently their ability to copulate (Meisel, 1983). One important male behavior involved in copulation is the act of **mounting** the female. Gray and Brooks (1984) found that lesions anywhere in the continuum between the anterior hypothalamus (AH) and MPOA would disrupt mounting but that AH lesions had a somewhat greater effect. The interesting thing is that MPOA lesions also disrupt female maternal behaviors of nest building, nursing, and retrieving pups that have crawled out of the nest. The pups of the mothers having bilateral MPOA lesions died from lack of care (Numan, 1985).

Both male sexual and female maternal behaviors, then, depend on the MPOA. This seems a trifle strange in that one would expect that if any female behaviors were controlled by the same area of the brain that runs male sexual behaviors then they would be female sexual, not maternal, responses. It has been suggested that the common thread between maternal responses and male sexual behaviors is that they are both relatively complex sequences. In contrast, female sexual behavior in the rat consists of two simple responses: moving close to a male and lordosing when the male attempts to mount. **Lordosis** is a posture adopted by the female in which she arches her back and moves her tail to one side to facilitate mounting (Figure 12.13). This female receptive behavior can be elicited very easily if the **ventromedial nucleus** of the hypothalamus has been exposed to a dose of estrogen (Floody et al., 1987). The ventromedial is the same nucleus that we found to be involved in satiety in Chapter 11. The hunger-related cells are probably mixed together

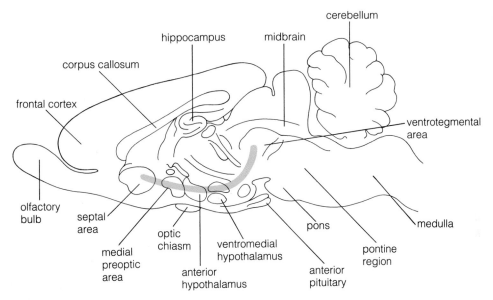

Figure 12.12 A sagittal section of the rat brain cut near the midline showing the hypothalamic areas most important to sexual function. The medial preoptic and anterior hypothalamus contain circuits for male sexual behaviors and female maternal responses, as well as the controls for secretion of gonadotropins from the anterior pituitary. The ventromedial nucleus contains cells that run female sexual responses. Coursing through these areas is a large cable of axons called the medial forebrain bundle (shown as a color line) that connects midbrain areas like the ventrotegmental area with limbic structures such as the septal area. It is an important part of the reinforcement mechanism and presumably mediates the pleasure of sexual activities. Other brain structures are shown as landmarks. (Note that because the rat brain does not have a temporal lobe, the hippocampus is up under the corpus callosum.)

Figure 12.13 Copulation in rats. The male has mounted the female, who has assumed the position called lordosis. (Adapted from Barnett, 1963)

with those that are sex-related, but why both should occupy that same region of the brain is not known.

Axons of MPOA neurons involved in maternal and male sexual behaviors run toward the brain stem in a major tract called the **medial forebrain bundle (MFB)**. Their destination is a group of midbrain neurons called the **ventrotegmental area (VTA)**. As we will see in Chapter 14, the MFB and VTA appear to be two of the most important components in the reinforcement system of the brain—the origin of the experience we call pleasure. A link between the circuits that produce reproductive behaviors and the circuits that produce pleasure would seem to be a good way of ensuring that these very important behaviors have a high probability of occurring. Because the survival of the species depends on reproduction behaviors, these responses must lead to pleasure.

The need for a link between sex and pleasure might explain the results of studies in which lesions in the MFB or VTA eliminated or reduced maternal behaviors (Numan & Smith, 1984). It could be that mother rats were still able to perform the responses when the correct stimuli appeared but no longer were motivated to care for their pups because maternal behavior was no longer pleasurable. This same reasoning should apply to male sexual behaviors controlled by MPOA; they are performed because they lead to pleasure. Axons of VTA neurons entering MPOA from the MFB are dopaminergic, and there is evidence that these fibers are involved in reinforcement (see Chapter 14). Chemicals that selectively stimulate the dopaminergic synapses in MPOA increase the number of times a male rat will ejaculate during mating and decrease the time between attempts to mount a female (Pehek et al., 1988). Careful knife-cut lesions that sever the fibers of the MFB without damaging MPOA reduce sexual behavior in the rat (Edwards & Einhorn, 1986). Results such as these are probably caused by increasing or decreasing a reinforcement effect from VTA.

If our thinking here is correct, then sexual behaviors are produced by one part of the brain (MPOA) and the resulting pleasure by another (VTA), and the implication is that it should be possible to separate them experimentally. That is, a lesion of the MPOA might make it impossible for an experienced adult animal to perform reproductive behaviors but still be able to anticipate pleasure from such behaviors. Edwards and Einhorn (1986) lesioned their male rats in MPOA and then placed them in a preference test (Figure 12.14) in which they could choose between two female rats, one of whom was in estrus (sexually receptive) and another who was not. If the male lacked a sex drive (anticipated no pleasure in copulation), then it should not show the normal preference that unlesioned males have for receptive females. On the other hand, if the male chose the receptive female, the implication would be that it

still was capable of anticipating sexual pleasure even though it could no longer copulate. The results did show that the MPOA-lesioned males had a preference for the receptive female (although significantly smaller than in normals). The fact that there was still a preference may mean that the pleasure–reinforcement circuitry of sex had not been destroyed along with the cells that generate sexual behaviors.

The MPOA is one of the areas of the brain that is sexually differentiated by testosterone. The effect of prenatal testosterone (which becomes estrogen) is to increase the size of the MPOA. Thus the MPOAs of rats, like the spinal nuclei and the song nuclei of birds, is larger in the male (Arnold & Gorski, 1984). If a newborn male rat is castrated, the adult has an MPOA–AH region that is 50 percent smaller than normal (Arnold & Gorski, 1984).

What then is the behavioral result of masculinizing the hypothalamus? Part of the answer to this question has come by way of studies that prevented this organizational effect from occurring. A genetically male rat that has been castrated shortly after birth will not have undergone masculinization of MPOA. If this rat is given estrogen as an adult, he shows the female sexual response of lordosis when another rat attempts to mount him (Figure 12.15). His brain was **feminized** simply by default. That is, any rat brain not subjected to the influence of gonadal hormones prenatally develops a female organization (McEwen, 1976). On the other hand, a newborn, genetically female rat given testosterone differentiates neurally as a male. When she reaches adulthood, she fails to show lordosis for a male and attempts to mount females instead (Levine, 1966). Her hypothalamus has been **masculinized** by the early hormone injection (Figure 12.16). Perhaps even stranger is the fact that a normally differentiated adult male rat reacts to a dose of estrogen by increasing its attempts to mount females (Nordeen & Yahr, 1983). (Don't forget that the hypothalamic neurons will treat testosterone as estrogen by converting it to the "female" hormone before using it.) In summary, both male and female rats have both male and female circuitry in their hypothalami, but the male circuitry grows stronger with masculinization and the female with feminization.

How well do these findings concerning mascu-

Figure 12.14 Sexual preference test for a male rat. The male is placed in one end of a long box. At the other end are two females, each tethered to the back wall of her own compartment. The female in the right-hand compartment is in estrus and is therefore sexually receptive; the female in the left side is not. Odors inform the male which female is receptive. The experimental question is, Will the male *care* which female is in estrus? A normal male would, but these males have MPOA lesions that make it impossible for them to mate. The results of this test showed that the lesioned males still moved into the compartment of the sexually receptive female despite their disability. (From Edwards & Einhorn, 1986)

linization and feminization apply to the human? Notice that masculinization and feminization of the rat brain are not generalized processes with all sorts of yet-to-be-discovered alterations involved. The idea of brain differentiation applies specifically to a few well-defined reproductive behaviors such as mounting and lordosis. Human reproduction depends very little, if at all, on genetically determined responses of this sort; thus, in the human, there simply aren't any specific male and female behaviors to differentiate (Feder, 1984). There are no stereotyped mating rituals or behavior sequences and no species-typical copulatory positions. The few reflexive movements that humans employ in copulation (pelvic thrusts, e.g.) are most likely of spinal cord origin rather than being organized by brain circuits. This is an impor-

tant idea to keep in mind later in this chapter when we discuss the possibility that human homosexuality might have a biological basis.

■ Do Gonadal Hormones Influence Adult Human Behavior?

Obviously, hormones have a profound effect on the behavior of the adult rat, but what about humans? There are three questions about hormonal influences that seem particularly interesting: Do hormones control our sexual motivation, our levels of aggression, or our choice of sexual partner?

Figure 12.15 Early brain organization determines the adult's reaction to gonadal hormones. (**a**) An adult male castrated at birth reacts to an injection of estrogen by exhibiting lordosis, a female sexual response. (**b**) A normal male injected with estrogen shows no lordosis response because the presence of testosterone in his brain shortly after birth established male circuits and inhibited the development of female circuits. The black dot within the rat represents the testes. (Adapted from Levine, 1966)

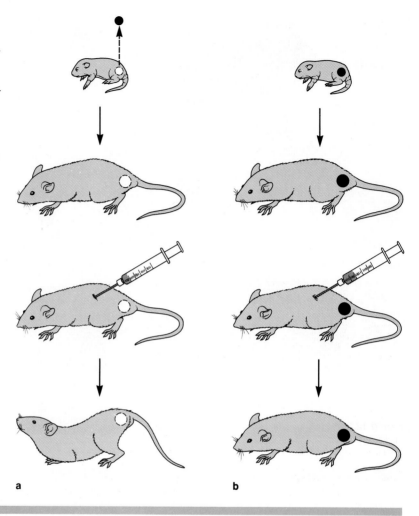

a   b

Do Hormone Levels Determine Sexual Motivation?

Neurons in and around the preoptic area of the hypothalamus have membrane receptor sites for molecules of gonadal hormones (Nordeen & Yahr, 1983). The circuits that produce elements of sexual behavior are apparently activated at puberty by the increased quantities of gonadal hormones available then (Meisel, 1983). Would these circuits still function if the hormones were not present? Studies of animals castrated as adults show that male sexual motivation declines after the gonads are removed and hormone levels drop. The decline can be quite

slow, however, and an experimenter usually has to wait for at least 3 weeks after the animal has been castrated to see an effect on sexual behavior. When the effect finally shows up, it may appear in a male as either noninterest in the female or impotency. In the latter case, the male attempts to copulate but fails to achieve an erection or intromission (insertion of penis).

In some species, prior experience at copulation has a great influence on sexual motivation after castration (Hart, 1974). A male cat that has copulated frequently before castration loses sexual motivation and potency much more slowly than does a cat without experience. Perhaps the use of the brain circuits

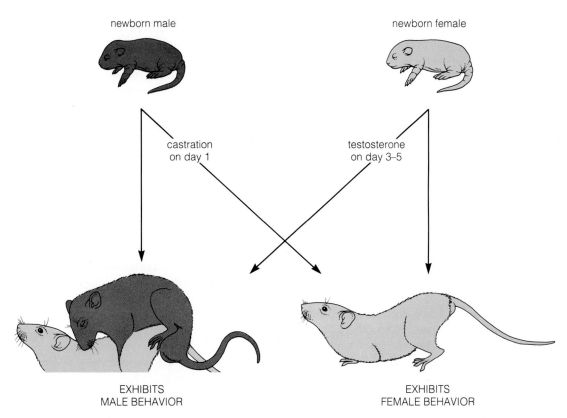

newborn male

newborn female

castration
on day 1

testosterone
on day 3–5

EXHIBITS
MALE BEHAVIOR

EXHIBITS
FEMALE BEHAVIOR

Figure 12.16 Adult sexual behavior in the rat depends on whether the brain was organized by gonadal hormones during the first few days after birth. Normal adult males display
mounting behavior because their brains were subjected to a dose of testosterone from their
gonads just after birth. The same effect can be produced in females by injecting the hormone. Depriving the male pups of testosterone by castrating them at birth results in a
female brain organization. As adults these feminized males, like normal females, display
very few attempts to mount but a high frequency of lordosis when mounted.

that produce the behavior strengthens the synapses
in those circuits and makes them less dependent on
help from the hormones.

In human males castrated after puberty, the ability
to ejaculate is usually the first component to be lost
(Money & Ehrhardt, 1972). After a period of dry
orgasms, erections are also lost. For some males,
these changes occur within weeks of surgery,
whereas others maintain some sexual motivation for
years. Although data are sparse, it seems likely that
sexual motivation is heavily influenced by levels of
gonadal hormones even in humans. In fact, some

law-enforcement agencies use an antiandrogen drug
(medroxyprogesterone acetate) to lower sexual
motivation in convicted sex offenders, and they claim
some success for its use (Money & Ehrhardt, 1972).

One might suspect that sexual motivation in
females would depend on estrogen, but this does
not seem to be the case. Without proper amounts of
estrogen, the vagina does not lubricate properly during intercourse, but this problem is not sufficient to
inhibit desire. In a recent experiment (Chambers &
Phoenix, 1987), adult female rhesus monkeys were
observed as they interacted with males in a large

group. They were categorized as either HLP (showing a high level of sexual performance) or LLP (low level of performance), based on how often and readily they sought contact with a male and permitted copulation. Their ovaries were then removed, and their performance again measured under varying doses of estrogen. The hormone seemed to have little effect on frequency of copulation. The HLP females always maintained a higher level of sexual performance than did the LLPs, regardless of the dosage. In fact, the HLP females maintained a higher level even when they were at zero estrogen dose and the LLP females were at the highest dose. The past experience of the animals seemed to be far more important than the presence or absence of the estrogen.

If sexual motivation in female primates is related to any hormones, androgens are the most likely candidates. We know that androgen sensitizes the clitoris and that an increase in desire is reported by some women receiving androgen therapy (Zuckerman, 1971). However, this would lead to the prediction that female HLP monkeys should have higher androgen levels than do female LLPs, and in the study mentioned above, this did not turn out to be the case (Chambers & Phoenix, 1987). As one moves up the phylogenetic scale from rats to primates, there is a decrease in the degree to which behavior is influenced by hormones (Chambers & Phoenix, 1987).

In summary, there is important evidence for male sex drive being dependent to some extent on levels of testosterone, but for the female sex drive, the idea of steroid dependence is still entirely hypothetical.

Does Testosterone Determine Aggressiveness?

Everyday observation of animals suggests that sex and aggression are related. Combat between males competing for the same female is common to many species, and in the case of cats, the aggression may even carry over to male–female interactions. During copulation the male bites the loose fold of skin at the back of the female's neck while the female growls and snarls. Does any experimental evidence exist for a connection between sex and aggression?

In many species from rodents to ring doves, aggression between males is heavily dependent on testosterone levels in the blood (Albert et al., 1988; Hart, 1974). The specific movements displayed in adult aggression may have their origin in the aggressive-play behavior of juveniles. In rats and monkeys, aggressive play occurs in both sexes but is significantly more frequent in males (Meaney, 1988). Such play usually begins when one animal pounces on another and ends, following a period of wrestling, with one of the pair standing over the other. Male rat pups that are castrated before postnatal day 6 show less play–fighting than do normal males; but if castration occurs following day 6, the loss of testosterone has no effect on this form of aggression (Meaney, 1988). This suggests that testosterone acts during a critical period of development to organize brain circuits underlying the play–fighting. That interpretation would explain why injecting female rat pups with testosterone during the critical period raises their later frequency of aggressive play to the male level.

Aggressive play in lower primates also seems to depend on androgen levels, but the critical period for their action seems to be prior to birth rather than during the first few postnatal days. This difference from rats occurs because primates are born at a later stage of development than are rat pups. Goy has found that juvenile female monkeys, exposed to androgens prenatally, engage in the same kind of rough-and-tumble, aggressive play with their siblings as do the male monkeys (cited in Miller, 1980). Data for humans are scarce, coming only from cases of endocrine disorders. For example, children who were exposed prenatally to androgen-based drugs exhibited significantly higher levels of aggression than did their siblings of the same sex (Reinisch, 1981). The same sort of effect is seen in female pseudohermaphrodites who frequently become aggressive "tomboys," presumably because of their exposure to androgens prenatally. These children feel strongly that they are girls but also feel quite comfortable with boys' games.

In conclusion, some kinds of aggression are determined in part by levels of androgens in rats and lower primates. The hormone has an organizational (rather than an activational) effect on the brain during a critical period. Some evidence suggests that the human brain may also become differentiated for aggression, but a definite conclusion is not yet warranted.

Is Homosexuality the Result of Hormonal Error? Ellis and Ames

Most behavior patterns common to humans are in some way traceable, directly or indirectly, to a survival advantage they once bestowed on our ancestors at some point in the course of evolution. Male and female homosexuality is widespread in the world, yet seems to work in opposition to the survival of the species. Considerations of this sort have led many people to suspect that homosexuality might be the result of a biological error early in life rather than being a natural result of experiences and upbringing. Might the accidental masculinization of a female fetal brain or the feminization of a male brain lead to sexual behaviors appropriate to the opposite sex later in life? In other words, could homosexuality be the result of a hormonal mistake during the prenatal period when the brain is being sexually differentiated?

Recent surveys conducted in the United States showed that about one quarter of the nonscientists sampled believed homosexuality to be the result of some inborn factor rather than the result of experience (Ellis & Ames, 1987). Most adult Americans have heard of estrogen and testosterone, and many may have formed the opinion that male homosexuals possess too little testosterone, female homosexuals too little estrogen. There does not seem to be any evidence for this notion. A study of five male transsexuals, who were awaiting surgical and hormonal treatments that would transform them to some degree into the females they desired to be, showed that before the estrogen injections were given testosterone was at normal male levels (Money & Ehrhardt, 1972). When testosterone levels were compared between heterosexual and homosexual college males, no difference could be found. If incorrect hormone concentrations are responsible for homosexuality, it is most likely that the error occurs during the organizational phase before birth rather than the activational phase of adulthood.

Ellis and Ames (1987) have proposed a biological theory of homosexuality that centers around the organizational phase, which they identify as the time between the sixth week following conception to the middle of the fifth month. Although Ellis and Ames acknowledge that **sexual orientation** (the choice of sexual partner) is determined to some extent by experience, their theory places a much heavier weight on the importance of intrauterine sexual differentiation of the brain. That is, they proposed that your eventual adult choice of a male versus a female sexual partner was determined for the most part before you were born. For example, male homosexuality would be the result of low testosterone levels during the organizational phase.

Animal Evidence If a biological error before birth can lead to a **sexual inversion** (choice of same-sexed partner), then homosexuality should not be an exclusively human behavior. Hormonal accidents can occur in other species, and therefore sexual inversions should also be observable in other species. Male rats castrated at birth show little interest in female rats but may seek to attract males, allow them to mount, and then display lordosis. Female rats injected with testosterone just after birth may, as adults, try to mount other females and resist the attempts of males to mount them. If such behaviors can be thought of as sexual inversion, then it does occur in animals strictly as a result of hormonal disruption around the time of birth.

There is, however, another way to interpret the behavior of the feminized male rat. When the male displays lordosis for another male, is he really choosing to copulate with a *male* rat? A simpler explanation might be that the neonatal feminization of his brain gave him the wrong set of sexual responses to use with female partners. When he feels sexually motivated, the only responses available to him are ones like lordosis, and the only partners that respond to these behaviors are male. Does the feminized male realize that he is attempting to copulate with another male, or is he simply making his particular type of sexual response with a rat that accepts it? If these questions prove to be pertinent, then it does not seem that these particular rat behaviors are very similar to the highly complex choices involved when a human male consciously selects a male for a sexual partner. When the term *sexual inversion* is taken to mean *homosexual*, then its application to rat behavior may represent a drastic distortion of the concept. We must be cautious in applying these particular experimental results to an interpretation of human homosexuality.

The sexual inversion experiments with rats do lead to an important question, however. What sort of natural biological accidents can lead to sexual inversion? Ward and Ward (1985) discovered that exposure of the mother rat to stress during the last week of pregnancy affects the unborn male pups. As adults they display a syndrome that includes a strong tendency toward lordosis if mounted and a reduced ability to ejaculate. There is no complete explanation of this effect yet, but it has been observed that male pups from stressed mothers show a testosterone deficiency for a few days after birth during which some brain differentiation might be taking place in normal males. After this, testosterone levels return to normal.

Normal male levels of aggressive play can also be affected by stress or by adrenal hormones naturally secreted during stress situations (glucocorticoids). If a 2-day-old pup is injected with stress hormones, it later fails to play–fight as frequently as most males (Meaney, 1988). The same injection at 10 days has no effect, nor does it lower frequency of aggressive play in females. Apparently, stress during the critical period counters a part of the organizing effect of testosterone on the male brain and reduces the "maleness" of behavior.

In some of the prenatal stress experiments, the mothers were stressed by being tied up so tightly that they could not move and then being placed in a brightly lighted box. This was a convenient way for the experimenter to induce stress but revealed little about how the prenatal stress syndrome might occur under natural conditions. In other experiments (Ward & Ward, 1985), stress was produced simply through overcrowding, a condition that could occur in a natural environment. The same demasculinization of male pups occurred, leaving them largely incapable of mating as adults. This cause-and-effect sequence seems a little too important for the health of the species to have occurred by chance. Whenever overcrowding endangers the whole group (because

of the limitations of food supplies), a set of males are born that cannot reproduce. Is sexual inversion nature's answer to overcrowding?

In summary, animal data have led to some important hypotheses about stress, crowding, and sexual inversion, but showing that these ideas apply to human homosexuality would require much more evidence.

Human Evidence The three most interesting sources of human evidence discussed by Ellis and Ames focus on the LH surge, sexual inversions associated with neonatal hormonal dysfunction, and data suggesting that homosexuality might be inherited.

Recall from our earlier discussion of the menstrual cycle (in animals, the estrous cycle) that the cycle begins as the hypothalamus secretes LH–RF. This releasing factor, however, is not the sole cause of ovulation. In rats very little LH is released in response to LH–RF unless the ovaries have begun secreting extra estrogen. Apparently, it is a combination of estrogen and releasing factor that induces the surge of LH that initiates the estrous cycle. The estrogen sensitizes the cells of the anterior pituitary, enhancing their response to the releasing factor. Without the estrogen, the pituitary fails to release enough LH to produce ovulation (McEwen, 1976). The normal rise in LH resulting from the combined effects of estrogen and LH–RF is called the **LH surge.**

An LH surge can be triggered in females simply by injecting a large enough dose of estrogen (Norman & Spies, 1979). Most males, however, do not show this response to estrogen. In one recent study on humans, about one half of the homosexuals tested with estrogen injections displayed an LH surge, a response that Ellis and Ames argue indicates that many male homosexuals have feminized brains. The female hypothalamus needs to secrete LH in bursts (once every 28 days for humans) so that the ovulation part of the cycle will occur; the male hypothalamus needs to secrete LH tonically (i.e., in a steady, continuous fashion). Ellis and Ames suggest that a prenatal hormone accident in some males feminized their brains so that they would become homosexual, and this fact is revealed by their female response to an estrogen injection—namely, an LH surge.

Critics of this type of interpretation point out that

there is evidence that primates do not have the same degree of sex differentiation of the hypothalamus as one sees in rodents (Byne & Bleier, 1987). They suggest that it is not abnormal for human males to secrete LH in bursts. LH surges in response to estrogen have been demonstrated in male rhesus monkeys (cited in Södersten, 1987), and ovaries transplanted into normal male monkeys continue to cycle all by themselves. Apparently, LH surges in human males do not necessarily mean that those males have feminized brains. This weakens the evidence for a biological interpretation of homosexuality and suggests that research on LH surges in human males needs to be pursued until some more definite conclusion can be drawn.

The second line of human evidence reported by Ellis and Ames comes from a study purportedly showing sexual inversion in males with 5α-reductase syndrome (Imperato-McGinley et al., 1974). The cases occurred in the tiny village of Salinas, located in such an isolated region of the Dominican Republic that considerable inbreeding has occurred within its population. The researchers discovered 24 cases of "male hermaphrodites" involving 13 families. All were genetically male (XY) but had such ambiguous external genitalia at birth that the first group of babies was assigned as females. Recall that the testosterone metabolite DHT is necessary for full prenatal development of the male external genitalia. These children lack the enzyme 5α-reductase, which converts the testosterone into DHT. The fact that they had no deficiency of testosterone itself became evident as the children began reaching puberty. Because of the normal male upsurge in testosterone secretion at that time, their voices deepened, facial hair darkened, muscle mass increased, and their penises (which at birth resembled large clitorises) grew enough to become unmistakably male sex organs. They showed strong male sexual orientation; that is, they considered themselves male and preferred female partners. Here then were a group of people raised for more than a decade as females, taught to think of themselves all of their previous lives as girls, who now expressed a male sexual orientation. Ellis and Ames suggest that this is due to the fact that the presence of testosterone during the critical prenatal period masculinized their brains, giving them an inevitable male orientation too strong to be overcome by experiences. The missing DHT, they say, won't prevent male brain differentiation because the metabolite is not used in the process. If their analysis is correct, this is strong evidence for their theory that sexual orientation is determined prenatally by hormones rather than through learning and experience.

Money (1987) disagrees with Ellis and Ames's interpretation of the Dominican Republic study. He points out that there were overwhelming social reasons for the children to switch to a male sexual orientation at puberty, and these reasons make it completely unnecessary to postulate an explanation dependent on hormones. The fact that the children developed such obvious male characteristics at puberty disqualified them for treatment as females in the tiny rural society of Salinas. They were forever denied the right to become wives and mothers. If they did not become recognized as males, they had no place at all in the rather rigid structure of the village society. Further, this Spanish-based culture is heavily macho-oriented. If given the choice, it is far more potentially rewarding to be a male than a female. Men command more respect and have far more rights than do any of the women. It would seem that the development of a male orientation among the children whose gender was suddenly in doubt could easily be explained from social causes without any need to speculate about possible prenatal brain differentiation. Not only does the Dominican Republic study fail to strongly support a biological interpretation of gender preference, the basic assumption about DHT not being involved in brain differentiation may be incorrect. Earlier in this chapter, evidence was presented that it is important in some species of birds. The possibility remains that it is also important in primates.

Another group of genetic males often raised as females are those suffering from the androgen-insensitivity syndrome. The inability to use testosterone not only left them with feminized external genitalia but also, presumably, with feminized brains. Ellis and Ames note that these people have a female sexual orientation, preferring males as partners, just as the theory would predict. However, this finding provides only weak support for the theory because the orientation can so easily be explained by the fact that the children were raised as girls and, unlike the males of Salinas, have no disturbing male features that conflict with this gender assignment. They are accepted completely as females and are usually happy to function in that role. Again, there is no need to search for underlying hormonal causes to explain their orientation.

In the adrenogenital syndrome, genetic females are masculinized prenatally by androgens secreted by a malfunctioning adrenal cortex. The hormonal theory of homosexuality would state that these girls have had their brains masculinized by the excessive androgen levels and should consequently display male behaviors. When compared with normal females, these girls tend to prefer competitive sports and seem to care little for dolls and feminine clothing (Ehrhardt & Meyer-Bahlburg, 1981). They have more masculine gestures and report fewer fantasies about romance and marriage. Over one third of the sample in one study stated a preference either for sexual relations with females only or did not prefer males over females (cited in Ellis & Ames, 1987). Some of these genetic females are assigned a male gender at birth, and this is allowed to stand when later it is discovered that they are XX. They are raised as boys, are happy with this role, and, when they are attracted to girls, are judged by society to be heterosexual. The adjustment of those raised as female can be much more difficult. Money (1987) cites the following case:

> One young woman in this . . . follow-up study who did develop a lesbian orientation said, after having had two different boyfriends with whom she attempted in vain to relate in sexual intercourse, that she had to admit that she could fall in love only with a chick, not a guy. She became lovesick over a girlfriend who, though her close companion, was unable to fall in love homosexually, only heterosexually. Driven to the despair of love unrequited, worsened by adversarial parents, the . . . girl drove her car into isolated swamp country, and there was found, two weeks later, dead of self-inflicted gunshot wounds.

The observations from adrenogenital cases represent the strongest evidence favoring the hormonal theory that we have yet explored. However,

it is possible that the only direct effect of the hormones is to produce a more aggressive approach to life rather than homosexuality. The aggressive approach creates the tomboy style, which in turn might lead to an overall male perspective on life with a resulting inverted sexual orientation. That would be a much more indirect chain of cause and effect from the hormone to the homosexuality. But even this interpretation, which is completely speculative, still assumes that androgens masculinize the brain prenatally, even if they do not make it inevitable that the girl will become homosexual. Thus, the hormonal theory seems to have found a source of support in this one hormonal dysfunction.

Other avenues of proof are less convincing. Recall that when a mother rat is stressed during pregnancy the male pups show a deficiency of testosterone during the few days immediately after birth when much brain differentiation is still going on. Later as adults, these male rats tend to display female behaviors. Could stress be a cause of homosexuality in human males? Some attempts have been made to test this by asking mothers about how much stress was experienced during pregnancy. Only 10 percent of the mothers of heterosexuals were able to recall episodes of stress, whereas nearly two thirds of the mothers of male homosexuals were able to recall such episodes. Rather than constituting clear proof, however, data such as these merely serve as a stimulus for further research. Is male homosexuality the result of being raised by a neurotic mother who finds most of life's events stressful? Did a tougher, more stressful pregnancy alter the attitude and affections of the mother toward her son in such a way as to predispose homosexuality? Dozens of alternative explanations will have to be examined before we can feel confident that stress during pregnancy causes sexual inversion in the offspring.

The third line of evidence presented by Ellis and Ames (1987) concerns the possibility that homosexuality is inherited. It was discovered in one sample that nearly one quarter of all brothers of male homosexuals were also homosexual (cited in Ellis & Ames, 1987). Of course, if homosexuality is the result of experience rather than prenatal hormones, then it is easy to see that a boy with a homosexual older brother may have had more opportunity to have acquired homosexual experiences prior to adolescence than would a boy with a heterosexual brother. Much more pertinent are the results of identical-twins studies. The chance that one twin will be homosexual if the other is turns out to be much higher in identical twins (with identical inheritance) than in fraternal twins (with different inheritance). This appears to be strong evidence for the hormonal theory. Regarding the question of what factor is inherited, one possibility is that some males may not inherit enough copies of the genes for enzymes such as 5α-reductase. This could perhaps lead to a shortage of an androgen or estrogen.

In summary then, Ellis and Ames presented the latest version of the hormonal theory of homosexuality. Their contention is that hormone deficiencies or excesses during the embryonic or fetal period of development organize the brain to produce behaviors inappropriate for the genetic sex of the person and that this brain organization cannot be fully overcome by socializing influences during childhood. However, much of the evidence offered for a hormonal theory of homosexuality is weak and inconclusive. The two most interesting lines of evidence are the data on sexual inversions in females with adrenogenital syndrome and the data from identical-twin studies suggesting that some cases of homosexuality might be inherited. However, neither line of evidence is strong, and there are some possibly conflicting data from cases of adrenogenital syndrome (Slijper, 1984).

If homosexuality could be explained entirely by biological factors, one would expect the effect to show up much more clearly than it has. Perhaps environmental factors such as the person's history of reinforcement and punishment are also potent contributing factors. A person who, by chance, has not been reinforced for heterosexual behaviors but has been reinforced in homosexual situations will be more likely to seek homosexual experiences in the future. If this is the case, then a person's choice of a homosexual orientation would be influenced by both biological predispositions and personal experiences. At this point in the history of research on homosexuality, an interactional theory that allows for both biological and learning factors is probably the best interpretation.

■ Summary

1. Sexual dimorphism in mammals depends on the genes to establish whether the gonads will become ovaries or testes and the gonadal hormones to determine whether the sex-related brain circuits and body features will be male or female. Because both males and females have X chromosomes, the genetic factor in gender is really the presence or absence of the Y chromosome.

2. All human embryos have both a Müllerian duct and a Wolffian duct. If the male Y chromosome is present, the gonads become testes and secrete testosterone, the hormone that stimulates the Wolffian duct to develop into the male internal genitalia. The Y chromosome also produces Sertoli cells that induce withering of the female Müllerian duct. In the female, the Y chromosome is supplanted by an X chromosome, and the Müllerian duct develops into the female internal genitalia.

3. A second wave of sex differentiation occurs at puberty when the preoptic area (POA) of the hypothalamus begins to secrete gonadotropin-releasing factor (GRF). This hormone is carried by the bloodstream to the anterior pituitary where it encourages the release of luteinizing hormone (LH) and follicle-stimulating hormone (FSH). The effect of these pituitary hormones is to bring about a much greater release of estrogen from the ovaries and testosterone from the testes. These gonadal hormones in turn produce the male and female secondary sex characteristics. In the female, a monthly upsurge in FSH acts on the ovaries to develop a follicle and matures the ovum it contains. LH releases the egg, allowing the follicle to mature into a corpus luteum that secretes the third reproductive hormone, progesterone.

4. A person's gender identity and gender assignment may not always agree with the genetic gender. A genetic male (XY chromosomes) may be assigned and reared as a female if the body tissues are unable to use the testosterone secreted from the testes, a condition called androgen-insensitivity syndrome. A genetic female (XX) may be mistaken for a male in the syndrome known as androgen-induced hermaphroditism. A malfunctioning adrenal cortex in the mother secretes great quantities of androgens during the prenatal period, and the fetus is mas-

culinized. When the infant's own adrenal cortex produces the excessive androgens through a lack of the enzyme 21-hydroxylase, the disorder is called adrenogenital syndrome. In the 5α-reductase syndrome, the lack of the reductase enzyme prohibits the production of dihydrotestosterone (DHT), the androgen responsible for the development of the external genitalia. The result is a feminized XY individual. All these syndromes produce people with unclear gender who are best categorized as intersexual.

5. Genes alone are not enough to determine the person's gender identity. There are six important factors: genetic, prenatal hormonal, type of internal genitalia, type of external genitalia, gender assignment, and socialization.

6. The developmental processes that lead to gender-specific brain circuits are called brain differentiation. Parts of the brain of the finch and canary are highly differentiated because only the males sing. For this reason, those species have been the subjects of much research on brain differentiation. The genes appear to establish the circuitry for both male and female behaviors in many of the species so far studied, but it is the gonadal hormones present during the prenatal period that determine which of these circuits will develop enough to command behavior in the adult. This determination is called an organizational effect. For an adult male to sing, it must experience a high level of testosterone prenatally (organizational effect) and again as an adult (activational effect).

7. Inside the neurons of the fetal male, testosterone is converted to estrogen, the hormone that actually masculinizes the brain. Females are protected against masculine brain organization by alpha fetoprotein that deactivates the estrogen in the bloodstream of the fetus.

8. Masculinization of the mammalian nervous system has been studied in the spinal nucleus of the bulbocavernosus, a group of spinal cord neurons that controls the bulbocavernosus and levitor ani muscles that are involved in penile erection. In the male rat, this cell group is much larger than in the female, and the neurons themselves are larger. Another group of sexually differentiated neurons lies in the medial preoptic area (MPOA) of the hypothalamus, an area that controls the PNS. Circuits in this area appear to control male sexual responses in the rat, such as mounting and erection, as well as female reproductive behaviors like nest building, nursing, and retrieving pups. Female sexual behaviors such as lordosis stem from the action of circuits in the ventromedial hypothalamus.

9. The hormonal activation effect appears to be present in adult humans as well as animals. Loss of testosterone in the male eventually leads to loss of ejaculation and erections. However, neither estrogen nor testosterone levels seem to influence sexual receptivity in the primate female, human or otherwise.

10. Considerable evidence exists linking aggression to testosterone levels in rats and lower primates. Some evidence suggests that this link may also exist in humans.

11. It has been repeatedly suggested that human homosexuality might be the result of a hormonal error during the critical prenatal period that differentiated the brain for the wrong gender, thus predisposing males toward female behavior and vice versa (sexual inversions). Such inversions can be readily produced in rats but may not be relevant to human homosexuality.

12. The hormonal theory of Ellis and Ames finds some support in the fact that genetic females with adrenogenital syndrome who are raised as girls frequently display strong lesbian leanings. Some interesting but inconclusive evidence exists that suggests that homosexuality might be inherited, presumably by way of an enzyme deficiency that would result in incorrect brain differentiation. The evidence that Ellis and Ames present from 5α-reductase cases can easily be explained on the basis of social influences rather than hormonal. Data showing a female hormonal pattern in male homosexuals (the LH surge) turn out not to be distinctive of homosexuals after all. One way to interpret the data involves a possible biological predisposition toward homosexual orientation that can be suppressed or amplified by reinforcement and punishment experiences.

Glossary

activational effect The production of a gender-specific behavior in the adult animal by the action of hormones on existing brain circuits that were organized prenatally. (494)

adrenogenital syndrome Masculinization of an XX fetus by overproduction of androgens from the fetus's adrenal cortexes; caused by lack of the enzyme 21-hydroxylase. (492)

alpha feto-protein A chemical that circulates in the blood of neonates and binds estrogen so that it cannot affect the nervous system. (494)

androgen-induced hermaphroditism Masculinization of an XX fetus by maternal oversecretion of adrenal androgens (usually because of a tumor of the adrenal cortex). (492)

androgen-insensitivity syndrome A syndrome in which the tissues of an XY fetus are unable to use androgens; the result is an intersexual person. (490)

androgens A family of hormones involved in reproduction. (483)

anterior hypothalamus Region that contains circuits controlling the erection reflex. (498)

anterior pituitary gland A lobe of the "master gland" that provides a hormonal link between the hypothalamus and the rest of the endocrine system. (485)

brain differentiation The developmental processes that lead to sex-specific brain circuits. (493)

bulbocavernosus muscle A muscle that aids the levator ani in the ejaculation of sperm and in the maintenance of an erection. (496)

cholesterol A type of fat from which the androgens and estrogens are derived. (483)

chromosomes Strands of DNA containing thousands of genes. (483)

corpus luteum A group of ovarian endocrine cells that secrete progesterone. (488)

critical period A short period during the course of prenatal development during which androgens or estrogens can have an organizing effect on the brain. (494)

dihydrotestosterone (DHT) An androgen responsible for the development of the external male genitalia in the fetus. (492)

dimorphism Having two different shapes; sexual dimorphism refers to body differences between the sexes. (483)

embryo The early stages of development after fertilization; in humans, usually the period from the third week through the twelfth week postconception. (483)

estrogens A group of ovarian and adrenal cortex hormones involved in reproduction. (483)

estrus The portion of the estrous cycle (the term used for the menstrual cycle in all mammals other than primates) in which the animal is sexually receptive. (489)

external genitalia Labia, clitoris, penis, and scrotum. (493)

fallopian tubes Ducts that connect the ovaries to the uterus. (485)

feminization Organization of the brain that promotes female behavior circuits over male. (500)

5α-reductase An enzyme that converts testosterone to DHT. (492)

5α-reductase syndrome Feminization of an XY fetus because the enzyme 5α-reductase is missing. (492)

follicle One of the small pockets of cells within the ovaries that contain an ovum. (488)

follicle-stimulating hormone (FSH) Stimulates the follicles of the ovaries and increases estrogen secretion. (485)

gender assignment The gender specified by the physician at birth. (490)

gender identity The sex that any person considers herself or himself to be. (489)

genes Individual segments of DNA; the units of reproduction. (483)

genetic factor The presence or absence of a Y chromosome as a gender determinant. (493)

gonadotropic hormones Pituitary hormones (LH and FSH) that stimulate the gonads. (485)

gonadotropin-releasing factors (GRFs) Hypothalamic hormones (FSH-RF and LH-RF) that stimulate the anterior pituitary gland to release gonadotropic hormones. (485)

gonads Reproductive glands; ovaries in the female, testes in the male. (482)

hermaphroditic Having both sexes in one body. (482)

internal genitalia Gonads and structures that develop from the Wolffian and Müllerian ducts. (493)

intersexual Designation for a person whose six determinants of gender identity conflict to produce unclear sexual morphology. (491)

levator ani muscle A muscle that aids the bulbocavernosus in the ejaculation of sperm and in the maintenance of an erection. (496)

LH surge The normal rise in LH resulting from the combined effects of estrogen and gonadotropin-releasing factor. (506)

lordosis A posture adopted by the female mammal in which she arches her back and moves her tail to one side to facilitate mounting. (498)

luteinizing hormone (LH) Induces ovulation and increases secretion of estrogen. (485)

masculinization Induction of male morphology (in the brain or the rest of body) by hormones. (500)

medial forebrain bundle (MFB) A major tract connecting the brain stem with the striatum and the limbic system; contains fibers of the reinforcement system. (499)

medial preoptic area (MPOA) The region just anterior to the hypothalamus proper that contains circuits important for reproductive behaviors such as erection and mounting. (498)

menstrual cycle The female reproductive cycle of ovulation and changes in the lining of the uterus that is governed by gonadotropic hormones. (487)

morphology Shape, structure, or appearance. (483)

mounting The male coital position. (498)

Müllerian duct An embryonic structure that can develop into the uterus, vagina, and fallopian tubes. (485)

Müllerian-inhibiting factor (MIF) A defeminizing hormone that prevents the development of the Müllerian duct. (485)

organizational effect Prenatal determination of gender-specific brain circuitry by androgens or estrogens. (494)

ovaries Female gonads. (483)

ovulation Release of the ovum from the ovarian follicle. (488)

prenatal hormonal balance The predominance of fetal androgens or estrogens as a gender determinant. (493)

preoptic area (POA) Portion of the hypothalamus containing groups of cells responsible for sexual behaviors. (485)

progesterone Ovarian hormone that helps prepare the lining of the uterus for the implantation of the ovum. (489)

progestin-induced hermaphroditism Accidental masculinization of XX fetuses by the drug progestin. (491)

puberty The period that begins adolescence and during which a person acquires the ability to reproduce. (485)

secondary impotence A condition in which anxiety renders a man incapable of having or keeping an erection during intercourse. (498)

secondary sex characteristics Bodily changes that occur at puberty such as the development of pubic hair, external sex organs, and so forth. (487)

seminal vesicle The sac that holds sperm until they are ejaculated. (485)

Sertoli cells Type of testicular cell that secretes MIF. (485)

sexual inversion Choice of same-sex partner. (505)

sexual orientation Preferred gender for one's sexual partner. (505)

socialization The influence of one's culture on attitudes and behavior. (493)

spinal nucleus of the bulbocavernosus Spinal motor neurons that control the bulbocavernosus and levator ani muscles. (496)

testes Male gonads. (483)

testosterone An androgen-type hormone secreted by the testes. (483)

21-hydroxylase An enzyme that converts progesterone to cortisol. (492)

uterus The female reproductive organ in which the embryo and fetus mature. (485)

vas deferens Tubes that carry the sperm from the testes to the seminal vesicles. (485)

ventromedial hypothalamic nucleus Region of the brain containing circuits for lordosis. (498)

ventrotegmental area (VTA) Group of dopaminergic neurons in the midbrain that form part of the reinforcement system. (499)

Wolffian duct An embryonic structure that can develop into vas deferens and seminal vesicles. (485)

X chromosome One of the two sex chromosomes; in primates two X chromosomes determine a female. (483)

Y chromosome One of the two sex chromosomes; in primates an XY chromosome pair determines a male. (483)

13

Emotions and Stress

P hysiological psychologists have two major research interests related to emotions: understanding what they are and how they work and finding out how they impact on a person's mental and physical health. We look first at the neural basis for emotions and then discuss the brain's system for reacting to stress situations.

■ The Problem of Emotions

While personality and clinical psychologists are busy studying how a person learns emotions and how emotions can influence adjustment, physiological psychologists pursue the most basic question of all: What is emotion? More specifically stated this question becomes, What sorts of brain mechanisms are emotions, and where in the nervous system are they located? Answering these questions is difficult because the concept of emotion is not the simple, clearcut idea that it might appear to be at first glance.

How many emotions are humans capable of experiencing? Without a complete listing of all possible emotional states, we cannot find the boundaries of the concept *emotion* and work up a clear definition for it. Anger, fear, pleasure, joy, love, sadness, dislike, and disgust might be a good start toward such a list. Should we add terror, sorrow, grief, anguish, guilt, happiness, euphoria, excitement, depression, boredom, delight, interest, envy, jealousy, thrill, hate, embarrassment, and anxiety? Does that leave out some? Of course it does. The list may be nearly endless, and any one person's list is different than anyone else's. There is no set list of emotions agreed on by everyone. In other words, the concept has no clear boundaries.

Why, then, after decades of research hasn't psychology produced a clear definition of emotion? The problem is that emotion is not a scientific category drawn from experimental data; it is a loose, hazy, everyday idea that people use to explain each other's behavior. "What's wrong with Ann today?" "She's mad at Joe. That's why she's acting so strange." The idea of emotion seems to be applied to explain any different or unusual conscious state or behavior tendency. But there are too many exceptions to that generalization to make it a good definition. Society has lumped all sorts of behavioral and conscious states into the bin called "emotions" without caring about whether they really have anything in common. It is possible that they do, but if there is a common denominator, it has not yet been accepted as such by the majority of psychologists.

As you can see, there really isn't much hope of finding a single structure within the brain that produces all emotional states, or even a single emotional state. As McCleary (1966) notes, just because a conceptual category is useful in talking about behavior doesn't mean that category will be found in the brain. What some theorists argue is that certain underlying dimensions consistently emerge in emotional behavior and these dimensions may represent real brain processes. The differences that we see between various emotional states result from different combinations of these same few dimensions rather than from having a separate psychological mechanism for each emotion. We discuss three of these proposed emotional dimensions: level of arousal, approach–avoidance, and appetitiveness–aversiveness.

In conscious experience, **level of arousal** refers to how awake you are. Arousal can vary all the way from the lowest levels in sleep through awake-alert to maximum excitement. **Approach–avoidance** refers more to a response tendency than to conscious experience, a motivation to move toward some stimuli and away from others. The word **appetitive** means something good, desirable, something for which you have an appetite. The opposite, **aversive**, means bad, undesirable, unwanted.

Most of the states that we label as emotions contain these three dimensions (and perhaps other dimensions as well). Fear, for example, falls toward the avoidance end of the approach–avoidance continuum, often involves high levels of arousal, and is induced by stimuli that are usually thought of as aversive. Anger is similar to fear in having a high arousal level and involving aversive stimuli but differs in having an approach tendency rather than avoidance. In rage and terror, the arousal level is increased over anger and fear. A higher arousal level would also distinguish joy from pleasure. These last two emotions would incorporate an approach tendency as in anger but would involve appetitive stimuli rather than aversive.

The interesting idea about the three dimensions of emotion is the possibility that they represent real mechanisms that can actually be located within brain circuitry. Levels of arousal are controlled by the **reticular formation** of the midbrain (MBRF) (Chapter 10). Recall that the reticular formation is a column of gray matter extending up through the center of the brain stem and that it contains cells that send their axons throughout the cortex.

The appetitive–aversive dimension may stem from the interplay of two systems of nuclei and fibers that extend from the midbrain up through the hypothalamus and into the limbic system (Figure 13.1). The **medial forebrain bundle** (MFB) is the system suspected of being responsible for reward (Chapter 14). Its task seems to be to detect stimuli that are useful to the organism and to label them as appetitive. The **periventricular system** lies just medial to the MFB and apparently can label stimuli as aversive (Schenberg et al., 1983). One of the nuclei within this system is the ventromedial hypothalamus (VMH), which seems to play a part in satiety for food (Chapter 11). When you have eaten to satiety, food becomes aversive. The periventricular system was also mentioned in Chapter 8 as a part of the pain system. The appetitiveness or aversiveness of a stimulus, then, may be found in the balance of activity between these two opposed systems.

When approach or avoidance behaviors are examined with brain lesions or stimulation experiments, the amygdala is repeatedly shown to be relevant. Because of its strong connections down into the hypothalamus and out into the neocortex, the amygdala is ideally located to use the sensory information generated by the cortical sensory areas in determining what emotional responses should be released from the hypothalamus and brain stem. Whereas the hypothalamus ties the emotions to the internal environment of the body, the amygdala associates them with the organism's external envi-

Reward

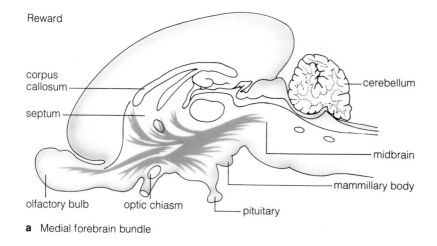

corpus
callosum

septum

olfactory bulb

optic chiasm

pituitary

cerebellum

midbrain

mammillary body

a Medial forebrain bundle

Punishment

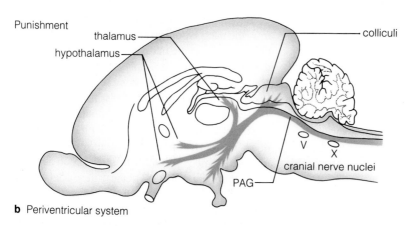

thalamus

hypothalamus

colliculi

V   X
cranial nerve nuclei

PAG

b Periventricular system

Figure 13.1 The systems central to appetitiveness and aversiveness are shown on a generalized mammalian brain. Both systems are collections of tracts interconnecting limbic structures, hypothalamic nuclei, and midbrain nuclei. (**a**) The reward system is the medial forebrain
bundle. (**b**) The punishment–aversion system centers around the periventricular system, which
lies medial to the MFB. (**a** Adapted from Stein, 1968; **b** adapted from LeGros Clark et al., 1938)

ronment by way of its connections with the hippocampus (memories of events) and neocortex
(sensory analysis).

This pivotal role of the amygdala appears clearly
in studies that record from amygdala neurons during
a conditioning task. Some neurons in the monkey
amygdala respond when an appetitive stimulus like
a slice of orange is consumed and when the same
stimulus is first seen at the start of a trial. Such a
neuron must be associating taste and visual stimuli

coming to it from the temporal cortex. Now, if the
orange slice is made unpalatable (aversive) with salt,
the cell stops firing when the monkey tastes it, suggesting that the neuron is associating the visual–
gustatory stimuli with the appetitive–aversiveness of
the stimulus. This interpretation is supported when
the monkey has experienced the orange on enough
trials for learning to have occurred and the neuron
stops responding to an orange when it is first seen
(Nishijo et al., 1988). In the next section, we look at

further reasons for thinking that the amygdala contains the approach–avoidance circuitry that can select the appropriate emotional responses using past experience.

■ Two Basic Emotions

Many human emotions such as joy and grief may have no certain counterpart in rat, cat, or monkey behavior and have attracted extremely little brain research. So far, there exist no research tools capable of discovering which human brain areas are active during such emotional states. The two emotions that do clearly exist in lower mammals and are amenable to research are fear and aggression.

In discussing these two emotions, we will examine a set of interconnected structures in the brain that seem to be linked together into an **aversion system**. This hypothetical system begins in the orbitofrontal cortex and continues through the amygdala into the anterior and ventromedial hypothalamic areas. From there the periventricular system continues the network down to the periaqueductal gray (PAG) and other midbrain areas. It is the structures linked by this system that apparently decide whether a particular stimulus is undesirable (aversive) and whether it should be avoided (fear or disgust) or attacked (aggression).

Anxiety and Fear

There are many shadings to the emotion of fear. Clinical psychologists deal most with the variety of fear termed *anxiety*. Although there is no perfect distinction between fear and anxiety, it is frequently useful to think of fear as a response to some immediate threat and anxiety as the anticipation of some undesired, threatening event. Thus, fear is typically a short-term state dependent on the presence of a particular stimulus, whereas anxiety is generated by anticipation and so can occur continually, no matter what stimuli are present. Because anticipation of a fearful stimulus is the key to anxiety and anticipation seems to be a prefrontal function (see Chapter 3), we can surmise that anxiety may originate in the frontal cortex.

Anxiety and the Orbitofrontal Cortex In 1934 Carlyle Jacobsen and colleagues were investigating the prefrontal regions of the chimpanzee brain. One female regularly displayed temper tantrums during the training procedures. Her task was to remember for a few seconds where a piece of food had been placed. As she watched one of a set of overturned cups being baited with a bit of food, she would whimper softly to herself; when an opaque screen came down between her and the cups to start the waiting period, she would fly into a rage—screaming, defecating, and urinating. When Jacobsen removed a large portion of her prefrontal cortex on both sides, however, the tantrums vanished. Her performance on the memory task was unhampered, and she appeared to be content with the whole arrangement, even when she chose the wrong cup and failed to find the food (cited in Valenstein, 1973).

Egaz Moniz, a Portuguese psychiatrist, was in the audience of the International Neurology Congress of 1935 when Jacobsen reported his chimpanzee experiments. Upon hearing of the calming effect of prefrontal removal, he asked if the surgery couldn't be used to relieve the debilitating anxiety of psychotic patients. Jacobsen was somewhat shocked at the suggestion, but Moniz went home to put the idea into effect. After a false start using alcohol to kill prefrontal tissue, he settled on simply cutting the connections from the orbitofrontal cortex to the limbic structures important to anxiety (Valenstein, 1973). These were the first attempts at **prefrontal lobotomy** (*tom* means to cut; and hence, *lobotomy* means to cut the lobe off from the rest of the brain).

During the 1940s, the prefrontal lobotomy became an accepted method of treating psychiatric patients in the United States. Freeman and Watts introduced their widely employed method in which a long, semiblunt knife was introduced through a hole in the region of the temple. Simply moving the knife back and forth severed the appropriate connections (Figure 13.2). By 1950 Freeman had given over 3,500 people prefrontal lobotomies (Valenstein, 1973). With the appearance of antipsychotic drugs and tranquilizers during the 1950s, use of the operation became much less frequent.

Prefrontal lobotomy does appear to have relieved anxiety to some extent in some patients. It typically

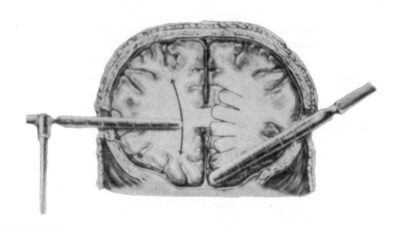

Figure 13.2 A frontal section through the head showing the Freeman–Watts technique for prefrontal lobotomy. Connections between the prefrontal cortex (including orbitofrontal) and other brain areas are cut by inserting a blunt knife through a hole in the skull at the temple. (From Freeman & Watts, 1950)

also cripples the person's motivation to plan ahead and to be concerned about the judgments of others. Without anxiety the person may fail to get to work on time or complete an important task. Lobotomy patients are careless about the things they say and have little control over angry reactions to minor frustrations. Anxiety appears to be critical for civilization; it is frequently the motive that makes us care what others think of us. It seems to me that there are only two kinds of college students who experience no anxiety over grades: those who make straight As with no effort and those who make Fs—with no effort. Much of human effort stems from anxiety.

The **orbitofrontal cortex** is often considered to be "limbic frontal lobe" (Smith & DeVito, 1984). Its role may be to connect the emotional areas of the limbic system into the planning areas of the prefrontal cortex. One of the most important limbic structures in anxiety is the amygdala, and some of the fibers cut in prefrontal lobotomy are axons of orbitofrontal neurons projecting to that structure (Crosby et al., 1962).

Amygdala The **amygdala** (am-IGG-duh-la) is a cluster of nuclei located just beneath the cortex near the tip of the temporal lobe (Figure 13.3). Its parts can be separated into three divisions: **basolateral nuclear group**, **central nucleus**, and **corticomedial nuclear group** (Figure 13.4). There are strong

connections between these nuclei and the orbitofrontal cortex (Smith & DeVito, 1984). One of the first hints that the amygdala was important to emotions came from the experiments of Klüver and Bucy (1938, 1939), in which the amygdala was removed from both hemispheres of rhesus monkey subjects. Adult rhesus monkeys are typically aggressive and hostile toward humans. They do not make good pets and are very likely to bite any hand that touches them. Removing the amygdalas of these animals converted them from wild animals to the equivalent of domestic house pets. They seemed to have lost most of the fear that lay behind the normal aggressive attitude.

This association of the amygdala with fear has also been demonstrated in the rat. Rats with lesioned amygdalas never learn to pause in what they are doing and become alert when given a cue that a frightening stimulus is about to occur (Spevack et al., 1975), nor do they learn to avoid such a stimulus (Hitchcock & Davis, 1986). Blanchard and Blanchard (1972) discovered that rats without amygdalas would accept the presence of a sedated cat in their cage and even climb onto its back. One animal was attacked by the cat after chewing briefly on its ear. (The cat apparently was too groggy to retaliate effectively.) When released again by the experimenter, the rat crawled up the cat's back once more with no hesitation!

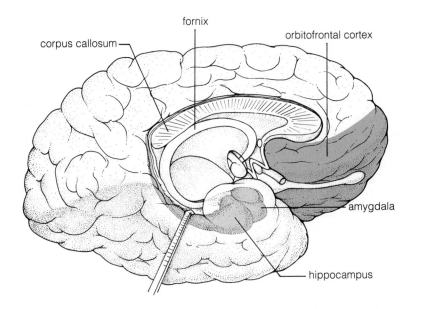

fornix

corpus callosum

orbitofrontal cortex

amygdala

hippocampus

Figure 13.3 A midsagittal view of the human brain with the thalamus, hypothalamus, and brain stem removed to reveal the medial surface of the temporal lobe. The temporal lobe is transparent to show the positions of the hippocampus and amygdala beneath the temporal cortex.

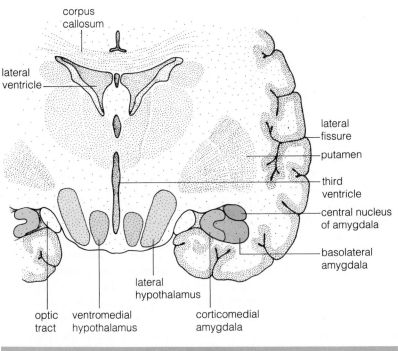

corpus callosum

lateral ventricle

lateral fissure

putamen

third ventricle

central nucleus of amygdala

basolateral amygdala

optic tract

ventromedial hypothalamus

lateral hypothalamus

corticomedial amygdala

Figure 13.4 A frontal section of the human brain just posterior to the optic chiasm showing the amygdala and two hypothalamic nuclei.

What if the amygdala is stimulated rather than removed? In the few rare cases of epilepsy in which the seizures are limited to the temporal lobes, the patient may become involuntarily aggressive and attack bystanders (Mark & Ervin, 1970). When seizures invade the region in and around the amygdala, patients often report experiencing intense emotions at the start of the seizure (MacLean, 1968), with feelings of sadness, fear, dread, terror, and rage. The seizure pattern of one patient typically began with a feeling of sadness accompanied by tears and followed by a feeling of hunger. (The amygdala is involved in the control of eating.) Electrical stimulation of the human amygdala has been reported to elicit fear without anger (cited in Blanchard & Blanchard, 1988).

More recently, researchers have selectively lesioned or stimulated individual nuclei within the amygdala. Stimulation of the central nucleus of cats produced fear and attempts to escape (Moyer, 1976). Stimulation of the basolateral nuclear group also elicits fear as well as inhibition of aggression (Niehoff & Kuhar, 1983; Smythies, 1966). Lesions of this nuclear group make it difficult for mice to learn to avoid a fearful stimulus like shock (Swartzwelder, 1981). Basolateral amygdala stimulation during human neurosurgery elicits feelings of fear and anxiety together with physical signs of fear such as increased heart rate, blood pressure, and pupillary dilation (Niehoff & Kuhar, 1983).

Is the amygdala then some sort of "fear center" in the brain, the sole location of that emotion? This is not likely because the hypothalamus, brain stem and sympathetic nervous system (SNS) also have important roles in the experiencing of fear. The contribution of the amygdala probably concerns the learning of appropriate emotional responses for various situations. Every sense system of the cortex sends information to the amygdala (Smith & DeVito, 1984), thus making it the perfect place to associate stimuli with emotional responses. Threatening stimuli (especially another individual bent on doing you harm) put you into a decision situation in which the major emotional factor is the approach–avoidance dimension ("Do I fight or run?"). Thus, the associations learned in the amygdala are usually characterized as approach–avoidance decisions.

The approach–avoidance conflict between anger and fear has been examined in the context of aggression between competing male cats (Moyer, 1976). The choice of an aggressive-approach response is promoted by the corticomedial group of the amygdala, whereas the central and basolateral nuclear group dictate a hasty avoidance. These two opposing areas of the amygdala are apparently balanced against one another in a state of continuing mutual inhibition (Moyer, 1976). Perhaps input from other brain areas tips the balance toward either fight or flight by triggering learned associations combined with predictions of anticipated outcome drawn from the orbitofrontal cortex.

Hypothalamus and Brain Stem The role of the amygdala may be to connect relevant memories to the appropriate emotional response, but the response circuits themselves appear to be located in the brain stem and spinal cord. The amygdala exerts its control over them by way of its connections to the hypothalamus (Smith & DeVito, 1984). The hypothalamus sends commands to the brain stem, calling for fear or relaxation or anger, and the brain stem interprets each of these as a different collection of stem and cord reflexes. Many of the cord reflex circuits belong to the autonomic nervous system (ANS) and have the task of adjusting heart rate, blood vessel constriction, adrenalin secretion, muscle tone in the stomach and intestines, and a host of other internal changes.

The heart-rate and blood vessel changes, called **cardiovascular responses**, are an easy way to objectively measure the presence of fear or anxiety in an animal. Smith and colleagues discovered that they could electrically elicit these cardiovascular responses by stimulating a small zone surrounding the descending fibers of the fornix where they course through the hypothalamus on their way to the mammillary bodies (cited in Smith & DeVito, 1984) (Figure 13.5). They designated this region **HACER** (hypothalamic area for conditioned emotional responses) and showed that the cardiovascular responses to conditioned emotional stimuli were lost when it was lesioned. The neurons in HACER project directly to the SNS cells of the spinal cord that control the cardiovascular reflexes and to all

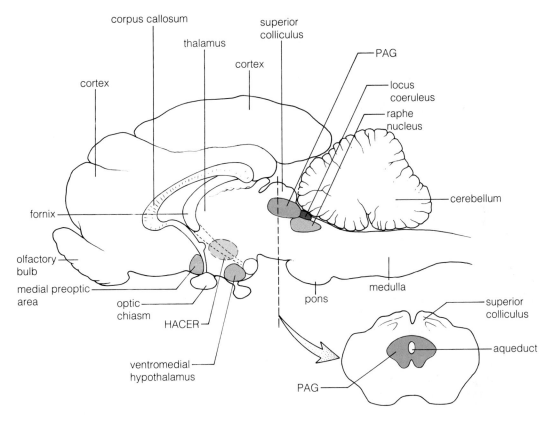

Figure 13.5 A medial view of the cat brain with a cross section of the midbrain to show location of the PAG. The dotted line on the medial view indicates the location of the cross section.

brain-stem emotion areas. Apparently, HACER may be limited to control of autonomic responses.

The **medial hypothalamus**, an area just medial to HACER and probably overlapping it, appears to be an organizer of striate muscle fear behaviors, especially escape responses (Siegel & Pott, 1988). Stimulation of this area makes a rat run around its cage in what appears to be flight. When it reaches a corner, it frequently attempts to jump over the wall of the cage (Lammers et al., 1988). This same sort of reaction has been elicited from the medial hypothalamus of the cat (Fuchs & Siegel, 1984). The medial hypothalamus sends axons to the **periaqueductal gray (PAG)** of the brain stem, an area that probably contains the motor circuits for many species-typical behavior patterns (see Chapter 8).

For example, the rabbit's fear response of freezing into immobility at the occurrence of certain threatening stimuli seems to be organized in the PAG (Fontani & Meucci, 1983). Both cardiovascular fear responses and flight behavior can be elicited by electrical stimulation of the PAG (Carobrez et al., 1983). Figure 13.6 summarizes the anxiety portions of the aversion system. Many of the connections between the hypothalamic parts and lower structures are made by way of the periventricular system.

Sympathetic Nervous System Fear and anxiety produce a collection of visceral responses including increased heart rate and stroke volume, increased respiration, constriction and dilation of arteries, inhibition of stomach and intestinal contractions, sweat-

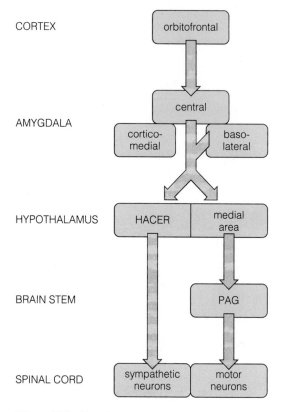

CORTEX — orbitofrontal

AMYGDALA — central — cortico-medial — baso-lateral

HYPOTHALAMUS — HACER — medial area

BRAIN STEM — PAG

SPINAL CORD — sympathetic neurons — motor neurons

Figure 13.6 Neural structures important in the production of anxiety and fear.

self in a face-off with a half-ton shaggy brute with 2-inch claws and more teeth than you knew existed. Your whole body reacts to this threat. As you swing your stone-tipped club with all your strength, your muscles need a sudden huge increase in blood supply. The SNS immediately begins to raise the heart rate and stroke volume and to contract the smooth muscles lining the blood vessels in the stomach and intestines, thus forcing blood out of the viscera toward the muscles and brain. Claws rake your arm, but you bleed much less than you would have if the injury had been sustained in an unemotional situation. The SNS has contracted the smooth muscles of the skin arteries, and the skin has relatively little blood in it at the moment. That is why it looks white and feels cold to the touch. Another SNS reflex has released a chemical that causes your blood to clot more rapidly than usual. Your palms begin to sweat, moistening the handle of your club and improving your grip. You feel a glancing blow to your left shoulder, but your sweaty skin is slick enough to help turn the claws a little so that they gouge less deeply. The bear maneuvers for another swing, and your brain swiftly calculates the expected trajectory. Your speed of thinking has been momentarily improved as blood vessels throughout your brain dilate, increasing the blood supply there. All your resources are being mobilized to make you momentarily the fastest, strongest, and most alert that you will ever be.

Psychopharmacology of Anxiety Fear was a highly effective protective device for our ancestors, but like a drug, it can have unfortunate side effects. Some people suffer from chronic fear and anxiety that interferes with their ability to function normally in their vocations or social interactions. In trying to help these people by altering their brain function with drugs, much has been learned about how the neural systems for anxiety work.

Most drugs are discovered more or less accidentally, their discoverers usually having no idea how the drug achieves its effect. The **anxiolytic drugs**, those that relieve anxiety, are no exception. The **barbiturates** were discovered in 1864 by Adolf von Bayer (of Bayer aspirin) and have been used for decades as sedatives and anxiolytics (Feldman &

ing, and release of liver glucose. The "white" face typical of strong fear results from the sympathetic constriction of blood vessels in the skin and the "butterflies" in the stomach from cessation of the continuous peristaltic contractions that are normal for that organ. What value do such internal adjustments have, and why should they be a part of fear and anxiety?

Fear and anger evolved as survival mechanisms. Fear makes you tend to avoid life-threatening situations. Anger helped your distant ancestors overcome obstacles, especially in social situations involving competition for scarce resources. For example, the paleolithic cave dwellers of France and Germany sometimes competed for shelter with gigantic cave bears. Imagine entering a dark cave and finding your-

Quenzer, 1984). All are derivatives of the chemical barbituric acid. Some of the most common are phenobarbital (trade name, Luminal), pentobarbital (Nembutal), and secobarbital (Seconal). Although their effects have different durations, all these drugs have a depressant effect on the CNS, which lingers for more than 24 hours. (In street language, they are called "downers.") Longer-acting varieties such as pentobarbital can be used as anesthetics. In moderate doses, they cause drowsiness, decreased mental acuity, poor coordination, impaired judgment, confusion, and sometimes depression. These symptoms are very similar to those of alcohol intoxication.

Barbiturates impede transmission at synapses apparently by interfering with sodium channels, thus blocking the EPSPs that presynaptic impulses should elicit (Feldman & Quenzer, 1984). Although such interference with transmission should depress CNS function if it occurs at any one of dozens of locations, the place where it can have the greatest effect is in the midbrain reticular formation (see Chapters 3 and 10). Barbiturates probably relieve anxiety only as a secondary effect of their depressive action; a person who is drowsy and relaxed cannot be simultaneously anxious. The depressive action, however, makes these drugs a poor solution to the problem of anxiety.

A better set of anxiolytic drugs, the **benzodiazepines,** were discovered in 1957. Two of these, **chlordiazepoxide** (trade name, Librium) and **diazepam** (Valium), are frequently called "tranquilizers" in reference to their superior anxiolytic capability. These two benzodiazepines have less sedative effect than do the barbiturates. (However, another benzodiazepine, Dalmane, is most frequently prescribed as a "sleeping pill.") Furthermore, it is possible that they act directly on the anxiety circuits of the brain. Gray (1988) suggests that benzodiazepines inhibit the noradrenergic neurons of the locus coeruleus and the serotonergic cells of the raphe nuclei (Figure 13.5) both of which are involved in arousing the cortex and limbic system during stress.

The serotonergic system has attracted most of the research. In a typical experiment, rats were trained to press a lever to get water under the condition that if they pressed more than four times per minute they would get a footshock. They had to learn to press at a pace much slower than their thirst dictated. Control rats learned to inhibit their tendency to press too often and received very few shocks, but rats given chlordiazepoxide earned frequent shocks. This implies that the drugged rats were less anxious about receiving shocks. The same effect was obtained when they were given drugs that blocked serotonin receptor sites (cited in Feldman & Quenzer, 1984). It would make sense for serotonin to be involved because most of the serotonergic neurons in the brain are located in the raphe nuclei, which probably make up the caudal end of that chain of medial structures (PAG, periventricular system, and medial hypothalamic nuclei) that we have been calling the aversion system. However, the evidence linking benzodiazepine action to serotonergic cells is full of conflicts (File, 1987) and hints that other transmitter systems are probably involved as well.

We may not be certain whether the benzodiazepines have their effects exclusively on serotonergic cells, but we are certain that their effect is an inhibitory one. The drugs provide inhibition indirectly by potentiating the action at GABA synapses. When GABA activates a $GABA_A$ receptor site on the postsynaptic neuron, chloride channels open, and the membrane hyperpolarizes, thus inhibiting the neuron by making it harder to initiate an action potential (see Chapter 4). Benzodiazepines are able to help GABA induce inhibition because of the way the receptor site is constructed (Figure 13.7). Attached to the GABA receptor area are **satellite receptors** designed for a chemical called **GABA-modulin.** When the GABA-modulin sites are occupied, the $GABA_A$ receptor is blocked, preventing the transmitter from inhibiting the postsynaptic cell. If there were a way to keep GABA-modulin molecules out of satellite receptor sites, the GABA receptors would be open to receive GABA, and inhibition of the postsynaptic cell would be possible. Benzodiazepines produce their effect by blocking satellite receptors so that GABA-modulin cannot block GABA. In other words, the benzodiazepines allow GABA to bind with its receptors and induce inhibition. Because the behavioral outcome of this inhibition is relief from anxiety, we must conclude that the postsynaptic cells that the drug helps inhibit must be producers of anxiety. Some of these cells appear to be in the anxiety system we have been discussing.

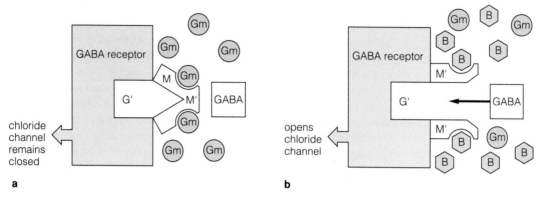

Figure 13.7 A single GABA$_A$ receptor with its satellite receptor (M) attached. Binding of GABA to this type of receptor opens chloride channels in the membrane producing inhibition. (**a**) Binding of GABA is prevented when GABA-modulin (Gm) binds with the satellite receptor sites (M'), thus blocking the GABA receptor sites (G'). (**b**) Benzodiazepines (B) block GABA-modulin sites and allow GABA to inhibit the postsynaptic cell. (Adapted from Feldman & Quenzer, 1984)

If chlordiazepoxide is injected directly into the rat PAG, significantly higher levels of shock are needed to induce fleeing, an effect identical to that obtained with injections of GABA (Schenberg et al., 1983). The implication is that GABA inhibits the fear responses available from the PAG, and that benzodiazepines (or, at least, chlordiazepoxide) facilitate this inhibition. Benzodiazepines also reduce fear responses when they are injected into the amygdala (Hitchcock & Davis, 1986). Receptors have been discovered in that structure with the highest concentrations being in the basolateral nuclear group (Niehoff & Kuhar, 1983).

Aggression

A phenomenon as complex as aggression is more easily understood in simpler mammals than it is in humans. The best system of categorizing all varieties of mammalian aggressive behavior was devised by K. E. Moyer (1976) and includes seven types: predatory, intermale, fear-induced, maternal, irritable, sex-related, and instrumental. **Predatory aggression** is the set of responses that a mammal uses to kill prey for food. These responses are typically different from

those seen in **intermale aggression**, which occurs when a strange male roams into the territory of a resident male. **Fear-induced aggression** occurs when a stimulus has frightened an animal, and it is trying to escape. **Maternal aggression** is displayed by a mother in the nesting area just before delivering the young and afterward until the offspring are able to defend themselves. **Irritable aggression** probably is accompanied by the conscious experience we call anger or rage and usually occurs as the result of frustration, pain, or deprivation. **Sex-related aggression** occurs between male and female as a normal part of the mating process. These are all genetically endowed types of aggression with species typical–response patterns in most mammals, but any of the behaviors can become more frequent or extreme if they are reinforced by circumstances. It is this increase that constitutes the last category, **instrumental aggression**. We examine only the types of aggression that have received enough research attention to yield some understanding of the underlying brain mechanisms.

Fear-Induced Aggression The distinguishing characteristic of this type of aggression is that it is almost always preceded by attempts to escape some potentially threatening stimulus (Moyer, 1976). A cat in this state exhibits hissing, spitting, and yowling. Its ears are flattened back against the skull, tail stiff, and fur fluffed. The back is arched, claws extended, and the hair on the neck is standing straight up. Internally, there is a host of sympathetic responses including adrenaline secretion, increased heart rate, blood vessel constriction in the digestive tract, and dilation in the brain and muscles.

The hissing and yowling very likely constitute frightening stimuli and have evolved as a means of winning before the fight even begins. Flattening the ears against the head gives them some protection against bites. The projection of a frightening image is enhanced by **piloerection**, a reflexive fluffing up of the fur, because it makes the cat appear larger. Fur-fluffing might seem to the reader to be a pretty thin disguise for the animal's true size, but when human observers unfamiliar with the purpose of the experiment were asked to judge the relative sizes of two rats, one of which was piloerecting, they tended to overestimate the latter's weight by about 50 percent (Blanchard et al., 1981).

Because fear-induced aggression is triggered by a fear state, it probably has its origins in the central nucleus and basolateral group of the amygdala. From those areas, general avoidance commands flow to the hypothalamus to be translated into specific behaviors and visceral responses. As with all aversive-stimulus situations, it is the periventricular system that is involved. Thus, in the hypothalamus, it is medial structures like the ventromedial nucleus and medial parts of the anterior nuclei and medial preoptic area (MPOA) that control the responses (Barrett et al., 1987; Maeda et al., 1985). At the caudal end of the periventricular system lies the PAG, the structure that apparently stores many of the motor patterns for species-typical behaviors, including flight movements and attack responses associated with flight. These defensive attack responses differ from other forms of attack. For example, a male rat intruding on the domain of a resident male will meet his attack defensively by biting mainly at the face and snout—in other words, directing his attack at the resident's weapons—whereas the resident male will aim bites at any part of the intruder's body (Blanchard et al.,

1981). The intruder is displaying fear-induced aggression, but the resident is showing intermale aggression (discussed below). The object of the resident male's aggression would appear to be to inflict as much pain as possible, while the intruder's object is to block those attacks with facial bites. Lesions of the PAG decrease the ability of rats to make fear-induced aggressive attacks (Blanchard et al., 1981).

Thus, the neural system for fear-induced aggression appears to begin in the central and basolateral portions of the amygdala; project down into the anterior, MPO, and ventromedial nuclei of the hypothalamus; and reach into the brain stem at least as far as the PAG (Figure 13.8). The structures are organized into a hierarchy of control in which each emotional response is directly produced by circuits in the spinal cord and brain stem, which are organized into behavior patterns by the PAG. Aggression can be elicited electrically from hypothalamic nuclei (Chi & Flynn, 1971) but only if the PAG is intact (Roberts, 1970). Thus, the hypothalamus issues orders that are interpreted by the PAG and actually carried out by reflex arcs in the brain stem and spinal cord. At the top of this hierarchy is the amygdala, which probably has the function of determining and remembering which type of aggression is most appropriate for each stimulus situation.

Intermale Aggression In the rat, intermale aggression occurs when a strange rat enters the territory of a group of females, subordinate males, and dominant male. The intruder is met by one of the resident males who sniffs him to establish identity as male or female, young or adult. If the new male is an adult, the resident male displays piloerection, threat, and attack (Blanchard et al., 1981). In the threat posture, called **lateral attack**, the resident male places his body at right angles across the front of the stranger, pushing and shoving belligerently. If the stranger then submits by retreating, there may be no further aggression; but if he braces and shoves back, the resident male will whirl to get around his side to position for a bite to the back of the neck. Because one source of this aggression seems to be competition over females, you might expect it to be affected by androgens, the male sex hormones.

In rodents and monkeys, higher androgen levels

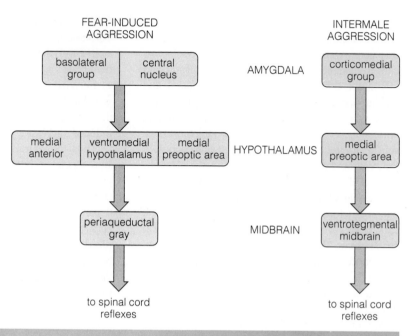

Figure 13.8 Structures that have been shown to be related to fear-induced and intermale aggression. They are both parts of the aversion system but seem to form separate hierarchies within that system. Although the arrows suggest that information flows only from the upper levels of each hierarchy down to the spinal cord, there probably is also a flow up from the brain stem and hypothalamus to the amygdala.

are associated with increased aggression and castration with lower levels (Moyer, 1976). When two castrated male rats were placed together in the same cage for the first time, only the rat with a testosterone implant displayed the typical intermale aggression behaviors (Albert et al., 1988). This androgen effect, however, generalizes beyond defending a territory that might be the scene of mating. It also appears in any situation involving scarce resources. When only a single water spout was available to pairs of thirsty male rats, those with testosterone implants were successful in obtaining access significantly more of the time than did rats without implants (Albert et al., 1987).

A primate study shows that the dominance ranking of male monkeys in a colony correlated with their testosterone levels (Moyer, 1976). A male with high testosterone levels is more likely to rise in the social hierarchy, and one who falls in the hierarchy after several defeats shows a drop in androgen concentration. Thus, the cause and effect appears to work in both directions; high testosterone concentrations enhance the chances of displaying aggression, and unsuccessful aggression reduces testosterone concentration. There is a good adaptive, evolutionary

reason for the effect of experience on levels of testosterone. If you are strongly predisposed by your hormones to fight every time someone gets in your way, but you keep losing fights, then a reduction in hormone concentration increases your chances of living long enough to pass along your genes.

Testosterone masculinizes the brain of the newborn male rat, and one of the sites of its action is the amygdala (see Chapter 12). During their first week of life (the critical period for sexual organization of the brain), male rat pups secrete and use more testosterone than do female pups, and these sex differences show most strongly in the amygdala (Meaney, 1988). When female pups received testosterone implants in the amygdala, they later engaged in more aggressive play–fighting than did normal females (Meaney, 1988). However, one experiment in which the amygdala was lesioned bilaterally showed no change in intermale aggression (Blanchard & Takahashi, 1988). In contrast, Vochteloo and Koolhaas (1987) did find a decrease in intermale aggression following small lesions within the corticomedial group but only in rats that had been given experience at exerting their aggressiveness. In the inexperienced group, the lesioned animals made just as many lateral threats as did the controls. We can see the hierarchical organization of the aversion system again in these data. Amygdalar lesions failed to eliminate the intermale-aggression response of lateral threat, implying that it is organized at a lower level in the hierarchy. What the lesions did appear to disrupt was the memories of how and when to employ the behavior. Thus, lower levels of the aversion system are responsible for innate responses like reflexes, whereas higher levels such as the amygdala focus on learning new behavior patterns.

The lateral threat can also be suppressed to some extent by lesions in the MPOA (Albert et al., 1986). In Chapter 12, we learned that the MPOA contains circuits for the male erection response and mounting behavior. The importance of the MPOA for sexual behaviors suggests that this nucleus might contain androgen-sensitive cells that mediate the effects of male hormones on the aggression system; it has been established that testosterone binds to its receptors more readily in the MPOA than in most other brain areas (cited in Blanchard & Blanchard, 1988). The brain-stem end of the intermale-aggression hierarchy appears to be in the ventrotegmental area (VTA) of the midbrain, an area just ventral to the PAG and next to one of the raphe nuclei. Lesions there abolish intermale aggression but have no effect on other kinds of aggression (Adams, 1986). Thus, intermale aggression appears to be mediated by a system that traces from the corticomedial amygdala to the MPOA to the ventrotegmental midbrain (Figure 13.8).

Predatory Aggression Stimulation of the lateral hypothalamus in cats produces a form of aggression with very little vocalization and none of the back arching, hissing, and other threat behaviors symptomatic of fear-induced and intermale aggression (Hutchinson & Renfrew, 1966). Predatory aggression in the cat starts with a sequence of crouching, slinking, tail twitching, and pouncing. It ends with a blow from the paw and/or a killing bite to the back of the neck. All of this is done with so little outward display of emotionality that it is referred to as **quiet-biting attack**. This contrasts vividly with the attack that can be elicited from stimulation of the medial hypo-

thalamus with its connections into the aversion system. Under medial hypothalamic stimulation, the cat attacks with slashes of the claws rather than bites and will ignore a rat in its cage to attack the experimenter instead (Moyer, 1976). If the experimenter is unavailable, the rat is attacked but with ragelike behavior rather than quiet biting.

Bilateral removal of a cat's amygdalas eliminates predatory aggression. Furthermore, some cells in the amygdala begin to fire when a rat is placed into a cat's cage and continue to fire until the rat is removed (cited in Moyer, 1976). Some rats will attack and kill a mouse introduced into their cage, using a quiet-biting attack similar to that of the cat. This attack is eliminated by lesions to the central nucleus of the amygdala. In the cat, however, the lateral portions of the amygdala have been associated with predatory aggression, so the exact location of the relevant area is still unresolved. To complicate the picture, other parts of the amygdala may inhibit predatory aggression (cited in Moyer, 1976). We can conclude that the amygdala is involved with predatory aggression but cannot say yet exactly which parts are critical.

A part of the role of the hypothalamus in aggression might be to help the amygdala select which pattern of aggression is appropriate to each situation. If the animal is hungry, it needs one set of aggressive responses; if facing a male rival, it needs quite a different pattern. During hunger the lateral hypothalamus becomes active (Chapter 11), but in sex-related conflict (intermale), the MPOA of the hypothalamus is activated. Thus, the hypothalamus can help determine which type of aggression to release.

Another reason for the involvement of the lateral hypothalamus in predatory aggression is that lateral hypothalamus provides connections with the appetitive–reward medial forebrain bundle system, which courses through it. Thus, predatory aggression may be accompanied by feelings of pleasure that help motivate and maintain hunting skills. This pleasure is in sharp contrast to the fear and hostility that appear to be a part of intermale and fear-induced aggression.

From the lateral hypothalamus, the system for predatory aggression extends down to the PAG and a midbrain zone called the VTA, which is associated with reward (Shaikh et al., 1987; Siegel & Pott, 1988)

Figure 13.9 Structures that have been shown to be related to predatory and irritable aggression. Those related to irritable aggression are parts of the aversion system, but the ones related to predatory aggression are linked to the medial forebrain bundle reward system.

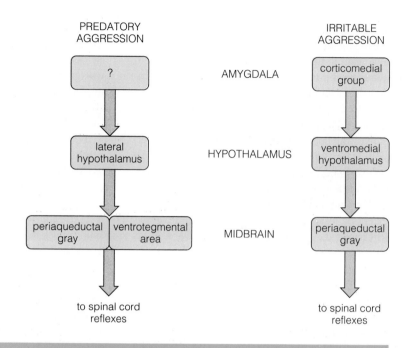

(Figure 13.9). The PAG probably has the task of organizing the motor patterns for the species-typical behaviors such as crouching, stalking, and biting.

The predatory attack may look very simple to a casual observer, but on close analysis, it can be seen to be a relatively complex series of mechanical reflex responses to definite stimuli. In the last few steps of the series, the cat reaches the prey and contacts it with its face. Stimulation to the facial area around the mouth reflexively turns the head so that the jaws are aligned properly for an effective bite. This head turn results in stimulation of a small area immediately surrounding the mouth and a resulting reflexive opening of the jaws. Now the body of the prey is partly inside the mouth of the cat, and the simulation it provides to mouth receptors triggers the final step in the sequence, the jaw closure (Siegel & Pott, 1988).

A primary task for the hypothalamus seems to be to enhance the probability that each of these reflexes in the sequence will be triggered. Normally, if you try to trigger the head-turn reflex by touching a cat's cheek, it will most likely just move away from you.

However, if the cat's lateral hypothalamus is being stimulated during the touch, the reflex will be elicited (McDonnell & Flynn, 1966). The stronger the stimulus to the hypothalamus, the larger the facial area from which the reflex can be elicited (Figure 13.10). Similarly, touching the underside of one forelimb rarely elicits more than moving away from the stimulus. With concurrent hypothalamic stimulation, however, the touch brings a quick, reflex striking motion that serves to catch and hold escaping prey. The size of the receptive field on the forelimb within which this reflex can be elicited expands with increased stimulation to the hypothalamus (Bandler, 1982). So during hunger, the lateral hypothalamus becomes active, thus making available the reflexes employed in predatory attack.

Irritable Aggression This emotional state appears to correspond to human anger and rage. In cats it can be elicited with hypothalamic stimulation. In contrast to fear-induced aggression, there are no attempts to escape prior to attacking, but the same overt emotionality is displayed. If a rat is present

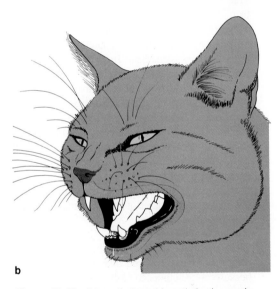

Figure 13.10 When the lateral hypothalamic area is active, as it is during hunger, reflex responses used in predation can be elicited from these zones around the mouth. **(a)** Trigger zone within which touch will elicit head turning toward the tactile stimulus. **(b)** Trigger zone within which a tactile stimulus will elicit the jaw-opening reflex. (Adapted from McDonnell & Flynn, 1966)

when the cat is stimulated, the cat leaps to its feet, arches its back and advances, hissing and snarling. It may stand poised over the rat for a moment, but then any slight movement triggers a ferocious attack with claws. The high-pitched screams of the cat during this attack give the behavior an entirely different appearance from the quiet-biting attack of predatory aggression (Moyer, 1976).

As in all forms of aggression, the amygdala and periventricular system are the important regions. Stimulation within the corticomedial group of the amygdala triggers irritable aggression (Figure 13.11), as do lesions of the central nucleus. This suggests that the fear circuitry of the central nucleus can inhibit an aggressive attack that a stimulus might otherwise elicit through the corticomedial group. These two interconnected areas of the amygdala probably represent the neural mechanism for deciding between an aggressive attack or fearful retreat from any threatening stimulus. Complete ablation of the amygdala disables both the fear and aggression circuits so badly that an amygdalectomized cat can be treated very roughly, even hung by its tail, without displaying fear-induced or irritable aggression (Schreiner & Kling, 1953).

We have some data from humans concerning the involvement of the amygdala in irritable aggression. Robert Heath at Tulane University has performed a unique series of experiments with volunteer patients suffering from epilepsy, brain damage, or psychosis in which electrodes were implanted for long periods of time. EEG recordings through deep electrodes during aversive emotions, rage in particular, revealed a consistent pattern of spindlelike bursts in the hippocampus and nearby medial amygdala. These were high-amplitude waves with a frequency of 12–18 Hz. (See Chapter 5 for an explanation of EEG waves.) If the patient was distracted from the emotional outburst and the conversation redirected to something else, the EEG spindles disappeared (Heath, 1981). If the amygdala or hippocampus was stimulated while the patient was engaged in normal conversation, either fear or anger immediately resulted. The anger was frequently at the level of rage and could quickly lead to the beginnings of violent, even homicidal, behavior before the stimu-

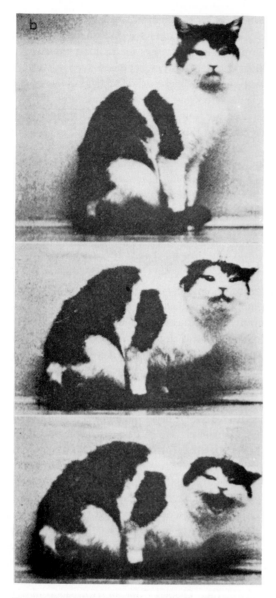

Figure 13.11 Threat behavior elicited by electrical stimulation of the corticomedial region of the amygdala. (From Hunsperger & Bucher, 1967)

cerebellum. In animal studies, this cerebellar activity led to a quieting of the spindling in the hippocampus and amygdala, so Heath decided to try cerebellar stimulation as a form of therapy for cases of violent behavior. A group of violent patients was selected in which standard drug therapy had failed. These people were given cerebellar pacemakers—that is, implanted electrodes sealed under the scalp together with an automatic stimulator pack able to give 5-minute bursts of stimulation to the cerebellum intermittently throughout the day (Heath, 1981). Heath reports that many of his patients were completely relieved of their violent episodes. The following is a sample case report:

This 19-year-old man was selected because he was considered to be the most severely ill patient in our state hospital system at that time. Slightly retarded from birth, he was first hospitalized when he was 13 years old. Following private treatment, he was hospitalized at several state institutions and, finally, at the East Louisiana State Hospital, where he was confined on a ward for severely disturbed patients. He had slashed his wrists and arms on numerous occasions during episodes of violence, and on one occasion, he had attempted to kill his sister. Despite administration of huge quantities of numerous drugs (lithium, imipramine, thioridazine, chlorpromazine, trihexyphenidyl, diazepam, phenobarbital, and anti-Parkinsonism medication), he had to be kept in physical restraints much of the time. All attending physicians had declared it hopeless that he would ever return to his home. A cerebellar pacemaker was implanted in March, 1976. The patient's post-operative course was turbulent because of the necessary withdrawal of large quantities of drugs and because of drug-induced tardive dyskinesia. Before the pacemaker was activated, it was necessary to use large quantities of sedatives and to continue to use restraints. He was so disturbing to the entire ward that other patients petitioned to have him removed.

From the day the pacemaker was activated, one month after its implantation, the patient had no further outbursts of violence. His tardive dyskinesia gradually diminished, and his behavior continued to improve. He became a pleasant and sociable young man. Psychological tests, including intelligence quotient, showed significant improvement, and he was able to cope adequately with the vicissitudes of everyday life. Clinically, the patient had a complete

lus ceased. The moment the current stopped, however, the patient lost the emotional state and could converse about it quite objectively.

During the spindle periods in the EEG, Heath's patients also displayed an increase in firing in the

remission and required no medication. He was enlisted in a vocational rehabilitation program.

The pattern of improvement continued until the Spring of 1978, when he began to be irritable and negativistic, both at home and at school. A check of the external power source—at that time techniques were not available to check the implanted equipment—failed to reveal a problem. But the patient grew more irascible until he viciously assaulted both parents, severely injuring his father. A neighbor who intervened was also severely injured before the police arrived. The patient was subdued with great difficulty and taken to a local hospital, where he injured some of the personnel and destroyed furniture before adequate sedation was achieved. Transferred to the University Hospital, roentgenograms showed a break in the wires between the receiver and the brain electrodes. In June, 1978, the original electrodes were removed and a new system was implanted. Symptoms again promptly remitted, and improvement has continued without further episodes of violence to the present time. (Heath, 1981)

The rage exhibited by Heath's patients probably arose in the corticomedial group of the amygdala that connects with the ventromedial hypothalamus (VMH), another area in which electrical stimulation yields irritable aggression (Moyer, 1976). The periventricular system connects the VMH to the zones within the midbrain that control the species-typical behavior patterns employed in aggression (Figure 13.9). Most of these zones appear to be within the PAG and are probably exactly the same circuits employed by higher brain structures during fear-induced and intermale aggression. In other words, the reflexes that unsheathe the claws of a cat or arch its back may play a part in several different types of aggression. The PAG seems to represent sort of a "toolbox" for use in any emotional state that requires those particular reflex responses as parts of the total behavior pattern.

▪ Stress

Deep within the liver of Robert Brown, a strand of DNA was suddenly altered—a mutation had occurred. The cell lost its normal inhibitions and began to replicate itself, splitting into two daughter cells. They in turn divided, and their daughters divided, and the daughters' daughters divided. The division process accelerated as more and more copies of the abnormal cell copied themselves. A once microscopic colony of cells gone wild had become the seed of a tumor, visible to the naked eye. Cancer had struck Robert Brown.

This process was not new to his body. Many times before in recent years, cells had turned cancerous and tumors had begun, but until now his natural defenses had arrested the criminal growth before it could gain a real foothold. This time the defense response was slower and weaker. During the past year, Robert had been retired from his job (he was forced out); his daughter and her husband had divorced after a bitter legal battle over the children; and his wife had suffered a series of strokes, leaving her helplessly dependent on him for her every need. Three months after the tumor began to grow, Robert Brown was dead of liver cancer.

Our fictitious character, Robert Brown, typifies what we know about the influence of stress on disease processes. Here we examine what stress is and how emotional processes within the brain can have such a profound influence on the physical and chemical functions of the rest of the body.

Nature of Stress

The term **stress** refers to much more than emotional states of the mind. As demonstrated in the pioneering work of Canadian researcher Hans Selye, stress includes a wide variety of life conditions that range from emotional states through disease and injury to simply being too cold or too hot. Poisons are stressors, as are sleep loss, exercise, tumors, prolonged tension, excitement, and getting a traffic ticket. What common denominator links all these widely differing conditions? Selye's brilliant insight was that a stressor of any sort initiates the same set of processes within the body. If these processes continue long enough, they produce a set of conditions called the **general adaptation syndrome (GAS)**.

Symptoms of the GAS include a shrunken thymus gland, enlarged adrenal glands, weight loss, and gastric ulcers (Selye, 1956). The thymus, a gland lying under the collarbone, is a part of the **immune system**, the body's apparatus for resisting diseases and tumors. The reason for its shrinking remains unclear. The **adrenal cortex** (the outside layer of the adrenal gland) secretes the hormones involved in resisting stress, and if the stress is long-term, the cortex enlarges in its efforts to meet the demands on it. Some of the weight loss in prolonged stress occurs because the stress hormones promote the use of muscle tissue for fuel.

The gastric ulcer symptom of the GAS seems to be an accidental side effect of activating the body's stress defenses. The hydrochloric acid secreted by the stomach to digest food can also digest the muscles that form the stomach if it can reach them. The stomach, however, protects itself with a mucosal lining that forms a barrier for the acid. This lining must be constantly maintained by a heavy flow of blood through the tissue. Ulcers can occur within just hours if this blood flow is impeded. If a rat is left for 4 hours in a restraint tube that allows no limb movements, ulcers frequently result (Henke, 1988). The central nucleus of the amygdala becomes quite active during restraint stress. Furthermore, direct electrical stimulation of this nucleus produces ulcers unless the connections to the hypothalamus are cut. Because we know that the amygdala can alter a number of vascular responses controlled by the hypothalamus by way of the SNS, one hypothesis for ulcer formation is that restraint stress arouses the fear circuitry in the central nucleus that then commands a state of emergency arousal (Henke, 1988). During such arousal, the SNS shifts blood from the digestive tract to the muscles and brain, thus leaving the stomach mucosa with an inadequate supply. In the short term, this does no damage; over hours of continuous stress, however, the acid eats through the lining and attacks the underlying muscle of the stomach to create an ulcer.

In reacting to a prolonged stress, your body goes through three stages, claims Selye: an **alarm reaction** lasting only a few hours during which the stress hormones are mobilized; a stage of **resistance**, which can go on for days or weeks, that represents full mobilization; and **exhaustion** in which defenses have been used up. If the stress continues after the stage of exhaustion has been reached, death results. This apparently occurs only rarely in a society with modern medical care. A possible example would be death from "exposure" among airplane crash victims stranded at sea or in the mountains.

During the stage of resistance, continuing stress can affect your ability to cope with the physical causes of disease such as bacteria, virus, and tumors. Thomas Holmes, a psychiatrist at the University of Washington, has used this knowledge to help in predicting the onset of serious illnesses. His *Life Schedule of Recent Events* (Holmes & Rahe, 1967) assigns a point value to life events that involve some amount of stress (Table 13.1). To find your score, check each event on the list that you have experienced within the last year and then add up all the points. A score of 300 or more means that you run a strong risk of developing some serious illness—such as heart or vascular problems, arthritis, or cancer—within the next 2 years. This is a very crude predictor, of course, and thus would falsely predict illness for a number of people who will stay healthy, but the scale has enough predictive validity that it is widely used in research on psychosomatic illness.

Psychosomatic Illness

Physicians are becoming more and more aware that the onset of disease can be strongly influenced by psychological variables, and this awareness has led to the idea of psychosomatic illness. The term *psychosomatic* has no standard definition yet, but most psychologists would agree that **psychosomatic disorders** are conditions of organic damage stemming in part from emotional problems. This definitely excludes the common everyday misuse of the term that confuses psychosomatic illness with the emotional disorders of hypochondria and conversion reaction, neither of which involve organic damage. Thus, a person whose emotional problems have been converted into the physical symptom of blindness without any organic damage to the visual system is suffering from the disorder called conversion reaction, not from a psychosomatic disorder. On the other hand, diseases such as gastric ulcer that involve serious organic problems (an untreated, bleeding

Table 13.1   The Holmes Life Scale of Recent Events

Life Events	Value	Life Events	Value
Death of spouse	100	In-law troubles	29
Divorce	73	Outstanding personal achievement	28
Marital separation	65	Wife starts or stops work outside home	26
Jail term	63	Begin or end school	26
Death of close family member	63	Change living conditions	25
Personal injury or illness	53	Revised personal habit	24
Marriage	50	Trouble with boss	23
Fired at work	47	Change in work hours or conditions	20
Marital reconciliation	45	Change in residence	20
Retirement	45	Change in schools	20
Change in health of family member	44	Change in recreation	19
Pregnancy	40	Change in church activities	19
Sex difficulties	39	Change in social activities	18
Business readjustment	39	Change in sleeping habits	16
Change in financial state	38	Change in number of family get-togethers	15
Death of close friend	37	Change in eating habits	15
Change line of work	36	Vacation	13
Change in number of arguments with spouse	35	Christmas	12
Foreclosure of mortgage	30	Minor violations of the law	11

From Holmes & Rahe, 1967.

gastric ulcer can result in death) often appear to be caused largely by emotional problems. Discoveries about stress in the last 30 years seem to point to the idea of **multiple causation** for almost all diseases. That is, an emotional cause must act together with a physical cause to produce the illness. Suppose that two people are exposed equally to the same virus, but only one of them shows signs of infection. The difference between the two might be a genetic factor or their diet plus how much emotional stress they were under. Four or five physical factors might interact with stress to determine whether you actually catch a cold to which you are exposed and, if you do, how bad the symptoms will be. This is the idea of multiple causation. There probably is no such thing as a purely psychosomatic disease, because that would be a disease with a single cause, but it is likely that almost all diseases have a psychosomatic component.

Effect of Emotions on Body Chemistry

The heart of your nervous system's stress-response mechanism lies in the hypothalamus, that central regulator of body chemistry. Physical stressors like overheating and exercise signal their presence to the hypothalamus through the sensory system and bloodborne chemicals. Emotional stress acts through the limbic system, which has strong connections with the hypothalamus. The hypothalamus monitors the sensory systems, the bloodstream, and the output of the limbic system and is apparently set to trigger a stress response when it detects emotional or physical stressors. Thus, both physical stress in the body and emotional stress in the limbic system have their effects by way of the hypothalamus, and both elicit the same response.

But how could the hypothalamus, a few cubic centimeters of gray matter at the base of your brain, have anything to do with the growth of a deadly tumor in your liver? How could grief and worry possibly have anything to do with catching a viral infection? A few decades ago, the suggestion of such associations would have seemed absurd or quackish. Over the last 20 years, however, we have learned that the hypothalamus involves itself in nearly every aspect of body chemistry. The functioning of every internal organ, the entire physiology of the body, lies open to the modulating commands from this tiny link between our emotions and our health. It derives its tremendous influence from two major connections with the rest of the body: the SNS route that comes into play during emotions and a route through the pituitary gland that reacts during emotional or physical stress.

During any kind of stress, the **anterior pituitary** secretes the hormone **adrenocorticotropic hormone (ACTH)** (uh-DREEN-oh-KORT-ik-oh-TRO-pick). ACTH travels by way of the bloodstream to the adrenal cortex where it stimulates the release of hormones called **glucocorticoids** (GLUE-ko-KORT-ik-oids). The glucocorticoids circulate in the blood to all body cells where they have a number of effects

on cell chemistry important to stress resistance. This pituitary–adrenal cortex response is the major mechanism of Selye's stage of resistance. It can be triggered by as little as 20 minutes of treadmill exercise done at 85 percent maximum effort (Funder, 1987).

The pituitary–adrenal cortex response is under the control of various parts of the body under different circumstances, but the example we understand the best involves the **paraventricular nucleus (PVN)** of the hypothalamus (Reisine et al., 1986). PVN is strongly connected to the aversion system by way of VMH. So during anxiety or aggression, certain cells in PVN are stimulated to secrete a hormone called **corticotropin-releasing factor (CRF)**, which stimulates the anterior pituitary to release ACTH. Figure 13.12 summarizes the path by which emotional stress affects the body using the ACTH–adrenal cortex mechanism. Physical stressors, by contrast, may

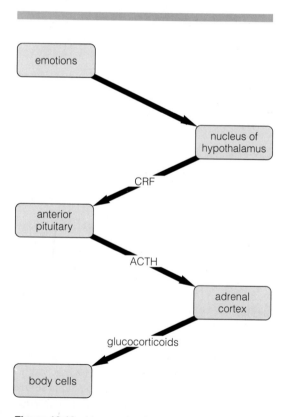

Figure 13.12 Hormonal pathway controlling the body's reaction to stress.

release ACTH directly by means of cholecystokinin or some other chemical circulating in the blood, thus bypassing the route through PVN (Reisine et al., 1986).

Glucocorticoids secreted during stress have a number of beneficial effects that include increasing the tone of the muscles in heart and blood vessels; releasing more nutrients into the blood; and decreasing inflammation and inhibiting the metabolically costly production of new proteins, including those used by the immune system (Sapolsky & Pulsinelli, 1985). This combination is appropriate for emergency situations. One can afford to break down proteins to use as fuel and secrete high levels of insulin to ensure that the extra nutrients enter the cells as long as these processes are reversed after a short while. So for relatively short-duration stresses such as a battle or several days of extreme physical effort or losing several nights' sleep, these changes do more good than harm. However, if the stress continues chronically week after week, as is frequently the case with emotional stressors, the harm may outweigh the benefits. The most serious problem arises in connection with the immune system.

Stress and the Immune System

Your body is a zoo. It literally swarms with microorganisms that share your food, set up housekeeping in your intestines, gobble up your skin secretions, and even take over the RNA machinery of your cells to make copies of themselves. Every breath you draw may be inviting in thousands of airborne virus particles. Each time you lick your finger, the bacteria that you picked up from a door handle or railing swim into their new home and start to multiply in the "leftovers" from your last meal. Fungus spores settle on your skin and sprout roots that spread rapidly between your cells. Amoebas, mycoplasms, and parasites of every description revel in your comfortable climate and good growing conditions.

Without the immune system, our body's life processes would soon be overwhelmed by these invaders and suffer a fatal breakdown. Essentially, you are always infected, but the immune system usually kills off most of these unwanted organisms as fast as they appear. This conflict goes on beneath your level of awareness. If an infection gets a rapid start and builds a fairly large population of organisms before it is brought under control, you may suffer a few days of feeling tired and "out-of-sorts" without actually deciding to call it an illness. It is only when the immune system reacts so slowly that the microorganism flourishes unchecked for hours or days that you develop obvious disease symptoms. Because it is possible for you to be infected without being "sick," let's refer to the condition with obvious symptoms as a **clinical level infection** and any weaker infection as a **subclinical infection**.

How the Immune System Combats Disease The body's first task in rooting out disease organisms is to identify them as something that is not a part of the body—something foreign. How does the body tell a bacterium from one of its own cells or know that a virus particle is foreign? The answer lies in the individualized structure of the proteins embedded in the surfaces of virus particles and microorganisms. For example, all herpes simplex type 2 virus particles have a particular protein in their outer jacket that is different from any you have in your cells. If your immune system can recognize that protein, it can kill anything bearing that label and spare all the cells around it that belong to you.

Any foreign protein that can act as a label is called an **antigen** (ANT-uh-jen). These proteins have distinctive shapes that can act as receptor sites for any other protein shaped to fit. For every antigen, your body must make a corresponding recognition protein shaped so that it can bind to the antigen and tag it for destruction. These recognition proteins are called **antibodies**. Antigens, then, bear the same resemblance to antibodies that receptor sites do to neurotransmitters. Antibodies are manufactured in the bone marrow and thymus and circulate in the blood and lymph. Once a bacterium or virus is tagged with an antibody, it can be eaten by one of the millions of **leucocytes** (LOO-ko-sights) that swarm through the body continually scavenging dead or tagged tissue. Some leucocytes, called **lymphocytes** (LIMF-oh-sights), are made with antibodies embedded in their cell membrane, and each lymphocyte is specialized for identifying and destroying anything bearing one specific antigen.

Production of any particular antibody is triggered by the arrival of an organism bearing the matching antigen and continues until the population of the organism has reached a very low level. Thereafter, antibodies persist in the blood for some amount of time (which varies with different diseases). If the body is reinvaded by the same organism, the immune system is ready with the appropriate antibody and can stifle the infection before it can reach clinical level. Thus, if you already have antibodies for some infective organism, you are said to have **immunity** to the disease. Vaccination involves exposing you to antigens prepared in such a way that you will start manufacturing antibodies without becoming infected.

It is the lymphocytes of the immune system that are of particular interest to stress researchers. Will these cells be fully available and active when you need them, or might your life-style hamper them in their battle against infecting microorganisms? As midterm exams approach and all those papers and projects begin to come due, will your infections stay at a subclinical level, or will they develop into full-blown clinical level diseases?

Emotional Stress and Infection Inject a laboratory mouse with a small dose of Coxsackie B virus—the one responsible for many of your colds—and then measure the symptoms the mouse exhibits as it fights off the disease. Next, take another mouse and teach it a shock-avoidance response before the Coxsackie B injection. Learning to avoid shock involves getting shocked a number of times and experiencing considerable fear. The shocked mouse develops worse cold symptoms than does the unshocked control mouse (Sklar & Anisman, 1981). This result is readily understandable. The immune system must synthesize great quantities of protein during an infection. Antibodies are protein, as are many other parts of leucocytes. Yet glucocorticoids—the stress hormones of the adrenal cortex—suppress protein formation and inhibit the working of the immune system.

Taking this type of research out of the laboratory, Jacobs and colleagues (1969) randomly selected a sample of male college students who had suffered a respiratory infection and compared them to a group of students who had not been sick for a year. Questionnaire data show that during the preceding year the sick students had experienced a significantly greater number of events involving personal failure or some crisis of self-esteem. This suggests that the emotional stress from personal problems can create susceptibility to disease and supports the laboratory studies.

The herpes virus that produces cold sores has a partial defense against the human immune system. For some reason, the body can never quite rid itself of herpes virus after the initial infection, so a clinical level infection recurs from time to time and antibodies are always present in the blood whether or not the person has any clinical symptoms. Katcher and colleagues (1973) made use of these facts to study the effects of stress on the frequency of herpes reinfections. Students entering nursing school were given a questionnaire to find out how typically happy or unhappy they felt. They were also given a blood test for presence or absence of antibodies for herpes simplex virus. Students with antibodies were then asked how frequently their symptoms recurred. Some students might have an attack only once a year, whereas for others the disease might reappear as frequently as once a month. The questionnaire showed that the less happy students experienced more frequent recurrences of the clinical symptoms. One interpretation of this result is that the unhappiness represented stress that diminished the capability of the immune system to keep the disease in check.

The same research tactic was used in a study of West Point cadets who were given blood tests to detect antibodies for Epstein–Barr virus, the infective agent in mononucleosis (Kasl et al., 1979). About two thirds of the entering cadets already showed antibodies for Epstein–Barr, indicating that they had already had the disease at some time and had acquired some immunity. The remaining one third were fully susceptible. Each year thereafter, about one fifth of the susceptible students began showing antibodies for mononucleosis, but only about one quarter of these actually developed clinical infections. (Those with subclinical infections probably just had several weeks during the semester when they felt really lousy without knowing why.) Why could some students hold the disease down to the subclinical level while others gave in to it completely? Records and questionnaire data from the preceding months showed that the students experiencing clinical symptoms had been making poorer grades and/or were among those most highly motivated toward a military career. Either situation would likely be a strong emotional stressor in an atmosphere as intense as West Point. Again, the best explanation of these data is that limbic arousal of PVN triggered release of ACTH and glucocorticoids with resulting suppression of antibody and leucocyte production—a process known as **immunosuppression.**

Because one of civilization's most stressful circumstances is warfare, the military has conducted some research on immunosuppression in simulated battle conditions. Subjects in one such study (Palmblad et al., 1976) had to be continually alert for enemy tanks, which they "destroyed" with electronic rifles. Once this ultimate in arcade games began, though, it went on nonstop for 77 hours (more than 3 days) during which the subjects were bombarded continually with recorded battle sounds played at high volume. High levels of glucocorticoids, epinephrine, and norepinephrine verified that the mock battle was a powerful stressor. Periodic blood samples showed that leucocytes became more and more impaired in their ability to find and destroy foreign protein.

Research of this sort points strongly to the conclusion that medical treatment by itself is a weak approach to disease control. It appears that help in solving and eliminating emotional problems could do more toward minimizing the effects of the common cold than anything the medical community has come up with yet.

Emotional Stress and Cancer Studies comparing cancer patients with healthy controls reveal that the former had experienced more stressful incidents in the year or two preceding the onset of the cancer symptoms (Sklar & Anisman, 1981). Many of the cancer victims had recently lost some important emotional relationship; that is, more of them were newly widowed, divorced, or separated. The people with the best statistical chance of getting cancer apparently are those who react to such a loss with feelings of hopelessness and inability to cope.

Unfortunately, human studies of this sort are always very poor experiments because the results can usually be explained in a number of different ways. For example, tumors may grow in the body for months before they begin to create the symptoms that signal their presence. Perhaps the feelings of hopelessness and inability to cope were emotional exaggerations of normal grief brought about by chemical alterations from the growing tumor or the body's reaction to it. In other words, we don't know from these studies whether stress caused the cancer or cancer caused the stress. Clear-cut experiments simply cannot ethically be done with humans. To get at cause and effect, we must turn to laboratory experiments on animals.

Literally hundreds of experiments exploring the link between stress and cancer have been done on mice. A study by Riley (1981) is typical. Two groups of mice were implanted with bits of lymphosarcoma tumors and observed daily to see whether these cancer tissues would grow in the new host. When a tumor is very small, before it has attracted blood vessels to help it grow, it is more vulnerable to attack from the immune system. If the lymphocytes can recognize it as unnatural protein, they will destroy the cancer cells. If the cells are destroyed faster than they can multiply, the tumor gradually dwindles and disappears. The body has cured itself. But, of course, this cure depends on plenty of highly active lymphocytes.

After Riley's mice had received the tumor implant, the experimental group was taken to an apparatus designed especially to stress mice, a high-walled box whose floor is a turntable. In the stress box, they were rotated continuously for 2 or 3 days. Both the experimental and control groups showed measurable tumor growth over the next 10 or 15 days, but then the tumors in the control mice began to shrink. Apparently, their immune systems had begun to manufacture lymphocytes with antibodies that fit the antigen on the cancer cells. While most of the control group grew healthier by the day, the experimental group grew closer to death as their tumors thrived, enlarged, and spread to every vital organ.

Was it really the stress that killed these mice? Our theory says that they were unable to combat the cancer because their lymphocytes were suppressed by glucocorticoids, secreted when the adrenal cortex received an ACTH signal from the pituitary. If this process really caused the failure of the immune defense, then couldn't the same effect be achieved without ever stressing the experimental group? Couldn't immunosuppression be produced just by injecting ACTH? The answer turned out to be yes (Riley, 1981), and the theory was supported. So much evidence of this sort has accumulated that researchers have now changed their focus to the details of how the stress system interacts with the immune system.

Factors That Interact with Stress Two identical stressors may produce quite different levels of immunosuppression, depending on factors such as timing, duration, degree of social–emotional content, and the ability of the organism to cope with the stress.

The timing of the stress strongly influences the outcome. If mice are first stressed and then inoculated with bacteria, they are much more likely to show immunosuppression than if they are first inoculated and then 2 days later given the stress (Sklar & Anisman, 1981). Apparently, during the 2 days, the immune system has time to develop antibodies to the virus and produce enough lymphocytes to balance the immunosuppression from the stress.

The duration of the stressor is also important. **Acute stress** comes and goes in a relatively short time. For a human, this could be an emotional argument with a fiancé or involvement in an automobile accident without suffering injury. **Chronic stress** continues over days, weeks, or even years. A married couple on the brink of divorce but still living together or a married person caring for a spouse who is slowly dying would be in chronic stress situations. The "weekend athlete" who exercises at a high level only 1 or 2 days a week is repeatedly subjecting himself to acute stress, whereas someone who exercises every day is under chronic stress. For a lab animal in a research study, acute stress might be a single session of shock-avoidance training, whereas

chronic stress might be daily shock sessions for several weeks. In general, the longer a stress lasts, the greater immunosuppression. A single disagreement with your boss will probably activate your pituitary–adrenal cortex system only briefly, but constant friction constitutes chronic stress and most likely induces dangerous immunosuppression. There is, however, a very important exception to this rule of thumb.

Our stress-response mechanism is capable of **adaptation** to continuing stressors. ACTH and glucocorticoid levels often return toward normal after a number of days or weeks of daily exposures to the stressor (Monjan & Collector, 1977). This means that daily exercises are not likely to be stressful after the first week or so. Exercising only once or twice a week, however, does not permit adaptation and probably yields strong immunosuppression even when it is undertaken every week for months. The rule is that a series of acute stressors cannot produce adaptation, whereas chronic stressors sometimes can. We have to qualify the rule about chronic stressors because adaptation does not occur to all types of chronic stress. Physical stressors such as cold, mild electric shock, and exercise permit adaptation, whereas many instances of social–emotional stress apparently do not. Subjecting rats to overcrowding, social isolation, and fear suppresses immune function as long as the stress lasts (Sklar & Anisman, 1981). Thus, repeated occasional reprimands from your supervisor might produce less immunosuppression than daily disagreements with that person. One generally doesn't adapt to the latter type of stress even though it is chronic.

The final factor influencing the effects of stress is the degree to which the organism feels able to cope with the situation. In a typical experiment on stress coping, pairs of rats were trained on a shock-avoidance task (Weiss, 1971). In each "yoked" pair, both rats received each shock delivered, but one rat (the experimental subject) was able to stop the shock from occurring by making the avoidance response to the shock-warning signal. Having the rats thus "yoked" ensures that the control subject receives exactly the same number of shocks as does the experimental subject and at precisely the same time. The only difference between experimental and control rats, then, was that the experimentals had an opportunity to learn a coping response to the shock, while the controls were helpless. As training progressed, the experimental subjects generated significantly lower glucocorticoid levels than did the helpless controls.

Lower glucocorticoid levels should mean that the immune system is better able to combat infections and tumors, but does this improved health actually occur? Sklar and Anisman (1979) implanted tumor tissue into healthy mice and 24 hours later subjected them to 60 shock trials separated by 1-minute intervals. Mice in the "coping" group were allowed to run to a safe compartment to escape the shocks, but the yoked controls were able to make no coping response and received shock at any time their yoked mates did. Despite experiencing no more shock than did the coping mice, the controls developed significantly larger tumors and had a higher mortality. In a similar study, only 27 percent of the rats receiving inescapable shock were able to reject their implanted tumors, whereas 63 percent of those allowed a coping response survived the cancer (Visintainer et al., 1982). These findings suggest that human disease control might be greatly improved by offering more people training in stress-coping techniques.

Are Humans Poorly Designed for Modern Civilization?

It is now very well established that stress increases glucocorticoids that under many conditions suppress the immune system and promote disease. But why would the body have evolved such a seemingly self-destructive response to stress? Perhaps a hypothetical answer can be drawn from what we have already learned about adaptation to stress.

Consider that our stress-resistance mechanism (the GAS) must have come into existence millions of years ago when the most typical stress situations were those of extreme cold, battle, physical injury, or prolonged physical exertion. Such stressors are usually acute rather than chronic. The sacrifice of some immune capability to gain increased strength and endurance is a good trade-off for a short while. Civilization, however, has found many ways to mini-mize acute physical stressors while accidentally creating more and more chronic emotional stress situations. Nowadays typical sources of stress are job-related deadlines, competition for job security, social isolation, and loss of personal relationships that provide emotional support. Primitive humans lived in extended families in which division of labor was determined by tradition (reducing job competition) and emotional support did not depend on one or two people (spouse or parents). One suspects that deadlines were infrequent events in most lives. These modern, emotional sources of stress, of course, seem not to yield to adaptation and can presumably induce chronic immunosuppression. If this hypothesis has any validity, the health of the human race may be deteriorating over the decades despite the minimizing of many physical risks and the rise of modern medicine.

Stress Chemistry and Emotions

How aggressive you feel or how depressed you are may depend to some extent on how much you have been stressed lately. The stress hormones, ACTH and the glucocorticoids, have direct and indirect effects on the emotional circuitry in your brain.

In an animal-dominance hierarchy, the "underdogs," who are subject to the aggressive whims of the more dominant animals, have higher levels of glucocorticoids (Schuhr, 1987) and ACTH, suggestive of greater stress. Glucocorticoids were elicited by ACTH, which not only affects the adrenal cortex but also the brain, where it apparently has a hand in reducing the secretion of the aggression-inducing androgens from the testes and adrenal cortex. As we saw earlier, being defeated in an aggressive competition situation tends to reduce the circulating testosterone, thus ensuring that aggressive emotions are less likely to determine future behavior. On the other hand, if you give male mice a drug that blocks ACTH, there will be an increase in the number of fights (Brain et al., 1971). Apparently, evolution has adjusted males to maximize their chances of obtaining food and procreation by predisposing them to aggression in competitive situations, but not to the extent of getting themselves killed because of it—a perfect blend of the emotional with the practical, but all determined at the chemical level of function. (How many of our human decisions are really the result of our rational thought processes, and how many times are we just using those thoughts to rationalize what has already been determined chemically?)

Other forms of stress have the same effect. An animal suffering from a serious injury tends to avoid aggressive confrontations, and this avoidance may be the result of stress hormones. If ACTH lowers the levels of androgen in the injured animal, then ACTH secretion helps to prevent aggression and further injury. In humans this effect can be seen as a decrease in androgens following surgery (which to the body is just another form of injury) (Matsumoto et al., 1970). ACTH also appears to inhibit aggression more directly by stimulating the prefrontal cortex and hippocampus, both of which are parts of the anxiety system of the brain (cited in Blanchard & Blanchard, 1988). Anxiety inhibits aggression.

Stress from being defeated also elicits secretion of endogenous opioids, chemicals used by the pain-suppression system (see Chapter 8). After a severe defeat, a rat simply stands still in the face of further attack and takes the punishment, squealing when approached but making no defensive movements (cited in Blanchard & Blanchard, 1988). This freezing may be defensive in that the lack of motion may reduce the probability of being attacked. In this condition, the opioids ensure the animal of significantly reduced ability to perceive pain.

Defeat also increases the density of benzodiazepine receptors in the anxiety system of the brain (Miller et al., 1987), which suggests that the GABA-secreting neurons are able to inhibit that system more effectively at such a time. Over the short term, this anxiety reduction is probably beneficial, but if stress continues chronically, it may be overdone. A breakdown product of glucocorticoids, **THDOC** ($3\alpha,5\alpha$-tetrahydrodeoxycorticosterone), mimics a barbiturate drug by binding with $GABA_A$ receptors to enhance inhibition (Barnes, 1986b). This stress chemical may be the origin of that groggy, depressed feeling you get when you have an infection. Long-term emotional stress may induce a state of psychiatric depression through the buildup of THDOC in the blood, but this hypothesis hangs on the untested question of whether the chemical can reach the brain through the blood–brain barrier.

We see then that a brain under stress not only alters the chemistry of the body it controls but also, indirectly, its own function.

■ Summary

1. Three dimensions appear to underlie all emotions: arousal, approach–avoidance, and appetitiveness–aversiveness. A key brain structure for the arousal dimension is the midbrain reticular formation (MBRF); for approach–avoidance, the amygdala; for appetitiveness, the medial forebrain bundle (MFB) system; and for aversiveness, the periventricular system.

2. Anxiety and aggression originate in the circuitry of the brain's aversion system, a set of interconnected structures including orbitofrontal cortex, amygdala, hypothalamus, and certain midbrain regions.

3. The anxiety–fear portion of the aversion system starts in the orbitofrontal cortex and continues through central and basolateral amygdala through the medial hypothalamus to the periaqueductal gray (PAG) of the midbrain. Species-typical behavior patterns used in fear situations appear to be organized in the PAG. Another route from the amygdala connects through the HACER to the SNS to provide the cardiovascular responses of the fear state. Prefrontal lobotomy performed to relieve anxiety involves cutting the fibers connecting the prefrontal and orbitofrontal cortex to the amygdala and hypothalamus. Bilateral removal of the amygdalas tames wild animals.

4. Anxiolytic drugs (those that relieve anxiety) include the barbiturates and the benzodiazepines. Barbiturates seem to produce their depressive effect on the nervous system by interfering with sodium channels. Benzodiazepines potentiate the inhibition induced by GABAergic neurons, apparently by preventing GABA-modulin from blocking GABA receptor sites. These sites may be on serotonergic neurons in the raphe nuclei of the brain stem.

5. Fear-induced aggression occurs when escape from an aversive stimulus is hindered. It depends on the central–basolateral amygdala, medial areas of the hypothalamus, and the PAG. Intermale aggression occurs when males compete for mating territory or other scarce resources. It is potentiated by testosterone, and levels of this hormone are lowered in the loser of an aggressive competition. The structures involved are the corticomedial amygdala, MPOA, and ventrotegmental midbrain.

6. Predatory aggression uses a sequence of species-typical responses, called the quiet-biting attack, which usually ends in a bite to the back of the neck. The neural system starts in the amygdala, continues caudally through the lateral hypothalamus, and ends in the PAG and ventrotegmental area (VTA) of the midbrain. Irritable aggression probably corresponds to human anger and rage. It appears to originate in the corticomedial amygdala, and excesses of violence in humans may be correlated with aberrant activity in this nuclear group. The rest of the system for irritable aggression includes the ventromedial hypothalamus and the PAG.

7. Selye discovered that any stressor of any type triggers the same set of responses in the body. He called these symptoms the general adaptation syndrome (GAS). In resisting stressors, the body goes through three stages: the alarm reaction, resistance, and exhaustion.

8. Stress appears to increase the susceptibility to diseases. It is proposed that most diseases can have a "psychosomatic" component. That is, the disease is caused by some physical agent acting together with stress.

9. Emotional stress begins with neural activity within the limbic system, which influences the hypothalamus. The paraventricular nucleus (PVN) of the hypothalamus reacts by secreting CRF, a hormone that triggers the release of ACTH from the anterior pituitary. ACTH is a hormone that induces the adrenal cortex to release their hormones, the glucocorticoids. Every cell of the body is affected by glucocorticoids as they reduce inflammation, increase available glucose, start the breakdown of body proteins, and suppress the immune system.

10. To control viruses, bacteria, and other parasites, the immune system creates antibodies to bind with antigens on each parasite's surface. It can also "tag" cancer cells with antibodies. Antibody-tagged parasites or cancer cells can be destroyed by cells called lymphocytes. Glucocorticoids hinder the action of lymphocytes, thus producing immunosuppression. The increased susceptibility to infections and cancer during prolonged stress is the result of immunosuppression.

11. Physical and emotional stressors differ in that adaptation can occur to chronic physical stressors but not to chronic emotional stress. The best defense against an emotional stressor is to learn some coping response that will lower the stress level.

12. The stress of defeat in an aggressive interaction stimulates the secretion of ACTH, which then circulates to the brain. Thus, it may be ACTH that lowers testosterone output by inhibiting the release of gonadotropin from the hypothalamus. Defeat also increases the secretion of opioid transmitters in the pain-suppression system and speeds the production of benzodiazepine receptors, thus instilling a quieting inhibition that may develop into depression.

Glossary

acute stress The type of stress that comes and goes in a relatively short time. (538)

adaptation The return of ACTH and glucocorticoid levels toward normal after a number of days or weeks of daily exposures to the stressor. (538)

adrenal cortex The outside layer of the adrenal gland. (532)

adrenocorticotropic hormone (ACTH) A hormone of the anterior pituitary that stimulates glucocorticoid secretion from the adrenal cortexes. (534)

alarm reaction Initial stress response of a few hours during which the stress hormones are mobilized. (532)

amygdala A cluster of nuclei located just beneath the cortex near the tip of the temporal lobe; part of the limbic system involved in approach–avoidance decisions. (518)

anterior pituitary The part of the "master" gland that secretes, among other hormones, ACTH. (534)

antibody Proteins created by the body's immune system to recognize foreign proteins. (535)

antigen Any protein for which an antibody can be formed. (535)

anxiolytic drugs Drugs that relieve anxiety. (522)

appetitive Something good, desirable; something you have an appetite for. (515)

approach–avoidance tendency One aspect of emotion; a motivation to move toward some stimuli and away from others. (515)

aversion system A set of nuclei and tracts that (hypothetically) decide whether or not a particular stimulus is undesirable (aversive) and whether it should be avoided (fear or disgust) or attacked (aggression); includes the paraventricular system. (517)

aversive Bad, undesirable, unwanted. (515)

barbiturates A class of sedative drugs derived from barbituric acid. (522)

basolateral nuclear group A set of amygdalar nuclei important for fear and aggression. (518)

benzodiazepines A class of anxiolytic drugs frequently called "tranquilizers." (523)

cardiovascular responses Heart-rate and blood-vessel changes. (520)

central nucleus A nucleus of the amygdala important to choosing escape and avoidance behavior or fear-induced aggression. (518)

chlordiazepoxide A benzodiazepine. (523)

chronic stress Stress that continues over days, weeks, or even years. (538)

clinical level infection An infection that has progressed far enough to have obvious disease symptoms. (535)

corticomedial nuclear group A set of amygdalar nuclei important to choosing aggressive approach behavior. (518)

corticotropin-releasing factor (CRF) A hypothalamic hormone secreted by PVN that stimulates the secretion of ACTH from the anterior pituitary. (534)

diazepam A benzodiazepine. (523)

exhaustion The final stage of the stress response in which defenses are used up and death ensues. (532)

fear-induced aggression The behaviors of a frightened animal that is trying to escape but is trapped. (524)

GABA-modulin A chemical that can prevent GABA from occupying GABA$_A$ receptor sites. (523)

general adaptation syndrome (GAS) A set of symptoms consisting of shrunken thymus gland, enlarged adrenal glands, weight loss, and gastric ulcers. (531)

glucocorticoids A set of adrenal cortex hormones that have numerous effects throughout the body related to stress resistance. (534)

HACER Hypothalamic area for conditioned emotional responses. (520)

immune system The body's apparatus for resisting diseases and tumors. (532)

immunity A condition in which antibodies for a disease have already been acquired in sufficient quantities to prevent a clinical level infection. (536)

immunosuppression Any condition that inhibits the immune system. (537)

instrumental aggression Attack behavior, associated with a particular stimulus, that has been reinforced previously in the presence of that stimulus. (524)

intermale aggression The responses of a resident male rat to a male intruder rat. (524)

irritable aggression Attack responses elicited by frustration, pain, or deprivation. (524)

lateral attack A form of aggression that occurs when a resident male places his body at right angles across the front of a male intruder, pushing and shoving belligerently. (525)

leucocyte Immune system cell found in the blood and lymph. (535)

level of arousal How awake, excited, or bored you are; one aspect of emotion. (515)

lymphocyte A type of leucocyte found in the lymph; many carry antibodies and are phagocytic. (535)

maternal aggression Attack responses displayed by a mother in the nesting area. (524)

medial forebrain bundle A large bundle of tracts connecting parts of the brain stem with limbic system and striatum; contains parts of the reinforcement system. (515)

medial hypothalamus An area just medial to HACER and probably overlapping it; apparently an organizer of striate muscle fear behaviors, especially escape responses. (521)

multiple causation The principle that a disease usually is caused by two factors working concurrently; especially a physical factor interacting with a stressor. (533)

orbitofrontal cortex Region of frontal cortex anterior, medial, and ventral to the prefrontal areas (see Chapter 3 for figure). (518)

paraventricular nucleus (PVN) The part of the hypothalamus that secretes CRF. (534)

periaqueductal gray (PAG) A midbrain area that probably contains the motor circuits for many species typical behavior patterns. (521)

periventricular system A collection of tracts and nuclei lying along the midline of the brain from the brain stem through the hypothalamus; may be the system responsible for the perception of aversiveness. (515)

piloerection A reflexive fluffing up of the fur. (525)

predatory aggression The set of responses that a mammal uses to kill prey for food. (524)

prefrontal lobotomy Cutting the connections from the prefrontal and/or orbitofrontal cortex to the limbic system and diencephalon. (517)

psychosomatic disorders Conditions of organic damage stemming in part from emotional problems. (532)

quiet-biting attack A part of predatory aggression; involves a killing bite to the back of the neck unaccompanied by emotional responses. (527)

resistance The full mobilization stage of the stress response, which can go on for days or weeks. (532)

reticular formation A column of gray matter extending up through the center of the brain stem; its cells send nonspecific facilitation and inhibition to the cortex and spinal cord. (515)

satellite receptors Receptor sites that are attached to and can modulate other receptors; for example, satellite receptors that bind GABA-modulin can block the $GABA_A$ receptor from binding GABA. (523)

sex-related aggression Biting, snarling, and other responses usually associated with attack that occur between male and female as a normal part of the mating process. (524)

stress A somewhat ambiguous term that is used both for a class of stimuli (more properly called "stressors") and the emotional–physiological response to stimuli of that class. (531)

subclinical infection An infection that has not yet progressed far enough to have obvious disease symptoms. (535)

THDOC A breakdown product of glucocorticoids that may create a groggy, depressed condition; $3\alpha,5\alpha$-tetrahydrodeoxycorticosterone. (540)

Learning

T he concept of learning is man-made. It does not refer to one, single, particular capacity we possess but rather to a group of related abilities, all of which have one thing in common. When an organism undergoes an experience that changes the way it typically responds to its environment, we say that "learning" has occurred. It is quite unlikely that the same sort of change occurring at the same place in the nervous system underlies all the different ways in which we are capable of altering our behavior through experience. Let's begin by listing some of these ways.

■ Types of Learning

Starting with the simplest forms, types of learning include habituation, sensitization, classical conditioning, instrumental conditioning, perceptual learning, motor learning, and cognitive and verbal learning. This is not an exhaustive list agreed on by all psychologists because such a list does not yet exist. The various types may overlap with each other to some extent and fail to cover all possible learning situations, but at least it provides us with a starting place for our discussion. It suggests that an answer to the question "what is learning?" is more likely to be found if we start with the simplest cases of learning and work up toward the more complex rather than trying to cope with the exclusively human forms at the beginning.

The origins of our human capacities and abilities lie millions of years in the past. The ability to learn almost certainly began in the simplest of our marine ancestors, for even a creature as uncomplex as a bottom-dwelling worm needs to be able to modify its behavior patterns when the environment changes. To fully understand what learning is, we should delay our discussion of those highly elaborate and human forms like cognitive and verbal learning until we have explored the simplest types.

Habituation and Sensitization

The evolution of better and better sensory equipment in the early creatures of the ocean produced a problem for them. All sense receptor output was fed immediately to motor neurons through simple reflex arcs, an arrangement that can leave an organism entirely at the mercy of environmental stimulus conditions. For example, picture yourself as a tube worm with your tail attached to the seafloor and your feeding cilia poking out of the top of your tube, combing the water for tiny bits of organic matter. Your neighbors are strands of seaweed, swaying back and forth in the currents. You possess an important defensive reflex that allows you to pull your vulnerable feeding cilia back into the protection of the tube whenever something too large to be food contacts one of them. After a wait of a minute or two, you re-extend your cilia once more and resume feeding. This really cuts down on the loss of cilia due to nibbling by passing fish, but you have a problem with your neighbors. The slight current causes the seaweed to bump into your cilia every few minutes. If you reflexively respond to each bump with a cilia withdrawal, you will starve to death and fail to pass along your genes to a next generation.

Fortunately, you are blessed with a slight mutation not possessed by your brethren worms. After the 40th or 50th bump, your defensive reflex begins to diminish in strength, and within a day you are feeding continually, despite repeated contacts from the seaweed. Your mutation has provided you with what is probably the very first form of learning to appear on the face of this planet. We call this tendency to ignore meaningless stimuli, **habituation**, and define it as the ability to stop responding to a repetitive stimulus that is meaningless in terms of any existing need such as mating, feeding, or safety. Your increased feeding time makes it more likely that you will live to produce a host of offspring that will carry the genes for the ability to habituate. Habituation is a relatively short-duration form of memory that outlasts the stimulus by only minutes or hours. So, when the troublesome seaweed breaks off in a large wave surge and floats away to festoon some distant beach, your defensive reflex eventually recovers and continues to protect you from predators.

Is habituation too simple a form of learning for humans, or has the evolving vertebrate nervous system carried this bit of behavioral baggage along with it down through the ages? Picture this scene. You are studying in a very quiet library. The person at the table behind you has covered the table top with books and, during the process of shuffling through the stacks, knocks one to the floor with a resounding crash. Your reaction is to freeze in midmovement, your pupils dilate, your heart slows momentarily, and all your senses are suddenly wide open. You have experienced the **startle response**, a mammalian reflex to a sudden, unexpected loud noise.

A minute later, your clumsy colleague again loses control of his heap, and another massive volume slams to the floor. Your head comes up and your heart slows slightly, but the complete startle reaction you experienced on the first occasion is muted this time. Five minutes later, when the third book goes, your only reaction is a quick decision to gather your things and seek a quieter environment. With repeated stimulation, your startle reflex habituated.

In a sense, the startle reaction is an extreme version of a more fundamental response, the **orienting reflex** that consists of a collection of reactions all aimed at rapid analysis of the stimulus and preparation for a proper response to it. When you discover that no response is required, habituation sets in. Orienting can vary in intensity all the way from the extreme activation of the startle reaction to the very weak activation you experience when something appears of mild interest to you. The orienting reflex is always elicited by a novel stimulus, with the repetition of that stimulus leading to habituation. In humans, then, habituation still plays the same role that it does in the simplest organisms; it is a mechanism for allowing us to withhold a reflex response when the stimulus no longer warrants a response. In everyday terms, we refer to habituation as boredom or loss of interest.

Habituation has its opposite in the phenomenon

of **sensitization**, the enhancement of a reflex following a number of recent experiences with strong or noxious stimuli. This was discovered during conditioning experiments. For example, if you are planning on conditioning a dog to flex its leg to the sound of a bell by associating the bell with a shock on the paw and you have presented the paw shock a few times already, you may find that the dog flexes its leg the very first time it hears a bell. Obviously, the bell didn't elicit a flexion through a learned association with the shock because the two had never been paired. The best explanation is that the experience of being shocked had sensitized the dog to any unusual or unexpected stimulus by increasing its general level of arousal for all stimuli. In humans we refer to this state as being "jumpy" or "nervous," and it comes from experience with any strongly aversive stimulus, not just shock.

Let's say that you had decided to remain seated near the book-dropper in the library after all because you had habituated to the occasional crashes behind you and were no longer startled. You reach down to pull another text from your book bag, and as you pull your hand out, you see a huge black spider crawling up your wrist. After frantically shaking it off onto the floor and watching it crawl away, you calm down and go back to studying. A moment later another book hits the floor, and you nearly jump out of your chair. The startle reflex has been fully reinstated by way of the sensitization produced by the spider experience. Because the sensitization in this case served to reawaken an habituated response, we term it **dishabituation**.

Conditioning

Both habituation and sensitization appear to be accomplished through the simple modification of an existing reflex pathway in some relatively minor way. If so, these forms of learning could occur in a very primitive organism with minimal neural circuitry. The types of learning categorized as conditioning are more complex in that they seem to involve completely new connections in the nervous system. Conditioning is a form of **associative learning**, that is, one in which associations are formed between two stimuli or between a stimulus and a response. There are two types: classical and instrumental.

Classical Conditioning   During the course of investigating the salivary reflex in dogs, Ivan Pavlov, a Russian physiologist, discovered that the stimulus control of the reflex could be shifted from its natural stimulus to some new stimulus that had nothing whatever to do with the digestive process. The normal stimulus for salivating is food in the mouth. Pavlov called this the **unconditioned stimulus (UCS)**. He used the term *unconditioned* to indicate that food would automatically elicit the response of salivating (the **unconditioned response—UCR**) without learning. In other words, the connection between UCS and UCR was a genetically determined, built-in reflex arc.

What Pavlov discovered was that a neutral stimulus (one that did not elicit the UCR) that occurred repeatedly a moment or two prior to the arrival of the UCS would come to be associated with the UCR so that it would gradually come to elicit that response (Figure 14.1). Sounding a bell, for example, about

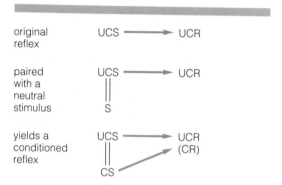

Figure 14.1   Model for classical conditioning. If a neutral stimulus (one that does not elicit the response in question) occurs repeatedly at the same time that a reflex (UCS → UCR) is elicited, then the previously neutral stimulus will gain the ability to evoke the reflex response. At the conclusion of conditioning, the neutral stimulus is called the CS (conditioned stimulus). The reflex response is termed the UCR (unconditioned response) when evoked by the UCS (unconditioned stimulus) and CR (conditioned response) when elicited by the CS. Note that all cases of classical conditioning begin with a reflex.

1 second before food delivery trained the dog to salivate at the sound of the bell. When the reflex response was elicited by a previously neutral stimulus such as the bell, that stimulus was termed the **conditioned stimulus (CS)**, and the response was called the **conditioned response (CR)**.

Instrumental Conditioning Although the fact is by no means yet established to everyone's satisfaction, it seems plausible that instrumental conditioning involves higher-level neural mechanisms than does classical conditioning. Every instance of classical conditioning involves eliciting a reflex. Instrumental conditioning, on the other hand, concerns the learning of **emitted responses**, ones that cannot be elicited directly by any stimulus. A 2-year-old child learning to say the word *please* would be learning an instrumental response. There is no stimulus anywhere in the universe that can elicit the word *please* from a child; the response only occurs when the child determines that it will. In other words, an emitted response is not a reflex. Emitted responses form the bulk of our behavior repertoire and range from walking and door opening to speaking and singing.

The most significant difference between classically conditioned responses and instrumentally conditioned responses, however, is that the latter are goal-oriented. That is, they are instrumental in getting us something that we want. The child learns to say *please* because doing so leads to obtaining something desirable from parents or friends. In other words, this form of learning occurs because of the **consequences** of the response. The rat in an operant chamber learns to press the bar, but this learning occurs only if the bar-press results in the delivery of food or water or some other desirable outcome.

Several forms of instrumental conditioning are possible because there are a number of different ways in which consequences can be arranged. If a response is emitted that is followed by a desirable stimulus, like food for a hungry organism, then the probability that the response will be emitted again increases. This is called **positive reinforcement**. If the rat in the operant chamber receives food when it accidentally presses the bar, then the probability of a second bar-press increases. You know that the rat is learning when you see its rate of bar-pressing

(i.e., number of presses per minute) increasing. A different sort of consequence would be to follow the response with an aversive stimulus. After the rat has learned to press the bar, change the rules on it by substituting a foot shock for the food it had been receiving. This consequence is termed **punishment** because the rate of bar-pressing now decreases. The type of learning is called **passive-avoidance conditioning** because a passive response (in this case, not pressing the bar) is learned.

The same aversive stimulus, foot shock, could be used to produce a type of reinforcement also. If the rat is placed in a chamber having a shock grid for a floor and a door in one wall that leads to a safe (no-shock) chamber, the animal learns to escape through the door to get away from the shock. The consequence of escaping an aversive stimulus is quite reinforcing, and the response is learned just as readily as bar-pressing. The consequence in this case is called **negative reinforcement**. If we give the rat a warning signal that appears a moment or two before shock onset, then the animal can learn to move out of the shock chamber before receiving any shock; in other words, it can avoid rather than escape. This sort of instrumental conditioning is called **active-avoidance learning**. In each of these types, we see learning occurring by the increase or decrease in the rate of an emitted response. Figure 14.2 summarizes these types.

In yet another form of instrumental conditioning called **discrimination learning**, the organism learns to make the response only in the presence of a particular stimulus (termed S^+). In learning to drive a stick-shift car, for example, you learn to move the gearshift lever only when you can sense that the clutch pedal is depressed (S^+). Doing it with the pedal up (S^-) is not very reinforcing. As a very young child, you earned your mother's gratitude by learning to make the response of releasing urine only in the presence of certain bathroom fixtures (S^+) rather than on the living room sofa (S^-).

Learning, as you can tell by now, is not a single mechanism. Instead, the concept refers to a whole variety of situations in which a more or less permanent behavior change occurs as the result of experience. Other forms of learning, more complex than conditioning, could be added to our growing list

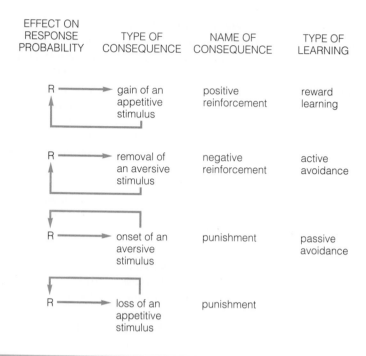

Figure 14.2 The four types of possible consequences in an operant-conditioning situation. Appetitive refers to something desirable; aversive means something unpleasant. The type of learning that occurs from loss of an appetitive stimulus has no technical name. An arrow aimed upward at the R indicates that the consequence *increased* the response rate; a downward arrow indicates that the consequence *depressed* the rate.

EFFECT ON RESPONSE PROBABILITY	TYPE OF CONSEQUENCE	NAME OF CONSEQUENCE	TYPE OF LEARNING
R →	gain of an appetitive stimulus	positive reinforcement	reward learning
R →	removal of an aversive stimulus	negative reinforcement	active avoidance
R →	onset of an aversive stimulus	punishment	passive avoidance
R →	loss of an appetitive stimulus	punishment	

(cognitive, verbal, etc.), but most of the research we have available to discuss concerns the simpler types already mentioned. Accordingly, we will go on at this time to see if we can understand what it is that takes place within the nervous system as learning occurs.

Where in the Nervous System Does Learning Take Place?

During the 1940s, Karl Lashley mounted an ambitious research program aimed at locating the place in the nervous system where memory traces, termed **engrams**, were formed during learning. In one series of experiments, Lashley trained rats to run a maze and then placed lesions in their brains to see whether the rats would lose their memory of the maze. Hopefully, the learning would be lost only with lesions to some particular part of the brain, and this would reveal the location of the engram. Behaviorism was a very strong influence at that time; however, little work had been done on forms of learning other than conditioning, so there was a tendency to try to

understand all types of learning as examples of conditioning. Lashley pictured the engram as an association between the visual cortex, where the stimuli were analyzed, and the motor cortex, where he thought the response was produced. Accordingly, he removed strips of cortex between these two cortical areas.

The results were not what he expected. No one area of cortex proved to be critical to remembering the maze pattern. No matter where the lesion was placed, the amount of memory that each rat had lost was determined simply by how much cortex was missing. Lashley decided that most of the cortex works, not as a collection of separate and discrete areas each with its own job, but as an undifferentiated whole and that the engram was distributed more or less evenly throughout. He called this the principle of **equipotentiality** (Lashley, 1950).

If Lashley had known what we know now about how extremely specific is the function of each tiny area of cortex (see, for example, the section on visual cortex in Chapter 6), he would probably not have drawn that conclusion. His results were most likely due to the complex nature of his maze task, which on close analysis contains many bits and pieces of behavior to be learned. For example, there are numerous ways for the rat to remember to turn right as it leaves the start box. The engram might be to turn toward a darker part of the ceiling above or in the general direction of the odor coming from the experimenter who happens to always station himself in the direction of the correct choice. Or, it might be the kinesthetic feel of making a right turn rather than a left, and so forth. Each of those possibilities uses a different part of the brain. Rather than one engram, the rats were storing dozens; and the more engrams lost in the lesion, the worse the rats performed.

The moral of this story is that it is going to be difficult to find a learning situation simple enough to produce just one type of engram that can then be tracked down to its location in one single brain structure. Let's see how psychologists have responded to this need to find the simplest possible learning situation as their starting point in the quest to locate the engram.

Site of Habituation

Habituation seems like a reasonable starting point because it is probably the simplest form of learning. Would the memory formed during habituation—the engram—be located in the cortex where Lashley searched? It seems unlikely because animals too primitive to have a cerebral cortex can still habituate. The same reasoning applies to the thalamus or brain stem. Can an animal that lacks even a spinal cord— an invertebrate—still habituate?

Habituation and Sensitization at *Aplysia* Synapses
The *Aplysia* (ah-PLEE-zee-uh) is a rather large marine snail (Figure 14.3) that has found itself to be almost as popular a subject for physiological psy-

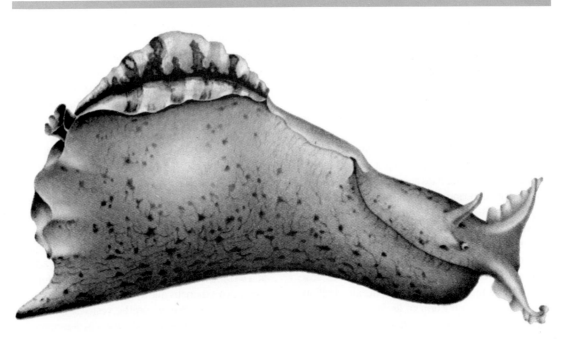

Figure 14.3 The marine snail *Aplysia*. If the two dorsal skin flaps are pulled apart, the gill is revealed. The end of the siphon tube, where the water drawn over the gill is expelled, can be seen just posterior to the skin flaps. (From Barnes, 1986a)

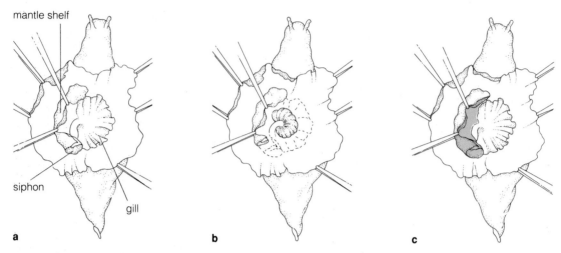

Figure 14.4 The gill-withdrawal reflex in the *Aplysia*. (**a**) Retractors are seen holding back the dorsal skin flaps to reveal the gill and mantle shelf. The gill is fully extended. (**b**) The gill is fully retracted after the withdrawal reflex has occurred. (**c**) The dark-shaded zone is the best area for eliciting the reflex. Stimuli to the light-shaded zone generate a weaker response. (Adapted from Castellucci & Kandel, 1976)

chologists as the monkey or pigeon. Because it is an invertebrate, it has no brain or spinal cord. In fact, its nervous system is so simple and contains so few neurons (about 15,000) that researchers can actually recognize one specific cell from animal to animal (Castellucci & Kandel, 1976). Accordingly, many of *Aplysia*'s neurons have been named and their connections listed in a catalog of cells. *Aplysia* respires through a gill that is hidden between two large flaps of skin that come together along its dorsal surface (Figure 14.3). If these flaps are separated, the siphon, gill, and its covering the mantle shelf are revealed (Figure 14.4). Oxygen-bearing water is drawn in between the leading edges of the skin flaps, flows across the gill, and is expelled through the siphon at the back. The animal has a defensive reflex designed to protect its delicate gill against damage. If anything touches the siphon or mantle shelf, the gill contracts to a fraction of its full size and withdraws under the mantle shelf (Figure 14.4b). This reflex is controlled by 13 motor neurons located within the abdominal ganglion, and these individual neurons are recognizable from one *Aplysia* to the

next. Figure 14.5 shows the reflex arc for the gill-withdrawal reflex.

Can an organism this simple learn? Kandel has found it capable of a number of types of simple learning, including habituation (Kandel, 1979). If a jet of water is repeatedly squirted on the siphon, the gill withdrawal becomes smaller and smaller with each succeeding stimulus. Microelectrode recordings from the motor neurons of the reflex arc showed that the response decreased in magnitude because the EPSPs generated in these cells by the sensory neurons from the siphon became progressively smaller. The sensory neurons released smaller quantities of transmitter, presumably because of decreased calcium ion influx in their terminals. Recall from Chapter 4 that a nerve impulse arriving at a terminal initiates the release of transmitter from the vesicles there by allowing Ca^{++} into the terminal; it is these ions that act on the vesicles. Habituation can last for hours, and its duration is determined by how long it takes for the calcium current to recover; exactly why the calcium current stays depressed during this time has yet to be discovered.

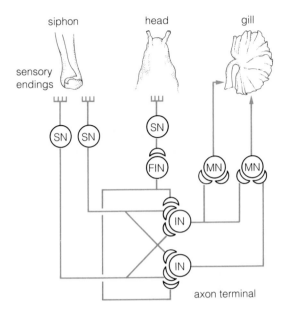

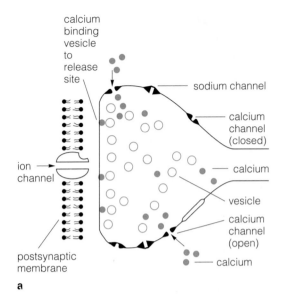

Figure 14.5 Reflex arc for the gill-withdrawal reflex in the *Aplysia*. The sensory neurons (SN) with receptor endings in the siphon synapse with interneurons (IN) that synapse with the motor neurons (MN) controlling gill muscles. Habituation occurs at the SN–IN synapse when the reflex is repeatedly elicited and the SN terminals run out of calcium. Sensitization occurs at those same synapses but involves other sensory neurons such as those in the head, which react to aversive stimuli. These aversive-stimulus sensory neurons excite a facilitative interneuron (FIN) that sends its terminals to synapse on the terminals of the siphon sensory cells. Serotonin released by the FIN terminal facilitates the action of the SN terminal, resulting in the secretion of a greater than normal amount of transmitter at the SN–IN synapse and intensification of the reflex.

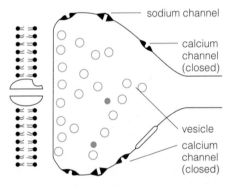

Figure 14.6 Habituation in the *Aplysia*. (**a**) The terminal is in normal operating condition. A nerve impulse has just arrived, and two of the four calcium channels have opened to admit calcium ions. Some of these ions have bound vesicles to the membrane sites where their transmitter molecules can be released. (**b**) The terminal has been exposed to many impulses recently, and this heavy usage has resulted in fewer openable calcium channels. The lower calcium influx yields the condition called habituation. If this terminal belongs to one of the sensory cells of the siphon, then it is the gill-withdrawal reflex that is habituating.

So, we have discovered that learning in the *Aplysia* turns out to be a change at certain synapses. The engram for this particular instance of habituation is a depression of calcium influx into the presynaptic terminals of the sensory neurons of the siphon (Figure 14.6). This decrease in calcium current is called **synaptic depression**. Perhaps learning in your own brain is a matter of changes at synapses.

The nervous system of the *Aplysia* is also capable of sensitization. If a weak stimulus is applied to the siphon, a partial gill withdrawal occurs; but if the

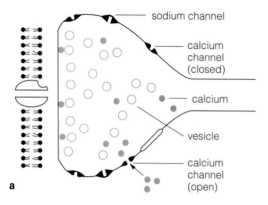

sodium channel

calcium channel (closed)

calcium

vesicle

calcium channel (open)

a

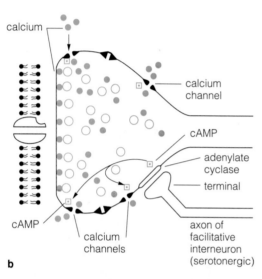

calcium

calcium channel

cAMP

adenylate cyclase

terminal

cAMP

calcium channels

axon of facilitative interneuron (serotonergic)

b

Figure 14.7 One explanation of how sensitization may work in the gill-withdrawal reflex of the *Aplysia*. (**a**) A terminal of one of the sensory cells of the mantle in its normal condition. (**b**) Noxious stimulation applied to some other part of the snail's body results in firing of the small serotonergic interneuron. The serotonin activates the enzyme adenylate cyclase, which manufactures more cAMP. The cAMP opens more calcium channels, allowing more calcium ions to enter the terminal. The result is a greater number of vesicles bound to the membrane, ready to eject transmitter into the synaptic gap with the arrival of the next impulse.

animal has just had an electric shock to its head several minutes before, the weak jet of water to the siphon triggers a full-sized gill reflex. Is sensitization, like habituation, produced by some change at the synapse—a change that outlasts the stimulus that evoked it? Kandel and his colleagues (Kandel, 1979) have found one site of sensitization at the synapses between the siphon sensory neurons and the interneurons that connect with the gill motor neurons (Figure 14.5). The facilitative interneuron that produces sensitization receives input from sensory cells such as those that react to the shock. Its terminals synapse not, as you might expect, on dendrites or cell bodies of the siphon sensory cells but on their terminals. Its action is called **presynaptic facilitation** because it helps the sensory neurons have a greater effect on the motor neurons of the reflex arc. This is why a small stimulus to the siphon can bring about an unexpectedly large withdrawal response; the presynaptic sensory neurons are receiving help from the facilitative interneurons. The chemical nature of this facilitation is important because it is a process that we find at many mammalian synapses.

The transmitter released by the facilitative interneuron is serotonin, one of the monoamine group (which includes dopamine, epinephrine, and norepinephrine). Figure 14.7 shows an enlarged view of the sensory neuron's terminal. The mechanism by which the transmitter molecules have their action is far more complex in the case of monoamine synapses, such as this one, than it is for the acetylcholine-type synapses that you learned about in Chapter 4. In the case of acetylcholine, receptor sites are in direct contact with the gate molecules on ion channels. When a transmitter molecule locks into a receptor site, the gates respond by opening and an EPSP current flows through the channels—very simple and direct.

In contrast to that simplicity, when a molecule of serotonin fits into a receptor site on the terminal of a sensory neuron, the receptor molecule responds by activating another molecule to which it is attached. This second molecule, an enzyme called **adenylate cyclase** (ah-DEEN-ul-ate SIGH-klase), is located on the inside surface of the cell membrane where it is in contact with all chemicals floating around in the intracellular fluid. Enzymes are proteins that enable

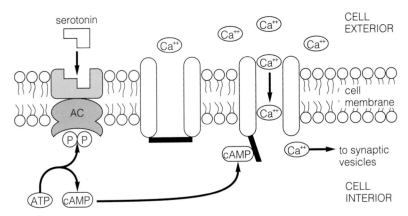

Figure 14.8 A section of membrane in the terminal of the sensory cell shown in Figure 14.7. At left a molecule of serotonin secreted from the terminal of the interneuron is moving into a receptor site in the membrane of the sensory neuron's terminal. When it binds to the receptor site, the underlying molecule of adenylate cyclase (AC) will be activated and begin to strip phosphate groups (P) off ATP molecules, converting them to cAMP. This cAMP reacts with calcium channels in such a way as to hold open the gates longer and allow more calcium ions (Ca^{++}) into the sensory neuron. This greater than normal amount of calcium will bind more vesicles to the membrane and result in an increased release of transmitter when an impulse arrives in this terminal. This picture is a magnified view of the area of sensory cell membrane under and around the terminal of the facilitative interneuron in Figure 14.7.

other molecules to split or combine with one another, and the role of adenylate cyclase at this location is to react with a chemical found in large quantities in most cells, **adenosine triphosphate (ATP)** (uh-DEEN-uh-sin try-FOSS-fate). As you can see from Figure 14.8, adenylate cyclase picks up a molecule of ATP and splits off two of its phosphate groups, leaving a molecule called **cyclic adenosine monophosphate (cAMP)**. It is important to keep in mind that normally the cyclase cannot produce cAMP; this reaction can only occur after the adenylate cyclase has been "activated" by a molecule of serotonin reacting with its receptor site. In other words, cAMP is made in the postsynaptic terminal only in response to an impulse arriving at the synapse between the interneuron and the sensory neuron terminal.

Now that it has been manufactured, cAMP can diffuse through the intracellular fluid to combine with other molecules; by doing so, it can influence how the terminal responds to any nerve impulse

arriving from the axon. Recall that a nerve impulse releases transmitter when it arrives in the terminal, but to do this it must act indirectly by way of opening the calcium channels and allowing Ca^{++} into the cell. It is calcium that opens synaptic vesicles and releases transmitter. The more calcium there is, the more transmitter will be released (Berridge, 1979). It is at this point that the cAMP produced by the action of the interneuron can influence events in this sensory neuron terminal. Through a chain of reactions, cAMP acts on the calcium channels to hold them open longer than normal, thus allowing more Ca^{++} into the terminal, with the result that more transmitter is released into the synaptic gap (Byrne, 1985). In this way, the facilitative interneuron increases the effectiveness of each impulse in the sensory neuron, allowing it to produce a larger EPSP in the motor neuron. In other words, the facilitative interneuron sensitizes the gill-withdrawal reflex arc so that it can produce a large contraction even to a small stimulus; it produces this sensitization only when its sensory input tells it that some dangerous stimulus event has occurred somewhere else on the body of the *Aplysia*.

Why does nature take such a complicated and roundabout way to increase calcium concentration inside the terminal? The answer lies in the duration of the effect. To serve the animal's survival needs, the sensitization process must establish a short type of memory. That is, it won't do for the effect to dissipate as soon as the noxious stimulus that produced it has ceased. The animal should remain activated and wary for minutes after the stimulus incident. But how can the short burst of impulses produced in the sensory neurons of the head by the electric shock keep the synapses in the withdrawal reflex arc sensitized long after the initial danger stimulus? If serotonin from the interneuron opened the calcium channels directly without the intermediate steps involving cAMP, its facilitation would last only as long as the electric shock. This would not be a memory effect but rather a short-lived arousal state. Prolonging this facilitation for minutes afterward is up to the adenylate cyclase–cAMP mechanism. As long as the cyclase is activated (probably less than 1 second), it is manufacturing cAMP, and each of these molecules can float around in the fluid for minutes afterward until they either arrive at the place on the membrane where they influence the calcium channels or until they are changed into something else by another enzyme. The result of this arrangement is sort of an amplifier effect (Gilman & Ross, 1979) that can extend the influence of a momentary stimulus over many succeeding minutes, that is, create a short-term memory.

Both habituation and sensitization then appear to be changes taking place at synapses. In the case of a very simple organism, we can find the specific area of the nervous system involved (the abdominal ganglion, in the case of *Aplysia*'s gill withdrawal) and even the specific synapses; in a mammal, however, we find that localizing the learning may be a much more difficult task. Part of Lashley's difficulties stemmed from beginning with an inadequate behavior analysis of a behaviorally complicated learning situation. Would localization of learning in the mammalian nervous system be simpler for a less complicated type of learning such as habituation?

Locating Habituation in the Mammalian Nervous System Lashley's work suggests that various bits of learning might be accomplished at different places in the nervous system, and this idea seems to apply to research on habituation. Thompson, for example, found that the spinal cord of the cat could habituate even after being entirely cut off from the brain (Thompson & Glanzman, 1976). Small electric shocks to the cat's hind leg elicited a flexion response that habituated in less than 20 minutes of repeated stimulation. Once habituated the flexion response required over 100 minutes to fully recover. This may not seem like a long time for a memory to persist, but keep in mind that the organism usually cannot afford for habituation to last more than minutes. Many cases of habituation occur in the reflex arcs of defensive reflexes, and turning off such a reflex for more than minutes at a time could lead to real trouble.

So learning (at least of the simplest sort) can apparently occur within the spinal cord. We must be careful not to overgeneralize this, however. For example, it would be unwise to say that this indicated that all forms of habituation were localized within the cord. In the case of the spinal cat, Thompson and Glanzman were employing a somatosensory stimulus (shock to the leg) and measuring a response in a limb. No cranial nerves are involved, only spinal nerves. The entire reflex arc is within the cord, and that is why it is possible for the habituation to take place there. But what about a reflex involving an auditory stimulus, such as the **acoustic startle reflex?** This is a defensive reflex that tends to curl the body into a hunched-over, protective posture with the head down when a sudden, loud noise occurs. A strong orienting response is a part of it. The pathway for the acoustic startle reflex branches off from the auditory projection fibers in the brain stem and runs through the pontine reticular formation and back down into the cord to end on the motor neurons of the ventral horn. A likely spot for the habituative changes to take place would be the synapse in the pontine reticular formation, but there are complications that must be dealt with.

The startle reflex is a defensive response, and we have said that it usually is not good for the organism's welfare to habituate that kind of reflex for more than a few minutes. However, there may be exceptions. What about a street construction worker who spends hours every day leaning over a jackhammer or the operator of a pile driver? They might benefit from startle-reflex habituation of a more durable variety than that lasting only minutes at a time. In fact, there does seem to exist two varieties of habituation: short- and long-term, the former lasting minutes, the latter days or weeks (Leaton & Supple, 1986). The short-term type appears to take place within the reflex arc itself, just as in the case of *Aplysia*'s gill-withdrawal habituation, and the mechanism may be the same, that is, synaptic depression (Groves & Thompson, 1970).

In a series of experiments aimed at finding the locus of the habituation engram for acoustic startle, Leaton discovered that lesions of the midbrain reticular formation (MBRF) in the rat had no effect on short-term habituation but did impair the long-term variety (Jordan & Leaton, 1982). The same was true of lesions to the midline portion of the cerebellum, the **cerebellar vermis** (Leaton & Supple, 1986). It looks as though long-term habituation is brought about by brain areas outside of the startle reflex arc itself. The cerebellar vermis receives input from the auditory system, and it sends output to the MBRF that connects to the pontine reticular formation, thus, it may be this pathway that is responsible for the long-term habituation. This would be typical of the way in which the nervous system is arranged. We can speculate that evolution first improved the original pontine startle reflex arc by making it more adaptive—giving it the ability to habituate—and then, as new brain structures evolved above the pontine level, used them to provide still more flexibility. The new structures such as the MBRF had to make their influence felt indirectly by modulating the workings of the original reflex arc in the pontine reticular formation rather than sending axons directly to the motor neurons. It was this evolution of modulators and then modulators of the modulators that produced the present hierarchical structure of our nervous systems.

The human, of course, has the highest structures and largest hierarchy of any known nervous system, and the bulk of the brain is above the level of the brain stem. Is it possible that, in the course of evolution, so many levels of control were layered onto the human brain stem that it no longer has enough independence for even the simplest type of learning? Although habituation can occur in the pontine brain stem of a rat, perhaps humans use the cortex even for such simple learning. We cannot say for sure that this is not the case, but some contradictory evidence does exist. Berntson and colleagues have attempted to establish habituation in five cases of children having little or no brain above the level of the stem (Berntson et al., 1983; Tuber et al., 1980). Three of the children suffered from hydroencephaly, a birth disorder in which the cerebral hemispheres fail to develop and the skull simply fills with cerebrospinal fluid (CSF). The other two subjects had hydrocephalus. In their brains the system of ventricles and chambers through which the CSF normally circulates had failed to develop the proper drains, but the tissue that generated the fluid kept on making CSF despite the fact that there was nowhere for it to go. What little brain tissue there was present at birth was crushed and distorted by the pressure from the buildup of CSF. Most of the subjects had no apparent cortex visible in a CT scan, and the basal ganglia and thalamus were either absent or badly distorted. It is unlikely that they had much, if any, functional brain tissue above the brain-stem level. Yet they could still learn.

A pair of stimuli, a tone followed immediately by a light, was presented repeatedly through several experimental sessions on different days. Eventually, the orienting response, measured by a brief slowing of the heart rate, habituated to a significant level below the initial baseline for three of the children. In a further test, a number of trials were given in which the tone was sounded but the light omitted. The result was a dramatic orienting response that resembled the startle response to a loud noise. Not only had habituation occurred but also an expectancy had developed. Apparently, even in the human, simple forms of learning are handled by the lower levels of the brain.

Site of Classical Conditioning

Habituation, we discovered, could occur in the spinal cord or brain stem, depending on the location of the

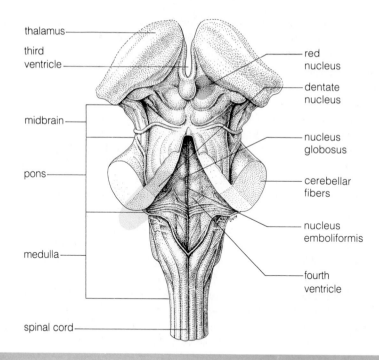

Figure 14.9 Location of conditioning circuits in a dorsal view of the brain stem. The cerebral hemispheres have been completely removed except for the thalamus on either side. The cerebellar hemispheres have also been cut away leaving just their input and output tracts. The cerebellar nuclei are clumped at the base of each hemisphere of the cerebellum, just above the fourth ventricle and pons. The human equivalent of the nucleus interpositus is the combination of nucleus globosus and the emboliform nucleus. (Adapted from Fowler, 1984)

thalamus

third ventricle

midbrain

pons

medulla

spinal cord

red nucleus

dentate nucleus

nucleus globosus

cerebellar fibers

nucleus emboliformis

fourth ventricle

reflex circuit in which it took place. Is classical conditioning exclusively the function of one particular brain area, or is it also a type of modification that can be made in synapses anywhere in the nervous system?

In most cases of classical conditioning, the CS involves a different sensory system than that of the UCS. Pavlov's dog, for example, learned to salivate to an auditory stimulus after it had been paired with a taste–somesthetic stimulus (i.e., food in the mouth). This kind of learning, then, is more complicated than habituation simply by the fact that it cannot occur strictly within a reflex arc; sensory inputs from several senses must somehow come together at the same point in the nervous system.

Paw Flexion: The Red Nucleus A light shock to the paw of a cat causes it to reflexively jerk its foreleg away from the place in which the paw was shocked. This is a defensive reflex similar to the one you demonstrate in jerking your hand from a hot stove. (The biggest difference is that your response

removes you from the source of the stimulus, whereas the cat's response does not do the same for it because the shock electrode is taped to its paw.) If an auditory stimulus (the CS) is presented a moment before the shock (the UCS) and this stimulus pairing is repeated over many trials, conditioning will occur, as signaled by the fact that the auditory stimulus comes to elicit the paw flexion. This conditioned response can be eliminated in the trained cat by lesioning a small part of its upper brain stem, the red nucleus (Smith, 1970).

The **red nucleus** is a part of the motor system located near the substantia nigra at the top of the midbrain (Figure 14.9). It receives input from the cerebellum and cortex (motor and somatosensory), and its fibers project down into the cord to the motor neurons of the ventral horn (Nieuwenhuys et al., 1981). Tsukahara became interested in this particular example of conditioning because the red nucleus had been shown to be a site in which the phenomenon of sprouting occurred. When a CNS tract is damaged, its axons fail to regenerate and reestablish their original connections. Receptor sites on the target neurons are left without any incoming transmitter, and somehow this condition must produce a chemical "distress" message because axons of neighboring tracts respond by growing branches to make connections with the neurons that had lost their input (Crutcher & Davis, 1981). This process, called **sprouting**, establishes new synapses that are functional (although this new input may not be able to accomplish the same results as the original correct input). The important factor for Tsukahara was that sprouting can sometimes occur even in the absence of damage, and this suggests that it might be involved in the formation of the new connections that supposedly underlie learning (Tsukahara, 1981a).

Tsukahara began by demonstrating that sprouting could occur in the red nucleus following damage to one of its chief inputs, the tract from interpositus nucleus of the cerebellum. The sprouts came from the undamaged tract connecting the sensory–motor cortex to the red nucleus (Figure 14.10). The next step was to show that the synapses between the corticorubral fibers (the ones coming from the sensory–motor cortex) and the cells in the red nucleus could be the site of learning in the case of the paw-flexion response. To do this, Tsukahara switched from an auditory CS to a direct stimulation of the corticorubral fibers by way of an implanted electrode (Figure 14.10). Each conditioning trial proceeded as follows: CS (stimulus to tract) followed immediately by the UCS (shock to forepaw) and response (leg flexion). Despite the fact that the CS was an internal rather than a normal external stimulus, conditioning occurred.

Measurements show that the synaptic change that represented the learned connection was not in the path from the red nucleus to spinal cord. The only connections that showed an improvement were those between the corticorubral path and neurons of the red nucleus (Tsukahara, 1981a). The improvement in these connections could have come about because the existing synapses grew stronger—a possibility that has yet to be proved or disproved—or because of the sprouting of new connections between the tract from the cortex and cells of the red nucleus. Tsukahara (1984) favors this latter interpretation and notes that the time taken to establish the

conditioned response (roughly 1 week) was very similar to the time required for sprouting (1 week). This leaves us wondering how more rapid forms of classical conditioning can possibly occur, but that is a matter that we take up in detail in Chapter 16 where we examine how memory is stored. Let us note here that the significant synaptic changes in paw-flexion conditioning do seem to take place within the red nucleus.

Nictitating Membrane Reflex: The Cerebellum The cerebellum is a likely site for lower-level types of learning such as classical conditioning, which probably appeared early in evolutionary history when vertebrate brains had only rudimentary beginnings of cerebrums. The fact that it receives inputs from most of the sensory systems and has strong connections with the motor circuitry of the brain stem suggests that it could function as a mechanism for associating stimuli with each other or with responses.

To examine these possibilities, Richard Thompson and colleagues needed a simple, easily controlled example of classical conditioning that they could use as a standard throughout a long series of ablation and single-cell recording experiments. For the UCR, they chose the defensive reflex of closing the eyelid and retracting the eyeball that occurs when something touches the very sensitive cornea of the eye. In the human, this is called the blink reflex, but in Thompson's experimental subjects, rabbits, it is termed the **nictitating membrane reflex (NMR)**.

Cats, rabbits, and a number of other animals have an inner eyelid, called the nictitating membrane, which can slide across the cornea for extra protection against dust, branches, claws, and so forth. Besides closing the outer lid, the full defensive reflex involves a slight retraction of the eyeball back into the skull. This withdrawal allows the elastic nictitating membrane to expand over the surface of the eye. Among this package of responses, the movement of the nictitating membrane is the most convenient to measure in the lab, so the entire phenomenon is referred to as the NMR (Farley & Alkon, 1985). It is a simple matter to repeatedly elicit the NMR without damaging the eye by using a mild puff of air to the cornea. A tone or slight increase in illumination can

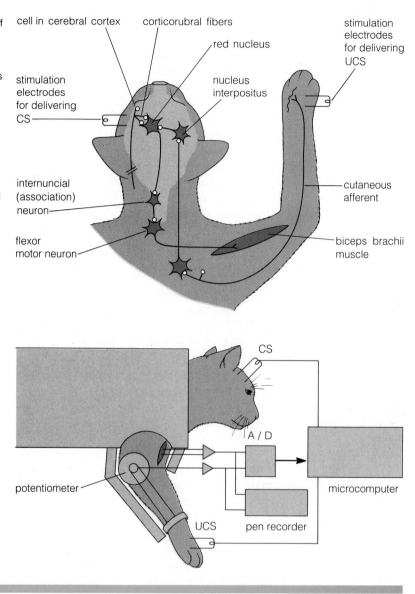

Figure 14.10 Arrangement of experimental setup in Tsuka-hara's study of conditioning in red nucleus. The conditioned stimulus is a shock to the fibers connecting cortex with red nucleus. The muscle that produces the unconditioned leg flexion is the biceps brachii. Wires from the leg muscle and from the potentiometer that senses the leg movement lead to amplifiers (the triangle symbols), which send the amplified electronic signals into an EEG recorder (pen recorder) and into a computer for analysis. (Adapted from Tsukahara, 1984)

be employed as a CS. As one trial follows another, the NMR gradually appears earlier and earlier so that it comes to precede the UCS and is elicited instead by the CS.

What parts of the brain are required if the NMR is to be learned? A number of studies have now shown that the CR still occurs if the hippocampus (cited in Farley & Alkon, 1985) or even the entire cortex (Thompson et al., 1983) has been removed.

Lesions to certain motor nuclei of the brain stem block the development of the CR, but this is because they contain the motor neurons that retract the eyeball and blink the eyelid. The structures that seem to be most involved in the development of an association itself are the **dentate nucleus** and **nucleus interpositus** of the cerebellum. (In the human, the nucleus interpositus becomes two structures: the nucleus globosus and nucleus emboliformis; see Fig-

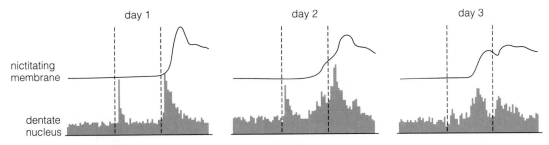

Figure 14.11 Nerve impulse histograms showing how activity of dentate nucleus neurons correlates with the movement of the nictitating membrane in NMR conditioning. The oscilloscope trace labeled nictitating membrane shows the movement of the membrane; the histograms show the number of nerve impulses in each 9-ms time period. The total duration of each of the three records is 750 ms. The first vertical line indicates the start of the CS (tone); the second line marks the UCS (air puff). Each histogram represents the average from 1 day of training. On the first day, the response follows the appearance of the UCS, as one would expect of a reflex, but by day 2, the membrane is beginning to twitch to the CS, and day 3 shows a good CR that delays a bit following the CS but definitely precedes the UCS. Except for a transitory brief response to the CS early in training, the firing pattern in neurons of the dentate nucleus is exactly the same shape as the NMR but precedes the reflex by a few milliseconds. (Adapted from McCormick et al., 1982)

ure 14.9.) Microelectrodes placed in these nuclei showed clusters of neurons changing their firing patterns as the CR developed; eventually, their changes in firing rates came to mimic the changes in the position of the nictitating membrane (Thompson et al., 1984) (Figure 14.11). When these nuclei were stimulated through the implanted electrodes, the NMR was elicited; when they were destroyed electrolytically (i.e., by passing a destructive current through the electrodes), the CR was lost, but the UCR was not (McCormick & Thompson, 1984). In other words, the loss of the response cannot be explained with the notion that the lesions destroyed the original reflex arc itself; the continued presence of the UCR ensures that the reflex arc is still intact. Therefore, it must have been the association that was lost.

One pair of investigators report finding a weak, infrequent CR surviving lesions of the nucleus interpositus, so there may be more yet to discover about the location of the NMR engram (Welsh & Harvey, 1989). However, the conflicting data came from unilateral lesions and might not have been obtained had the nucleus been removed in both hemispheres.

Marr and Albus made use of the circuitry of the

cerebellar cortex in their theory of NMR conditioning (Gellman & Miles, 1985). From an anatomical standpoint, the cortex seems ideal for forming associations between stimuli and reflexes. It receives visual, auditory, somesthetic, kinesthetic, and vestibular input, and the arrangement of neurons suggests an associational device. We can see in Figure 14.12 how associations might form in the cerebellar cortex. Note that the original reflex circuit on which the conditioning is built starts with the corneal somatosensory neuron that reacts to the air puff. This cell synapses with a brain-stem association neuron that excites the retractor muscle motor neuron. These three cells—receptor, association neuron, and motor neuron—form the basic reflex arc. However, the association neuron sends an axon branch to the inferior olivary nucleus of the brain stem that in turn projects up to the **Purkinje cells** of the cerebellar cortex. These same Purkinje cells also receive afferents from the cochlea carrying auditory information about the CS tone. The cortical Purkinje neurons project down to the dentate and interpositus nuclei, which send their output to the motor neurons for the retractor muscles of the eyes. Purkinje cells then

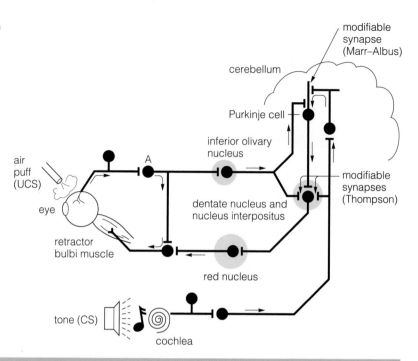

Figure 14.12 Circuit diagram illustrating the Marr–Albus and Thompson theories of NMR conditioning. The reflex arc begins with a sensory ending in the cornea that reacts to the air puff (UCS). An association neuron (A) in the brain stem carries the excitation to the motor neuron for the retractor bulbi muscle, which pulls the eye inward, allowing the nictitating membrane to slip over the eye. Marr and Albus thought that the CS–UCS association was made at the dendrites of Purkinje cells in the cerebellar cortex. Thompson has good evidence that they are formed in the nucleus interpositus. (Adapted from Gellman & Miles, 1985)

seem to be the place where the association between the CS and UCS might take place. The **Marr–Albus theory** holds that Purkinje cells do not begin to react to the cochlear input (the CS) until after this input has occurred together with the somatosensory input (the UCS) a number of times (Gellman & Miles, 1985).

Despite the fact that Purkinje cells are anatomically a connecting point for the CS and UCS, the basic association may not be made there. Thompson showed that NMR conditioning could still occur after the cerebellar cortex had been lesioned (McCormick & Thompson, 1984). Yeo, however, failed to obtain conditioning after cortical removal and supported the Marr–Albus theory (cited in Thompson, 1988). Subsequently, Thompson replicated his early study and again found that conditioning could occur despite the missing cortex (Thompson, 1988). Thompson notes that the auditory and somatosensory inputs can get together in the nucleus interpositus and thus, he places the site of the essential association in that nucleus. There are now consid-

erable data for this interpretation (Thompson, 1988), but Yeo's conflicting results suggest that the cerebellar cortex might still be involved in NMR conditioning in some other fashion. Let's examine that possibility.

A standard phenomenon observed in the development of the CR as conditioning trials progress is that the CR delays its appearance until just before the occurrence of the UCS rather than coming immediately after the CS. Behaviorally, this makes sense; the organism shouldn't blink right after the tone goes on or the blink will be finished too soon, and the lid will be opening just in time to get the blast of air that the animal could have avoided with a correctly timed CR. There are two things to be learned then: the association between the tone and the air puff (or between the tone and the blink) and the timing of the blink. It could be that the basic associative learning, linking CS to UCS, takes place in the interpositus and dentate nuclei but that the activity in these neurons that would trigger a CR is briefly held back by the cerebellar cortex circuits that have calculated the correct time for the CR to occur (McCormick & Thompson, 1984; Thompson, 1983). Recall from Chapter 9 that studies of motor functions have collected impressive evidence that one of the more important functions of the cerebellar cortex is the timing of responses. If this is true, the loss of NMR conditioning observed by Thompson following the lesioning of the cerebellar nuclei would be explainable. The conflicting data from studies that lesioned cerebellar cortex probably means that the circuit through cerebellar nuclei can function without the cerebellar cortex but only with difficulty.

Another structure important to NMR conditioning is the red nucleus (Chapman et al., 1988). Lesions of this structure eliminate the conditioned NMR but not the UCR (Rosenfield et al., 1985). Does this mean that the NMR is a change at synapses in both the cerebellum and red nucleus? Not necessarily. Haley and colleagues (1988) have found that the conditioned NMR depends on a pathway from the nucleus interpositus of the cerebellum to the red nucleus and then back down the brain stem to the motor neurons that produce the NMR. Lesions of the red nucleus cut the CR pathway to the retractor bulbi muscle but leave the UCR path untouched. Why don't interpositus neurons send axon branches directly to motor nuclei for the retractor bulbi? Perhaps, changes at this seemingly superfluous synapse in the red nucleus constitute yet another engram that produces some aspect of NMR behavior that has been ignored so far. For example, it might integrate the eye blink with a defensive head turn away from the aversive stimulus.

As you can see, the engram is almost as slippery and difficult to pin down now as it was in Lashley's day. We are left wondering, for the time, if changes have to occur at both the red nucleus and cerebellar synapses in order for NMR conditioning to occur; we should also wonder if it won't turn out that the cerebellum is involved in the conditioning of the paw-flexion response. There does seem to be one safe conclusion, however: Several types of classical conditioning involve changes at the brain-stem level and do not require any higher areas of the brain.

Thus far at least two brain areas have been implicated in the learning of the NMR, each making its own unique contribution: the development of the

association in the path that includes cerebellar nuclei and the red nucleus and the development of the correct timing for the CR in the cerebellar cortex. A third part of the learning seems to involve the pontine brain stem. When the first conditioned blink occurs to the CS, it usually is accompanied by a diffuse, nonspecific collection of reactions that are defensive in nature, many of which are run by the autonomic nervous system. The animal freezes into a crouch, the heart rate changes, all components of the orienting reflex appear, and the NMR occurs. It has been suggested that the more specific and precise eyeblink slowly emerges from this package of defensive responses as the animal experiences dozens of trials. In other words, at first the NMR may just be one part of an overall emotional reaction that some have called the **conditioned emotional response (CER)**, which occurs to any novel aversive stimulus (Thompson, 1983; Thompson et al., 1984). As the UCS slowly loses its novelty and the nervous system habituates to it, the final residue is the one response that is most appropriate for a stimulus to the cornea—a protective eyeblink. This is not the original, crude, all-purpose NMR but a learned, fine-tuned NMR especially designed for this particular stimulus situation (i.e., the appearance of the tone that signals that the air puff is coming).

Special Features of Conditioning: The Hippocampus Typically, the time between the beginning of the CS and the occurrence of the UCS is less than 1 second. Aversive classical conditioning can be interpreted as a way for the nervous system to learn to start up a defensive-reflex response a moment before the appearance of the harmful stimulus that would otherwise normally elicit the response. In that way, some or all of the harmful effects of the UCS might be avoided. This is a valuable survival device, and the ability to extend the interval into several seconds would make it even more valuable. Conditioning can occur when there are several seconds between the beginning of the CS and UCS, a procedure called **delay conditioning**, but many more trials are needed to establish the CR. An even more difficult type is **trace conditioning** in which there is a gap between the CS and UCS. That is, the tone is sounded briefly, a few seconds of silence pass, and then the air puff occurs. In the delay procedure, the tone continues to sound until the air puff occurs. Trace conditioning seems as though it might exceed the capacity of the brain stem. It calls for the association of two stimuli that do not even occur together at the same time. Would this very difficult type of conditioning call for a more highly evolved, later addition to the nervous system—perhaps a structure designed to encompass lengthy samples of time?

Animals with their hippocampi removed cannot learn a trace-conditioned response even though the loss of those structures does not prevent the learning of a basic, short-delay CR (Lavond et al., 1981). Furthermore, hippocampal neurons increase and decrease their response rate in synchrony with the beginning and end of each conditioned NMR (Thompson et al., 1983). Perhaps then, the hippocampus comes to the rescue of the brain stem learning mechanisms whenever the conditioning situation is extremely difficult. This idea has been examined in some detail for the case of classical **discrimination-reversal learning**. Discrimination conditioning occurs when the subject learns to make the CR following one stimulus (called the **CS**$^+$) but not to make it following another similar stimulus (**CS**$^-$). For example, the rabbit could be taught to blink following a high-pitched tone (CS$^+$) but not after a low-pitched tone (CS$^-$). This is accomplished by pairing CS$^+$ with the UCS, while presenting CS$^-$ alone, without the UCS. As you can see, discrimination conditioning is more complicated than simple conditioning, but it is closer to a normal, everyday sort of learning that the rabbit is likely to need in the natural environment. (If you were a rabbit, you should learn to freeze when you hear an owl hoot but ignore the coo of a dove.) Adding a reversal to this basic discrimination complicates learning even more.

Reversal learning occurs when you must unlearn old habits that no longer work and learn new ones that sometimes directly contradict the old ones. Taking this idea into the lab, we can train our rabbit on a discrimination NMR task with two tones, and then when learning is complete, we reverse the stimuli so that what used to be the CS$^+$ is now the CS$^-$ and vice versa. If the rabbit is still in possession of its hippocampi, it takes this reversal right in stride and learns the new rules. Without the hippocampus, it is

lost. The new CS$^+$ is learned, but the old one is never unlearned and the rabbit responds to both tones, even though the one that is now CS$^-$ never is followed by the air puff (Berger & Orr, 1982). Perhaps, without the hippocampus, the animal cannot recall which of the two stimuli is the *current* CS$^+$.

Microelectrode recordings from hippocampal cells during discrimination-reversal learning show these neurons gradually increasing their firing rate during the interval between the CS and UCS in which the CR occurs (Berger, 1984). On each trial, after conditioning has been established, hippocampal cells start firing just before the blink begins and fire continually throughout the movement. When the CS$^-$ is added to the trials, hippocampal neurons ignore it and reserve their response for the correct tone (Figure 14.13). If the rabbit does mistakenly respond to the CS$^-$, the record shows that neurons in the hippocampus fired before the response began just as though the tone had been the CS$^+$. Apparently, if the animal makes a mistake, it is because its hippocampus hadn't learned the discrimination yet. When the stimulus reversal takes place, hippocampal neurons alter their firing so that they ignore the old CS$^+$ and gradually come to respond only to the new. The behavior of these cells faithfully predicts what the rabbit will do a moment later (Berger, 1984).

In summary then, our example of a "simple" classical conditioning type of learning appears to have at least four aspects: an initial, possibly pontine phase of CR development in which a generalized emotional response is learned (of which the NMR may be one component); a specific NMR that seems to be located at synapses in the interpositus and dentate nuclei (and perhaps, red nucleus); and the correct timing of the CR with reference to the UCS, which seems to develop in the cerebellar cortex. Last, the hippocampus appears to be involved in enabling the organism to use classical conditioning in the more natural circumstances that one would find outside the controlled environment of the lab, as when the CS–UCS interval is lengthy or when conditions change so that a prior habit must be unlearned.

The general principle that these ideas illustrate is that learning is not the function of one specific place in the nervous system. It seems to be distributed throughout many structures according to what

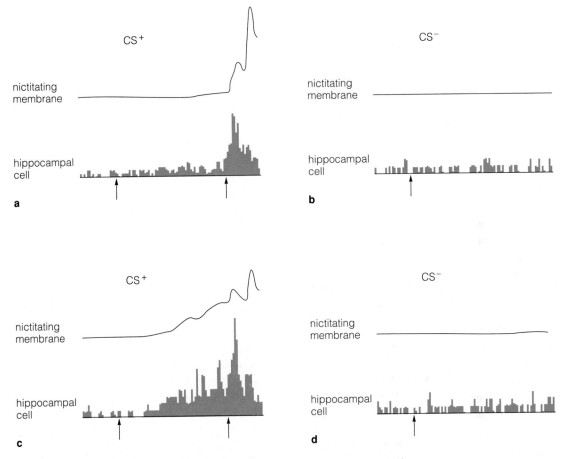

Figure 14.13 Responses of two hippocampal pyramidal cells recorded from a rabbit during discrimination NMR conditioning: (**a** and **b**) a neuron observed during the early stages of learning; (**c** and **d**) a different cell in the final stages. The left arrow indicates the onset of the CS (a tone); the right arrow is the UCS (air puff to eye). The trace labeled nictitating membrane is a record of the response—the movement of the nictitating membrane. The histograms show number of impulses per time unit. Each record shown is 1,250 ms long. (Adapted from Berger, 1984)

sort of change the learning represents (Bloch & Laroche, 1984; Cohen, 1985; Thompson et al., 1984). One possible reason for this is that the simplest circuits evolved first and the higher capacities (like the reversal ability) evolved later through the addition of new brain structures to the existing structure. Thus, NMR conditioning produces changes at a variety of levels in the brain, each level being responsible for a different aspect of the conditioning. Another

reason for the distributed nature of learning in the nervous system is that different responses are run by different basic circuits located anywhere from the medulla (breathing) to the M1 cortex (typing). If, for example, we had chosen to look at heart-rate conditioning instead of the nictitating response, we would have found ourselves involved with the workings of the amygdala (Kapp et al., 1984) or lateral geniculate nucleus (Cohen, 1985).

Site of Instrumental Conditioning

The problem of understanding instrumental conditioning is far more complex than that of classical for several reasons. For one thing, it comes in a great variety of forms. Instrumental learning includes any situation in which there is an increase or decrease in the probability of an emitted response because that response was followed by reinforcement or punishment. For example, learning to bar-press is a type of instrumental learning called **operant conditioning** in which there are no trials and the subject is free to make the response at any time when it is in the operant chamber. Sensory-discrimination problems usually involve discrete trials, as do instances of motor learning such as improving your golf swing or learning to shift gears. Avoidance-conditioning examples range all the way from a rat learning to avoid poisoned bait to children learning not to quarrel for fear of losing TV privileges.

Another source of complexity is the fact that any instance of avoidance conditioning seems to be a composite of many interlocked fragments of learning, each of which may be localized in a different part of the brain. (Recall the analysis of bar-press learning earlier in this chapter in which it was broken down into incentive learning, habituation, motor learning, and associative learning.) This is the same problem that we encountered with classical conditioning, but in the case of instrumental, it seems to be even worse. For these reasons, researchers who have made an effort to track down the location of engrams in the nervous system have generally avoided instrumental tasks so far and have chosen to begin their hunt with simpler forms of learning. For that reason, our discussion is limited to more global types of experimental analyses, and the generalizations we can draw may be considerably fuzzier.

An Operant Response: The Bar-Press In trying to localize classical conditioning in the nervous system, early research eliminated the entire neocortex from consideration by simply removing it and demonstrating that the learning could still take place. The same approach was tried with certain varieties of instrumental conditioning with the same result.

Decorticate rats learned a bar-press response just as readily as did rats with intact cortex (Oakley, 1979). These animals still had their limbic cortex; only the neocortex had been removed. Neodecorticates also were able to learn a visual-discrimination task in which they had to choose to enter a door with horizontal stripes rather than one with vertical stripes to get food. With no visual cortex, the animals probably could not tell vertical stripes from horizontal but solved the problem on the basis of how the total amount of reflected light varied as they moved their heads up and down or back and forth. If the stimuli had been altered to eliminate this possibility but to still allow a pattern discrimination, the rats probably would not have been able to learn.

The decorticate rats also failed to keep up their bar-press conditioning if the ratio of responses to reinforcements was raised too high. A normal rat can learn to press the bar 50 or more times to get a pellet of food, but the decorticates were unable to go beyond a ratio of 8-to-1 (Oakley, 1979). A possible explanation of this was that the loss of cortex left the animals too easily distracted by the food cup so that, instead of first pressing 8 times and then looking for the food in the cup, the rats checked the cup after each press and eventually forgot to return to the bar for more presses. This interpretation would agree with the idea presented in Chapter 3 that frontal cortex stores memories of long behavior sequences and inhibits end-of-the-sequence behaviors until all responses have been made. Oakley (1979) attempted to minimize the distraction factor by eliminating the bar and making the response-to-be-learned an opening of the cover of the food cup. Decorticate rats were then able to perform more than 8 responses for a single reinforcement, thus lending support to the distraction hypothesis.

Primates have considerably more cortex than do rodents and probably are more dependent on it for much of their learning. As we learned in Chapter 6, very few visual discriminations are possible for the primate without cortex. In fact, any type of sensory discrimination (auditory, somatic, etc.) seems to be cortically dependent in the primate. In Chapter 9, we saw that some motor sets and sequences seem to be located in the premotor and M2 cortex. The human, of course, cannot learn language or reasoning without temporal and frontal lobes. Unfortunately, however, these statements are all at the level of crude generalizations and are in sharp contrast with the specificity of our knowledge of classically conditioned engrams.

Avoiding Perseveration: The Hippocampus Another feature of the bar-press and visual-discrimination situations is the phenomenon of **extinction**, the loss of the conditioned response. In instrumental conditioning, the **extinction procedure** (the way in which extinction is produced) is to stop reinforcing the learner for the correct response; in classical conditioning, it is to repeatedly present the CS without the UCS. You might guess that extinction is the process of forgetting or unlearning the conditioning, but this seems unlikely because, after an interval of a day or so away from the learning situation, the animal again exhibits the CR (a phenomenon called spontaneous recovery). Extinction seems to be a process of constructing a new engram rather than disassembling an old one. In the classical situation, the subject is perhaps learning that the CS no longer has anything to do with the reflex; in the instrumental case, the response no longer has anything to do with obtaining the reinforcer. Does extinction learning depend more on any one part of the brain than on any other?

A great deal of data points to the hippocampus. For example, rats with hippocampal lesions had trouble extinguishing their bar-press response (Kimble & Kimble, 1965), their learned response in a straight runway (Jarrard et al., 1964), and conditioned brightness discrimination in a Y maze (Kimble, 1968). In the Y-maze experiment, the rat had to learn to choose the brighter of the two maze arms in order to obtain water. Rats with damaged hippocampi can learn this problem without much trouble, but they have great difficulty in unlearning it. The data in Figure 14.14 indicate that they had made little progress in 50 trials, and some of the animals still continued to run the maze without reinforcement after 100 trials (Kimble, 1968). Kimble interpreted these results as meaning that the rats without hippocampi were lacking a mechanism for inhibiting useless responses.

Much of the behavior of hippocampally lesioned animals appears to be one form or another of **per-**

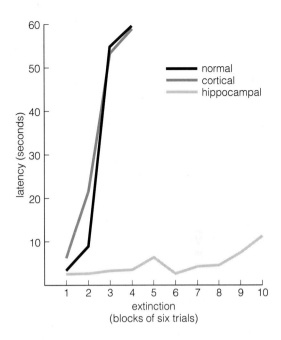

Figure 14.14 Data showing inability of hippocampally lesioned rats to extinguish a response that is no longer reinforced. Latency (the time taken to make a response once the stimulus is presented) should increase as extinction occurs. This increase in latency occurs for the normal rats and for a control group with lesions in the cortex, but the hippocampally lesioned rats continue to respond with no hesitation at all. (Adapted from Kimble, 1968)

severation—continuing to make a response long after it has ceased to serve any purpose. This describes very well what the hippocampally lesioned rat does in certain kinds of avoidance situations (Isaacson et al., 1966). Passive-avoidance conditioning involves training the animal to withhold a response that used to be reinforced but now leads to punishment. For example, a bar-press that used to deliver food now yields a shock to the feet through the floor grid. Not having a hippocampus makes it very difficult to learn not to press the bar, and the rat perseverates through a long series of shocks that any normal animal would have avoided.

Recall from our discussion of classical conditioning that the hippocampus appears not to be the originator of the basic association itself but rather functions only in particularly difficult situations such as discrimination-reversal conditioning. Is this also true of instrumental conditioning? Visual brightness discrimination is one form of instrumental conditioning, and we have seen that Kimble's rats achieved the discrimination without the use of a hippocampus. Kimble also tested his hippocampally lesioned rats on a discrimination-reversal task in which they had to learn to avoid the arm of the Y maze that they had been taking to the water reinforcer and choose instead the opposite arm that now led to water. Rats without a hippocampus never learned this (Kimble, 1968). They perseverated in choosing the arm in which they had been previously reinforced. The concept of perseveration seems not only to explain all the instrumental conditioning data but also to apply to the classical conditioning results. Failure of discrimination reversal in the NMR situation can be seen as perseverative responding to the old CS^+ after it had become the CS^-.

The hippocampus also comes into play in another difficult sort of operant-conditioning situation called a DRL schedule. A **schedule** is a set of rules for when reinforcement will be delivered. A **continuous reinforcement schedule** provides one reinforcer each time the response is made, whereas other schedules may require a number of responses before one reinforcer is given. (Decorticate rats, you will recall, have trouble with high-ratio schedules.) A **DRL schedule** is one that demands patience and waiting from the hungry rat; DRL stands for "differential reinforcement of low rates of responding." The first lever-press is reinforced, but the delivery of the reinforcement starts a waiting period during which the rat must not touch the bar. If a press is made during the waiting period, no food is given for the response, and the timer is reset to start the delay again. The subject will never receive another reinforcement unless the waiting period is allowed to finish.

Normal rats working on a DRL schedule learn to inhibit their tendency to press the bar too soon after the last reinforcement and adjust to a low rate that rarely resets the clock, thus ensuring them of obtaining nearly every reinforcement possible. Hippocampally damaged rats cannot seem to withhold their responses and wind up pressing the bar many more times for far fewer payoffs. Could they be having this

trouble because they are perseverating in some fashion? A study by Schmaltz and Isaacson (1966) suggests that this was the case. These experimenters knew that the standard procedure for training rats on a DRL schedule is to start the animals with a few days of continuous reinforcement to get the basic bar-press response well established before moving to the more difficult schedule. They suspected that the problems experienced by the lesioned rats might stem from this experience of obtaining a reinforcement following each press; therefore, they trained a group of normals and a group of hippocampally lesioned rats to bar-press on a DRL schedule, with neither group having prior experience on bar-pressing. With continuous reinforcement omitted, the lesioned animals learned on a DRL schedule, and their rate of acquisition was the same as that of the normals.

How can we interpret the DRL results? In a hungry animal, continuous reinforcement can produce a high rate of bar-pressing. To move from this schedule to a DRL, the animals had to learn that the rules had changed and that now a slow rate was demanded. Normal rats were able to suppress their old rate and learn the new rate, but the lesioned animals perseverated in their old rate. Hippocampally lesioned rats that had not been given the opportunity to acquire an "old rate" simply learned the rate appropriate to DRL. (The number of reinforcements available in DRL are too few to build the strong associations needed to produce a high rate.) Again, the hippocampus has been shown to be necessary for learning to occur in a situation where previous learning interferes with the acquisition of a new habit.

To summarize, the hippocampus is needed not to establish the basic associations in conditioning but to suppress responses that used to be associated with the reinforcement. Examples included extinction, passive avoidance, reversal learning, and DRL-schedule responding following continuous reinforcement.

Instrumental Conditioning in Other Brain Structures The hippocampus sends its output to over a dozen brain areas (Figure 14.15), but the one that is probably most important is the **cingulate gyrus** (SING-gyoo-let) of the limbic system (Swanson, 1979). Not only does it send fibers directly to this

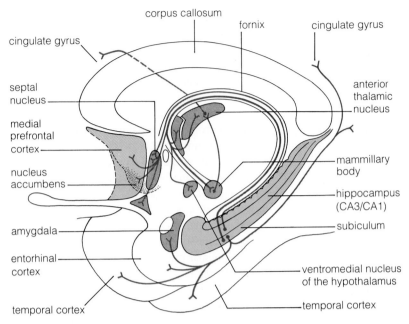

Figure 14.15 Diagram showing the destinations of fibers leaving the hippocampus. The medial prefrontal cortex is shown as transparent in order to reveal the nucleus accumbens behind it. (Adapted from Nieuwenhuys et al., 1981)

gyrus by way of the medial temporal lobe, it also has an important indirect link by way of the **mammillary bodies** of the hypothalamus and the **anterior nucleus of the thalamus**. Human clinical data suggest that both the mammillary bodies (Lhermitte & Signoret, 1976) and the anterior thalamus (Markowitsch & Pritzel, 1985) are involved in memory, but not enough data exist to enable us to guess at whether any sort of engram might be stored in those locations. In the case of the cingulate gyrus, experiments on animals have shown that lesions to that structure impair active-avoidance learning (McCleary & Moore, 1965). An example of this sort of task for a rat employs a two-chamber box with a shock-grid floor on one side and a safe, no-shock floor on the other. A small barrier separates the two chambers, and when the rat is placed in the shock chamber, it must react to a warning stimulus by climbing over the barrier to the safe side before the shock comes on. Like most cases of instrumental conditioning, this situation has never been explored in the fashion that Thompson analyzed NMR conditioning; thus, we have no idea of what fragment of the engram (if any)

might be stored in the cingulate. Recall from our discussion of the hippocampus that lesions to that part of the brain impair passive-avoidance learning, so it may be important that cingulate lesions have no effect on passive avoidance.

Another recipient of hippocampal output is the **septal nucleus** (Figure 14.15). Damage to the septal nucleus mimics hippocampal damage by making passive-avoidance learning more difficult (McCleary & Moore, 1965), but septal lesions can also impair active avoidance (Sagvolden & Johnsrud, 1982). With regard to active avoidance, some hints are emerging about what part of the engram might be involved. The active-avoidance task must involve quite a few elements to be learned, among which would be habituation to the apparatus, learning which chamber is associated with shock and how to get from one chamber to the other, learning that the warning signal will be followed by shock, and learning to be motivated by that warning signal. Each of these fragments of the engram probably is developed by a different brain structure.

It is the learning to be motivated by the signal

that may be occurring in a part of the septal nucleus. The motivation must be learned because the signal for action is simply some previously neutral stimulus such as a warning light that comes on 10 seconds before the shock. The light itself is not enough to produce the escape response, so during the early trials of the training, the rat is learning to associate the light with the shock. Through classical conditioning, the light (CS) comes to evoke the same fear (CR) that the shock (UCS) reflexively evokes. As soon as the rat has come to fear the light, it can then learn to escape the warning light by crossing the barrier. Its response is negatively reinforced by the decrease in fear that it experiences upon arriving in the safe chamber. What appears at first glance to be a case of instrumental learning then turns out to be a sequence of classical, then instrumental conditioning. Sagvolden and Holth (1986) speculate from their data that septal lesions interfere with the first half, the motivational or **incentive-learning** aspect.

Just because septal lesions interfere with avoidance learning doesn't mean that the septal nucleus contains the association between fear and warning stimulus, however. If we examine the connections of the septal nucleus, we find that it not only communicates with the hippocampus but with the amygdala as well. The **amygdala** (uh-MIG-duh-luh) is a collection of nuclei in the anterior temporal lobe at the forward tip of the hippocampus (Figure 14.15). It has very strong connections with the motivational–emotional areas of the hypothalamus (Chapter 13) and seems to be involved with making associations between environmental stimuli and internal motivational states like hunger and fear. The rat, foraging constantly for new sources of food, depends on its sense of taste to keep it out of trouble. Rats are very difficult animals to poison because of their ability to associate flavors with sickness and their habit of nibbling very small samples of any new substance. It is probably the amygdala that provides the engram linking the novel flavor with fear and avoidance. Years of research now clearly show that taste aversions are lost if the basolateral portion of the amygdala is lesioned (Sarter & Markowitsch, 1985). With regard to other types of avoidance, the data are conflicting and, so far, lead to no clear conclusions

(Sarter & Markowitsch, 1985). Engrams associating environmental events with reinforcement may also be located within the amygdala. Single-cell recordings from monkeys working on a bar-pressing task reveal many cells that increased their firing rates when reinforcement (food) occurred and decreased their rates during extinction (Nakano et al., 1987).

A major projection from the amygdala goes to the **dorsomedial nucleus of the thalamus (DMT)**, a site that neurosurgeons have often deliberately lesioned in humans for the relief of psychotic symptoms. The operation, called a **thalamotomy** (thal-uh-MOT-oh-me), is supposed to reduce emotional tension, anxiety, and agitation (Smythies, 1966), which certainly sounds like the human equivalent of what the animal must be experiencing in a shock avoidance–learning task. However, the DMT seems to be involved with more than just avoidance learning. Means discovered that DMT-lesioned rats were severely impaired in their ability to learn a discrimination task employing a combination visual and somatic S^+ (Means et al., 1973). Furthermore, if the lesions were made after training (rather than before), the rats apparently forgot what they had learned (i.e., the engram had been wiped out). In Chapter 16, we will see that humans with DMT lesions suffer severe amnesia.

In summary, the data from studies of instrumental condition are not as refined as those from habituation and classical conditioning, and the learning situations are far more varied and complex. We get hints that various structures might be involved in certain types or portions of learning, but the data are not definite enough to draw firm conclusions. We still suspect, as we have for many decades, that the limbic structures are the site of incentive and emotional learning (approach, avoidance, what to eat, what not to eat, etc.) and that the cortex stores specific sensory-discrimination learning and motor plans. The hippocampus seems to be related in some way to almost every case of learning. We have proposed that it does not contain basic associations such as CS to UCS but instead stores some sort of engram that allows the learner to avoid perseveration. In the coming sections, we develop this idea further.

One idea does seem to clearly emerge from the

mass of experiments in this area of research: the concept of **distributed learning**. Learning is not a specialized function of a single brain area or even of a select few. It appears that most of the areas of the nervous system are modifiable to some degree. The difference between cord and cortex seems not to be that the one cannot learn and the other can; rather, it is that the type of learning that can occur is different in the two structures.

Reinforcement

In an operant-conditioning situation, no response is learned unless it is followed by **reinforcement**. However, despite its obvious importance to learning, we still do not have a generally agreed-on definition of reinforcement. Some theorists use the term within the context of classical conditioning to denote the occurrence of the UCS following the CS and CR, whereas others limit the use of the term to instrumental conditioning. Behavior managers find it necessary to distinguish positive from negative reinforcement, but many brain researchers have disregarded this need and treated reinforcement as though it were equivalent with reward. The reason for all the various usages of the term is the fact that we still do not know quite enough to have produced a good, workable theory of reinforcement, and without this understanding to place limits on the concept, many different phenomena can be placed within its boundaries. For example, everyone seems to agree that some form of reinforcement is involved when a 4-year-old brushes her teeth and is praised by a parent, but can it possibly be the same thing that is happening in the rat's brain when food is delivered following a bar-press? Another problem is how reinforcement affects learning. Does it direct behavior by strengthening stimulus-response associations, or does it act by producing a state of pleasure (called "hedonic tone"), or by doing both? All these ideas and many more have been suggested, and we are far from resolving the problem. In the following section, you will see that a start has been made toward understanding the phenomenon, mostly in terms of locating reward circuits in the brain that are related to basic drives. We use the term *reinforcement* here as equivalent to reward and thus exclude negative reinforcement.

The Nature of SSB

The majority of our data concerning the brain mechanisms of reinforcement have come from work with chronically implanted electrodes, a technique discussed in Chapter 5. In 1954 the technique of implanting electrodes into the brains of animals so that they could be stimulated while moving about was very new. Several studies had discovered that an electric current to various parts of the brain stem seemed to have a punishing effect, and it was speculated that the pain system was being stimulated in those cases. The reticular formation was one such spot, and it was this site that a team of researchers at McGill University aimed their electrodes. James Olds and Peter Milner (1954) allowed their implanted rats time to recover from the surgery and then began testing their responses to reticular stimulation in a large, open box. Unknown to the researchers, the electrodes in one rat had slipped off their course and wound up in a different structure, the septal area. This rat behaved in a remarkable way when stimulated.

Olds and Milner decided to deliver a brain shock whenever the rat ran to one particular corner of the box. They soon found that the rat returned more and more often to this corner. They reasoned that the rat might be curious about the strange experience of brain stimulation but also realized that the animal acted as though the shock was a reward, so they arranged a different test. The animal was first deprived of food for 24 hours and then placed in a T maze in which both arms contained food in their goal boxes. If the animal turned into the right arm, however, a brief brain stimulation was given half way down the arm. Whenever the rat reached the food in the left arm or the shock-point in the right arm, it was returned to the start box for another trial. Gradually, learning occurred, but it was not a left turn toward food that grew more frequent from trial to trial. The rat learned to choose a right turn each time, and then it ran as far as the stimulation point and stopped there, ignoring the food that was waiting for it only inches away at the end of the arm. The best interpretation seemed to be that the electric current triggered a reward effect in the rat's brain.

These results inspired Olds to explore other areas of the brain. Was there one structure that served the function of reinforcement, a "reward center," or could the reward effect be obtained from many electrode locations? To simplify testing, Olds shifted the testing to an operant chamber and arranged the circuitry so that a bar-press would trigger a train of electrical pulses to the electrodes. In other words, the rat could learn to stimulate its own brain by pressing the lever. This technique has been used in hundreds of experiments over the last 30 years and is referred to as **self-stimulation of the brain (SSB)**.

Is There a Reward Center in the Brain? Reward sites have been found in many places including the amygdala, hippocampus, septal area, entorhinal cortex, caudate nucleus, hypothalamus, and substantia nigra (Olds & Fobes, 1981). These sites are not all equally potent, however. Locations in the limbic system typically yielded bar-press rates of about 200 per hour while stimulation of the best area, the **lateral hypothalamus** (LH), could produce 500–5,000 presses per hour. If allowed, some rats would spend the better part of 24 hours in pressing (Olds, 1956).

Why are there so many reward sites? Is it because there is no single reward center, or is it because these brain locations all feed into a single center so that stimulating them triggers activity in that center? Many experiments were run in which lesions were made in one or more of the various reward sites and the effect on SSB was recorded. It was found that most of the lesions anterior to the lateral hypothalamus (which includes all sites on the above list except for the substantia nigra) had little effect on SSB delivered to LH; the rats learned to stimulate their own lateral hypothalamus regardless of the lesion, thus showing that they were still being rewarded by the brain stimulation (reviewed in Olds & Fobes, 1981). For example, removing the amygdala would not prevent LH stimulation from being rewarding. In one set of experiments, almost all these sites were removed in one giant lesion. The

entire brain above the level of the thalamus and hypothalamus was removed without affecting the rats' ability to learn a simple postural response for LH stimulation (Huston & Borbély, 1973; Pritzel et al., 1983). Apparently, if there is a reward center, it is not in the higher levels of the cerebrum. If you wish to eliminate the SSB effect with lesions, the place to make them is in the regions posterior to the lateral hypothalamus. A number of experiments have been successful at disabling the reward mechanism with brain-stem lesions (Olds & Fobes, 1981). We will return later to the implications of this fact.

Is SSB Related to Natural Reinforcers? The lateral hypothalamus is the best area of the brain for obtaining a reward effect from electrical stimulation, and this nucleus is also heavily involved in hunger. Olds found neurons in LH that became active during food deprivation and stopped firing shortly after the animal ate (reviewed in Olds & Fobes, 1981). Rolls (1982) found that there were neurons in the lateral hypothalamus that responded to taste stimuli when the animal was hungry and that these cells also fired when SSB was delivered. In a microelectrode study, Nakamura and Ono (1986) found that about 50 percent of the cells that fired during SSB also responded when the reward was glucose. If a rat was made hungry by depriving it of food or injecting insulin (which speeds the depletion of nutrients from the blood), the animal increases its rate of responding for LH stimulation. On the other hand, a rat that has been force fed and is highly satiated for food decreases its SSB (Olds & Fobes, 1981). Some experimenters have also noted the same sort of relationship between SSB and thirst (reviewed in Stellar & Stellar, 1985).

It is tempting to hypothesize that the rewarding effect of LH stimulation comes from the fact that circuits involved in eating and drinking are being stimulated, but unfortunately not all data fit this interpretation. Both eating and drinking can be elicited by stimulating the hypothalamus at the correct locations (see Chapter 11 for details), and one might expect that an electrode site at which stimulation produced eating might also be an SSB site. This is frequently true, and that would lead you to expect that making the animal hungry would increase the

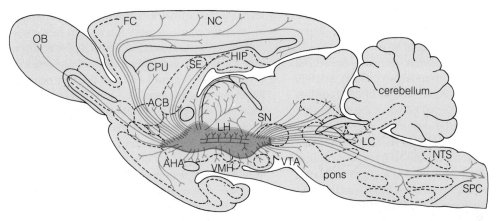

Figure 14.16 Midsagittal section of rat brain showing structures in which fibers of the medial forebrain bundle (MFB) terminate. For ease of illustration, the segment of the bundle in the hypothalamus is depicted as a solid mass. On either end of the hypothalamus, the bundle fans out into a wider array of smaller tracts. Abbreviations: ACB = nucleus accumbens, AHA = anterior hypothalamic area, LH = lateral hypothalamus, OB = olfactory bulb, CPU = caudate and putamen, FC = frontal cortex, HIP = hippocampus, LC = locus coeruleus, NC = neocortex, NTS = nucleus of tractus solitarius, SE = septal nucleus, SN = substantia nigra, SPC = spinal cord, VMH = ventromedial hypothalamus, VTA = ventrotegmental area. (Adapted from Nieuwenhuys et al., 1982)

SSB rate at this site. That also occurs. The problem is that hunger also increases SSB at sites from which eating cannot be elicited, and it is difficult to see how this could occur if the SSB site is tapping the eating circuitry (Frutiger, 1986). Mogenson (1969) found that water deprivation had no effect on SSB at sites from which drinking could be electrically elicited. Olds and Fobes (1981) conclude that we cannot decide at this time if SSB works because it activates the same circuits as those activated by food or water. It can safely be said, however, that the hunger and thirst mechanisms of the hypothalamus tie into the reward circuitry underlying SSB in some way that we have yet to discover.

Olds: The Medial Forebrain Bundle

The reward-mapping experiments of Olds led to the discovery that reward sites did not belong to any particular group of cells. There is no such thing as

a "reward center." The relevant structure turned out to be a tract called the **medial forebrain bundle (MFB)**. The bundle sends branches to every one of the areas from which SSB can be obtained when using LH electrodes. (Later we will see, however, that there are other weaker SSB sites in the cortex that are not a part of this system.) This bundle contains millions of axons of brain-stem neurons projecting up into the limbic system, striatum, and neocortex plus axons of neurons in those structures projecting back down into the stem. In a map of the nervous system, it resembles a very large, complex interstate highway connecting the two coasts of a continent (Figure 14.16). Reinforcement signals are probably only a fraction of the information the MFB carries between the higher and lower analyzers of the brain. In fact, the MFB contains approximately 50 fiber systems, and each of these presumably carries different information to and from different analyzers (Gratton & Wise, 1985). For example, in

Chapter 9, you learned about the nigrostriatal pathway connecting the substantia nigra with the corpus striatum; this path is a part of MFB.

The lateral hypothalamus seems to be a focal point for much of the up-and-down traffic in the MFB. Not only does the bundle send its fibers threading their way between the cell bodies of the nucleus but also many axons drop out of the tract in LH and synapse on the neurons there. Many neurons within LH send their axons into the MFB to make connections with higher- or lower-level structures. Because the business of the hypothalamus is to monitor and control the chemistry of the body (including water and nutrient supply), these connections in and out of LH must be for the purpose of allowing bodily needs to have some control over events in the brain stem and cerebrum. The most obvious form of control would be the reinforcement mechanism because that mechanism ensures that responses that have led to the satisfaction of some drive will be remembered and, in the future, will be selected in preference to responses that have not satisfied any bodily need. Perhaps then, reinforcement is the interplay between the internal chemistry of the body (hunger, thirst, sex, emotional and stress hormones, etc.) represented by the firing patterns of hypothalamic cells and the engrams for perception and responding that appear to be stored throughout brain stem, striatum, hippocampus, amygdala, cortex, and elsewhere. At this point in our discussion, this concept of reinforcement is vague and very general, but somewhat more clarity will emerge as we continue.

Olds developed a theory of reward and punishment that placed the reward function in the activation of the medial forebrain bundle and punishment (aversive stimulation) in a tract lying alongside the MFB, the **periventricular system**, which runs through the medial hypothalamus. This latter bundle of axons also connects brain-stem areas with higher structures such as the amygdala in the cerebrum. Presumably, it would be activated by painful stimuli and would be responsible for escape and avoidance learning. Stimulation of this system through implanted electrodes appears to be aversive to the animal and leads to responses that turn off the stimulation (Olds & Fobes, 1981).

In Olds's theory, the primary event in reinforce-

ment was the activation of interneurons with somas in LH that connect sensory inputs with motor outputs. Now, 20 years later, we know that it is impossible for all conceivable sensory–motor associations to take place at synapses with hypothalamic neurons. Recall that we have examined specific cases of such engrams forming in the cerebellum, cortex, and hippocampus and concluded that other types of engrams probably form in many other structures of the brain. Probably, the only responses directly controlled by LH neurons are feeding and drinking behaviors. It is quite possible, however, that the firing of LH interneurons is under the control of internal, chemical events within the body (e.g., nutrient shortage and water scarcity) and that they can control output cells, which in turn can influence all brain areas in which associations can be learned. Also, it is true that axons entering LH carry sensory information from smell and taste organs concerning food, water, sex, dangers, and novel stimuli; thus, Olds seems to have been correct in seeing LH as a point in which sensory, motivational, and motor factors are all brought together. We will see later that he was also correct as to the importance of LH neurons in reward.

Stein: The Norepinephrine Hypothesis

Many of the ascending axons in the MFB secrete norepinephrine (noradrenaline) at their terminals. The family of drugs called the **amphetamines** has the ability to stimulate the nervous system, and it accomplishes this through its effects on **noradrenergic neurons** (NOR-ad-dren-URGE-ik) (cells that use norepinephrine as a transmitter). Stein (1968) found that the rate of responding for SSB was enhanced by a dose of amphetamine and concluded that noradrenergic axons of the MFB were the ones involved in reward.

Anatomy of the Noradrenergic System If noradrenergic axons were responsible for the reinforcement effect of SSB, then it became important to know more about these cells. Specifically, where were their somas and terminals? With the histofluorescence method (Chapter 5), neurochemists have established that there are five clusters of noradrenergic cells in

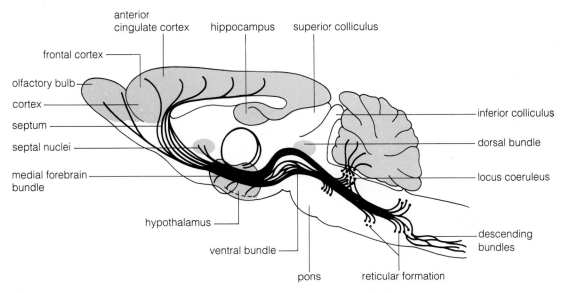

Figure 14.17 A midsagittal section of a rat brain showing the major noradrenergic (noradrenalin) paths. Noradrenergic cell clusters throughout the brain stem (the most outstanding of which is the locus coeruleus) send their fibers up through the MFB to many areas in the limbic system and neocortex (in color). (Adapted from Ungerstedt, 1971)

the brain and all lie within the brain-stem reticular formation (Figure 14.17). Most send axons up to higher centers by way of the MFB with some fibers reaching the neocortex (Moore & Bloom, 1979). The largest cell group is the **locus coeruleus** (suh-ROO-lee-us)—literally, the "blue spot" because of the deep blue color it takes on when stained for cell bodies. Stein proposed that part or all of this system is responsible for the brain mechanism of reinforcement.

Evidence For and Against the Norepinephrine Hypothesis Cocaine is a drug that acts as a stimulant. It is known to exert its effects through its influence on the **catecholamine** (KAT-uh-KOLE-uh-meen) transmitters—norepinephrine and dopamine. Specifically, it decreases the reuptake of catecholamine transmitters, thus enabling them to have greater effects on the postsynaptic neurons because of increased concentration in the synaptic gaps (Julien, 1981). This relates to reward because cocaine, like amphetamine, increases the rate of SSB

(cited in Fibiger, 1978). This fact was interpreted to mean that if a small release of norepinephrine (NE) at the axon terminals is reinforcing then a larger dose should be even more so and produce a higher response rate. Related evidence came from the findings showing that **chlorpromazine** (klor-PRO-muh-zeen), an antipsychotic drug, prevented SSB apparently by diminishing the reward effect. It is well known that chlorpromazine has its effect by blocking the receptor sites for catecholamine transmitters such as norepinephrine and dopamine. The problem with this evidence is that neither amphetamine, cocaine, nor chlorpromazine is selective for norepinephrine; they also facilitate or block dopamine transmission. This is important because the MFB contains a strong complement of **dopaminergic fibers** (axons using dopamine as a transmitter) and SSB should be exciting these axons just as much as the NE (noradrenergic) fibers. The possibility exists that the dopaminergic fibers, rather than the noradrenergic, might be producing or at least sharing in the production of the reward effects.

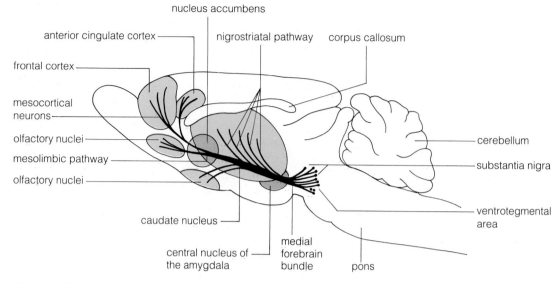

Figure 14.18 A midsagittal section of a rat brain showing the major dopaminergic paths. The two most important cell groupings are in the ventrotegmental area and substantia nigra of the midbrain. Their axons project forward through the MFB into the limbic structures. (Adapted from Ungerstedt, 1971)

Stein and Wise (1969) tried to establish which transmitter was involved by sampling the cerebrospinal fluid after SSB to see if the concentration of NE (norepinephrine) had increased. They found NE levels following brain stimulation to be significantly higher at reward sites than at nonreward sites. Nakano and colleagues (1987) found neurons in the amygdala that were inhibited by NE and that decreased their firing rate during rewarding events. Despite such positive evidence, the outcome of other research makes it doubtful that the NE system is related to reinforcement in any simple way. For example, compounds were discovered that could selectively block noradrenergic receptors while leaving dopaminergic transmission alone; when these NE blockers were given to rats, they failed to prevent the development of SSB. Furthermore, drugs that selectively blocked dopaminergic transmission did prevent SSB (reviewed in Wise & Bozarth, 1984). Data of this sort led Wise to propose the dopamin-ergic theory of reward as an alternative to the NE theory.

Wise: The Dopamine Theory

The two major dopaminergic pathways of the brain are the **nigrostriatal** (NIG-row-stry-ATE-ul) and the **mesolimbic** (MEE-zo-LIM-bik) (Moore & Bloom, 1978). These are shown in Figure 14.18. The mesolimbic pathway originates in a group of cells located in the **ventrotegmental area (VTA)** of the midbrain, and the axons project up through the MFB to terminate mainly in the limbic structures of the cerebrum and in the prefrontal cortex. Dopaminergic cells of the VTA (Figure 14.19) lie immediately medial to the DA (dopaminergic) neurons of substantial nigra, which projects through the MFB to the striatum (see Chapter 9). The nigrostriatal system appears to be more concerned with motor control, whereas the mesolimbic system relates to motivation

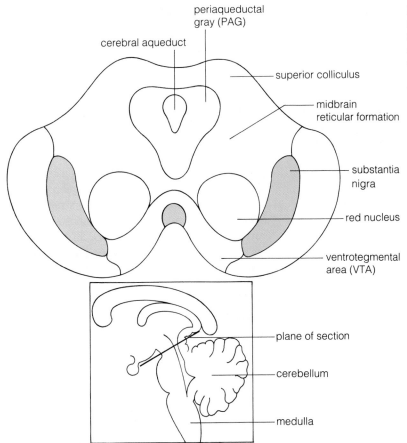

Figure 14.19 A cross section of the brain stem at the level of the midbrain showing the VTA and substantia nigra. The small, midsagittal view in the box indicates the plane in which the cross section was cut.

and reinforcement. Whenever dopamine is manipulated in an experiment, the effects on both systems must be kept in mind.

Evidence Favoring the Dopamine Theory Many cells have been found in the amygdala of the monkey that increase their rate of firing when an animal is being rewarded for making a correct response, and these neurons were shown to be sensitive to dopamine (Nakano et al., 1987). Rats will self-administer dopamine to their brains, and humans will take drugs like cocaine and amphetamine that stimulate dopamine synapses (cited in Stellar & Stellar, 1985). In humans, the state of euphoria (feelings of pleasure

and extreme well-being) induced by amphetamine can be eliminated with a DA-blocking drug but not with a drug that selectively blocks NE (Wise, 1980a). Blocking DA receptor sites also decreases the rewarding quality of food and water (Wise, 1980a). Under the influence of these drugs, rats will no longer press for SSB.

There is a problem in interpreting the DA-blocker data, however. Because a DA-blocking drug would work just as well on the nigrostriatal motor projection as it would on the mesolimbic path, the negative effect of the drug on SSB might not have anything at all to do with loss of reward effect. Instead, the rat may simply have trouble making the movements involved in responding (Mason et al., 1980). A variety of attempts have been made to surmount this problem. One such procedure is the **double-extinction method** that involves training a rat to press in two different operant chambers and then administering the DA blocker. The rat is returned to the first chamber where it begins to press for brain stimulation (usually to the lateral hypothalamus), but the rate quickly drops to zero as the drug takes effect. At this point, it is impossible to tell if the pressing has stopped because of motor problems or loss of the reward effect. The rat is then taken to the second operant chamber where it immediately begins pressing again. Apparently, the animal's movements have *not* been disabled by the drug. However, extinction again quickly occurs, revealing that the brain stimulation has indeed lost its rewarding effect (cited in Stellar & Stellar, 1985).

A different approach to this problem of motor disability interfering with the interpretation of DA-blocker experiments is that of Spyraki and co-workers (1982) who solved the problem by shifting from bar-pressing to place-learning. Their rats were repeatedly exposed to two compartments while under the influence of a DA-blocker drug. They were always fed in one compartment and never in the other. Normal rats would learn this simple place discrimination rapidly, but the DA theory would have to say that learning was not possible for these animals because the drug had disabled the reward circuit and the food could have no reinforcing effect. The animals were allowed to recover from the drug and then were given a choice of which compartment to enter. Controls that experienced food in one of the compartments without being under the influence of the drug spent significantly more time in that chamber than did the drugged group. Blocking dopamine transmission severely retarded place-learning despite the fact that the drugged rats had eaten all the food they had found in the one compartment. This use of place-learning clearly shows that motor problems caused by the DA blocker cannot explain the failure to learn. The rats were always able to express a preference for which compartment to enter and how much time they would explore it. The best way to interpret the results seems to be that the drug affected motivation, just as the DA theory suggests.

Apparently, DA blockers produce somewhat depressed rats that are still willing to eat food (out of habit?) but not interested enough to learn where to find it.

Modifying the DA Theory If dopamine cells are the ones involved in reward, then they should be the ones fired when the rat self-stimulates. This is probably true, but it is clear from recent evidence that DA neurons are not the only ones involved. The dopaminergic fibers of the MFB all originate in the brain stem and travel up into the cerebrum, but evidence has been found that the fibers stimulated in SSB that produce the reward effect descend from cerebrum to brain stem (Shizgal et al., 1980). This was discovered in a clever SSB experiment in which each rat had an electrode implanted into the VTA, along with the usual LH electrode. The electric currents in the LH electrode were of the usual variety, designed to fire the axon. In other words, the current made the outside of the cell membranes more negative, thus depolarizing them. Such depolarization opens the voltage-controlled ion gates and allows the transmembrane current to flow, thus initiating a nerve impulse. The current in the VTA electrode, however, was set in the opposite direction so that it would *hyperpolarize* the membrane and make it impossible for a nerve impulse traveling down the axon and into that area to open the ion gates. Any impulses triggered by the LH electrode, in axons going to the VTA, would be blocked by the hyperpolarization and never reach the terminals in the VTA. If the reward effect was the responsibility of ascending axons traveling to the cerebrum, this hyperpolarization block wouldn't matter; but if reward depends on the arrival of impulses in the VTA, then the bar-presses would not be rewarded. The results showed that hyperpolarization of the descending fibers to VTA stopped the SSB; reward is dependent on a descending route. Other data are also in agreement with this interpretation (Stellar & Stellar, 1985).

Where do these descending fibers originate? Lesions of the anterior hypothalamus and a nearby area called the **diagonal band of Broca** have been reported to hinder the SSB effect (Yeomans, 1982); this could be explained if the cell bodies of reward neurons were located in those areas. Another possible source for reward fibers is the lateral hypothalamus itself. Examining this possibility is a bit tricky because a lesion there, made in the usual manner, would burn out the tissue and make it impossible to test for SSB with LH electrodes. However, a recent development in neurochemistry has given us a neurotoxin (nerve poison) called **ibotenic acid** (EYE-bo-TEN-ik) that selectively kills the cell bodies in the region where it is injected without harming the axons passing through that area. In a recent experiment, this toxin was employed to kill LH cells on one side of the brain. Electrodes were then implanted into LH on both sides, and the rats were tested for SSB effect using each electrode in turn. It was found that the rats would press for stimulation on the unlesioned side but did poorly for stimulation on the lesioned side (Velley et al., 1983). This means that the fibers remaining in the MFB after the lesion were not enough to constitute the entire reward system. Apparently, fibers from the dead LH cells normally make a very important contribution to the downward path to VTA. Our conclusion is that reward fibers probably originate in the anterior hypothalamus, diagonal band of Broca, and, especially, in the lateral hypothalamus. The LH cells are the same ones that Olds made central to the reinforcement process in his theory.

Descending reward fibers flow into the brain stem, many of them ending in the VTA. Wise (1980a) has found a zone in which an SSB effect can be obtained that matches the boundaries of VTA. He concluded that the electrodes were triggering activity in the dopaminergic cells of VTA, but Arbuthnott (1980) presented evidence that suggests that the self-stimulation was actually triggering impulses in the telodendria of the descending reward fibers coming from cells in LH. No one knows what transmitter these descending fibers secrete, but there is reason to believe that it is not dopamine (Gallistel, 1983; Wise, 1980b), and recent evidence suggests that it could be acetylcholine (Gratton & Wise, 1985). This seems to conflict with the pharmacological data that strongly implicate dopamine in the reward process. Wise tried to synthesize these two sets of results by hypothesizing that the reward system consists of a descending projection through LH and a returning ascending projection from VTA (Figure 14.20). If this is true, then anything that makes VTA cells easier to fire should produce a stronger SSB effect from electrodes in LH. VTA cells are normally under a certain level of inhibition that can be decreased by some of the input neurons to VTA that use opioid transmitters (Kelly et al., 1980). Morphine mimics opioid transmitters; thus, injecting morphine into VTA should make it much easier to fire the DA neurons there. Following this logic, Broekkamp and colleagues injected morphine into the VTA region of rats barpressing for LH stimulation and found that the drug significantly enhanced the rate of responding (cited in Stellar & Stellar, 1985). This fits with Wise's idea that the descending neurons from LH have their reward effect by stimulating the DA cells of VTA. Further evidence comes from the fact that direct injection of opioids into VTA is rewarding (Wise & Bozarth, 1984).

A major target of VTA neurons is the nucleus accumbens (Figure 14.20), a structure that lies next to the head of the caudate nucleus and that is sometimes called the limbic striatum. Because of its close ties with both VTA and striatum, the nucleus accumbens might be the point in the nervous system where motivational factors like reinforcement select which behaviors the striatum will elicit (Taghzouti et al., 1985). Rats will self-stimulate for electrical stimulation of this nucleus (West & Wise, 1988) and for direct microinjections of amphetamine into the nucleus. It is clear that the DA fibers are involved because the amphetamine reinforcement can be reduced with DA-blocking drugs (Wise & Bozarth, 1984). Wise feels that nucleus accumbens is the place where cocaine and amphetamines have their effect on the reward system.

In summary, there is much evidence that dopamine neurons are central to the reinforcing effect that underlies SSB but that these cells are not the ones directly stimulated by the electric currents. Instead, the currents from the implanted electrodes trigger impulses in lateral hypothalamus, diagonal band of Broca, and anterior hypothalamus. These axons descend into the midbrain and synapse with the dopaminergic neurons of the VTA. The VTA neurons project back up into such limbic areas as the nucleus accumbens (the probable site from which

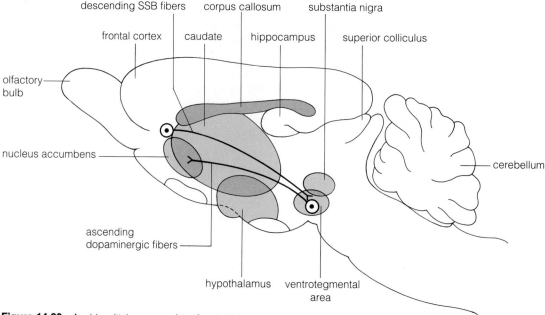

Figure 14.20 A midsagittal cross section of rat brain showing the descending fibers that are stimulated by SSB, their destination in the VTA of the midbrain, and the ascending fibers of the VTA dopaminergic neurons that connect to the nucleus accumbens and adjoining regions.

amphetamines elicit euphoria). Thus, the reinforcement system has at least a descending and an ascending limb.

SSB in the Medial Frontal Cortex

Most of the SSB sites in the cerebrum are cell groups that connect to VTA through the MFB, but there is one notable exception: the medial prefrontal cortex (Figures 14.16 and 14.20). When rats self-stimulate in this cortical region, they do not elicit activity in the reward system running through MFB to the nucleus accumbens. We know this because radioactive 2-deoxyglucose injected into rats while they were self-stimulating in their medial prefrontal regions shows up in places like the lateral septal nucleus, amygdala, and medial nucleus of the thalamus, but not in the nucleus accumbens. On the other hand, 2-DG injected during SSB in the lateral hypo-

thalamus did appear in the nucleus accumbens (Gallistel, 1983).

This difference in brain structures activated shows up in behavioral differences. SSB in the medial frontal cortex produces a lower rate of bar-pressing with fewer signs of arousal and excitement than does hypothalamic SSB. Further, the rats take much longer to learn to self-stimulate and must be given some preparatory sessions in which the stimulation is turned on by the experimenter before they begin to show any interest in obtaining the shocks by pressing the bar (Stellar & Stellar, 1985). This suggests that they have to learn the reward value of the stimulation much in the same way a rat learns to value a conditioned reinforcer because of its continued association with a primary reward.

As one might predict from autoradiographic studies, lesions of the MFB do not affect the SSB effect from prefrontal electrodes, nor do lesions in nucleus

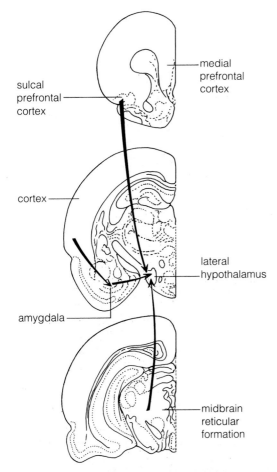

Figure 14.21 Sections of a rat brain showing location of the sulcal cortex and medial prefrontal cortex. The top section is the most anterior; the bottom, most posterior. The proposed secondary reward system would lead from the medial prefrontal cortex across to the sulcal cortex and then down to connect with the primary SSB system in the lateral hypothalamus. (Adapted from Rolls, 1977)

accumbens. However, cutting the paths that extend out laterally from medial prefrontal cortex does suppress cortical SSB, and this leads Stellar and Stellar (1985) to suggest that the prefrontal reward path may lead into the lateral prefrontal cortex, an area in the rat brain called the **sulcal cortex**. From the sulcal cortex, there are connections down to the entorhinal cortex, a major gateway into the hippocampus. The

hippocampus is one of the areas where electrodes will yield SSB, as is the sulcal cortex; thus, it is possible that further research may reveal a second reward system, perhaps connected more with secondary reinforcement than with primary. The two systems could connect with each other at the lateral hypothalamus (Figure 14.21), as proposed by Rolls (cited in Stellar & Stellar, 1985).

Summing Up

Two reward systems have been located in the brain. The MFB system has at least two stages, the first being a group of cells with their somas in lateral hypothalamus, diagonal band of Broca, and anterior hypothalamus and whose axons project down into the VTA of the midbrain. The second stage is the dopaminergic neurons of VTA that respond to the first-stage cells. These project back up through the MFB into limbic and cortical areas. The receiving area of greatest interest is nucleus accumbens because this seems to be the region responsible for the euphoric effects of drugs that work by amplifying dopamine transmission. The second reward system is speculative, the only hard facts being that a group of structures in the cerebrum support SSB but do this independently of the MFB and that the starting point seems to be the medial prefrontal cortex.

Evidence exists suggesting that the noradrenergic system may also be involved in reinforcement; but if it does play a role, the nature of the relationship is not yet clear. A clue from research on the amygdala, however, leads to one possible explanation. The central nucleus of the amygdala receives inputs from both the mesolimbic DA and NE systems. During reinforcement the dopamine input facilitates the cells of the central nucleus, while the NE input inhibits (Jiang & Oomura, 1988). Recall from Chapter 13 that the central nucleus seems to be involved with the approach–avoidance dimension of emotion. Thus, the DA input to the amygdala may be facilitating the neurons that generate an approach tendency, while the NE input inhibits the cells responsible for an avoidance. A positive reaction to a potentially reinforcing stimulus then may depend on both the initiation of an approach and prevention of avoidance.

Loss of these changes when food is the reinforcer should make food unreinforcing; indeed, lesions of the central nucleus produce aphagia or hypophagia (Jiang & Oomura, 1988). If this interpretation is correct, then Stein was correct about NE having a role in reinforcement, and Wise was also correct about dopamine.

◼ Summary

1. Habituation, probably the most basic form of learning, involves learning to ignore repetitive, meaningless stimuli. An example would be the loss of the orienting reflex to a novel unimportant stimulus. The opposite of habituation is sensitization, the enhancement of defensive reflexes following experience with some aversive stimulus.

2. Conditioning is a somewhat higher form of learning because it establishes an association between two stimuli or between a stimulus and response. In classical conditioning, the association is between a neutral stimulus (CS) and a reflex (UCS–UCR).

3. Instrumental conditioning involves the altering of emitted rather than reflexive responses. The association develops in this case because of the consequences of the response. Types of consequence include punishment, positive reinforcement, and negative reinforcement. The latter is the consequence employed in escape and active-avoidance learning. In discrimination learning, another form of instrumental conditioning, responses to one stimulus (S^+) are positively reinforced, while responses to any other stimulus (S^-) receive no reinforcement.

4. We infer that learning creates memory traces in the nervous system, which we call engrams. Lashley searched for the engram in the rat brain but found that it seemed to be distributed more or less evenly throughout the cortex, a principle Lashley called equipotentiality. In reality, Lashley was using a complex learning problem with many things to be learned, so that many fractional engrams were learned in many parts of the brain. This was the first hint that learning does not occur just in one place in the brain.

5. To find the simplest possible learning situation with the fewest complications, some researchers have turned to invertebrate species such as the *Aplysia* for subjects.

6. A study of the *Aplysia*'s gill-withdrawal reflex showed that habituation can occur in that system and that the engram probably consists of a temporary depression of the calcium current into the presynaptic terminals (synaptic depression). Sensitization is another learning process that can occur in the gill-reflex circuit. The sensitizing stimulus fires interneurons that employ serotonin as a transmitter. Serotonin acts on receptors that trigger an enzyme system employing adenylate cyclase, ATP, and cAMP to enhance calcium influx into the sensory cell axon terminal. The result is a prolonged increase in the quantity of transmitter released with each nerve impulse. This "memory" lasts until all enzymes have been inactivated.

7. Habituation has been demonstrated in mammals and is thought to be so basic a form of learning that it may even occur within the spinal cord. Short-term habituation of the acoustic startle reflex seems to take place in the pontine reticular formation (PFR), whereas long-term habituation may require the midbrain reticular formation (MBRF) and cerebellum.

8. Tsukahara found evidence that the engram for the conditioned paw-flexion response in the cat may be established within the red nucleus. Thompson found that conditioning of the rabbit's nictitating membrane reflex (NMR) takes place in the nucleus interpositus of the cerebellum. Because this nucleus sends output to the red nucleus, both types of classical conditioning seem to take place in the same circuit. Correct timing of the CR, in relation to the UCS, is probably learned in the cerebellar cortex.

9. Special forms of conditioning, such as trace-conditioning and discrimination-reversal, appear to depend more on the hippocampus than on the basic circuit in the cerebellum and brain stem. As conditioning occurs, the engram is apparently established simultaneously at several levels in the brain. The hippocampus seems especially important whenever a CR needs to be unlearned or inhibited.

10. Cortical ablation experiments show that operant conditioning can take place below the level of the cortex as long as none of the sensory analysis or motor capabilities of the cortex are needed for performance of the task. Cortex was needed if the learning task required the rat to resist distractions during an extended period of performance such as pressing the bar 10 times to get a pellet. In primates any type of sensory discrimination appears to depend on the presence of the cortex.

11. Extinction, which involves learning not to make a response that no longer is reinforced, depends on the hippocampus. Rats with hippocampal damage tend to perseverate in making unreinforced responses in extinction, passive-avoidance learning, discrimination reversal, and DRL performance.

12. Also involved in instrumental conditioning are two brain areas that receive output from the hippocampus: the cingulate gyrus and septal nucleus. The hippocampus connects to the cingulate gyrus by way of the mammillary bodies and anterior thalamic nuclei. Lesions of the cingulate cortex impair active-avoidance learning. The septal nucleus appears to be involved with incentive learning.

13. The amygdala connects with the septal nucleus and hypothalamus. This position makes it important for the conditioning of associations between environmental stimuli and internal motivational states such as hunger and fear. Consequently, it plays a part in the learning of preferences and aversions concerning choice of what to eat, what to drink, and who to mate.

14. Most of our knowledge of brain mechanisms responsible for reinforcement comes from studies of self-stimulation of the brain (SSB). Electrical stimulation of the brain through implanted electrodes is reinforcing at many brain sites, but the spot yielding the highest rates of SSB in rats is the lateral hypothalamus.

15. Some evidence suggests that one reason for the lateral hypothalamus being an excellent site for SSB is the possibility that stimulation there may elicit activity in eating and drinking circuits. More important, however, is the fact that the medial forebrain bundle (MFB) courses through that area of the hypothalamus and the current triggers impulses in fibers descending into the ventrotegmental area (VTA) of the brain stem.

16. Stein proposed that the reinforcement effect depended on the excitation of noradrenergic cells within the brain stem, especially those of the locus coeruleus, but considerable evidence has ruled out this possibility. A more recent theory by Wise holds that the descending nerve impulses triggered in the MFB produce a reinforcing effect by exciting dopaminergic cells in VTA. The dopaminergic axons ascend into such limbic structures as the nucleus accumbens, nucleus of the diagonal band of Broca, and septal nucleus. Drugs such as amphetamine and cocaine have their reinforcing effects by modulating dopaminergic synaptic transmission in these areas of the brain.

17. There is the possibility of a secondary reinforcement system involving the medial frontal cortex and some of the lateral frontal cortex (sulcal cortex in the rat). These areas yield lower rates of SSB than are obtained from lateral hypothalamus or other structures along the route of the MFB. Little is known of this system at this time, but there is the possibility that it may relate to secondary (learned) reinforcement rather than primary.

Glossary

acoustic startle reflex See startle response. (556)

active-avoidance learning A form of instrumental conditioning in which one learns to make a particular response in order not to experience an aversive stimulus. The consequence involved is negative reinforcement. (549)

adenosine triphosphate (ATP) A molecule produced by the mitochondria that can provide energy for chemical reactions by losing phosphate groups. (555)

adenylate cyclase An enzyme located on the inside surface of the cell membrane but connected to a neurotransmitter receptor on the outside; when activated by receptor binding it converts ATP to cyclic AMP. (554)

amphetamines A family of drugs whose chief action is stimulation of the nervous system through the noradrenergic neurons. (574)

amygdala A collection of limbic nuclei in the anterior temporal lobe at the forward tip of the hippocampus that is involved in motivational and incentive learning. (570)

anterior nucleus of the thalamus A brain structure that may be involved in memory. (569)

Aplysia A large marine snail widely used as a subject in neuroscience labs. (551)

associative learning Learning in which associations are formed between two stimuli or between a stimulus and a response. (548)

catecholamines The neurotransmitters: dopamine, epinephrine, and norepinephrine. (575)

cerebellar vermis A midline portion of the cerebellum that may be important to long-term habituation. (557)

chlorpromazine An antipsychotic drug that can block SSB, perhaps through its action on catecholamines. (575)

cingulate gyrus The area of the limbic cortex that forms the dorsal border of the corpus callosum. (568)

cocaine A drug that acts as a stimulant; its major site of action appears to be the nucleus accumbens in the reinforcement system. (575)

conditioned emotional response (CER) A set of somatic and autonomic responses (crouching, increased heart rate) that occur to any novel or aversive stimulus. (563)

conditioned response (CR) The reflex when elicited by the CS. (549)

conditioned stimulus (CS) A stimulus that is neutral prior to conditioning but through pairing with the UCS gains the ability to elicit the reflex. (549)

consequence Any event immediately following a response that alters the subsequent probability of that response. (549)

continuous reinforcement schedule A reinforcement schedule that provides one reinforcer each time a response is made. (568)

CS^+ The conditioned stimulus that is paired with the unconditioned stimulus (UCS). (564)

CS^- The conditioned stimulus that is not paired with the unconditioned stimulus. (564)

cyclic adenosine monophosphate (cAMP) A form of phosphorolated adenosine having only one phosphate group; frequently plays the role of a "messenger" within the cell by carrying the information that receptors have been activated. (555)

delay conditioning A conditioning procedure in which there are several seconds between the beginning of the CS and UCS. (563)

dentate nucleus A cerebellar nucleus that may be involved in forming the association between a CS and UCS in NMR conditioning. (560)

diagonal band of Broca A part of the septal nucleus that is related to reinforcement. (578)

discrimination learning A form of instrumental conditioning in which one learns to make the response only in the presence of a particular stimulus (termed CS^+). (549)

discrimination-reversal learning Discrimination procedure involving a second stage in which the subject learns to treat the previous CS^- as a CS^+, and vice versa. (564)

dishabituation The process in which an aversive stimulus sensitizes a reflex that has already undergone habituation. (548)

distributed learning The idea that engrams are spread throughout the nervous system rather than concentrated in one structure devoted exclusively to memory. (571)

dopaminergic fibers The axons of dopamine neurons. (575)

dorsomedial nucleus of the thalamus (DMT) A structure forming part of the route from the amygdala to the frontal lobes that appears to be critical for some forms of memory. (570)

double-extinction method A procedure for demonstrating that a drug that can induce extinction of a conditioned response does so because of its negative effect on the reinforcement system rather than through the production of interfering motor symptoms. (578)

DRL schedule A procedure in which reinforcement can only be obtained by waiting a while after each response before making another. (568)

emitted responses Those that cannot be elicited but that occur spontaneously. (549)

engram The neural representation of a memory. (550)

equipotentiality Lashley's principle that any engram is distributed more or less evenly throughout the cortex. (550)

extinction The loss of the conditioned response when the CR is unreinforced (instrumental conditioning) or when the CS occurs without the UCS (classical conditioning). (567)

extinction procedure Either the cessation of reinforcement (instrumental conditioning) or the presentation of the CS without the UCS (classical conditioning). (567)

habituation Form of learning in which a repeated stimulus having no appetitive or aversive force comes to be disregarded. (547)

ibotenic acid A neurotoxin important for lesion research because it selectively kills the cell bodies in the region where it is injected without harming the axons passing through that area. (579)

incentive learning Associating motivation with stimulus cues (as in learning that a reinforcer is present under certain conditions). (570)

lateral hypothalamus (LH) The brain site that yields the highest rates of SSB; probably because it contains the fibers of the medial forebrain bundle. (572)

locus coeruleus A collection of noradrenergic cells at the pontine-midbrain border that send their axons widely throughout the cortex as a part of the ascending reticular formation. (575)

mammillary bodies Hypothalamic nuclei that may be involved in memory. (569)

Marr–Albus theory The theory that the association

formed in NMR conditioning is found in the cerebellar cortex. (562)

medial forebrain bundle (MFB) A collection of tracts, some of which connect brain-stem areas with limbic structures involved in reinforcement. (573)

mesolimbic tract The axons of dopaminergic cells in the VTA that project to nucleus accumbens and other limbic structures; an important part of the reinforcement system. (576)

negative reinforcement An event in which the probability of a response is increased because the response leads to the removal of an aversive stimulus. (549)

nictitating membrane reflex (NMR) Closure of the inner eyelid in response to any stimulus potentially harmful to the eye. (559)

nigrostriatal tract The axons of dopaminergic cells in the substantia nigra that project to the striatum through the medial forebrain bundle. (576)

noradrenergic neurons Cells that use norepinephrine as a transmitter. (574)

nucleus interpositus A cerebellar nucleus that may be the site of the auditory-somatic association in NMR conditioning. (560)

operant conditioning A form of instrumental conditioning in which there are no trials and the subject is free to make the response at any time. (566)

orienting reflex A collection of reactions (including receptor organ aiming and cortical arousal) all aimed at rapid analysis of the stimulus and readying you for a proper response to it. (547)

passive-avoidance conditioning A form of instrumental conditioning in which one learns not to make a particular response in order not to experience an aversive stimulus. The consequence involved is punishment. (549)

periventricular system A collection of tracts connecting brain-stem areas with limbic structures apparently related to punishment and aversion. (574)

perseveration Continuing to make a response long after it has ceased to serve any purpose. (567)

positive reinforcement An event in which the probability of a response is increased because the response is followed by an appetitive stimulus. (549)

presynaptic facilitation An increase in the efficacy of a synapse induced by a third neuron that has a terminal synapsing on the terminal of the presynaptic cell. (554)

punishment An event that lowers the subsequent probability of the response it follows. (549)

Purkinje cells A layer of cells in the cerebellar cortex where the association between a CS and UCS might take place. (561)

red nucleus A part of the motor system located near the substantia nigra at the top of the midbrain. (558)

reinforcement Increasing the probability of a response by following it with the removal of an aversive stimulus (negative reinforcement) or the addition of an appetitive one (positive reinforcement). (571)

S$^+$ The stimulus that signals that the response will be reinforced. (549)

S$^-$ The stimulus that signals that the response will not be reinforced. (549)

schedule A set of rules for when reinforcement will be delivered. (568)

self-stimulation of the brain (SSB) An arrangement whereby the subject can provide a brief, non-injurious electrical current or drug dose to its own brain. (572)

sensitization The enhancement of a defensive reflex following a number of recent experiences with strong or noxious stimuli. The opposite of habituation. (548)

septal nucleus A limbic structure near the midline; apparently involved in transferring emotional-

motivational information in and out of the hippocampus. (569)

sprouting A response to brain damage in which cells that have lost some inputs make new synapses with nearby axons through their growth of new telodendria and terminals. (559)

startle response A defensive reflex that tends to curl the body into a hunched-over, protective posture with the head down when a sudden, loud noise occurs; same as acoustic startle reflex. (547)

sulcal cortex An area of lateral prefrontal cortex in the rat brain that may be a part of a second reward system apart from the mesolimbic system. (581)

synaptic depression A decrease in calcium influx into the presynaptic terminal, which reduces the release of transmitter. (553)

thalamotomy Ablation of a portion of the thalamus. (570)

trace conditioning A conditioning procedure in which there is a gap between the CS and UCS. (563)

unconditioned response (UCR) Any reflex response. (548)

unconditioned stimulus (UCS) Any stimulus that can automatically elicit a reflex prior to conditioning. (548)

ventrotegmental area (VTA) A midbrain nucleus with dopaminergic cells whose axons form the mesolimbic portion of the medial forebrain bundle; an important part of the reinforcement system. (576)

The Hippocampus
in Learning and Memory

We have seen that the hippocampus is involved at some higher level in both classical and instrumental conditioning and that one way to characterize this involvement might be as a mechanism for decreasing useless response perseveration. In this chapter, however, we find that the task of decreasing response perseveration is just one aspect of hippocampal function. The study of hippocampal EEG and single-cell recordings made as animals move freely through their environments has begun to reveal the nature of the memories formed in the hippocampus and has contributed to the development of the idea that there is more than one kind of memory system in the brain.

■ Hippocampal EEG: Theta Rhythm

So far we have tried to understand the hippocampus by discovering what happens when it is lesioned and what individual hippocampal neurons do as the animal is undertaking some bit of learning. Another approach is to implant macroelectrodes into the structure and record the simultaneous voltage variations from thousands of neurons there. A macroelectrode is usually a length of wire having roughly the same thickness as the wire in twist ties, and it is insulated except for 1 mm at the tip. The uninsulated tip picks up a blended combination of EPSP and IPSP fields from thousands of nearby neurons, all merged into one continuous series of up-and-down voltage changes. When these voltage variations are amplified and written out by a machine, they are called an **electroencephalogram** or simply, an **EEG** record. (See Chapter 5 for an explanation of EEG recording.)

Two such EEG records taken from the hippocampus are shown in Figure 15.1. The two records look so different that you might think they were recorded at two different brain sites, but they actually were taken from the same region at two different times. Whereas the EEG in the top line is small and highly irregular in its ups and downs, the bottom record shows a relatively regular, rhythmical series of waves that have a frequency of about 4–5 Hz (cycles per

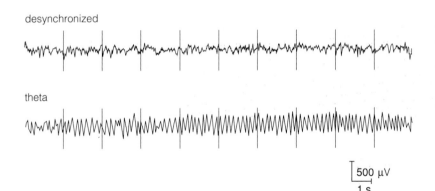

second). These waves are called **theta rhythm**. Much can be learned from theta's appearance and disappearance in the EEG records from the behaving animal.

Theta rhythm appears during the early stages of conditioning when the animal is still getting used to the situation and is orienting to the conditioned stimulus (CS), unconditioned stimulus (UCS), and extraneous stimuli (Grastyán et al., 1959; Smythies, 1966). Bennett's research indicated that theta rhythm accompanies the process of attention in operant conditioning (Bennett, 1975). After reviewing all related research, Bland (1986) concluded that there were two types of occasion in which theta rhythm would occur: when the animal is engaged in voluntary movements like walking or swimming and when the subject is immobile but attending to a novel stimulus. Bland also recorded from single cells in the hippocampus while simultaneously recording EEG and found that the nerve impulses within a single neuron correspond to troughs of theta waves during walking. The same correspondence (in the same neuron) appeared when the animal was hearing a novel sound but disappeared following habituation. Habituated stimuli do not elicit theta and neither do reflexive behaviors like scratching, licking, and sneezing (Bland, 1986). The behavior of theta rhythm shows us that the hippocampus systematically monitors all ongoing sensory and motor events that are being attended and that demand, or may demand, voluntary adjustments. At first glance, this monitoring function would not seem to be related to the task of limiting response perseveration, but as we review the research on hippocampus, we find that a good explanation can be devised.

Spatial Memory or Context?

The most exciting results in hippocampal research have come from studies in which microelectrode recordings were made from single neurons. This approach, more than any other, has inspired the creation of theories to explain hippocampal function. We first examine the theory of O'Keefe and Nadel and then see how their ideas might be incorporated into the larger framework of context theory.

Place Cells of the Hippocampus

The hippocampus contains a number of different cell types, and not all are related to theta rhythm. O'Keefe and colleagues have studied a type of neuron in rat hippocampus that they call a **place cell**. Amazingly enough, the receptive fields (RFs) of these neurons are actually *places* in the rat's environment. Figure 15.2 shows a diagram of the lab in which the data were collected. The rat's task was to learn how to find its way to the food at the end of one arm of the

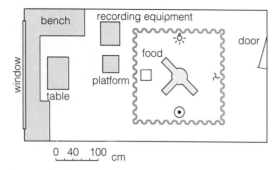

Figure 15.2 Floor plan of O'Keefe's lab and apparatus. The wavy lines represent the curtains around the maze. Each side of the curtained enclosure was made distinctive with one stimulus source. These sources were (clockwise from the top) a light, fan, buzzer, and cardboard square. (Adapted from O'Keefe & Conway, 1978)

T maze. The maze was located inside a square, curtained enclosure containing four stimulus objects—one placed near each of the four sides to give the rat a locational cue. Two sides were marked by auditory cues (fan and buzzer) and the other two by visual cues (square card and light). On each trial, the rat was placed at the end of the middle arm of the T and allowed to find which one of the other arms contained the food. The particular variation of this experiment had the food located toward the corner between the light and the card. Ordinarily, a rat might solve this problem by learning to always turn left at the choice point, but the experimenters wanted the subject to use the locational cues. To prevent turn learning, they rotated the maze between trials so that the starting arm was sometimes pointed toward the corner between the light and the fan, sometimes toward the card/buzzer corner. On every trial, however, the food was placed in the arm pointed at the light–card corner so that reaching it meant a right turn on some trials and a left on others. Microelectrodes were implanted in the rat's hippocampi and single-cell recordings were made as the subject traversed the maze. It was in this way that place cells were discovered.

A place cell is quiet as the rat runs up the starting arm toward the choice point of the maze but comes to life as the animal runs down the correct arm toward the food. The cells are not excited by the reinforcer, however, but by the location in the enclosure. Because the enclosure is a deliberately limited-stimulus environment, there is hardly any way for the rat to perceive one location versus another except by the use of the four cues provided by the experimenters. So, location boils down to designations like "toward the light" or "between the light and the fan." Apparently, various place neurons are turned on by the rat's proximity to one or another of these locations (places), and there seems to be a different set of neurons for each location (O'Keefe & Black, 1978; O'Keefe & Nadel, 1978).

To make the rat's behavior easier to visualize, a tiny LED was fastened to each subject's head and programmed to light up whenever a place cell began to fire. A typical record from one cell, as recorded by an overhead camera, is summarized in Figure 15.3. The first four frames in the figure (a–d) show the response of the place cell on four trials. Both the locational cues and the maze were rotated between each pair of trials so that no cues from outside the enclosure (e.g., traffic noise) would be reliably associated with any place and so that neither a right or left turn would be associated with the food. The food location did remain constant with regard to the four cues, however. The reinforcer was always on the arm pointed at the card/light corner. To make the results easier to understand, frames a–d of Figure 15.3 were each rotated to put the card/light corner at the same place in the pictures, and then the data points from all four were superimposed on one maze diagram. The result is shown in frame E which reveals clearly that the neuron tended to fire most often in the arm leading to the card/light corner (O'Keefe & Black, 1978).

According to O'Keefe and Nadel (1978), the function of the hippocampus is to provide the animal with a spatial memory (a "map") of its environment, and the learner's acquisition of this map depends on the place cells. In their theory, the hippocampus uses the sensory input it receives to calculate the organism's location in the environment with reference to the places identified by place neurons. It is apparent from the data that these cells are somehow specific to places as such and not merely to individual stim-

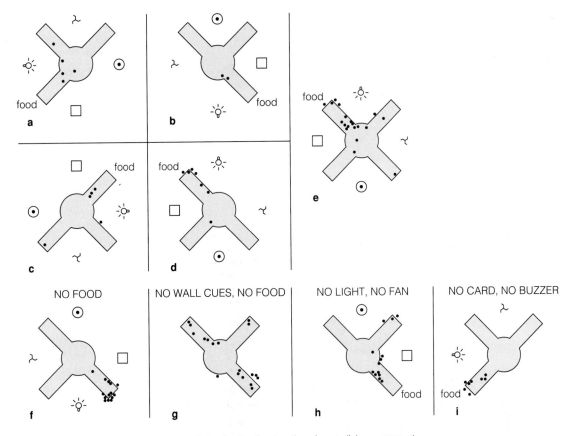

Figure 15.3 Data from experiment by O'Keefe showing locations in a radial arm maze at which one particular hippocampal place cell fired as the rat moved about. Each dot is one firing location. Frame **e** condenses the data from frames **a–d**. (Adapted from O'Keefe & Black, 1978)

ulus cues. For example, when one or two of the four cues used in O'Keefe's experiment were removed, place cells were still just as accurate in detecting the location of food in the maze (Figure 15.3, h and i). Each corner was apparently recognized not by just one or two stimuli but by its position relative to all available cues. For these cells to have this property, each would have to receive information about all outstanding environmental stimuli that could be used to recognize a location, and then all these sensory inputs would have to be cross correlated or associated with one another. Assuming that a rat possesses that sort of neural mechanism, then as it runs

down the correct arm of the T maze, its place cell for that location is using information about the approach of the light on its right and the card on its left, as well as the receding fan noise at its back right and the buzzer to its back left. Apparently, all these facts help determine the firing of this one neuron but in such a way that not all of them have to be present for the cell to detect the place it has learned. Its firing can be elicited by a partial pattern. If all cues are removed, of course, the cell can no longer respond *selectively* to just one part of the environment; as you can see from Figure 15.3g, it begins to respond no matter where the rat is in the maze.

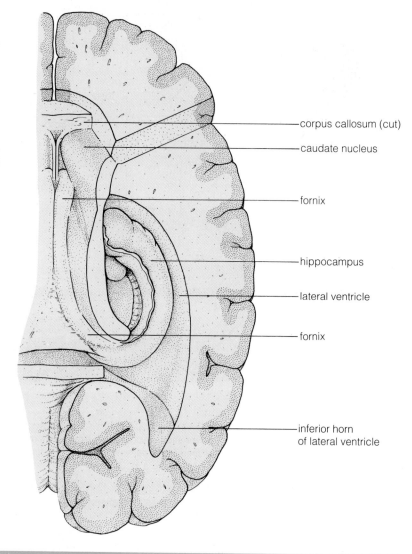

Figure 15.4 Horizontal view of the human brain with the cortex dissected away down to the level of the temporal lobe. On the left, the fornix and caudate nucleus swing up out of the lateral ventricle and curve forward into the frontal lobe. The hippocampus lies along the floor of the anterior arm of the lateral ventricle, its tip curving medially within the temporal lobe. (Adapted from Moyer, 1980)

corpus callosum (cut)

caudate nucleus

fornix

hippocampus

lateral ventricle

fornix

inferior horn of lateral ventricle

(Some cells found by O'Keefe & Black [1978], however, stopped firing altogether when all locational cues were removed.)

Anatomical Considerations

O'Keefe and Nadel relate the mapping function to one part of the hippocampus and the novelty detection to another. The hippocampus (Figure 15.4) appears to be a three-stage analyzer. Sensory infor-

mation from neocortical areas of the temporal lobe enters the **entorhinal cortex** (see hippocampal cross section in Figure 15.5) and is passed along through the **perforant path** into the first stage, the **dentate gyrus. Granule cells** of the dentate gyrus send their fibers into the second stage, a crescent of pyramidal-shaped cells called **CA3. Pyramidal cells of CA3** send one set of axon branches through the fimbria and into the fornix, while the other set of branches goes to the third stage, another zone of pyramidal cells called **CA1** (Swanson, 1979).

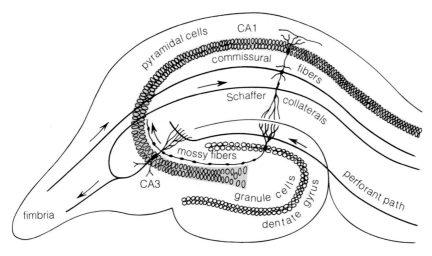

Figure 15.5 A cross section of rat hippocampus showing the major pathways. The perforant path consists of axons of entorhinal cortex cells (out of the picture to the right). They synapse with the dendrites of the granule cells in the dentate gyrus, a C-shaped structure that fits around the end of the CA3 region. Axons of granule cells are the mossy fibers, which synapse with CA3 neurons. Pyramidal cells of CA3 send one branch of each axon into the fimbria and, by way of the fornix, into the lateral septal area. The other axon branch, the Schaffer collaterals, makes connections with the pyramidals of CA1. Also synapsing with these CA1 cells are the commissural fibers crossing the midline from the hippocampus of the other hemisphere. (Adapted from Bliss & Dolphin, 1982)

To make a map that includes all four cues in O'Keefe and Black's experiment, the rat would have to establish associative links between four stimulus inputs to the hippocampus (card, fan, buzzer, light). The theory holds that the dentate gyrus receives all the sensory inputs needed to create the cognitive map and passes them to CA3 and CA1 where the map is located. Various places in the environment and the associative links between them are found in CA3, whereas CA1 is organized to detect changes in the map (novelty) and focus attention on them (orienting response). If this theory is correct, destruction of CA3 should make spatial learning impossible. This was shown by Handelmann and Olton (1981). Animals with lesions that specifically destroyed CA3 neurons were unable to learn the maze when correct responding depended on the ability to discriminate places in the environment.

Cognitive Maps and Reversal Learning

Recall that Chapter 14 reviewed a number of experiments that seem to link the hippocampus with the prevention of perseveration or the elimination of responses that have become useless because of changing stimulus conditions (e.g., an extinction situation). We must now ask if this control over out-of-date responses is an additional function of the hippocampus or one that grows out of its ability to generate cognitive maps. To answer this question, let's consider one type of learning situation in which perseveration can occur—discrimination reversal of the nictitating membrane response (NMR). Hippocampal neurons change their firing patterns as NMR conditioning takes place (Thompson, 1988), suggesting that some sort of memory is being formed there, and the ability to accomplish reversal learning is lost if the hippocampus is destroyed (Berger & Orr, 1982).

In discrimination-reversal conditioning (Chapter 14), the subject has been conditioned to two CSs, an old one (such as a 200-Hz tone), and a new one (a 600-Hz tone) but must now respond only to the new one. To solve the problem, the subject must be able to discriminate the situation in which the 200-Hz tone is the CS^+ from a situation in which a 600-Hz tone becomes the CS^+. Despite more recent training on the 600-Hz tone, the subject finds it difficult to avoid responding to the incorrect stimulus (200 Hz) because of the original association between this stimulus and the UCS. As a result of the reversal, the subject has acquired two competing associations to the same UCS, and this conflict could seriously impair performance. Apparently, the hippocampal engram is used in the suppression of the out-of-date response to the previous CS. But what mechanism decides that it is the 200-Hz tone rather than the 600-Hz tone that must be suppressed? Could a spatial map engram provide the basis for knowing which CS is the current one? Although O'Keefe and Nadel do not specifically address this problem in their theory, it is possible to see how their ideas might be extended to handle the problem.

It is not immediately apparent how the learning of a spatial map could be of any use to the subject in NMR-reversal conditioning because all stimulus cues seem to come from the same point in space. The solution to this problem lies in the fact that all 200-Hz trials came at one time and all 600-Hz trials at a different, later time. They were never intermixed. This means that the spatial map present during the 200-Hz trials on, for example, Tuesday could be different than that of the 600-Hz trials on Wednesday. The spatial map is a set of locations for specific stimuli, and if these stimuli change, the map changes. For example, let's say that on Tuesday there are faint sounds of a very large introductory psychology class getting out filtered in from the hall outside. One lab assistant, who always stands on the rabbit's left, had a cold and sneezed persistently. On Wednesday (with the new CS^+) no classes were changing, the head cold had cleared up, and the ventilator fan in the ceiling had begun to develop a squeak. Each of these stimuli had a particular *location* in the lab, thus we

can assume that hippocampal place cells altered their firing patterns to include all of them. The resulting cognitive map of these extraneous stimuli gave the animal different stimulus *contexts* in which to place the two CSs. The 200-Hz tone was associated (entirely without the experimenter's knowledge or approval) with the sneezing and student noises, whereas the 600-Hz tone became linked instead to the quiet hall and noisy fan.

Thus, the cerebellum can build up two conditioned responses (CRs), one to the 200-Hz tone and the other to the 600, and the hippocampus can say, "Don't blink to that 200-Hz tone. There isn't any sneezing or noisy students. The fan is squeaking, so blink when you hear a 600-Hz tone." We are suggesting that the hippocampus is able to suppress a response that has become associated with one cognitive map while allowing a CR that is associated with another. The map becomes a context that provides a "date stamp" for any bit of learning and tells the rest of the brain whether the current CS is the one that was correct on the current set of trials or the previous set. Each time the animal's environment shifts, a different map is established in the hippocampus, and it is the responses that are associated with this map that the hippocampus will allow.

Beyond Cognitive Maps

There seems to be little question that the CA3–CA1 region of the hippocampus can act in certain situations as a cognitive map, but the suggestion has been made that this map is only a single facet of that structure's true function (Hirsh, 1980). A recent set of experiments casts new light on the mapping idea and enables us to broaden the theory considerably.

Kubie and Ranck (1983), like O'Keefe, used microelectrode recordings to find place cells in the hippocampus but studied these cells in a variety of environments rather than just one. Recordings were made from a single cell as the rat was successively exposed to a radial arm maze, operant chamber, and home box, all placed at exactly the same point in the room so that the environmental cues would be identical. A **radial arm maze** (Figure 15.6) has a number of arms radiating out from a central circular platform like spokes from the hub of a wheel. The rat's task in Kubie and Ranck's experiment was to learn to run down each arm of the radial maze to reach the food at the end. Because rats, when they exit an arm, do not systematically enter the next arm, proceeding around the maze in perfect clockwise or counterclockwise order, they had to learn to keep track of which arms they had already entered and which still contained food. In the operant chamber, they learned to bar-press on a DRL schedule; in the home cage, they were given pups to retrieve and food to find at various locations. All these learning problems were designed to invoke the participation of the hippocampus.

A number of place cells were found, some of which only became active in one of the three environments (24 percent), some in two of them (33 percent), and some in all three (43 percent). The behaviors of a two-environment and a three-environment cell are illustrated in Figure 15.6. In Figure 15.6a, one of the neurons has a split receptive field (RF) that includes two different arms of the maze, while the other neuron is specific to only one place in the maze. These places, however, are not exactly "in" the maze because they seem to be based heavily on far cues (from outside the maze). This is illustrated in Figure 15.6b, which shows that the cell responds at exactly the same spot in the room despite the fact that the maze has been rotated so that a different arm now occupies this space. This is not too surprising because all arms of a radial arm maze are deliberately designed to look alike and do not have sides, thus forcing the animal to use distant cues. In the operant chamber and home cage, however, the RFs rotated with the environments, indicating that near cues from within the apparatus were dominating the cell's response.

The really surprising finding in these results was that the same neuron would simultaneously develop selectivity for a different place in each different apparatus. Neuron 227–8 fired within two places in the maze but only one in the home cage, and the cage location seemed to have nothing in common with either of the maze locations. In the operant chamber, it had still two other places. Kubie and Ranck were unable to find any organizing principle that could be used to predict which place a cell would pick when exposed to a new environment. This is defi-

nitely not what we would expect of a cognitive map. If O'Keefe and Nadel are correct in their theory, then the mapping going on in the hippocampus is certainly not a simple one-to-one correspondence such that each cell becomes specific to a single place in a particular environment. Although these results certainly do not refute O'Keefe and Nadel's theory, they do suggest that the theory needs to be broadened from its original limits.

Deciding that a neuron's activity is specific to a particular place is not quite as easy as we have made it sound. For example, a cell that is assigned an RF near the water bottle in the home cage may fire continually as the rat moves around other areas of the cage, but it fires at a noticeably higher rate in the vicinity of the water bottle. Any activity lower than the high level associated with a particular place was designated as "background" and was considered to be random firing. This supposedly random background displayed some interesting behavior, however. In a number of cells, it was present only in certain environments. A cell with an RF plus a strong background level of firing in the maze might not emit a single nerve impulse during 10 minutes of recording in the operant chamber. Other cells have strong background rates in one apparatus and weaker rates in another environment. In other words, the background rate seems to be a product of which environment the animal is currently experiencing. Kubie and Ranck (1984) took this fact to mean that the background firing was somehow specific to the environmental **context**, that is, to all the surrounding stimuli.

A possible reason for background firing is that each pyramidal cell in CA3–CA1 may influence hundreds of its neighbors via **basket cells** whose short axons stay within this one region of the hippocampus. They receive input from the pyramidals, and their axons spread over a wide area of the hippocampus, contacting 200–500 other pyramidal cells (Shepherd, 1979). This suggests that each environment produces a different level of background firing because the cell is getting inputs from many neighboring place cells as well as many different stimuli. Such an arrangement would seem to be ideal if the job of the hippocampus was to associate everything that occurred at one particular time in the animal's

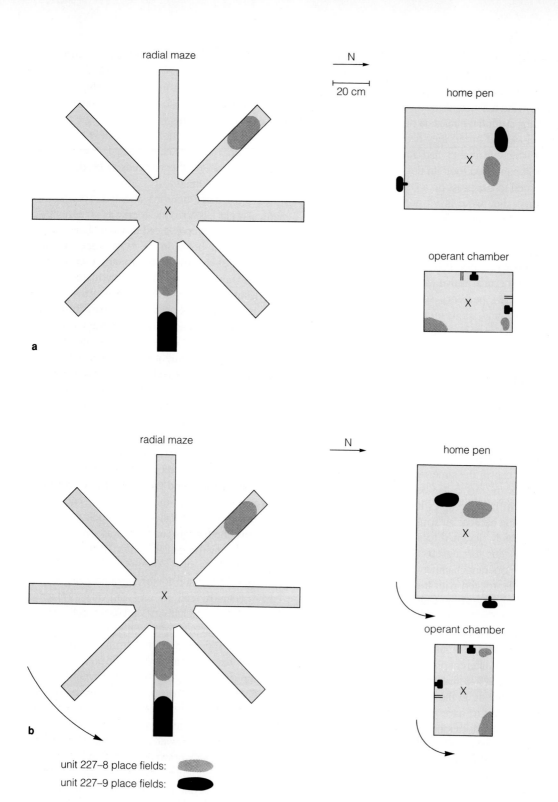

radial maze

N

20 cm

home pen

operant chamber

a

radial maze

N

home pen

operant chamber

b

unit 227–8 place fields:

unit 227–9 place fields:

Figure 15.6 **(a)** Place fields of the same two neurons (227–8 and 227–9) in three different environments. A water bottle is indicated on the side of the home pen. The operant chamber has two bars, each with a pellet dispenser. Unit 227–9 does not have a place field in the operant chamber. Room cues were equated between environments by placing the center of each apparatus (marked with X) at the same place in the room during recording sessions. **(b)** Rotating the environments 90° revealed that place fields were defined by room cues for the maze but by cues within the apparatus in the case of home pen and operant chamber. (Adapted from Kubie & Ranck, 1983)

life with everything else that happened then. Thus, as the rat enters and runs down arm B of the maze, all stimuli present are associated with one another to produce a network of connections, which could be called a context.

Associational Context Theory

Context theory was first suggested by Hirsh (1974) and has been elaborated by Wicklegren (1979), Kesner (1980), and Teyler and DiScenna (1986). Kubie and Ranck (1984) employ it to explain their data on background firing in place cells. The version of context theory presented here, best called associational context theory, is a synthesis of these variations.

The Basic Theory Our synthesis agrees with O'Keefe and Nadel that the hippocampus assembles "cognitive maps" but generalizes that idea to go beyond mere spatial maps of the environment. Wible and colleagues (1986) discovered that nonspatial stimuli (such as brightness changes) are also coded by hippocampal neurons. In another study (Best & Thompson, 1984), it was found that hippocampal cells responsive to particular places in a radial maze also fired selectively for a tone stimulus in a classical conditioning task (a presumably nonspatial stimulus). Selective firing was even demonstrated in response to a particular sequence of odors, a completely nonspatial event (Eichenbaum & Cohen, 1988). Drive states, such as hunger and thirst (Hirsh, 1980), motor programs, frontal lobe output (Teyler & DiScenna, 1986) representing intentions, and limbic system output representing emotions are also "mapped." All these studies indicate that more than spatial mapping is going on in the hippocampus.

According to context theory, the hippocampus

becomes the "secretary" of the brain, recording all environmental stimuli, internal stimuli, emotions, drives, and responses that occurred during any one episode of time. It then associates these events with one another so that they form a memory of the context in which the primary stimulus and response occurred. If most of the stimuli in a learning situation are related to spatial locations (as in O'Keefe and Nadel's testing situations), then the context is nothing more than a spatial map of the environment; but if nonspatial stimuli are involved, the engram within the hippocampus shows itself to be a record of the full context within which the organism's behavior took place. Because the hippocampal engram consists of associations between the CS's, UCS's, S^+'s, and S^-'s (the primary stimuli), and all the context stimuli from a learning experience, the entire experience can be recalled later if just a few of the stimuli recur together.

Using Context Theory Context theory offers an explanation of some place cell recordings that are very puzzling in the framework of the spatial mapping idea. Eichenbaum and colleagues (1987) placed their rats in a large box with a goal cup at one end, where food reinforcement was delivered, and a stimulus-sampling port at the other end, where odors representing S^+'s and S^-'s were delivered. Recording electrodes located some hippocampal cells that responded to a particular place in this box. However, the correlation between firing rate and any particular place in the box was not very good. On close examination of the sequence of neural and behavioral events, the experimenters found that the firing of these presumed place cells could be predicted better by factors other than place. Some cells only fired when the rat was moving *through* the place (as opposed to sitting there) and only when the direction of movement was toward the goal cup. If the rat traversed the same place on its way to the odor-sampling port, then the cell would not fire. Other cells were specific to the odor-sampling port rather than the goal cup. Movement through the particular place in the direction of the sampling port fired these "port" cells, whereas movement through that same area in the direction of the goal cup did not.

Activity in these cells seemed to be time-locked to the moment of arrival at some significant feature of the box (like the goal cup or sampling port), in the sense that firing would begin just before the rat arrived there. Cells seemed to be specific to one place in the box because the rat had to traverse that area on its way to the goal cup (or port) and was always in that region of the box about 1 second or so before arriving at its destination. The cells really appeared to be firing in anticipation of the goal.

Context theory could explain these results in the following way. As the rat approaches some significant portion of the environment (such as the goal cup), some stimuli from that area are perceived. In prior experiences with the goal cup, the hippocampus has associated all stimuli in that area with each other so that receiving a few of them elicits the whole context memory. In other words, before the rat arrives at the goal cup, it catches sight of it, and that visual stimulus is enough to elicit the whole context of stimuli that had become associated with the cup. Thus, the rat remembers the previous experiences with the cup, such as finding food there, eating, and so forth. The increase in firing rate found in certain hippocampal cells as the rat approaches the goal cup may represent the triggering of the entire context memory through associations with a few of the stimuli it includes.

This interpretation seems to fit the behavior of these particular hippocampal neurons better than an explanation drawn from cognitive mapping theory. However, this does not mean that the hippocampus does not construct cognitive maps of the environment. Many contexts would include spatial memories, and those spatial parts of the contexts would constitute cognitive maps. Because many rat experiments reduce the important stimuli to those that are spatial, the context in such a case would consist

entirely of a cognitive map. We continue to use the idea with the understanding that it is regarded here as a limited form of context.

Improving Context Theory: Indexing Teyler & Di-Scenna (1986) have recently proposed a form of context theory in which the hippocampus functions as a **memory indexing system.** The theory, an elaboration on basic context theory, holds that the associated stimuli are not stored as traces within the hippocampus. The stimulus engrams are stored in portions of the cortex and subcortical brain devoted to the particular sense. For example, in a visual learning situation, the engram of a visual stimulus would probably be stored in occipital visual cortex and inferotemporal cortex (shape aspects) as well as parietal cortex and superior colliculus (spatial location aspects). Because the engram within the hippocampus is an association between stimulus elements, it would consist of a set of connections between occipital visual cortex, inferotemporal cortex, parietal cortex, and colliculus. Furthermore, a major part of most learning situations is the presence of a reinforcer following the response, so another part of the context engram would be connections linking reinforcer engrams in the amygdala and hypothalamus to the visual cortex, inferotemporal cortex, and superior colliculus. Another part of the context might involve connections to auditory engram circuits in the auditory system that represent any persistent, extraneous noises that were present during the learning episode (e.g., fans, traffic, experimenters, building noises). Still another part would be connections to cortical and brain-stem motor engrams that produced the response used to obtain the reinforcer and the particular response topography employed (corpus striatum engrams). Connections to olfactory engrams in the frontal cortex would provide the context with the smells that were distinctive at the time of learning and associate them, too, with all the rest of this enormous network of memories that constitutes the whole context. When the hippocampal synapses have made the appropriate connections, the whole network (context plus primary stimuli and response) can be reevoked by the appearance of just one or two parts ("Oh! That odor reminds me of that trip to the beach last summer when we . . .").

According to indexing theory, the only thing contained within the hippocampus itself is a record of where engrams for any particular episode can be found in the rest of the brain. The record is like a library card catalog that contains information about where to go in the brain to find the individual scraps of memory. However, it is more than an index because every engram in the context leads, through associations in the hippocampus, to every other engram.

The concept of a hippocampal indexing mechanism has an important implication. The associational context it provides may be the origin of our ability to remember our past experience as a sequence of separate events. When you study this page, you are probably only aware of learning the *ideas* it contains; but if asked to recall, you may also be able to remember the place on the page where a certain term was discussed, that is, its context. You may be able to further recall whether anyone else was present in the room when you did your studying. These context elements can be used as a "time tag" for *when* the primary associations were learned. In other words, you not only learn this page but also learn that you studied it *under certain conditions* (e.g., in your dorm room while your roommate was playing a record you hate). It is these context elements that enable you to later recall that "I studied that chapter last Thursday night." You can remember having done it then because this particular chapter is associated with certain context stimuli that were not present during any of your other activities (including studying other chapters). So, as you study, you may be building two kinds of memories: concept memories of the material you studied and event memories of the studying process itself. **Event memories** may be a product of an associational context mechanism in the hippocampus.

◼ Putting Motivation into the Context

We have examined research suggesting that the hippocampus can associate most of the environmental stimuli available at any moment with one another to provide a contextual memory of an entire situation or event. Internal states such as emotions and motivations can also be represented in this contextual memory, and it is to these aspects that we now turn our attention.

Motivational Input to the Hippocampus

A good record of events should include memories of which stimuli are important enough to command attention and which previously reinforced responses no longer lead to reward. These two kinds of motivational memories apparently depend on two separate mechanisms.

The Septal Nucleus and Attention Lesions of the **medial septal nucleus** mimic lesions of CA3; both lesions damage spatial memory (Mitchell et al., 1982). This is not surprising because the medial septal nucleus is one of the two major inputs to CA3 (Figure 15.7). Drive-related arousal apparently enters the hippocampus by way of this route, coming from the hypothalamus and brain stem. This arousal may be in the form of an attention or orienting signal because the reticular activating system accounts for the major portion of the brain stem input to the septal nucleus. Furthermore, the medial septal nucleus is the source of one type of theta rhythm in the hippocampus (Bland, 1986), and we noted earlier that theta is associated with attention. So septal input seems to keep CA3 cells appraised of the relative importance of stimuli present in the environment and may relate to directing attention toward particular parts of the context residing in CA3. Probably, the reason that the loss of this input appears to impair memory is that a rat's memory is always tested by using a reinforcer or punisher. If the rat can no longer remember to pay close attention to stimuli associated with reinforcement and punishment, those consequences lose their influence on its behavior, and learning is impaired.

A second major input to CA3 pyramidal cells comes from entorhinal cortex (Figure 15.7) and carries specific sensory information about the environment (Van Hoesen et al., 1975). If the perforant path from the entorhinal cortex is cut, hippocampal neurons stop responding to environmental stimuli (Foster et al., 1988). Neither the septal input nor the

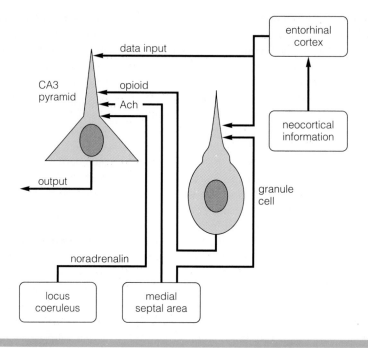

Figure 15.7 Diagram showing some of the internal circuitry of the hippocampus. Note that input from the entorhinal cortex can reach the pyramidal cells of CA3 directly and indirectly by way of granule cells of the dentate gyrus (perforant path). (Adapted from Routtenberg, 1984)

entorhinal input alone can fire CA3 pyramidals; it requires both acting together (Routtenberg, 1984). CA3 pyramidals then seem to be the point where the cognitive map, or context, acquires emotional coloration. Without the septal input, the entorhinal information is just cold, sterile facts about what stimuli are present in the environment. After the septal information has been read in, the map is apparently transformed into *fearful* areas to avoid, *interesting* zones to explore, and *good* places in which one can eat or drink.

Can Some Memories Be Erased? The motivational arousal from the septal nucleus also reaches the granule cells of the dentate gyrus, which project to CA3 (Deadwyler et al., 1981). Figure 15.7 shows that sensory information reaches CA3 both directly through the perforant path from entorhinal cortex (Brankack & Buzsáki, 1986) and indirectly from entorhinal cortex by way of the dentate gyrus, but these two routes to the pyramidal cells do not carry identical sets of information. Input from granule cells of the dentate gyrus has already been modified by septal data concerning which stimuli are motivation-

ally significant and worthy of attention. What is the reason for this granule cell path?

Routtenberg suggests that the side path through the dentate gyrus is for the process of forgetting rather than remembering. He claims that the synapse between granule cells and CA3 pyramidals uses an opioid transmitter (perhaps enkephalin); hence, it can be disabled with the opiate blocker naloxone. (See Chapter 8 for a discussion of opiates and naloxone.) This fact led Routtenberg to see if memory formation could be stopped with an injection of naloxone. When the drug was tried, however, no amnesia could be produced, and this implies that granule cells do not participate in creating engrams. In fact, Routtenberg thinks that they may be involved in just the opposite—the process of forgetting. Evidence for this idea comes from an experiment in which stimulating electrodes were implanted in the dentate gyrus.

The rat was placed on the central platform of a radial maze and allowed to search until it found the single piece of food that the experimenters had placed at the end of one of the arms. Normally, as a rat gains experience with the maze from day to day, it finds this food faster and faster. The improvement comes from shortening its search pattern by eliminating arms that have already been entered that day and found empty. After a certain amount of experience, the rat will enter each arm only once on any particular search. The learning that must take place for this to happen is the development of a cognitive map identifying each arm with its distinctive location in the room. Once the rat can identify every arm by its location, it can then remember which ones it has entered that day.

The training procedure started each day by giving the rat one search for a piece of food, then after a 20-minute wait, a second search with the food located in the same arm. The point was to see how well the rat recalled the location of the first piece of food. Each day the rat got a pair of trials, but every day the food was left in a different arm. The results showed that the animals could find the food on trial 2 with a minimum of wrong-arm entries; normal rats are quite capable of relearning the location of food that shifts position from day to day. This memory was destroyed, however, if the subjects received 10 seconds of dentate gyrus stimulation during the 20 minutes between trials. The electrical stimulation did not disrupt the cognitive map; the rats could still eliminate arms one by one as they searched for food, but it did seem to erase the memory of which arm had been baited on the first trial of the day. This erasure effect was probably dependent on the synapse between granule cells and CA3 pyramidals, rather than being the result of some general process like fear or arousal. This was established by giving each animal a dose of naloxone before the stimulation. Rats with naloxone could remember the food location from the first trial, whereas those without the drug had amnesia for the first trial experience. By preventing conduction at the synapse in CA3, naloxone apparently prevented erasure and allowed the memory to survive the stimulation (Collier & Routtenberg, 1984). This might lead you to wonder if naloxone would prevent forgetting even without stimulation of the dentate gyrus. Several animal studies have shown a mild improvement in memory following naloxone administration (cited in Collier et al., 1987).

Now we can see why two routes exist between the entorhinal cortex and CA3; the direct route to CA3 through the perforant path brings in sensory information for the establishment of the cognitive map (Routtenberg, 1984), while the indirect route through dentate gyrus produces a quick form of forgetting by means of an **erasure mechanism**. It is important to understand that the dentate gyrus is erasing the memory of where food is located in the cognitive map rather than the map itself. In the animal's natural environment, food locations themselves may remain fairly constant, but occurrence of food within those locations could vary a great deal. Thus, it is important for survival to have an erasure mechanism that can produce quick changes in the reinforcement aspect of cognitive maps. This rapid memory suppression appears to be the way in which the hippocampus prevents response perseveration in all those situations we have discussed in which the previously reinforced response no longer produces reward. In other words, it may be the action of the dentate granule cells on the cognitive map in CA3–CA1 that makes possible rapid extinction and reversal learning.

Memory for Reinforcement Events

One way to examine the role of the dentate gyrus as an erasure mechanism is to feed the brain a stimulus (such as a tone) and follow it with reinforcement. When the connection has been learned, remove the reinforcer (start an extinction procedure) and see what happens to the electrical activity in the gyrus. Deadwyler and associates trained rats to make a simple response to obtain water whenever a tone sounded and recorded the EEG potentials in the dentate gyrus that were evoked by the tone (Deadwyler et al., 1981). Rather than focusing on the individual responses of single neurons, this **evoked response technique** uses a macroelectrode to record the composite activity of thousands of neurons simultaneously. All surrounding nerve impulses, IPSPs, and EPSPs within range of the electrode tip are blended into a single voltage level that fluctuates from moment to moment as the pattern of action potentials and postsynaptic potentials changes. At the beginning of the record in Figure 15.8, there is a short length (about one tenth of a

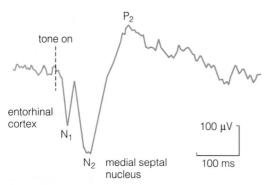

Figure 15.8 Representative averaged evoked potential in dentate gyrus based on 50 tone presentations. N_1 and N_2 waves represent negative voltage changes, whereas P_2 is a positive wave. N_1 is imposed on the granule cells by the perforant path fibers from the entorhinal cortex; N_2 comes from the medial septal nucleus. When the tone becomes CS⁻, N_1 becomes larger with each succeeding trial. (Adapted from Deadwyler, 1985)

second's worth) of regular EEG waves indicating that nothing out of the usual is occurring around the electrode. Then, the tone that has come to mean that water is available in payment for a response made at this time is sounded. The composite voltage immediately goes strongly negative, recovers almost to normal, and then drops to an even greater negativity before swinging all the way back into the positive region and then drifting slowly back to normal. As you can see in the figure, the first negative wave of this evoked potential is labeled $\mathbf{N_1}$ and the second $\mathbf{N_2}$.

Both negative waves represent the synaptic events involved in the transfer of information about the tone, response, and reinforcement. N_2 increases its amplitude (size) throughout the learning trials, reaching its full height as the task is completely learned and then dwindling away during extinction. N_1 displays exactly the opposite behavior, being associated with the *absence* of reward rather than its presence. It is either missing or very small in the dentate gyrus of a fully trained rat but starts to grow as soon as extinction begins (Deadwyler et al., 1981). It can also be seen strongly in a variation of the learning task in which two tones are used: one an

S⁺ and the other an S⁻. On a trial in which the tone is S⁺, the response will be reinforced; on an S⁻ trial, it will not. The two tones are presented in a random sequence so that the animal never knows which condition to expect on any trial. If S⁺ is presented on a particular trial and the rat receives the water after making the response, the size of N_1 *decreases* on the next trial. If the tone is an S⁻ indicating that the response will not be reinforced, N_1 *increases* on the following trial (Deadwyler, 1985).

Neither N_1 nor N_2 is generated by cells of the hippocampus even though the dentate gyrus is the site at which they can be recorded. The N_2 wave represents input from the medial septal nucleus (Foster et al., 1988). N_1, on the other hand, is a product of the impulses from the entorhinal cortex arriving at the gyrus by way of the perforant path plus the EPSPs they evoke in granule cell dendrites (Deadwyler et al., 1981). Thus, both waves are generated outside the hippocampus and relayed to that structure.

The N_1 wave occurs about 20–35 ms after the tone onset; this amount of time is apparently required for the auditory information to pass through the synapses of the auditory projection system (about 2 ms per synapse plus a smaller amount of conduction time), to be processed by the limbic system, and then be relayed to granule cells of the dentate gyrus. At this point in the nervous system, the evoked potential apparently carries information about a lack of association between the response and reinforcement. This association or lack thereof is probably decided by the amygdala, which receives sensory information plus notification of the existence of hunger or other drive states as well as the occurrence of an incentive (Figure 15.9).

The information contained in N_1 is ideal for preventing perseverative responses because it always seems to signal the probability of not getting reinforced for making a response to the stimulus that triggered it. This trait is displayed in Figure 15.10, which shows the changes in N_1 amplitude throughout a sequence of discrimination trials in which S⁺ and S⁻ were randomly mixed. Thus, on the first four trials, the rat was reinforced on the first trial, and the size of N_1 dropped on the second trial. There was no reinforcement on the second trial, so N_1 was

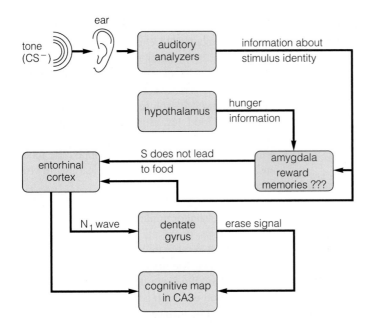

tone
(CS⁻)

ear

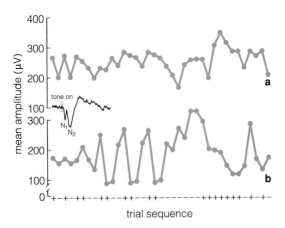

Figure 15.9 Flowchart of proposed influences on the hippocampus in a reversal-learning or extinction situation. The signal from the dentate gyrus erases the previously established association between the tone and the food, formed when the tone was a positive stimulus rather than negative. The auditory system tells the amygdala and entorhinal cortex which tone it is that is sounding, and the amygdala labels it as "not leading to food." The N_1 wave carries this information to granule cells that can erase the food association to this tone that was stored in the cognitive map.

Figure 15.10 Trial-to-trial fluctuations in the amplitudes of N_1 and N_2. The pluses (+) and minuses (−) at the bottom indicate whether the stimulus for that trial was a CS⁺ or CS⁻. (a) The N_2 amplitudes are not related to the sign of the CS. (b) N_1 amplitudes increase following unreinforced trials (CS⁻) and drop after reinforced (CS⁺) trials. (Adapted from Deadwyler, 1985)

larger on the third. When two unreinforced trials occurred together, N_1 grew much larger than for just one unreinforced trial, and a sequence of seven consecutive unreinforced trials yielded a huge potential that was quickly eroded by a sequence of six reinforced trials.

N_1 input from the entorhinal cortex signaling nonreinforcement experiences feeds into granule cells of the dentate gyrus. There it combines with N_2 input from the medial septal nucleus representing reinforcement experiences. The firing of granule cells in response to any combination of environmental stimuli represents both of these influences (Foster et al., 1988). It is possible at this point to see a way in which Routtenberg's erasure idea might be combined with Deadwyler's evoked potential data. Let us suggest hypothetically that whenever N_1 input overwhelms N_2 input the granule cells respond by sending an erasure signal to the context in CA3 to remove the memory of reinforcement availability. In other words, a string of nonreinforcement experiences generates a larger and larger N_1, which creates a growing erasure signal. If it is not counteracted by N_2 input from reinforced trials, this erasure signal will quickly remove the tendency to respond fruitlessly in a situation in which reinforcement is no longer available. Response perseveration is prevented.

Working Memory

In trying to sort out the contribution of the hippocampus from all other areas of the brain that contribute to the overall engram, Olton proposed that there were two forms of memory, reference and working, and that the task of the hippocampus was to provide working memory (Olton, 1983). **Reference memory** contains all the constant, stable engrams like the knowledge you learn in this course, the ability to recognize your car or notebook, and the words to a song. For our distant ancestors who evolved this ability, reference memory might have included engrams for the smell of food, the shape of a tree, how to crack a nut, where berries grow in the woods, the shape of a face or the look of one's mate, and the fact that a right turn at the stream takes you to the lake, whereas a left turn takes you to the pool with the fish in it. **Working memory** is a short-lived record of events that need to be remembered only for a limited period of time. It would include the memory of having attended class today, of having driven your car downtown, or of having sung a particular song in music class.

Working Memory and the Hippocampus

Reference memories are developed by structures throughout the brain from stem to cortex and include such examples as NMR conditioning, visual discrimination learning, and bar-pressing that we have discussed throughout the chapter. Working memory is chiefly a function of the hippocampus (Olton, 1983). Because this interpretation of hippocampal function appears to be in competition with the cognitive map idea of O'Keefe and Nadel, Olton has conducted a number of experiments to compare the predictive ability of the two concepts.

Olton cleverly brought the natural foraging situation into the laboratory where it could be examined under controlled conditions in a radial arm maze (Olton, 1979). Recall that this maze has a number of arms, radiating out from a central circular platform. Food is placed at the end of each arm, and the rat is allowed to explore the entire structure until it locates all food. Just as in a natural foraging situation, the rat wastes a great deal of effort if it reenters arms from which it has already stripped the food, and it responds to the situation by learning to visit each arm only once in each trial.

In one radial arm–maze experiment, Olton deliberately eliminated or minimized as many room cues (fans, windows, doors, etc.) as possible so that the rat would not be able to construct a spatial map of its environment. The maze was surrounded by high gray walls, and the room lights were dimmed. This enabled Olton to set up a test in which the hippocampus could be involved in the learning if it were functioning as a working memory device but not if it were a cognitive mapping mechanism. Each maze arm was made distinctive with internal cues, and a light was turned on within each arm to make these visible. A door was positioned at the entrance to each arm, and after the rat had visited any one of the arms, the doors were all closed so that the rat was confined to the center disk. To completely eliminate any spatial room cues, the arms were then detached and traded around so that when the doors opened again the arm that had been to the rat's right might now be on its left or behind it. Despite having to use just the cues within each arm, the rat nevertheless learned to visit each of the four arms without returning to any that had already been stripped of food.

Because there was little chance to learn a cognitive map of the environment here, the O'Keefe and Nadel theory would presumably have to say that the hippocampus was not involved in learning not to reenter arms. However, after the rats had been given lesions in which the fornix was cut on both sides, they were no longer able to perform this task. Remember that the fornix is a major output path of CA3 and CA1 so that even if the hippocampus itself is still functioning it will have lost much of its ability to influence the rest of the brain. Furthermore, it is likely that the output through the fornix to lateral septal nucleus returns to the hippocampus by way of medial septal nucleus, which projects to dentate gyrus and CA3. If that is an important feedback path, then the hippocampus itself cannot function properly without the fornix. Olton's experiment appears to demonstrate that the hippocampus is still necessary to performance on a radial arm maze even when a cognitive map cannot be a part of what is learned (Olton et al., 1980). On the other hand, a working memory, if such a thing exists, would be a great help because it would allow the rat to remember which arms had already been entered recently.

In a second study, Olton and Papas (1979) set up a situation in which cognitive maps, working memory, and reference memory might all develop. The apparatus was a 17-arm radial maze in which room cues were readily available. Food was placed in only 8 of the arms (the same 8 on each trial), the remaining 9 arms always being empty. As the rats gained experience with this environment, they should learn which arms always contained food at the beginning of a trial and which never did (reference memory). According to Olton, reference memory should enable them to ignore the 9 unbaited arms, and working memory would tell them which of the baited arms to avoid because the food there had already been eaten. The rats in the experimental group were given fornix lesions, and their performance compared with that of the controls. With no hippocampus to aid the rats, the cognitive map theory would have to predict that the subjects would no longer remember any of the places in the maze and should randomly enter as many of the 9 never-baited arms as the 8 food arms. The working memory concept, however, would predict that the lesioned rats should keep right on avoiding the 9 never-baited arms because this engram was a part of reference memory and was thus outside the hippocampus and still intact. Only working memory had been injured, and the only errors predicted by this loss would be those in which a baited arm is reentered after the food there had already been eaten.

The results showed that after poor performance on all arms for a few trials, the rats quickly recovered their ability to avoid the unbaited arms, whereas performance on the food arms remained at chance. If spatial memories used in avoiding the unbaited arms had been stored in the disabled hippocampus,

the animals should have erroneously entered those arms as well. The logical conclusion to draw is that spatial memories must be stored elsewhere (perhaps in the cortex). This is an outcome that the cognitive map theory would have a hard time explaining. However, the data are entirely consistent with the idea that working memory but not reference memory had been lost.

Primate data also support the idea that the hippocampus serves working memory rather than spatial memory. Monkeys in one study (Friedman & Goldman-Rakic, 1988) were trained on a spatial delayed alternation or a delayed object alternation task (Figure 15.11). In the **delayed spatial alternation** task, the monkey must choose between two stimuli that cover food wells, only one of which is baited on any trial. If the animal pushes away the correct stimulus and reaches into the well, it will find food. If it chooses incorrectly, the table with food wells and stimuli are quickly withdrawn and a screen lowered to prevent the animal from also trying the other stimulus. This noncorrection procedure ensures that the subject will be reinforced only on trials in which it chooses correctly. The screen is also lowered immediately after the monkey has obtained the food reinforcer after a correct choice. It stays down for the length of the delay period (e.g., 30 seconds) during which the experimenter baits one of the wells and replaces stimulus cards over them. At the end of the delay, the screen is again raised, and the monkey must choose the stimulus that was *not* correct on the previous trial. In other words, during the delay it must keep a memory of which stimulus was correct so that it can choose the alternate stimulus on the next trial— hence, the name delayed alternation. It is a spatial task because the alternation is between the stimulus on the right *side* and the one on the left.

The **delayed object alternation** task is exactly like the delayed spatial alternation except that the animal must alternate between two different stimulus objects no matter what side they are on. Thus, if a square covered the correct well on the first trial and a circle covered the incorrect well, then the circle must be chosen on the second trial regardless of whether it is covering the right or left food well. Both delayed alternation tasks require working

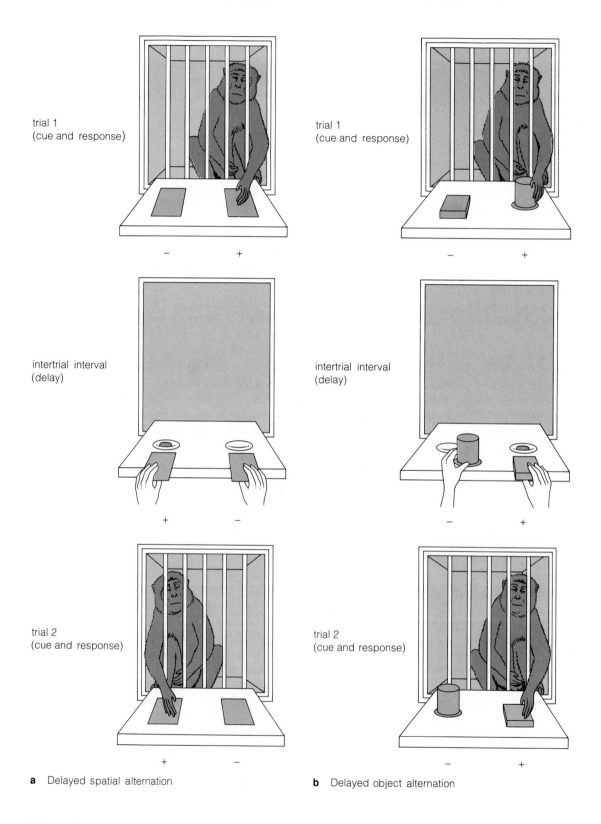

trial 1
(cue and response)

trial 1
(cue and response)

intertrial interval
(delay)

intertrial interval
(delay)

−   +

−   +

+   −

−   +

trial 2
(cue and response)

trial 2
(cue and response)

+   −

−   +

a Delayed spatial alternation

b Delayed object alternation

Figure 15.11 Two learning tasks that can be used to study working memory in primates. (a) Delayed spatial alternation. During the delay, a screen comes down between the monkey and the stimuli, and the experimenter baits one of the food wells and covers both wells with stimulus objects. The subject must choose the side that was incorrect on the previous trial. (b) Delayed object alternation. The same procedure is used as in the spatial alternation but the subject must choose the *object* that was incorrect on the previous trial. (Adapted from Friedman & Goldman-Rakic, 1988)

memory to keep track of the previous response, but the one task is spatial and the other (object alternation) is not.

Friedman and Goldman-Rakic (1988) reasoned that the hippocampus should be critical to both tasks if the working memory theory is correct and should be critical only for the delayed spatial alternation if the spatial map theory is right. They then applied the 2-deoxyglucose technique (see Chapter 5) during the learning of the two tasks in order to measure the amount of neural activity in the hippocampus at that time. The hippocampus showed significantly higher levels of activity during both tasks than were found in control animals working on nonmemory learning tasks. This is exactly what the working memory theory would predict. Furthermore, there was no difference in activity levels between the spatial and nonspatial tasks. This is contrary to what the spatial map theory would predict. The results clearly support the working memory interpretation of hippocampal function.

Mishkin partially disagrees with this conclusion. His primate research with Murray suggested that a major memory deficit could be obtained from a hippocampal lesion only when the amygdala was also removed (Murray & Mishkin, 1984b, 1986). The amygdala, like the hippocampus, receives input from all the sensory analyzer systems and sends output to the cortex, thus putting it in a good position to integrate information into memories. Its close proximity to the anterior hippocampus makes it seem almost an extension of that structure and suggests that it may be involved in anything the hippocampus is doing. However, its internal anatomy is completely different; it has nothing comparable to a dentate gyrus, CA3, or CA1. Furthermore, no memory defect appears when the amygdala is carefully ablated in such a way that the surrounding cortex is not dam-

aged (Zola-Morgan et al., 1989). Thus, Squire and Zola-Morgan claim that the memory function Mishkin attributed to the amygdala is really a property of the adjacent cortex. However, this does not explain why Mishkin failed to find a memory deficit when the hippocampus alone was destroyed. That question is still unresolved.

More recently, Mishkin's lab did find a memory loss in monkeys with pure hippocampal lesions, but the defect appeared when the memory task involved remembering *where* a stimulus object had been located a few seconds before (Parkinson et al., 1988). Could it be that the hippocampus is limited to spatial memory? This is doubtful in light of all the other research supporting a nonspatial interpretation (discussed earlier). Furthermore, Squire has recently reported a patient with hippocampal damage who showed a completely nonspatial memory loss (specifically, a failure to recall events of the day and sentences heard a few minutes before). The patient, a 57-year-old man, had suffered anoxic brain damage during open heart surgery and had lost the entire CA1 field of pyramidal cells in both hippocampi. Moreover, there was no detectable damage to the amygdala or any other memory-related structure (Squire & Zola-Morgan, 1988). Although there are still some questions to be answered, no research currently offers completely convincing evidence against the hypothesis that the hippocampus is the site of working memory.

Working Memory Versus Context Theory

If the associational context explanation of hippocampal function is an extension of O'Keefe and Nadel's theory, do Olton's results cast doubt on the context interpretation? No, a context memory is more general than a spatial map because it contains many nonspatial stimuli present at the time of learning. It also allows for the development of spatial reference memories. If the context memory is actually an index that links reference engrams stored elsewhere in the brain, then cutting the fornix would destroy those links but still leave the rat with its reference memories for which maze arms were never baited.

The theory that the hippocampus provides a working memory is not really in conflict with the idea that it provides an associational context (or index). Working memory is a record of experience as a series of *events* or episodes (Squire, 1987), and we saw earlier that an event memory might arise from having a series of different *context* memories with which to discriminate one episode of stimulation from the next. Future research may show that working memory derives directly from the context formation ability of the hippocampus.

■ Summary

1. In the early stages of learning or whenever the animal is orienting to some stimulus, a distinctive EEG wave appears in the hippocampus. This 4–8-Hz wave has been named theta rhythm, and its pattern of occurrence suggests that the hippocampus systematically monitors all ongoing sensory and motor events that are being attended and that demand, or may demand, voluntary adjustments.

2. In the O'Keefe and Nadel theory, the task of the hippocampus is to store all spatial memories tied together into a cognitive map of the animal's environment. Recordings showed that individual neurons in the hippocampus become active only when the animal is in a specific place in the environment. These place cells are the major elements of the cognitive map.

3. More recent experiments have shown that the hippocampus stores more than spatial information. Context theory seems to assimilate more of the data than does spatial mapping theory. Context theory contends that the hippocampus is a device for associating all background stimuli and responses that occur in a learning situation with the stimulus and response being learned. These associations provide a context that facilitates later recall of the learned response. In rats much of this associative context consists of the spatial stimuli around the animal during learning, and this is why there are place cells in the hippocampus. Discrimination-reversal learning depends on the hippocampus because the rat can only discriminate the current CS by the change in context. The most highly developed version of context theory is Teyler and DiScenna's indexing theory that likens the multiple associations formed by the hippocampus to an index of all other parts of the brain.

4. Context information (such as the cognitive map) seems to be stored in the CA3 portion of the hippocampus, and this zone receives input from the medial septal nucleus, the brain area responsible for generating theta rhythm. The medial septal nucleus probably modifies the cognitive map so that some parts of the environment are perceived as important or unimportant, worthy or not worthy of attention.

5. Another part of the hippocampus, the dentate gyrus, may act as an erasure mechanism, altering the cognitive map (context) whenever there are changes in the circumstances of reinforcement. Rapid extinction, for example, would depend on this mechanism. An evoked potential called N_1 can be recorded in the dentate gyrus in response to an auditory stimulus. N_1 grows in size with each successive unreinforced trial; thus, its size reflects the probability that a response will not be followed by reinforcement. It may be this signal that triggers the erasure mechanism to remove a reinforcement association from some part of the cognitive map.

6. Olton has inspired much hippocampal research with his distinction between working memory (a rapidly fading set of engrams that stores just recent events) and reference memory (all the relatively unchangeable facts that have been learned). It is working memory that is the business of the hippocampus. In a radial arm maze that remains the same from day to day, the knowledge of where each arm leads would be in reference memory, whereas the memory of which arms have already been stripped of food on any particular day would be working memory.

7. The constantly changing context engrams generated by the hippocampus might provide a basis for event memory, in which case working memory becomes one product of the hypothesized associational context mechanism.

Glossary

basket cells A type of interneuron (Golgi II cells) found in the CA1 and CA3 fields of the hippocampus. (595)

CA1 A field of cells in the hippocampus that receives from CA3 and sends output to limbic cortex. (592)

CA3 A field of cells in the hippocampus that receives from the entorhinal cortex and dentate gyrus and sends output to CA1. (592)

context (environmental) All the stimuli present during learning other than the cues directly involved in the association under study. (595)

context theory The idea that the function of the hippocampus is to develop a context memory for all the significant events of the animal's life. (597)

delayed object alternation A learning task in which the monkey is shown the same two stimuli on each trial and must learn to choose the one not chosen in the previous trial, no matter what side it is on. (605)

delayed spatial alternation A learning task in which the monkey is shown two stimuli on each trial and must learn to choose the one that is on the opposite side from the one chosen in the previous trial. (605)

dentate gyrus A group of cells in the hippocampus that receives input from the entorhinal cortex and medial septal nucleus and that sends its output to the CA3 field. (592)

electroencephalogram (EEG) A record of voltage changes that represents an aggregate of all the EPSPs, IPSPs, and nerve impulses between the two electrodes. (588)

entorhinal cortex A part of the parahippocampal gyrus that overlies the hippocampus and that supplies that structure with information from all the sense systems. (592)

erasure mechanism Routtenberg's idea that the dentate gyrus can quickly alter the contextual engram in the hippocampus following an environmental event such as nonreinforcement. (601)

event memories Memories of events. (599)

evoked response technique A method for examining the impact of a single stimulus on the brain by examining short segments of EEG record. (601)

granule cells The major neurons of the dentate gyrus. (592)

medial septal nucleus A midline structure near the anterior end of the corpus callosum; provides one of the two major inputs to the dentate gyrus. (599)

memory indexing system A variation of context theory in which the hippocampal engram is thought to be a set of links connecting sensory engrams in various parts of the cortex. (598)

N_1 The first large negative wave in a tone-evoked potential recorded from the perforant path; its size increases with nonreinforced trials. (602)

N_2 The second large negative wave in a tone-evoked potential recorded from the perforant path; its size increases with learning. (602)

perforant path Axons of neurons in the entorhinal cortex that extend into the dentate gyrus. (592)

place cell A type of hippocampal neuron that responds selectively to different places in the environment. (589)

pyramidal cells of CA3 The major neurons in CA3. (592)

radial arm maze An apparatus for testing animal memory that consists of a circular central platform with arms radiating out like spokes from the hub of a wheel. (594)

reference memory The part of memory that contains facts, concepts, and ideas. (604)

theta rhythm A regular, fairly synchronized EEG rhythm of about 4–5 Hz. (589)

working memory The part of memory that contains records of events. (604)

Memory

How good is your memory? Do you think you could remember the nonsense syllable CZL 1 minute from now if you were asked to recall it at that time? Your chances of success depend on how that scrap of information is stored when you attempt to remember it. Cognitive psychologists have marshaled considerable evidence in favor of the idea that there are two separate stages in storing a stimulus such as the nonsense syllable CZL. The first stage is called **short-term memory (STM)** and is temporary. Under some circumstances, it can hold information for only 15–30 seconds. If the nonsense syllable is to be recalled 5 minutes later, it would have to be transferred to the second stage, **long-term memory (LTM)**, which can last days or years. This transfer is usually accomplished by repeating the information a number of times.

If you are having a hard time imagining how anyone could possibly forget a nonsense syllable in only 30 seconds, consider the experimental conditions under which STM is typically tested. You, the subject, are shown one three-letter nonsense syllable and are then instructed to immediately begin counting backward from 300 by three's. Thirty seconds later, your counting is interrupted, and you are asked to spell the nonsense syllable. Why must you do the counting? The problem for the experimenter is to obtain an accurate measurement of how long your brain can hold that nonsense syllable *following a single input to memory*. Now, if you don't count during the retention interval, how will you spend that 30 seconds? Most people will fill the interval by repeating the nonsense syllable over and over (rehearsal). Each repetition (even a silent, mental one) is another separate input to the memory system. This rehearsal then could keep the experimenter from ever finding the limit of your memory; hence, the counting task. When people are forced to perform an interfering mental task that prevents rehearsal, they usually have considerable difficulty in remembering a simple verbal stimulus after 30 seconds (Peterson & Peterson, 1959). Try this experiment as a game the next time you throw a party and see just how amazingly short STM is.

Physiological psychologists are interested in discovering how memories are stored in the brain. The implication of the STM–LTM division is that they must look for two separate mechanisms rather than one. Most of their research has been devoted to the mechanism of LTM, and the bulk of the chapter concerns our knowledge in that area. Let's begin then by finding out what hypotheses have been advanced to explain STM.

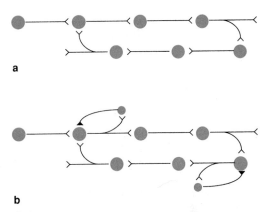

a

b

Figure 16.1   Schematic diagrams of reverberatory circuits. Circles represent cell bodies; synaptic terminals are shown as forks at the ends of axons. (**a**) If we assume that each neuron can fire its postsynaptic cell, then an impulse in the axon of the cell at top left would trigger activity in the loop that would continue until one of the cells fatigued. (**b**) A more realistic arrangement shows some neurons have inhibitory side loops. The smaller neurons secrete an inhibitory transmitter and have the function of limiting the amount of firing in the larger neuron. The widespread existence of such feedback inhibitory loops makes it unlikely that activity in the reverberatory circuit could continue for more than a few seconds. Note that real reverberatory circuits would probably involve thousands of neurons working in parallel.

The Physiological Basis of Short-Term Memory

The most frequently suggested basis for STM is the activity of a **reverberatory circuit** (Figure 16.1a). If each cell in the circuit can excite its postsynaptic cell, then activity in the loop will continue after the input neuron has quit firing. This continued **reverberation** means that the circuit will provide an output to the rest of the nervous system after the original stimulus event is over. Does your viewing of the nonsense syllable set up reverberation in some language circuit specific to that stimulus? Neuroanatomy shows that loop circuits do exist. Most of the thalamic nuclei not only send axons to a particular area of cortex but also receive a return from that area, sometimes by way of another thalamic nucleus. Bishop proposed that reverberation in thalamocortical loops produced the waves of the EEG (reviewed in Tsukahara, 1981b). The anatomical existence of loops, however, doesn't tell us whether reverberation is possible in those circuits and whether such reverberation could last for as long as 30 seconds (which is a long time for a neural event).

The anatomy of the cortex has revealed loop circuits that are contained completely within that structure, and this fact made possible a rather dramatic experiment by Burns (1950) who sought evidence for reverberation. This experimenter completely isolated a section of cortex by cutting all around it and then undercutting it. This removed all sources of input to these cortical neurons. Burns then provided a single "input" for them in the form of a momentary

electrical stimulation through an electrode. He found that the single shock triggered activity (EEG waves) in the isolated section that sometimes lasted as long as 30 minutes. Apparently, neurons within the isolated slab were reexciting each other repeatedly. Reverberation seems to be a physiological reality as well as an anatomical possibility. Tsukahara (1981b) has also found evidence for a possible reverberatory circuit in the cerebellar region with links to the dentate and interpositus nuclei, two cell groups that are apparently involved in classical conditioning (see Chapter 14). This is very sparse evidence, however, and we will see as we explore the basis of LTM and amnesia that the whole idea of splitting memory into two stages may need to be reinterpreted.

The Physiological Basis of Long-Term Memory

No one suggests that LTM also could be stored as continued activity in reverberatory circuits. Most loop circuits contain negative feedback, side loops that should quickly damp the activity in the circuit. For example, in the cortex, many neurons have a main axon that is a part of the loop circuit but also have a side branch that provides input to a small inhibitory neuron. This inhibitory cell feeds back to the original neuron in a tiny, two-cell loop (Figure 16.1b). Tsukahara (1981b) notes that such inhibitory side loops are found in many places throughout the nervous system and make reverberation a somewhat questionable explanation even for STM, let alone LTM, because their action would seem to be one of stopping the reverberation almost as soon as it starts. For a memory to persist for as long as a month or year, some chemical or structural change must occur in the nervous system.

Let's assume that each engram is a different circuit (pathway) in the nervous system. When you remember an idea from physiological psychology, one such pathway fires; recalling the appearance of an apple would fire a different circuit. In this interpretation, the first time you see an apple the sensory input would fire a collection of neurons consisting of a sample of all possible cells that might have responded to that stimulus. This particular collection happened to be those that were best able to respond at that moment. To recognize an apple the next time you see one, the same collection of cells must be activated. But how could this chance collection ever be simultaneously activated again? Some change must occur during the first experience that binds this particular collection together so that when some of them fire, they all will become active as a group.

Thus, the question of memory formation becomes the problem of how these neurons come to reliably fire one another so that the whole engram can become active at one time. The answer lies in the connections between cells. In the human cortex, there are about 38,000 synapses on each neuron, and each cell receives input from roughly 600 axons (Cragg, 1980). This strongly suggests that any one neuron can participate in hundreds of different circuits at different times. But some circuits may be more reliable than others because synaptic connections vary in strength. Recall that the neurotransmitter at a synapse elicits an EPSP in the postsynaptic cell, and this EPSP is usually too weak to trigger an impulse. The stronger the connections between two cells, the larger the EPSPs will be and the greater the chance that the first cell will be able to fire the second cell. To get a collection of cells to function as an engram—to fire reliably together—each time the appropriate stimulus appears, some connections between those cells must be strengthened. At the physiological level then, learning seems to be the strengthening of synaptic connections.

Hebb (1949) proposed that a connection between cells is strengthened whenever it is used. We now examine some evidence in favor of this idea.

Long-Term Potentiation

How would a neuroscientist be able to tell if the connections between two sets of neurons had been strengthened? One approach would be the electrophysiological method in which EPSPs are recorded before and after a synapse has been used. If Hebb is correct, the EPSPs in the postsynaptic cells should grow a little larger with each train of impulses in the presynaptic cells. This is much more difficult to demonstrate than it sounds, however. Locating one electrode on the presynaptic axons and the other in the postsynaptic cells is not something that can be done easily with a stereotaxic instrument and brain atlas. The **hippocampal slice method** has been very helpful in this circumstance because it has enabled electrophysiologists to guide their electrodes to the correct sites with just the aid of a microscope. In that method, the brain is removed, the structure of interest is dissected out (e.g., the hippocampus) and sliced into thick sections. The sections are placed in a solution that keeps neurons alive long enough for the experiment to be completed (Andersen, 1981). With the help of a binocular microscope, the experimenter can now place electrodes into the zone of interest without the difficulty and imprecision of implanting them stereotaxically. Furthermore, chemicals can easily be added to or subtracted from the

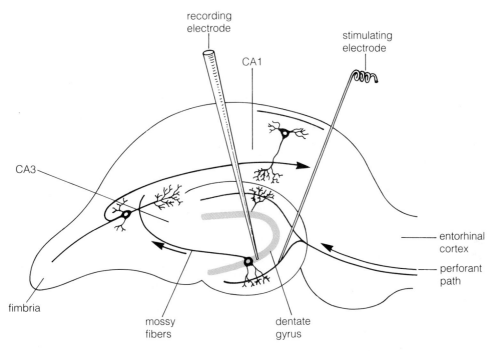

Figure 16.2 Experimental arrangement for recording long-term potentiation from the dentate gyrus of the hippocampus. The stimulating electrode is on one branch of the perforant path within the dentate gyrus, and the recording electrode is on the granule cell bodies. The fimbria connects to the fornix; mossy fibers, axons of the dentate granule cells, synapse with the dendrites of CA3 pyramidal cells. (Adapted from Green & Greenough, 1986)

solution bathing the tissue in order to assess their effect on transmission.

Figure 16.2 shows a typical experimental arrangement with stimulating electrodes on the fibers of the perforant path and recording electrodes on granule cell dendrites in the dentate gyrus of the hippocampus (see Chapter 15 for hippocampal anatomy). A series of tiny, very brief shocks are sent through the stimulating electrodes, triggering a train of nerve impulses in the perforant path axons. The recording electrode collects a composite of all granule cell EPSPs elicited as the synapses between the axons and granule cell dendrites are activated. The composite EPSP grows in voltage after each series of stimulations. That is, the last shock in a series of shocks gets a bigger response from the dendrites than did the first shock. This increase in EPSP size

following extended use of the synapses is termed **long-term potentiation (LTP)**. Some change has occurred at the synapses that allows the same number of presynaptic nerve impulses to produce a greater effect in postsynaptic cells.

This phenomenon has caused considerable excitement among memory researchers because of its durability. EPSPs last only about 15/1,000 of a second, and activity in reverberatory circuits probably cannot last more than a few seconds (if that long). LTP, however, has been observed to linger for as long as days and weeks (Teyler & DiScenna, 1984). It is the first neural phenomenon ever found with sufficient duration to put it within the range of long-term memory, and it provides strong evidence for the idea that the use of a synapse increases the strength of the connections between neurons. LTP mimics the changes in behavior that we call learned responses; it is strengthened by repetition, growing larger with each training experience (Bliss, 1979; Lynch & Baudry, 1984a).

There are some cautions about concluding that LTP is a part of the LTM mechanism. The phenomenon was discovered under highly artificial laboratory conditions. Much of the work has been done on slices of hippocampus, and these pieces of tissue are always in the process of slowly dying despite the careful physiological adjustment of the fluids in which they are bathed. The original observation of LTP by Bliss, however, was made in living rabbits; thus, the phenomenon is not itself artificial (Bliss & Gardner-Medwin, 1973; Bliss & Lomo, 1973). The stimulus used by Bliss consisted of 10-second trains of electrical pulses at 15 pulses per second delivered to axons of the perforant path. If the frequency was set too low, LTP would not occur regardless of how many times the synapses were used in the course of a day.

You may wonder if this electrical stimulation of the perforant path could possibly mimic any natural stimulus. The frequency of 15 Hz is not an unnaturally high frequency for impulses in hippocampal axons (Teyler & DiScenna, 1984), but the fact that LTP is being triggered through only one pathway probably is unnatural. Granule cells normally do not fire unless they receive some combination of inputs from at least two sources: the perforant path and the path from medial septal nucleus. In addition, there are dopaminergic and noradrenergic inputs from the medial forebrain bundle as well as commissural fibers coming from the hippocampus in the other hemisphere. Most likely, several of these pathways cooperate when LTP is produced naturally. In experiments LTP is much easier to obtain if stimulus trains are generated in both the perforant path and septal nucleus (Abraham & Goddard, 1984).

Fortunately, synaptic enhancement looking very much like LTP has been produced in unstimulated animals by behavioral training procedures alone. In one of these experiments, the perforant path was given occasional test shocks while EPSPs and postsynaptic impulses were recorded from dentate gyrus. The shocks were too few to produce LTP themselves and were simply a way of measuring the respon-

siveness of postsynaptic neurons. The experimenters hoped to produce LTP behaviorally through nictitating membrane reflex (NMR) conditioning. They were quite successful at this, obtaining posttraining EPSPs as much as 200 percent larger than those recorded before training (Weisz et al., 1982). The case for claiming LTP to be a natural phenomenon is growing stronger.

In another study, hippocampal slices were taken from rats raised in standard, individual lab cages and from rats raised in complex environments designed to produce a greater amount of learning. When test shocks were given to the perforant path in these slices, granule cells from the complex environment yielded significantly more impulses than were obtained from the control (standard environment) slices (Green & Greenough, 1986). Again, a natural learning situation produced a change in the hippocampus strongly resembling LTP.

There is also evidence that LTP can be demonstrated at synapses outside the hippocampus (cited in Teyler & DiScenna, 1984), which means it is not just some curiosity limited to one of the many places where learning can occur in the nervous system. So far, however, we do not know that LTP can occur at all brain regions demonstrated to be learning sites. I am satisfied that, at least within the hippocampus, LTP is a part of the memory-formation process.

Now that we have evidence that neurons do indeed strengthen connections between them we need to find out what sort of structural change might underlie this strengthening and see if there is any evidence for such a process. There are two general types of structural change that have been proposed: the formation of new synapses and the strengthening of existing synapses (Greenough, 1984). Let's explore what has been discovered about each possibility.

LTM: New Synapses?

In the brain of the developing fetus and infant, axons grow, sprouting branches and telodendria and continually creating new synapses. These growth processes appear to be turned off in the adult brain, but the possibility exists that they might still be available, waiting to be switched on again by the proper stim-

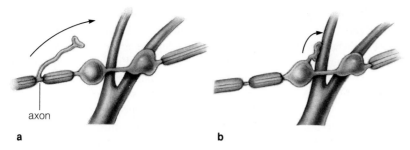

axon

a   b

Figure 16.3 Two varieties of sprouting. The structure looking like a tree trunk with two main branches is a branching dendrite. An axon is passing in front of it and making a synapse with each branch as it passes. The axon loses its myelin sheath in the vicinity of the dendrite and regains it on the other side. (**a**) Axon collateral sprouting. Because the creation of a whole new branch on an axon is a larger enterprise than the creation of new synapses on already existing branches, this collateral type of sprouting is observed only when damage has caused denervation of nearby neurons. (**b**) Terminal sprouting. This involves much less growth and is the variety most likely to be involved in learning. (Adapted from Cotman & Nieto-Sampedro, 1982)

ulus conditions. Damage to the brain might elicit new growth as an attempt to compensate for the loss. It is also possible that learning situations produce the relatively permanent structural changes underlying memory in the adult brain by temporarily switching developmental growth processes back on. If learning involves the growth of new synaptic connections, then anatomists should be able to find some evidence of this as they examine electron micrographs of nerve tissue. The best evidence that such growth does occur in the mature brain comes from studies of sprouting.

Sprouting and Synapse Turnover The growth of new telodendria and/or terminals in the mature brain is called **sprouting**. It has most frequently been studied as a response to injury in the hippocampus of the rat. In a typical experiment, the growth process would be stimulated by ablating the entorhinal cortex on one side of the brain. To follow the process of sprouting, several animals would be killed every few days and their hippocampal tissue stained for microscopic examination. In the dentate gyrus (the destination of many of the dying axons from the ablated entorhinal cortex), the first change is a 60 percent loss of synapses in the zone where entorhinal axons would normally terminate. After 3 days,

however, new synapses begin to appear, and the new terminals are from entorhinal cortex neurons on the opposite, unlesioned side of the brain (Cotman & Nieto-Sampedro, 1982). Apparently, these surviving neurons were among those that normally send axon branches ("collaterals") across the midline of the brain to connect the two entorhinal cortexes and the new synapses sprouted from these collaterals. Sprouting can also occur from nearby axons and terminals that have survived a lesion (Figure 16.3).

There are several possible explanations for how sprouting is triggered. The denervated postsynaptic cells (i.e., the ones that lost their input) may secrete some sort of chemical signal that turns on the growth process in surrounding axons and guides the growth to the vacated synaptic site (Tsukahara, 1981b). Another possibility is that under normal conditions terminals may manufacture a growth inhibitor, which prevents sprouting. As long as a terminal is present, no new growth occurs, but if the axon dies, the inhibition is removed, and nearby axons can then sprout to form terminals for the vacated synapses (Tsukahara, 1981b). These two ideas are not mutually exclusive; both mechanisms may be present.

The production of new synapses to replace lost ones following damage to the nervous system is called **reactive synaptogenesis**. There is reason to suspect that this synapse formation is a continuation of the original growth process that produced the brain because it apparently occurs even when there is no damage. Synapses seem to suffer from "wear and tear" simply through regular use and must be replaced periodically. Cotman refers to this process as **synapse turnover** and describes it as a "normal operation and maintenance" function of the brain (Cotman & Nieto-Sampedro, 1982). It is difficult to obtain a realistic estimate of the typical "life expectancy" of a synapse, but Cotman reasons that the half-life of a group of synapses in the dentate gyrus may be on the order of 1 week (Cotman & Nieto-Sampedro, 1982). (A half-life is the amount of time required for half of the synapses to be replaced.)

Sprouting, then, can occur in reaction to the loss from a lesion (reactive synaptogenesis) or simply as a part of the normal maintenance of the brain. The question that intrigues memory researchers is whether the organism's experiences (learning) can influence normal synaptogenesis. If, for example, a synapse that has been in heavy use recently not only is replaced but is given several "neighbors" that connect the same axon to the same dendrite, then Hebb's idea would be correct. Learning would be the establishment of stronger connections between neurons of a potential circuit so that the circuit could be reevoked at a later time. Such an increase in number of synapses was found by Rutledge, who stimulated corpus callosum fibers electrically and examined the area of cortex in which those fibers synapsed (cited in Cotman & Nieto-Sampedro, 1982). The increase in number of synapses suggests that sprouting occurred because of nerve impulse activity in the excited fibers.

Dendritic Changes in Learning Axons are not the only cell parts that may change in the establishment of engrams. Rats trained in a series of mazes were found to have more dendrite branches on some types of cortical neurons, and the same was true of rats trained in a task in which they had to reach into a tube for food (Greenough, 1985). More dendritic branches could mean increased area for new synapses. In fact, one could reason that as synapses are acquired it would be absolutely necessary to provide more dendritic surface to accommodate them. Fur-

thermore, if memories are held in the form of synaptic connections, then the number of synapses should increase with age as more and more memories are acquired. Indeed, there is evidence that dendrites of cortical cells increase the number and complexity of their smallest terminal branches as rats and people age. Parahippocampal gyrus neurons from elderly people with normal brains had markedly more dendritic branching than did such neurons in young adults but seemed to have atrophy of dendrites in cases of senile dementia, a disorder that involves memory loss (Buell & Coleman, 1979). However, there is a question that should be asked about these results: Were the increases in dendritic branching the result of learning or of some unknown effect of aging that has nothing to do with the establishment of more synapses?

The amount of experience (i.e., opportunities for learning) can be manipulated in rats by increasing or decreasing the complexity of their environment. Rosenzweig and Bennett performed a classic series of experiments in which they compared the brains of rats raised in standard lab cages containing only food and water with those raised in an "enriched" environment full of movable, chewable, climbable, and manipulable objects. In other words, the standard environment contained very few learning experiences, while the enriched environment presumably provided a continuing source of new things to learn. Neurons in the occipital cortexes of rats from the enriched environment had significantly larger dendritic "trees" with longer branches and more divisions into smaller branchlets (cited in Greenough, 1985; Cotman & Nieto-Sampedro, 1982). So, the rats that aged in an environment that allowed lots of learning showed much more of the dendritic growth associated with aging than did the animals that aged without many opportunities for learning. The best interpretation of the results on dendritic branching still seems to be that the growth provides more area for new synaptic contacts to form.

We have seen that learning might involve the manufacture of new terminals ending on newly formed areas of dendrites. This leads to the thought that several years' worth of learning might produce a severe case of overcrowding in the brain. New telodendria, terminals, and dendritic branches all take up space. We will see later that much of memory formation may not necessitate the formation of new structures, but one cannot overlook the evidence that some new growth does appear to take place; this seems to lead to the conclusion that the brain actually must grow in size as months and years of experience pile up. The housing studies comparing enriched and standard environments bear this out. Brains of rats from the learning-rich environments had cerebral cortexes that were both heavier and thicker than those of the controls (cited in Greenough, 1985).

Protein Synthesis and Learning Brain structures such as telodendria, terminals, and dendrites are largely composed of protein. If engrams consist of newly formed brain tissue, then the rate of protein synthesis in neurons must increase as memories are formed. Evidence for this interpretation was obtained by injecting the drug **anisomycin**, a **protein synthesis inhibitor (PSI)**, directly into the brains of rats that had just learned a task (Rosenzweig & Bennett, 1984b). A retention test the next day showed that the controls, who received an injection of a neutral saline solution, remembered the task, whereas the experimental subjects, who received anisomycin, showed amnesia. Apparently, the inability to synthesize proteins prevented the formation of LTM.

A problem with the results of PSI experiments was that the more training trials an animal received, the less effect the anisomycin had on retention (Rosenzweig & Bennett, 1984a). This is understandable, however, if we adopt Rosenzweig and Bennett's (1984b) suggestion that the training experience sets up some sort of template (perhaps equivalent to STM) that maintains the engram until protein synthesis has occurred and LTM has been formed. The template is presumed to be quite temporary, fading away within minutes, but each training trial would presumably renew this template and extend the time during which LTM could be forming. Now, if we can assume that protein synthesis takes place within minutes of training, then a subject that had received, for example, 20 training trials could have already synthesized some of the needed proteins before the trials were completed and the drug administered. Once the engram is formed, the PSI drug should not

be able to harm it; thus, the animal with lengthy training should display some memory despite the drug. This interpretation does, however, rest on the idea that protein synthesis begins immediately, within minutes of training.

PSI experiments could be more easily interpreted if the learning task could be completed before any new protein could be synthesized. Then, if protein synthesis is critical, PSI drugs should always produce amnesia. For this reason, researchers shifted to a **passive-avoidance** task in which a rat is placed on a small wooden pedestal in the middle of a shock grid. The animal's natural inclination is to step down off the block, but when it does so, it receives a foot shock. Most rats learn to avoid stepping down onto the grid after just one such experience. The PSI drug can be administered just before this one-trial training or at any time following.

Such PSI experiments showed clearly that protein synthesis is needed for learning to occur (Davis & Squire, 1984). Inhibition soon after practice blocked learning. It was also found that if the drug was not injected until 1 hour after training, it had no effect on performance (Barondes & Cohen, 1968). The rats remembered their training despite the protein synthesis inhibition. This suggests that the proteins involved in the engram are already synthesized shortly after training. However, animals that received PSI injections just prior to learning could remember just as well as the controls for a period of time following training (about 3 hours in the rat). Then they began to show a permanent loss of memory for the task. This could mean that the early stages of memory do not depend on making new proteins. These results lead some researchers to postulate the existence of a temporary form of storage from which LTM is normally built. This fast-fading memory might be STM, but it appears to last longer than the 15–30 seconds that are usually thought to be the limits of STM. Rosenzweig and Bennett simply call it a memory template and do not try to define it further.

Recall from our earlier discussion that electrophysiologists have produced data that strongly suggest LTP to be the synaptic equivalent of LTM. A logical conclusion at this point would be that protein synthesis is necessary for LTP. That does not seem to be entirely the case, however. In at least one study,

PSI failed to block the development of LTP during the first 3 hours following the beginning of stimulation (cited in Davis & Squire, 1984). Another study found that anisomycin did block the persistence of LTP but only after the fourth hour (Frey et al., 1988). If early LTP is independent of protein synthesis, then we must find some other mechanism to explain how it is maintained until new structures have sprouted. We return to this problem in a later section.

Summary   In this section, we explored the possibility that LTMs are acquired through the formation of new synapses, a physiological process that might be identical to the growth process that originally builds all the synapses of the fetal brain. Formation of new synapses in the adult brain was not thought to be possible until it was discovered that a lesion that deprives some surviving neurons of a part of their normal input stimulated the growth of new telodendria and terminals from remaining, undamaged axons. This process is called sprouting, and it may also occur in undamaged brains on a smaller scale because synapses wear out and must be replaced regularly. It would be an extension of this replacement process (called synapse turnover) that would produce the engrams of LTM.

Dendritic growth is probably also involved in memory formation. Some types of dendrites show more profuse branching following learning experiences. The added branches would provide more area for contact with terminals of presynaptic cells. The constant addition of dendritic branches and terminals should result in an increase in the overall size of the brain, and this has been shown to occur in the experiments contrasting enriched with standard environments.

New growth requires synthesis of proteins, and PSI studies show that memory formation can be prevented by the administration of drugs that inhibit protein synthesis during training and the period immediately following. Because PSI drugs do not stop the animal from learning the task and from remembering it for a few hours afterward, some temporary memory process (perhaps STM) must maintain the engram for a short while. If proteins can be made during this time, they apparently enable the brain to construct a long-term engram to replace the fading "template" or STM.

LTM: Strengthening of Old Synapses

PSI experiments showed us that some "template" or short-range storage mechanism must hold the memory for a few hours until the more permanent storage mechanisms (construction of new synapses, etc.) are able to come into play. We hesitate to label this temporary template as STM because it far outlasts the 20–30 seconds specified by cognitive psychologists as the duration of STM. Some theorists have argued that there is an "intermediate-term" memory that links STM to LTM. This idea of three memory stages rather than two seems like a good solution, but it probably doesn't go far enough. The data presented above and the ideas examined below suggest that memory formation is a complex process with many stages, only the last of which is the actual building of new structures (Gibbs & Ng, 1977).

Having examined the potential longer-duration, memory-storage mechanisms in the last section, we should now examine the evidence for "intermediate-memory" mechanisms. What processes might maintain the engram between the end of reverberation and the construction of new connections between neurons? This hypothetical process would have to involve existing synapses, and if Hebb was correct in his postulate, the process would have to be one that resulted in the strengthening of these old synapses.

Ependymins and Synaptic Strengthening   Shashoua (1985) has generated a clever hypothesis in which proteins formed early after training could be used in an immediate but temporary template that would guide the slower process of building new structure. The hypothesis came from Shashoua's work on goldfish. The task he devised for the fish was to learn how to swim upright after a float had been attached at the ventral midline. The buoyancy of the float was sufficient to flip the fish over on its back and pull it up to the surface of the water (Figure 16.4). Most fish learned to overcome the problem in about 3 hours and were able to remain right-side up there-

Figure 16.4 To study protein formation in learning, Shashoua gave his subjects (goldfish) the task of learning to swim right-side up despite wearing a float attached ventrally. (**a**) Typical postures right after the float is attached. (**b**) The fish on the left has learned to partially compensate, and the fish on the right shows an example of complete learning. (Adapted from Shashoua, 1985)

a

b

after. At the end of 4 hours, the floats were removed, and each fish received an injection of radioactive valine, an amino acid precursor for certain proteins. One hour was allowed for the valine to be absorbed and incorporated into proteins, and the brains were extracted, homogenized, and analyzed for various proteins. There were three proteins found in greater quantity in the trained experimental subjects than in the untrained controls. Furthermore, when the brains of controls were compared with those of trained fish that failed to learn the task, there was no difference in the concentrations of those three proteins. Apparently, only certain proteins are synthesized as a result of a learning experience.

Two of the proteins, called β and γ, were isolated

and studied. They turned out to be a type found highly concentrated in an area of midbrain called the zona ependyma and hence were given the tentative names β and γ **ependymin** (beta and gamma eh-PEN-di-min). These are normal brain proteins that are manufactured by cells and then released into the extracellular fluid that circulates between neurons and glia.

The question arose about whether these proteins were actually involved in creating an engram or were just some coincidental side effect of the process. To answer this, Shashoua needed to somehow disable the ependymins and see if the fish still retained their training. Accordingly, he devised an antiserum composed of antibody molecules that were designed to

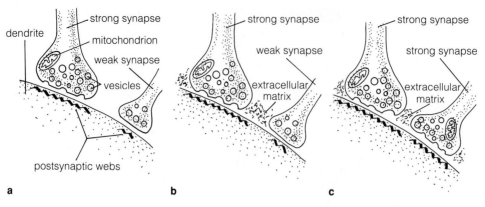

Figure 16.5 Shashoua's proposed role of ependymins in engram formation. (**a**) Two terminals ending on the same postsynaptic cell. One of them is a strong synapse, the other is weak. (**b**) During the learning experience, both terminals fire together or nearly simultaneously. This activity depletes calcium in the region between them and triggers the polymerization of the ependymins there to form a matrix that will guide synaptic growth. (**c**) The growth has occurred, making the weak synapse stronger, thus increasing the influence of a presynaptic cell on a postsynaptic. (Adapted from Shashoua, 1985)

react specifically with β and γ ependymins (see the section on immunological methods in Chapter 5). The immune reaction with the antibodies changed the shape of the protein molecules enough that they were unable to play their usual role. The result was that fish injected with the antiserum were unable to retain what they learned. Three days after successful training, the floats were reattached, and the injected fish had to learn again how to stay upright. Uninjected controls had no trouble at all in remembering how to swim right-side up. You can see that this "protein-disablement" experiment resembles the protein synthesis–inhibition experiments we discussed earlier, and the similarity extends to the fact that interference with proteins can only produce amnesia if done around the time of training. If Shashoua injected the antiserum 48 hours after training, it had no influence on the memory for the task. Apparently, ependymins are part of a temporary type of engram that precedes LTM. The same sort of results were also obtained with a shock-avoidance task (Pirong & Schmidt, 1988).

Shashoua's hypothesis hinges on the way ependymins are controlled by calcium ions. If the concentration of calcium ions in the extracellular fluid

is lowered below normal, the proteins begin to bind to one another in a reaction called polymerization. Large clumps of ependymin protein are formed this way. Figure 16.5 shows a strong synapse next to a weak synapse, presumably both from the same presynaptic cell. If the weak synapse could be strengthened, the presynaptic cell would have established stronger connections with the postsynaptic cell—a change that fits our theoretical definition for an engram. When nerve impulses in the presynaptic cell reach the two terminals, a large quantity of calcium ions enters the terminals to initiate the release of transmitter (see Chapter 4). This influx of calcium ions lowers the calcium concentration in the area between the terminals, thus initiating the polymerization of ependymins in that small region (Figure 16.5b). Shashoua proposes that this clumping of protein forms a matrix to guide the subsequent growth of the smaller terminal (Figure 16.5c). In this hypothesis, ependymins play the part of the template proposed by Rosenzweig and Bennett, marking the spot where other proteins will eventually form more membrane in the terminal and dendrite.

A great deal of research will be required to evaluate Shashoua's proposal, but already a few

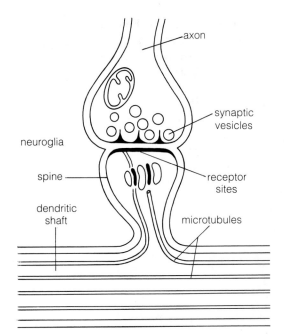

Figure 16.6 Synapse showing dendritic spine (with receptor sites) and axon terminal (with synaptic vesicles). (Adapted from Gray, 1982)

experiments seem relevant. In one such study, electronmicrographs of brains of imprinted chicks were compared with those with no imprinting experience. Measurements of the lengths of synapses showed that the imprinted chicks tended to have significantly larger synapses in an area of the brain thought related to that type of learning (Horn et al., 1985). This broadening of synapses is the sort of synaptic change that Shashoua's hypothesis proposes. Recently, Shashoua has extended his work to mice, finding the same sorts of protein changes that he found in goldfish (reviewed in Thompson et al., 1983).

Dendritic Spines Shashoua's theory emphasizes events on the presynaptic side of the synapse. The most interesting data, however, come from the postsynaptic side. Recall from Chapter 2 that dendrites of most cortical neurons and many hippocampal neurons are covered with tiny protrusions called dendritic spines (Figure 16.6) and that most of the excitatory synapses are made on these structures (Wilson et al., 1983). They come in a variety of sizes and shapes (Figures 16.7 and 16.8) but seem to fall roughly into three classes (Wilson et al., 1983). The thin, pinched-in stalks of some spines are a source of resistance for EPSPs initiated by the synapse at the spine tip. Because the circumference of the stalk is less than that of the tip of the spine, there is less membrane at the stalk to provide the ions that must flow toward the opening ion channels when an EPSP is initiated (Crick, 1982; Wilson et al., 1983). An EPSP in a spine with a long, thin stalk comes out weaker than it would in a shorter, fatter-stalked spine. One can surmise then that the short, stubby spines would yield the largest EPSPs (all other factors held constant). Because learning seems to be a matter of improving the size of the EPSP that a synapse can generate, the shape of spines might be a factor worthy of our attention.

Francis Crick (1982) has proposed that spines may change their shapes and that this change may underlie memory. He notes that dendritic spines appear to be filled with fine filaments that give the insides a fluffy appearance at high magnifications and suggests that these may be protein fibers such as actin, a muscle protein, which could contract to change the shape of the spine. After studying these filaments, other researchers agree and have begun to speak of the **cytoskeleton**, a network of protein fibers that holds the rather flimsy cell membrane into a stable shape (Wilson et al., 1983).

Not only is Crick's idea a possibility, it might help explain intermediate-term memory. Actin fibers within the spine should be able to react quite swiftly to the kind of stimulus train that evokes LTP (Crick, 1982). Some experimenters have induced LTP in the hippocampus and then examined the tissue for spine changes. They have found a rounding of the spine heads from mushroom shape to stubby (cited in Lynch & Baudry, 1984a), just the sort of change that should lower the electrical resistance of the spine to EPSPs. Greenough (1984) also found a greater number of stubby spines in tissue in which LTP had been induced. The rounding of the spine heads occurred within 10 minutes of the stimulation but (note this!) lasted for only 2 hours. Tissue that had

Figure 16.7 Varieties of dendritic spine shapes. It is possible that the largest EPSPs can be produced in the stubby types that do not impede the current with a narrow "bottle neck." (Adapted from Crick, 1982)

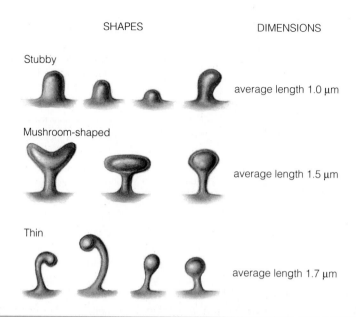

SHAPES

Stubby

Mushroom-shaped

Thin

DIMENSIONS

average length 1.0 μm

average length 1.5 μm

average length 1.7 μm

been stimulated without producing LTP showed no changes in the spines. The clarity of these results is blurred by the problem of how they should be interpreted. Greenough believes that the stubby spines he found after LTP are brand new spines rather than the ones on which the active synapses were located. However, this leaves him in the awkward position of insisting that synapses (spines plus terminals) can sprout within 15 minutes of the stimulus (Greenough, 1985). It seems more reasonable to me that the stubby spines that are more prevalent after LTP are the spines with synapses that are active in producing the LTP and that have changed their shapes. The lowered resistance from the shape change would be a part of the increased EPSP size that constitutes LTP. The disappearance of the rounding effect within 2 hours leads us to associate this change with intermediate-term memory rather than LTM.

Evidence for a relation between learning and changes in the diameter of spine shafts comes from a rearing study in fish (Coss & Globus, 1978). Dendritic spines from jewel fish raised in the company of other jewel fish were compared with those from fish reared in isolation. Because there is considerable social interaction in this species, it is fairly certain that much less learning was possible in the

isolated rearing condition than in the social. The socially reared subjects had more dendritic branches and spines (Figure 16.9a) as well as having an average difference in spine shape (Figure 16.9b). The spines of socially reared fish had shorter stalks. That is, more of the total spine length was taken up by the swollen tip. This extra tip-membrane area would provide a greater supply of ions near the synapse, thus increasing the size of any EPSP elicited (Coss & Globus, 1978). Studies of one-trial avoidance learning in chicks also found enlargement of spine heads and shortening of stems as well as an increase in the density of spines on the dendrites (Patel et al., 1988; Patel & Stewart, 1988).

At this point in our review then, we have drawn several tentative conclusions. LTM is represented in the nervous system by a semipermanent increase in the size of the EPSPs that a particular synapse can produce (LTP). When we seek the causes of LTP, we find a variety of hypothetical mechanisms, no one of which has the correct timing to do the job alone. Sprouting has the permanence needed to maintain LTP for years, but it probably takes days to reach the point where there is enough growth to account for the enhancement. Shashoua's protein matrix seems to simply provide a guide for the sprouting. Changes

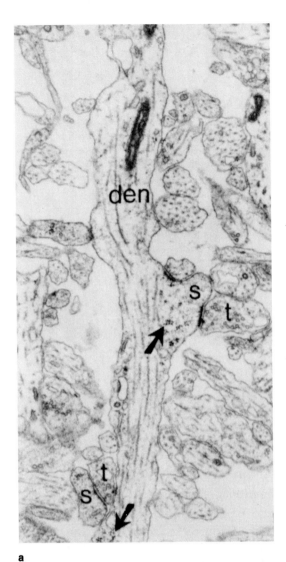

a

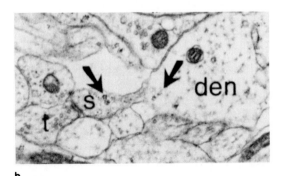

b

Figure 16.8 Electron micrographs of dendrites and terminals. (**a**) The shaft in the center is a dendrite (den). Most of the roughly circular objects are cross sections of telodendria or axon terminals. The hump on the right side of the dendrite (S) is a "stubby" dendritic spine, which forms a separate synapse with each of three adjacent axon terminals. The arrow at the base of the spine points at a cluster of polyribosomes, the structures in which protein molecules are assembled from the RNA template. (**b**) This shows a dendrite (in cross section) bearing a mushroom-shaped spine having a long, thin stalk. Our knowledge of ion gradients suggests that this type of spine would produce weaker EPSPs at the synapse on its tip than would be the case for a stubby spine. (From Steward & Falk, 1986)

in dendritic spine shape can occur within 10 minutes but seem to fade out within 2–3 hours. There seems to be a time gap between the stimulus and a point roughly 10 minutes later, with no mechanism to explain the storage of the engram. Reverberation might account for the first 15 seconds or so of this, but serious objections have been raised for even this length of time. Another gap seems to exist between roughly 3 hours poststimulus and 2–3 days poststimulus. Let us now see if we can explain how memory is stored during the first 10 minutes.

The Calpain–Fodrin Theory Lynch and Baudry (1984a) have advanced a theory that may meet this need. They started with the idea that the transmitter for most of the major types of synapses in the hippocampus is **glutamate**. Using hippocampal slices, they evoked LTP and then measured the capability of the tissue to bind glutamate. The slices in which LTP had occurred bound significantly more glutamate than did the unstimulated control slices. This indicated that there were more glutamate receptors in the LTP slices. Because too little time was involved for new synapses to have grown, Lynch and Baudry reasoned that the extra receptors must have been present in the dendritic spines all along but, prior to LTP, not in a usable condition (Lynch & Baudry, 1984b).

Calcium ions also seemed to be involved because increasing the concentration at the synapse not only made it easier to elicit LTP (Teyler & DiScenna, 1984)

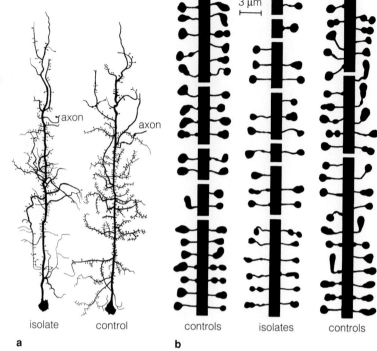

Figure 16.9 Learning-induced changes in dendrites and dendritic spines of jewel fish neurons. (**a**) Drawings of typical neurons from experimental and control groups. The controls lived in a normal social environment in which considerable learning could occur, whereas the experimental subjects were reared in isolation and were denied social learning experiences. Neurons of control fish had more dendritic branches and more spines. (**b**) Each spine was drawn from a microphotograph model onto a black bar representing the dendrite. Spines from isolates have smaller heads (meaning less area for synapses) and, on the average, longer stems (which could mean weaker EPSPs). (Adapted from Coss & Globus, 1978)

but also increased the amount of glutamate that would bind to hippocampal tissue (Baudry & Lynch, 1984). It is easy to guess that LTP enhancement was not caused directly by calcium ions but came about because the calcium made more glutamate receptors available. Having more receptors available would bind more transmitter, with the result that a larger EPSP would be produced. If this potentiation lasts for as long as minutes, you have LTP. This reasoning leads immediately to the question of how calcium ions could make more glutamate receptors available.

The key to calcium's effect may be a group of enzymes of the proteinase variety, collectively called **calpain,** that become active only after reacting with calcium ions. A proteinase enzyme makes it possible for changes to occur in protein molecules, and the particular protein that appears to be altered in the dendritic spine is **fodrin.** In Figure 16.10a, fodrin is seen as one of the proteins making up the microtubules and microfilaments of the cytoskeleton. A number of studies have shown that fodrin has a role in allowing the cytoskeleton to change so that the

cell structure can alter its shape (Nixon, 1986). It could be fodrin that is responsible for the reshaping of the dendritic spines into a configuration with less electrical resistance (i.e., rounding of spine tip and broadening of the spine stalk). But there is another, even more important facet to Lynch and Baudry's theory. Note in Figure 16.10b that some receptor sites for the glutamate neurotransmitter are positioned on the outside of the cell membrane where they are accessible to the transmitter molecules, while others are buried deep in the membrane and inaccessible. Lynch and Baudry propose that calpain and fodrin act to make these buried receptors available to glutamate.

The sequence of events begins with a series of nerve impulses in the presynaptic axon. Because we are trying to explain the origin of LTP, this train of impulses must be fairly long and have a high frequency. After the released glutamate diffuses across the synaptic gap and binds to the receptors on the spine, two events occur: the sodium gates open to initiate an EPSP, and calcium-channel gates open to

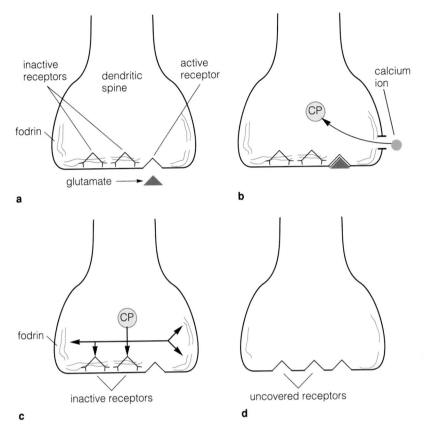

Figure 16.10 Lynch and Baudry's theory of memory storage. (**a**) Dendritic spines at glutamate synapses contain active (uncovered) and inactive (covered) receptors. Transmitter can only bind with active receptors. (**b**) Binding of the transmitter not only opens the usual sodium channels to produce an EPSP but also calcium channels. When calcium ions flow inward, they combine with molecules of calpain (CP), triggering calpain to begin degrading the protein fodrin. (**c**) Some fodrin molecules are covering glutamate receptors, thus keeping them inactive. (**d**) The degrading of fodrin uncovers receptors and increases the spine's receptivity to glutamate. It may be this increase in receptors that underlies the increase in EPSP size that is LTP.

allow calcium ions into the dendritic spine. We have already discussed the fact that calcium enters the presynaptic terminal to make possible the release of transmitter from the vesicles, but we have not mentioned that calcium also enters the postsynaptic cell during transmission. Calcium entry does occur at a number of types of synapses (Roufogalis, 1980), and one of its effects in the spine is to bind with the calpain found there. This addition of calcium activates the calpain, enabling it to act as an enzyme.

In the next step, calpain finds a molecule of fodrin and breaks it down into other molecules (Figure 16.10c). The theory proposes that fodrin was holding onto the glutamate receptors, thus keeping them inaccessible. Breaking down a part of the fodrin network releases some of the receptors that then add themselves to those on the outside of the membrane. This uncovering of hidden receptors increases the dendrite's ability to receive neurotransmitter (Figure 16.10d) and results in a larger EPSP following the next presynaptic impulse. When a long train of presynaptic impulses occurs in a brief time span (the stimulus condition needed to produce LTP), greater than normal amounts of calcium enter the spine, and the effect of the calpain becomes widespread throughout the spine (Lynch & Baudry, 1984a). Significant numbers of glutamate receptors are uncovered, and enough fodrin is broken up to change the cytoskeleton and alter the shape of the spine to make it stubbier (resembling those in the top row of Figure 16.7). The uncovering of receptors would be a rapid effect that could explain why LTP arises within seconds of the stimulus: the spine-shape change would add to LTP but presumably take somewhat longer to occur. Thus, the Lynch–Baudry theory gives us a mechanism that fills in the time gaps we discussed earlier. The calpain–fodrin mechanism should take care of storing the engram until the slower growth processes dependent on protein synthesis have had time to take place. A number of studies have produced evidence that fits well with this theory (Horn et al., 1985; Lynch and Baudry, 1984a).

The cAMP–Kinase Theory We have seen that learning experiences appear to be able to trigger RNA changes and the formation of new protein, with the resulting growth of new tissue (terminals, dendrites, etc.). The idea that these processes really are initiated by learning would be easier to accept if we could picture some concrete set of chemical steps by which heavy use of a synapse could increase protein synthesis. We now know that one possible chemical link does exist (Nathanson & Greengard, 1977).

Figure 16.11 shows a postsynaptic membrane with a receptor site binding a neurotransmitter molecule. Another molecule, **adenylate cyclase**, is on the inside of the membrane but in close association with the receptor. This enzyme then reacts to this binding by becoming chemically activated. Having been activated, it can bind with and alter **adenosine triphosphate (ATP)** (see Chapter 2), which is available inside the cell. Activated adenylate cyclase can strip two of the three phosphate groups from an ATP molecule, producing a chemical called **cyclic AMP (cAMP)**, which it releases into the cytoplasm. Cyclic AMP can perform all sorts of tasks such as initiating the opening of ion gates (as is the case in sensiti-

zation of the *Aplysia*'s gill reflex described in Chapter 14), but our present interest in this molecule concerns its effect on RNA and protein formation.

After diffusing into the cytoplasm from the adenylate cyclase, the cAMP molecule eventually encounters a molecule of **protein kinase**. This enzyme specializes in transferring phosphate groups to protein molecules to bring about changes in their function, a process called **phosphorylation**. The kinase is held in an inactivated condition by a molecular fragment called an inhibitory subunit. Cyclic AMP can activate the kinase by removing this inhibitory subunit (Figure 16.11). The remainder of the kinase molecule is the active enzyme. This active kinase diffuses into the nucleus of the cell where it finds the protein on which it is designed to act—a **nuclear regulatory protein**. This regulatory protein is bound to a stretch of DNA, preventing that gene fragment from producing RNA until needed.

To activate the gene, cAMP must remove the regulatory protein, which it does by obtaining a phosphate group from a passing ATP molecule and giving it to the regulatory protein. Once it has accepted the phosphate group, the protein can no longer bind to the DNA molecule and the gene is now free to manufacture a "replica" of itself in the form of messenger RNA (mRNA). Messenger RNA diffuses out to the ribosomes and initiates the manufacture of proteins for various cell parts like receptor sites needed for strengthening synapses (Nathanson & Greengard, 1977). Some evidence has accrued for this theory. For example, inhibition of protein kinase shortens the persistence of LTP to a few minutes—too short a time for it to underlie LTM (Lovinger et al., 1987).

Some cAMP is used to open ion channels and produce EPSPs (see Chapter 14 for the chemistry). Thus, when the transmitter binds to its receptor site, two processes are evoked: facilitation (EPSPs) and protein synthesis. The facilitation is quickly stopped, which prevents a runaway EPSP, but lingering quantities of cAMP can again open ion channels, initiating more EPSP activity. This will continue until cAMP has been disabled by an enzyme. The amount of time cAMP persists following one presynaptic impulse is uncertain, but it could easily be for enough seconds to account for STM. Thus, cAMP may be involved in both STM and LTM.

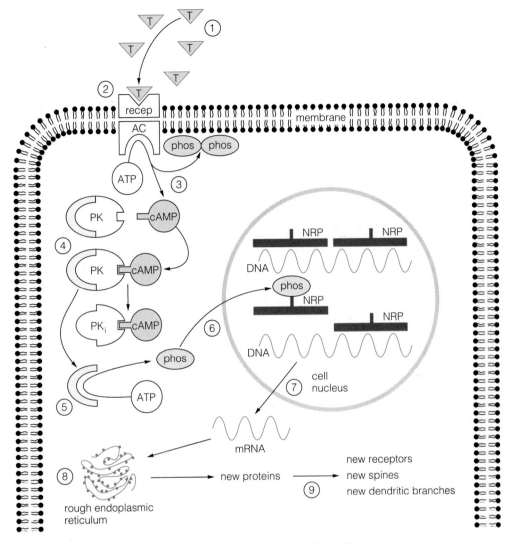

Figure 16.11 The cAMP–kinase theory of how a synapse is strengthened by use.
(1) Transmitter (T) molecules from the presynaptic terminal diffuse across the synaptic gap
and (2) bind to a receptor (recep) in the postsynaptic membrane. This binding activates
the enzyme adenylate cyclase (AC), which (3) strips two phosphate groups (phos) from a
molecule of ATP, creating cyclic AMP (cAMP). The cAMP (4) binds to a molecule of protein
kinase (PK), which responds by breaking into two parts. The inhibitory subunit of the kinase
(PK$_i$) stays bound to the cAMP, leaving the enzyme portion free to react with ATP (5). ATP
is stripped of one phosphate that is taken to the nucleus of the cell (6) and combined with
a nuclear regulatory protein (NRP). The phosphorylated NRP releases a stretch of DNA to
make mRNA (7). The mRNA leaves the nucleus for the rough endoplasmic reticulum (8)
where it is used to create proteins that will be incorporated (9) into receptors, spines, and
dendritic branches, thus strengthening the connections between cells.

The proposed cAMP–kinase mechanism should not be viewed as competing with the calpain–fodrin theory because the two ideas relate to different transmitter systems. The monoamine transmitters seem, at this time, to be the only ones whose receptors are linked to adenylate cyclase, the enzyme that manufactures cAMP. Within the hippocampus, synapses involved in processing the information flowing through that structure probably use glutamate as a transmitter. There are, however, monoaminergic synapses on pyramidal cells and other neurons within the dentate gyrus. These are noradrenergic synapses of axons coming from the locus coeruleus in the pontine brain stem, and evidence strongly indicates that they have their effect by way of cAMP (Moore & Bloom, 1979). Monoamines seem to be used by systems that modulate the flow of information in other systems rather than in the direct processing of information itself (i.e., emotion, mood, reinforcement systems). It would seem that different functional systems in the brain may employ different memory mechanisms to store their engrams.

NMDA Receptors and Associative Learning Much of your everyday learning is associative in nature. You learn to link a name with a face, a definition with a term, or a stimulus with a response. In the nervous system, this would require linking two engrams (e.g., associating the engram for a face with the engram for a name). Such linking could be achieved if some of the cells in one engram were fired at exactly the same moment that they received stimulation from cells in the other engram. In other words, the association between the two engrams could only be formed if both engrams become active simultaneously. However, this calls for a mechanism that strengthens the synapses between the engrams when both engrams are simultaneously active but *not* when only one is active. In our discussion so far, we have stipulated only that a synapse be *used* for it to strengthen. Now we have a situation where the synapse could be used many times without strengthening it but must be able to grow stronger whenever the postsynaptic cell receives a simultaneous input from another synapse. This arrangement is called a **Hebbian synapse** (after the originator of

the idea, Donald Hebb) and has been suggested as the basis for associative learning.

How might a Hebbian synapse work? Our hypothesis employs the calpain–fodrin mechanism at glutamate synapses. (Amino acid transmitters like glutamate are the most widely used excitatory transmitters in the CNS [Cotman & Iversen, 1987].) According to the Lynch–Baudry theory (see previous sections), glutamate synapses strengthen when calcium channels are opened by glutamate. At a Hebbian synapse, these channels should open only when the cell gets two nearly simultaneous EPSPs. This is exactly what happens at a particular type of calcium channel that is opened by **NMDA receptors** (NMDA is N-methyl-D-aspartate). NMDA receptors normally do not react to glutamate. However, if the membrane has already been depolarized by an EPSP just prior to the release of transmitter at the glutamate synapse, the NMDA receptors respond to the binding of glutamate by opening their calcium channels (Cotman & Monaghan, 1988). Presumably, the calcium influx could then trigger the calpain–fodrin mechanism, leading to the strengthening of the glutamate synapse. Thus, simultaneous activity at some other synapse could decide whether strengthening will occur at the NMDA glutamate synapse. The new connection is formed only when two events occur in association. In support of this hypothesis, NMDA receptors are found throughout the brain (Cotman et al., 1987) and have been strongly linked to the occurrence of LTP (Collingridge & Bliss, 1987; Cotman & Monaghan, 1988). Blocking NMDA receptors in the hippocampus stops theta rhythm (Leung & Desborough, 1988).

Summary Our survey of possible memory-storage mechanisms suggests that the old distinction between STM and LTM may be inadequate. Instead there seems to be a wide variety of starting and ending times for the various mechanisms. I suspect that memory-storage mechanisms overlap in time in such a way that during the early phases the engram is continually shifting from one form of storage to another. However, the summary of mechanisms in Table 16.1 stays within the STM–LTM tradition, allowing for its problems by adding two other memory stages.

Table 16.1 Proposed Physiological Bases of Memory

	Sensory	Short Term	Intermediate	Long Term
Approximate duration	0.5 s	0.5–30 s	30 s–hours	Hours–years
Possible mechanisms	Reverberation	AMP persistence Receptor uncovering	Receptor uncovering Ependymin matrix Spine-shape changes	New:* Terminals Dendrites Receptors Larger synapses

*Building these new structures depends on cAMP activation of DNA, RNA transcription, and protein synthesis.

The concept of sensory memory comes from cognitive psychology. It is a very brief store, lasting only about half a second following the stimulus. Considering how fragile the process of reverberation likely is, it seems probable that reverberation would be better employed explaining sensory memory rather than STM. When you study Table 16.1, remember how tentative is our evidence for all proposed mechanisms and their timing.

Amnesia

A completely different approach to the understanding of memory comes from the study of traumatic memory loss (amnesia), both in human clinical cases and in laboratory animals. We will see that the results of these studies have completely remodeled our views on what categories of memory exist.

The Amnesic Syndrome

Memory loss from brain damage has been portrayed so frequently in an erroneous fashion in popular fiction that some people may have come to doubt the reality of its existence. When the story's hero regains consciousness following a blow to the head, he either is able to recall immediately the incident in which he was struck (highly improbable) or is unable to recall *any* of his life history (even more improbable). In some cases, his missing life history

is conveniently restored with a second blow to the head (outrageously improbable). Let's examine the facts of the amnesic syndrome and then see what they can add to our understanding of memory.

Almost anything that can cause brain damage can bring about loss of memory: impaired blood supply (as in a stroke), infections (such as herpes encephalitis or meningitis), and accidents. Memory loss is one symptom of senile dementia and Alzheimer's disease. A **concussion**, a blow to the head that throws the brain against the inside of the skull, can cause blood vessels to rupture and cells to die, with resulting **concussive amnesia**. Alcoholism produces a variety of amnesia called **Korsakoff's syndrome**, which has been very important as a source of subjects for neuropsychologists studying memory. The damage in Korsakoff's syndrome seems to result from the poor diet of the chronic alcoholic rather than directly from the drug itself. The alcohol provides so many calories that the alcoholic fails to eat foods that provide a sufficient supply of vitamin B_1. The deficiency is responsible for the brain damage and amnesia.

Because the damage in Korsakoff's syndrome accumulates very slowly over years, there is no clear onset to the amnesia. By contrast, concussive amnesia has a very clear beginning and thus has provided the model traditionally used to describe the symptomatology. A case history presented by Barbizet (1970) illustrates the important ideas (Figure 16.12). The concussion occurred at the point on the time line labeled *trauma* (a term meaning injury).

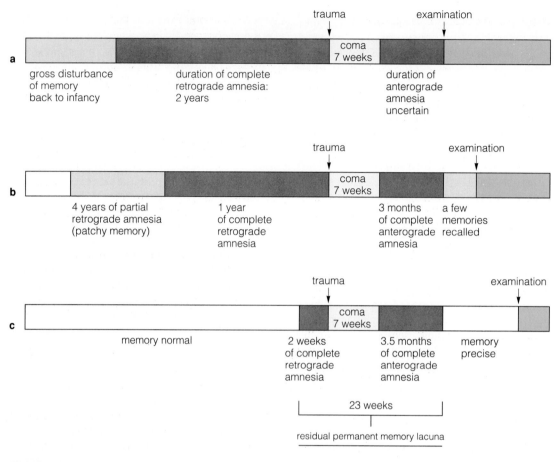

Figure 16.12 Time lines showing the results of Mr. G.'s memory examinations at (**a**) 5, (**b**) 8, and (**c**) 16 months posttrauma. (Adapted from Barbizet, 1970)

The patient, Mr. G., stayed in a coma for 7 weeks following his injury. Fourteen weeks later, an attempt to establish the extent of his amnesia revealed that he could remember no events occurring during roughly the preceding 2 years. This sort of difficulty in recalling events preceding the trauma is called **retrograde amnesia**. Not all amnesia patients display noticeable retrograde amnesia beyond the few minutes leading up to the concussion, but all suffer from some degree of memory loss for things that happen after the trauma. For a time after awakening from the coma, a patient appears highly confused. Rela-

tives and friends are recognized when they come to visit, but the next day the visit itself will probably be forgotten. Memory span has been shortened to the events of the preceding minutes. Perhaps, STM is still available, but the ability to transfer information to LTM is badly impaired. This inability to remember events that took place *after* the trauma is termed **anterograde amnesia**. Another way to view anterograde amnesia is as a deficit in learning; one cannot remember that which has not been learned.

Figure 16.12b indicates that Mr. G.'s memory had improved by the time of the second examination.

There was now total retrograde amnesia only for 1 year preceding the accident, and the anterograde amnesia had diminished enough that he was able to recall some of the events that occurred from day to day. None of the events from the first 3 months following the coma were recovered, however. Such anterograde amnesia is permanent, suggesting that the engrams were never stored. The final examination (Figure 16.12c) revealed almost complete recovery from the retrograde amnesia, with the exception of the 2 weeks just prior to the accident. It is likely that Mr. G. will always have a lingering memory gap—a **lacuna**—totaling roughly 23 weeks.

Mr. G.'s case is typical in that most of his retrograde amnesia was temporary while the anterograde amnesia was permanent. Barbizet (1970) described a case of a 27-year-old man studying to be a veterinary surgeon whose severe cranial trauma wiped out an entire 3 years of veterinary training. After coming out of the coma, he believed that he was still preparing for his entrance exam. Following his recovery from the injury, his friends worked with him steadily for 3 months, aiding him to recover enough of his knowledge to continue his education. Apparently, the brain injury had not erased the engrams; it simply made them harder to activate. In other words, the problem was one of difficulty in **retrieval**.

The retrieval of memories "lost" in retrograde amnesia is aided by reexperiencing stimuli associated in the past with the missing ideas. For example, a patient, 5 months after brain injury who is unable to recall anything from the preceding 20 years of his life, goes home for a visit and immediately begins to remember. Standing in one room, he is suddenly able to visualize the contents and arrangement of adjoining rooms without looking. While walking down the street, the sight of a neighbor's house evokes the memory of the neighbor's name. Bit by bit, association by association, most of the missing memories are retrieved simply by experiencing stimuli linked to the lost engrams.

Amnesia is a frightening, emotional experience. Some patients appear to be unable to accept the fact that they cannot recall certain episodes from their lives and, consciously or unconsciously, let their imaginations fill in the lacunae. This motivation may be partly responsible for **confabulation**, the creation of pseudomemories out of the patient's deductions about what must have happened during the forgotten episode. Sometimes these confabulations involve deductions that are more imaginative than logical. Consider the case of Mr. Gue, a French amnesia patient:

On the night of December 24, 1961, Mr. Gue, a workman aged 42, had an automobile accident in which his companion was killed and he suffered a cranial trauma with coma. . . . His memory for former facts was still good, although he was unsure about the few months preceding the accident. His account of the accident was confabulatory, as the following will show.

"At six o'clock on Friday evening I bought an airplane for 25,000 francs. My wife knew nothing about it. I took off with a friend for Roye, where my brother lives. We came down on the road and we had lunch. We got on our way and were taking off from the runway when I met an automobile that I could not avoid, for my reflexes were not quick enough to enable me to pull the stick in time. Although injured, for my feet had gone through the floor, I managed to bring the aircraft to the 'Place du Père Lachaise.' The police report found the driver of the car to have been in the wrong, since he should not have been on the runway." (It is interesting to note that Mr. Gue had never piloted an aircraft in his life!)

Going over with the patient the hour-by-hour events of the evening of the accident, it was found that he could remember the details of the dinner and the number of persons there, but there followed a total lacuna covering about two hours up to the accident. When he was shown a photograph of his car, he replied that it was impossible, because he was piloting his aircraft and therefore, could not have been in his car at the same time. This started him off again, entirely convinced of the story he had just told, with another recital, which, although enriched with a few additional details, remained perfectly coherent and in conformity with the initial account. This delirious conviction persisted for long months, but little by little he began to acknowledge that he really had had a car accident, without in any way denying his airplane accident. When he was seen again in November 1963, he told us once more and with great precision of detail all about his aircraft accident, then, linking the two together, he said: "Would you believe my luck? On leaving the police station I had a second accident, in which my car was completely wrecked!" (Barbizet, 1970)

Confabulation is quite characteristic of Korsakoff's syndrome, a disorder that usually ends in massive anterograde amnesia. The following case shows the extent to which the memory loss can go:

Victor, aged 59, . . . has extensive memories of his past and can, for example, give a detailed account of his military service in Indochina in 1903 during the Annam campaign and of the conditions of his service during the 1914–1918 war. For more than a year, however, Victor has been progressively forgetting everything he has just perceived or accomplished. He can carry on a conversation, but as soon as one leaves him he states that he has seen nobody: if his questioner returns, Victor does not recognize him and this behavior is repeated each time Victor sees him. After some months at Sainte-Anne he is unable to recognize either the doctors or the nurses; he loses his way in the hospital wing, of which he cannot recall the geography any more than the name of the ward or the number of his bed. He reads the paper but immediately forgets what he has read and will show the same surprise he originally showed upon reading the same news again. Victor cannot recognize his place at table and cannot remember if he has actually eaten what has only just been served to him. He plays cards, but as soon as the game is over he forgets that he had been playing. His amnesia extends with the same intensity to all perceptions: visual, auditory, and tactile, and even the polyneuritic pains provoked by the pressure of the calf muscles are immediately forgotten. (Delay, 1942)

The Anatomy of Amnesia

In 1957 W. B. Scoville, a neurosurgeon, reported that one of his patients had suffered a dramatic loss of memory following surgery for the removal of the diseased areas of his brain that were causing continuous, prolonged epileptic seizures (Scoville & Milner, 1957). In the first (and last) operation of its kind, Scoville removed the medial portions of both temporal lobes, including the hippocampi and amygdalas. The patient, H.M., obtained considerable relief from the seizures but only at the cost of forgetting

everything that happened to him only minutes after experiencing it. If you were to walk into his room, introduce yourself and leave, he would have no recollection of your name or face when you returned 5 minutes later. H.M. showed a little retrograde amnesia, but his major symptom was a pervasive anterograde loss. He had little trouble recalling the events of his life up to the time of his surgery, but from then on he had no sense of time passing. Each moment of each day existed as an island of experience with no idea of what has gone before and no memory of what should happen next.

H.M. has been cared for all this time by his mother, who usually accompanies him wherever he goes. It so happened, however, that in 1966 the mother was in Hartford Hospital, recovering from a minor operation, just when H.M. was about to leave for Boston. It was his father, therefore, who packed H.M.'s clothes for him and brought him to meet us at Dr. Scoville's office prior to the journey. The father had also taken the patient to visit his mother in [the] hospital that very morning, the third such visit within a week. Yet when we questioned H.M., he seemed not to remember any of these visits, although he expressed a vague idea that something might have happened to his mother. On the journey to Boston, he kept saying that he felt a little uneasy and wondered if something might be wrong with one of his parents, though he could not be sure which one. On being asked who had packed his bag for the trip, he said "Seems like it was my mother. But then that's what I'm not sure about. If there is something wrong with my mother, then it could have been my father." Despite our explaining the situation to him repeatedly during the journey, H.M. was never able to give a clear account of what had happened, and was still feeling "uneasy" when he reached Boston, wondering if something was "wrong" with one of his parents. Gradually, this uneasiness wore off, and although he was told repeatedly that he could telephone home any time he wished, he no longer seemed to know why he should do so. Next day he appeared completely unaware that there had been any question of illness in his family. (Milner et al., 1968)

H.M.'s amnesia appears to have stemmed from the loss of both hippocampi, but other parts of the brain may also be involved in memory formation. These other parts lie within the **diencephalon**, a region just above and anterior to the midbrain that consists chiefly of the thalamus, subthalamus, and hypothalamus. Anatomically then, there may be two kinds of amnesia: **diencephalic** and **medial temporal** (hippocampal), with H.M. being the best example of the latter. Patients with Korsakoff's psychosis represent the diencephalic variety.

Some autopsy reports on patients with memory problems have revealed destruction to the **mammillary bodies** of the hypothalamus. Because these lesions were caused by vascular problems (bursting blood vessels or clots that shut off blood flow) or tumors, the extent of the damage was by no means localized to the mammillary bodies. This allows us to make only tentative conclusions. It may be significant, however, that one of the major outputs from the hippocampus is through the fornix to the mammillary bodies. Unfortunately, some cases of damage to the mammillary bodies have been reported in which the patients supposedly showed no amnesia at all (Victor, 1964). Another diencephalic structure that seems to be relevant to amnesia is the **dorsomedial nucleus of the thalamus (DMT)**. Several cases of tumors and other types of lesion in the region of the DMT have been found during autopsy of brains from amnesia patients (Markowitsch & Pritzel, 1985). Research with rats given DMT lesions showed that the animals had considerable difficulty in remembering from trial to trial what responses they had just made (Means et al., 1970).

Autopsies of brains from Korsakoff's syndrome patients clearly show that the focus of their problem was diencephalic lesions, but beyond that the picture is foggy. Some studies emphasize destruction in the mammillary bodies, whereas others discount these changes or fail to find them, insisting instead that DMT destruction produced the amnesia symptoms (Markowitsch & Pritzel, 1985). To confuse matters still further, neurosurgeons who deliberately set out to destroy the DMT or mammillary bodies bilaterally in order to relieve other problems frequently report that the patients demonstrated no memory changes at all as a result of the loss (Markowitsch & Pritzel, 1985). However, the surgeon's chances of accurately placing an electrode directly within the DMT, using only the very loose stereotaxic coordinates available for the human brain plus X-ray pictures, are not good

at all. Without evidence from autopsy, we cannot be sure that it was the DMT that was destroyed.

The best working hypothesis is that Korsakoff's syndrome patients probably suffer anterograde amnesia because of destruction of either the DMT or mammillary bodies or some combination of both. That there are two places in the brain where damage can cause amnesia suggests that there might be two types of amnesia. Squire is currently investigating the possibility that diencephalic amnesia might be different from medial temporal amnesia (Squire, 1987).

The Consolidation-Failure Hypothesis

The major symptom of anterograde amnesia is the inability to recall events that happened just minutes before, coupled with a relatively normal STM. This failure to maintain a memory beyond the span of STM suggested to early researchers that the basic problem in anterograde amnesia might be a failure to store information into LTM. This theoretical process of shifting information from STM to LTM is called **consolidation**; thus, the first explanation of anterograde amnesia was termed the **consolidation-failure hypothesis**.

The Early Version In the original statement of his two-stage theory of memory, Hebb (1949) proposed that when you experience an event the stimuli set up a pattern of firing in the brain that is specific to that particular set of stimuli and to no other. Reverberation within this collection of neurons keeps the pattern together as a unit for a short time but only long enough to serve as STM. If this engram is to persist as LTM, the pattern must be consolidated; that is, relatively permanent changes must occur at the synapses so that firing some of the neurons will reevoke activity in all of them. Presumably, the reverberation keeps all cells active just long enough that permanent, LTM changes can occur (or begin to occur) at the synapses, that is, until consolidation can occur. As you can see, Hebb's ignorance of the storage mechanisms we discussed in the first half of this chapter led him to oversimplify the events of consolidation, but let's set this problem aside long enough to see what research his idea provoked.

Hebb reasoned that, because of the dependence on reverberation, the STM period represents a time in the life of an engram when it is a very fragile, easily disrupted pattern of activity. To disrupt the pattern and prevent consolidation, all one would have to do is to get some neurons in the reverberating circuit to fire out of turn or fail to fire when their turn came. That alteration of the pattern of active cells would represent a disruption of the information stored in the pattern. Accordingly, Mahut taught rats a visual discrimination and then stimulated their reticular activating systems during the period right after a choice. In other words, they were stimulated during the time in which their brains were trying to consolidate the sensory information about which stimulus had been chosen and whether reinforcement had been forthcoming. Because the reticular activating system sends nerve impulses to neurons all over the entire cortex, it is likely that this sudden wave of impulses, representing non-sense rather than a stimulus event, must have been enough to fire some neurons of the discrimination engram at the wrong time or to inhibit them when they should have been participating in a reverberatory circuit. That learning was severely impaired supports the idea that the engram was disrupted before consolidation could occur (cited in Mahut & Moss, 1984).

Some areas of the brain may be more critical for consolidation than are others, the two most likely regions being the diencephalon and the hippocampus. H.M., who lost both hippocampi, exhibits the symptoms one would expect from a failure of consolidation. When H.M. was examined, Milner et al. (1968) found that his STM seemed unimpaired. That is, he was able to recall items of information for a few minutes as long as he was not distracted by some new event. His memory problem appeared to be a complete failure to transfer material from STM to LTM, in other words, a failure of consolidation. H.M. could look at a collection of pictures and, with about 60 percent accuracy, identify those he had *not* seen 6 months before (Freed & Corkin, 1988). That performance was as good as could be obtained from a normal subject. However, H.M. had to look at each picture much longer than did the normals if he was to remember it 6 months later. His extra viewing

time might have been enough to compensate for a very slow rate of consolidation.

The fact that H.M. has retained STM means that it cannot reside within the hippocampus. Furthermore, H.M. showed relatively little retrograde amnesia. That is, his LTM from before the surgery was largely intact. This suggests that neither STM nor LTM are contained in the hippocampus. The consolidation-failure hypothesis gives the hippocampus the role of creating long-term memories out of short-term memories, both of which lie elsewhere in the brain.

Seizure-Induced Amnesia Much of what we have learned about amnesia comes from people and animals subjected to strong electric currents passed through the brain from outside the skull. Psychiatrists have discovered that a series of shocks to the brain, strong enough to produce convulsions, is the fastest way to relieve the symptoms of depression. When there is the possibility that the depressed patient may commit suicide during the week required for antidepressant drugs to start having an effect, shock treatment may save the person's life. **Electroconvulsive therapy (ECT)** usually consists of a course of four to five sessions spread over 2 weeks. The patient is given muscle-relaxant drugs to minimize the convulsive contractions of the muscles; electrodes are pasted to the skull; and a brief, carefully measured current is passed through the brain. There is an immediate loss of consciousness, which lasts for a number of minutes following the shock. The patient awakes groggy and confused, frequently with some retrograde amnesia for the treatment. There have been anecdotal reports of more extensive retrograde loss—reports of patients who have forgotten their children, who have forgotten how to cook certain familiar dishes, or who are unable to recognize their own clothes hanging in the closet—but there is little hard, objective data to substantiate such sweeping losses (Friedberg, 1977).

However, there have been a few experiments in which patients were tested after the convulsion as soon as the confusion had abated (about 90 minutes following ECT), and some amount of anterograde amnesia has been found (Wetzel & Squire, 1982). Psychotherapists have noted that in the days following ECT there may also be some signs of a limited anterograde amnesia. One psychiatrist remarked that psychotherapy for depression was wasted on such patients because they couldn't remember what was discussed from one session to the next (Friedberg, 1977).

Squire (1977) has collected some evidence of retrograde loss in ECT patients. He had them learn some material either 18 hours or 10 minutes prior to ECT and then tested them for retention after recovery. There was significantly more loss of the material learned 10 minutes before shock than that learned 18 hours before. It would seem that the closer the experience is to the traumatic, amnesia-producing event, the greater the amnesia for that event. This is called **Ribot's law** (or, sometimes, the last-in, first-out principle). It is easily explained by the principle of consolidation failure. The 18-hour memories had time to consolidate before ECT, whereas the 10-minute memories suffered an interruption of consolidation.

The convulsion produced by ECT seems to be just a side effect and is not needed to induce amnesia. Apparently, any event that disrupts normal firing patterns of cerebral neurons may be sufficient. This is probably what occurs immediately after a blow to the head severe enough to produce concussion. Such concussive injuries are fairly common in football where the effect is known as a "ding." Immediately after being struck, the player has complete recall of the play and the concussive impact, but a few minutes later the memory of both is lost (Newcombe, 1980). STM memory seems to be functioning, but there is apparently no consolidation to LTM.

Researchers have sought to mimic the human ECT effects by using **electroconvulsive shock (ECS)** with animal subjects. In one of the classic studies, Duncan (1949) placed his rats in a shock-avoidance apparatus in which they had 10 seconds to run out of the shock compartment into the "safe" compartment in order to avoid a shock to their feet. As each rat in the experimental group finished its training, it was given an ECS. This is done by clipping an electrode on each ear and switching on a current through the head strong enough to produce a seizure (abnormal neuron firing) in the brain, as evidenced by muscular convulsions. After 24 hours, the rat is placed in the apparatus again to see if it remembers the avoidance response. Experimental group animals received ECS and lost their avoidance response, whereas control animals, who went through exactly the same experience except for the ECS, suffered no amnesia. The ECS experience seems to duplicate the effects of concussive amnesia; both the shock and a blow to the head produce retrograde amnesia for the events immediately preceding the trauma. Such memory loss is readily explained as an interruption of the consolidation process that prevents the formation of LTM for the foot-shock event.

Later ECS experiments varied the amount of time between the end of training and the occurrence of ECS, reasoning that if ECS were delayed long enough the consolidation process should be complete so that the engram would not be lost during the seizure. This prediction proved true; usually, ECS delivered more than 30 minutes after the completion of training failed to produce amnesia. Further, the sooner ECS was given following training, the greater the amnesia (cited in Deutsch, 1973), a finding that suggests that an engram for the foot-shock event gets stronger as the minutes pass. Experimenters sought to discover exactly how many minutes were required for the consolidation process by giving different groups ECS at different intervals following training. Unfortunately, different studies found different amounts of time. While some experimenters found no amnesia when ECS was delayed by only minutes, others found that some amnesia could be produced even when the ECS came 3 hours after training (Deutsch, 1973).

An Alternative: Retrieval-Failure Theory The consolidation-failure theory soon found itself under attack by experimenters who were rerunning the old ECS studies with an added twist—a reminder cue. **Reminder-cue studies** began by training the rats to make an avoidance response and then delivered ECS, just as in the older studies. Two hours later, however, when the rat had regained consciousness and recovered from the ECS, it was taken to a new apparatus and given a brief foot-shock. No avoidance was allowed, and every precaution was taken to prevent this additional experience from becoming a second avoidance-training trial. Instead, it was intended to serve as a reminder of the original foot-shock experience. The next day when the animals were placed again in the original avoidance apparatus and tested for memory of the avoidance response, the control rats that had been given ECS without a reminder showed the typical amnesia, whereas those that received the reminder shock following ECS were able to perform the avoidance as well as controls that never experienced ECS at all (Miller & Springer, 1972). These results were interpreted to mean that ECS had not prevented consolidation at all but had simply made retrieval of the memory difficult.

Research on human amnesia patients shows a similar "reminder" effect. When patients were asked to recall a list of words they had been shown earlier, they scored very badly, as would be expected with amnesia. However, if they were shown the first three letters in the word (e.g., STO __ = store), as a cue, their scores improved significantly (cited in Warrington & Weiskrantz, 1973). In this **cued-recall task** words were chosen so that many different completions were possible and that mere guessing would produce a very low score. The patients obviously had stored some engram of the previous experience with the word. The results suggest that the memory had been consolidated but, for some reason, was difficult to retrieve. This also agrees with the fact that much of the retrograde amnesia demonstrated in concussive amnesia disappears as the person reexperiences familiar stimuli. Some of the retrograde amnesia was due to a failure to retrieve still existing engrams.

Consolidation Failure Versus Retrieval Failure We must not rush to give up consolidation failure as a viable explanation, however. The retrieval hypothesis has problems of its own. Wicklegren (1979) has pointed out that it cannot explain anterograde amnesia because there is never any recovery of these memories comparable to the gradual reinstatement of pretrauma memories so common with retrograde amnesia. The retrieval-failure hypothesis may also have trouble with Ribot's law. If a head injury has made it difficult to retrieve some of your memories from the past, why isn't the difficulty spread more or less evenly over your whole past? Why are the most recent events the hardest to retrieve and the oldest ones the easiest? The answer that is apt to occur intuitively to that question is that the most recent are the hardest to retrieve because they are the weakest. But, then, why are they the weakest? Perhaps because they have had less time to consolidate. Could it be that both ideas are needed for a complete explanation?

How well does the consolidation-failure hypothesis explain Ribot's law? Hebb's original expression of the hypothesis saw the consolidation process as a transfer of the engram from the temporary, delicate, and easily disrupted form of reverberation in loop circuits (STM) to the relative permanency of structural changes at synapses (LTM). Data from human studies indicate that STM lasts only about 15–20 seconds. This suggests that if something (injury, shock, etc.) is going to interrupt consolidation it has only about 20 seconds in which to do so. If you consider that for a moment, you will realize that this implies that retrograde amnesia can stretch back only 20 seconds into the person's past. All memories older than that supposedly have already been transferred to LTM. This, of course, does not agree with the data about retrograde amnesia; it is known to reach back weeks, months, even years (Barbizet, 1970; Squire, 1982). For example, several patients with medial temporal lobe damage similar to that of H.M. were examined by Milner and found to have extensive anterograde amnesia with retrograde amnesia limited to a period of 3 months to 3 years prior to the damage. Milner noted that if the amnesia is caused by loss of a hippocampal consolidation mechanism then consolidation must continue for far longer than the original hypothesis proposed (cited in Mahut & Moss, 1984). Loss of memories already 1 or 2 years old would mean that consolidation takes years, not seconds, and this is exactly what has been proposed by Squire (1987).

Prolonged consolidation is not so far-fetched if one considers the ideas presented in the first half of this chapter. It is no longer so simple to defend the idea that memory has only two stages: STM and LTM. Researchers have discovered possible memory-storage mechanisms ranging all the way from very fast-acting, fast-fading changes like an increase in cAMP to slow-acting, long-lasting changes such as axon branch sprouting. It is possible that consolidation may start with receptor uncovering (Lynch–Baudry theory), go from there to changes in dendritic spine shape, to the development of ependymin matrices and larger synaptic area, to an increase in newly constructed receptor sites, and finally to a growth of new terminals and even axon branches. All these processes can be considered possible stages of consolidation. Although they would surely overlap in time with one another, they certainly would not all run to completing within 30 seconds of the memory event. It seems reasonable to hypothesize that, when all these mechanisms are considered, consolidation may require much more than seconds to reach completion—perhaps even years. If memories do slowly strengthen over years, then Ribot's gradient of forgetting can be explained; recent memories have been through fewer of the various stages in consolidation and are therefore more easily disrupted by traumatic events. In other words, a trauma may stop the consolidation process and leave memories only partly consolidated. Presumably, the older a memory is, the more it has been consolidated and the greater its resistance to amnesia. These various degrees of consolidation would yield the gradient of Ribot's law.

If consolidation is thought of as a lengthy process that can be interrupted long before it is complete, then consolidation failure can be used to explain the results of the reminder-cue experiments. The rat is given a single training trial with the foot shock. Presumably, consolidation begins immediately but is interrupted before many of the more permanent changes can occur, thus leaving a very weak engram. When the animal is returned to the test chamber, the memory of the foot shock exists but is too weak (too poorly consolidated) to influence behavior (Schneider & Plough, 1983). The experimenter concludes that the rat has amnesia for the foot shock. If some of the rats are given a reminder shock before their test, the stimulus is distinctive enough to elicit activity in many of the same neurons that were activated by the training foot shock. Despite the experimenter's precautions against making the reminder shock into a second training trial, that is precisely what it becomes. The rat now goes into the test situation with a more strongly consolidated memory of the

original foot-shock, thanks to the reminder cue. Retrieval theorists have never given us any alternative explanation of why the reminder shock should make retrieval easier. They have never shown that the enhanced retrieval is not due to increased consolidation.

We must ask, then, what is being manipulated in a reminder-cue study: retrieval or consolidation? When analyzed carefully, the differences between the two ideas seem much fuzzier than they appeared at first. We must ask, Why should the interruption of consolidation produce amnesia? We know that an interruption doesn't wipe out the partially consolidated engram. The answer must be that partial engrams are more difficult to *retrieve*. But, according to that analysis, we are dealing with retrieval failure. In fact, amnesia appears to stem from retrieval failure resulting from a partial consolidation failure. The two hypotheses may not really represent alternative explanations at all. Both may be required for a complete explanation.

Let's try to collect what we have learned so far. Consolidation failure explains anterograde amnesia and does a reasonable job of explaining retrograde amnesia and Ribot's law if the hypothesis is extended to allow for a very lengthy period of consolidation, probably involving multiple, physiological memory mechanisms. The reminder-cue studies, which provided important evidence for retrieval-failure theory, can be explained in terms of consolidation failure if one assumes that there are degrees of consolidation (Squire, 1980). The earlier the process is interrupted by the trauma, the weaker the consolidation. The reminder experience is similar enough to the original experience to further reinforce the weak engram and make it strong enough to influence behavior. In other words, retrieval failed because of consolidation failure. It may not be possible to separate the two explanations in any real situation.

■ Many Types of Memory

Most psychologists would agree that the end result of learning something is the production of a memory. However, if that holds true for all the types of learning we explored in Chapter 14, then we may have to expand our understanding of what the term *memory* means. Does classical conditioning create memories? Presumably so, but apparently these memories have no conscious aspect. How does one "recall" a conditioned response? You can remember an occasion in which you made a conditioned response, but what you recall is the fact that you responded. The response itself is unconscious.

In the last decade, memory theorists have come to grips with this problem and with the fact that amnesia patients really can learn and remember things, and they have produced the beginnings of a classification scheme that allows for a variety of memory types.

Memory Sparing in Amnesia

Even in the early 1960s, it was known that there were a few things that H.M. was able to learn. For example, when he was given daily practice at **mirror tracing** (tracing a path with a pencil while viewing everything in a mirror), H.M. steadily improved over 3 days. He showed some improvement in a tactile maze and considerable improvement in a **pursuit-tracking** task in which the object was to hold a pointer on a moving target (Cohen, 1984; Corkin, 1965, 1968). This is termed **perceptual–motor learning**, and other amnesics as well as H.M. show that they are still capable of developing this type of memory. Understand that simply because H.M. learned the pursuit-tracking task doesn't mean that he can learn that he had ever practiced it. One amnesic patient spent most of one afternoon practicing a new piano piece, but when he was asked to play it the next day, he had no memory of ever having heard the song or of ever having practiced it. However, as soon as he heard the first few bars, he immediately sat down and played the piece (Hirst, 1982). This suggests that there are two varieties of memory: one that stores the skill acquired through practice and another for remembering the practice experiences as events. Amnesia would affect the event memory but not the skill memory.

The discovery that amnesia spared perceptual–motor memories motivated investigators to look for other tasks that might also reveal memory sparing. Perceptual-learning tasks like mirror reading

Figure 16.13   The tower of Hanoi puzzle. The object is to move all of the disks from the left post to the right post so that they are in the same ascending order. Only one disk can be moved at a time and a larger disk may never be placed on top of a smaller disk. The center post may be used in the process of shuttling the disks. There is no limit on the number of times a disk can be moved. The most direct solution to the puzzle involves a series of 31 moves.

showed improvement from day to day at a rate equal to that of normal controls. Cognitive problem solving, using the **tower of Hanoi puzzle** (Figure 16.13), was also acquired by amnesics (Cohen, 1984). Amnesics could never recall having solved the puzzle on a previous day, but at each session with the puzzle they became faster at finding the solution. Again, an event memory seems to be missing while a skill memory is retained.

A third case of memory sparing is similar to the verbal cued-recall task described earlier. In a **priming task**, the memory test uses fragments of the original stimuli. For example, if the subject was first shown a list of words to remember, then the test will supply the first two or three letters of each of these words. The same technique can also be used for visual memory (Figure 16.14). If the fragments were used as a cued-recall task, the subjects would be told that the word (or picture) is one of those shown earlier and the task is to recall which one. Normal and amnesic subjects improve their recall of the word list when given these "hints," but normals remember considerably more than amnesics (Figure 16.15). However, if the instructions are changed to those of a priming task, the results are quite different. Now the subjects are simply asked to fill in the missing letters with the first word that comes to their mind. No mention is made of the list of words they viewed earlier, and there is no hint that this is a memory test. So, the only difference between the cued-recall task and the priming task is the instructions. The astounding result is that the amnesics

Figure 16.14 Examples of **(a)** fragmented pictures and **(b)** words of the sort used in some cued-recall experiments. The subject is shown the most fragmented view first and asked to recall it from an earlier viewing. Progressively easier versions are shown until identification is made. (Adapted from Iversen, 1983)

a   b PORCH

score just as well as the normals at filling in the words from the list (Figure 16.15). Their memory defect shows only when they are making a conscious effort to remember (Cohen, 1984; Squire, 1986). Are there then two kinds of memory: one that employs conscious retrieval (and that is missing in the amnesic) and one that does not (and that the amnesic still has)?

Types of Memory

Perhaps the best way to understand memory is to recall what we know about the process that generates memories—the learning process. As the mammalian brain evolved, it started with only a few primitive ways to learn (habituation, sensitization, conditioning) and was thus only able to generate a few prim-

itive types of memory. As higher structures were added to the brain during the course of evolution, mammals obtained more and more ways to acquire knowledge about any situation, and this meant that the memory of that situation would not be one, single, unified engram but rather a collection of engrams, each in its own set of brain structures and each with its own properties. Thus, one type of engram might represent a situation as an event, while another extracted a memory of the perceptual–motor skill practiced in that situation.

In the last decade, nearly a dozen hypotheses have been offered about how memory should be divided into constituent parts. Because this is not the place to discuss all these possibilities, we will look at just one such scheme—the one I hope is the best in terms of encompassing the most experimental data.

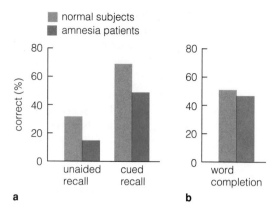

Figure 16.15 Comparisons of normal subjects versus amnesic patients on (**a**) a cued-recall task and (**b**) a priming (word completion) task. The large difference between normals and amnesics that is evident in normal and cued recall disappears when the task instructions are changed to require completion rather than recall. (Adapted from Squire, 1986)

Squire and Zola-Morgan (1988) have suggested that we should begin by splitting memory into two compartments: declarative and nondeclarative. **Declarative memory** is the type that most people think of when speaking about memory. Your declarative memories are conscious. They consist of events (episodes), facts, and general information about your experiences. Almost all your college education comes under this heading. **Nondeclarative memory** is not available to the conscious mind. You activate nondeclarative memories by *doing something* rather than by consciously trying to remember. Your memories of how to type or speak words or swing a golf club are nondeclarative, as are your feelings of dislike for a certain person or your remembered interest in a favorite college course. Remembering how to ride a bike is a nondeclarative memory, but remembering that you *can* ride a bike is declarative.

Squire (1986) distinguishes between several types of nondeclarative memories: skill, priming, classical conditioning, and others. **Skill memories** contain the plans for making the movements involved in walking, eating, driving, speaking, and so forth. These are largely unconscious and very likely

exist mostly within the basal ganglia (see Chapter 9). When H.M. learned the pursuit-tracking task and when the other patient learned to play the piano piece, they were building skill memories. (Some psychologists refer to such memories as "perceptual–motor.") **Classical conditioning memories** are automatic reactions to conditioned stimuli. Most of these would be emotional or motivational. All your learned likes, dislikes, and preferences for various stimuli are likely conditioning memories. All stimuli that function as conditioned reinforcers in your life do so because they elicit memories of pleasure or desire. **Priming memory** is the brief type of retention seen in a priming task. Squire also includes adaptation level effects, which we will not discuss, and an "other" category, realizing that it would be impossible to achieve a complete listing at our current level of knowledge. I feel that a category called **orienting memories** should be added, which would include habituation and sensitization engrams.

Declarative memory can also be subdivided but only into two parts: working memory and reference memory, terms borrowed from Olton (1979). **Working memory** is an episodic type of memory, a memory for events. Your working memory would include recollections of where you parked your car in the theater lot, what classes you attended today, what you had for lunch, what friend you saw at 10:00, and how the weather was in the morning. **Reference memory** contains all the constant, stable engrams like the knowledge you learn in this course, the ability to recognize your car or notebook, and the words to a song. The recognition of a particular food by its odor, a friend by her face, or a tree by its shape are all reference memories, as are the memories of where your classroom is located, whether you must make a right or left turn at the top of the stairs, and which row contains your seat. As the name suggests, these memories are like entries in an encyclopedia. These are facts that remain reasonably constant from one time to another, whereas working memories are specific to single occurrences. (See Figure 16.16 for a summary of memory types.)

It is easier to maintain reference memories for months and years than it is to keep working memories. Try to remember exactly what you ate for dinner on January 21, 1985. That would be a working

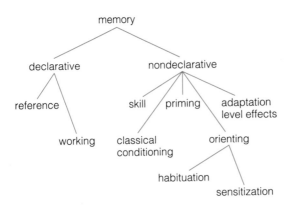

Figure 16.16 A scheme for classifying memory into its components. This was adapted from Squire's classification by substituting "orienting" for "other."

memory, and you probably cannot retrieve it. If we had asked you to retrieve it on January 23, 1985, you probably could have, but not now. During the intervening years, you have eaten so many other dinners, each producing their own working memory, that interference between memories makes the task of retrieval like looking for a needle in a haystack. However, if we asked you to remember if you ate pizza for breakfast on the morning of January 21, 1985, you could probably answer with no trouble at all that you most certainly did not. You do not need to draw on your fast-fading working memory to answer this question; your reference memory contains the knowledge that you do not eat pizza for breakfast so you would not have done so on the morning of January 21. Reference memory appears to have more permanence than working memory, and the temporary nature of working memory is probably due to a greater opportunity for interference between similar memories.

Recall from Chapter 15 that there is some evidence that working memory is largely located in the hippocampus, whereas reference memory seems to be a cortical type of storage. Nondeclarative memories would center mostly within such subcortical structures as the basal ganglia (skills) and brain stem (classical conditioning and orienting). Now we can see why it is that H.M. exhibits sparing of skill memories. He lost his medial temporal lobes and with

them his working memory, but his basal ganglia, with its store of skill memories, are intact and apparently still able to function.

The difference between reference and working memory should also help us explain the priming experiments. In those studies amnesics showed significantly less retrieval than did normals if they were required to recall the words they had seen earlier, but they scored just as well as normals at retrieving those same words if the memory task was disguised as a word-completion task. This suggests that when the person deliberately attempts to recall an event, the hippocampal–diencephalic system is activated. Because this is the system that is damaged in amnesia patients, they find it difficult to retrieve the correct words. Another way of saying the same thing is that the instructions to *recall* the word list refer to the memory of a specific event or episode, and it is this working type of memory that the amnesic has lost. However, all items on the word list are common, everyday English words, and the patients have no trouble using them in their communications, no matter how amnesic they are. This means that those same words are stored away separately in some other memory that the amnesic may still retain undamaged. This other store would, of course, be reference memory. It is not the memory of each word that has been lost but rather the memory of having seen those words *at that particular time* on the list presented by the experimenter—an episodic, working memory. So when the amnesic is tested in such a way that the instructions do not activate the damaged working memory circuits, the retrieval can be made from reference memory. Presumably, when the subjects were exposed to the word list, that set of stimuli activated the reference memories of those words, and this activation persists for a number of minutes during which it can be tapped by the correct instructions (Graf & Mandler, 1984). This relatively short-lived activation of reference memory circuits is what we have been calling "priming," and Squire (1986) found in one experiment that it faded completely within 120 minutes. Squire separates priming memory as a form of nondeclarative memory, but it might better be considered simply as a characteristic of reference memory.

The division of memory into various types does

not mean that the categories are completely independent of one another. To the contrary, reference memory appears to be so interdependent with working memory that amnesics may not be able to form new reference memories despite retaining the parts of the nervous system in which those engrams seem to be stored. This is not surprising. We have known for decades that the cortex does not function independently from other structures such as the hippocampus. Damage to one is bound to limit the function of the surviving part. Experimenters will have to develop much more precise methods to find out exactly how each type of memory functions.

We have said little, so far, about reference memory amnesia. The reason is that loss of reference memories (word engrams, perceptual engrams, etc.) has not traditionally been thought of as a form of amnesia and has been categorized under a variety of other headings such as aphasia, agraphia, and agnosia—topics that we will examine in the last chapter.

Conclusions

We began this chapter within the framework of the old separate-stores model of memory that divided it into long-term memory and short-term memory. A review of the possible physiological processes involved in memory storage, however, leads to the suspicion that an engram goes through a succession of many changes in form: ionic currents, protein shifts, receptor unveiling, dendritic-shape changes, and, finally, sprouting of new terminals and axon branches. The LTM–STM division does not seem to be very realistic in light of those data. Work with amnesia patients has led to a new and more extensive division of memory into functions that seem to be more closely related to actual brain structures. Much of the data on which we base the LTM–STM distinction may be reinterpreted in the future as the result of the interplay between working memory and reference memory. Working memory shares a temporary nature with STM, but its fading with time is explained as the piling up of interference between memories, and this gives it a duration that can be anywhere from 20 seconds or so on up to weeks or months. What we have been calling STMs may just

be those engrams that faded very rapidly because they happened to be followed by events that produced maximal interference. Rather than continuing the search for a mechanism that transfers memories from STM to LTM, brain researchers should perhaps turn their attention to discovering how working memories become reference memories.

■ Summary

1. Cognitive psychologists have long held that there are two separate memories: long term (LTM) and short term (STM). Activity in reverberatory circuits might be the physiological basis of STM.

2. LTM may be formed as a circuit (representing a memory) reverberates. Hebb proposed that each time the synapses between the circuit neurons are used they grow stronger, thus binding neurons into a more and more permanent combination. The physiological basis of LTM then would be some more or less permanent change at synapses to make them stronger.

3. Stronger synaptic connections should produce larger EPSPs in the postsynaptic neurons. This seems to be the case because stimulation of circuits in places like the hippocampus alters the synapses there so that they produce steadily larger EPSPs. This effect is called long-term potentiation (LTP) because it outlasts the stimulation that caused it by days or weeks. LTP apparently is an indication that an LTM has been established.

4. Two types of physiological change have been proposed as the basis of LTP (i.e., as a basis for memory storage): the formation of new synapses and the strengthening of existing synapses. Evidence for the formation of new synapses comes from three sources: experiments on sprouting, dendrite growth, and protein synthesis. Evidence for the strengthening of existing synapses derives from studies of ependymins, dendritic spines, the calpain–fodrin mechanism, and cyclic AMP (cAMP).

5. When damage occurs in the brain and the remaining neurons lose some of the terminals that previously synapsed on them, a process called reactive synaptogenesis occurs in which neighboring axons

sprout new terminals to fill in for the missing ones. This sort of sprouting may also be stimulated by a learning situation so that neurons of the engram come to be more firmly connected by way of sharing more synapses.

6. There is also evidence that new dendritic branches may be formed as a result of the learning experience so that there is room on postsynaptic neurons for more synapses. Sprouting and dendrite branching require protein synthesis. Experiments in which protein synthesis is inhibited during or after the learning suggest that protein manufacture is necessary for the establishment of LTM. However, it does not seem to be needed for recall of the memory for a few hours after training. Some other storage mechanism (an intermediate-term memory?) must come into play rapidly after the learning experience and act as a temporary holding mechanism until the construction of new connections can begin.

7. Intermediate-term memory might be explained by mechanisms that are able to come into play sooner because they merely modify existing synapses rather than create new ones. The first of these mechanisms discussed was the idea that the use of a synapse creates a protein matrix out of intercellular ependymins and that this matrix guides the expansion of the existing synapse. A larger synapse would create larger EPSPs (i.e., LTP).

8. Many axon terminals synapse on dendritic spines, many of which have narrow necks. A synapse on a spine could be strengthened if the neck were thickened because the increase in membrane would provide more ions for a larger EPSP.

9. A very rapid-acting storage mechanism involves the uncovering of unused receptor sites in the postsynaptic neuron. Calcium is admitted to the cell when the synapse is activated, and once inside it causes calpain to alter a protein called fodrin. This alteration allows latent receptors to come to the surface of the membrane and strengthen the synapse by increasing its receptivity to transmitter. This may, however, only work at glutamate synapses.

10. At monoaminergic synapses, memory may be stored briefly in the form of increased concentrations of cyclic AMP. Monoamine transmitter activates adenylate cyclase when it binds to its receptor site.

The cyclase converts ATP to cAMP, which then initiates the opening of ion channels (i.e., triggers an EPSP). Thus, the postsynaptic cell will remain facilitated until the cAMP is used up. The cAMP may also participate in more permanent memory storage by triggering the transcription of RNA that could be used in the construction of additional receptor sites.

11. Difficulty in recalling events prior to a brain trauma is called retrograde amnesia; difficulty with events following the trauma is anterograde amnesia. The memory gap caused by a trauma is called a lacuna, and the amnesia patient may try to fill this gap by reconstructing memories or by confabulation.

12. Two places in the brain seem to be involved with amnesia: the medial temporal lobes (especially the hippocampus) and the diencephalon (in particular, the mammillary bodies and dorsomedial nucleus of the thalamus).

13. The shift of memory from STM to LTM has been termed consolidation, and one theory of amnesia explains the loss as a failure of consolidation. Trauma would interrupt the activity in a reverberatory circuit and stop the consolidation process. Electroconvulsive therapy (ECT) should have the same effect as trauma, and this would explain why ECT produces some amnesia.

14. The observation that more recent memories suffer more amnesia than do earlier memories is called Ribot's law.

15. Electroconvulsive shock (ECS) studies in animals found that if ECS were given shortly after training the animal exhibited amnesia for the event. This supported the consolidation-failure hypothesis. Later studies that added a reminder cue, however, suggested that consolidation had not been prevented by the shock and that the amnesia could be better explained as retrieval failure.

16. The retrieval-failure hypothesis, however, also has problems such as not being able to explain Ribot's law. If it can be assumed that consolidation is a long-term process, perhaps spanning years, and that interruptions of the process produce partial consolidation, then the best conclusion seems to be that amnesia is a product of *both* consolidation *and* retrieval problems.

17. Recent experiments have demonstrated memory sparing in amnesics in tasks such as mirror tracing,

problem-solving tests (tower of Hanoi), and priming tasks. The fact that amnesics can demonstrate the ability to develop new memories has led to a revised classification of memory functions.

18. Squire divides memory into declarative versus nondeclarative. The latter includes skill (perceptual motor), classical conditioning, priming, and other memories. Orienting memories (habituation and sensitization) probably belong in this category as well. Declarative memories are of two types: reference and working. The former include facts, perceptual images, and concepts; the latter consists of events and episodes.

19. Reference memories appear to typically be of much greater duration than are working memories. Working memories are most likely a product of the hippocampus or of a hippocampal–diencephalic system, whereas reference memories are probably thalamocortical.

Glossary

adenosine triphosphate (ATP) The energy-carrying molecule of the cell; supplies phosphate groups in many chemical reactions. (628)

adenylate cyclase An intracellular enzyme that can be activated by a neurotransmitter receptor to create cyclic AMP. (628)

anisomycin An antibiotic drug that acts through the inhibition of protein synthesis. (619)

anterograde amnesia An inability to remember events that took place after a brain trauma. (632)

calpain A group of enzymes of the proteinase variety that are activated by calcium ions and that can degrade fodrin. (626)

classical conditioning memories Associations linking CRs to CS's. (642)

concussion A blow to the head that throws the brain against the inside of the skull. (631)

concussive amnesia Amnesia resulting from a blow to the head. (631)

confabulation The creation of pseudomemories out of the patient's deductions about what must have happened during a lacuna. (633)

consolidation The theoretical process of shifting information from STM to LTM. (635)

consolidation-failure hypothesis The idea that anterograde amnesia can be explained as a failure to form LTMs out of STMs. (635)

cued-recall task A memory test that suggests a retrieval-failure explanation of amnesia. (638)

cyclic AMP (cAMP) A "second messenger" molecule that can activate protein kinase. (628)

cytoskeleton A network of protein filaments and microtubules that holds the cell membrane into a stable shape. (623)

declarative memory Memories of events, facts, and information. (642)

dendritic spine A tiny protrusion on a dendrite on which a synapse is likely to be found. (623)

diencephalic amnesia Memory loss originating in damage to the diencephalon. (635)

diencephalon A region just above and anterior to the midbrain that consists chiefly of the thalamus, subthalamus, and hypothalamus. (634)

dorsomedial nucleus of the thalamus (DMT) A thalamic nucleus that may be involved in memory; damage there appears to produce amnesia. (635)

electroconvulsive shock (ECS) An electric shock to the head that is strong enough to produce convulsions. (637)

electroconvulsive therapy (ECT) The use of an electric shock to the brain to relieve depression. (636)

ependymins Proteins found in the extracellular fluid that may be involved in the formation of engrams. (621)

fodrin One of the proteins making up the microtubules and microfilaments of the cytoskeleton. (626)

glutamate A transmitter found throughout the brain. (625)

Hebbian synapse A synapse that can be used many times without becoming stronger but that is able to grow stronger whenever the postsynaptic cell receives a simultaneous input from another synapse. (630)

hippocampal slice method A research technique in which the hippocampus is studied by removing it, sectioning it, and preserving the sections in nutrient solution; this allows microscopic visual positioning of electrodes. (614)

Korsakoff's syndrome A form of brain damage caused by alcoholism and having amnesia as its main symptom. (631)

lacuna An amnesic memory gap. (633)

long-term memory (LTM) A more or less permanent information store created when memories in STM are rehearsed. (612)

long-term potentiation (LTP) An increase in EPSP size following extended use of a synapse. (615)

mammillary bodies Hypothalamic nuclei that receive the terminations of the fornix and that may be sites of some amnesia-causing lesions. (635)

medial temporal amnesia Memory loss originating in damage to the limbic structures of the temporal lobe (hippocampus and, perhaps, the amygdala). (635)

mirror tracing Learning task that involves tracing a path with a pencil while viewing everything in a mirror. (640)

NMDA receptors Transmitter receptors that do not react to glutamate unless the membrane has already been depolarized; possible basis for a Hebbian synapse. (630)

nondeclarative memory Unconscious memory routines for doing things; includes skills, habituation, and conditioned responses. (642)

nuclear regulatory protein A protein bound to a stretch of DNA, preventing that gene fragment from producing RNA until needed. (628)

orienting memories Engrams for habituations and sensitizations. (642)

passive avoidance Instrumental learning in which the subject learns not to make a response because the response is followed by punishment. (619)

perceptual–motor learning Learning to guide movements with sensory feedback. (640)

phosphorylation The transfer of a phosphate group to a protein molecule to bring about some change in its function (such as opening an ion channel). (628)

priming memory The temporary persistence in the activation of a reference memory. (642)

priming task A memory test similar to the cued-recall task except for the instructions. (640)

protein kinase An enzyme that specializes in transferring phosphate groups to protein molecules to bring about changes in their function. (628)

protein synthesis inhibitor (PSI) A chemical that inhibits the production of proteins. (619)

pursuit tracking A learning task in which the object is to hold a pointer on a moving target. (640)

reactive synaptogenesis The production of new synapses to replace ones lost through damage to the nervous system. (617)

reference memory Knowledge of facts and information; a form of declarative memory. (642)

reminder-cue studies The experiments that sought to show that memories were retained despite electroconvulsive shock but were not as available to retrieval. (637)

retrieval The reactivation of already stored engrams. (632)

retrograde amnesia A difficulty in recalling events preceding a brain trauma. (632)

reverberation The continuation of activity in a reverberatory circuit after the input stimulus has ceased. (613)

reverberatory circuit A chain of neurons that forms a loop, so that the last cell excites the first. (613)

Ribot's law The last-in, first-out principle; that is, the closer the experience is to the traumatic, amnesia-producing event, the greater the amnesia for that event. (637)

short-term memory (STM) A temporary information store lasting less than 30 seconds. (612)

skill memories Unconscious motor routines for movement sequences (as in walking, forming word sounds, eating, and so on). (642)

sprouting The growth of new telodendria and/or terminals in the mature brain. (617)

synapse turnover The regular, periodic replacement of synapses because of wear. (618)

tower of Hanoi puzzle A test for cognitive problem solving. (640)

working memory The form of declarative memory that contains events or episodes. (642)

17

Brain Dysfunction

Schizophrenia
Concepts: psychotic, organic mental disorders, insanity

THE CONCEPT OF SCHIZOPHRENIA
Concepts: multiple personality, hallucinations, delusions, catatonia, thought disorder, flattened affect

IS SCHIZOPHRENIA INHERITED?
Concepts: monozygotic and dizygotic twins, vulnerability model, genetic factor, stress factor, moderating factors

NEUROPATHOLOGY IN SCHIZOPHRENIA
Concept: neuropathology

Findings from Neurological Exams and Autopsies
Concepts: neurological soft signs, atrophy

Radiological Evidence
Concept: hypofrontality

Type I Versus Type II Schizophrenia
Concepts: prognosis, positive and negative symptoms, type I and type II schizophrenia

ATTENTION AND AROUSAL IN SCHIZOPHRENIA
Concepts: continuous performance test (CPT), P300, Yerkes–Dodson law, overinclusion

HYPERAROUSAL IN THE MESOLIMBIC SYSTEM
Concepts: ventrotegmental area (VTA), neostriatum, limbic striatum, septal area, nucleus accumbens, mesolimbic system, paranoia

AMPHETAMINES AND PSYCHOSIS
Concepts: amphetamines, monoamine

THE DOPAMINE HYPOTHESIS
Antipsychotic Drugs and DA Receptors
Concepts: antipsychotic drugs, phenothiazines, chlorpromazine

Problems with the Dopamine Hypothesis

Mood Disorders

DESCRIPTION AND CLASSIFICATION
Concepts: grief reactions, mood disorder, depressive disorder, bipolar disorder

HEREDITY AND MOOD DISORDER

CATECHOLAMINE THEORY OF DEPRESSION
Monoamines and Depression
Concepts: monoamine transmitters, locus coeruleus

Drugs and Monoamines
Concepts: monoamine oxidase (MAO), MAO-inhibitors, tricyclic antidepressants (TADs)

Problems with the Catecholamine Theory

Presynaptic Regulation of NE Release
Concepts: alpha presynaptic receptors, autoreceptors, up-regulation, down-regulation

Postsynaptic Repercussions

Serotonin Involvement

LITHIUM AND ELECTROCONVULSIVE THERAPY
Concepts: lithium, electroconvulsive therapy (ECT), seizure, convulsions

Alzheimer's Disease
Concepts: senility, senile dementia, Alzheimer's disease

THE ALZHEIMER'S SYNDROME

BRAIN ALTERATIONS IN ALZHEIMER'S DISEASE
Concepts: neurofibrillary tangle, β-amyloid, neuritic plaque, β-amyloid precursor protein, nucleus basalis of Meynert

ALZHEIMER'S DISEASE AND HEREDITY
Concept: Down syndrome

Epilepsy

Concept: hypersynchrony

TYPES OF EPILEPSY

Concepts: epileptic focus, generalized seizures, grand mal, convulsions, aura, tonic seizures, atonic seizures, absence attacks, partial seizures (simple and complex), fugue state

DO SEIZURES PROMOTE FURTHER SEIZURES?

Concepts: kindling, long-term potentiation (LTP)

CAUSES OF EPILEPSY

Concepts: neuropathological factors, triggering process

The Epileptic Focus and Paroxysmal Depolarization Shift

Concepts: paroxysmal depolarization shift (PDS), GABA

Triggering a Seizure

TREATMENT OF EPILEPSY

Concepts: phenytoin, carbamazepine, ethosuximide

Summary

The brain, like any other organ of the body, can malfunction in a number of ways. It can be damaged mechanically, grow tumors, or contract infections just like the liver or muscles but with one enormous difference. The brain is several orders of magnitude more complex than any other human organ, both structurally and chemically, and it continually alters its specific reactions through a process, not present in any other organ, called learning. This complexity and alterability make the understanding of many brain dysfunctions extremely difficult. In fact, it even becomes a major scientific struggle just to discover whether a particular set of human behaviors represents a symptom of brain dysfunction or is simply the result of a peculiar set of past experiences in which odd habits, perceptions, and attitudes were learned through normal processes. Is schizophrenic behavior the product of brain chemistry gone amiss, or does it stem from emotional conflicts learned in an unhappy childhood?

In this chapter, we try to sort out a little clarity in the nearly overwhelming mass of confusing clinical observation and experimental data. However, no final theories yet exist to explain the major disorders. The topics addressed—schizophrenia, mood disorders, Alzheimer's disease, and epilepsy—represent only a small sample of the ways in which the brain can dysfunction. They were selected over other dysfunctions because they are probably of greater interest to more readers.

■ Schizophrenia

A person whose behaviors are strange and socially inappropriate, whose thoughts are disordered, who may sometimes hallucinate and suffer from delusions is said to be **psychotic**. The outstanding symptom of psychosis is a loss of contact with reality. Schizophrenia, paranoia, and some forms of mood and organic disorders involve psychotic symptomatology. Some types of psychosis, the **organic mental disorders**, have readily identifiable causes. These are the disorders in which there is some clear evidence of brain damage or disruption. Examples of organic mental disorders would be delirium (caused by such factors as head injury, toxic substances, liver or kidney disease, and infections of the nervous system), dementia (the loss of memory, judgment, and reasoning most often found in elderly persons), and alcohol amnesic disorder (Korsakoff's disease) in which chronic dietary deficiency of vitamin B_1 has damaged temporal lobe limbic structures and affected memory.

The causes of other psychotic disorders like schizophrenia and mood disorders are still unknown; thus, even though the crucial causal factors may be biological rather than social, these psychoses are still not classed as organic. Some psychologists feel that it may be impossible to separate organic causes from experiential because of the complex interplay between the two. A brain enzyme deficiency, for example, might decrease the person's ability to tolerate psychological stress. This stress cannot be separated from biological factors because the brain reacts to stressful emotional situations by secreting hormones that circulate back to the brain where they alter neural function at a purely biological level. Some researchers have spent great portions of their lives collecting data in an attempt to demonstrate that schizophrenia is strictly the result of early family experiences or has purely organic origins. The data collected were valuable, but the efforts to separate organic and psychological factors were probably a waste of time. Before we discuss the specific symptoms of schizophrenia, one more idea needs clarification; the word **insanity** is a legal term that is used to categorize people who are mentally and emotionally incapable of being held responsible for their actions. It is not a psychological or psychiatric category and will not appear again in this chapter.

The Concept of Schizophrenia

Various forms of "madness" have been recognized throughout human history, but it wasn't until 1896 that medicine achieved some agreement on definite categories and names. The concept of schizophrenia was devised by Swiss psychiatrist Eugen Bleuler in 1911 (Kendell, 1978). Bleuler decided that some cases of "madness" could be distinguished from others by the presence of one outstanding symptom: the splitting apart of emotions from intellect. This idea led Bleuler to label these cases with the term *schizo* (split) *phrenia* (mind). To understand the sort of behavior Bleuler had in mind when he spoke of emotions split from intellect, picture the following conversation between a psychologist and a schizophrenic patient:

PSYCHOLOGIST: Good morning, Mr. Smith.

PATIENT: Hello.

PSYCHOLOGIST: Did you remember to take your medication this morning?

PATIENT: Sure.

PSYCHOLOGIST: How are you feeling?

PATIENT: Oh, all right, I guess. I'm OK.

PSYCHOLOGIST: Did you enjoy the pancakes this morning? I know they are your favorite.

PATIENT: Yeah. They were good. Only thing those cooks really get right.

PSYCHOLOGIST: But you said the other day you really liked the beef stew, didn't you?

PATIENT: Oh yeah. Right, right. That too. Pretty good stuff. [Drops his head and begins crying.]

PSYCHOLOGIST: What's wrong?

PATIENT: The bed is rotten. You know? They put the bed in it, and I'm gonna wash tonight. The food shoudn't do that, but it is. And I'm red. I'm stewed. [Goes back to crying.]

The patient's emotional responses seem to have little to do with the conversation or the disconnected stream of nonsensical associations. A more modern view might interpret the splitting of schizophrenia as a separation of the emotions from reality. In either case, it is important to understand that the idea of "split mind" has nothing to do with another emotional disorder called **multiple personality** in which the personality has fragmented into two or more distinct persons that compete for control of conscious processes, with the loser lying latent at an unconscious level until the next opportunity to emerge. Multiple personality is not a psychosis and bears no resemblance to schizophrenia at all. Each of the various personalities seems fully attached to reality when it appears and would never generate the type of responses or conversation shown above. The U.S. popular press has been confused for years about this because "split mind" *seems* as though it *should* refer to multiple personality; thus, you will constantly be subjected to erroneous use of the term *schizophrenia*. This barrage of misinformation is so constant and consistent that it may be difficult for you to remember not to confuse the two even after reading this.

Schizophrenia does not begin suddenly. Family and friends gradually become aware that the person has changed in a variety of subtle ways. Typically, there is a diminishing interest in being with other people and a loss of concern for personal hygiene and appearance. Job or school performance becomes worse and worse as the person finds it harder to maintain motivation toward any goal. Every week more time is spent wrapped in subjective fantasies, and less attention is paid to reality. Communication becomes difficult as the person begins to respond more to individualistic perceptions of the situation that others do not share and starts to slip into a way of thinking that is bizarre and impossible for anyone else to follow. Emotional responses are frequently absent when one would expect them and inappropriate when they do appear.

Finally, the person's behavior becomes too bizarre for others to cope with and steps are taken to secure medical help. By this time, the patient may be exhibiting **hallucinations** (strange, incorrect sensory perceptions such as hearing voices that are not there and feeling worms crawling under the skin); **delusions** (incorrect beliefs frequently involving feelings of persecution, sometimes of grandeur); and odd movements or postures, the most extreme of which, **catatonia**, involves remaining absolutely motionless and speechless for hours at a time. **Thought disorder** involving strange, wild mental associations becomes common, and there is a loss of appropriate emotional responses, a condition called **flattened affect**.

Schizophrenia frequently has its onset during adolescence or early adulthood. Chances of a full recovery are rather poor although most patients do not have to remain hospitalized. With the help of antipsychotic drugs and psychotherapy, many victims of schizophrenia can find a useful place in society despite our inability to do more than treat symptoms. Between episodes some individuals show no symptoms at all.

Is Schizophrenia Inherited?

If schizophrenia arises from defective brain chemistry, as is widely suspected, then it is a good guess that the defect may be wholly or partially inherited. There is no longer any doubt that inherited brain disorders are possible. Brady (1982) describes over 25 different hereditary brain metabolism disorders, and this list includes only those involving a problem in the storage of a metabolite. Knowing how many enzymes the brain needs to function properly, it would really be surprising if no human had ever been born with a genetic enzyme deficiency. The odds are simply too strongly in favor of such genetic accidents.

One way to discover an inheritance factor in the causation of a disorder is to survey families of schizophrenic patients to see if there are any relatives diagnosed as schizophrenic and, if there are, to see if there are more than would be found in the families of nonschizophrenics. One study (cited in Henderson, 1982) established that 11.3 percent of the children of schizophrenic patients also developed schizophrenia, whereas only 2.7 percent of the patient's nieces and nephews did. The percentage fell to 1.6 for first cousins of the patient. A brother or sister had an 8.4 percent chance of becoming schizophrenic. The obvious problem with these data is that they can be explained very easily by family interactions. If schizophrenia has no genetic cause at all, then the next most likely hypothesis would be that it originates in the childhood interactions with the parents; if one of the parents is definitely schizophrenic, those interactions are not likely to engender normal behavior and thought.

More convincing evidence for a genetic factor in schizophrenia comes from studies of twins. There are two types of twins: **monozygotic** (identical), in which one fertilized ovum (zygote) splits to form two embryos, and **dizygotic** (fraternal), in which each twin comes from a different ovum and sperm. Thus, the monozygotic pair, arising from one ovum and one sperm, have exactly the same set of genes, whereas the dizygotic twins, coming from two separate ova and sperm, have different genes. Dizygotics are like an ordinary pair of siblings who happen to have been born at the same time. Monozygotics, of course, must always be the same sex, whereas dizygotics may be opposite sexed. According to the data surveyed by Faraone and Tsuang (1985), if you have a dizygotic twin who is schizophrenic, then your chances of also becoming schizophrenic are 5.6 percent if the twin is of the opposite sex and 12 percent if of the same sex. However, if that schizophrenic twin is monozygotic with you, then your chances of developing the disorder are 57.7 percent. That is an astounding leap from 12 percent to a nearly 60 percent chance and very difficult to explain on the basis of differences in upbringing or childhood experiences.

A third approach to unearthing hereditary influences involves the surveying of adopted children. A study by Heston (cited in Faraone & Tsuang, 1985) investigated a group of children adopted by normal parents. Some of these children were born of normal biological parents, and the others had biological parents who were schizophrenic. Both sets of children had spent most of their early childhood in the normal home life of their adoptive parents; the only major difference was in their inheritance. None of the children of normal parents were schizophrenic at the time of the survey, whereas 11 percent of the children with a schizophrenic biological parent were also schizophrenic themselves. If the survey had been done after the children had reached adulthood, the percentage might have been even higher because, as stated, the onset of the disorder often occurs during adolescence or early adulthood.

Combining this adoption approach with the twin method, Slater and Cowie (cited in Pincus & Tucker, 1978) managed to find 12 pairs of monozygotic twins who had been separated during the first year of life to be reared in separate foster homes and in which at least one of the pair became schizophrenic. In 9 out of the 12 cases (75 percent), the remaining twin

also became schizophrenic. The fact of identical genes apparently far outweighed the differences in upbringing and parent–child interactions.

The cumulated evidence for a genetic factor in schizophrenia is very strong, and few researchers bother to try to challenge the idea anymore. However, the evidence also suggests that the hereditary factor is not going to be a single gene but rather something more complex (Loehlin et al., 1988). One reason for this may be that we are not dealing with a single disorder in schizophrenia. No single schizophrenic patient exhibits all symptoms used to identify the disorder. Instead, the diagnostician is offered a "menu" of symptoms, and the person is categorized as having schizophrenia if a certain proportion of those symptoms are present. One patient will have a certain combination, whereas another may have quite a different set with only a limited amount of overlap with those of the first patient. Thus, it would not be surprising if we were really dealing with a variety of disorders, all of which produce some symptoms in common but that stem from different gene problems.

Another interesting feature of the genetic survey data is the *lack* of concordance between monozygotic twins. If there was a single defective gene at the root of schizophrenia, then there should never be any cases in which only one of two identical twins living together becomes schizophrenic. This strongly argues for some kind of interaction between the genetic factor and other environmental variables. A modern theory of schizophrenic causation produced by Zubin and Steinhauer (1982), the **vulnerability model** of schizophrenia, proposes that there must be at least two causal factors at work to produce the disorder: a **genetic factor**, which creates a predisposition or vulnerability for developing schizophrenia, and a **stress factor**, which can act as the agent that triggers the actual development of the disorder. In addition, Zubin and Steinhauer postulate the existence of a set of **moderating factors** that either help or hinder the development of the disorder. These might include such things as socioeconomic status and intelligence level. Gruenberg (1988) hazards an educated guess that genes may account for about 60–70 percent of the probability that a person will develop schizophrenia.

Because there is now little doubt about the genetic influence in schizophrenia, it is interesting to note that Erlenmeyer-Kimling and colleagues found evidence that the rate of reproduction in schizophrenic women is rising faster than the reproductive rate of the general population (cited in Henderson, 1982). The implication seems to be that schizophrenia is going to become a greater and greater problem in our society.

Neuropathology in Schizophrenia

Genetic studies imply that the brains of schizophrenic patients may have physical deformities or damage either structurally, chemically, or both (technically termed **neuropathology**). A number of lines of evidence indicate that this hypothesis is probably valid.

Findings from Neurological Exams and Autopsies

A neurologist can examine you for neuropathology without ever looking directly at your nervous system. Reflexes and other behaviors observed in a standardized fashion can reveal malfunctions in the brain. Neurological "hard signs," such as the failure of the pupil to adjust to a beam of light from a flashlight, are cues to the neurologist about the existence and possible location of damage in the nervous system. **Neurological soft signs**, on the other hand, are much less specific and give only weak clues about the type and location of the malfunction. Hard signs are rarely found in schizophrenia, whereas soft signs, such as right–left disorientation, failure to maintain balance, tremor, and an inability to identify numbers drawn on the palm of the hand, are quite prevalent (Pincus & Tucker, 1978).

A rather direct way of seeking signs of neuropathology is to examine the brains of schizophrenic patients in autopsy. It would have made theory construction a great deal easier if all schizophrenic brains showed a defect in one particular brain structure, but that is too much to ask of nature. There does appear to be a fairly consistent finding of atrophy in the cerebral cortex and in a part of the cerebellum called the vermis (Seidman, 1983). **Atrophy**, in the case of the brain, is a condition in which the tissue is shrunken from loss of cells. The atrophy of the cerebellar vermis is interesting because a number of the neurological soft signs associated with schizophrenia (like difficulty with gait and coordination, loss of balance, and poorly functioning vestibulo-ocular reflexes) relate to the function of the vestibular–cerebellar circuits. When Crow and colleagues performed postmortem examinations of the brains from 232 schizophrenic and mood-disorder patients, the temporal horns of the lateral ventricles were found to be 97 percent larger in schizophrenics than in mood-disorder patients (cited in Tyrer & Mackay, 1986). This was probably because of the loss of tissue in the parahippocampal gyrus that was significantly smaller in the schizophrenic brains. Recall from Chapter 15 that the parahippocampal gyrus (which includes the entorhinal cortex) is the major sensory input channel to the hippocampus. Such loss might be relevant to the thought disorders of schizophrenia.

Radiological Evidence What psychiatrists need is a way to peer inside the living brain of a schizophrenic patient to check it for neuropathology and observe the metabolic responses of its various parts. It is now possible to do those things with three new radiological techniques: CT scan (computerized tomographic X-ray scan), PET scan (positron-emission tomographic scan), and ,CBF scan (regional cerebral blood flow scan) (see Chapter 5 for descriptions).

A number of CT studies of schizophrenic brains (reviewed in Seidman, 1983) reveal enlarged ventricles, atrophy of the cortex, and atrophy of the cerebellar vermis. In other words, the findings from a small, possibly biased sample of autopsy cases is verified in a large sample of living schizophrenic brains. Enlargement of the ventricles can only come about through loss of tissue in the brain surrounding the ventricles; thus, all these findings point to extensive loss of brain tissue in at least some cases of schizophrenia.

In the schizophrenic brain, PET shows that the frontal cortex has lower than normal activity (Figure 17.1). This is also true of the corpus striatum and the thalamus (both of which have two-way connections with the prefrontal cortex). Figure 17.1 compares the PET scans of two normals (on the right) with four schizophrenics (Buchsbaum et al., 1982).

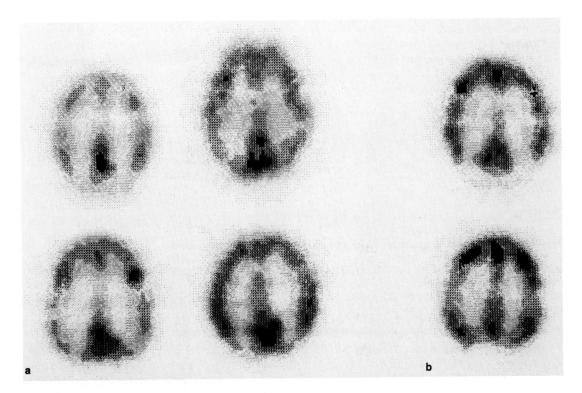

Figure 17.1 PET scans showing the relative rate of glucose use in (**a**) four schizophrenic patients and (**b**) two normals. The pictured slices were high in the brain, above the level of the ventricles. The darkest areas are those with the highest glucose use-rate; lightest areas are those with the lowest. Because the white matter has a lower normal use-rate than does the cortex, it shows as the lightest area in all the brains. Note that the two normal brains have highest glucose use (most neural activity) in the frontal cortex, whereas schizophrenic brains tend to show a very quiet frontal cortex but heavy activity in the posterior cortex. (From Buchsbaum et al., 1982)

The horizontal section is high in the brain, just above the level of the ventricles, so most of the activity shown is cortical. The areas of highest activity in the normals is frontal, whereas most of the active areas in the schizophrenics are parietal or occipital. Another study shows the premotor portions of the frontal lobe to be low in metabolic activity, and these regions are also connected to the corpus striatum (cited in Seidman, 1983). It is worth noting that the prefrontal cortex and striatum are the target areas for the major dopamine systems that run through the medial forebrain bundle (MFB) from the brain stem into the anterior cerebrum. We will return to the importance of dopamine later in this chapter.

This same lack of frontal lobe activity was also found using $_r$CBF scans (Weinberger, 1988). Figure 17.2 pictures an average $_r$CBF scan from eight normal brains on the left and seven schizophrenic brains on the right. During a blood flow test, the typical pattern for a normal brain is to show more blood flow in the frontal lobes than anywhere else in the cortex. But Ingvar (1982) found that schizophrenics have abnormally low blood flow in the frontal lobes (Figure 17.2). Instead of the normal frontal activation pattern, they develop areas of increased blood flow in the sensory and sensory-related areas of the parietal, occipital, and temporal lobes. This pattern of blood flow in the cortex is called **hypofrontality**.

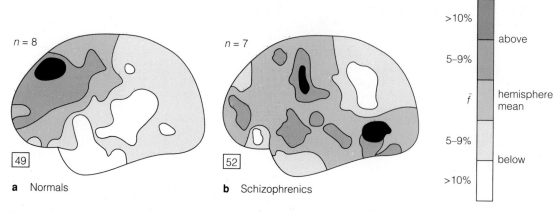

Figure 17.2 These two brain diagrams display the average cerebral blood flow reading of (**a**) eight normal subjects and (**b**) seven schizophrenic patients. The numbers 49 and 52 are indices of overall flow rate and show no significant difference. The shading from black to white indicates variations in regional flow rates, with the darker shades for above-normal rates. The schizophrenic brains show lack of blood flow in the frontal lobes and increased flow in the posterior regions. (Adapted from Ingvar, 1982)

The lack of normally functioning frontal lobes that is implied by all three radiological techniques may have implications for the schizophrenic's ability to focus attention and carry out ordered sequences of behavior. In keeping with this interpretation, it has been found (Weinberger, 1988) that schizophrenics perform very poorly on attention-demanding behavioral tests of frontal lobe function such as the Wisconsin Card Sort task (described in Chapter 18).

Type I Versus Type II Schizophrenia Throughout the history of research on schizophrenia, attempts have been made to differentiate two types of the disorder, but no agreement has been reached on exactly how to characterize the distinction. Accruing evidence indicates that there may be an important difference in neuropathology between categories, with a chronic, long-term type showing more signs of brain damage than an acute episodic type. In some studies, diagnosticians were shown to have trouble distinguishing the chronic type from cases of organic psychosis (in which there is clear-cut, known brain damage). Cerebral blood flow appeared normal in acute cases but below normal in chronic schizophrenia (Seidman, 1983).

A recently proposed categorization system (Crow, 1982) seems to encompass most of the modern research. Crow notes that some cases of schizophrenia have a much better **prognosis** (chance of recovery or improvement in symptoms) than do others. The acute patients who have been exhibiting psychotic symptoms for only a few months rather than for years and whose symptoms tend to fall in the "positive" rather than the "negative" category have the best prognosis. By **positive symptoms**, Crow means hallucinations, delusions, and thought disorders, whereas **negative symptoms** include flattened affect, refusal to speak, catatonia, and loss of motivation. The term *positive* is used because these are the symptoms associated with a positive prognosis. Table 17.1 summarizes the differences between **type I** and **type II schizophrenia**, which are Crow's designations for his two categories. The designation "intellectual impairment" refers to the inability of the patient to answer such questions as, How old are you? How long have you been hospitalized here? and What year is this?

Crow proposes that type II schizophrenic symptoms arise from loss of brain tissue and that type I is related to a chemical error, probably in the dopa-

Table 17.1 Crow's Classification Criteria for Schizophrenic Types

Criteria	Type I	Type II
Typical symptoms	Positive (hallucinations, delusions, thought disorders)	Negative (affective flattening, poverty of speech and movement, loss of drive)
Most frequently seen in	Acute cases	Chronic cases
Intellectual impairment	Absent	Sometimes present
CBF scan	Normal	Hypofrontal
CT scan	Normal	Ventricular enlargement (suggesting atrophy)
Response to antipsychotics	Good	Poor
Prognosis	Good	Poor
Suggested pathology	Too many dopamine receptors	Neuron loss, especially in frontal lobes

Adapted in part from "Two Syndromes in Schizophrenia?" by T. J. Crow, 1982, *Trends in Neuro-Science, 5*, 352. Copyright 1982 by Elsevier Biomedical Press.

mine systems of the brain. CT scan data support this interpretation by revealing a greater incidence of enlarged ventricles (indicative of tissue loss) in patients exhibiting negative symptoms (Waddington, 1985). Type I would have a better prognosis because a chemical defect is possibly correctable with drug therapy, whereas brain damage is irreversible.

In support of his contention that dopamine transmission is involved in type I schizophrenia, Crow (1982) made a postmortem examination of 14 patients, discovering that the number of dopamine receptors in the brains correlated with the degree of symptomatology displayed in the type I brains but not in the type II.

Attention and Arousal in Schizophrenia

Most symptoms displayed by a patient with type II schizophrenia may be explainable on the basis of the extensive brain damage that appears to accompany that condition. But what of type I cases? It could

be that type I symptoms stem from a neurotransmitter defect originating in a portion of the brain called the mesolimbic system (to be discussed shortly) and that this defect disrupts arousal and attention.

Researchers are in fair agreement that schizophrenics suffer an impairment in attention. For example, when tested on their ability to memorize and retain word lists, they were not able to recall as well as normals, although they performed like normals when all they had to do was to recognize the memorized words. The difference between successful recognition performance and recall performance can be determined by how much attention the learner pays to organizing and categorizing the material as it is memorized. While simply reading the list over and over may do well for a recognition test, good performance on recall demands that the learner actively think about the words. Research results suggest that schizophrenics get worse scores on recall tests because they fail to devote enough attention either to organizing their memory of the words for future use (Gjerde, 1983) or to employing their memories during the recall test (Lutz & Marsh, 1981).

Another way of measuring attention is the **continuous performance test (CPT)** in which the subject must monitor a series of stimuli for periods up to 20 minutes and be scored for those he fails to report and for any he reports incorrectly. The CPT is widely used in drug studies and in examining patients with suspected neurological, psychiatric, and metabolic problems (Seidman, 1983). As you might predict from the results of the short-term memory experiments, schizophrenics do poorly on the CPT. Of course, the poor performance may have very little to do with schizophrenia itself, simply being a reflection of an "I don't care" attitude born of too many life-shattering emotional and adjustment problems. A study by Stammeyer (cited in Seidman, 1983), however, controlled for this problem by comparing schizophrenics to hospitalized neurotics; even in this comparison, the schizophrenics still performed significantly more poorly on the CPT. Furthermore, schizophrenics' performance improved after they had been on antipsychotic medication for a while.

Averaged evoked potentials also reveal an attention deficit. Recall from Chapter 5 that a short, discrete stimulus such as a click or a flash produces a series of waves in the EEG that is seen most clearly when records are combined ("averaged") from several hundred occurrences of the stimulus. The large, positive wave occurring 300–400 ms after the beginning of the stimulus, called **P300**, has been found to correlate with the degree of attention to the stimulus, and this wave is consistently smaller and often later in schizophrenics than in normals (Mirsky & Duncan, 1986; Pritchard, 1986). However, P300 reduction may be more strongly associated with negative symptoms than positive and be indicative of permanent brain damage rather than a neurotransmitter problem. It is still abnormal in patients whose delusions and hallucinations have been relieved by antipsychotic medication (Pritchard, 1986).

What causes the attention deficit so characteristic of schizophrenia? One explanation focuses on arousal. Investigators have established that acute schizophrenics maintain a higher-than-normal level of autonomic arousal as seen in higher heart rates (Gjerde, 1983). Another indication of high chronic arousal in schizophrenics is the fact that they take so long to habituate to repetitive, nonmeaningful stimuli like a bell that sounds every 60 seconds. Normal people are able to raise their sensory thresholds to such unimportant stimuli and partially block them out—in other words, to quit paying attention to them.

As you learned in the chapter on sleep, attention and arousal are linked together. Arousal is one part of paying attention. It seems to be involved with amplifying the effect that the chosen stimulus can have on the nervous system and diminishing the effect that all unattended stimuli can have. To use a concept that you learned in the vision chapter, arousal appears to increase the signal-to-noise ratio, making the attended stimulus stand out from the background of unwanted stimuli. EEG recordings, as you may recall, show a shift from alpha rhythm to beta rhythm as the person becomes attentive, and this same shift also signals an increase in general level of arousal. In some studies, schizophrenics have shown a predominance of betalike, fast EEGs with little or no alpha rhythm, indicating high arousal (Seidman, 1983).

How does chronic high arousal fit together with a deficit in attention? Generally, attention tends to focus in and improve as arousal increases. This principle, however, is true only up to a point. Mirsky and Kornetsky (cited in Seidman, 1983) both point out that the Yerkes–Dodson law would explain why excessive activation leaves schizophrenics with attention problems. The **Yerkes–Dodson law** states that the capacity of the organism to perform well increases as arousal increases, up to a point, and further increases in arousal produce worse and worse performance. Thus, the relation between performance and arousal is an inverted U-shaped curve with attention first increasing and then decreasing with higher and higher levels of arousal. If schizophrenics suffer what might be termed *hyperarousal*, then they should have continual problems with maintaining their attention. Gjerde (1983) cites a study by Orzack in which patients improved their performance on a CPT after receiving antipsychotic medication (phenothiazine). The drug is known to reduce activity in the reticular activating system, the brain-stem structure responsible for producing arousal.

Hyperarousal alone may not explain the attention deficit. If you look at Figure 17.2, you will see that cerebral blood flow is depressed in the frontal lobes and unusually high in the posterior temporal regions. Because blood flow reflects activity levels in a brain area, we can assume that the pattern of arousal in the cortex mimics the blood flow pattern. In other words, schizophrenics appear to have too little activity in the frontal lobes and too much in the temporal regions. EEG data agree with these findings; unusually slow brain waves (delta) are dominant in the frontal lobes of schizophrenics. Beta waves, indicative of arousal, are strong only in parietal and temporal lobes (Morstyn et al., 1983).

The frontal lobes are known to be involved in planning and organizing sequences of behavior. To do this, they must help determine which stimuli fit with the ongoing plan and should be amplified and which do not fit and should be inhibited. In other words, the frontal lobes must be an important part of the mechanism of attention. The blood flow data indicate that the frontal lobes probably are not functioning properly, and the CT scans show that in type II schizophrenia they do not even have all the cells they should have. If the frontal lobes are not functioning as they should, the schizophrenic should have difficulty attending to the stimuli that are relevant to the situation (such as a list of nonsense syllables to memorize) and find it difficult not to be distracted by irrelevant stimuli and irrelevant associations.

The Yerkes–Dodson law suggests that an attention disorder could be caused either by too little arousal or by too much. Thus, the schizophrenic attention disorder may be the result of both *hypo*-arousal in the frontal lobes and *hyper*arousal in the posterior cortex. Both frontal and posterior cortex may be involved in the process of attention but responsible for different aspects of the phenomenon. Posterior cortex is probably responsible for selecting among possible sensory inputs, whereas frontal cortex may be the selector of internal associations.

Pincus and Tucker (1978) note that one of the characteristics of schizophrenics is a thought defect

they call **overinclusion**, which refers to the tendency to include all sorts of mental associations in their speech that most people suppress as irrelevant to the conversation. Bleuler (cited in Pincus & Tucker, 1978) gave the example of a statement from a patient that showed this inability to inhibit associations: "My last teacher in that subject was Professor A. He was a man with black eyes. I also like black eyes. There are also blue and gray eyes and other sorts too. I have heard it said that snakes have green eyes. All people have eyes." This sort of speech has usually been interpreted as indicating a thought disorder in schizophrenia, but, as Gjerde (1983) suggests, the problem may be more one of attention than of thought. If it is this sort of useless association that patients have while trying to organize a list of words for later recall, it is not surprising that they fail to build memory structures that will be useful to them.

While frontal lobe dysfunction might explain the failure of the attention process to select meaningfully among all the mental associations available and suppress the irrelevant ones, the hyperarousal of the posterior cortex shown in the blood flow and EEG studies might bear on the failure of the attention mechanism to select among environmental stimuli. The posterior cortex contains all cortical sensory areas except those for olfaction; thus, arousal of posterior sensory areas without guidance from the frontal lobes probably should produce an inability "to selectively attend to relevant environmental cues owing to the intrusion of irrelevant stimuli" (Kokkinidis & Anisman, 1980). The schizophrenic seems to be unable to think clearly because the frontal lobes are failing to direct his attention through a logical sequence of associations, and the sensory areas are apparently aroused to the point where the filtering of environmental stimuli should be impaired.

The idea of hyperarousal in the sensory areas leads one to wonder if that arousal might not so intensify the experience of particular stimuli that they develop hallucinatory qualities. Could it be that the schizophrenic in the grip of catatonia (mute immobility) is simply so overwhelmed by the feel of clothes against the skin or of rumblings from the stomach that there is no attention left over for the physician trying to elicit the answer to a question, or even for the fact that he has not moved his body

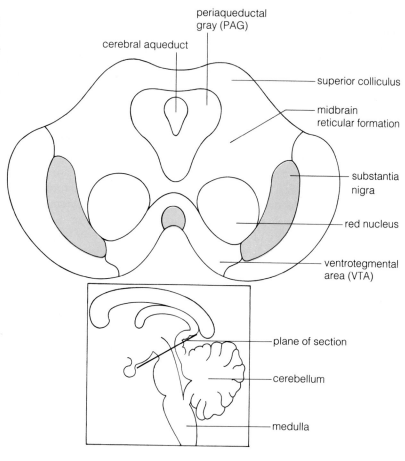

Figure 17.3 A cross section of the brain stem at the level of the midbrain. The small midsagittal view in the box shows the plane in which the cross section was cut.

periaqueductal gray (PAG)

cerebral aqueduct

superior colliculus

midbrain reticular formation

substantia nigra

red nucleus

ventrotegmental area (VTA)

plane of section

cerebellum

medulla

in the last 4 hours? There are interesting hypotheses here for future explorations.

Hyperarousal in the Mesolimbic System

The evidence of hyperarousal in schizophrenia has led many investigators to speculate that the midbrain reticular formation (MBRF) is misfunctioning in this disorder. That may well be the case, but it cannot be the whole story. There is now considerable evidence implicating another area of the midbrain close to the reticular formation, the **ventrotegmental area (VTA)**. Figure 17.3 is a cross section through the brain stem at the level of the midbrain. At the top is the dorsal surface with the twin bulges of the superior colliculi. On the ventral side is a band of cells

making up the VTA. Notice that the VTA is just medial to another nucleus, the substantia nigra. In reality, the border between these two is indistinct, and they appear to overlap considerably (Moore & Bloom, 1978). These two nuclei, substantia nigra and VTA, hold the cell bodies of the two most important dopamine projection systems of the brain, the nigrostriatal path and the mesolimbic path, both of which send their axons coursing forward into the anterior structures of the brain by way of that major tract, the medial forebrain bundle (Figure 17.4).

In the chapter on motor functions, you studied the nigrostriatal path in detail and learned about how it may be involved in modulating the functions of the striatum (caudate and putamen). The caudate and putamen have an "ancestral" set of structures to

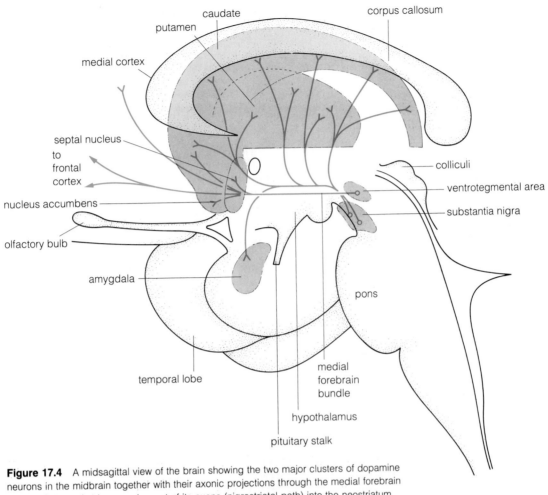

Figure 17.4 A midsagittal view of the brain showing the two major clusters of dopamine neurons in the midbrain together with their axonic projections through the medial forebrain bundle. Substantia nigra sends most of its axons (nigrostriatal path) into the neostriatum (caudate and putamen), whereas the ventrotegmental area sends its axons (mesolimbic path) to neocortex and to limbic structures such as the septal nucleus and nucleus accumbens. In the figure, the shaded areas represent brain structures buried beneath the visible surface. (Adapted from Nieuwenhuys et al., 1981)

which they are closely related but which evolved much earlier along with the old limbic cortex. So, let us distinguish between the **neostriatum** (caudate and putamen) and the **limbic striatum**, which consists mainly of the **septal area** and the **nucleus accumbens** (Figure 17.5). The dopaminergic neurons of the substantia nigra project into the neostriatum as the nigrostriatal path; those of the VTA project to the limbic striatum as the mesolimbic path.

The **mesolimbic system** includes the dopaminergic neurons of the ventrotegmental area, the mesolimbic path, and all neurons to which they send their axons in the nucleus accumbens, septal area, prefrontal cortex, and other limbic sites. It also includes the descending pathways from the limbic structures back to the VTA (Figure 17.6).

Is the mesolimbic system involved in the hyperarousal and attentional problems of schizophrenia?

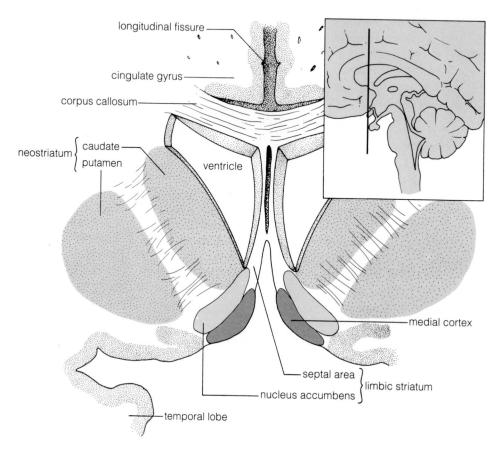

longitudinal fissure

cingulate gyrus

corpus callosum

neostriatum { caudate
putamen

ventricle

medial cortex

septal area } limbic striatum
nucleus accumbens }

temporal lobe

Figure 17.5 A frontal section of a human brain through the septal area and nucleus accumbens. The inset shows the anterior–posterior position of the cross section (heavy vertical line running from the cingulate gyrus to the pituitary gland). Only the core of the hemispheres near the midline is shown. Notice how close the structures of the limbic striatum are to those of the neostriatum, suggesting that their functions are related. (Adapted from DeArmond et al., 1976)

A number of researchers feel that it is. Stress seems to increase the rate of firing of VTA neurons (Trulson & Preussler, 1984). VTA-lesioned rats do poorly in some types of learning tasks, apparently because they have trouble attending to the task stimuli. They constantly stop or turn back to examine irrelevant stimuli, giving every appearance of being too distractible to perform well (Oades, 1982). You may recall the problems schizophrenics have when trying to learn word lists—a phenomenon also interpretable as distractibility.

Stevens (1979) cites research in which stimulation of the mesolimbic system (either in the VTA or in the limbic striatum) elicited hyperactivity, fearfulness, or exploratory behavior. During stimulation, the animals acted as though they suspected some-

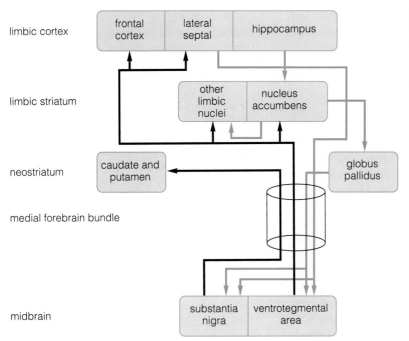

limbic cortex

limbic striatum

neostriatum

medial forebrain bundle

midbrain

Figure 17.6 A block diagram of the mesolimbic system and nigrostriatal pathway. Black arrows are upward routes from the midbrain; color arrows are downward paths. Only selected nuclei and projections are shown.

thing amiss somewhere in their environment but couldn't find the source of the discomfort. Tame, affectionate cats changed their behavior dramatically when stimulated in the VTA, backing into corners, searching every nook and cranny of the room, and slinking along the walls in an apparent avoidance of open areas. The effect on monkeys was increased pacing and searching behavior as well as stereotyped submissive posturing as though there were some threatening male that had to be appeased. Iversen characterized the effects of mesolimbic stimulation as producing a "search for meaning" in the environment (cited in Stevens, 1979). For some researchers, this agitated examination of the environment as though it were a potential source of threat is very reminiscent of the human psychotic symptom of paranoia.

Paranoia is a set of delusional beliefs, usually of persecution. The person is deeply suspicious of his whole environment, believing that every thing relates to himself and every behavior of the other peo-

ple around him (who are usually strangers) is all part of a plot to do him some harm. Frequently, paranoia is a symptom of schizophrenia. If paranoia really can be produced in animals by stimulating their mesolimbic systems, then this strongly suggests that the ventrotegmental projection might be the part of the brain most directly involved in schizophrenia. Additional evidence for this interpretation could be obtained if we could stimulate the dopaminergic systems of human subjects and see if they developed psychotic behavior. In fact, such experiments have been carried out both spontaneously by people using drugs recreationally and in the laboratory. The drugs used to stimulate the mesolimbic system are amphetamines.

Amphetamines and Psychosis

Amphetamines are a class of drugs whose major effect is arousal. They are widely used as stimulants by truck drivers and students. Dextroamphetamine ("speed" in street jargon) is frequently the chief ingredient in so-called diet pills that attempt to suppress appetite. Other "uppers" are methamphetamine and destroamphetamine but this short list by no means exhausts the category.

Drugs almost always have more than one effect, and the price of amphetamine-produced arousal are symptoms such as irritability, increased heart rate, sweating, pupil dilation, insomnia, increased blood pressure, and loss of appetite (Bokar, 1976). (The suppression of appetite works only for a few days and is totally unsuitable for solving an obesity problem.) Together with the increased attentiveness and arousal induced by amphetamine, there may be other effects such as euphoria, increased sex drive and excitement, or fearfulness and psychotic symptoms, depending on the size of the dose and the degree of dependency. Even one dose seems to produce withdrawal symptoms: lethargy, fatigue, and depression being the most common. If amphetamines have been taken regularly for several weeks and a strong dependency established, withdrawal symptoms are more severe. Besides extreme fatigue and depression, there are sleep disturbances with REM-sleep abnormalities and nightmares. Headaches, profuse sweating, and severe muscle cramps are common, and feelings of anxiety from terrifying thoughts may dominate consciousness (Bokar, 1976). The paranoid thinking that accompanies all these other symptoms is illustrated in the following case:

Jessica was a 41-year-old divorced pharmacist who took advantage of her easy access to amphetamine. She used the drug to counteract lethargy and boredom. Eventually, she became addicted. Jessica had always been friendly and open, but now she became hostile and suspicious. She accused her son of spying on her and hiring detectives to follow her. One day she told her son that the announcer on the evening news had sent her brain messages in secret code that would enable her to outwit the detectives. At first, Jessica's son was irritated at her suspiciousness. Later, he became angry. Finally, her son realized that his mother was seriously ill. Like most people suddenly confronted with serious mental illness he had no idea what might be wrong or how to get help. He knew nothing of her amphetamine abuse. It took much wheedling to get Jessica to a psychiatrist, and once she did meet with him, she successfully concealed her drug use. The psychiatrist thought she had schizophrenia and needed antipsychotic therapy, but Jessica refused to enter the hospital. Because initiating antipsychotic therapy on outpatients is risky, the psychiatrist could not offer her much help.

Several days later, Jessica walked into a camera store and smashed a movie camera that she believed had been spying on her from the window. She was then hospitalized on a two-physician certificate. (In many states, a person can be involuntarily committed to a psychiatric hospital for a few days if two physicians certify that the person is a danger to himself or others or cannot care for himself.) In the hospital, Jessica had no access to amphetamine and was given antipsychotics. Her symptoms cleared up unusually fast. When medication was removed, she did not relapse. As soon as Jessica stopped taking amphetamine, she stopped suffering from "schizophrenia." (Lickey & Gordon, 1983, pp. 113–114)

Amphetamine psychosis has been known since 1938 when patients with narcolepsy (see Chapter 10) were treated with amphetamine. The symptoms these patients displayed prompted some researchers to see if they could deliberately produce a psychotic state in a normal volunteer through amphetamine intoxication. In several of these studies, amphetamine was administered hourly for several days. Paranoid delusions seemed to be the first symptoms to appear (Figure 17.7). With more doses, hallucinations and signs of thought disorder also were noted (reviewed in Angrist & van Kammen, 1984). Many investigators now accept the amphetamine-type psychotic disorder as roughly the same as schizophrenia (Angrist & van Kammen, 1984; Kokkinidis & Anisman, 1980).

If prolonged amphetamine use produces a form of schizophrenia, then giving the drug to schizophrenic patients should increase the intensity of their symptoms. That is exactly what happens. Janowsky and colleagues (cited in Lickey & Gordon, 1983) reported that they treated a patient with schizophrenic delusions centering on the idea that spirits talked to him and that the spirits rose up out of peoples' heads. Antipsychotic drugs brought the person out of his delusional state and to the point where he admitted that his references to spirits was just "crazy talk." However, within just 1 minute of an injection of amphetamine, he was claiming that spir-

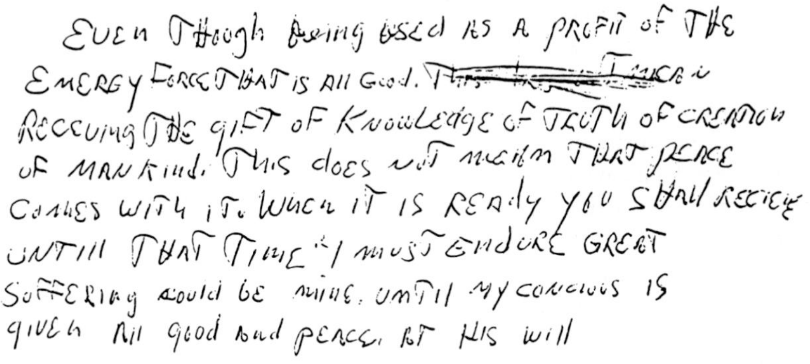

Figure 17.7 The influence of amphetamine on thought and writing. This passage was written by a normal subject who had been given doses of amphetamine periodically for 4–6 hours. At the time this was written, 575 mg of amphetamine had been consumed. (From Angrist & van Kammen, 1984)

Even though being used as a profit of the energy force that is all good. This ~~_____ there~~ is receving the gift of Knowledge of truth of creation of mankind. This does not mean that peace comes with it. When it is ready you shall recieve until that time I must endure great suffering would be mine, until my concious is given all good and peace, at His will

its were rising out of the physician's head. It is interesting that this amphetamine effect is limited mostly to those patients that Crow would classify as type I, the ones who presumably have something wrong with the dopamine systems of their brains. Type II patients (brain-damaged) show little response to the drug (Angrist & van Kammen, 1984).

Is there any evidence then that amphetamines affect the dopamine brain systems? There are three neurotransmitters in the category called catecholamines: epinephrine, norepinephrine, and dopamine. It is well known that amphetamines act to increase the availability of DA (dopamine) and norepinephrine at catecholaminergic synapses by blocking reuptake and (in high doses) stimulating the increased release of transmitter (Cooper et al., 1974). Several decades ago, Randrup (cited in Crow, 1979) and others conducted amphetamine tests on rodents, first noting the behavioral effects of the drug and then trying to block these effects with other drugs. They found that the amphetamine effects were stopped by a substance that inhibited the synthesis of catecholamines. When the researchers selectively depleted the neural stores of norepinephrine (NE), the amphetamine-provoked behaviors could still be seen, so NE apparently was not involved. Epinephrine is used as a transmitter only by a very few cells in the brain stem, and it is very unlikely that it is involved importantly in the brain's response to amphetamine. By elimination it would seem that dopamine is the transmitter of greatest importance in the neural response to amphetamine. However, Trulson and Jacobs (1979a) have discovered that

amphetamines also affect a related transmitter, serotonin. Catecholamines and serotonin both belong to the **monoamine** group of transmitters. Because prolonged use of amphetamines appears to deplete the available quantities of serotonin and it is through serotonin depletion that LSD produces hallucinations, the possibility exists that serotonin problems may compound the DA problem in some cases of schizophrenia.

In summary, amphetamine is a drug whose main effect is arousal and which produces symptoms resembling many of those in schizophrenia. Furthermore, this drug seems to act mostly on dopamine systems of the brain. Findings of this sort have led to the development of the most widely held theory of schizophrenic brain dysfunction, the dopamine hypothesis.

The Dopamine Hypothesis

Because the mesolimbic system seems to be involved in arousal and schizophrenia is categorized by hyperarousal, it was logical that the mesolimbic system should be suspected of being hyperactive. By hyperactive we mean that the DA neurons are overactive in their inhibition of postsynaptic cells. There are a number of forms that this hyperactivity could take. The simplest idea is that the mesolimbic cells are firing too frequently and thus releasing too much DA at their synapses and that it is the excess transmitter causing the overcontrol of the postsynaptic cells. In other words, the defect in schizophrenia may be too much dopamine released. Evidence for this idea comes from autopsy studies in which abnormally high concentrations of DA were found in the brains of schizophrenics (Iverson, 1979). The clinical observation that few patients with Parkinson's disease ever develop schizophrenia also concurs with the excess dopamine hypothesis. Recall that Parkinson's disease is a disorder of the neostriatum in which there is too *little* DA available. If too little DA is associated with Parkinson's disease and having Parkinson's disease lowers the chances of becoming schizophrenic, then schizophrenia might be associated with too *much* dopamine.

Antipsychotic Drugs and DA Receptors Other evidence comes from the study of **antipsychotic drugs**. The largest category of antipsychotics is **phenothiazines** among which **chlorpromazine** (trade name, Thorazine) was the first to be developed and the best known. Phenothiazines and other antipsychotic drugs have their effect on dopaminergic transmission by blocking receptor sites for the transmitter (Lickey & Gordon, 1983). The drug molecule fits into the receptor molecule ("binds" with it) well enough to prevent DA molecules from binding there, but not well enough to trigger the opening of ion channels. Thus, the antipsychotic drug fails to stimulate the postsynaptic cell and prevents the transmitter from stimulating it as well. By blocking DA receptor sites, the drug could counteract the effects of too much dopamine.

A problem with this simple interpretation soon became apparent, however. When the rate of DA usage was measured in schizophrenics, it turned out to be at a lower level than in other patients, rather than at a higher level as you would expect. Autopsy studies discovered that schizophrenic brains possessed far too many DA receptors in the neostriatum and in the nucleus accmbens of the limbic striatum (Crow, 1979). Presumably, additional receptors would make the postsynaptic neurons supersensitive to dopamine by providing more sites for its action. Some researchers suspected that this proliferation of DA receptor sites might have been caused by antipsychotic drugs taken by the patients before their deaths because animal data showed that chronic administration of antipsychotic drugs produced supersensitivity to dopamine. However, it is doubtful that the rat data are relevant because the action of the drug on a *normal* rat brain is most likely quite different than its action on a schizophrenic human brain. Unfortunately, no animal model of schizophrenia exists (i.e., no schizophrenic rats) on which to test our drugs. Most important to this argument, however, are data from schizophrenics who had never taken antipsychotic drugs but who still showed an excess of DA receptors (Crow, 1979; Wong et al., 1986).

Apparently, schizophrenia may be a disorder characterized by too much dopamine transmission because of an excess of DA receptors. Antipsychotic drugs probably work not by keeping excessive amounts of DA out of postsynaptic receptors but rather by blocking some of the excessive numbers of receptors, thus preventing normal amounts of DA from having an abnormally large effect (Feldman & Quenzer, 1984). In keeping with this interpretation, antipsychotic drugs with the greatest potency are also the best at blocking DA receptors (Lickey & Gordon, 1983). Amphetamine psychosis, like schizophrenia, is apparently the result of too much DA transmission but seems to be caused by excessive release of DA (especially in the nucleus accumbens), rather than by too many receptors (Robinson et al., 1988).

Although other transmitter systems may yet prove to also be involved in schizophrenia, psychiatry now has more than 40 antischizophrenic drugs at its disposal, and they all affect dopamine transmission (Barnes, 1987). The dopamine hypothesis constitutes our best available explanation of schizophrenia.

Problems with the Dopamine Hypothesis Many observations still do not fit into the DA hypothesis. One problem concerns timing. Chlorpromazine and other antipsychotic drugs begin blocking DA receptors as soon as they reach the brain, but the effect on schizophrenic symptoms is far from immediate. There may be some change in behavior within 1 hour of administration, but the change is small compared to what will be obtained over 4 weeks if the medication is given regularly (Baldessarini, 1977; Crow, 1979). In other words, our hypothesis would predict that antipsychotics would have their maximum effect immediately, but clinical data are clear that this maximum is reached only after the drug has been taken repeatedly for days. There seems to be a delay in the therapeutic effect of the drugs that remains to be explained.

A beginning of an explanation might be found in the observation that the mesolimbic neurons themselves gradually slow their firing during several weeks of drug administration. Bunney (1984) has made recordings of individual nerve cell activity in the VTA during antipsychotic drug administration (in rats). He found that the drugs had an immediate effect of increasing the firing rate of the mesolimbic neurons, but after 2 weeks or so of continuous dosing, the cells eventually dropped their firing to zero.

Another problem is that we know too little about how antipsychotic drugs affect dopaminergic neurons. These cells are covered with DA receptors, making them sensitive to their own transmitter (Feldman & Quenzer, 1984). Are these receptors also blocked by drugs? If so, what is the effect on transmission at the synapse? Do other transmitters (such as cholecystokinin) influence the events at the DA synapse (Chiodo & Bunney, 1987)? Still another problem stems from the fact that antipsychotic drugs appear to relieve the emotional, hallucinatory, and delusional symptoms but appear to have no effect on the problem of attention (Medalia et al., 1988). If this is true, it suggests that a defect in DA transmission (supposedly corrected by the drug) could not be responsible for the arousal and attention deficit discussed above. Many years of research separate us from a comprehensive understanding of schizophrenia.

In summary then, schizophrenia seems to divide into at least two types: one kind the result of brain damage, especially in the frontal regions, and the other type possibly the product of hyperarousal in the mesolimbic system. The second type is treatable with antipsychotic drugs that alter dopaminergic transmission apparently by blocking DA receptors. This type may result from some biochemical defect that produces an overabundance of DA receptors, resulting in excessive influence from the mesolimbic system. The major problem with this dopamine theory is that there is no explanation for the 2-week lag between the beginning of drug therapy and the relief from symptoms. Thus, our explanation of schizophrenia as a dopamine problem is not complete at this time.

Schizophrenia is not the only brain dysfunction related in part to a disturbance in one of the brain's neurotransmitter systems. Considerable evidence implicates the noradrenergic and serotonergic systems in the genesis of mania and depression, the two aspects of mood disorders.

■ Mood Disorders

These disorders used to be called *affective psychosis* or *manic–depressive psychosis*. Their origin is unclear despite decades of research, but at least we can now be sure that many cases have a very strong physiological component and in some the causes may be entirely chemical.

Description and Classification

Abnormalities of mood apparently can arise from a tremendous variety of causes, and it is likely that few such disorders have one single origin. **Grief reactions** are normal reactions to life events (such as death of a spouse or loss of employment), characterized by a temporary depression (1–6 months) (Pincus & Tucker, 1978). Grief reactions are very different from depressive episodes that occur repeatedly and fail to correlate with any discernible change in the person's environment. The American Psychiatric Association (1987) categorizes this sort of emotional problem as a **mood disorder**. Much evidence now suggests that the causes of mood disorders are to be found mainly within the physiology of the nervous system.

Psychiatry now recognizes two types of mood disorder: depressive disorder and bipolar disorder. In **depressive disorder**, the person often enjoys a normal range of activation (i.e., from quiet to excited) but has periods during which activation level gradually falls to a depressed level and stays there for days or weeks before it rises again. During these depressed periods, there is a total loss of interest in people or events. No activity seems capable of providing enjoyment, and the mood is one of pervasive gloom and despair. Sleep, appetite, and sex drive are all disturbed. Although the person feels restless and agitated, there seems to be too little energy to accomplish even the simplest task. Thinking through a problem or reaching a decision involves immense effort and demands more concentration than can be mustered. In some people at the bottom of their depressions, feelings of pessimism and self-reproach become overwhelming, and they may attempt suicide.

The onset of a depressive episode cannot usually be traced to any environmental, psychosocial factor. This frequent failure to find any outside cause for depression in the events of the person's life suggests an internal, chemical cause.

The "poles" in **bipolar disorder** are the opposite extremes on the activation continuum: mania at one end and depression at the other. As the name implies, episodes of extremely high activation (mania) are involved, usually alternating with periods of depression. The depression of the bipolar disorder is much like that of depressive disorder. In the manic phase of the bipolar disorder, the patient may be overactive, expansive, irritable, and overtalkative. Tremendous energy is displayed, and ideas appear to come too fast to allow time for expressing them all. There may be feelings of grandiosity, recklessness, and even delusions if the mania is severe. Manic episodes tend to develop over a few days and last for as long as several months. Frequently, manic episodes are followed quickly by depressive episodes, and vice versa (American Psychiatric Association, 1987).

Heredity and Mood Disorder

Mood disorders (the ones that seem to have a stronger biological than environmental origin) seem to run in families. In studies of patients who were adopted children, it was found that the biological parent had a higher probability of also having mood disorder than did the adoptive parent (Gershon & Nurnberger, 1982). Inheritance seems to be more important as a determinant than family environment and rearing. When twins were compared, it was found that the chances of the second of a pair of dizygotic twins contracting depression after the first had was only 13 percent; but if one monozygotic twin was diagnosed as having mood disorder, the other twin had a 69 percent chance of also developing mood disorder (Sachar & Baron, 1979). Because childhood family experiences and rearing were nearly identical for both kinds of twins, the most likely explanation for the difference in risk is that monozygotic twins are genetically identical, whereas dizygotic twins are not. Note, however, that in *only* 69 percent of monozygotic twins in which one twin was ill did the other also become depressed. The remaining 31 percent of cases in which only one twin contracted mood disorder strongly indicates that a genetic factor is not the only cause of depression. If it were the sole cause, then *all* monozygotic twins with mood disorder should have a twin with mood disorder. Room is left for the possibility of environmental causes, both physical and psychological, that could act together with the genetic factor.

The nature of the genetic factor has been very difficult to isolate, and no clear theory has emerged. The clinical distinction between bipolar disorder and depressive disorder suggests two separate genetic defects, but attempts to find evidence for this idea have been negative. It has been found that relatives of a patient with bipolar disorder have a greater chance of developing depression than do relatives of a depressive disorder patient; but when attempts were made to find biological differences between the two types of disorder, few emerged. The most likely way for a genetic difference to be expressed in a different pattern of emotional disorder would be for each type to have a different missing enzyme. For example, MAO and catechol-o-methyltransferase (an enzyme that inactivates norepinephrine in the synapse) have been studied, but levels are similar in both depressive disorder and bipolar disorder (Sachar & Baron, 1979). Geneticists have generally concluded that the present data best fit the idea that the two types of disorder arise from the same causes and that the bipolar variety is simply a more extreme set of symptoms than is the depressive disorder. Some genetic research suggests a connection between mood disorders and a region of the sixth chromosome close to or among the genes involved in the immune system, but no one has any idea yet of how this might relate to the generation of the disorder (Matthysse & Kidd, 1982). Other studies have purportedly discovered a "depression gene" on the X chromosome. However, none of these claims has been able to stand the test of replication (Barnes, 1989), and at this time no one knows which gene or genes are at fault.

Catecholamine Theory of Depression

The closest thing we have to a theory of depression had its origins in an observation made in the 1950s about the side effects of a new drug. The drug was reserpine, and it was being used to treat hypertension (high blood pressure). The problem with reserpine was that in 10–15 percent of the patients, it produced a serious state of depression. This suggested that much could be learned about the origins of depression if it could be discovered how reserpine acted on the brain. In another area of medicine, the drug isoniazid was being used to treat tuberculosis, and this drug was found to have a mood-elevating effect. These two side effects, depression and activation, were seen to be related when someone discovered that both drugs affected an important group of neurotransmitters, the monoamines. Reserpine reduced the levels of the monoamines, whereas isoniazid raised them (Maas, 1979). Each monoamine is a transmitter for a separate system of neurons in the brain. Could it be that one of these monoamine systems is the focus of the apparent chemical defect underlying depressive disorders?

Monoamines and Depression   There are two types of **monoamine transmitters** that are of interest to us, the indolamines and the catecholamines. The indolamines include serotonin; the catecholamines are dopamine, norepinephrine, and epinephrine. Of these four monoamines, norepinephrine (NE) was the most interesting in relation to depression because of its well-known relation to activation. As a hormone, NE is secreted by the adrenal medulla and circulates through the bloodstream to activate organs throughout the body in situations calling for greater-than-normal energy expenditure, alertness, and fast

reaction times. NE also functions as a neurotransmitter in the sympathetic nervous system and thus plays a part in the neural activation of the same organs that it affects as a hormone. Within the brain stem are small clusters of neurons that employ NE as a transmitter. The most interesting of these nuclei is a small area near the pontine–midbrain border called the **locus coeruleus** (suh-RULE-ee-us), which sends its axons threading up the base of the brain through the hypothalamus, branching and rebranching into enormous areas of cortex that are the final destinations of these neurons. The anatomy of this system suggests an influence on brain function disproportionately large for the size of its nucleus of origin. Here is an ideal place to look for the disruptions underlying depression—a system that seems linked to the activation of nearly the entire forebrain and that uses NE, a transmitter linked to activation. The discovery concerning isoniazid and reserpine led to the proposal that depression was the result of too little NE in the brain, whereas mania resulted from too much. This was the earliest and simplest version of the catecholamine theory.

Drugs and Monoamines   If depression occurs because of a shortage of norepinephrine, then one means of treating it might involve the enzyme called **monoamine oxidase (MAO)**, which destroys NE. As soon as NE is manufactured, it is immediately stored in synaptic vesicles where it is safe from the destructive influence of MAO. However, after being released into the synaptic gap and having its effect on the receptors of the postsynaptic neuron, the left-over NE is taken back up into the presynaptic terminal. Between the time when the NE re-enters the terminal and the time it is re-stored in another vesicle, it remains vulnerable to being converted by MAO. If for some reason NE is in short supply, then one way of increasing the supply would be to interfere with the enzymatic action of MAO. The idea that depression might involve a shortage of NE led to the development of a class of antidepressants called **MAO-inhibitors**. It now becomes clear why the drug isoniazid made the tuberculosis patients so energetic and happy. As one of its actions, isoniazid is an MAO-inhibitor. Taking it was like taking a shot of norepinephrine, epinephrine, and dopamine. Reserpine, on the other hand, produced depression because it interferes with the storage of NE in vesicles and thus leaves the transmitter unprotected from the destructive effect of MAO (Baldessarini, 1977).

MAO-inhibitors like isoniazid and its relatives were discovered to be antidepressants without anyone understanding why they worked. The discovery that they could elevate the concentration of NE in the neurons by slowing its destruction became a cornerstone of the catecholamine theory of depression. Further evidence for the theory came with the discovery of still another class of drugs, the **tricyclic antidepressants (TADs)** (such as amitriptyline and imipramine), that may have their action by blocking reuptake of catecholamines. By preventing the transmitter from re-entering the cell, these drugs would leave more NE available in the synaptic gap. If depression involves a deficiency of NE, this additional transmitter would help compensate for inadequate amounts of NE released from the terminal during nerve impulses.

Problems with the Catecholamine Theory It may have occurred to you that amphetamines might make good antidepressants. These drugs raise the person's activation level both by interfering with reuptake of NE and by facilitating its release (Feldman & Quenzer, 1984). A possible problem for the catecholamine theory is that amphetamines are not very effective at relieving depression, and they are no longer used therapeutically (Pincus & Tucker, 1978). However, a probable explanation has been found for this apparent contradiction. There is some evidence that with continued use amphetamine begins to interfere with the synthesis of NE from dopamine, eventually depleting the transmitter enough to produce depression in a normal person. This is the best explanation at this time for the fact that long-term users of amphetamines cannot stay "high" indefinitely. Eventually they "crash" into a condition strongly resembling depressive disorder.

The catecholamine theory has a much more difficult time explaining the matter of timing in TAD therapy. It ordinarily requires anywhere from 7–14 days of continuous treatment with TADs before there is any alleviation of the depression, despite the fact that reuptake of NE is inhibited almost immediately

(Peroutka & Snyder, 1980; Sachar & Baron, 1979). If the drugs can raise the level of available NE without any delay, then why doesn't the depression lift immediately? A possible answer to this is that several weeks are required for the level of NE to increase in the synapse. This is precisely what Crews and Smith (1978) discovered; a slow increase in NE concentration occurred within the synapse throughout 3 weeks of TAD treatment. Now the question becomes, Why should synaptic NE concentrations rise so slowly when TADs block reuptake immediately?

Presynaptic Regulation of NE Release If the expected immediate buildup in NE concentration fails to materialize, one possible reason could be that less and less NE is being released into the synapse with each nerve impulse. This idea is reasonable because a mechanism for limiting the release of NE does exist—an inhibitory feedback mechanism triggered by **alpha presynaptic receptors**. At catecholaminergic synapses (those using a catecholamine transmitter), there are receptors on both sides of the synapse. The NE synapse sports at least five receptor types: alpha and beta presynaptic sites plus alpha, beta 1, and beta 2 postsynaptic sites. Because presynaptic receptors are located in the membrane of the cell that released the transmitter, they are frequently called **autoreceptors**.

Beta autoreceptors are the first step in a positive-feedback control mechanism that increases the release of NE, and alpha autoreceptors are the first link in a negative-feedback system that decreases the amount of NE released (Langer, 1980; McNeal & Cimbolic, 1986). Beta receptors "turn the faucet on," and the alphas "turn it off." When an impulse arrives at a NE terminal and some vesicles spill their transmitter into the synaptic gap, some NE molecules find their way into beta autoreceptors. Apparently, this immediately produces the release of more NE (Figure 17.8). The few data that are available about this mechanism suggest that beta and alpha receptors work in sequence, so that alpha receptors always react after beta receptors. Perhaps the alpha feedback device has a higher threshold than the beta (Berridge, 1979). In any case, the fact that the alphas lag a few microseconds behind the betas means that NE molecules released into the synaptic gap will first result

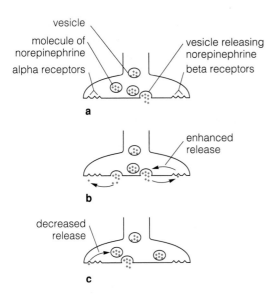

vesicle
molecule of norepinephrine
alpha receptors
vesicle releasing norepinephrine
beta receptors

a

enhanced release

b

decreased release

c

Figure 17.8 Regulation of transmitter release by positive- and negative-feedback mechanisms triggered by alpha and beta receptor sites. (**a**) Axon terminal with vesicles, one of which is releasing molecules of NE into the synaptic gap. (**b**) One of the NE molecules has entered a beta receptor and stimulated an increased rate of release. (**c**) An alpha receptor has been stimulated and the inhibitory mechanism that it controls is slowing the rate of release.

in an increased rate of NE release and then a sudden decrease. If the alphas can shut off the outflow of NE rapidly, then the two feedback mechanisms constitute a biological measuring device for ensuring that the terminal releases exactly the same amount of NE following each impulse (Berridge, 1979).

So, let us assume that alpha autoreceptors can diminish the release of NE (even though beta receptors are also being stimulated). It also seems plausible that greater amounts of NE in the synaptic gap will stimulate the alpha feedback system more strongly, inducing an even greater reduction of NE. Now picture what will happen when a TAD is added to this picture. The TAD blocks the reuptake of NE so that the concentration in the synaptic gap rises. This means that there is more NE to stimulate alpha receptors. That in turn means a greater suppression of NE release with each succeeding impulse. Now we can answer the question that introduced this sec-

tion: If TADs can begin blocking NE reuptake as soon as they are administered, then why don't synaptic NE levels begin to rise immediately? The answer apparently is that the positive effect of blocking reuptake is canceled by the negative effect of overstimulating the alpha autoreceptor system so that with every impulse, less and less NE is released. If this analysis is correct, reuptake blocking by itself cannot explain how TADs can slowly increase the amount of NE in the synapse.

We may be able to explain the increase in NE with a known synaptic mechanism. It has become clear to researchers that synaptic membranes regulate their sensitivity to neurotransmitter molecules by way of a feedback mechanism that depends on the number of transmitter molecules received (Friedhoff & Miller, 1983). Decreasing the number of transmitter molecules will lead to a gradual increase in the number of receptors (both presynaptic and postsynaptic), and increasing the number of transmitter molecules will reduce the receptor density. In this way, the cell keeps the strength of its response fairly constant for each impulse in the synaptic neuron (Figure 17.9). The increase in receptor density during times when transmitter is scarce is now called **up-regulation**, whereas the opposite effect is termed **down-regulation** (Friedhoff & Miller, 1983). These adjustments are comparatively slow by nervous system standards and could require as much as 2 weeks. Thus, if the major effect of TADs is the down-regulation of alpha presynaptic receptors, then the amount of NE released should slowly increase over several weeks as the inhibitory control over release is slowly lifted. As evidence for this hypothesis, Garcia-Sevilla and colleagues (1981) showed that in depressed patients the density of binding sites on blood cells comparable to alpha presynaptic receptors decreased throughout several weeks of treatment with antidepressants.

If the major effect of TADs is to decrease the number of alpha autoreceptors, then the chemical defect responsible for the depressive state must be the overproduction of alpha autoreceptors (Harrison-Read, 1981). An abnormally high density of alpha autoreceptors would explain why there is not enough NE. The more alpha autoreceptors there are, the greater the inhibition of transmitter release. TADs

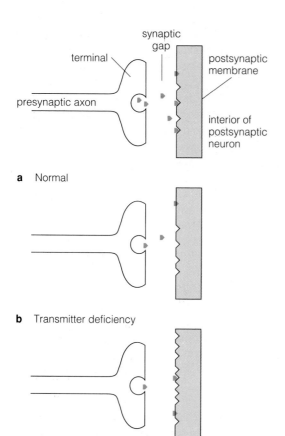

synaptic gap

terminal

presynaptic axon

postsynaptic membrane

interior of postsynaptic neuron

a Normal

b Transmitter deficiency

c Up-regulation

Figure 17.9 Up-regulation of postsynaptic receptor sites. (**a**) An axon terminal in the normal condition with adequate amounts of transmitter and receptors. (**b**) A synapse in a state of transmitter deficiency. The inadequate amounts of transmitter released cannot maintain the postsynaptic neuron at a normal level of function. (**c**) The postsynaptic cell attempts to compensate for the deficiency by increasing the number of receptors (up-regulation).

would have a therapeutic effect because of their ability to constrain the alpha feedback system and thus allow the presynaptic neurons to release normal amounts of NE with each impulse.

In summary, the catecholamine theory states that depression occurs when there is too little NE available at noradrenergic synapses. One elaboration of

this theory hypothesizes that an overabundance of alpha autoreceptors is the cause of NE shortage and that TADs relieve depression by decreasing the number of alpha presynaptic receptors while also blocking reuptake of NE.

Postsynaptic Repercussions If we are correct about a NE shortage in depression, then we can also deduce that postsynaptic cells will react to this lack of NE. Postsynaptic membranes will undergo up-regulation of noradrenergic receptor sites in an attempt to compensate for the lack of transmitter. In the early stages of a depressive episode, the increase in sensitivity to NE induced by this increase in density of postsynaptic receptors probably is enough to prevent the symptoms of depression from appearing. As the shortage of NE becomes more severe, however, the cell must reach a point where up-regulation can no longer fully compensate and postsynaptic cell activity begins to diminish. That is when depressive symptoms should begin to appear. Some evidence for this idea is found in the fact that chronic treatment with TADs induces down-regulation in the postsynaptic cell (Friedhoff & Miller, 1983). This decrease in post-synaptic-receptor density could result indirectly from the action of the drug on alpha autoreceptors (Cohen et al., 1982). As the TAD decreases the number of autoreceptors, the amount of NE released rises, thus making the extra postsynaptic receptors unnecessary and initiating down-regulation. Thus, the TAD brings both the presynaptic- and postsynaptic-receptor density back to normal. Cohen and co-workers (1982) have provided evidence that down-regulation of postsynaptic beta receptor sites does indeed begin a number of days after the antidepressant has already begun to decrease the number of presynaptic alpha receptors.

Serotonin Involvement Glassman (1969) proposed that the noradrenergic system might not be the only one involved in depression. The brain-stem reticular formation sends serotonergic fibers as well as noradrenergic fibers up into the hypothalamic-limbic regions, and Glassman noted that much of the data for the noradrenergic theory of depression also implicated serotonin. For example, MAO-inhibitors increase the supply of serotonin (a monoamine) in the same way that they increase NE levels; they prevent its enzymatic breakdown. Reserpine may induce depression because it depletes the supply of NE; however, it also depletes serotonin supplies and does so in the same way (McNeal & Cimbolic, 1986).

As more and more types of TADs were synthesized, it became evident that some antidepressants have more effect on the NE systems of the brain, whereas others have greater influence on serotonergic transmission. Feldman and Quenzer (1984) note that the "noradrenergic" antidepressants are better at increasing activity levels, whereas the "serotonergic" antidepressants are better at improving mood. Some therapists came to suspect that there were separate "serotonergic" and "noradrenergic depressions" (Mendels et al., 1975) and tried to treat their patients with drugs to match their symptoms. No conclusive evidence exists for this division (van Praag et al., 1987), but the interest has spurred the search for TADs that are more specific to serotonin or NE.

Van Praag and colleagues (1987) compared the degree of improvement in patients treated with tryptophan (the amino acid from which serotonin is made) with those treated with tyrosine (the amino acid precursor of NE). Tyrosine by itself had little influence on depressive symptoms or on brain NE levels. Tryptophan by itself had only a weak antidepressant effect. When the two precursors were combined, however, there was a measurable relief from symptoms accompanied by an increase in catecholamine levels in the brain. The suggestion is strong that at least some types of depression could involve both the adrenergic and serotonergic systems. One experiment shows how the two systems might interact. The brains of rats treated with a drug that increases serotonin transmission had fewer than normal beta adrenergic receptors (Byerley et al., 1987). Apparently, serotonin may control transmission at NE synapses.

Lithium and Electroconvulsive Therapy

The treatment of mood disorders involves more than antidepressant drugs. Patients with bipolar disorder are usually treated with the basic element **lithium** (usually in the form of lithium carbonate). Roughly 80 percent of manic patients respond to lithium treatment. Not only does the substance prevent the occurrence of manic episodes, but it also controls the depression of bipolar disorders. Typically, a bipolar patient not being treated with lithium can be expected to have about one episode of mania every 14 months and one depressive episode every 17 months. When taking lithium on a constant basis, however, the risk goes down to an average of one manic episode in 9 years and one depression in 4 years (Lickey & Gordon, 1983). Interestingly enough, lithium, like antidepressants, requires about 2 weeks of chronic treatment to achieve full effectiveness.

Lithium seems to interact in some way with calcium in the brain. It also enhances the reuptake of NE and, in one experiment, reduced the rate of release from vesicles (cited in Feldman & Quenzer, 1984). Calcium controls the release of transmitter from vesicles; so it may be that lithium inhibits calcium from doing this. It seems reasonable to assume that less NE transmission would help decrease arousal and that this might be the basis of lithium's therapeutic effect.

It would be convenient if we could explain the therapeutic effects of lithium on the basis of changes it produces in the NE system of the brain, but the evidence is not available. Studies in which lithium is given for several weeks show slight effects on NE or none at all (Sheard, 1980). Interpreting these studies is difficult, however, because the subjects were not only nonhuman (rats) but also nonmanic as well. If it is behavior that is to be measured rather than brain chemicals, then humans can be used as subjects, and such research has turned up at least one very interesting side note. A study of prisoners with a history of hostile, aggressive behavior showed that lithium significantly lowered the incidence of violent threats and assaults. This was a well-controlled experiment in which some of the prisoners were given the lithium while the rest were given a placebo and in which neither the subjects nor the physicians administering the substances knew which each prisoner was getting (Sheard, 1980).

Electroconvulsive therapy (ECT) is widely employed in the treatment of mood disorder, especially with the depressive disorder cases where it is most effective. Convulsive therapies date back to the turn of the century, but they found their first really widespread use in Budapest during the 1930s under Meduna in the treatment of schizophrenia. Meduna thought he noticed some improvement in schizophrenic patients who had had seizures and hypothesized that epilepsy and schizophrenia were mutually antagonistic. This led him to try convulsive therapy with his patients. Meduna used a drug called metrazol to produce the convulsions, but other therapists shifted to electrically produced convulsions that could be more carefully controlled. This became a very popular therapy and was tried out on just about every psychiatric symptom ever diagnosed. As objective data were gradually collected concerning the efficacy of convulsive therapy, it became clear that only a very select group of patients really showed any measurable benefit: those with mood disorder. At this time, ECT and TADs are probably the two most important methods of treating depression.

Over the years, the procedure for ECT has changed extensively. At its inception, the technique simply involved running a controlled current through electrodes attached to each side of the head. Such a current through the brain induces millions of brain cells to fire together in massive volleys—a condition known as **seizure**. Because many of those neurons are within the motor system, the seizure produced intense muscle spasms called **convulsions**. These convulsions could be strong enough to occasionally break bones, so physicians learned to employ a drug (usually succinylcholine) that would insulate the muscles from the effects of the seizure in the brain. Nowadays, patients are not only given a muscle relaxant but may also be anesthetized or sedated. Because the seizure lasts several seconds and breathing is interrupted during that time, oxygen has been added to the regimen in many clinics. Furthermore, the drug atropine is given to quiet the circulatory system's response, thus preventing severe changes in cardiac rate or blood pressure. What used to be simply an electric shock is now a carefully planned and coordinated form of therapy (Fink, 1980).

Many changes were tried in the hopes of achieving a greater therapeutic effect or of minimizing any discomfort the patient might have. Electric current

levels below the threshold for seizure (and thus convulsion) were tried but with no success. The seizure, rather than the electricity, is the therapeutic agent. In fact, there are many chemicals that cause seizures and work just as well as ECT. Drugs, however, always have side effects and in some cases the control of their main effect is more difficult. Incomplete seizures are ineffective, and longer seizures are more effective than short ones (Fink, 1980).

Even ECT has some side effects. Some patients complain of either headache, confusion, or memory loss (Crow & Johnstone, 1978). The memory loss is rather subtle, and most of it seems to dissipate with time. The effect is lessened with the administration of oxygen during therapy and the use of an electrode placement that produces a seizure in only one hemisphere.

A few patients actually die during ECT; the rate is 9 deaths in 100,000 treatments (Crow & Johnstone, 1978). If the use of ECT is reserved for patients with which it works best, however, their mortality rate is lowered. Severely depressed people are the ones who produce most of the suicides in our society, and ECT is the best known treatment when the risk of suicide is present. It can have its effect somewhat faster than drugs, and it has been shown to be more effective that either MAO-inhibitors or TADs (Scovern & Kilmann, 1980). In fact, a study in Iowa showed that mortality was lower in depressives who received ECT than in those who received low doses of antidepressants.

ECT shares one intriguing feature with antidepressant drugs and lithium therapy. One ECT treatment is no better at relieving depression than 1 day's worth of drugs. To be effective, ECT must be administered at least four times and occasionally as many as nine over a period of 6–14 days (Fink, 1980). Four to eight convulsions in 1 day are better than just one but do not relieve the depression. Apparently, each seizure produces a brain condition that lasts for hours or days, and if this brain state is continued for more than a week, a more or less permanent change is effected. The possibility that up- or down-regulation is taking place at various synapses comes immediately to mind, but as of yet, there are very few data. Friedhoff and Miller (1983) report that in one study, electroconvulsive shock did decrease the density, but not the sensitivity, of beta receptors. It remains a possibility that MAO-inhibitors, TADs, lithium, and ECT all have their major antidepressant effect at the same place—the NE synapse.

Alzheimer's Disease

It is not unusual for elderly people to begin to lose their memory and for sight and hearing to dim. We attribute these changes to an hypothetical process called senility. As a syndrome, **senility** includes memory loss, inability to reason, slow reaction time, poor motor control, and sensory loss. When medical researchers first began to attempt an explanation of senility, one obvious possibility was loss of brain cells. Up until the 1970s, physicians assumed that senility was brought about by a series of "mini-strokes" happening over many years. A stroke occurs when a cerebral blood vessel bursts or occludes (closing so that blood flow is stopped). Occlusion occurs as the result of "hardening" of the arteries, a syndrome in which the arterial walls expand into the inside cavity of the artery (thus narrowing it) and fill up with deposits of cholesterol, a fat. Although there is no doubt that many elderly people do suffer strokes that kill parts of their brains, it is doubtful that strokes can explain all cases of senility. Post-mortem studies on the brains of people who died in their 70s and 80s reveal no difference in the number of neurons between normal and senile cases (Terry & Davies, 1980).

Some of the changes seen in senility do occur to a lesser degree in normals, apparently as a part of the normal aging process. For example, there is a pervasive downward shift in the dominant frequencies of the EEG associated with aging (Spydell & Sheer, 1983), and slower EEG rhythms are generally interpreted to indicate lower levels of activation. For example, beta waves occupy a range of frequencies above 20 Hz and are associated with alertness and concentration. A young person might have an average beta frequency of 35 Hz, whereas a 70-year-old might average 20 Hz. Given that sort of change in the EEG, one would expect elderly people to show

slower reaction time and reasoning; those functions need higher activation levels. These lower activation levels might in part be the indirect result of cellular loss in sensory receptors. Sensory loss does occur normally in aging, probably because receptor cells in the cochlea, retinas, tongue, and so on simply wear out (Smith, 1984). But sensory input to the reticular formation is one of the prime sources of activation for the cortex. Thus, if sensory input is reduced, it is logical to expect reductions in functions dependent on activation, such as reasoning, concentration, and reaction time. Presumably, senility would be associated with extreme slowing of EEG frequencies because the degree of slowing exhibited by normal elderly people is not enough to significantly impair their ability to perform normal everyday tasks such as driving, working, and learning.

However, during the 1970s it gradually became clear to medical workers that about 50 percent of the cases diagnosed as **senile dementia** (loss of mental functions in old age) were not the victims of sensory loss or multiple strokes but suffered instead from a heretofore unsuspected disorder now called **Alzheimer's disease**. Although it rarely strikes before the age of 60, Alzheimer's disease is not equivalent to aging. The progress is faster in people who contract it earlier in life (i.e., before age 65) and slowest when it begins after age 70 (Goldsmith, 1984b). There is no cure for the disease; the prognosis is a slow decline (over 3–15 years) into total loss of mental function and death.

The Alzheimer's Syndrome

The onset of Alzheimer's disease is inconspicuous and difficult to distinguish from any number of other problems that beset humans. The person finds it increasingly difficult to concentrate. There is a tendency toward irritability, withdrawal, anxiety, and agitation. As the disease progresses, the mental losses, subtle at first, become obvious; there is an inability to make change, add and subtract, and guess the approximate time of day. There are lapses in judgment, depression, occasional delusions and temper tantrums, and difficulties with basics such as remembering how to dress. The final stages of the disease are marked by almost total amnesia, apathy, disorientation, and loss of concern about the opinion of others. Death is frequently from pneumonia, pulmonary problems, or some other disorder unrelated to the brain.

When a physician interviews a patient suspected of having Alzheimer's disease, a list of questions is frequently used to assess the level of disorientation. Typical are, Where are we now? What is today's date? Where were you born? Who is president? Relatives may be asked if the patient can travel alone; shop; cook; do housework; dress without help; take care of hair, teeth, washing self; and so forth.

A neurological examination may reveal a stooped posture and slow walk with no arm swing and hands held cupped at the sides. The patient usually takes small, mincing steps with the feet spread wide apart, perhaps to guard against falls. The electroencephalogram shows a general slowing of frequencies toward delta waves, but some frequencies are affected more than others. The greatest difference between normal controls and early-stage Alzheimer's patients is the significantly greater amount of theta wave (5–8 Hz) activity in the dementia cases (Coben et al., 1985; Penttilä et al., 1985). Spydell and Sheer (1983) also found that the upward shift in frequency into the 35–44-Hz band that normals make when they are working on a mental problem was mostly missing in Alzheimer's patients. This would suggest that they might have a very hard time focusing on the stimuli and memories relevant to dealing with the problem.

Bayles (1982) gives us samples of language production in the various stages of Alzheimer's disease. The following is from a patient in the early stages:

E: Tell me everything you can about this. (button)

S: It's a button, a large button with two little holes in it. (extended pause)

E: Can you tell me any more about it?

S: Well, not much. It's just two little holes in the button. I'd have to say it fast with two little holes in it.

In the advanced stages, the description of a button becomes unrecognizable:

Right yes, on a button, very pretty. Well a man, I used to when I uh, but nobody would hardly (*unintelligible word*) that. This has got a two things. Very much. This you mean that hold that back. Well it is a the first day of a child's doesn't carry it very good. An uh, but, as time goes on it becomes a very (*unintelligible word*). (Bayles, 1982)

Brain Alterations in Alzheimer's Disease

Postmortem examinations of brains from Alzheimer's patients reveal degeneration (cell loss) in the hippocampus (as well as other limbic structures). The cerebral cortex is also severely affected, mostly in the temporal, occipital, and parietal lobes (Corkin, 1981).

Most of the surviving nerve cells in the cortex appear to be normal, but some are filled with a dense thicket of strange filaments called a **neurofibrillary tangle**. The origin of these tangles is not fully understood, and no one has a good idea of what effect such an abnormality may have on function. Tangles are present in at least four other neurological diseases and may represent a standard cellular response to a variety of dysfunctions (Selkoe, 1989). A second symptom is the deterioration of dendrites, especially of those of the large output cells in the hippocampus and cortex. Fewer dendrites mean fewer available synapses—the points at which memories are apparently formed.

Squeezed in between the neurons and glial cells are grotesque, intrusive clusters of peculiar dendrite and axon tips all gathered around central clumps of abnormal protein called β-amyloid. The whole tangled mass is referred to as a **neuritic plaque** (Selkoe, 1989; Wisniewski & Iqbal, 1980). Neurofibrillary tangles are more prevalent in senile dementia, whereas neuritic plaques are more common in Alzheimer's disease, but so far there is no way to interpret the meaning of this difference.

The β-amyloid protein is a short strand of only 39 amino acids cleaved from a molecule called β-**amyloid precursor protein**. Another part of the precursor protein is a chemical that (theoretically) can inhibit the enzyme that cleaves out the β-amyloid. However, some of the RNA that codes for β-amyloid precursor protein fails to create the enzyme-inhibiting portion of the molecule, leaving the enzyme free to create β-amyloid. This type of RNA that lacks the inhibitor sequence is found in much greater abundance in the parts of the brain particularly relevant to Alzheimer's disease (Tanzi et al., 1989).

Alzheimer's disease may also involve a transmitter defect. Acetylcholine (Ach) is an important brain transmitter, and the enzyme responsible for its production, choline acetyltransferase (chAT), is present in abnormally small quantities in Alzheimer's disease (Corkin, 1981). The level of the patient's chAT (and therefore Ach) has been found to correlate with the severity of the behavioral symptoms and with the number of neuritic plaques (Terry & Davies, 1980). That is, the less chAT there is in the brain, the greater the behavioral deficit and the more plaques there are. Ach deficiency arises from a loss of cholinergic cells in the medial septal nucleus and in a small adjacent region at the ventromedial boundary of the globus pallidus called the **nucleus basalis of Meynert** (Allen et al., 1988). Nucleus basalis neurons project to the entire cerebral cortex as part of an arousal system involved in attention and memory (Richardson & DeLong, 1988).

Current attempts at drug therapy for Alzheimer's patients center around drugs that can increase cholinergic transmission to compensate for the cell loss in nucleus basalis. The use of cholinergic agonists (substances that mimic Ach) has met with little therapeutic success, probably because the agonists bind with both the postsynaptic Ach receptors and with Ach presynaptic receptors that reduce the release of Ach (Sarter et al., 1988). Activation of postsynaptics produces the desired increase in cholinergic transmission that would probably reduce Alzheimer's symptoms if the increase weren't canceled out by the activation of presynaptics that produce a loss of cholinergic transmission. A more promising set of drugs are those that prevent GABAergic inhibition of Ach release in the cortex, but not enough data are yet available to judge their worth (Sarter et al., 1988).

Alzheimer's Disease and Heredity

There appears to be a genetic factor that predisposes an individual to the disease under the proper environmental conditions. The disease seems to some-

times cluster in families and, in those selected cases, has been judged to be a dominant trait (Tanzi et al., 1989). In some families, there are records across six generations showing that in each generation, 50 percent of the children of an Alzheimer's patient went on to develop Alzheimer's disease themselves (Goldsmith, 1984a). It should be noted, however, that such a genetic relationship is not found in all cases of Alzheimer's disease. It is quite possible that the syndrome may have many different causes so that different patients may have arrived at the same symptoms through different routes.

There is an interesting resemblance between Alzheimer's disease and **Down syndrome**, a congenital brain disorder characterized by mental retardation. At about age 30 or 40, Down syndrome patients develop neuritic plaques embedded with β-amyloid and probably show indications of Alzheimer-like dementia (although this is difficult to test in these patients) (Marx, 1989). One of the abnormalities of Down syndrome is the presence of an extra copy of chromosome 21, and it is on this chromosome that the gene for the β-amyloid precursor protein is found. Does dementia occur when too much β-amyloid is manufactured because of an extra copy of this gene? Disappointingly, three separate studies showed that Alzheimer's patients do not have an extra copy of this gene (Tanzi et al., 1989). A suspected "Alzheimer gene" does occur on chromosome 21, but it is definitely not located in the same region as the β-amyloid precursor protein gene that is apparently involved in Down syndrome (Marx, 1987). Although β-amyloid is definitely involved in Alzheimer's disease, we still do not know whether it is a cause or an effect.

Research on Alzheimer's disease is increasing in the U.S. but there is some question about whether the knowledge can be generated in time to prevent a health catastrophe. At this time, about 5 percent of Americans over age 64 are severely demented, and this adds up to over 1 million people (Terry & Davies, 1980). Some 60,000 younger people in their 40s and 50s are also affected (Goldsmith, 1984a). In another 40 years, there will be over 58 million Americans in the age group of 65-and-over. Unless something can be done to stop it, the result will be 3–4 million cases of Alzheimer's disease.

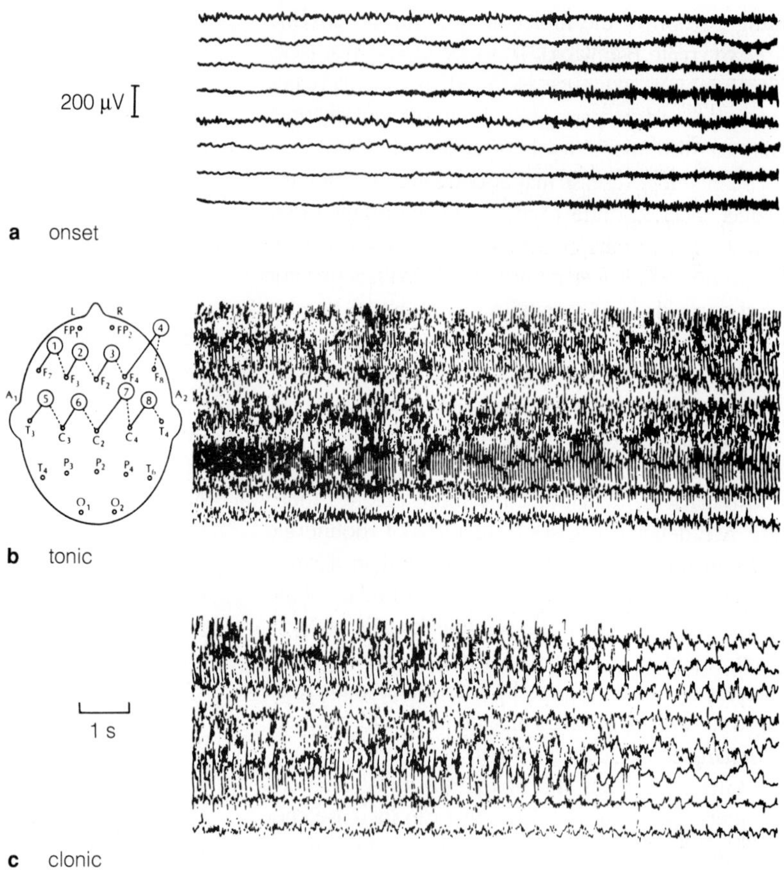

Figure 17.10 An EEG record of a grand mal seizure. Placement of the electrodes is shown on the view of the head at left. Eight channels of encephalogram are displayed, each record showing the voltage changes between the pair of electrodes indicated on the head diagram. Each of the three segments of record (**a–c**) is about 12 seconds long. (**a**) The seizure begins; (**b**) is taken from the tonic stage; (**c**) is from the clonic stage. (From Pincus & Tucker, 1978)

200 μV

a onset

b tonic

1 s

c clonic

Epilepsy

About 2 million people in the United States suffer from epilepsy, and none can be cured of it. Epilepsy is not a disease; it is a collection of different brain dysfunction symptoms all involving *seizure* activity. A seizure is a brain state involving the organization of massive numbers of neurons into patterns of abnormal activity. The abnormality of these patterns can be readily seen in an EEG record. The most outstanding feature of seizure activity is hypersynchrony, which shows up on the EEG as very large, slow waves.

Hypersynchrony (*hyper-*, too much; *-syn-*, together; *-chron*, time) refers to a condition in which there is too much simultaneous facilitation. There

are too many EPSPs occurring together at the same time. Figure 17.10 shows the EEG evidence of the drastic reorganization occurring in the brain as an epileptic seizure begins. The high-amplitude waves in the seizure imply that literally millions of neurons are firing together in gigantic volleys. This activity resembles the sort one finds in some forms of coma. Thus, it is not surprising that such waves are usually accompanied by total loss of consciousness. The small, fast activity of the normal waking brain probably indicates the firing of relatively small assemblies of neurons, each of which represents a particular thought or perception. The huge waves of a seizure suggest that neurons that would normally participate in patterns of activity underlying thoughts or percepts are being forced to fire in giant groups that

Table 17.2 Standard Classification of Seizures

I. Partial Seizures

    A. Simple partial seizures (focal, no impairment of consciousness)
        1. With motor symptoms
        2. With sensory symptoms
    B. Complex partial seizures (consciousness impaired)
        1. With delayed loss of consciousness, automatisms
        2. With immediate unconsciousness, automatisms

II. Generalized seizures

    A. Absence attacks (petit mal)
    B. Tonic
    C. Atonic
    D. Tonic-clonic (grand mal)

represent nothing at all, that convey no meaning because they are assembled by some defective internal process rather than by meaningful external or internal events. In other words, seizure waves contain no information; they are nonsense events and are therefore unable to produce a conscious state.

Types of Epilepsy

We noted above that epilepsy is a collection of various dysfunctions all involving seizures. Table 17.2 lists the major varieties. Once a seizure begins, it tends to spread outward from its point of origin (the **epileptic focus**), and some seizures spread throughout the entire neocortex as well as into parts of the old (limbic) cortex. Epileptic activity is never found in the cerebellum or brain stem. **Generalized seizures** are those that include the entire cortex, whereas **partial seizures** are localized to a particular area such as the temporal lobes.

When the term *epilepsy* comes up in everyday conversation, the image it evokes for most people is that of one type of generalized seizure, the tonic-clonic, or **grand mal** (GRAWN MAHL). This type (pictured in Figure 17.10) strongly invades the motor areas and produces patterns of muscular contraction called **convulsions**. A grand mal seizure begins with a conscious experience called an **aura**, which may simply be a vague feeling of things not being right

or it may be a specific sensory experience. One patient's seizures always began with a visual hallucination of himself throwing a stick to his dog. The aura lasts only for a few seconds and is followed by loss of consciousness as the convulsions begin. In the first, or tonic, phase of the convulsion, extreme muscle tone is induced in the entire striate muscle system. With flexors pulling against extensors, the person goes completely rigid and breathing stops. (The circuits that move the muscles of the diaphragm to produce breathing are in the unaffected brain stem but, thanks to the need for diaphragmatic control during speech, the cortex also controls the same muscles. Thus, the epileptic storm in the cortex can stop respiration.) After a moment of extreme rigidity, the flexors and extensors get out of phase with one another so that the convulsions become an alternation of the two. In this clonic phase, the arms and legs alternately flex and extend with gradually lessening intensity as the seizure slowly loses intensity and dies away. As the cortex releases its control over the diaphragm, breathing is restored. Consciousness is regained, but the person is quite sluggish and confused.

If you happen to be a bystander when someone falls into convulsions, it is important for you to act swiftly to help the person get to the floor without sustaining head injury. The greatest danger in a grand mal seizure is that the person will fall against a hard

Figure 17.11 An EEG record of petit mal (absence) seizure. This type of seizure is characterized by a record showing a series of fast, sharp "spike" waves alternating with slow, rolling "dome" waves. In this particular record, the spike is seen on the falling side of each dome. These waves appear much slower than those of the grand mal seizure in Figure 17.10 partly because this record was made at a faster speed, which stretched out the voltage fluctuations across the paper. (From Pincus & Tucker, 1978)

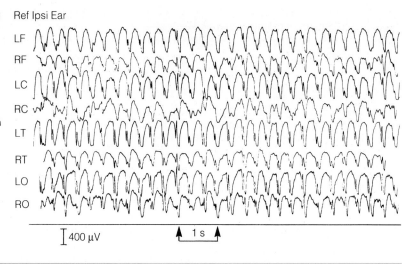

Ref Ipsi Ear

LF
RF
LC
RC
LT
RT
LO
RO

400 µV   1 s

object. Once the person is in a relatively safe position on the floor, all you need do is to cushion the head against contact with the floor. Do not try to place an object in the mouth to "prevent the tongue from being swallowed," as was advised by some people in the past. Don't expect the person to be able to answer questions readily during the period of confusion after the seizure. If it is a first seizure, then the person should visit a physician and find out if the seizure indicates some more serious condition. If the person is already being treated for epilepsy, then all that is usually needed is to help the person get to where she can rest for a few hours. The occurrence of a seizure is usually a medical emergency only when the first one is immediately followed by another.

Some generalized seizures are not as severe as the grand mal and exhibit only half of the tonic-clonic combination. In **tonic seizures**, the convulsion is limited to a sudden stiffening of all muscles, frequently accompanied by impairment of consciousness. **Atonic seizures** seem to involve a loss of all muscle tone, especially in the "antigravity" muscles of the back and legs that hold a person upright. The result of the seizure is a fall to the floor with no effect on consciousness.

The French term, *grand mal*, means *big sickness*,

and *petit mal* (PETTY MAHL) denotes *little sickness*. **Absence attacks** (petit mal) involve only a loss of awareness and last for about 10 seconds. They are extremely rare in anyone over the age of 15 and are far more frequent in children than in teenagers. Petit mal seizures do not leave the conscious mind clouded and depressed as do grand mal; thus, recovery is almost instantaneous. As the seizure starts, the person stops whatever he was doing and simply stares into space, blinking now and then, and not responding to any stimulus. In a classroom setting, this behavior in a child not yet diagnosed is frequently mistaken for simple inattentiveness. The child might possibly guess from the discontinuities in his perception (i.e., the teacher sitting at the desk one moment and standing at the board the next) that he has suffered a lapse of consciousness, but such an insight is really too much to expect at that age. More likely, he will not have any idea that anything is wrong. The EEG in a petit mal seizure is quite distinctive, each wave consisting of a large, slow "dome" with sharp spike added (Figure 17.11).

Unlike the generalized seizure types we have just reviewed, partial seizures (see Table 17.2) tend to affect only one portion of the cerebrum. In the past, these types have often been grouped under the heading of "psychomotor" seizures or have been termed "temporal lobe seizures" because so many of them have their focus in the limbic structures of the medial temporal lobes. There are two major differences between the **simple** and **complex partial seizures**. First, automatic behavior sequences occur in the complex types but not in the simple. Second, impairment of consciousness occurs only in the complex type (Theodore, 1985). During a simple partial seizure, the person may either experience sensory symptoms (such as auditory distortions, shrinking vision, taste hallucinations, or severe abdominal pain) or motor symptoms (paralysis or twitching in one or more limbs on one side of the body), and there is no loss of consciousness.

In the complex partial seizures, consciousness is affected without being entirely lost. The result is a peculiar, semiconscious condition in which the person responds only to those external stimuli that fit into the automatic behavior that is being executed. Typical automatisms are fumbling with buttons, picking at clothing, lip smacking, chewing, assuming some bizarre posture, or repeating a phrase over and over. The patient makes no response to other people even when her own name is called, yet some sensory input is obviously used (such as somatosensory stimuli, which guide the fingers in buttoning or unbuttoning clothes). In rare cases, this dissociation of the conscious state is so extreme that the person experiences a **fugue state**—a condition involving travel to a different location in a trancelike state with amnesia for the episode after the seizure ends. This may simply mean that the person gets up and walks out of the room, with no later memory for having done so, or it may involve a half-hour drive in a car. Very rarely (perhaps when the seizure hyperstimulates the amygdala), the automatic behavior is aggressive in nature and can have tragic consequences. One such case has been described in detail:

In Julia's case, the relationship between brain disease and violent behavior was very clear. Her history of brain disease went back to the time when, before the age of 2, she had a severe attack of encephalitis following mumps. When she was 10, she began to have epileptic seizures; occasionally these attacks were grand mal seizures. Most of the time, they consisted of brief lapses of consciousness, staring, lip smacking, and chewing. Often after such a seizure she would be overcome by panic and run off as fast as she could without caring about destination. Her behavior between seizures was marked by severe temper tantrums followed by extreme remorse. Four of these depressions ended in serious suicide attempts. The daughter of a professional man, she was an attractive, pleasant, cherubic blonde who looked much younger than her age of 21.

On twelve occasions, Julia had seriously assaulted other people without any apparent provocation. By far the most serious attack had occurred when she was 18. She was at a movie with her parents when she felt a wave of terror pass over her body. She told her father that she was going to have another one of her "racing spells" and agreed to wait for her parents in the ladies' lounge. As she went to it, she automatically took a small knife out of her hand bag. She had gotten into the habit of carrying this knife for protection because her "racing spells" often took her into dangerous neighborhoods where she would come out of her fuguelike state to find herself helpless, alone, and confused. When she got to the lounge, she looked in the mirror and perceived the left side of her face and trunk (including the left arm) as shriveled, disfigured, and "evil." At the same time, she noticed a drawing sensation in her face and hands. Just then another girl entered the lounge and inadvertently bumped against Julia's left arm and hand. Julia, in a panic, struck quickly with her knife, penetrating the other girl's heart, and then screamed loudly. Fortunately, help arrived in time to save the life of her victim.

The next serious attack occurred inside the mental hospital to which Julia had been sent. Julia's nurse was writing a report and when Julia said "I feel another spell coming on, please help me," the nurse replied, "I'll be with you in just a minute." Julia dragged a pair of scissors out of the nurse's pocket and drove the point into the unfortunate woman's lungs. Luckily, the nurse recovered. (Mark & Ervin, 1970)

To locate the focus of Julia's seizures, electrodes were implanted deep within several brain regions, and EEG recordings made. These indicated abnormal activity within both amygdalas. (Recall from the chapter on emotion that the amygdala is more heavily involved than any other brain region in the regulation of aggressive behavior.) The electrodes were then used to make lesions in both amygdalas in hopes of burning out the damaged tissue that was generating the seizures. Julia's seizure frequency was reduced during the next year, and in the second year after surgery, she had no seizures at all (Mark & Ervin, 1970).

Do Seizures Promote Further Seizures?

The possibility exists that seizure sensitivity may be increased through a process strongly resembling the physiological events underlying learning. If you implant electrodes in the amygdala of a rat and then stimulate at a low intensity for a few seconds each day, there will be no behavioral sign that the stimulation is having any effect until the second week of daily sessions. Then, seizure activity will begin to appear on the EEG, and as the days pass, what begins as a small, focal seizure will grow to a full-blown, generalized seizure with clonic convulsions (Goddard et al., 1969). This phenomenon is termed **kindling** and has been studied extensively since its discovery by Goddard in 1969.

Although there are many regions of the neocortex and limbic system that can be stimulated to evoke kindling, the area that seems most sensitive is the amygdala. This may be because of the possibility that the hippocampus plays a central role in the development of the kindled seizure activity and the fact that the amygdala has such strong inputs to the hippocampus. Neurophysiologists interested in synaptic events responsible for learning and memory development have discovered a phenomenon within the hippocampus that seems to be related to kindling. If you implant an electrode in one of the tracts leading into the hippocampus and then stimulate with a brief train of electrical pulses, some change occurs that sensitizes the hippocampal synapses. This increase in sensitivity is called **long-term potentiation (LTP)** because it lingers for hours after the brief stimulus that instigated it. This sort of enhanced transmission at specific synapses is exactly what theory predicts should be the basis of memory; thus, LTP is widely regarded as a brain change that is probably the basis for some forms of learning (Abraham & Goddard, 1984). LTP lasts long enough in most cases (i.e., 24 hours) that it could serve as at least

part of the explanation of kindling (Goddard, 1983). In this interpretation, the daily stimulation sessions that produce the kindling would trigger LTP that accumulates from day to day until some synapses have been strengthened past the normal level. Seizure activity would be the result. Thus, in epilepsy a seizure might provide an input to the hippocampus that is similar to the train of pulses that the experimenter uses. If so, then each seizure would produce LTP and kindling. In this way, a series of seizures would drive the brain deeper and deeper into epilepsy, making it more and more seizure-prone.

Causes of Epilepsy

We know that epilepsy that begins in adulthood often follows brain injury resulting from automobile accidents, drug use, or infection. However, when the onset of epilepsy occurs between the ages of 2 and 20, a genetic predisposition usually plays a part (Pincus & Tucker, 1978). The occurrences of seizures before 6 months of age can usually be traced to brain injury incurred during or just prior to birth. During birth, the oxygen supply to all or part of the brain can be cut off either through strangulation when the umbilical cord wraps around the neck or through injury to blood vessels that occurs when the infant's head is squeezed through the narrow birth canal. One of the most common *apparent* causes of seizures that appear during the first year of life is hypoxia (oxygen deprivation) from interruption of circulation during birth (Holmes & Weber, 1985). Recent research, however, has indicated that it may be the loss of blood supply to the brain (ischemia) rather than hypoxia that does the damage (Moshé & Albala, 1985).

The real key to understanding epilepsy, however, lies in discovering how the primary causes (accidents, infections, anoxia, etc.) alter brain function in such a way as to produce seizures. We refer to these seizure-producing brain alterations as the **neuropathological factors** underlying epilepsy. (The term *pathology* refers to disease processes or knowledge about disease; so neuropathology refers to nervous system disease.) In the search for the neuropathology of epilepsy one thing becomes immediately apparent. Two factors must be present to cause a seizure: some form of brain damage brought about by the primary cause plus some type of **triggering process** that actually starts the seizure. If the neuropathological defects could cause a seizure all by themselves, the brain would lapse into a seizure state and stay there until death. So the entire causal sequence must look like this:

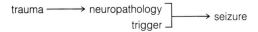

The real heart of current research efforts on epilepsy then is directed at discovering the neuropathological factors and as many of the triggering factors as possible. Keep in mind that epilepsy is just a symptom, not a disease, and that means that there may be dozens of different neuropathological conditions and hundreds of different trigger conditions that can produce seizures. We can anticipate, at the very least, a half-century of epilepsy research before we can say that we have a reasonably complete knowledge of its causes.

The Epileptic Focus and Paroxysmal Depolarization Shift

One of the most important tools in the research on seizure neuropathology is the use of penicillin to produce artificial epilepsy in animals. In this procedure, a portion of the skull is removed and the cortex revealed. A small, open-bottomed cup is set on the cortex and filled with a solution of the antibiotic. The result is the development of an epileptic focus in the area contacted by the penicillin. Cells in this focus produce the same sort of EEG waves seen in natural seizures; so, in some way, the drug has apparently damaged the brain in a mimicry of an accident or infection. If microelectrodes are inserted into cells within the focus to record what each individual neuron does during a seizure, a huge shift in membrane potential is found, and this shift is toward depolarization. Riding on top of this potential (which strongly resembles a giant EPSP) is a train of nerve impulses, which it has triggered. Because the depolarization induces a paroxysm of firing in the neuron, the phenomenon has been termed a **paroxysmal depolarization shift (PDS)**.

Some understanding of the PDS might come from reports that cells within the epileptic focus have been stripped of their GABA end bulbs (Ribak et al., 1982). Neurons using **GABA** as their transmitter constitute one of the most important inhibitory systems in the cortex. This suggests that a major loss of inhibition underlies epilepsy. If we try to deliberately deprive the cortex of inhibition by giving rats daily injections of a drug that blocks GABA, no effect is seen until about the fifth day, and on that day convulsions are triggered by the drug. This clearly seems to be a drug-induced kindling effect involving loss of inhibition (Nutt et al., 1982).

To summarize then, some research suggests that the neuropathological result of the initial brain damage may be some sort of malfunction in the GABA-inhibitory system in the cortex, which allows neurons to become hyperactive. Although this hyperactivity in the affected cells may not be sufficient to overwhelm the normal functioning of the remaining neurons to begin with, the defect probably grows larger each time there is a PDS because of the kindling process.

Triggering a Seizure As was noted earlier, neuropathology alone is not sufficient to produce a seizure; it must be supplemented by some sort of trigger event. Table 17.3 shows how diverse such triggers can be. Two of them, hyperventilation and visual stimuli, are frequently used in an attempt to deliberately elicit a seizure in a patient suspected of having epilepsy. An EEG record of a seizure not only confirms the diagnosis of epilepsy but also can help categorize the type involved. Hyperventilation refers to overbreathing. A minute or so of rapid, shallow breathing lowers the level of carbon dioxide and raises the level of oxygen in the blood to a point where both gasses are outside normal limits. Severe hyperventilation tends to promote convulsions even in nonepileptic individuals.

Flashing lights (like those in a disco club) should be avoided by anyone who is seizure-prone. A frequency of about 15–18 flashes per second is the most likely to elicit a seizure, probably because the flashes trigger firing in the visual cortex at a rate very favorable to the development of synchrony (Binnie et al., 1985). The frequency sensitivity of the visual system to hypersynchrony seems to be greater than for any other part of the brain, and minor seizures can be

Table 17.3 Causes of Epilepsy		
Source of Defect	Possible Neuropathology	Triggers*
Genetic factor	Potassium and/or calcium imbalance	Hyperventilation
Perinatal hypoxia and ischemia		Sleep
	Loss of activity in inhibitory systems (especially, GABA)	Sleep deprivation
Brain infections (meningitis, encephalitis)		Sensory stimuli (flashing lights, sound, touch, pain)
	Kindling	
Mechanical brain injury (accidents, wounds, etc.)		Injury
		Hormonal changes (menses, puberty, etc.)
		Fever
		Emotional stress
		Drugs (antihistamines, alcohol, etc.)

*This column was modified from Pincus and Tucker, 1978, p. 5.

elicited with flashing lights even in subjects who have never had a seizure (Scott & Elian, 1980). I have succeeded in producing convulsions in a squirrel monkey with no history of convulsions simply by electrically stimulating the visual cortex from implanted electrodes for about 2 minutes at a rate of around 10 pulses per second. In some cases of epilepsy, the person is so sensitive to alternations of light and dark on the retina that merely blinking the eyes for a minute brings on a seizure (Darby et al., 1980). There has been one case reported in which all the patient had to do to elicit a seizure was to scan across the alternating light and dark squares of a chess board (Kogeorgos et al., 1980).

Treatment of Epilepsy

In most cases of epilepsy, the seizures can be controlled reasonably well with appropriate drugs in the correct doses. For years, the drug of choice was **phenytoin** (trade name, Dilantin), and this is still used as second choice for grand mal and some types of partial seizure. The first choice has shifted to **car-**bamazepine** for grand mal and **ethosuximide** for petit mal (Theodore, 1985). When drugs fail, surgery may be attempted if brain scans indicate an area of damage that might be providing an epileptic focus. The strategy of the surgery is to remove the entire focus of damaged cells with minimal disturbance to the surrounding healthy tissue; the usual procedure is to spend an hour or so electrically stimulating the region in and around the focus with the patient awake and reporting on the effects. In this way, language areas, for example, can be located, with the intent of sparing as much of them as possible. In cases in which synchrony builds up through a process of back-and-forth stimulation between the hemispheres, some portion of the corpus callosum is cut to prevent the seizure spread, but this is rare. At the present time, and for decades to come, the best method we possess for handling epilepsy as a medical problem is to prevent its occurrence. Decreasing the incidence of prenatal and infantile diseases, brain damage during birth, automobile accidents, and brain infections is a strategy well within our grasp. There are no drugs or any form of surgery that can replace brain tissue once it has been lost.

Summary

1. Psychosis is a condition characterized by strange and socially unacceptable behavior, inappropriate or extreme moods, disordered thought, and, sometimes, hallucinations and delusions. The varieties of psychoses known as organic mental disorders clearly stem from brain damage or malfunction. The causes of the remaining psychoses, schizophrenia and mood disorder, are unknown.

2. Schizophrenia is a complex syndrome in which the patient may show some or all of the following symptoms: social withdrawal, hallucinations, delusions, catatonia, thought disorder, and flattened affect.

3. Studies of monozygotic twins strongly suggest the presence of a genetic factor in schizophrenia, but probably only as one of several causes, all of which have to act together to bring about the disease. The vulnerability model proposes that environmental stress must interact with a genetic predisposition in order for the brain disorder to develop and that the chances that schizophrenia will actually occur are increased or decreased by other moderating factors.

4. Examinations of schizophrenic patients rarely reveal the presence of hard signs, but soft signs such as tremor, right-left disorientation, and difficulty with balance are quite prevalent. Autopsies of schizophrenic brains frequently reveal atrophy of the cerebral cortex. Many schizophrenics have abnormally low frontal lobe blood flow and metabolism (revealed by PET scans). CT scans show enlarged lateral ventricles in the frontal regions, indicating a loss of brain tissue from the frontal lobes.

5. Crow has proposed that there are two forms of schizophrenia. Type I schizophrenics display symptoms like hallucinations, delusions, and thought disorder. Their ,CBF and CT scans are normal, their response to antipsychotic medication is good, and their prognosis is good. Type II schizophrenics show emotional flattening, poverty of speech and movement, and loss of drive. Intellectual impairment is often present. CT scans and blood flow records show frontal lobe atrophy and hypofrontality. The response to drugs is poor, as is the prognosis for recovery. Crow suggests that type I is the result of a problem in the dopamine systems of the brain, whereas type II is the product of neuronal loss, especially in the frontal lobes.

6. The continuous performance test (CPT) shows that schizophrenics have trouble maintaining attention. Other measures indicate that schizophrenics suffer from chronically high levels of arousal. The Yerkes–Dodson law predicts that both excessive and insufficient arousal have a negative effect on attention; hyperarousal in the posterior regions of the cortex and hypoarousal in the frontal cortex are probably together responsible for the attention deficit.

7. A part of the brain likely to be malfunctioning in both types of schizophrenia is the mesolimbic system which has cell bodies in the ventrotegmental area (VTA) and sends axons via the MFB to terminate in the limbic striatum (septal area and nucleus accumbens) and prefrontal cortex.

8. The amphetamines are a class of drugs whose major effect is arousal induced by increasing the levels of catecholamines, including dopamine (DA). The fact that prolonged use leads to a paranoid form of emotional disorder resembling schizophrenia suggests that it may be excessive DA that causes schizophrenia.

9. The dopamine theory holds that schizophrenia is the result of excessive DA transmission at the terminals of the VTA neurons in limbic structures like the nucleus accumbens. That antipsychotic drugs block DA receptor sites, thus limiting dopaminergic transmission, supports the theory. The excessive transmission results from an overabundance of DA receptors.

10. A major problem with the DA theory is that antipsychotic drugs take about 2 weeks to significantly reduce schizophrenic symptomatology, but their receptor-blocking action begins almost immediately.

11. There are two categories of mood disorder: depressive disorders and bipolar disorders. The patient with a depressive disorder varies from normal mood to deep depression in which there is a total loss of interest in people or events, together with disturbance of sleep, appetite, and sex drive. The bipolar disorder patient alternates between periods of depression and hyperactivation (mania), in which the person is overactive, irritable, expansive, and overtalkative.

12. Mood disorders seem to run in families. In studies of patients who were adopted children, it was found that inheritance was a more important determinant than family environment and rearing. However, the nature of the genetic factor has been very difficult to isolate, and no clear understanding of its nature has emerged.

13. The catecholamine theory holds that the cause of depression is a shortage of norepinephrine (NE) in the brain. Drugs that increase NE levels by inhibiting monoamine oxidase (MAO) act as antidepressants. The catecholamine theory is also supported by the fact that tricyclic antidepressant drugs (TADs) block reuptake of NE. Thus, TADs may compensate for an inadequate release of NE from the terminals by holding the transmitter in the synaptic gap longer, allowing it more chance to have its effect.

14. The catecholamine theory has a number of problems, the most important of which is that TADs begin blocking reuptake almost immediately yet must be taken steadily for 1 or 2 weeks before the depression is relieved.

15. The problem of the 2-week delay in the therapeutic effect of TADs might depend on their effects on autoreceptors. NE release at the synapse is governed by alpha and beta autoreceptors located on the presynaptic membrane. Beta sites are hooked to a feedback system within the terminal that increases release of the transmitter, whereas alphas inhibit release. One hypothesis to explain depression holds that the defect is one of hyperactivity (too many receptors) in the alpha system—the effect of which is to shut off NE release prematurely, thus depriving the postsynaptic neuron of enough transmitter. TADs apparently inhibit this alpha autoreceptor system (probably by down-regulating alpha receptors) and bring about an increase in NE release. The reason that 2 weeks are required for a therapeutic effect is that every increase in NE release provides a greater stimulus to the alpha inhibitory system, which works to decrease the amount of transmitter released per impulse. It is equivalent to taking three steps forward and two backward.

16. Antidepressant therapy also induces a decrease (down-regulation) in postsynaptic beta receptors, which could be interpreted as a return to normal.

Prior to therapy, the postsynaptic cell would have up-regulated to compensate for the shortage of NE.

17. Serotonergic neurons may also be involved in depression.

18. Antidepressant drugs are not the only means of treating mood disorders. Lithium is effective against mania and electroconvulsive therapy (ECT) is the fastest way of relieving depression. Because of its speed, it is the therapy of choice against depression with strong suicidal tendencies. ECT has not been shown to be effective against schizophrenia or any other mental disorder.

19. Some cases of senile dementia (loss of mental functions in old age) are apparently due to loss of neurons from strokes and loss of cells in the receptor organs, but about 50 percent of these cases are instead a product of a brain disease called Alzheimer's disease.

20. Alzheimer's disease symptoms include irritability, withdrawal, and agitation (in the early stages); temporal disorientation, depression, and delusions (in the middle stages); and total amnesia, apathy, disorientation, and lack of concern (in the final stage).

21. The brains of Alzheimer's patients reveal extensive neuropathology in the hippocampus and temporal, parietal, and occipital lobes. Neurons are frequently filled with neurofibrillary tangles and are interspersed with neuritic plaques, composed in part of an abnormal protein called β-amyloid.

22. Some of the memory loss and attention problem in Alzheimer's disease is probably due to the loss of cholinergic neurons in the nucleus basalis of Meynert, a structure located just below the globus pallidus. These cells serve to arouse the cerebral cortex. Drug therapy is aimed at amplifying cholinergic transmission from the remaining basalis neurons.

23. Epilepsy is a collection of different brain dysfunction symptoms all involving seizure activity in the brain. A seizure is a condition in which neurons become organized into abnormal patterns of activity, the most outstanding of which is hypersynchrony. In EEG recordings, hypersynchrony is revealed by very large, slow waves.

24. Generalized seizures are those that include the entire cortex, whereas partial seizures are localized

to a particular area such as the temporal lobes. Tonic-clonic seizures (grand mal) are generalized with loss of consciousness. Through their involvement of the motor areas, they produce convulsions. Atonic seizures produce a loss of muscle tone but no loss of consciousness. Absence attacks (petit mal seizures) involve a loss of consciousness (for a few seconds) with no convulsions or automatic behaviors.

25. Among the partial seizures are those of the temporal lobe, "psychomotor" variety that involve automatic behavior sequences or paralysis or sensory symptoms such as distortions and hallucinations. Complex partial seizures may produce a dissociative state called fugue, in which the person is only partially conscious and flees his normal surroundings.

26. Brief, daily periods of electrical stimulation in certain brain areas will gradually lower the threshold for seizure in a normal animal, a phenomenon called kindling. This increase in epileptic tendency may be based on a synaptic change termed long-term potentiation (LTP).

27. Although there may be a genetic factor that increases the likelihood of developing epilepsy, equally important is the occurrence of some form of brain damage. This trauma leaves the brain with a type of neuropathology that makes it susceptible to seizures when a triggering stimulus occurs. Rapid, deep breathing and flashing lights are common triggers.

28. Penicillin applied directly to the surface of the brain is used to produce an experimental type of epilepsy in which the cells in the epileptic focus suffer paroxysmal depolarization shift (PDS). This depolarization induces a paroxysm of firing in the neuron as long as it lasts. The cortex seems to acquire a tendency for PDSs by losing many of the inhibitory GABA terminals that normally prevent hyperactivity in cortical neurons.

29. Epilepsy is treated with drugs like phenytoin or carbamazepine. If these fail to control the seizures, surgery may be used in an attempt to remove the diseased neural tissue in which the seizures start.

Glossary

absence attacks Seizures that involve only a loss of awareness; also called petit mal epilepsy. (680)

alpha presynaptic receptors Autoreceptors that inhibit transmitter release at catecholaminergic synapses. (670)

Alzheimer's disease A brain disease that produces symptoms of senility. (675)

amphetamines A class of drugs whose major effect is arousal. (663)

antipsychotic drugs Those that are used to treat schizophrenia. (666)

atonic seizures Those that involve a loss of all muscle tone, especially in the "antigravity" muscles. (680)

atrophy A condition in which the tissue has shrunk from loss of cells. (654)

aura A brief sensory experience that immediately precedes a grand mal seizure. (679)

autoreceptors Receptors in the presynaptic membrane that bind the terminal's own transmitter. (670)

β-amyloid An abnormal type of protein frequently seen in the brains of Alzheimer's patients. (676)

β-amyloid precursor protein The molecule from which β-amyloid is created. (676)

bipolar disorder A form of mood disorder in which mood may swing from normal to depressed and back or from mania to depression. (668)

carbamazepine A drug used to control grand mal (tonic–clonic) seizures. (684)

catatonia Remaining immobile and uncommunicative for hours, usually in some peculiar posture. (652)

chlorpromazine The first of the phenothiazines to be developed. (666)

complex partial seizures Seizures that impair consciousness but, unlike generalized seizures, do not involve the entire cortex. (681)

continuous performance test (CPT) A situation in which the subject must monitor a series of stimuli for periods up to 20 minutes and must be scored for those he or she fails to report and for any he or she reports incorrectly. (658)

convulsions Muscle spasms produced by a seizure. (674, 679)

delusions Incorrect beliefs frequently involving feelings of persecution, sometimes of grandeur. (652)

depressive disorder A form of mood disorder characterized by periods of abnormally low activation in which there is a loss of all interest and pleasure. (667)

dizygotic twins Twins derived from two different zygotes. (653)

down-regulation The decrease in receptor density during times when transmitter is abundant. (671)

Down syndrome A congenital brain disorder characterized by mental retardation. (677)

electroconvulsive therapy (ECT) The widely employed treatment for mood disorder that involves passing an electric current through the head. (673)

epileptic focus The small area of brain in which a seizure starts. (679)

ethosuximide A drug used to control absence attacks (petit mal epilepsy). (684)

flattened affect Loss of emotional responses. (652)

fugue state An epileptic condition involving travel to a different location in a trancelike seizure state with amnesia for the episode. (681)

GABA An inhibitory neurotransmitter that may be depleted in an area of the brain subject to seizures. (683)

generalized seizures Those that include the entire cortex. (679)

genetic factor One of the two causal factors in a vulnerability theory of schizophrenia or mood disorder. (653)

grand mal seizure A seizure that produces tonic–clonic convulsions. (679)

grief reactions A temporary depression that is a normal reaction to distressing life events such as death of a spouse or loss of employment. (667)

hallucination A perceptual experience for which there is no stimulus. (652)

hypersynchrony A condition in which an abnormal number of impulses and EPSPs occur simultaneously in large waves. (678)

hypofrontality The lower-than-normal rate of blood flow often seen in schizophrenia. (655)

insanity A legal term for people who are mentally and emotionally incapable of being held responsible for their actions. (651)

kindling The production of seizures by repeatedly,

over a period of days, restimulating the same place in the brain with below-threshold electrical impulses. (682)

limbic striatum A group of cell groups anterior to the hypothalamus that receive projections from VTA; mainly the septal area and the nucleus accumbens. (661)

lithium One of the elements; used to treat mania. (673)

locus coeruleus A small group of noradrenergic cells at the pontine–midbrain border. (669)

long-term potentiation (LTP) An increase in EPSP size following extended use of a synapse. (682)

MAO-inhibitors A class of antidepressant drugs that have their action by inhibiting the destruction of monoamines (especially norepinephrine) by MAO. (669)

mesolimbic system The dopaminergic neurons of the ventrotegmental area, the mesolimbic path, and all the neurons to which they send their axons in nucleus accumbens, septal area, prefrontal cortex, and other limbic sites as well as the descending pathways from the limbic structures back to the VTA. (661)

moderating factors Possible causal factors in schizophrenia or mood disorder that are secondary in importance to the two major factors of stress and heredity. (653)

monoamine oxidase (MAO) The enzyme that destroys norepinephrine. (669)

monoamines A group of transmitters including serotonin and the catecholamines. (665, 669)

monozygotic twins Two indiviuals derived from the same zygote. (652)

mood disorder A psychiatric illness characterized by prolonged and excessive mood elevation or depression that does not stem from life events or some other physical disorder. (667)

multiple personality A disorder in which the personality has fragmented into two or more distinct persons that compete for control of conscious processes. (651)

negative symptoms Those symptoms of schizophrenia that respond poorly to therapy; they include flattened affect, refusal to speak, catatonia, and loss of motivation. (656)

neostriatum The caudate and putamen. (661)

neuritic plaque A tangled mass of telodendria, dendrite branches gathered about clumps of β-amyloid. (676)

neurofibrillary tangle The dense thicket of strange

filaments often seen in cortical neurons of Alzheimer's patients. (676)

neurological soft signs Subtle behavioral abnormalities that suggest that some part of the brain is dysfunctional but that are too vague and nonspecific to point clearly to any specific region of the nervous system. (654)

neuropathological factors (in epilepsy) Brain damage or chemical changes that lead to seizures. (682)

neuropathology Structural or chemical abnormalities of, or damage to, the brain. (654)

nucleus accumbens A limbic system cell group just lateral to the septal area. (661)

nucleus basalis of Meynert A nucleus near the globus pallidus that contains the cells of the cholinergic arousal system for the cortex. (677)

organic mental disorders Psychotic states for which there is some clear evidence of brain damage or disruption of brain function. (650)

overinclusion The tendency of schizophrenic patients to include all sorts of mental associations in their speech that most people suppress as irrelevant to the conversation. (659)

P300 The large, positive EEG wave occurring 300–400 ms into an auditory evoked potential. (658)

paranoia A set of delusional beliefs, usually of persecution. (663)

paroxysmal depolarization shift (PDS) The abnormally large wave of depolarization in the cortex that triggers the excessive firing of neurons in a seizure. (683)

partial seizures Those that are localized to a particular area. (679)

phenothiazines The largest family of antipsychotic drugs. (666)

phenytoin A drug used to control tonic–clonic and partial seizures. (684)

positive symptoms Symptoms of schizophrenia amenable to treatment; specifically, hallucinations, delusions, and thought disorders. (656)

prognosis The chance of recovery from an illness (or improvement in symptoms). (656)

psychotic A state characterized by behaviors that are strange and socially inappropriate, thoughts that are disordered, and, sometimes, hallucinations or delusions. (650)

seizure Large waves of synchronized firing that temporarily destroy normal electrical patterns in some part of the brain. (674)

senile dementia The loss of mental functions in old age. (675)

senility The loss of mental functions and motor control with aging. (675)

septal area A limbic system cell group anterior to the hypothalamus and ventral to the septum. (661)

simple partial seizures Seizures that do not impair consciousness and, unlike generalized seizures, do not involve the entire cortex. (681)

stress factor One of the two causal factors in a vulnerability theory of schizophrenia or mood disorder. (653)

thought disorder A psychotic symptom involving strange, illogical associations. (652)

tonic seizures Those in which the convulsion is limited to a sudden stiffening of all the muscles and that is frequently accompanied by impairment of consciousness. (680)

tricyclic antidepressants (TADs) A group of antidepressant drugs that block reuptake of catecholamines. (670)

triggering process (in epilepsy) An electrical event in the brain that initiates a seizure. (683)

type I and type II schizophrenia Crow's two categories of schizophrenia. (656)

up-regulation The increase in receptor density during times when transmitter is scarce. (671)

ventrotegmental area (VTA) A group of dopaminergic neurons in the midbrain adjacent to the substantia nigra. (660)

vulnerability model The theory that schizophrenia is predisposed by certain genes that leave the individual vulnerable to environmental factors. (653)

Yerkes–Dodson law The capacity of the organism to perform well increases as arousal increases, up to a point, and further increases in arousal produce worse and worse performance. (658)

18

Neuropsychology of Cortical Function

Prefrontal Cortex
Concept: neuropsychology

SYMPTOMS OF PREFRONTAL DAMAGE
Frontal Lobe Anatomy
Neuropsychological Tests
Concepts: Prisco delayed-comparison task, Corsi recency-discrimination task, set, Stroop test, Wisconsin card-sorting task, perseveration, maze-learning task
Animal Studies
Concepts: delayed-response task, delayed-alternation task, delayed matching-to-sample task

A THEORY OF PREFRONTAL FUNCTION
Concept: goal set

ORBITOFRONTAL CORTEX
Concepts: Phineas Gage, frontal lobe personality

Occipital Lobes

A SURVEY OF VISUAL SYSTEM LESIONS
Concepts: visual field, optic chiasm, lateral geniculate nucleus (LGN), ipsilateral projection, contralateral projection
Projection-System Damage
Concepts: optic nerve, optic tract, optic radiations
Cortical Lesions
Concepts: scotoma, hemianopsia, visual agnosia, fovea, frontal eye fields
Therapy for Agnosia
Concept: visual scanning

Parietal Lobes

SOMATIC SYMPTOMS
Concepts: anosognosia, pain asymbolia, autotopagnosia, apraxia

SPATIAL ORIENTATION AND NEGLECT
Concepts: spatial orientation, Weinstein maps, visuospatial agnosia, unilateral neglect, covert orienting

The Language Areas
Concepts: Broca's area, Wernicke's area, expressive aphasia, receptive aphasia

VARIETIES OF APHASIA
Expressive Aphasia
Concepts: Broca's aphasia, telegraphic speech, dysarthria, paraphrasia, phonemic paraphrasia, semantic paraphrasia, circumlocution
Receptive Aphasia
Concepts: Wernicke's aphasia, neologisms, word salad
Other Aphasias
Concepts: conduction aphasia, anomic aphasia, transcortical motor aphasia, mutism, transcortical sensory aphasia

THE SITE OF DAMAGE IN APHASIA
Concept: stroke
Damage Underlying Broca's Aphasia
Interpreting the Function of Broca's Area
Anterior Versus Posterior Lesions
The Disconnection Syndromes
Concepts: Heschl's gyrus, planum temporale, arcuate fasciculus

When the brain suffers physical damage, two medical specialties come into play: neurosurgery and neurology. The neurosurgeon's task is to clean the wound and stop the bleeding after an accident or to remove a tumor. The neurologist is more likely to deal with less obvious cases in which the patient's behavior suggests the possibility of brain damage, and medical tests are needed to confirm and pinpoint the problem. The neurologist tests reflexes, looks at the retinas (for signs of brain tumors), and asks about dizziness, memory, sensory function, and movement problems. Diagnostic tests may be ordered, such as an EEG, blood tests, CT scan, EMG, $_r$CBF or NMR imaging (see Chapter 5). From all these bits and pieces, the neurologist arrives at the most likely disease (if there is one) and the most likely site of brain damage. It turns out, however, that neurological tests for non-infective damage to specific areas of the brain are best at detecting lesions below the level of the cerebral cortex. Cortical lesions come in such an array of complexity and are frequently so subtle that they slip through the neurologist's diagnostic net. It is at this point that the unique skills of the neuropsychologist enter.

Neuropsychology is a branch of clinical psychology aimed at diagnosing brain damage and studying dysfunctions of the nervous system from the viewpoint of a psychologist. This professional is trained to apply various psychological tests to patient behavior and to make diagnostic reports, frequently for the benefit of the medical team handling the patient. As a therapist, the neuropsychologist can suggest how the patient might best adjust to the loss of brain function and, perhaps, design a rehabilitation program. As a researcher, the neuropsychologist is interested in using clinical data from patients to draw conclusions about normal brain function. For example, neuropsychologists who worked with epileptic neurosurgery patients undergoing brain bisection gave us tremendous insights into the way in which the two hemispheres divide the total work load of the brain. Many research-oriented neuropsychologists carry this interest in normal function one step further and perform experiments on normal subjects, but the fact that the hypotheses tested stem from clinical observations keeps these experiments within the realm of neuropsychology. Moreover, in almost all situations, the neuropsychologist is oriented toward higher cognitive function rather than basic processes such as learning, hunger, or vision. For these reasons, the neuropsychologist deals more with the cerebral cortex than with any other part of the brain. One could think of the field as a blend of cognitive psychology with clinical and physiological psychology. Very recently, neuropsychologists with stronger interest in basic research on language, attention, and hemispheric differences have formed a subfield known as cognitive neuropsychology. The first half of this chapter focuses more on the clinical aspects of neuropsychology, and the second half, with its discussion of hemispheric specialization, is more within the realm of cognitive neuropsychology.

Prefrontal Cortex

Nancy and her husband are in a car traveling down the highway at 55 miles per hour. Nancy's husband, who is driving, is tailgating the car ahead, and Nancy has failed to fasten her seat belt. The driver of the car in front of them slams on his brakes as a dog runs across the road, and Nancy's husband, distracted for a fraction of a second by conversation, is unable to brake in time to avoid a collision. Inevitably, Nancy's forehead smashes into the windshield. Inside her head, her prefrontal cortex smashes against the inside of the skull. The promptness of the rescue squad ensures her survival, but nothing can be done about the massive loss of neural tissue. What effect will this have on her life? What are the effects of losing prefrontal cortex?

Symptoms of Prefrontal Damage

At the supermarket, Nancy wheels her shopping cart up to the checkout counter. Her basket contains several types of meat but nothing else, despite the fact that her grocery list is full of other items. She pays,

loads her bag into her car, and drives home. Carrying the groceries into the house, she sets the bag on the counter next to the refrigerator and turns as the mail carrier's truck stops out front. When her husband comes home that evening, the meat is sitting on the counter, spoiling. The vacuum cleaner resides in the middle of the living room floor. Dirty laundry is spread around the entryway in piles, and one washer load waits to be put in the dryer. Nancy is lying on the bed, reading a magazine. The husband bites his lip in frustration but says nothing. It has been only 3 months since her release from the hospital, and before her frontal lobe injury, his wife had always been a conscientious, well-organized, reliable person. Perhaps her present scatterbrained, unmotivated unreliability is just a passing symptom?

Unfortunately, Nancy's symptoms are probably not some psychological reaction to her hospitalization that might respond to psychotherapy. They are typical of damage to particular parts of the frontal lobes and are most likely permanent.

Frontal Lobe Anatomy There are five major divisions of the frontal lobes: M1, premotor cortex, M2, prefrontal cortex, and orbitofrontal cortex (Figure 18.1). In the motor chapter, we discussed the first three. The two most anterior areas are very important for human intellect and personality, and it is these that we discuss in this chapter. The homemaker described previously showed symptoms of damage to both prefrontal and orbitofrontal cortex. To understand her behavior, we need to find, by means of neuropsychological testing, what functions have been localized in these cortical areas.

Neuropsychological Tests Imagine yourself as a neuropsychologist working in a large hospital. The neurosurgery unit has just discharged an accident victim who had received severe head wounds and considerable frontal damage. Your task is to use your available psychological tests to assess the extent of the patient's remaining capacities. These data can then be used by the counselors and occupational therapists when they attempt to help the patient adjust to home and work situations. What functions

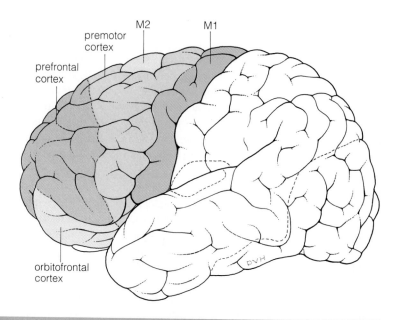

Figure 18.1 The five regions of the frontal lobes.

have been damaged, and how much can the person still do despite the disability?

Let's say that you begin testing your patient with the **Prisco delayed-comparison task** (Milner & Petrides, 1984). You present flashes of light at a slow rate, wait for 60 seconds and present another series of flashes at a different rate. You ask the patient, Was the second stimulus the same or different from the first? A normal person has little trouble with this task, but your patient makes a very poor score. Has the person's short-term memory been damaged? Let's not be hasty in drawing that conclusion.

Now you change the task, using nonsense figures rather than flashes. A new pair of nonsense figures is employed on each trial. With this change, your patient's score improves to near normal and is much better than the scores of your patients with damage to the memory areas of the temporal lobe. (See the section on the hippocampus.) This suggests that the problem uncovered in the first Prisco task may not be a memory defect. Perhaps it arose in the first version because the same rates were used over and over in different pairs, thus creating interference between trials. When the subject recognized a particular rate there may have been confusion over

when that rate had been previously experienced. The subject might not know if it had been seen a moment before as the first member of this pair or as either member of some previous pair. In the nonsense-figures version of the task, this interference could not arise because all the figures were different. Success on the second task after failure on the first implies that the patient has trouble handling interference between stimuli.

You proceed to the **Corsi recency-discrimination task** (Milner & Petrides, 1984). The patient is shown a series of cards, each having two pictures (Figure 18.2). Some of the pictures reappear from trial to trial on different cards, paired with different pictures. Occasionally, a card also displays a question mark to indicate to the subject that it is time to respond. The person must answer two questions at this point: Have these pictures been shown before, and which one was shown most recently?

Your patient responds easily to the first question, correctly identifying the pictures viewed before, and this is something that patients with memory problems from medial temporal lobe damage can only do very poorly, if at all. However, your frontal lobe patient runs aground on the second part of the Corsi

Figure 18.2 One of the cards used in the Corsi recency-discrimination task. This one has question marks, indicating that the patient should state whether these two pictures have been displayed previously and, if so, which one was shown most recently. (From Milner & Petrides, 1984)

task—deciding which picture had been shown most recently. By contrast, whenever a temporal lobe patient is able to recognize a pair of pictures, he can also tell which he saw last. As we saw in the chapter on memory, there are many varieties of memory; it is not a unitary ability. The type of memory loss revealed by this task seems to be related to deciding about the relative recency of several stimulus events. In other words, the stimuli were remembered, but the *sequence* of stimuli was not. The Prisco task, on the other hand, shows a deficit in the ability to minimize interference between memories.

Deciding to further check on the problem of interference, you first instruct the patient to count to 16 and stop. This is accomplished with no trouble. The next step is to continue counting from that point to 22. This is also done without hesitation. The patient can remember what the task is long enough to finish it and seems to have no trouble with the counting itself. The rest of the dialogue is the following:

PSYCHOLOGIST: I want you to count up to 6. While you are counting, I will ask you to stop and do something else for me. After I have done this, I will ask you to continue counting up to 6. (Pause.) Now count up to 6.

PATIENT: 1, 2, 3, 4 . . .

PSYCHOLOGIST: Stop. What letter comes after *B*?

PATIENT: *C*

PSYCHOLOGIST: All right. Now finish counting.

PATIENT: What am I supposed to do? *D, E, F, G* . . .

With even a momentary distraction, the person loses track of the task. This symptom has been described as an inability to maintain a **set** toward a goal.

Another task designed to measure the patient's ability to minimize interference and maintain a response set is the **Stroop test**, which consists of a page of color names printed in different colors. Interference arises because the names are not printed in the colors they name; for example, the word *red* might appear in blue or the word *yellow* in green. The subject must ignore the interfering color words and name the colors of the ink in which the words are printed and do it as fast as possible. The task is so similar to reading that the tendency is to respond to the words rather than the colors and to make errors. Your patient responds to the Stroop test by naming the first three inks correctly, then blocking on the fourth for several seconds before finding the correct answer. After getting the fifth ink correct, three consecutive errors are made; in each case, the word is read and the ink ignored rather than vice versa. The patient seems to have forgotten the instructions and slipped into responding the easiest way, but when you ask about this, the person is able to repeat the instructions accurately. The preferred mode of responding (reading words) seems to have

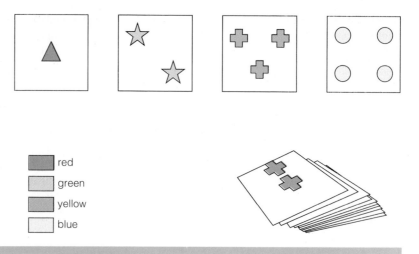

Figure 18.3 The Wisconsin card-sorting test. The cards can be sorted into piles of similar cards according to the shape of each figure, its color, or the number of figures on each card. After rewarding the patient for sorting according to one rule, the psychologist switches to a different rule. Frontal patients have difficulty switching and tend to perseverate at following the old rule. (From Milner, 1963)

red
green
yellow
blue

commanded the patient's behavior despite the realization that it led to the wrong responses.

You seek to confirm this observation by administering the **Wisconsin card-sorting task** (Figure 18.3). You lay out four cards with colored figures in front of the patient and state that each of the remaining cards in the deck must be placed in the correct pile, but you don't say what you mean by "correct." You will indicate the correctness of each choice by saying yes or no, and the patient must discover the rule. At first, you "reward" the patient each time a choice is based on matching the color of the new card with the color of the card already on the table. You continue with this unspoken rule until the patient makes a series of 10 correct guesses, indicating that the rule has been learned. Now, without warning, you change the rule and start rewarding the subject for ignoring color and placing crosses with crosses, triangles with triangles, and so forth. Normal people experience difficulty with this shift but can adjust and learn the new rule. Your patient, like others with prefrontal injury, is unable to make the shift and continues to match color with color. The term most often applied to this symptom of prefrontal damage is **perseveration**. Examples of this are seen in a drawing task in which the patients were asked to draw a series of forms, with changes from one form to another occurring at random points in the series. Figure 18.4 shows what the

patients drew versus what they were asked to draw. They were frequently unable to make the switch from one form to another.

The startling thing about perseveration is that it frequently seems to embarrass the patient. Jouandet and Gazzaniga (1979) report that one of their patients was quite puzzled by his perseveration. He had already discovered that he needed to shift to a different rule and could verbalize it but seemed unable to follow it in the actual behavior of placing each card. Although he was able to comment on this discrepancy between what he thought he should do and what he really did, he had no explanation for his inability to put the new plan into action. This discrepancy between verbally comprehending the concept and using it to control behavior is a common observation in prefrontal cases (Luria, 1973; Milner & Petrides, 1984).

Perseveration is also apparent in your patient when you introduce a **maze-learning task** (Milner & Petrides, 1984). The person must push a metal stylus along a metal-lined groove in a wooden board hidden from view. Every time a blind alley is entered, an error buzzer sounds, warning the patient to go back and take a different choice at the last choice point. Although you have explained the rules clearly and had the patient repeat them back, the stylus now continues down a blind alley despite the continuing warning from the buzzer. At the end of the alley,

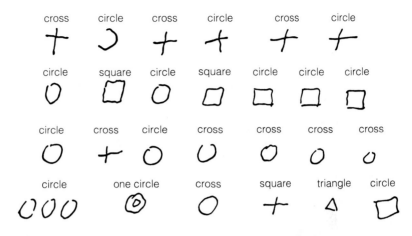

Figure 18.4 Perseveration is evident in the drawings made by four frontal lobe patients. The third line was done by a patient with an abscess of the right frontal lobe. The other three lines were the responses of tumor patients. The printed words indicate what the patients were asked to draw. (From Luria, 1970)

there is no place to go but back, but this doesn't bother your patient. The stylus is simply lifted out of the groove for a moment and "hopped" over a wall into an adjoining groove. You point out that this is definitely against the rules, and the patient agrees in an embarrassed manner but then proceeds to do the same thing at the next blind alley. Once a wrong alley has been entered, perseveration seems to carry the patient forward regardless of the knowledge that it is against the rules to proceed. This discrepancy doesn't seem to overly concern the person, however, despite the fact that it indicates a loss of conscious control over behavior. Frontal lobe patients show very little self-criticism and a great lack of concern about the consequences of their behavior (Stuss & Benson, 1984).

As a final test, you ask your patient to place one hand flat on the table, fingers extended and together, then clench his fist and finally, turn his hand on edge with fingers extended again (Goodglass & Kaplan, 1979). The patient does as requested, and you then ask that he repeat this sequence until told to stop. At first, performance is accurate, but it quickly breaks down as the patient seems to lose the memory of which posture comes next in the sequence.

From your tests, it has become apparent that the patient has lost considerable frontal lobe function. Deficits were shown in the ability to act out sequences; to recall stimulus sequences (Corsi task); to use verbal concepts to command behavior se-

quences (maze task and card sorting); to maintain a behavioral set, or plan of action, in the face of interfering stimuli (Stroop test and Prisco task); and to relinquish an out-of-date set and avoid perseveration (maze task and card sorting). These losses will seriously impair the person's ability to create daily plans of action and carry them out (e.g., I must get up at 6:30, take a shower, eat breakfast, and drive to work). Rehabilitation demands a situation in which the patient works only under close supervision in an environment having stimuli that aid the recall of the next step in the job rather than acting as distractions. The ideal might be a job in which a supervisor is constantly present saying, "Do this. Now do that." Leaving the patient to plan the workday or to follow through a sequence of tasks without help is doomed to failure.

Animal Studies Monkeys with prefrontal lesions have been tested on a wide variety of learning and memory tasks. They show little, if any, impairment on conditioning or discrimination learning, but they consistently reveal a large deficit on a type of memory task called the delayed-response problem.

In the simplest form of the **delayed-response task**, the monkey is shown a piece of food being placed under one of two stimulus objects. A screen is moved in front of the stimulus objects for a brief time (e.g., 60 seconds) and then is taken away to allow the animal to make a choice (Figure 18.5).

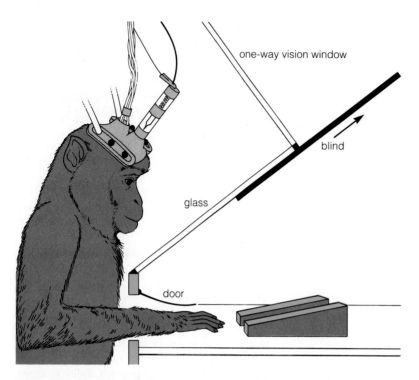

Figure 18.5 Experimental arrangement for the delayed-response task. The monkey watches through the glass as food is placed beneath one of two blocks. The door is fastened to prevent a response at this time. The blind is lowered for a designated amount of time (the delay period) and then raised as the door is unlocked. The monkey can now reach through and make a choice. If the choice is wrong, the blocks are withdrawn out of reach before a second choice can be made and a new trial begun. Attached to the monkey's head are permanent sockets allowing an outside-of-the-skull electrical connection with the electrodes permanently implanted in the brain. Plugged into the front socket is a microelectrode driver that can move the microelectrode in fractions of a millimeter. The assembly causes no pain and, thanks to the permanent socket, the cables and driver can be removed at the end of each experimental session without exposing the brain. (From Fuster, 1984)

Moving the correct block reveals the food; an incorrect choice is followed immediately by the lowering of the screen. Normal monkeys have little trouble bridging short time gaps between the stimulus and the response, but those without prefrontal cortex are severely impaired. It seems as though during the delay they forget which response to make. At first glance, the problem appears to be a lack of short-term memory, but our experience with the Prisco task should warn us that this appearance may be deceptive. Recall that the poor memory performance

on the Prisco task actually revealed an inability to disregard interfering stimuli. Similarly, when prefrontal monkeys were given delayed-response training in which the lights were turned out during the delay, their scores improved greatly. Interfering stimuli were minimized in the dark (Malmo, 1942).

Several similar tasks have also been found to be sensitive to prefrontal lesions. Figure 18.6 shows the **delayed-alternation task** in which the animal must choose to respond to either the right or left button, wait through a delay, and then choose the alternate

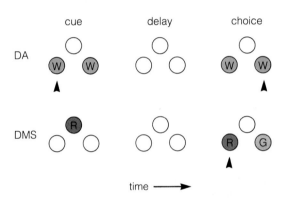

cue   delay   choice

time ⟶

Figure 18.6 A monkey performing a delayed-alternation or delayed matching-to-sample task. Reinforcement in the form of fruit juice is provided by way of a metal "straw." There are three steps in both tasks. In the delayed-alternation task (DA), two white keys (W) are lighted, and the monkey must press one of them. The lights are turned off for a short delay period. When the keys are lighted again, the subject must avoid the key chosen last and select the other key in order to obtain reinforcement. In the delayed matching-to-sample task (DMS) a light above the two keys appears during the cue period. Its color is the "sample" and indicates which of the two keys should be pushed after the delay is over. In this example, the cue light is red (R) and, after the delay, the monkey must press the red key rather than the green (G). (Adapted from Fuster, 1984)

button. In the **delayed matching-to-sample task**, the trial starts with the display of the S^+ (the correct stimulus). After the delay period, S^+ and S^- are displayed, and the monkey must choose S^+ in order to receive food. If microelectrode recordings are made of single neurons during any of these tasks, cells can be found in the prefrontal cortex that appear to be related to the solution of the problem (Fuster, 1984) (Figure 18.7). A number of prefrontal cell types seem to "bridge" the delay by firing steadily from the moment the stimulus appears to the moment the response is finally allowed.

A Theory of Prefrontal Function

There are a number of ways to characterize the general function to which all the observed prefrontal symptoms point. Hopefully, the concept suggested here will help explain more of the data than is explained by the previously proposed hypotheses. A

number of experimenters have suggested that the most fundamental ability of the prefrontal cortex is to provide the animal with goal sets. A **goal set** is a neural mechanism that prepares a set of response circuits for action. For example, a track runner waiting in the blocks for the start of the 100-meter dash demonstrates a very strong goal set. Her whole motor system is primed to send her hurtling down the track at top speed the moment the starting gun fires. The prefrontal cortex presumably is responsible for her ability to maintain this waiting readiness. Rather than creating the responses, the prefrontal cortex prepares the way for a response to be made at an appropriate time (at the sound of the gun). It *sets* the response mechanism for some expected future opportunity to make a particular response. The monkey in the delayed-response situation watches the food being slipped under the right-hand object and sets itself to grab that object rather than the left-hand object as soon as it is given the opportunity.

The prefrontal cortex was a relatively recent addition to the vertebrate brain, and this suggests that its evolution must have bestowed some new, fairly high-level function that would give the animal a capacity to go beyond the basic forms of learning and memory. What would that function be? In lower forms of learning, such as classical conditioning, the learned response must immediately follow the stimulus that cues it. This is a severe limitation that had to be overcome in any animal that survived as a predator.

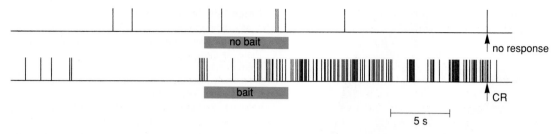

Figure 18.7 A record of the activity in a single neuron of the prefrontal cortex made during delayed-response performance. Time is along the horizontal axis. Each vertical mark represents a single nerve impulse. The heavy dark bar shows the period during which the monkey observed food being placed under one of the two stimuli. The delay period occupies the interval beginning at the end of the heavy bar and lasting until the arrow indicating the lifting of the screen. In the upper record, a control trial is shown in which no food was hidden. When no food was involved, the prefrontal cell was quiet during the delay, and no response occurred at the end of that period. When the monkey had been shown the bait, however (as in the bottom record), a "set" was initiated in prefrontal cortex, as can be seen in the firing of the prefrontal neuron all during the delay. This activity lasts until the response has been made. (From Fuster, 1984)

In the successful stalking of prey, the predator's initial inclination to attack the moment the prey is sighted must be inhibited. The successful predator waits, unsensed, until the conditions are just right or the attack will be unsuccessful. This patient waiting through a long delay in order to release a response when the correct stimulus condition arises represents a magnificent evolutionary step. The response has been freed of its bondage to the immediate stimulus situation. A goal set allows a person to imagine a future set of stimuli (the goal) and to prepare an appropriate response to be used when the stimuli actually occur. It is this temporal disconnection of stimulus and response that gives rise to the ideas of "will" and "intention." It is the basis of our ability to plan for the future. The act of "willing" or "intending" to do something involves two steps: choosing a response and selecting the set of stimulus conditions that must arise before the response will be made. There really isn't any difference between an intention and a plan. The prefrontal cortex then is the seat of intentions and plans.

There are corollaries to this hypothesis. Because a goal set means that a response is being held in readiness for a particular stimulus, the implication is that other responses that might conflict with the chosen response are being suppressed and that attention to interfering stimuli is being inhibited. Loss of the ability to form goal sets then would make a person vulnerable to interfering stimuli during the period between the start of the set and the occurrence of the relevant stimulus. Thus, prefrontal monkeys could perform a delayed response if the lights were turned off. The human patient could count to 22 providing you did not interrupt with a letter-naming task midway through the counting.

The homemaker with prefrontal damage set out to buy every item on her supermarket list, but as she rounded the second aisle, the checkout counter was immediately in front of her; the strongest association with this stimulus was the response of entering the line and proceeding with the checkout process. She had no strong goal set for finishing the list that would suppress this "checkout" behavior and no goal set to turn her attention away from the interfering checkout stimuli and back to her list. The result was that she wound up "forgetting" the remainder of the list and buying only meat. When she arrived home and put the meat on the counter, a strong goal set for the task of bringing in the groceries from the car and storing them correctly would have prevented her from being distracted by the arrival of the mail carrier or would have returned her to the interrupted task after his departure. Without the set, the meat was forgotten on the counter. The idea of cleaning the house produced the behavior of getting out the vacuum cleaner and beginning the task, but the lack of a goal set for completion of the job allowed distractions to prevent her from finishing.

What of the other symptoms displayed by prefrontal patients? Can they also be explained as the result of damage to a goal-set mechanism? The difficulty in applying verbal instructions to control behavior seems understandable. Comprehension of instructions, such as "do not lift your stylus from the groove in the maze," would take place in the temporal language cortex, which is not damaged. In a normal brain, the activity in the temporal lobes would presumably establish a goal set in the prefrontal cortex that would prepare the appropriate motor circuits in the corpus striatum and posterior frontal lobes and suppress inappropriate response tendencies. In the prefrontal patient, we must presume that only a weak, partially effective goal set can be established by the temporal lobe verbal concepts. Hence, the patient has difficulty in following rules and even in obeying his own comprehension of the task. In card sorting, for example, the subject comes to understand that the rule that worked for the first few minutes has been changed and is able eventually to express the new rule out loud. However, because no goal set can be created, his behavior remains uninfluenced by this temporal lobe input, and the result is perseveration. The original sorting plan is probably being directed by the striatum.

There is one other important aspect to the concept of goal set that allows this function to fit itself into the general plan of the frontal lobes. Recall from the chapter on the motor system that the M1 cortex at the posterior edge of the frontal lobes produces plans for individual movements. Movements can be considered to be sequences of muscle contractions. Anterior to M1 is the premotor cortex that apparently contains the plans for sequences of movements. Extending this idea to the cortex anterior to the premotor cortex—that is, to the prefrontal areas—we hypothesize that these areas contain the plans for the longest behavior sequences. Returning to our idea of goal sets, we can see that some sets (like the

runner waiting for the gun) focus on a single response, whereas others (like the idea of going grocery shopping) involve a long *sequence* of behaviors. Loss of a goal-set mechanism then should disturb the ability to organize sequences of behavior such as the hand-positions test of the clinical psychologist. Because behavior sequences usually involve stimulus cues for the release of the individual behaviors, the loss of sequencing circuitry might also impair the ability to recall stimulus sequences. This seems to be the problem in the Corsi task.

In summary then, the symptoms we have reviewed suggest that the prefrontal cortex provides goal sets that organize behaviors into sequences, inhibit competing responses, and suppress interfering stimuli. Without such sets, one frequently cannot put ideas into action.

Orbitofrontal Cortex

The most famous case of frontal lobe damage on record is that of Phineas Gage, a worker on a blasting crew in the mid-1800s. Gage had the job of ramming charges of dynamite into the holes drilled in the rock for them. A stray spark or too hard a shove set off the blast while Gage was leaning over the hole. His yard-long, steel tamping rod shot out of the hole and through his head, entering his cheek and exiting through the top of the skull (Figure 18.8). Amazingly enough, he survived the injury, albeit as a radically changed person. From the reliable, industrious, sober individual he had been, he became obstinate and capricious, devising and abandoning plans in a childish way. He was impatient with anything that blocked his desires and cared little about the feelings of his associates.

Judging from the holes in Gage's skull, the injury must have been especially severe in the area at the base of the frontal lobes—the orbitofrontal cortex. This area seems to be the major meeting point between the limbic system and neocortex. Apparently, this is where the planning mechanism of the prefrontal cortex obtains its information about the motives and emotional evaluations of the brain. It is likely that this connection from limbic system through orbitofrontal cortex into prefrontal cortex is a two-way street, with the planning ability of the

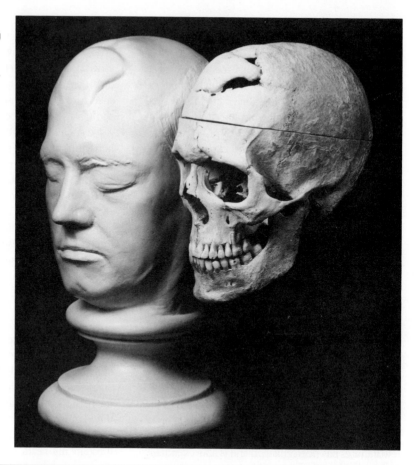

Figure 18.8 Phineas Gage: his bust and skull. The tamping iron entered the cheek and exited the left forehead, passing chiefly through the left frontal lobe. (From Blakemore, 1977)

cortex controlling the more primitive circuits of amygdala and hypothalamus (Jouandet & Gazzaniga, 1979). Without this control, most of the knowledge stored in the cortex is probably lost to the limbic circuits, and they are free to modify behavior without constraints. In other words, Gage might have been able to verbalize the social concept "don't hit someone simply because they don't want to do you a favor," but that circuit probably was no longer able to make connections with the limbic circuits and to temper their influence over the motor system. Apparently, if he felt the urge to hit, he did just that.

Patients with prefrontal damage often show symptoms of orbitofrontal cortex damage as well. Stuss and Benson (1984) describe a **frontal lobe personality** that includes traits such as "unrestrained and tactless behavior; mood changes including jocularity and bawdy, puerile joking . . . blunted feeling; callous unconcern; boastfulness; and grandiose, obstinate, and childishly egocentric behavior." Not every patient displays all these traits, of course.

■ Occipital Lobes

Although we discussed these cortical areas in the chapter on vision, there was no opportunity in that context to see their function through the eyes of the neuropsychologist. Consider, for example, the case of a 60-year-old man reported by Bay (cited in Williams, 1979) who "woke from a sleep unable to find his clothes, though they lay ready for him close by. As soon as his wife put the garments into his hands, he recognized them, dressed himself correctly and went out. In the streets he found he could not recognize people—not even his own daughter. He could see things but could not tell what they were." The sudden visual problem most likely resulted from a minor stroke during the night. But how could the loss of a part of the brain leave the person with the ability to "see" without being able to understand what was seen and what part of the brain could produce such a defect? Let us begin our answer to these questions by surveying the results of lesions throughout the visual projection system and see how the symptoms stem from the anatomy.

A Survey of Visual System Lesions

How would it affect your vision if you lost your right occipital lobe? You might guess that such a lesion would make you blind in the left eye, but this is not the case. Instead, you would be blind in the left visual *field* in both eyes. To see why this is the case, look carefully at the diagram of the visual projection system in Figure 18.9. At the top of the picture are the visual fields for right and left eyes. The **visual field** of each eye is the area of the environment visible to that eye at any one moment. The visual fields for the two eyes overlap, except for a small area on the extreme outside of each, so we speak of them collectively as a single visual field. As the light image of the visual field passes through the lens of the eye, it is reversed (right and left and upside down). That is why the lines in the picture cross as they lead from the field to the retina. The result of this reversal is that the objects in the left field are imaged on the right side of each retina and the right field is represented on the left sides.

The optic nerve leaving each eye is divided into two bundles of fibers, one of which crosses to the opposite side of the brain at the **optic chiasm** (Figure 18.9) while the other remains on the same side. All fibers (axons) in both bundles extend on into the thalamus where they synapse in the **lateral geniculate nucleus (LGN)** (see Chapter 6). The fibers that stay on the same side as their origin (e.g., left retina to left LGN) are called an **ipsilateral pro-**

jection (*ipsi* = same; *lateral* = side), whereas the fibers that cross at the chiasm and run to the LGN on the opposite side of the brain are termed a **contralateral projection** (*contra* = opposite).

Now imagine an object in the right side of the visual field and then trace the path taken by information. The light rays from an object in the right visual field would cross at the lens and fall on the left side of the retinas. Notice that this puts both images of our object into the LGN on the left side of the brain. This is because the image in the right eye falls on the part of the retina that projects contralaterally, whereas the image in the left eye falls on the part of that retina that projects ipsilaterally (check this with Figure 18.9). Thus, each LGN receives two overlapping images of one-half of the visual field (one from each eye), which it sends on to the occipital lobe on its side of the brain. In other words, your visual field is split right down the middle with the left half represented in the right hemisphere and the right half in the left hemisphere.

This system creates a strange problem for anyone interested in the nature of consciousness. If you close one eye and stare straight ahead while moving a finger across your visual field from left to right, the image of the finger will induce activity first in your right occipital lobe, and then, as the image of the finger crosses the midline of your retina, the activity will leap to the occipital lobe of your left hemisphere. Despite this enormous neural discontinuity, there is no "jump" in your conscious experience of the image; the finger appears to move smoothly from one side of the field to the other without even a hint of a break. At this time, there is no good explanation for this fact. (We older folk have to leave something for the next generation to chew on.)

Now that you understand how the visual projection system (or, at least, the geniculostriate part) is organized, a question may have occurred to you. Why does it have to be so complicated? Why doesn't the right eye simply project to the left hemisphere and vice versa? The answer is that a simpler system of that sort would fail to give each hemisphere the overlapping images that enable it to extract information about depth. The slight difference between the right and left image, produced by the fact that the right eye sees slightly more of the right side of

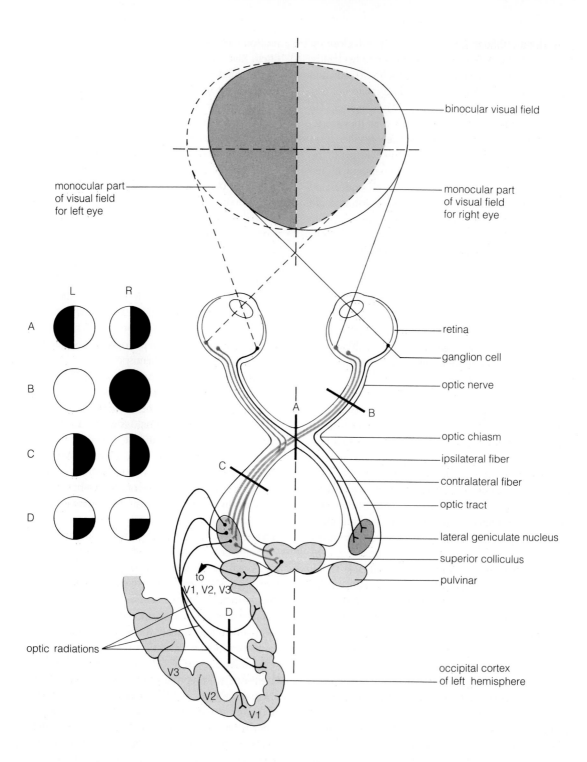

binocular visual field

monocular part
of visual field
for left eye

monocular part
of visual field
for right eye

L   R

A

B

C

D

retina

ganglion cell

optic nerve

A

B

optic chiasm

ipsilateral fiber

contralateral fiber

optic tract

lateral geniculate nucleus

superior colliculus

pulvinar

C

to
V1, V2, V3

D

optic radiations

V3

V2

V1

occipital cortex
of left hemisphere

Figure 18.9 Diagram of the major subcortical and some of the cortical parts of the visual system. Note that the temporal half of each retina (the half closest to the temple) sends its optic nerve fibers ipsilaterally (i.e., to the same side of the brain). The nasal half of each retina sends its optic nerve fibers across the optic chiasm to the contralateral (opposite) side of the brain. Thus, each occipital lobe receives from half of each retina: the temporal half of the ipsilateral retina and the nasal side of the contralateral retina. Verify this by tracing the paths taken by the pictured fibers, noting which half of the retina contains their somas. Because the lens reverses the image, the right side of each retina is looking at the left side of each field and vice versa. Thus, the left occipital cortex "sees" the right side of each visual field; the right hemisphere "sees" the left side. Lesions at various points along the projection system are indicated by lettered bars. Circles at the left, representing right and left visual fields, show the areas of the field in which vision is lost for each type of lesion. A lesion that cuts the optic chiasm (A) severs only the optic nerve fibers coming from the nasal side of each retina, thus eliminating vision in the outside of each field. The result is tunnel vision. Cutting the nerve on one side (B) yields blindness in that eye. A lesion of the left optic tract (C) produces blindness on the right side of *both* visual fields. A lesion in the radiations (axons of LGN cells) rarely cuts all the fibers because they are so spread out. Typically, as in D, vision is lost in roughly one quadrant of each field contralateral to the lesioned hemisphere. (Adapted from Nieuwenhuys et al., 1981)

any solid object while the left eye sees slightly more of the left side, can be used by the cortex to calculate the distance of the object (see Chapter 6).

Projection-System Damage Now let's see what happens to vision when a part of the system is damaged. Figure 18.9 indicates the visual loss following lesions at various points. The circles represent the visual fields of the right and left eye, and the dark areas indicate blindness. Cutting the right **optic nerve** (the section of the optic fibers between their origin in the retina and the optic chiasm) would produce the same result as loss of the right eye. However, loss of the right **optic tract** (the section of optic fibers between the chiasm and the LGN) would produce blindness in the left visual field of each eye. (Verify this by tracing the path in Figure 18.9.) Losing the **optic radiations** (the axons of LGN cells that run from LGN to the visual cortex) in one hemisphere would produce blindness in the contralateral field of each eye. A tumor growing at the midline could invade the optic chiasm, killing all the fibers in the contralateral projections, and result in tunnel vision.

Cortical Lesions To understand the complex results of occipital cortex damage, recall (from Chapter 6) that the visual cortex is a crazy quilt of different

visual analyzer areas, each performing a different visual function or set of functions. The visual radiations synapse in the area called V1, which appears to analyze the input for line and edge orientation, color, depth, and perhaps other aspects of vision. V1 passes its analysis on to a number of interconnected areas such as V2, V3, V4, MT, MST, and 7. Motion information is extracted by the analyzers in MT and MST. Location of an object in relation to the viewer is pinpointed by area 7, and so forth. It is clear that each patient with an occipital lesion is going to have a slightly different set of symptoms because no two injuries are going to damage exactly the same collection of analyzers. We can also see that vision is not a single function but a collection of dozens of functions, and selectively damaging certain of these analyzers while leaving others intact will produce completely unexpected visual experiences.

V1 is a crucial area in that it seems to be somewhat of a bottleneck in the system; almost all information from the retina must flow through this one zone. It is not unexpected then that the loss of a part of V1 causes a loss of all visual functions for the particular patch of the visual field handled by that portion of V1. Such an area of blindness is called a **scotoma** (sko-TOE-mah) and is experienced by the patient as a black area in a zone of vision. If the entire V1 area is lost in one hemisphere, the person is blind for the entire contralateral visual field. That is, loss of the right occipital lobe leaves one blind in the left visual field and vice versa, a disorder called **hemianopsia** (HEM-ee-an-AHP-see-uh).

When the lesion occurs farther forward in the occipital lobe, outside of V1, however, blindness does not result. An area such as MT, for example, receives input from V4 but is not absolutely dependent on that route. It also gets information from V1 and V3, as well as several other areas. Although the loss of V4 input must hamper MT in performance of its analysis, the input coming from other areas contains much of the same information as would have come from V4, so MT is not totally incapacitated. This means that the patient with a lesion in V4 will show visual peculiarities but not blindness. What are some of these peculiarities? That is, what are some of the symptoms of visual cortex damage outside of V1?

Stauffenberg described a patient with this sort of lesion. The woman "could see objects, and avoid them when they constituted obstacles in her way, but she could not identify them surely, without recourse to the aid of hearing, touch, smell, or taste. At first, indeed, she could not identify objects by touch, but gradually lost this disability. She could not recognize a sponge held before her until she felt it with her finger. She could not recognize a cigar until she put it into her mouth. A spoon was occasionally recognized, less often a knife and fork. A key, pocket knife, and wash basin were not recognized, or at any rate, their use was not described. Nevertheless, after looking for a long time at a watch, she named the numbers correctly and told the time correctly" (cited in Williams, 1979, p. 66). Such a loss of visual abilities without blindness is called **visual agnosia** (*a* = lack of; *gnosis* = knowledge). Damage to V1 causes blindness; damage to other areas of visual cortex (e.g., V2, V3, MT, etc.) causes agnosia. Some insight into how a patient with visual agnosia sees the world might be obtained from the drawings of such a patient (Figure 18.10).

Another patient could not name the object on the table in front of him (a glass of water) and could not describe its function. However, a few more minutes into the interview, he reached over and took a drink from it. This does not mean he was lying when he claimed not to recognize what it was; it simply means that the routes from the visual analyzers to his language cortex (the part of the brain that would answer the psychologist's question) were damaged, whereas the pathways carrying visual information to the motivational circuits in the limbic system were still working. The patient may have been more surprised by his behavior than was the interviewer.

Small areas of damage may disrupt the function of only a few analyzers and leave the patient with a highly specific problem. Stengel, for example, reported on a patient (cited in Williams, 1979) with no visual problems other than color identification. In a standard color test, the patient was given a collection of colored yarns and asked to pick out the one that was the same color as grass (he chose a light green), sky (he chose a dark green), blood (red yarn), tomato (he hesitates, points to purple, then to orange, adding that the latter was probably more correct).

Bodamen described a patient for whom faces appeared

> strangely flat; white with very dark eyes, as if in one plain, like white oval plates . . . all the same. He could see but not interpret facial movements and grimaces. Gazing in a mirror, he described the delineaments of what he saw, but could not recognize the face as his. Together with three other soldiers, he had his photograph taken, but he afterwards failed to recognize his face in the print. The features of his closest relatives, either in snaps or in real life, appeared quite foreign to him. He walked past his mother in the street, and he never got to know the looks of the other patients in the ward. (Critchley, 1953)

Visual attention also seems to suffer from occipital damage. When shown a set of overlapping line drawings (Figure 18.11) and asked to describe what he sees, the patient may pick out one of the objects and completely disregard the rest. If asked about the remaining objects, he may deny that there are any others. This seems to be a problem in separating the figure (the visual elements to which one is attending) from the ground (all of the unattended, background elements). Either the patient could extract only one figure from the confusion of overlapping images, or, having chosen one set of lines to use as a figure and

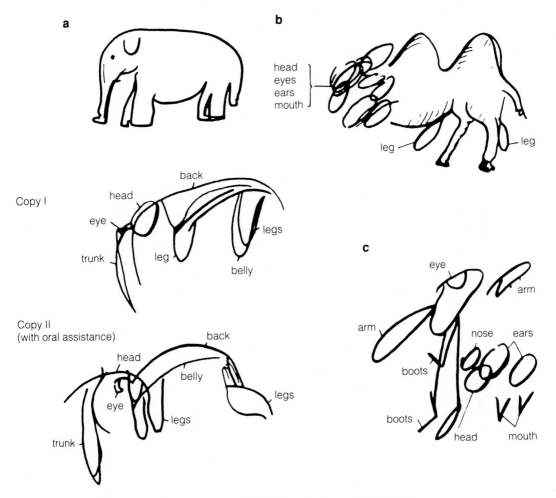

a

b

head
eyes
ears
mouth

leg

leg

Copy I

back

head

eye

trunk

leg

legs

belly

c

eye

arm

arm

nose   ears

Copy II
(with oral assistance)

back

head

belly

legs

eye

legs

trunk

boots

boots

head   mouth

Figure 18.10   Drawings made by an agnosia patient. (**a**) The patient was asked to copy the drawing of an elephant. Two attempts are shown below the specimen. (**b**) The patient's task was to complete the unfinished drawing of a camel. (**c**) The patient's attempt to draw a person from memory. (From Luria, 1973)

relegating all others to the status of ground, he was unable to shift attention to a different figure.

A somewhat different form of attention problem also appears in some agnosia cases. The patient is shown two objects (e.g., two pencils side by side), and she can see only one of them. Faces can be recognized but only one at a time. The right-hand face or object is usually identified first, and in reading a long sentence, only the words farthest to the right

would be read. The problem underlying these symptoms may be an inability to coordinate visual scanning.

You may recall from the chapter on vision that most of your fine, detailed vision is accomplished with one tiny central area of the retina called the **fovea**. To view any scene, you must move your fovea around, capturing first one, then another portion of the whole. Your perception of the entire scene is a

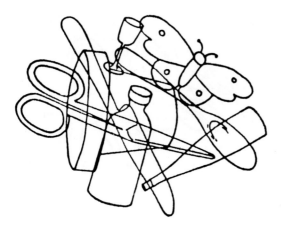

Figure 18.11 Drawing used in the overlapping-figures test. When asked to name all objects pictured, an agnosia patient can usually name one of them but cannot seem to perceive any of the others. (From Williams, 1979)

composite of dozens of these momentary, foveal "snapshots" sandwiched between the eye movements that shifted the fovea from one fixation point to the next. As you stare at the scene in front of you right now, you may feel as though you are perceiving all of it simultaneously, but this is probably just an illusion. Most of your perception of the parts of the scene outside of your present fixation point consists of memories of what your foveas took in when you last fixated on those parts of your environment rather than what your retina is receiving at the moment. It is your memory, rather than the visual image, that gives clarity to the peripheral parts of the visual field. Visual perception then may be inextricably tied up with the eye-movement patterns that shifted your foveas around as you became familiar with the scene.

Could the attentional problems of agnosia indicate a problem with scanning (eye movements)? Perhaps patients who fail to report the left ends of printed sentences simply never move their eyes to the point on the page where the beginning of the sentence would fall on their foveas. Peculiarities of scanning are fairly clear in some patients. For example, some patients have been observed to enter an unfamiliar room with unusual caution, turning head from side to side and peering about. Head

movements might be taking the place of missing eye movements. An important part of scanning is the fixation at the end of each eye movement. One patient failed to fixate objects normally, and his eyes could be pulled away from a needed fixation by any new stimulus entering the field of view (Williams, 1979). Scanning problems of this sort could arise because the motor "machinery" that allows cortical circuits to direct eye movements is no longer connected to the visual system. Voluntary eye movements are directed by the **frontal eye fields** of the frontal cortex, just posterior to the prefrontal cortex. It is likely that some lesions of the occipital lobes might have severed the connections between the visual processors and those eye fields.

Therapy for Agnosia   Luria, a famous Russian neuropsychologist, has devoted much of his career to finding ways to help brain-damage patients. In the case of agnosia, he has discovered some useful strategies for the patient that can help compensate for the loss of visual functions. Frequently, there is more than one way to accomplish a perceptual task, and just because one method has been lost to brain damage doesn't mean that all have been. Because brain-damage patients may feel so defeated by their loss of abilities that they fail to find ways to compensate, one of the most important things a neuropsychologist can do is to motivate the patient to discover alternate strategies and use them. For example, if someone shows you some common object, they will expect you to identify it in a fraction of a second and make some intelligent reply immediately. Having behaved this way for years, the agnosia patient tries to make the identification faster than his limited processing capacity is able, and this haste frequently produces a mislabeling of the object.

If you show a drawing of a spider, for example, the patient may call it a crab. A narrowing of the focus of attention, similar to that seen in the overlapping-images test, has led the patient to focus on the legs and kept him from seeing the body. Perhaps the eye movements needed to shift the foveas away from the "leg" region of the picture never occurred. Having perceived legs but little else, the patient names the first creature that comes to mind that has six or eight legs. When shown a picture of eyeglasses, one patient called them scissors. He had perceived the two circles at the ends of the handles but little else.

The task of the therapist then is to get the patient to slow down and persist in his attempts to recognize the object. According to Luria, this frequently pays off with an eventual correct identification. He quotes from the response of a patient, interviewed by Gelb and Goldstein, who at first claimed to be completely unable to understand the test picture at all: "Something pink . . . on top of it there's something black, and underneath something white, and then more black . . . and the pink on top is probably a face . . . and the black . . . well, of course, it is quite obvious, it's a man!" (cited in Luria, 1963). Persistence pays.

Another basic strategy is to relearn how to scan a scene. One of Luria's patients could write sentences easily from dictation but could not copy them from printed form. Obviously, this was a visual problem rather than a language disability. Luria had the patient practice tracing letters with his finger and following his finger with his eyes. Because tracing activated the unharmed kinesthetic sense in the muscles and joints, the patient was immediately able to perceive the letters with that method. Making the eye movements simultaneously seemed to create new associations between these perceptions and the visual sense, for he became faster and faster at letter identifications. Finally, Luria had the patient drop the finger tracing and rely solely on tracing the letters with eye movements (a detailed form of **visual scanning**). Eventually, the patient was able to recognize each letter without even the eye-movement tracing.

There is an interesting similarity between this example of relearning visual perceptions and the original learning of such perceptions reported by von Senden (described in Hebb, 1949) who examined surgery patients (without brain damage) who had just been given the ability to see for the first time in their lives. These people had been born with cataracts (clouded lenses) that allowed only diffuse light to reach their retinas. They had never experienced a visual image prior to the surgery that removed the cataracts. They strongly resembled agnosia patients in their inability to identify faces and objects visually even after several days of experience. One interviewer observed that the only way his

patient eventually learned to perceive the difference between a triangle and a square was to move his eyes around the shape, counting the corners. In a few days, however, this detailed scanning apparently became unnecessary, and the object could be immediately perceived as a whole as soon as it was presented. It is possible that Luria's teaching of scanning may represent a retraining procedure that mimics the way in which the brain originally built up the visual engrams lost when the occipital lobes were damaged.

■ Parietal Lobes

At their anterior ends, the parietal lobes contain S1 and S2, the somatosensory areas responsible for many mechanoreceptive, thermoreceptive, nociceptive, and kinesthetic perceptual abilities. Visually related functions are found at their posterior borders where they meet the occipital and temporal lobes. Functions that depend on both visual and somatosensory input are located in between. Very little work has been done on the visual parts of the parietal lobes, and damage there produces some dysfunctions that remain quite mysterious. Cleland and coworkers, for example, report the case of a woman who suffered a stroke in the right posterior parietal region that left her with a tendency toward perseverative perception of movement sequences. The first time this happened

a man walked in front of her window and she continued to see him in her left field of vision but his walking was speeded up. She described the sensation as though she was watching a film being shown at the wrong speed, that speed being about twice normal. The amplitude of the movements was unchanged. On the second occasion she continued to see a child waving but, as on the previous occasion, the action was speeded up. On the third occasion, her brother put his hand through his hair. She continued to see him repeatedly perform this action at a faster rate. Each episode of perseveration lasted about ten minutes with the image gradually fading although there was no diminution of the movement (Cleland et al., 1981)

In examining parietal lobe symptoms, let us start at the anterior end of the lobe and work back to the occipital border.

Somatic Symptoms

In Chapter 8, we discussed the postcentral gyrus, the most anterior part of the parietal lobe, and its contribution to the somatic senses. Lesions there produce somatic sensory deficits such as difficulties in localizing objects that are touching the skin. Apparently, the parietal lobes contain a "body image" that the brain uses in this localization process; if the body image is damaged, parts of the body may "disappear" perceptually for the patient. The result of some cases of right-side parietal injury is the disorder, **anosognosia** (a-NOSE-ahgh-NOSE-ee-uh), the inability to recognize a defect in some part of the body. The *a* at the beginning of this term refers to a "lack of," and *gnosia* means "knowledge." *Noso* refers to "disease"; so the term, taken as a whole, tells you that the patient with this disorder has a lack of knowledge (perception) of her disease. It would seem that the patient is missing parts of her body image but cannot perceive that fact. For example, the lesion may have also invaded the hand area of M1 in the precentral gyrus and given the patient a partial paralysis of that extremity; but when asked about her difficulty with the left hand, the patient denies that she has a problem. Apparently, the paralysis doesn't bother her because she is no longer aware of her left hand. As a result of the parietal lobe injury, the left hand has been lost from the image, and any remarks you make about it will only be met with confusion or denial. (PSYCHOLOGIST: "Would you mind handing me the cup you have in your left hand?" PATIENT: "What cup? I don't have any cup.")

Extreme anosognosia produces some severe conflicts between the various senses. When the patient looks at his left side and sees his left hand, his vision tells him that there is a hand there, attached to his arm, but his somatic senses firmly deny that this is true. The patient appears to trust the somatic senses more than the visual and denies that the hand is his. No concern at all is shown for the disowned limb, and it may be allowed to dangle out of the bed or placed carelessly where it can obviously come to

harm. Cases have been recorded in which the patient called the nurse repeatedly to complain of a "foreign" arm or leg in his bed, requesting its immediate removal (Beaumont, 1983).

Disturbance of body image can also result in **pain asymbolia** (a-simm-BOLE-ee-uh) in which the act of ignoring a particular body part spreads from mechanoreception to nociception. The patient seems to be unable to appreciate painful stimuli in that part of the body, and the outcome frequently is neglect, carelessness, and injury to the "disowned" limb. The left hand, for example, having come to rest accidentally on a hot radiator, might be left there until the smell of burning flesh arouses someone to investigate.

Ogden (1985) reported the case of a 59-year-old man with left parietal lobe injury from a tumor (Figure 18.12). This patient displayed **autotopagnosia** (auto-TOPE-ag-NOSE-ee-uh), a disorder in which the patient seemed to have lost the location of his body parts (*auto* = self; *top* = location; *gnosia* = knowledge). He was unable to point to his left arm or to his nose or to any other body part when requested. Furthermore, this condition generalized to an inability to point to the examiner's body parts. However, when the psychologist pointed to one of the parts of the patient's body, it was named with no difficulty at all. Autotopagnosia is clearly not a language problem; rather it seems to be a spatial difficulty. The patient can no longer think in terms of body "geography."

This same patient also exhibited various apraxias. An **apraxia** is the inability to perform some set of movements despite lack of paralysis or any other obvious damage to the motor system. Ogden's patient showed difficulty in dressing. He couldn't tell which arm or leg to put into which hole, even when the garment was held in place for him. He was also unable to mimic stirring a cup of coffee, waving goodbye, or pounding a nail into a board (Ogden, 1985). Writing gave him a terrible time. When trying to write a *J*, for example, he would form a *B* instead, and then say, "That's not what I wanted to write. I wanted a *J*, not a *B*." When asked to print the sentence, "I will be very pleased when I can go home," he printed "I will be evey lleased wenw I can go hoem."

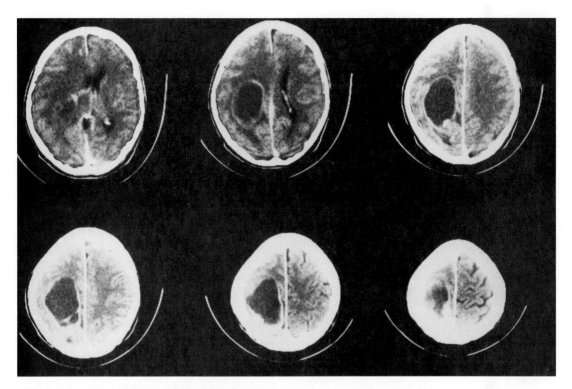

Figure 18.12 CT scans of a patient with the symptoms of autotopagnosia. The lowest section is shown at the upper left, the highest at lower right. The scan reveals a large tumor in the parietal region of the left parietal lobe. (From Ogden, 1985)

Spatial Orientation and Neglect

It is difficult to generalize accurately about parietal injury at a time when there is still so little data available, but a general principle may be emerging. It seems that the farther back the lesion is in the parietal lobe, the less the defect is directly related to the body parts themselves and the more the loss has to do with perceiving the space around the body. **Spatial orientation** is the ability to perceive where objects are in space in relation to self and in relation to other objects. This ability usually requires input from both the somatic senses and vision: the former to locate one's own body parts and the latter to perceive the space in which the body and other objects are situated. The **Weinstein maps** (Semmes et al., 1955) test for loss of a form of spatial orientation that probably resides closer to the postcentral gyrus

than to the occipital lobes because it seems to have a larger somatic than visual component. The patient places one hand into a flat box in order to feel a raised line on a board inside. The object is to use the turns that the line makes on the board as a map to guide himself through an identical series of turns paced out on a grid painted on the floor of the room (Figure 18.13). His feet must imitate the route that his finger is tracing inside the box. Normal people have little trouble with this, but parietal lobe patients perform very poorly. It is likely that it is your parietal lobes that guide you as you drive through town from one location to another or as you leave this room to go to your next class. The loss of this spatial orientation ability is called **visuospatial agnosia**.

In our study of visual processes (see Chapter 6), we saw that the visual areas at the back of the parietal lobe are responsible for locating the position of

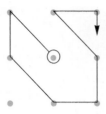

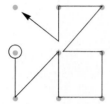

Figure 18.13 Weinstein maps. The dots represent spots painted on the floor of the room and the lines show the subject the route that must be followed from dot to dot. The map can be read either visually or tactually. In the latter case, the lines are made by gluing a string to a board and putting the map in a box where it can be touched but not seen. (From Beaumont, 1983)

objects in space. It is not surprising then to discover that the posterior parietal cortex is important to spatial attention. Damage in this region on one side of the brain (especially in the right hemisphere) results in **unilateral neglect** in which the patient forgets the side of his body contralateral to the lesion. He may fail to shave on the neglected side or forget to dress that side of the body. If you stand on that side of him when you ask him a question, you may find that you are completely ignored (Baynes et al., 1986). Food may be eaten off one side of the tray but not off the "forgotten" side. Patients with right-hemisphere damage fail to read the left half of each line of print in a book (Mesulam, 1983).

This syndrome differs from anosognosia in that calling attention to the neglected side brings the patient's attention to it and produces a normal response. Neglect can occur on either side, but the two parietal lobes do not perform exactly the same functions; so right-hemisphere symptoms are a bit different than are left-hemisphere symptoms. If the psychologist measures neglect of ambient vision (see Chapter 6), which covers the entire visual field, then the rule seems to be that right-hemisphere lesions create neglect of visual stimuli in the left visual field, whereas left-hemisphere lesions make for neglect of the right visual field (Gainotti et al., 1986). If the test is for focal vision, however, so that all stimuli are in the center of the field, then neglect of the contralesional field (the part of the visual field opposite the lesion) occurs only with right-hemisphere damage. This might mean that the right hemisphere is slightly more specialized for perceiving spatial relations than is the left hemisphere. (The comparable area of cortex in the left hemisphere is probably specialized for functions relating to language.)

The directing of attention to one side or the other of the visual field sounds as though it ought to be linked to the frontal eye fields and their mechanism for directing gaze to one side or the other, and it would appear that this is true of the posterior parietal regions. However, the *overt* moving of the eyes is not the only way to direct one's attention. Posner and colleagues (1984, 1987) have been studying the mechanism of covert orienting that depends on this part of the cortex. In **covert orienting,** the person directs his attention to another part of the visual field despite keeping the head and eyes fixed. Apparently, this process requires at least three processors. First, there must be a disengage mechanism that allows one to stop paying attention to some previous stimulus. Second, one needs a shift mechanism that calculates where in visual space the current locus of attention is and where the new locus will be. Third, there is an engage mechanism that allows one to focus on the new location. Posner has evidence that at least the disengage processor is located in posterior parietal cortex. All three parts are probably required to direct your eye movements as you think about one part of your environment, then another.

In summary then, the neuropsychological evidence suggests that the parietal cortex posterior to the somatosensory areas of the postcentral gyri provide the ability to perceive visuosomatic spatial orientation and body image. In other words, it tells you where objects are in space, including the parts of your own body.

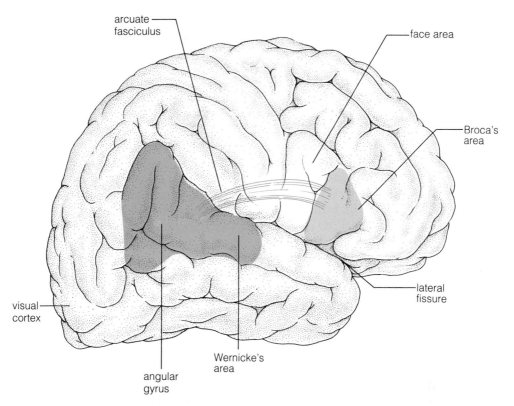

Figure 18.14 The major language areas of the cortex. The face area of the precentral gyrus (M1) controls movements of the lips, tongue, and jaws. Broca's area is more involved in speech production, whereas Wernicke's area has less to do with speech, more to do with language comprehension. The angular gyrus is in a position to connect visual and language functions, as in reading and writing. The arcuate fasciculus is a tract that connects Wernicke's area with Broca's area.

■ The Language Areas

Our first knowledge that the cortex contained separate areas for language came through the acute observations of the French physician Paul Broca. In the 1860s, Broca was an official in a hospital for the retarded and insane, and it befell him to treat a patient named Leborgne who apparently had a serviceable degree of intelligence but who was unable to speak. Broca saw that the problem was not with the speech muscles or nerves leading to them and reasoned that Leborgne was brain-damaged. When

Leborgne died of an infection, Broca removed the brain and located the lesion. By 1861 he had gathered several brains of people showing the same loss of speech syndrome and published his observations together with the hypothesis that the speech center of the brain was an area of cortex in the frontal lobes just anterior to the precentral gyrus (Figure 18.14). Subsequent observations by others confirmed that this area of cortex is indeed involved with speech; consequently, it has come to be called **Broca's area**. Another publication by Broca in 1865 revealed (from a study of eight other brains) that the comparable area in the right hemisphere did not serve speech (Geschwind, 1972). Apparently, the speech cortex was exclusively in the left hemisphere.

Broca's discoveries generated great excitement in the infant science of brain function and led to the 1874 article by an unknown, 26-year-old junior assistant of neurological services at Breslau that filled in the other half of the puzzle of language localization in the cortex (Geschwind, 1972). Carl Wernicke realized that language has two elements: speech and comprehension. Broca had discovered only the location of the speech portion. Wernicke, in his 1874 paper, established the location of the language-comprehension function in the posterior end of the left temporal lobe, a zone now known as **Wernicke's area** (Figure 18.14).

The language disorder resulting from loss of left-hemisphere language areas is termed **expressive aphasia** if the speech function is the one suffering the greatest loss and **receptive aphasia** if the greater loss is that of language comprehension.

Varieties of Aphasia

The person who tries to classify various cases of aphasia into clear-cut types encounters the same problem we saw in studying visual agnosia. The frontal, parietal, and temporal cortex areas that contribute to language apparently consist of dozens of separate analyzers, each with its own small, poorly understood function. Until we have mapped these separate neural functions and understood each, we cannot generate a realistic system of categories for the symptoms of their loss. Despite the inadequacy of our present classification scheme, it must be discussed, however. The alternative is to leave the reader with the task of making sense out of what appears to be a hopeless muddle of symptoms.

Expressive Aphasia This disorder is also known as **Broca's aphasia** and sometimes as "nonfluent aphasia." Goldberg and Benjamins (1982) give us some samples of speech productions by patients with expressive aphasia. When asked to describe a picture showing a farm scene, the patient replied, "She's going to school. That girl ... other one. Watching him. The man is watching ... I can't say it. The house.

I can't say it. [Points.] The house. The house. Um ... that's it." When shown a harbor scene, the patient said, "Boats. The house. The bridge. The girl. The sun. They're using them. I don't know. Holding a barrel. Whatever." In describing pictures of a man embracing a woman, clothes on a line, and a shovel, the patient said, "The man. The lady. I can't say no more. Arm. I can't say nuthin! The clothes. I ... out and dry. You use the shovel ... to ... in the ... I can't say it."

You can see from this sample that the speech remaining to the patient was compressed in that it omitted many of the linking words of grammar and syntax. For this reason, it is called **telegraphic speech** because it consists mainly of nouns, verbs, and short common phrases. The patient is able to comprehend speech, however, and can tell when a needed word is blocked or unavailable. As you would expect, this condition is highly frustrating for the speaker. Another frequent symptom of expressive aphasia is **dysarthria** (dis-ARE-three-uh), a problem in pronunciation and fluency. Speech is choppy and halting rather than free-flowing, and the lips and tongue may not respond properly to form the syllables. For example, when asked to describe a picture of children stealing cookies while the mother is washing dishes, the patient said, "Well ... mess ... uh 'sgga ... dder' cookie, uh-oh, fall down ... wife spill water ... and uh 'dis ... ez' ... and, uh 'tsups' and saucer and plate ... I, uh ... no ... done" (Naeser, 1982). The words were only articulated with great effort, and the dysarthria was evident in the word *scatter*, which came out as "sgga ... dder" and *dishes*, which was pronounced "dis ... ez."

When a missing word cannot be found, the aphasic patient frequently makes some sort of substitution. The substitution of one word for another is called a **paraphrasia** (PAIR-uh-PHRASE-ee-uh), and there are two ways in which this can be done. In **phonemic paraphrasia**, the substituted word simply *sounds* similar to the desired word, although the meaning may be quite different. The patient searches for *frog* but *cog* is pronounced instead, or *band* is substituted for *hand*. When describing a fire, one patient wanted *smolder* but came up with *snowbar*. If the substituted word is similar to the blocked word in meaning rather than sound, it is called a **semantic paraphrasia**. Examples would be *lizard* for *frog*, *arm* rather than *hand*, *smoke* instead of *smolder*, and *ashtray* for *plate*.

Another way of "getting around" a missing word is to substitute a rough description or a phrase that is associated with the word, a process called **circumlocution** (SIR-come-low-CUE-shun). For example, if shown a picture of a match and asked to name it, the patient might say, "Rub it on something rough . . . it's hot." When shown a car, "This is around town. And if you go far also."

Receptive Aphasia This is also called **Wernicke's aphasia**, and it differs dramatically from expressive aphasia. There is no dysarthria, slowness, or difficulty in articulation. Speech flows freely just as though there were nothing at all wrong. In describing the "cookie-stealing" picture, a patient with receptive aphasia said, "I would say the little boy was hooking some cookies and was going to fall off, his girl wanted a piece of the cookies, too. . . . His mother was washing clothes, and spilt on the . . . up over the, the 'shring' . . ." (Naeser, 1982). Although the speech is fluent, much of what the patient says doesn't sound quite right or make much sense. Paraphrasias are common to this syndrome, and examples would be *hooking* for *stealing*, *clothes* for *dishes*, and *girl* for *sister*. This example also shows a third type of substitution in which the patient creates her own word to fill the blank in her word memory. This is typical of receptive aphasia, and the substituted words are called **neologisms**. The word *shring* was an example.

Apparently, these neologisms and paraphrasias occur partly because the patient no longer can comprehend exactly what words she is uttering. An inability to comprehend the meaning of speech sounds is the fundamental symptom of receptive aphasia. A patient will frequently be able to follow some of what is said, but much of it apparently sounds like gibberish. In listening to her own speech, the patient has the same inability to comprehend, hence no ability to check on the correctness of her utterances. Combined with this is some amount of the same word-finding difficulties seen in expressive aphasia. Although the receptive aphasic has syntactical words like conjunctions and adjectives available, the lack

of comprehension apparently leads to a misuse of these speech elements, and the result is a jumble called **word salad**. In the following quote from a receptive aphasic, the psychologist has just interrupted the patient's ramblings to begin a question.

"Thank you, Mr. Gorgan. I want to ask you a few . . ."

"Oh, sure, go ahead, any old think you want. If I could I would. Oh, I'm taking the word the wrong way to say, all of the barbers here whenever they stop you it's going around and around, if you know what I mean, that is tying and tying for repucer, repuceration, well, we were trying the best that we could while another time it was with the beds over there the same thing. . . ." (Gardner, 1976)

In summary then, receptive aphasia is characterized by good fluency and poor comprehension, with paraphrasias, neologisms, and word salad.

Other Aphasias The defect in **conduction aphasia** is far more subtle than either of the other aphasias we have discussed. There is good comprehension of speech and writing (unlike receptive aphasia) and reasonably good speech with adequate fluency (unlike expressive aphasia). The major problem is that the patient cannot *repeat* what he hears or reads. This might eventually turn out to be a limited type of amnesia, selective for language (Kolb & Wishaw, 1985), but we see in the next section that there is an anatomical way of explaining it that would make it a pure language phenomenon.

The problem in **anomic aphasia** seems to be the loss of reference memory for words. There is good language comprehension, and speech is intact except for the absence of many nouns. The person's only real difficulty comes in trying to name things. The result is speech peppered with semantic paraphrasias and circumlocutions.

The patient with **transcortical motor aphasia** comprehends language well and is capable of repeating most of what is said to her. Reading out loud is also no problem. The major symptom is **mutism**; the patient, left on her own, will say nothing at all. There is no spontaneous speech.

Transcortical sensory aphasia, on the other hand, is similar to receptive aphasia in that language comprehension has been lost. Spontaneous speech is disorganized word salad, but the patient can *repeat*

Table 18.1 Types of Language-Related Brain Disorders

Disorder	Symptoms	Site of Lesion
Broca's aphasia (expressive)	Telegraphic speech, dysarthria, phonemic paraphrasias, semantic paraphrasias, circumlocution	Usually involves some of Broca's area and underlying white matter, the operculum, and some of the superior temporal gyrus
Wernicke's aphasia (receptive)	Good fluency, poor comprehension, paraphrasias, neologisms, word salad	Planum temporale and posterior end of superior temporal gyrus
Conduction aphasia	Good comprehension of speech and writing, adequate fluency, cannot repeat what is heard or read	Arcuate fasciculus
Anomic aphasia	Cannot recall and use nouns	Anterior language areas
Transcortical motor aphasia	Difficulty in initiating speech	Prefrontal cortex or M2
Mutism	Complete absence of speech	Tracts from M2 and anterior cingulate
Transcortical sensory aphasia	Poor comprehension and speech but can repeat what is heard	Tracts connecting language areas to rest of cortex
Agraphia	Inability to write words	Left parietal lobe?
Acquired alexia	Inability to read	Angular gyrus or tracts connecting it to visual areas

with great accuracy whatever is heard or read—an ability not available to the receptive aphasic.

With these various sets of aphasic symptoms in mind (Table 18.1), let us discover what the causes of these syndromes might be.

The Site of Damage in Aphasia

Aphasia more often results from a stroke than any other form of brain damage. A **stroke**, in medical parlance, is known as a type of cardiovascular acci-

dent (CVA). *Cardio-* refers to the heart; *-vascular* refers to the blood vessels. A CVA in the brain typically occurs either when an artery is occluded (blocked) by a blood clot or when a vessel bursts. In either case, some of the brain tissue served by that artery will be cut off from oxygen long enough to die. Figure 18.15 shows that the area served by the middle cerebral artery includes almost all the cortex that participates in language function. Most of the strokes that result in aphasia involve CVAs in the middle cerebral artery. An occlusion in one of its

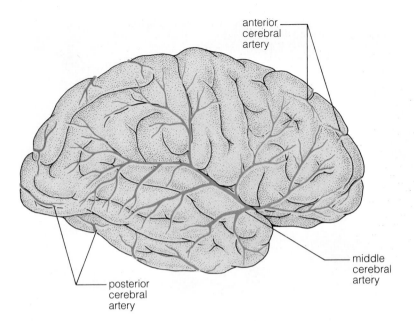

anterior cerebral artery

posterior cerebral artery

middle cerebral artery

Figure 18.15 The three major arteries of the brain. The language areas are served mainly by the middle cerebral artery, which is usually the one involved in aphasia-producing strokes.

minor branches might kill cortex in quite a limited area, leaving the person with a very specific, limited defect; an occlusion of the artery near the anterior end of the lateral fissure would deprive nearly the entire language cortex of oxygen and probably produce a "global" aphasia with severe disruption of comprehension and speech, as well as writing and reading.

Damage Underlying Broca's Aphasia According to Broca, expressive aphasia will result from damage to the third frontal convolution of the left hemisphere—the area now known as Broca's area. This idea gained so much acceptance during the 19th century that it became a commonplace fixture in any textbook dealing with the nervous system. Neurosurgeons, however, realized that the truth could not possibly be that simple. Too many excisions of cortex including parts of Broca's area had been done in the course of surgery without producing aphasia (Pribram & Roberts, 1970). Could Broca have been incorrect about his observations? In the late 1970s, a group of French physicians recalled that Broca

had kept one of the two original brains—that of Leborgne—and donated it to a museum. The brain was found in a cellar and subjected to modern scrutiny with computerized axial tomography (Signoret et al., 1984).

Figure 18.16 is a photograph of the left hemisphere of Leborgne's brain. It reveals that the greatest obvious loss of cortical tissue was in Broca's area, as Broca stated. It also shows, however, what appears to be damage to the lower borders of the frontal and parietal lobes just above the lateral fissure, an area known as the operculum. The dorsal view allows one to compare the relative size of the two hemispheres and to see that a great deal of tissue underlying the cortex must be missing from the left hemisphere. It is clear from the horizontal section that passes through Wernicke's area (Figure 18.17) that there is only a hole where much of the white matter should be. The remaining temporal cortex is like an empty shell.

Broca, of course, did not have the benefit of modern CT scanning. Yet he appears to have ignored the obvious fact that the temporal lobe was severely

Figure 18.16 Leborgne's brain. (From Signoret et al., 1984)

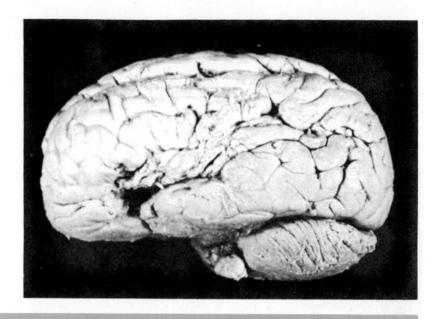

reduced in size (and therefore probably damaged within). Why did he leap to pinpoint the lesion in the third frontal convolution when the actual extent of the lesion seems to have involved the parietal and temporal lobes as well? Pribram (1971) notes that Broca had been much influenced by the phrenologists of the early 1800s who were the first to promote the idea of localization of function. Their reasoning was that the prefrontal cortex was the latest evolutionary development (an incorrect premise) and that therefore it must contain the highest-level, most human of the various brain functions. This would include language. Broca then must have viewed the evidence of Leborgne's brain through the prejudice that damage outside the frontal lobes could not possibly be relevant to language, and this led him to place all language function in what we now know to be just one little "corner" of the language cortex.

What can we conclude? Is Broca's area really necessary for speech as most textbooks would have us believe, or is Broca's aphasia actually the result of a much wider lesion involving white matter and portions of other lobes? In his review of this question, Mohr (1976) concludes that the operculum, the cor-

pus striatum, and much white matter were also lost in Broca's cases and that this damage was important to the aphasia Leborgne showed. He adds that damage to Broca's area alone seems to produce little or no persistent deficit, and others agree (Damasio & Geschwind, 1984). Poeck and colleagues (1984) did CT scans of the brains of eight aphasia patients having the same symptoms as Leborgne, and instead of finding that they all had lesions of Broca's area, they observed a variety of lesion locations within the language areas. Lesser and co-workers (1984) had the opportunity in connection with surgery to electrically stimulate Broca's area and obtained evidence that it was involved in the integration of several types of complex behavior including writing and movements of the fingers, tongue, and toes. Broca's area may not be exclusively devoted to language functions.

The most interesting research on Broca's area was conducted in 1948 by Mettler and Rowland who were interested in prefrontal lobotomy (cited in Pribram, 1971). There are a number of ways in which the prefrontal areas can be cut off from the rest of the brain, but the technique of Freeman and Watts (1950)

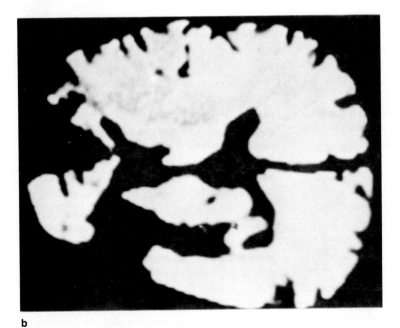

a

b

Figure 18.17 CT scan of Leborgne's brain. **(a)** The level at which the cut was made. **(b)** The scan represents a horizontal section through both hemispheres at that level. Notice how badly the left hemisphere cortex is undermined. Considering the amount of missing white matter in the temporal lobe, it is doubtful that the language areas of the temporal lobe could have been intact and functioning normally. (From Signoret et al., 1984)

had become so widely used at that time that it was almost a standard procedure. The cutting instrument in the Freeman–Watts technique was always inserted through a hole in the skull at the temple, through the cortex, and into the white matter, which was then cut by rotating the knife (Figure 13.2). What struck Mettler was that the cortex underlying the temple—the cortex that was damaged in a prefrontal lobotomy only because it lay between the surgeon and the white matter that was to be cut—was none other than Broca's area. To confirm this, Mettler and Rowland examined scores of cadaver heads, marking the spot that would be used for prefrontal lobotomy and

then opening the skull to check that Broca's area lay beneath. Their positive results meant that literally thousands of psychiatric patients had received lesions in Broca's area without one case of aphasia ever being reported as a result. In an experiment that surely would no longer be permitted under the guidelines of modern medical ethics, Mettler then removed Broca's area in two schizophrenic patients who were catatonic and had not spoken in 20 years. The amazing result was that they began speaking shortly after recovering from surgery and continued to speak for years thereafter (cited in Pribram, 1971). The best conclusion we can draw from all this is that

Broca overgeneralized from biased observation and that the third frontal convolution is not necessary to the production of speech. Damage to Broca's area alone will not cause Broca's aphasia, and it is wrong to call it "*the* speech area" of the brain.

Interpreting the Function of Broca's Area Recall that expressive aphasia consists of a group of symptoms, each of which may depend on damage to a slightly different brain area. Dysarthria, for example, seems to be purely a motor loss, and this suggests that it will appear as a part of expressive aphasia if the lesion extends into the part of the operculum at the base of the precentral gyrus. This region is a part of M1, which commands the muscles of the lips, tongue, and other speech organs. When it is stimulated electrically, speech is blocked until the stimulus is removed (Ojemann, 1983).

A second symptom of expressive aphasia—the slow, halting nature of the speech—suggests that it is difficult for the damaged brain to find the words and get them into correct order, or sequence. This problem of sequencing may also be related to the symptom of telegraphic speech, which results from leaving out all the linking and pointing words such as conjunctions and prepositions. If you consider the nature of such words as *after* and *into*, you realize that they reveal the *sequence* of cause and effect in a sentence. In Chapter 8, we saw that the major task of the premotor cortex (the zone immediately anterior to M1) was that of organizing sequences of responses. Because Broca's area is simply the most ventral part of the premotor area, it would seem reasonable that its contribution to language might lie in arranging sequences.

Bradley and colleagues (1980) took this sequencing hypothesis one step further. Broca's aphasia is classically regarded as a purely expressive disorder. According to these researchers, the reason that the patient repeats the sentence "Bill goes out of the door after walking down the stairs" as "Bill goes ... door ... walking the stairs" is not because he can't *say* the linking words but because he can no longer understand them. The concepts underlying the words may have been lost. The patient may no longer comprehend sequences of cause and effect in language. Does Bill go out of the door after he walks

down the stairs or before? The expressive aphasic may not know from listening to your sentence. This hypothesized deficit in comprehension would remain undetected most of the time because the context of knowledge available to the patient fills in so many of the gaps. For example, the patient may hear the sentence "the apple that the boy is eating is red" as "the apple ... boy ... eating ... red" but not experience any confusion regarding the direction of cause and effect. Common knowledge rules out the sequence "apple is eating the boy" and makes it very likely that the apple is the one that is red and the boy is the one doing the eating.

Bradley and colleagues designed a test aimed at finding out if expressive aphasics really did comprehend the words they tend to leave out in telegraphic speech. Sentences were presented to the patients, and their understanding of the meaning was then tested. The sentences were carefully chosen to be ambiguous unless one understood and used the pointing words. An example was "the girl that the boy is chasing is tall." If the expressive aphasic hears this as "the girl ... boy ... chasing ... tall," general knowledge will not tell her the cause-and-effect sequence. Is the tall boy chasing the girl, or is the girl chasing the tall boy, or the tall girl being chased, and so forth? As predicted, expressive aphasics showed poor comprehension of such sentences while doing well on ones that could be understood without pointing words (Bradley et al., 1980). The theory that Broca's area aids in language sequencing is supported. This research suggests that our division of aphasias into receptive and expressive may not be as realistic as it first sounded. At the present, however, there are not enough data to throw out this useful distinction.

Anterior Versus Posterior Lesions There does seem to be enough data to support a rough rule of thumb about lesion location and type of aphasia: Expressive aphasia is usually associated with more anterior lesions, whereas receptive aphasia is typical of more posterior damage (Basso et al., 1985; Ludlow et al., 1986; Pribram, 1971). The word *usually* should be taken seriously. For example, Ludlow and colleagues (1986) found that Broca's area was damaged in only 77 percent of Ludlow's cases of expressive aphasia, whereas Basso and colleagues (1985) found seven cases of receptive aphasia resulting from *anterior* lesions and six cases of expressive aphasia with *posterior* lesions. These authors have suggested that individual differences between brains might account for some of these results. Broca's area, for example, is not always exactly in the same place in every brain. The third frontal convolution, like much of the cortex, takes varying twists and turns in different brains so that common landmarks are difficult to distinguish.

Another reason why so much variability seems to occur between the type of aphasia and the lesion site is that too many of the studies done so far have neglected a serious consideration of subcortical damage. The cortical language areas do not operate independently of the rest of the brain. Essentially, they are only processing stations along a network of circuitry in which information is shuttled from cortex to thalamus to cortex to basal ganglia, and so on. Good evidence exists that damage to the thalamus or corpus striatum can result in aphasia (Crosson, 1985). Mohr and co-workers (1978) stated the opinion that damage to the white matter underlying Broca's area was more likely to result in Broca's aphasia than damage to the cortex itself. This seems reasonable given the fact that a little damage to the white matter can cut the inputs and outputs from a wide area of cortex. Many cases of brain damage may have been misinterpreted if the examiner assumed an area of cortex to still be functional without verifying that the input-and-output links to the rest of the brain were still intact. Some of these problems may be reduced as radiological techniques like PET scanning (see Chapter 5) come into widespread use, allowing researchers to examine the functioning of subcortical areas as the patient works on some verbal task.

The Disconnection Syndromes The symptoms of conduction aphasia (good comprehension and reasonably fluent speech) strongly suggest that the lesion is not interfering with the speech-production circuits or those involved in comprehension. Apparently, although these facilities still exist in the patient's brain, they are in some way disconnected so that their functions are no longer available for use in some circumstances. Recall that the patient

with conduction aphasia is unable to repeat what is heard or read. Wernicke produced an hypothesis to explain this condition, which is shown in Figure 18.14. When you listen to speech, the auditory input arrives in the cortex through the primary auditory projection area located in **Heschl's gyrus**, a strip of cortex that forms the floor of the lateral fissure (Figure 18.18). This area provides the input for Wernicke's area that lies partly in the **planum temporale** (also hidden within the lateral fissure) and partly in the superior temporal gyrus (which forms the lower border of the lateral fissure). Figure 18.14 shows a tract, called the **arcuate fasciculus**, looping out of Wernicke's area and running forward through the white matter to connect with the frontal lobe speech areas, including Broca's. After the posterior language area translates the speech sounds into word meanings, the arcuate fasciculus carries this language information to the anterior speech areas to be converted into motor programs that will produce speech. If the whole route is intact, you are able to repeat speech to which you have listened.

As you can now guess, it is the arcuate fasciculus that has been damaged in conduction aphasia, thus disconnecting the comprehension areas from the speech areas (Damasio & Geschwind, 1984; Geschwind, 1972). You can see from Figure 18.14 that Wernicke's hypothesis of language function includes the assumption that speech is produced by Broca's area alone. Fortunately, however, that weakness does not entirely invalidate the theory. We can simply generalize Wernicke's idea to include the whole anterior language area, and the hypothesis still works nicely to explain conduction aphasia.

Transcortical motor aphasia, in close analysis, turns out to be two different defects frequently confused with one another (Ardila & Lopez, 1984). The major symptom, difficulty in initiating speech, can come about from a lesion to the prefrontal zone anterior to Broca's area or from damage to M2, the supplementary motor area lying on the medial surface of the frontal lobe. Lesions in the prefrontal zone may disconnect the language areas from the plans and programs within the rest of the prefrontal cortex that direct behavior. It is not speech that is lost but the intention to speak. Damage to M2, on the other hand, probably disconnects the language mecha-

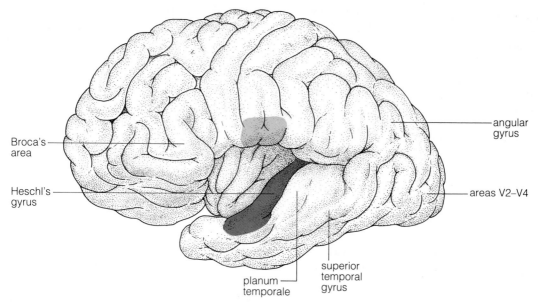

Figure 18.18 A lateral view of the brain with the temporal lobe pulled down to expose the cortex lying within the lateral fissure. This reveals Heschl's gyrus and the planum temporale, both of which are normally hidden from view. Wernicke's area consists of the planum temporale plus some of the posterior part of the superior temporal gyrus. (Adapted from Geschwind, 1972)

nisms from some critical part of the motor system. Patients with M2 damage are mute until you ask them to repeat something, and then their speech seems slow and difficult to produce, apparently requiring considerable effort (Ardila & Lopez, 1984). Recalling the suggestion in Chapter 9 that M2 acts to divide the labor between right and left hemispheres, it is intriguing to consider that with the left M2 missing the nonlanguage areas of the right hemisphere might be interfering with the linguistic tasks of the remaining left-hemisphere cortex. White matter lesions that disconnect M2 and anterior cingulate gyrus from the motor circuits of the caudate nucleus and the area of M1 that controls the speech muscles also results in mutism (Naeser et al., 1989).

Another disconnection syndrome is transcortical sensory aphasia that is characterized by poor comprehension and speech. This combination of symptoms might sound like the result of massive damage to both anterior and posterior language zones until

you recall that the patient is able to repeat much of what is said to him with only a few paraphrasias and neologisms. Geschwind (1972) reported a case of transcortical sensory aphasia in a woman who had suffered considerable brain damage from prolonged carbon monoxide poisoning. Because of the greater vulnerability of the tissue way out at the farthest reaches of an arterial field, a circle of cortex lying at the borders of the middle cerebral artery lost the most cells. The language cortex was completely surrounded by areas of damage. Comprehension of speech was impossible for the patient because the lesions had cut the tracts carrying the language information to other parts of the cortex. Repetition of speech was still possible because the language cortex itself was largely intact, together with its internal connections (such as the arcuate fasciculus). This patient could not only repeat perfectly what was said to her but could also finish common phrases such as "roses are red. ..." However, she had no way to

Figure 18.19 An agraphia patient's attempts to write and print. (**a**) From top to bottom, the patient tried to write "small form" (printing), "small form" (cursive), "antique dealer" (printing), and "antique dealer" (cursive). (**b**) An attempt to print the alphabet. (From Margolin & Binder, 1984)

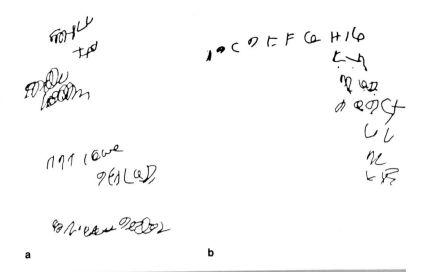

a   b

use her undamaged language cortex in her daily life and, being totally helpless, required full-time nursing care.

Language-Related Syndromes

As you might expect, most aphasic conditions also affect the ability to write words to some extent. However, because writing disability can occasionally occur without aphasia, it is considered by many to be a separate syndrome and given the name **agraphia** (*a* = lack of; *graphia* = writing). Some samples of writing from a patient plus his attempt to print the alphabet are shown in Figure 18.19. Although this patient also had some symptoms of visual agnosia that may have contributed to his inability to form letters, other patients have been reported who were able to copy letters quite legibly despite the fact that spontaneous writing was so poor as to be unreadable (Margolin & Binder, 1984). Apparently, agraphia is not simply an inability to perceive what one is writing. Agraphia has been studied very little, and all that can be said for sure about the site of the lesion is that it usually involves a part of the left parietal lobe (Margolin & Binder, 1984).

The inability to read is termed **alexia**. When an adult loses the ability to read through brain damage,

the disorder is frequently called **acquired alexia**. The adjective *acquired* is intended to separate this disorder from **developmental dyslexia**, which refers to difficulties in *learning* to read seen in some children. (The *dys-* prefix indicates that there is some but not total loss of the function. This is far more common than the total loss suggested by the term *alexia*.) When pure alexia is seen (without agraphia), it is associated with damage to the part of the left parietal lobe just behind Wernicke's area called the **angular gyrus** (Figures 18.14 and 18.18). Perhaps this is the area of cortex in which visual stimuli (i.e., words and letters) are interpreted for their linguistic meaning.

Most cases of acquired alexia involve a lesion that disconnects the visual from the language areas so that the latter are deprived of information about the words on the page (Damasio & Geschwind, 1984). The lesion pictured in Figure 18.20 encroaches on the angular gyrus, but as you can see from the horizontal section, it also slices through much of the white matter leading from the occipital lobe to the more anterior language areas. Loss of white matter disconnects areas of the cortex. Dejerine described a case of pure alexia in which the angular gyrus was undamaged but disconnected from its visual input. The left visual cortex had been destroyed by a stroke

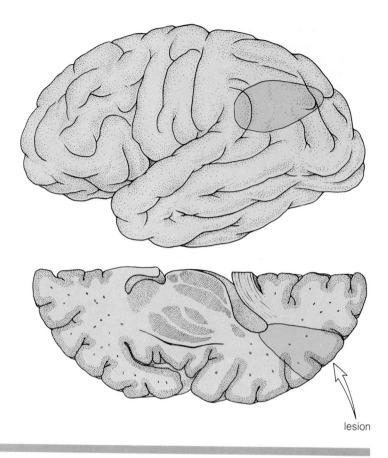

Figure 18.20 Site of a brain lesion that produced alexia and agraphia. The angular gyrus is involved, along with some occipital cortex. The horizontal section through the same brain shows that the lesion ran deep, extending completely through the white matter. (From Henderson, 1986)

lesion

along with the most posterior portion of the corpus callosum (Figure 18.21). Consequently, the patient's language cortex was unable to get any visual information from the missing left occipital lobe and was likewise unable to use input from the remaining right occipital lobe because the connections carrying that information had been lost in the destruction of the visual corpus callosum fibers. The man could see the print very well and had no other language problems, but when it came to reading, he was as helpless as though he were blind (cited in Damasio, 1983). The importance of the corpus callosum in the transfer of information from the processors of the right hemisphere across to the language cortex of the left hemisphere is a topic that we now look at in detail in the next section.

Lateralization of Function

Clinical experience with victims of brain damage strongly suggests that the language functions are localized to the left hemisphere. This sort of hemispheric specialization is called **lateralization** (*lateral* = to one side). Anatomical studies have found evidence that this functional difference may relate to a difference in the sizes of certain cortical areas. The most important of these is the planum temporale, the part of Wernicke's area buried inside of the lateral fissure (see Figure 18.18). The planum temporale is right next to Heschl's gyrus (which is the primary auditory area), and this would seem to be an obvious location for a processor of speech sounds. Figure 18.22 is the result of Geschwind's

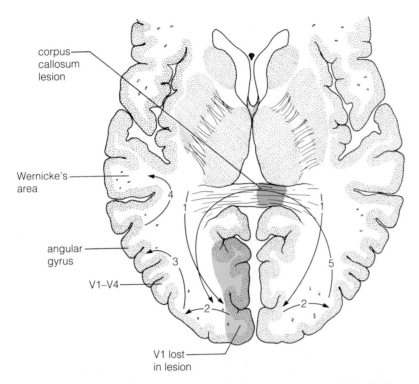

corpus callosum lesion

Wernicke's area

angular gyrus

V1–V4

4

1

1

3

5

2

2

V1 lost in lesion

Figure 18.21 A horizontal brain-section diagram explaining the combination of lesions that produced Dejerine's case of alexia without agraphia. The flow of visual information in a normal brain is indicated by the numbered arrows. In both hemispheres, the input from LGN (1) goes to V1 (the optic radiations). (2) Information from V1 is sent to V2, V3, and V4 and, in the left hemisphere, from there to the angular gyrus (3). From the angular gyrus it goes (4) to Wernicke's area. Information coming into the right hemisphere can normally reach the left by way of the corpus callosum (5). Dejerine's patient could copy written records with no problem but could not read. Because he had lost the V1 area of the left occipital lobe, the only source of visual input for the left hemisphere was by way of the corpus callosum from the right hemisphere. Because visual fibers of the corpus callosum were also lesioned, no visual input reached the language areas. The patient still had vision in the left visual field because the right hemisphere was undamaged. Thus, he could perceive and copy letters and words even if they made no verbal sense to him. The lesions in V1 and corpus callosum are indicated in color.

survey of 100 brains and indicates that the human brain typically (but not always!) has a significantly larger planum temporale in the left hemisphere than in the right (Geschwind & Levitsky, 1968). However, the planum temporale does definitely exist in the right hemisphere, albeit in a smaller version. This suggests that both hemispheres might have language-comprehension areas but that the left hemisphere should be better at comprehending than the right hemisphere. Is this really the case, or is language

Figure 18.22 A brain dissected to show the difference in size between right and left planum temporale. (**a**) A horizontal cut was made from the occipital cortex, forward to the posterior end of the lateral fissure; (**b**) This is what the brain looked like with the upper half and frontal lobes removed. You are viewing the tops of the temporal lobes and the insides of the occipital lobes. The planum temporale (the shaded area on the upper surface of the temporal lobe) was larger in the left hemisphere in 65 percent of the brains examined in this study. (Adapted from Geschwind & Levitsky, 1968)

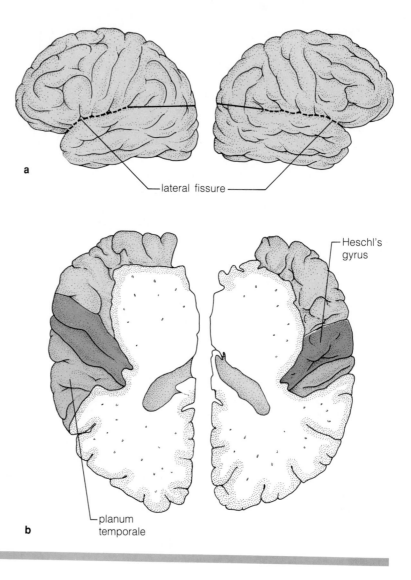

a

lateral fissure

Heschl's gyrus

b

planum temporale

completely lateralized to the left? Are any other functions lateralized, or is language alone in this hemispheric division of labor? It has not been easy to gain answers to questions of this sort. Researchers have run afoul of several obstacles stemming from the way in which the nervous system is organized and have responded by inventing and discovering a number of very clever techniques for surmounting those roadblocks to knowledge. Let's see what the problems have been and how they were solved.

Studying Lateralization

How do you go about testing each hemisphere separate from the other to see if its abilities differ from that of its counterpart? The answer, at least in part, would be to find a way to present stimuli exclusively to the hemisphere being tested. For example, let first the right then the left hemisphere look at a set of visual stimuli and see which is better at identifying them. This sounds much easier than it really is.

Visual Studies Presenting a word or picture exclusively to the right hemisphere is an easy matter, isn't it? All you have to do is to cover the right eye. Correct? If you agree with that erroneous statement, it is time to go back to Figure 18.9 for a very thorough look at how the visual fields are represented in the cortex. That figure shows you that the visual *field* of each eye (the part of your environment seen at any one moment by that eye) is split vertically down the middle through the foveal region so that the image from the left visual field falls on the right side of each retina and is sent to the right occipital lobe; the image from the left field is processed by the right occipital lobe. (It is a good idea to verify this in Figure 18.9 because much of the following discussion depends on a very clear understanding of these ideas.)

So, the anatomy of the visual system tells us that it is possible to restrict the initial visual input to one hemisphere or the other by presenting the stimulus to one side of the midline of the visual field. Any stimulus to the right of the midline enters the left occipital lobe and anything to the left of the midline is handled by right hemisphere. However, this method of stimulus presentation is not easily accomplished; human reflexes keep interfering. If a word is flashed on a screen in front of you but to one side of your fixation point, you will reflexively move your eyes so that the image falls on your fovea. Of course, when you do that, the image is then sent to both hemispheres, and the experimental procedure is ruined. To prevent this, visual stimuli are presented with an instrument called a **tachistoscope** (tah-KISS-tah-scope), which allows one to view the stimulus for a limited amount of time. A 100-ms presentation is short enough to be over before an eye movement can be made but long enough that the visual system can perceive the stimulus if attention is focused. This procedure has become a standard method, called **hemifield** (half-field) **tachistoscopy** (TACK-is-TAH-sko-pee), and has been used in literally hundreds of experiments. Currently, most tachistoscopy is done with a computer.

Tachistoscopy experiments in which the subject must repeat a word presented to either the right or left visual field reveal a slight bias in favor of the right field. Thus, fewer errors are made in identifying words when they are presented in the right field than in the left. This right-field preference also shows up for identifying letters, digits, and nonsense syllables (Beaumont, 1982) and is interpreted to mean that language is better represented in the left hemisphere. However, the small size of the typical difference between fields does not support the idea that language is very highly lateralized. The problem with hemifield tachistoscopy is that it can guarantee only to *deliver* the stimulus to one hemisphere; there is no way to keep it there as long as the corpus callosum is intact. Presumably, any information coming into the right hemisphere will be available to the left hemisphere within a second, and this clouds the interpretation of these experiments. In fact, it becomes difficult to understand why there should be any difference at all, even if the language cortex turns out to be exclusively in the left hemisphere. This is still a mystery, but the tachistoscope studies cannot be abandoned because they do keep producing hemispheric differences that must be understood.

Auditory Studies Is there any way to present auditory stimuli exclusively to one hemisphere? Unfortunately for researchers, the auditory projection system sends information from the right ear up both sides of the brain stem to reach Heschl's gyrus in both temporal lobes. Thus, a stimulus to either ear reaches both hemispheres. However, the **contralateral projection**—the one that crosses to the opposite side—is considerably stronger than the **ipsilateral** (same side) **projection**, and there is a widely used research technique that apparently takes advantage of this. In a **dichotic-listening** experiment (dye-COT-ick), the subject (wearing earphones) hears a separate string of digits in each ear and tries to repeat them. The right ear might receive "38, 81, 94" while the left ear is simultaneously hearing "46, 12, 67." Few subjects can repeat all numbers with complete accuracy, and more errors are made on the stimuli for the left ear. Why does this right-ear preference occur? It could be because contralateral projections are stronger than ipsilateral projections and the contralateral projection from the *right* ear leads to the left hemisphere. If we are correct about language being lateralized to the left hemisphere, then the dichotic-listening experiment makes sense. The language hemisphere "hears better out of the right ear," so to speak. (Remember that spoken digits are *words*.)

Note that this right-ear preference only occurs when there is a conflict between the two inputs. For example, if the digits are presented alternately between the two ears, the effect fails to show.

Doreen Kimura, the first scientist to study lateralization using dichotic listening, became curious about what functions might be lateralized to the right hemisphere. She knew that patients with lesions of the right anterior temporal lobe found it difficult to discriminate between different tone qualities and patterns but that left temporal lobe lesions produced no such deficit (Milner, 1975). She guessed that music perception might be a right temporal lobe function and set up a dichotic-listening experiment using short, melodic segments. Her subjects heard a different melody in each ear and then were asked to identify the two from a multiple choice set of melodies. There was, as Kimura predicted, a significant left-ear preference, suggesting a right-hemisphere specialization for music (Kimura, 1964). Later research showed us that the division between hemispheres cannot be characterized quite this easily. Both hemispheres are involved in processing the rhythmic aspect of familiar music as well as the phrasing. The right hemisphere seems more important for remembering the correct sequence of pitches (Shapiro et al., 1981). It may also be superior to the left for recognizing natural noises and various sound qualities (such as the difference between voices or musical instruments) (Ardila & Ostrosky-Solis, 1984).

However, along with a great number of interesting experimental results, researchers using dichotic listening have encountered the same problem that is seen in the hemifield tachistoscopy studies; the right-left differences are quite small. In the case of the digits, 15 subjects showed a right-ear preference, whereas only 3 favored the left ear—excellent results—but when all the errors were totalled up, digits presented to the right ear were incorrectly reported 6 percent of the time and those to the left ear 10 percent of the time. The lateralization effect showed as a 4 percent difference. Does this represent the degree to which the two hemispheres are specialized, or have we again run up against the problem of interhemispheric transfer? That is, were the left-ear, right-hemisphere responses more accurate than expected because the digits presented to the left ear were transferred across the corpus callosum to the language cortex of the left hemisphere? It would seem that the existence of the corpus callosum prevents a really definitive answer to the question of hemispheric specialization. Is there any way to eliminate its influence?

Studies of Bisected Brains A little over 40 people in the United States have undergone a form of neurosurgery in which the corpus callosum is cut in order to prevent the spread of epileptic seizure activity from the hemisphere of its origin into the "good" hemisphere. Such surgery is a last desperate measure, undertaken after drug control has failed, but it is amazingly successful. It not only eliminates the spread of seizures but seems to also diminish or eliminate the epilepsy in the "bad" hemisphere as well (Gazzaniga, 1967). With the callosum eliminated, the only connections remaining between the hemispheres above the level of the brain stem are the relatively small anterior, posterior, and hippocampal commissures (Figure 18.23). Even these were cut in the early versions of the operation.

Amazingly enough, the patient's everyday behavior seems little affected by this drastic splitting of the brain. There is no noticeable alteration in personality, temperament, or intelligence (Gazzaniga, 1967). Roger Sperry, at Cal Tech, began working with these patients in 1961, using an experimental arrangement like the one in Figure 18.24. The subject is asked to fixate on a point in the middle of the projection screen and report what he sees. The experimenter flashes six spots of light onto the screen too rapidly for eye movements, and the spots are arranged in a row so that three are to the left of the fixation point and three to the right. The subject reports seeing three lights, not six! If a single light is flashed to one side or other of the fixation point, it is reported when it appears in the right visual field but not in the left. Is the patient blind in the left field? Not at all; if you ask him to point whenever

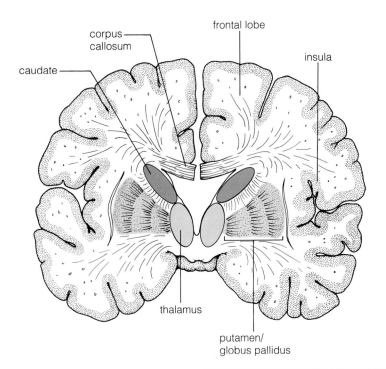

Figure 18.23 A frontal brain section showing the surgical cut made in hemispheric disconnection. Early operations cut the entire corpus callosum plus anterior and posterior commissures (not shown here). Later cases showed that epilepsy could be halted even though the commissures and much of the corpus callosum is left intact. (From Sperry, 1975)

he sees a light flashed, he points at both the right- and left-field flashes. When the word *heart* is presented so that the fixation falls between the *e* and the *a* (HE*ART) the subject reports seeing the word *art*. However, if after seeing the word, he is asked to point with his left hand to one of two cards, one of which has *he* and the other *art*, the patient points to *he*.

All these results make sense if you assume that surgery has left the person with two nearly separate brains that function with considerable independence under the rather unusual conditions of the experiment. Remember that the right hemisphere is seeing only the left field and the left hemisphere only the right field. If we are correct in proposing that the left hemisphere is the only one in control of the speech apparatus, then all verbal answers must be made by that hemisphere. When you ask the subject, "how many lights were there?" you are really only asking the left hemisphere, and that hemisphere saw

only three lights, not six. The same reasoning explains why a single light would be reported in the right field but not in the left. The hemisphere to which you are talking—the left—saw only the lights in the right field. However, when you allowed the patient to point to any light seen, then the right hemisphere could also get into the act by way of its control over the left hand; thus, the light was indicated no matter what side of the field it was on if the response was one available to both hemispheres. When the stimulus is the word "HE*ART," the left hemisphere reports verbally exactly what it saw ("ART") but the right hemisphere can use the left hand to point to what it saw ("HE").

This same apparently paradoxical result occurs when the patient is asked to name objects from touch. An object placed in the right hand can be named without trouble but an object in the left hand cannot. However, if the response requested of the subject is not one of naming but rather of selecting

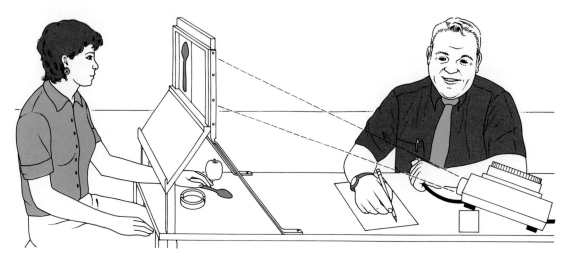

Figure 18.24 An experimental arrangement for collecting data from hemispheric-disconnection patients. The slide projector at the right has a tachistoscopic shutter that allows the images to be projected for measured fractions of a second. The subject focuses on the dot at the center of the screen on which the images will appear. This ensures that stimuli on the right side of the screen will be sent to the left hemisphere and vice versa. (Adapted from Gazzaniga, 1983)

a previously felt object from a row of objects by touch, then the left hand is as good as the right. During the original touching with the left hand, the somatosensory information went to the right hemisphere; so even though that hemisphere knows what was touched, no verbal reply can be expected. However, it can reveal this knowledge by manually selecting the correct object.

Clinical reports from cases of brain damage suggested that spatial perception was more a function of right than of left parietal lobes, so tests were devised by Sperry and Gazzaniga to see if spatial functions were lateralized. A split-brain patient was shown a colored design such as the one in Figure 18.25 and asked to create a duplicate of it from blocks. The patient, W. J., rapidly assembled the blocks with his left hand (right hemisphere) to form the pattern; but when the task was given to the right hand (left hemisphere), there was great hesitation and impression of difficulty (cited in Springer & Deutsch, 1981). At one point, the right hemisphere apparently became frustrated with the rate of prog-

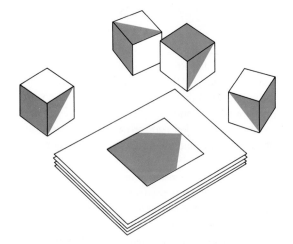

Figure 18.25 The block-design test used to measure spatial abilities. The subject is shown a series of designs, each of which must be duplicated by assembling the blocks into the correct pattern. (From Springer & Deutsch, 1981)

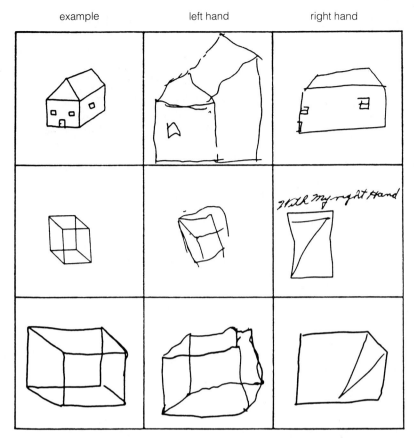

example	left hand	right hand

Will my right Hand

Figure 18.26 Drawings made by a hemispheric-disconnections patient. The first column shows the examples to be copied. Column 2 contains the productions of left hand–right hemisphere and column 3 the drawings by the right hand–left hemisphere. There is a greater precision and regularity of line in the right-handed drawings (reflecting the years of practice at eye–hand coordination stored in the left hemisphere), but comprehension of spatial form is very poor compared to that demonstrated by the left hand–right hemisphere. (From Gazzaniga, 1967)

ress, for the left hand crept in and began to make corrections. The experimenter had to restrain it. While L. B. (another patient) was performing on this task with his right hand, his left hand also attempted to speed the job, but in this case the patient's right hand slapped the interfering left and the patient was heard to say, "that will keep it quiet for a while" (Bogen, 1985).

In another test of spatial understanding, the patient had to copy the same drawing with his left hand and then his right. He was normally right-handed, and Figure 18.26 shows that his left-handed productions were shaky with clumsy, wavy lines, whereas his right-handed drawings were reasonably neat and had straight lines. However, the drawings done by the right hand resembled the original pic-

tures only vaguely (Gazzaniga et al., 1965). Compare the two drawings at the bottom; the left hand's drawing, although clumsy, is recognizable as a cube, whereas the drawing done by the right hand makes no sense at all. Although the left-hemisphere M1 area probably had benefited from years of practice at coordinating eye and hand in moving a pencil over paper, it had apparently been the *right*-hemisphere parietal lobe that had been deciding the shape of what was to be drawn.

When these results are put together with data from patients with unilateral brain damage and with data from normals, they suggest an hypothesis: The right hemisphere may store information about visual forms as pure shapes, whereas the left stores verbal descriptions of shapes (Ardila & Ostrosky-Solis,

1984). Thus, a particular face might be stored in the right hemisphere as a collection of geometric forms but in the left hemisphere as a collection of verbal concepts. However, hemispheric specialization for face recognition occurs even when there are no verbal functions in the left hemisphere, as in the monkey. A study of 25 split-brain monkeys revealed significantly better scores for the right hemisphere than the left in a face-discrimination task (Hamilton & Vermeire, 1988). Early in the history of this research, it was thought that engrams of faces were stored exclusively in the right hemisphere, but this simplistic interpretation has been challenged (Sergent & Bindra, 1981). Brain-damage patients who completely lose the ability to discriminate one face from another have damage in both hemispheres rather than just in right hemisphere (Ardila & Ostrosky-Solis, 1984). Sergent (1985) concluded that the right hemisphere seems to take care of perceiving the gross outlines of facial features, whereas the left hemisphere fills in the details of surface texture, hair, and so forth.

The right hemisphere also seems better at some auditory discriminations (Sidtis & Gazzaniga, 1981) and the identification of objects by active touch (LeDoux, 1979).

Early in the history of split-brain research, there was considerable doubt that the mind could stay integrated into just one consciousness when the brain was so badly split. The symptom of **intermanual conflict** in which one hand opposes what the other is doing seemed to be very convincing evidence for the existence of two separate minds in one head. When a patient is observed buttoning her shirt with one hand while the other (unobserved) tries to unbutton it, the idea of a double consciousness springs readily to mind. Intermanual conflict, however, turned out to be a transitory phenomenon, usually disappearing within 2–3 weeks (Bogen, 1985). It seems that as the brain adjusts to its new condition, during the weeks following surgery, it reorganizes to take maximum advantage of its subcortical interhemispheric connections in order to maintain a single consciousness as much as possible. Perhaps that is why the everyday behavior of split-brain patients seems so normal in almost every respect.

Right-Hemisphere Language Abilities

In some of the experiments with split-brain patients previously described, the right hemisphere made responses requested by the experimenter. Apparently, the right hemisphere can follow verbal instructions, and this fact implies some sort of language ability. We have explained many of the experimental results by reasoning based on the premise that the right hemisphere cannot speak, but this doesn't mean that it cannot comprehend spoken or written language. When children lose their left hemisphere early in life, they still can develop language abilities that appear quite normal unless special tests are applied. They have adequate comprehension but inferior speech and syntax (Zaidel, 1985). Apparently, the right hemisphere is not genetically different enough from the left that it cannot take over basic language functions when the left hemisphere is absent. Yet similar damage in adulthood can produce global aphasia.

Among the researchers who work with split-brain patients, there is sharp conflict over the extent to which language abilities exist in the right hemisphere. Zaidel finds language abilities in almost all right hemispheres of his patient group (Zaidel, 1983), whereas Gazzaniga claims that only a handful of patients have ever shown any sign of right-hemisphere language (Gazzaniga, 1983). Controversy of this sort arises to fill vacuums created by lack of good data. Split-brain patients are extremely rare. There are only two groups of them in the nation: the "California series" consisting of 11 patients examined by Sperry, Zaidel, and others and Gazzaniga's group of 29 patients in the East and Midwest (Zaidel, 1983). All data, of course, are collected on a volunteer basis, and with so few subjects, our knowledge of hemispheric function in bisected brains has crept forward at a snail's pace during the quarter of a century since the first operation.

Studying right-hemisphere language comprehension is a tricky business because there is no way to speak to the right brain without the left "listening in." Zaidel tries to get around this problem by presenting visual stimuli in the left visual field and then asking questions about the stimuli verbally or presenting the instructions visually to just one hemisphere (Zaidel, 1985). For example, one method calls for him to present a word visually to the right hemisphere and then ask the subject to pick that word out of a list of spoken words. Theoretically, the left brain cannot interfere with this test because only the right hemisphere saw the printed word. As we'll see shortly, however, Gazzaniga disagrees with this reasoning and demonstrates a way in which the left hemisphere might still determine the response.

To examine language functions more complex than simple word recognition, Zaidel uses the **token test** in which the subject must follow complex instructions like "put the red circle between the green square and the yellow triangle." The subject can manipulate objects on the table in front of her while viewing the scene with only the right hemisphere, thanks to a special apparatus invented by Zaidel. A contact lens and viewer are used to throw the entire image from right and left visual fields onto just one-half of the retina—the half that projects to the right hemisphere. This eliminates the need for tachistoscopic viewing. However, contact lenses must be made specially for each individual subject, and it is not entirely clear that Zaidel has used this apparatus with more than two subjects. In any case, Zaidel claims that tests such as the token test show that the "typical" right hemisphere can comprehend printed and spoken language to some extent. On the token test, subjects score about as well as a 4-year-old, whereas other tests indicate relatively poor grasp of grammar and syntax (Levy, 1979; Zaidel, 1985). Concrete nouns are easier for the right hemisphere than are abstract nouns, and it seems to have considerable ability to comprehend spatial prepositions (*on, under, in*). However, it has considerable trouble with numbers and words about quantities (*middle, many, two*). Zaidel sums up by stating that, for most components of language, the right hemisphere has the competence of a normal 3- to 6-year-old (Zaidel, 1985).

Gazzaniga claims that almost all of Zaidel's data indicating right-hemisphere language came from two subjects. In his own subject set, Gazzaniga has found only 3 people out of 28 who had any evidence at all of language capability on the right side of the brain (Gazzaniga, 1983). Two of the 3 (V. P. and P. S.) can actually control speech from the right hem-

isphere, but this capacity developed slowly over several years following surgery. Interestingly, both these patients underwent two-stage operations in which one-half of the corpus callosum (e.g., the anterior portion) was cut several months before the final stage of complete bisection. It is conceivable that some reorganization of the brain occurred during the time when half the corpus callosum still functioned that allowed the right hemisphere to take on a speech ability. The three patients with right-hemisphere language showed in Gazzaniga's tests that their right hemispheres varied considerably in how much vocabulary and syntax were available and that none of them possess language or cognitive skills equal to those of the left hemispheres (Gazzaniga et al., 1984; Gazzaniga & Smylie, 1984).

One of the findings that makes Gazzaniga extremely wary about interpreting experimental results to mean that the right hemisphere of a particular patient possesses language ability is the fact that the left hemisphere gets so clever at picking up subtle cues from the behavior controlled by the right brain and using them to correctly infer what was shown to the right. Gazzaniga and Hillyard (1971) discovered this phenomenon early in the history of split-brain research and dubbed it **cross cueing**. An example occurred when some patients began to name objects held out of sight in the left hand. They could not do this before because in a bisected brain the left-hemisphere speech areas get information only from the *right* hand. Had the right hemisphere suddenly developed speech? No, it was merely that the left hand was cueing the left hemisphere by making distinctive sounds with the object (e.g., running the finger down the teeth of a comb or stroking the bristles of a brush). This sort of cross cueing is fairly obvious and more easily controlled than some of the subtle forms. One patient who showed no ability to name objects held in his left hand or pictures flashed to his left field (i.e., no sign of right-hemisphere speech) was able to repeat digits shown to the right hemisphere. The right brain could probably read the digit, but it was highly unlikely that it could speak the word because there were no other indications of right-brain speech. The experimenters suspected cross cueing to the left brain, but how was it being accomplished? Apparently, when the right brain received a digit, the left hemisphere started counting silently. The right hemisphere, feeling the slight movements of the speech muscles, knew when the left had reached the correct digit and would make some movement to signal that it should stop counting. The left brain then reported the last digit in its count. The experimenters noted that the higher the digit, the longer it took the subject to respond.

Cross cueing may be done without the patient deliberately striving to fool the experimenters. It is simply a natural, human response to try everything possible to win in a challenging situation. All these considerations created great difficulties for anyone trying to clearly demonstrate right-hemisphere language, and Gazzaniga, having several decades of experience with this problem, is suspicious of the data from the California series. He believes that the five patients who clearly show right-hemisphere language capabilities are exceptions to the rule because of brain damage. Keep in mind that all these people had such bad cases of epilepsy that the radical brain-bisection operation was finally deemed warranted. Early (infantile) brain damage in the left-hemisphere language areas may shift language development in the right hemisphere. So Gazzaniga cautions us that their right-hemisphere language is probably not typical for people without brain damage in the left hemisphere.

Levy, who has worked with many of the California patients, agrees with Gazzaniga about this but disagrees that the right hemisphere has no ability at all to recognize words visually and in spoken form (Levy, 1983). She argues that words can be treated as simple visual stimuli apart from their semantic meanings and be associated with other stimuli in a nonlinguistic fashion. This is why the right hemisphere can follow simple verbal directions. It has had years to associate the sounds of the words *raise* and *hand* with an upward direction and a particular part of the body. So, when the experimenter informs the right hemisphere that it should "raise your hand," the simple associations stored in that part of the cortex are sufficient to get the job done.

Perhaps the ideal source of data to bring to bear on this problem can be found in a clinical procedure used prior to cortical surgery for the relief of epilepsy. When a surgeon has decided that seizures can be reduced or eliminated by removing troublesome areas of diseased cortex, it becomes very important to find where the language cortex is. A person can function reasonably well after removal of somatosensory or motor areas, but to deprive a person of language ability is to seriously impair that person's chances to function in our society. So, a test is made prior to surgery to see if language is in this patient's right or left hemisphere. A very short-acting barbiturate, **sodium amytal**, is injected directly into one of the major arteries going up the neck to the brain, the external carotid. This artery serves only one hemisphere, so the drug puts one side of the brain to sleep while the other side remains awake. This is called the **Wada test** after the man who devised it in 1949. The Wada test can tell us whether speech can be controlled by either hemisphere or just by one. The results of testing showed that the vast majority of patients are able to continue speaking as the right hemisphere is drugged but lose speech for a few minutes when the amytal is sent to the left side of the brain. Milner found disturbance of speech from right carotid injection in 17 out of 117 left-handed or ambidextrous patients and in one out of 95 right-handers (cited in Roberts, 1969). In another report, 2 patients out of 30 showed bilateral representation of speech. This is very similar to the frequency that Gazzaniga claims for right-hemisphere language in bisected brains and, as he suggests, could be the result of early brain damage shifting the speech cortex from the damaged left hemisphere to the healthy right.

More recent use of Wada data, however, shows that language lateralization may not be an either/or phenomenon. McGlone (1984) found that patients who showed speech blocking when the left hemisphere was drugged were able to follow simple commands, such as "raise your hand," but were unable to follow the directions on the token test. This fits Levy's suggestion that the right hemisphere has a stimulus–response level of word comprehension rather than a full linguistic understanding. It enables the right side to make many intelligent responses to words but treats them more as sounds or pictures than verbal concepts. This idea fits with the data on prosody.

Prosody is the intonation aspect of speech that

gives it a rhythm and musical quality. If someone calls your name and you answer yes?, the sounds you have uttered are quite different than if you are asked whether you like something and you reply yes! The difference does not involve syntax, grammar, or choice of words. It is a difference between a rising inflection in the questioning yes versus a descending pitch at the end of the emphatic yes—in other words, a prosodic difference. Ross (1981, 1984) has collected evidence for the hypothesis that prosody is the right hemisphere's contribution to speech (Figure 18.27). This would fit with the evidence mentioned earlier in this chapter that musical abilities are represented in right hemisphere. However, it appears that the syllable-emphasis aspect of prosody that allows us to tell the difference between *OBject* (a thing) and *obJECT* (disagree) is located in left hemisphere (Emmorey, 1987). Prosody also includes the emotional tone of speech (e.g., the difference between angry and frightened), and this aspect apparently is right hemisphere (Ross, 1984).

To sum up what we have found: It seems that most people use their left hemisphere for all their speech processing and much of language comprehension (except for some aspects of prosody and some word associations). However, those who suffer left-hemisphere damage in infancy may develop more reliance on right-brain language, the amount varying with the individual case all the way from limited comprehension to good comprehension plus speech capability.

Development of Lateralization and Handedness

The probability that infants with left-hemisphere damage develop right-hemisphere language leads us to wonder whether we are born with our brains fully lateralized or acquire hemispheric specialization gradually through experience. A great number of experiments have been directed at answering this question, and two major theoretical views have emerged (Hahn, 1987). Lenneberg holds that the hemispheres are equipotential for language during infancy (until about age 2) and that lateralization occurs slowly throughout childhood. In other words, language learning is going on in both hemispheres early in life but tapers off in the right hemisphere

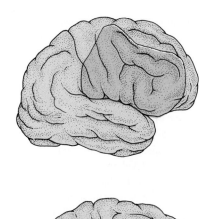

a

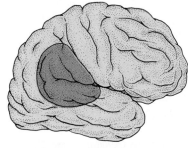

b

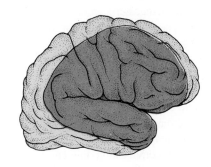

c

Figure 18.27 Locations of lesions of the right hemisphere associated with deficits in prosody (aprosodia). More anterior lesions (**a**) produce motor aprosodia, an inability to use emotional gestures or tones in speech. More posterior lesions (**b**) are associated with sensory aprosodia, a deficit in comprehending the gestures or prosody of other people. Global aprosodia (**c**) includes both sensory and motor deficits. (From Ross, 1984)

as lateralization is acquired. Kinsbourne, on the other hand, contends that children are born already lateralized and that no changes occur with development. If you have taken a course in the psychology of childhood, you may recognize this difference of opinion as a variation on the old nature–nurture argument: are the child's abilities the result of heredity or environment? It is somewhat surprising that neuropsychologists should still be stuck at this level of theory when developmental psychologists outgrew this sort of black-white conceptualization decades ago. Experience has taught most psychologists that both genetic and experiential factors are *always* at work in any human phenomenon. Let us look first at some of the evidence favoring each extreme position and then attempt to put together a reasonable compromise. We will begin with Lenneberg's idea that lateralization is entirely the result of development.

Does Lateralization Develop During Childhood?

Lenneberg's idea is that the specialization of one hemisphere for language is acquired slowly through experience. The role of the genes would be to provide the left hemisphere some slight, built-in superiority at birth that would gradually, over the first 4 or 5 years, give it more and more dominance for this function. Just as the "rich get richer," the left brain would obtain a larger and larger share of any language learning available in each new daily experience until it reached the point (somewhere in late childhood) of commanding the entire language function.

One can deduce from this hypothesis that there should be some residue of this early right-hemisphere language learning. Because comprehension learning begins much earlier in infancy than does speech learning, the right hemisphere's theoretical language residue should be biased toward word recognition rather than toward speech. This is pretty much what Zaidel seems to find in his split-brain patients. He stated that his tests revealed right hemispheres to have the language capacity of a normal child between the ages of 3 and 6 and that this was best explained by the idea that in early childhood both hemispheres were learning language (Zaidel,

1985). The reason that none of the right brains function beyond the 6-year level is that lateralization may have been completed by that time and that the right hemispheres were shut off from further language learning.

Also in favor of Lenneberg's hypothesis is the fact that some of the split-brain patients definitely exhibit right-hemisphere speech, even though this function was clearly not present immediately after the operation. Recall that one split-brain patient first demonstrated right-brain language ability a full year after surgery and required many months for it to develop to its current level of proficiency. This means that it was *not* present prior to the surgery, and that is evidence that the right hemisphere is not excluded by the genes from learning language. Given this fact, it is not clear exactly what Kinsbourne means when he says that language is "lateralized" at birth. If lateralization does not involve prohibiting the right brain from learning language by building it to perform other functions, then to what does it refer?

A supporter of Kinsbourne's **invariance hypothesis** (the idea that lateralization is present at birth and does not increase with experience) could argue that Lenneberg contradicts himself. He claims that the hemispheres are equipotential at birth for language learning and yet must postulate some genetic factor to give the left hemisphere a slightly greater language-acquisition ability at birth that makes it possible for it to slowly acquire dominance. Clearly, there cannot be complete equipotentiality. In fact, we know that the language areas of the left hemisphere are not even the same size as the comparable areas in the right brain. Recall Geschwind's data showing the much greater size of the planum temporale in the left hemisphere. Recent studies show that these anatomical differences between the hemispheres are there at birth and, even before that, in fetuses (LeMay, 1982). Perhaps, the genetic predisposition toward left-brain language acquisition is nothing more than simply providing that hemisphere with more space in which to do the learning.

To explore language lateralization in children, Kinsbourne has used an interesting technique called **time sharing**. The subject is given two tasks to perform simultaneously, such as reciting something out loud plus balancing a dowel rod on one hand. It turned out that the dowel could be balanced much better in the left hand than in the right, but only when the person was speaking at the same time (Hicks, 1975). In a more common variation of time sharing, children (from the ages of 3½ to 12½ years) are asked to name animals or recite nursery rhymes while tapping a key as fast as possible with one hand. The rate of tapping is measured and is found to be slowed below normal during the recitation. Usually, the right hand can tap faster than the left, but this advantage is lost during the recitation (Hiscock & Kinsbourne, 1980; White & Kinsbourne, 1980). The best interpretation of these results appears to be that a hemisphere is best at doing just one thing at once. When the right hand is required to balance a dowel or tap a key as the person speaks, the left hemisphere must control both a manual and speech output simultaneously. In a fully lateralized brain, the left hand can balance the dowel better because it has no other task to perform that could interfere. The term *time sharing* comes from computer vocabulary where it refers to the method of rapidly alternating back and forth between work on two tasks to give the appearance of performing both simultaneously. It is doubtful that the human brain really "time shares" in this original sense, but the data do suggest that each hemisphere does have some sort of capacity for controlling output that has definite limits, for whatever reason.

Kinsbourne uses the time-sharing technique to show that the disruptive effect that speaking has on tapping was just as strong in the youngest children as in the oldest tested. This suggests to him that brains are fully lateralized in the youngest children and that development did not increase hemispheric specialization, as Lenneberg would have it (White & Kinsbourne, 1980). Studies using hemifield tachistoscopy, dichotic-listening, and other techniques with normal subjects also support the idea that lateralization does not increase during childhood (Hahn, 1987). The problem with the time-sharing studies is their exceptionally naïve measurement of language ability. So far they have tested none of the higher-level language processes (such as the prepositional logic of *under, around, in front of,* etc.) and have chosen to test functions (like naming) that are among those most likely to be learned by both hemispheres (if both are learning). In other words, with language tasks designed for 3-year-olds, you will never be able to demonstrate any greater lateralization than that possessed by a 3-year-old. It is not surprising that Kinsbourne finds invariance.

One way to address this problem is to ask, What should happen to lateralization if normal language experience were prevented? Lenneberg would have to predict that less-than-expected degrees of lateralization would be present in older children, whereas the invariance hypothesis would say that lateralization should still be found because it was inborn. Children with severe hearing impairments who have learned to read should provide us with a test for these predictions. Kelly and Tomlinson-Keasey (1981), using hemifield tachistoscopy, showed words to such children (third- to fifth-grade reading levels) and found that reaction times for word recognition were no different between right and left hemispheres. In contrast, normal-hearing children showed a marked right-field (left-hemisphere) preference, as would be expected. This suggests that lack of experience at hearing words impaired lateralization, and this in turn suggests that lateralization is something that has to develop with experience.

In trying to draw some conclusions from this controversy, we should keep in mind the decades of experience that developmental psychologists have had with similar nature–nurture arguments. The final resolution has always been that both genetic and developmental factors interact to produce the final product—in this case, lateralization of language. If one asks, Is language lateralization completely genetic or completely the product of experience?, the controversy can rage for years because neither answer is correct.

Considering how much good evidence has accrued for both hereditary and environmental determination of lateralization, it seems reasonable to conclude that

1. There must be some genetic factor that *predisposes* the left hemisphere (in most people)

toward language learning and "inhibits" the right hemisphere from duplicating that learning unless the left brain is damaged. [Although he is a supporter of the invariance hypothesis, Woods (1983) agrees that the data support this limited role for heredity.]

2. That this inherited predisposition is not for all of language but for specific elements of linguistic function, especially speech and complex syntactical and grammatical parts of comprehension. Zaidel (1985) has marshaled considerable evidence for this very reasonable compromise.

There is one other very important factor to consider: individual differences. Why have only five split-brain patients acquired clear-cut evidence of right-hemisphere language? Do some people inherit a weaker predisposition to lateralize than others and wind up with more right-brain language ability? These questions are best answered as we move on to consider the matter of handedness.

The Development of Handedness   It is difficult to be a left-handed person in a world that considers all left-handers to be sinister by nature. If you are left-handed, you are, quite literally, sinister. If you don't believe that, look up the word *sinister* in any dictionary. The definition in *The American College Dictionary* (Random House) says "of or on the left side; left" and "threatening, bad, unfortunate." The ideas of *left hand* and *bad* have been linked for centuries in our culture and that probably traces back to the simple fact that the majority always has the privilege of defining what is considered right. (Notice that when we mean *correct* we say *right.*) Because the term *left-handed* is somewhat clumsy to use, many researchers favor the technical terms **sinistral** (left-hander) and **dextral** (right-hander); we will employ those designations below.

An idea that has been around for some time without much of any evidence favoring it is the **contralateral rule** that claims that the speech hemisphere is always the one contralateral to the preferred hand. Dextrals would have left-hemisphere language and sinistrals, right-hemisphere language. This notion has often been extended to another doubtful idea— that of **hemispheric dominance** that holds that the

hemisphere containing language and the motor area for the preferred hand is in some way stronger than the other hemisphere and dominates brain function. Data from Wada testing should help us evaluate the truth of the contralateral rule because it reveals which hemisphere contains the speech areas. Roughly 89 percent of the general population is right-handed, and of these, 99 percent have the language cortex in the left hemisphere, according to Wada testing (cited in Levy, 1974). Approximately 11 percent of the population is left-handed, and of these 56 percent also have left-hemisphere speech. The remaining 44 percent either have right-hemisphere speech or seem to have speech in both hemispheres ("bilaterality"). Not even the Wada test is foolproof, however, and it is not surprising that other sources yield somewhat different figures. Satz (1979), using data from aphasia studies, estimates that 70 percent of sinistrals have speech bilaterally represented. Apparently, there is little evidence that the contralateral rule holds. Even sinistrals tend to have left-hemisphere speech, and of those who don't, the tendency is toward *lack* of lateralization rather than right-hemisphere language.

Lack of lateralization for language is matched by incomplete handedness in the so-called left-handers. Upon close inspection, it turns out that only dextrals are clearly handed. Some sinistrals may write with their left hand but cut with scissors using their right hand. Or they may cut paper, catch balls, and hold forks with their left hands but write with the right. All possible combinations of lateralized motor activities seem to be present, and the business of classifying a person for handedness often leads the investigator to ask a whole series of questions about which hand is used in particular activities and then calling a person sinistral if they get a left-hand score over a certain arbitrary number. In fact, some researchers have given up talking about sinistrals and simply refer to "right-handers" versus "non–right-handers." There is some question then about whether there really is a true category of left-handedness. It appears that both language and handedness may be incompletely lateralized in some brains.

The lack of language lateralization in sinistrals also shows up in the fact that they tend to recover to a greater degree from aphasia and tend to do it more rapidly than do dextrals (Curtiss, 1985; Levy, 1974). In accordance with this are the findings in dichotic-listening and hemifield tachistoscopy studies that frequently fail to show ear preferences and right-field preferences for sinistrals when such preferences are clearly present for dextrals (cited in Springer & Deutsch, 1981). Such evidence suggests that there is a large group of humans that are clearly right-handed and have left-hemisphere speech and that a smaller group (about 11 percent) shows a range of lateralization from slightly left hemisphere through bilateral to slightly right hemisphere and strongly right hemisphere.

How does this arrangement come about? One suggestion is that sinistrality is an error—the result of brain damage (Bakan, 1977). If the left hemisphere is damaged early in life, functions located there would have to shift to the right hemisphere. The more extensive the damage, the greater the shift; thus, varying degrees of early damage would produce varying degrees of handedness and language lateralization. It is unfortunate that such a clear explanation should receive so little experimental confirmation, but that is the case (Beaumont, 1983; Springer & Deutsch, 1981). There does seem to be a small number of sinistrals who could be said to have **pathological sinistrality** (left-handedness based on brain damage), but they account for only a small percentage of sinistrals.

Most left-handers are **familial sinistrals**, that is, they have a number of sinistrals in their immediate family. Having a number of sinistrals in the same family suggests that sinistrality can be inherited but not in any simple way as with dominant and recessive traits. Annett (1981) has made a careful genetic analysis of the data and suggests an explanation she calls the **right-shift theory**. She postulates that there is no gene for handedness itself, but there is one that creates a left-hemisphere advantage for language (perhaps, determining the size of the planum temporale?), and in the process of establishing left-hemisphere language, the bias toward left-hemisphere hand control is also created as an accidental by-product. The "natural" condition of the brain, when this gene is missing, is to make the hemispheres equivalent. Thus, sinistrals are missing a gene that acts in dextrals to bias the brain toward

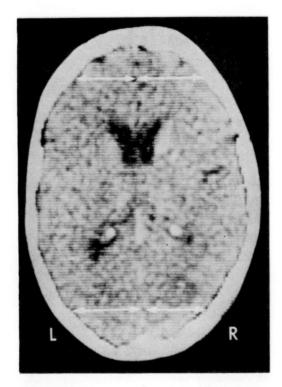

Figure 18.28 A CT scan of a typical, normal human brain showing the lack of symmetry between the hemispheres. This is a horizontal section with the frontal lobes at the top of the picture, occipital at the bottom. The right frontal lobe is slightly wider than the left, whereas the left occipital area is wider and appears to extend back farther. These alterations in the left hemisphere may result from the larger planum temporale pushing the posterior structures toward the back of the skull. (From LeMay, 1982)

left-hemisphere control. In this theory, the degree of left-handedness exhibited by the sinistral is largely a matter of learning experiences.

If many sinistrals are relatively unlateralized, is this reflected in brain structures? CT scans show that most left hemispheres, especially in dextrals, have larger posterior regions that are wider and extend back a bit farther than those of the right hemisphere (Figure 18.28). The percentage of cases that does not show this bias is larger in sinistrals than in dextrals (LeMay, 1982). A second possible difference between sinistrals and dextrals in brain structures is in the

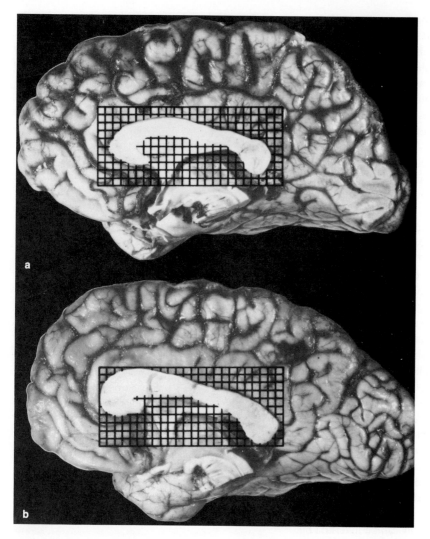

Figure 18.29 Two human brains with a grid superimposed for accurate measurement of the corpus callosum: brain from (**a**) a right-handed female and from (**b**) a non–right-handed female. The latter measures 824 mm² versus only 580 mm² for the right-hander. It is from data on 42 such brains that Witelson concluded that non–right-handers have, on the average, larger corpus callosums. (From Witelson, 1985)

size of the corpus callosum. Witelson (1985) found the anterior and midportions of that structure to average 11 percent larger in sinistrals (Figure 18.29), and it is these regions of the corpus callosum that carry fibers from the areas serving hand and language. The sinistral-dextral difference in callosal size probably relates to the fact that during early development millions of neurons die in the cortex. Apparently, many more are originally generated than are needed, and those that fail in some way are eliminated. Many of these neurons send axon branches across the corpus callosum. So, if lateralization depends on normal developmental brain processes, then it may involve the loss of axon collaterals in the corpus callosum. Perhaps, the more the lateralization progresses, the smaller the corpus callosum becomes, especially that part of it that carries fibers from the language and hand areas. Because dextrals theoretically undergo more lateralization during development, they have on the average smaller corpus callosums. All of this, however, is very speculative until Witelson's data can be replicated. Research on hemispheric anatomical differences has a very poor history of replicability (Bleier et al., 1986).

Conclusions

To some extent, the two hemispheres of the brain divide up the labor of the cortex and take up separate processing tasks. The degree to which each is specialized depends on which task is being considered. The most heavily lateralized function appears to be speech (usually left hemisphere). Probably also lateralized to some extent are handedness (usually left), syntactic and grammatical aspects of language comprehension (usually left), and attention to space on and around the body (right). Possibly somewhat lateralized are spatial comprehension, visual and auditory perceptual functions, and the nonsyntactic parts of prosody (all usually right hemisphere). However, it may turn out that all of these functions, like face perception, have a different aspect in each hemisphere.

Some researchers propose that lateralization is controlled entirely by genes and is complete at birth, whereas others argue that the process is a product of experience and develops slowly through childhood. This question is unsettled, but a synthesis seems the most reasonable approach to solving the dilemma. Genes provide an anatomical bias that must be supported by experience with language over a number of years in order for lateralization to be realized. The same genetic factor may, as a side effect, account for right-handedness (or, when it is missing, for left-handedness).

On a final note: Early experimental results from Sperry's lab in the 1960s led to the oversimplified generalization that the right hemisphere was "hol-

istic" in nature, whereas the left was "analytic." Claims were made in the 1960s that each hemisphere operated with its own "style" and that our culture tends to suppress the right-hemisphere holism in favor of a left-hemisphere analytic approach to life. In keeping with the general rebelliousness of the 1960s, educators were told to rework their curricula so that the right hemisphere could *also* be educated! Personally, I feel that such advice goes well beyond what is reasonable. If you are interested in reading a level-headed discussion of the implications of these research results, see Corballis's (1980) article. The safest conclusion that can be drawn at this time is that there seem to be some real differences in the way in which the two hemispheres operate on their inputs but that the difference is not on the gross level of "words in one hemisphere, pictures and sounds in the other." Instead, there seem to be small, subtle input-processing differences that may or may not represent important divisions of labor. At this time, the only truly clear-cut hemispheric specialization is the control of speech. Furthermore, the differences found in experiments are typically very small, suggesting that the two hemispheres are more similar in their function than they are different. Although some hemispheric differences seem to be real phenomena, the popularization of this research topic has led to completely unrealistic notions of how the two hemispheres work together to produce behavior and conscious experience (Springer, 1987).

▇ Summary

1. Neuropsychology is a branch of clinical psychology that focuses on the function of the damaged brain but also is involved with normal function of the cortex.

2. Symptoms of prefrontal damage include a loss of the ability to act out sequences, recall stimulus sequences (Corsi task), use verbal concepts to command behavior sequences (maze task and card sorting), maintain a behavioral set—plan of action—in the face of interfering stimuli (Stroop test and Prisco task), and relinquish an out-of-date set in order to avoid perseveration (maze task and card sorting).

3. Monkeys with prefrontal damage have trouble solving delayed-response, delayed-alternation, and delayed match-to-sample tests. Both human and animal data support the hypothesis that prefrontal areas provide goal sets that organize behaviors into sequences, inhibit competing responses, and suppress interfering stimuli.

4. Orbitofrontal lesions have a greater effect on personality characteristics than on goal sets because this area of cortex links the prefrontal cortex to the limbic system.

5. Lesions anywhere in the visual system from retina through V1 cause areas of blindness. Lesions in higher-level visual processors anterior to V1 cause some form of visual agnosia. A patient with agnosia does not complain of blindness yet cannot use the visual input in a normal fashion. Many of the problems of agnosia seem related to defects of visual scanning and attention.

6. Lesions of parietal cortex just posterior to S1 yield the symptoms of anosognosia, pain asymbolia, and autotopagnosia, all of which relate to a disturbance of body image. Apraxia is also common. Lesions of the posterior parietal lobes damage processors that integrate visual input with somatic input to yield spatial orientation. The symptoms include visuospatial agnosia and unilateral neglect.

7. Broca's area, the first language area discovered, was thought to be responsible for speech production. Wernicke located a second zone in the posterior-superior temporal lobe that is important for verbal comprehension. Recently, it has been established that most of the cortex of the frontal, parietal, and temporal lobes surrounding the lateral fissure in the left hemisphere is language cortex. Anterior regions tend to be more involved with the speech aspect of language, whereas posterior regions tend to be more relevant to comprehension.

8. Lesions in the language area at the base of M1 yield dysarthria, whereas those in the planum temporale and posterior temporal lobe produce Wernicke's aphasia with its word salad, neologisms, good fluency, and poor comprehension. Anterior lesions tend to produce a type of aphasia characterized by paraphrasias, telegraphic speech, and circumlocutions. Broca's aphasia usually involves a wide area

of damage to frontal, parietal, and temporal lobes and seems to be a combination of speech and comprehension deficits.

9. Conduction aphasia involves good comprehension, reasonable fluency, but no ability to repeat what is heard. The lesion appears to be in the arcuate fasciculus. Transcortical motor aphasia, characterized by mutism, is produced by lesions of either the prefrontal cortex or M2. The lesion in transcortical sensory aphasia (poor comprehension and speech coupled with the ability to repeat) is one that surrounds the language areas and disconnects them from the rest of the brain.

10. Syndromes related to language include agraphia (an inability to write) and alexia (inability to read). The lesion site for agraphia is uncertain; that for alexia is probably in the angular gyrus and the posterior end of the lateral fissure.

11. Hemifield tachistoscopy can be used to present visual stimuli to a single hemisphere in order to discover what functions are lateralized to that side of the brain. A comparable method for the auditory sense is the dichotic-listening technique. Both methods suggest that many language functions are lateralized to some extent to the left hemisphere. Some functions that appear to be better handled by the right hemisphere include the recognition of musical sequences of notes as well as natural sounds.

12. All research techniques aimed at finding hemispheric differences suffer from the fact that information fed selectively into one hemisphere is almost immediately transferred to the other side of the brain by way of the corpus callosum. For this reason, split-brain patients have provided a fascinating source of information about hemispheric lateralization. Their data confirm the findings of research on normals and also show a slightly stronger representation of spatial abilities and visual spatial attention in the right hemisphere.

13. Researchers disagree about the extent that the right hemisphere can control language functions. Zaidel maintains that the right hemisphere demonstrates roughly a 4-year-old's grasp of grammar and syntax. Gazzaniga, on the other hand, holds that split-brain patients showing right-hemisphere language func-

tions are so scarce that this ability is best explained as the result of early brain damage to the left hemisphere. (Keep in mind that all split-brain patients had suffered brain damage prior to their surgery.) He warns that cross cueing can fool an experimenter into thinking that the response is being produced by the right hemisphere when actually it was generated by the left.

14. The Wada test provides evidence bearing on the problem of right-hemisphere language. The results suggest that the right hemisphere may have a stimulus–response level of language comprehension but not complete language ability.

15. Prosody, the rhythm and intonation of speech, seems largely right hemisphere, especially the emotional-expression aspect and variations in melodic quality.

16. Another controversy focuses on whether lateralization is genetically determined or slowly developed as the result of learning experiences. In support of his genetic theory (the invariance hypothesis), Kinsbourne conducted a number of experiments on time sharing, which seemed to show that trying to do two left-hemisphere tasks simultaneously will produce interference no matter how young the child is. A developmental theory should predict that older children, who would have to be more lateralized, should show more interference.

17. Lenneburg supports the developmental theory of lateralization with data showing that children with less-than-normal developmental experience with language because of hearing impairment showed little evidence of lateralization in a language test. The best synthesis of these two positions seems to be to assume that there is a genetic factor, but that it only provides a predisposition for language experience to more strongly affect the left rather than the right hemisphere.

18. Originally, it was thought that the speech hemisphere was always opposite the preferred hand (the contralateral rule), but more recent data show that most sinistrals have their language cortex in the left hemisphere, just as do dextrals. The relation between handedness and language lateralization is further complicated by the difficulty in finding true sinistrals (people who are *completely* left-handed). Instead, people seem to divide up as right-handers and non–right-handers, the latter being a mix containing all degrees of ambidexterity and sinistrality.

19. Annett's right-shift theory of handedness proposes a gene that biases the left hemisphere toward language learning and hand control. When the gene is absent, chance factors of the individual's experience determine whether right- or left-handedness is learned as a set of habits. There is also the possibility that some sinistrals were biased toward right-hemisphere control by early left-hemisphere brain damage.

Glossary

acquired alexia A loss of the ability to read because of brain damage. (723)

agraphia A loss of the ability to write. (723)

alexia An inability to read. (723)

angular gyrus The part of the left parietal lobe just behind Wernicke's area; damage causes alexia. (723)

anomic aphasia A loss of memory for nouns. (715)

anosognosia Parietal-lobe damage symptom characterized by an inability to recognize a defect in some part of the body. (710)

apraxia The inability to perform some set of movements despite lack of paralysis or any other obvious damage to the motor system. (710)

arcuate fasciculus A tract connecting Wernicke's area with parts of the frontal lobe. (721)

autotopagnosia Parietal-lobe damage symptom characterized by a loss of body parts from memory and conscious attention. (710)

Broca's aphasia A language loss that is usually more expressive than receptive. (714)

Broca's area A portion of the ventral premotor area of the frontal lobes that is important for speech and language. (713)

circumlocution A symptom of aphasia in which a rough description or phrase is substituted for the missing word. (715)

conduction aphasia A disorder in which there is good comprehension of speech and writing and reasonably good speech with adequate fluency but an inability to repeat what is heard or read. (715)

contralateral projection Axons that cross to the opposite side of the brain from their cell bodies. (703, 727)

contralateral rule The (fallacious) idea that the speech cortex is always contralateral to the preferred hand. (738)

Corsi recency-discrimination task A neuropsychological test for memory. (694)

covert orienting The act of directing attention to a part of the visual field without moving the eyes to that location. (712)

cross cueing A method whereby the left hemisphere of a split-brain patient surreptitiously obtains information about the stimulus presented to the right hemisphere. (733)

delayed-alternation task A memory task for animals in which the subject must choose on each trial the response not chosen on the previous trial. (698)

delayed matching-to-sample task A memory task for animals in which the subject must choose on each trial the member of the stimulus pair shown just before a delay interval. (699)

delayed-response task A memory task for animals in which the subject must keep in mind which response to make until the chance for making the response occurs. (697)

developmental dyslexia Difficulty in learning to read. (723)

dextral A right-handed person. (738)

dichotic listening An experimental method in which different auditory stimuli are presented to the two hemispheres. (727)

dysarthria A symptom of aphasia characterized by problems in pronunciation and general lack of verbal fluency. (714)

expressive aphasia Brain-damage symptom involving loss of speaking abilities. (714)

familial sinistrals Left-handed people who have a number of sinistrals in their immediate families. (739)

fovea A tiny central area of the retina in which most of the detailed vision takes place. (707)

frontal eye field Region of the frontal lobe (within the premotor area) devoted to conscious control of eye movements. (708)

frontal lobe personality The tactlessness, egocentricity, boastfulness, and lack of concern that seems somewhat characteristic of patients with frontal lobe damage. (702)

goal set See *set*. (699)

hemianopsia Blindness in either the right or left visual half-field. (706)

hemifield tachistoscopy An experimental method for presenting visual stimuli to just one hemisphere at a time. (727)

hemispheric dominance The idea that the hemisphere that contains the language area and the motor area for the preferred hand is in some way stronger than the other hemisphere and dominates brain function. (738)

Heschl's gyrus A strip of temporal lobe cortex that forms part of the floor of the lateral fissure; contains the auditory projection area A1. (721)

intermanual conflict A split-brain symptom in which one hand opposes what the other is doing. (732)

invariance hypothesis Kinsbourne's idea that lateralization is present at birth and does not increase with experience. (736)

ipsilateral projection Axons that stay on the same side of the brain as their cell bodies. (703, 727)

lateral geniculate nucleus (LGN) Portion of the thalamus where the optic tract terminates. (703)

lateralization A form of brain organization that divides labor by having the two hemispheres specialize in different aspects of information processing. (724)

maze-learning task A neuropsychological test for perseveration. (696)

mutism An unwillingness or inability to speak. (715)

neologisms The creation of a new "word" when the correct word is missing from memory because of brain damage; symptom of aphasia. (715)

neuropsychology A branch of clinical psychology aimed at diagnosing brain damage and studying dysfunctions of the nervous system from the viewpoint of a psychologist. (692)

optic chiasm The point where the nasal fibers of each optic nerve cross to the opposite side of the brain to join the contralateral optic tract. (703)

optic nerve The section of the optic fibers between their origin in the retina and the optic chiasm. (705)

optic radiations The axons of LGN cells that run from LGN to the visual cortex. (705)

optic tract The section of the optic fibers between the chiasm and LGN. (705)

pain asymbolia Parietal-lobe damage symptom characterized by the inability to appreciate painful stimuli. (710)

paraphrasia The substitution of one word for another; symptom of aphasia. (714)

pathological sinistrality Left-handedness based on brain damage. (739)

perseveration To continually make a response after it is no longer appropriate. (696)

phonemic paraphrasia A word substitution based on sound similarities rather than similarities of meaning. (714)

planum temporale A strip of temporal lobe cortex lying immediately posterior to Heschl's gyrus and forming part of the floor of the lateral fissure; contains much of Wernicke's area. (721)

Prisco delayed-comparison task A light-flash test used by neuropsychologists to detect frontal lobe damage. (694)

prosody The intonation aspect of speech that gives it a rhythm and musical quality. (734)

receptive aphasia Brain-damage symptom that involves loss of language comprehension. (714)

right-shift theory Annett's idea that the bias toward left hemisphere hand control is created as an accidental byproduct of gene action that structures the left hemisphere to be the speech cortex. (739)

scotoma An area of blindness in the visual field. (705)

semantic paraphrasia A word substitution based on similarities of meaning rather than sound similarities. (715)

set A behavioral readiness to make a particular response to a particular stimulus whenever that stimulus should appear. (699)

sinistral A left-handed person. (738)

sodium amytal A very short-acting barbiturate drug used in the Wada test. (734)

spatial orientation The ability to perceive where objects are in space in relation to self and in relation to other objects. (711)

stroke Brain damage resulting from loss of blood supply to a part of the brain; a "cardiovascular accident." (716)

Stroop test A color-naming task used for assessing the person's ability to maintain a set. (695)

tachistoscope An instrument that can present visual stimuli for very brief, measured intervals. (727)

telegraphic speech A condition in which speech consists mainly of verbs, nouns, and short, common phrases; symptom of Broca's aphasia. (714)

time sharing An experimental method for studying language lateralization; the subject's ability to perform a motor task using one hand while speaking is compared between the two hands. (736)

token test A test (involving the manipulation of tokens following verbal instructions) that measures complex language abilities. (733)

transcortical motor aphasia A loss of will to speak that results in long periods of mutism. (715)

transcortical sensory aphasia A loss of language comprehension resulting in word-salad speech but with retention of the ability to repeat accurately anything heard or read. (715)

unilateral neglect Symptom of parietal-lobe damage in which the patient forgets the side of his or her body contralateral to the lesion. (712)

visual agnosia A brain-damage symptom in which the patient can see but cannot understand what is seen. (706)

visual field The area of the environment visible to the eyes at any one moment. (703)

visual scanning The sequence of eye movements used in constructing a visual image. (709)

visuospatial agnosia The loss of spatial orientation ability. (711)

Wada test A test in which a sedative drug is injected into an artery serving one side of the brain in order to discover which hemisphere contains the speech cortex. (734)

Weinstein maps A test for the loss of spatial orientation resulting from parietal lobe damage. (711)

Wernicke's aphasia A form of aphasia in which the greater part of the deficit is in the inability to comprehend language rather than in its expression. (715)

Wernicke's area A region around the posterior end of the lateral fissure that is important to language (especially to comprehension). (714)

Wisconsin card-sorting task A test for the person's ability to shift from one set of rules to another; that is, it measures the tendency to perseverate. (696)

word salad An aphasic symptom in which speech consists of a meaningless jumble of words and neologisms. (715)

References

Abraham, W. C., & Goddard, G. V. (1984). Functions of afferent coactivity in long-term potentiation. In G. Lynch, J. L. McGaugh, & N. M. Weinberger (Eds.), *Neurobiology of learning and memory.* New York: Guilford Press.

Adams, D. B. (1986). Ventromedial tegmental lesions abolish offense without disturbing predation or defense. *Physiology & Behavior, 38,* 165–168.

Adams, P. R. (1978). Molecular aspects of synaptic transmission. *Trends in NeuroSciences, 1,* 141–143.

Ad Hoc Committee on Animals in Research. (1983). Taub case update. *Neuroscience Newsletter, 14*(5), 3–5.

Ad Hoc Committee on Animals in Research. (1984). The Taub case: A final report. *Neuroscience Newsletter, 15*(5), 6–7.

Adkins-Regan, E. (1985). Nonmammalian psychosexual differentiation. In N. Adler, D. Pfaff, & R. W. Goy (Eds.), *Handbook of behavioral neurobiology: Vol. 7. Reproduction.* London: Plenum.

Aitkin, L. (1979). The auditory midbrain. *Trends in Neurosciences, 2,* 308–310.

Aitkin, L. (1986). *The auditory midbrain.* Clifton, NJ: Humana Press.

Akil, H., Watson, S. J., Young, E., Lewis, M. E., Khachaturian, J., & Walker, J. M. (1984). Endogenous opioids: Biology and function. *Annual Review of Neuroscience, 7,* 223–255.

Albert, D. J., Dyson, E. M., & Walsh, M. L. (1987). Competitive behavior in male rats: Aggression and success enhanced by medial hypothalamic lesions as well as by testosterone implants. *Physiology & Behavior, 40,* 695–701.

Albert, D. J., Dyson, E. M., Walsh, M. L., & Wong, R. (1988). Defensive aggression and testosterone-dependent intermale social aggression are each elicited by food competition. *Physiology & Behavior, 43,* 21–28.

Albert, D. J., Walsh, M. L., Gorzalka, B. B., Mendelson, S., & Zalys, C. (1986). Intermale social aggression: Suppression by medial preoptic area lesions. *Physiology & Behavior, 38,* 169–173.

Aldrich, R. W. (1986). Voltage-dependent gating of sodium channels: Towards an integrated approach. *Trends in NeuroSciences, 9,* 82–86.

Allen, S. J., Dawbarn, D., & Wilcock, G. K. (1988). Morphometric immunochemical analysis of neurons in the nucleus basalis of Meynert in Alzheimer's disease. *Brain Research, 454,* 275–281.

American Psychiatric Association. (1987). *Diagnostic and statistical manual of mental disorders* (3rd rev. ed.). Washington, DC: APA.

Amoore, J. E., Johnston, J. W., Jr., & Rubin, M. (1964). The stereochemical theory of odor. *Scientific American, 210*(2), 42–49.

Anand, B. K., & Brobeck, J. R. (1951). Localization of a feeding center in the hypothalamus of the rat. *Proceedings of the Society of Experimentation and Medicine, 77,* 323–324.

Anand, B. K., & Pillai, R. V. (1967). Activity of single neurones in the hypothalamic feeding centres: Effect of gastric distension. *Journal of Physiology, 192,* 63–77.

Andersen, P. (1981). Brain slices—a neurobiological tool of increasing usefulness. *Trends in NeuroSciences, 4,* 53–56.

Andersen, P. (1982). Cerebellar synaptic plasticity—putting theories to the test. *Trends in NeuroSciences, 5,* 324–325.

Andersson, B., & McCann, S. M. (1955). A further study of polydipsia evoked by hypothalamic stimulation in the goat. *Acta Physiologica Scandinavia, 33,* 333–346.

Andersson, B., & Rundgren, M. (1982). Thirst and its disorders. *Annual Review of Medicine, 33,* 231–239.

Andres, K. H., & von Düring, M. (1973). Morphology of cutaneous receptors. In A. Iggo (Ed.), *Handbook of sensory physiology: Vol. II. Somatosensory system.* Heidelberg: Springer-Verlag.

Angrist, B., & van Kammen, D. P. (1984). CNS stimulants as tools in the study of schizophrenia. *Trends in Neuro-Sciences, 7,* 388–390.

Annett, M. (1981). The genetics of handedness. *Trends in NeuroSciences, 4,* 256–258.

Aravich, P. F., & Sclafani, A. (1983). Paraventricular hypothalamic lesions and medial hypothalamic knife cuts produce similar syndromes. *Behavioral Neuroscience, 97,* 970–983.

Arbuthnott, G. W. (1980). The dopamine synapse and the notion of "pleasure centres" in the brain. *Trends in NeuroSciences, 3,* 199–200.

Ardila, A., & Lopez, V. (1984). Transcortical motor aphasia: One or two aphasias? *Brain and Language, 22,* 350–353.

Ardila, A., & Ostrosky-Solis, F. (1984). The right hemisphere and behavior: A review of the problem. In A. Ardila & F. Ostrosky-Solis (Eds.), *The right hemisphere: Neurology and neuropsychology.* New York: Gordon & Breach.

Arnold, A. P., & Gorski, R. A. (1984). Gonadal steroid induction of structural sex differences in the central nervous system. *Annual Review of Neuroscience, 7,* 413–442.

Arshavsky, Yu. I., Gelfand, I. M., & Orlovsky, G. N. (1983). The cerebellum and control of rhythmical movements. *Trends in NeuroSciences, 6,* 417–422.

Ashford, J. W., & Fuster, J. M. (1985). Occipital and inferotemporal responses to visual signals in the monkey. *Experimental Neurology, 90,* 444–466.

Atwood, H. L., & Lnenicka, G. A. (1986). Structure and function in synapses: Emerging correlations. *Trends in NeuroSciences, 9,* 248–250.

Bakan, P. (1977). Left handedness and birth order revisited. *Neuropsychologia, 15,* 837–840.

Baldessarini, R. J. (1977). *Chemotherapy in psychiatry.* Cambridge: Harvard University Press.

Bandler, R. (1982). Neural control of aggressive behaviour. *Trends in NeuroSciences, 5,* 390–394.

Barbizet, J. (1970). *Human memory and its pathology.* San Francisco: Freeman.

Barend ter Haar, M. (1978). Ancient Chinese art of medicine—acupuncture. *Trends in NeuroSciences, 1,* 19–20.

Barlow, H. B. (1982). David Hubel and Torsten Wiesel: Their contributions towards understanding the primary visual cortex. *Trends in NeuroSciences, 5,* 145–152.

Barnes, D. M. (1986a). Lessons from snails and other models. *Science, 231,* 1246–1249.

Barnes, D. M. (1986b). Steroids may influence changes in mood. *Science, 232,* 1344–1345.

Barnes, D. M. (1987). Biological issues in schizophrenia. *Science, 235,* 430–433.

Barnes, D. M. (1989). Troubles encountered in gene linkage land. *Science, 243,* 313–314.

Barnett, S. A. (1963). *The rat: A study in behavior.* Chicago: Aldine.

Barondes, S. H., & Cohen, H. D. (1968). Memory impairment after subcutaneous injection of acetoxycycloheximide. *Science, 160,* 556–557.

Barrett, J. A., Shaikh, M. B., Edinger, H., & Siegel, A. (1987). The effects of intrahypothalamic injections of norepinephrine upon affective defense behavior in the cat. *Brain Research, 426,* 381–384.

Bartoshuk, L. M., Dateo, G. P., Vandenbelt, D. J., Butterick, R. L., & Long, L. (1969). Effects of Gymnesma Sylvestre and Synsepalum Dulcificum on taste in man. In C. Pfaffman (Ed.), *Olfaction and taste.* New York: Rockefeller University Press.

Basbaum, A. I., & Fields, H. L. (1984). Endogenous pain control systems: Brainstem spinal pathways and endorphin circuitry. *Annual Review of Neuroscience, 7,* 309–338.

Basso, A., Lecours, A. R., Moraschini, S., & Vanier, M. (1985). Anatomoclinical correlations of the aphasias as defined through computerized tomography: Exceptions. *Brain and Language, 26,* 201–229.

Batini, C., Moruzzi, G., Palestini, M., Rossi, B. F., & Zanchetti, A. (1958). Persistent patterns in the pretrigeminal midpontine preparation. *Science, 128,* 30–32.

Baudry, M., & Lynch, G. (1984). Glutamate receptor regulation and the substrates of memory. In G. Lynch, J. L. McGaugh, & N. M. Weinberger (Eds.), *Neurobiology of learning and memory.* New York: Guilford Press.

Bayles, K. A. (1982). Language function in senile dementia. *Brain and Language, 16,* 265–280.

Baynes, K., Holtzman, J. D., & Volpe, B. T. (1986). Components of visual attention: Alterations in response pattern to visual stimuli following parietal lobe infarction. *Brain, 109,* 99–114.

Beaumont, J. G. (1982). Studies with verbal stimuli. In J. G. Beaumont (Ed.), *Divided visual field studies of cerebral organization.* São Paulo: Academic Press.

Beaumont, J. G. (1983). *Introduction to neuropsychology.* New York: Guilford Press.

Becker, W. M. (1986). *The world of the cell.* Redwood City, CA: Benjamin/Cummings.

Beidler, L. M. (1978). Biophysics and chemistry of taste. In E. C. Carterette & M. P. Friedman (Eds.), *Handbook of perception: Vol. VIa. Tasting and smelling*. San Francisco: Academic Press.

Bennett, T. L. (1975). The electrical activity of the hippocampus and the process of attention. In R. L. Isaacson & K. H. Pribram (Eds.), *The hippocampus: Vol. 2. Neurophysiology and behavior*. New York: Plenum.

Bennett, T. L. (1977). *Brain and behavior*. Pacific Grove, CA: Brooks/Cole.

Berger, T. W. (1984). Neural representation of associative learning in the hippocampus. In L. R. Squire & N. Butters (Eds.), *Neuropsychology of memory*. New York: Guilford Press.

Berger, T. W., & Orr, W. B. (1982). Role of the hippocampus in reversal learning of the rabbit nictitating membrane response. In C. D. Woody (Ed.), *Conditioning: Representation of involved neural functions*. New York: Plenum.

Bergstrom, L., & Thompson, P. (1976). Ototoxicity. In J. L. Northern (Ed.), *Hearing disorders*. Boston: Little, Brown.

Berland, T. (1964, March 7). Botulism: The killer who came to dinner. *Saturday Evening Post*.

Bernardis, L. L., & Frohman, L. (1970). Effect of lesion size in the ventromedial hypothalamus on growth hormone and insulin levels in weanling rats. *Neuroendocrinology, 6,* 319–328.

Berntson, G. G., Tuber, D. S., Ronca, A. E., & Bachman, D. S. (1983). The decerebrate human: Associative learning. *Experimental Neurology, 81,* 77–88.

Berridge, M. J. (1979). Modulation of nervous activity by cyclic nucleotides and calcium. In F. O. Schmitt & F. G. Worden (Eds.), *The neurosciences: Fourth study program*. Cambridge: MIT Press.

Best, P. H., & Thompson, R. F. (1984). Hippocampal cells which have place field activity also show changes in activity during classical conditioning. *Society for Neuroscience Abstracts, 10A,* 125. (Abstract No. 36.18)

Binnie, C. D., Findlay, J., & Wilkins, A. J. (1985). Mechanisms of epileptogenesis in photosensitive epilepsy implied by the effects of moving patterns. *Electroencephalography and Clinical Neurophysiology, 61,* 1–6.

Bird, E. D. (1978). Huntington's disease (chorea). *Trends in NeuroSciences, 1,* 57–59.

Björklund, A., & Stenevi, U. (1979). Reconstruction of brain circuitries by neural transplants. *Trends in NeuroSciences, 2,* 301–306.

Björklund, A., & Stenevi, U. (1984). Intracerebral neural implants: Neuronal replacement and reconstruction of damaged circuitries. *Annual Review of Neuroscience, 7,* 179–308.

Blakemore, C. B. (1977). *Mechanics of the mind*. Cambridge: Cambridge University Press.

Blanchard, D. C., & Blanchard, R. J. (1972). Innate and conditioned reactions to threat in rats with amygdaloid lesions. *Journal of Comparative and Physiological Psychology, 81,* 281–290.

Blanchard, D. C., and Blanchard, R. J. (1988). Ethoexperimental approaches to the biology of emotion. *Annual Review of Psychology, 39,* 43–68.

Blanchard, D. C., & Takahashi, S. N. (1988). No change in intermale aggression after amygdala lesions which reduce freezing. *Physiology & Behavior, 42,* 613–616.

Blanchard, D. C., Williams, G., Lee, E. M. C., & Blanchard, R. J. (1981). Taming of wild *Rattus norvegicus* by lesions of the mesencephalic central gray. *Physiological Psychology, 9,* 157–163.

Bland, B. H. (1986). The physiology and pharmacology of hippocampal formation theta rhythms. *Progress in Neurobiology, 26,* 1–54.

Blasdel, G. G. (1986). Voltage-sensitive dyes reveal the modular organization of the visual cortex. *IBRO News, 14,* 5.

Blasdel, G. G., & Salama, G. (1986). Voltage-sensitive dyes reveal a modular organization in monkey striate cortex. *Nature, 321,* 579–585.

Blass, E. M., & Hall, W. G., (1976). Drinking termination: Interactions among hydration, orogastric and behavioral controls in rats. *Psychological Review, 83,* 356–374.

Bleier, R., Houston, L., & Byne, W. (1986). Can the corpus callosum predict gender, age, handedness, or cognitive differences? *Trends in NeuroSciences, 9,* 391–394.

Bliss, T. V. P. (1979). Synaptic plasticity in the hippocampus. *Trends in NeuroSciences, 2,* 42–45.

Bliss, T. V. P., & Dolphin, A. C. (1982). What is the mechanism of long-term potentiation in the hippocampus? *Trends in NeuroSciences, 5,* 289–290.

Bliss, T. V. P., & Gardner-Medwin, A. (1973). Long-lasting potentiation of synaptic transmission in the dentate area of the unanesthetized rabbit following stimulation of the perforant path. *Journal of Physiology (London), 232,* 357–374.

Bliss, T. V. P., & Lomo, T. (1973). Long-lasting potentiation of synaptic transmission in the dentate area of the anesthetized rabbit following stimulation of the perforant path. *Journal of Physiology (London), 232,* 331–356.

Bloch, V., & Laroche, S. (1984). Facts and hypotheses related to the search for the engram. In G. Lynch, J. L. McGaugh, & N. M. Weinberger (Eds.), *Neurobiology of learning and memory*. New York: Guilford Press.

Bloom, W., & Fawcett, D. W. (1975). *A textbook of histology*. Philadelphia: Saunders.

Blout, E. R. (1967). Conformation of proteins. In G. C. Quarton, R. Melnechuk, & F. O. Schmitt (Eds.), *The neurosciences: A study program*. New York: Rockefeller University Press.

Bloxham, C. A., Mindel, T. A., & Firth, C. D. (1984). Initiation and execution of predictable and unpredictable movements in Parkinson's disease. *Brain, 107,* 371–384.

Bodian, D. (1967). Neurons, circuits, and neuroglia. In G. C. Quarton, R. Melnechuk, & F. O. Schmitt (Eds.), *The neurosciences: A study program*. New York: Rockefeller University Press.

Bogen, J. E. (1985). The stabilized syndrome of hemisphere disconnection. In D. F. Benson & E. Zaidel (Eds.), *The dual brain: Hemispheric specialization in humans*. New York: Guilford Press.

Bokar, J. A. (1976). *Primer for the nonmedical psychotherapist*. New York: Spectrum.

Bolles, R. C., & Fanselow, M. S. (1982). Endorphins and behavior. *Annual Review of Psychology, 33,* 87–103.

Bonnet, K. A. (1982). Neurobiological dissection of Tourette Syndrome: A neurochemical focus on a human neuroanatomical model. *Advances in Neurology, 35,* 77–82.

Boring, E. G. (1950). *A history of experimental psychology*. New York: Appleton-Century-Crofts.

Bormann, J. (1988). Electrophysiology of GABAA and g receptor subtypes. *Trends in Neurosciences, 11,* 112–116.

Boycott, B. B. (1974). Aspects of the comparative anatomy and physiology of the vertebrate retina. In R. Bellairs & E. G. Gray (Eds.), *Essays on the nervous system: A festschrift for Professor J. Z. Young*. Oxford: Clarendon Press.

Bradbury, M. (1979). Why a blood–brain barrier? *Trends in NeuroSciences, 2,* 36–38.

Bradley, D. C., Garrett, M. F., & Zurif, E. B. (1980). Syntactic deficits in Broca's aphasia. In D. Caplan (Ed.), *Biological studies of mental processes*. Cambridge: MIT Press.

Brady, R. O. (1982). Inherited metabolic storage disorders. *Annual Review of Psychology, 5,* 33–56.

Brain, P. F., Nowell, N. W., & Wouters, A. (1971). Some relationships between adrenal function and effectiveness of a period of isolation in inducing intermale aggression in albino mice. *Physiology & Behavior, 6,* 27–29.

Brainard, G. C., Lewy, A. L., Menaker, M., Fredrickson, R. H., Miller, L. S., Weleber, R. G., Cassone, V., & Hudson, D. (1988). Dose-response relationship between light irradiance and the suppression of plasma melatonin in human volunteers. *Brain Research, 354,* 212–218.

Brankack, J., & Buzsáki, G. (1986). Hippocampal responses evoked by tooth pulp and acoustic stimulation: Depth profiles and effect of behavior. *Brain Research, 378,* 303–314.

Brazier, M. A. B. (1962, June). The analysis of brain waves. *Scientific American, 206,* 142–153.

Brazier, M. B. (1959). The historical development of neurophysiology. In J. Field, H. W. Magoun, & V. E. Hall (Eds.), *Handbook of physiology: Sec. 1, Vol. 1. Neurophysiology*. Baltimore: Williams & Wilkins.

Bremer, F. (1937). L'activité cérébrale au cours de sommeil et de la narcose. Contribution a l'étude du mécanisme du sommeil. *Bulletin de l'Académie Royale de Belgique, 4,* 68–86.

Bremer, F. (1954). The neurophysiological problem of sleep. In J. F. Delafresnaye (Ed.), *Brain mechanisms and consciousness*. Springfield: Charles C. Thomas.

Bremer, F. (1970). Preoptic hypnogenic focus and mesencephalic reticular formation. *Brain Research, 21,* 132–134.

Brinkman, C. (1984). Supplementary motor area of the monkey's cerebral cortex: Short- and long-term deficits after unilateral ablation and the effects of subsequent callosal section. *The Journal of Neuroscience, 4,* 918–929.

Brismar, T. (1982). Distribution of K^+-channels in the axolemma of myelinated fibers. *Trends in NeuroSciences, 5,* 179–181.

Brobeck, J. R. (1973). Neural control systems. In J. R. Brobeck (Ed.), *Best & Taylor's Physiological basis of medical practice* (9th ed.). Baltimore: Williams & Wilkins.

Brobeck, J. R., Tepperman, J., & Long, C. N. H. (1943). Experimental hypothalamic hyperphagia in the albino rat. *Yale Journal of Biology and Medicine, 15,* 831–853.

Brodal, A. (1957). *The reticular formation of the brainstem. Anatomical aspects and functional correlates*. Edinburgh: Oliver.

Brooks, D. C. (1967). Localization of the lateral geniculate nucleus monophasic waves associated with paradoxical sleep in the cat. *Electroencephalography and Clinical Neurophysiology, 23,* 123–133.

Brooks, V. (1986). *The neural basis of motor control*. New York: Oxford University Press.

Browman, C. P. (1980). Sleep following sustained exercise. *Psychophysiology, 17,* 577–580.

Brown, T. S. (1975). General biology of sensory systems. In B. Scharf (Ed.), *Experimental sensory psychology*. Glenview, IL: Scott, Foresman.

Brownell, W. E., Bader, C. R., Bertrand, D., & Ribaupierre, Y. D. (1985). Evoked mechanical responses of isolated cochlear outer hair cells. *Science, 227,* 194–196.

Brugge, J. F. (1975). Progress in neuroanatomy and neurophysiology of auditory cortex. In E. A. Eagles (Ed.), *The nervous system: Vol. 3. Human communication and its disorders*. New York: Raven Press.

Buchsbaum, M. S., Ingvar, D. H., Kessler, R., Waters, R. N., Cappelletti, J., van Kammen, D. P., King, A. C., Johnson, J. L., Manning, R. G., Flynn, R. W., Mann, L. S., Bunney, W. E., & Sokoloff, L. (1982). Cerebral glucography with positron tomography. *Archives of General Psychiatry, 39,* 251–259.

Buell, S. J., & Coleman, P. D. (1979). Dendritic growth in the aged human brain and failure of growth in senile dementia. *Science, 206,* 854–856.

Buguet, A., Roussel, R., Angus, R., Sabiston, B., & Radomski, M. (1980). Human sleep and adrenal individual reactions to exercise. *Electroencephalography and Clinical Neurophysiology, 49,* 515–523.

Bunge, R. P. (1968). Glial cells and the central myelin sheath. *Physiological Review, 48,* 197–251.

Bunney, B. S. (1984). Antipsychotic drug effects on the electrical activity of dopaminergic neurons. *Trends in NeuroSciences, 7,* 212–215.

Burgess, P. R. (1973). Cutaneous mechanoreceptors. In E. C. Carterette & M. P. Friedman (Eds.), *Handbook of perception: Vol. III. Biology of perceptual systems.* New York: Academic Press.

Burgess, P. R., & Perl, E. R. (1973). Cutaneous mechanoreceptors and nociceptors. In A. Iggo (Ed.), *Handbook of sensory physiology: Vol. II. Somatosensory system.* Heidelberg: Springer-Verlag.

Burke, D. (1978). The fusimotor innervation of muscle spindle endings in man. *Trends in NeuroSciences, 1,* 89–92.

Burns, B. D. (1950). Some properties of the cat's isolated cerebral cortex. *Journal of Physiology (London), 11,* 50–68.

Busswell, B. T. (1935). *How people look at pictures.* Chicago: University of Chicago Press.

Byerley, W. F., McConnell, E. J., McCabe, T. R., Dawson, T. M., Brosser, B. I., & Wamsley, J. K. (1987). Chronic administration of sertraline, a selective serotonin uptake inhibitor, decreased the density of β-adrenergic receptors in rat frontoparietal cortex. *Brain Research, 421,* 377–381.

Byne, W., & Bleier, R. (1987). How different are male and female brains? *Trends in NeuroSciences, 10,* 198–199.

Byrne, J. H. (1985). Neural and molecular mechanisms underlying information storage in *Aplysia:* Implications for learning and memory. *Trends in NeuroSciences, 8,* 478–482.

Caballero, A., & DeAndrés, I. (1986). Unilateral lesions in locus coeruleus area enhance paradoxical sleep. *Electroencephalography and Clinical Neurophysiology, 64,* 339–346.

Carlson, A. J. (1916). *The control of hunger in health and disease.* Chicago: University of Chicago Press.

Carlson, N. R. (1981). *Physiology of Behavior* (2nd ed.). Boston: Allyn & Bacon.

Carobrez, A. P., Schenberg, L. C., & Graeff, F. G. (1983). Neuroeffector mechanisms of the defense reaction in the rat. *Physiology & Behavior, 31,* 439–444.

Carpenter, R. G., & Grossman, S. P. (1982). Plasma fat metabolites and hunger. *Physiology & Behavior, 30,* 57–63.

Casey, K. L. (1978). Neural mechanisms of pain. In E. C. Carterette & M. P. Friedman (Eds.), *Handbook of perception: Vol. VIb. Feeling and hurting.* New York: Academic Press.

Casey, K. L. (1982). Neural mechanisms in pain and analgesia: An overview. In A. L. Beckman (Ed.), *The neurological basis of behavior.* New York: SP Medical and Scientific Books.

Castellucci, V., & Kandel, E. R. (1976). An invertebrate system for the cellular study of habituation and sensitization. In T. J. Tighe & R. N. Leaton (Eds.), *Habituation: Perspectives from child development, animal behavior, and neurophysiology.* Hillsdale, NJ: Lawrence Erlbaum.

Caviness, V. S., Jr., & Rakic, P. (1978). Mechanisms of cortical development: A view from mutations in mice. *Annual Review of Neuroscience, 1,* 297–326.

Celesia, G. C., Archer, C. R., & Chung, H. D. (1981). Hyperphagia and obesity: Relationship to medial hypothalamic lesions. *Journal of the American Medical Association, 246,* 151–153.

Chafetz, M. D., Parko, K., Diaz, S., & Leibowitz, S. F. (1986). Relationships between medial hypothalamic α2-receptor binding, norepinephrine, and circulating glucose. *Brain Research, 384,* 404–408.

Chambers, K. C., & Phoenix, C. H. (1987). Differences among ovariectomized female rhesus macaques in the display of sexual behavior without and with estradiol treatment. *Behavioral Neuroscience, 101,* 303–308.

Chambers, M. R., Andres, K. H., von Düring, M., & Iggo, A. (1972). Structure and function of the slowly adapting type II mechanoreceptor in hairy skin. *Quarterly Journal of Experimental Physiology, 57,* 417–445.

Chapman, P. F., Steinmetz, J. E., & Thompson, R. F. (1988). Classical conditioning does not occur when direct stimulation of the red nucleus or cerebellar nuclei is the unconditioned stimulus. *Brain Research, 442,* 97–104.

Chase, M. H. (1982). New perspectives in sleep research. *Trends in NeuroSciences, 5,* 105–107.

Chi, C. C., & Flynn, J. P. (1971). Neural pathways associated with hypothalamically-elicited attack behavior in cats. *Science, 171,* 703–705.

Chiodo, L. A., & Bunney, B. S. (1987). Population response of midbrain dopaminergic neurons to neuroleptics: Further studies on time course and nondopaminergic neuronal influences. *The Journal of Neuroscience, 7,* 629–633.

Chudler, E., Dong, W. K., & Kawakami, Y. (1986). Cortical nociceptive responses and behavioral correlates in the monkey. *Brain Research, 397,* 47–60.

Churchland, P. S. (1988). The significance of neuroscience for philosophy. *Trends in Neurosciences, 11,* 304–307.

Cleland, P. G., Saunders, M., & Rosser, R. (1981). An unusual case of visual perseveration. *Journal of Neurology, Neurosurgery, and Psychiatry, 44,* 262–263.

Clemente, C. D., & Chase, M. H. (1973). Neurological substrates of aggressive behavior. *Annual Review of Physiology, 35,* 329–356.

Coben, L. A., Danziger, W., & Storandt, M. (1985). A longitudinal EEG study of mild senile dementia of the Alzheimer type: Changes at 1 year and at 2.5 years. *Electroencephalography and Clinical Neurophysiology, 61,* 101–112.

Coburn, K. L., Garcia, J., Kiefer, S. W., & Rusiniak, K. W. (1984). Taste potentiation of poisoned odor by temporal contiguity. *Behavioral Neuroscience, 98,* 813–819.

Cohen, D. B. (1979). *Sleep and dreaming: Origins, nature and functions.* New York: Pergamon Press.

Cohen, D. H. (1985). Some organizational principles of a vertebrate conditioning pathway: Is memory a distributed property? In N. M. Weinberger, J. L. McGaugh, & G. Lynch (Eds.), *Memory systems of the brain.* New York: Guilford Press.

Cohen, N. J. (1984). Preserved learning capacity in amnesia: Evidence for multiple memory systems. In L. R. Squire & N. Butters (Eds.), *Neuropsychology of memory.* New York: Guilford Press.

Cohen, R. M., Ebstein, R. P., Daly, J. W., & Murphy, D. L. (1982). Chronic effects of a monoamine oxidase-inhibiting antidepressant: Decreases in functional alpha-adrenergic autoreceptors precede the decrease in norepinephrine-stimulated cyclic adenosine 3′:5′-monophosphate systems in rat brain. *The Journal of Neuroscience, 2,* 1588–1595.

Collier, T. J., Gash, D. M., & Sladek, J. R., Jr. (1988). Transplantation of norepinephrine neurons into aged rats improves performance of a learned task. *Brain Research, 449,* 77–87.

Collier, T. J., Quirk, G. J., & Routtenberg, A. (1987). Separable roles of hippocampal granule cells in forgetting and pyramidal cells in remembering spatial information. *Brain Research, 409,* 316–328.

Collier, T. J., & Routtenberg, A. (1984). Selective impairment of declarative memory following stimulation of dentate gyrus granule cells: A naloxone-sensitive effect. *Brain Research, 310,* 384–387.

Collingridge, G. L., & Bliss, T. V. P. (1987). NMDA receptors—their role in long-term potentiation. *Trends in Neurosciences, 10,* 288–293.

Committee on Care and Use of Laboratory Animals. (1985). *Guide for the care and use of laboratory animals* (NIH Publication No. 85-23, Contract No. 1-RR-2-2135). Bethesda, MD: National Institutes of Health.

Cools, A., van den Bercken, J., Horstink, M., van Spaendonck, K., & Berger, H. (1981). The corpus striatum and the programming of behaviour. *Trends in NeuroSciences, 4,* 124.

Cooper, J. R., Bloom, F. E., & Roth, R. H. (1974). *The biochemical basis of neuropharmacology.* New York: Oxford University Press.

Cooper, R., Osselton, J. W., and Shaw, J. C. (1980). *EEG technology* (3rd ed.). Durban: Butterworths.

Corballis, M. C. (1980). Laterality and myth. *American Psychologist, 35,* 284–295.

Corkin, S. (1965). Tactually-guided maze learning in man: Effects of unilateral cortical excisions and bilateral hippocampal lesions. *Neuropsychologia, 3,* 339–351.

Corkin, S. (1968). Acquisition of motor skill after bilateral medial temporal lobe excision. *Neuropsychologia, 6,* 255–265.

Corkin, S. (1978). The roles of different cerebral structures in somesthetic perception. In E. C. Carterette & M. P. Friedman (Eds.), *Handbook of perception: Vol. VIb. Feeling and hurting.* New York: Academic Press.

Corkin, S. (1981). Acetylcholine, aging and Alzheimer's disease: Implications for treatment. *Trends in NeuroSciences, 4,* 287–290.

Coss, R. G., & Globus, A. (1978). Spine stems on tectal interneurons in jewel fish are shortened by social stimulation. *Science, 200,* 787–790.

Cotman, C. W., & Iversen, L. L. (1987). Excitatory amino acids in the brain—focus on NMDA receptors. *Trends in Neurosciences, 10,* 263–265.

Cotman, C. W., & Monaghan, D. T. (1988). Excitatory amino acid neurotransmission: NMDA receptors and Hebb-type synaptic plasticity. *Annual Review of Neuroscience, 11,* 61–80.

Cotman, C. W., Monaghan, D. T., Ottersen, O. P., & Storm-Mathisen, J. (1987). Anatomical organization of excitatory amino acid receptors and their pathways. *Trends in Neurosciences, 10,* 273–280.

Cotman, C. W., & Nieto-Sampedro, M. (1982). Brain function, synapse renewal, and plasticity. *Annual Review of Psychology, 33,* 371–401.

Cox, J. E., & Smith, G. P. (1986) Sham feeding in rats after ventromedial hypothalamic lesions and vagotomy. *Behavioral Neuroscience, 100,* 57–63.

Coyle, J. T. (1978). Neuronal mapping with kainic acid. *Trends in NeuroSciences, 1,* 132–135.

Cragg, B. (1980). Re: Realistic hardware for brain modeling. *Trends in NeuroSciences, 3,* viii.

Creager, J. G. (1983). Human anatomy and physiology. Belmont, CA: Wadsworth.

Crews, F. T., & Smith, C. B. (1978). Presynaptic alpha-receptor subsensitivity after long-term antidepressant treatment. *Science, 202,* 322–324.

Crick, F. (1982). Do dendritic spines twitch? *Trends in NeuroSciences, 5,* 44–46.

Critchley, Mc. (1953). *The parietal lobes.* London: Edward Arnold.

Crosby, E. C., Humphrey, T., & Lauer, E. W. (1962). *Correlative anatomy of the nervous system.* New York: Macmillan.

Crosson, B. (1985). Subcortical functions in language: A working model. *Brain and Language, 25,* 25–29.

Crow, T. J. (1979). What is wrong with dopaminergic transmission in schizophrenia? *Trends in NeuroSciences, 2,* 52–55.

Crow, T. J. (1982). Two syndromes in schizophrenia? *Trends in NeuroSciences, 5,* 351–354.

Crow, T. J., & Johnstone, E. C. (1978). ECT—Does it work? *Trends in NeuroSciences, 1,* 51–53.

Crutcher, K. A., & Davis, J. N. (1981). Sympathetic noradrenergic sprouting in response to central cholinergic denervation. *Trends in NeuroSciences, 4,* 70–72.

Cunningham, V. J., & Cremer, J. E. (1985). Current assumptions behind the use of PET scanning for measuring glucose utilization in brain. *Trends in NeuroSciences, 8,* 96–99.

Curtiss, S. (1985). The development of human cerebral lateralization. In D. F. Benson & E. Zaidel (Eds.), *The dual brain: Hemispheric specialization in humans.* New York: Guilford Press.

Dallos, P. (1985). Response characteristics of mammalian cochlear hair cells. *The Journal of Neuroscience, 5,* 1591–1608.

Dallos, P. (1988). Cochlear neurobiology: Revolutionary developments. *Asha, 30,* 50–56.

Damasio, A. R. (1983). Pure alexia. *Trends in NeuroSciences, 6,* 93–96.

Damasio, A. R., & Geschwind, N. (1984). The neural basis of language. *Annual Review of Neuroscience, 7,* 127–148.

Damasio, A. R., & van Hoesen, G. W. (1983). Emotional disturbances associated with focal lesions of the limbic frontal lobe. In K. M. Heilman & P. Satz (Eds.), *Neuropsychology of human emotion.* New York: Guilford Press.

Darby, C. E. deKorted, R., Binnie, C. D., & Wilkins, A. (1980). Self-induction of epileptic seizures by blinking: Its incidence and recognition. *Electroencephalography and Clinical Neurophysiology, 49,* 100p.

Darien-Smith, I. (1982). Touch in primates. *Annual Review of Psychology, 33,* 155–194.

Davidson, T. L., Flynn, F. W., & Grill, H. J. (1988). Comparison of the interoceptive sensory consequences of CCK, LiCl, and satiety in rats. *Behavioral Neuroscience, 102,* 134–140.

Davis, H., & Silverman, S. R. (1978). *Hearing and deafness.* New York: Holt, Rinehart & Winston.

Davis, H. P., & Squire, L. R. (1984). Protein synthesis and memory: A review. *Psychological Bulletin, 96,* 518–559.

Davson, H. (1978). The environment of the neurone. *Trends in NeuroSciences, 1,* 39–41.

Deadwyler, S. A. (1985). Involvement of hippocampal systems in learning and memory. In N. M. Weinberger, J. L. McGaugh, & G. Lynch (Eds.), *Memory systems of the brain.* New York: Guilford Press.

Deadwyler, S. A., West, M. O., & Robinson, J. H. (1981). Entorhinal and septal inputs differentially control sensory-evoked responses in the rat dentate gyrus. *Science, 211,* 1181–1183.

DeArmond, S. J., Fusco, M. M., & Dewey, M. M. (1976). *Structure of the human brain: A photographic atlas* (2nd ed.). New York: Oxford University Press.

Delay, J. (1942). *Les dissolutions de la mémoire.* Paris: Presses Universitaires de France. [Quoted in English translation in Barbizet, J. (1970). *Human memory and its pathology.* San Francisco: Freeman.]

Delcomyn, F. (1980). Neural basis of rhythmic behavior in animals. *Science, 210,* 492–498.

Della-Fera, M. A., & Baile, C. A. (1979). Cholecystokinin octapeptide: Continuous picomole injections into the cerebral ventricles of sheep suppress feeding. *Science, 206,* 471–473.

Dement, W., Zarcone, V., Ferguson, J., Cohen, H., Pivik, T., & Barches, J. (1969). Some parallel findings in schizophrenic patients and serotonin-depleted cats. In D. V. Siva Sanker (Ed.), *Schizophrenia: Great concepts and research.* Westbury, NY: PJD.

Dement, W. C. (1972). *Some must watch while some must sleep.* San Francisco: Freeman.

Dement, W. C. (1979). The relevance of sleep pathologies to the function of sleep. In R. Drucker-Colin, M. Shkurovich, & M. B. Sterman (Eds.), *The functions of sleep.* New York: Academic Press.

Dement, W. C., & Kleitman, N. (1957). Cyclic variations in EEG during sleep and their relation to eye movements, body motility, and dreaming. *Electroencephalography and Clinical Neurophysiology, 9,* 673–690.

Denes, P. B., & Pinson, E. N. (1973). *The speech chain: The physics and biology of spoken language.* Garden City, NY: Anchor Press/Doubleday.

Desimone, R., Albright, T. D., Gross, C. G., & Bruce, C. (1984). Stimulus-selective properties of inferior temporal neurons in the macaque. *The Journal of Neuroscience, 4,* 2051–2062.

Desmedt, J. E. (1980). Patterns of motor commands during various types of voluntary movement in man. *Trends in NeuroSciences, 3,* 265–268.

Deutsch, J. A. (1973). Electroconvulsive shock and memory. In J. A. Deutsch (Ed.), *The physiological basis of memory.* London: Academic Press.

Deutsch, J. A., Young, W. G., & Kalogeris, T. J. (1978). The stomach signals satiety. *Science, 201,* 165–167.

Diamond, I. T., & Neff, W. D. (1957). Ablation of temporal cortex and discrimination of auditory patterns. *Journal of Neurophysiology, 20,* 300–315.

Dionne, V. E. (1988). How do you smell? Principle in question. *Trends in Neurosciences, 11,* 188–189.

Dowling, J. E. (1967). The site of visual adaptation. *Science, 155,* 273–279.

Dowling, J. E. (1979). Information processing by local circuits: The vertebrate retina as a model system. In F. O. Schmitt & F. G. Worden (Eds.), *The neurosciences: Fourth study program.* Cambridge: MIT Press.

Dowling, J. E., & Boycott, B. B. (1966). Organization of the primate retina. *Proceedings of the Royal Society of London* (Series B), *166,* 80–111.

Drewnowski, A., Cohen, A. E., Faust, I. M., & Grinker, J. A. (1984). Meal-taking behavior is related to predisposition to dietary obesity in the rat. *Physiology & Behavior, 32,* 61–67.

Drucker-Colin, R. (1979). Protein molecules and the regulation of REM sleep: Possible implications for function. In R. Drucker-Colin, M. Shkurovich, & M. B. Sterman (Eds.), *The functions of sleep.* New York: Academic Press.

Drugan, R. C., Ader, D. N., & Maier, S. F. (1985). Shock controllability and the nature of stress-induced analgesia. *Behavioral Neuroscience, 99,* 791–801.

Drugan, R. C., Moye, T. B., & Maier, S. F. (1982). Opioid and non forms of stress-induced analgesia: Some environmental determinants and characteristics. *Behavioral and Neural Biology, 35,* 251–264.

Dudel, J. (1976). Excitation of nerve and muscle. In R. F. Schmidt (Ed.), *Fundamentals of neurophysiology.* Heidelberg: Springer-Verlag.

Duggan, A. W. (1982). Brainstem control of the responses of spinal neurones to painful skin stimuli. *Trends in NeuroSciences, 1,* 21–23.

Duncan, C. P. (1949). The retroactive effect of electroshock on learning. *Journal of Comparative and Physiological Psychology, 42,* 32–44.

Durrant, J. D., & Lovrinic, J. H. (1977). *Bases of hearing science.* Baltimore: Williams & Wilkins.

Duvoisin, R. (1976). Parkinsonism. *Clinical Symposia, 28*(1). Summit, NJ: CIBA Pharmaceutical Co.

Easter, S. S. (1984). Lifelong neurogenesis. *Trends in NeuroSciences, 7,* 105–109.

Ebbesson, S. O. E., & Rubison, K. (1969). A simplified Nauta procedure. *Physiology & Behavior, 4,* 281–282.

Eccles, J. C. (1977). *The understanding of the brain.* Düsseldorf: McGraw-Hill.

Eccles, J. C. (1982). The synapse: From electrical to chemical transmission. *Annual Review of Neuroscience, 5,* 325–340.

Edwards, D. A., & Einhorn, L. C. (1986). Preoptic and midbrain control of sexual motivation. *Physiology & Behavior, 37,* 329–355.

Efron, R., Crandall, P. H., Koss, B., Divenyi, P. L., & Yund, E. W. (1983). Central auditory processing: III. The "cocktail party" effect and anterior temporal lobectomy. *Brain and Language, 19,* 254–263.

Ehrhardt, A. A., & Meyer-Bahlburg, H. F. L. (1981). Effects of prenatal sex hormones on gender-related behavior. *Science, 211,* 1312–1318.

Eichenbaum, H., & Cohen, N. J. (1988). Representation in the hippocampus: What do hippocampal neurons code? *Trends in Neurosciences, 11,* 244–248.

Eichenbaum, H., Kuperstein, M., Fagan, A., & Nagode, J. (1987). Cue-sampling and goal-approach correlates of hippocampal unit activity in rats performing an odor-discrimination task. *The Journal of Neuroscience, 7,* 716–732.

Ellis, L., & Ames, M. A. (1987). Neurohormonal functioning and sexual orientation: A theory of homosexuality–heterosexuality. *Psychological Bulletin, 101,* 233–258.

Emmorey, K. D. (1987). The neurological substrates for prosodic aspects of speech. *Brain and Language, 30,* 305–320.

Erickson, R. P. (1963). Sensory neural patterns and gustation. In Y. Zotterman (Ed.), *Olfaction and taste.* New York: Macmillan.

Evans, E. F. (1975). Neural processes for the detection of acoustic patterns and for sound localization. In G. Werner (Ed.), *Feature extraction by neurons and behavior.* Cambridge: MIT Press.

Evarts, E. V. (1967). Unit activity in sleep and wakefulness. In G. C. Quarton, T. Melnechuk, & F. O. Schmitt (Eds.). *The neurosciences: A study program.* New York: Rockefeller University Press.

Evarts, E. V. (1979). Brain mechanisms of movement. *Scientific American, 241,* 164–179.

Evarts, E. V., Kimura, M., Wurtz, R. H., & Hikosaka, O. (1984). Behavioral correlates of activity in corpus striatum neurons. *Trends in NeuroSciences, 7,* 447–453.

Everhart, T. E., & Hayes, T. L. (1972, January). The scanning electron microscope. *Scientific American, 226,* 54–69.

Fanselow, M., & Helmstetter, F. J. (1988). Conditional analgesia, defensive freezing and benzodiazepines. *Behavioral Neuroscience, 102,* 233–243.

Faraone, S. V., & Tsuang, M. T. (1985). Quantitative models of the genetic transmission of schizophrenia. *Psychological Bulletin, 98,* 41–66.

Farley, J., & Alkon, D. L. (1985). Cellular mechanisms of learning, memory, and information storage. *Annual Review of Psychology, 36,* 419–494.

Favorov, O., & Whitsel, B. L. (1988a). Spatial organization of the peripheral input to area 1 cell columns: I. The detection of segregates. *Brain Research Reviews, 13,* 25–42.

Favorov, O., & Whitsel, B. L. (1988b). Spatial organization of the peripheral input to area 1 cell columns: II. The forelimb representation achieved by a mosaic of segregates. *Brain Research Reviews, 13,* 43–56.

Fay, R. R., & Popper, A. N. (1980). Structure and function in teleost auditory systems. In A. N. Popper & R. R. Fay (Eds.), *Comparative studies of hearing in vertebrates*. Heidelberg: Springer-Verlag.

Feder, H. H. (1984). Hormones and sexual behavior. *Annual Review of Psychology, 33,* 165–200.

Feldman, R. S., & Quenzer, L. F. (1984). *Fundamentals of neuropsychopharmacology.* Sunderland, MA: Sinauer Associates.

Ferguson, N. B. L., & Keesey, R. E. (1975). Effect of a quinine-adulterated diet upon body-weight maintenance in male rats with ventromedial hypothalamic lesions. *Journal of Comparative and Physiological Psychology, 89,* 478–488.

Fibiger, H. C. (1978). Drugs and reinforcement mechanisms: A critical review of the catecholamine theory. *Annual Review of Pharmacology and Toxicology, 18,* 37–56.

File, S. (1987). The search for novel anxiolytics. *Trends in Neurosciences, 10,* 461–463.

Fine, A. (1986). Transplantation in the central nervous system. *Scientific American, 255,* 52–58B.

Fink, M. (1980). A neuroendocrine theory of convulsive therapy. *Trends in NeuroSciences, 3,* 25–27.

Fishbein, W., Kastaniotis, C., & Chattman, D. (1974). Paradoxical sleep: Prolonged augmentation following learning. *Brain Research, 79,* 61–75.

Fisher, A. E. (1964). Chemical stimulation of the brain. *Scientific American, 211,* 66–74.

Flament, D., Vilis, T., & Hore, J. (1984). Dependence of cerebellar tremor on proprioceptive but not visual feedback. *Experimental Neurology, 84,* 314–325.

Flier, J. S. (1983). Insulin receptors and insulin resistance. *Annual Review of Medicine, 34,* 145–160.

Floody, O. R., Blinn, N. E., Lisk, R. D., & Vomachka, A. J. (1987). Localization of hypothalamic sites for the estrogen-priming of sexual receptivity in female hamsters. *Behavioral Neuroscience, 101,* 309–314.

Fontani, G., & Meucci, M. (1983). Dorsolateral PAG neurons: Tonic immobility and morphine effect in freely moving rabbits. *Physiology & Behavior, 31,* 213–218.

Fornal, C., Auerback, S., & Jacobs, B. L. (1985). Activity of serotonin-containing neurons in nucleus raphe magnus in freely moving cats. *Experimental Neurology, 88,* 590–608.

Foster, T. C., Hampson, R. E., West, M. O., & Deadwyler, S. A. (1988). Control of sensory activation of granule cells in the fascia dentata by extrinsic afferents: Septal and entorhinal inputs. *The Journal of Neuroscience, 8,* 3869–3878.

Fowler, I. (1984). *Human anatomy.* Belmont, CA: Wadsworth.

Fox, J. L. (1984). The brain's dynamic way of keeping in touch. *Science, 225,* 820–821.

Freed, D. M., & Corkin, S. (1988). Rate of forgetting in H.M.: 6-month recognition. *Behavioral Neuroscience, 102,* 823–827.

Freed, W. J., Morihisa, J. M., Spoor, E., Hoffer, B. J., Olson, L., Seiger, A., & Wyatt, R. J. (1981). Transplanted adrenal chromaffin cells in the rat brain reduce lesion-induced rotational behavior. *Nature, 292,* 351–352.

Freeman, W., & Watts, J. W. (1950). *Psychosurgery in the treatment of mental disorders and intractable pain* (2nd ed.). Springfield, IL: Charles C. Thomas.

French, J. D. (1957, May). The reticular formation. *Scientific American, 200.*

Freund, H. (1984). Premotor areas in man. *Trends in NeuroSciences, 7,* 481–483.

Freund, T. F., Bolam, J. P., Björklund, A., Stenevi, U., Dunnett, S. B., Powell, J. F., & Smith, A. D. (1985). Efferent synaptic connections of grafted dopaminergic neurons reinnervating the host neostriatum: A tyrosine hydroxylase immunocytochemical study. *The Journal of Neuroscience, 5,* 603–616.

Frey, U., Krug, M., Reymann, K. G., & Matthies, H. (1988). Anisomycin, an inhibitor of protein synthesis, blocks late phases of LTP phenomena in the hippocampal CA1 region in vitro. *Brain Research, 452,* 57–65.

Friedberg, J. (1977). Shock treatment, brain damage, and memory loss: A neurological perspective. *American Journal of Psychiatry, 134,* 1010–1014.

Friedhoff, A. J., & Miller, J. C. (1983). Clinical implications of receptor sensitivity modification. *Annual Review of Neuroscience, 6,* 121–148.

Friedlander, M. J., & Sherman, S. M. (1981). Morphology of physiologically identified neurons. *Trends in NeuroSciences, 4,* 211–214.

Friedman, H. R., & Goldman-Rakic, P. (1988). Activation of the hippocampus and dentate gyrus by working-memory: A 2-deoxyglucose study of behaving rhesus monkeys. *The Journal of Neuroscience, 8,* 4693–4706.

Friedman, M. I., & Stricker, E. M. (1976). The physiological psychology of hunger: A physiological perspective. *Psychological Review, 83,* 409–431.

Frommer, G. P. (1985). Tactile discrimination following analgesia-producing brain stem stimulation in the rat. *Physiological Psychology, 13,* 63–69.

Frutiger, S. A. (1986). Changes in self-stimulation at stimulation-bound eating and drinking sites in the lateral hypothalamus during food or water deprivation, glucoprivation, and intracellular or extracellular dehydration. *Behavioral Neuroscience, 2,* 221–229.

Fuchs, S. A. G., & Siegel, A. (1984). Neural pathways mediating hypothalamically elicited flight behavior in the cat. *Brain Research, 306,* 263–281.

Fulton, J. F. (1943). *Physiology of the nervous system* (2nd ed.). New York: Oxford.

Funder, J. W. (1987). Adrenal steroids: New answers, new questions. *Science, 237,* 236–237.

Fuster, J. M. (1984). Behavioral electrophysiology of the prefrontal cortex. *Trends in NeuroSciences, 7,* 408–414.

Fuster, J. M., & Jervey, J. P. (1981). Inferotemporal neurons distinguish and retain behaviorally relevant features of visual stimuli. *Science, 212,* 952–955.

Gademann, G. (1984). *NMR—Tomography of the normal brain.* Berlin: Springer-Verlag.

Gainotti, G., d'Erme, P., Monteleone, D., & Silveri, M. C. (1986). Mechanisms of unilateral spatial neglect in relation to laterality of cerebral lesions. *Brain, 109,* 599–612.

Galambos, R., & Davis, H. (1943). The response of single auditory-nerve fibers to acoustic stimulation. *Journal of Neurophysiology, 6,* 39–57.

Galanter, E. (1962). Contemporary psychophysics. In *New directions in psychology.* New York: Holt, Rinehart & Winston.

Gallistel, C. R. (1983). Self-stimulation. In J. A. Deutsch (Ed.), *The physiological basis of memory.* New York: Academic Press.

Garcia-Sevilla, J. A., Zis, A. P., Zelnic, T. C., & Smith, C. B. (1981). Tricyclic antidepressant drug treatment decreases α_2-adrenoreceptors on human platelet membranes. *European Journal of Pharmacology, 69,* 121–123.

Gardner, E. (1975). *Fundamentals of neurology.* Philadelphia: Saunders.

Gardner, H. (1976). *The shattered mind.* New York: Random House.

Gardner, W. D., & Osburn, W. A. (1968). *Structure of the human body.* Philadelphia: Saunders.

Garelik, G. (1986). Exorcising a damnable disease. *Discover, 7*(12), 74–85.

Gastaut, H., & Roger, A. (1960). Les mécanismes de l'activité nerveuse supérieure au niveau des grandes structures fonctionelles du cerveau. In H. H. Jasper & G. D. Smirnov (Eds.), *Moscow colloquium on electroencephalogy of higher nervous activities. Electroencephalography and clinical neurophysiology* (Suppl. 13).

Gazzaniga, M. S. (1967). The split brain in man. *Scientific American, 218,* 24–29.

Gazzaniga, M. S. (1983). Right hemisphere language following brain bisection: A 20-year perspective. *American Psychologist, 38,* 525–538.

Gazzaniga, M. S., Bogen, J. E., & Sperry, R. W. (1965). Observations on visual perception after disconnexion of the cerebral hemispheres in man. *Brain, 88,* 221–236.

Gazzaniga, M. S., & Hillyard, S. A. (1971). Language and speech capacity of the right hemisphere. *Neuropsychologia, 9,* 273–280.

Gazzaniga, M. S., & Smylie, C. S. (1984). Dissociation of language and cognition. *Brain, 107,* 145–153.

Gazzaniga, M. S., Smylie, C. S., Baynes, K., Hirst, W., & McCleary, C. (1984). Profiles of right hemisphere language and speech following brain bisection. *Brain and Language, 22,* 206–220.

Geffard, M., McRae-Degeuerce, A., & Souan, M. L. (1985). Immunocytochemical detection of acetylcholine in the rat central nervous system. *Science, 229,* 77–79.

Geldard, F. A. (1953). *The human senses.* New York: John Wiley.

Geldard, F. A. (1972). *The human senses* (2nd ed.). New York: John Wiley.

Geliebter, A., Westreich, S., Hashim, S. A., & Gage, D. (1987). Gastric balloon reduced food intake and body weight in obese rats. *Physiology & Behavior, 39,* 399–402.

Gellman, R. S., & Miles, F. A. (1985). A new role for the cerebellum in conditioning? *Trends in NeuroSciences, 8,* 181–182.

Gergen, J. A., & MacLean, P. D. (1962). *A stereotaxic atlas of the squirrel monkey's brain.* Bethesda, MD: U.S. Department of Health, Education and Welfare.

Gershon, E. S., & Nurnberger, J. I., Jr. (1982). Inheritance of major psychiatric disorders. *Trends in NeuroSciences, 5,* 241–242.

Geschwind, N. (1972). Language and the brain. *Scientific American, 226,* 76–83.

Geschwind, N., & Levitsky, W. (1968). Human brain: Left–right asymmetries in temporal speech region. *Science, 161,* 186–187.

Gibbs, M. E., & Ng, K. T. (1977). Psychobiology of memory: Towards a model of memory formation. *Biobehavioral Reviews, 1,* 113–136.

Gilman, A. G., & Ross, E. M. (1979). Regulation of adenylate cyclase activity. In F. O. Schmitt & F. G. Worden (Eds.), *The neurosciences: Fourth study program.* Cambridge: MIT Press.

Gjerde, P. F. (1983). Attentional capacity dysfunction and arousal in schizophrenia. *Psychological Bulletin, 93,* 57–72.

Glassman, A. (1969). Indoleamines and affective disorder. *Psychosomatic Medicine, 31,* 107–114.

Glickstein, M., & Gibson, A. R. (1976, November). Visual cells in the pons of the brain. *Scientific American, 235,* 90–98.

Goddard, G. V. (1983). The kindling model of epilepsy. *Trends in NeuroSciences, 6,* 275–279.

Goddard, G. V., McIntyre, D. C., & Leech, C. K. (1969). A permanent change in brain functioning resulting from daily electrical stimulation. *Experimental Neurology, 25,* 295.

Goetz, R. R., Goetz, D. M., Hanlon, C., Davies, M., Weitzman, E. D., & Puig-Antich, J. (1983). Spindle characteristics in prepubertal major depressives during an episode and after sustained recovery: A controlled study. *Sleep, 6,* 369–375.

Gold, R. M. (1973). Hypothalamic obesity: The myth of the ventromedial nucleus. *Science, 182,* 488–491.

Goldberg, T., & Benjamins, D. (1982). The possible existence of phonemic reading in the presence of Broca's aphasia: A case report. *Neuropsychologia, 20,* 547–558.

Goldsmith, M. (1984a). Attempts to vanquish Alzheimer's disease intensify, take new paths. *Journal of the American Medical Association, 251,* 1805–1812.

Goldsmith, M. (1984b). Steps toward staging, therapy of dementia. *Journal of the American Medical Association, 251,* 1812–1840.

Goldstein, E. B. (1984). *Sensation and perception* (2nd ed.). Belmont, CA: Wadsworth.

Goldstein, E. B. (1989). *Sensation and perception* (3rd ed.). Belmont, CA: Wadsworth.

Gonzalez, M. F., & Deutsch, J. A. (1981). Vagotomy abolishes cues of satiety produced by gastric distension. *Science, 212,* 1283–1284.

Goodglass, H., & Kaplan, E. (1979). Assessment of cognitive deficit in the brain-injured patient. In M. S. Gazzaniga (Ed.), *Handbook of behavioral neurobiology: Vol. 2. Neuropsychology.* London: Plenum.

Gore, R. (1971, October 22). The brain: Part II. *Life, 117,* 42–64.

Graf, P., & Mandler, G. (1984). Activation makes words more accessible, but not necessarily more retrievable. *Journal of Verbal Learning and Verbal Behavior, 23,* 553–568.

Graff, H., & Stellar, E. (1962). Hyperphagia, obesity and finickiness. *Journal of Comparative and Physiological Psychology, 55,* 418–424.

Grastyán, E. (1959). The hippocampus and higher nervous activity. In M. A. Brazier (Ed.), *The central nervous system and behavior.* New York: Macy.

Grastyán, E., Lissak, K., Madarasz, I., & Donhoffer, H. (1959). *Electroencephalography and Clinical Neurophysiology, 11,* 409–430.

Gratton, A., & Wise, R. A. (1985). Hypothalamic reward mechanism: Two first-stage fiber populations with a cholinergic component. *Science, 227,* 545–548.

Grau, J. W. (1987). The central representation of an aversive event maintains the opioid and non forms of analgesia. *Behavioral Neuroscience, 101,* 272–288.

Gray, E. G. (1982). Rehabilitating the dendritic spine. *Trends in NeuroSciences, 5,* 5–6.

Gray, J. A. (1988). Behavioral and neural-system analyses of the actions of anxiolytic drugs. *Pharmacology, Biochemistry & Behavior, 29,* 767–769.

Gray, P., & Brooks, P. J. (1984). Effect of lesion location within the medial preoptic-anterior hypothalamic continuum on maternal and male sexual behaviors in female rats. *Behavioral Neuroscience, 98,* 703–711.

Green, E. J., & Greenough, W. T. (1986). Altered synaptic transmission in dentate gyrus of rats reared in complex environments: Evidence from hippocampal slices maintained in vitro. *Journal of Neurophysiology, 55,* 739–750.

Greenough, W. T. (1984). Possible structural substrates of plastic neural phenomena. In G. Lynch, J. L. McGaugh, & N. M. Weinberger (Eds.), *Neurobiology of learning and memory.* New York: Guilford Press.

Greenough, W. T. (1985). The possible role of experience-dependent synaptogenesis, or synapses on demand, in the memory process. In N. M. Weinberger, J. L. McGaugh, & G. Lynch (Eds.), *Memory systems of the brain.* New York: Guilford Press.

Greenstein, B. D. (1978). Steroid hormone receptors in the brain. *Trends in NeuroSciences, 1,* 4–6.

Grillner, S. (1981). Control of locomotion in bipeds, tetrapods and fish. In V. B. Brooks (Ed.), *Handbook of physiology: Sec. 1, Vol. 2. The nervous system: Motor control.* American Physiological Society, MD: Waverly Press.

Grillner, S., & Wallén, P. (1985). Central pattern generators for locomotion, with special reference to vertebrates. *Annual Review of Neuroscience, 8,* 233–261.

Grillner, S., & Zangger, P. (1984). The effect of dorsal root transection on the efferent motor pattern in the cat's hindlimb during locomotion. *Acta Physiologica Scandinavia, 120,* 393–405.

Gross, C. G., Bruce, C. J., Desimone, R., Fleming, J., & Gattass, R. (1981). Cortical visual areas of the temporal lobe: Three areas in the macaque. In C. N. Woolsey (Ed.), *Cortical sensory organization: Vol. 2. Multiple visual areas.* Clifton, NJ: Humana Press.

Grossman, S. P. (1960). Eating or drinking elicited by direct adrenergic or cholinergic stimulation of the hypothalamus. *Science, 132,* 301–302.

Grossman, S. P. (1979). The biology of motivation. *Annual Review of Psychology, 30,* 209–242.

Grossman, S. P., Dacey, D., Halaris, A. E., Collier, T., & Routtenberg, A. (1978). Aphagia and adipsia after preferential destruction of nerve cell bodies in hypothalamus. *Science, 202,* 537–539.

Groves, P. M., & Thompson, R. F. (1970). Habituation: A dual-process theory. *Psychological Review, 77,* 419–450.

Grüsser, O.-J. (1979). Cat ganglion-cell receptive fields and the role of horizontal cells in their generation. In F. O. Schmitt & F. G. Worden (Eds.), *The neurosciences: Fourth study program.* Cambridge: MIT Press.

Guillemin, R., & Burgus, R. (1972, November). The hormones of the hypothalamus. *Scientific American, 227,* 24–33.

Gulick, W. L. (1971). *Hearing: Physiology and psychophysics.* New York: Oxford University Press.

Hagenmeyer-Houser, S. H., & Sanberg, P. R. (1987). Locomotor behavior changes induced by E-17 striatal transplants in normal rats. *Pharmacology, Biochemistry & Behavior, 27,* 583–586.

Hagins, W. A. (1979). Excitation in vertebrate photoreceptors. In F. O. Schmitt & F. G. Worden (Eds.), *The neurosciences: Fourth study program.* Cambridge: MIT Press.

Hahn, W. K. (1987). Cerebral lateralization of function: From infancy through childhood. *Psychological Bulletin, 101,* 376–392.

Haley, D. A., Thompson, R. F., & Madden, J., IV. (1988). Pharmacological analysis of the magnocellular red nucleus during classical conditioning of the rabbit nictitating membrane response. *Brain Research, 454,* 131–139.

Hallonquist, J. D., & Brandes, J. S. (1981). Ventromedial hypothalamic lesions and weight gain in rats: Absence of a static phase. *Physiology & Behavior, 27,* 709–713.

Hallonquist, J. D., & Brandes, J. S. (1984). Ventromedial hypothalamic lesions in rats: Gradual elevation of body weight set-point. *Physiology & Behavior, 33,* 831–836.

Halpern, M., & Kubie, J. L. (1984). The role of the ophidian vomeronasal system in species-typical behavior. *Trends in NeuroSciences, 7,* 472–477.

Hamba, M., & Toda, K. (1985). Effects of electroacupuncture on the neuronal activity of the arcuate nucleus of the rat hypothalamus. *Experimental Neurology, 87,* 118–128.

Hamilton, C. R., & Vermeire, B. A. (1988). Complementary hemispheric specialization in monkeys. *Science, 242,* 1691–1694.

Hamilton, J. M., Heller, H. W., & Wade, G. N. (1984). Adipose tissue lipoprotein lipase activity in rats maintained at a reduced body weight. *Physiology & Behavior, 33,* 373–378.

Hammer, R. P. (1982). A brain for all seasons. *Trends in NeuroSciences, 5,* 183.

Handelmann, G. E., & Olton, D. S. (1981). Spatial memory following damage to hippocampal CA3 pyramidal cells with Kainic acid: Impairment and recovery with preoperative training. *Brain Research, 217,* 41–58.

Harrison, J. M. (1978). Functional properties of the auditory system of the brain stem. In R. B. Masterton (Ed.), *Handbook of behavioral neurobiology: Vol. 1. Sensory integration.* New York: Plenum.

Harrison-Read, P. E. (1981). Synaptic and behavioural actions of antidepressant drugs. *Trends in NeuroSciences, 4,* 32–34.

Hart, B. L. (1969). *Experimental neuropsychology: A laboratory manual.* San Francisco: Freeman.

Hart, B. L. (1974). Gonadal androgen and sociosexual behavior of male mammals: A comparative analysis. *Psychological Bulletin, 81,* 383–400.

Hartmann, W. K. (1987). *Astronomy: The cosmic journey.* Belmont, CA: Wadsworth.

Harvey, J. A., & Hunt, H. F. (1965). Effect of septal lesions on thirst in the rat as indicated by water consumption and operant responding for water reward. *Journal of Comparative and Physiological Psychology, 59,* 49–56.

Hatton, G. I. (1976). Nucleus circularis: Is it an osmoreceptor in the brain? *Brain Research Bulletin, 1,* 123–131.

Hatton, G. I., & Armstrong, W. E. (1981). Hypothalamic function in the behavioral and physiological control of body fluids. In P. J. Morgane & J. Panksepp (Eds.), *Handbook of the hypothalamus: Vol. 3, Part B. Behavioral studies of the hypothalamus.* Basel: Marcel Dekker.

Hausberger, F. X., & Volz, J. E. (1984). Feeding in infancy, adipose tissue cellularity and obesity. *Physiology & Behavior, 33,* 81–87.

Heath, R. G. (1981). The neural basis for violent behavior: Physiology and anatomy. In L. Valzelli & L. Mogese (Eds.), *Aggression and violence: A psychobiological and clinical approach.* Saint Vincent, West Indies: Edizioni.

Hebb, D. (1949). *The organization of behavior.* New York: John Wiley.

Heffner, H., & Masterton, R. B. (1975). Contribution of auditory cortex to sound localization in the monkey (*Macaca mulatta*). *Journal of Neurophysiology, 38,* 1340–1359.

Heffner, H. E., & Heffner, R. S. (1986). Hearing loss in Japanese macaques following bilateral auditorycortex lesions. *Journal of Neurophysiology, 55,* 256–270.

Heimer, L. (1971, July). Pathways in the brain. *Scientific American, 225,* 48–64.

Henderson, N. D. (1982). Human behavior genetics. *Annual Review of Psychology, 33,* 403–440.

Henderson, V. W. (1986). Anatomy of posterior pathways in reading: A reassessment. *Brain and Language, 29,* 119–133.

Hendricks, J. C., Morrison, A. R., & Mann, G. L. (1982). Different behaviors during paradoxical sleep without atonia depend on pontine lesion site. *Brain Research, 239,* 81–105.

Hendrickson, A. E. (1985). Dots, stripes and columns in monkey visual cortex. *Trends in NeuroSciences, 8,* 406–410.

Hendrickson, C. W., Kimble, R. J., & Kimble, D. P. (1969). Hippocampal lesions and the orienting response. *Journal of Comparative and Physiological Psychology, 67,* 220–227.

Henke, P. G. (1988). Electrophysiological activity in the central nucleus of the amygdala: Emotionality and stress ulcers in rats. *Behavioral Neuroscience, 102,* 77–83.

Hensel, H. (1973). Cutaneous thermoreceptors. In A. Iggo (Ed.), *Handbook of sensory physiology: Vol. II. Somatosensory system.* Heidelberg: Springer-Verlag.

Hervey, G. R. (1959). The effects of lesions in the hypothalamus in parabiotic rats. *Journal of Physiology, 145,* 336–352.

Hicks, R. E. (1975). Intrahemispheric response competition between vocal and unimanual performance in normal adult human males. *Journal of Comparative and Physiological Psychology, 89,* 50–60.

Hinman, D. J., & Okamoto, M. (1984a). Sleep patterns in cats during chronic low-dose barbiturate treatment and withdrawal. *Sleep, 1,* 69–76.

Hinman, D. J., & Okamoto, M. (1984b). Cortical and subcortical EEG patterns during moderate-intensity barbiturate withdrawal. *Experimental Neurology, 83,* 555–567.

Hirsh, J., & Knittle, J. L. (1970). Cellularity of obese and nonobese human adipose tissue. *Federation Proceedings, 29,* 1516–1521.

Hirsh, R. (1974). The hippocampus and contextual retrieval of information from memory: A theory. *Behavioral Biology, 12,* 421–444.

Hirsh, R. (1980). The hippocampus, conditional operations, and cognition. *Physiological Psychology, 8,* 175–182.

Hirst, W. (1982). The amnesic syndrome: Descriptions and explanations. *Psychological Bulletin, 91,* 435–460.

Hiscock, M., & Kinsbourne, M. (1980). Asymmetry of verbal-manual time sharing in children: A follow-up study. *Neuropsychologia, 18,* 151–162.

Hitchcock, J., & Davis, M. (1986). Lesions of the amygdala, but not of the cerebellum or red nucleus, block conditioned fear as measured with the potentiated startle paradigm. *Behavioral Neuroscience, 100,* 11–22.

Hobson, J. A., McCarley, R. W., & Wyzinski, P. W. (1975). Sleep cycle oscillation: Reciprocal discharge by two brainstem neuronal groups. *Science, 189,* 55–58.

Hodgson, E. S. (1977). The evolutionary origin of the brain. In S. J. Dimond & D. A. Blizard (Eds.), *Evolution and lateralization of the brain.* New York: New York Academy of Sciences.

Hoebel, B. G., & Teitelbaum, P. (1962). Hypothalamic control of feeding and self-stimulation. *Science, 135,* 375–377.

Hoebel, B. G., & Teitelbaum, P. (1966). Weight regulation in normal and hypothalamic hyperphagic rats. *Journal of Comparative and Physiological Psychology, 61,* 189–193.

Holmes, G. (1939). The cerebellum of man. *Brain, 62,* 11–30.

Holmes, G. L., & Weber, D. A. (1985). Effects of hypoxicischemic encephalopathies on kindling in the immature brain. *Experimental Neurology, 90,* 194–203.

Holmes, T. H., & Rahe, R. H. (1967). The social readjustment rating scale. *Journal of Psychosomatic Medicine, 11,* 213–218.

Horn, G., Bradley, P., & McCabe, B. J. (1985). Changes in the structure of synapses associated with learning. *The Journal of Neuroscience, 5,* 3161–3168.

Horridge, G. A. (1968). *Interneurons: Their origin, action, specificity, growth, and plasticity.* London: Freeman.

Hosubuchi, Y., Rossier, J., Bloom, F. E., & Guillemin, R. (1979). Stimulation of human periaqueductal gray for pain relief increases immunoreactive beta-endorphin in ventricular fluid. *Science, 203,* 279–280.

Hotton, N., III. (1968). *The evidence of evolution.* New York: American Heritage.

Hubel, D. H. (1963). The visual cortex of the brain. *Scientific American, 209,* 54–62.

Hubel, D. H. (1979). The brain. *Scientific American, 241,* 44–53.

Hubel, D. H., & Livingstone, M. S. (1983). The 11th J. A. F. Stevenson Memorial Lecture: Blobs and color vision. *Canadian Journal of Physiology and Pharmacology, 61,* 1433–1441.

Hubel, D. H., & Livingstone, M. S. (1987). Segregation of form, color, and stereopsis in primate area 18. *The Journal of Neuroscience, 7,* 3378–3415.

Hubel, D. H., & Wiesel, T. N. (1959). Receptive fields of single neurons in the cat's striate cortex. *Journal of Physiology, 148,* 574–591.

Hubel, D. H., & Wiesel, T. N. (1962). Receptive fields, binocular interaction, and functional architecture in the cat's visual cortex. *Journal of Physiology, 160,* 106–154.

Hubel, D. H., & Wiesel, T. N. (1965a). Receptive fields and functional architecture in two nonstriate visual areas (18 and 19) of the cat. *Journal of Neurophysiology, 28,* 229–289.

Hubel, D. H., & Wiesel, T. N. (1965b). Binocular interaction in striate cortex of kittens reared with artificial squint. *Journal of Neurophysiology, 28,* 1041–1059.

Hubel, D. H., Wiesel, T. N., & Lam, D. M.-K. (1974). Autoradiographic demonstration of ocular-dominance columns in the monkey striate cortex by means of transneuronal transport. *Brain Research, 79,* 273–279.

Hubel, D. H., Wiesel, T. N., & Stryker, M. P. (1978). Anatomical demonstration of orientation columns in macaque monkeys. *Journal of Comparative Neurology, 177,* 361–380.

Hudspeth, A. J. (1982). Extracellular current flow and the site of transduction by vertebrate hair cells. *The Journal of Neuroscience, 2,* 1–10.

Hudspeth, A. J. (1983). Mechanoelectrical transduction by hair cells in the acousticolateralis sensory system. *Annual Review of Neuroscience 6,* 187–216.

Hudspeth, A. J. (1985). The cellular basis of hearing: The biophysics of hair cells. *Science, 230,* 745–752.

Hunsperger, R. W., & Bucher, V. M. (1967). Affective behavior produced by electrical stimulation in the forebrain and brainstem of the cat. In W. R. Adey & T. Tokizane (Eds.), *Structure and function of the limbic system*. Amsterdam: Elsevier.

Hunt, D. D., Adamson, R., Egan, K., & Carr, J. E. (1988). Opioids: Mediators of fear or mania. *Biological Psychiatry, 23,* 426–428.

Huston, J. P., & Borbély, A. A. (1973). Operant conditioning in forebrain ablated rats by use of rewarding hypothalamic stimulation. *Brain Research, 50,* 467–472.

Hutchinson, R. R., & Renfrew, J. W. (1966). Stalking attack and eating behaviors elicited from the same sites in the hypothalamus. *Journal of Comparative and Physiological Psychology, 61,* 360–367.

Hyvärinen, J., & Poranen, A. (1978). Movement-sensitive and direction and orientation-selective cutaneous receptive fields in the hand area of the post-central gyrus in monkeys. *Journal of Physiology, 283,* 523–537.

Iggo, A., & Andres, K. H. (1982). Morphology of cutaneous receptors. *Annual Review of Neuroscience, 5,* 1–32.

Ikeda, H. (1979). Physiological basis of amblyopia. *Trends in NeuroSciences, 2,* 209–213.

Imperato-McGinley, J., Guerrero, L., Gautier, T., & Peterson, R. E. (1974). Steroid 5α-reductase deficiency in man: An inherited form of male pseudohermaphroditism. *Science, 186,* 1213–1215.

Ingvar, D. H. (1982). Mental illness and regional brain metabolism. *Trends in NeuroSciences, 5,* 199–201.

Isaacson, R. L., Douglas, R. J., Lubar, J. F., & Schmaltz, L. W. (1971). *A primer of physiological psychology.* New York: Harper & Row.

Isaacson, R. L., Olton, D. S., Bauer, B., & Swart, P. (1966). The effect of training trials on passive avoidance deficits in the hippocampectomized rat. *Psychonomic Science, 5,* 419–420.

Ito, M. (1974). The control mechanisms of cerebellar motor systems. In E. V. Evarts (Ed.), *Central processing of sensory input leading to motor output.* Cambridge: MIT Press.

Iversen, L. L. (1979). The chemistry of the brain. *Scientific American, 241,* 134–149.

Iversen, S. D. (1983). Brain lesions and memory in animals: A reappraisal. In J. A. Deutsch (Ed.), *The physiological basis of memory* (2nd ed.). London: Academic Press.

Iwai, E., & Mishkin, M. (1968). Two visual foci in the temporal lobe of monkeys. *Japan–United States Joint Seminar on Neurophysiological Basis of Learning.*

Jacklet, J. W. (1978). The cellular mechanisms of circadian clocks. *Trends in NeuroSciences, 1,* 117–119.

Jackson, R. L., Maier, S. F., & Coon, D. J. (1979). Long-term analgesic effects of inescapable shock and learned helplessness. *Science, 206,* 91–92.

Jacobs, B. L., & Trulson, M. E. (1979). Dreams, hallucinations and psychosis—the serotonin connection. *Trends in NeuroSciences, 2,* 276–280.

Jacobs, M. A., Spilken, A., & Norman, M. (1969). Relationship of life change, maladaptive aggression, and upper respiratory infection in male college students. *Psychosomatic Medicine, 31,* 31–44.

Jarrard, L. E., Isaacson, R. L., & Wicklegren, W. O. (1964). Effects of hippocampal ablation and intertrial interval on runaway acquisition and extinction. *Journal of Comparative and Physiological Psychology, 57,* 442–444.

Jasper, H. H. (1954). Functional properties of the thalamic reticular system. In J. F. Delafresnaye (Ed.), *Brain mechanisms and consciousness.* Springfield, IL: Charles C. Thomas.

Jeannerod, M., Michel, F., & Prablanc, C. (1984). The control of hand movements in a case of hemianaesthesia following a parietal lesion. *Brain, 107,* 899–920.

Jensen, W., Heinrich, B., Wake, D. B., Wake, M. H., & Wolfe, S. L. (1979). *Biology.* Belmont, CA: Wadsworth.

Jiang, L. H., & Oomura, Y. (1988). Effect of catecholamine-receptor antagonists on feeding-related neuronal activity in the central amygdaloid nucleus of the monkey: A microiontophoretic study. *Journal of Neurophysiology, 60,* 536–548.

Johansson, R. S., & Vallbo, Å. B. (1983). Tactile sensory coding in the glabrous skin of the human hand. *Trends in NeuroSciences, 6,* 27–32.

Johnson, R. E., & Rasmussen, K. (1984). Individual recognition of female hamsters by males: Role of chemical cues and of the olfactory and vomeronasal systems. *Physiology & Behavior, 33,* 95–104.

Jollie, M. (1977). The origin of the vertebrate brain. In S. J. Dimond & D. A. Blizard (Eds.), *Evolution and lateralization of the brain.* New York: New York Academy of Sciences.

Jones, B. E., Harper, S. T., & Halaris, A. E. (1977). Effects of locus coeruleus lesions upon cerebral monoamine content, sleep-wakefulness states and the responses to amphetamine in the cat. *Brain Research, 124,* 473–496.

Jones, E. G., & Hartman, B. K. (1978). Recent advances in neuroanatomical methodology. *Annual Review of Neuroscience, 1,* 215–296.

Jones, E. G., & Powell, T. P. S. (1973). Anatomical organization of the somatosensory cortex. In A. Iggo (Ed.), *Handbook of sensory physiology: Vol. II. Somatosensory system.* Heidelberg: Springer-Verlag.

Jones, R. (1977). Anomalies of disparity in the human visual system. *Journal of Physiology, 264,* 621–640.

Jonsson, G. (1980). Chemical neurotoxins as denervation tools in neurobiology. *Annual Review of Neuroscience, 3,* 169–187.

Jordan, W. P., & Leaton, R. N. (1982). Startle habituation in rats after lesions in the brachium of the inferior colliculus. *Physiology & Behavior, 28,* 253–258.

Jouandet, M., & Gazzaniga, M. S. (1979). The frontal lobes. In M. S. Gazzaniga (Ed.), *Handbook of behavioral neurobiology: Vol. 2. Neuropsychology.* London: Plenum.

Jouvet, M. (1967a). Neurophysiology of the states of sleep. In G. C. Quarton, T. Melnechuk, & F. O. Schmitt (Eds.), *The neurosciences: A study program.* New York: Rockefeller University Press.

Jouvet, M. (1967b, February). The states of sleep. *Scientific American, 216,* 62–72.

Jouvet, M. (1979). What does a cat dream about? *Trends in NeuroSciences, 2,* 280–282.

Jouvet-Mounier, D., Astic, L., & Lacote, D. (1970). Ontogenesis of the states of sleep in the rat, cat and guinea pig during the first post-natal month. *Developmental Psychobiology, 2,* 216–239.

Julien, R. M. (1981). *A primer of drug action.* San Francisco: Freeman.

Kaars, C., & Faber, D. S. (1981). Myelinated central vertebrate axon lacks voltage-sensitive potassium conductance. *Science, 212,* 1063–1265.

Kaas, J. H. (1987). The organization of neocortex in mammals: Implications for theories of brain function. *Annual Review of Psychology, 38,* 129–152.

Kaas, J. H., Merzenich, M. M., & Killackey, H. P. (1983). The reorganization of somatosensory cortex following peripheral nerve damage in adult and developing mammals. *Annual Review of Neuroscience, 6,* 325–356.

Kaas, J. H., Nelson, R. J., Sur, M., Chia-Cheng, L., & Merzenich, M. M. (1979). Multiple representations of the body within the primary somatosensory cortex of primates. *Science, 204,* 521–523.

Kahn, A. U., & Cataio, J. (1984). *Men and women in biological perspective.* Eastbourne, UK: Praeger.

Kaitin, K. I. (1984). Preoptic area unit activity during sleep and wakefulness in the cat. *Experimental Neurology, 83,* 347–357.

Kamil, A. C., & Roitblat, H. L. (1985). The ecology of foraging behavior: Implications for animal learning and memory. *Annual Review of Psychology, 36,* 141–169.

Kandel, E. R. (1976). *Cellular basis of behavior.* San Francisco: Freeman.

Kandel, E. R. (1979, September). Small systems of neurons. *Scientific American, 241,* 67–76.

Kandel, E. R. (1982). The origins of modern neuroscience. *Annual Review of Neuroscience, 5,* 299–330.

Kapp, B. S., Pascoe, J. P., & Bixler, M. A. (1984). The amygdala: A neuroanatomical systems approach to its contribution to aversive conditioning. In L. R. Squire & N. Butters (Eds.), *Neuropsychology of memory.* New York: Guilford Press.

Kasl, S. V., Evans, A. S., & Niederman, J. C. (1979). Psychosocial risk factors in the development of infectious mononucleosis. *Psychosomatic Medicine, 41,* 445–466.

Katcher, A. H., Brightman, B., Luborsky, L., & Ship, I. (1973). Prediction of the incidence of recurrent herpes labiales and systemic illness from psychological measurements. *Journal of Dental Research, 52,* 49–58.

Katz, B. (1966, August). How cells communicate. *Scientific American, 205,* 209–221.

Kaufman, L. (1974). *Sight and mind: An introduction to visual perception.* New York: Oxford University Press.

Keesey, R. E., & Powley, T. L. (1986). The regulation of body weight. *Annual Review of Psychology, 37,* 109–134.

Kelley, A., Stinus, L., & Iversen, S. D. (1980). Interactions between d-ala-met-enkephalin, A10 dopaminergic neurons, and spontaneous behavior in the rat. *Behavioral Brain Research, 1,* 3–24.

Kelly, D. B. (1986). The genesis of male and female brains. *Trends in NeuroSciences, 9,* 499–502.

Kelly, R. R., & Tomlinson-Keasey, C. (1981). The effect of auditory input on cerebral laterality. *Brain and Language, 13,* 67–77.

Kemp, D. T. (1978). Stimulated acoustic emissions from within the human auditory system. *Journal of the Acoustic Society of America, 64,* 1386–1391.

Kendell, R. E. (1978). Schizophrenia—the disease concept refined. *Trends in NeuroSciences, 1,* 24–26.

Kennedy, G. C. (1953). The role of depot fat in the hypothalamic control of food intake in the rat. *Proceedings of the Royal Society* (Series B), *140,* 578–592.

Kenshalo, D. R. (1972). Cutaneous senses. In L. Riggs & J. W. Kling (Eds.), *Experimental psychology* (Vol. I). New York: Holt, Rinehart & Winston.

Kenshalo, D. R. (1978). Biophysics and psychophysics of feeling. In E. C. Carterette & M. P. Friedman (Eds.), *Handbook of Perception: Vol. VIb. Feeling and hurting.* New York: Academic Press.

Kerr, F. W. L., & Wilson, P. R. (1978). Pain. *Annual Review of Neuroscience, 1,* 83–102.

Kesner, R. P. (1977). A neural system approach to the study of memory storage and retrieval. In R. R. Drucker-Colin & J. L. McGaugh (Eds.), *Neurobiology of sleep and memory.* New York: Academic Press.

Kesner, R. P. (1980). An attribute analysis of memory: The role of the hippocampus. *Physiological Psychology, 8,* 189–197.

Kety, S. S. (1979). Disorders of the human brain. *Scientific American, 241,* 202–214.

Keverne, E. B. (1978). Olfaction and taste—dual systems for sensory processing. *Trends in NeuroSciences, 1,* 32–34.

Keverne, E. B. (1983). Pheromonal influences on the endocrine regulation of reproduction. *Trends in NeuroSciences, 6,* 381–384.

Keynes, R. D. (1979, March). Ion channels in the nerve-cell membrane. *Scientific American, 240,* 126–135.

Kiefer, S. W., Rusiniak, K. W., & Garcia, J. (1982). Flavor-illness aversions: Gustatory neocortex ablations disrupt taste but not taste-potentiated odor cues. *Journal of Comparative and Physiological Psychology, 96,* 540–548.

Kiester, E., Jr. (1986). Spare parts for damaged brains. *Science86, 7,* 32–38.

Kimble, D. P. (1968). Hippocampus and internal inhibition. *Psychological Bulletin, 70,* 285–295.

Kimble, D. P., & Kimble, R. J. (1965). Hippocampectomy and response perseveration in the rat. *Journal of Comparative and Physiological Psychology, 60,* 474–476.

Kimura, D. (1964). Left-right differences in the perception of melodies. *Quarterly Journal of Experimental Psychology, 16,* 355–358.

Kirchgessner, A., & Sclafani, A. (1988). PVN-hindbrain pathway involved in the hypothalamic hyperphagia-obesity syndrome. *Physiology & Behavior, 42,* 517–528.

Kissileff, H. R., Pi-Sunyer, F. X., Thornton, J., & Smith, G. P. (1981). C-terminal octopeptide of cholecystokinin decreases food intake in man. *American Journal of Clinical Nutrition, 34,* 154–160.

Klein, M. V., Lovaas, K. M., Terman, G. W., & Liebeskind, J. C. (1983). The effects of decerebration and spinal transection on three discrete forms of stress-induced analgesia. *Society for Neuroscience Abstracts, 9,* 795.

Kleitman, N. (1960, November). Patterns of dreaming. *Scientific American, 203,* 82–88.

Klüver, H., & Bucy, P. C. (1938). An analysis of certain effects of bilateral temporal lobectomy in the rhesus monkey with special reference to "psychic blindness." *Journal of Psychology, 5,* 33–54.

Klüver, H., & Bucy, P. C. (1939). Preliminary analysis of functions of the temporal lobes in monkeys. *Archives of Neurology and Psychiatry, 42,* 979–1000.

Knab, B., & Engel, R. R. (1988). Perception of waking and sleeping: Possible implications for the evaluation of insomnia. *Sleep, 11,* 265–272.

Knittle, J. L., & Hirsh, J. (1968). Effect of early nutrition on the development of rat epididymal fat pads: Cellularity and metabolism. *Journal of Clinical Investigation, 47,* 2091.

Knudsen, E. I. (1982). Auditory and visual maps of space in the optic tectum of the owl. *The Journal of Neuroscience, 2,* 1177–1194.

Knudsen, E. I. (1984). The role of auditory experience in the development and maintenance of sound localization. *Trends in NeuroSciences, 7,* 326–330.

Knudsen, E. I., du Lac, S., & Esterly, S. D. (1987). Computational maps in the brain. *Annual Review of Neuroscience, 10,* 41–65.

Knudsen, E. I., & Konishi, M. (1977). A neural map of auditory space in the owl. *Science, 200,* 795–797.

Kogeorgos, J., Henson, R. A., & Scott, D. F. (1980). Pattern sensitive epilepsy. *Electroencephalography and Clinical Neurophysiology, 49,* 101p.

Kokkinidis, L., & Anisman, H. (1980). Amphetamine models of paranoid schizophrenia: An overview and elaboration of animal experimentation. *Psychological Bulletin, 88,* 551–579.

Kolata, G. (1985). Obesity declared a disease. *Science, 227,* 1019–1020.

Kolata, G. (1986a). Obese children: A growing problem. *Science, 232,* 20–21.

Kolata, G. (1986b). Maleness pinpointed on Y Chromosome. *Science, 234,* 1076–1077.

Kolb, B., & Wishaw, I. Q. (1985). *Fundamentals of human neuropsychology.* New York: Freeman.

Komisaruk, B. R. (1980). Pain and pleasure. *Science News, 118,* 185.

Konishi, M., & Gurney, M. E. (1982). Sexual differentiation of brain and behaviour. *Trends in NeuroSciences, 5,* 20–23.

Krieg, W. J. S. (1966). *Functional neuroanatomy* (3rd ed.). Evanston, IL: Brain Books.

Krinsky, R., Lotter, E. C., & Woods, S. C. (1979). Appetite suppression caused by CCK is diet-specific in VMH-lesioned rats. *Physiological Psychology, 7,* 67–69.

Kristensson, K., & Olsson, Y. (1971). Retrograde axonal transport of protein. *Brain Research, 29,* 363–365.

Kubie, J. L., & Ranck, J. B., Jr. (1983). Sensory-behavioral correlates in individual hippocampus neurons in three situations: Space and context. In W. Seifert (Ed.), *Neurobiology of the hippocampus.* London: Academic Press.

Kubie, J. L., & Ranck, J. B., Jr. (1984). Hippocampal neuron firing, context, and learning. In L. R. Squire & N. Butters (Eds.), *Neuropsychology of memory.* New York: Guilford Press.

Kuffler, S. W., Nicholls, J. G., & Martin, A. R. (1984). *From neuron to brain.* Sunderland, MA: Sinauer Associates.

Kuhar, M. J. (1981). Autoradiographic localization of drug and neurotransmitter receptors in the brain. *Trends in NeuroSciences, 4,* 60–64.

Kurata, K., Fujimoto, K., Sakata, T., Etou, H., & Fukagawa, K. (1986). D-glucose suppression of eating after intra-third ventricle infusion in the rat. *Physiology & Behavior, 37,* 615–620.

Kurata, K., & Tanji, J. (1985). Contrasting neuronal activity in supplementary and precentral motor cortex of monkeys: II. Responses to movement triggering vs. nontriggering sensory signals. *Journal of Neurophysiology, 53,* 142–152.

Lammers, J. H. C. M., Kruk, M. R., Meelis, W., & van der Poel, A. M. (1988). Hypothalamic substrates for brain stimulation-induced patterns of locomotion and escape jumps in the rat. *Brain Research, 449,* 294–310.

Lancet, D. (1984). Molecular view of olfactory reception. *Trends in NeuroSciences, 7,* 35–36.

Langer, S. Z. (1980). Presynaptic receptors and modulation of neurotransmission: Pharmacological implications and therapeutic relevance. *Trends in NeuroSciences, 3,* 110–112.

Langston, J. W. (1985). MPTP and Parkinson's disease. *Trends in NeuroSciences, 8,* 79–83.

Larsen, T. A., & Calne, D. B. (1982). Recent advances in the study of Parkinson's disease. *Trends in NeuroSciences, 5,* 10–12.

Lashley, K. (1950). In search of the engram. *Symposia of the Society of Experimental Biology, 4,* 478–505.

Lasiter, P. S., & Glanzman, D. L. (1985). Cortical substrates of taste aversion learning: Involvement of dorsolateral amygdaloid nuclei and temporal neocortex in taste aversion learning. *Behavioral Neuroscience, 99,* 257–276.

Lassen, N. A., Ingvar, D. H., & Skinhøj, E. (1978, October). Brain function and blood flow. *Scientific American, 239,* 62–71.

Lavond, D. G., McCormick, D. A., Clark, G. A., Holmes, D. T., & Thompson, R. F. (1981). Effects of ipsilateral rostral pontine reticular lesions on retention of classically conditioned nictitating membrane and eyelid responses. *Physiological Psychology, 9,* 335–339.

Leaton, R. N., & Supple, W. F. (1986). Cerebellar vermis: Essential for long-term habituation of the acoustic startle response. *Science, 232,* 513–515.

Le Doux, J. E. (1979). Parietooccipital symptomology: The split-brain perspective. In M. S. Gazzaniga (Ed.), *Handbook of behavioral neurobiology: Vol. 2. Neuropsychology.* London: Plenum.

Le Gros Clark, W. E., Beattie, J., Riddoch, G., & Dott, N. M. (1938). *The hypothalamus.* Edinburgh: Oliver & Boyd.

Leibowitz, S. F., Roland, C. R., Hor, L., & Squillari, V. (1984). Noradrenergic feeding elicited via the paraventricular nucleus is dependent upon circulating corticosterone. *Physiology & Behavior, 22,* 857–864.

Leksell, L. (1971). *Stereotaxic and radio surgery. An operative system.* Springfield, IL: Charles C. Thomas.

LeMay, M. (1982). Morphological aspects of human brain asymmetry: An evolutionary perspective. *Trends in NeuroSciences, 5,* 273–275.

Lemeshow, S. (1982). *The handbook of clinical types in mental retardation.* Boston: Allyn & Bacon.

Lennie, P. (1984). Recent developments in the physiology of color vision. *Trends in NeuroSciences, 7,* 243–248.

Leon, G. (1976). Current directions in the treatment of obesity. *Psychological Bulletin, 83,* 557–578.

Leonard, C. M. (1979). Degeneration methods in neurobiology. *Trends in NeuroSciences, 2,* 156–159.

Lesser, R. P., Lueders, H., Dinner, D. S., Hahn, J., & Cohen, L. (1984). The location of speech and writing functions in the frontal language area. *Brain, 107,* 275–291.

Lester, L. S., & Fanselow, M. S. (1985). Exposure to a cat produces opioid analgesia in rats. *Behavioral Neuroscience, 99,* 756–759.

Lettvin, J. Y., Maturana, H. R., Pitts, W. H., & McCulloch, W. S. (1961). Two remarks on the visual system of the frog. In W. A. Rosenblith (Ed.), *Sensory communication.* Cambridge: MIT Press.

LeVay, S., Connolly, M., Houde, J., & Van Essen, D. C. (1985). The complete pattern of ocular dominance stripes in the striate cortex and visual field of the macaque monkey. *The Journal of Neuroscience, 5,* 486–501.

Levine, S. (1966). Sex differences in the brain. *Scientific American, 215,* 67–75.

Levitan, I. B. (1988). Modulation of ion channels in neurons and other cells. *Annual Review of Neuroscience, 11,* 119–136.

Levy, J. (1974). Psychological implications of biological asymmetry. In S. J. Dimond & J. G. Beaumont (Eds.), *Hemisphere function in the human brain.* London: Elek Science.

Levy, J. (1979). Human cognition and lateralization of cerebral function. *Trends in NeuroSciences, 2,* 222–225.

Levy, J. (1983). Language, cognition and the right hemisphere: A response to Gazzaniga. *American Psychologist, 38,* 538–541.

Lewin, R. (1985). Clinical trials for Parkinson's disease? *Science, 230,* 527–528.

Lewin, R. (1987). Brain grafts benefit Parkinson's patients. *Science, 236,* 149.

Lewin, R. (1988). Cloud over Parkinson's therapy. *Science, 240,* 390–392.

Lewis, E. R., Everhart, T. E., & Zeevi, Y. Y. (1969). Studying neural organization in Aplysia with the scanning electron microscope. *Science, 165,* 1142.

Lewis, J. W., Cannon, J. T., & Liebeskind, J. C. (1980). Opioid and non mechanisms of stress analgesia. *Science, 208,* 623–625.

Lhermitte, F., & Signoret, J.-L. (1976). The amnesic syndromes and the hippocampal–mammillary system. In E. L. Bennett & M. R. Rosenzweig (Eds.), *Neural mechanisms of learning and memory.* Cambridge: MIT Press.

Libassi, P. T. (1975). To sleep the good sleep. *The Sciences, 15,* 24–28.

Libet, B. (1973). Electrical stimulation of cortex in human subjects, and conscious sensory aspects. In A. Iggo (Ed.), *Handbook of sensory physiology: Vol. II. Somatosensory system.* Heidelberg: Springer-Verlag.

Lickey, M. E., & Gordon, B. (1983). *Drugs for mental illness: A revolution in psychiatry.* New York: Freeman.

Light, K. C., Koepke, J. P., Obrist, P. A., & Willis, P. W. (1983). Psychological stress induces sodium and fluid retention in men at high risk for hypertension. *Science, 220,* 429–431.

Lima, F. B., Hill, N. S., Timo-Iaria, C., Dolnikoff, M. S., & Pupo, A. A. (1982). Carbohydrate metabolism and food intake in food restricted rats: Effects of an unexpected meal. *Physiology & Behavior, 29,* 931.

Lindsley, D. B. (1957). Psychophysiology & motivation. *Nebraska Symposium on Motivation, 5,* 44–105.

Lippe, W. R. (1986). Recent developments in cochlear physiology. *Ear and Hearing, 7,* 233–239.

Livingston, W. K. (1943). *Pain mechanisms.* New York: Macmillan.

Livingstone, M. S., & Hubel, D. H. (1982). Thalamic inputs to cytochrome oxidase-rich regions in monkey visual cortex. *Proceedings of the National Academy of Science, USA (Neurobiology), 79,* 6098–6101.

Livingstone, M. S., & Hubel, D. H. (1984a). Anatomy and physiology of a color system in the primate visual cortex. *The Journal of Neuroscience, 4,* 309–356.

Livingstone, M. S., & Hubel, D. H. (1984b). Specificity of intrinsic connections in primate primary visual cortex. *The Journal of Neuroscience, 4,* 2830–2835.

Livingstone, M. S., & Hubel, D. H. (1987a). Connections between layer 4B of area 17 and the thick cytochrome oxidase stripes of area 18 in the squirrel monkey. *The Journal of Neuroscience, 7,* 3371–3377.

Livingstone, M. S., & Hubel, D. H. (1987b). Psychophysical evidence for separate channels for the perception of form, color, movement, and depth. *The Journal of Neuroscience, 7,* 3416–3468.

Loeb, G. E. (1985). The functional replacement of the ear. *Scientific American, 252,* 104–111.

Loehlin, J. C., Willerman, L., & Horn, J. M. (1988). Human behavior genetics. *Annual Review of Psychology, 39,* 101–133.

Lohr, J. B., & Wisniewski, A. A. (1987). *Movement disorders: A neuropsychiatric approach.* New York: Guilford Press.

Lovinger, D. M., Wong, K. M., & Routtenberg, A. (1987). Protein kinase C inhibitors eliminate hippocampal long-term potentiation. *Brain Research, 436,* 177–183.

Lucas, F., Bellisle, F., & Di Maio, A. (1987). Spontaneous insulin fluctuations and the preabsorptive insulin response to food ingestion in humans. *Physiology & Behavior, 40,* 631–636.

Luce, G. G. (1970). *Biological rhythms in psychiatry and medicine.* NIMH Public Health Service (Bulletin No. 2088). Washington, DC: U.S. Government Printing Office.

Lucero, M. (1970). Lengthening of REM sleep duration consecutive to learning in the rat. *Brain Research, 20,* 319–322.

Ludlow, C. L., Rosenberg, J., Fair, C., Buck, D., Schesselman, S., & Salazar, A. (1986). Brain lesions associated with nonfluent aphasia fifteen years following penetrating head injury. *Brain, 109,* 55–80.

Lueng, L.-W. S., & Desborough, K. A. (1988). APV, an N-methyl-D-aspartate receptor antagonist, blocks the hippocampal theta rhythm in behaving rats. *Brain Research, 463,* 148–152.

Luiten, P. G. M., ter Horst, G. J., & Steffens, A. B. (1986). The hypothalamus, intrinsic connections and outflow pathways to the endocrine system in relation to the control of feeding and metabolism. *Progress in Neurobiology, 28,* 1–54.

Luria, A. R. (1963). *Restoration of function after brain injury.* New York: Macmillan.

Luria, A. R. (1970). The functional organization of the brain. *Scientific American, 222,* 66–79.

Luria, A. R. (1973). The frontal lobes and the regulation of behavior. In K. H. Pribram & A. R. Luria (Eds.), *Psychophysiology of the frontal lobes.* New York: Academic Press.

Lutz, J., & Marsh, T. K. (1981). The effect of a dual level word list on schizophrenic free recall. *Schizophrenia Bulletin, 7,* 509–515.

Lynch, G., & Baudry, M. (1984a). The biochemistry of memory: A new and specific hypothesis. *Science, 224,* 1057–1063.

Lynch, G., & Baudry, M. (1984b). Between model systems and memory: The use of physiological plasticity in hippocampus to identify cellular chemistries involved in memory storage. In L. R. Squire & N. Butters (Eds.), *Neuropsychology of memory.* New York: Guilford Press.

Lynn, R. (1966). *Attention, arousal and the orienting reaction.* Oxford: Pergamon Press.

Maas, J. W. (1979). Neurotransmitters and depression: Too much, too little, or too unstable? *Trends in NeuroSciences, 2,* 306–308.

MacKay, W. A. (1980). The motor program: Back to the computer. *Trends in NeuroSciences, 3,* 97–100.

Mackie, G. O. (1980). Jellyfish neurobiology since Romanes. *Trends in NeuroSciences, 3,* 13–16.

MacLean, P. D. (1949). Psychosomatic disease and the "visceral brain": Recent developments bearing on the Papez theory of emotion. *Psychosomatic Medicine, 11,* 338–353.

MacLean, P. D. (1965). New finding relevant to the evolution of psychosexual functions of the brain. In J. Money (Ed.), *Sex research: New developments.* New York: Holt, Rinehart and Winston.

MacLean, P. D. (1968). Contrasting functions of limbic and neocortical systems of the brain and their relevance to psychophysiological aspects of medicine. In E. Gellhorn (Ed.), *Biological foundations of emotion.* Glenview, IL: Scott, Foresman.

MacLusky, N. J., & Naftolin, F. (1981). Sexual differentiation in the central nervous system. *Science, 211,* 1294–1303.

Maeda, H., Sato, T., & Maki, S. (1985). Effects of dopamine agonists on hypothalamic defensive attack in cats. *Physiology & Behavior, 35,* 89–92.

Maggio, C. A., Haraczkiewicz, E., & Vasselli, J. R. (1988). Diet composition alters the satiety effect of cholecystokinin in lean and obese Zucher rats. *Physiology & Behavior, 43,* 485–491.

Mahut, H., & Moss, M. (1984). Consolidation of memory: The hippocampus revisited. In L. R. Squire & N. Butters (Eds.), *Neuropsychology of memory.* New York: Guilford Press.

Malmo, R. B. (1942). Interference factors in delayed response in monkeys after removal of frontal lobes. *Journal of Neurophysiology, 5,* 295–308.

Mann, J. J., Stanley, M., Gershon, S., & Rossor, M. (1980). Mental symptoms in Huntington's disease and a possible primary aminergic neuron lesion. *Science, 210,* 1369–1372.

Margolin, D. I., & Binder, L. (1984). Multiple component agraphia in a patient with atypical cerebral dominance: An error analysis. *Brain and Language, 22,* 26–40.

Mark, V. H., & Ervin, F. R. (1970). *Violence and the brain.* Evanston: Harper & Row.

Mark, V. H., Ervin, F. R., & Yakovlev, P. I. (1963). Stereotaxic thalamotomy III: The verification of anatomical lesion sites in the human thalamus. *Archives of Neurology, 8,* 528–538.

Markowitsch, H. J., & Pritzel, M. (1985). The neuropathology of amnesia. *Progress in Neurobiology, 25,* 189–287.

Marsden, C. D. (1980). The enigma of the corpus striatum and movement. *Trends in NeuroSciences, 3,* 284–287.

Marx, J. L. (1979). Parkinson's disease: Search for better therapy. *Science, 203,* 737–738.

Marx, J. L. (1987). Role of Alzheimer's protein is tangled. *Science, 238,* 1352–1353.

Marx, J. L. (1989). Brain protein yields clues to Alzheimer's disease. *Science, 243,* 1664–1666.

Mason, S. T., Beninger, R. J., Fibiger, H. C., & Phillips, A. G. (1980). Pimozide-induced suppression of responding: Evidence against a block of food reward. *Pharmacology and Biochemistry of Behavior, 12,* 917–923.

Mastaglia, F. L., & Cala, L. A. (1980). Computed tomography of the brain in multiple sclerosis. *Trends in NeuroSciences, 3,* 16–20.

Masterton, B. R., & Glendenning, K. K. (1978). Phylogeny of the vertebrate sensory systems. In R. B. Masterton (Ed.), *Handbook of neurobiology: Vol. 1. Sensory integration.* New York: Plenum.

Matsumoto, K., Takeyasu, K., Mitzutiani, Y., Hamanaka, Y., & Vozumi, T. (1970). Plasma testosterone levels following surgical stress in male patients. *Acta Endocrinologica, 65,* 11–17.

Matthysse, S., Kidd, K. K. (1982). HLA-linkage in affective disorders. *Trends in NeuroSciences, 5,* 104–105.

Mayer, J. (1952). The glucostatic theory of regulation of food intake and the problem of obesity. *Bulletin of the New England Medical Center, 14,* 43–49.

Mayer, J. (1977, February). Should you starve yourself thin? *Family Health/Today's Health Magazine.*

McCleary, R. A. (1966). Response-modulation functions of the limbic system: Initiation and suppression. In E. Stellar & J. M. Sprague (Eds.), *Progress in physiological psychology* (Vol. 1). New York: Academic Press.

McCleary, R. A., & Moore, R. Y. (1965). *Subcortical mechanisms of behavior.* New York: Basic Books.

McClintock, M. K. (1971). Menstrual synchrony and suppression. *Nature, 229,* 244–245.

McCloskey, D. I. (1980). Knowledge about muscular contractions. *Trends in NeuroSciences, 3,* 311–314.

McCormick, D. A., Clark, G. A., Lavond, D. G., & Thompson, R. F. (1982). Initial localization of the memory trace for a basic form of learning. *Proceedings of the National Academy of Sciences, USA, 79,* 2731–2742.

McCormick, D. A, & Thompson, R. F. (1984). Cerebellum: Essential involvement in the classically conditioned eyelid response. *Science, 223,* 296–299.

McDonnell, M. F., & Flynn, J. P. (1966). Control of sensory fields by stimulation of hypothalamus. *Science, 152,* 1406–1408.

McEwen, B. S. (1976). Interactions between hormones and nerve tissue. *Scientific American, 235,* 48–58.

McGinty, D., & Szymusiak, R. (1988). Neuronal unit activity patterns in behaving animals. *Annual Review of Psychology, 39,* 135–168.

McGinty, D. J. (1979). Ontogenetic and clinical studies of sleep state organization and dissociation. In R. Drucker-Colin, M. Shkurovich, & M. B. Sterman (Eds.), *The functions of sleep.* New York: Academic Press.

McGinty, D. J. (1985). Physiological equilibrium and the control of sleep states. In D. McGinty, R. Drucker-Colin, A. Morrison, & P. L. Parmeggiani (Eds.), *Brain mechanisms of sleep.* New York: Raven Press.

McGinty, D. J., & Siegel, J. M. (1977). Neuronal activity patterns during rapid-eye movement sleep: Relation to waking patterns. In R. R. Drucker-Colin & J. L. McGaugh (Eds.), *Neurobiology of sleep and memory.* New York: Academic Press.

McGlone, J. (1984). Speech comprehension after unilateral injection of sodium amytal. *Brain and Language, 22,* 150–157.

McLaughlin, C. L., Baile, C. A., & Della-Fera, M. A. (1986). Changes in brain CCK concentrations with peripheral CCK injections in Zucker rats. *Physiology & Behavior, 36,* 477–482.

McLaughlin, C. L., Baile, C. A., Della-Fera, M. A., & Kasser, T. G. (1985). Meal-stimulated increased concentrations of CCK in the hypothalamus of Zucker obese and lean rats. *Physiology & Behavior, 35,* 215–220.

McMinn, M. R. (1984). Mechanisms of energy balance in obesity. *Behavioral Neuroscience, 98,* 375–393.

McNeal, E. T., & Cimbolic, P. (1986). Antidepressants and biochemical theories of depression. *Psychological Bulletin, 99,* 361–374.

Meaney, M. J. (1988). The sexual differentiation of social play. *Trends in Neurosciences, 11,* 54–58.

Means, L. W., Huntley, D. H., Anderson, H. P., & Harrel, T. H. (1973). Deficient acquisition and retention of a visual-tactile discrimination task in rats with medial thalamic lesions. *Behavioral Biology, 9,* 435–450.

Means, L. W., Walker, D. W., & Isaacson, R. L. (1970). Facilitated single-alternation go, no-go acquisition following hippocampectomy in the rat. *Journal of Comparative and Physiological Psychology, 72,* 278–285.

Medalia, A., Gold, J., & Merriam, A. (1988). The effects of neuroleptics on neuropsychological test results of schizophrenics. *Archives of Clinical Neuropsychology, 3,* 249–371.

Meisel, R. L. (1983). Recovery of masculine copulatory behavior from lesions of the medial preoptic area: Effects of age vs. hormonal state. *Behavioral Neuroscience, 309,* 1136–1137.

Melzack, R. (1972). The perception of pain. In R. F. Thompson (Ed.), *Physiological psychology: Readings from Scientific American.* San Francisco: Freeman.

Melzack, R. (1973). *The puzzle of pain.* New York: Basic Books.

Melzack, R., & Wall, P. D. (1965). Pain mechanisms: A new theory. *Science, 150,* 971–979.

Mendels, J., Stinnett, J. L., Burns, D., & Frazer, A. (1975). Amine precursors and depression. *Archives of General Psychiatry, 32,* 22–30.

Mersky, J. (1975). Psychological aspects of pain. In M. Weisenberg (Ed.), *Pain: Clinical and experimental perspectives.* St. Louis: Mosby.

Merzenich, M. M., & Kaas, J. H. (1982). Reorganization of mammalian somatosensory cortex following peripheral nerve injury. *Trends in NeuroSciences, 5,* 434–436.

Merzenich, M. M., & Reid, M. D. (1974). Representation of the cochlea within the inferior colliculus of the cat. *Brain Research, 77,* 397–415.

Mesulam, M.-M. (1983). The functional anatomy and hemispheric specialization for directed attention: The role of the parietal lobe and its connectivity. *Trends in NeuroSciences, 6,* 384–387.

Miceli, M. O. (1985). Role of gastric distention in cholecystokinin's satiety effect in golden hamsters. *Physiology & Behavior, 35,* 945–953.

Michael, R. P. (1972). Role of olfaction in sexual response. *Medical Aspects of Human Sexuality, 6,* 63–69.

Middlebrooks, J. C., & Knudsen, E. I. (1984). A neural code for auditory space in the cat's superior colliculus. *The Journal of Neuroscience, 4,* 2621–2634.

Millar, J. B., Tong, Y. C., & Clark, G. M. (1984). Speech processing for cochlear implant prostheses. *Journal of Speech and Hearing Research, 27,* 280–296.

Miller, J. A. (1980). Breaking down "boyish" behavior. *Science News, 118,* 344.

Miller, J. A. (1983). Molecular hardware of cell communication: Describing the acetylcholine receptor. *Neuroscience Commentaries, 1,* 93–98.

Miller, L. G., Thompson, M. L., Greenblatt, D. J., Deutsch, S. I., Shader, R. I., & Paul, S. M. (1987). Rapid increase in brain benzodiazepine receptor binding following defeat stress in mice. *Brain Research, 414,* 395–400.

Miller, R. R., & Springer, A. D. (1972). Induced recovery of memory in rats following electroconvulsive shock. *Physiology & Behavior, 8,* 645–651.

Milner, B. (1963). Effects of different brain lesions on card sorting. *Archives of Neurology, 9,* 90–100.

Milner, B. (1975). Hemispheric specialization: Scope and limits. In B. Milner (Ed.), *Hemispheric specialization and interaction.* Cambridge: MIT Press.

Milner, B., Corkin, S., & Teuber, H.-L. (1968). Further analysis of the hippocampal amnesic syndrome: 14-year follow-up study of H. M. *Neuropsychologia, 6,* 215–234.

Milner, B., & Petrides, M. (1984). Behavioural effects of frontal-lobe lesions in man. *Trends in NeuroSciences, 7,* 403–407.

Mirsky, A. F., & Duncan, C. C. (1986). Etiology and expression of schizophrenia: Neurobiological and psychosocial factors. *Annual Review of Psychology, 37,* 291–319.

Mirsky, R. (1980). Cell-type-specific markers in nervous system cultures. *Trends in NeuroSciences, 3,* 190–192.

Mishkin, M. (1966). Visual mechanisms beyond the striate cortex. In R. W. Russel (Ed.), *Frontiers in physiological psychology.* New York: Academic Press.

Mishkin, M., & Ungerleider, L. G. (1982). Contribution of striate inputs to the visuospatial functions of parieto-preoccipital cortex in monkeys. *Behavioral Brain Research, 6,* 57–77.

Mishkin, M., Ungerleider, L. G., and Macko, K. A. (1983). Object vision and spatial vision: Two cortical pathways. *Trends in NeuroSciences, 6,* 414–417.

Mitchell, S. J., Rawlins, J. N. P., Steward, O., & Olton, D. S. (1982). Medial septal area lesions disrupt θ rhythm and cholinergic staining in medial entorhinal cortex and produce impaired radial arm maze behavior in rats. *The Journal of Neuroscience, 2,* 292–302.

Mogenson, G. J. (1969). Water deprivation and excessive water intake during self-stimulation. *Physiology & Behavior, 4,* 393–397.

Mohr, J. P. (1976). Broca's area and Broca's aphasia. In H. Whitaker & H. A. Whitaker (Eds.), *Studies in neurolinguistics*. New York: Academic Press.

Mohr, J. P., Pessin, M. S., Finkelstein, S., Funkenstein, H. H., Duncan, G. W., & Davis, K. R. (1978). Broca aphasia: Pathological and clinical. *Neurology, 28,* 311–324.

Moldofsky, H., & Lue, F. A. (1980). The relationship of alpha and delta EEG frequencies to pain and mood in "fibrositis" patients treated with chlorpromazine and L-tryptophan. *Electroencephalography and Clinical Neurophysiology, 50,* 71–80.

Moldofsky, H., & Scarisbrick, P. (1976). Induction of neurasthenic musculoskeletal pain syndrome by selective sleep stage deprivation. *Psychosomatic Medicine, 38,* 35–44.

Moncrieff, R. W. (1951). *The chemical senses.* London: Leonard Hill.

Money, J. (1987). Sin, sickness, or status?: Homosexual gender identity and psychoneuroendocrinology. *American Psychologist, 42,* 384–399.

Money, J., & Ehrhardt, A. A. (1972). *Man and woman, boy and girl.* Baltimore: Johns Hopkins University Press.

Monjan, A. A., & Collector, M. I. (1977). Stress-induced modulation of the immune response. *Science, 196,* 307–308.

Montagna, W. (1965). The skin. *Scientific American, 11,* 58–59.

Moore, B. C. J. (1984). Electrical stimulation of the auditory nerve in man. *Trends in NeuroSciences, 7,* 274–277.

Moore, D. R. (1983). Development of inferior colliculus and binaural audition. In R. Romand (Ed.), *Development of auditory and vestibular systems*. Sydney: Academic Press.

Moore, R. Y., & Bloom, F. E. (1978). Central catecholamine neuron systems: Anatomy and physiology of the dopamine systems. *Annual Review of Neuroscience, 1,* 129–169.

Moore, R. Y., & Bloom, F. E. (1979). Central catecholamine neuron systems: Anatomy and physiology of the norepinephrine and epinephrine systems. *Annual Review of Neuroscience, 2,* 113–168.

Morgane, P. J. (1961). Alterations of feeding and drinking behavior of rats with lesions in globi pallidi. *American Journal of Physiology, 201,* 410–428.

Morrison, A. R. (1979). Brainstem regulation of behavior during sleep and wakefulness. In J. M. Sprague & A. N. Epstein (Eds.), *Progress in psychobiology and physiological psychology* (Vol. 8). New York: Academic Press.

Morrison, A. R. (1983, April). A window on the sleeping brain. *Scientific American, 248,* 94–103.

Morstyn, R., Duffy, F. H., & McCarley, R. W. (1983). Altered topography of EEG spectral content in schizophrenia. *Electroencephalography and Clinical Neurophysiology, 56,* 263–271.

Moshé, S. L., & Albala, B. J. (1985). Perinatal hypoxia and subsequent development of seizures. *Physiology & Behavior, 35,* 819–823.

Moss, M. S., & Basbaum, A. I. (1983). The peptidergic organization of the cat periaqueductal gray: II. The distribution of immunoreactive substance P and vasoactive intestinal peptide. *The Journal of Neuroscience, 3,* 1437–1439.

Motter, B. C., & Mountcastle, V. B. (1981). The functional properties of the light-sensitive neurons of the posterior parietal cortex studied in waking monkeys: Foveal sparing and opponent vector organization. *The Journal of Neuroscience, 1,* 3–26.

Mountcastle, V. B. (1978). An organizing principle for cerebral function: The unit module and the distributed system. In B. M. Edelman and V. B. Mountcastle (Eds.), *The mindful brain*. Cambridge: MIT Press.

Mountcastle, V. B. (1979). An organizing principle for cerebral function: The unit module and the distributed system. In F. O. Schmitt & F. G. Worden (Eds.), *The neurosciences: Fourth study program*. Cambridge: MIT Press.

Moyer, K. E. (1976). *The psychobiology of aggression*. New York: Harper & Row.

Moyer, K. E. (1980). *Neuroanatomy*. New York: Harper & Row.

Mrosovsky, N. (1986). Body fat: What is regulated? *Physiology & Behavior, 38,* 407–414.

Munson, J. B., & Graham, R. B. (1971). Lateral geniculate spikes in sleeping, awake, and reserpine-treated cats: Correlated excitability changes in superior colliculus and related structures. *Experimental Neurology, 31,* 326–336.

Munson, J. B., & Graham, R. B. (1973). Localization of lateral geniculate spikes in alert, sleeping and reserpine-treated cats. *Electroencephalography and Clinical Neurophysiology, 35,* 323–326.

Munson, J. B., & Schwartz, K. S. (1972). Lateral geniculate and occipital cortex spikes with eye movements in awake and sleeping cats: Temporal and functional correlations. *Experimental Neurology, 35,* 300–304.

Murray, E. A., & Mishkin, M. (1984a). Relative contributions of SmII and area 5 to tactile discrimination of monkeys. *Behavioral Brain Research, 11,* 67–84.

Murray, E. A., & Mishkin, M. (1984b). Severe tactual as well as visual memory deficits follow combined removal of the amygdala and hippocampus in monkeys. *The Journal of Neuroscience, 4,* 2565–2580.

Murray, E. A., & Mishkin, M. (1986). Visual recognition in monkeys following rhinal cortical ablations combined with either amygdalectomy or hippocampectomy. *The Journal of Neuroscience, 6,* 1991–2003.

Murzi, E., Hernandez, L., & Baptista, T. (1986). Lateral hypothalamic sites eliciting eating affect medullary taste neurons in rats. *Physiology & Behavior, 36,* 829–834.

Musiek, F. E. (1983). The evaluation of brainstem disorders using ABR and central auditory tests. *Monographs in Contemporary Audiology, 4*(2), 1–24.

Mytilineou, C., & Cohen, G. (1984). 1-Methyl-4-Phenyl-1,2,3,6-Tetrahydropyridine destroys dopamine neurons in explants of rat embryo mesencephalon. *Science, 225,* 529–531.

Naeser, M. A. (1982). Language behavior in stroke patients: Cortical vs. subcortical lesion sites on CT scans. *Trends in NeuroSciences, 5,* 53–59.

Naeser, M. A., Palumbo, C. L., Helm-Estabrooks, N., Stiassny-Eder, D., & Albert, M. L. (1989). Severe nonfluency in aphasia: Role of the medial subcallosal fasciculus and other white matter pathways in recovery of spontaneous speech. *Brain, 112,* 1–38.

Nakamura, K., & Ono, T. (1986). Lateral hypothalamus neuron involvement in integration of natural and artificial rewards and cue signals. *Journal of Neurophysiology, 55,* 163–181.

Nakano, Y., Lénárd, L., Oomura, Y., Nishino, H., Aou, S., & Yamamoto, T. (1987). Functional involvement of catecholamines in reward-related neuronal activity of the monkey amygdala. *Journal of Neurophysiology, 57,* 72–91.

Nathan, P. W. (1978). Acupuncture analgesia. *Trends in NeuroSciences, 1,* 21–23.

Nathanson, J. A., & Greengard, P. (1977). "Second messengers" in the brain. *Scientific American, 237,* 108–119.

Nauta, W., & Fiertag, M. (1979, September). The organization of the brain. *Scientific American, 241,* 88–111.

Nauta, W. J. H. (1946). Hypothalamic regulation of sleep in rats: Experimental study. *Journal of Neurophysiology, 9,* 285–316.

Nauta, W. J. H. (1979, June). The Nauta–Gygax stain. *Trends in NeuroSciences, 2,* xiii–xiv.

Nauta, W. J. H., & Fiertag, M. (1986). *Fundamental neuroanatomy.* New York: Freeman.

Neff, W. D. (1961). Neural mechanisms of auditory discrimination. In W. A. Rosenblith (Ed.), *Sensory communication.* New York: John Wiley.

Netter, F. (1962). *The CIBA collection of medical illustration: Vol. I. The nervous system.* Summit, NJ: CIBA Pharmaceutical.

Newcombe, F. (1980). Memory: A neuropsychological approach. *Trends in NeuroSciences, 3,* 179–182.

Newsome, W. T., Wurtz, R. H., Dürsteler, M. R., & Mikami, A. (1985). Deficits in visual motion processing following ibotenic acid lesions of the middle temporal visual areas of the macaque monkey. *The Journal of Neuroscience, 5,* 825–840.

Niehoff, D. L., & Kuhar, M. J. (1983). Benzodiazepine receptors: Localization in rat amygdala. *The Journal of Neuroscience, 3,* 2091–2097.

Nieuwenhuys, R., Geeraedts, L. M. G., & Veening, J. G. (1982). The medial forebrain bundle of the rat. I. General introduction. *Journal of Comparative Neurology, 206,* 49–81.

Nieuwenhuys, R., Voogd, J., and Huijzen, C. van (1981). *The human central nervous system: A synopsis and atlas* (2nd rev. ed.). Heidelberg: Springer-Verlag.

Nirenberg, M. W. (1963, March). The genetic code: II. *Scientific American, 208,* 80–95.

Nisbett, R. E. (1972). Hunger, obesity and the ventromedial hypothalamus. *Psychological Review, 79,* 433–453.

Nishijo, H., Ono, T., & Nishino, H. (1988). Single neuron responses in amygdala of alert monkey during complex sensory stimulation with affective significance. *The Journal of Neuroscience, 8,* 3570–3583.

Nishino, H., Oomura, Y., Aou, S., & Lénárd, L. (1987). Catecholaminergic mechanisms of feeding-related lateral hypothalamic activity in the monkey. *Brain Research, 405,* 56–67.

Nixon, R. A. (1986). Fodrin degradation by calcium-activated neutral proteinase (CANP) in retinal ganglion cell neurons and optic glia: Preferential localization of CANP activities in neurons. *Journal of Neuroscience, 6,* 1264–1271.

Nordeen, E. J., & Yahr, P. (1983). A regional analysis of estrogen binding to hypothalamic cell nuclei in relation to masculinization and defeminization. *Journal of Neuroscience, 3,* 933–941.

Nordeen, K. W., Nordeen, E. J., & Arnold, A. P. (1986). Estrogen establishes sex differences in androgen accumulation in zebra finch brain. *Journal of Neuroscience, 6,* 734–738.

Norman, R. L., & Spies, H. G. (1979). Central nervous control of reproduction in female primates. *Trends in NeuroSciences, 2,* 64–66.

Northcutt, R. G. (1981). Evolution of the telencephalon in nonmammals. *Annual Review of Neuroscience, 4,* 301–350.

Nottebohm, F. (1981). A brain for all seasons: Cyclical anatomical changes in song control nuclei of the canary brain. *Science, 214,* 1368–1370.

Numan, M. (1985). Brain mechanisms and parental behavior. In N. Adler, D. Pfaff, & R. W. Goy (Eds.), *Handbook of behavioral neurobiology: Vol. 7. Reproduction.* London: Plenum.

Numan, M., & Smith, H. G. (1984). Maternal behavior in rats: Evidence for the involvement of preoptic projections to the ventral tegmental area. *Behavioral Neuroscience, 98,* 712–727.

Nutt, D. J., Cowen, P. J., Batts, C. C., Grahame-Smith, D. G., & Green, A. R. (1982). Repeated administration of subconvulsant doses of GABA antagonist drugs: I. Effect on seizure threshold (Kindling). *Psychopharmacology, 76*, 84–87.

Oades, R. D. (1982). Search strategies on a hole-board are impaired in rats with ventral tegmental damage: Animal model for tests of thought disorder. *Biological Psychiatry, 17*, 243–250.

Oakley, D. A. (1979). Neocortex and learning. *Trends in NeuroSciences, 2*, 149–152.

Öberg, R. G. E., & Divac, I. (1981). Levels of motor planning: Cognition and the control of movement. *Trends in NeuroSciences, 4*, 122–124.

Ogden, J. A. (1985). Autotopagnosia: Occurrence in a patient without nominal aphasia and with an intact ability to point to parts of animals and objects. *Brain, 108*, 1009–1022.

Ojemann, G. A. (1983). The intrahemispheric organization of human language, derived with electrical stimulation techniques. *Trends in NeuroSciences, 6*, 184–189.

O'Keefe, J., & Black, A. H. (1978). Single unit and lesion experiments on the sensory inputs to the hippocampal cognitive map. In L. Weiskrantz (Ed.), *Functions of the septo-hippocampal system. Ciba Foundation Symposium 58*. Amsterdam: Elsevier.

O'Keefe, J., & Conway, D. H. (1978). Hippocampal place units in the freely moving rat: Why they fire where they fire. *Experimental Brain Research, 31*, 573–590.

O'Keefe, J., & Nadel, L. (1978). *The hippocampus as a cognitive map*. Oxford: Clarendon Press.

O'Keefe, J., Nadel, L., & Willner, J. (1979). Tuning out irrelevancy? Comments on Solomon's temporal mapping view of the hippocampus. *Psychological Bulletin, 86*, 1280–1289.

Olds, J. (1956). Pleasure centers in the brain. *Scientific American, 195*, 105–116.

Olds, J., & Milner, P. (1954). Positive reinforcement produced by electrical stimulation of septal area and other regions of the rat brain. *Journal of Comparative and Physiological Psychology, 47*, 419–427.

Olds, M. E., & Fobes, J. L. (1981). The central basis of motivation: Intracranial self-stimulation studies. *Annual Review of Psychology, 32*, 523–574.

Olsson, Y., & Malmgren, L. T. (1978). Histochemical localization of horseradish peroxidase in neurones. *Trends in NeuroSciences, 1*, 105–107.

Olton, D. S. (1979). Mazes, maps, and memory. *American Psychologist, 34*, 583–596.

Olton, D. S. (1983). Memory functions and the hippocampus. In W. Seifert (Ed.), *Neurobiology of the hippocampus*. London: Academic Press.

Olton, D. S., Becker, J. T., & Handelmann, G. E. (1980). Hippocampal function: Working memory or cognitive mapping? *Physiological Psychology, 8*, 239–246.

Olton, D. S., & Papas, B. C. (1979). Spatial memory and hippocampal function. *Neuropsychologia, 17*, 669–682.

O'Malley, B. W., & Schrader, W. T. (1976, February). The receptors of steroid hormones. *Scientific American, 234*, 32–43.

Ommanney, F. D. (1963). *The fishes*. New York: Time.

Orbach, H. S., Cohen, L. B., & Grinvald, A. (1985). Optical mapping of electrical activity in rat somatosensory and visual cortex. *The Journal of Neuroscience, 5*, 1886–1895.

Oswald, I. (1966). *Sleep*. Baltimore: Penguin Books.

Ottersen, O. P., & Storm-Mathisen, J. (1979). "Ghost from the sea" helps neuroscientists perform selective brain lesions. *Trends in NeuroSciences, 2*(6), xv–xvi.

Palmblad, H., Cantell, K., Strander, H., Froberg, J., Karlson, C., Levi, L., Gronstrom, M., & Unger, P. (1976). Stressor exposure and immunological response in man: Interferon producing capacity and phagocytosis. *Journal of Psychosomatic Research, 20*, 193–199.

Pansky, B., & Allen, D. J. (1980). *Review of neuroscience*. New York: Macmillan.

Parkinson, J. K., Murray, E. A., & Mishkin, M. (1988). A selective mnemonic role for the hippocampus in monkeys: Memory for the location of objects. *The Journal of Neuroscience, 8*, 4159–4167.

Parmeggiani, P. L., Morrison, A., Drucker-Colin, R., & McGinty, D. (1985). Brain mechanisms of sleep: An overview of methodological issues. In D. McGinty, R. Drucker-Colin, A. Morrison, & P. L. Parmeggiani (Eds.), *Brain mechanisms of sleep*. New York: Raven Press.

Pasik, T., & Pasik, P. (1971). The visual world of monkeys deprived of striate cortex: Effective stimulus parameters and the importance of the accessory optic system. *Vision Research* (Supp. 3), 419–435.

Patel, S. N., Rose, S. P. R., & Stewart, M. G. (1988). Training induced dendritic spine density changes are specifically related to memory formation processes in the chick, *Gallus domesticus. Brain Research, 463*, 168–173.

Patel, S. N., & Stewart, M. G. (1988). Changes in the number and structure of dendritic spines 25 hours after passive avoidance training in the domestic chick, *Gallus domesticus. Brain Research, 449*, 34–46.

Patterson, D. (1987, August). The causes of Down syndrome. *Scientific American, 257*, 52–61.

Pearlman, C. A. (1982). Negative transfer abolished by REM sleep deprivation in rats. *Physiology & Behavior, 28*, 73–75.

Pearson, K. (1976). The control of walking. *Scientific American, 235*, 72–86.

Pehek, E. A., Warner, R. K., Bazzett, T. J., Bitran, D., Band, L. C., Eaton, R. C., & Hull, E. M. (1988). Microinjection of *cis*-flupenthixol, a dopamine antagonist, into the medial preoptic area impairs sexual behavior of male rats. *Brain Research, 443,* 70–76.

Penfield, W., & Roberts, L. (1959). *Speech and brain-mechanisms.* Princeton, NJ: Princeton University Press.

Penny, J. B., & Young, A. B. (1983). Speculations on the functional anatomy of corpus striatum disorders. *Annual Review of Neuroscience, 6,* 73–94.

Penttilä, M., Partanen, J. V., Soininen, H., & Riekkinen, P. J. (1985). Quantitative analysis of occipital EEG in different stages of Alzheimer's disease. *Electroencephalography and Clinical Neurophysiology, 60,* 1–6.

Perenin, M. T., & Jeannerod, M. (1979). Subcortical vision in man. *Trends in NeuroSciences, 2,* 204–207.

Perlow, M. J., Freed, W. J., Hoffer, B. J., Seiger, A., Olson, L., & Wyatt, R. J. (1979). Brain grafts reduce motor abnormalities produced by destruction of nigrostriatal dopamine system. *Science, 204,* 643–647.

Peroutka, S. J., & Snyder, S. (1980). Long-term antidepressant treatment decreases spiroperidol-labeled serotonin receptor binding. *Science, 210,* 88–90.

Perry, J. W., & Morton, D. (1989). *Laboratory manual for Starr and Taggart's Biology: The unity and diversity of life* (5th ed.). Belmont, CA: Wadsworth.

Peterson, L. R., & Peterson, M. J. (1959). Short-term retention of individual verbal items. *Journal of Experimental Psychology, 58,* 193–198.

Pettigrew, J. D. (1972). The neurophysiology of binocular vision. *Scientific American, 227,* 84–95.

Phelps, M. E., & Mazziotta, J. C. (1985). Positron emission tomography: Human brain function and biochemistry. *Science, 228,* 799–809.

Phoenix, C. H., Goy, R. W., Gerall, A. A., & Young, W. C. (1959). Organizing action of prenatally administered testosterone propionate on the tissues mediating mating behavior in the female guinea pig. *Endocrinology, 93,* 1129–1139.

Pickles, J. O. (1982). *An introduction to the physiology of hearing.* San Diego: Academic Press.

Pickles, J. O. (1985). Recent advances in cochlear physiology. *Progress in Neurobiology, 24,* 1–42.

Pincus, J. H., & Tucker, G. H. (1978). *Behavioral neurology* (2nd ed.). New York: Oxford University Press.

Pirong, M.-L., & Schmidt, R. (1988). Inhibition of long-term memory formation by anti-ependymin antisera after active shock-avoidance learning in goldfish. *Brain Research, 442,* 53–62.

Poeck, K., de Bleser, R., & von Keyserlingk, D. G. (1984). Neurolinguistic status and localization of lesion in aphasic patients with exclusively consonant-vowel recurring utterances. *Brain, 107,* 199–217.

Poggio, G. F., & Fischer, B. (1977). Binocular interaction and depth sensitivity in striate and prestriate cortex of behaving rhesus monkey. *Journal of Neurophysiology, 40,* 1392–1405.

Poggio, G. F., & Poggio, T. (1984). The analysis of stereopsis. *Annual Review of Neuroscience, 7,* 379–412.

Pohl, W. (1973). Dissociation of spatial discrimination deficits following frontal and parietal lesions in monkeys. *Journal of Comparative and Physiological Psychology, 82,* 227–239.

Pollock, M., & Harris, A. J. (1981). Accuracy in peripheral nerve regeneration. *Trends in NeuroSciences, 4,* 18–20.

Pompeiano, O. (1970). Mechanisms of sensorimotor integration during sleep. In E. Stellar & J. M. Sprague (Eds.), *Progress in physiological psychology* (Vol. 3). New York: Academic Press.

Popper, A. N., Platt, C., & Saidel, W. M. (1982). Acoustic functions in the fish ear. *Trends in NeuroSciences, 5,* 276–280.

Popper, D. R., & Eccles, J. C. (1977). *The self and its brain.* New York: Springer International.

Porter, K. R., Byers, H. R., & Ellisman, M. H. (1979). The cytoskeleton. In F. O. Schmitt & F. G. Worden (Eds.), *The neurosciences: Fourth study program.* Cambridge: MIT Press.

Porter, R. H., & Cernoch, J. M. (1983). Maternal recognition of neonates through olfactory cues. *Physiology & Behavior, 30,* 151–154.

Posner, M. I., Walker, J. A., Friedrich, F. J., & Rafal, R. D. (1984). Effects of parietal injury on covert orienting of attention. *The Journal of Neuroscience, 4,* 1864–1874.

Posner, M. I., Walker, J. A., Friedrich, F. J., & Rafal, R. D. (1987). How do the parietal lobes direct covert attention? *Neuropsychologia, 25,* 135–145.

Powley, T. L. (1977). The ventromedial hypothalamic syndrome, satiety and a cephalic phase hypothesis. *Psychological Review, 84,* 89–126.

Preuss, P. (1983, December). The shape of things to come. *Science 83, 4,* 80–89.

Pribram, K. (1971). *Languages of the brain: Experimental paradoxes and principles in neuropsychology.* Englewood Cliffs, NJ: Prentice-Hall.

Pribram, K., & Roberts, L. (1970). Personal communications during a conference on brain function.

Prichard, J. W., & Shulman, R. G. (1986). NMR spectroscopy of brain metabolism in vivo. *Annual Review of Neuroscience, 9,* 61–86.

Pritchard, W. S. (1986). Cognitive event-related potential correlates of schizophrenia. *Psychological Bulletin, 100,* 43–66.

Pritzel, M., Huston, J. P., & Buscher, W. (1983). Hypothalamic self-stimulation in rats with one hemisphere isolated anterior to the midbrain and the other hemisphere devoid of the telencephalon. *Experimental Neurology, 81,* 426–435.

Puel, J.-L., Bonfils, P., & Pujol, R. (1988). Selective attention modifies the active micromechanical properties of the cochlea. *Brain Research, 447,* 380–383.

Raichle, M. E. (1980, August). Cerebral blood flow and metabolism in man: Past, present and future. *Trends in NeuroSciences, 3,* vi–x.

Raichle, M. E. (1983). Positron emission tomography. *Annual Review of Neuroscience, 6,* 249–267.

Rakic, P. (1979). Genetic and epigenetic determinants of local circuit neurons in the mammalian central nervous system. In F. O. Schmitt & F. G. Worden (Eds.), *The neurosciences: Fourth study program.* Cambridge: MIT Press.

Ravizza, R. J., & Belmore, S. M. (1978). Auditory forebrain: Evidence from anatomical and behavioral experiments involving human and animal subjects. In R. B. Masterton (Ed.), *Handbook of neurobiology: Vol. 1. Sensory integration.* New York: Plenum.

Raybould, H. E., Gayton, R. J., & Dockray, G. J. (1988). Mechanisms of actions of peripherally administered cholecystokinin octapeptide on brain stem neurons in the rat. *The Journal of Neuroscience, 8,* 3018–3024.

Rechtschaffen, A. (1971). Discussion of *Experimental dream studies* by W. C. Dement. In J. H. Masserman (Ed.), *Science and psychoanalysis* (Vol. 1). New York: Grune & Stratton.

Rechtschaffen, A., & Kales, A. (1968). *A manual of standardized terminology, techniques and scoring system for sleep stages of human subjects.* Washington, DC: Public Health Service, U.S. Government Printing Office.

Reichardt, L. F., & Matthew, W. D. (1982). Monoclonal antibodies: Applications to studies on the chemical synapse. *Trends in NeuroSciences, 5,* 24–31.

Reinisch, J. M. (1981). Prenatal exposure to synthetic progestins increases potential for aggression in humans. *Science, 211,* 1171–1173.

Reisine, R., Affolter, H.-U., Rougon, G., & Barbet, J. (1986). New insights into the molecular mechanisms of stress. *Trends in NeuroSciences, 9,* 574–579.

Reivich, M. (1982). The use of cerebral blood flow and metabolic studies in cerebral localization. In R. A. Thompson & J. R. Green (Eds.), *New perspectives in cerebral localization.* New York: Raven Press.

Rendell, M., McGrane, D., & Cuesta, M. (1978). Fatal compulsive water drinking. *Journal of the American Medical Association, 240,* 2557–2559.

Renehan, W. E., Stansel, S. S., McCall, R. D., Rhoades, R. W., & Jacquin, M. R. (1988). An electron microscopic analysis of the morphology and connectivity of individual HRP-labeled slowly adapting vibrissa primary afferents in the adult rat. *Brain Research, 462,* 396–400.

Ribak, C. E., Bradburne, R. M., & Harris, A. B. (1982). A preferential loss of GABAergic, symmetric synapses in epileptic foci: A quantitative ultrastructural analysis of monkey neocortex. *The Journal of Neuroscience, 2,* 1725–1735.

Rich, A. (1967). The ribosome—A biological information translator. In G. C. Quarton, R. Melnechuk, & F. O. Schmitt (Eds.), *The neurosciences: A study program.* New York: Rockefeller University Press.

Richardson, R. T., & DeLong, M. R. (1988). A reappraisal of the functions of the nucleus basalis of Meynert. *Trends in Neurosciences, 11,* 264–267.

Riggs, L. A. (1965). Visual acuity. In C. Graham (Ed.), *Vision and visual perception.* Summerset, NJ: John Wiley.

Riley, V. (1981). Psychoneuroendocrine influences on immunocompetence and neoplasia. *Science, 212,* 1100–1109.

Roberts, L. (1969). Aphasia, apraxia and agnosia in abnormal states of cerebral dominance. *Handbook of clinical neurology* (Vol. IV). Amsterdam: North-Holland.

Roberts, W. W. (1970). Hypothalamic mechanisms for motivational and species-typical behavior. In R. E. Whalen, R. F. Thompson, M. Verzeano, & N. M. Weinberger (Eds.), *The neural control of behavior.* New York: Academic Press.

Robertson, M., Evans, K., Robinson, A., Trimble, M., & Lascelles, P. (1987). Abnormalities of copper in Gilles de la Tourette syndrome. *Biological Psychiatry, 22,* 968–978.

Robinson, C. J., & Burton, J. (1980). Somatic submodality distribution within the second somatosensory (SII), 7b, retroinsular, post-auditory, and granular insular cortical areas of M. fascicularis. *Journal of Comparative Neurology, 192,* 43–67.

Robinson, T. E., Jurson, P. A., Bennett, J. A., & Bentgen, K. M. (1988). Persistent sensitization of dopamine neurotransmission in ventral striatum (nucleus accumbens) produced by prior experience with (+)-amphetamine: A microdialysis study in freely moving rats. *Brain Research, 462,* 211–222.

Roby-Brami, A., Bussel, B., Willer, J. C., & LeBars, D. (1987). An electrophysiological investigation into the pain-relieving effects of heterotopic nociceptive stimuli. *Brain, 110,* 1497–1508.

Roffwarg, H. P., Musio, J., & Dement, W. C. (1966). The ontogenetic development of the· human sleep dream cycle. *Science, 152,* 604–618.

Rogers, Q. R., & Leung, M. B. (1977). The control of food intake: When and how are amino acids involved? In M. R. Kare & O. Maller (Eds.), *The chemical senses and nutrition.* New York: Academic Press.

Rojas-Ramirez, J. A., & Drucker-Colin, R. R. (1977). Phylogenetic correlations between sleep and memory. In R. R. Drucker-Colin & J. L. McGaugh (Eds.), *Neurobiology of sleep and memory.* New York: Academic Press.

Roland, P. E. (1984). Metabolic measurements of the working frontal cortex in man. *Trends in NeuroSciences, 7,* 430–435.

Rolls, B. J., Wood, R. J., & Rolls, E. T. (1980). Thirst: The initiation, maintenance and termination of drinking. In J. M. Sprague & A. N. Epstein (Eds.), *Progress in psychobiology and physiological psychology* (Vol. IX). New York: Academic Press.

Rolls, E. T. (1977). Neural activity during natural and brain stimulation reward. In R. W. Hall, F. E. Bloom, & J. Olds (Eds.), *Neuroscience research program bulletin.* Cambridge: MIT Press.

Rolls, E. T. (1978). Neurophysiology of feeding. *Trends in NeuroSciences, 1,* 1–3.

Rolls, E. T. (1982). Feeding and reward. In B. G. Hoebel & D. Novin (Eds.), *The neural basis of feeding and reward.* Brunswick, ME: Haer Institute.

Rolls, E. T., Burton, M. J., & Mora, F. (1976). Hypothalamic neuronal responses associated with the sight of food. *Brain Research, 111,* 53–66.

Romer, A. S. (1968). *The procession of life.* Cleveland: World.

Rosen, S., Bergman, M., Plester, D., El-Mofty, A., & Satti, M. H. (1962). Presbycusis study of a relatively noise-free population in the Sudan. *Annals of Otology, Rhinology and Laryngology, 71,* 727.

Rosenblatt, J. S. (1983). Olfaction mediates developmental transition in the altricial newborn of selected species of mammals. *Developmental Psychobiology, 16,* 347–375.

Rosenfield, M. E., Dovydaitis, A., & Moore, J. W. (1985). Brachium conjuctivum and rubrobulbar tract: Brain stem projections of red nucleus essential for the conditioned nictitating membrane response. *Physiology & Behavior, 34,* 751–759.

Rosenstein, J. M. (1987). Adrenal medulla grafts produce blood–brain barrier dysfunction. *Brain Research, 414,* 192–196.

Rosenzweig, M. R., & Bennett, E. L. (1984a). Basic processes and modulatory influences in the stages of memory formation. In G. Lynch, J. L. McGaugh, & N. M. Weinberger (Eds.), *Neurobiology of learning and memory.* New York: Guilford Press.

Rosenzweig, M. R., & Bennett, E. L. (1984b). Studying stages of memory formation with chicks and rodents. In L. R. Squire & N. Butters (Eds.), *Neuropsychology of memory.* New York: Guilford Press.

Rosenzweig, M. R., Bennett, E. L., & Diamond, M. C. (1972, February). Brain changes in response to experience. *Scientific American, 226,* 22–29.

Ross, E. D. (1981). The aprosodias. *Archives of Neurology, 38,* 561–569.

Ross, E. D. (1984). Right hemisphere's role in language, affective behavior and emotion. *Trends in NeuroSciences, 7,* 342–345.

Roufogalis, B. D. (1980). Calmodulin: Its role in synaptic transmission. *Trends in NeuroSciences, 3,* 238–241.

Routtenberg, A. (1984). The CA3 pyramidal cell in the hippocampus: Site of intrinsic expression and extrinsic control of memory formation. In L. R. Squire & N. Butters (Eds.), *Neuropsychology of memory.* New York: Guilford Press.

Ruch, T. C. (1965). The cerebral cortex: Its structure and motor functions. In T. C. Ruch & H. D. Patton (Eds.), *Physiology and biophysics* (19th ed.). Philadelphia: Saunders.

Ruch, T. C., & Patton, H. D. (1965). *Physiology and biophysics.* Philadelphia: Saunders.

Rusak, B., & Groos, G. (1982). Suprachiasmatic stimulation phase shifts rodent circadian rhythms. *Science, 215,* 1407–1409.

Russek, M. (1970). Demonstration of the influence of an hepatic glucosensitive mechanism on food-intake. *Physiology & Behavior, 5,* 1207–1209.

Russell, M. J., Switz, G. M., & Thompson, K. (1980). Olfactory influences on the human menstrual cycle. *Pharmacology and Biochemistry of Behavior, 13,* 737–738.

Ryan, A., & Dallow, P. (1976). Physiology of the inner ear. In J. L. Northern (Ed.), *Communicative disorders: Hearing loss.* Boston: Little, Brown.

Sachar, E. J., & Baron, M. (1979). The biology of affective disorders. *Annual Review of Neuroscience, 2,* 505–518.

Sagvolden, T., & Holth, P. (1986). Slower acquisition of positively reinforced behavior following medial, but not dorsolateral, septal lesions in rats. *Behavioral Neuroscience, 100,* 330–336.

Sagvolden, T., & Johnsrud, G. (1982). Two-way active avoidance learning following medial, dorsolateral, or total septal lesions in rats: Effect of intensity of discontinuous shock. *Behavioral and Neural Biology, 35,* 17–32.

Saito, H., Yukie, M., Tanaka, K., Hikosaka, K., Fukada, Y., & Iwai, E. (1986). Integration of direction signals of image motion in the superior temporal sulcus of the macaque monkey. *The Journal of Neuroscience, 6,* 145–157.

Sakai, K. (1984). Central mechanisms of paradoxical sleep. In A. Borbély & J.-L. Valatx (Eds.), *Sleep mechanisms.* Berlin: Springer-Verlag.

Sakai, K. (1985a). Anatomical and physiological basis of paradoxical sleep. In D. J. McGinty, R. Drucker-Colin, A. Morrison, & P. L. Parmeggiani (Eds.), *Brain mechanisms of sleep.* New York: Raven Press.

Sakai, K. (1985b). Neurons responsible for paradoxical sleep. In A. Wauquier, J. M. Gaillard, J. M. Monti, & M. Radulovacki (Eds.), *Sleep: Neurotransmitters and neuromodulators.* New York: Raven Press.

Salk Institute Newsletter, The, Fall, 1983.

Sallanon, C., Buda, C., Janin, M., & Jouvet, M. (1985). In A. Wauquier, J. M. Gaillard, J. M. Monti, & M. Radulovacki (Eds.), *Sleep: Neurotransmitters and neuromodulators*. New York: Raven Press.

Sapolsky, R. M., & Pulsinelli, W. A. (1985). Glucocorticoids potentiate ischemic injury to neurons: Therapeutic implications. *Science, 220,* 1397–1400.

Sarter, M., & Markowitsch, H. J. (1985). Involvement of the amygdala in learning and memory: A critical review, with emphasis on anatomical relations. *Behavioral Neuroscience, 99,* 342–380.

Sarter, M., Schneider, H. H., & Stephens, D. N. (1988). Treatment strategies for senile dementia: Antagonist β-carbolines. *Trends in Neurosciences, 11,* 13–17.

Sassin, J. F. (1977). Sleep-related hormones. In R. R. Drucker-Colin & J. L. McGaugh (Eds.), *Neurobiology of sleep and memory*. New York: Academic Press.

Satz, P. (1979). A test of some models of hemispheric speech organization in the left- and right-handed. *Science, 203,* 1131–1133.

Schallert, T. (1983). Sensorimotor impairment and recovery of function in brain-damaged rats: Reappearance of symptoms during old age. *Behavioral Neuroscience, 97,* 159–164.

Scheibel, A. B. (1980). Anatomical and physiological substrates of arousal. In S. A. Hobson & A. M. Brazier (Eds.), *The reticular formation revisited: Specifying function for a nonspecific system*. New York: Raven Press.

Scheibel, M. E., & Scheibel, A. B. (1967). Anatomical basis of attention mechanisms in vertebrate brains. In G. C. Quarton, T. Melnechuk, & F. O. Schmitt (Eds.), *The neurosciences: A study program*. New York: Rockefeller University Press.

Scheibel, M. E., & Scheibel, A. B. (1970). Elementary processes in selected thalamic and cortical subsystems—the structural substrates. In G. C. Quarton, T. Melnechuk, & G. Adelman (Eds.), *The neurosciences: Second study program*. New York: Rockefeller University Press.

Schenberg, L. C., de Aguiar, J. C., & Graeff, F. G. (1983). GABA modulation of the defense reaction induced by brain electrical stimulation. *Physiology & Behavior, 31,* 429–437.

Schiffman, H. R. (1976). *Sensation and perception: An integrated approach*. Toronto: John Wiley.

Schiffman, S. S. (1974a). Physiochemical correlates of olfactory quality. *Science, 185,* 112–117.

Schiffman, S. S. (1974b). Contributions to the physiochemical dimensions of odor: A psychophysical approach. *Annals of the New York Academy of Science, 237,* 164–183.

Schiffman, S. S., & Dackis, C. (1975). Taste of nutrients: Amino acids, vitamins, and fatty acids. *Perception & Psychophysics, 17,* 140–146.

Schiffman, S. S., & Erickson, R. P. (1971). A theoretical review: A psychophysical model for gustatory quality. *Physiology & Behavior, 7,* 617–633.

Schiffman, S. S., Orlandi, M., & Erickson, R. P. (1979). Changes in taste and smell with age: Biological aspects. In J. M. Ordy & K. R. Brizzie (Eds.), *Sensory systems and communication in the elderly* (Aging, Vol. 10). New York: Raven Press.

Schmaltz, L. W., & Isaacson, R. L. (1966). The effects of preliminary training conditions upon DRL performance in the hippocampectomized rat. *Physiology & Behavior, 1,* 175–182.

Schmidt, R. F. (1973). Control of the access of afferent activity to somatosensory pathways. In A. Iggo (Ed.), *Handbook of sensory physiology: Vol. II. Somatosensory system*. Heidelberg: Springer-Verlag.

Schmidt, R. F. (1976). Synaptic transmission. In R. F. Schmidt (Ed.), *Fundamentals of neurophysiology*. Heidelberg: Springer-Verlag.

Schmitt, F. O. (1970). *The neurosciences: Second study program*. New York: Rockefeller University Press.

Schneider, A. M., & Plough, M. (1983). Electroconvulsive shock and memory. In J. A. Deutsch (Ed.), *The physiological basis of memory*. London: Academic Press.

Schneider, A. M., & Tarshish, B. (1976). *An introduction to physiological psychology*. New York: Random House.

Schneider, G. E. (1967). Contrasting visuomotor functions of tectum and cortex in the golden hamster. *Psychologische Forschung, 31,* 52–62.

Schreiner, L., & Kling, A. (1953). Behavioral changes following rhinencephalic injury in the cat. *Journal of Neurophysiology, 16,* 643–659.

Schuhr, B. (1987). Social structure and plasma corticosterone level in female albino mice. *Physiology & Behavior, 40,* 689–693.

Schultz, H., Salzarulo, P., Fagioli, I., & Massetani, R. (1983). REM latency: Development in the first year of life. *Electroencephalography and Clinical Neurophysiology, 56,* 316–322.

Schwartz, D. G., Weinstein, L. N., & Arkin, A. M. (1978). Qualitative aspects of sleep mentation. In A. M. Arkin, J. S. Antrobus, & S. J. Ellman (Eds.), *The mind in sleep: Psychology and psychophysiology*. Hillsdale, NJ: Lawrence Erlbaum.

Schwartz, E. A. (1985). Phototransduction in vertebrate rods. *Annual Review of Neuroscience, 8,* 339–367.

Schwartz, W. J., & Gainer, H. (1977). Suprachiasmatic nucleus: Use of (14)C-labeled deoxyglucose uptake as a functional marker. *Science, 197,* 1089–1091.

Sclafani, A. (1971). Neural pathways involved in the ventromedial hypothalamic lesion syndrome in the rat. *Journal of Comparative and Physiological Psychology, 77,* 70–96.

Scott, D. F., & Elian, M. (1980). Photo-convulsive responses in patients over 30 years of age. *Electroencephalography and Clinical Neurophysiology, 49,* 90p.

Scovern, A. W., & Kilmann, P. R. (1980). Status of electro-convulsive therapy: Review of the outcome literature. *Psychological Bulletin, 87,* 260–303.

Scoville, W. B., & Milner, B. (1957). Loss of recent memory after bilateral hippocampal lesions. *Journal of Neurology, Neurosurgery and Psychiatry, 20,* 11–21.

Seidman, L. J. (1983). Schizophrenia and brain dysfunction: An integration of recent neurodiagnostic findings. *Psychological Bulletin, 94,* 195–238.

Sekuler, R., & Blake, R. (1985). *Perception.* New York: Knopf.

Selkoe, D. J. (1989). Biochemistry of altered brain proteins in Alzheimer's disease. *Annual Review of Neuroscience, 12,* 463–490.

Sellick, P. M. (1979). Recordings from single receptor cells in the mammalian cochlea. *Trends in NeuroSciences, 2,* 114–116.

Selye, H. (1956). *The stress of life.* New York: McGraw-Hill.

Semmes, J. (1973). Somesthetic effects of damage to the central nervous system. In A. Iggo (Ed.), *Handbook of sensory physiology: Vol. II. Somatosensory system.* Heidelberg: Springer-Verlag.

Semmes, J., Weinstein, S., Ghent, L., & Teuber, H.-L. (1955). Spatial orientation in man after cerebral injury: Analysis by locus of lesion. *Journal of Psychology, 39,* 227–244.

Sergent, J. (1985). Influence of task and input factors on hemispheric involvement in face processing. *Journal of Experimental Psychology: Human Perception and Performance, 11,* 846–861.

Sergent, J., & Bindra, D. (1981). Differential hemispheric processing of faces: Methodological considerations and reinterpretation. *Psychological Bulletin, 89,* 541–554.

Shaikh, M. B., Barrett, J. A., & Siegel, A. (1987). The pathways mediating affective defense and quiet biting attack behavior from the midbrain central gray of the cat: An autoradiographic study. *Brain Research, 437,* 9–25.

Shapiro, B. E., Grossman, M., & Gardner, H. (1981). Selective musical processing deficits in brain damaged populations. *Neuropsychologia, 19,* 161–169.

Shapiro, D. Y. (1980). Serial female sex changes after simultaneous removal of males from social groups of a coral reef fish. *Science, 209,* 1136–1137.

Shapley, R., & Lennie, P. (1985). Spatial frequency analysis in the visual system. *Annual Review of Neuroscience, 8,* 547–583.

Shashoua, V. E. (1985). The role of extracellular proteins in learning and memory. *American Scientist, 73,* 364–370.

Sheard, M. H. (1980). The biological effects of lithium. *Trends in NeuroSciences, 3,* 85–86.

Shelburne, S. A., Jr. (1978). Visual evoked potentials to language stimuli in children with reading disabilities. In D. Otto (Ed.), *Multidisciplinary perspective in event-related brain potential research.* Washington, DC: U.S. Environmental Protection Agency.

Shepherd, G. M. (1979). *The synaptic organization of the brain* (2nd ed.). New York: Oxford University Press.

Shepherd, G. M. (1983). *Neurobiology.* Oxford: Oxford University Press.

Sherman, S. M. (1979). The functional significance of X and Y cells in normal and visually deprived cats. *Trends in NeuroSciences, 2,* 192–195.

Sherman, S. M., Wilson, J. R., Kaas, J. H., & Webb, S. V. (1976). X- and Y-cells in the dorsal lateral geniculate nucleus of the owl monkey (*Aotus trivirgatus*). *Science, 192,* 475–477.

Shizgal, P., Bielajew, C., & Kiss, I. (1980). Anodal hyperpolarization block technique provides evidence for rostrocaudal conduction of reward related signals in the medial forebrain bundle. *Society for Neuroscience Abstracts, 6,* 422.

Shor-Posner, G., Azar, A. P., Insinga, S., & Leibowitz, S. F. (1985). Deficits in the control of food intake after hypothalamic paraventricular nucleus lesions. *Physiology & Behavior, 35,* 883–890.

Sidtis, J. J., & Gazzaniga, M. S. (1981). *Complex pitch perception after callosal section: Further evidence for a right hemisphere mechanism.* Paper presented at the meeting of the Acoustical Society of America.

Siegel, A., & Pott, C. B. (1988). Neural substrates of aggression and flight in the cat. *Progress in Neurobiology, 31,* 261–283.

Siegel, J. M. (1985). Ponto-medullary interactions in the generation of REM sleep. In D. J. McGinty, R. Drucker-Colin, A. Morrison, & P. L. Parmeggiani (Eds.), *Brain mechanisms of sleep.* New York: Raven Press.

Signoret, J.-L., Castaigne, P., Lhermitte, F., Abelanet, R., & Lavorel, P. (1984). Rediscovery of Leborgne's brain: Anatomical description with CT scan. *Brain and Language, 22,* 303–319.

Silber, S. J. (1981). *The male from infancy to old age.* New York: Scribner's.

Simon, C., Schlienger, J. L., Sapin, R., & Imler, M. (1986). Cephalic phase insulin secretion in relation to food presentation in normal and overweight subjects. *Physiology & Behavior, 36,* 465–469.

Sims, E. A., Kelleher, P. E., Horton, E. S., Gluck, C. M., Goodman, R. F., & Rowe, D. A. (1968). Experimental obesity in man. *Excerpta Medical Monographs.*

Sinclair, D. (1981). *Mechanisms of cutaneous stimulation.* Oxford: Oxford University Press.

Singer, W. (1979). Central-core control of visual-cortex functions. In F. O. Schmitt & F. G. Worden (Eds.), *The neurosciences: Fourth study program*. Cambridge: MIT Press.

Sinsheimer, R. L. (1962, July). Single-stranded DNA. *Scientific American, 207,* 109–116.

Sklar, L. S., & Anisman, H. (1979). Stress and coping factors influence tumor growth. *Science, 205,* 513–515.

Sklar, L. S., & Anisman, H. (1981). Stress and cancer. *Psychological Bulletin, 89,* 369–406.

Sladek, J. R., Jr., & Shoulson, I. (1988). Neural transplantation: A call for patience rather than patients. *Science, 240,* 1386–1388.

Slijper, F. M. E. (1984). Androgens and gender role behavior in girls with congenital adrenal hyperplasia (CAH). *Progress in Brain Research, 61,* 417–422.

Smith, A. M. (1970). The effects of rubral lesions and stimulation on conditioned forelimb flexion responses in the cat. *Physiology & Behavior, 5,* 1121–1126.

Smith, C. A. (1968). Ultrastructure of the organ of Corti. *The Advancement of Science, 122,* 419–433.

Smith, C. A. (1975). The inner ear: Its embryological development and microstructure. In E. L. Eagles (Ed.), *The nervous system: Vol. 3. Human communication and its disorders*. New York: Raven Press.

Smith, C. B. (1984). Aging and changes in cerebral energy metabolism. *Trends in NeuroSciences, 7,* 203–208.

Smith, G. P., Jerome, C., Cushin, B. J., Eterno, R., & Simansky, K. J. (1981). Abdominal vagotomy blocks the satiety effect of cholecystokinin in the rat. *Science, 213,* 1036–1037.

Smith, K. R. (1947). The problem of stimulation deafness: II. Histological changes in the cochlea as a function of tonal frequency. *Journal of Experimental Psychology, 37,* 304–317.

Smith, K. R., & Wever, E. G. (1949). The problem of stimulation deafness: III. The functional and histological effects of high frequency stimulus. *Journal of Experimental Psychology, 39,* 238–241.

Smith, O. A., & DeVito, J. L. (1984). Central neural integration for the control of autonomic responses associated with emotion. *Annual Review of Neuroscience, 7,* 43–65.

Smith, R. J. (1979). Study finds sleeping pills overprescribed. *Science, 204,* 287–288.

Smythies, J. R. (1966). *The neurological foundations of psychiatry*. New York: Academic Press.

Snyder, S. H. (1977, March). Opiate receptors and internal opiates. *Scientific American, 236,* 44–67.

Sochurek, H., & Miller, P. (1987, January). Medicine's new vision. *National Geographic, 171,* 2–41.

Södersten, P. (1987). How different are male and female brains? *Trends in Neurosciences, 10,* 197–198.

Sokoloff, L. (1978). Mapping cerebral functional activity with radioactive deoxyglucose. *Trends in NeuroSciences, 1,* 75–79.

Sokolov, E. N. (1963). *Perception and the conditioned reflex*. Oxford: Pergamon Press.

Solodkin, M., Cardona, A., & Corsi-Cabrera, M. (1985). Paradoxical sleep augmentation after imprinting in the domestic chick. *Physiology & Behavior, 35,* 343–348.

Sperry, R. W. (1975). Lateral specialization in the surgically separated hemispheres. In B. Milner (Ed.), *Hemispheric specialization and interaction*. Cambridge: MIT Press.

Spevack, A. A., Campbell, C. T., & Drake, L. (1975). Effect of amygdalectomy on habituation and CER in rats. *Physiology & Behavior, 15,* 199–207.

Spoor, A. (1967). Presbycusis values in relation to noise induced hearing loss. *International Audiology, 6,* 48–57.

Springer, S. P. (1987). Educating the left and right sides of the brain. *National Forum: The Phi Kappa Phi Journal, 67,* 25–28.

Springer, S. P., & Deutsch, G. (1981). *Left brain, right brain*. San Francisco: Freeman.

Spydell, J. D., & Sheer, D. E. (1983). Forty hertz EEG activity in Alzheimer's dementia. *Psychophysiology, 20,* 313–323.

Spyraki, C., Fibiger, H. C., & Phillips, A. G. (1982). Attenuation by haloperidol of place preference conditioning using food reinforcement. *Psychopharmacology, 77,* 379–382.

Squire, L. R. (1977). ECT and memory loss. *American Journal of Psychiatry, 134,* 997–1001.

Squire, L. R. (1980). Specifying the defect in human amnesia: Storage, retrieval and semantics. *Neuropsychologia, 19,* 368–372.

Squire, L. R. (1982). The neuropsychology of human memory. *Annual Review of Neuroscience, 5,* 241–273.

Squire, L. R. (1986). Mechanisms of memory. *Science, 232,* 1612–1619.

Squire, L. R. (1987). *Memory and brain*. Oxford: Oxford University Press.

Squire, L. R., & Zola-Morgan, S. (1988). Memory: Brain systems and behavior. *Trends in Neurosciences, 11,* 170–175.

Starr, C., & Taggart, R. (1987). *Biology: The unity and diversity of life* (4th ed.). Belmont, CA: Wadsworth.

Steffens, A. B., Morgenson, G. J., & Stevenson, J. (1972). Blood glucose, insulin and free fatty acids after stimulation and lesions of the hypothalamus. *American Journal of Physiology, 222,* 1446–1452.

Stein, J. F. (1982). *An introduction to neurophysiology*. Edinburgh: Blackwell Scientific.

Stein, L. (1968). Chemistry of reward and punishment. In D. H. Efron (Ed.), *Psychopharmacology: A review of progress, 1957–1967*. (Public Service Publication No. 1836, pp. 105–135). Washington, DC: U.S. Government Printing Office.

Stein, L. (1975). Norepinephrine reward pathways: Role in self-stimulation, memory consolidation, and schizophrenia. In J. Cole & T. Sonderegger (Eds.), *Nebraska symposium on motivation, 1974*. Lincoln, NE: University of Nebraska Press.

Stein, L., & Wise, C. D. (1969). Release of norepinephrine from hypothalamus and amygdala by rewarding medial forebrain bundle stimulation and amphetamine. *Journal of Comparative and Physiological Psychology, 67,* 189–198.

Stein, P. S. G. (1978). Motor systems, with specific reference to the control of locomotion. *Annual Review of Neuroscience, 1,* 61–81.

Steinbusch, H. W. M., DeVente, J., & Schipper, J. (1986). Immunohistochemistry of monoamines in the central nervous system. In D. E. MacMallan & A. C. Cuello (Eds.), *Neurohistochemistry: Modern methods and applications.* New York: Alan Liss.

Stellar, E. (1954). The physiology of motivation. *Psychological Review, 61,* 5–22.

Stellar, J. R., & Stellar, E. (1985). *The neurobiology of motivation and reward.* New York: Springer-Verlag.

Stent, A. J. (1963). *Molecular biology of bacterial viruses.* San Francisco: Freeman.

Steriade, M., Ropert, N., Kitsikis, A., & Oakson, G. (1980). Ascending activating neuronal networks in midbrain reticular core and related rostral systems. In S. A. Hobson & A. M. Brazier (Eds.), *The reticular formation revisited: Specifying function for a nonspecific system.* New York: Raven Press.

Sterman, M. B., & Clemente, C. D. (1962). Forebrain inhibitory mechanisms: Cortical synchronization induced by basal forebrain stimulation. *Experimental Neurology, 6,* 91–102.

Stern, W. C., & Morgane, P. J. (1977). Sleep and memory: Effects of growth hormone on sleep, brain neurochemistry and behavior. In R. R. Drucker-Colin & J. L. McGaugh (Eds.), *Neurobiology of sleep and memory.* New York: Academic Press.

Stevens, C. F. (1979). The neuron. *Scientific American, 241,* 54–65.

Stevens, J. C., & Green, B. G. (1978). History of research on feeling. In E. C. Carterette & M. P. Friedman (Eds.), *Handbook of perception: Vol. VIb. Feeling and hurting.* New York: Academic Press.

Stevens, J. R. (1979). Schizophrenia and dopamine regulation in the mesolimbic system. *Trends in NeuroSciences, 2,* 102–105.

Stevens, S. S., & Davis, H. (1938). *Hearing: Its psychology and physiology.* New York: John Wiley.

Steward, O., & Falk, P. M. (1986). Protein-synthetic machinery at postsynaptic sites during synaptogenesis: A quantitative study of the association between polyribosomes and developing synapses. *The Journal of Neuroscience, 6,* 412–423.

Stone, J. (1983). *Parallel processing in the visual system.* New York: Plenum.

Storlien, L. H., Smith, D. J., Atrens, D. M., & Lovinbond, P. F. (1985). Development of hypoglycemia and hyperglycemia as a function of number of trials in insulin conditioning. *Physiology & Behavior, 35,* 603–606.

Stricker, E. M. (1969). Osmoregulation and volume regulation in rats: Inhibition of hypovolemic thirst by water. *American Journal of Physiology, 217,* 98–105.

Stroud, R. M. (1983). Acetylcholine receptor structure. *Neuroscience Commentaries, 1,* 139–157.

Strumwasser, F. (1967). Neurophysiological aspects of rhythms. In G. C. Quarton, T. Melnechuk, & F. O. Schmitt (Eds.), *The neurosciences: A study program.* New York: Rockefeller University Press.

Stuss, D. T., & Benson, D. F. (1984). Neuropsychological studies of the frontal lobes. *Psychological Bulletin, 95,* 3–28.

Swanson, L. W. (1979). The hippocampus—new anatomical insights. *Trends in NeuroSciences, 2,* 9–12.

Swanson, L. W., Mogenson, G. J., Simerly, R. B., & Wu, M. (1987). Anatomical and electrophysiological evidence for a projection from the medial preoptic area to the "mesencephalic and subthalamic locomotor regions" in the rat. *Brain Research, 405,* 108–122.

Swanson, L. W., & Sawchenko, P. E. (1983). Hypothalamic integration: Organization of the paraventricular and supraoptic nuclei. *Annual Review of Neuroscience, 6,* 269–324.

Swartzwelder, H. S. (1981). Deficits in passive avoidance and fear behavior following bilateral and unilateral amygdala lesions in mice. *Physiology & Behavior, 26,* 323–326.

Székely, G. (1979). Order and plasticity in the nervous system. *Trends in NeuroSciences, 2,* 245–248.

Taghzouti, K., Louilot, A., Herman, J. P., LeMoal, M., & Simon, H. (1985). Alternation behavior, spatial discrimination, and reversal disturbances following 6-hydroxydopamine lesions in the nucleus accumbens of the rat. *Behavioral and Neural Biology, 44,* 354–363.

Takagi, S. F. (1979). Dual systems for sensory olfactory processing in higher primates. *Trends in NeuroSciences, 2,* 313–315.

Takahashi, Y. (1979). Growth hormone secretion related to the sleep and waking rhythm. In R. Drucker-Colin, M. Shkurovich, & M. B. Sterman (Eds.), *The functions of sleep.* New York: Academic Press.

Tanaka, K., Hikosaka, K., Saito, H., Yukie, M., Fukada, Y., & Iwai, E. (1986). Analysis of local and wide-field movements in the superior temporal visual areas of the macaque monkey. *The Journal of Neuroscience, 6,* 134–144.

Tanelian, D. L., & Beuerman, R. W. (1984). Responses of rabbit corneal nociceptors to mechanical and thermal stimulation. *Experimental Neurology, 84,* 165–178.

Tanji, J. (1984). The neuronal activity in the supplementary motor area of primates. *Trends in NeuroSciences, 7,* 282–285.

Tanji, J., & Kurata, K. (1985). Contrasting neuronal activity in supplementary and precentral motor cortex of monkeys: I. Responses to instructions determining motor responses to forthcoming signals of different modalities. *Journal of Neurophysiology, 53,* 129–141.

Tanzi, R. E., St. George-Hyslop, P. H., & Gusella, J. F. (1989). Molecular genetic approaches to Alzheimer's disease. *Trends in Neurosciences, 12,* 152–158.

Teitelbaum, P., & Epstein, A. N. (1962). The lateral hypothalamic syndrome. *Psychological Review, 69,* 74–90.

Terman, G. W., Shavit, Y., Lewis, J. W., Cannon, J. T., & Liebeskind, J. C. (1984). Intrinsic mechanisms of pain inhibition and their activation by stress. *Science, 226,* 1270–1277.

Terry, R. D., & Davies, P. (1980). Dementia of the Alzheimer type. *Annual Review of Neuroscience, 3,* 77–95.

Teyler, T. J., & DiScenna, P. (1984). Long-term potentiation as a candidate mnemonic device. *Brain Research Reviews, 7,* 15–28.

Teyler, T. J., & DiScenna, P. (1986). The hippocampal memory indexing theory. *Behavioral Neuroscience, 100,* 147–154.

Theodore, W. H. (1985). Recent advances in the diagnosis and treatment of seizure disorders. *Trends in Neuro-Sciences, 8,* 144–147.

Thomas, G. J., & Gash, D. M. (1985). Mammillothalamic tracts and representational memory. *Behavioral Neuroscience, 99,* 621–630.

Thompson, R. F. (1983). Neuronal substrates of simple associative learning: Classical conditioning. *Trends in NeuroSciences, 6,* 270–275.

Thompson, R. F. (1988). The neural basis of basic associative learning of discrete behavioral responses. *Trends in Neurosciences, 11,* 152–155.

Thompson, R. F., Berger, T. W., & Madden, J. (1983). Cellular processes of learning and memory in the mammalian CNS. *Annual Review of Neuroscience, 6,* 447–491.

Thompson, R. F., Clark, G. A., Donegan, N. H., Lavond, D. G., Lincoln, J. S., Madden, J., IV, Mamounas, L. A., Mauk, M. D., McCormick, D. A., & Thompson, J. K. (1984). Neuronal substrates of learning and memory: A "multiple-trace" view. In G. Lynch, J. L. McGaugh, & N. M. Weinberger (Eds.), *Neurobiology of learning and memory.* New York: Guilford Press.

Thompson, R. F., & Glanzman, D. L. (1976). Neural and behavioral mechanisms of habituation and sensitization. In T. J. Tighe & R. N. Leaton (Eds.), *Habituation: Perspectives from child development, animal behavior, and neurophysiology.* Hillsdale, NJ: Lawrence Erlbaum.

Thompson, W. G. (1979). *The irritable gut: Functional disorders of the alimentary canal.* Baltimore: University Park Press.

Tonndorf, J. (1960). Shearing motion in scala media of cochlear models. *Journal of the Acoustical Society of America, 32,* 238–244.

Tonndorf, J. (1962). Time/frequency analysis along the partition of cochlear models: A modified place concept. *Journal of the Acoustical Society of America, 34,* 1337–1350.

Townes-Anderson, E., Dacheux, R. F., & Raviola, E. (1988). Rod photoreceptors dissociated from the adult rabbit retina. *The Journal of Neuroscience, 8,* 320–331.

Towns, L. C. (1984, September). An outline of the use of horseradish peroxidase in neuroanatomical tract-tracing. *Kopf Carrier.* Tujunga, CA: David Kopf Instruments.

Tracey, D. (1978). Joint receptors—changing ideas. *Trends in NeuroSciences, 1,* 63–65.

Travers, J. B., Travers, S. P., & Norgren, R. (1987). Gustatory neural processing in the hindbrain. *Annual Review of Neuroscience, 10,* 595–632.

Trevarthen, C. B. (1968). Two mechanisms of vision in primates. *Psychologische Forschung, 31,* 299–337.

Truex, R. C., & Carpenter, M. B. (1964). *Strong and Elwyn's human neuroanatomy* (5th ed.). Baltimore: Williams & Wilkins.

Trulson, M. E., & Jacobs, B. L. (1979a). Long-term amphetamine treatment decreases brain serotonin metabolism: Implications for theories of schizophrenia. *Science, 205,* 1295–1297.

Trulson, M. E., & Jacobs, B. L. (1979b). Raphe unit activity in freely moving cats: Correlation with level of behavioral arousal. *Brain Research, 163,* 135–150.

Trulson, M. E., & Preussler, D. W. (1984). Dopamine-containing ventral tegmental area neurons in freely moving cats: Activity during the sleep-waking cycle and effects of stress. *Experimental Neurology, 83,* 367–377.

Tsukahara, N. (1981a). Sprouting and the neuronal basis of learning. *Trends in NeuroSciences, 4,* 234–237.

Tsukahara, N. (1981b). Synaptic plasticity in the mammalian central nervous system. *Annual Review of Neuroscience, 4,* 351–379.

Tsukahara, N. (1984). Classical conditioning mediated by the red nucleus: An approach beginning at the cellular level. In G. Lynch, J. L. McGaugh, & N. M. Weinberger (Eds.), *Neurobiology of learning and memory.* New York: Guilford Press.

Tuber, D. S., Berntson, G. G., Bachman, D. S., & Allen, J. N. (1980). Associative learning in premature hydranencephalic and normal twins. *Science, 210,* 1035–1037.

Tyrer, P., & Mackay, A. (1986). Schizophrenia: No longer a functional psychosis. *Trends in NeuroSciences, 9,* 537–538.

Ungerleider, L. G., & Mishkin, M. (1982). Two cortical visual systems. In D. J. Ingle, M. A. Goodale, & R. J. W. Mansfield (Eds.), *Analysis of visual behavior*. Cambridge: MIT Press.

Ungerstedt, U. (1971). Stereotaxic mapping of the monoamine pathway in the rat brain. *Acta Physiologica Scandinavia, 82* (Suppl. 367), 1–48.

Uttal, W. R. (1973). *The psychobiology of sensory coding.* New York: Harper & Row.

Valenstein, E. S. (1973a). *Brain control: A critical examination of brain stimulation and psychosurgery.* New York: John Wiley.

Valenstein, E. S. (1973b). History of brain stimulation: Investigations into the physiology of motivation. In E. S. Valenstein (Ed.), *Brain stimulation and motivation.* Glenview, IL: Scott, Foresman.

Vallbo, Å. B., Olsson, K. Å. K., Westberg, K.-G., & Clark, F. J. (1984). Microstimulation of single tactile afferents from the human hand: Sensory attributes related to unit type and properties of receptive fields. *Brain, 107,* 747–749.

van Bergeijk, W. A. (1967). The evolution of vertebrate hearing. In W. D. Neff (Ed.), *Contributions to sensory physiology* (Vol. 2). New York: Academic Press.

van Bergeijk, W. A., Pierce, J. R., & David, E. E., Jr. (1960). *Waves and the ear.* Garden City, NY: Anchor Books (Doubleday).

Van den Hoofdakker, R. H., & Beersma, D. G. M. (1984). Sleep deprivation, mood, and sleep physiology. In A. Borbély & J.-L. Valatx (Eds.), *Sleep mechanisms.* Berlin: Springer-Verlag.

Van Essen, D. C. (1979). Visual areas of the mammalian cerebral cortex. *Annual Review of Neuroscience, 2,* 227–264.

Van Essen, D. C. (1985). Functional organization of the primate visual cortex. In A. Peters & E. G. Jones (Eds.), *Cerebral cortex: Vol. 3. Visual cortex.* New York: Plenum.

Van Essen, D. C., & Maunsell, J. H. R. (1983). Hierarchical organization and functional streams in the visual cortex. *Trends in NeuroSciences, 6,* 370–375.

Van Essen, D. C., Maunsell, J. H. R., & Bixby, J. L. (1981). Organization of extrastriate visual areas in the macaque monkey. In C. N. Woolsey (Ed.), *Cortical sensory organization: Vol. 2. Multiple visual areas.* Clifton, NJ: Humana Press.

Van Heyningen, W. E. (1965). Bacterial exotoxins. In *Encyclopedia of life sciences: Vol. IV. The world of microbes.* Garden City, NY: Doubleday.

Van Hoesen, G. W. (1982). The parahippocampal gyrus: New observations regarding its cortical connections in the monkey. *Trends in NeuroSciences, 5,* 345–350.

Van Hoesen, G. W., Pandya, D. N., & Butters, N. (1975). Some connections of the entorhinal (area 28) and perirhinal (area 35) cortices of the rhesus monkey: II. Frontal lobe afferents. *Brain Research, 95,* 25–38.

van Hulzen, Z. J. M., & Coenen, A. M. L. (1982). Effects of paradoxical sleep deprivation on two-way avoidance acquisition. *Physiology & Behavior, 29,* 581–587.

van Praag, H. M., Kahn, R., Asnis, G. M., Lemus, C. Z., & Brown, S. L. (1987). Therapeutic indications for serotonin-potentiating compounds: A hypothesis. *Biological Psychiatry, 22,* 205–212.

Velley, L., Chaminade, C., Roy, M. T., Kempf, E., & Cardo, B. (1983). Intrinsic neurons are involved in lateral hypothalamic self-stimulation. *Brain Research, 268,* 79–86.

Verbalis, J. G., McCann, M. J., McHale, C. M., & Stricker, E. M. (1986). Oxytocin secretion in response to cholecystokinin and food: Differentiation of nausea from satiety. *Science, 232,* 1417–1419.

Verzeano, M. (1977). The activity of neuronal networks in memory consolidation. In R. R. Drucker-Colin & J. L. McGaugh (Eds.), *Neurobiology of sleep and memory.* New York: Academic Press.

Vibulsreth, S., Hefti, F., Ginsberg, M. D., Dietrich, W. D., & Busto, R. (1987). *Brain Research, 422,* 303–311.

Victor, M. (1964). Observations on the amnestic syndrome in man and its anatomical basis. In M. A. B. Brazier (Ed.), *Brain function: Vol. II. RNA and brain function, memory and learning.* Berkeley: University of California Press.

Vieth, J. L., Buck, M., Getzlaf, S., Van Dalfsen, P., & Slade, S. (1983). Exposure to men influences the occurrence of ovulation in women. *Physiology & Behavior, 31,* 313–315.

Visintainer, M. A., Volpicelli, J. R., & Seligman, M. E. P. (1982). Tumor rejection in rats after inescapable or escapable shock. *Science, 216,* 438–439.

Vochteloo, J. D., & Koolhaas, J. M. (1987). Medial amygdala lesions in male rats reduce aggressive behavior: Interference with experience. *Physiology & Behavior, 41,* 99–102.

Vogt, B. A., Rosene, D. L., & Pandya, D. N. (1979). Thalamic and cortical afferents differentiate anterior from posterior cingulate cortex in the monkey. *Science, 204,* 205–207.

von Békésy, G. (1960). *Experiments in hearing.* New York: McGraw-Hill.

von Békésy, G. (1967). *Sensory inhibition.* Princeton, NJ: Princeton University Press.

Waddington, J. L. (1985). Further anomalies in the dopamine receptor supersensitivity hypothesis of tardive dyskinesia. *Trends in NeuroSciences, 8,* 200.

Wagner, E. M., & Scow, R. O. (1957). Effect of insulin on growth in force fed hypophysectomized rats. *Endocrinology, 61,* 419–424.

Wagner, H. N., Jr., Burns, H. D., Dannals, R. F., Wong, D. F., Langstron, B., Duelfer, T., Front, J. J., Ravert, H. T., Links, J. M., Rosenbloom, S. B., Lukas, S. E., Kramer, A. V., & Kuhar, M. J. (1983). Imaging dopamine receptors in the human brain by positron tomography. *Science, 221,* 1262–1266.

Wald, G., & Brown, P. K. (1965). Human color vision and color blindness. *Cold Spring Harbor Symposia on Quantitative Biology, 30,* 345–359.

Walter, G. (1954, June). The electrical activity of the brain. *Scientific American, 197,* 71–79.

Ward, I. L., & Ward, O. B. (1985). Sexual behavior differentiation: Effects prenatal manipulations in rats. In N. Adler, D. Pfaff, & R. W. Goy (Eds.), *Handbook of behavioral neurobiology: Vol. 7. Reproduction.* London: Plenum.

Warkentin & Carmichael. (1939). *Journal of Genetic Psychology, 55,* 77.

Warrington, E. K., & Weiskrantz, L. (1973). In J. A. Deutsch (Ed.), *The physiological basis of memory.* London: Academic Press.

Webb, W. B. (1978). Sleep and dreams. *Annual Review of Psychology, 29,* 223–252.

Webb, W. B. (1979). Theories of sleep function and some clinical implications. In R. Drucker-Colin, M. Shkurovich, & M. B. Sterman (Eds.), *The functions of sleep.* New York: Academic Press.

Webb, W. B. (1981). *Sleep disorders and modes of treatment.* Riverside, CA: Psychological Seminars.

Webster, W. R., & Aitkin, L. M. (1975). Central auditory processing. In M. S. Gazzaniga & C. Blakemore (Eds.), *Handbook of psychobiology.* New York: Academic Press.

Weinberger, D. R. (1988). Schizophrenia and the frontal lobe. *Trends in Neurosciences, 11,* 367–370.

Weinrich, M., & Wise, S. P. (1982). The premotor cortex of the monkey. *Journal of Neuroscience, 2,* 1329–1445.

Weinrich, M., Wise, S. P., & Mauritz, J.-H. (1984). A neurophysiological analysis of the premotor cortex of the monkey. *Brain, 107,* 385–414.

Weiskrantz, L. (1975). The interaction between occipital and temporal cortex in vision: An overview. In K. Pribram (Ed.), *Central processing of sensory input.* Cambridge: MIT Press.

Weiss, J. M. (1971). Effects of coping behavior with and without a feedback signal on stress pathology in rats. *Journal of Comparative and Physiological Psychology, 77,* 22–30.

Weisz, D. J., Clark, G. A., Yang, B., Thompson, R. F., & Solomon, P. R. (1982). Activity of dentate gyrus during NM conditioning in rabbit. In C. D. Woody (Ed.), *Conditioning: Representation of involved neural functions.* New York: Plenum.

Weitzman, E. D. (1981). Sleep and its disorders. *Annual Review of Neuroscience, 4,* 381–417.

Weller, R. E., & Kaas, J. H. (1981). Cortical and subcortical connections of visual cortex in primates. In C. N. Woolsey (Ed.), *Cortical sensory organization: Vol. 2. Multiple visual areas.* Clifton, NJ: Humana Press.

Welsh, J. P., & Harvey, J. A. (1989). Cerebellar lesions and the nictitating membrane reflex: Performance deficits of the conditioned and unconditioned response. *The Journal of Neuroscience, 9,* 299–311.

Wenzel, B. M. (1973). Chemoreception. In E. C. Carterette & M. P. Friedman (Eds.), *Handbook of perception: Vol. III. Biology of perceptual systems.* New York: Academic Press.

Werblin, F. S. (1973). The control of sensitivity in the retina. *Scientific American, 228,* 71–79.

Werblin, F. S. (1979). Integrative pathways in local circuits between slow-potential cells in the retina. In F. O. Schmitt & F. G. Worden (Eds.), *The neurosciences: Fourth study program.* Cambridge: MIT Press.

Werner, G., & Whitsel, B. L. (1973). Functional organization of the somatosensory cortex. In A. Iggo (Ed.), *Handbook of sensory physiology: Vol. II. Somatosensory system.* Heidelberg: Springer-Verlag.

Wersäll, J., & Bagger-Sjöbäck, D. (1974). Morphology of the vestibular sense organ. In H. H. Kornhuber (Ed.), *Handbook of sensory physiology: Vol. VI/1, Vestibular system part 1: Basic mechanisms.* New York: Springer.

West, R. E. G., & Wise, R. A. (1988). Effects of naltrexone on nucleus accumbens, lateral hypothalamic and ventral tegmental self-stimulation rate-frequency functions. *Brain Research, 462,* 126–133.

Wetzel, C. D., & Squire, L. R. (1982). Cued recall in anterograde amnesia. *Brain and Language, 15,* 70–81.

Wetzel, M. C., & Stuart, D. G. (1976). Ensemble characteristics of cat locomotion and its neural control. *Progress in Neurobiology, 7,* 1–98.

Wever, E. G. (1949). *Theory of hearing.* New York: John Wiley.

Whalen, R. E., & Simon, N. G. (1984). Biological motivation. *Annual Review of Psychology, 35,* 257–276.

White, N., & Kinsbourne, M. (1980). Does speech output control lateralize over time? Evidence from verbal-manual time-sharing tasks. *Brain and Language, 10,* 215–223.

White, R., & Lalouel, J.-M. (1988). Chromosome mapping with DNA markers. *Scientific American, 258,* 40–48.

Wible, C. G., Findling, R. L., Shapiro, M., Lang, E. J., Crane, S., & Olton, D. S. (1986). Mnemonic correlates of unit activity in the hippocampus. *Brain Research, 399,* 97–110.

Wicklegren, W. A. (1979). Chunking and consolidation: A theoretical synthesis of semantic networks, configuring in conditioning, S–R versus cognitive learning, normal forgetting, the amnesic syndrome, and the hippocampal arousal system. *Psychological Review, 86,* 44–60.

Williams, M. (1979). *Brain damage, behaviour, and the mind.* New York: John Wiley.

Wilson, C. J., Groves, P. M., Kitai, S. T., & Linder, J. C. (1983). Three-dimensional structure of dendritic spines in the rat neostriatum. *Journal of Neuroscience, 3,* 383–398.

Wilson, J. D., George, F. W., & Griffin, J. E. (1981). The hormonal control of sexual development. *Science, 211,* 1278–1284.

Wise, R. A. (1980a). The dopamine synapse and the notion of "pleasure centers" in the brain. *Trends in Neuro-Sciences, 3,* 91–95.

Wise, R. A. (1980b). "Yes, but! . . . " A response to Arbuthnott from Roy Wise. *Trends in NeuroSciences, 3,* 200.

Wise, R. A., & Bozarth, M. A. (1984). Brain reward circuitry: Four circuit elements "wired" in apparent series. *Brain Research Bulletin, 12,* 203–208.

Wise, S. P. (1985). The primate premotor cortex: Past, present, and preparatory. *Annual Review of Neuroscience, 8,* 1–19.

Wise, S. P., & Evarts, E. V. (1981). The role of the cerebral cortex in movement. *Trends in NeuroSciences, 4,* 297–300.

Wise, S. P., & Strick, P. L. (1984). Anatomical and physiological organization of the nonprimary motor cortex. *Trends in NeuroSciences, 7,* 442–446.

Wisniewski, H. M., & Iqbal, K. (1980). Ageing of the brain and dementia. *Trends in NeuroSciences, 3,* 226–228.

Witelson, S. F. (1985). The brain connection: The corpus callosum is larger in left-handers. *Science, 229,* 665–668.

Wolfe, S. L. (1983). *Introduction to cell biology.* Belmont, CA: Wadsworth.

Wong, D. F., Wagner, H. N., Jr., Tune, L. E., Dannals, R. F., Pearlson, G. D., Links, J. M., Tamminga, C. A., Broussolle, E. P., Ravert, H. T., Wilson, A. A., Toung, J. K., Malat, J., Williams, J. A., O'Tauma, L. A., Snyder, S. H., Kuhar, M. J., & Gjedde, A. (1986). Positron emission tomography reveals elevated D2 dopamine receptors in drug-naive schizophrenics. *Science, 234,* 1558–1563.

Wong-Riley, M. T. T. (1979). Changes in the visual system of monocularly sutured or enucleated cats demonstrable with cytochrome oxidase histochemistry. *Brain Research, 171,* 11–28.

Woodburne, L. S. (1967). *The neural basis of behavior.* Columbus, OH: Merrill.

Woodruff, M. L., Baisden, R. H., Whitington, D. L., & Benson, A. E. (1987). Embryonic hippocampal grafts ameliorate the deficit in DRL acquisition produced by hippocampectomy. *Brain Research, 408,* 97–117.

Woods, B. T. (1983). Is the left hemisphere specialized for language at birth? *Trends in NeuroSciences, 6,* 115–117.

Woods, S. C., Decke, E., & Vasselli, J. R. (1974). Metabolic hormones and regulation of body weight. *Psychological Review, 81,* 26–43.

Woolsey, T. A., & Van der Loos, H. (1970). The structural organization of layer IV in the somatosensory region (SI) of the mouse cerebral cortex. The description of a cortical field composed of discrete cytoarchitectonic units. *Brain Research, 17,* 205–242.

Wurtz, R. H., Goldberg, M. E., & Robinson, D. L. (1982). Brain mechanisms of visual attention. *Scientific American, 246*(6), 124–135.

Yeomans, J. S. (1982). The cells and axons mediating medial forebrain bundle reward. In B. G. Hoebel & D. Novin (Eds.), *The neural basis of feeding and reward.* Brunswick, ME: Haer Institute.

Yingling, C. (1978). Neurobiology of pain. In *Eleventh Winter Conference on Brain Research: Summaries of symposia* (BIS Conference Report No. 47). Los Angeles: Brain Information Service/BRI Publications Office, UCLA.

Zaidel, E. (1983). A response to Gazzaniga: Language in the right hemisphere. *American Psychologist, 38,* 542–546.

Zaidel, E. (1985). Language in the right hemisphere. In D. F. Benson & E. Zaidel (Eds.), *The dual brain: Hemispheric specialization in humans.* New York: Guilford Press.

Zeki, S. M. (1980). The representation of colours in the cerebral cortex. *Nature, 284,* 412–418.

Zemanick, M. C., Walker, P. D., & McAllister, J. P., II. (1987). Quantitative analysis of dendrites from transplanted neostriatal neurons. *Brain Research, 414,* 149–152.

Zhang, D.-M., Bula, W., & Stellar, E. (1986). Brain cholecystokinin as a satiety peptide. *Physiology & Behavior, 36,* 1183–1186.

Zigmond, M. J., & Stricker, E. M. (1972). Deficits in feeding behavior after intraventricular injection of 6-Hydroxy-dopamine in rats. *Science, 177,* 1211–1214.

Zohar, J., & Insel, T. R. (1987). Obsessive-compulsive disorder: Psychobiological approaches to diagnosis, treatment, and pathophysiology. *Biological Psychiatry, 22,* 667–687.

Zola-Morgan, S., Squire, L. R., & Amaral, D. G. (1989). Lesions of the amygdala that spare adjacent cortical regions do not impair memory or exacerbate the impairment following lesions of the hippocampal formation. *The Journal of Neuroscience, 9,* 1922–1936.

Zubenko, G. S. (1987). Water homeostasis in psychiatric patients. *Biological Psychiatry, 22,* 121–125.

Zubin, J., & Steinhauer, S. (1982). How to break the logjam in schizophrenia: A look beyond genetics. *Journal of Nervous and Mental Disease, 169,* 477–492.

Zucker, I. (1968). Biphasic effects of progesterone on sexual receptivity in the female guinea pig. *Journal of Comparative and Physiological Psychology, 65,* 472–478.

Zuckerman, M. (1971). Physiological measures of sexual arousal in the human. *Psychological Bulletin, 75,* 297–329.

Zuckerman, S. (1957, March). Hormones. *Scientific American, 199,* 56–65.

Davis, H. P., 619, 620
Davis, J. N., 559
Davis, K. R., 721
Davis, M., 518, 524
Davson, H., 38
Dawbarn, D., 677
Dawson, T. M., 673
Deadwyler, S. A., 599, 600, 601, 602, 603
de Aguiar, J. C., 515, 524
DeAndrés, I., 419
DeArmond, S. J., 662
de Bleser, R., 718
Decke, E., 464
deKorted, R., 684
de la Tourette, G. G., 3
Delay, J., 634
Delcomyn, F., 369
Della-Fera, M. A., 448, 458
DeLong, M. R., 677
Dement, W. C., 412, 416, 423, 430, 433, 434
Denes, P. B., 256
d'Erme, P., 712
Desborough, 630
Desimone, R., 214, 225, 226, 227, 228
Deutsch, G., 730, 739
Deutsch, J. A., 447, 637
Deutsch, S. I., 540
DeVente, J., 177
DeVito, J. L., 518, 520
Dewey, M. M., 662
Diaz, S., 459
Dietrich, W. D., 36
Di Maio, A., 465
Dinner, D. S., 718
Dionne, V. E., 289
DiScenna, P., 597, 598, 615, 616, 625
Divac, I., 371
Dockray, G. J., 447
Dolnikoff, M. S., 464
Dolphin, A. C., 593
Donegan, N. H., 561, 563, 565
Dong, W. K., 324
Donhoffer, H., 589
Dott, N. M., 516
Dowling, J. E., 205, 206, 210, 211
Drake, L., 518
Drewnowski, A., 464
Drucker-Colin, R., 421, 424, 430
Drugan, R. C., 333
Dudel, J., 117
Duffy, F. H., 659
Duggan, A. W., 328
du Lac, S., 272
Duncan, C. C., 658

Duncan, C. P., 637
Duncan, G. W., 721
Dunn, E., 10
Dunnett, S. B., 12
Durrant, J. D., 277
Dursteler, M. R., 239
Duvoisin, R., 373, 376
Dyson, E. M., 526

Easter, S. S., 288
Ebbesson, S. O. E., 175
Ebstein, R. P., 672
Eccles, J. C., 3, 4, 360, 361
Edinger, H., 525
Edwards, D. A., 500, 501
Egan, K., 335
Ehrhardt, A. A., 408, 491, 492, 503, 505
Eichenbaum, H., 597
Einhorn, L. C., 500, 501
Elian, M., 684
Ellis, L., 492, 505, 506, 507, 508, 509
Ellisman, M. H., 24
El-Mofty, A., 276
Emmorey, K. D., 735
Engel, R. R., 432
Epstein, A. N., 451
Erickson, R. P., 281, 282, 284, 285
Ervin, F. R., 164, 165, 324, 520, 681, 682
Esterly, S. D., 272
Eterno, R., 447
Evans, A. S., 536
Evans, E. F., 275
Evans, K., 6
Evarts, E. V., 378, 383, 386, 430
Everhart, T. E., 44

Fagan, A., 597
Fagioli, I., 411
Fair, C., 720, 721
Falk, P. M., 625
Fanselow, M. S., 328, 335
Faraone, S. V., 653
Farley, J., 559, 560
Faust, I. M., 464
Favorov, O., 313, 315
Fawcett, D. W., 343
Feder, H. H., 501
Feldman, R. S., 38, 145, 458, 522, 523, 524, 666, 667, 670, 673
Ferguson, N. B., 455
Fibiger, H. C., 575, 578
Fields, H. L., 328, 330, 333, 334
Fiertag, M., 73, 82, 83
File, S., 523

Findlay, J., 683
Findling, R. L., 597
Fine, A., 10, 12, 13, 14
Fink, M., 674
Finkelstein, S., 721
Firth, C. D., 380
Fischer, B., 232
Fishbein, W., 429
Fisher, A. E., 168
Flament, E., 363
Fleming, J., 214
Flier, J. S., 457
Floody, O. R., 498
Flynn, F. W., 448
Flynn, J. P., 525, 528
Flynn, R. W., 654, 655
Fobes, J. L., 572, 573, 574
Fontani, G., 521
Fornal, C., 419
Foster, T. C., 599, 602, 603
Fowler, I., 22, 24, 25, 29, 31, 36, 37, 71, 201, 259, 261, 359, 362, 382, 442, 558
Fox, J. L., 317, 318
Frazer, A., 673
Fredrickson, R. H., 428
Freed, D. M., 636
Freed, W. J., 11, 12
Freeman, W., 517, 718, 719
French, J. D., 405
Freund, T. F., 12, 388, 390, 391, 392
Friedberg, J., 636, 637
Friedhoff, A. J., 671, 672, 674, 675
Friedlander, M. J., 219
Friedman, H. R., 605, 607
Friedman, M. I., 445, 453, 456
Friedrich, F. J., 712
Fritsch, G., 155
Froberg, J., 537
Frohman, L., 457
Frommer, G. P., 329
Frutiger, S. A., 573
Fuchs, S. A. G., 521
Fukada, Y., 239, 242
Fulton, J. F., 349
Funder, J. W., 534
Funkenstein, H. H., 721
Fusco, M. M., 662
Fuster, J. M., 139, 220, 225, 698, 699, 700

Gademann, G., 187
Gage, D., 447
Gage, P., 701
Gainer, H., 428
Gainotti, G., 712

Galambos, R., 267
Galanter, E., 210, 305
Gallistel, C. R., 579, 580
Galvani, L., 4
Garcia, J., 286
Garcia-Sevilla, J. A., 671
Gardner, E., 58, 302, 307
Gardner, H., 715, 728
Gardner, W. D., 489
Gardner-Medwin, A., 616
Garelik, G., 6
Garrett, M. F., 720
Gash, D. M., 14, 166
Gastaut, H., 426
Gattass, R., 214
Gautier, T., 507
Gayton, R. J., 447
Gazzaniga, M. S., 696, 702, 728, 730,
    731, 732, 733, 734
Geffard, M., 178
Geldard, F. A., 263, 288, 348
Gelfand, I. M., 360
Geliebter, A., 447
Gellman, R. S., 561, 562
Gerall, A. A., 494
Gergen, J. A., 161
Gershon, E. S., 668
Gershon, S., 373
Geschwind, N., 88, 714, 718, 721,
    722, 723, 724, 725, 726
Getzlaf, S., 292
Ghent, L., 711
Gibbs, M. E., 620
Gilman, A. G., 556
Ginsberg, M. D., 36
Gjedde, A., 666
Gjerde, P. F., 658, 659
Glanzman, D. L., 281, 556
Glassman, A., 672
Globus, A., 624, 626
Gluck, C. M., 462
Goddard, G. V., 616, 682
Goetz, D. M., 425
Goetz, R. R., 425
Gold, J., 667
Gold, R. M., 458
Goldberg, M. E., 239, 243, 378
Goldberg, T., 714
Goldman-Rakic, P., 605, 607
Goldsmith, M., 675, 677
Goldstein, E. B., 205, 207, 208, 209,
    222, 223, 234, 257, 259, 260, 264,
    266, 271
Gonzalez, M. F., 447
Goodglass, H., 697
Goodman, R. F., 462

Gordon, B., 664, 666, 673
Gorski, R. A., 493, 494, 495, 497, 500
Gorzalka, B. B., 527
Goy, R. W., 494
Graeff, F. G., 515, 521, 524
Graf, P., 643
Graff, H., 455
Graham, R. B., 416, 417
Grahame-Smith, D. G., 683
Grastyán, E., 408, 589
Gratton, A., 573, 579
Grau, J. W., 333, 334
Gray, E. G., 623
Gray, J. A., 523
Gray, P., 498
Green, A. R., 683
Green, B. G., 318
Green, E. J., 615, 616
Greenblatt, D. J., 540
Greengard, P., 132, 628
Greenough, W. T., 615, 616, 618, 619,
    623, 624
Greenstein, B. D., 494
Grill, H. J., 448
Grillner, S., 70, 365, 367, 369, 370,
    386
Grinker, J. A., 464
Grinvald, A., 181
Gronstrom, M., 537
Groos, G., 428
Gross, C. G., 214, 225, 226, 227, 228
Grossman, M., 728
Grossman, S. P., 445, 452, 453, 456
Groves, P. M., 483, 557, 623
Grüsser, O. J., 211
Guerrero, J., 507
Guillemin, R., 326, 328
Gulick, W. L., 260
Gurney, M. E., 494, 496
Gusella, J. F., 677
Gygax, P., 175

Haar, B., 330
Hagenmeyer-Houser, S. H., 14
Hagins, W. A., 204, 206
Hahn, J., 718
Hahn, W. K., 735, 737
Halaris, A. E., 419, 452
Haley, D. A., 563
Hall, W. G., 475
Hallonquist, J. D., 455
Halpern, M., 290
Hamanaka, Y., 540
Hamba, M., 331
Hamilton, C. R., 732
Hamilton, J. M., 462

Hammer, R. P., 495
Hampson, R. E., 599, 602, 603
Handelmann, G. E., 593, 605
Hanlon, C., 425
Harper, S. T., 419
Harrel, T. H., 570
Harris, A. B., 683
Harris, A. J., 59, 60
Harrison, J. M., 271
Harrison-Read, P. E., 671
Hart, B. L., 162, 166, 498, 502, 504
Hartman, B. K., 176, 177, 178, 428
Hartmann, W. K., 199
Harvey, J. A., 475, 561
Hashim, S. A., 447
Hatton, G. I., 470, 472
Hausberger, F. X., 462
Heath, R. G., 529, 530
Hebb, D., 4, 614, 618, 620, 630, 635,
    636, 709
Heffner, H. E., 273
Heffner, R. S., 273
Heimer, L., 42
Heinrich, B., 30, 121, 130, 467
Heller, H. W., 462
Henderson, N. D., 652, 654, 724
Hendricks, J. C., 414, 415
Hendrickson, 236, 237
Henke, P. G., 532
Hensel, H., 319, 320
Henson, R. A., 684
Herman, J. P., 579
Hernandez, L., 281
Hervey, G. R., 457
Hicks, R. E., 737
Hikosaka, K., 239, 242
Hikosaka, O., 378
Hill, N. S., 464
Hillyard, S. A., 733
Hinman, D. J., 433
Hirsh, J., 462
Hirsh, R., 594, 597
Hirst, W., 640
Hiscock, M., 737
Hitchcock, J., 518, 525
Hitzig, E., 155
Hobson, J. A., 419, 420, 421, 429
Hodges, F. J., III, 185
Hodgson, E. S., 97, 98
Hoebel, B. G., 449, 455
Hoffer, B. J., 11, 12
Holmes, D. T., 564
Holmes, G., 361
Holmes, G. L., 682
Holmes, T. H., 532, 533
Holth, P., 570

approach–avoidance conditioning of, 291
and instrumental conditioning, 570
and irritable aggression, 529
and olfactory input, 289
and predatory aggression, 527
Amyloid precursor protein, 676
Anabolism, 26
  energy, 26–27
  protein, 27–32
Analgesia, 328, 338
Analgesics, 326, 338
Analyzers, in vision, 210–11, 248
Androgen-induced hermaphroditism, 492, 511
Androgen-insensitivity syndrome, 490–91, 507–8, 511
Androgens, 483, 511
Angiotensin, 469, 478
Angular gyrus, 723, 743
Animal care and use committee, 189
Animal care and use program, 189
Animal electricity, 4
Animal model, 167, 194
Animal research
  ethics in, 154–55
  guidelines for, 192–93
  in neuroscience, 187, 189–93, 697–99
Animal Welfare Act, 187, 189
Anisomycin, 619, 646
Anomic aphasia, 715, 716, 743
Anosognosia, 710, 743
Anoxia, 36, 46
Antagonist, 329, 338, 361, 395
Anterior, 50, 105
Anterior hypothalamus, 498, 511
Anterior lesions, versus posterior lesions, 720–21
Anterior nucleus of the thalamus, 569, 584
Anterior pituitary gland, 79, 105, 459–60, 485, 511, 534, 542
Anterograde amnesia, 632–33, 646
Anterograde tracing, 176, 194
Antibodies, 177–78, 194, 535, 542
Antidiuretic hormone (ADH), 470, 478
Antigen, 177, 194, 535, 542
Antipsychotic drugs, 6, 16, 687
  and DA receptors, 666
Anvil, 258, 296
Anxiety, 517–24
  and amygdala, 518, 520
  and brain stem, 520–21
  and fear, 517–24

and hypothalamus, 520–21
and orbitofrontal cortex, 517–18
psychopharmacology of, 522–24
and sympathetic nervous system, 521–22
Anxiolytic drugs, 522–23, 542
Aphagia, 449, 478
Aphasia
  anomic, 715, 716
  Broca's, 714, 716
  conduction, 715, 716
  damage underlying Broca's, 717–20
  expressive, 714, 720
  receptive, 714, 715, 721
  site of damage in, 716–23
  transcortical motor, 715, 716, 721–22
  transcortical sensory, 715–16, 722
  varieties of, 714–16
  Wernicke's, 715, 716
Aplysia, 551, 584
Aplysia synapses, habituation and sensitization at, 551–56
Appetite-suppressant drugs, 463
Appetitive, 515, 542
Approach–avoidance tendency, 515, 542
Apraxia, 710, 743
Arcuate fasciculus, 721, 743
Area 7a, 242, 248–49
Area 18. See V2
Area 19, 249. See also V2
Area postrema, 38, 46
Arousal, 400, 403, 436
  and attention, 658
  and habituation, 402–8
  and reticular formation, 403–6
  in schizophrenia, 657–60
  and sleep, 409–13
Aspiration, 155, 194
Associational context theory, 597–99
Association neurons, 63, 105
Associative learning, 548, 584
  and NMDA receptors, 630
Astigmatism, 202, 249
Astrocytes, 33, 35–36, 46
Asymbolia, pain, 710
Ataxia, 360, 395
Atomic nuclei, 111, 147
Atoms, 111, 147
Atonia, 436
  and REM sleep, 414–16
Atonic seizures, 680, 687
ATP (adenosine triphosphate), 26–27

Atrophy, 654, 687
Atropine, 674
Attention, 400
  and arousal, 658
  in schizophrenia, 657–60
  and septal nucleus, 599–600
Attractants, 290, 296
Audiometer, 277, 296
Audition, 87–88, 105, 254–55, 296
  and anatomy of ear, 257–62
  auditory projection system, 269–75
  detecting sound waves, 255–62
  difficulties in hearing, 275–79
  neural correlates of sensation, 262–69
Auditory cortex, 273, 275, 295
Auditory evoked potential, 169, 194, 277–78, 295
Auditory nerve fiber, 259, 295
Auditory projection system, 269–75, 295
Aura, 679, 687
Auricles, 257, 295
Autoimmune disease, 374, 395
Automatic behavior episodes, 434, 436
Autonomic fibers, 53, 105
Autonomic nervous system (ANS), 64–66, 105
Autoradiographic method, 176, 194
Autoradiography, 176
Autoreceptors, 670, 687
Autotopagnosia, 710, 743
Averaged evoked potentials, 171, 194
Aversion system, 517, 542
Aversive, 515, 542
Axon, 10, 16, 33, 46, 52
  absolute refractory period, 263
  following, in brain mapping, 175–76
Axon hillock, 121, 147
Axon threshold, 127, 147–48

Background firing, reason for, 595, 597
Bamazepine, in treating epilepsy, 684
Barbiturates, 432, 433, 436, 522–23, 542
Baroreceptors, 471, 478
Bar-press, 566–67
Barrels, 313, 338
Bases, 29, 46
Basilar membrane, 259, 296
  tuning, 267–69

Dark adaptation, 209, 249
Dark current, 204, 249
D cells, 239, 249
Deafferentation, 365, 396
Decibel, 257, 296
Declarative memory, 642, 646
Decomposition of movements, 360, 396
Decremental conduction, 134, 148
Deep somatic receptors, 301, 338
Degeneration, 55, 106
Delay conditioning, 563, 584
Delayed-alternation task, 698–99, 744
Delayed matching-to-sample task, 699, 744
Delayed match-to-nonsample task, 225, 249
Delayed object alternation, 605, 607, 609
Delayed-response task, 697, 744
Delayed spatial alternation, 605, 609
Delirium, 651
Delta waves, 401–2, 436
Delusions, 652, 688
Dementia, 651
Dendrites, 14, 16, 33, 46, 52
Dendritic changes, in learning, 618–19
Dendritic spines, 43, 47, 623–25, 646
Dentate gyrus, 592, 609
Dentate nucleus, 560, 584
Deoxyglucose, 428, 436
Deoxyribonucleic acid (DNA), 23, 47
    replication of, 28–30
Depolarization, 125–28, 148
Depression
    catecholamine theory of, 669–73
    clinical, 432
    and monoamines, 669
    synaptic, 553
Depressive disorder, 667–68, 688
Descending pain-control system, 328–30
Destroamphetamine, 664
Desynchronization, 410, 436
Desynchrony, 401, 436
Developmental dyslexia, 723, 744
Dexamethasone, 9, 16
Dextral, 738, 744
Dextroamphetamine, 663–64
Diabetes insipidus, 471, 478
Diabetes mellitus, 444, 478
Diagonal band of Broca, 578–79, 584
Diazepam, 523, 542
Dichotic listening, 727, 744
Diencephalic amnesia, 635, 646

Diencephalon, 634–35, 646
Dieting, 464–66
Diffusion, 115, 148
Diffusion pressure, 115
Dihydrotestosterone (DHT), 492, 511
Dilantin, in treating epilepsy, 684
Dimorphism, 483, 511
Disconnection syndromes, 721–23
Discrimination learning, 549, 584
Discrimination-reversal conditioning, 594
Discrimination-reversal learning, 564, 584
Disease, role of immune system in combating, 535–36
Dishabituation, 548, 584
Distributed learning, 571, 584
Disynaptic arc, 345, 396
Dizygotic twins, 653, 688
    and study of schizophrenia, 653
DNA (deoxyribonucleic acid), 23, 47
    replication of, 28–30
Doctrine of specific nerve energies, 4, 16
DOPA, 166
Dopamine, 6, 16, 136, 141, 142, 145, 148, 166, 177, 373, 554
Dopaminergic fibers, 575, 585
Dopamine theory, 576–77
    evidence favoring, 577–78
    modifying, 578–80
    problems with, 666–67
Dorsal, 50, 106
Dorsal horn, 62, 106, 310, 338
Dorsal root, 62, 106, 309–10, 338
Dorsal root ganglion, 62, 106, 310, 338
Dorsomedial nucleus of thalamus (DMT), 585, 635, 646
    and instrumental learning, 570
Double-extinction method, 578, 584
Downers, 523
Down-regulation, 671, 688
Down syndrome, 677, 688
Dreams, 414–16
DRL schedule, 568, 585
Drugs
    effect of, on transmitters, 140
    and monoamines, 669–70
Dualism, 2–3, 16
    interactional, 3
Dual-processing theory of taste coding, 285–86, 296
Dual-projection model, 218
Dual-projection theory, 219

Dual visual projection system, 217, 249
Dumping, 447
Duodenum, 441, 478
Dura mater, 72, 106
Dynamic phase of hyperphagia, 454–55, 478
Dysarthria, 714, 720, 744
Dyslexia, developmental, 723
Dysmetria, 361, 396

Ear, anatomy of, 257–62
ECT. See Electroconvulsive therapy
EEG waves
    amplitude of, 401–2
    frequency of, 401–2
Efferent fibers, 53
Efferents, 63
Electroconvulsive shock (ECS), 637, 646
    effect of, on amnesia, 637
Electroconvulsive therapy (ECT), 636, 673–74, 688
    side effects of, 674
Electrode, 111, 148
    implanting, in brain research, 160–64
    surface, in brain research, 169–73
Electroencephalograph (EEG), 156–60, 194, 588, 609
    and identification of sleep stages, 409–10
    in petit mal seizure, 680
Electrolytic lesion, 164, 194
Electromagnetic radiation, 199, 249
Electromagnetic spectrum, 199, 249
Electromyogram (EMG), 365, 396, 413, 436
Electronic currents, 121–22, 148
Electron micrography, 41, 43
Electro-oculogram (EOG), 413, 436
Electrostatic attraction, 116, 148
Electrostatic forces, 115–16
Electrostatic repulsion, 115, 148
Embedding, 39, 47
Embryo, 483, 511
Emergent stage 1, 410, 436
Emitted responses, 549, 585
Emotional stress, and infection, 536
Emotions. See also Stress
    aggression, 524–31
    anxiety and fear, 517–24
    effect of, on body chemistry, 534–35
    problem of, 514–17
    stress chemistry and, 539–40

Encephalization, 97–99, 106
End bulb. *See* Terminal
Endocrine glands, 76–77, 106
Endocrine system, 76, 106
    control of internal environment
        through, 76–77, 79
Endogenous opioids, 330, 338
Endoplasmic reticulum, 23–24, 47
Endorphins, 330, 338
Endothelial cells, 38, 47
End-stopped cells, 238–39, 249
Energy anabolism, 26–27
Engrams, 550, 585
Enkephalins, 330, 338
Entorhinal cortex, 592, 609
Entrainment, 428, 436
Enzyme deactivation, 142–45
Enzymes, 27, 47, 441, 478
Ependymal cells, 33, 37, 47
Ependymins, 621, 646
Epilepsy, 156, 678–79
    causes of, 682–84
    diagnosis and treatment of, 160
    seizures in, 682, 683–84
    treatment of, 684
    types of, 679–82
Epileptic focus, 679, 688
    and paroxysmal depolarization
        shift, 683
Epinephrine, 142, 148, 177, 554
Epstein–Barr virus, 536
Equilibrium point, 116, 148
Equipotentiality, 550, 585
Erasure mechanism, 601, 609
Estrogen, 77, 483, 511
Estrus, 489, 511
Ethosuximide, 684, 688
Euphoria, 328, 338
Event memories, 599, 609
Evoked response technique, 601, 609
Excitability, 125–28, 148
Excitation, 136, 148, 194
Excitatory postsynaptic potential
    (EPSP), 133, 148
    versus nerve pulse, 133–34
Excitotoxins, 167
Exhaustion, 532, 542
Exocrine glands, 76, 106
Explanation, 3
Expressive aphasia, 714, 744
Extensor muscle, 350, 396
Extensor thrust reflex, 364, 396
External genitalia, 493, 511
Extinction, 567, 585
Extinction procedure, 567, 585

Extracellular microelectrode
    technique, 174, 194
Extracellular space, 466, 478

FA I, 304, 338
FA II, 304, 338
Face cells, 228, 249
Facilitation, 136, 148
Fallopian tubes, 485, 511
Familial sinistrals, 739, 744
Far disparity, 231, 249
Fast adapter (FA), 303, 338
Fasting, 463, 478
Fasting phase, 441
Fear. *See also* Anxiety
    and stress, 334–36
Fear-induced aggression, 524–25, 542
Female hermaphroditism syndromes,
    491–92
Feminization, 500, 511
Fibers, 53, 106
    somatic versus autonomic, 53, 55
Fibrositis, 425, 436
Field neuron, 241, 249
Figure, 239, 249
Figure neurons, 241, 249
Filaments, 24, 47
Fissure, 85, 106
5α-reductase, 492, 511
5α-reductase syndrome, 492–93, 511
Fix, 39
Fixation, 39, 47
Flaccid paralysis, 141, 148, 383, 396
Flattened affect, 652, 688
Flavor, 286, 296
Flexor muscle, 350, 396
Florida "walking" catfish, 94
Flower-pot technique, 429–30
Fluid bilayer membrane, 22–23.
    See also Cell membrane
Flurazepam, 432, 436
Focal vision, 218, 249
Fodrin, 626, 646
Follicles, 488, 511
Follicle-stimulating hormone (FSH),
    485, 511
Formalin, 39
Form analysis, 224–28
Fourth ventricle, 72, 106
Fovea, 202, 207, 249, 707–8, 744
Fractionation, 387, 396
    and motor hierarchy, 385–87
Free fatty acids, 441, 478
Free nerve endings, 302, 338

Frequency
    of EEG waves, 158, 194
    of sound waves, 256–57, 296
Frequency following, 263, 296
Frequency matching, 309, 338
Frequency theory, 262–63
Frontal eye fields (FEF), 219, 243,
    249, 708, 744
Frontal lobe, 85, 106
    anatomy of, 693
Frontal lobe personality, 702, 744
FTG (gigantocellular tegmental
    field), 419, 436
Fuels, use and storage of, 441, 443
Fugue state, 681, 688
Functional obesity, 462, 478

GABA (gamma-aminobutyric acid),
    137–38, 148, 523, 683, 688
GABA$_A$ receptor, 138, 148
GABA$_B$ receptor, 138, 148
GABA-modulin, 523, 542
Gamma-aminobutyric acid (GABA),
    137–38, 523, 693
Gamma efferent, 352, 396
    tuning the stretch reflex with,
        352–54
Gamma radiation, 200
Ganglion, 59, 106
Ganglion cells, 202, 203, 249
Gastric ulcer symptom of GAS, 532
Gender, problems in determining,
    489–93
Gender assignment, 490, 493, 511
Gender identity, 489–90, 511
Gene, 23, 31, 47, 483, 511
General adaptation syndrome (GAS),
    531, 542
    symptoms of, 531–32
Generalization of habituation, 408,
    436
Generalized seizures, 679, 688
Genetic factor, 493, 511, 653, 688
Genetic obesity, 462, 478
Geniculostriate path, 217, 249
Geniculostriate system
    parallel paths outside, 219
    parallel paths within, 218–19
Gigantocellular tegmental field
    (FTG), 419, 436
Glia, 33. *See also* Neuroglia
Glial cells, 33, 35–37
Globus pallidus, 79, 106, 371, 396,
    451, 478
Glucagon, 443, 479

Glucocorticoids, 77, 106, 460, 478, 534, 535, 542
Glucose, 26, 47, 441, 478
Glucostatic theory of hunger, 444–45, 478
Glutamate, 167, 194, 625, 646
Glycerol, 441, 478
Glycine, 30
Glycogen, 27, 47, 441–42, 478
Goal set, 699–701. *See also* Set
Golgi complex, 24, 47
Golgi–Cox method, 40, 47
Golgi tendon organ, 348, 396
Golgi type I neurons, 33, 47
Golgi type II neurons, 33, 47
Gonadal hormones, influence of, on adult human behavior, 501–9
Gonadotropic hormones, 485, 511
Gonadotropin-releasing factor (GRF), 485, 511
Gonads, 77, 106, 482, 511
Graded potentials, 203. *See also* Local currents
Grand mal seizure, 679, 680, 688
Granule cells, 592, 609
Gravitational sense, 354, 396
Gravity, and linear acceleration, 354–57
Gray matter, 58–59, 66, 106
Grief reactions, 667, 688
Grip control, 309
Ground, 239, 249
Growth hormone (GH), 430, 436
Guanine, 29
Gustation, 88, 106
Gustatory cortex, 281, 296
Gyrus, 85, 106

[³H]proline, 235, 249
Habituation, 408, 436, 547, 585
and arousal, 402–8
locating, in mammalian nervous system, 556–57
and sensitization at Aplysia synapses, 551–56
site of, 551–57
Habituation hypothesis, 426, 436
HACER (hypothalamic area for conditioned emotional responses), 520–21, 542
Hair cells, 259, 296
Hair follicle, 302, 338
Hallucinations, 652, 688
Haloperidol, 6, 16
Hammer, 258, 296
Hand, human, 303–4

Hand cell, 228, 249
Handedness, 735–36, 738
Hearing impairment, 275–77
measuring, 277–78
relieving, 278–79
Hearing prosthesis, 279, 296
Hebbian synapse, 630, 646–47
Helicotrema, 259, 296
Hemianopsia, 706, 744
Hemifield tachistoscopy, 727, 744
Hemiplegia, 383, 396
Hemispheric coordination, and M2, 390
Hemispheric dominance, 738, 744
Heredity
and Alzheimer's disease, 677
and mood disorder, 668–69
and schizophrenia, 652–54
Hermaphroditic, 482, 511
Heroin, 327, 338
Hertz (Hz), 256, 296
Heschl's gyrus, 273, 296, 721, 744
Hierarchical motor system, 377, 396
Hippocampal EEG, 588–89
Hippocampal slice method, 614–31, 647
Hippocampus, 14, 82, 84, 106
motivational input to, 599–601
place cells of, 589–92
role of, in avoiding perseveration, 567–68
role of, in conditioning, 563–65
role of, in learning and memory, 589–608
and working memory, 604–7
Histidine, 30
Histofluorescence, 177, 194
Hobson–McCarley theory, 419–21, 436
Homeostasis, 440, 478
Homeostatic mechanisms, 440, 478
Homosexuality, as result of hormonal error, 505–9
Horizontal cells, 202, 249
Hormones, 76, 106, 483, 485
Horseradish peroxidase (HRP) technique, 176, 194
Humans, weight control in, 461–66
Hunger, 441–66, 527
and hypothalamus, 448–54
turning hunger on, 444
turning off, 445–48
use and storage of fuels, 441, 443
Huntington's chorea, 167
Huntington's disease, 371, 373–74, 396

Hyperactivity, 665
Hyperarousal, 658–60
in mesolimbic system, 660–63
Hyperdipsia, 475, 478
Hyperopia, 202, 249
Hyperphagia
and hypothalamus, 454–61
and satiety, 458–61
Hyperpolarization, 137, 148
Hypersynchrony, 678, 688
Hypertension, 471, 478
Hyperventilation, 683
Hypoalgesia, 331, 338
Hypodipsia, 471, 478
Hypofrontality, 655, 688
Hypothalamic area for conditioned emotional responses (HACER), 520–21
Hypothalamic hyperphagia, 448–49, 479
Hypothalamic theory of hunger, 451
Hypothalamus, 59, 74, 76–77, 79, 83, 106, 448, 479, 520–21
approach–avoidance conditioning of, 291
and fear-induced aggression, 525
and hunger, 448–54
and hyperphagia, 454–61
Hypovolemic (extracellular) thirst, 475, 479

Ibotenic acid, 167, 194, 579, 585
Ice-cube model, 237, 249
Imipramine, 670
Immune system, 177, 194, 532, 542
role of, in combating disease, 535–36
and stress, 535–39
Immunity, 536, 542
Immunohistochemical method, 177–78, 194
Immunosuppression, 537, 542
Incentive, 291, 296
Incentive learning, 570, 585
Indexing theory on context theory, 599
Inertia, 354, 396
Infection, and emotional stress, 536–37
Inferior, 50, 106
Inferior colliculus, 71, 106, 272, 296
Inferotemporal (IT) cortex, 214, 250
Infrared radiation, 200
Ingestion, 440
Inhibition, 137, 148

Inhibitory postsynaptic potential (IPSP), 136–37, 148
Inhibitory receptors, 136–38
Initial segment, 121, 148
Initial stage 1, 410, 436
Injured nerves, 55–56, 58
Inner ear, 258, 262, 296
Insanity, 651, 688
Insomnia, 431–33, 436
   acute versus chronic, 431–32
   drug treatment of, 432–33
   and use of EEG, 158–60
Instrumental aggression, 524, 542
Instrumental conditioning
   in other brain structures, 568–71
   site of, 566–71
Insula, 87
Insulin, 444, 479
Insulin hypothesis, 457
Intensity of sound waves, 256–57, 296
Intention tremor, 363, 396
Interactional dualism, 3, 16
Interaural intensity difference, 271, 296
Interaural time difference, 269, 296
Interblobs, 236. 250
Intercellular space, 32–33, 47
Interconnected analyzers, network of, 245–46
Intermale aggression, 524–27, 542
Intermanual conflict, 732, 744
Internal capsule, 371, 396
Internal genitalia, 493, 512
International Society for Neuro-science, 5
Interneurons, 33, 47, 63, 106
Interosseous, 366–67
Interrupt signal, 379, 396
Intersexual, 491, 512
Interstripe cells, 239, 250
Intestinal bypass, 463, 479
Intracellular microelectrode technique, 174, 194
Intracellular space, 466, 479
Intralaminar nucleus, 323, 338
Invariance hypothesis, 736, 744
In vitro autoradiographic technique, 177, 194
In vivo technique, 177
Ions, 112, 148
   movement of, during nerve impulse, 117, 119
Ion channels, 115, 148
Ion pump, 117

Ipsilateral projection, 703, 727, 744
Iris, 201, 250
Irritable aggression, 524, 528–31, 542
Isometric contraction, 347, 396
Isoniazid, 669–70
Isotonic contractions, 347, 396
Isotopes, 185, 194

Kainic acid, 167, 194, 452, 479
K-complex, 410, 436
Ketones, 441, 464, 479
Kidney function, 467–69
Kindling, 682, 688
Kinesthesia, 88, 106
Kinesthesis, 347–49, 396
Korsakoff's disease, 651
Korsakoff's syndrome, 631, 635, 647

Labeled, 176
Labeled-line theory of taste coding, 283, 296
Labeled molecule, 176, 194
Lacuna, 633, 647
Landmark discrimination, 244, 250
Language areas, 90–91, 713–14
Language-related syndromes, 723–24
   auditory studies of lateralization, 727–28
   right-hemisphere language abilities, 732–35
   studies of bisected brains in lateralization, 728–32
   visual studies of lateralization, 727
Lateral, 50, 106
Lateral attack, 525, 542
Lateral fissure, 85, 106
Lateral geniculate nucleus (LGN), 214, 250, 703, 744
Lateral hypothalamic nucleus, 449, 479
Lateral hypothalamus, 527, 585
   as hunger center, 451–53
   as reward center in brain, 572
   role of, in hunger, 453–54
Lateralization, 724–26, 744
   development of, 735–38
   visual studies of, 727
Lateral preoptic area of hypothalamus, 472, 479
Lateral superior olive, 269, 296
Lateral ventricles, 72, 106
l-DOPA, 145, 148, 376, 396
Learned helplessness, 333, 338
Learning, 650. *See also* Reinforcement
   dendritic changes in, 618–19
   discrimination-reversal, 564

distributed, 571
and nervous system, 550–71
NMDA receptors and associative, 630
perceptual-motor, 640
and protein synthesis, 619–20
reversal, 564, 593–94
role of hippocampus in, 589–608
types of, 546–50
Lens, 201, 250
Lesion, 153–54, 194
Lesioning, 154
Lesion research, 155
Leucocytes, 535, 542
Levator ani, 496, 512
Level of arousal, 515, 542
LH surge, 506–7, 512
Librium, 432, 523
Light, nature of, 199–200
Light adaptation, 209, 250
Light microscopy
   staining, 39–40
   tissue preparation, 39
Limbic striatum, 661, 688
Limbic system, 82–84, 106
Linear acceleration, 354, 396
   and gravity, 354–57
Line-orientation analyzers, 222, 250
Lipids, 445, 479
Lipocytes, 441, 479
Lipoprotein lipase (LPL), 462, 479
Lipostatic theory, 445, 479
Lithium, 673–74, 688
Load, 350, 396
Local currents, 202, 250
Localization, of stimulus, 307, 338
Lock-and-key theory of olfaction, 288, 296
Locomotion, 364
   central pattern generators, 365–70
   roots of walking, 364–65
Locus coeruleus, 419, 436, 575, 585, 669, 688
Locus coeruleus-α, 422, 436
Longitudinal fissure, 87, 106
Long-term memory, 612, 647
   physiological basis of, 614–31
Long-term potentiation (LTP), 614–16, 647, 682, 689
Lordosis, 498, 512
Loudness, 257, 296
Luminal, 523
Luteinizing hormone (LH), 485, 512
Lymphocytes, 535, 542
Lynch–Baudry theory, 639

M1 (primary motor cortex), 91, 106, 380, 383–90, 396
M2 (supplementary motor cortex), 91, 106, 383, 387–90, 396
Macula, 354, 396
Magnocellular layers, 219, 250
Mammalian class, 96, 107
Mammalian reproductive behavior, 496–501
Mammals, 96
Mammillary bodies, 569, 585, 635, 647
Manic–depressive psychosis. *See* Mood disorder
MAO inhibitors, 143, 148, 669–70, 688
Marr–Albus theory, 562, 585
Masculinization, 494, 500, 512
Maternal aggression, 524, 542
Maze-learning task, 696–97, 744
Mechanoreception, 88, 107
  in central nervous system, 309–18
Mechanoreceptive threshold, 305–7, 338
Mechanoreceptors, 300, 338
Medial, 50, 107
Medial area of hypothalamus, 472
Medial forebrain bundle (MFB), 451, 479, 499–500, 512, 515, 542, 573–74, 585
Medial frontal cortex, self-stimulation of brain in, 580–81
Medial geniculate body (MGB), 273, 296
Medial hypothalamus, 521, 542
Medial preoptic area (MPOA), 479, 498–500, 512
  and fear-induced aggression, 525
  and intermale aggression, 527
Medial septal nucleus, 599, 609
Medial superior olive, 269, 296
Medial temporal amnesia, 635, 647
Medial thalamic nucleus, 323, 338
Medroxyprogesterone acetate, 503
Medulla oblongata, 66, 107
Meissner's corpuscles, 302, 303, 338
Membrane, 21–23
  fluid bilayer, 22–23
Membrane reflex, nictitating, and cerebellum, 559–63
Memory. *See also* Amnesia
  classical conditioning, 642
  declarative, 642
  erasing, 600–1
  event, 599

long-term, 614–31
nondeclarative, 642, 643
orienting, 642
priming, 642
reference, 604, 642–43
for reinforcement events, 601–4
research on, 14
role of hippocampus in, 589–608
short-term, 613
skill, 642
spatial, 589–99
types of, 641–44
working, 604–8, 642, 643–44
Memory indexing system, 598–99, 609
Memory sparing in amnesia, 640–41
Menstrual cycle, 487–88, 512
Mentation, 413, 436
Merkel endings, 302, 303, 338
Mesencephalic locomotor area, 370, 396, 472–73, 479
Mesolimbic system, 451, 479, 661, 688
  hyperarousal in, 660–63
Mesolimbic tract, 576, 585
Messenger RNA (mRNA), 31, 47
Metabolism, 26, 47
Methamphetamine, 664
Microelectrodes, 174, 194
Microelectrode technique, 225
Microglia, 33, 36, 47
Micrography, scanning electron, 43, 45
Microsleeps, 425
Microtome, 39, 47
Microtubules, 24, 47, 176
Midbrain, 70–72, 107
Midbrain reticular formation (MBRF), 403–4, 436
  and habituation, 557
Middle ear, 258, 296
Mind, link between brain and, 2–3
Mineralocorticoids, 77, 107
Minicolumn, 84. *See also* Module
Mirror tracing, 640, 647
Mitochondria, 24, 27, 47
Moderating factors, 653, 688
Module, 84, 107
Molar, 3, 16
Molecular, 3–4, 16
Molecules, 111, 148
Monism, 3, 16
Monoamine group of transmitters, 665
Monoamine oxidase (MAO), 142, 148, 669, 688

Monoaminergic synapses, 142, 148, 396
Monoamines, 142, 148, 688
  and depression, 669
  and drugs, 669–70
Monoamine transmitters, 669
Monosynaptic arc, 345
Monozygotic twins, 652
  and study of schizophrenia, 652–53
Mood disorder, 432, 667, 688
  causes of, 651
  description and classification, 667–68
  heredity and, 668–69
  therapy for, 673–74
Morphine, 327, 330, 338
Morphology, 483, 512
Motivational input to the hippo-campus, 599–601
Motor–action areas, 91
Motor cortex, 380–83, 396
  premotor cortex, 390–93
Motor fibers, 53, 107
Motor hierarchy and fractionation, 385–87
Motor nucleus of the vagus, 453, 479
Motor unit, 343, 397
Mounting, 498, 512
Movement
  and corpus striatum, 370–80
  and locomotion, 364–70
  and motor cortex, 380–93
  perceiving, 239, 241–42
  preparation for, 391–93
  role of cerebellum in, 359–64
  role of muscles in, 342–47
  sensory control of, 347–59
Movement sequencing, 391
MPTP (1-methyl-4-phenyl-1,2,3,6-tetrahydropyridine), 12, 16
MST, 239, 250
MT, 239, 250
Müllerian duct, 485, 512
Müllerian-inhibiting factor (MIF), 485, 512
Multiple causation, 533, 542
Multiple parallel processing pathways, 219, 250
Multiple personality, 651–52, 688
Multisynaptic arcs, 345, 397
Muscle fibers, 343, 397
Muscles, 342–43
  cardiac, 342

neural control of, 343–45
smooth, 342
striate, 342
Muscle spindles, 348, 397
Muscle tone, 353–54, 397
Mutism, 387, 397, 715, 716, 744
Myelin, 35, 47
Myelin sheath, 35, 47
Mygdala, and fear-induced
aggression, 525
Myopia, 201, 250

N_1, 602, 609
N_2, 602, 609
Naloxone, 329, 338
Nanometers, 206, 250
Narcolepsy, 433–34, 437, 664
Nauta–Gygax method, 175–76, 194
Near disparity, 231, 250
Negative reinforcement, 549, 585
Negative symptoms, 656, 688
Nembutal, 523
Neocortex, 84–85, 107
anatomy of, 85, 87
language areas, 90–91
motor–action areas, 91
sensory–perceptual areas of,
87–90
Neologisms, 715, 744
Neostriatum, 661, 688
NE release, presynaptic regulation of,
670–72
Nerve cells, 4, 16, 33, 52
Nerve fiber, 35, 47
Nerve impulse, 4, 16, 110, 119,
148–49
bioelectricity, 111–12
conduction of, 119, 121–23
creating resting potential, 114–17
excitatory postsynaptic potentials
versus, 133–34
measuring action potentials,
123–29
movements of ions during, 119
nature of, 110–11
resting potential, 112–14
triggering, 134–36
Nerves, 52–53, 107
cranial, 53
injured, 55–56, 58
spinal, 53
Nervous system
autonomic, 64–66
brain stem, 66–72
cerebrospinal fluid, 72

control of internal environment
through, 74, 76
corpus striatum, 79–82
hypothalamus, 74, 76–77, 79
and learning, 550–71
organizational principles, 58–60
organization of, 50, 52
parasympathetic, 66
peripheral, 52–53, 55–56, 58
role of, in thirst, 471–75
sympathetic, 66, 521–22
thalamus, 72, 74
ventricles, 72
Nervous system tissue, 32
blood–brain barrier, 37–39
neurons, 32–33
Neural control of muscles, 343–45
Neuritic plaque, 676, 688
Neurofibrillary tangle, 676, 688–89
Neuroglia, 33, 47
of brain and spinal cord, 35–37
of peripheral nervous system, 33,
35
Neurological soft signs, 654, 689
Neuroma, 47, 56, 58, 107
Neuromuscular junctions, 141, 149
Neuromyal junction, 343, 397
Neuron, 4, 6, 17, 32–33
probing single, in brain research,
173–74
transmission of information
between, 129–38
viewing, 39–43, 45
Neuron doctrine, 4, 17
Neuropathological factors underlying
epilepsy, 682–83, 689
Neuropathology, 5, 17, 689
in schizophrenia, 654–57
Neuropil, 33, 47
Neuropsychological tests, 693–97
Corsi recency-discrimination task,
694–95
maze-learning task, 696–97
Prisco delayed-comparison task,
694
Stroop test, 695–96
Wisconsin card-sorting task, 696
Neuropsychologist, 153, 194
Neuropsychology, 5, 692–93, 744
Neuroscience, 5, 17
use of animals in, 187, 189–90,
192–93
Neurotic pain, realness of, 325
Neurotoxins, 11, 17, 164, 166–67, 194
effect of, on transmitters, 140
Neurotransmitter, 4, 6, 8, 17, 130, 149

Neurotransmitter antagonists, 9, 17
Neurotransmitter system, 8, 17
Nictitating membrane reflex (NMR),
559, 585
Nigrostriatal neurons, 10, 17
Nigrostriatal path, 660–61
Nigrostriatal pathway, 376, 397
Nigrostriatal tract, 451, 479, 576, 585
NMDA receptors, 630, 647
and associative learning, 630
Nociception, 88, 107
Nociceptors, 300, 338
Nodes of Ranvier, 122–23, 149
Nondeclarative memory, 642, 643,
647
Nondecremental conduction, 122,
149
Nonspecific facilitation, 405, 437
Noradrenalin, 77, 107, 149
Noradrenergic neurons, 574, 585
Noradrenergic system, anatomy of,
574–75
Noradrenergic theory of depression,
672–73
Norepinephrine, 136, 142, 177, 554
Norepinephrine hypothesis, 574–75
evidence for and against, 575–76
NREM sleep, 411, 437
role of, 423–29
Nuclear magnetic resonance (NMR),
187, 194–95
Nuclear regulatory protein, 628, 647
Nuclei, 111. See also Atomic nuclei
Nucleolus, 23, 47
Nucleus, 23, 47, 107
in nervous system, 59
Nucleus accumbens, 82, 661, 689
Nucleus basalis, 82
Nucleus basalis of Meynert, 677, 689
Nucleus circularis, 470, 479
Nucleus interpositus, 560, 585
Nucleus of tractus solitarius (NTS),
66–67, 107, 281, 296–97, 453,
479
Nucleus raphe magnus, 328, 338
Nucleus reticularis magnocellularis
(NRMC), 422, 437

Obesity, types of, 462
Object vision pathway, 221, 250
Obsessions, 8, 17
Obsessive–compulsive disorder
(OCD), 6–9, 17
and serotonin, 9
symptoms of, 8–9

Occipital lobe, 87, 107, 702–3
  survey of visual system lesions, 703–9
Occlusion, 675
Ocular dominance, 228, 250
Ocular dominance bands, 235–36, 250
Ocular dominance slabs, 237
Odorants, 286. *See also* Olfactory stimulus
  receiving and identifying, 286–89
Olfaction, 286, 297
  receiving and identifying odorants, 286–89
  use of input by the brain, 289–93
Olfactory bulb, 287, 297
Olfactory epithelium, 286, 297
Olfactory nerve, 286–87, 297
Olfactory stimulus, 286, 297
Olfactory tract, 289, 297
Olfactory transduction, 288, 297
Oligodendrocytes, 37, 47
Oligodendroglia, 33, 36–37
One-way conduction, 111, 149
Operant conditioning, 566, 585
Operant response, 566–67
Opiate, 327, 339
Opiate analgesia, 327–28
Opiate antagonist, 329, 339
Opiate blocker, 329, 339
Opium, 327, 337
Opponent processes, 232, 250
Opponent vector cells, 242, 250
Opsin, 206, 250
Optic chiasm, 703, 744
Optic disc, 202, 204, 250
Optic nerve, 204, 705, 744
  fibers in, 703
Optic radiations, 705, 745
Optic tract, 705, 745
Orbitofrontal areas, 91, 107
Orbitofrontal cortex, 289, 297, 518, 543, 701–2
  and anxiety, 517–18
Orders, 96, 107
Organ, 20, 47
Organelles, 23, 47
Organic mental disorders, 650–51, 689
Organism, 20, 47
Organizational effect, 494, 512
Organ of Corti, 259, 260, 297
Orientation columns, 235, 250
Orienting memories, 642, 647
Orienting reaction, 402–3, 437
Orienting reflex, 547, 585

Oscilloscope, 124, 149
Osmoreceptors, 470, 479
Osmotic pressure, 466, 479
Osmotic thirst, 471–73, 479
Otoliths, 354, 397
Otosclerosis, 275, 297
Outer ear, 257–58, 297
Outer hair cells, 267–68, 297
Outer segments, 204, 250
Output neurons, 203, 250
Oval window, 258, 297
Ovaries, 483, 512
Overinclusion, 659, 689
Ovulation, 488, 512

P300, 658, 689
Pacinian corpuscles, 302, 303, 339
PAG, and fear-induced aggression, 525
Pain, 322–36
  analgesia from brief versus prolonged, 333–34
  analgesia of avoidable and unavoidable, 332–33
  chronic, 326–28
  effect of pain on, 331–32
  nature of, 322–23
  problems in understanding, 323
  reasons for experiencing, 325–26
Pain asymbolia, 710, 745
Pain-control pathway, 329–30
Pain-control system
  anatomy of, 328–29
  descending, 328–30
Pain-projection system, 323–24
Pain suppression pathway, 339
Pancreas, 77, 107, 443, 479
Papillae, 280, 297
Parabiotic-twins technique, 456–57, 479
Paradoxical cold, 319, 339
Parahippocampal gyrus, 82, 84, 107
Parallelism, 3
Parallel processing pathways, 218–20
Paranoia, 663, 689
Paraphrasia, 714, 745
  phonemic, 714
  semantic, 715
Parasympathetic nervous system, 66, 107
Paraventricular nucleus (PVN), 458–61, 479, 534, 543
Paresis, 383, 397
Parietal lobe, 85, 107, 709–10
  somatic symptoms, 710

  spatial orientation and neglect, 711–12
Parkinson's disease, 10, 17, 374–77, 397, 666
  problems for transplant therapy, 12–14
  symptoms of, 10–11
  transplants for, 11–12
Paroxysmal depolarization shift (PDS), 683, 689
  epileptic focus, 683
Partial seizures, 679, 689
Parvocellular layers, 219, 250
Passive-avoidance, 619, 647
Passive-avoidance conditioning, 549, 585
Patella, 350, 397
Patellar tendon reflex, 350, 397
Pathological obesity, 462, 479
Pathological sinistrality, 739, 745
Pattern theory, 303
Paw flexion, 558–59
Pentobarbital, 523
Perceptual–motor learning, 640, 647
Perforant path, 592, 609
Periaqueductal gray (PAG), 326, 339, 521, 543
Peripheral, 50, 107
Peripheral nervous system, 52–53, 55–56, 58, 107
  neuroglia of, 33, 35
Peripheral retina, 207, 250
Peristalsis, 343, 397
Peristriate cortex, 214, 250
Periventricular system, 515, 543, 574, 585
  and irritable aggression, 529
Perseveration, 567–68, 585, 696, 745
  avoiding, 567–68
Petit mal seizure, 680
PET (positron-emission tomography), 184–87, 195, 654, 721
PGO waves, 416–17, 437
Phagocytosis, 36, 47
Phantom limb, 323, 339
Phase, of wave, 269, 297
Phenobarbital, 523
Phenothiazine, 658–59, 666, 689
Phenytoin, in treating epilepsy, 684, 689
Pheromones, 290–93, 297
Phonemic paraphrasia, 714, 745
Phospholipid, 21, 47
Phosphorylation, 628, 647
Photochemicals, 204, 250

Serotonin, 8, 17, 142, 149, 177, 416, 437. *See also* Monoamines
  involvement of, in mood disorder, 672–73
  obsessive–compulsive disorder and, 9
Sertoli cells, 485, 512
Servomechanisms, 352, 397
Set, 695, 699, 745
Set point, 352, 397, 440, 480
Set-point theory, 455–56
Sex-related aggression, 524, 543
Sexual dimorphism and gender, development of, 483–501
Sexual inversion, 505, 512
Sexual motivation, effect of hormones on, 502–4
Sexual orientation, 505, 512
Shape recognition, 307, 339
Shearing action, 260, 297
Short-term memory, 612, 647
  physiological basis of, 613
Signal averaging, 171, 195
Simple cortical neuron, 223, 251
Simple partial seizure, 681, 689
Sinistral, 738, 745
6-hydrozydopamine (6-OHDA), 1, 11, 17, 166–67, 195
Skill memories, 642, 647
Sleep
  architecture of typical, 410–13
  nature of, 408–22
  as part of brain's circadian rhythm, 427–29
  reasons for, 423–31
Sleep-associated disorders, 431
  insomnia, 431–33
  narcolepsy, 433–34
Sleep center, location of, 422–23
Sleep spindles, 410, 437
Sleep stages, EEG identification of, 409–10
Slow adapters (SA), 303, 339
Smooth muscles, 53, 108, 342, 397
Socialization, 493, 512
Society for Neuroscience
  ethical codes of, 155
  and ethics for animal research, 187, 192–93
Sodium amytal, 734, 745
Sodium equilibrium potential, 117, 149
Sodium–potassium pump, 117, 149
Soma, 33, 48, 52
  as decision mechanism, 138–40
Somatic fibers, 53, 108

Somatic projection areas, 310, 339
Somatic senses, 300, 339
  cutaneous somatic mechano-receptors, 301–18
  contributions of receptors, 305–9
  human hand, 303–4
  cutaneous thermoreception, 318–22
  nature of somatic sensitivity, 300–1
  pain, 322–36
Somatosensory projection system, 309–18, 339
Sound, 255, 297
Sound shadow, 271, 297
Sound waves, 297
  detecting, 255–62
  nature of, 255–57
Spatial acuity, 307–8, 339
Spatial attention mechanism, 244, 251
Spatial memory, 589–99
Spatial orientation, 711, 745
Spatial vision and visual attention, 242–44
Spatial vision pathway, 221, 239–44, 251
Species-typical behaviors, 377, 397
Spike potential, 127, 149
Spinal cord, 62–64
  neuroglia of, 35–37
Spinal nerves, 53, 108
Spinal nucleus of the bulbocavernosus, 496, 512
Spinal reflexes, 139
Sprouting, 559, 586, 617–18, 620, 647
Squid, nerve impulse of, 124–25
SSB (self-stimulation of brain), 571–73
  and natural reinforcement, 571–73
Startle response, 547, 586
Static phase of hyperphagia, 455, 480
Statocyst, 97, 108
Stepping reflex, 364, 397
Stereo blindness, 232, 251
Stereocilia, 259–60, 297, 354, 358, 397
Stereognosis, 311–12, 339
Stereopsis, 229–32, 251
Stereotaxic brain atlas, 160, 195
Stereotaxic instrument, 160, 195
Stimulator, 124
Stimulus, 300, 339
Stirrup, 258, 297
Stress, 531, 543. *See also* Emotions
  acute, 538
  and cancer, 537–38

chronic, 538
emotional, and infection, 536–37
factors that interact with, 538
and fear, 334–36
and immune system, 535–39
nature of, 531–32
Stress chemistry and emotions, 539–40
Stress factor, 653, 689
Stress response, and obsessive–compulsive disorder, 9
Stretch reflex, 349–54, 397, 414, 437
  mechanics of, 350
  tuning the, with gamma efferent, 352–54
Striate muscles, 53, 108, 342, 397
Striatum, 10, 17, 79, 108, 371, 397
Stroke, 716, 745
Stroop test, 695–96, 745
Subclinical infection, 535, 543
Subfornical organ, 475, 480
Subroutine, 370, 397
Substantia gelatinosa, 328, 339
Substantia nigra, 10, 17, 371, 397, 451, 480
Succinylcholine, 674
Sugar phosphate groups, 29, 48
Sulcal cortex, 581, 586
Sulcus, 85, 108
Summated potential, 138, 149
Summation, 138, 149
Superior, 50, 108
Superior colliculi, 71, 108
Superior olivary complex, 269, 297
Supplementary motor cortex (M2), 91, 106, 380, 383–90, 396, 397
Suprachiasmatic nucleus (SCN), 428, 437
Supraoptic nucleus, 470, 480
Surgical lesions, 153–55
Sympathetic chain ganglia, 65, 108
Sympathetic nervous system, 66, 108, 521–22
Synapse, 4, 17, 33, 48, 130, 149
Synapse turnover, 618, 620, 647
Synaptic cleft, 43, 48, 149
Synaptic depression, 553, 586
Synaptic gap, 130, 149
Synaptic vesicles, 43, 48
Synchrony, 401, 437
Synergists, 366–67, 397
Synthesis, 431

Tachistoscope, 727, 745
Tail-flick latency, 331, 339

and the receptor organ, 200–2
    retina, 202–12
Visual agnosia, 214, 251, 706, 745
Visual attention, and spatial vision,
    242–44
Visual field, 703, 745
Visual projection system, 214, 251
Visual scanning, 709, 745
Visual sensory projection area, 87,
    108
Visual system lesions, 703–9
Visuospatial agnosia, 711, 745
Volatile, 286, 298
Volley principle, 263–64, 298
Volt, 113, 150
Voltage-regulated channel, 133, 150
Voltage-sensitive dye, 181–82, 195
Voluntary muscles, 55

Vomeronasal organ, 289–90, 298
Vulnerability model of schizophrenia,
    653, 689

Wada test, 734, 738, 745
Waking nightmares, 434, 437
Walking, roots of, 364–65
Water, and salt conservation,
    469–71
Wavelength, 158
Weight control, in humans, 461–66
Weinstein maps, 711, 745
Wernicke's aphasia, 715, 716, 745
Wernicke's area, 714, 717, 745
White matter, 58, 66, 108
Wisconsin Card Sort task, 656, 696,
    745
Wolffian duct, 485, 512

Word salad, 715, 745
Working memory, 609, 642, 643–44,
    647
    and hippocampus, 604–7
    versus context theory, 607–8

X area, 422, 437
X cells, 218–19, 251
X chromosome, 483, 512
    depression gene on, 669
Xenon, 178, 180
X rays, 183, 195

Y cells, 218–19, 251
Y chromosome, 483, 512
Yerkes–Dodson law, 658–59, 689
Young–Helmholtz theory, 207, 251

Acknowledgments

Fig. 1.2 from *Acta Physiologica Scandinavica, 82,* Supplement 367, 1–48. Reprinted by permission of Blackwell Scientific Publications, Ltd.

Fig. 1.3 reprinted by permission of Ed Kiester.

Fig. 1.4 illustration by Carol Donner from "Transplantation in the Central Nervous System," by Alan Fine. © 1986 by Scientific American, Inc. All rights reserved.

Figs. 2.1, 2.5 from *Introduction to Cell Biology* by Stephen L. Wolfe. © 1983 by Wadsworth, Inc. Reprinted by permission of the publisher.

Figs. 2.2, 2.3, 2.4, 2.9, 2.11, 2.16, 3.19, 6.2, 7.6a, 7.8, 9.13, 9.16, 9.27, 11.1, 14.9 from *Human Anatomy* by Ira Fowler. © 1984 by Wadsworth, Inc. Reprinted by permission of the publisher.

Figs. 2.6, 2.12, 2.19, 2.21, 2.26, 3.3, 3.16, 3.32, 4.7, 4.10, 4.13, 4.23 from *Biology: The Unity and Diversity of Life,* fourth edition, by Cecie Starr and Ralph Taggart. © 1987 by Wadsworth, Inc. Reprinted by permission of the publisher.

Figs. 2.10, 4.8, 4.16, 11.15 from *Biology* by William A. Jensen, Bernd Heinrich, David B. Wake, and Marvalee H. Wake. © 1979 by Wadsworth, Inc. Reprinted by permission of the publisher.

Fig. 2.14 from Boycott, B. B. (1974), "Aspects of the Comparative Anatomy and Physiology of the Vertebrate Retina," in R. Bellairs and E. G. Gray (Eds.), *Essays on the Nervous System: A Festschrift for Professor J. Z. Young.* Reprinted by permission of Oxford University Press.

Fig. 2.15 reprinted by permission of Arthur Nitz, Ph.D.

Fig. 2.17 from Bunge, R. P., "Glial Cells and the Central Myelin Sheath," *Physiological Reviews, 48,* 197–251. Reprinted by permission of The American Physiological Society.

Fig. 2.20 from Schmitt, F. O., and Worden, F. G. (Eds.), *Neurosciences: Fourth Study Program,* p. 118. © 1979 by The MIT Press. Reprinted by permission of the publisher.

Fig. 2.22 from Renehan, W. E., et al., *Brain Research, 462,* 399. Reprinted by permission of Elsevier Science Publishers and Dr. W. E. Renehan.

Fig. 2.23 from Heimer, L. (1971), "Pathways in the Brain," *Scientific American, 225* (July), 48–64. Reprinted by permission of the author.

Fig. 2.25 from Gore, R. (1971), "The Brain, Part II," *Life.* Reprinted by permission of Bonnier Fakta Bokforlag AB.

Fig. 2.27 from *Science, 165,* 1142, 1969, "Studying Neural Organization in Aplysia with the Scanning Electron Microscope," E. R. Lewis et al. Reprinted by permission of The American Association for the Advancement of Science, and the author.

Fig. 3.5 from Keynes, R. D. (1979), "Ion Channels in the Nerve-Cell Membrane," *Scientific American, 240* (March), 126–135. Reprinted by permission of Dr. Alexander von Muralt.

Figs. 3.6, 3.12, 3.14, 3.17, 3.22, 3.28, 7.14, 7.25, 7.28, 7.30, 9.2, 9.10, 9.11 from *Human Anatomy and Physiology* by Joan G. Creager. © 1983 by Wadsworth, Inc. Reprinted by permission of the publisher.

Fig. 3.7 © 1983 Nelva Richardson. Reprinted by permission.

Fig. 3.8 from *Fundamentals of Neurology,* sixth edition, by E. Gardner. © 1975 by W. B. Saunders Company, reprinted by permission of the publisher.

Figs. 3.9, 3.10 from Pollock, M., and Harris, A. J. (1981), "Accuracy in Peripheral Nerve Regeneration," *Trends in NeuroSciences, 4,* 18–20. Reprinted by permission of Elsevier Publications Cambridge and Dr. A. J. Harris.

Figs. 3.11, 3.15, 3.18, 3.24, 3.25, 6.14, 11.8, 14.15, 18.9 from *The Human Central Nervous System,* third edition, by Nieuwenhuys, R., Voogd, J., and von Huijzen, C. © 1988 by Springer-Verlag New York, Inc.

Fig. 3.20 from *Fundamental Neuroanatomy* by Walle J. H. Nauta and Michael Feirtag. © 1986 by W. H. Freeman and Company. Reprinted with permission.

Figs. 3.21, 6.13, 9.21, 11.5, 11.6 © 1962 by CIBA-GEIGY Corporation. Reproduced with permission from *CIBA Collection of Medical Illustrations* by Frank Netter, M.D. All rights reserved.

Fig. 3.27 illustration by Carol Donner from "Opiate Receptors and Internal Opiates," by Solomon Snyder. © 1977 by Scientific American, Inc. All rights reserved.

Fig. 3.29 illustration by Bunji Tagawa from "Language and the Brain," by Norman Geschwind. © 1972 by Scientific American, Inc. All rights reserved.

Fig. 3.33 © 1973 Tom McHugh, Photo Researchers, Inc.

Fig. 3.34 from *Darwin After Darwin* by George John Romanes. © 1968 by American Heritage Publishing Company. Adapted with permission of Open Court Publishing Company.

Fig. 3.35 from Mackie, G. O. (1980), "Jellyfish Neurobiology Since Romanes," *Trends in NeuroSciences, 3,* 13–16. Reprinted by permission of Elsevier Science Publishers and Dr. G. O. Mackie.

Fig. 3.36 from Hodgson, E., and Jollie, M. (1977), "Evolution and Lateralization of the Brain," *Annals of the New York Academy of Sciences, 299,* 23, 75. Reprinted by permission of the authors and publisher.

Fig. 3.37 from *Strong and Elwyn's Human Neuroanatomy,* fifth edition. © 1964 by the Williams & Wilkins Co., Baltimore. Reprinted by permission of the publisher.

Fig. 3.38 from *A Primer of Physiological Psychology* by Robert L. Isaacson et al. © 1971 by Harper & Row, Publishers, Inc. Reprinted by permission of the publisher.

Fig. 4.6 from Dudel, J. (1976), "Excitation of Nerve and Muscle," in R. F. Schmidt (Ed.), *Fundamentals of Neurophysiology.* Reprinted by permission of Springer-Verlag New York, Inc.

Fig. 4.18 by Jamie Simon from the *Salk Institute Newsletter,* Fall, 1983. Reprinted by permission of the Salk Institute.

Fig. 4.19 reprinted by permission of Dr. Robert Stroud.

Figs. 5.2, 5.3 from Wilder Penfield, Lamar Roberts, *Speech and Brain Mechanisms.* © 1959 by Princeton University Press. Figs. VII-2, VII-3, VII-5 reprinted with permission of literary executors, Princeton University Press, and The McGill Archive.

Fig. 5.4 courtesy of Grass Instrument.

Figs. 5.8, 5.14 from *Experimental Psychobiology* by Benjamin L. Hart. © 1969, 1976 by W. H. Freeman and Company. Reprinted by permission.

Figs 5.9, 5.10 reprinted by permission of Dr. Marianne Olds.

Figs. 5.11, 5.13 from *Violence and the Brain,* 1970. Reprinted by permission of Dr. Vernon H. Mark.

Fig. 5.12 from Leksell, L., *Stereotaxic and Radio Surgery.* Reprinted by permission of Charles C. Thomas, Publisher, Springfield, IL.

Fig. 5.15 from Thomas, G. J., and Gash, D. M. (1985), "Mammillothalamic Tracts and Representational Memory," *Behavioral Neuroscience, 99,* 621–630. Reprinted by permission of The American Psychological Association and the author.

Fig. 5.16 from Valenstein, E. S. (1973), *Brain Control: A Critical Examination of Brain Stimulation and Psychosurgery.* © 1973 by John Wiley & Sons, Inc. Reprinted by permission of the publisher.

Fig. 5.17 courtesy of Dr. Alan E. Fisher.

Fig. 5.18 from Delafresnaye, *Brain Mechanisms and Consciousness.* Reprinted by permission of Charles C. Thomas, Publisher, Springfield, IL.

Fig. 5.20 by David Linton, *Scientific American,* June 1962. Reprinted by permission of Ann H. Linton.

Fig. 5.21 from Otto, D. (Ed.), *Multidisciplinary Perspective in Event-Related Brain Potential Research.* U.S. Environmental Protection Agency.

Fig. 5.22 from Ebbeson, S. O. E., and Rubison, K., "A Simplified Nauta Procedure," *Physiology and Behavior, 4,* 281–282. Reprinted by permission of Pergamon Press, Inc.

Figs. 5.23, 5.24 from Lassen, N. A., et al. (1978), "Brain Function and Blood Flow," *Scientific American, 239,* 62–71. Reprinted by permission of Dr. Niels A. Lassen.

Fig. 5.25 from Hubel, D. A., et al. (1978), *Journal of Comparative Neurology, 177,* 361–380. Reprinted by permission of Alan R. Liss, Inc. and Dr. David A. Hubel.

Fig. 5.26 from Blasdel, G. G. (1986), "Voltage-Sensitive Dyes Reveal the Modular Organization of the Visual Cortex," *IBRO News, 14,* 5. Reprinted by permission of Andree Blakemore.

Fig. 5.27 from Mastaglia, F. L., and Cala, L. A. (1980), "Computed Tomography of the Brain in Multiple Sclerosis," *Trends in NeuroSciences, 3,* 16–20. Reprinted by permission of Elsevier Publications Cambridge, and Dr. L. A. Cala.

Fig. 5.28 from Kety, S. S. (1979), "Disorders of the Human Brain," *Scientific American, 241,* 202–214. Reprinted by permission of Dr. Fred J. Hodges III.

Fig. 5.29 from "Positron Emission Tomography: Human Brain Functions and Biochemistry," *Science, 228,* 799–809, May 17, 1985. © 1985 by The AAAS. Reprinted by permission of Dr. Michael E. Phelps and the publisher.

Fig. 5.30 from *Journal of Neuroscience,* vol. 7, no. 8, 1987. © 1987 by the Society for Neuroscience. Reprinted by permission of Oxford University Press and Dr. Antonio Damasio.

Fig. 5.31 redrawn by permission of *National Geographic* from original artwork by Davis Meltzer. © National Geographic Society.

Fig. 6.1 from *Astronomy: The Cosmic Journey,* 1987 edition, by William K. Hartmann. © 1987 by Wadsworth, Inc. Reprinted by permission of the publisher.

Fig. 6.4 from Kaufman, L., *Philosophical Transactions,* vol. 194 (1901). Reprinted by permission of The Royal Society, London.

Fig. 6.5 from Townes-Anderson, E., et al. (1988), "Rod Photoreceptors Disassociated from the Adult Rabbit Retina," *The Journal of Neuroscience, 8,* 320–331. Reprinted by permission of Dr. Ellen Townes-Anderson, Elsevier Science Publishers, and Oxford University Press.

Figs. 6.6, 6.10, 7.6b, 7.7a, 7.12 from *Sensation and Perception,* third edition, by E. Bruce Goldstein. © 1989 by Wadsworth, Inc. Reprinted by permission.

Fig. 6.7 from Schmitt, F. O., and Worden, F. G. (Eds.), *Neurosciences: Fourth Study Program,* p. 118. © 1979 by The MIT Press. Reprinted by permission of the publisher.

Fig. 6.8 from *Symposium Cold Spring Harbor Laboratory of Quantitative Biology, 30,* 345–359. Reprinted by permission of the publisher and Dr. George Wald.

Fig. 6.9 from Riggs, L. A. (1965), "Visual Acuity," in C. Graham (Ed.), *Vision and Visual Perception.* © 1965 by John Wiley & Sons, Inc. Reprinted by permission of the publisher.

Fig. 6.15 from Schneider, G. E. (1967), "Contrasting Visuomotor Functions of Tectum and Cortex in the Golden Hamster," *Psychologische Forschung, 31,* 52–62. Reprinted by permission of Springer-Verlag Heidelberg and Dr. Gerald E. Schneider.

Fig. 6.16 from Van Essen, D. C., "Functional Organization of the Primate Visual Cortex," in *Cerebral Cortex,* Vol. 3, 1985. Reprinted by permission of Dr. David C. Van Essen and Plenum Publishing Corporation.

Fig. 6.17 from Mishkin, M., et al. (1983), "Object Vision and Spatial Vision: Two Cortical Pathways," *Trends in Neuro-Sciences, 6,* 414–417. Reprinted by permission of Elsevier Science Publications and Dr. Mortimer Mishkin.

Figs. 6.18, 6.19 from Hubel, D. H., and Wiesel, T. N. (1962), "Receptive Fields, Binocular Interaction, and Functional Architecture in the Cat's Visual Cortex," *Journal of Physiology, 160,* 106–154. Reprinted by permission of Oxford University Press and Dr. David Hubel.

Figs. 6.21, 6.22 from Desimone, R., et al. (1984), "Stimulus-Selective Properties of Inferior Temporal Neurons in the Macaque," *Journal of Neuroscience, 4,* 2051–2062. Reprinted by permission of Dr. Robert Desimone and Oxford University Press.

Fig. 6.23 adapted from Barlow, H. B., et al. (1982), *Trends in NeuroSciences, 5,* 145–152. Reprinted by permission of Elsevier Science Publications and H. B. Barlow.

Fig. 6.24 from Sekuler, R., and Blake, R. (1985), *Perception,* New York: McGraw-Hill.

Fig. 6.27 from Poggio, G. F., and Poggio, T. (1984), "The Analysis of Steropsis," *The Annual Review of Neuroscience,* Vol. 7, pp. 379–412. © 1984 Annual Reviews, Inc. Reprinted by permission of the publisher.

Fig. 6.29 from Livingstone, M. S., and Hubel, D. H. (1984), "Anatomy and Physiology of a Color System in the Primate Visual Cortex," *The Journal of Neuroscience, 4,* 309–356. Reprinted by permission of Oxford University Press.

Fig. 6.30 from *Sensation and Perception,* second edition, by E. Bruce Goldstein. © 1984 by Wadsworth, Inc. Reprinted by permission.

Fig. 6.31 from LeVay, S., Connolly, M., Houde, J., and Van Essen, D. C. (1985), "The Complete Pattern of Ocular Dominance Stripes in the Striate Cortex and Visual Field of the Macaque Monkey," *The Journal of Neuroscience, 5,* 486–501. Reprinted by permission of Oxford University Press.

Fig. 6.32 from Hubel, D. H., and Livingstone, M. S. (1987), "Segregation of Form, Color, and Steropsis in Primate Area 18," *The Journal of Neuroscience, 7,* 3378–3415. Reprinted by permission of Dr. David Hubel and Oxford University Press.

Fig. 6.33 from Hubel, D. H., and Livingstone, M. S. (1983), the 11th JAF Stevenson Memorial Lecture: "Blobs and Color Vision," *Canadian Journal of Physiology and Pharmacology, 61,* 1433–1441. Reprinted by permission of The National Research Council of Canada.

Fig. 6.36 from Van Essen, D. C. (1979), "Visual Areas of the Mammalian Cerebral Cortex," *Annual Review of Neuroscience, 2,* 227–264. Reprinted by permission of the publisher. © 1979 Annual Reviews, Inc.

Figs. 6.39, 6.40 from *Behavioral Brain Research, 11,* 67–83. Adapted with permission of Dr. Elisabeth A. Murray and Elsevier Science Publishers BV.

Fig. 7.2 from *The Speech Chain* by Peter B. Denes and Elliot N. Pinson. © 1963 by Bell Telephone Laboratories, Incorporated. Reprinted by permission of Doubleday, a division of Bantam, Doubleday, Dell Publishing Group, Inc.

Fig. 7.3 from Schiffman, H. R., *Sensation and Perception.* © 1976 by John Wiley & Sons, Inc. Reprinted by permission of the publisher.

Fig. 7.4 from Stevens, S. S., and Davis, H., *Hearing: Its Psychology and Physiology.* Copyright 1938 by John Wiley & Sons, Inc. Reprinted by permission of the publisher.

Fig. 7.5 from *Hearing and Deafness,* ninth edition, by Hallowell Davis and S. Richard Silverman. © 1978 by Holt, Rinehart and Winston, Inc., reprinted by permission of the publisher.

Fig. 7.7b from Gulick, W. L. (1971), *Hearing: Physiology and Psychophysics.* Reprinted by permission of Oxford University Press.

Fig 7.10 from "Cochlear Neurobiology: Revolutionary Developments," by Peter Dallos, 1988, *ASHA, 30,* 50. © 1988 by The American Speech-Language Hearing Association. Reprinted by permission of the publisher and the author.

Fig. 7.11 from Wever, E. G. (1949), *Theory of Hearing.* Copyright 1949 by John Wiley & Sons, Inc. Reprinted by permission of the publisher.

Fig. 7.13 from Tonndorf, J. (1962), *Journal of the Acoustical Society of America, 34,* 1337–1350. Reprinted by permission of the publisher and the author.

Fig. 7.16 from Galambos, R., and Davis, H. (1943), *Journal of Neurophysiology, 6,* 39–57. Reprinted by permission of The American Physiological Society.

Fig. 7.17 from Pickles, J. O. (1985), "Recent Advances in Cochlear Physiology," *Progress in Neurobiology, 24,* 1–42. Reprinted by permission of Pergamon Press, Inc. and the author.

Fig. 7.18 from Smith, C. A. (1975), "The Inner Ear: Its Embryological Development and Microstructure," in E. L. Eagles (Ed.), *The Nervous System, Vol. 3: Human Communication and Its Disorders.* Reprinted by permission of Dr. Catherine A. Smith and The Raven Press.

Figs. 7.20b, c from Brugge, J. F. (1975), "Progress in Neuroanatomy and Neurophysiology of Auditory Cortex," in E. A. Eagles (Ed.), *The Nervous System, Vol. 3: Human Communication and Its Disorders.* Reprinted by permission of Dr. John F. Brugge and The Raven Press.

Fig. 7.21 from Spoor, A. (1967), *Internal Audiology, 6,* 48–57. Reprinted by permission of S. Karger AG.

Fig. 7.22 from Rosen, S., Bergman, M. , et al. (1962), "Prebycusis Study of a Relatively Noise-Free Population in the Sudan," *Annals of Otology, Rhinology and Laryngology, 71,* 727. Reprinted by permission of the publisher.

Figs. 7.27, 7.29 from Erickson, R. P., "Sensory Neural Patterns and Gestation," in Y. Zotterman (Ed.), *Olfaction and Taste.* Reprinted by permission of Dr. Robert Erickson and Macmillan Publishing Company.

Fig. 7.31 illustration by Bunji Tagawa from "The Stereochemical Theory of Odor," by John F. Amoore, James W. Johnston, Jr., and Martin Rubin, February 1964. © 1964 by Scientific American, Inc. All rights reserved.

Fig. 7.32 adapted from Keverne, E. B. (1978), "Olfaction and Taste: Dual Systems for Sensory Processing," *Trends in NeuroSciences, 1,* 33. Reprinted by permission of Elsevier Publications Cambridge.

Fig. 7.34 adapted from Halpern, M., and Kubie, J. L. (1984), "The Role of the Ophidian Vomeronasal System in Species-Typical Behavior," *Trends in NeuroSciences, 7,* 473. Reprinted by permission of Elsevier Science Publications.

Fig. 7.35 adapted from Keverne, E. B. (1983), "Pheromonal Influences on the Endocrine Regulation of Reproduction," *Trends in NeuroSciences, 6,* 381–384. Reprinted by permission of Dr. E. B. Keverne and Elsevier Science Publications.

Fig. 8.1 illustration by Bunji Tagawa from "The Skin," by William Montagna, February 1965. © 1965 by Scientific American, Inc. All rights reserved.

Fig. 8.2 adapted from figures 11.1 and 11.2 from *Fundamentals of Neurology* by Ernest D. Gardner. © 1965 by Saunders College Publishing, a division of Holt, Rinehart and Winston, Inc. Reprinted by permission of the publisher.

Fig. 8.4 and Table 8.1 from Johansson, R. S., and Vallbo, A. B. (1983), *Trends in NeuroSciences, 6,* 27–32. Reprinted by permission of Elsevier Science Publications and Roland S. Johansson.

Fig. 8.5 from Andres, K. H., and von Düring, M. V. (1973), "Morphology of Cutaneous Receptors," in A. Iggo (Ed.), *Handbook of Sensory Physiology, Vol. 2: Somatosensory System.* Reprinted by permission of Dr. Karl H. Andres.

Fig. 8.6 from *Journal of Physiology,* 1969, p. 224. Reprinted by permission of Oxford University Press and Professor A. Iggo.

Fig. 8.7 from Darien-Smith, I., *Annual Review of Psychology, 33.* © 1982 by Annual Reviews, Inc. Reprinted by permission of the publisher and the author.

Fig. 8.8 adapted from Chambers, M. R., et al. (1972), "Structure and Function of the Slowly Adapting Type II Mechanoreceptor in Hairy Skin," *Quarterly Journal of Experimental Physiology, 57,* 417–445. Reprinted by permission of Professor A. Iggo and Oxford University Press.

Figs. 8.12, 8.13 from Merzenich, M., and Kaas, J. (1982), *Trends in NeuroSciences, 5,* 434–436. Reprinted by permission of Dr. M. Merzenich, Dr. John Kaas, and Elsevier Publications Cambridge.

Fig. 8.14 from *Science, 225,* 820–821, August 24, 1984, "The Brain's Dynamic Way of Keeping in Touch," by Dr. Jeffrey L. Fox. © 1984 by the AAAS.

Fig. 8.15 from Stevens, J. C., and Green, B. G. (1978), "History of Research on Feeling," in E. C. Carterette and M. P. Friedman (Eds.), *Handbook of Perception: Vol. 6-B, Feeling and Hurting.* Reprinted by permission of Academic Press and the authors.

Figs. 8.16, 8.17 from Iggo, A. (Ed.), *Handbook of Sensory Physiology, Vol. 2: Somatosensory System.* Reprinted by permission of Springer-Verlag Publishers.

Fig. 8.18 from Kenshalo, D. R. (1978), "Biophysics and Psychophysics of Feeling," in E. C. Carterette and M. P. Friedman (Eds.), *Handbook of Perception: Vol. 6-B, Feeling and Hurting.* Reprinted by permission of Academic Press and the author.

Fig. 8.19 from *Experimental Psychology,* Vol. I. © 1972 by Academic Press. Reprinted by permission of the publisher.

Fig. 8.22 from Roby-Brami, A., et al. (1987), "An Electrophysiological Investigation," *Brain, 110,* 1497–1508. Reprinted by permission of Oxford University Press.

Fig. 8.25 from Basbaum, A. I., and Fields, H. L. (1984), *The Annual Review of Neuroscience, Vol. 7,* p. 320. © 1984 by Annual Reviews, Inc. Reprinted by permission of the author and the publisher.

Fig. 9.1 from *A Textbook of Histology.* Reprinted by permission of Don W. Fawcett, M.D.

Fig. 9.4 from Shepherd, G. M. (1983), *Neurobiology.* Reprinted by permission of Oxford University Press.

Fig. 9.5 adapted from Fulton, J. F. (1943), *Physiology of the Nervous System,* second edition, p. 101. Reprinted by permission of Oxford University Press.

Figs. 9.12a, b from Buss, A. (1973), *Psychology: Man in Perspective.* Reprinted by permission of John Wiley & Sons, Inc.

Fig. 9.14 from Caviness, V. S., Jr., and Rakic, P. (1978), "Mechanisms of Cortical Development: A View from Mutations in Mice," *The Annual Review of Neuroscience,* Vol. 1, pp. 297–326. © 1978 by Annual Reviews, Inc. Reprinted by permission of the publisher and the authors.

Figs. 9.17a, b reprinted by permission of Blackwell Scientific Publications, Ltd.

Fig. 9.17c from Wetzel, M. C., and Stuart, D. G. (1976), "Ensemble Characteristics of Cat Locomotion and Its Neural Control," *Progress in Neurobiology, 7,* 1–98. Reprinted by permission of Pergamon Press, Oxford University Press, and the authors.

Fig. 9.18 reprinted by permission of Elsevier Publications Cambridge.

Fig. 9.20 from MacKay, W. A. (1980), "The Motor Program: Back to the Computer," *Trends in NeuroSciences, 3,* 97–100. Reprinted by permission of Elsevier Publications Cambridge and the author.

Figs. 9.22, 9.23, 9.24 © 1962 CIBA-GEIGY Corporation. Reproduced with permission of The Curtis Publishing Company. All rights reserved.

Fig. 9.28 reprinted by permission of The Guilford Press.

Figs. 9.29, 9.30 reprinted by permission of Oxford University Press.

Fig. 9.32 reprinted by permission of Dr. Niels A. Lassen.

Fig. 9.33 from Freund, H. J. (1984), "Premotor Areas in Man," *Trends in NeuroSciences, 7,* 481–483. Reprinted by permission of Professor H. J. Freund and Elsevier Science Publications.

Fig. 10.5 from Scheibel, M. E., and Scheibel, A. B. (1970), in M. A. B. Brazier (Ed.), *The Electrical Activity of the Brain,* third edition. Reprinted by permission of Longman Group, Ltd., United Kingdom.

Fig. 10.7 reprinted by permission of William Vandivert.

Fig. 10.9 from Kleitman, N. (1960), "Patterns of Dreaming," *Scientific American, 203* (November), 82–88. © 1960 by Scientific American, Inc. All rights reserved. Reprinted by permission of Dr. William Dement and the publisher.

Fig. 10.10 from Brooks, D. C. (1967), *Electroencephalography and Clinical Neurophysiology, 23,* 123–133. Reprinted by permission of Elsevier Scientific Publishers Ireland, Ltd.

Fig. 10.16 from *Science, 189,* 55–58, July 4, 1975, "Sleep Cycle Oscillation: Reciprocal Discharge by Two Brainstem Neuronal Groups." © 1975 by the AAAS. Reprinted by permission of Dr. J. A. Hobson and the publisher.

Fig. 10.18 from *Science, 197,* 1089–1091, September 9, 1977, "Suprachiasmiatic Nucleus: Use of (14) C-Labeled Deoxyglucose Uptake as a Functional Marker." © 1977 by the AAAS. Reprinted by permission of Dr. William J. Schwartz and the publisher.

Fig. 11.7 from *Science, 112,* 256–259, September 1, 1950, "Decreased Hunger but Increased Food Intake Resulting from Hypothalamic," N. E. Miller. Copyright © 1950 by the AAAS. Reprinted by permission of the publisher and the author.

Fig. 11.10 from Hallonquist, J. D., and Brandes, J. S. (1984), "Ventromedial Hypothalamic Lesions in Rats," *Physiology and Behavior, 33,* 831–836. Reprinted by permission of Pergamon Press, Inc.

Fig. 11.14 from Simon, C., et al., "Cephalic Phase Insulin Secretion in Relation to Food Presentation in Normal and Overweight Subjects," *Physiology and Behavior, 36,* 465–469. Reprinted by permission of Pergamon Press, Inc.

Fig. 12.1 from O'Malley, B. W., and Schrader, W. T. (1976), "Steroid Hormones," *Scientific American, 234,* 32–43. Reprinted by permission of George V. Kelvin Science Graphics.

Fig. 12.2 from Money, J. (1987), "Sin, Sickness, or Status?: Homosexual Gender Identity and Psychoneuroendocrinology," *American Psychologist, 42,* 384–399. Adapted by permission of the American Psychological Association.

Fig. 12.3 reprinted by permission of Charles Scribner's Sons, an imprint of Macmillan Publishing Company from *The Male: From Infancy to Old Age* by Sherman J. Silber, M.D. Illustrations by Scott Barrows. © 1981 by Sherman J. Silber, M.D.

Figs. 12.5, 12.11 from *Structure of the Human Body* by W. D. Gardner and W. A. Osburn. © 1968 by Saunders College Publishing, a division of Holt, Rinehart and Winston, Inc., reprinted by permission of the publisher.

Figs. 12.6, 12.7 from Money, J., and Ehrhardt, A. (1972), *Man and Woman, Boy and Girl: Differentiation and Dimorphism of Gender Identity from Conception to Maturity,* Johns Hopkins University Press. Reprinted by permission of the publisher.

Figs. 12.8, 12.10 from Konishi, M. (1982), "Sexual Differentiation of Brain and Behavior," *Trends in NeuroSciences, 5,* 20–23. Reprinted by permission of Elsevier Science Publications and Dr. M. Konishi.

Fig. 12.13 from Barnett, S. A., *The Rat: A Study in Behavior.* © 1963 by S. A. Barnett, © 1975 by The University of Chicago. All rights reserved. Used by permission of the publisher.

Fig. 12.14 from Edwards, D. A., and Finhorn, I. C. (1986), "Preoptic and Midbrain Control of Sexual Motivation," *Physiology and Behavior, 37,* 329–355. Reprinted by permission of Pergamon Press, Inc. and the authors.

Fig. 13.7 from Feldman, R. S., and Quenzer, L. F. (1984), *Fundamentals of Neuropsychopharmacology,* fig. 15, p. 348. Reprinted by permission of Sinauer Associates, Inc.

Fig. 13.10 from *Science, 152,* 1406–1408, June 8, 1966, "Control of Sensory Fields by Stimulation of Hypothalamus," M. F. MacDonnel. © 1966 by the AAAS. Reprinted by permission of the publisher.

Excerpt on p. 530 from Heath, R. G. (1981), "The Neural Basis for Violent Behavior," *Physiology and Anatomy,* in L. Valzelli and L. Mogese (Eds.), *Aggression and Violence: A Psychobiological and Clinical Approach.* Reprinted by permission of Dr. Robert Heath.

Fig. 13.11 from Hunsperger, R. W., and Bucher, V. M. (1967), in W. R. Adey and T. Tokizane (Eds.), *Structure and Function of the Limbic System.* Reprinted by permission of Elsevier Science Publishers BV.

Table 13.1 from Holmes, T. H., and Rahe, R. H. (1967), "The Holmes Life Scale of Recent Events," *Psychosomatic Medicine 11,* 213–218. Reprinted by permission of Elsevier Science Publications and the authors.

Fig. 14.3 from *Science, 231,* 1246–1249, May 19, 1986, "Lessons from Snails and Other Models," Deborah M. Barnes. © 1986 by the AAAS. Reprinted by permission of the publisher and the California Academy of Sciences.

Fig. 14.10 reprinted by permission of The Guilford Press.

Fig. 14.11 adapted from McCormick, David A., *Biological Science Proceedings of the National Academy of Sciences of the USA, 79,* 2731–2742. Reprinted by permission of the author.

Fig. 14.12 from Gellman, R. S., et al. (1985), *Trends in NeuroSciences, 8,* 181–182. Reprinted by permission of The Guilford Press and the author.

Fig. 14.13 from Berger, T. W., and Orr, W. B. in C. D. Woody (Ed.), *Conditioning: Representation of Involved Neural Functions.* © 1982 Plenum Publishing Corporation. Reprinted by permission of the publisher and the authors.

Fig. 14.14 from Kimble, D. P. (1968), "Hippocampus and Internal Inhibition," *Psychological Bulletin, 70,* 285–295. © 1968 by The American Psychological Association. Reprinted by permission of the publisher.

Fig. 14.16 reprinted by permission of Alan R. Liss, Inc.

Figs. 14.17, 14.18 from Ungerstedt, U. (1971), "Stereotaxic Mapping of the Monoamine Pathway in the Rat Brain," *Acta Physiologica Scandinavia, 82,* Supplement 367, 1–48. Reprinted by permission of Blackwell Scientific Publications, Ltd.

Fig. 14.21 from Rolls, E. T. (1977), "Neural Activity During Natural and Brain Stimulation Reward," in Hall et al. (Eds.), *Neuroscience Research Program Bulletin.* Reprinted by permission of The MIT Press.

Fig. 15.1 from Bennett, T. L. (1977), *Brain and Behavior.* Reprinted by permission of Brooks/Cole Publishing Co.

Fig. 15.2 from O'Keefe, J., and Conway, D. H. (1978), "Hippocampal Place Units in the Freely Moving Rat: Why They Fire Where They Fire," *Experimental Brain Research, 33,* 573–590. Reprinted by permission of Springer-Verlag, Heidelberg and the authors.

Fig. 15.3 from O'Keefe, J., et al. (1978), "Single Unit and Lesion Experiments on the Sensory Inputs to the Hippocampal Cognitive Map," in L. Weiskrantz (Ed.), *Functions of the Septo-Hippocampal System,* CIBA Foundation Symposium 58. Reprinted by permission of Elsevier Science Publishers BV and the authors.

Fig. 15.4 from *Neuroanatomy* by K. E. Moyer. © 1980 by K. E. Moyer. Reprinted by permission of Harper & Row, Publishers, Inc.

Fig. 15.5 from Bliss, T. V. P. et al. (1982), "What Is the Mechanism of Long-Term Potentiation in the Hippocampus?" *Trends in NeuroSciences, 5,* 289–290. Reprinted by permission of the authors and Elsevier Science Publications.

Fig. 15.6 from Kubie, J. L., and Ranck, J. B., Jr., (1983), "Sensory-Behavioral Correlates in Individual Hippocampus Neurons in Three Situations: Space and Context," in W. Seifert (Ed.), *Neurobiology.* Reprinted by permission of The Academic Press.

Fig. 15.7 from Routtenberg, A. (1984), "The CA3 Pyramidal Cell in the Hippocampus: Site of Intrinsic Expression and Extrinsic Control of Memory Formation," in L. R. Squire and N. Butters (Eds.), *Neuropsychology of Memory.* Reprinted by permission of The Guilford Press.

Figs. 15.8, 15.10 from Deadwyler, S. A. (1985), "Involvement of Hippocampal Systems in Learning and Memory," in N. M. Weinberger, J. L. McGaugh, and G. Lynch (Eds.), *Memory Systems of the Brain.* Reprinted by permission of The Guilford Press and the author.

Fig. 15.11 from Friedman, H. R., and Goldman-Rakic, P. S., "Activation of the Hippocampus and Dentate Gyrus by Working Memory: A 2-Deoxyglucose Study of Behaving Rhesus Monkeys," *The Journal of Neuroscience, 8,* 4693–4706. Reprinted by permission of Oxford University Press and Harriet R. Friedman.

Fig. 16.2 reprinted by permission of Elsevier Science Publications.

Fig. 16.3 from Cotman, C. W., and Nieto-Sampedro, M. (1982), "Brain Function, Synapse Renewal, and Plasticity," *The Annual Review of Psychology,* Vol. 33, pp. 371–401. © 1982 by Annual Reviews, Inc. Reproduced by permission of the publisher and the authors.

Figs. 16.4, 16.5 from Shashoua, V. E. (1985), "The Role of Extracellular Proteins in Learning and Memory," *American Scientist, 73,* 364–370. Reprinted by permission of The Scientific Research Society and the author.

Fig. 16.6 from Gray, E. G. (1982), "Rehabilitating the Dendritic Spine," *Trends in NeuroSciences, 5,* 5–6. Reprinted by permission of Elsevier Science Publications.

Fig. 16.7 from Crick, F. (1982), "Do Dendritic Spines Twitch?" *Trends in NeuroSciences, 5,* 44–46. Reprinted by permission of Boston University Medical School.

Fig. 16.8 from Steward, O., et al. (1986), "Protein-Synthetic Machinery at Postsynaptic Sites During Synaptogenesis," *The Journal of Neuroscience, 6,* 412–423. Reprinted by permission of Elsevier Science Publications and Dr. Oswald Steward.

Fig. 16.9 from *Science, 200,* 787–790, May 19, 1978, "Spine Stems on Tectal Interneurons in Jewel Fish Are Shortened by Social Stimulations." © 1978 by the AAAS. Reprinted by permission of The Academic Press and Dr. Richard Cross.

Fig. 16.14 from *The Physiological Basis of Memory,* second edition, reprinted by permission of The Academic Press and Dr. S. D. Iversen.

Figs. 16.15, 16.16 from *Science, 232,* 1612–1619, June 27, 1986, "Mechanisms of Memory," Dr. Larry Squire. Copyright © 1986 by the AAAS. Reprinted by permission of the publisher and the author.

Fig. 17.1 from Buschbaum, M. S., et. al. (1982), "Cerebral Glucography with Positron Tomography," *Archives of General Psychiatry, 39,* 251–259. Reprinted by permission of the American Medical Association and the author.

Fig. 17.2 from Ingvar, D. H. (1982), "Mental Illness and Regional Brain Metabolism," *Trends in NeuroSciences, 5,* 199–201. Reprinted by permission of Dr. David H. Ingvar and Elsevier Science Publications.

Fig. 17.5 from *Structure of the Human Brain: A Photographic Atlas,* second edition, by Stephen J. DeArmond, Madeline M. Fusco, and Maynard M. Dewey. © 1976 by Oxford University Press. Reprinted by permission of the publisher.

Fig. 17.7 from Angrist, B., and van Kammen, D. (1984), "CNS Stimulants as Tools in the Study of Schizophrenia," *Trends in NeuroSciences, 7,* 388–390. Reprinted by permission of Elsevier Science Publications and the authors.

Figs. 17.10, 17.11 from Pincus, J. H., and Tucker, G. H., *Behavioral Neurology.* © 1978 by Oxford University Press. Reprinted by permission of the publisher.

Fig. 18.2 from Milner, B., and Petrides, M. (1984), "Behavioral Effects of Frontal-Lobe Lesions in Man," *Trends in NeuroSciences, 7,* 403–407. Reprinted by permission of The American Medical Association and Elsevier Science Publications.

Fig. 18.3 from Milner, B. (1963), "Effects of Different Brain Lesions on Card Sorting," *Archives of Neurology, 9,* 90–100. Reprinted by permission of The MIT Press.

Figs. 18.4, 18.10 from *The Working Brain: An Introduction to Neuropsychology* by A. R. Luria. © 1973 Penguin Books, Ltd. Reprinted by permission of the publisher.

Figs. 18.5, 18.6, 18.7 adapted from Fuster, J. M. (1984), "Behavioral Electrophysiology of the Prefrontal Cortex," *Trends in NeuroSciences, 7,* 408–414. Reprinted by permission of Elsevier Science Publications and the author.

Fig. 18.8 used by permission of Warren Museum, Harvard Medical School.

Fig. 18.11 from Williams, M. (1979), *Brain Damage, Behavior, and the Mind.* Reprinted by permission of John Wiley & Sons, Inc.

Fig. 18.12 from Ogden, J. A. (1985), *Brain, 108,* 1009–1022. Reprinted by permission of Oxford University Press and the author.

Fig. 18.13 reprinted by permission of The Guilford Press.

Figs. 18.16, 18.17 from Signoret, J.-L., et al. (1984), "Rediscovery of Leborgne's Brain: Anatomical Deception with CT Scan," *Brain and Language, 22,* 303–319. Reprinted by permission of Academic Press, Inc. and the authors.

Fig. 18.19 from Margolin, D. I., et al. (1984), "Multiple Component Agraphia in a Patient with Atypical Cerebral Dominance: An Error Analysis," *Brain and Language, 22,* 26–40. Reprinted by permission of Academic Press, Inc. and the authors.

Fig. 18.20 from Henderson, V. W. (1986), "Anatomy of Posterior Pathways in Reading: A Reassessment," *Brain and Language, 29,* 119–133. Reprinted by permission of Academic Press, Inc. and the author.

Fig. 18.24 from Gazzaniga, M. S. (1983), "Right Hemisphere Language Following Brain Bisection: A 20-Year Perspective," *American Psychologist, 38,* 525–538. Copyright 1983 by the American Psychological Association. Reprinted by permission of the publisher.

Fig. 18.26 reprinted by permission of Dr. Michael Gazzaniga.

Fig. 18.27 from Ross, E. D. (1984), "Right Hemisphere's Role in Language, Affective Behavior and Emotion," *Trends in NeuroSciences, 7,* 342–345. Reprinted by permission of Elsevier Science Publications.

Fig. 18.28 from LeMay, M. (1982), "Morphological Aspects of Human Brain Asymmetry: An Evolutionary Perspective," *Trends in NeuroSciences, 5,* 273–275. Reprinted by permission of Elsevier Science Publications and Dr. Marjorie LeMay.

Fig. 18.29 from *Science, 229,* 665–668, August 16, 1985, "The Brain Connection: The Corpus Callosum Is Larger in Left-Handers," Dr. Sandra F. Witelson. © 1985 by the AAAS. Reprinted by permission of the publisher and Dr. Sandra F. Witelson.